ANNOTATED
INSTRUCTOR'S
EDITION

THE
BLAIR
READER

EDITED BY

LAURIE G. KIRSZNER
Philadelphia College of Pharmacy and Science

STEPHEN R. MANDELL
Drexel University

LAURIE G. KIRSZNER

STEPHEN R. MANDELL

with

MICHAEL G. MORAN

ROBERT W. CROFT

SUZANNE GILBERT

RUSSELL A. GREER

KAREN S. RADFORD

KRISTINE L. SIELOFF

ALL OF THE
UNIVERSITY OF GEORGIA

A BLAIR PRESS BOOK

PRENTICE HALL, ENGLEWOOD CLIFFS, NJ 07632

Library of Congress Cataloging-in-Publication Data
The Blair reader / edited by Laurie G. Kirszner and Stephen R.
  Mandell.—Annotated instructor's ed.
      p.   cm.
    "A Blair Press book."
    Includes index.
    ISBN 0-13-094897-7 (annotated instructor's ed.).—ISBN
0-13-085325-9
    1. College readers. 2. English language—Rhetoric. I. Kirszner.
  Laurie G. II. Mandell, Stephen R.
  PE1417.B54   1992
  808'.0427—dc20   91-32589
                                                                 CIP

Cover design: Ben Santora
Cover photo: Garrett Kalleberg
Interior design: Sally Steele
Prepress buyer: Herb Klein
Manufacturing buyer: Patrice Fraccio
Acknowledgments appear on pages 1111–1115, which
constitute a continuation of the copyright page.
Blair Press
The Statler Building
20 Park Plaza, Suite 1113
Boston, MA 02116-4399.

Printed in the United States of America
10 9 8 7 6 5 4 3 2 1

ISBN 0-13-085325-9
      0-13-094897-7 (Annotated Instructor's Edition)

Prentice-Hall International (UK) Limited, *London*
Prentice-Hall of Australia Pty. Limited, *Sydney*
Prentice-Hall of Canada Inc., *Toronto*
Prentice-Hall Hispanoamericana, S.A., *Mexico*
Prentice-Hall of India Private Limited, *New Delhi*
Prentice-Hall of Japan, Inc., *Tokyo*
Simon & Schuster Asia Pte. Ltd., *Singapore*
Editora Prentice-Hall do Brasil, Ltda., *Rio de Janeiro*

PREFACE

After more than twenty years of teaching composition, we have come to believe that students should view reading and writing as a way of participating in a public discussion about subjects that matter. Being involved in this manner enables students not only to discover their own ideas but also to see how these ideas fit into a larger social context, where ideas gain additional meaning and value. Because we feel so strongly about this view of reading and writing, we decided to create *The Blair Reader*, a reader designed to encourage students to make their own contribution to the public discussion and to help them see that ideas take shape only in response to other ideas.

Another reason we decided to create *The Blair Reader* was that we could not find a reader that actually addressed our needs as teachers. Most readers available to us seemed to include a selection of "classic" essays with a few "relevant" ones mixed in. Some included no questions, no writing suggestions, and no context for teaching the material. Others offered no more than cookie-cutter questions about content, style, and structure. The instructor's manuals that accompanied these texts seemed to us no better. They typically supplied the one "correct" answer to each question and occasionally suggested a possible interpretation of an essay. Regardless of their approach, few readers did much to engage students or instructors.

We—like you—expect (and believe we are entitled to) more than such readers offer. We expect compelling reading selections that engage both instructors and students in a spirited dialogue. We also expect selections that reflect the cultural diversity that characterizes our schools and our society. We expect writers to speak in distinctive voices, to treat issues that concern us deeply, and to use language that challenges and provokes us. In addition, we expect questions that ask not "What does this mean?" but "What does this mean *to you*?" In short, we expect a book that stimulates discussion and encourages students to see new ideas and to see familiar ideas from new perspectives.

These expectations led us to the decision to assemble a reader that would not push the same old buttons—for us or for our students. This decision did not mean, though, that we wanted to overwhelm instructors with flavor-of-the-month gimmicks masquerading as pedagogy, or readings that were so idiosyncratic as to be unteachable, or apparatus that had the intellectual depth of sound bites. What we wanted was a book that we could sink our teeth into, one that we could use as a resource. We think that this is the book we have created.

The Selections

We began *The Blair Reader* determined that the book would include the readings that composition instructors really enjoyed teaching. To accomplish this goal, we surveyed hundreds of instructors and asked them what essays they thought were the most readable and the most teachable. To their selections we added our favorite contemporary essays, fiction, and poetry. After assembling our table of contents, we had both essays and apparatus class tested by teachers all over the country. The result of this effort is a reader that contains 150 of the most readable and teachable essays, stories, and poems—many by minorities, women, and writers from other cultures. Throughout the text, an "Authors-in-Depth" feature spotlights five distinguished writers—Annie Dillard, Joan Didion, Stephen Jay Gould, George Orwell, and Alice Walker—enabling students to see a single author's range of styles and treatment of a variety of subjects.

We arranged the readings in *The Blair Reader* into twelve large thematic units ("Reading and Writing," "Thinking and Learning," "A Sense of the Past," "Nature and the Environment," "Making Choices," and so on). These broad thematic groupings, representing subjects requested most often by composition instructors, are diverse enough to allow plenty of options yet focused enough for meaningful discussion and writing. In addition, we provided at the back of the book a separate list of topical clusters of readings that focus on the narrower issues. Within these clusters, we included some selections that speak directly to each other (such as John Hope Franklin's response to The Declaration of Independence in "The Moral Legacy of the Founding Fathers") and others that exchange ideas indirectly (such as Norman Cousins's and Joyce Carol Oates's analyses of boxing and Paul Fussell's and Shelby Steele's discussions of class in the United States). Thus the book's flexible organizing scheme provides many options for reading and writing and suggests a variety of alternative perspectives from which to view an issue.

The selections in *The Blair Reader* represent a variety of rhetorical patterns and many different types of discourse. In addition to essays, *The Blair Reader* contains speeches, meditations, journalistic pieces, short stories, and poems. The level of diction ranges from the relaxed formality of E. B. White's "Once More to the Lake" to the biting satire of Marge Piercy's "The Secretary Chant." Every effort has been made, too, to include a wide variety of voices, because we believe that the only way students can discover their own voices is by becoming acquainted with the voices of others.

Resources for Students

We designed the apparatus in *The Blair Reader* to engage students and to encourage them to react to what they read. Their reactions can then become the basis for more focused thinking and writing. In order to facilitate this process, we included the following special features:

- An **Introduction** to the entire book discusses the interactive process of reading and writing that helps students formulate varied and original responses.

- **Chapter Introductions** place each thematic unit in a more immediate social or political context, highlighting a specific idea or issue with which students can connect.

- **"Preparing to Read and Write" Questions** at the end of each chapter introduction help students to sharpen their intellectual and emotional reactions to individual selections in the context of the chapter's larger issues.

- **Headnotes** that accompany each selection provide useful biographical information and often offer insight into the writer's motivation or purpose.

- **"Responding to Reading" Questions** that follow each selection engage students on a personal level so that they have incentive to write about the ideas they have encountered. At the same time, these questions encourage students to respond critically to the material they have read. By asking students to move beyond the level of reading essays simply for facts or information, the "Responding to Reading" questions help them realize that reading is an interactive and intellectually stimulating process and that they have something valuable to contribute.

- **Writing Suggestions** at the end of each chapter ask students to respond in writing to the various ideas they have encountered. These questions encourage students to explore relationships among readings and to connect readings to their own lives.

Resources for Instructors

Because we wanted *The Blair Reader* to be a rich and comprehensive resource for instructors, we developed an **Annotated Instructor's Edition**. This annotated edition, designed to serve as a useful and accessible classroom companion, assembles teaching techniques drawn from our more than twenty years in the classroom; reactions of our own students to the essays, stories, and poems; and approaches to the material developed by Michael Moran and the graduate teaching assistants at the University of Georgia, one of the composition programs in which the book was class tested.

In addition to the full student text, the Annotated Instructor's Edition includes the following features:

- **Confronting the Issues**, an interactive classroom exercise at the beginning of each chapter designed to heighten student awareness of the social and political issues related to the chapter's theme.

- **For Openers**, a provocative strategy for encouraging a dialogue about each selection.

- **Teaching Strategies**, innovative suggestions for eliciting responses to readings and stimulating class discussions.

- **Collaborative Activities**, group activities that enable students to develop insight and understanding by exchanging ideas with others.

- **Background on Readings and Authors**, additional information about the author or the context of a reading.

- **Suggested Answers to Responding to Reading Questions**

- **Additional Responding to Reading Questions**, alternate questions for those instructors who want more editorial apparatus than the book includes.

- **Writing Suggestions**, engaging writing topics for every essay, story, and poem in the book.

We encourage you to use the Annotated Instructor's Edition to complement your own proven strategies. We also encourage you to let us know your reactions to the Annotated Instructor's Edition and your suggestions for making it better. We are especially interested in hearing about classroom strategies that you use successfully and reading selections that have consistently appealed to your students. In future editions of the Annotated Instructor's Edition, we would like to include these suggestions along with the names of the individuals who submitted them. Just write us in care of Blair Press (The Statler Building, 20 Park Plaza, Suite 1113, Boston, MA 02116), and we will personally respond to your letters.

Acknowledgments

The Blair Reader is the result of a fruitful collaboration between the two of us, between us and our students, between us and Blair Press, and between us and you—our colleagues who told us what you wanted in a reader. Because we worked so closely with so many generous people, we have a long list of thank yous.

First, we wish to express our gratitude to Nancy Perry for doing her usual thorough, professional job—and for somehow always managing to see both the forest and the trees. Also at Blair Press, we want to thank Leslie "grace under pressure" Arndt, who always knew where everything was. At Prentice Hall, we thank Phil Miller and Kate Morgan for their support for the project and Ann Knitel for coordinating the Annotated Instructor's Edition. We are especially grateful for the contributions of Michael Moran, Director of Composition at the University of Georgia, and his graduate teaching assistants—Robert Croft, Suzanne Gilbert, Russell Greer, Karen Radford, and Kristine Sieloff—which helped make the Annotated Instructor's Edition the rich collection of resources that it is. We also appreciate the organizational skills of Geraldine McGowan of Editorial Services of New England, who guided the book through production. Finally, we would like once again to thank the reference and interlibrary loan staff at the Joseph W. England Library of the Philadelphia College of Pharmacy and Science—particularly Leslie Bowman, Sue Brizuela, Susan Joseph, Kathleen Smith, Carol Tang, and Robert Woodley—

for their patience and imagination in tracking down readings and information for headnotes and footnotes.

In creating *The Blair Reader*, we benefited at every stage from the assistance and suggestions of colleagues from across the country. We extend our thanks to the hundreds of instructors who responded to our original survey. Space does not permit us to list them all by name, but we are nonetheless grateful for their advice. We would like to thank, too, the many instructors who reviewed the manuscript or tried out chapters in their classrooms: Lynn Dianne Beene, University of New Mexico; Robinson Blann, Trevecca Nazarene College; Lisa Cohen, University of Georgia; Patricia E. Connors, Memphis State University; George A. Cox, North Carolina State University; Dawn Daemon, North Carolina State University; Robert W. Funk, Eastern Illinois University; Lauren M. Jones, North Carolina State University; Frank Kelley, University of Houston—University Park; Michelle LeBeau, University of New Mexico; Janet Madden-Simpson, El Camino College; Robert Mayberry, University of Nevada—Las Vegas; Ruth Meyers, Wichita State University; Susan J. Miller, Santa Fe Community College; Betty Mitchell, Southern Illinois University; Michael G. Moran, University of Georgia; Robert G. Noreen, California State University—Northridge; Kathleen O'Fallon, Butler University; Edward A. Shannon, North Carolina State University; Kathleen Shannon, North Carolina State University; Agatha Taormina, Northern Virginia Community College; Ronald Tranquilla, Saint Vincent College; Elizabeth Ruth Webb, Memphis State University; Lana White, West Texas State University; William F. Woods, Wichita State University; and William Young, Lynchburg College. *The Blair Reader* is a better book because of their contributions.

On the home front, we once again round up the usual suspects to thank—Mark, Adam, and Rebecca Kirszner and Demi, David, and Sarah Mandell. And, of course, we thank each other: It really has been "a beautiful friendship."

Laurie G. Kirszner
Stephen R. Mandell

CONTENTS

♦   AUTHOR IN DEPTH

CHAPTER 10   SCIENCE AND MEDICINE   834

CHAPTER 11   NATURE AND THE ENVIRONMENT   934

CHAPTER 12 MAKING CHOICES 1002

THE
BLAIR
READER

Introduction to Reading and Writing

READING TEXTS

In some ways being in college is like visiting a country that you have never seen before. You make new, interesting observations, and, if you are lucky, you even make some unexpected and exciting discoveries. Throughout your years at college you are exposed to new worlds of ideas—some from conversations with your friends, others from instructors, but most from the books and articles you read. In spite of predictions to the contrary, reading has not been overwhelmed by new technologies like computers, laser disks, and digital tape. In fact, it seems to be alive and well in American colleges and universities. It is safe to say, therefore, that, without reading, much of what we call education simply would not take place.

Reading is an activity that seems simple enough. After all, you have been doing it for years. Even so, it makes sense to examine what many students mean when they say they are going to "read." Much of the reading they do is assigned. For example, students will be asked to read a chapter of a textbook written by an expert in a particular field of study. Typically, they will approach such texts by looking for the writer's main ideas. Once they figure out what the writer is trying to say, they may mark key passages in the text or even jot down a few notes. Whether the text is concerned with modern American poetry, principles of corporate management, or quantum mechanics, the students' goal is the same: to search for specific information.

In addition to reading textbooks, students also read essays, fiction, and poetry. These forms present their own challenges. With these, you read not just to acquire information but also to discover your own ideas about the text: what it means to you, how you react

1

to it, why you react as you do, and how your reactions differ from the responses of other readers.

When you read a textbook, you assume its ideas will be accessible, free of ambiguity, and easily retrievable. If the book is clearly written and organized, these expectations will be met. But reading essays, fiction, and poetry is not usually this straightforward. Because these have no one true "meaning," your role as a reader must be more active than it is when you read a textbook. Even so, the difference between textbooks and essays, fiction, and poetry is primarily one of degree. All texts—that is, all of the things you read—are open to interpretation.

Like many readers, you may assume that the meaning of a text is hidden somewhere between the lines and that if you only ask the right questions or unearth the appropriate clues, you will be able to discover exactly what the writer is getting at. But reading is not a game of hide-and-seek in which you must find ideas that have been hidden by the writer. This way of thinking incorrectly assumes that the author is in complete control of the words on the page and that the only "correct" meaning of a text is the one that the author intended. It also assumes that there *is* only one "correct meaning." As current reading theory demonstrates, this model oversimplifies the reading process by failing to recognize the complex interaction that takes place between a reader and a text.

READING AND MEANING

Current models of reading hold that meaning is not contained within a text but is rather created by the interaction of a reader with a text. In other words, readers *actively* create meanings as they read. The easiest way to explain this concept is to draw an analogy between a text and an individual word. A word is not the natural equivalent of the thing it signifies. *Dog*, for example, does not call forth the image of a furry, four-legged animal in all parts of the world. In Spain the word *perro* has the same power to elicit a mental picture as *dog* does in English-speaking countries. Not only does the word *dog* have meaning only in a specific cultural context, but it also evokes different images in different people. Some people may picture a collie, others a poodle, and still others a specific dog that they owned when they were children. Moreover, in some cultural contexts a word from another culture may have no equivalent. How, for example, can you translate *simpatico* from Spanish into English? Loosely speaking, the word means "pleasing" or "compatible," but it also implies much more; therefore, it has no exact English equivalent.

Like an individual word, a text can have different meanings in different cultures—or even in different historical time periods. Each reader brings to the text associations that come from the cultural community in which he or she lives. These associations are determined by experience and education as well as by ethnic group, class, religion, gender, and many other factors that contribute to the way in which a person views the world. A reader also brings to the text a host of expectations, desires, and prejudices—to say nothing of a knowledge of literature—that influence how he or she reacts to and interprets it. Therefore, it is entirely possible for two readers to have very different, yet equally valid, interpretations of the same text.

In "Once More to the Lake" E. B. White tells a story about his visit to a lake in Maine. White compares a visit he made with his father in 1904 to one he made much later with his own son. Throughout the essay the changes that have occurred since White was there as a boy frustrate his desire to "revisit old haunts." Memories from the past flood his consciousness and lead him to remember things he did when he was a boy. At one point, after he and his son have been feeding worms to fish, he remembers doing the same thing with his father and has trouble separating the past from the present. As a result, White realizes that he will soon be just a memory in his son's mind—as his father is just a memory in his.

As he wrote his essay, White had certain specific goals in mind. His title, "Once More to the Lake," indicates that he intended to compare his childhood and adult visits to the lake. The organization of ideas in the essay and the use of flashbacks and transitional phrases reinforce this structure. In addition, imagery—such as the tarred road that replaced the dirt road—reminds readers, as well as the narrator, that the years have made the lake site different from what it once was. The essay ends not on an idyllic note but with the image of the son standing on the dock in cold, dripping bathing trunks and the father suddenly feeling the "chill of death."

Despite White's intentions, each person reading "Once More to the Lake" will respond to it differently. Male readers might identify with the boy in the essay. If they have ever spent a summer vacation camping, they might have experienced the "peace and goodness and jollity" of the whole summer scene. Female readers might also want to share these experiences, but they might feel excluded because only males are described in the essay. Urban readers who have never been on a camping trip might not feel the same nostalgia for the woods that White feels. To them camping in the woods away from the comforts of home might seem to be an unthinkably uncomfortable ordeal. Older readers might identify with White. They might sympathize with his efforts to recapture the past and see his son as naively innocent of the hardships of life.

Thus although each person who reads White's essay will read the same words, each will be likely to *interpret* it differently and to see different things as important. This is because much is left open to interpretation. All essays leave *blanks* or *gaps*—missing words, phrases, or images—that readers have to fill in. In "Once More to the Lake," for example, readers must imagine what happened in the years that separated the narrator's last visit to the lake and the trip he takes with his son.

In addition to gaps, texts also contain *ambiguities*—words, phrases, descriptions, or ideas so broad that they need to be interpreted by the reader. For instance, when you read the words "One summer, along about 1904, my father rented a camp on a lake," how do you picture the camp? When White describes the setting, he paints a picture that contains a great deal of detail. No matter how many sensory impressions he conveys, however, he cannot begin to provide a complete verbal representation of the specific area he visited. He must rely on the reader's ability to visualize the setting and supply details from his or her own experience.

Readers also bring their own *emotional associations* to individual words. For example, how readers react to White's statement above depends, in part, on their reactions to the word *father*. Does this word bring to mind a parent who is loving, strong, protective, and considerate, or one who is distant, bad-tempered, excitable, or even abusive?

In more general terms, each reader may see a different *emphasis* in "Once More to the Lake." Some might see nature as the primary element in the essay and believe that White's purpose is to condemn the gradual encroachment of human beings on the environment. Others might see the passage of time as the central focus. Still others might see the initiation theme as being the most important element of the essay: Each boy is brought to the wilderness by his father, and each eventually passes from childhood innocence to adulthood.

Finally, each reader may *evaluate* the essay differently. Some readers might think "Once More to the Lake" is impossibly boring because it has little action and deals with a subject in which they have no interest. Others might believe the essay is a brilliant meditation that makes an impact through vivid description and a highly imaginative use of figurative language. Still others might see the essay as a mixed bag—admitting, for example, that although White is an excellent stylist, he is also self-centered and self-indulgent. After all, the experiences he describes are available only in certain relatively privileged segments of society and are irrelevant to those who must struggle every day with unemployment, discrimination, or poverty. Beyond the denotative meaning of words on a page, then, an essay, short story, or poem will elicit different responses and different judgments from its readers.

THINKING CRITICALLY

Your awareness of the reader's role in creating meaning should help you see the need to develop a reading strategy. Think of reading as a dialogue—one that takes place between you and the text. Sometimes the author will assert himself or herself, and at other times you will dominate the conversation. Knowing that your voice enters into the dialogue should encourage you to open your mind to a text's possibilities. As you read, try asking questions like the ones that follow. They will help you to become aware of the relationships that exist between the text's perspective and your view of the world.

What audience does the writer address? Does the work itself offer any clues to this audience? In "Who Killed Benny Paret?" for example, Norman Cousins seems to address an audience that takes the sport of boxing for granted and does not see it as brutal or extremely dangerous. The title, the word choice, and the lurid descriptions of what happens in the ring clearly indicate that Cousins is trying to shock this audience out of its complacency.

What emotional response is the writer trying to evoke? In "The Stolen Party," Liliana Heker uses the poignant story of a young girl to suggest the insidiousness of the class structure in Argentina. Throughout the story Heker supports her point by eliciting sympathy for the child.

What is the writer's purpose? For example, is he or she attempting to explain, persuade, justify, evaluate, suggest, describe, entertain, preach, browbeat, threaten, or frighten? What strategies does the writer use to achieve this purpose? Is the writer, like Gary Snyder in "Mother Earth: Her Whales," trying to move people to action? Does the writer use logic, emotion, or a combination of the two to achieve his or her end? Does the writer appeal to the prejudices or fears of readers, engage in name calling, or in any other way attempt to influence readers unfairly?

Does the text display any ideology or bias? Just a quick glance at the title of Barbara Tuchman's "The Persistence of Unwisdom in Government," for example, reveals her bias; similarly, W. H. Auden clearly conveys a bias against modern technology when, in "Moon Landing," he expresses a wish that the astronauts had never landed on the moon. Keep in mind, however, that a bias or ideology does not automatically render a work's ideas invalid. A work may express ideas that have been shaped by a writer's geographical, cultural, religious, historical, or ethnic context. This helps to explain why ideas that are considered shocking or absurd in one historical time and place are readily accepted in another. Virginia Woolf strikingly illustrates this discrepancy in "If Shakespeare Had a Sister" when she compares the roles of male and female writers in Elizabethan England. Rather than limiting or discouraging you, the realization that the essays and stories you read have certain built-in biases should enable you to understand them more fully and to place them in their larger cultural and historical context.

What kind of voice does the writer use? Is the writer close to his or her subject? Does the writer seem to talk directly to you? Does the writer's subjectivity get in the way, or does it have a positive effect on you? Is the writer distant or formal? Is the writer's tone appropriate for his or her subject?

What beliefs, assumptions, or habits of thought do you have that color your response to a work? Do you have any ideas that you accept as "natural" but that the writer is challenging? For example, does Garrett Hardin's stand in "Lifeboat Ethics: The Case Against Helping the Poor" that we should not attempt to help the poor shock you or violate your sense of fair play? Does the fact that you do not like baseball prevent you from appreciating the perspective of the essay "Fathers, Daughters, and the Magic of Baseball?" Is the writer like or unlike you in terms of age, ethnic background, and social class? How do the similarities or differences affect your reaction to the work?

What experiences have you had that enable you to understand or interpret the text? Do these experiences give you any special insights? In one class, two students discussing "The Fear of Losing a Culture" by Richard Rodriguez had very different responses. An Anglo student said he did not understand why Rodriguez felt that he was in danger of losing his culture. After all, he argued, Rodriguez is an American. Another student, born in Mexico City and now living in a U.S. suburb, said she agreed with Richard Rodriguez and expressed great concern that she and her brother were being cut off from their roots. She told the class how, like Rodriguez, she had felt alone when she first entered an American school and could not speak English. She could not tell her problems to her teacher or to her parents because she thought that neither would understand. Eventually things got better, but she still felt as if she had one foot in each culture and that she was not fully a part of either. Her unique cultural perspective enabled her to explain in highly personal and compelling terms the frustration Rodriguez expresses in his essay.

What kind of support does the writer use? Does the writer use a series of individual examples, as Robin Lakoff does in "You Are What You Say," or an extended example, as E. B. White does in "Once More to the Lake?" Does the writer use statistics, as Carolyn Bird does in "College Is a Waste of Time and Money," or personal anecdotes, as Brent Staples does in "Just Walk on By?" Does he or she use quotations by experts, as Jessica Mitford does in "The American Way of Death," or informal conversation, as Lorrie Moore does in "How to Become a Writer"? Why does the writer choose a particular kind of support? Does the writer supply enough evidence to support his or her assertions? Is the evidence relevant to the issues being discussed? Are the writer's concerns valid, or do they seem forced or unrealistic? Are any references in the work unfamiliar to you? If so, do they arouse your curiosity or discourage you?

RECORDING YOUR REACTIONS

As you read and reread, you interact with a text and develop ideas that will help you interpret it. You should read a work at least twice: the first time to get a general sense of the ideas suggested by the text and the second to think critically about them. As you read, you should record your responses, because if you do not, you will forget many of your best ideas. Two activities can help you keep a record of the insights you gain as you read: *highlighting*—using a system of symbols and underlining to identify key ideas—and *annotating*—writing down your responses and interpretations. These techniques helped a student interpret the poem on page 8. The combination of highlighting and annotating helped the student identify Mora's key assumptions, make connections, and eventually arrive at her own conclusions. She underlined key ideas of the poem, used arrows to show the relationship of one idea to another, and wrote down definitions of unfamiliar words, phrases, and names (*sonrisas, tamales,* and *mucho ruido*). Finally, she recorded questions that she could expand on later in her writing.

When you react to a text, you should not be afraid to go against the grain of a text and challenge its assumptions. As you read and make annotations, you might find that you are bothered by or disagree with some of the ideas within the text. Do not ignore these misgivings. Jot your responses down in the margin of the text and later try to analyze them. These ideas may be the beginning of a thought process that will lead you to an original insight—and an interesting piece of writing. You could, for example, read Martin Luther King, Jr.'s "Letter

[handwritten annotation: 2 cultures? Anglo vs Mexican-American?]

SONRISAS *[handwritten: ⟩ smiles]*

I live in a doorway

between two rooms, I hear

quiet clicks, cups of black

coffee, *click, click* like facts   *[handwritten: ? College]*

[handwritten: Instructors?] budgets, tenure, curriculum,

from careful women in crisp beige

suits, quick beige smiles

that seldom sneak into their eyes.

I peek   *[handwritten: Why "peek"?]*

in the other room señoras

in faded dresses stir sweet   *[handwritten: Poor?]*

[handwritten: Sweet vs bitter] milk coffee, laughter whirls

with steam from fresh *tamales* *[handwritten: ⟩ Food]*

  sh, sh, mucho ruido, *[handwritten: ⟩ "Too much noise"]*

they scold one another,

press their lips, trap smiles

in their dark, Mexican eyes.

Pat Mora

from Birmingham Jail" and think that King is being too easy on his opposition. You might ask why he takes such pains to placate individuals who want to maintain a segregated society. You may feel that King should have aggressively condemned these individuals instead of trying to calm their fears. As you record your responses, however, you may also begin to think about the social, political, and racial contexts of King's ideas. As a result, you may decide that his ability to respond to his opponents was severely limited by the type of society in which he lived.

READING TO WRITE

Much of the reading you will do will prepare you for writing. Writing helps you focus your ideas about particular issues; the process of writing can lead you in new and interesting directions and enable you to discover unexpected insights. In fact, the most rewarding way to examine a particular text is not just to read and think about it but also to write about it. This book has a number of special features that can help you in this endeavor.

The readings in the book are arranged thematically, with each chapter providing a number of vantage points from which to view a theme. Short fiction and poetry further expand the theme, enabling you to become acquainted with a range of intellectual perspectives. Throughout the book, the work of five writers—Joan Didion, Annie Dillard, Stephen Jay Gould, George Orwell, and Alice Walker—is presented in depth, with several selections by each. (Essays by these writers are indicated in the table of contents by an ◆.) This Authors-in-Depth feature enables you to consider how a writer adapts his or her voice and style to different subjects, audiences, and purposes.

Each chapter in the book has a brief introduction that provides a context for the theme being discussed. Following each introduction are "Preparing to Read and Write" questions designed to guide your thinking about the essays, short stories, and poems in the chapter. These questions encourage you to see the readings from many different angles and thus enable you to sharpen your critical skills and apply them in a way that will become natural to you as you become accustomed to reading in an academic environment.

Following each reading selection is a series of questions designed to help you think about and respond—in discussion and perhaps in writing—to what you have read. These "Responding to Reading" questions focus on the reader's side of the interaction, encouraging you to make personal connections with the writer's ideas or to reexamine your own values and beliefs. In "A Life for a Life: What That Means Today," for example, Margaret Mead says that capital punishment makes "a cold mockery of our very real concern for human rights and our serious efforts to bring peace . . . among nations." A question following this essay asks you to consider your own thoughts about capital punishment in light of the concern the United States expresses for human rights violations in other countries.

You should consider keeping a record of your responses to these questions—as well as any other ideas you get as you read and highlight each selection—in a writing journal. Your journal will not only help you maintain a record of your reactions but will also serve as a sourcebook for ideas that you can use later in your writing.

Concluding each chapter are writing suggestions that expand upon the ideas developed by the "Preparing to Read and Write" and "Responding to Reading" questions. Writing suggestions are designed to further the interaction between reader and text: they invite you to relate the chapter's theme to your own experiences and encourage you to make connections among different works in the chapter.

As you read the selections in this book and write about the ideas they suggest, remember that you are learning ways of thinking about yourself and the world. By considering and reconsidering the ideas of others, by rejecting easy answers and set conclusions, by considering a problem from many different angles, and by appreciating the many factors that can influence and determine your responses, you develop critical thinking skills that will shape the ideas you will use throughout your life. In addition, you participate in an ongoing conversation that has been taking place for centuries within the community of scholars and writers who care deeply about the issues that shape our world.

1

READING AND WRITING
AS DISCOVERY

CONFRONTING THE ISSUES

Some students may have difficulty understanding the fuss the writers in this section make about reading and writing. Today, when the written word seems to have been devalued by advertising, television, and movies, students may find it hard to understand that there are some ideas to which only reading and writing can provide access. For this reason, students are not likely to see books as having an almost magical power to open doors to new worlds. They may also have difficulty understanding how reading and writing can empower oppressed or disadvantaged people.

To help students understand the way reading and writing can not only give pleasure but also enlighten and inspire, divide the class into groups of three or four students. Ask each group to read a different pair of selections from the following list:

- "Learning to Read and Write" and "The Joys of Reading"
- "The Library Card" and "From the Poets in the Kitchen"
- "On Keeping a Notebook" and "How to Become a Writer"
- "The Library Card" and "A Summer's Reading"
- "Why I Write" and "One Writer's Beginnings"
- "Saving the Life That Is Your Own" and "Why I Write"
- "Learning to Read and Write" and "Why I Write"

As they read, have students imagine a dialogue between each pair of writers (or between a writer and a character or speaker). What could each learn from the other? How would each writer react to the other's ideas? What would each find startling? Exciting? Challenging? Upsetting? Subversive? Where might a writer react with disbelief? Anger? Envy? Sympathy? Why?

"I lived in Master Hugh's family about seven years. During this time, I succeeded in learning to read and write." With these words Frederick Douglass, former slave, abolitionist, and statesman, begins the chapter of his autobiography in which he describes how he learned to read and write. To many of us, learning these skills was as natural as breathing and eating, but to Douglass it marked the beginning of his transformation from a slave into an individual who was able to chart his own destiny. Like Douglass, the other writers in this section recall the empowerment they felt when they discovered the ideas that books opened up to them. In some cases enlightenment came when an individual discovered the library, as it did for Richard Wright; in other cases it came as a result of keeping a notebook, as it did for Joan Didion. Reading and writing gave these writers the skills with which to analyze, judge, and perhaps even reject the complex cultures in which they lived.

For other writers coming into contact with literature—even in a cursory way—is profoundly disconcerting. In the story "A Summer's Reading," for example, Bernard Malamud tells about a young man who lies about reading only to find that by doing so he has inadvertently changed the course of his life. Lorrie Moore writes a rather droll set of instructions that illustrate the pain and sacrifice that are part of becoming a writer.

Perhaps the most important idea expressed by writers represented in this chapter is that reading—and eventually writing—gives individuals access to realms previously unknown to them. Both Alice Walker in "Saving the Life That Is Your Own" and Paule Marshall in "From the Poets in the Kitchen," for example, describe the thrill of discovering African-American writers who enabled them to dream that perhaps one day they too could write about their lives and their culture.

The common thread that runs through all the selections in this chapter is the idea that reading and writing, because they have the power to so deeply affect those who engage in them, are potentially subversive activities. Even as these activities enable us to unlock our deepest thoughts, they also challenge the assumptions that many of us accept as true. Great writing encourages us to reject the commonplace and the clichéd and to read with a conscious awareness of the influences of language, history, and culture on our ideas.

PREPARING TO READ AND WRITE

As you read and prepare to write about the selections in this chapter, consider the following questions:

- How does reading change the writer's or character's view of himself or herself? Of society?

- In what ways are the writer's new viewpoints different from his or her former ones? Are the changes positive or negative?

- In what way does the writer's society play a part in shaping his or her ideas about literature and writing?

- Does the writer distinguish between the literature of his or her culture and that of another culture?

- If the writer is from another culture, do his or her ideas about reading and writing differ from yours?

- What function does the selection suggest writing should serve? For example, should writing serve any political ends? Is it a form of education?

- Do you think the selection overstates (or understates) the value of literature?

- According to the selection, what motivates reading? Writing?

- Can you recall any experiences you had that were similar to any of those described in this chapter?

- What audience do you think the writer is aiming at? Do you think the writer's arguments about the value of writing and reading would appeal to his or her audience regardless of ethnic or religious background?

Learning to Read and Write

FREDERICK DOUGLASS

Frederick Douglass (1818–1895)—editor, author, lecturer, U.S. minister to Haiti—was born a slave in agricultural Maryland and later served a family in Baltimore. In the city, he had opportunities for personal improvement—and the luck to escape to the North in 1838. He settled in New Bedford, Massachusetts, where he became active in the abolitionist movement. In 1845, Douglass wrote his most famous work, *Narrative of the Life of Frederick Douglass*. Like other such narratives, extensions of the storytelling oratory and drama of former slaves in the abolitionist movement, it was distributed to large and diverse audiences. In the following excerpt from his *Narrative*, Douglass writes of outwitting his owners to become literate and find "the pathway from slavery to freedom."

I lived in Master Hugh's family about seven years. During this 1
time, I succeeded in learning to read and write. In accomplishing this, I was compelled to resort to various stratagems. I had no regular teacher. My mistress, who had kindly commenced to instruct me, had, in compliance with the advice and direction of her husband, not only ceased to instruct, but had set her face against my being instructed by any one else. It is due, however, to my mistress to say of her, that she did not adopt this course of treatment immediately. She at first lacked the depravity indispensable to shutting me up in mental darkness. It was at least necessary for her to have some training in the exercise of irresponsible power, to make her equal to the task of treating me as though I were a brute.

My mistress was, as I have said, a kind and tender-hearted woman; 2
and in the simplicity of her soul she commenced, when I first went to live with her, to treat me as she supposed one human being ought to treat another. In entering upon the duties of a slaveholder, she did not seem to perceive that I sustained to her the relation of a mere chattel,[1] and that for her to treat me as a human being was not only wrong, but dangerously so. Slavery proved as injurious to her as it did to me. When I went there, she was a pious, warm, and tender-hearted woman. There was no sorrow or suffering for which she had not a tear. She had bread for the hungry, clothes for the naked, and comfort for every mourner that came within her reach. Slavery soon proved its ability to divest her of these heavenly qualities. Under its influence, the tender heart became stone, and the lamblike disposition gave way to one of

---

[1]Property. [Eds.]

tigerlike fierceness. The first step in her downward course was in her ceasing to instruct me. She now commenced to practise her husband's precepts. She finally became even more violent in her opposition than her husband himself. She was not satisfied with simply doing as well as he had commanded; she seemed anxious to do better. Nothing seemed to make her more angry than to see me with a newspaper. She seemed to think that here lay the danger. I have had her rush at me with a face made all up of fury, and snatch from me a newspaper, in a manner that fully revealed her apprehension. She was an apt woman; and a little experience soon demonstrated, to her satisfaction, that education and slavery were incompatible with each other.

From this time I was most narrowly watched. If I was in a separate 3 room any considerable length of time, I was sure to be suspected of having a book, and was at once called to give an account of myself. All this, however, was too late. The first step had been taken. Mistress, in teaching me the alphabet, had given me the *inch*, and no precaution could prevent me from taking the *ell*.

The plan which I adopted, and the one by which I was most 4 successful, was that of making friends of all the little white boys whom I met in the street. As many of these as I could, I converted into teachers. With their kindly aid, obtained at different times and in different places, I finally succeeded in learning to read. When I was sent on errands, I always took my book with me, and by going one part of my errand quickly, I found time to get a lesson before my return. I used also to carry bread with me, enough of which was always in the house, and to which I was always welcome; for I was much better off in this regard than many of the poor white children in our neighborhood. This bread I used to bestow upon the hungry little urchins, who, in return, would give me that more valuable bread of knowledge. I am strongly tempted to give the names of two or three of those little boys, as a testimonial of the gratitude and affection I bear them; but prudence forbids;—not that it would injure me, but it might embarrass them; for it is almost an unpardonable offence to teach slaves to read in this Christian country. It is enough to say of the dear little fellows, that they lived on Philpot Street, very near Durgin and Bailey's ship-yard. I used to talk this matter of slavery over with them. I would sometimes say to them, I wished I could be as free as they would be when they got to be men. "You will be free as soon as you are twenty-one, *but I am a slave for life!* Have not I as good a right to be free as you have?" These words used to trouble them; they would express for me the liveliest sympathy, and console me with the hope that something would occur by which I might be free.

I was now about twelve years old, and the thought of being *a* 5 *slave for life* began to bear heavily upon my heart. Just about this

ADDITIONAL QUESTIONS FOR RESPONDING TO READING

1. Which "stratagems" of Douglass's proved most effective in helping him learn to read? Which were least effective? Why?
2. What books did Douglass read? How did they help him develop his ideas about the world?
3. Douglass says that slavery was as harmful to the slaveowner as to the slave. Do you agree? Why or why not?
4. The white boys on Philpot Street are sympathetic to Douglass. Is their sympathy sincere? Can someone who has not experienced slavery firsthand truly understand it?
5. Douglass seems to think that education is a basic human right. Do you agree? Why or why not?
6. Douglass writes with a distinctive, descriptive style. Find examples of the images he uses in describing the change in Mrs. Hugh, his dilemma upon realizing his condition as a slave, and his "stratagems" for learning to read.

TEACHING STRATEGIES

1. Discuss the background of slavery with students. Point out to them that slaveholders did not consider slaves human beings. In addition, let students know that slaves were thought to be incapable of learning or of embracing moral values. (To grant them these attributes would be to accept their humanness and thereby undercut the rationale for keeping them in bondage.) Throughout his life as a free man these attitudes haunted Douglass. Many contemporaries considered him a freak of nature, anomalous to what they knew to be the actual nature of enslaved African-Americans.

2. What is freedom? Can a person be free when he or she is in chains? How? When did Douglass become free? When he escaped to the North? Or earlier, when he achieved intellectual freedom?

time, I got hold of a book entitled "The Columbian Orator."[2] Every opportunity I got, I used to read this book. Among much of other interesting matter, I found in it a dialogue between a master and his slave. The slave was represented as having run away from his master three times. The dialogue represented the conversation which took place between them, when the slave was retaken the third time. In this dialogue, the whole argument in behalf of slavery was brought forward by the master, all of which was disposed of by the slave. The slave was made to say some very smart as well as impressive things in reply to his master—things which had the desired though unexpected effect; for the conversation resulted in the voluntary emancipation of the slave on the part of the master.

In the same book, I met with one of Sheridan's mighty speeches on and in behalf of Catholic emancipation.[3] These were choice documents to me. I read them over and over again with unabated interest. They gave tongue to interesting thoughts of my own soul, which had frequently flashed through my mind, and died away for want of utterance. The moral which I gained from the dialogue was the power of truth over the conscience of even a slaveholder. What I got from Sheridan was a bold denunciation of slavery, and a powerful vindication of human rights. The reading of these documents enabled me to utter my thoughts, and to meet the arguments brought forward to sustain slavery; but while they relieved me of one difficulty, they brought on another even more painful than the one of which I was relieved. The more I read, the more I was led to abhor and detest my enslavers. I could regard them in no other light than a band of successful robbers, who had left their homes, and gone to Africa, and stolen us from our homes, and in a strange land reduced us to slavery. I loathed them as being the meanest as well as the most wicked of men. As I read and contemplated the subject, behold! that very discontentment which Master Hugh had predicted would follow my learning to read had already come, to torment and sting my soul to unutterable anguish. As I writhed under it, I would at times feel that learning to read had been a curse rather than a blessing. It had given me a view of my wretched condition, without the remedy. It opened my eyes to the horrible pit, but to no ladder upon which to get out. In moments of agony, I envied my fellow-slaves for their stupidity. I have often

6

---

[2]A popular textbook that taught the principles of effective public speaking. [Eds.]

[3]Richard Brinsley Sheridan (1751–1816), British playwright and statesman who made speeches supporting the right of English Catholics to vote. Full emancipation was not granted to Catholics until 1829. [Eds.]

wished myself a beast. I preferred the condition of the meanest reptile to my own. Any thing, no matter what, to get rid of thinking! It was this everlasting thinking of my condition that tormented me. There was no getting rid of it. It was pressed upon me by every object within sight or hearing, animate or inanimate. The silver trump of freedom had roused my soul to eternal wakefulness. Freedom now appeared, to disappear no more forever. It was heard in every sound, and seen in every thing. It was ever present to torment me with a sense of my wretched condition. I saw nothing without seeing it, I heard nothing without hearing it, and felt nothing without feeling it. It looked from every star, it smiled in every calm, breathed in every wind, and moved in every storm.

I often found myself regretting my own existence, and wishing myself dead; and but for the hope of being free, I have no doubt but that I should have killed myself, or done something for which I should have been killed. While in this state of mind, I was eager to hear any one speak of slavery. I was a ready listener. Every little while, I could hear something about the abolitionists. It was some time before I found what the word meant. It was always used in such connections as to make it an interesting word to me. If a slave ran away and succeeded in getting clear, or if a slave killed his master, set fire to a barn, or did any thing very wrong in the mind of a slaveholder, it was spoken of as the fruit of *abolition*. Hearing the word in this connection very often, I set about learning what it meant. The dictionary afforded me little or no help. I found it was "the act of abolishing"; but then I did not know what was to be abolished. Here I was perplexed. I did not dare to ask any one about its meaning, for I was satisfied that it was something they wanted me to know very little about. After a patient waiting, I got one of our city papers, containing an account of the number of petitions from the north, praying for the abolition of slavery in the District of Columbia, and of the slave trade between the States. From this time I understood the words *abolition* and *abolitionist*, and always drew near when that word was spoken, expecting to hear something of importance to myself and fellow-slaves. The light broke in upon me by degrees. I went one day down on the wharf of Mr. Waters; and seeing two Irishmen unloading a scow of stone, I went, unasked, and helped them. When we had finished, one of them came to me and asked me if I were a slave. I told him I was. He asked, "Are ye a slave for life?" I told him that I was. The good Irishman seemed to be deeply affected by the statement. He said to the other that it was a pity so fine a little fellow as myself should be a slave for life. He said it was a shame to hold me. They both advised me to run away to the north; that I should find friends there, and that I should be free. I pretended not to be inter-

7

COLLABORATIVE ACTIVITY

Divide students into groups and ask them to retell Douglass's story of how he learned to read from one of the following perspectives: Mrs. Hugh, Mr. Hugh, Thomas Hugh, a fellow slave on the Hugh plantation, a freed slave after the Civil War, and Douglass himself (in one of his later autobiographies).

WRITING SUGGESTIONS

1. Write an essay in which you discuss the books that have changed the way you look at the world and at yourself.
2. Write an essay in which you examine how your life would be different if you could not read or write.
3. Both Frederick Douglass and Richard Wright ("The Library Card," page 26) used reading as a means of overcoming restrictions placed upon them by society. Write an essay in which you discuss a means you used to overcome restrictions placed on you by society.

ested in what they said, and treated them as if I did not understand them; for I feared they might be treacherous. White men have been known to encourage slaves to escape, and then, to get the reward, catch them and return them to their masters. I was afraid that these seemingly good men might use me so; but I nevertheless remembered their advice, and from that time I resolved to run away. I looked forward to a time at which it would be safe for me to escape. I was too young to think of doing so immediately; besides, I wished to learn how to write, as I might have occasion to write my own pass. I consoled myself with the hope that I should one day find a good chance. Meanwhile, I would learn to write.

The idea as to how I might learn to write was suggested to me 8 by being in Durgin and Bailey's ship-yard, and frequently seeing the ship carpenters, after hewing, and getting a piece of timber ready for use, write on the timber the name of that part of the ship for which it was intended. When a piece of timber was intended for the larboard side, it would be marked thus—"L." When a piece was for the starboard side, it would be marked thus—"S." A piece for the larboard side forward, would be marked thus—"L. F." When a piece was for starboard side forward, it would be marked thus—"S. F." For larboard aft, it would be marked thus—"L.A." For starboard aft, it would be marked thus—"S. A." I soon learned the names of these letters, and for what they were intended when placed upon a piece of timber in the ship-yard. I immediately commenced copying them, and in a short time was able to make the four letters named. After that, when I met with any boy who I knew could write, I would tell him I could write as well as he. The next word would be, "I don't believe you. Let me see you try it." I would then make the letters which I had been so fortunate as to learn, and ask him to beat that. In this way I got a good many lessons in writing, which it is quite possible I should never have gotten in any other way. During this time, my copy-book was the board fence, brick wall, and pavement; my pen and ink was a lump of chalk. With these, I learned mainly how to write. I then commenced and continued copying the Italics in Webster's Spelling Book, until I could make them all without looking on the book. By this time, my little Master Thomas had gone to school, and learned how to write, and had written over a number of copy-books. These had been brought home, and shown to some of our near neighbors, and then laid aside. My mistress used to go to class meeting at the Wilk Street meetinghouse every Monday afternoon, and leave me to take care of the house. When left thus, I used to spend the time in writing in the spaces left in Master Thomas's copy-book, copying what he had written. I continued to do this until I could write a hand very similar to that of Master Thomas. Thus, after a long, tedious effort for years, I finally succeeded in learning how to write.

RESPONDING TO READING

1. Douglass escaped from slavery in 1838 and became a leading figure in the antislavery movement. In what ways did reading and writing help him form his ideas about slavery? Do you think it is fair to say that without reading and writing Douglass could not have developed his ideas?   **2.** Do you think education and slavery are compatible or incompatible? Why do you think slaveholders did not want slaves to learn to read and write?   **3.** What ideas about education does Douglass have that are different from yours? Which of his ideas have relevance for the society in which you live? How do you account for the similarities and differences between his ideas and yours?

One Writer's Beginnings

EUDORA WELTY

After beginning her career as a journalist and copywriter, Eudora Welty (1909–   ) soon turned to short stories and novels, writing about the people of her native Mississippi, where she has lived all her life, with familiarity, sensitivity, and a keen sense of place. During the Depression, she worked for the Works Progress Administration. The photographs she took of Southern rural poverty were later published in a book and exhibited at the Museum of Modern Art in New York City. Among Welty's novels are *The Robber Bridegroom* (1942), *Delta Wedding* (1946), and *The Optimist's Daughter* (1969). Her stories are in *The Collected Stories of Eudora Welty* (1980). "One Writer's Beginnings" is a chapter from the book of the same title, which Welty originally presented at Harvard University in 1983 as a series of lectures about the people and events that have influenced her literary life.

I learned from the age of two or three that any room in our house, at any time of day, was there to read in, or to be read to. My mother read to me. She'd read to me in the big bedroom in the mornings, when we were in her rocker together, which ticked in rhythm as we rocked, as though we had a cricket accompanying the story. She'd read to me in the diningroom on winter afternoons in front of the coal fire, with our cuckoo clock ending the story with "Cuckoo," and at night when I'd got in my own bed. I must have given her no peace. Sometimes she read to me in the kitchen while she sat churning, and

1

ANSWERS TO RESPONDING TO READING

1. Douglass's ideas about slavery were formed by his actual experiences with it, but learning to read and write made him aware of the possibilities of achieving freedom both physically and intellectually. Although Douglass knew slavery was wrong even before he learned to read and write, these skills focused his ideas and enabled him to become a powerful spokesperson for the abolitionist movement.

2. Because it makes a person aware of himself or herself as an individual with certain inherent rights, education is inimical to slavery. Slaveholders feared that slaves would organize and revolt if they were educated.

3. Answers will vary. Douglass's ideas are based on his experience as a slave and as someone who was deprived of an education. Many students, because they live in a society where education is universal, may feel that his ideas have no relevance to their world. Others may believe that people with disadvantages or handicaps may face similar struggles to Douglass's.

BACKGROUND ON READING

When published in book form in 1983, *One Writer's Beginnings* remained on the *New York Times* best-seller list for forty-six weeks. In this book, Welty explores the influences that made her a writer. The book has three chapters—"Listening," "Learning to See," and "Finding a Voice"—in which she explains how a growing understanding of time and point of view was crucial to her development.

FOR OPENERS

In "One Writer's Beginnings" Welty explains how her mother and father each passed unique gifts on to her. Ask the class to discuss their childhood literary influences. What unique gifts did their parents pass on to them?

ADDITIONAL QUESTIONS
FOR RESPONDING TO READING

1. Discuss your favorite childhood book characters. Why did they appeal to you? What you think you learned from them? Do they still appeal to you?

2. Did you ever misunderstand something as a child and carry that misunderstanding forward into your teen and adult years? How did you learn of your misconception?

3. Critic Hershel Brickell tells Welty, "Always be sure you get your moon in the right part of the sky." What does he mean, and what effect does his statement have on Welty's development as a writer?

the churning sobbed along with *any* story. It was my ambition to have her read to me while *I* churned; once she granted my wish, but she read off my story before I brought her butter. She was an expressive reader. When she was reading "Puss in Boots," for instance, it was impossible not to know that she distrusted *all* cats.

It had been startling and disappointing to me to find out that story books had been written by *people*, that books were not natural wonders, coming up of themselves like grass. Yet regardless of where they came from, I cannot remember a time when I was not in love with them—with the books themselves, cover and binding and the paper they were printed on, with their smell and their weight and with their possession in my arms, captured and carried off to myself. Still illiterate, I was ready for them, committed to all the reading I could give them.

Neither of my parents had come from homes that could afford to buy many books, but though it must have been something of a strain on his salary, as the youngest officer in a young insurance company, my father was all the while carefully selecting and ordering away for what he and Mother thought we children should grow up with. They bought first for the future.

Besides the bookcase in the livingroom, which was always called "the library," there were the encyclopedia tables and dictionary stand under windows in our diningroom. Here to help us grow up arguing around the diningroom table were the Unabridged Webster, the Columbia Encyclopedia, Compton's Pictured Encyclopedia, the Lincoln Library of Information, and later the Book of Knowledge. And the year we moved into our new house, there was room to celebrate it with the new 1925 edition of the Britannica, which my father, his face always deliberately turned toward the future, was of course disposed to think better than any previous edition.

In "the library," inside the mission-style bookcase with its three diamond-latticed glass doors, with my father's Morris chair and the glass-shaded lamp on its table beside it, were books I could soon begin on—and I did, reading them all alike and as they came, straight down their rows, top shelf to bottom. There was the set of Stoddard's Lectures, in all its late nineteenth-century vocabulary and vignettes of peasant life and quaint beliefs and customs, with matching halftone illustrations: Vesuvius erupting, Venice by moonlight, gypsies glimpsed by their campfires. I didn't know then the clue they were to my father's longing to see the rest of the world. I read straight through his other love-from-afar: the Victrola Book of the Opera, with opera after opera in synopsis, with portraits in costume of Melba, Caruso, Galli-Curci, and Geraldine Farrar, some of whose voices we could listen to on our Red Seal records.

My mother read secondarily for information; she sank as a hedo-   6
nist into novels. She read Dickens in the spirit in which she would
have eloped with him. The novels of her girlhood that had stayed on
in her imagination, besides those of Dickens and Scott and Robert
Louis Stevenson, were *Jane Eyre, Trilby, The Woman in White, Green
Mansions, King Solomon's Mines.* Marie Corelli's name would crop up
but I understood she had gone out of favor with my mother, who
had only kept *Ardath* out of loyalty. In time she absorbed herself in
Galsworthy, Edith Wharton, above all in Thomas Mann of the *Joseph*
volumes.

St. Elmo was not in our house; I saw it often in other houses. This   7
wildly popular Southern novel is where all the Edna Earles in our
population started coming from. They're all named for the heroine,
who succeeded in bringing a dissolute, sinning roué[1] and atheist of
a lover (St. Elmo) to his knees. My mother was able to forgo it. But
she remembered the classic advice given to rose growers on how to
water their bushes long enough: "Take a chair and *St. Elmo.*"

To both my parents I owe my early acquaintance with a beloved   8
Mark Twain. There was a full set of Mark Twain and a short set of
Ring Lardner in our bookcase, and those were the volumes that in
time united us all, parents and children.

Reading everything that stood before me was how I came upon   9
a worn old book without a back that had belonged to my father as a
child. It was called *Sanford and Merton.* Is there anyone left who recognizes it, I wonder? It is the famous moral tale written by Thomas
Day in the 1780s, but of him no mention is made on the title page of
this book; here it is *Sanford and Merton in Words of One Syllable* by Mary
Godolphin. Here are the rich boy and the poor boy and Mr. Barlow,
their teacher and interlocutor, in long discourses alternating with
dramatic scenes—danger and rescue allotted to the rich and the poor
respectively. It may have only words of one syllable, but one of them
is "quoth."[2] It ends with not one but two morals, both engraved on
rings: "Do what you ought, come what may," and "If we would be
great, we must first learn to be good."

This book was lacking its front cover, the back held on by strips   10
of pasted paper, now turned golden, in several layers, and the pages
stained, flecked, and tattered around the edges; its garish illustrations
had come unattached but were preserved, laid in. I had the feeling
even in my heedless childhood that this was the only book my father
as a little boy had had of his own. He had held onto it, and might

TEACHING STRATEGY

One of the more interesting ways to approach this selection is to study Welty's style, specifically her use of repetition, parallel structure, and imagery. After identifying examples of these strategies, ask students how they affect their response to the essay.

COLLABORATIVE ACTIVITY

Divide the class into groups and have them search the text for figurative language. How does Welty create figures of speech? Ask a spokesperson from each group to discuss the way Welty constructs and uses metaphors and similes and how they help her make her point.

have gone to sleep on its coverless face: he had lost his mother when he was seven. My father had never made any mention to his own children of the book, but he had brought it along with him from Ohio to our house and shelved it in our bookcase.

My mother had brought from West Virginia that set of Dickens; 11 those books looked sad, too—they had been through fire and water before I was born, she told me, and there they were, lined up—as I later realized, waiting for *me*.

I was presented, from as early as I can remember, with books of 12 my own, which appeared on my birthday and Christmas morning. Indeed, my parents could not give me books enough. They must have sacrificed to give me on my sixth or seventh birthday—it was after I became a reader for myself—the ten-volume set of Our Wonder World. These were beautifully made, heavy books I would lie down with on the floor in front of the diningroom hearth, and more often than the rest volume 5, *Every Child's Story Book*, was under my eyes. There were the fairy tales—Grimm, Andersen, the English, the French, "Ali Baba and the Forty Thieves"; and there was Aesop and Reynard the Fox; there were the myths and legends, Robin Hood, King Arthur, and St. George and the Dragon, even the history of Joan of Arc; a whack of *Pilgrim's Progress* and a long piece of *Gulliver*. They all carried their classic illustrations. I located myself in these pages and could go straight to the stories and pictures I loved; very often "The Yellow Dwarf" was first choice, with Walter Crane's Yellow Dwarf in full color making his terrifying appearance flanked by turkeys. Now that volume is as worn and backless and hanging apart as my father's poor *Sanford and Merton*. The precious page with Edward Lear's "Jumblies"[3] on it has been in danger of slipping out for all these years. One measure of my love for Our Wonder World was that for a long time I wondered if I would go through fire and water for it as my mother had done for Charles Dickens; and the only comfort was to think I could ask my mother to do it for me.

I believe I'm the only child I know of who grew up with this 13 treasure in the house. I used to ask others, "Did you have Our Wonder World?" I'd have to tell them The Book of Knowledge could not hold a candle to it.

I live in gratitude to my parents for initiating me—and as early 14 as I begged for it, without keeping me waiting—into knowledge of the word, into reading and spelling, by way of the alphabet. They taught it to me at home in time for me to begin to read before starting

---

[3]Lear (1812–88) wrote *Nonsense Songs, Stories, Botany and Alphabets* (1871), which contains "The Owl and the Pussy-Cat" and "The Jumblies," a long narrative poem about creatures who went to sea in a sieve. [Eds.]

to school. I believe the alphabet is no longer considered an essential piece of equipment for traveling through life. In my day it was the keystone to knowledge. You learned the alphabet as you learned to count to ten, as you learned "Now I lay me" and the Lord's Prayer and your father's and mother's name and address and telephone number, all in case you were lost.

My love for the alphabet, which endures, grew out of reciting it but, before that, out of seeing the letters on the page. In my own story books, before I could read them for myself, I fell in love with various winding, enchanting-looking initials drawn by Walter Crane at the heads of fairy tales. In "Once upon a time," an "O" had a rabbit running it as a treadmill, his feet upon flowers. When the day came, years later, for me to see the Book of Kells,[4] all the wizardry of letter, initial, and word swept over me a thousand times over, and the illumination, the gold, seemed a part of the word's beauty and holiness that had been there from the start.

Learning stamps you with its moments. Childhood's learning is made up of moments. It isn't steady. It's a pulse.

In a children's art class, we sat in a ring on kindergarten chairs and drew three daffodils that had just been picked out of the yard; and while I was drawing, my sharpened pencil and the cup of the yellow daffodil gave off whiffs just alike. That the pencil doing the drawing should give off the same smell as the flower it drew seemed a part of the art lesson—as shouldn't it be? Children, like animals, use all their senses to discover the world. Then artists come along and discover it the same way, all over again. Here and there, it's the same world. Or now and then we'll hear from an artist who's never lost it.

In my sensory education I include my physical awareness of the *word*. Of a certain word, that is; the connection it has with what it stands for. At around age six, perhaps, I was standing by myself in our front yard waiting for supper, just at that hour in a late summer day when the sun is already below the horizon and the risen full moon in the visible sky stops being chalky and begins to take on light. There comes the moment, and I saw it then, when the moon goes from flat to round. For the first time it met my eyes as a globe. The word "moon" came into my mouth as though fed to me out of a silver spoon. Held in my mouth the moon became a word. It had the roundness of a Concord grape Grandpa took off his vine and gave me to suck out of its skin and swallow whole, in Ohio.

15

16

17

18

---

[4]An eighth-to ninth-century manuscript of the four Gospels which contains magnificent colored illustrations consisting of intricate patterns made up of abstract and animal forms. [Eds.]

This love did not prevent me from living for years in foolish error 19 about the moon. The new moon just appearing in the west was the rising moon to me. The new should be rising. And in early childhood the sun and moon, those opposite reigning powers, I just as easily assumed rose in east and west respectively in their opposite sides of the sky, and like partners in a reel they advanced, sun from the east, moon from the west, crossed over (when I wasn't looking) and went down on the other side. My father couldn't have known I believed that when, bending behind me and guiding my shoulder, he positioned me at our telescope in the front yard and, with careful adjustment of the focus, brought the moon close to me.

The night sky over my childhood Jackson[5] was velvety black. I 20 could see the full constellations in it and call their names; when I could read, I knew their myths. Though I was always waked for eclipses, and indeed carried to the window as an infant in arms and shown Halley's Comet in my sleep, and though I'd been taught at our diningroom table about the solar system and knew the earth revolved around the sun, and our moon around us, I never found out the moon didn't come up in the west until I was a writer and Herschel Brickell, the literary critic, told me after I misplaced it in a story. He said valuable words to me about my new profession: "Always be sure you get your moon in the right part of the sky."

My mother always sang to her children. Her voice came out just 21 a little bit in the minor key. "Wee Willie Winkie's" song was wonderfully sad when she sang the lullabies.

"Oh, but now there's a record. She could have her own record 22 to listen to," my father would have said. For there came a Victrola record of "Bobby Shafftoe" and "Rock-a-Bye Baby," all of Mother's lullabies, which could be played to take her place. Soon I was able to play her my own lullabies all day long.

Our Victrola stood in the diningroom. I was allowed to climb onto 23 the seat of a diningroom chair to wind it, start the record turning, and set the needle playing. In a second I'd jumped to the floor, to spin or march around the table as the music called for—now there were all the other records I could play too. I skinned back onto the chair just in time to lift the needle at the end, stop the record and turn it over, then change the needle. That brass receptable with a hole in the lid gave off a metallic smell like human sweat, from all the hot needles that were fed it. Winding up, dancing, being cocked to start and stop the record, was of course all in one the act of *lis-*

WRITING SUGGESTIONS
1. Write an essay in which you discuss some books you read as a child and what they taught you about yourself.
2. Define Welty's concept of the reader-voice. How did she find it? Write an essay in which you discuss your reader-voice and how it is important to you as a writer.

[5]Welty grew up and continues to make her home in Jackson, Mississippi. [Eds.]

tening—to "Overture to *Daughter of the Regiment*," "Selections from *The Fortune Teller*," "Kiss Me Again," "Gypsy Dance from *Carmen*," "Stars and Stripes Forever," "When the Midnight Choo-Choo Leaves for Alabam," or whatever came next. Movement must be at the very heart of listening.

Ever since I was first read to, then started reading to myself, there has never been a line read that I didn't *hear*. As my eyes followed the sentence, a voice was saying it silently to me. It isn't my mother's voice, or the voice of any person I can identify, certainly not my own. It is human, but inward, and it is inwardly that I listen to it. It is to me the voice of the story or the poem itself. The cadence, whatever it is that asks you to believe, the feeling that resides in the printed word, reaches me through the reader-voice. I have supposed, but never found out, that this is the case with all readers—to read as listeners—and with all writers, to write as listeners. It may be part of the desire to write. The sound of what falls on the page begins the process of testing it for truth, for me. Whether I am right to trust so far I don't know. By now I don't know whether I could do either one, reading or writing, without the other. 24

My own words, when I am at work on a story, I hear too as they go, in the same voice that I hear when I read in books. When I write and the sound of it comes back to my ears, then I act to make my changes. I have always trusted this voice. 25

RESPONDING TO READING

1. Eudora Welty says she cannot remember a time when she was not in love with books. Describe your own youthful introduction to books and to reading. How does it compare with Welty's experience?   **2.** In paragraph 14 Welty says that, along with her parents, books initiated her into "knowledge of the world." What does she mean? Do other media—for example, newspapers and magazines—serve the same function for you that books do for Welty?   **3.** Why does Welty see reading as a writer's beginnings? What do you think reading has to do with becoming a writer? In what ways might the essays you are reading in this book help or hinder your effort to become a writer?

ANSWERS TO RESPONDING TO READING

1. Answers will vary. Some students will have no trouble with this question, whereas others will say that they do not feel the way Welty does about books. Introduce students to the idea of the life of the mind and illustrate how only books enable individuals to enter into the conversation that has been taking place between readers and writers for thousands of years.

2. Books give Welty her first glimpse of a reality beyond her own home. Even though modern media commonly serve this same function for children today, they do so in a watered-down, simplistic way. Because they are commercial entities, they tend to shy away from challenging comfortable preconceptions in a way that great books do not.

3. Reading begins the writer's engagement with words. All reading helps provide a model for developing writers, enabling them to define the connection that exists between themselves and the world.

The Library Card

RICHARD WRIGHT

Born on a plantation near Natchez, Mississippi, Richard Wright (1908–1960) spent much of his childhood in an orphanage or with various relatives. He moved to Chicago in 1934 and worked at various unskilled jobs before joining the Federal Writer's Project. Wright's politics became radical at this time, and he wrote poetry for leftist publications. In 1938 he published his first book, *Uncle Tom's Children: Four Novellas*. His 1940 novel *Native Son* made him famous. After World War II, Wright lived as an expatriate in Paris, where he wrote his autobiography, *Black Boy* (1945), a book that celebrates black resilience and courage much as nineteenth-century slave narratives do. In this excerpt from *Black Boy*, Wright tells how he took advantage of an opportunity to feed his hunger for an intellectual life.

FOR OPENERS

1. Have you ever felt isolated from a group? Describe the circumstances.
2. Are books pathways to other worlds? If so, is this sort of escapism positive or negative? Is the escapism books offer different from the escapism offered by television and films?
3. Can a person change inside without the world noticing the change?

ADDITIONAL QUESTIONS FOR RESPONDING TO READING

1. How do books make "the world look different" for Wright? Is the difference good or bad? Or is it both?
2. Wright's hunger for books is actually a deeper hunger for something else. What do you think he really wants?
3. Wright also feels isolated from his fellow blacks. How and why?
4. Wright writes of "the problem of being black." Is *this* a problem? If so, in what ways?
5. Wright includes several lengthy passages of dialogue. Are these more effective than more strictly narrative passages would be? Why or why not?

One morning I arrived early at work and went into the bank lobby where the Negro porter was mopping. I stood at a counter and picked up the Memphis *Commercial Appeal* and began my free reading of the press. I came finally to the editorial page and saw an article dealing with one H. L. Mencken.[1] I knew by hearsay that he was the editor of the *American Mercury*, but aside from that I knew nothing about him. The article was a furious denunciation of Mencken, concluding with one hot, short sentence: Mencken is a fool. 1

I wondered what on earth this Mencken had done to call down upon him the scorn of the South. The only people I had ever heard denounced in the South were Negroes, and this man was not a Negro. Then what ideas did Mencken hold that made a newspaper like the *Commercial Appeal* castigate him publicly? Undoubtedly he must be advocating ideas that the South did not like. Were there, then, people other than Negroes who criticized the South? I knew that during the Civil War the South had hated northern whites, but I had not encountered such hate during my life. Knowing no more of Mencken than I did at that moment, I felt a vague sympathy for him. Had not the South, which had assigned me the role of a non-man, cast at him its hardest words? 2

Now, how could I find out about this Mencken? There was a huge library near the riverfront, but I knew that Negroes were not allowed to patronize its shelves any more than they were the parks and playgrounds of the city. I had gone into the library several times to get 3

---

[1]Henry Louis Mencken (1880–1956), journalist, critic, and essayist who was known for his pointed, outspoken, and satirical comments about the blunders and imperfections of democracy and the cultural awkwardness of Americans. [Eds.]

books for the white men on the job. Which of them would now help me to get books? And how could I read them without causing concern to the white men with whom I worked? I had so far been successful in hiding my thoughts and feelings from them, but I knew that I would create hostility if I went about this business of reading in a clumsy way.

I weighed the personalities of the men on the job. There was Don, 4 a Jew; but I distrusted him. His position was not much better than mine and I knew that he was uneasy and insecure; he had always treated me in an offhand, bantering way that barely concealed his contempt. I was afraid to ask him to help me to get books; his frantic desire to demonstrate a racial solidarity with the whites against Negroes might make him betray me.

Then how about the boss? No, he was a Baptist and I had the 5 suspicion that he would not be quite able to comprehend why a black boy would want to read Mencken. There were other white men on the job whose attitudes showed clearly that they were Kluxers or sympathizers, and they were out of the question.

There remained only one man whose attitude did not fit into an 6 anti-Negro category, for I had heard the white men refer to him as a "Pope lover." He was an Irish Catholic and was hated by the white Southerners. I knew that he read books, because I had got him volumes from the library several times. Since he, too, was an object of hatred, I felt that he might refuse me but would hardly betray me. I hesitated, weighing and balancing the imponderable realities.

One morning I paused before the Catholic fellow's desk. 7

"I want to ask you a favor," I whispered to him. 8

"What is it?" 9

"I want to read. I can't get books from the library. I wonder if 10 you'd let me use your card?"

He looked at me suspiciously. 11

"My card is full most of the time," he said. 12

"I see," I said and waited, posing my question silently. 13

"You're not trying to get me into trouble, are you, boy?" he asked, 14 staring at me.

"Oh, no, sir." 15

"What book do you want?" 16

"A book by H. L. Mencken." 17

"Which one?" 18

"I don't know. Has he written more than one?" 19

"He has written several." 20

"I didn't know that." 21

"What makes you want to read Mencken?" 22

"Oh, I just saw his name in the newspaper," I said. 23

TEACHING STRATEGIES

1. Ask students if they believe a class structure exists in the United States. If they do, ask how they think the various classes relate to one another. How does Wright's dilemma illustrate these relationships?

2. Ask the students to consider changes that have occurred in their own views. What prompted these changes in their beliefs, values, and goals?

3. Isolation is a dominant theme in African-American literature. What reasons might prompt any person to become isolated from those around him or her? What causes Wright's increasing isolation from both whites and blacks and from himself?

COLLABORATIVE ACTIVITIES

1. Wright uses dialogue in several scenes in this selection. Have students work in groups to create dialogue for some of the scenes that have no dialogue.

2. In groups, analyze the key episodes in which Wright changes in some way. What prompts each transformation? Which changes are the most significant?

"It's good of you to want to read," he said. "But you ought to 24 read the right things."

I said nothing. Would he want to supervise my reading? 25

"Let me think," he said. "I'll figure out something." 26

I turned from him and he called me back. He stared at me quiz- 27 zically.

"Richard, don't mention this to the other white men," he said. 28

"I understand," I said. "I won't say a word." 29

A few days later he called me to him. 30

"I've got a card in my wife's name," he said. "Here's mine." 31

"Thank you, sir." 32

"Do you think you can manage it?" 33

"I'll manage fine," I said. 34

"If they suspect you, you'll get in trouble," he said. 35

"I'll write the same kind of notes to the library that you wrote 36 when you sent me for books," I told him. "I'll sign your name."

He laughed. 37

"Go ahead. Let me see what you get," he said. 38

That afternoon I addressed myself to forging a note. Now, what 39 were the names of books written by H. L. Mencken? I did not know any of them. I finally wrote what I thought would be a foolproof note: *Dear Madam: Will you please let this nigger boy*—I used the word "nigger" to make the librarian feel that I could not possibly be the author of the note—*have some books by H. L. Mencken?* I forged the white man's name.

I entered the library as I had always done when on errands for 40 whites, but I felt that I would somehow slip up and betray myself. I doffed my hat, stood a respectful distance from the desk, looked as unbookish as possible, and waited for the white patrons to be taken care of. When the desk was clear of people, I still waited. The white librarian looked at me.

"What do you want, boy?" 41

As though I did not possess the power of speech, I stepped for- 42 ward and simply handed her the forged note, not parting my lips.

"What books by Mencken does he want?" she asked. 43

"I don't know, ma'am," I said, avoiding her eyes. 44

"Who gave you this card?" 45

"Mr. Falk," I said. 46

"Where is he?" 47

"He's at work, at the M—Optical Company," I said. "I've been 48 in here for him before."

"I remember," the woman said. "But he never wrote notes like 49 this."

Oh, God, she's suspicious. Perhaps she would not let me have 50
the books? If she had turned her back at that moment, I would have
ducked out the door and never gone back. Then I thought of a bold
idea.

"You can call him up, ma'am," I said, my heart pounding.   51

"You're not using these books, are you?" she asked pointedly.   52

"Oh, no, ma'am. I can't read."   53

"I don't know what he wants by Mencken," she said under her 54
breath.

I knew now that I had won; she was thinking of other things and 55
the race question had gone out of her mind. She went to the shelves.
Once or twice she looked over her shoulder at me, as though she was
still doubtful. Finally she came forward with two books in her hand.

"I'm sending him two books," she said. "But tell Mr. Falk to come 56
in next time, or send me the names of the books he wants. I don't
know what he wants to read."

I said nothing. She stamped the card and handed me the books. 57
Not daring to glance at them, I went out of the library, fearing that
the woman would call me back for further questioning. A block away
from the library I opened one of the books and read a title: *A Book of
Prefaces*. I was nearing my nineteenth birthday and I did not know
how to pronounce the word "preface." I thumbed the pages and saw
strange words and strange names. I shook my head, disappointed. I
looked at the other book; it was called *Prejudices*. I knew what that
word meant; I had heard it all my life. And right off I was on guard
against Mencken's books. Why would a man want to call a book
Prejudices? The word was so stained with all my memories of racial
hate that I could not conceive of anybody using it for a title. Perhaps
I had made a mistake about Mencken? A man who had prejudices
must be wrong.

When I showed the books to Mr. Falk, he looked at me and 58
frowned.

"That librarian might telephone you," I warned him.   59

"That's all right," he said. "But when you're through reading 60
those books, I want you to tell me what you get out of them."

That night in my rented room, while letting the hot water run 61
over my can of pork and beans in the sink, I opened *A Book of Prefaces*
and began to read. I was jarred and shocked by the style, the clear,
clean, sweeping sentences. Why did he write like that? And how did
one write like that? I pictured the man as a raging demon, slashing
with his pen, consumed with hate, denouncing everything American,
extolling everything European or German, laughing at the weaknesses of people, mocking God, authority. What was this? I stood

up, trying to realize what reality lay behind the meaning of the words
. . . Yes, this man was fighting, fighting with words. He was using
words as a weapon, using them as one would use a club. Could
words be weapons? Well, yes, for here they were. Then, maybe,
perhaps, I could use them as a weapon? No. It frightened me. I read
on and what amazed me was not what he said, but how on earth
anybody had the courage to say it.

Occasionally I glanced up to reassure myself that I was alone in   62
the room. Who were these men about whom Mencken was talking
so passionately? Who was Anatole France? Joseph Conrad? Sinclair
Lewis, Sherwood Anderson, Dostoevski, George Moore, Gustave
Flaubert, Maupassant, Tolstoy, Frank Harris, Mark Twain, Thomas
Hardy, Arnold Bennett, Stephen Crane, Zola, Norris, Gorky,
Bergson, Ibsen, Balzac, Bernard Shaw, Dumas, Poe, Thomas Mann,
O. Henry, Dreiser, H. G. Wells, Gogol, T. S. Eliot, Gide, Baudelaire,
Edgar Lee Masters, Stendhal, Turgenev, Huneker, Nietzsche, and
scores of others? Were these men real? Did they exist or had they
existed? And how did one pronounce their names?

I ran across many words whose meanings I did not know, and I   63
either looked them up in a dictionary or, before I had a chance to do
that, encountered the word in a context that made its meaning clear.
But what strange world was this? I concluded the book with the
conviction that I had somehow overlooked something terribly important in life. I had once tried to write, had once reveled in feeling, had
let my crude imagination roam, but the impulse to dream had been
slowly beaten out of me by experience. Now it surged up again and
I hungered for books, new ways of looking and seeing. It was not a
matter of believing or disbelieving what I read, but of feeling something new, of being affected by something that made the look of the
world different.

As dawn broke I ate my pork and beans, feeling dopey, sleepy.   64
I went to work, but the mood of the book would not die; it lingered,
coloring everything I saw, heard, did. I now felt that I knew what
the white men were feeling. Merely because I had read a book that
had spoken of how they lived and thought, I identified myself with
that book. I felt vaguely guilty. Would I, filled with bookish notions,
act in a manner that would make the whites dislike me?

I forged more notes and my trips to the library became frequent.   65
Reading grew into a passion. My first serious novel was Sinclair Lewis's *Main Street*.[2] It made me see my boss, Mr. Gerald, and identify

---

[2]*Main Street*, published in 1920, examines the smugness, intolerance, and lack of imagination
that characterizes small-town American life. [Eds.]

him as an American type. I would smile when I saw him lugging his golf bags into the office. I had always felt a vast distance separating me from the boss, and now I felt closer to him, though still distant. I felt now that I knew him, that I could feel the very limits of his narrow life. And this had happened because I had read a novel about a mythical man called George F. Babbitt.[3]

The plots and stories in the novels did not interest me so much 66
as the point of view revealed. I gave myself over to each novel without reserve, without trying to criticize it; it was enough for me to see and feel something different. And for me, everything was something different. Reading was like a drug, a dope. The novels created moods in which I lived for days. But I could not conquer my sense of guilt, my feeling that the white men around me knew that I was changing, that I had begun to regard them differently.

Whenever I brought a book to the job, I wrapped it in news- 67
paper—a habit that was to persist for years in other cities and under other circumstances. But some of the white men pried into my packages when I was absent and they questioned me.

"Boy, what are you reading those books for?" 68

"Oh, I don't know, sir." 69

"That's deep stuff you're reading, boy." 70

"I'm just killing time, sir." 71

"You'll addle your brains if you don't watch out." 72

I read Dreiser's *Jennie Gerhardt* and *Sister Carrie*[4] and they revived 73
in me a vivid sense of my mother's suffering; I was overwhelmed. I grew silent, wondering about the life around me. It would have been impossible for me to have told anyone what I derived from these novels, for it was nothing less than a sense of life itself. All my life had shaped me for the realism, the naturalism of the modern novel, and I could not read enough of them.

Steeped in new moods and ideas, I bought a ream of paper and 74
tried to write; but nothing would come, or what did come was flat beyond telling. I discovered that more than desire and feeling were necessary to write and I dropped the idea. Yet I still wondered how it was possible to know people sufficiently to write about them. Could I ever learn about life and people? To me, with my vast ignorance, my Jim Crow station in life, it seemed a task impossible of achievement. I now knew what being a Negro meant. I could endure the

[3]A character in Sinclair Lewis's *Babbitt* (1922) who believed in the virtues of home, the Republican party, and middle-class conventions. To Wright, Babbitt symbolizes the mindless complacency of white middle-class America. [Eds.]

[4]Both *Jennie Gerhardt* (1911) and *Sister Carrie* (1900) tell the stories of working women who struggle against poverty and social injustice. [Eds.]

hunger. I had learned to live with hate. But to feel that there were feelings denied me, that the very breath of life itself was beyond my reach, that more than anything else hurt, wounded me. I had a new hunger.

In buoying me up, reading also cast me down, made me see what 75 was possible, what I had missed. My tension returned, new, terrible, bitter, surging, almost too great to be contained. I no longer *felt* that the world about me was hostile, killing; I *knew* it. A million times I asked myself what I could do to save myself, and there were no answers. I seemed forever condemned, ringed by walls.

I did not discuss my reading with Mr. Falk, who had lent me his 76 library card; it would have meant talking about myself and that would have been too painful. I smiled each day, fighting desperately to maintain my old behavior, to keep my disposition seemingly sunny. But some of the white men discerned that I had begun to brood.

"Wake up there, boy!" Mr. Olin said one day. 77

"Sir!" I answered for the lack of a better word. 78

"You act like you've stolen something," he said. 79

I laughed in the way I knew he expected me to laugh, but I 80 resolved to be more conscious of myself, to watch my every act, to guard and hide the new knowledge that was dawning within me.

If I went north, would it be possible for me to build a new life 81 then? But how could a man build a life upon vague, unformed yearnings? I wanted to write and I did not even know the English language. I bought English grammars and found them dull. I felt that I was getting a better sense of the language from novels than from grammars. I read hard, discarding a writer as soon as I felt that I had grasped his point of view. At night the printed page stood before my eyes in sleep.

Mrs. Moss, my landlady, asked me one Sunday morning: "Son, 82 what is this you keep on reading?"

"Oh, nothing. Just novels." 83

"What you get out of 'em?" 84

"I'm just killing time," I said. 85

"I hope you know your own mind," she said in a tone which 86 implied that she doubted if I had a mind.

I knew of no Negroes who read the books I liked and I wondered 87 if any Negroes ever thought of them. I knew that there were Negro doctors, lawyers, newspapermen, but I never saw any of them. When I read a Negro newspaper I never caught the faintest echo of my preoccupation in its pages. I felt trapped and occasionally, for a few days, I would stop reading. But a vague hunger would come over me for books, books that opened up new avenues of feeling and seeing, and again I would forge another note to the white librarian.

Again I would read and wonder as only the naïve and unlettered can read and wonder, feeling that I carried a secret, criminal burden about with me each day.

That winter my mother and brother came and we set up house- 88 keeping, buying furniture on the installment plan, being cheated and yet knowing no way to avoid it. I began to eat warm food and to my surprise found that regular meals enabled me to read faster. I may have lived through many illnesses and survived them, never suspecting that I was ill. My brother obtained a job and we began to save toward the trip north, plotting our time, setting tentative dates for departure. I told none of the white men on the job that I was planning to go north; I knew that the moment they felt I was thinking of the North they would change toward me. It would have made them feel that I did not like the life I was living, and because my life was completely conditioned by what they said or did, it would have been tantamount to challenging them.

I could calculate my chances for life in the South as a Negro fairly 89 clearly now.

I could fight the southern whites by organizing with other 90 Negroes, as my grandfather had done. But I knew that I could never win that way; there were many whites and there were but few blacks. They were strong and we were weak. Outright black rebellion could never win. If I fought openly I would die and I did not want to die. News of lynchings were frequent.

I could submit and live the life of a genial slave, but that was 91 impossible. All of my life had shaped me to live by my own feelings and thoughts. I could make up to Bess and marry her and inherit the house. But that, too, would be the life of a slave; if I did that, I would crush to death something within me, and I would hate myself as much as I knew the whites already hated those who had submitted. Neither could I ever willingly present myself to be kicked, as Shorty had done. I would rather have died than do that.

I could drain off my restlessness by fighting with Shorty and 92 Harrison. I had seen many Negroes solve the problem of being black by transferring their hatred of themselves to others with a black skin and fighting them. I would have to be cold to do that, and I was not cold and I could never be.

I could, of course, forget what I had read, thrust the whites out 93 of my mind, forget them; and find release from anxiety and longing in sex and alcohol. But the memory of how my father had conducted himself made that course repugnant. If I did not want others to violate my life, how could I voluntarily violate it myself?

I had no hope whatever of being a professional man. Not only 94 had I been so conditioned that I did not desire it, but the fulfillment

WRITING SUGGESTIONS

1. Like Frederick Douglass ("Learning to Read and Write," page 14), Wright used several strategies to gain an education. Compare and contrast the educational strategies of these two individuals.

2. In seeking to educate himself, Wright relies almost exclusively on books by white authors. Write an essay in which you argue for or against the proposition that by doing this Wright isolates himself further.

**ANSWERS TO RESPONDING
TO READING**

1. Wright realizes that he has been restricted and deprived all his life. This realization creates a distance between him and others, both black and white. The changes are good insofar as they cause him to grow intellectually; they are perhaps bad in the degree to which they make him more isolated. Like Mark Twain in "Reading the River" (Chapter 2), Wright's education has caused him to gain something and to lose something.
2. Wright's "station in life" is that of a second-class citizen. He presents a passive, subservient image to the whites around him in order to survive in a culture hostile to blacks.
3. Wright's feelings of increasing isolation make his decision to leave the United States seem inevitable. Answers will vary. Those who believe in confronting injustice might suggest that he should have stayed. Those more interested in Wright's personal happiness might applaud his decision to leave.

of such an ambition was beyond my capabilities. Well-to-do Negroes lived in a world that was almost as alien to me as the world inhabited by whites.

What, then, was there? I held my life in my mind, in my consciousness each day, feeling at times that I would stumble and drop it, spill it forever. My reading had created a vast sense of distance between me and the world in which I lived and tried to make a living, and that sense of distance was increasing each day. My days and nights were one long, quiet, continuously contained dream of terror, tension, and anxiety. I wondered how long I could bear it. 95

RESPONDING TO READING

1. What changes occurred in Wright as a result of his reading? Did these changes bring Wright closer to or farther from other African-Americans? Do you think Wright was better or worse off after learning about books?   **2.** In paragraph 74 Wright mentions his "Jim Crow station in life." The term *Jim Crow*, derived from a character in a minstrel show, refers to laws enacted in Southern states that legalized racial segregation. What is Wright's "station in life"? In what ways does he adapt his behavior to accommodate this Jim Crow image? In what ways does he not? How would you describe your "station in life"?   **3.** After World War II Wright left the United States to live in Paris. Given what you have read in this essay, does his decision surprise you? Do you agree with his decision? If you had been he, would you have stayed and fought the injustices he discusses?

The Joys of Reading

ANNIE DILLARD

BACKGROUND ON AUTHOR

Raised in Pittsburgh, Dillard later became attached to the natural environment around Roanoke, Virginia. Since *Pilgrim at Tinker Creek* she has written a great deal in addition to lecturing and teaching at Western Washington University and Wesleyan University. Some have characterized her as a transcendental naturalist, others as a Christian mystic. "The Joys of Reading" was first published in the *New York Times Magazine*, May 16, 1982.

Known as a naturalist and essayist, Annie Dillard (1945–   ) won the Pulitzer Prize in 1974 for her first book, *Pilgrim at Tinker Creek*, a nonfiction work in which she records her explorations in the Roanoke Valley of Virginia. Dillard calls herself a "stalker" of nature and its mysteries and delights in both the wonders and terrors it inspires. She contributes to periodicals, such as *Harper's* and *The Atlantic*, and has also written *Teaching a Stone to Talk* (1982), *An American Childhood* (1987), and *The Writing Life* (1989). In her 1982 essay "The Joys of Reading," Dillard takes readers on a ramble through the books she read as a child and remembers how they affected her then.

By 1955, when I was 10, my father's reading had gone to his head. 1

My father's reading during that time, and for many years after, 2 consisted, for the most part, of Mark Twain's *Life on the Mississippi*. He traveled up and down the East Coast for the family firm; he traveled alone. He would check into a hotel, find a bookstore, and choose for the night's reading, after what I fancy to have been long deliberation, yet another copy of *Life on the Mississippi*. He brought all these books home. There were dozens of them on the living-room shelves. From time to time, I read one.

When all this reading went to his head, he took action. He quit 3 the family firm, bade farewell to his wife and his daughters—10 and 7 years old and 6 months old—loaded his 24-foot cabin cruiser with canned food, and took off down the Allegheny River. It was only a few miles to the Ohio River at Pittsburgh's Point. He continued down the Ohio to the Mississippi at Cairo, Ill., and down the Mississippi to Memphis. Although he had intended to go on to New Orleans, he actually found the river rather lonesome, so he sold the boat at Memphis, and flew home.

I scarcely remember my father's brief absence for, during that 4 same time, my own reading was giving me a turn. I had found the Homewood Library, stumbled across *The Field Book of Ponds and Streams*, and discovered that the things you learned from a library were not all in the library's books. During those years, I never knew where my next revelation was coming from, but I knew it was coming—some hairpin curve, some stray bit of romance or information that would turn my life around in a twinkling.

The Homewood branch of Pittsburgh's Carnegie library system 5 was in a black section of town. I understood that our maid, Elizabeth, had friends there. I never saw her there, but I did see Henry, my grandmother's chauffeur. I was getting out of my mother's car in front of the library when Henry appeared on the sidewalk; he was walking with some other old men. I had never before seen him at large. It would embarrass him, I thought, if I said hello to him in front of his friends. I was wrong. He spied me, picked me up—books and all—and introduced my mother and me to his friends. Later, as we were climbing the long stone steps to the library's door, my mother said to me, "That's what I mean by good manners."

Mark Twain accused Andrew Carnegie[1] of purchasing fame. As 6 far as I was concerned, it worked. You could join free drawing classes

---

[1]Andrew Carnegie (1835–1919), a Scottish-born industrialist who made a fortune in the steel industry. He gave large amounts of money to educational institutions, including the Carnegie Institute in Pittsburgh. He also made large endowments to construct libraries all over the United States. [Eds.]

across town in his extremely famous Carnegie hall. After class you could look at his dinosaur skeletons, or at his Abstract Expressionist paintings; you could buy labeled rocks, foreign stamps and mounted butterflies at his museum store; you could make lightning on his Van de Graaff generator. Andrew Carnegie, who had started out as a tiny bobbin boy, had gone on, I thought, to invent free libraries, the arts and the sciences. Across the enormous stone facade of the main Carnegie library were graven the words: FREE TO THE PEOPLE.

The kindly Homewood librarians, after a trial period, had given 7 me a card to the adult section. This was an enormous, silent room with marble floors. Nonfiction was on the left.

Next to the farthest wall, and under leaded windows set 10 feet from 8 the floor, so that no human being could ever see anything from them— next to the wall, and at the farthest remove from the idle librarians at their curved wooden counter, and from the oak bench where my mother sat in her camel's hair coat chatting with the librarians or reading— stood the last and most obscure of the tall nonfiction stacks: NEGRO HISTORY and NATURAL HISTORY. It was in Natural History, in the darkness of a bottom shelf, that I found *The Field Book of Ponds and Streams*.

The Field Book of Ponds and Streams was, and is, a small blue-bound 9 book printed in fine type on thin paper like The Book of Common Prayer. Its third chapter explained how to make sweep nets, plankton nets, glass-bottomed buckets and killing jars. It specified how to mount slides, how to label insects on their pins, and how to set up a freshwater aquarium. One was to go into "the field" wearing hip boots and perhaps a head net for mosquitoes; one carried in a "rucksack" half a dozen corked test tubes, a smattering of screw-top baby-food jars, a white enamel tray, assorted pipettes and eyedroppers, an artillery of cheesecloth nets, a notebook, a hand lens, perhaps a map, and *The Field Book of Ponds and Streams*. There, in this field, which was apparently well watered, one would find and distinguish among daphnia, planaria, water pennies, stonefly larvae, dragonfly nymphs, salamanders, tadpoles, snakes and turtles, all of which one could carry home.

That anyone had lived the fine life described in Chapter Three 10 astonished me. I imagined the book's author as a man, though his name was clearly Ann Haven Morgan. It would be good to write him, the lonely man, and assure him that someone had found his book, in the dark near the floor at the Homewood Library. I would, in the same letter, or in a subsequent one, ask him a question outside the scope of his book, which was where I personally might find a pond or a stream. But I did not know how to address such a letter, of course, or how to learn if he was still alive. I was afraid, too, that my letter would disappoint him by betraying my ignorance, which was just beginning to attract my own notice. What, for example, was cheesecloth, and where do scientists get it? What, when you really got down to it, was enamel? Where might a sixth-grade student at the Ellis School on Fifth Avenue obtain such a legendary item as a bucket?

The Field Book of Ponds and Streams was a shocker from beginning 11 to end. The greatest shock came at the end.

When you checked out a book from the Homewood Library, the 12 librarian wrote your number on the book's card and stamped the due date on a sheet glued to the book's last page. When I checked out *The Field Book of Ponds and Streams* for the second time, I noticed the book's card. It was almost full. There were numbers on both sides. Mr. Morgan and I were not entirely alone in the world. With us, and sharing our secret life, were many Negro adults.

Who were these people? Had they, in Pittsburgh's Homewood 13 section, found ponds? Had they found streams? At home, I read the book again; I studied the drawings; I reread Chapter Three, and then I settled in to study the due-date slip. Seven or eight people were reading this book every year. People read this book in every season. People had read this book during the recent war.

Every year, I reread *The Field Book of Ponds and Streams*. Often when 14 I was in the library I simply visited it. I sat on the marble floor and studied the book's card. There we all were. There was my number. There was the number of someone else who had checked it out more than once. Might I contact this person, and cheer him up? Homewood was apparently full of dreaming maids and chauffeurs. All this explained, perhaps, why our maid, the diminutive Elizabeth, was so sullen.

None of us had suspected Elizabeth's interest in ponds and 15 streams. She had never let slip the faintest clue. For what would have been the use? She was rarely off, and when she was, she saw her friends. By day she polished silver; by night, I understood, she fashioned plankton nets in her attic bedroom. She was saving to buy hip boots. But it was all in vain. She had no car. There was neither pond nor stream on the streetcar routes.

The marble floor was beginning to chill me. I returned the book's 16 card to its flap. It was not fair.

I had been driven into nonfiction against my wishes. I wanted to 17 read fiction, but I had learned to be cautious about fiction.

"When you open a book," the library posters said, "anything can 18 happen." This was so. A book of fiction was a bomb. It was a land mine you wanted to go off. You wanted it to blow your whole day. Unfortunately, hundreds of thousands of books were duds. They had

TEACHING STRATEGIES

1. "The Joys of Reading" tells the story of how Dillard came to know the power of books. Outline the process on the board, listing the discoveries that accompanied each step she describes.

2. Examine the peculiarities of Dillard's style. For example, the entire last section of the essay gives a sense of increasing speed and volume. She strings together parallel clauses; she lists books with seeming randomness, interspersing references into a terse chronology of her teenage life; she piles quotation upon quotation, without stopping to analyze them; and, in the last sentence, she jumps frenetically into the future: "In New Orleans— if you could get to New Orleans—would the music be loud enough?"

COLLABORATIVE ACTIVITY

Dillard is known for her powers of observation. Divide the class into groups, and have each group find passages in different essays by Dillard in this book that illustrate her descriptive skills. Ask students to pay particular attention to Dillard's use of adjectives and figurative language. In class discussion, have a spokesperson from each group read a passage the group thinks is particularly appealing.

been rusting out of everyone's way for so long that they no longer worked. There was no way to distinguish the duds from the live mines except to throw oneself at them, one by one.

The suggestions of adults were uncertain and incoherent. Any 19 book that contained children, or short adults, or animals, was felt to be a children's book. So also was any book about the sea, or any book by Charles Dickens or Mark Twain. Suited to female children were love stories set in any century but this one. Consequently, one had read, exasperated, *Pickwick Papers, Wuthering Heights, Lad: A Dog, Gulliver's Travels, Gone With the Wind, Robinson Crusoe*, Nordoff and Hall's *Bounty* trilogy, *Moby Dick, The Five Little Peppers, The Mysterious Stranger, Lord Jim, Désirée, Old Yeller.*

Virtually all British books, in particular, were children's books. 20 No one understood children like the British, who were in most ways children themselves—with their badgers and dormice, their Tiny Tims, Peter Pans, Pushmi-Pullyus and Heffalumps—but who nevertheless had recently been rallied from their piddling by the spectacle of Hitler at their shores.

A many-volumed set, bound in black leather and calling itself 21 *Journeys Through Bookland*, appeared at home on our sun-porch shelves. I judged from its title that its British editors subscribed to the flying-carpet theory of children's reading. Its selections confirmed my notion that adults mixed good stories and bad stories together simply because they could not distinguish between them. Buried in one of the volumes of *Journeys Through Bookland*, for instance, was a stratum of Norse myths about Balder, Freya, Loki and a wolf. This was grand stuff. But the same volume also contained those British children's classics *The Water Babies* and *The Swiss Family Robinson*. These were botched jobs. Tom the Water Baby looked wonderful in the picture: a naked, cheerful baby who lived down among fishes and bubbles. Why was this book not better? There was nothing in it but this picture, nothing at all. Similarly, *The Swiss Family Robinson* sounded so good when you heard about it. But, alas, the Swiss Family Robinson had struggled not. If they needed a thing such as a ham, a cask of butter, some silver plate or a window shutter, they simply fetched it from their wrecked boat.

The adults who compiled *Journeys Through Bookland* gave me to 22 understand that generations of British children had loved *The Water Babies* and *The Swiss Family Robinson*. Generations of British children could go hang. Apparently, even dead bombs were effective on the British. No wonder they had been losing the war.

The fiction stacks at the Homewood Library, their volumes alpha- 23 betized by author, continued to baffle me. How could I learn to choose a novel? That I could not easily reach the top two shelves helped limit choices a little. Still, on the lower shelves I saw too many books: Mary Johnson, *Sweet Rocket*; Samuel Johnson, *Rasselas*; James Jones, *From Here to Eternity*. I checked out the last because I had heard of it. It was good. I decided to check out books I had heard of. I had heard, for instance, of *The Mill on the Floss*. I checked it out, and it was good. On its binding was printed a dancing figure, a man in silhouette. I had noticed this man before. On the title page of *The Mill on the Floss*, I found the same figure printed in greater detail. The man was not dancing; he was running flat out and carrying something that was smoking terribly. He was looking for a place to put this smoky thing down. He was carrying it high over his head because, if he carried it lower, sparks would blow onto him, and he wasn't wearing a stitch.

For many years I tested the theory that those short gray or green 24 books with the running-man colophon[2]—Modern Library books— were good. The going was often rocky. *Native Son* was good, *Walden* was good. *The Interpretation of Dreams* was O.K., and *The Education of Henry Adams* was awful. *Ulysses*, a very famous book, was also awful. *Confessions*, by Jean-Jacques Rousseau, was much better, though it fell apart halfway through.

In fact, most books fell apart halfway through, as their protago- 25 nists left, without any apparent reluctance, the most interesting part of their lives, and entered upon decades of unrelieved tedium. *Jude the Obscure* was the type case. It started out so well. Halfway through, the author forgot how to write. After Jude got married, his life was over, but the book went on for hundreds of pages while he stewed in his own juices. The same thing happened in *The Little Shepherd of Kingdom Come*. This was simply a hazard of reading. Only an appalled loyalty to the protagonists of the early chapters kept me reading chronological narratives to their bitter ends.

We moved to a different house; I had my own room. Books wan- 26 dered in and out of my hands, as they had always done—but now most of them had a common theme. It was, essentially, a time and a series of places to which I returned almost nightly; so also must have thousands, or millions, of us who grew up in the 1950s reading what came to hand. What came to hand in those years were books about the war: the war in England, France, Belgium, Norway, Italy, Greece; the war in Africa; the war in the Pacific, in Guam, New Guinea, the Philippines; the war, Hitler and the camps.

We read Leon Uris, *Exodus*, and, better, his *Mila Eighteen*, about 27 the Warsaw ghetto. We read *The Wall*—again, the Warsaw ghetto.

---

[2]An identifying device or picture used by a printer or publisher. [Eds.]

We read *Time* magazine and *Life* and *Look*. It was in the air, that there had been these things. We read, above all, and over and over, Anne Frank's *The Diary of a Young Girl*. This was where we belonged; here we were at home. I say "we," but in fact I did not know anyone else who read these things. Perhaps my parents did, for they had brought the books home. What were my friends reading? We did not talk about books; our reading was private. Still, I say, there must have been millions of us.

We read *The Bridge Over the River Kwai, The Young Lions*. In the 28 background sang the librarians' chorus:

> The world of books is a child's land of enchantment.
> When you open a book and start reading
> You enter another world—the world
> Of make-believe—where anything can happen.

We read *Thirty Seconds Over Tokyo, To Hell and Back*. We read *The* 29 *Naked and the Dead, Run Silent, Run Deep,* and *Tales of the South Pacific*, in which American GIs saw native victims of elephantiasis pushing their own enlarged testicles before them in wheelbarrows. We read *The Caine Mutiny, Some Came Running*.

I was a skilled bombardier; I could run a submarine with my eyes 30 closed, evading torpedoes and mines. I could disembowel a soldier with a bayonet, survive under a tarp in a lifeboat, and parachute behind enemy lines. I could contact the Resistance with my high-school French and eavesdrop on the Nazis with my high-school German.

"*Du! Kleines Mädchen! Bist du französisches Mädchen oder bist du* 31 *amerikanischer* spy?"

"*Je suis une jeune fille de la belle France, Herr S.S.* Officer." 32
"Prove it!" 33
"*Je suis, tu es, il est, nous sommes, vous êtes, ils sont.*" 34
"Very gut. Run along and play." 35
One librarian pressed upon me a copy of *Look Homeward, Angel*. 36 "How I envy you," she said, "having a chance to read this for the very first time." But it was several years too late.

We read *On the Beach, A Canticle for Liebowitz*; we read *Hiroshima*. 37

At school, we had air-raid drills. We took the drills seriously; 38 surely Pittsburgh, which had the country's iron, steel, coal, aluminum and libraries, would be the enemy's primary target.

During the war, my father (who was 4-F because of a collapsing 39 lung) had "watched the skies." We all knew that people still watched the skies. But when the watcher spotted the bomber over Pittsburgh what, precisely, would be his moves? Surely, he would only calculate, just as we in school did, what good it would do him to get under something.

When the alarm sounded, our teachers stopped talking and led 40
us to the basement. There, the gym teachers lined us against the
cement walls and lockers, and showed us how to tuck in and fold
our arms over our heads. Our school was a small school, but it ran
from kindergarten through 12th grade. We had air-raid drills in small
groups, only three or four grades together, because there was not
room for all of us against the walls. The teachers had to stand in the
middle of the basement rooms: those bright Pittsburgh women who
taught English, Latin, science and art, and those educated, beautifully
mannered, bewildered European women who taught French, history
and German, who had landed in Pittsburgh at the end of their flights
from Hitler and who baffled us by their common insistence on tidi-
ness, above all, in our written work.

The teachers stood in the middle of the rooms, not talking to one 41
another. We tucked against the walls and lockers, dozens of girls
wearing green jumpers, green knee socks and saddle shoes. We
folded our skinny arms over our heads, raising to the enemy a clatter
of gold scarab bracelets and gold bangle bracelets. If the bomb actually
came, should we not let the little kids—the kindergarteners and the
first- and second-graders—stand against the wall? We older ones
would occupy the middle with the teachers. The European teachers
were almost used to this sort of thing. We would help them keep
everyone's spirit up, we would sing "Frère Jacques."

Our house was stone. In the basement was a room furnished with 42
a long wooden bar, tables and chairs, a leather couch, a refrigerator,
a sink, an ice maker, a fireplace, a piano, a record player and a set
of drums. There was another, larger set of basement rooms that held
a washer and dryer, a workbench, shelves of canned food and, especially, a chest freezer. We would live in this basement. We would live
there for many years, like the Swiss Family Robinson, like the Franks,
until the radiation outside blew away. My two younger sisters would
grow up there; I would teach them all I knew, and entertain them on
the piano. My father would build a radiation barrier for the basement's
sunken windows; he would play the drums. Mother would feed us
and tend to us. We would grow close.

I had spent the equivalent of years of my life, I thought, in con- 43
centration camps, in ghettos, in prison camps and in lifeboats. I knew
from my reading how to ration food and water. We would each have
four ounces of food a day and eight ounces of water. I knew how to
stretch my rations by hoarding food in my shirt, by chewing slowly,
by sloshing water around in my mouth and wetting my tongue well
before I swallowed. If the water gave out in the taps, we could suck
ice; we could drink club soda and tonic water; we could live on the

juice in canned food. I figured the five of us could live for many years on the food in the basement—but I was not sure.

"Mother—how long could we last on the food in the basement?" 44 She did not know what I had been reading.

"The food in the basement? In the freezer and on the shelves? 45 Oh, about a week and a half. Two weeks."

She knew there were legs of lamb in the freezer, turkeys, chickens, 46 pork roasts, shrimp and steaks; there were pounds of frozen vegetables, quarts of ice cream, dozens of Popsicles. How many family dinners was that? A leg of lamb one night, rice and vegetables; steak the next night, potatoes and vegetables.

"Two weeks! We could live much longer than two weeks." 47

"There's really not very much food down there. About two weeks' 48 worth."

I let it go. What did I know about feeding a family? On the other 49 hand, I considered that, if it came down to it, I might have to take charge.

I had been 14 when the Ellis School moved to its new building; 50 my classmates and I had access to the new Upper School library.

It was there, in that plush open library room—with its orange 51 upholstered chairs, its maple coffee tables and its abstract graphics on the walls—that I tried to kill time until high school should be over. It was there, for instance, that I found *Penn's Woods West*, a coffee-table book of color photographs of western Pennsylvania woods, ponds and streams. And it was there that I began a poetry collection.

The poetry collection consisted of poems copied into a notebook 52 labeled "Poetry Collection." To lend distinction to the collection, I copied the poems as neatly as I could manage, using peacock-blue ink. Further, I did not cross the "t's" at the ends of words, but instead used what I fancied to be the French final "t."

This collection, which is extant—as my collections of rocks, bee- 53 tles and stamps are not—contains great illegible hunks of Edna St. Vincent Millay, Rupert Brooke, Wilfred Owen, Isaiah, and Rimbaud and Verlaine in simple French. It contains the first four lines of "The Wasteland," the first stanza of Francis Thompson's "The Hound of Heaven," the end of "Intimations of Immortality," Pound's "River Merchant's Letter to His Wife," the dreary whole of Coleridge's "Dejection: An Ode," and page after peacock-blue page of haiku.[3] It

---

[3]A Japanese lyric poem that presents the poet's impressions of an object or scene in exactly seventeen syllables. [Eds.]

also contains "Adlestrop," by Edward Thomas, which begins so ludi-
crously, "Ah yes, I remember Adlestrop," and ends so grandly, "all
the birds of Oxfordshire and Gloucestershire."

Under the spell of Rimbaud, I wrote a poem that began with a   54
line from "Une Saison en Enfer": "Once, if I remember well," and
continued, "My flesh did lay confined in hell." I wrote other poems
in the manner of "The Song of Songs."

In Oscar Williams's *A Little Treasury of Modern Poetry*, I had found   55
a photograph of Rupert Brooke; it may have been this photograph
that attracted me to poetry. Rupert Brooke was wearing a loose, soft
collar; he was looking into the distance and, surely, murmuring in
an inward sort of way, "If I should die, think only this of me." This
photograph so smote me that I drew a large pencil portrait of it and
taped the portrait to my bedroom mirror. I hoped that my family, if
by accident anyone got into my room, would think this was only a
drawing of Ralph, my current boyfriend, who in fact greatly resembled Rupert Brooke.

So in the long school afternoons I plundered the fancy new Upper   56
School library, copying unthinkably lovely passages from Hubert
Creekmore's *A Little Treasury of World Poetry*, looking at color photographs of western Pennsylvania forests, ponds and streams, and
making lists of things I would need if I ran away. After school was
basketball practice. In the evenings, I talked on the phone with Ralph;
together we were reading the works of Robert Ruark.

You could not take part in the conversation at home until you   57
had all of Thurber at your finger tips: "They are here with the reeves";
"Who has noticed the sores on the tops of the horses in the animal-
husbandry building?" "I think that what you have is a cast-iron lawn
dog." Next to Thurber was Benchley: *My Ten Years in a Quandary and
How They Grew*. Benchley was my favorite; Thurber's classical status
made him less human than Benchley, who was an admitted self-
convulser. Up there with Benchley, but muffled in a halo of nostalgia,
so that he partook somewhat of the legendary aura of Ty Cobb or
Honus Wagner, was Ring Lardner, author of the finest single English
sentence, " 'Shut up,' he explained."

For my father, the hero of American literature was the man who   58
wandered unencumbered by family ties: Chandler's Marlowe, going,
as a man must, down these mean streets; Huck Finn, lighting out for
the Territories; Jack Kerouac, on the road.

"Turn that record player down!" Someone was shouting from the   59
dining room. Father turned it down a notch. "Remember that line in

On the Road?"[4] He was addressing me, because I was there by the record player, dancing: "Kerouac's in a little bar in Mexico. He says the only time he ever got to hear music played loud enough was in that little Mexican bar. It was in *On the Road.* The only time he ever got to hear music played loud enough. I always remember that." He laughed, shaking his head; he turned it down some more. Did he think of himself as I thought of him, as the man who had cut out of town and headed down the river? Between us, we had read *On the Road* a dozen times.

My father explained things. He explained how people built cof- 60
ferdams to set bridge pilings in a river. He explained how pumps worked, how river locks worked, how water got up to the second floor of houses. He explained American economics. Money, it turned out, worked the way locks on the river worked, the way water flowed down from water towers into our upstairs bathrooms, the way the Allegheny and the Monongahela flowed into the Ohio, and the Ohio flowed into the Mississippi and out into the Gulf of Mexico at New Orleans. The money, once you got enough of it high enough, would flow by gravitation over everybody.

"It doesn't work," my mother said. "Remember those shacks we 61
see in Georgia? Those barefoot little children who have to quit school to work in the fields, their poor mothers not able to feed them enough, not even able to keep them warm?"

We were, by now, all dancing in front of the record player, so 62
we could hear the music. They shouldn't have so many kids, my father said. They must be crazy.

It was clear that adults approved of children who were "readers," 63
but it was not at all clear why this was so. Our reading was subversive, and we knew it. Did they think we read to improve our vocabularies?

We who had grown up in the Warsaw ghetto, who had seen all 64
our relatives gassed in the death chambers, who had shipped before the mast, had hunted the sperm whale in Antarctic seas; we who had battled the Germans and the Japanese in the North Atlantic, in North Africa, in New Guinea and Burma and Guam, in the air over London, in the Greek and Italian hills; we who had learned to man mine sweepers before we learned to walk in high heels; we who knew how to dislocate our senses with sleeplessness and absinthe in order to write great poetry, and who suspected the secret lives of maids and chauffeurs; we who knew by heart every snag and sand bar on the

---

[4]*On the Road* (1957), by Jack Kerouac (1922–1969), is a quasi-autobiographical tale of bohemians driving across America to Mexico to gain experience and fulfillment. [Eds.]

Mississippi River south of Cairo, and the prelude to "Evangeline," and the "Poet and Peasant" Overture—were we going to marry Holden Caulfield's roommate, buy a house in Pittsburgh, and send our children to dancing school?

I was gaining momentum; I was approaching escape velocity.   65

I was a junior, a senior. The sleepy old Homewood Library was   66 behind me; ponds and streams were behind me. I was smoking cigarettes on the sly. This forced me into the basement, where there was nothing to do but read and play the piano. I read *On the Road* again. I learned to play "Shake, Rattle and Roll."

I started reading books people were talking about. *The Ugly American; Rabbit Run; How to Live on 24 Hours a Day*. The latter knocked   67 me for a loop; it described how I wanted to live. I would learn all the world languages at the bus stop. Why waste time?

Why, indeed? Ralph never seemed to sleep. "When do you   68 sleep?" "I can sleep when I'm dead," he said. So said Nick Romano in *Knock on Any Door*: "Live fast, die young and have a good-looking corpse." Was this not grand? But for those of us who grew up reading, things will never, I suspect, be fast enough, or the world real enough, short of war.

I was learning French, German and Latin, applying to college,   69 writing a term paper on Emerson. What would you do if you had 15 minutes to live before the bomb went off? Things were converging; I wrote a paper on Rupert Brooke; I wrote a paper on peace; I learned to drink coffee.

There was much driving around, playing the radio, there were   70 many dances. I wore black turtlenecks and took up the guitar. At home, I smoked in the basement, reading, looking up and out of the sunken basement windows. In New Orleans—if you could get to New Orleans—would the music be loud enough?

RESPONDING TO READING

1. What does Dillard mean when she says, "Our reading was subversive"? Can you give examples of "subversive reading"? What reading have you done that is "subversive"?   **2.** Much of Dillard's professional writing focuses on nature. Does her early reading show any indication of this interest? Why is the sight of the other readers of *The Field Book of Ponds and Streams* shocking?   **3.** Do you think Dillard overstates the effect reading can have on someone's life? If not, why? What part did reading play in your life during your childhood? What effect has it had on your adult life?

WRITING SUGGESTIONS

1. "The Joys of Reading" is an affirmation of the power of the written word. Write an essay that uses as its thesis Dillard's recurrent theme, "When you open a book, . . . anything can happen."
2. Write an essay comparing the influence of reading on Dillard's generation, as detailed in her essay, with the influence of reading on your own generation. How do you account for the differences?

ANSWERS TO RESPONDING TO READING

1. According to Dillard, reading "subverts" our thinking, causing us to go in directions contrary to our intentions and to reevaluate basic assumptions continually. Dillard reports in detail the changes (the erroneous as well as the instructive) wrought on her imagination by reading.
2. Dillard's early exposure to *The Field Book of Ponds and Streams* and Thoreau's *Walden* contributed directly to the perspective of *Pilgrim at Tinker Creek* as well as to numerous other works about nature. She was also influenced by her father's obsession with books about travel, particularly Twain's *Life on the Mississippi*. Dillard was shocked to discover that many others, like her, read *The Field Book of Ponds and Streams*. Until that time she had felt isolated. After her discovery she realized that she was part of a community of readers and writers who had a set of interests in common.
3. Answers will vary. Dillard's purpose is to show that firing the imagination with ideas from the printed page can and does influence people to change their lives.

From the Poets in the Kitchen

PAULE MARSHALL

Born in Brooklyn, New York of parents from Barbados, Paule Marshall (1929–   ) began writing before she was ten. Today, Marshall is best known for the authentic West Indian–African-American dialogue and expressions that characterize her novels and stories. As she has written in the *Los Angeles Times*, "My work asks that you become involved, that you think." Marshall's first novel, *Brown Girl, Brownstones* (1959), has autobiographical elements. She has also written *Praisesong for the Widow* (1983) and *Reena and Other Stories* (1985). In the following essay, which appeared in *The New York Times Book Review* in 1983, Marshall pays tribute to the women in her mother's kitchen, who used language as a refuge from an America that overwhelmed them.

BACKGROUND ON WRITER

Marshall's occupation as a journalist afforded her the opportunity to travel to the Caribbean and to observe firsthand the traditions and language that so enriched her childhood. Marshall's writing demonstrates how attention to one's heritage can enhance one's creativity.

FOR OPENERS

Discuss levels of diction (formal, informal, colloquial), and address attitudes associated with the "appropriateness" of different dialects and language styles. Should one dialect be "standard" for all Americans? If so, who (or what) should determine what constitutes "standard" English? Should this standard apply to spoken language or only to written language?

Some years ago, when I was teaching a graduate seminar in fiction   1
at Columbia University, a well-known male novelist visited my class to speak on his development as a writer. In discussing his formative years, he didn't realize it but he seriously endangered his life by remarking that women writers are luckier than those of his sex because they usually spend so much time as children around their mothers and their mothers' friends in the kitchen.

What did he say that for? The women students immediately forgot   2
about being in awe of him and began readying their attack for the question and answer period later on. Even I bristled. There again was that awful image of women locked away from the world in the kitchen with only each other to talk to, and their daughters locked in with them.

But my guest wasn't really being sexist or trying to be provocative   3
or even spoiling for a fight. What he meant—when he got around to examining himself more fully—was that, given the way children are (or were) raised in our society, with little girls kept closer to home and their mothers, the woman writer stands a better chance of being exposed, while growing up, to the kind of talk that goes on among women, more often than not in the kitchen; and that this experience gives her an edge over her male counterpart by instilling in her an appreciation for ordinary speech.

It was clear that my guest lecturer attached great importance to   4
this, which is understandable. Common speech and the plain, workaday words that make it up are, after all, the stock in trade of some of the best fiction writers. They are the principal means by which a character in a novel or story reveals himself and gives voice sometimes to profound feelings and complex ideas about himself and the world. Perhaps the proper measure of a writer's talent is his skill in rendering

everyday speech—when it is appropriate to his story—as well as his ability to tap, to exploit, the beauty, poetry and wisdom it often contains.

"If you say what's on your mind in the language that comes to 5 you from your parents and your street and friends you'll probably say something beautiful." Grace Paley tells this, she says, to her students at the beginning of every writing course.

It's all a matter of exposure and a training of the ear for the would- 6 be writer in those early years of his or her apprenticeship. And, according to my guest lecturer, this training, the best of it, often takes place in as unglamorous a setting as the kitchen.

He didn't know it, but he was essentially describing my experi- 7 ence as a little girl. I grew up among poets. Now they didn't look like poets—whatever that breed is supposed to look like. Nothing about them suggested that poetry was their calling. They were just a group of ordinary housewives and mothers, my mother included, who dressed in a way (shapeless housedresses, dowdy felt hats and long, dark, solemn coats) that made it impossible for me to imagine they had ever been young.

Nor did they do what poets were supposed to do—spend their 8 days in an attic room writing verses. They never put pen to paper except to write occasionally to their relatives in Barbados. "I take my pen in hand hoping these few lines will find you in health as they leave me fair for the time being," was the way their letters invariably began. Rather, their day was spent "scrubbing floor," as they described the work they did.

Several mornings a week these unknown bards would put an 9 apron and a pair of old house shoes in a shopping bag and take the train or streetcar from our section of Brooklyn out to Flatbush. There, those who didn't have steady jobs would wait on certain designated corners for the white housewives in the neighborhood to come along and bargain with them over pay for a day's work cleaning their houses. This was the ritual even in the winter.

Later, armed with the few dollars they had earned, which in their 10 vocabulary became "a few raw-mouth pennies," they made their way back to our neighborhood, where they would sometimes stop off to have a cup of tea or cocoa together before going home to cook dinner for their husbands and children.

The basement kitchen of the brownstone house where my family 11 lived was the usual gathering place. Once inside the warm safety of its walls the women threw off the drab coats and hats, seated themselves at the large center table, drank their cups of tea or cocoa, and talked. While my sister and I sat at a smaller table over in a corner doing our homework, they talked—endlessly, passionately, poeti-

ADDITIONAL QUESTIONS FOR
RESPONDING TO READING

1. Marshall describes many functions that language served for the women she observed. What are these functions?
2. How could Marshall justify labeling the women "poets"?
3. Why does Marshall call the idea of becoming a writer "dangerous"? Do you agree?

cally, and with impressive range. No subject was beyond them. True, they would indulge in the usual gossip: whose husband was running with whom, whose daughter looked slightly "in the way" (pregnant) under her bridal gown as she walked down the aisle. That sort of thing. But they also tackled the great issues of the time. They were always, for example, discussing the state of the economy. It was the mid and late 30s then, and the aftershock of the Depression, with its soup lines and suicides on Wall Street, was still being felt.

Some people, they declared, didn't know how to deal with adver- 12 sity. They didn't know that you had to "tie up your belly" (hold in the pain, that is) when things got rough and go on with life. They took their image from the bellyband that is tied around the stomach of a newborn baby to keep the navel pressed in.

They talked politics. Roosevelt was their hero. He had come along 13 and rescued the country with relief and jobs, and in gratitude they christened their sons Franklin and Delano and hoped they would live up to the names.

If F.D.R. was their hero, Marcus Garvey was their God. The name 14 of the fiery, Jamaican-born black nationalist of the 20s was constantly invoked around the table. For he had been their leader when they first came to the United States from the West Indies shortly after World War I. They had contributed to his organization, the United Negro Improvement Association (UNIA), out of their meager salaries, bought shares in his ill-fated Black Star Shipping Line, and at the height of the movement they had marched as members of his "nurses' brigade" in their white uniforms up Seventh Avenue in Harlem during the great Garvey Day parades. Garvey: He lived on through the power of their memories.

And their talk was of war and rumors of wars. They raged against 15 World War II when it broke out in Europe, blaming it on the politicians. "It's these politicians. They're the ones always starting up all this lot of war. But what they care? It's the poor people got to suffer and mothers with their sons." If it was *their* sons, they swore they would keep them out of the Army by giving them soap to eat each day to make their hearts sound defective. Hitler? He was for them "the devil incarnate."

Then there was home. They reminisced often and at length about 16 home. The old country. Barbados—or Bimshire, as they affectionately called it. The little Caribbean island in the sun they loved but had to leave. "Poor—poor but sweet" was the way they remembered it.

And naturally they discussed their adopted home. America came 17 in for both good and bad marks. They lashed out at it for the racism they encountered. They took to task some of the people they worked for, especially those who gave them only a hard-boiled egg and a few spoonfuls of cottage cheese for lunch. "As if anybody can scrub floor on an egg and some cheese that don't have no taste to it!"

Yet although they caught H in "this man country," as they called 18 America, it was nonetheless a place where "you could at least see your way to make a dollar." That much they acknowledged. They might even one day accumulate enough dollars, with both them and their husbands working, to buy the brownstone houses which, like my family, they were only leasing at that period. This was their consuming ambition: to "buy house" and to see the children through.

There was no way for me to understand it at the time, but the talk 19 that filled the kitchen those afternoons was highly functional. It served as therapy, the cheapest kind available to my mother and her friends. Not only did it help them recover from the long wait on the corner that morning and the bargaining over their labor, it restored them to a sense of themselves and reaffirmed their self-worth. Through language they were able to overcome the humiliations of the work-day.

But more than therapy, that freewheeling, wide-ranging, exu- 20 berant talk functioned as an outlet for the tremendous creative energy they possessed. They were women in whom the need for self-expression was strong, and since language was the only vehicle readily available to them they made of it an art form that—in keeping with the African tradition in which art and life are one—was an integral part of their lives.

And their talk was a refuge. They never really ceased being baffled 21 and overwhelmed by America—its vastness, complexity and power. Its strange customs and laws. At a level beyond words they remained fearful and in awe. Their uneasiness and fear were even reflected in their attitude toward the children they had given birth to in this country. They referred to those like myself, the little Brooklyn-born Bajans (Barbadians), as "these New York children" and complained that they couldn't discipline us properly because of the laws here. "You can't beat these children as you would like, you know, because the authorities in this place will dash you in jail for them. After all, these is New York children." Not only were we different, American, we had, as they saw it, escaped their ultimate authority.

Confronted therefore by a world they could not encompass, which 22 even limited their rights as parents, and at the same time finding themselves permanently separated from the world they had known, they took refuge in language. "Language is the only homeland," Czeslaw Milosz, the emigré Polish writer and Nobel Laureate, has said. This is what it became for the women at the kitchen table.

It served another purpose also, I suspect. My mother and her 23 friends were after all the female counterpart of Ralph Ellison's invisible

COLLABORATIVE ACTIVITY

Divide the class into groups. Then identify idiomatic phrases from Marshall's essay and assign one or two to each student group. Ask students to define the phrases and to determine the meanings of unfamiliar words. In class discussion, ask students to share their definitions and to explain how they formulated them. Do other groups see these definitions as accurate?

man.[1] Indeed, you might say they suffered a triple invisibility, being black, female and foreigners. They really didn't count in American society except as a source of cheap labor. But given the kind of women they were, they couldn't tolerate the fact of their invisibility, their powerlessness. And they fought back, using the only weapon at their command: the spoken word.

Those late afternoon conversations on a wide range of topics were a way for them to feel they exercised some measure of control over their lives and the events that shaped them. "Soully-gal, talk yuk talk!" they were always exhorting each other. "In this man world you got to take yuh mouth and make a gun!" They were in control, if only verbally and if only for the two hours or so that they remained in our house. 24

For me, sitting over in the corner, being seen but not heard, which was the rule for children in those days, it wasn't only what the women talked about—the content—but the way they put things—their style. The insight, irony, wit and humor they brought to their stories and discussions and their poet's inventiveness and daring with language—which of course I could only sense but not define back then. 25

They had taken the standard English taught them in the primary schools of Barbados and transformed it into an idiom, an instrument that more adequately described them—changing around the syntax and imposing their own rhythm and accent so that the sentences were more pleasing to their ears. They added the few African sounds and words that had survived, such as the derisive suck-teeth sound and the word "yam," meaning to eat. And to make it more vivid, more in keeping with their expressive quality, they brought to bear a raft of metaphors, parables, Biblical quotations, sayings and the like: 26

"The sea ain't got no back door," they would say, meaning that it wasn't like a house where if there was a fire you could run out the back. Meaning that it was not to be trifled with. And meaning perhaps in a larger sense that man should treat all of nature with caution and respect. 27

"I has read hell by heart and called every generation blessed!" They sometimes went in for hyperbole. 28

A woman expecting a baby was never said to be pregnant. They never used that word. Rather, she was "in the way" or, better yet, "tumbling big." "Guess who I butt up on in the market the other day tumbling big again!" 29

---

[1] *The Invisible Man* is a 1952 novel by Ralph Ellison that traces the life of a young African-American trying to find himself as an individual and in relation to his race and society. [Eds.]

And a woman with a reputation of being too free with her sexual 30
favors was known in their book as a "thoroughfare"—the sense of
men like a steady stream of cars moving up and down the road of
her life. Or she might be dubbed "a free-bee," which was my favorite
of the two. I liked the image it conjured up of a woman scandalous
perhaps but independent, who flitted from one flower to another in
a garden of male beauties, sampling their nectar, taking her pleasure
at will, the roles reversed.

And nothing, no matter how beautiful, was ever described as 31
simply beautiful. It was always "beautiful-ugly:" the beautiful-ugly
dress, the beautiful-ugly house, the beautiful-ugly car. Why the word
"ugly," I used to wonder, when the thing they were referring to was
beautiful, and they knew it. Why the antonym, the contradiction, the
linking of opposites? It used to puzzle me greatly as a child.

There is the theory in linguistics which states that the idiom of a 32
people, the way they use language, reflects not only the most fundamental views they hold of themselves and the world but their very
conception of reality. Perhaps in using the term "beautiful-ugly" to
describe nearly everything, my mother and her friends were
expressing what they believed to be a fundamental dualism in life:
the idea that a thing is at the same time its opposite, and that these
opposites, these contradictions make up the whole. But theirs was
not a Manichean[2] brand of dualism that sees matter, flesh, the body,
as inherently evil, because they constantly addressed each other as
"soully-gal"—soul: spirit; gal: the body, flesh, the visible self. And
it was clear from their tone that they gave one as much weight and
importance as the other. They had never heard of the mind/body
split.

As for God, they summed up His essential attitude in a phrase. 33
"God," they would say, "don' love ugly and He ain't stuck on pretty."

Using everyday speech, the simple commonplace words—but 34
always with imagination and skill—they gave voice to the most complex ideas. Flannery O'Connor would have approved of how they
made ordinary language work, as she put it, "double-time,"
stretching, shading, deepening its meaning. Like Joseph Conrad they
were always trying to infuse new life in the "old old words worn thin
. . . by . . . careless usage." And the goals of their oral art were the
same as his: "to make you hear, to make you feel . . . to make you
see." This was their guiding esthetic.

---

[2]A religious philosophy which asserts that the forces of good and evil are engaged in an
eternal cosmic struggle. This cosmic struggle also takes place in each individual, with the body
belonging to Satan and the spirit belonging to God. The elect succeed in freeing the light of the
spirit from the darkness of the material body. [Eds.]

By the time I was 8 or 9, I graduated from the corner of the kitchen   35
to the neighborhood library, and thus from the spoken to the written
word. The Macon Street Branch of the Brooklyn Public Library was
an imposing half block long edifice of heavy gray masonry, with glass-
paneled doors at the front and two tall metal torches symbolizing the
light that comes of learning flanking the wide steps outside.

The inside was just as impressive. More steps—of pale marble   36
with gleaming brass railing at the center and sides—led up to the
circulation desk, and a great pendulum clock gazed down from the
balcony stacks that faced the entrance. Usually stationed at the top
of the steps like the guards outside Buckingham Palace was the custodian, a stern-faced West Indian type who for years, until I was old
enough to obtain an adult card, would immediately shoo me with
one hand into the Children's Room and with the other threaten me
into silence, a finger to his lips. You would have thought he was the
chief librarian and not just someone whose job it was to keep the
brass polished and the clock wound. I put him in a story called "Barbados" years later and had terrible things happen to him at the end.

I was sheltered from the storm of adolescence in the Macon Street   37
library, reading voraciously, indiscriminately, everything from Jane
Austen to Zane Grey, but with a special passion for the long, full-
blown, richly detailed 18th- and 19th-century picaresque tales:[3] *Tom
Jones. Great Expectations. Vanity Fair.*

But although I loved nearly everything I read and would enter   38
fully into the lives of the characters—indeed, would cease being
myself and become them—I sensed a lack after a time. Something I
couldn't quite define was missing. And then one day, browsing in
the poetry section, I came across a book by someone called Paul
Laurence Dunbar, and opening it I found the photograph of a wistful,
sad-eyed poet who to my surprise was black. I turned to a poem at
random. "Little brown-baby wif spa'klin'/eyes/Come to yo' pappy an'
set on his knee." Although I had a little difficulty at first with the
words in dialect, the poem spoke to me as nothing I had read before
of the closeness, the special relationship I had had with my father,
who by then had become an ardent believer in Father Divine[4] and
gone to live in Father's "kingdom" in Harlem. Reading it helped to
ease somewhat the tight knot of sorrow and longing I carried around
in my chest that refused to go away. I read another poem. "Lias! Lias!

---

[3]An episodic novel in which a rascal who lives by his wits has a long, loosely connected series
of adventures. The genre emerged in sixteenth-century Spain. [Eds.]

[4]Father Divine (George Baker, 1882–1965) founded the Peace Mission Movement, an interracial
religious organization. Many of his followers believed he was God. [Eds.]

Bless de Lawd!/Don' you know de day's/erbroad?/Ef you don' get up, you scamp/Dey'll be trouble in dis camp.'' I laughed. It reminded me of the way my mother sometimes yelled at my sister and me to get out of bed in the mornings.

And another: ''Seen my lady home las' night/Jump back, 39 honey, jump back./Hel' huh han' an' sque'z it tight . . .'' About love between a black man and a black woman. I had never seen that written about before and it roused in me all kinds of delicious feelings and hopes.

And I began to search then for books and stories and poems about 40 ''The Race'' (as it was put back then), about my people. While not abandoning Thackeray, Fielding, Dickens and the others, I started asking the reference librarian, who was white, for books by Negro writers, although I must admit I did so at first with a feeling of shame—the shame I and many others used to experience in those days whenever the word ''Negro'' or ''colored'' came up.

No grade school literature teacher of mine had ever mentioned 41 Dunbar or James Weldon Johnson or Langston Hughes.[5] I didn't know that Zora Neale Hurston existed and was busy writing and being published during those years. Nor was I made aware of people like Frederick Douglass and Harriet Tubman—their spirit and example— or the great 19th-century abolitionist and feminist Sojourner Truth. There wasn't even Negro History Week when I attended P.S. 35 on Decatur Street!

What I needed, what all the kids—West Indian and native black 42 American alike—with whom I grew up needed, was an equivalent of the Jewish shul, someplace where we could go after school—the schools that were shortchanging us—and read works by those like ourselves and learn about our history.

It was around that time also that I began harboring the dangerous 43 thought of someday trying to write myself. Perhaps a poem about an apple tree, although I had never seen one. Or the story of a girl who could magically transplant herself to wherever she wanted to be in the world—such as Father Divine's kingdom in Harlem. Dunbar— his dark, eloquent face, his large volume of poems—permitted me to dream that I might someday write, and with something of the power with words my mother and her friends possessed.

When people at readings and writers' conferences ask me who 44 my major influences were, they are sometimes a little disappointed when I don't immediately name the usual literary giants. True, I am

WRITING SUGGESTIONS

1. Describe the women who inhabit your ''kitchen.'' Take into account their mode of living, their relationships to one another, and their attitudes.
2. According to both Marshall and Annie Dillard, writing is a ''subversive'' activity. After explaining what these writers mean when they apply such terms, write an essay in which you describe a time when your writing was dangerous or subversive.

---

[5]Important African-American literary figures and thinkers who influenced later writers and who were active in the Harlem Renaissance, an American cultural movement of the 1920s. [Eds.]

indebted to those writers, white and black, whom I read during my formative years and still read for instruction and pleasure. But they were preceded in my life by another set of giants whom I always acknowledge before all others: the group of women around the table long ago. They taught me my first lesson in the narrative art. They trained my ear. They set a standard of excellence. This is why the best of my work must be attributed to them; it stands as testimony to the rich legacy of language and culture they so freely passed on to me in the wordshop of the kitchen.

RESPONDING TO READING

1. As you look back on your own childhood experiences, how would you describe "the talk that filled the kitchen" in your own family when adults got together? Was it the way Paule Marshall describes it—a kind of therapy, an outlet for creative energy and self-expression—or was it different? Explain.   **2.** Explain what the statement "Language is the only homeland" (paragraph 22) means. Do you feel this is a valid statement? Why?   **3.** Who were the major influences on Marshall's life as a writer? Who are her models? Why? If you became a writer, whom would you name as your major influences or models?

On Keeping a Notebook

JOAN DIDION

Joan Didion (1934–   ), a native of California, is an essayist, novelist, and screenwriter. She is best known for her nonfiction, which is reflective and personal and, at the same time, journalistic and spare in style. Her nonfiction books include two essay collections, *Slouching Toward Bethlehem* (1968) and *The White Album* (1979), and two works of reportage, *Salvador* (1983) and *Miami* (1987). She has said of her writing, "There is always a point in the writing of a piece where I sit in a room literally papered with false starts and cannot put one word after another." In the following essay, characteristically full of personal anecdotes and introspection, Didion explores what her notebooks are really about.

" 'That woman Estelle,' " the note reads, " 'is partly the reason 1 why George Sharp and I are separated today.' *Dirty crepe-de-Chine wrapper, hotel bar, Wilmington RR, 9:45 a.m. August Monday morning.*"

Since the note is in my notebook, it presumably has some meaning 2 to me. I study it for a long while. At first I have only the most general notion of what I was doing on an August Monday morning in the bar of the hotel across from the Pennsylvania Railroad station in Wilmington, Delaware (waiting for a train? missing one? 1960? 1961? why Wilmington?), but I do remember being there. The woman in the dirty crepe-de-Chine wrapper had come down from her room for a beer, and the bartender had heard before the reason why George Sharp and she were separated today. "Sure," he said, and went on mopping the floor. "You told me." At the other end of the bar is a girl. She is talking, pointedly, not to the man beside her but to a cat lying in the triangle of sunlight cast through the open door. She is wearing a plaid silk dress from Peck & Peck, and the hem is coming down.

Here is what it is: the girl has been on the Eastern Shore, and 3 now she is going back to the city, leaving the man beside her, and all she can see ahead are the viscous summer sidewalks and the 3 A.M. long-distance calls that will make her lie awake and then sleep drugged through all the steaming mornings left in August (1960? 1961?). Because she must go directly from the train to lunch in New York, she wishes that she had a safety pin for the hem of the plaid silk dress, and she also wishes that she could forget about the hem and the lunch and stay in the cool bar that smells of disinfectant and malt and make friends with the woman in the crepe-de-Chine wrapper. She is afflicted by a little self-pity, and she wants to compare Estelles. That is what that was all about.

Why did I write it down? In order to remember, of course, but 4 exactly what was it I wanted to remember? How much of it actually happened? Did any of it? Why do I keep a notebook at all? It is easy to deceive oneself on all those scores. The impulse to write things down is a peculiarly compulsive one, inexplicable to those who do not share it, useful only accidentally, only secondarily, in the way that any compulsion tries to justify itself. I suppose that it begins or does not begin in the cradle. Although I have felt compelled to write things down since I was five years old, I doubt that my daughter ever will, for she is a singularly blessed and accepting child, delighted with life exactly as life presents itself to her, unafraid to go to sleep and unafraid to wake up. Keepers of private notebooks are a different breed altogether, lonely and resistant rearrangers of things, anxious malcontents, children afflicted apparently at birth with some presentiment of loss.

My first notebook was a Big Five tablet, given to me by my mother 5 with the sensible suggestion that I stop whining and learn to amuse myself by writing down my thoughts. She returned the tablet to me a few years ago; the first entry is an account of a woman who believed herself to be freezing to death in the Arctic night, only to find, when

Of course I stole the title for this talk from George Orwell. One reason I stole it was that I like the sound of the words: Why I Write. There you have three short unambiguous words that share a sound, and the sound they share is this:

I

I

I

In many ways writing is the act of saying *I*, of imposing oneself upon other people, of saying *listen to me*, *see it my way*, *change your mind*. It's an aggressive, even a hostile act. You can disguise its aggressiveness all you want with veils of subordinate clauses and qualifiers and tentative subjunctives, with ellipses and evasions—with the whole manner of intimating rather than claiming, of alluding rather than stating—but there's no getting around the fact that setting words on paper is the tactic of a secret bully, an invasion, an imposition of the writer's sensibility on the reader's most private space.

**ADDITIONAL QUESTIONS FOR
RESPONDING TO READING**

1. Do you see evidence of Didion's worldview in "On Keeping a Notebook"? What does she see as the role of the individual in a fragmented world?
2. Didion says that the purpose of her notebook is not "to have an accurate factual record." What does she mean when she says, "Not only have I always had trouble distinguishing between what happened and what merely might have happened, but I remain unconvinced that the distinction, for my purposes, matters"? What are her purposes? Do you believe journalists like Didion have an obligation to make clear distinctions between what actually happened and what might have happened? Or do her purposes here excuse her? (You might tell students that lawsuits over journalistic inaccuracies—in particular, misquoting sources or quoting them out of context—have become increasingly common in recent years. If Didion's notebook is a source for future articles, she may have to be more careful than she might like to be.)
3. Didion says we are "taught to be diffident, just this side of self-effacing." What does she mean, and what is her response to this attitude? How does keeping a notebook "give us away"?

day broke, that she had stumbled onto the Sahara Desert, where she would die of the heat before lunch. I have no idea what turn of a five-year-old's mind could have prompted so insistently, "ironic" and exotic a story, but it does reveal a certain predilection for the extreme which has dogged me into adult life; perhaps if I were analytically inclined I would find it a truer story than any I might have told about Donald Johnson's birthday party or the day my cousin Brenda put Kitty Litter in the aquarium.

So the point of my keeping a notebook has never been, nor is it 6 now, to have an accurate factual record of what I have been doing or thinking. That would be a different impulse entirely, an instinct for reality which I sometimes envy but do not possess. At no point have I ever been able successfully to keep a diary; my approach to daily life ranges from the grossly negligent to the merely absent, and on those few occasions when I have tried dutifully to record a day's events, boredom has so overcome me that the results are mysterious at best. What is this business about "shopping, typing piece, dinner with E, depressed?" Shopping for what? Typing what piece? Who is E? Was this "E" depressed, or was I depressed? Who cares?

In fact I have abandoned altogether that kind of pointless entry; 7 instead I tell what some would call lies. "That's simply not true," the members of my family frequently tell me when they come up against my memory of a shared event. "The party was *not* for you, the spider was *not* a black widow, *it wasn't that way at all*." Very likely they are right, for not only have I always had trouble distinguishing between what happened and what merely might have happened, but I remain unconvinced that the distinction, for my purposes, matters. The cracked crab that I recall having for lunch the day my father came home from Detroit in 1945 must certainly be embroidery, worked into the day's pattern to lend verisimilitude; I was ten years old and would not now remember the cracked crab. The day's events did not turn on cracked crab. And yet it is precisely that fictitious crab that makes me see the afternoon all over again, a home movie run all too often, the father bearing gifts, the child weeping, an exercise in family love and guilt. Or that is what it was to me. Similarly, perhaps it never did snow that August in Vermont; perhaps there never were flurries in the night wind, and maybe no one else felt the ground hardening and summer already dead even as we pretended to bask in it, but that was how it felt to me, and it might as well have snowed, could have snowed, did snow.

How it felt to me: that is getting closer to the truth about a notebook. 8 I sometimes delude myself about why I keep a notebook, imagine that some thrifty virtue derives from preserving everything observed. See enough and write it down, I tell myself, and then some morning when the world seems drained of wonder, some day when I am only going through the motions of doing what I am supposed to do, which is write—on that bankrupt morning I will simply open my notebook and there it will all be, a forgotten account with accumulated interest, paid passage back to the world out there: dialogue overheard in hotels and elevators and at the hat-check counter in Pavillon (one middle-aged man shows his hat-check to another and says, "That's my old football number"); impressions of Bettina Aptheker[1] and Benjamin Sonnenberg[2] and Teddy ("Mr. Acapulco") Stauffer[3]; careful *aperçus*[4] about tennis bums and failed fashion models and Greek shipping heiresses, one of whom taught me a significant lesson (a lesson I could have learned from F. Scott Fitzgerald,[5] but perhaps we all must meet the very rich for ourselves) by asking, when I arrived to interview her in her orchid-filled sitting room on the second day of a paralyzing New York blizzard, whether it was snowing outside.

I imagine, in other words, that the notebook is about other people.   9 But of course it is not. I have no real business with what one stranger said to another at the hat-check counter in Pavillon; in fact I suspect that the line "That's my old football number" touched not my own imagination at all, but merely some memory of something once read, probably "The Eighty-Yard Run." Nor is my concern with a woman in a dirty crepe-de-Chine wrapper in a Wilmington bar. My stake is always, of course, in the unmentioned girl in the plaid silk dress. *Remember what it was to be me*: that is always the point.

It is a difficult point to admit. We are brought up in the ethic that   10 others, any others, all others, are by definition more interesting than ourselves; taught to be diffident, just this side of self-effacing ("You're the least important person in the room and don't forget it," Jessica Mitford's[6] governess would hiss in her ear on the advent of any social occasion; I copied that into my notebook because it is only recently that I have been able to enter a room without hearing some such phrase in my inner ear.) Only the very young and the very old may recount their dreams at breakfast, dwell upon self, interrupt with memories of beach picnics and favorite Liberty lawn dresses and the rainbow trout in a creek near Colorado Springs. The rest of us are

Ask students to keep a notebook for a specific period of time. Encourage them to observe carefully and write frequently. At the end of this period, have students talk in class about the nature of their observations and the form their entries took. An interesting follow-up would be to collect the notebooks, return them a month later, and have students record their reactions to the entries.

COLLABORATIVE ACTIVITY

Didion is renowned for her no-nonsense style and her clean, precise sentences. In "Why I Write," she describes the "infinite power" of grammar:

> To shift the structure of a sentence alters the meaning of that sentence, as definitely and inflexibly as the position of a camera alters the meaning of the object photographed. Many people know about camera angles now, but not so many know about sentences. The arrangement of the words matters, and the arrangement you want can be found in the picture in your mind. The picture dictates the arrangement. The picture dictates whether this will be a sentence with or without clauses, a sentence that ends hard or a dying-fall sentence, long or short, active or passive. The picture tells you how to arrange the words and the arrangement of the words tells you, or tells me, what's going on in the picture.

Break students into groups, and read aloud the preceding passage. Then, have each group examine one or two sentences from "On Keeping a Notebook." Have each group analyze the sentences to see how Didion achieves her effect.

---

[1] A leader of the 1960's free speech movement at the University of California-Berkeley. [Eds.]

[2] Well-known public relations expert who once described himself as "a cabinetmaker who fashioned large pedestals for small statues." [Eds.]

[3] Big band leader who retired to Acapulco and opened his own nightclub.

[4] Observations. [Eds.]

[5] American author (1896–1940) who wrote stories and novels about the manners and morals of the rich. His most famous works are set in the 1920s and deal with the ironies of the American dream. [Eds.]

[6] British-born (1917–   ) self-styled muckraker who exposes unfair and unscrupulous methods in business and government. [Eds.]

expected, rightly, to affect absorption in other people's favorite dresses, other people's trout.

And so we do. But our notebooks give us away, for however 11 dutifully we record what we see around us, the common denominator of all we see is always, transparently, shamelessly, the implacable "I." We are not talking here about the kind of notebook that is patently for public consumption, a structural conceit for binding together a series of graceful *pensées*,[7] we are talking about something private, about bits of the mind's string too short to use, an indiscriminate and erratic assemblage with meaning only for its maker.

And sometimes even the maker has difficulty with the meaning. 12 There does not seem to be, for example, any point in my knowing for the rest of my life that, during 1964, 720 tons of soot fell on every square mile of New York City, yet there it is in my notebook, labeled "FACT." Nor do I really need to remember that Ambrose Bierce liked to spell Leland Stanford's name "£eland $tanford" or that "smart women almost always wear black in Cuba," a fashion hint without much potential for practical application. And does not the relevance of these notes seem marginal at best?:

> In the basement museum of the Inyo County Courthouse in Independence, California, sign pinned to a mandarin coat: "This MANDARIN COAT was often worn by Mrs. Minnie S. Brooks when giving lectures on her TEAPOT COLLECTION."

> Redhead getting out of car in front of Beverly Wilshire Hotel, chinchilla stole, Vuitton bags with tags reading:
> MRS LOU FOX
> HOTEL SAHARA
> VEGAS

Well, perhaps not entirely marginal. As a matter of fact, Mrs. 13 Minnie S. Brooks and her MANDARIN COAT pull me back into my own childhood, for although I never knew Mrs. Brooks and did not visit Inyo County until I was thirty, I grew up in just such a world, in houses cluttered with Indian relics and bits of gold ore and ambergris and the souvenirs my Aunt Mercy Farnsworth brought back from the Orient. It is a long way from that world to Mrs. Lou Fox's world, where we all live now, and is it not just as well to remember that? Might not Mrs. Minnie S. Brooks help me to remember what I am? Might not Mrs. Lou Fox help me to remember what I am not?

But sometimes the point is harder to discern. What exactly did 14 I have in mind when I noted down that it cost the father of someone I know $650 a month to light the place on the Hudson in

---

[7]Thoughts, maxims. [Eds.]

which he lived before the Crash? What use was I planning to make of this line by Jimmy Hoffa:[8] "I may have my faults, but being wrong ain't one of them?" And although I think it interesting to know where the girls who travel with the Syndicate have their hair done when they find themselves on the West Coast, will I ever make suitable use of it? Might I not be better off just passing it on to John O'Hara?[9] What is a recipe for sauerkraut doing in my notebook? What kind of magpie keeps this notebook? *"He was born the night the Titanic went down."* That seems a nice enough line, and I even recall who said it, but is it not really a better line in life than it could ever be in fiction?

But of course that is exactly it: not that I should ever use the line, 15 but that I should remember the woman who said it and the afternoon I heard it. We were on her terrace by the sea, and we were finishing the wine left from lunch, trying to get what sun there was, a California winter sun. The woman whose husband was born the night the *Titanic* went down wanted to rent her house, wanted to go back to her children in Paris. I remember wishing that I could afford the house, which cost $1,000 a month. "Someday you will," she said lazily. "Someday it all comes." There in the sun on her terrace it seemed easy to believe in someday, but later I had a low-grade afternoon hangover and ran over a black snake on the way to the supermarket and was flooded with inexplicable fear when I heard the checkout clerk explaining to the man ahead of me why she was finally divorcing her husband. "He left me no choice," she said over and over as she punched the register. "He has a little seven-month-old baby by her, he left me no choice." I would like to believe that my dread then was for the human condition, but of course it was for me, because I wanted a baby and did not then have one and because I wanted to own the house that cost $1,000 a month to rent and because I had a hangover.

It all comes back. Perhaps it is difficult to see the value in having 16 one's self back in that kind of mood, but I do see it; I think we are well advised to keep on nodding terms with the people we used to be, whether we find them attractive company or not. Otherwise they turn up unannounced and surprise us, come hammering on the mind's door at 4 A.M. of a bad night and demand to know who deserted them, who betrayed them, who is going to make amends. We forget all too soon the things we thought we could never forget.

---

[8]United States labor leader (1913–   ) who was president of the Teamsters Union. Convicted of jury tampering and sentenced to a thirteen-year prison term. After his release in 1971, he mysteriously disappeared and was rumored to have been murdered by rival union leaders. [Eds.]

[9]American novelist (1905–70). [Eds.]

WRITING SUGGESTIONS

1. Write a personal essay about a moment when your present collided with your past—when your present self was forced to reexamine the actions of a past self.
2. Discuss similarities and differences between Didion's concept of self and those expressed by George Orwell in "Why I Write" (page 61).

ANSWERS TO RESPONDING TO READING

1. According to Didion, it is a good idea to "keep on nodding terms with the people we used to be," or they will "turn up unannounced." One either recognizes or is made a victim of the past. For Didion, the notebook also reinforces the sense of self, affirming its importance and beating down the voice that tells her she is the "least important person in the room."
2. Answers will vary. Students may find some of Didion's revelations melodramatic and therefore self-indulgent. Encourage them, however, to recognize her honesty and to emulate it in their own entries. Another issue to men-

We forget the loves and the betrayals alike, forget what we whispered and what we screamed, forget who we were. I have already lost touch with a couple of people I used to be; one of them, a seventeen-year-old, presents little threat, although it would be of some interest to me to know again what it feels like to sit on a river levee drinking vodka-and-orange-juice and listening to Les Paul and Mary Ford and their echoes sing "How High the Moon" on the car radio. (You see I still have the scenes: but I no longer perceive myself among those present, no longer could even improvise the dialogue.) The other one, a twenty-three-year-old, bothers me more. She was always a good deal of trouble, and I suspect she will reappear when I least want to see her, skirts too long, shy to the point of aggravation, always the injured party, full of recriminations and little hurts and stories I do not want to hear again, at once saddening me and angering me with her vulnerability and ignorance, an apparition all the more insistent for being so long banished.

It is a good idea, then, to keep in touch, and I suppose that 17 keeping in touch is what notebooks are all about. And we are all on our own when it comes to keeping those lines open to ourselves: your notebook will never help me, nor mine you. *"So what's new in the whiskey business?"* What could that possibly mean to you? To me it means a blonde in a Pucci bathing suit sitting with a couple of fat men by the pool at the Beverly Hills Hotel. Another man approaches, and they all regard one another in silence for a while. "So what's new in the whiskey business?" one of the fat men finally says by way of welcome, and the blonde stands up, arches one foot and dips it in the pool, looking all the while at the cabaña where Baby Pignatari is talking on the telephone. That is all there is to that, except that several years later I saw the blonde coming out of Saks Fifth Avenue in New York with her California complexion and a voluminous mink coat. In the harsh wind that day she looked old and irrevocably tired to me, and even the skins in the mink coat were not worked the way they were doing them that year, not the way she would have wanted them done, and there is the point of the story. For a while after that I did not like to look in the mirror, and my eyes would skim the newspapers and pick out only the deaths, the cancer victims, the premature coronaries, the suicides, and I stopped riding the Lexington Avenue IRT because I noticed for the first time that all the strangers I had seen for years—the man with the seeing-eye dog, the spinster who read the classified pages every day, the fat girl who always got off with me at Grand Central—looked older than they once had.

It all comes back. Even that recipe for sauerkraut: even that brings 18 it back. I was on Fire Island when I first made that sauerkraut, and

it was raining, and we drank a lot of bourbon and ate the sauerkraut and went to bed at ten, and I listened to the rain and the Atlantic and felt safe. I made the sauerkraut again last night and it did not make me feel any safer, but that is, as they say, another story.

RESPONDING TO READING

1. Why do you think it is so important for Joan Didion to remember "what it was to be me?"   **2.** If you were keeping a notebook of the kind Didion describes, what would you record in today's entry? Why?   **3.** In paragraph 16 Didion says, "I have already lost touch with a couple of people I used to be." What does she mean? Do you think it is possible for someone to change as completely as Didion claims to have done? Have you experienced the kind of changes Didion describes?

tion is that a justification of the indulgence of self, the "implacable 'I,'" just may be Didion's point.

3. Didion may have consciously lost touch with her former personae, but they still exist deep inside her, as she indicates when she refers to one of them: "I suspect she will reappear when I least want to see her." If she is aware of her past, she can control it; she also can write about it, making the past part of her present. Certainly it is possible for people to change quite a bit during the course of a life, but some vestiges of their past personalities will always remain. According to Didion, all aspects of a personality must be integrated—in her case, in her notebook—if a writer is to maintain a sense of self.

Why I Write

GEORGE ORWELL

Eric Blair (1903–1950) was an Englishman, born in Bengal, India, who took the pen name George Orwell. He attended school in England and then became a member of the Indian Imperial Police in Burma, where he came to question the British methods of colonialism. Orwell was an enemy of totalitarianism and spokesman for the opressed; his most famous novels are *Animal Farm* (1945) and *1984* (1949), both satires of totalitarian political systems. Some other titles are *Down and Out in Paris and London* (1933), *Keep the Aspidistra Flying* (1936), *The Road to Wigan Pier* (1937), and *Homage to Catalonia* (1938), his memoir of the Spanish civil war. In his essay "Why I Write," Orwell reveals the events and motivations that led to his literary career, and he tells how he eventually strove to "make political writing into an art."

BACKGROUND ON READING

"Why I Write" first appeared in a small English literary magazine, *Gangrel* (no. 4), in the summer of 1946. Because of its value for helping readers to understand Orwell's approach to writing, the essay later appeared at the beginning of his collected essays.

From a very early age, perhaps the age of five or six, I knew that 1 when I grew up I should be a writer. Between the ages of about seventeen and twenty-four I tried to abandon this idea, but I did so with the consciousness that I was outraging my true nature and that sooner or later I should have to settle down and write books.

I was the middle child of three, but there was a gap of five years 2 on either side, and I barely saw my father before I was eight. For this and other reasons I was somewhat lonely, and I soon developed disagreeable mannerisms which made me unpopular throughout my

FOR OPENERS

Examine the definition of propaganda, and cite some examples of its use in this century. Some contemporary critics might argue that all literature has a political or ideological bias, whether intentional or not. Discuss the political consequences of language choice, such as using plural forms instead of the traditional masculine singular to discuss a subject ("Students must study. *They* should approach *their* studies with zeal" instead of "A student must study. *He* should approach *his* studies with zeal.")

ADDITIONAL QUESTIONS FOR RESPONDING TO READING

1. When you were a child, what did you want to be when you grew up? Has that career choice changed over the years? If so, how?
2. To what extent does the age in which you live influence your thoughts and attitudes? What is its greatest influence? Would you be a different person if you lived in a different time?
3. Why, according to Orwell, does he write? Do you believe his explanation? Why or why not?
4. What does Orwell mean when he says he spent five years in an unsuitable profession? Did his years with the Indian Imperial Police affect his writing? How? Was that effect positive or negative?

schooldays. I had the lonely child's habit of making up stories and holding conversations with imaginary persons, and I think from the very start my literary ambitions were mixed up with the feeling of being isolated and undervalued. I knew that I had a facility with words and a power of facing unpleasant facts, and I felt that this created a sort of private world in which I could get my own back for my failure in everyday life. Nevertheless the volume of serious—*i.e.* seriously intended—writing which I produced all through my childhood and boyhood would not amount to half a dozen pages. I wrote my first poem at the age of four or five, my mother taking it down to dictation. I cannot remember anything about it except that it was about a tiger and the tiger had "chair-like teeth"—a good enough phrase, but I fancy the poem was a plagiarism of Blake's "Tiger, Tiger." At eleven, when the war of 1914–18 broke out, I wrote a patriotic poem which was printed in the local newspaper, as was another, two years later, on the death of Kitchener.[1] From time to time, when I was a bit older, I wrote bad and usually unfinished "nature poems" in the Georgian style. I also, about twice, attempted a short story which was a ghastly failure. That was the total of the would-be serious work that I actually set down on paper during all those years.

However, throughout this time I did in a sense engage in literary 3 activities. To begin with there was the made-to-order stuff which I produced quickly, easily and without much pleasure to myself. Apart from school work, I wrote *vers d'occasion*, semi-comic poems which I could turn out at what now seems to me astonishing speed—at fourteen I wrote a whole rhyming play, in imitation of Aristophanes, in about a week—and helped to edit school magazines, both printed and in manuscript. These magazines were the most pitiful burlesque stuff that you could imagine, and I took far less trouble with them than I now would with the cheapest journalism. But side by side with all this, for fifteen years or more, I was carrying out a literary exercise of a quite different kind: this was the making up of a continuous "story" about myself, a sort of diary existing only in the mind. I believe this is a common habit of children and adolescents. As a very small child I used to imagine that I was, say, Robin Hood, and picture myself as the hero of thrilling adventures, but quite soon my "story" ceased to be narcissistic in a crude way and became more and more a mere description of what I was doing and the things I saw. For minutes at a time this kind of thing would be running through my

---

[1] Horatio Herbert Kitchener, 1st Earl (1850–1916) was a British field marshal and statesman who served in India as commander and chief of British forces. He died when his ship hit a German mine and sank off the Orkney Islands. [Eds.]

head: "He pushed the door open and entered the room. A yellow beam of sunlight, filtering through the muslin curtains, slanted on to the table, where a matchbox, half open, lay beside the inkpot. With his right hand in his pocket he moved across to the window. Down in the street a tortoiseshell cat was chasing a dead leaf," etc., etc. This habit continued till I was about twenty-five, right through my non-literary years. Although I had to search, and did search, for the right words, I seemed to be making this descriptive effort almost against my will, under a kind of compulsion from outside. The "story" must, I suppose, have reflected the styles of the various writers I admired at different ages, but so far as I remember it always had the same meticulous descriptive quality.

When I was about sixteen I suddenly discovered the joy of mere 4 words, *i.e.* the sounds and associations of words. The lines from *Paradise Lost*—

> So hee with difficulty and labour hard
> Moved on: with difficulty and labour hee,

which do not now seem to me so very wonderful, sent shivers down my backbone; and the spelling "hee" for "he" was an added pleasure. As for the need to describe things, I knew all about it already. So it is clear what kind of books I wanted to write, in so far as I could be said to want to write books at that time. I wanted to write enormous naturalistic novels with unhappy endings, full of detailed descriptions and arresting similes, and also full of purple passages in which words were used partly for the sake of their sound. And in fact my first completed novel, *Burmese Days*, which I wrote when I was thirty but projected much earlier, is rather that kind of book.

I give all this background information because I do not think one 5 can assess a writer's motives without knowing something of his early development. His subject matter will be determined by the age he lives in—at least this is true in tumultuous, revolutionary ages like our own—but before he ever begins to write he will have acquired an emotional attitude from which he will never completely escape. It is his job, no doubt, to discipline his temperament and avoid getting stuck at some immature stage, or in some perverse mood: but if he escapes from his early influences altogether, he will have killed his impulse to write. Putting aside the need to earn a living, I think there are four great motives for writing, at any rate for writing prose. They exist in different degrees in every writer, and in any one writer the proportions will vary from time to time, according to the atmosphere in which he is living. They are:

TEACHING STRATEGY

Examine what Orwell is saying about literature and propaganda. Is he arguing for a greater acceptance of political writing by the literary establishment? How would such an acceptance serve his own interests?

COLLABORATIVE ACTIVITY

Divide the class into groups to discuss the poem that appears in "Why I Write." Why does Orwell include it in the essay? What does it mean? Examine its importance to Orwell's development.

1. Sheer egoism. Desire to seem clever, to be talked about, to be remembered after death, to get your own back on grownups who snubbed you in childhood, etc., etc. It is humbug to pretend that this is not a motive, and a strong one. Writers share this characteristic with scientists, artists, politicians, lawyers, soldiers, successful businessmen—in short, with the whole top crust of humanity. The great mass of human beings are not acutely selfish. After the age of about thirty they abandon individual ambition—in many cases, indeed, they almost abandon the sense of being individuals at all—and live chiefly for others, or are simply smothered under drudgery. But there is also the minority of gifted, wilful people who are determined to live their own lives to the end, and writers belong in this class. Serious writers, I should say, are on the whole more vain and self-centered than journalists, though less interested in money.

2. Esthetic enthusiasm. Perception of beauty in the external world, or, on the other hand, in words and their right arrangement. Pleasure in the impact of one sound on another, in the firmness of good prose or the rhythm of a good story. Desire to share an experience which one feels is valuable and ought not to be missed. The esthetic motive is very feeble in a lot of writers, but even a pamphleteer or a writer of textbooks will have pet words and phrases which appeal to him for non-utilitarian reasons; or he may feel strongly about typography, width of margins, etc. Above the level of a railway guide, no book is quite free from esthetic considerations.

3. Historical impulse. Desire to see things as they are, to find out true facts and store them up for the use of posterity.

4. Political purpose—using the word "political" in the widest possible sense. Desire to push the world in a certain direction, to alter other people's idea of the kind of society that they should strive after. Once again, no book is genuinely free from political bias. The opinion that art should have nothing to do with politics is itself a political attitude.

It can be seen how these various impulses must war against one another, and how they must fluctuate from person to person and from time to time. By nature—taking your "nature" to be the state you have attained when you are first adult—I am a person in whom the first three motives would outweigh the fourth. In a peaceful age I might have written ornate or merely descriptive books, and might have remained almost unaware of my political loyalties. As it is I have been forced into becoming a sort of pamphleteer. First I spent five years in an unsuitable profession (the Indian Imperial Police, in

Burma), and then I underwent poverty and the sense of failure. This
increased my natural hatred of authority and made me for the first
time fully aware of the existence of the working classes, and the job
in Burma had given me some understanding of the nature of imperialism: but these experiences were not enough to give me an accurate
political orientation. Then came Hitler, the Spanish civil war, etc. By
the end of 1935 I had still failed to reach a firm decision. I remember
a little poem that I wrote at that date, expressing my dilemma:

> A happy vicar I might have been
> Two hundred years ago,
> To preach upon eternal doom
> And watch my walnuts grow;
>
> But born, alas, in an evil time,   5
> I missed that pleasant haven,
> For the hair has grown on my upper lip
> And the clergy are all clean-shaven.
>
> And later still the times were good,
> We were so easy to please,   10
> We rocked our troubled thoughts to sleep
> On the bosoms of the trees.
>
> All ignorant we dared to own
> The joys we now dissemble;
> The greenfinch on the apple bough   15
> Could make my enemies tremble.
>
> But girls' bellies and apricots,
> Roach in a shaded stream,
> Horses, ducks in flight at dawn,
> All these are a dream.   20
>
> It is forbidden to dream again;
> We maim our joys or hide them;
> Horses are made of chromium steel
> And little fat men shall ride them.
>
> I am the worm who never turned,   25
> The eunuch without a harem;
> Between the priest and the commissar
> I walk like Eugene Aram;

And the commissar is telling my fortune
While the radio plays,   *30*
But the priest has promised an Austin Seven,
For Duggie always pays.

I dreamed I dwelt in marble halls,
And woke to find it true;
I wasn't born for an age like this;   *35*
Was Smith? Was Jones? Were you?

The Spanish war and other events in 1936–7 turned the scale and thereafter I knew where I stood. Every line of serious work that I have written since 1936 has been written, directly or indirectly, *against* totalitarianism and *for* democratic socialism, as I understand it. It seems to me nonsense, in a period like our own, to think that one can avoid writing of such subjects. Everyone writes of them in one guise or another. It is simply a question of which side one takes and what approach one follows. And the more one is conscious of one's political bias, the more chance one has of acting politically without sacrificing one's esthetic and intellectual integrity.

What I have most wanted to do throughout the past ten years is 7 to make political writing into an art. My starting point is always a feeling of partisanship, a sense of injustice. When I sit down to write a book, I do not say to myself, "I am going to produce a work of art." I write it because there is some lie that I want to expose, some fact to which I want to draw attention, and my initial concern is to get a hearing. But I could not do the work of writing a book, or even a long magazine article, if it were not also an esthetic experience. Anyone who cares to examine my work will see that even when it is downright propaganda it contains much that a full-time politician would consider irrelevant. I am not able, and I do not want, completely to abandon the world-view that I acquired in childhood. So long as I remain alive and well I shall continue to feel strongly about prose style, to love the surface of the earth, and to take a pleasure in solid objects and scraps of useless information. It is no use trying to suppress that side of myself. The job is to reconcile my ingrained likes and dislikes with the essentially public, non-individual activities that this age forces on all of us.

It is not easy. It raises problems of construction and of language, 8 and it raises in a new way the problem of truthfulness. Let me give just one example of the cruder kind of difficulty that arises. My book about the Spanish civil war, *Homage to Catalonia*, is, of course, a frankly political book, but in the main it is written with a certain detachment and regard for form. I did try very hard in it to tell the whole truth

WRITING SUGGESTIONS

1. Is Orwell's essay literature or propaganda? Write an essay in which you explain your answer.
2. In his essay Orwell defines four motivations for writing. Choose one of the authors in this chapter and discuss which motivation most clearly explains the reason for which he or she writes.

without violating my literary instincts. But among other things it contains a long chapter, full of newspaper quotations and the like, defending the Trotskyists[2] who were accused of plotting with Franco. Clearly such a chapter, which after a year or two would lose its interest for any ordinary reader, must ruin the book. A critic whom I respect read me a lecture about it. "Why did you put in all that stuff?" he said. "You've turned what might have been a good book into journalism." What he said was true, but I could not have done otherwise. I happened to know, what very few people in England had been allowed to know, that innocent men were being falsely accused. If I had not been angry about that I should never have written the book.

In one form or another this problem comes up again. The problem of language is subtler and would take too long to discuss. I will only say that of late years I have tried to write less picturesquely and more exactly. In any case I find that by the time you have perfected any style of writing, you have always outgrown it. *Animal Farm* was the first book in which I tried, with full consciousness of what I was doing, to fuse political purpose and artistic purpose into one whole. I have not written a novel for seven years, but I hope to write another fairly soon. It is bound to be a failure, every book is a failure, but I do know with some clarity what kind of book I want to write. 9

Looking back through the last page or two, I see that I have made it appear as though my motives in writing were wholly public-spirited. I don't want to leave that as the final impression. All writers are vain, selfish and lazy, and at the very bottom of their motives there lies a mystery. Writing a book is a horrible, exhausting struggle, like a long bout of some painful illness. One would never undertake such a thing if one were not driven on by some demon whom one can neither resist nor understand. For all one knows that demon is simply the same instinct that makes a baby squall for attention. And yet it is also true that one can write nothing readable unless one constantly struggles to efface one's own personality. Good prose is like a window pane. I cannot say with certainty which of my motives are the strongest, but I know which of them deserve to be followed. And looking back through my work, I see that it is invariably where I lacked a *political* purpose that I wrote lifeless books and was betrayed into purple passages, sentences without meaning, decorative adjectives and humbug generally. 10

---

[2]Followers of Leon Trotsky (1879–1940), one of the principal leaders in the establishment of the USSR, who developed a theory of permanent communist revolution that would spread throughout the world. [Eds.]

ANSWERS TO RESPONDING TO READING

1. Interpreted broadly, Orwell's definitions include most motives. Eudora Welty's aesthetic enthusiasm figures prominently in her motivation, and Malamud implies in his short story "A Summer's Reading" that pride, "sheer egoism," is a powerful motivating force for writing as well as reading. Answers will vary. You might narrow the question further by choosing specific essays or stories to compare.

2. The conflict between Orwell's literary instincts and his need "to tell the truth" centers on what kind of truth he is trying to tell: the transitory, politically motivated truth of his propaganda, or those unchanging truths about human nature and the universe that we associate with the best literature. Orwell says *Animal Farm* is his first successful fusion of artistic and political purpose.

3. Whereas literature tries to convey the complex ambiguities of human experience, propaganda tries to persuade by presenting ideas in strictly black and white terms. Although one may resemble the other, propaganda is usually too simplistic and one-sided to be considered literature.

RESPONDING TO READING

1. Orwell lists four motives for writing, asserting that these motives exist in every writer. Do the other writers you have read in this chapter support Orwell's claim?   **2.** In what way does Orwell's need to "tell the whole truth" (paragraph 8) clash with his literary instincts? Does Orwell ever resolve this dilemma? Do you think a writer has an obligation to "tell the truth"?   **3.** Do you think a book can be "journalism" and still be "a good book" in the critic's sense? Do you think propaganda can be literature? Explain.

Saving the Life That Is Your Own: The Importance of Models in the Artist's Life

ALICE WALKER

Alice Walker (1944–   ) was born in Eatonton, Georgia, where her parents were sharecroppers. A writer of stories since childhood, she is today known as a poet, fiction writer, essayist, biographer, and editor. Walker writes mostly about the experiences of poor black women and the effects of racism and sexism. An advocate of African-American women writers, she helped revive the literary reputation of writer and folklorist Zora Neale Hurston by editing a collection of her writing, *I Love Myself When I Am Laughing* (1979). Walker is also the author of three novels, including the Pulitzer-Prize-winning *The Color Purple* (1982), and several collections of poetry, stories, and essays. In the following essay from her collection *In Search of Our Mothers' Gardens*, she talks about the early influences and models in her writing life.

FOR OPENERS

Walker claims that certain books were "indispensable" to her life and to her growth as a writer. Are these claims exaggerated?

There is a letter Vincent Van Gogh[1] wrote to Emile Bernard that is very meaningful to me. A year before he wrote the letter, Van Gogh had had a fight with his domineering friend Gauguin, left his company, and cut off, in desperation and anguish, his own ear. The letter was written in Saint-Remy, in the South of France, from a mental institution to which Van Gogh had voluntarily committed himself.

I imagine Van Gogh sitting at a rough desk too small for him, looking out at the lovely Southern light, and occasionally glancing

---

[1]Vincent Van Gogh (1853–90) was a Dutch impressionist painter. The majority of his works were produced in twenty-nine months of frenzied activity and bouts of depression that eventually ended in suicide. He has become the epitome of the tortured genius. [Eds.]

critically next to him at his own paintings of the landscape he loved so much. The date of the letter is December 1889. Van Gogh wrote:

> However hateful painting may be, and however cumbersome in the times we are living in, if anyone who has chosen this handicraft pursues it zealously, he is a man of duty, sound and faithful.
>
> Society makes our existence wretchedly difficult at times, hence our impotence and the imperfection of our work.
>
> . . . I myself am suffering under an absolute lack of models.
>
> But on the other hand, there are beautiful spots here. I have just done five size 30 canvasses, olive trees. And the reason I am staying on here is that my health is improving a great deal.
>
> What I am doing is hard, dry, but that is because I am trying to gather new strength by doing some rough work, and I'm afraid abstractions would make me soft.

Six months later, Van Gogh—whose health was "improving a great deal"—committed suicide. He had sold one painting during his lifetime. Three times was his work noticed in the press. But these are just details. 3

The real Vincent Van Gogh is the man who has "just done five size 30 canvasses, olive trees." To me, in context, one of the most moving and revealing descriptions of how a real artist thinks. And the knowledge that when he spoke of "suffering under an absolute lack of models" he spoke of that lack in terms of both the intensity of his commitment and the quality and singularity of his work, which was frequently ridiculed in his day. 4

The absence of models, in literature as in life, to say nothing of painting, is an occupational hazard for the artist, simply because models in art, in behavior, in growth of spirit and intellect—even if rejected—enrich and enlarge one's view of existence. Deadlier still, to the artist who lacks models, is the curse of ridicule, the bringing to bear on an artist's best work, especially his or her most original, most strikingly deviant, only a fund of ignorance and the presumption that, as an artist's critic, one's judgment is free of the restrictions imposed by prejudice, and is well informed, indeed, about all the art in the world that really matters. 5

What is always needed in the appreciation of art, or life, is the larger perspective. Connections made, or at least attempted, where none existed before, the straining to encompass in one's glance at the varied world the common thread, the unifying theme through immense diversity, a fearlessness of growth, of search, of looking, that enlarges the private and the public world. And yet, in our particular society, it is the narrowed and narrowing view of life that often wins. 6

Recently, I read at a college and was asked by one of the audience what I considered the major difference between the literature written 7

ADDITIONAL QUESTIONS FOR
RESPONDING TO READING

1. Walker has written that one of her concerns as a writer, and as a human being, is the "spiritual survival, the survival *whole* of my people." In what way is this statement applicable to this particular essay?
2. In paragraphs 14 and 15 Walker makes several observations about what she sees as the misguided concerns of education today. What are these observations? Do you agree with her that much "accepted literature" is racist or sexist (paragraph 20)?
3. How can even a rejected model "enrich and enlarge one's view of existence" (paragraph 5)?
4. Walker asserts that it is difficult for an African-American to completely identify with Jane Eyre (paragraph 21). Do you agree? Would Richard Wright?
5. What, according to Walker, do we learn from art?

TEACHING STRATEGY

Much of this essay may seem abstract to your class. Try to have your students express in their own words what Walker might mean by such phrases as "acquiring a sense of essence, of timelessness, and of vision" (paragraph 19).

by black and by white Americans. I had not spent a lot of time considering this question, since it is not the difference between them that interests me, but, rather, the way black writers and white writers seem to me to be writing one immense story—the same story, for the most part—with different parts of this immense story coming from a multitude of different perspectives. Until this is generally recognized, literature will always be broken into bits, black and white, and there will always be questions, wanting neat answers, such as this.

Still, I answered that I thought, for the most part, white American 8 writers tended to end their books and their characters' lives as if there were no better existence for which to struggle. The gloom of defeat is thick.

By comparison, black writers seem always involved in a moral 9 and/or physical struggle, the result of which is expected to be some kind of larger freedom. Perhaps this is because our literary tradition is based on the slave narratives, where escape for the body and freedom for the soul went together, or perhaps this is because black people have never felt themselves guilty of global, cosmic sins.

This comparison does not hold up in every case, of course, and 10 perhaps does not really hold up at all. I am not a gatherer of statistics, only a curious reader, and this has been my impression from reading many books by black and white writers.

There are, however, two books by American women that illustrate 11 what I am talking about: *The Awakening*, by Kate Chopin, and *Their Eyes Were Watching God*, by Zora Neale Hurston.

The plight of Mme Pontellier is quite similar to that of Janie Craw- 12 ford.[2] Each woman is married to a dull, society-conscious husband and living in a dull, propriety-conscious community. Each woman desires a life of her own and a man who loves her and makes her feel alive. Each woman finds such a man.

Mme Pontellier, overcome by the strictures of society and the 13 existence of her children (along with the cowardice of her lover), kills herself rather than defy the one and abandon the other. Janie Crawford, on the other hand, refuses to allow society to dictate behavior to her, enjoys the love of a much younger, freedom-loving man, and lives to tell others of her experience.

When I mentioned these two books to my audience, I was not 14 surprised to learn that only one person, a young black poet in the

---

[2]Mme Pontellier is the main character of Chopin's *The Awakening*, and Janie Crawford is the main character of Hurston's *Their Eyes Were Watching God*. [Eds.]

first row, had ever heard of *Their Eyes Were Watching God* (*The Awakening* they had fortunately read in their "Women in Literature" class), primarily because it was written by a black woman, whose experience—in love and life—was apparently assumed to be unimportant to the students (and the teachers) of a predominantly white school.

Certainly, as a student, I was not directed toward this book, which   15 would have urged me more toward freedom and experience than toward comfort and security, but was directed instead toward a plethora of books by mainly white male writers who thought most women worthless if they didn't enjoy bullfighting or hadn't volunteered for the trenches in World War I.

Loving both these books, knowing each to be indispensable to   16 my own growth, my own life, I choose the model, the example, of Janie Crawford. And yet this book, as necessary to me and to other women as air and water, is again out of print.[3] But I have distilled as much as I could of its wisdom in this poem about its heroine, Janie Crawford:

> I love the way Janie Crawford
> left her husbands
> the one who wanted to change her
> into a mule
> and the other who tried to interest her   5
> in being a queen.
> A woman, unless she submits,
> is neither a mule
> nor a queen
> though like a mule she may suffer   10
> and like a queen pace the floor.

It has been said that someone asked Toni Morrison[4] why she   17 writes the kind of books she writes, and that she replied: Because they are the kind of books I want to read.

This remains my favorite reply to that kind of question. As if   18 anyone reading the magnificent, mysterious *Sula* or the grim, poetic *The Bluest Eye* would require more of a reason for their existence than for the brooding, haunting *Wuthering Heights*, for example, or the melancholy, triumphant *Jane Eyre*. (I am not speaking here of the most famous short line of that book, "Reader, I married him," as the triumph, but, rather, of the triumph of Jane Eyre's control over her own sense of morality and her own stout will, which are but reflec-

---

[3]Reissued by the University of Illinois Press, 1979.
[4]American writer (1931–   ) whose works *Sula* (1973) and *The Bluest Eye* (1969) explore the theme of being African-American in the United States. [Eds.]

COLLABORATIVE ACTIVITY

Ask groups of students to discuss what they think Walker means when she writes that America, "being America," did not recognize the greatness of Zora Neale Hurston's novel. What are the implications of this assertion? Do they agree with Walker?

tions of her creator's, Charlotte Brontë, who no doubt wished to write the sort of book *she* wished to read.)[5]

Flannery O'Connor[6] has written that more and more the serious 19 novelist will write, not what other people want, and certainly not what other people expect, but whatever interests her or him. And that the direction taken, therefore, will be away from sociology, away from the "writing of explanation," of statistics, and further into mystery, into poetry, and into prophecy. I believe this is true, *fortunately true*, especially for "Third World Writers"; Morrison, Marquez, Ahmadi, Camara Laye make good examples. And not only do I believe it is true for serious writers in general, but I believe, as firmly as did O'Connor, that this is our only hope—in a culture so in love with flash, with trendiness, with superficiality, as ours—of acquiring a sense of essence, of timelessness, and of vision. Therefore, to write the books one wants to read is both to point the direction of vision and, at the same time, to follow it.

When Toni Morrison said she writes the kind of books she wants 20 to read, she was acknowledging the fact that in a society in which "accepted literature" is so often sexist and racist and otherwise irrelevant or offensive to so many lives, she must do the work of two. She must be her own model as well as the artist attending, creating, learning from, realizing the model, which is to say, herself.

(It should be remembered that, as a black person, one cannot 21 completely identify with a Jane Eyre, or with her creator, no matter how much one admires them. And certainly, if one allows history to impinge on one's reading pleasure, one must cringe at the thought of how Heathcliff, in the New World far from Wuthering Heights, amassed his Cathy-dazzling fortune.)[7] I have often been asked why, in my own life and work, I have felt such a desperate need to know and assimilate the experiences of earlier black women writers, most of them unheard of by you and by me, until quite recently; why I felt a need to study them and to teach them.

I don't recall the exact moment I set out to explore the works of 22 black women, mainly those in the past, and certainly, in the beginning, I had no desire to teach them. Teaching being for me, at that

---

[5]Charlotte Bronte (1816–55) wrote *Jane Eyre* (1847), and her sister Emily (1818–48) wrote *Wuthering Heights* (1847). Both novels present powerful portraits of their characters and realistic descriptions of life in nineteenth-century rural England. [Eds.]

[6]American author (1925–64) who combines the grotesque and the gothic in her treatment of contemporary Southern life. [Eds.]

[7]Heathcliff is the famous romantic hero of Emily Brontë's *Wuthering Heights*. After being rejected by Catherine because of his low social class, Heathcliff goes to America and amasses a fortune. He returns three years later and flaunts his wealth to Cathy, who has since married a dull but wealthy man. [Eds.]

time, less rewarding than star-gazing on a frigid night. My discovery of them—most of them out of print, abandoned, discredited, maligned, nearly lost—came about, as many things of value do, almost by accident. As it turned out—and this should not have surprised me—I found I was in need of something that only one of them could provide.

Mindful that throughout my four years at a prestigious black and 23 then a prestigious white college I had heard not one word about early black women writers, one of my first tasks was simply to determine whether they had existed. After this, I could breathe easier, with more assurance about the profession I myself had chosen.

But the incident that started my search began several years ago: 24 I sat down at my desk one day, in a room of my own, with key and lock, and began preparations for a story about voodoo, a subject that had always fascinated me. Many of the elements of this story I had gathered from a story my mother several times told me. She had gone, during the Depression, into town to apply for some government surplus food at the local commissary, and had been turned down, in a particularly humiliating way, by the white woman in charge.

My mother always told this story with a most curious expression 25 on her face. She automatically raised her head higher than ever—it was always high—and there was a look of righteousness, a kind of holy *heat* coming from her eyes. She said she had lived to see this same white woman grow old and senile and so badly crippled she had to get about on *two* sticks.

To her, this was clearly the working of God, who, as in the old 26 spiritual," . . . may not come when you want him, but he's right on time!" To me, hearing the story for about the fiftieth time, something else was discernible: the possibilities of the story, for fiction.

What, I asked myself, would have happened if, after the crippled 27 old lady died, it was discovered that someone, my mother perhaps (who would have been mortified at the thought, Christian that she is), had voodooed her?

Then, my thoughts sweeping me away into the world of hexes 28 and conjurings of centuries past, I wondered how a larger story could be created out of my mother's story; one that would be true to the magnitude of her humiliation and grief, and to the white woman's lack of sensitivity and compassion.

My third quandary was: How could I find out all I needed to 29 know in order to write a story that used *authentic* black witchcraft?

Which brings me back, almost, to the day I became really interested in black women writers. I say "almost" because one other thing, 30 from my childhood, made the choice of black magic a logical and irresistible one for my story. Aside from my mother's several stories about root doctors she had heard of or known, there was the story I had often heard about my "crazy" Walker aunt.

Many years ago, when my aunt was a meek and obedient girl 31 growing up in a strict, conventionally religious house in the rural South, she had suddenly thrown off her meekness and had run away from home, escorted by a rogue of a man permanently attached elsewhere.

When she was returned home by her father, she was declared 32 quite mad. In the backwoods South at the turn of the century, "madness" of this sort was cured not by psychiatry but by powders and by spells. (One can see Scott Joplin's *Treemonisha*[8] to understand the role voodoo played among black people of that period.) My aunt's madness was treated by the community conjurer, who promised, and delivered, the desired results. His treatment was a bag of white powder, bought for fifty cents, and sprinkled on the ground around her house, with some of it sewed, I believe, into the bodice of her nightgown.

So when I sat down to write my story about voodoo, my crazy 33 Walker aunt was definitely on my mind.

But she had experienced her temporary craziness so long ago that 34 her story had all the excitement of a might-have-been. I needed, instead of family memories, some hard facts about the *craft* of voodoo, as practiced by Southern blacks in the nineteenth century. (It never once, fortunately, occurred to me that voodoo was not worthy of the interest I had in it, or was too ridiculous to study seriously.)

I began reading all I could find on the subject of "The Negro and 35 His Folkways and Superstitions." There were Botkin and Puckett and others, all white, most racist. How was I to believe anything they wrote, since at least one of them, Puckett, was capable of wondering, in his book, if "The Negro" had a large enough brain?

Well, I thought, where are the *black* collectors of folklore? Where 36 is the *black* anthropologist? Where is the *black* person who took the time to travel the back roads of the South and collect the information I need: how to cure heat trouble, treat dropsy, hex somebody to death, lock bowels, cause joints to swell, eyes to fall out, and so on. Where was this black person?

And that is when I first saw, in a *footnote* to the white voices of 37 authority, the name Zora Neale Hurston.

Folklorist, novelist, anthropologist, serious student of voodoo, 38 also all-around black woman, with guts enough to take a slide rule

---

[8]Joplin (1868–1917) was an African-American ragtime pianist and composer. *Treemonisha* (1911), an opera that he produced at his own expense, failed to gain recognition. Today Joplin is considered a composer of great innovation and genius. [Eds.]

and measure random black heads in Harlem; not to prove their inferiority, but to prove that whatever their size, shape, or present condition of servitude, those heads contained all the intelligence anyone could use to get through this world.

Zora Hurston, who went to Barnard[9] to learn how to study what she really wanted to learn: the ways of her own people, and what ancient ritual, customs, and beliefs had made them unique.   39

Zora, of the sandy-colored hair and the daredevil eyes, a girl who escaped poverty and parental neglect by hard work and a sharp eye for the main chance.   40

Zora, who left the South only to return to look at it again. Who went to root doctors from Florida to Louisiana and said, "Here I am. I want to learn your trade."   41

Zora, who had collected all the black folklore I could ever use.   42
That Zora.   43

And having found *that Zora* (like a golden key to a storehouse of varied treasure), I was hooked.   44

What I had discovered, of course, was a model. A model, who, as it happened, provided more than voodoo for my story, more than one of the greatest novels America had produced—though, being America, it did not realize this. She had provided, as if she knew someday I would come along wandering in the wilderness, a nearly complete record of her life. And though her life sprouted an occasional wart, I am eternally grateful for that life, warts and all.   45

It is not irrelevant, nor is it bragging (except perhaps to gloat a little on the happy relatedness of Zora, my mother and me), to mention here that the story I wrote, called "the Revenge of Hannah Kemhuff," based on my mother's experiences during the Depression, and on Zora Hurston's folklore collection of the 1920s, and on my own response to both out of a contemporary existence, was immediately published and was later selected, by a reputable collector of short stories, as one of the *Best Short Stories of 1974*.   46

I mention it because this story might never have been written, because the very bases of its structure, authentic black folklore, viewed from a black perspective, might have been lost.   47

Had it been lost, my mother's story would have had no historical underpinning, none I could trust, anyway. I would not have written the story, which I enjoyed writing as much as I've enjoyed writing anything in my life, had I not known that Zora had already done a thorough job of preparing the ground over which I was then moving.   48

---

[9]Located in New York City, Barnard College for women (est. 1889) is part of Columbia University. [Eds.]

In that story I gathered up the historical and psychological threads 49 of the life my ancestors lived, and in the writing of it I felt joy and strength and my own continuity. I had that wonderful feeling writers get sometimes, not very often, of being *with* a great many people, ancient spirits, all very happy to see me consulting and acknowledging them, and eager to let me know, through the joy of their presence, that, indeed, I am not alone.

To take Toni Morrison's statement further, if that is possible, in 50 my own work I write not only what I want to read—understanding fully and indelibly that if I don't do it no one else is so vitally interested, or capable of doing it to my satisfaction—I write all the things *I should have been able to read*. Consulting, as belatedly discovered models, those writers—most of whom, not surprisingly, are women—who understood that their experience as ordinary human beings was also valuable, and in danger of being misrepresented, distorted, or lost:

Zora Hurston—novelist, essayist, anthropologist, autobiographer;

Jean Toomer—novelist, poet, philosopher, visionary, a man who cared what women felt;

Colette—whose crinkly hair enhances her French, part-black face; novelist, playwright, dancer, essayist, newspaperwoman, lover of women, men, small dogs; fortunate not to have been born in America;

Anaïs Nin—recorder of everything, no matter how minute;

Tillie Olson—a writer of such generosity and honesty, she literally saves lives;

Virginia Woolf—who has saved so many of us.

It is, in the end, the saving of lives that we writers are about. 51 Whether we are "minority" writers or "majority." It is simply in our power to do this.

We do it because we care. We care that Vincent Van Gogh muti- 52 lated his ear. We care that behind a pile of manure in the yard he destroyed his life. We care that Scott Joplin's music *lives*! We care because we know this: *the life we save is our own.*

RESPONDING TO READING

1. Walker argues that the work of Zora Neale Hurston would have been more valuable to her education than the work of white authors. Do you agree? What implications does Walker's view have for the college literature curriculum?   **2.** In paragraphs 8 and 9, Walker mentions a basic difference between the work of African-American and white writers. She goes on to illustrate this contrast in two novels. Does this example convince you that a difference exists? Do you agree with her explanation for this difference? Consider your own reading and observations as you form your conclusion.   **3.** In paragraph 50 Walker says that most of her models, "not surprisingly," are women. Do you agree that this fact is not surprising? Do you believe it is possible for people to have role models of different sexes and races?

ences of African-American women, whose stories tend to be discounted in "accepted" literature.

A Summer's Reading

BERNARD MALAMUD

Bernard Malamud (1914–1986) was born in Brooklyn to Russian-Jewish immigrants and was educated in New York City. From 1961 until his death, he taught writing at Bennington College. Most of Malamud's fiction explores the interplay between suffering and humor. His early stories of the struggles of poor Jews and the possibility of miracles are collected in *The Magic Barrel* (1958). Malamud wrote several novels, among them *The Natural* (1952), a semirealistic story about baseball and the mythic hero, and *The Fixer* (1966), a story set in anti-Semitic czarist Russia. For the latter, he won the Pulitzer Prize. In "A Summer's Reading," the short story that follows, Malamud presents a character who seems to be a loser but who gradually responds to the positive effects of his own lies.

George Stoyonovich was a neighborhood boy who had quit high 1 school on an impulse when he was sixteen, run out of patience, and though he was ashamed everytime he went looking for a job, when people asked him if he had finished and he had to say no, he never went back to school. This summer was a hard time for jobs and he had none. Having so much time on his hands, George thought of going to summer school, but the kids in his classes would be too young. He also considered registering in a night high school, only he didn't like the idea of the teachers always telling him what to do. He felt they had not respected him. The result was he stayed off the streets and in his room most of the day. He was close to twenty and had needs with the neighborhood girls, but no money to spend, and he couldn't get more than an occasional few cents because his father was poor, and his sister Sophie, who resembled George, a tall bony girl of twenty-three, earned very little and what she had she kept for herself. Their mother was dead, and Sophie had to take care of the house.

Very early in the morning George's father got up to go to work 2 in a fish market. Sophie left at about eight for her long ride in the subway to a cafeteria in the Bronx. George had his coffee by himself, then hung around in the house. When the house, a five-room railroad flat above a butcher store, got on his nerves he cleaned it up—mopped

BACKGROUND ON READING

"A Summer's Reading" first appeared in *The New Yorker* on September 22, 1956, and was later collected in *The Magic Barrel* (1958).

FOR OPENERS

This short story demonstrates the power of the imagination to transform life. Begin the discussion by examining what books mean to George's community and why his community honors him for reading.

ADDITIONAL QUESTIONS FOR RESPONDING TO READING

1. Is reading valued in your community in the same way it is valued in George's? Explain.
2. Do you think it is possible for someone like George, who is a nonreader, to turn into a reader? Why or why not?
3. What separates childhood from adulthood? Is there a single moment or action in the story that signals that George has matured? Discuss the transition.

the floors with a wet mop and put things away. But most of the time he sat in his room. In the afternoons he listened to the ball game. Otherwise he had a couple of old copies of the *World Almanac* he had bought long ago, and he liked to read in them and also the magazines and newspapers that Sophie brought home, that had been left on the tables in the cafeteria. They were mostly picture magazines about movie stars and sports figures, also usually the *News* and *Mirror*. Sophie herself read whatever fell into her hands, although she sometimes read good books.

She once asked George what he did in his room all day and he 3 said he read a lot too.

"Of what besides what I bring home? Do you ever read any 4 worthwhile books?"

"Some," George answered, although he really didn't. He had 5 tried to read a book or two that Sophie had in the house but found he was in no mood for them. Lately he couldn't stand made-up stories, they got on his nerves. He wished he had some hobby to work at— as a kid he was good in carpentry, but where could he work at it? Sometimes during the day he went for walks, but mostly he did his walking after the hot sun had gone down and it was cooler in the streets.

In the evening after supper George left the house and wandered 6 in the neighborhood. During the sultry days some of the storekeepers and their wives sat in chairs on the thick, broken sidewalks in front of their shops, fanning themselves, and George walked past them and the guys hanging out on the candy store corner. A couple of them he had known his whole life, but nobody recognized each other. He had no place special to go, but generally, saving it till the last, he left the neighborhood and walked for blocks till he came to a darkly lit little park with benches and trees and an iron railing, giving it a feeling of privacy. He sat on a bench here, watching the leafy trees and the flowers blooming on the inside of the railing, thinking of a better life for himself. He thought of the jobs he had had since he had quit school—delivery boy, stock clerk, runner, lately working in a factory—and he was dissatisfied with all of them. He felt he would someday like to have a good job and live in a private house with a porch, on a street with trees. He wanted to have some dough in his pocket to buy things with, and a girl to go with, so as not to be so lonely, especially on Saturday nights. He wanted people to like and respect him. He thought about these things often but mostly when he was alone at night. Around midnight he got up and drifted back to his hot and stony neighborhood.

One time while on his walk George met Mr. Cattanzara coming 7 home very late from work. He wondered if he was drunk but then could tell he wasn't. Mr. Cattanzara, a stocky, bald-headed man who worked in a change booth on an IRT station, lived on the next block after George's, above a shoe repair store. Nights, during the hot weather, he sat on his stoop in an undershirt, reading the *New York Times* in the light of the shoemaker's window. He read it from the first page to the last, then went up to sleep. And all the time he was reading the paper, his wife, a fat woman with a white face, leaned out of the window, gazing into the street, her thick white arms folded under her loose breast, on the window ledge.

Once in a while Mr. Cattanzara came home drunk, but it was a   8
quiet drunk. He never made any trouble, only walked stiffly up the street and slowly climbed the stairs into the hall. Though drunk, he looked the same as always, except for his tight walk, the quietness, and that his eyes were wet. George liked Mr. Cattanzara because he remembered him giving him nickels to buy lemon ice with when he was a squirt. Mr. Cattanzara was a different type than those in the neighborhood. He asked different questions than the others when he met you, and he seemed to know what went on in all the newspapers. He read them, as his fat sick wife watched from the window.

"What are you doing with yourself this summer, George?" Mr.   9
Cattanzara asked. "I see you walkin' around at nights."

George felt embarrassed. "I like to walk."   10

"What are you doin' in the day now?"   11

"Nothing much just right now. I'm waiting for a job." Since it   12
shamed him to admit he wasn't working, George said, "I'm staying home—but I'm reading a lot to pick up my education."

Mr. Cattanzara looked interested. He mopped his hot face with   13
a red handkerchief.

"What are you readin'?"   14

George hesitated, then said, "I got a list of books in the library   15
once, and now I'm gonna read them this summer." He felt strange and a little unhappy saying this, but he wanted Mr. Cattanzara to respect him.

"How many books are there on it?"   16

"I never counted them. Maybe around a hundred."   17

Mr. Cattanzara whistled through his teeth.   18

"I figure if I did that," George went on earnestly, "it would help   19
me in my education. I don't mean the kind they give you in high school. I want to know different things than they learn there, if you know what I mean."

The change maker nodded. "Still and all, one hundred books is   20
a pretty big load for one summer."

"It might take longer."   21

"After you're finished with some, maybe you and I can shoot the   22
breeze about them?" said Mr. Cattanzara.

"When I'm finished," George answered.   23

TEACHING STRATEGY

List on the board all those qualities associated with reading by George, his family, and his community. Use this list of qualities to determine what role books play in the neighborhood's concept of the world and whether their view is distorted or accurate by your standards.

COLLABORATIVE ACTIVITY

Divide the class into groups. Each group should discuss whether or not George will actually read one hundred books, citing specific support from the story. After a representative from each group presents its respective position to the class, use the groups' responses to help the class decide whether the story should be read ironically.

Mr. Cattanzara went home and George continued on his walk. After that, though he had the urge to, George did nothing different from usual. He still took his walks at night, ending up in the little park. But one evening the shoemaker on the next block stopped George to say he was a good boy, and George figured that Mr. Cattanzara had told him all about the books he was reading. From the shoemaker it must have gone down the street, because George saw a couple of people smiling kindly at him, though nobody spoke to him personally. He felt a little better around the neighborhood and liked it more, though not so much he would want to live in it forever. He had never exactly disliked the people in it, yet he had never liked them very much either. It was the fault of the neighborhood. To his surprise, George found out that his father and Sophie knew about his reading too. His father was too shy to say anything about it— he was never much of a talker in his whole life—but Sophie was softer to George, and she showed him in other ways she was proud of him.

As the summer went on George felt in a good mood about things. 25 He cleaned the house every day, as a favor to Sophie, and he enjoyed the ball games more. Sophie gave him a buck a week allowance, and though it still wasn't enough and he had to use it carefully, it was a helluva lot better than just having two bits now and then. What he bought with the money—cigarettes mostly, an occasional beer or movie ticket—he got a big kick out of. Life wasn't so bad if you knew how to appreciate it. Occasionally he bought a paperback book from the newsstand, but he never got around to reading it, though he was glad to have a couple of books in his room. But he read thoroughly Sophie's magazines and newspapers. And at night was the most enjoyable time, because when he passed the storekeepers sitting outside their stores, he could tell they regarded him highly. He walked erect, and though he did not say much to them, or they to him, he could feel approval on all sides. A couple of nights he felt so good that he skipped the park at the end of the evening. He just wandered in the neighborhood, where people had known him from the time he was a kid playing punchball whenever there was a game of it going; he wandered there, then came home and got undressed for bed, feeling fine.

For a few weeks he had talked only once with Mr. Cattanzara, 26 and though the change maker had said nothing more about the books, asked no questions, his silence made George a little uneasy. For a while George didn't pass in front of Mr. Cattanzara's house anymore, until one night, forgetting himself, he approached it from a different direction than he usually did when he did. It was already past midnight. The street, except for one or two people, was deserted, and George was surprised when he saw Mr. Cattanzara still reading his newspaper by the light of the street lamp overhead. His impulse was to stop at the stoop and talk to him. He wasn't sure what he wanted to say, though he felt the words would come when he began to talk; but the more he thought about it, the more the idea scared him, and he decided he'd better not. He even considered beating it home by another street, but he was too near Mr. Cattanzara, and the change maker might see him as he ran, and get annoyed. So George unobtrusively crossed the street, trying to make it seem as if he had to look in a store window on the other side, which he did, and then went on, uncomfortable at what he was doing. He feared Mr. Cattanzara would glance up from his paper and call him a dirty rat for walking on the other side of the street, but all he did was sit there, sweating through his undershirt, his bald head shining in the dim light as he read his *Times,* and upstairs his fat wife leaned out of the window, seeming to read the paper along with him. George thought she would spy him and yell out to Mr. Cattanzara, but she never moved her eyes off her husband.

George made up his mind to stay away from the change maker 27 until he had got some of his softback books read, but when he started them and saw they were mostly story books, he lost his interest and didn't bother to finish them. He lost his interest in reading other things too. Sophie's magazines and newspapers went unread. She saw them piling up on a chair in his room and asked why he was no longer looking at them, and George told her it was because of all the other reading he had to do. Sophie said she had guessed that was it. So for most of the day, George had the radio on, turning to music when he was sick of the human voice. He kept the house fairly neat, and Sophie said nothing on the days when he neglected it. She was still kind and gave him his extra buck, though things weren't so good for him as they had been before.

But they were good enough, considering. Also his night walks 28 invariably picked him up, no matter how bad the day was. Then one night George saw Mr. Cattanzara coming down the street toward him. George was about to turn and run but he recognized from Mr. Cattanzara's walk that he was drunk, and if so, probably he would not even bother to notice him. So George kept on walking straight ahead until he came abreast of Mr. Cattanzara and though he felt wound up enough to pop into the sky, he was not surprised when Mr. Cattanzara passed him without a word, walking slowly, his face and body stiff. George drew a breath in relief at his narrow escape, when he heard his name called, and there stood Mr. Cattanzara at his elbow, smelling like the inside of a beer barrel. His eyes were sad as he gazed at George, and George felt so intensely uncomfortable he was tempted to shove the drunk aside and continue on his walk.

But he couldn't act that way to him, and, besides, Mr. Cattanzara 29 took a nickel out of his pants pocket and handed it to him.

"Go buy yourself a lemon ice, Georgie." 30

"It's not that time anymore, Mr. Cattanzara," George said, "I am 31 a big guy now."

"No, you ain't," said Mr. Cattanzara, to which George made no 32 reply he could think of.

"How are all your books comin' along now?" Mr. Cattanzara 33 asked. Though he tried to stand steady, he swayed a little.

"Fine, I guess," said George, feeling the red crawling up his face. 34

"You ain't sure?" The change maker smiled slyly, a way George 35 had never seen him smile.

"Sure I'm sure. They're fine." 36

Though his head swayed in little arcs, Mr. Cattanzara's eyes were 37 steady. He had small blue eyes which could hurt if you looked at them too long.

"George," he said, "name me one book on that list that you read 38 this summer, and I will drink to your health."

"I don't want anybody drinking to me." 39

"Name me one so I can ask you a question on it. Who can tell, 40 if it's a good book maybe I might wanna read it myself."

George knew he looked passable on the outside, but inside he 41 was crumbling apart.

Unable to reply, he shut his eyes, but when—years later—he 42 opened them, he saw that Mr. Cattanzara had, out of pity, gone away, but in his ears he still heard the words he had said when he left: "George, don't do what I did."

The next night he was afraid to leave his room, and though Sophie 43 argued with him he wouldn't open the door.

"What are you doing in there?" she asked. 44

"Nothing." 45

"Aren't you reading?" 46

"No." 47

She was silent a minute, then asked, "Where do you keep the 48 books you read? I never see any in your room outside of a few cheap trashy ones."

He wouldn't tell her. 49

"In that case you're not worth a buck of my hard-earned money. 50 Why should I break my back for you? Go on out, you bum, and get a job."

He stayed in his room for almost a week, except to sneak into 51 the kitchen when nobody was home. Sophie railed at him, then begged him to come out, and his old father wept, but George wouldn't budge, though the weather was terrible and his small room stifling.

WRITING SUGGESTIONS

1. Write an essay in which you discuss Mr. Cattanzara's role in the story. Why is he so important to George, and what part does he play in George's maturation?

2. Books help George achieve the respect he could not find in school. Write an essay in which you discuss what actions or qualities help you achieve respect in school.

3. A community is a body of people who live in close proximity or who share a set of values. The community in which George lives plays a part in his decision to begin reading. In an essay, discuss how a community with which you associate—people in a neighborhood, a dormitory, or a club, for example—plays a part in defining your values and aspirations.

He found it very hard to breathe, each breath was like drawing a flame into his lungs.

One night, unable to stand the heat anymore, he burst into the 52 street at one A.M., a shadow of himself. He hoped to sneak to the park without being seen, but there were people all over the block, wilted and listless, waiting for a breeze. George lowered his eyes and walked, in disgrace, away from them, but before long he discovered they were still friendly to him. He figured Mr. Cattanzara hadn't told on him. Maybe when he woke up out of his drunk the next morning, he had forgotten all about meeting George. George felt his confidence slowly come back to him.

That same night a man on a street corner asked him if it was true 53 that he had finished reading so many books, and George admitted he had. The man said it was a wonderful thing for a boy his age to read so much.

"Yeah," George said, but he felt relieved. He hoped nobody 54 would mention the books anymore, and when, after a couple of days, he accidentally met Mr. Cattanzara again, *he* didn't, though George had the idea he was the one who had started the rumor that he had finished all the books.

One evening in the fall, George ran out of his house to the library, 55 where he hadn't been in years. There were books all over the place, wherever he looked, and though he was struggling to control an inward trembling, he easily counted off a hundred, then sat down at a table to read.

RESPONDING TO READING

1. Why do you suppose George is not a reader? Consider his family, his age, his education, and your own experience.   **2.** Why does George lie? In what way does his lying affect the community in which he lives? What effect does his lying have on him? What other options do you think he had?   **3.** What kind of future do you think George will have? Will he continue to read? Will reading change his life? Why or why not?

ANSWERS TO RESPONDING TO READING

1. George comes from a very poor neighborhood and has few opportunities. He is not a reader because that activity is not encouraged by his family and friends and because George has few role models who are readers.
2. George lies to enhance his self-image. His lie, however, strikes a sympathetic chord in his community. His family and neighbors look to George as someone who will escape the community's limited possibilities through education. George, in turn, feels their sympathy and respect, something he has never been able to find in school, and responds by trying to live up to his community's hopes. His other option is to deny their collective encouragement and sink into despair.
3. Although one interpretation of this story suggests that George will read those books, that he will escape his neighborhood through education, another reading might see George as incapable of escape, unprepared to take on the task he sets for himself. Ultimately, though, many students will see the story as hopeful and feel that George will change his beliefs and values as he reads more.

How to Become a Writer

LORRIE MOORE

Lorrie Moore (1957–   ), author of novels, short stories, essays, and a children's book, teaches at the University of Wisconsin. She won critical praise for her first book of short stories, *Self-Help* (1985), in which several stories parody the form of self-help manuals. Her novel *Anagrams* (1986) is unusual in its overlapping stories and shifts in point of view and tense. This experimental approach is in keeping with Moore's comments in the *Contemporary Literary Criticism Yearbook*: "I think that when you write you should have the feeling that you're creating something brand new, something that doesn't already exist in the world." She recently published a collection of stories called *Like Life* (1990). In the following story, the narrator speaks in the second person and tells how ending up in a creative writing class because the lines were long at the registrar changed her life.

First, try to be something, anything, else. A movie star/astronaut. 1
A movie star/missionary. A movie star/kindergarten teacher. President of the World. Fail miserably. It is best if you fail at an early age—say, fourteen. Early, critical disillusionment is necessary so that at fifteen you can write long haiku[1] sequences about thwarted desire. It is a pond, a cherry blossom, a wind brushing against sparrow wing leaving for mountain. Count the syllables. Show it to your mom. She is tough and practical. She has a son in Vietnam and a husband who may be having an affair. She believes in wearing brown because it hides spots. She'll look briefly at your writing, then back up at you with a face blank as a donut. She'll say: "How about emptying the dishwasher?" Look away. Shove the forks in the fork drawer. Accidentally break one of the freebie gas station glasses. This is the required pain and suffering. This is only for starters.

In your high school English class look at Mr. Killian's face. Decide 2
faces are important. Write a villanelle[2] about pores. Struggle. Write a sonnet. Count the syllables: nine, ten, eleven, thirteen. Decide to experiment with fiction. Here you don't have to count syllables. Write a short story about an elderly man and woman who accidentally shoot each other in the head, the result of an inexplicable malfunction of a shotgun which appears mysteriously in their living room one night. Give it to Mr. Killian as your final project. When you get it back, he

---

[1]A Japanese poetic form that presents the poet's impression of a natural object or scene in exactly seventeen syllables. [Eds.]

[2]A poetic form consisting of five three-line stanzas and a four-line stanza, using only two rhymes, and with repetitions of lines one and three. [Eds.]

has written on it: "Some of your images are quite nice, but you have no sense of plot." When you are home, in the privacy of your own room, faintly scrawl in pencil beneath his black-inked comments: "Plots are for dead people, pore-face."

Take all the babysitting jobs you can get. You are great with kids. 3
They love you. You tell them stories about old people who die idiot deaths. You sing them songs like "Blue Bells of Scotland," which is their favorite. And when they are in their pajamas and have finally stopped pinching each other, when they are fast asleep, you read every sex manual in the house, and wonder how on earth anyone could ever do those things with someone they truly loved. Fall asleep in a chair reading Mr. McMurphy's *Playboy*. When the McMurphys come home, they will tap you on the shoulder, look at the magazine in your lap, and grin. You will want to die. They will ask you if Tracey took her medicine all right. Explain, yes, she did, that you promised her a story if she would take it like a big girl and that seemed to work out just fine. "Oh, marvelous," they will exclaim.

Try to smile proudly. 4

Apply to college as a child psychology major. 5

As a child psychology major, you have some electives. You've 6
always liked birds. Sign up for something called "The Ornithological Field Trip." It meets Tuesdays and Thursdays at two. When you arrive at Room 134 on the first day of class, everyone is sitting around a seminar table talking about metaphors. You've heard of these. After a short, excruciating while, raise your hand and say diffidently, "Excuse me, isn't this Bird-watching One-oh-one?" The class stops and turns to look at you. They seem to all have one face—giant and blank as a vandalized clock. Someone with a beard booms out, "No, this is Creative Writing." Say: "Oh—right," as if perhaps you knew all along. Look down at your schedule. Wonder how the hell you ended up here. The computer, apparently, has made an error. You start to get up to leave and then don't. The lines at the registrar this week are huge. Perhaps you should stick with this mistake. Perhaps your creative writing isn't all that bad. Perhaps it is fate. Perhaps this is what your dad meant when he said, "It's the age of computers, Francie, it's the age of computers."

Decide that you like college life. In your dorm you meet many 7
nice people. Some are smarter than you. And some, you notice, are dumber than you. You will continue, unfortunately, to view the world in exactly these terms for the rest of your life.

ADDITIONAL QUESTIONS FOR
RESPONDING TO READING

1. What is the value of "pain and suffering"? Why does the narrator say that it is required?
2. What sort of support or encouragement does the narrator receive toward her goal to become a writer? How does she view the attitudes that confront her? What is her response, and why does she continue her efforts?
3. How does the narrator describe her desire to write? How is it possible that she finds all these labels appropriate?
4. Why is the narrator unable to write about her brother?

TEACHING STRATEGIES

1. Ask students how Moore violates the conventions that characterize self-help books. Tell them to point to particular aspects of the narrative that they found departed from their preconceptions of what self-help books should say.
2. Discuss the style of "How to Become a Writer," particularly the use of the pronoun *you.* Also point to variations in sentence length, patterns of repetition, similes, recurring phrases, and diction. What effects do such techniques create, and how does the style contribute to the meaning of the story?
3. Note the style of paragraph 34. The repetition of "Perhaps" to begin sentences serves to introduce alternative possibilities, and the listing climaxes with the least pleasing and yet most likely possibility of them all. Also, what attitude does the language of "sooner or later you have a finished manuscript more or less" convey?

The assignment this week in creative writing is to narrate a violent 8 happening. Turn in a story about driving with your Uncle Gordon and another one about two old people who are accidentally electrocuted when they go to turn on a badly wired desk lamp. The teacher will hand them back to you with comments: "Much of your writing is smooth and energetic. You have, however, a ludicrous notion of plot." Write another story about a man and a woman who, in the very first paragraph, have their lower torsos accidentally blitzed away by dynamite. In the second paragraph, with the insurance money, they buy a frozen yogurt stand together. There are six more paragraphs. You read the whole thing out loud in class. No one likes it. They say your sense of plot is outrageous and incompetent. After class someone asks you if you are crazy.

Decide that perhaps you should stick to comedies. Start dating 9 someone who is funny, someone who has what in high school you called a "really great sense of humor" and what now your creative writing class calls "self-contempt giving rise to comic form." Write down all of his jokes, but don't tell him you are doing this. Make up anagrams of his old girlfriend's name and name all of your socially handicapped characters with them. Tell him his old girlfriend is in all of your stories and then watch how funny he can be, see what a really great sense of humor he can have.

Your child psychology advisor tells you you are neglecting courses 10 in your major. What you spend the most time on should be what you're majoring in. Say yes, you understand.

In creative writing seminars over the next two years, everyone 11 continues to smoke cigarettes and ask the same things: "But does it work?" "Why should we care about this character?" "Have you earned this cliché?" These seem like important questions.

On days when it is your turn, you look at the class hopefully as 12 they scour your mimeographs for a plot. They look back up at you, drag deeply, and then smile in a sweet sort of way.

You spend too much time slouched and demoralized. Your boy- 13 friend suggests bicycling. Your roommate suggests a new boyfriend. You are said to be self-mutilating and losing weight, but you continue writing. The only happiness you have is writing something new, in the middle of the night, armpits damp, heart pounding, something no one has yet seen. You have only those brief, fragile, untested moments of exhilaration when you know: you are a genius. Understand what you must do. Switch majors. The kids in your nursery project will be disappointed, but you have a calling, an urge, a delusion, an unfortunate habit. You have, as your mother would say, fallen in with a bad crowd.

Why write? Where does writing come from? These are questions to ask yourself. They are like: Where does dust come from? Or: Why is there war? Or: If there's a God, then why is my brother now a cripple? 14

These are questions that you keep in your wallet, like calling cards. These are questions, your creative writing teacher says, that are good to address in your journals but rarely in your fiction. 15

The writing professor this fall is stressing the Power of the Imagination. Which means he doesn't want long descriptive stories about your camping trip last July. He wants you to start in a realistic context but then to alter it. Like recombinant DNA. He wants you to let your imagination sail, to let it grow big-bellied in the wind. This is a quote from Shakespeare. 16

Tell your roommate your great ideas, your great exercise of imaginative power: a transformation of Melville[3] to contemporary life. It will be about monomania and the fish-eat-fish world of life insurance in Rochester, New York. The first line will be "Call me Fishmeal," and it will feature a menopausal suburban husband named Richard, who because he is so depressed all the time is called "Mopey Dick" by his witty wife Elaine. Say to your roommate: "Mopey Dick, get it?" Your roommate looks at you, her face blank as a large Kleenex. She comes up to you, like a buddy, and puts an arm around your burdened shoulders. "Listen, Francie," she says, slow as speech therapy. "Let's go out and get a big beer." 17

The seminar doesn't like this one either. You suspect they are beginning to feel sorry for you. They say: "You have to think about what is happening. Where is the story here?" 18

The next semester the writing professor is obsessed with writing from personal experience. You must write from what you know, from what has happened to you. He wants deaths, he wants camping trips. Think about what has happened to you. In three years there have been three things: you lost your virginity; your parents got divorced; 19

---

[3]Herman Melville (1819–91) was an American author most famous for his novel *Moby Dick* (1851). Its famous first line is "Call me Ishmael."

COLLABORATIVE ACTIVITY

What is the narrator really like? Break students into groups and have each group write a character sketch, including family, hobbies, geographical and ethnic background, and physical characteristics. Ask them to compare their sketches and to explain the reasons for their choices.

and your brother came home from a forest ten miles from the Cambodian border with only half a thigh, a permanent smirk nestled into one corner of his mouth.

About the first you write: "It created a new space, which hurt 20 and cried in a voice that wasn't mine, 'I'm not the same anymore, but I'll be okay.' "

About the second you write an elaborate story of an old married 21 couple who stumble upon an unknown land mine in their kitchen and accidentally blow themselves up. You call it: "For Better or for Liverwurst."

About the last you write nothing. There are no words for this. 22 Your typewriter hums. You can find no words.

At undergraduate cocktail parties, people say, "Oh, you write? 23 What do you write about?" Your roommate, who has consumed too much wine, too little cheese, and no crackers at all, blurts: "Oh, my god, she always writes about her dumb boyfriend."

Later on in life you will learn that writers are merely open, helpless 24 texts with no real understanding of what they have written and therefore must half-believe anything and everything that is said of them. You, however, have not yet reached this stage of literary criticism. You stiffen and say, "I do not," the same way you said it when someone in the fourth grade accused you of really liking oboe lessons and your parents really weren't just making you take them.

Insist you are not very interested in any one subject at all, that 25 you are interested in the music of language, that you are interested in—in—syllables, because they are the atoms of poetry, the cells of the mind, the breath of the soul. Begin to feel woozy. Stare into your plastic wine cup.

"Syllables?" you will hear someone ask, voice trailing off, as they 26 glide slowly toward the reassuring white of the dip.

Begin to wonder what you do write about. Or if you have anything 27 to say. Or if there even is such a thing as a thing to say. Limit these thoughts to no more than ten minutes a day; like sit-ups, they can make you thin.

You will read somewhere that all writing has to do with one's 28 genitals. Don't dwell on this. It will make you nervous.

Your mother will come visit you. She will look at the circles under 29 your eyes and hand you a brown book with a brown briefcase on the cover. It is entitled: *How to Become a Business Executive*. She has also brought the *Names for Baby* encyclopedia you asked for; one of your characters, the aging clown–school teacher, needs a new name. Your mother will shake her head and say: "Francie, Francie, remember when you were going to be a child psychology major?"

Say: "Mom, I like to write."   30

She'll say: "Sure you like to write. Of course. Sure you like to write."   31

Write a story about a confused music student and title it: 32
"Schubert Was the One with the Glasses, Right?" It's not a big hit, although your roommate likes the part where the two violinists accidentally blow themselves up in a recital room. "I went out with a violinist once," she says, snapping her gum.

Thank god you are taking other courses. You can find sanctuary   33
in nineteenth-century ontological snags and invertebrate courting rituals. Certain globular mollusks have what is called "Sex by the Arm." The male octopus, for instance, loses the end of one arm when placing it inside the female body during intercourse. Marine biologists call it "Seven Heaven." Be glad you know these things. Be glad you are not just a writer. Apply to law school.

From here on in, many things can happen. But the main one will   34
be this: you decide not to go to law school after all, and, instead, you spend a good, big chunk of your adult life telling people how you decided not to go to law school after all. Somehow you end up writing again. Perhaps you go to graduate school. Perhaps you work odd jobs and take writing courses at night. Perhaps you are working on a novel and writing down all the clever remarks and intimate personal confessions you hear during the day. Perhaps you are losing your pals, your acquaintances, your balance.

You have broken up with your boyfriend. You now go out with   35
men who, instead of whispering "I love you," shout: "Do it to me, baby." This is good for your writing.

Sooner or later you have a finished manuscript more or less.   36
People look at it in a vaguely troubled sort of way and say, "I'll bet becoming a writer was always a fantasy of yours, wasn't it?" Your lips dry to salt. Say that of all the fantasies possible in the world, you can't imagine being a writer even making the top twenty. Tell them you were going to be a child psychology major. "I bet," they always sigh, "you'd be great with kids." Scowl fiercely. Tell them you're a walking blade.

Quit classes. Quit jobs. Cash in old savings bonds. Now you have   37
time like warts on your hands. Slowly copy all of your friends' addresses into a new address book.

Vacuum. Chew cough drops. Keep a folder full of fragments.   38

WRITING SUGGESTION

Construct your own "how-to" paper, addressing your subject from an ironic angle as Moore does. For example, you might choose to write a survival guide for beginning composition students or for students learning to use a computer.

1. Answers will vary. Some students will be mystified, whereas others will realize that the unconventional point of view allows the narrator to distance herself from the subject matter of the story and to present ironically the obstacles she faces as she approaches her goal.
2. The narrator's description of her development makes the point that the urge to become a writer cannot be denied; the narrator is playful in the descriptions of her efforts to create plot, at times making herself appear ridiculous, yet she seems all the more admirable because she will not accept "helpful" advice from others and simply quit.
3. The main character is the narrator, who devotes herself completely to writing. She constantly tests new ideas and questions the nature of her craft. The selection is different from other stories in this book because of its unusual point of view and its experimental, episodic structure.

BACKGROUND ON AUTHOR

Keats died at twenty-six, succumbing to tuberculosis after watching both his mother and brother die of the disease. During his life, he published fifty-four poems in three volumes and a few magazines, producing a total of about fifteen thousand lines of poetry. "On First Looking into Chapman's Homer" is considered one of Keats's finest sonnets.

ADDITIONAL QUESTIONS FOR
RESPONDING TO READING

1. Modern-day readers may be unfamiliar with Keats's classical allusions. If Keats were writing today, what different allusions might he make?
2. Because Keats had a very sketchy classical education and could not have read Homer in the original Greek, his introduction to the epics through George Chapman's translation was especially exciting: it opened up the ancient world for the young poet. What passages suggest Keats's reaction to his discovery? How would you characterize the tone of these passages?
3. What are the "realms of gold" (line 1)? How does this metaphor suggest early Spanish explorers? How does the extended metaphor in lines 1–4 characterize the poet's previous discoveries in literature? What figurative lan-

An eyelid darkening sideways.
World as conspiracy.
Possible plot? A woman gets on a bus.
Suppose you threw a love affair and nobody came.

At home drink a lot of coffee. At Howard Johnson's order the 39 cole slaw. Consider how it looks like the soggy confetti of a map: where you've been, where you're going—"You Are Here," says the red star on the back of the menu.

Occasionally a date with a face blank as a sheet of paper asks you 40 whether writers often become discouraged. Say that sometimes they do and sometimes they do. Say it's a lot like having polio.

"Interesting," smiles your date, and then he looks down at his 41 arm hairs and starts to smooth them, all, always, in the same direction.

RESPONDING TO READING

1. Moore writes her story as if it were a set of instructions. How does this unusual style affect your reactions to her story?   **2.** Despite the unconventional aspect of this story and the way it pokes fun at "creative writers," what serious points does it make about the process of becoming a writer?   **3.** This selection is a work of fiction. How is it unlike other stories you have read? For example, who is the main character?

On First Looking into Chapman's Homer[1]

JOHN KEATS

One of England's most famous poets, John Keats (1795–1821) suffered poverty, illness, and tragedy in his short life, yet he wrote some of the most enduring romantic poetry in the English language—"Ode to a Nightingale," "Ode on a Grecian Urn," and "The Eve of St. Agnes." His father was a stablekeeper, and both his parents died by the time Keats was fifteen, at which time he was apprenticed to a physician. Eventually, Keats turned to literature and writing. He was first introduced to Greek literature when a former teacher gave him George Chapman's translation of Homer's *Iliad.* After spending the whole night reading it, Keats wrote the sonnet that follows.

---

[1]George Chapman's translations of Homer were famous during the Renaissance. [Eds.]

Much have I travell'd in the realms of gold,
And many goodly states and kingdoms seen:
Round many western islands have I been
Which bards in fealty to Apollo[2] hold.
Oft of one wide expanse had I been told
That deep-brow'd Homer ruled as his demesne;[3]
Yet did I never breathe its pure serene[4]
Till I heard Chapman speak out loud and bold:
Then felt I like some watcher of the skies
When a new planet swims into his ken;[5]
Or like stout Cortez[6] when with eagle eyes
He star'd at the Pacific—and all his men
Look'd at each other with a wild surmise—
Silent, upon a peak in Darien.[7]

RESPONDING TO READING

1. To what does the speaker compare his experience of reading Chapman's Homer? What ideas does he seek to convey with this comparison? How do you react to this comparison? Can you think of a more contemporary comparison that would work as well?   **2.** Has a work of literature ever opened a new world to you? Explain how and why it did so.   **3.** In the poem the speaker says that Cortez discovered the Pacific Ocean, but actually Balboa did. What effect, if any, does your awareness of this factual error have on your reading of the poem? Would you react the same way if you found an error like this in a history text? How do you account for any differences in your reactions?

guage is used to develop this metaphor?
4. Keats uses similes to express the way he is affected by his discovery of Homer's poetry. What are these similes? How are they related to one other? To the overall theme?
5. What qualities do you think help to explain this sonnet's continuing popularity?

TEACHING STRATEGIES

1. Explain the sonnet form and its conventions. Ask students why it might be significant that the sonnet form was originally used for love poems. Could Keats's poem be considered a love poem?
2. Keats uses the rhyme scheme of an Italian sonnet and the organization of a Shakespearean sonnet. What ideas are presented in the first eight lines of the sonnet? What conclusion or observation is made in the last six lines?
3. Ask students to identify words in the poem that have more than one denotation or connotation. Discuss how the multiple meanings of the words enrich the poem. (You may also want to consider the etymology of the words.)

WRITING SUGGESTION

Write a personal essay describing a discovery you have made in reading. Relate an experience that approximates, as closely as possible, the sense of epiphany, of awe, that Keats expresses in his poem.

ANSWERS TO RESPONDING
TO READING

1. Reading Chapman's Homer, Keats feels like a discoverer of a planet or an explorer who comes upon a great ocean previously unknown to him. The poem communicates a sense of personal discovery. Answers about personal reactions to the comparison will vary.
2. Given the modern loss of familiarity with classical literature, some readers may not immediately identify with Keats's reactions. But they probably have experienced a sudden insight.
3. A history book would be marred by this kind of error, but Keats's sense of discovery—the point of the poem—is preserved, no matter who discovers the ocean.

---

[2]Greek god of poetry and music. *Fealty* is literally the duty owed to a lord by his vassal. In other words, poets are sworn servants of Apollo. Keats identifies his exploration of Homer with Odysseus's exploration of the Aagean. Like Odysseus, Keats travels in "realms of gold" and explores the "western islands." [Eds.]
[3]Realm; estate. [Eds.]
[4]Atmosphere; a clear expanse of air. [Eds.]
[5]Field of vision. [Eds.]
[6]Hernando Cortez (1485–1547), Spanish general who conquered the Aztecs and Mexico. Keats apparently confused Cortez with Vasco Balboa (1475–1519), who was the first European to view the Pacific.
[7]Darien is the former name of the Isthmus of Panama [Eds.]

WRITING: READING AND WRITING AS DISCOVERY

1. In "The Joys of Reading" Annie Dillard recalls the books that shaped her life. Write your own version of Dillard's essay, mentioning the books, movies, and television shows that fired your youthful imagination and helped shape your present outlook on life.

2. Describe the effects of reading upon one of the authors in this chapter, and use this information to develop an argument for or against the statement, "Ignorance is bliss."

3. Both Frederick Douglass and Richard Wright had to face personal danger to satisfy their desire to read—and eventually to become writers. Write an essay comparing their respective struggles and examining each man's reasons for going to such lengths to gain access to books.

4. Basing your essay on the experiences of the writers in this chapter, write your own version of "How to Become a Writer." You can, if you like, experiment with Lorrie Moore's unusual style. You can write a humorous essay, or you can give serious advice.

5. Although both Richard Wright and Annie Dillard write about the magnetism of the library and both list books that inspired them, their memoirs are very different. After carefully considering their attitudes toward reading, write an essay that examines ways in which one of these writer's experiences is like your own.

6. In paragraph 55 Dillard hints at a basic discrepancy between her reading and her life, thereby suggesting a possible negative consequence of reading widely. Write an essay in which you identify differences between the content of your own leisure reading and the events of your daily life and discuss the significance of these differences.

7. The writers in this chapter draw their inspiration from a wide variety of sources: writers, books, family, culture, politics, and personal memories. If you were to become a writer, what sources would inspire you? What key events and experiences do you imagine would serve as your inspiration? Why?

8. In her essay Alice Walker talks about how books helped her develop a sense of her own heritage. Discuss a book, poem, play, or song that helped you discover your own heritage.

9. Economic status and social class play a significant part in determining an individual's access to and attitude toward writing and reading. Discuss the part these factors played in your attitudes toward reading and writing.

2

THINKING AND LEARNING

CONFRONTING THE ISSUES

Many students are not aware that a debate is taking place that will decide the direction of their education. On one side are those who claim that the standard core curriculum at most American schools, with its stress on Western values, does not reflect the reality of the United States today. They point out that the 1990 census shows the United States to be an increasingly diverse country, made up of not just white males of Northern European descent, but also of women; African-, Hispanic-, and Asian-Americans; and people of Eastern European descent. For this reason, the argument goes, the curriculum must be changed if it is to be relevant to students' lives and to connect their unique experiences to the learning process. In a high school with a diverse ethnic population, for example, the study of American history could treat topics such as Asian immigration, the role of African-American soldiers in the Civil War, and the effect of Jefferson's ideal vision of America on colonial women. According to Henry Louis Gates, Jr., W. E. B. Du Bois professor of the humanities at Harvard, "It's only when we are free to explore the complexities of our hyphenated culture that we can discover what a genuinely American culture may look like."

On the other side of the debate are those who reject the call for multicultural education, which they believe would ultimately fragment the curriculum into a multitude of separate ethnic enclaves. At its extreme, they charge, multicultural education rejects the values and beliefs of Western civilization. They maintain that this heritage has created a society that, however flawed, has influenced writers and thinkers of many backgrounds and given the world the idea of a government that champions the dignity, independence, and freedom of the individual. For this reason, says Donald Kagan, dean of Yale College, "It is necessary to place Western civilization and the culture to which it has given rise at the center of our studies, and we fail to do so at the peril of our students, country, and the hopes for a democratic, liberal society."

After you explain the two positions outlined above, ask students what they think of the idea of a multicultural curriculum. Have they been exposed to such a curriculum? What are its advantages and disadvantages? Is there a way of bridging the gap between the two positions? Do they see any value in studying history, literature, or even sciences in this way?

In "Reading the River" Mark Twain discusses two different ways of looking at the river. The boy who looks at the river sees its grace, poetry, and majesty. Because of his lack of knowledge, he sees only the surface, broken by the "boiling, tumbling rings, that were as many-tinted as an opal." The riverboat pilot, because of his knowledge, sees beneath the surface of the river. To him the swirling rings suggest the possibility of submerged dangers: a reef that can tear the bottom out of a boat or a changing channel line that can cause a boat to run aground. Of course it soon becomes evident that Twain is talking about more than looking at the river. He is also examining two different ways of looking at the world: one innocent and naive, the other experienced and educated; one accepting, the other questioning. For Twain both views of the world have their advantages and disadvantages.

It may seem odd to us in our time, when education is touted as a remedy for all the afflictions of modern society, that one hundred years ago Twain could celebrate—even obliquely—an innocent or uneducated view of the world. And he is not alone. In "When I Heard the Learn'd Astronomer" Walt Whitman also celebrates this view. For these writers becoming educated means paying a price: forfeiting youthful innocence and happiness. To both writers, education has the potential to separate an individual from nature and to some extent from other people.

It is this view of education—as a process that radically changes a person from an unthinking child to a cognizant adult—that is largely missing from today's educational systems. In fact, more stress seems to be placed on reinforcing familiar ideas and avoiding controversy than on challenging old theories and discovering new ways of thinking and learning. Thus ideas become sanitized, classic books are censored, and scientific theories become balanced. The result is an intellectual climate that has all the excitement of elevator music. Many people seem to have forgotten that ideas must be unsettling if they are to educate us. What is education, after all, but a process of challenging and restructuring our view of the world?

All the writers in this chapter see education as a process that challenges rather than confirms ideas. As a result, they are all concerned, directly or indirectly, with the importance of critical thinking—that is, with the ability to judge, evaluate, and analyze ideas and events—and with the part education plays in helping students develop this skill. Whether writers examine informal education—a personal process of learning from observation and experience—as Mark Twain does in "Reading the River," or formal education—a process connected with social and pedagogical institutions—as John Holt does in "School Is Bad for Children," they all see education as a process of intellectual growth, and they all see the value of education as something that helps us achieve a mature and healthy skepticism.

PREPARING TO READ AND WRITE

As you read and prepare to write about the selections in this chapter, you may consider the following questions:

- How does the writer define education? Is this definition consistent with yours?
- Does the writer believe that informal education is more important than formal education?
- What aspects of education does the writer value most? Do you share the writer's opinion?
- What obstacles to learning does the writer identify? How does the writer explain their presence? How does he or she suggest they be overcome?
- Does the writer present formal education as a positive or negative experience? Do you agree with this assessment?
- Is the writer's educational experience similar to or different from your own? Is it a positive one?
- What changes in the educational system does the writer recommend? Do you agree with the writer's recommendations?
- Does the writer's definition of the purpose of formal education coincide with yours?
- In what way does gender or race determine the perspective from which the writer views education?
- In what ways do your own ideas about the value of formal and informal education affect your reaction to each selection?

After this general discussion, divide the class into groups and ask each group to reexamine one of the reading selections in this text that the class has read. Their assignment is to evaluate the essay, poem, or story in light of its value to their college's student body, considering subject matter, style, date of publication, author's background, and any other criteria they like.

In further class discussion, debate the usefulness and educational value of the selections students have identified as particularly meaningful to—or particularly remote from—their experiences. Why should today's students read each selection? In short, does education mean reinforcing or challenging ways of thinking and learning about issues and ideas?

Reading the River

MARK TWAIN

Samuel Clemens (1835–1910) grew up in Hannibal, Missouri. He is known by his pen name, Mark Twain, a phrase, meaning "two fathoms deep," that indicates the navigating depth of a river. Twain became a riverboat pilot in 1859, but he practiced this trade only until 1861, when the Civil War ended commercial river transportation. His writing is known for its wit, satire, and irony. He wrote humorous sketches of his travels to Europe and the Holy Land (*Innocents Abroad*, 1869) and of his prospecting days in the Nevada Territory and California (*Roughing It*, 1872). After settling in Hartford, Connecticut, in 1871, Twain used the rich material of his midwestern childhood to write his best-known works, *The Adventures of Tom Sawyer* (1876) and *The Adventures of Huckleberry Finn* (1884). Later, Twain lived abroad for many years and traveled extensively as a lecturer. "Reading the River" is an excerpt from his autobiographical narrative, *Life on the Mississippi* (1883).

FOR OPENERS

Most students will come to this essay assuming that education is always beneficial. For this reason, Twain's ideas will seem foreign to them. A few minutes spent discussing what is lost as well as what is gained through education may be in order. Introduce the loss of innocence motif with the story of the Fall in the Garden of Eden. Ask students whether they believe that knowledge inevitably leads to disillusionment and a loss of innocence.

ADDITIONAL QUESTIONS FOR RESPONDING TO READING

1. Twain says that he lost something. What did he lose? Was he somehow able to retain at least part of that romantic view of life?
2. Twain says he pities doctors. Why? Are there any other professionals he might also pity? Any he might see as capable of keeping youthful imagination alive?
3. Do all professions have their romance and beauty? In what ways can knowledge add to rather than detract from the romance?
4. Is it possible for someone to remain innocent? What would a person gain? What would he or she give up?

Now when I had mastered the language of this water and had 1 come to know every trifling feature that bordered the great river as familiarly as I knew the letters of the alphabet, I had made a valuable acquisition. But I had lost something, too. I had lost something which could never be restored to me while I lived. All the grace, the beauty, the poetry, had gone out of the majestic river! I still kept in mind a certain wonderful sunset which I witnessed when steamboating was new to me. A broad expanse of the river was turned to blood; in the middle distance the red hue brightened into gold, through which a solitary log came floating, black and conspicuous; in one place a long, slanting mark lay sparkling upon the water; in another the surface was broken by boiling, tumbling rings, that were as many-tinted as an opal; where the ruddy flush was faintest, was a smooth spot that was covered with graceful circles and radiating lines, ever so delicately traced; the shore on our left was densely wooded and the somber shadow that fell from this forest was broken in one place by a long, ruffled trail that shone like silver; and high above the forest wall a clean-stemmed dead tree waved a single leafy bough that glowed like a flame in the unobstructed splendor that was flowing from the sun. There were graceful curves, reflected images, woody heights, soft distances, and over the whole scene, far and near, the dissolving lights drifted steadily, enriching it every passing moment with new marvels of coloring.

I stood like one bewitched. I drank it in, in a speechless rapture. 2 The world was new to me and I had never seen anything like this at home. But as I have said, a day came when I began to cease from noting the glories and the charms which the moon and the sun and the twilight wrought upon the river's face; another day came when I ceased altogether to note them. Then, if that sunset scene had been repeated, I should have looked upon it without rapture, and should have commented upon it inwardly after this fashion: "This sun means that we are going to have wind to-morrow; that floating log means that the river is rising, small thanks to it; that slanting mark on the water refers to a bluff reef which is going to kill somebody's steamboat one of these nights, if it keeps on stretching out like that; those tumbling 'boils' show a dissolving bar and a changing channel there; the lines and circles in the slick water over yonder are a warning that that troublesome place is shoaling up dangerously; that silver streak in the shadow of the forest is the 'break' from a new snag and he has located himself in the very best place he could have found to fish for steamboats; that tall dead tree, with a single living branch, is not going to last long, and then how is a body ever going to get through this blind place at night without the friendly old landmark?"

No, the romance and beauty were all gone from the river. All the value any feature of it had for me now was the amount of usefulness it could furnish toward compassing the safe piloting of a steamboat. Since those days, I have pitied doctors from my heart. What does the lovely flush in a beauty's cheek mean to a doctor but a "break" that ripples above some deadly disease?[1] Are not all her visible charms sown thick with what are to him the signs and symbols of hidden decay? Does he ever see her beauty at all, or doesn't he simply view her professionally and comment upon her unwholesome condition all to himself? And doesn't he sometimes wonder whether he has gained most or lost most by learning his trade? 3

RESPONDING TO READING

1. Which of the two ways of looking at nature that Twain describes does he seem to believe is more valuable? Why? Do you agree?   **2.** Would you define Twain's view of education as optimistic or pessimistic? What leads you to this conclusion?   **3.** As you have become more educated, have you found yourself seeing the "usefulness" of information and experiences instead of their "romance and beauty"? Explain.

TEACHING STRATEGY

Ask students for examples of how their views of a place, an object, or a person changed as they grew older. What caused the change?

COLLABORATIVE ACTIVITY

Divide the class into groups and distribute to each group a copy of a fairy tale. Have each group make two lists, one of details an innocent, unsophisticated reader (such as a child) would notice, and one of details an educated adult would see. In class discussion, compare each group's list. What can be inferred about the two ways of approaching a story?

WRITING SUGGESTIONS

1. Write an essay in which you compare how things looked to you the first day you saw your college campus and how they look to you now.
2. Write about an incident that taught you that things were not what you thought they were. Did you feel more mature or simply betrayed?

ANSWERS TO RESPONDING TO READING

1. Twain seems to prefer the innocent view, since it retains the mystery, beauty, and excitement of nature. Twain is, however, a realist. Even though he appreciates the romantic view of the river, he realizes that a realistic view is absolutely necessary if he is to navigate the river safely.
2. His attitude could be called resigned. Twain knows that education inevitably results in a loss of innocence, but he also knows that this loss is necessary.
3. Answers will vary. Most will agree that education often strips the world of its mystery, and yet some may think of situations in which the mystery simply deepens as one gains more knowledge. You might also ask students at what point holding on to a romantic view of life becomes a refusal to grow up, to participate in adult life.

---

[1]Red cheeks are one of the signs of tuberculosis. [Eds.]

Il Faut Travailler[1]

ANNIE DILLARD

In her autobiography, *An American Childhood* (1987), from which *"Il Faut Travailler"* is taken, Annie Dillard (see also p. 34) turns her skill as an observer of nature to her own childhood in Pittsburgh. She writes of small incidents, then probes them for their philosophical meanings. In the excerpt that follows, Dillard reflects on the work of Pasteur and Salk before attempting to define what a life's work means for her.

FOR OPENERS

Louis Pasteur said, "In the fields of observation, chance favors only the prepared mind." In what way do sentiments expressed by Dillard reflect Pasteur's ideas?

ADDITIONAL QUESTIONS FOR RESPONDING TO READING

1. Dillard was inspired by the life of Louis Pasteur. Whose life story has inspired you?
2. Dillard recounts the near panic during the polio epidemic. Do you see similarities and/or differences between that situation and the present AIDS epidemic?
3. One of the main points of Dillard's essay is that success rarely comes without great effort. Do you think the personal sacrifices are worth the success when it finally comes?
4. How do you define "good work"?

I intended to live the way the microbe hunters lived. I wanted to work. Hard work on an enormous scale was the microbe hunters' stock-in-trade. They took a few clear, time-consuming steps and solved everything. In those early days of germ theory, large disease-causing organisms, whose cycles traced straightforward patterns, yielded and fell to simple procedures. I would know just what to do. I would seize on the most casual remarks of untutored milkmaids. When an untutored milkmaid remarked to me casually, "Oh, everyone knows you won't get the smallpox if you've had the cowpox," I would perk right up.

Microbe Hunters[2] sent me to a biography of Louis Pasteur. Pasteur's was the most enviable life I had yet encountered. It was his privilege to do things until they were done. He established the germ theory of disease; he demonstrated convincingly that yeasts ferment beer; he discovered how to preserve wine; he isolated the bacillus in a disease of silkworms; he demonstrated the etiology of anthrax and produced a vaccine for it; he halted an epidemic of cholera in fowls and inoculated a boy for hydrophobia. Toward the end of his life, in a rare idle moment, he chanced to read some of his early published papers and exclaimed (someone overheard), "How beautiful! And to think that I did it all!" The tone of this exclamation was, it seemed to me, astonished and modest, for he had genuinely forgotten, moving on.

Pasteur had not used up all the good work. Mother told me again and again about one of her heroes, a doctor working for a federal agency who solved a problem that arose in the late forties. Premature babies, and only premature babies, were turning up blind, in enormous numbers. Why? What do premature babies have in common?

"Look in the incubators!" Mother would holler, and knock the

---

[1] One Must Work. [Eds.]

[2] A book by Paul DeKruif that presents narrative accounts of famous scientists and their battles against disease. [Eds.]

side of her head with the heel of her hand, holler outraged, glaring far behind my head as she was telling me this story, holler, "Look in the incubators!" as if at her wit's end facing a roomful of doctors who wrung their useless hands and accepted this blindness as one of life's tough facts. Mother's hero, like all of Mother's heroes, accepted nothing. She rolled up her sleeves, looked in the incubators, and decided to see what happened if she reduced the oxygen in the incubator air. That worked. Too much oxygen had been blinding them. Now the babies thrived; they got enough oxygen, and they weren't blinded. Hospitals all over the world changed the air mixture for incubators, and prematurity no longer carried a special risk of blindness.

Mother liked this story, and told it to us fairly often. Once she posed it as a challenge to Amy. We were all in the living room, waiting for dinner. "What would you do if you noticed that all over the United States, premature babies were blind?" Without even looking up from her homework, Amy said, "Look in the incubators. Maybe there's something wrong in the incubators." Mother started to whoop for joy before she realized she'd been had.

Problems still yielded to effort. Only a few years ago, to the wide-eyed attention of the world, we had seen the epidemic of poliomyelitis crushed in a twinkling, right here in Pittsburgh.

We had all been caught up in the polio epidemic: the early neighbor boy who wore one tall shoe, to which his despairing father added another two soles every year; the girl in the iron lung reading her schoolbook in an elaborate series of mirrors while a volunteer waited to turn the page; my friend who limped, my friend who rolled everywhere in a wheelchair, my friend whose arm hung down, Mother's friend who walked with crutches. My beloved dressed-up aunt, Mother's sister, had come to visit one day and, while she was saying hello, flung herself on the couch in tears; her son had it. Just a touch, they said, but who could believe it?

When Amy and I had asked, Why do we have to go to bed so early? Why do we have to wash our hands again? we knew Mother would kneel to look us in the eyes and answer in a low, urgent voice, So you do not get polio. We heard polio discussed once or twice a day for several years.

And we had all been caught up in its prevention, in the wild ferment of the early days of the Salk vaccine, the vaccine about which Pittsburgh talked so much, and so joyously, you could probably have heard the crowd noise on the moon.

In 1953, Jonas Salk's Virus Research Laboratory at the University of Pittsburgh had produced a controversial vaccine for polio. The small

5

6

7

8

9

10

TEACHING STRATEGY

Ask students the question "Why do people work?" List the reasons, and then have the class rank them according to importance. Is Dillard's view of work different from other people's? If so, how?

stories in the Pittsburgh *Press* and the *Post-Gazette* were coming out in *Life* and *Time*. It was too quick, said medical colleagues nationwide: Salk had gone public without first publishing everything in the journals. He rushed out a killed-virus serum without waiting for a safe live-virus one, which would probably be better. Doctors walked out of professional meetings; some quit the foundation that funded the testing. Salk was after personal glory, they said. Salk was after money, they said. Salk was after big prizes.

Salk tested the serum on five thousand Pittsburgh schoolchildren, 11 of whom I was three, because I kept changing elementary schools. Our parents, like ninety-five percent of all Pittsburgh parents, signed the consent forms. Did the other mothers then bend over the desk in relief and sob? I don't know. But I don't suppose any of them gave much of a damn what Salk had been after.

When Pasteur died, near a place wonderfully called Saint-Cloud, 12 he murmured to the devoted assistants who surrounded his bed, *"Il faut travailler."*

Il faut indeed *travailler*—no one who grew up in Pittsburgh could 13 doubt it. And no one who grew up in Pittsburgh could doubt that the great work was ongoing. We breathed in optimism—not coal dust—with every breath. What couldn't be done with good hard *travail*?

The air in Pittsburgh had been dirty; now we could see it was 14 clean. An enormous, pioneering urban renewal was under way; the newspapers pictured fantastic plans, airy artists' watercolors, which we soon saw laid out and built up in steel and glass downtown. The Republican Richard King Mellon had approached Pittsburgh's Democratic, Catholic mayor, David L. Lawrence, and together with a dozen business leaders they were razing the old grim city and building a sparkling new one; they were washing the very air. The Russians had shot Sputnik into outer space. In Shippingport, just a few miles down the Ohio River, people were building a generating plant that used atomic energy—an idea that seemed completely dreamy, but there it was. A physicist from Bell Laboratories spoke to us at school about lasers; he was about as wrought up a man as I had ever seen. You could not reasonably believe a word he said, but you could see that he believed it.

We knew that "Doctor Salk" had spent many years and many 15 dollars to produce the vaccine. He commonly worked sixteen-hour days, six days a week. Of course. In other laboratories around the world, other researchers were working just as hard, as hard as Salk and Pasteur. Hard work bore fruit. This is what we learned growing up in Pittsburgh, growing up in the United States.

Salk had isolated seventy-four strains of polio virus. It took him   16
three years to verify the proposition that a workable vaccine would
need samples of only three of these strains. He grew the virus in
tissues cultured from monkey kidneys. The best broth for growing
the monkey tissue proved to be Medium Number 199; it contained
sixty-two ingredients in careful proportion.

This was life itself: the big task. Nothing exhilarated me more   17
than the idea of a life dedicated to a monumental worthwhile task.
Doctor Salk never watched it rain and wished he had never been
born. How many shovelfuls of dirt did men move to dig the Panama
Canal? Two hundred and forty million cubic yards. It took ten years
and twenty-one thousand lives and $336,650,000, but it was possible.

I thought a great deal about the Panama Canal, and always con-   18
templated the same notion: You could take more time, and do it with
teaspoons. I saw myself and a few Indian and Caribbean co-workers
wielding teaspoons from our kitchen: Towle, Rambling Rose.[3] And
our grandchildren, and their grandchildren. Digging the canal across
the isthmus at Panama would tear through a good many silver spoons.
But it could be done, in theory and therefore in fact. It was like Mount
Rushmore, or Grand Coulee Dam. You hacked away at the landscape
and made something, or you did not do anything, and just died.

How many filaments had Thomas Edison tried, over how many   19
years, before he found one workable for incandescence? How many
days and nights over how many years had Marie Curie labored in a
freezing shed to isolate radium? I read a biography of George Washington Carver: so many years on the soybean, the peanut, the sweet
potato, the waste from ginning cotton. I read biographies of Abraham
Lincoln, Thomas Edison, Daniel Boone.

It was all the same story. You have a great idea and spend grinding   20
years at dull tasks, still charged by your vision. All the people about
whom biographies were not written were people who failed to find
something that took years to do. People could count the grains of
sand. In my own life, as a sideline, and for starters, I would learn all
the world's languages.

What if people said it could not be done? So much the better. We   21
grew up with the myth of the French Impressionist painters, and its
queer implication that rejection and ridicule guaranteed, or at any
rate signaled, a project's worth. When little George Westinghouse at
last figured out how to make air brakes, Cornelius Vanderbilt of the
New York Central Railroad said to him, "Do you mean to tell me with
a straight face that a moving train can be stopped with wind?" "They

COLLABORATIVE ACTIVITY

In small groups, identify three major scientific discoveries that have occurred in the world
during the past decade. Ask students to evaluate
which changes are positive and which are not,
and to explain why.

---

[3]Silver pattern. [Eds.]

laughed at Orville," Mother used to say when someone tried to talk her out of a wild scheme, "and they laughed at Wilbur."

I had small experience of the evil hopelessness, pain, starvation, and terror that the world spread about; I had barely seen people's malice and greed. I believed that in civilized countries, torture had ended with the Enlightenment. Of nations' cruel options I knew nothing. My optimism was endless; it grew sky-high within the narrow bounds of my isolationism. Because I was all untried courage, I could not allow that the loss of courage was a real factor to be reckoned in. I put my faith in willpower, that weak notion by which children seek to replace the loving devotion that comes from intimate and dedicated knowledge. I believed that I could resist aging by will-power.   22

I believed then, too, that I would never harm anyone. I usually believed I would never meet a problem I could not solve. I would overcome any weakness, any despair, any fear. Hadn't I overcome my fear of the ghosty oblong that coursed round my room, simply by thinking it through? Everything was simple. You found good work, learned all about it, and did it.   23

Questions of how to act were also transparent to reason. Right and wrong were easy to discern: I was right, and Amy was wrong. Many of my classmates stole things, but I did not. Sometimes, in a very tight spot, when at last I noticed I had a moral question on my hands, I asked myself, What would Christ have done? I had picked up this method (very much on the sly—we were not supposed really to believe these things) from Presbyterian Sunday school, from summer camp, or from any of the innumerable righteous orange-bound biographies I read. I had not known it to fail in the two times I had applied it.   24

As for loss, as for parting, as for bidding farewell, so long, thanks, to love or a land or a time—what did I know of parting, of grieving, mourning, loss? Well, I knew one thing; I had known it all along. I knew it was the kicker. I knew life pulled you in two; you never healed. Mother's emotions ran high, and she suffered sometimes from a web of terrors, because, she said, her father died when she was seven; she still missed him.   25

My parents played the Cole Porter song "It's All Right with Me." When Ella Fitzgerald sang, "There's someone I'm trying so hard to forget—don't you want to forget someone too?," these facile, breathy lyrics struck me as an unexpectedly true expression of how it felt to be alive. This was experience at its most private and inarticulate: longing and loss. "It's the wrong time, it's the wrong place, though your face is charming, it's the wrong face." I was a thirteen-year-old   26 child; I had no one to miss, had lost no one. Yet I suspect most children feel this way, probably all children feel this way, as adults do; they mourn this absence or loss of someone, and sense that unnamable loss as a hole or hollow moving beside them in the air.

Loss came around with the seasons, blew into the house when 27 you opened the windows, piled up in the bottom desk and dresser drawers, accumulated in the back of closets, heaped in the basement starting by the furnace, and came creeping up the basement stairs. Loss grew as you did, without your consent; your losses mounted beside you like earthworm castings. No willpower could prevent someone's dying. And no willpower could restore someone dead, breathe life into that frame and set it going again in the room with you to meet your eyes. That was the fact of it. The strongest men and women who had ever lived had presumably tried to resist their own deaths, and now they were dead. It was on this fact that all the stirring biographies coincided, concurred, and culminated.

Time itself bent you and cracked you on its wheel. We were 28 getting ready to move again. I knew I could not forever keep riding my bike backward into ever-older neighborhoods to look the ever-older houses in the face. I tried to memorize the layout of this Richland Lane house, but I couldn't force it into my mind while it was still in my bones.

I saw already that I could not in good faith renew the increasingly 29 desperate series of vows by which I had always tried to direct my life. I had vowed to love Walter Milligan forever; now I could recall neither his face nor my feeling, but only this quondam[4] urgent vow. I had vowed to keep exploring Pittsburgh by bicycle no matter how old I got, and planned an especially sweeping tour for my hundredth birthday in 2045. I had vowed to keep hating Amy in order to defy Mother, who kept prophesying I would someday not hate Amy. In short, I always vowed, one way or another, not to change. Not me. I needed the fierceness of vowing because I could scarcely help but notice, visiting the hatchling robins at school every day, that it was mighty unlikely.

As a life's work, I would remember everything—everything, against 30 loss. I would go through life like a plankton net. I would trap and keep every teacher's funny remark, every face on the street, every microscopic alga's sway, every conversation, configuration of leaves, every dream, and every scrap of overhead cloud. Who would remember Molly's infancy if not me? (Unaccountably, I thought that only I had noticed—

---

[4]Former; sometime. [Eds.]

WRITING SUGGESTIONS

1. What goals did you have when you were a child? Choose one of them and write an essay in which you discuss why it was or was not a realistic one. What do you now know about this goal that you did not know then?
2. Where do you see yourself in ten years? Write a job application letter in which you summarize your professional achievements and goals.

1. Answers will vary. Most students will admit that in some ways today's students are selfish, but they may point to a renewed concern for the homeless, the environment, and world peace. It might be interesting to discuss the difference between *concern* and *actions*—for example, between going to a concert to benefit victims of famine and working in a kitchen to feed the homeless.

2. Possibly, but she admits that her childish views changed, and so perhaps will these.

3. "Il faut travailler" is a statement by Pasteur on his deathbed. It is ironic because even on his deathbed Pasteur talks about work, expressing the idea that a constant struggle is necessary for any progress. This comment puts the work done by Pasteur and Salk into perspective. Both men kept going—even in the face of hopelessness, pain, and terror—until they achieved their respective goals.

not Molly, but time itself. No one else, at least, seemed bugged by it. Children may believe that they alone have interior lives.)

Some days I felt an urgent responsibility to each change of light 31 outside the sunporch windows. Who would remember any of it, any of this our time, and the wind thrashing the buckeye limbs outside? Somebody had to do it, somebody had to hang on to the days with teeth and fists, or the whole show had been in vain. That it was impossible never entered my reckoning. For work, for a task, I had never heard the word.

RESPONDING TO READING

1. The present generation of students has been called the "me generation." Do you think this label is accurate? In what ways are the values of today's college students like or unlike those described by Dillard?   **2.** Could Dillard be accused of taking a biased view of technology—that is, of celebrating the success of technology while ignoring its failures?   **3.** What is the significance of the essay's title? In what way is it ironic? How does the description of Pasteur and Salk relate to the section beginning with paragraph 22 on loss?

Thinking as a Hobby

WILLIAM GOLDING

William Golding (1911–   ) is an English novelist, poet, and playwright whose most famous work is *Lord of the Flies* (1954). This novel, about a group of schoolboys stranded on an island, became a cult classic in the 1960s. Winner of the Nobel Prize for Literature in 1983, Golding is the author of *The Inheritors* (1955), *The Brass Butterfly: A Play in Three Acts* (1958), *Darkness Visible* (1979), *A Moving Target* (1982), and *Fire Down Below* (1989). He has been described as a mystical, spiritual, and allegorical writer who is concerned with the struggle between the civilized self and the dark nature within. In *Talk: Conversations with William Golding*, he says, "I'm against the picture of the artist as a starry-eyed visionary not really in control or knowing what he does. I think I'd almost prefer the word 'craftsman'." In his essay "Thinking as a Hobby," Golding describes how he learned about thought in school.

While I was still a boy, I came to the conclusion that there were 1 three grades of thinking; and since I was later to claim thinking as my hobby, I came to an even stranger conclusion—namely, that I myself could not think at all.

I must have been an unsatisfactory child for grownups to deal 2
with. I remember how incomprehensible they appeared to me at first,
but not, of course, how I appeared to them. It was the headmaster
of my grammar school who first brought the subject of thinking before
me—though neither in the way, nor with the result he intended. He
had some statuettes in his study. They stood on a high cupboard
behind his desk. One was a lady wearing nothing but a bath towel.
She seemed frozen in an eternal panic lest the bath towel slip down
any farther; and since she had no arms, she was in an unfortunate
position to pull the towel up again. Next to her, crouched the statuette
of a leopard, ready to spring down at the top drawer of a filing cabinet
labeled A–AH. My innocence interpreted this as the victim's last,
despairing cry. Beyond the leopard was a naked, muscular gentleman,
who sat, looking down, with his chin on his fist and his elbow on
his knee. He seemed utterly miserable.

Some time later, I learned about these statuettes. The headmaster 3
had placed them where they would face delinquent children, because
they symbolized to him the whole of life. The naked lady was the
Venus of Milo. She was Love. She was not worried about the towel.
She was just busy being beautiful. The leopard was Nature, and he
was being natural. The naked, muscular gentleman was not miserable. He was Rodin's Thinker, an image of pure thought. It is easy
to buy small plaster models of what you think life is like.

I had better explain that I was a frequent visitor to the head- 4
master's study, because of the latest thing I had done or left undone.
As we now say, I was not integrated. I was, if anything, disintegrated;
and I was puzzled. Grownups never made sense. Whenever I found
myself in a penal position before the headmaster's desk, with the
statuettes glimmering whitely above him, I would sink my head,
clasp my hands behind my back and writhe one shoe over the
other.

The headmaster would look opaquely at me through flashing 5
spectacles.

"What are we going to do with you?" 6

Well, what *were* they going to do with me? I would writhe my 7
shoe some more and stare down at the worn rug.

"Look up, boy! Can't you look up?" 8

Then I would look up at the cupboard, where the naked lady was 9
frozen in her panic and the muscular gentleman contemplated the
hindquarters of the leopard in endless gloom. I had nothing to say
to the headmaster. His spectacles caught the light so that you could
see nothing human behind them. There was no possibility of communication.

"Don't you ever think at all?" 10

ADDITIONAL QUESTIONS FOR RESPONDING TO READING

1. Golding recounts several incidents in his essay. What do readers learn from these? Which is the most effective?
2. What kind of thinking does television advertising encourage in people? Can you give examples of commercials that encourage a higher level of thinking than most? (You may want to contrast commercial messages with public service announcements designed to raise awareness about the dangers of driving while intoxicated, drug abuse, smoking, and sexually transmitted diseases.)
3. Do you share Golding's opinions about the masses of people? Is Golding being fair? Accurate?
4. How would you characterize your own thinking? Give examples.

TEACHING STRATEGY

Begin by presenting students with a problem that faces contemporary society—the destruction of the environment, the validity of the death penalty, or world hunger, for example. Then ask students to examine the problem using each of Golding's three types of thinking. Ask students what insights they gain as they move from grade-three to grade-one thinking.

No, I didn't think, wasn't thinking, couldn't think—I was simply 11
waiting in anguish for the interview to stop.

"Then you'd better learn—hadn't you?" 12

On one occasion the headmaster leaped to his feet, reached up 13
and plonked Rodin's masterpiece on the desk before me.

"That's what a man looks like when he's really thinking." 14

I surveyed the gentleman without interest or comprehension. 15

"Go back to your class." 16

Clearly there was something missing in me. Nature had endowed 17
the rest of the human race with a sixth sense and left me out. This
must be so, I mused, on my way back to the class, since whether I
had broken a window, or failed to remember Boyle's Law, or been
late for school, my teachers produced me one, adult answer: "Why
can't you think?"

As I saw the case, I had broken the window because I had tried 18
to hit Jack Arney with a cricket ball and missed him; I could not
remember Boyle's Law because I had never bothered to learn it; and
I was late for school because I preferred looking over the bridge into
the river. In fact, I was wicked. Were my teachers, perhaps, so good
that they could not understand the depths of my depravity? Were
they clear, untormented people who could direct their every action
by this mysterious business of thinking? The whole thing was incomprehensible. In my earlier years, I found even the statuette of the
Thinker confusing. I did not believe any of my teachers were naked,
ever. Like someone born deaf, but bitterly determined to find out
about sound, I watched my teachers to find out about thought.

There was Mr. Houghton. He was always telling me to think. 19
With a modest satisfaction, he would tell me that he had thought a
bit himself. Then why did he spend so much time drinking? Or was
there more sense in drinking than there appeared to be? But if not,
and if drinking were in fact ruinous to health—and Mr. Houghton
was ruined, there was no doubt about that—why was he always
talking about the clean life and the virtues of fresh air? He would
spread his arms wide with the action of a man who habitually spent
his time striding along mountain ridges.

"Open air does me good, boys—I know it!" 20

Sometimes, exalted by his own oratory, he would leap from his 21
desk and hustle us outside into a hideous wind.

"Now, boys! Deep breaths! Feel it right down inside you—huge 22
draughts of God's good air!"

He would stand before us, rejoicing in his perfect health, an open- 23
air man. He would put his hands on his waist and take a tremendous
breath. You could hear the wind, trapped in the cavern of his chest
and struggling with all the unnatural impediments. His body would

reel with shock and his ruined face go white at the unaccustomed visitation. He would stagger back to his desk and collapse there, useless for the rest of the morning.

Mr. Houghton was given to high-minded monologues about the 24 good life, sexless and full of duty. Yet in the middle of one of these monologues, if a girl passed the window, tapping along on her neat little feet, he would interrupt his discourse, his neck would turn of itself and he would watch her out of sight. In this instance, he seemed to me ruled not by thought but by an invisible and irresistible spring in his nape.

His neck was an object of great interest to me. Normally it bulged 25 a bit over his collar. But Mr. Houghton had fought in the First World War alongside both Americans and French, and had come—by who knows what illogic?—to a settled detestation of both countries. If either country happened to be prominent in current affairs, no argument could make Mr. Houghton think well of it. He would bang the desk, his neck would bulge still further and go red. "You can say what you like," he would cry, "but I've thought about this—and I know what I think!"

Mr. Houghton thought with his neck. 26

There was Miss Parsons. She assured us that her dearest wish 27 was our welfare, but I knew even then, with the mysterious clairvoyance of childhood, that what she wanted most was the husband she never got. There was Mr. Hands—and so on.

I have dealt at length with my teachers because this was my 28 introduction to the nature of what is commonly called thought. Through them I discovered that thought is often full of unconscious prejudice, ignorance and hypocrisy. It will lecture on disinterested purity while its neck is being remorselessly twisted toward a skirt. Technically, it is about as proficient as most businessmen's golf, as honest as most politicians' intentions, or—to come near my own preoccupation—as coherent as most books that get written. It is what I came to call grade-three thinking, though more properly, it is feeling, rather than thought.

True, often there is a kind of innocence in prejudices, but in those 29 days I viewed grade-three thinking with an intolerant contempt and an incautious mockery. I delighted to confront a pious lady who hated the Germans with the proposition that we should love our enemies. She taught me a great truth in dealing with grade-three thinkers; because of her, I no longer dismiss lightly a mental process which for nine-tenths of the population is the nearest they will ever get to thought. They have immense solidarity. We had better respect them, for we are outnumbered and surrounded. A crowd of grade-three thinkers, all shouting the same thing, all warming their hands at the

COLLABORATIVE ACTIVITY

Golding met Einstein and was impressed by him. Group students and ask them to choose a famous modern thinker they would like to meet. Then ask them to write a list of questions they would ask that person.

fire of their own prejudices, will not thank you for pointing out the contradictions in their beliefs. Man is a gregarious animal, and enjoys agreement as cows will graze all the same way on the side of a hill.

Grade-two thinking is the detection of contradictions. I reached 30 grade two when I trapped the poor, pious lady. Grade-two thinkers do not stampede easily, though often they fall into the other fault and lap behind. Grade-two thinking is a withdrawal, with eyes and ears open. It became my hobby and brought satisfaction and loneliness in either hand. For grade-two thinking destroys without having the power to create. It set me watching the crowds cheering His Majesty and King and asking myself what all the fuss was about, without giving me anything positive to put in the place of that heady patriotism. But there were compensations. To hear people justify their habit of hunting foxes and tearing them to pieces by claiming that the foxes liked it. To hear our Prime Minister talk about the great benefit we conferred on India by jailing people like Pandit Nehru and Gandhi. To hear American politicians talk about peace in one sentence and refuse to join the League of Nations in the next. Yes, there were moments of delight.

But I was growing toward adolescence and had to admit that Mr. 31 Houghton was not the only one with an irresistible spring in his neck. I, too, felt the compulsive hand of nature and began to find that pointing out contradiction could be costly as well as fun. There was Ruth, for example, a serious and attractive girl. I was an atheist at the time. Grade-two thinking is a menace to religion and knocks down sects like skittles. I put myself in a position to be converted by her with an hypocrisy worthy of grade three. She was a Methodist—or at least, her parents were, and Ruth had to follow suit. But, alas, instead of relying on the Holy Spirit to convert me, Ruth was foolish enough to open her pretty mouth in argument. She claimed that the Bible (King James Version) was literally inspired. I countered by saying that the Catholics believed in the literal inspiration of Saint Jerome's *Vulgate*,[1] and the two books were different. Argument flagged.

At last she remarked that there were an awful lot of Methodists, 32 and they couldn't be wrong, could they—not all those millions? That was too easy, said I restively (for the nearer you were to Ruth, the nicer she was to be near to) since there were more Roman Catholics than Methodists anyway; and they couldn't be wrong, could they— not all those hundreds of millions? An awful flicker of doubt appeared in her eyes. I slid my arm around her waist and murmured breath-

---

[1]The version of the Bible used by Roman Catholics. [Eds.]

lessly that if we were counting heads, the Buddhists were the boys for my money. But Ruth had *really* wanted to do me good, because I was so nice. She fled. The combination of my arm and those countless Buddhists was too much for her.

That night her father visited my father and left, red-cheeked and 33 indignant. I was given the third degree to find out what had happened. It was lucky we were both of us only fourteen. I lost Ruth and gained an undeserved reputation as a potential libertine.

So grade-two thinking could be dangerous. It was in this knowl- 34 edge, at the age of fifteen, that I remember making a comment from the heights of grade two, on the limitations of grade three. One evening I found myself alone in the school hall, preparing it for a party. The door of the headmaster's study was open. I went in. The headmaster had ceased to thump Rodin's Thinker down on the desk as an example to the young. Perhaps he had not found any more candidates, but the statuettes were still there, glimmering and gathering dust on top of the cupboard. I stood on a chair and rearranged them. I stood Venus in her bath towel on the filing cabinet, so that now the top drawer caught its breath in a gasp of sexy excitement. "A-ah!" The portentous Thinker I placed on the edge of the cupboard so that he looked down at the bath towel and waited for it to slip.

Grade-two thinking, though it filled life with fun and excitement, 35 did not make for content. To find out the deficiencies of our elders bolsters the young ego but does not make for personal security. I found that grade two was not only the power to point out contradictions. It took the swimmer some distance from the shore and left him there, out of his depth. I decided that Pontius Pilate was a typical grade-two thinker. "What is truth?" he said, a very common grade-two thought, but one that is used always as the end of an argument instead of the beginning. There is still a higher grade of thought which says, "What is truth?" and sets out to find it.

But these grade-one thinkers were few and far between. They did 36 not visit my grammar school in the flesh though they were there in books. I aspired to them, partly because I was ambitious and partly because I now saw my hobby as an unsatisfactory thing if it went no further. If you set out to climb a mountain, however high you climb, you have failed if you cannot reach the top.

I *did* meet an undeniably grade-one thinker in my first year at 37 Oxford. I was looking over a small bridge in Magdalen Deer Park, and a tiny mustached and hatted figure came and stood by my side. He was a German who had just fled from the Nazis to Oxford as a temporary refuge. His name was Einstein.

But Professor Einstein knew no English at that time and I knew 38 only two words of German. I beamed at him, trying wordlessly to convey by my bearing all the affection and respect that the English felt for him. It is possible—and I have to make the admission—that I felt here were two grade-one thinkers standing side by side; yet I doubt if my face conveyed more than a formless awe. I would have given my Greek and Latin and French and a good slice of my English for enough German to communicate. But we were divided; he was as inscrutable as my headmaster. For perhaps five minutes we stood together on the bridge, undeniable grade-one thinker and breathless aspirant. With true greatness, Professor Einstein realized that my contact was better than none. He pointed to a trout wavering in midstream.

He spoke: *"Fisch."*   39

My brain reeled. Here I was, mingling with the great, and yet   40
helpless as the veriest grade-three thinker. Desperately I sought for some sign by which I might convey that I, too, revered pure reason. I nodded vehemently. In a brilliant flash I used up half of my German vocabulary.

"Fisch. Ja Ja."   41

For perhaps another five minutes we stood side by side. Then   42
Professor Einstein, his whole figure still conveying good will and amiability, drifted away out of sight.

I, too, would be a grade-one thinker. I was irreverent at the best   43
of times. Political and religious systems, social customs, loyalties and traditions, they all came tumbling down like so many rotten apples off a tree. This was a fine hobby and a sensible substitute for cricket, since you could play it all the year round. I came up in the end with what must always remain the justification for grade-one thinking, its sign, seal and charter. I devised a coherent system for living. It was a moral system, which was wholly logical. Of course, as I readily admitted, conversion of the world to my way of thinking might be difficult, since my system did away with a number of trifles, such as big business, centralized government, armies, marriage. . . .

It was Ruth all over again. I had some very good friends who   44
stood by me, and still do. But my acquaintances vanished, taking the girls with them. Young women seemed oddly contented with the world as it was. They valued the meaningless ceremony with a ring. Young men, while willing to concede the chaining sordidness of marriage, were hesitant about abandoning the organizations which they hoped would give them a career. A young man on the first rung of the Royal Navy, while perfectly agreeable to doing away with big business and marriage, got as rednecked as Mr. Houghton when I proposed a world without any battleships in it.

Had the game gone too far? Was it a game any longer? In those prewar days, I stood to lose a great deal, for the sake of a hobby.

WRITING SUGGESTION

Have you ever changed your mind about an important subject? Write an essay in which you describe your original position and what prompted you to adopt a new viewpoint.

Now you are expecting me to describe how I saw the folly of my 46
ways and came back to the warm nest, where prejudices are so often
called loyalties, where pointless actions are hallowed into custom by
repetition, where we are content to say we think when all we do is
feel.

But you would be wrong. I dropped my hobby and turned profes- 47
sional.

If I were to go back to the headmaster's study and find the dusty 48
statuettes still there, I would arrange them differently. I would dust
Venus and put her aside, for I have come to love her and know her
for the fair thing she is. But I would put the Thinker, sunk in his
desperate thought, where there were shadows before him—and at
his back, I would put the leopard, crouched and ready to spring.

RESPONDING TO READING

1. Would you describe thinking as a hobby? Why do you think Golding
characterizes thinking in this way?   **2.** Do you think Golding's three categories of thinking are accurate? Do you think they are simplistic? Can you
apply them to your own thinking? Explain.   **3.** What does Golding mean
when he says he went professional? What do you think is lost or gained
when someone abandons thinking as a hobby and becomes a professional?

ANSWERS TO RESPONDING TO READING

1. Answers will vary. Golding perhaps characterizes thinking as a hobby because he has
considered it a game all his life.
2. The three categories are accurate insofar as
they divide thought into higher and lower
orders, but it is perhaps limiting (or even simplistic) to accept the three as the only possible levels of thought.
3. By saying he went professional, Golding indicates that he now takes his thinking seriously.
As a professional he gained skill, efficiency,
and speed, but he lost spontaneity and innocence. In discussing the answer to this question, you may want to compare Golding's
evolution with Twain's (page 98) or Whitman's (p. 187).

My Built-in Doubter

ISAAC ASIMOV

Born in the Soviet Union, Isaac Asimov (1920–   ) came to the
United States as a child and became a citizen in 1928. He was introduced to science fiction in the magazines sold in his father's candy
store, and he began writing science fiction stories himself while
attending college. At one time a biochemistry professor at the Boston
University School of Medicine, Asimov now lives in New York and
writes full-time, and he has produced more than 200 books of fiction,
nonfiction, humor, and literary criticism. Among his most influential
science fiction books are *I, Robot* (1950) and the *Foundation* series,
published as a trilogy in 1964. Asimov is also a prolific science writer
for popular audiences, and he writes a science column for the *Isaac
Asimov Science Fiction Magazine.* "My Built-in Doubter," in which
Asimov argues that doubt helps advance science, is from *Fact and
Fancy* (1961).

BACKGROUND ON READING

Introduce your students to the concept of
skepticism. Many students will think it is dis-
respectful to doubt someone in authority. Ask
them under what conditions they should doubt
and whether doubting can ever be constructive.

FOR OPENERS

Begin by relating to the class some of the more outrageous theories of science—the hollow earth theory, the flat earth theory, and the lost continent theory, for example. Then point out that each of these theories was widely accepted by some very intelligent people. Ask if anyone in class doubts some contemporary theories—global warming or evolution, for example. Then ask the class to comment on the doubts that have been expressed.

ADDITIONAL QUESTIONS FOR RESPONDING TO READING

1. Do you have a built-in doubter? Give an example.
2. Asimov stresses the importance of doubt in science. Are there any other fields in which doubt is essential? Are there fields in which doubt is *never* necessary? Explain.
3. What criteria should one use to differentiate between acceptable and unacceptable ideas?
4. Explain Asimov's conclusion (paragraphs 75–79). In what way does it sum up the points he makes in his essay?

Once I delivered myself of an oration before a small but select audience of non-scientists on the topic of "What Is Science?" speaking seriously and, I hope, intelligently. 1

Having completed the talk, there came the question period, and, bless my heart, I wasn't disappointed. A charming young lady up front waved a pretty little hand at me and asked, not a serious question on the nature of science, but: "Dr. Asimov, do you believe in flying saucers?" 2

With a fixed smile on my face, I proceeded to give the answer I have carefully given after every lecture I have delivered. I said, "No, miss, I do not, and I think anyone who does is a crackpot!" 3

And oh, the surprise on her face! 4

It is taken for granted by everyone, it seems to me, that because I sometimes write science fiction, I believe in flying saucers, in Atlantis,[1] in clairvoyance and levitation, in the prophecies of the Great Pyramid, in astrology, in Fort's theories,[2] and in the suggestion that Bacon[3] wrote Shakespeare. 5

No one would ever think that someone who writes fantasies for pre-school children really thinks that rabbits can talk, or that a writer of hard-boiled detective stories really thinks a man can down two quarts of whiskey in five minutes, then make love to two girls in the next five, or that a writer for the ladies' magazines really thinks that virtue always triumphs and that the secretary always marries the handsome boss—but a science-fiction writer apparently *must* believe in flying saucers. 6

Well, I do not. 7

To be sure, I wrote a story once about flying saucers in which I explained their existence very logically. I also wrote a story once in which levitation played a part. 8

If I can buddy up to such notions long enough to write sober, reasonable stories about them, why, then, do I reject them so definitely in real life? 9

I can explain by way of a story. A good friend of mine once spent quite a long time trying to persuade me of the truth and validity of what I considered a piece of pseudo-science and bad pseudo-science at that. I sat there listening quite stonily, and none of the cited evidence and instances and proofs had the slightest effect on me. 10

Finally the gentleman said to me, with considerable annoyance, 11

---

[1]A city, mentioned by Plato in his Republic, which is said to be beneath the sea. [Eds.]

[2]Charles Fort (1874–1932), journalist and editor who formulated theories about psychic and other phenomena. [Eds.]

[3]Francis Bacon (1561–1626), English philosopher who some believe is the actual author of Shakespeare's works. [Eds.]

"Damn it, Isaac, the trouble with you is that you have a built-in doubter."

To which the only answer I could see my way to making was a 12 heartfelt, "Thank God."

If a scientist has one piece of temperamental equipment that is 13 essential to his job, it is that of a built-in doubter. Before he does anything else, he must doubt. He must doubt what others tell him and what he reads in reference books, and, *most of all*, what his own experiments show him and what his own reasoning tells him.

Such doubt must, of course, exist in varying degrees. It is impos- 14 sible, impractical, and useless to be a maximal doubter at all times. One cannot (and would not want to) check personally every figure or observation given in a handbook or monograph before one uses it and then proceed to check it and recheck it until one dies. *But*, if any trouble arises and nothing else seems wrong, one must be prepared to say to one's self, "Well, now, I wonder if the data I got out of the 'Real Guaranteed Authoritative Very Scientific Handbook' might not be a misprint."

To doubt intelligently requires, therefore, a rough appraisal of 15 the authoritativeness of a source. It also requires a rough estimate of the nature of the statement. If you were to tell me that you had a bottle containing one pound of pure titanium oxide, I would say, "Good," and ask to borrow some if I needed it. Nor would I test it. I would accept its purity on your say-so (until further notice, anyway).

If you were to tell me that you had a bottle containing one pound 16 of pure thulium oxide, I would say with considerable astonishment, "You have? Where?" Then if I had use for the stuff, I would want to run some tests on it and even run it through an ion-exchange column before I could bring myself to use it.

And if you told me that you had a bottle containing one pound 17 of pure americium oxide, I would say, "You're crazy," and walk away. I'm sorry, but my time is reasonably valuable, and I do not consider that statement to have enough chance of validity even to warrant my stepping into the next room to look at the bottle.

What I am trying to say is that doubting is far more important to 18 the advance of science than believing is and that, moreover, doubting is a serious business that requires extensive training to be handled properly. People without training in a particular field do not know what to doubt and what not to doubt; or, to put it conversely, what to believe and what not to believe. I am very sorry to be undemocratic, but one man's opinion is not necessarily as good as the next man's.

To be sure, I feel uneasy about seeming to kowtow to authority 19 in this fashion. After all, you all know of instances where authority

TEACHING STRATEGY

Assign the short story "Gryphon" by Charles Baxter (page 170). In class discussion, analyze some of the more outrageous statements that Miss Ferenczi makes. How do the different characters react to these statements? Why do some doubt and some believe?

COLLABORATIVE ACTIVITY

Ask students, working in groups, to identify the various examples Asimov gives to illustrate the function of doubt and the transitions he uses to connect one example to the next. In class discussion, analyze the effectiveness of his examples.

was wrong, dead wrong. Look at Columbus, you will say. Look at Galileo.

I know about them, and about others, too. As a dabbler in the history of science, I can give you horrible examples you may never have heard of. I can cite the case of the German scientist, Rudolf Virchow, who, in the mid-nineteenth century was responsible for important advances in anthropology and practically founded the science of pathology. He was the first man to engage in cancer research on a scientific basis. However, he was dead set against the germ theory of disease when that was advanced by Pasteur. So were many others, but one by one the opponents abandoned doubt as evidence multiplied. Not Virchow, however. Rather than be forced to admit he was wrong and Pasteur right, Virchow quit science altogether and went into politics. How much wronger could Stubborn Authority get? [20]

But this is a very exceptional case. Let's consider a far more normal and natural example of authority in the wrong. [21]

The example concerns a young Swedish chemical student, Svante August Arrhenius, who was working for his Ph.D. in the University of Uppsala in the 1880s. He was interested in the freezing points of solutions because certain odd points arose in that connection. [22]

If sucrose (ordinary table sugar) is dissolved in water, the freezing point of the solution is somewhat lower than is that of pure water. Dissolve more sucrose and the freezing point lowers further. You can calculate how many molecules of sucrose must be dissolved per cubic centimeter of water in order to bring about a certain drop in freezing point. It turns out that this same number of molecules of glucose (grape sugar) and of many other soluble substances will bring about the same drop. It doesn't matter that a molecule of sucrose is twice as large as a molecule of glucose. What counts is the number of molecules and not their size. [23]

But if sodium chloride (table salt) is dissolved in water, the freezing-point drop per molecule is twice as great as normal. And this goes for certain other substances too. For instance, barium chloride, when dissolved, will bring about a freezing-point drop that is three times normal. [24]

Arrhenius wondered if this meant that when sodium chloride was dissolved, each of its molecules broke into two portions, thus creating twice as many particles as there were molecules and therefore a doubled freezing-point drop. And barium chloride might break up into three particles per molecule. Since the sodium chloride molecule is composed of a sodium atom and a chlorine atom and since the barium chloride molecule is composed of a barium atom and two chlorine atoms, the logical next step was to suppose that these particular molecules broke up into individual atoms. [25]

Then, too, there was another interesting fact. Those substances 26
like sucrose and glucose which gave a normal freezing-point drop did
not conduct an electric current in solution. Those, like sodium chloride
and barium chloride, which showed abnormally high freezing-point
drops, *did* do so.

Arrhenius wondered if the atoms, into which molecules broke up 27
on solution, might not carry positive and negative electric charges. If
the sodium atom carried a positive charge, for instance, it would be
attracted to the negative electrode. If the chlorine atom carried a
negative charge, it would be attracted to the positive electrode. Each
would wander off in its own direction and the net result would be
that such a solution would conduct an electric current. For these
charged and wandering atoms, Arrhenius adopted Faraday's name
"ions" from a Greek word meaning "wanderer."

Furthermore, a charged atom, or ion, would not have the prop- 28
erties of an uncharged atom. A charged chlorine atom would not be
a gas that would bubble out of solution. A charged sodium atom
would not react with water to form hydrogen. It was for that reason
that common salt (sodium chloride) did not show the properties of
either sodium metal or chlorine gas, though it was made of those two
elements.

In 1884 Arrhenius, then twenty-five, prepared his theories in the 29
form of a thesis and presented it as part of his doctoral dissertation.
The examining professors sat in frigid disapproval. No one had ever
heard of electrically charged atoms, it was against all scientific belief
of the time, and they turned on their built-in doubters.

However, Arrhenius argued his case so clearly and, on the single 30
assumption of the dissolution of molecules into charged atoms, managed to explain so much so neatly, that the professors' built-in
doubters did not quite reach the intensity required to flunk the young
man. Instead, they passed him—with the lowest possible passing
grade.

But then, ten years later, the negatively charged electron was 31
discovered and the atom was found to be not the indivisible thing it
had been considered but a complex assemblage of still smaller particles. Suddenly the notion of ions as charged atoms made sense. If
an atom lost an electron or two, it was left with a positive charge; if
it gained them, it had a negative charge.

Then, the decade following, the Nobel Prizes were set up and in 32
1903 the Nobel Prize in Chemistry was awarded to Arrhenius for that
same thesis which, nineteen years earlier, had barely squeaked him
through for a Ph.D.

Were the professors wrong? Looking back, we can see they were. 33
But in 1884 they were *not* wrong. They did exactly the right thing and

they served science well. Every professor must listen to and appraise dozens of new ideas every year. He must greet each with the gradation of doubt his experience and training tells him the idea is worth.

Arrhenius's notion met with just the proper gradation of doubt. 34 It was radical enough to be held at arm's length. However, it seemed to have just enough possible merit to be worth some recognition. The professors *did* give him his Ph.D. after all. And other scientists of the time paid attention to it and thought about it. A very great one, Ostwald,[4] thought enough of it to offer Arrhenius a good job.

Then, when the appropriate evidence turned up, doubt receded 35 to minimal values and Arrhenius was greatly honored.

What better could you expect? Ought the professors to have fallen 36 all over Arrhenius and his new theory on the spot? And if so, why shouldn't they also have fallen all over forty-nine other new theories presented that year, no one of which might have seemed much more unlikely than Arrhenius's and some of which may even have appeared less unlikely?

It would have taken *longer* for the ionic theory to have become 37 established if overcredulity on the part of scientists had led them into fifty blind alleys. How many scientists would have been left to investigate Arrhenius's notions?

Scientific manpower is too limited to investigate everything that 38 occurs to everybody, and always will be too limited. The advance of science depends on scientists in general being kept firmly in the direction of maximum possible return. And the only device that will keep them turned in that direction is doubt; doubt arising from a good, healthy and active built-in doubter.

But, you might say, this misses the point. Can't one pick and 39 choose and isolate the brilliant from the imbecilic, accepting the first at once and wholeheartedly, and rejecting the rest completely? Would not such a course have saved ten years on ions without losing time on other notions?

Sure, if it could be done, but it can't. The godlike power to tell 40 the good from the bad, the useful from the useless, the true from the false, instantly and *in toto* belongs to gods and not to men.

Let me cite you Galileo as an example; Galileo, who was one of 41 the greatest scientific geniuses of all time, who invented modern science in fact, and who certainly experienced persecution and authoritarian enmity.

Surely, Galileo, of all people, was smart enough to know a good 42

---

[4]Wilhelm Ostwald (1853–1932), a German physical chemist and natural philosopher who received the 1909 Nobel Prize in Chemistry. [Eds.]

idea when he saw it, and revolutionary enough not to be deterred by its being radical.

Well, let's see. In 1632 Galileo published the crowning work of 43 his career, *Dialogue on the Two Principal Systems of the World*, which was the very book that got him into real trouble before the Inquisition. It dealt, as the title indicates, with the two principal systems; that of Ptolemy, which had the earth at the center of the universe with the planets, sun and moon going about it in complicated systems of circles within circles; and that of Copernicus, which had the sun at the center and the planets, earth, and moon going about *it* in complicated systems of circles within circles.

Galileo did not as much as mention a *third* system, that of Kepler, 44 which had the sun at the center but abandoned all the circles-within-circles jazz. Instead, he had the various planets traveling about the sun in ellipses, with the sun at one focus of the ellipse. It was Kepler's system that was correct and, in fact Kepler's system has not been changed in all the time that has elapsed since. Why, then, did Galileo ignore it completely?

Was it that Kepler had not yet devised it? No, indeed. Kepler's 45 views on that matter were published in 1609, twenty-seven years before Galileo's book.

Was it that Galileo had happened not to hear of it? Nonsense. 46 Galileo and Kepler were in steady correspondence and were friends. When Galileo built some spare telescopes, he sent one to Kepler. When Kepler had ideas, he wrote about them to Galileo.

The trouble was that Kepler was still bound up with the mystical 47 notions of the Middle Ages. He cast horoscopes for famous men, for a fee, and worked seriously and hard on astrology. He also spent time working out the exact notes formed by the various planets in creating the "music of the spheres" and pointed out that Earth's notes were mi, fa, mi, standing for misery, famine, and misery. He also devised a theory accounting for the relative distances of the planets from the Sun by nesting the five regular solids one within another and making deductions therefrom.

Galileo, who must have heard of all this, and who had nothing 48 of the mystic about himself, could only conclude that Kepler, though a nice guy and a bright fellow and a pleasant correspondent, was a complete nut. I am sure that Galileo heard all about the elliptical orbits and, considering the source, shrugged it off.

Well, Kepler was indeed a nut, but he happened to be luminously 49 right on occasion, too, and Galileo, of all people, couldn't pick the diamond out from among the pebbles.

Shall we sneer at Galileo for that? 50

Or should we rather be thankful that Galileo didn't interest him- 51 self in the ellipses *and* in astrology *and* in the nesting of regular solids *and* in the music of the spheres. Might not credulity have led him into wasting his talents, to the great loss of all succeeding generations?

No, no, until some supernatural force comes to our aid and tells 52 men what is right and what wrong, men must blunder along as best they can, and only the built-in doubter of the trained scientist can offer a refuge of safety.

The very mechanism of scientific procedure, built up slowly over 53 the years, is designed to encourage doubt and to place obstacles in the way of new ideas. No person receives credit for a new idea unless he publishes it for all the world to see and criticize. It is further considered advisable to announce ideas in papers read to colleagues at public gatherings that they might blast the speaker down face to face.

Even after announcement or publication, no observation can be 54 accepted until it has been confirmed by an independent observer, and no theory is considered more than, at best, an interesting speculation until it is backed by experimental evidence that has been independently confirmed and that has withstood the rigid doubts of others in the field.

All this is nothing more than the setting up of a system of "natural 55 selection" designed to winnow the fit from the unfit in the realm of ideas, in manner analogous to the concept of Darwinian evolution. The process may be painful and tedious, as evolution itself is; but in the long run it gets results, as evolution itself does. What's more, I don't see that there can be any substitute.

Now let me make a second point. The intensity to which the built- 56 in doubter is activated is also governed by the extent to which a new observation fits into the organized structure of science. If it fits well, doubt can be small; if it fits poorly, doubt can be intensive; if it threatens to overturn the structure completely, doubt is, and should be, nearly insuperable.

The reason for this is that now, three hundred fifty years after Galileo 57 founded experimental science, the structure that has been reared, bit by bit, by a dozen generations of scientists is so firm that its complete overturning has reached the vanishing point of unlikelihood.

Nor need you point to relativity as an example of a revolution 58 that overturned science. Einstein did not overturn the structure, he merely extended, elaborated, and improved it. Einstein did not prove Newton wrong, but merely incomplete. Einstein's world system contains Newton's as a special case and one which works if the volume of space considered is not too large and if velocities involved are not too great.

In fact, I should say that since Kepler's time in astronomy, since 59 Galileo's time in physics, since Lavoisier's[5] time in chemistry, and since Darwin's time in biology no discovery or theory, however revolutionary it has seemed, has actually overturned the structure of science or any major branch of it. The structure has merely been improved and refined.

The effect is similar to the paving of a road, and its broadening 60 and the addition of clover-leaf intersections, and the installation of radar to combat speeding. None of this, please notice, is the equivalent of abandoning the road and building another in a completely new direction.

But let's consider a few concrete examples drawn from contemporary life. A team of Columbia University geologists have been 61 exploring the configuration of the ocean bottom for years. Now they find that the mid-Atlantic ridge (a chain of mountains, running down the length of the Atlantic) has a rift in the center, a deep chasm or crack. What's more, this rift circles around Africa, sends an offshoot up into the Indian Ocean and across eastern Africa, and heads up the Pacific, skimming the California coast as it does so. It is like a big crack encircling the earth.

The observation itself can be accepted. Those involved were 62 trained and experienced specialists and confirmation is ample.

But why the rift? Recently one of the geologists, Bruce Heezen, 63 suggested that the crack may be due to the expansion of the earth.

This is certainly one possibility. If the interior were slowly 64 expanding, the thin crust would give and crack like an eggshell.

But why should Earth's interior expand? To do so it would have 65 to take up a looser arrangement, become less dense; the atoms would have to spread out a bit.

Heezen suggests that one way in which all this might happen is 66 that the gravitational force of the Earth was very slowly weakening with time. The central pressures would therefore ease up and the compressed atoms of the interior would slowly spread out.

But why should Earth's gravity decrease, unless the force of gravitation everywhere were slowly decreasing with time? Now this 67 deserves a lot of doubt, because there is nothing in the structure of science to suggest that the force of gravitation must decrease with time. However, it is also true that there is nothing in the structure of science to suggest that the force of gravitation might *not* decrease with time.[6]

---

[5]Antoine Laurent Lavoisier (1743–94), French chemist and physicist who is credited with founding modern chemistry. He was guillotined during the Reign of Terror. [Eds.]

[6]As a matter of fact, there have been cosmological speculations (though not, in my opinion, very convincing ones) that involve a steady and very slow decrease in the gravitational constant;

Or take another case. I have recently seen a news clipping con- 68 cerning an eighth-grader in South Carolina who grew four sets of bean plants under glass jars. One set remained there always, subjected to silence. The other three had their jars removed one hour a day in order that they might be exposed to noise: in one case to jazz, in another to serious music, and in a third to the raucous noises of sports-car engines. The only set of plants that grew vigorously were those exposed to the engine noises.

The headline was: BEANS CAN HEAR—AND THEY PREFER AUTO 69 RACING NOISE TO MUSIC.

Automatically, my built-in doubter moves into high gear. Can it 70 be that the newspaper story is a hoax? This is not impossible. The history of newspaper hoaxes is such that one could easily be convinced that nothing in any newspaper can possibly be believed.

But let's assume the story is accurate. The next question to ask 71 is whether the youngster knew what he was doing. Was he experienced enough to make the nature of the noise the only variable? Was there a difference in the soil or in the water supply or in some small matter, which he disregarded through inexperience?

Finally, even if the validity of the experiment is accepted, what 72 does it really prove? To the headline writer and undoubtedly to almost everybody who reads the article, it will prove that plants can hear and that they have preferences and will refuse to grow if they feel lonely and neglected.

This is so far against the current structure of science that my built- 73 in doubter clicks it right off and stamps it: IGNORE. Now what is an alternative explanation that fits in reasonably well with the structure of science? Sound is not just something to hear; it is a form of vibration. Can it be that sound vibrations stir up tiny soil particles making it easier for plants to absorb water, or putting more ions within reach by improving diffusion? May the natural noise that surrounds plants act in this fashion to promote growth? And may the engine noises have worked best on a one-hour-per-day basis because they were the loudest and produced the most vibration?

Any scientist (or eighth-grader) who feels called on to experiment 74 further, ought to try vibrations that do not produce audible sound, ultrasonic vibrations, mechanical vibrations and so on. Or he might also try to expose the plant itself to vibrations of all sorts while leaving the soil insulated; and vice versa.

Which finally brings me to flying saucers and spiritualism and 75

WRITING SUGGESTION

Write an essay in which you discuss a time when doubt played a crucial, though not necessarily helpful, role.

and there is also Kapp's theory, . . . which involves decreasing gravitational force on earth, without involving the gravitational constant.

the like. The questions I ask myself are: What is the nature of the authorities promulgating these and other viewpoints of this sort? And How well do such observations and theories fit in with the established structure of science?

My answers are, respectively, Very poor and Very poorly. 76

Which leaves me completely unrepentant as far as my double role 77 in life is concerned. If I get a good idea involving flying saucers and am in the mood to write some science fiction, I will gladly and with delight write a flying-saucer story.

And I will continue to disbelieve in them firmly in real life. 78

And if that be schizophrenia, make the most of it. 79

RESPONDING TO READING

1. At what audience is Asimov aiming his essay? How does he attempt to accommodate this audience? What does he sacrifice by doing this? **2.** Do you agree with Asimov about the value of doubts? In what sense, if any, can you see skepticism as a valid method of education? Is there a difference between *skepticism* and *cynicism*? **3.** Can you make the case that too much skepticism can actually hold science back? Consider, for example, how long it took the scientific community to accept Galileo. How does this example affect your reactions to Asimov's claims?

Graduation

MAYA ANGELOU

Maya Angelou (1928–   ) was born in St. Louis, where her mother lived, but was raised in Arkansas by her grandmother, who ran a general store. She began a theatrical career when she toured with *Porgy and Bess* in 1954–55, but now Angelou is a poet, writer, lecturer, civil rights leader, and teacher. A critic in *Southern Humanities Review* has said that ''her genius as a writer is in her ability to recapture the texture of the way of life in the texture of its idioms, its idiosyncracies, and especially its process of image-making.'' Angelou's many books include *Oh Pray My Wings Are Gonna Fit Me Well* (poetry, 1975) and *I Know Why the Caged Bird Sings* (autobiography, 1969). In ''Graduation,'' Angelou remembers the anger and pride of her high school graduation day in Stamps, Arkansas.

The children in Stamps trembled visibly with anticipation. Some 1 adults were excited too, but to be certain the whole young population had come down with graduation epidemic. Large classes were graduating from both the grammar school and the high school. Even those

1. How does Angelou convey a sense of community in this essay?
2. Opportunities were very limited for African-Americans in Angelou's early years. Do you think this situation has changed?
3. The last few paragraphs serve as both a conclusion and a commentary for the essay. What message does Angelou convey in her conclusion?

TEACHING STRATEGY

Ask students to identify examples of Angelou's use of figurative language throughout the story ("The man's dead words fell like bricks" [paragraph 42], for example). Ask them to discuss how these images affect their reactions to the story.

who were years removed from their own day of glorious release were anxious to help with preparations as a kind of dry run. The junior students who were moving into the vacating classes' chairs were tradition-bound to show their talents for leadership and management. They strutted through the school and around the campus exerting pressure on the lower grades. Their authority was so new that occasionally if they pressed a little too hard it had to be overlooked. After all, next term was coming, and it never hurt a sixth grader to have a play sister in the eighth grade, or a tenth-year student to be able to call a twelfth grader Bubba. So all was endured in a spirit of shared understanding. But the graduating classes themselves were the nobility. Like travelers with exotic destinations on their minds, the graduates were remarkably forgetful. They came to school without their books, or tablets or even pencils. Volunteers fell over themselves to secure replacements for the missing equipment. When accepted, the willing workers might or might not be thanked, and it was of no importance to the pregraduation rites. Even teachers were respectful of the now quiet and aging seniors, and tended to speak to them, if not as equals, as beings only slightly lower than themselves. After tests were returned and grades given, the student body, which acted like an extended family, knew who did well, who excelled, and what piteous ones had failed.

Unlike the white high school, Lafayette County Training School 2 distinguished itself by having neither lawn, nor hedges, nor tennis court, nor climbing ivy. Its two buildings (main classrooms, the grade school and home economics) were set on a dirt hill with no fence to limit either its boundaries or those of bordering farms. There was a large expanse to the left of the school which was used alternately as a baseball diamond or basketball court. Rusty hoops on swaying poles represented the permanent recreational equipment, although bats and balls could be borrowed from the P.E. teacher if the borrower was qualified and if the diamond wasn't occupied.

Over this rocky area relieved by a few shady tall persimmon trees 3 the graduating class walked. The girls often held hands and no longer bothered to speak to the lower students. There was a sadness about them, as if this old world was not their home and they were bound for higher ground. The boys, on the other hand, had become more friendly, more outgoing. A decided change from the closed attitude they projected while studying for finals. Now they seemed not ready to give up the old school, the familiar paths and classrooms. Only a small percentage would be continuing on to college—one of the South's A & M (agricultural and mechanical) schools, which trained Negro youths to be carpenters, farmers, handymen, masons, maids, cooks and baby nurses. Their future rode heavily on their shoulders, and blinded them to the collective joy that had pervaded the lives of the boys and girls in the grammar school graduating class.

Parents who could afford it had ordered new shoes and ready-made clothes for themselves from Sears and Roebuck or Montgomery Ward. They also engaged the best seamstresses to make the floating graduating dresses and to cut down secondhand pants which would be pressed to a military slickness for the important event.

Oh, it was important, all right. Whitefolks would attend the ceremony, and two or three would speak of God and home, and the Southern way of life, and Mrs. Parsons, the principal's wife, would play the graduation march while the lower-grade graduates paraded down the aisles and took their seats below the platform. The high school seniors would wait in empty classrooms to make their dramatic entrance.

In the Store I was the person of the moment. The birthday girl. The center. Bailey[1] had graduated the year before, although to do so he had had to forfeit all pleasures to make up for his time lost in Baton Rouge.

My class was wearing butter-yellow piqué dresses, and Momma launched out on mine. She smocked the yoke into tiny crisscrossing puckers, then shirred the rest of the bodice. Her dark fingers ducked in and out of the lemony cloth as she embroidered raised daisies around the hem. Before she considered herself finished she had added a crocheted cuff on the puff sleeves, and a pointy crocheted collar.

I was going to be lovely. A walking model of all the various styles of fine hand sewing and it didn't worry me that I was only twelve years old and merely graduating from the eighth grade. Besides, many teachers in Arkansas Negro schools had only that diploma and were licensed to impart wisdom.

The days had become longer and more noticeable. The faded beige of former times had been replaced with strong and sure colors. I began to see my classmates' clothes, their skin tones, and the dust that waved off pussy willows. Clouds that lazed across the sky were objects of great concern to me. Their shiftier shapes might have held a message that in my new happiness and with a little bit of time I'd soon decipher. During that period I looked at the arch of heaven so religiously my neck kept a steady ache. I had taken to smiling more often, and my jaws hurt from the unaccustomed activity. Between the two physical sore spots, I suppose I could have been uncomfortable, but that was not the case. As a member of the winning team

4

5

6

7

8

9

COLLABORATIVE ACTIVITY

Ask students, working in pairs, to discuss how one of the other characters (Donleavy, Henry, the narrator's mother, for example) might have reacted to the events of the story. (Assign different groups to focus on different characters.) In class discussion, identify similarities and differences among the characters' reactions.

---

[1]Angelou's brother. [Eds.]

(the graduating class of 1940) I had outdistanced unpleasant sensations by miles. I was headed for the freedom of open fields.

Youth and social approval allied themselves with me and we 10 trammeled memories of slights and insults. The wind of our swift passage remodeled my features. Lost tears were pounded to mud and then to dust. Years of withdrawal were brushed aside and left behind, as hanging ropes of parasitic moss.

My work alone had awarded me a top place and I was going to 11 be one of the first called in the graduating ceremonies. On the classroom blackboard, as well as on the bulletin board in the auditorium, there were blue stars and white stars and red stars. No absences, no tardinesses, and my academic work was among the best of the year. I could say the preamble to the Constitution even faster than Bailey. We timed ourselves often: "WethepeopleoftheUnitedStatesinorderto formamoreperfectunion . . ." I had memorized the Presidents of the United States from Washington to Roosevelt in chronological as well as alphabetical order.

My hair pleased me too. Gradually the black mass had lengthened 12 and thickened, so that it kept at last to its braided pattern, and I didn't have to yank my scalp off when I tried to comb it.

Louise and I had rehearsed the exercises until we tired out our- 13 selves. Henry Reed was class valedictorian. He was a small, very black boy with hooded eyes, a long, broad nose and an oddly shaped head. I had admired him for years because each term he and I vied for the best grades in our class. Most often he bested me, but instead of being disappointed I was pleased that we shared top places between us. Like many Southern Black children, he lived with his grandmother, who was as strict as Momma and as kind as she knew how to be. He was courteous, respectful and soft-spoken to elders, but on the playground he chose to play the roughest games. I admired him. Anyone, I reckoned, sufficiently afraid or sufficiently dull could be polite. But to be able to operate at a top level with both adults and children was admirable.

His valedictory speech was entitled "To Be or Not to Be." The 14 rigid tenth-grade teacher had helped him write it. He'd been working on the dramatic stresses for months.

The weeks until graduation were filled with heady activities. A 15 group of small children were to be presented in a play about buttercups and daisies and bunny rabbits. They could be heard throughout the building practicing their hops and their little songs that sounded like silver bells. The older girls (nongraduates, of course) were assigned the task of making refreshments for the night's festivities. A tangy scent of ginger, cinnamon, nutmeg and chocolate wafted around the home economics building as the budding cooks made samples for themselves and their teachers.

In every corner of the workshop, axes and saws split fresh timber 16
as the woodshop boys made sets and stage scenery. Only the graduates were left out of the general bustle. We were free to sit in the
library at the back of the building or look in quite detachedly, naturally, on the measures being taken for our event.

Even the minister preached on graduation the Sunday before. His 17
subject was, "Let your light so shine that men will see your good
works and praise your Father, Who is in Heaven." Although the
sermon was purported to be addressed to us, he used the occasion
to speak to backsliders, gamblers and general ne'er-do-wells. But since
he had called our names at the beginning of the service we were
mollified.

Among Negroes the tradition was to give presents to children 18
going only from one grade to another. How much more important
this was when the person was graduating at the top of the class.
Uncle Willie and Momma had sent away for a Mickey Mouse watch
like Bailey's. Louise gave me four embroidered handkerchiefs. (I gave
her crocheted doilies.) Mrs. Sneed, the minister's wife, made me an
undershirt to wear for graduation, and nearly every customer gave
me a nickel or maybe even a dime with the instruction "Keep on
moving to higher ground," or some such encouragement.

Amazingly the great day finally dawned and I was out of bed 19
before I knew it. I threw open the back door to see it more clearly,
but Momma said, "Sister, come away from that door and put your
robe on."

I hoped the memory of that morning would never leave me. 20
Sunlight was itself young, and the day had none of the insistence
maturity would bring it in a few hours. In my robe and barefoot in
the backyard, under cover of going to see about my new beans, I
gave myself up to the gentle warmth and thanked God that no matter
what evil I had done in my life He had allowed me to live to see this
day. Somewhere in my fatalism I had expected to die, accidentally,
and never have the chance to walk up the stairs in the auditorium
and gracefully receive my hard-earned diploma. Out of God's merciful
bosom I had won reprieve.

Bailey came out in his robe and gave me a box wrapped in 21
Christmas paper. He said he had saved his money for months to pay
for it. It felt like a box of chocolates, but I knew Bailey wouldn't save
money to buy candy when we had all we could want under our noses.

He was as proud of the gift as I. It was a soft-leather-bound copy 22
of a collection of poems by Edgar Allan Poe, or, as Bailey and I called
him, "Eap." I turned to "Annabel Lee" and we walked up and down
the garden rows, the cool dirt between our toes, reciting the beautifully sad lines.

Momma made a Sunday breakfast although it was only Friday. 23

After we finished the blessing, I opened my eyes to find the watch on my plate. It was a dream of a day. Everything went smoothly and to my credit. I didn't have to be reminded or scolded for anything. Near evening I was too jittery to attend to chores, so Bailey volunteered to do all before his bath.

Days before, we had made a sign for the Store, and as we turned 24 out the lights Momma hung the cardboard over the doorknob. It read clearly: CLOSED. GRADUATION.

My dress fitted perfectly and everyone said that I looked like a 25 sunbeam in it. On the hill, going toward the school, Bailey walked behind with Uncle Willie, who muttered, "Go on, Ju." He wanted him to walk ahead with us because it embarrassed him to have to walk so slowly. Bailey said he'd let the ladies walk together, and the men would bring up the rear. We all laughed, nicely.

Little children dashed by out of the dark like fireflies. Their crepe- 26 paper dresses and butterfly wings were not made for running and we heard more than one rip, dryly, and the regretful "uh uh" that followed.

The school blazed without gaiety. The windows seemed cold and 27 unfriendly from the lower hill. A sense of ill-fated timing crept over me, and if Momma hadn't reached for my hand I would have drifted back to Bailey and Uncle Willie, and possibly beyond. She made a few slow jokes about my feet getting cold, and tugged me along to the now-strange building.

Around the front steps, assurance came back. There were my 28 fellow "greats," the graduating class. Hair brushed back, legs oiled, new dresses and pressed pleats, fresh pocket handkerchiefs and little handbags, all homesewn. Oh, we were up to snuff, all right. I joined my comrades and didn't even see my family go in to find seats in the crowded auditorium.

The school band struck up a march and all classes filed in as had 29 been rehearsed. We stood in front of our seats, as assigned, and on a signal from the choir director, we sat. No sooner had this been accomplished than the band started to play the national anthem. We rose again and sang the song, after which we recited the pledge of allegiance. We remained standing for a brief minute before the choir director and the principal signaled to us, rather desperately I thought, to take our seats. The command was so unusual that our carefully rehearsed and smooth-running machine was thrown off. For a full minute we fumbled for our chairs and bumped into each other awkwardly. Habits change or solidify under pressure, so in our state of nervous tension we had been ready to follow our usual assembly pattern: the American national anthem, then the pledge of allegiance, then the song every Black person I knew called the Negro National

Anthem. All done in the same key, with the same passion and most often standing on the same foot.

Finding my seat at last, I was overcome with a presentiment of 30 worse things to come. Something unrehearsed, unplanned, was going to happen, and we were going to be made to look bad. I distinctly remember being explicit in the choice of pronoun. It was "we," the graduating class, the unit, that concerned me then.

The principal welcomed "parents and friends" and asked the 31 Baptist minister to lead us in prayer. His invocation was brief and punchy, and for a second I thought we were getting on the high road to right action. When the principal came back to the dais, however, his voice had changed. Sounds always affected me profoundly and the principal's voice was one of my favorites. During assembly it melted and lowed weakly into the audience. It had not been in my plan to listen to him, but my curiosity was piqued and I straightened up to give him my attention.

He was talking about Booker T. Washington, our "late great 32 leader," who said we can be as close as the fingers on the hand, etc. . . . Then he said a few vague things about friendship and the friendship of kindly people to those less fortunate than themselves. With that his voice nearly faded, thin, away. Like a river diminishing to a stream and then to a trickle. But he cleared his throat and said, "Our speaker tonight, who is also our friend, came from Texarkana to deliver the commencement address, but due to the irregularity of the train schedule, he's going to, as they say, 'speak and run.' " He said that we understood and wanted the man to know that we were most grateful for the time he was able to give us and then something about how we were willing always to adjust to another's program, and without more ado—"I give you Mr. Edward Donleavy."

Not one but two white men came through the door off-stage. The 33 shorter one walked to the speaker's platform, and the tall one moved to the center seat and sat down. But that was our principal's seat, and already occupied. The dislodged gentleman bounced around for a long breath or two before the Baptist minister gave him his chair, then with more dignity than the situation deserved, the minister walked off the stage.

Donleavy looked at the audience once (on reflection, I'm sure that 34 he wanted only to reassure himself that we were really there), adjusted his glasses and began to read from a sheaf of papers.

He was glad "to be here and to see the work going on just as it 35 was in the other schools."

At the first "Amen" from the audience I willed the offender to 36 immediate death by choking on the word. But Amens and Yes, sir's began to fall around the room like rain through a ragged umbrella.

He told us of the wonderful changes we children in Stamps had 37
in store. The Central School (naturally, the white school was Central)
had already been granted improvements that would be in use in the
fall. A well-known artist was coming from Little Rock to teach art to
them. They were going to have the newest microscopes and chemistry
equipment for their laboratory. Mr. Donleavy didn't leave us long in
the dark over who made these improvements available to Central
High. Nor were we to be ignored in the general betterment scheme
he had in mind.

He said that he had pointed out to people at a very high level 38
that one of the first-line football tacklers at Arkansas Agricultural and
Mechanical College had graduated from good old Lafayette County
Training School. Here fewer Amen's were heard. Those few that did
break through lay dully in the air with the heaviness of habit.

He went on to praise us. He went on to say how he had bragged 39
that "one of the best basketball players at Fisk sank his first ball right
here at Lafayette County Training School."

The white kids were going to have a chance to become Galileos 40
and Madame Curies and Edisons and Gauguins, and our boys (the
girls weren't even in on it) would try to be Jesse Owenses and Joe
Louises.

Owens and the Brown Bomber were great heroes in our world, 41
but what school official in the white-goddom of Little Rock had the
right to decide that those two men must be our only heroes? Who
decided that for Henry Reed to become a scientist he had to work
like George Washington Carver, as a bootblack, to buy a lousy microscope? Bailey was obviously always going to be too small to be an
athlete, so which concrete angel glued to what country seat had
decided that if my brother wanted to become a lawyer he had to first
pay penance for his skin by picking cotton and hoeing corn and
studying correspondence books at night for twenty years?

The man's dead words fell like bricks around the auditorium and 42
too many settled in my belly. Constrained by hard-learned manners
I couldn't look behind me, but to my left and right the proud graduating class of 1940 had dropped their heads. Every girl in my row
had found something new to do with her handkerchief. Some folded
the tiny squares into love knots, some into triangles, but most were
wadding them, then pressing them flat on their yellow laps.

On the dais, the ancient tragedy was being replayed. Professor 43
Parsons sat, a sculptor's reject, rigid. His large, heavy body seemed
devoid of will or willingness, and his eyes said he was no longer with
us. The other teachers examined the flag (which was draped stage
right) or their notes, or the windows which opened on our now-
famous playing diamond.

Graduation, the hush-hush magic time of frills and gifts and con- 44
gratulations and diplomas, was finished for me before my name was
called. The accomplishment was nothing. The meticulous maps,
drawn in three colors of ink, learning and spelling decasyllabic words,
memorizing the whole of *The Rape of Lucrece*[2]—it was for nothing.
Donleavy had exposed us.

We were maids and farmers, handymen and washerwomen, and 45
anything higher that we aspired to was farcical and presumptuous.

Then I wished that Gabriel Prosser and Nat Turner[3] had killed all 46
whitefolks in their beds and that Abraham Lincoln had been assassinated before the signing of the Emancipation Proclamation, and that
Harriet Tubman[4] had been killed by that blow on her head and Christopher Columbus had drowned in the *Santa Maria*.

It was awful to be a Negro and have no control over my life. It 47
was brutal to be young and already trained to sit quietly and listen
to charges brought against my color with no chance of defense. We
should all be dead. I thought I should like to see us all dead, one on
top of the other. A pyramid of flesh with the whitefolks on the bottom,
as the broad base, then the Indians with their silly tomahawks and
teepees and wigwams and treaties, the Negroes with their mops and
recipes and cotton sacks and spirituals sticking out of their mouths.
The Dutch children should all stumble in their wooden shoes and
break their necks. The French should choke to death on the Louisiana
Purchase (1803) while silkworms ate all the Chinese with their stupid
pigtails. As a species, we were an abomination. All of us.

Donleavy was running for election, and assured our parents that 48
if he won we could count on having the only colored paved playing
field in that part of Arkansas. Also—he never looked up to acknowledge the grunts of acceptance—also, we were bound to get some new
equipment for the home economics building and the workshop.

He finished, and since there was no need to give any more than 49
the most perfunctory thank-you's, he nodded to the men on the stage,
and the tall white man who was never introduced joined him at the
door. They left with the attitude that now they were off to something
really important. (The graduation ceremonies at Lafayette County
Training School had been a mere preliminary.)

The ugliness they left was palpable. An uninvited guest who 50
wouldn't leave. The choir was summoned and sang a modern arrangement of "Onward, Christian Soldiers," with new words pertaining

---

[2]*The Rape of Lucrece* is a long narrative poem by Shakespeare. [Eds.]
[3]Prosser and Turner both led slave rebellions. [Eds.]
[4]Harriet Tubman (1820–1913) was an African-American abolitionist who became one of the
most successful guides on the Underground Railroad. [Eds.]

to graduates seeking their place in the world. But it didn't work. Elouise, the daughter of the Baptist minister, recited "Invictus,"[5] and I could have cried at the impertinence of "I am the master of my fate, I am the captain of my soul."

My name had lost its ring of familiarity and I had to be nudged 51 to go and receive my diploma. All my preparations had fled. I neither marched up to the stage like a conquering Amazon, not did I look in the audience for Bailey's nod of approval. Marguerite Johnson, I heard the name again, my honors were read, there were noises in the audience of appreciation, and I took my place on the stage as rehearsed.

I thought about colors I hated: ecru, puce, lavender, beige and 52 black.

There was shuffling and rustling around me, then Henry Reed 53 was giving his valedictory address, "To Be or Not to Be." Hadn't he heard the whitefolks? We couldn't *be*, so the question was a waste of time. Henry's voice came out clear and strong. I feared to look at him. Hadn't he got the message? There was no "nobler in the mind" for Negroes because the world didn't think we had minds, and they let us know it. "Outrageous fortune"? Now, that was a joke. When the ceremony was over I had to tell Henry Reed some things. That is, if I still cared. Not "rub," Henry, "erase." "Ah, there's the erase." Us.

Henry had been a good student in elocution. His voice rose on 54 tides of promise and fell on waves of warnings. The English teacher had helped him to create a sermon winging through Hamlet's soliloquy. To be a man, a doer, a builder, a leader, or to be a tool, an unfunny joke, a crusher of funky toadstools. I marveled that Henry could go through with the speech as if we had a choice.

I had been listening and silently rebutting each sentence with my 55 eyes closed; then there was a hush, which in an audience warns that something unplanned is happening. I looked up and saw Henry Reed, the conservative, the proper, the A student, turn his back to the audience and turn to us (the proud graduating class of 1940) and sing, nearly speaking,

> "Lift ev'ry voice and sing
> Till earth and heavy ring
> Ring with the harmonies of Liberty . . ."

It was the poem written by James Weldon Johnson. It was the music composed by J. Rosamond Johnson. It was the Negro national anthem. Out of habit we were singing it.

Our mothers and fathers stood in the dark hall and joined the 56

---

[5]An inspirational poem written in 1875 by William Ernest Henley (1849–1903). Its defiant and stoic sentiments made it extremely popular with nineteenth-century readers. [Eds.]

hymn of encouragement. A kindergarten teacher led the small children onto the stage and the buttercups and daisies and bunny rabbits marked time and tried to follow:

> "Stony the road we trod
> Bitter the chastening rod
> Felt in the days when hope, unborn, had died.
> Yet with a steady beat
> Have not our weary feet
> Come to the place for which our fathers sighed?"

Each child I knew had learned that song with his ABC's and along 57 with "Jesus Loves Me This I Know." But I personally had never heard it before. Never heard the words, despite the thousands of times I had sung them. Never thought they had anything to do with me.

On the other hand, the words of Patrick Henry had made such 58 an impression on me that I had been able to stretch myself tall and trembling and say, "I know not what course others may take, but as for me, give me liberty or give me death."

And now I heard, really for the first time: 59

> "We have come over a way that with tears
> has been watered,
> We have come, treading our path through
> the blood of the slaughtered."

While echoes of the song shivered in the air, Henry Reed bowed 60 his head, said "Thank you," and returned to his place in the line. The tears that slipped down many faces were not wiped away in shame.

We were on top again. As always, again. We survived. The depths 61 had been icy and dark, but now a bright sun spoke to our souls. I was no longer simply a member of the proud graduating class of 1940; I was a proud member of the wonderful, beautiful Negro race.

Oh, Black known and unknown poets, how often have your auc- 62 tioned pains sustained us? Who will compute the lonely nights made less lonely by your songs, or the empty pots made less tragic by your tales?

If we were a people much given to revealing secrets, we might 63 raise monuments and sacrifice to the memories of our poets, but slavery cured us of that weakness. It may be enough, however, to have it said that we survive in exact relationship to the dedication of our poets (include preachers, musicians and blues singers).

WRITING SUGGESTION

Write a graduation address that you might deliver if you were the Stamps High School valedictorian the following year.

1. Some educators still have limited expectations for minority groups.
2. Donleavy's speech is really eye-opening: It shows the graduates the limits placed on them by the white culture. Angelou's optimism and hope for the future are shaken as she listens to him, but they return when Henry Reed sings the Negro national anthem.
3. The graduates have been taught many things, some practical, some esoteric; more subtly, they have been taught their expected place in life as laborers and housekeepers.

BACKGROUND ON READING

You may want to explain more fully the type of curriculum Holt is criticizing. According to Holt, children fail because they are afraid, bored, and confused. The strict lock-step curriculum only adds to these problems. An open curriculum that enables students to explore ideas freely and progress at their own pace will turn children into interested and motivated students. Ironically, many schools are returning to what they call "the basics," implementing curricula that have many of the faults Holt criticizes.

FOR OPENERS

Open by assigning a journal-writing topic on students' most memorable school lesson. Then, discuss why it stuck in their minds, and look for similar characteristics their memorable experiences share.

RESPONDING TO READING

1. Angelou's graduation took place in 1940. Do you think that mainstream educators still have limited expectations for minority groups? What expectations did the teachers in your high school have for you and your fellow students?   **2.** In what sense is Mr. Donleavy's speech an educational experience for the graduates? In what sense does Angelou's thinking change as she listens to him?   **3.** What has their formal education taught the graduates? What more subtle lessons have they learned as citizens of Stamps, Arkansas? Did your formal education teach you things beyond the subject matter?

School Is Bad for Children

JOHN HOLT

Teacher and education theorist John Holt (1923–1985) believed that schooling undermines the curiosity and love of life that children have naturally. In his writings about education, Holt suggests that there should be more than one path for learning and that students should be allowed to pursue only what interests them. Some of his many books include *How Children Fail* (1964), *How Children Learn* (1967), *Instead of Education* (1976), and *Learning All the Time* (1989). The following essay, first published in *The Saturday Evening Post* in 1969, makes a plea to free children from the classroom, a "dull and ugly place, where nobody ever says anything very truthful," and to "give them a chance to learn about the world at first hand."

Almost every child, on the first day he sets foot in a school building, is smarter, more curious, less afraid of what he doesn't know, better at finding and figuring things out, more confident, resourceful, persistent and independent than he will ever be again in his schooling—or, unless he is very unusual and very lucky, for the rest of his life. Already, by paying close attention to and interacting with the world and people around him, and without any school-type formal instruction, he has done a task far more difficult, complicated and abstract than anything he will be asked to do in school, or than any of his teachers has done for years. He has solved the mystery of language. He has discovered it—babies don't even know that language exists—and he has found out how it works and learned to use it. He has done it by exploring, by experimenting, by developing his own model of the grammar of language, by trying it out and seeing whether it works, by gradually changing it and refining it until it does work. And while he has been doing this, he has been learning other things as well, including many of the "concepts" that the schools think only they can teach him, and many that are more complicated than the ones they do try to teach him.

In he comes, this curious, patient, determined, energetic, skillful learner. We sit him down at a desk, and what do we teach him? Many things. First, that learning is separate from living. "You come to school to learn," we tell him, as if the child hadn't been learning before, as if living were out there and learning were in here, and there were no connection between the two. Secondly, that he cannot be trusted to learn and is no good at it. Everything we teach about reading, a task far simpler than many that the child has already mastered, says to him, "If we don't make you read, you won't, and if you don't do it exactly the way we tell you, you can't." In short, he comes to feel that learning is a passive process, something that someone else does *to* you, instead of something you do for yourself.

In a great many other ways he learns that he is worthless, untrustworthy, fit only to take other people's orders, a blank sheet for other people to write on. Oh, we make a lot of nice noises in school about respect for the child and individual differences, and the like. But our acts, as opposed to our talk, say to the child, "Your experience, your concerns, your curiosities, your needs, what you know, what you want, what you wonder about, what you hope for, what you fear, what you like and dislike, what you are good at or not so good at— all this is of not the slightest importance, it counts for nothing. What counts here, and the only thing that counts, is what we know, what we think is important, what we want you to do, think and be." The child soon learns not to ask questions—the teacher isn't there to satisfy his curiosity. Having learned to hide his curiosity, he later learns to be ashamed of it. Given no chance to find out who he is— and to develop that person, whoever it is—he soon comes to accept the adults' evaluation of him.

He learns many other things. He learns that to be wrong, uncertain, confused, is a crime. Right Answers are what the school wants, and he learns countless strategies for prying these answers out of the teacher, for conning her into thinking he knows what he doesn't know. He learns to dodge, bluff, fake, cheat. He learns to be lazy. Before he came to school, he would work for hours on end, on his own, with no thought of reward, at the business of making sense of the world and gaining competence in it. In school he learns, like every buck private, how to goldbrick, how not to work when the sergeant isn't looking, how to know when he is looking, how to make him think you are working even when he is looking. He learns that in real life you don't do anything unless you are bribed, bullied or conned into doing it, that nothing is worth doing for its own sake,

2

3

4

ADDITIONAL QUESTIONS FOR RESPONDING TO READING

1. What are some things children learn before they come to school?
2. How does passive learning differ from active learning? Is watching television passive or active learning?
3. Why were compulsory attendance laws passed? Are they still necessary?
4. What is the purpose of testing? Do most tests measure what we don't know? What kind of test would measure what we *do* know?

TEACHING STRATEGY

Ask students to discuss what they consider good education, examining how their ideas are similar to or different from Holt's.

COLLABORATIVE ACTIVITY

Holt proposes doing away with the fixed curriculum required in most schools. Ask students, working in groups, to list arguments for and against Holt's proposal.

or that if it is, you can't do it in school. He learns to be bored, to work with a small part of his mind, to escape from the reality around him into daydreams and fantasies—but not like the fantasies of his preschool years, in which he played a very active part.

The child comes to school curious about other people, particularly 5 other children, and the school teaches him to be indifferent. The most interesting thing in the classroom—often the only interesting thing in it—is the other children, but he has to act as if these other children, all about him, only a few feet away, are not really there. He cannot interact with them, talk with them, smile at them. In many schools he can't talk to other children in the halls between classes; in more than a few, and some of these in stylish suburbs, he can't even talk to them at lunch. Splendid training for a world in which, when you're not studying the other person to figure out how to do him in, you pay no attention to him.

In fact, he learns how to live without paying attention to anything 6 going on around him. You might say that school is a long lesson in how to turn yourself off, which may be one reason why so many young people, seeking the awareness of the world and responsiveness to it they had when they were little, think they can only find it in drugs. Aside from being boring, the school is almost always ugly, cold, inhuman—even the most stylish, glass-windowed, $20-a-square-foot schools.

And so, in this dull and ugly place, where nobody ever says 7 anything very truthful, where everybody is playing a kind of role, as in a charade, where the teachers are no more free to respond honestly to the students than the students are free to respond to the teachers or each other, where the air practically vibrates with suspicion and anxiety, the child learns to live in a daze, saving his energies for those small parts of his life that are too trivial for the adults to bother with, and thus remain his. It is a rare child who can come through his schooling with much left of his curiosity, his independence or his sense of his own dignity, competence and worth.

So much for criticism. What do we need to do? Many things. 8 Some are easy—we can do them right away. Some are hard, and may take some time. Take a hard one first. We should abolish compulsory school attendance. At the very least we should modify it, perhaps by giving children every year a large number of authorized absences. Our compulsory school-attendance laws once served a humane and useful purpose. They protected children's right to some schooling, against those adults who would otherwise have denied it to them in order to exploit their labor, in farm, store, mine or factory. Today the laws help nobody, not the schools, not the teachers, not the children. To keep kids in school who would rather not be there costs the schools an enormous amount of time and trouble—to say nothing of what it costs to repair the damage that these angry and resentful prisoners do every time they get a chance. Every teacher knows that any kid in class who, for whatever reason, would rather not be there not only doesn't learn anything himself but makes it a great deal tougher for anyone else. As for protecting the children from exploitation, the chief and indeed only exploiters of children these days *are* the schools. Kids caught in the college rush more often than not work 70 hours or more a week, most of it on paper busywork. For kids who aren't going to college, school is just a useless time waster, preventing them from earning some money or doing some useful work, or even doing some true learning.

Objections. "If kids didn't have to go to school, they'd all be out   9
in the streets." No, they wouldn't. In the first place, even if schools stayed just the way they are, children would spend at least some time there because that's where they'd be likely to find friends; it's a natural meeting place for children. In the second place, schools wouldn't stay the way they are, they'd get better, because we would have to start making them what they ought to be right now—places where children would *want* to be. In the third place, those children who did not want to go to school could find, particularly if we stirred up our brains and gave them a little help, other things to do—the things many children now do during their summers and holidays.

There's something easier we could do. We need to get kids out   10
of the school buildings, give them a chance to learn about the world at first hand. It is a very recent idea, and a crazy one, that the way to teach our young people about the world they live in is to take them out of it and shut them up in brick boxes. Fortunately, educators are beginning to realize this. In Philadelphia and Portland, Oregon, to pick only two places I happen to have heard about, plans are being drawn up for public schools that won't have any school buildings at all, that will take the students out into the city and help them to use it and its people as a learning resource. In other words, students, perhaps in groups, perhaps independently, will go to libraries, museums, exhibits, courtrooms, legislatures, radio and TV stations, meetings, businesses and laboratories to learn about their world and society at first hand. A small private school in Washington is already doing this. It makes sense. We need more of it.

As we help children get out into the world, to do their learning   11
there, we can get more of the world into the schools. Aside from their parents, most children never have any close contact with any adults except people whose sole business is children. No wonder they have no idea what adult life or work is like. We need to bring a lot more people who are *not* full-time teachers into the schools, and into contact

with the children. In New York City, under the Teachers and Writers Collaborative, real writers, working writers—novelists, poets, play-wrights—come into the schools, read their work, and talk to the children about the problems of their craft. The children eat it up. In another school I know of, a practicing attorney from a nearby city comes in every month or so and talks to several classes about the law. Not the law as it is in books but as he sees it and encounters it in his cases, his problems, his work. And the children love it. It is real, grown-up, true, not *My Weekly Reader*, not "social studies," not lies and baloney.

Something easier yet. Let children work together, help each other, 12 learn from each other and each other's mistakes. We now know, from the experience of many schools, both rich-suburban and poor-city, that children are often the best teachers of other children. What is more important, we know that when a fifth- or sixth-grader who has been having trouble with reading starts helping a first-grader, his own reading sharply improves. A number of schools are beginning to use what some call Paired Learning. This means that you let chil-dren form partnerships with other children, do their work, even including their tests, together, and share whatever marks or results this work gets—just like grownups in the real world. It seems to work.

Let the children learn to judge their own work. A child learning 13 to talk does not learn by being corrected all the time—if corrected too much, he will stop talking. *He* compares, a thousand times a day, the difference between language as he uses it and as those around him use it. Bit by bit, he makes the necessary changes to make his language like other people's. In the same way, kids learning to do all the other things they learn without adult teachers—to walk, run, climb, whistle, ride a bike, skate, play games, jump rope—compare their own performance with what more skilled people do, and slowly make the needed changes. But in school we never give a child a chance to detect his mistakes, let alone correct them. We do it all for him. We act as if we thought he would never notice a mistake unless it was pointed out to him, or correct it unless he was made to. Soon he becomes dependent on the expert. We should let him do it himself. Let him figure out, with the help of other children if he wants it, what this word says, what is the answer to that problem, whether this is a good way of saying or doing this or that. If right answers are involved, as in some math or science, give him the answer book, let him correct his own papers. Why should we teachers waste time on such donkey work? Our job should be to help the kid when he tells us that he can't find a way to get the right answer. Let's get rid of all this nonsense of grades, exams, marks. We don't know now, and we never will know, how to measure what another person knows or understands. We certainly can't find out by asking him questions. All we find out is what he doesn't know—which is what most tests are for, anyway. Throw it all out, and let the child learn what every educated person must someday learn, how to measure his own understanding, how to know what he knows or does not know.

We could also abolish the fixed, required curriculum. People 14 remember only what is interesting and useful to them, what helps them make sense of the world, or helps them get along in it. All else they quickly forget, if they ever learn it at all. The idea of a "body of knowledge," to be picked up in school and used for the rest of one's life, is nonsense in a world as complicated and rapidly changing as ours. Anyway, the most important questions and problems of our time are not *in* the curriculum, not even in the hotshot universities, let alone the schools.

Children want, more than they want anything else, and even 15 after years of miseducation, to make sense of the world, themselves, and other human beings. Let them get at this job, with our help if they ask for it, in the way that makes most sense to them.

RESPONDING TO READING

1. Notice that throughout this essay, Holt uses third-person masculine pronouns to refer to children—"every child . . . he," for example. If he were writing this essay today, what changes would you advise him to make?   **2.** Do Holt's ideas about education seem dated? In what ways do they or do they not apply to your educational experience?   **3.** Do you agree with Holt when he says, "Let's get rid of all this nonsense of grades, exams, marks" (paragraph 13)? What would be the positive or negative effects of this proposal?

College Pressures

WILLIAM ZINSSER

William Zinsser (1922–   ) is a critic, writer, editor, and teacher who advocates clear and simple prose. He was a columnist for *Look*, *Life*, and *The New York Times*; he taught at Yale University from 1970 to 1979; and he is currently general editor of the Book-of-the-Month Club. Zinsser has written nine books, including *Pop Goes America* (1963), *The Lunacy Boom* (1970), and *Writing with a Word Processor* (1983). One of his most popular books, which explains good writing to beginners, is *On Writing Well* (4th edition, 1991). Zinsser first published the following article in *Blair and Ketchum's Country Journal* (1979). In it, he defines four kinds of pressure that college students

FOR OPENERS

Ask students to list the reasons why they are enrolled in college. Follow with a discussion of the many reasons people attend college.

face and argues that most college students are rigidly goal-oriented young people too fearful "to imagine allowing the hand of God or chance to nudge them down some unforeseen trail."

Dear Carlos: I desperately need a dean's excuse for my chem midterm which will begin in about 1 hour. All I can say is that I totally blew it this week. I've fallen incredibly, inconceivably behind.

Carlos: Help! I'm anxious to hear from you. I'll be in my room and won't leave it until I hear from you. Tomorrow is the last day for . . .

Carlos: I left town because I started bugging out again. I stayed up all night to finish a take-home make-up exam & am typing it to hand in on the 10th. It was due on the 5th. P.S. I'm going to the dentist. Pain is pretty bad.

Carlos: Probably by Friday I'll be able to get back to my studies. Right now I'm going to take a long walk. This whole thing has taken a lot out of me.

Carlos: I'm really up the proverbial creek. The problem is I really *bombed* the history final. Since I need that course for my major I . . .

Carlos: Here follows a tale of woe. I went home this weekend, had to help my Mom, & caught a fever so didn't have much time to study. My professor . . .

Carlos: Aargh! Trouble. Nothing original but everything's piling up at once. To be brief, my job interview . . .

Hey Carlos, good news! I've got mononucleosis.

Who are these wretched supplicants, scribbling notes so laden with anxiety, seeking such miracles of postponement and balm? They are men and women who belong to Branford College, one of the twelve residential colleges at Yale University, and the messages are just a few of the hundreds that they left for their dean, Carlos Hortas— often slipped under his door at 4 A.M.—last year.

But students like the ones who wrote those notes can also be found on campuses from coast to coast—especially in New England and at many other private colleges across the country that have high academic standards and highly motivated students. Nobody could doubt that the notes are real. In their urgency and their gallows humor they are authentic voices of a generation that is panicky to succeed.

My own connection with the message writers is that I am master of Branford College. I live in its Gothic quadrangle and know the students well. (We have 485 of them.) I am privy to their hopes and fears—and also to their stereo music and their piercing cries in the dead of night ("Does anybody *ca-a-are*?"). If they went to Carlos to ask how to get through tomorrow, they come to me to ask how to get through the rest of their lives.

Mainly I try to remind them that the road ahead is a long one

ADDITIONAL QUESTIONS FOR RESPONDING TO READING

1. If you were not in college, what would you be doing?
2. What are the advantages and disadvantages of attending college? Of alternative options?

and that it will have more unexpected turns than they think. There will be plenty of time to change jobs, change careers, change whole attitudes and approaches. They don't want to hear such liberating news. They want a map—right now—that they can follow unswervingly to career security, financial security, Social Security and, presumably, a prepaid grave.

What I wish for all students is some release from the clammy grip 5 of the future. I wish them a chance to savor each segment of their education as an experience in itself and not as a grim preparation for the next step. I wish them the right to experiment, to trip and fall, to learn that defeat is as instructive as victory and is not the end of the world.

My wish, of course, is naïve. One of the few rights that America 6 does not proclaim is the right to fail. Achievement is the national god, venerated in our media—the million-dollar athlete, the wealthy executive—and glorified in our praise of possessions. In the presence of such a potent state religion, the young are growing up old.

I see four kinds of pressure working on college students today: 7 economic pressure, parental pressure, peer pressure, and self-induced pressure. It is easy to look around for villains—to blame the colleges for charging too much money, the professors for assigning too much work, the parents for pushing their children too far, the students for driving themselves too hard. But there are no villains; only victims.

"In the late 1960s," one dean told me, "the typical question that 8 I got from students was 'Why is there so much suffering in the world?' or 'How can I make a contribution?' Today it's 'Do you think it would look better for getting into law school if I did a double major in history and political science, or just majored in one of them?' " Many other deans confirmed this pattern. One said: "They're trying to find an edge—the intangible something that will look better on paper if two students are about equal."

Note the emphasis on looking better. The transcript has become 9 a sacred document, the passport to security. How one appears on paper is more important than how one appears in person. *A* is for Admirable and *B* is for Borderline, even though, in Yale's official system of grading, *A* means "excellent" and *B* means "very good." Today, looking very good is no longer good enough, especially for students who hope to go on to law school or medical school. They know that entrance into the better schools will be an entrance into the better law firms and better medical practices where they will make a lot of money. They also know that the odds are harsh. Yale Law School, for instance, matriculates 170 students from an applicant pool of 3,700; Harvard enrolls 550 from a pool of 7,000.

COLLABORATIVE ACTIVITY

Divide the class into four groups, one for each of the types of pressure Zinsser identifies. Then have each group identify the sources, manifestations, and coping strategies of one kind of pressure. Finally, ask groups to share their findings with the class.

It's all very well for those of us who write letters of recommen- 10
dation for our students to stress the qualities of humanity that will
make them good lawyers or doctors. And it's nice to think that admission officers are really reading our letters and looking for the extra
dimension of commitment or concern. Still, it would be hard for a
student not to visualize these officers shuffling so many transcripts
studded with *A*s that they regard a *B* as positively shameful.

The pressure is almost as heavy on students who just want to 11
graduate and get a job. Long gone are the days of the "gentleman's
C," when students journeyed through college with a certain relaxation, sampling a wide variety of courses—music, art, philosophy,
classics, anthropology, poetry, religion—that would send them out
as liberally educated men and women. If I were an employer I would
rather employ graduates who have this range and curiosity than those
who narrowly pursued safe subjects and high grades. I know countless students whose inquiring minds exhilarate me. I like to hear the
play of their ideas. I don't know if they are getting *A*s or *C*s, and I
don't care. I also like them as people. The country needs them, and
they will find satisfying jobs. I tell them to relax. They can't.

Nor can I blame them. They live in a brutal economy. Tuition, 12
room, and board at most private colleges now comes to at least $7,000,
not counting books and fees. This might seem to suggest that the
colleges are getting rich. But they are equally battered by inflation.
Tuition covers only 60 percent of what it costs to educate a student,
and ordinarily the remainder comes from what colleges receive in
endowments, grants, and gifts. Now the remainder keeps being swallowed by the cruel costs—higher every year—of just opening the
doors. Heating oil is up. Insurance is up. Postage is up. Health-
premium costs are up. Everything is up. Deficits are up. We are
witnessing in America the creation of a brotherhood of paupers—
colleges, parents, and students, joined by the common bond of debt.

Today it is not unusual for a student, even if he works part time 13
at college and full time during the summer, to accrue $5,000 in loans
after four years—loans that he must start to repay within one year
after graduation. Exhorted at commencement to go forth into the
world, he is already behind as he goes forth. How could he not feel
under pressure throughout college to prepare for this day of
reckoning? I have used "he," incidentally, only for brevity. Women
at Yale are under no less pressure to justify their expensive education
to themselves, their parents, and society. In fact, they are probably
under more pressure. For although they leave college superbly
equipped to bring fresh leadership to traditionally male jobs, society
hasn't yet caught up with this fact.

Along with economic pressure goes parental pressure. Inevitably, 14
the two are deeply intertwined.

I see many students taking pre-medical courses with joyless 15
tenacity. They go off to their labs as if they were going to the dentist.
It saddens me because I know them in other corners of their life as
cheerful people.

"Do you want to go to medical school?" I ask them. 16

"I guess so," they say, without conviction, or "Not really." 17

"Then why are you going?" 18

"Well, my parents want me to be a doctor. They're paying all this 19
money and . . ."

Poor students, poor parents. They are caught in one of the oldest 20
webs of love and duty and guilt. The parents mean well; they are
trying to steer their sons and daughters toward a secure future. But
the sons and daughters want to major in history or classics or philosophy—subjects with no "practical" value. Where's the payoff on
the humanities? It's not easy to persuade such loving parents that the
humanities do indeed pay off. The intellectual faculties developed by
studying subjects like history and classics—an ability to synthesize
and relate, to weigh cause and effect, to see events in perspective—
are just the faculties that make creative leaders in business or almost
any general field. Still, many fathers would rather put their money
on courses that point toward a specific profession—courses that are
pre-law, pre-medical, pre-business, or, as I sometimes heard it put,
"pre-rich."

But the pressure on students is severe. They are truly torn. One 21
part of them feels obligated to fulfill their parents' expectations; after
all, their parents are older and presumably wiser. Another part tells
them that the expectations that are right for their parents are not right
for them.

I know a student who wants to be an artist. She is very obviously 22
an artist and will be a good one—she has already had several modest
local exhibits. Meanwhile she is growing as a well-rounded person
and taking humanistic subjects that will enrich the inner resources
out of which her art will grow. But her father is strongly opposed.
He thinks that an artist is a "dumb" thing to be. The student vacillates
and tries to please everybody. She keeps up with her art somewhat
furtively and takes some of the "dumb" courses her father wants her
to take—at least they are dumb courses for her. She is a free spirit
on a campus of tense students—no small achievement in itself—and
she deserves to follow her muse.

Peer pressure and self-induced pressure are also intertwined, and 23
they begin almost at the beginning of freshman year.

TEACHING STRATEGIES

1. Using your college's course catalogue, discuss the range of course offerings. Ask students to consider what clues the catalogue
   gives to the purpose of a college education.
   According to the catalogue, what function
   does the college see itself as serving?
2. In the United States college is seen as something for everyone. In Europe college is only
   for the relatively few good students. Ask students to consider the positive and negative
   aspects of both systems.

"I had a freshman student I'll call Linda," one dean told me, 24 "who came in and said she was under terrible pressure because her roommate, Barbara, was much brighter and studied all the time. I couldn't tell her that Barbara had come in two hours earlier to say the same thing about Linda."

The story is almost funny—except that it's not. It's symptomatic 25 of all the pressures put together. When every student thinks every other student is working harder and doing better, the only solution is to study harder still. I see students going off to the library every night after dinner and coming back when it closes at midnight. I wish they would sometimes forget about their peers and go to a movie. I hear the clacking of typewriters in the hours before dawn. I see the tension in their eyes when exams are approaching and papers are due: *"Will I get everything done?"*

Probably they won't. They will get sick. They will get "blocked." 26 They will sleep. They will oversleep. They will bug out. *Hey Carlos, help!*

Part of the problem is that they do more than they are expected 27 to do. A professor will assign five-page papers. Several students will start writing ten-page papers to impress him. Then more students will write ten-page papers, and a few will raise the ante to fifteen. Pity the poor student who is still just doing the assignment.

Once you have 20 or 30 percent of the student population delib- 28 erately overexerting," one dean points out, "it's bad for everybody. When a teacher gets more and more effort from his class, the student who is doing normal work can be perceived as not doing well. The tactic works, psychologically."

Why can't the professor just cut back and not accept longer 29 papers? He can, and he probably will. But by then the term will be half over and the damage done. Grade fever is highly contagious and not easily reversed. Besides, the professor's main concern is with his course. He knows his students only in relation to the course and doesn't know that they are also overexerting in their other courses. Nor is it really his business. He didn't sign up for dealing with the student as a whole person and with all the emotional baggage the student brought along from home. That's what deans, masters, chaplains, and psychiatrists are for.

To some extent this is nothing new: a certain number of professors 30 have always been self-contained islands of scholarship and shyness, more comfortable with books than with people. But the new pauperism has widened the gap still further, for professors who actually like to spend time with students don't have as much time to spend. They also are overexerting. If they are young, they are busy trying to publish in order not to perish, hanging by their finger nails onto a shrinking profession. If they are old and tenured, they are buried under the duties of administering departments—as departmental chairmen or members of committees—that have been thinned out by the budgetary axe.

Ultimately it will be the students' own business to break the circles 31 in which they are trapped. They are too young to be prisoners of their parents' dreams and their classmates' fears. They must be jolted into believing in themselves as unique men and women who have the power to shape their own future.

"Violence is being done to the undergraduate experience," says 32 Carlos Hortas. "College should be open-ended: at the end it should open many, many roads. Instead, students are choosing their goal in advance, and their choices narrow as they go along. It's almost as if they think that the country has been codified in the type of jobs that exist—that they've got to fit into certain slots. Therefore, fit into the best-paying slot.

"They ought to take chances. Not taking chances will lead to a 33 life of colorless mediocrity. They'll be comfortable. But something in the spirit will be missing."

I have painted too drab a portrait of today's students, making 34 them seem a solemn lot. That is only half of their story; if they were so dreary I wouldn't so thoroughly enjoy their company. The other half is that they are easy to like. They are quick to laugh and to offer friendship. They are not introverts. They are unusually kind and are more considerate of one another than any student generation I have known.

Nor are they so obsessed with their studies that they avoid sports 35 and extracurricular activities. On the contrary, they juggle their crowded hours to play on a variety of teams, perform with musical and dramatic groups, and write for campus publications. But this in turn is one more cause of anxiety. There are too many choices. Academically, they have 1,300 courses to select from; outside class they have to decide how much spare time they can spare and how to spend it.

This means that they engage in fewer extracurricular pursuits than 36 their predecessors did. If they want to row on the crew and play in the symphony they will eliminate one; in the '60s they would have done both. They also tend to choose activities that are self-limiting. Drama, for instance, is flourishing in all twelve of Yale's residential colleges as it never has before. Students hurl themselves into these productions—as actors, directors, carpenters, and technicians—with a dedication to create the best possible play, knowing that the day will come when the run will end and they can get back to their studies.

They also can't afford to be the willing slave of organizations like 37 the *Yale Daily News*. Last spring at the one-hundredth anniversary banquet of that paper—whose past chairmen include such once and future kings as Potter Stewart,[1] Kingman Brewster,[2] and William F. Buckley, Jr.[3]—much was made of the fact that the editorial staff used to be small and totally committed and that "newsies" routinely worked fifty hours a week. In effect they belonged to a club; Newsies is how they defined themselves at Yale. Today's student will write one or two articles a week, when he can, and he defines himself as a student. I've never heard the word Newsie except at the banquet.

If I have described the modern undergraduate primarily as a 38 driven creature who is largely ignoring the blithe spirit inside who keeps trying to come out and play, it's because that's where the crunch is, not only at Yale but throughout American education. It's why I think we should all be worried about the values that are nurturing a generation so fearful of risk and so goal-obsessed at such an early age.

I tell students that there is no one "right" way to get ahead— 39 that each of them is a different person, starting from a different point and bound for a different destination. I tell them that change is a tonic and that all the slots are not codified nor the frontiers closed. One of my ways of telling them is to invite men and women who have achieved success outside the academic world to come and talk informally with my students during the year. They are heads of companies or ad agencies, editors of magazines, politicians, public officials, television magnates, labor leaders, business executives, Broadway producers, artists, writers, economists, photographers, scientists, historians—a mixed bag of achievers.

I ask them to say a few words about how they got started. The 40 students assume that they started in their present profession and knew all along that it was what they wanted to do. Luckily for me, most of them got into their field by a circuitous route, to their surprise, after many detours. The students are startled. They can hardly conceive of a career that was not pre-planned. They can hardly imagine allowing the hand of God or chance to nudge them down some unforeseen trail.

---

[1]Potter Stewart is an Associate Justice of the United States Supreme Court. [Eds.]
[2]Kingman Brewster is a former president of Yale. [Eds.]
[3]William F. Buckley, Jr., is a columnist and founder of the conservative journal the *National Review*.

WRITING SUGGESTIONS

1. Write a response to Zinsser in which you discuss how relevant you feel his pressures are to your own experience in college.
2. Write a letter to your college president offering a suggestion that would improve student life at your school.

RESPONDING TO READING

1. In his essay Zinsser defines four kinds of college pressures. Do you feel the same pressures? To what causes do you attribute these kinds of pressures?   **2.** Zinsser uses students who attend Yale University as his examples. How representative are these examples? Do you think that students from other types of colleges face the same pressures? What pressures, for example, might a student in a community college or a large urban university face that the students in Zinsser's sample might not?   **3.** Do you agree with Zinsser's characterization of today's undergraduate as "a driven creature who is largely ignoring the blithe spirit inside" (paragraph 38)? In your experience, is the current generation of college students really as fearful and goal-obsessed as Zinsser says?

ANSWERS TO RESPONDING
TO READING

1. Answers will vary. Causes range from family to society.
2. Students at Yale, a highly selective school, are perhaps not representative, but certainly most college students share some common goals and similar pressures to achieve those goals. Students in less elite institutions may face greater economic pressures or have to struggle harder to succeed academically.
3. Certainly this mood is exacerbated by the high tuition of many schools. The trend seems to be shifting, however. More students are seeing education as a process rather than a product.

The Recoloring of Campus Life

SHELBY STEELE

Shelby Steel (1945–   ), professor of English at San Jose State University, writes sensitively about African-Americans and his own experience growing up in a white world. He has published a collection of essays called *The Content of Our Character: A New Vision of Race in America* (1990). Steele says in a 1989 article in *American Scholar* that "the exhilaration of new freedom is followed by a shock of accountability." In this essay published in *Harper's* magazine in 1989, Steele tries to understand continuing racial unrest on campuses in post–civil rights America.

In the past few years, we have witnessed what the National Institute Against Prejudice and Violence calls a "proliferation" of racial incidents on college campuses around the country. Incidents of on-campus, "intergroup conflict" have occurred at more than 160 colleges in the last three years, according to the institute. The nature of these incidents has ranged from open racial violence—most notoriously, the October 1986 beating of a black student at the University of Massachusetts at Amherst after an argument about the World Series turned into a racial bashing, with a crowd of up to 3,000 whites chasing twenty blacks—to the harassment of minority students, to acts of racial or ethnic insensitivity, with by far the greatest number falling in the last two categories. At Dartmouth College, three editors of the *Dartmouth Review*, the off-campus right-wing student weekly, were suspended last winter for harassing a black professor in his lecture hall. At Yale University last year a swastika and the words "white power" were painted on the school's Afro-American cultural center.

1

FOR OPENERS

Read aloud from Martin Luther King, Jr.'s "I Have a Dream" speech (page 474) or Langston Hughes's frequently anthologized poem "Dream Deferred." Then discuss whether or not this dream has been realized.

ADDITIONAL QUESTIONS FOR
RESPONDING TO READING

1. In the 1960s universities were in the vanguard of social change. Where do you think they stand today?
2. Do various ethnic studies and women's studies programs serve a legitimate function in a university, or do they simply isolate one group from another?
3. Does Arab, Asian, or Hispanic anxiety differ from the "black anxiety" Steele describes?
4. Does an exclusively African-American college have a role in an integrated society? (You might point out to the class that African-American students at historically black colleges are less likely to drop out than their counterparts at predominantly white colleges.)
5. African-American filmmaker Spike Lee stated in a July 1991 *Playboy* magazine interview, "Black people can't be racist. Racism is an institution. Black people don't have the power to keep hundreds of people from getting jobs or the vote." What are your reactions to Lee's comments? How do you think Steele might react?

Racist jokes were aired not long ago on a campus radio station at the University of Michigan. And at the University of Wisconsin at Madison, members of the Zeta Beta Tau fraternity held a mock slave auction in which pledges painted their faces black and wore Afro wigs. Two weeks after the president of Stanford University informed the incoming freshman class last fall that "bigotry is out, and I mean it," two freshmen defaced a poster of Beethoven—gave the image thick lips—and hung it on a black student's door.

In response, black students around the country have rediscovered   2
the militant protest strategies of the Sixties. At the University of Massachusetts at Amherst, Williams College, Penn State University, UC Berkeley, UCLA, Stanford, and countless other campuses, black students have sat in, marched, and rallied. But much of what they were marching and rallying about seemed less a response to specific racial incidents than a call for broader action on the part of the colleges and universities they were attending. Black students have demanded everything from more black faculty members and new courses on racism to the addition of "ethnic" foods in the cafeteria. There is the sense in these demands that racism runs deep.

Of course, universities are not where racial problems tend to arise.   3
When I went to college in the mid-Sixties, colleges were oases of calm and understanding in a racially tense society; campus life—with its traditions of tolerance and fairness, its very distance from the "real" world—imposed a degree of broad-mindedness on even the most provincial students. If I met whites who were not anxious to be friends with blacks, most were at least vaguely friendly to the cause of our freedom. In any case, there was no guerrilla activity against our presence, no "mine field of racism" (as one black student at Berkeley recently put it) to negotiate. I wouldn't say that the phrase "campus racism" is a contradiction in terms, but until recently it certainly seemed an incongruence.

But a greater incongruence is the generational timing of this new   4
problem on the campuses. Today's undergraduates were born after the passage of the 1964 Civil Rights Act. They grew up in an age when racial equality was for the first time enforceable by law. This too was a time when blacks suddenly appeared on television, as mayors of big cities, as icons of popular culture, as teachers, and in some cases even as neighbors. Today's black and white college students, veterans of *Sesame Street* and often of integrated grammar and high schools, have had more opportunities to know each other— whites and blacks—than any previous generation in American history. Not enough opportunities, perhaps, but enough to make the notion of racial tension on campus something of a mystery, at least to me.

To try to unravel this mystery I left my own campus, where there have been few signs of racial tension, and talked with black and white students at California schools where racial incidents had occurred: Stanford, UCLA, Berkeley. I spoke with black and white students— and not with Asians and Hispanics—because, as always, blacks and whites represent the deepest lines of division, and because I hesitate to wander onto the complex territory of other minority groups. A phrase by William H. Gass—"the hidden internality of things"— describes with maybe a little too much grandeur what I hoped to find. But it *is* what I wanted to find, for this is the kind of problem that makes a black person nervous, which is not to say that it doesn't unnerve whites as well. Once every six months or so someone yells "nigger" at me from a passing car. I don't like to think that these solo artists might soon make up a chorus or, worse, that this chorus might one day soon sing to me from the paths of my own campus.

I have long believed that trouble between the races is seldom what it appears to be.[1] It was not hard to see after my first talk with students that racial tension on campus is a problem that misrepresents itself. It has the same look, the archetypal pattern, of America's timeless racial conflict—white racism and black protest. And I think part of our concern over it comes from the fact that it has the feel of a relapse, illness gone and come again. But if we are seeing the same symptoms, I don't believe we are dealing with the same illness. For one thing, I think racial tension on campus is the result more of racial equality than inequality.

How to live with racial difference has been America's profound social problem. For the first 100 years or so following emancipation it was controlled by a legally sanctioned inequality that acted as a buffer between the races. No longer is this the case. On campuses today, as throughout society, blacks enjoy equality under the law— a profound social advancement. No student may be kept out of a class or a dormitory or an extracurricular activity because of his or her race. But there is a paradox here: On a campus where members of all races are gathered, mixed together in the classroom as well as socially, differences are more exposed than ever. And this is where the trouble starts. For members of each race—young adults coming into their own, often away from home for the first time—bring to this site of freedom, exploration, and now, today, equality very deep fears and anxieties, inchoate feelings of racial shame, anger, and guilt.

[1]See my essay, "I'm Black, You're White, Who's Innocent? Race and Power in an Era of Blame," *Harper's Magazine*, June 1988.

TEACHING STRATEGIES

1. Writing on the op-ed page of the *New York Times* (2/3/91), Lawrence Otis Graham, a young African-American lawyer, describes a visit to his old high school, where he encountered something he thought he would never see again, "something that was a source of fear and dread for each school morning of [his] early adolescence: the all-black lunch table in the cafeteria of [his] predominantly white suburban junior high school." Ask students whether there were "black tables" in their high school cafeterias. Are there "black tables" in college? "Asian tables"? Why do they think these tables exist? Are they a sign of racism? Are they necessary? Desirable?

2. This is a good time to discuss the impact of the increase in minority college enrollment that has taken place in the last twenty years. One result has been more questions asked by faculty and students about the need to include the contributions of various minority groups in the curriculum. The "Confronting the Issues" section of this chapter addresses this issue.

These feelings could lie dormant in the home, in familiar neighborhoods, in simpler days of childhood. But the college campus, with its structures of interaction and adult-level competition—the big exam, the dorm, the "mixer"—is another matter. I think campus racism is born of the rub between racial difference and a setting, the campus itself, devoted to interaction and equality. On our campuses, such concentrated micro-societies, all that remains unresolved between blacks and whites, all the old wounds and shames that have never been addressed, present themselves for attention—and present our youth with pressures they cannot always handle.

I have mentioned one paradox: racial fears and anxieties among 8 blacks and whites bubbling up in an era of racial equality under the law, in settings that are among the freest and fairest in society. And there is another, related paradox, stemming from the notion of—and practice of—affirmative action. Under the provisions of the Equal Employment Opportunity Act of 1972, all state governments and institutions (including universities) were forced to initiate plans to increase the proportion of minority and women employees—in the case of universities, of students too. Affirmative action plans that establish racial quotas were ruled unconstitutional more than ten years ago in *University of California Regents v. Bakke*. But quotas are only the most controversial aspect of affirmative action; the principle of affirmative action is reflected in various university programs aimed at redressing and overcoming past patterns of discrimination. Of course, to be conscious of patterns of discrimination—the fact, say, that public schools in the black inner cities are more crowded and employ fewer top-notch teachers than white suburban public schools, and that this is a factor in student performance—is only reasonable. However, in doing this we also call attention quite obviously to difference: in the case of blacks and whites, racial difference. What has emerged on campus in recent years—as a result of the new equality and affirmative action, in a sense, as a result of progress—is a *politics of difference*, a troubling, volatile politics in which each group justifies itself, its sense of worth and its pursuit of power, through difference alone.

In this context, racial, ethnic, and gender differences become 9 forms of sovereignty, campuses become balkanized,[2] and each group fights with whatever means are available. No doubt there are many factors that have contributed to the rise of racial tension on campus: What has been the role of fraternities, which have returned to campus with their inclusions and exclusions? What role has the heightened notion of college as some first step to personal, financial success

---

[2] Broken up into smaller, usually hostile units. [Eds.]

played in increasing competition, and thus tension? Mostly what I sense, though, is that in interactive settings, while fighting the fights of "difference," old ghosts are stirred, and haunt again. Black and white Americans simply have the power to make each other feel shame and guilt. In the "real" world, we may be able to deny these feelings, keep them at bay. But these feelings are likely to surface on college campuses, where young people are groping for identity and power, and where difference is made to matter so greatly. In a way, racial tension on campus in the Eighties might have been inevitable.

I would like, first, to discuss black students, their anxieties and 10 vulnerabilities. The accusation that black Americans have always lived with is that they are inferior—inferior simply because they are black. And this accusation has been too uniform, too ingrained in cultural imagery, too enforced by law, custom, and every form of power not to have left a mark. Black inferiority was a precept accepted by the founders of this nation; it was a principle of social organization that relegated blacks to the sidelines of American life. So when today's young black students find themselves on white campuses, surrounded by those who historically have claimed superiority, they are also surrounded by the myth of their inferiority.

Of course it is true that many young people come to college with 11 some anxiety about not being good enough. But only blacks come wearing a color that is still, in the minds of some, a sign of inferiority. Poles, Jews, Hispanics, and other groups also endure degrading stereotypes. But two things make the myth of black inferiority a far heavier burden—the broadness of its scope and its incarnation in color. There are not only more stereotypes of blacks than of other groups, but these stereotypes are also more dehumanizing, more focused on the most despised of human traits—stupidity, laziness, sexual immorality, dirtiness, and so on. In America's racial and ethnic hierarchy, blacks have clearly been relegated to the lowest level— have been burdened with an ambiguous, animalistic humanity. Moreover, this is made unavoidable for blacks by the sheer visibility of black skin, a skin that evokes the myth of inferiority on sight. And today this myth is sadly reinforced for many black students by affirmative action programs, under which blacks may often enter college with lower test scores and high-school grade point averages than whites. "They see me as an affirmative action case," one black student told me at UCLA.

So when a black student enters college, the myth of inferiority 12 compounds the normal anxiousness over whether he or she will be good enough. This anxiety is not only personal but also racial. The families of these students will have pounded into them the fact that

COLLABORATIVE ACTIVITIES

1. Divide students into groups, and assign different groups to represent the interests of African-American, Hispanic, Asian, white, women's, and men's groups on a college campus. What legitimate concerns would each of these groups have? Is it possible to meet their individual needs without infringing upon the rights of the other groups?
2. Ask students, working in groups, to divide a fictitious $25,000 available in the student activities fund among the various African-American, white, Asian, Hispanic, men's, and women's programs on campus. Before they begin, tell each group the composition of its student body (make sure each group's student body has a different ethnic composition and gender ratio). Compare results.

blacks are not inferior. And probably more than anything, it is this pounding that finally leaves a mark. If I am not inferior, why the need to say so?

This myth of inferiority constitutes a very sharp and ongoing   13 anxiety for young blacks, the nature of which is very precise: It is the terror that somehow, through one's actions or by virtue of some "proof" (a poor grade, a flubbed response in class), one's fear of inferiority—inculcated in ways large and small by society—will be confirmed as real. On a university campus, where intelligence itself is the ultimate measure, this anxiety is bound to be triggered.

A black student I met at UCLA was disturbed a little when I asked   14 him if he ever felt vulnerable—anxious about "black inferiority"—as a black student. But after a long pause, he finally said, "I think I do." The example he gave was of a large lecture class he'd taken with more than 300 students. Fifty or so black students sat in the back of the lecture hall and "acted out every stereotype in the book." They were loud, ate food, came in late—and generally got lower grades than the whites in the class. "I knew I would be seen like them, and I didn't like it. I never sat by them." Seen like what? I asked, though we both knew the answer. "As lazy, ignorant, and stupid," he said sadly.

Had the group at the back been white fraternity brothers, they   15 would not have been seen as dumb *whites*, of course. And a frat brother who worried about his grades would not worry that he would be seen "like them." The terror in this situation for the student I spoke with was that his own deeply buried anxiety would be given credence, that the myth would be verified, and that he would feel shame and humiliation not because of who he was but simply because he was black. In this lecture hall his race, quite apart from his performance, might subject him to four unendurable feelings—diminishment, accountability to the preconceptions of whites, a powerlessness to change those preconceptions, and, finally, shame. These are the feelings that make up his racial anxiety, and that of all blacks on any campus. On a white campus a black is never far from these feelings, and even his unconscious knowledge that he is subject to them can undermine his self-esteem. There are blacks on every campus who are not up to doing good college-level work. Certain black students may not be happy or motivated or in the appropriate field of study—*just like whites*. (Let us not forget that many white students get poor grades, fail, drop out.) Moreover, many more blacks than whites are not quite prepared for college, may have to catch up, owing to factors beyond their control: poor previous schooling, for example. But the white who has to catch up will not be anxious that his being behind is a matter of his whiteness, of his being *racially* inferior. The black student may well have such a fear.

This, I believe, is one reason why black colleges in America turn 16
out 34 percent of all black college graduates, though they enroll only
17 percent of black college students. Without whites around on
campus the myth of inferiority is in abeyance and, along with it, a
great reservoir of culturally imposed self-doubt. On black campuses
feelings of inferiority are personal; on campuses with a white majority,
a black's problems have a way of becoming a "black" problem.

But this feeling of vulnerability a black may feel in itself is not as 17
serious a problem as what he or she does with it. To admit that one
is made anxious in integrated situations about the myth of racial
inferiority is difficult for young blacks. It seems like admitting that
one *is* racially inferior. And so, most often, the student will deny
harboring those feelings. This is where some of the pangs of racial
tension begin, because denial always involves distortion.

In order to deny a problem we must tell ourselves that the problem 18
is something different than what it really is. A black student at
Berkeley told me that he felt defensive every time he walked into a
class and saw mostly white faces. When I asked why, he said,
"Because I know they're all racists. They think blacks are stupid." Of
course it may be true that some whites feel this way, but the singular
focus on white racism allows this student to obscure his own underlying racial anxiety. He can now say that his problem—facing a class
full of white faces, *fearing* that they think he is dumb—is entirely the
result of certifiable white racism and has nothing to do with his own
anxieties, or even that this particular academic subject may not be his
best. Now all the terror of his anxiety, its powerful energy, is devoted
to simply *seeing* racism. Whatever evidence of racism he finds—and
looking this hard, he will no doubt find some—can be brought in to
buttress his distorted view of the problem, while his actual deep-
seated anxiety goes unseen.

Denial, and the distortion that results, places the problem *outside* 19
the self and in the world. It is not that I have any inferiority anxiety
because of my race; it is that I am going to school with people who
don't like blacks. This is the shift in thinking that allows black students
to reenact the protest pattern of the Sixties. Denied racial anxiety-
distortion-reenactment is the process by which feelings of inferiority
are transformed into an exaggerated white menace—which is then
protested against with the techniques of the past. Under the sway of
this process, black students believe that history is repeating itself,
that it's just like the Sixties, or Fifties. In fact, it is the not yet healed
wounds from the past, rather than the inequality that created the
wounds, that is the real problem.

This process generates an unconscious need to exaggerate the 20
level of racism on campus—to make it a matter of the system, not

just a handful of students. Racism is the avenue away from the true
inner anxiety. How many students demonstrating for a black "theme
house"—demonstrating in the style of the Sixties, when the battle
was to win for blacks a place on campus—might be better off spending
their time reading and studying? Black students have the highest
dropout rate and lowest grade point average of any group in American
universities. This need not be so. And it is not the result of not having
black theme houses.

It was my very good fortune to go to college in 1964, when the   21
question of black "inferiority" was openly talked about among blacks.
The summer before I left for college I heard Martin Luther King Jr.
speak in Chicago, and he laid it on the line for black students everywhere. "When you are behind in a footrace, the only way to get ahead
is to run faster than the man in front of you. So when your white
roommate says he's tired and goes to sleep, you stay up and burn
the midnight oil." His statement that we were "behind in a footrace"
acknowledged that because of history, of few opportunities, of racism,
we were, in a sense, "inferior." But this had to do with what had
been done to our parents and their parents, not with inherent inferiority. And because it was acknowledged, it was presented to us as
a challenge rather than a mark of shame.

Of the eighteen black students (in a student body of 1,000) who   22
were on campus in my freshman year, all graduated, though a number
of us were not from the middle class. At the university where I currently teach, the dropout rate for black students is 72 percent, despite
the presence of several academic-support programs; a counseling
center with black counselors; an Afro-American studies department;
black faculty, administrators, and staff; a general education curriculum that emphasizes "cultural pluralism"; an Educational Opportunities Program; a mentor program; a black faculty and staff
association; and an administration and faculty that often announce
the need to do more for black students.

It may be unfair to compare my generation with the current one.   23
Parents do this compulsively and to little end but self-congratulation.
But I don't congratulate my generation. I think we were advantaged.
We came along at a time when racial integration was held in high
esteem. And integration was a very challenging social concept for
both blacks and whites. We were remaking ourselves—that's what
one did at college—and making history. We had something to prove.
This was a profound advantage; it gave us clarity and a challenge.
Achievement in the American mainstream was the goal of integration,
and the best thing about this challenge was its secondary message—
that we *could* achieve.

There is much irony in the fact that black power would come   24 along in the late Sixties and change all this. Black power was a movement of uplift and pride, and yet it also delivered the weight of pride—a weight that would burden black students from then on. Black power "nationalized" the black identity, made blackness itself an object of celebration and allegiance. But if it transformed a mark of shame into a mark of pride, it also, in the name of pride, required the denial of racial anxiety. Without a frank account of one's anxieties, there is no clear direction, no concrete challenge. Black students today do not get as clear a message from their racial identity as my generation got. They are not filled with the same urgency to prove themselves, because black pride has said, You're already proven, already equal, as good as anybody.

The "black identity" shaped by black power most powerfully 25 contributes to racial tensions on campuses by basing entitlement more on race than on constitutional rights and standards of merit. With integration, black entitlement was derived from constitutional principles of fairness. Black power changed this by skewing the formula from rights to color—if you were black, you were entitled. Thus, the United Coalition Against Racism (UCAR) at the University of Michigan could "demand" two years ago that all black professors be given immediate tenure, that there be special pay incentives for black professors, and that money be provided for an all-black student union. In this formula, black becomes the very color of entitlement, an extra right in itself, and a very dangerous grandiosity is promoted in which blackness amounts to specialness.

Race is, by any standard, an unprincipled source of power. And 26 on campuses the use of racial power by one group makes racial or ethnic or gender *difference* a currency of power for all groups. When I make my difference into power, other groups must seize upon their difference to contain my power and maintain their position relative to me. Very quickly a kind of politics of difference emerges in which racial, ethnic, and gender groups are forced to assert their entitlement and vie for power based on the single quality that makes them different from one another.

On many campuses today academic departments and programs 27 are established on the basis of difference—black studies, women's studies, Asian studies, and so on—despite the fact that there is nothing in these "difference" departments that cannot be studied within traditional academic disciplines. If their rationale truly is past exclusion from the mainstream curriculum, shouldn't the goal now be complete inclusion rather than separateness? I think this logic is overlooked because these groups are too interested in the power their difference can bring, and they insist on separate departments and programs as a tribute to that power.

This politics of difference makes everyone on campus a member 28

of a minority group. It also makes racial tensions inevitable. To highlight one's difference as a source of advantage is also, indirectly, to
inspire the enemies of that difference. When blackness (and femaleness) becomes power, then white maleness is also sanctioned as
power. A white male student at Stanford told me, "One of my friends
said the other day that we should get together and start up a white
student union and come up with a list of demands."

It is certainly true that white maleness has long been an unfair 29
source of power. But the sin of white male power is precisely its use
of race and gender as a source of entitlement. When minorities and
women use their race, ethnicity, and gender in the same way, they
not only commit the same sin but also, indirectly, sanction the very
form of power that oppressed them in the first place. The politics of
difference is based on a tit-for-tat sort of logic in which every victory
only calls one's enemies to arms.

This elevation of difference undermines the communal impulse 30
by making each group foreign and inaccessible to others. When
difference is celebrated rather than remarked, people must think in
terms of difference, they must find meaning in difference, and this
meaning comes from an endless process of contrasting one's group
with other groups. Blacks use whites to define themselves as different, women use men. Hispanics use whites and blacks, and on
it goes. And in the process each group mythologizes and mystifies
its difference, puts it beyond the full comprehension of outsiders.
Difference becomes an inaccessible preciousness toward which outsiders are expected to be simply and uncomprehendingly reverential. But beware: In this world, even the insulated world of the
college campus, preciousness is a balloon asking for a needle. At
Smith College, graffiti appears: "Niggers, Spics, and Chinks quit
complaining or get out."

Most of the white students I talked with spoke as if from under a 31
faint cloud of accusation. There was always a ring of defensiveness in
their complaints about blacks. A white student I spoke with at UCLA
told me: "Most white students on this campus think the black student
leadership here is made up of oversensitive crybabies who spend all
their time looking for things to kick up a ruckus about." A white student at Stanford said: "Blacks do nothing but complain and ask for sympathy when everyone really knows they don't do well because they don't
try. If they worked harder, they could do as well as everyone else."

That these students felt accused was most obvious in their com- 32
pulsion to assure me that they were not racists. Oblique versions
of some-of-my-best-friends-are stories came ritualistically before or
after critiques of black students. Some said flatly, "I am not a racist,

but . . ." Of course, we all deny being racists, but we only do this compulsively, I think, when we are working against an accusation of bias. I think it was the color of my skin, itself, that accused them.

This was the meta-message that surrounded these conversations   33 like an aura, and in it, I believe, is the core of white American racial anxiety. My skin not only accused them, it judged them. And this judgment was a sad gift of history that brought them to account whether they deserved such an accounting or not. It said that wherever and whenever blacks were concerned, they had reason to feel guilt. And whether it was earned or unearned, I think it was guilt that set off the compulsion in these students to disclaim. I believe it is true that in America black people make white people feel guilty.

Guilt is the essence of white anxiety, just as inferiority is the   34 essence of black anxiety. And the terror that it carries for whites is the terror of discovering that one has reason to feel guilt where blacks are concerned—not so much because of what blacks might think but because of what guilt can say about oneself. If the darkest fear of blacks is inferiority, the darkest fear of whites is that their better lot in life is at least partially the result of their capacity for evil—their capacity to dehumanize an entire people for their own benefit, and then to be indifferent to the devastation their dehumanization has wrought on successive generations of their victims. This is the terror that whites are vulnerable to regarding blacks. And the mere fact of being white is sufficient to feel it, since even whites with hearts clean of racism benefit from being white—benefit at the expense of blacks. This is a conditional guilt having nothing to do with individual intentions or actions. And it makes for a very powerful anxiety because it threatens whites with a view of themselves as inhuman, just as inferiority threatens blacks with a similar view of themselves. At the dark core of both anxieties is a suspicion of incomplete humanity.

So the white students I met were not just meeting me; they were   35 also meeting the possibility of their own inhumanity. And this, I think, is what explains how some young white college students in the late Eighties can so frankly take part in racially insensitive and outright racist acts. They were expected to be cleaner of racism than any previous generation—they were born into the Great Society. But this expectation overlooks the fact that, for them, color is still an accusation and judgment. In black faces there is a discomforting reflection of white collective shame. Blacks remind them that their racial innocence is questionable, that they are the beneficiaries of past and present racism, and that the sins of the father may well have been visited on the children.

And yet young whites tell themselves that they had nothing to   36 do with the oppression of black people. They have a stronger belief in their racial innocence than any previous generation of whites, and a natural hostility toward anyone who would challenge that innocence. So (with a great deal of individual variation) they can end up in the paradoxical position of being hostile to blacks as a way of defending their own racial innocence.

I think this is what the young white editors of the *Dartmouth* 37 *Review* were doing when they shamelessly harassed William Cole, a black music professor.[3] Weren't they saying, in effect, I am so free of racial guilt that I can afford to ruthlessly attack blacks and still be racially innocent? The ruthlessness of that attack was a form of denial, a badge of innocence. The more they were charged with racism, the more ugly and confrontational their harassment became. Racism became a means of rejecting racial guilt, a way of showing that they were not ultimately racists.

The politics of difference sets up a struggle for innocence among 38 all groups. When difference is the currency of power, each group must fight for the innocence that entitles it to power. Blacks sting whites with guilt, remind them of their racist past, accuse them of new and more subtle forms of racism. One way whites retrieve their innocence is to discredit blacks and deny their difficulties, for in this denial is the denial of their own guilt. To blacks this denial looks like racism, a racism that feeds black innocence and encourages them to throw more guilt at whites. And so the cycle continues. The politics of difference leads each group to pick at the sore spots of the other.

Men and women who run universities—whites, mostly—also 39 participate in the politics of difference, although they handle their guilt differently than many of their students. They don't deny it, but still they don't want to *feel* it. And to avoid this *feeling* of guilt they have tended to go along with whatever blacks put on the table rather than work with them to assess their real needs. University administrators have too often been afraid of their own guilt and have relied on negotiation and capitulation more to appease that guilt than to help blacks and other minorities. Administrators would never give white students a racial theme house where they could be "more comfortable with people of their own kind," yet more and more universities are doing this for black students, thus fostering a kind of voluntary segregation. To avoid the anxieties of integrated situations,

---

[3]In 1990 the editors of the *Dartmouth Review*, an independently funded, conservative campus newspaper, were accused of racism, antisemitism, sexism, and of harassing William Cole, an African-American music professor. Cole resigned, stating that the constant criticism made it impossible for him to teach. [Eds.]

blacks ask for theme houses; to avoid guilt, white administrators give them theme houses.

When everyone is on the run from his anxieties about race, race relations on campus can be reduced to the negotiation of avoidances. A pattern of demand and concession develops in which each side uses the other to escape itself. Black studies department, black deans of student affairs, black counseling programs, Afro houses, black theme houses, black homecoming dances and graduation ceremonies—black students and white administrators have slowly engineered a machinery of separatism that, in the name of sacred difference, redraws the ugly lines of segregation.   40

Black students have not sufficiently helped themselves, and universities, despite all their concessions, have not really done much for blacks. If both faced their anxieties, I think they would see the same thing: Academic parity with all other groups should be the overriding mission of black students, and it should also be the first goal that universities have for their black students. Blacks can only *know* they are as good as others when they are, in fact, as good—when their grades are higher and their dropout rate lower. Nothing under the sun will substitute for this and no amount of concessions will bring it about.   41

Universities and colleges can never be free of guilt until they truly help black students, which means leading and challenging them rather than negotiating and capitulating. It means inspiring them to achieve academic parity, nothing less, and helping them see their own weaknesses as their greatest challenge. It also means dismantling the machinery of separatism, breaking the link between difference and power, and skewing the formula for entitlement away from race and gender and back to constitutional rights.   42

As for the young white students who have rediscovered swastikas and the word "nigger," I think they suffer from an exaggerated sense of their own innocence, as if they were incapable of evil and beyond the reach of guilt. But it is also true that the politics of difference creates an environment which threatens their innocence and makes them defensive. White students are not invited to the negotiating table from which they see blacks and others walk away with concessions. The presumption is that they do not deserve to be there because they are white. So they can only be defensive, and the less mature among them will be aggressive. Guerrilla activity will ensue. Of course this is wrong, but it is also a reflection of an environment where difference carries power and where whites have the wrong "difference."   43

I think universities should emphasize commonality as a higher value than "diversity" and "pluralism"—buzzwords for the politics   44

WRITING SUGGESTION

Write an editorial for publication in your college newspaper suggesting ways in which relations between the races at your college could be improved.

ANSWERS TO RESPONDING TO READING

1. Answers will vary. In integrated public schools students have contact with other races from kindergarten on.
2. Answers will vary. Steele questions the standard liberal viewpoint on affirmative action and uses common sense to challenge standard responses to the problem of African-American underachievement.
3. Answers will vary. Steele's essay is really about the struggle of all individuals to get an education and to succeed in life, no matter what their color.

of difference. Difference that does not rest on a clearly delineated foundation of commonality not only is inaccessible to those who are not part of the ethnic or racial group but is antagonistic to them. Difference can enrich only the common ground.

Integration has become an abstract term today, having to do with   45 little more than numbers and racial balances. But it once stood for a high and admirable set of values. It made difference second to commonality, and it asked members of all races to face whatever fears they inspired in each other. I doubt the word will have a new vogue, but the values, under whatever name, are worth working for.

RESPONDING TO READING

1. How accurate is Shelby Steele's assertion that today's African-American and white students have had more opportunities to know each other than any previous generation in America? Does your own experience confirm this idea or call it into question?   **2.** Steele has taken some controversial positions in his writing. His stand against affirmative action, for example, resulted in a storm of criticism. Does he voice opinions in this essay that you find upsetting? Does he succeed in making you reconsider any of your ideas?   **3.** How closely does Steele's description of the racial situation on American college campuses resemble the one that exists on your campus? Is Steele's essay primarily about race, or is its real subject something else? Explain.

College Is a Waste of Time and Money
CAROLINE BIRD

Caroline Bird (1915–   ) is a writer who often focuses on women's roles in the business world. In her book *Born Female: The High Cost of Keeping Women Down* (1968), she cites proof of job discrimination. *The Invisible Scar: The Great Depression and What It Did to American Life, from Then until Now* (1966) was named one of the year's best books by the American Library Association. Other titles include *The Two-Paycheck Marriage: How Women at Work Are Changing Life in America* (1979) and *The Good Years: Your Life in the Twenty-First Century* (1983). The essay that follows, from Bird's *The Case Against College* (1975), questions our notions about the necessity of a college education for everyone and suggests that college is "too expensive . . . to serve as a holding pen for large numbers of our young."

A great majority of our nine million college students are not in school because they want to be or because they want to learn. They are there because it has become the thing to do or because college is a pleasant place to be; because it's the only way they can get parents or taxpayers to support them without working at a job they don't like; because Mother wanted them to go, or some other reason entirely irrelevant to the course of studies for which college is supposedly organized.

As I crisscross the United States lecturing on college campuses, I am dismayed to find that professors and administrators, when pressed for a candid opinion, estimate that no more than 25 percent of their students are turned on by classwork. For the rest, college is at best a social center or aging vat, and at worst a young folks' home or even a prison that keeps them out of the mainstream of economic life for a few more years.

The premise—which I no longer accept—that college is the best place for all high-school graduates grew out of a noble American ideal. Just as the United States was the first nation to aspire to teach every small child to read and write, so, during the 1950s, we became the first and only great nation to aspire to higher education for all. During the '60s we damned the expense and built great state university systems as fast as we could. And adults—parents, employers, high-school counselors—began to push, shove and cajole youngsters to "get an education."

It became a mammoth industry, with taxpayers footing more than half the bill. By 1970, colleges and universities were spending more than 30 billion dollars annually. But still only half our high school graduates were going on. According to estimates made by the economist Fritz Machlup, if we had been educating every young person until age 22 in that year of 1970, the bill for higher education would have reached 47.5 billion dollars, 12.5 billion more than the total corporate profits for the year.

Figures such as these have begun to make higher education for all look financially prohibitive, particularly now when colleges are squeezed by the pressures of inflation and a drop-off in the growth of their traditional market.

Predictable demography has caught up with the university empire builders. Now that the record crop of postwar babies has graduated from college, the rate of growth of the student population has begun to decline. To keep their mammoth plants financially solvent, many institutions have begun to use hard-sell, Madison-Avenue techniques to attract students. They sell college like soap, promoting features they think students want: innovative programs, an environment con-

1
2
3
4
5
6

TEACHING STRATEGY

This essay is especially relevant given the cost of a college education. You might acquaint students with the range of tuitions now being charged across the country and ask them if it is useful to judge the value of a college education solely on the basis of financial return.

ducive to meaningful personal relationships, and a curriculum so free that it doesn't sound like college at all.

Pleasing the customers is something new for college administrators. Colleges have always known that most students don't like to study, and that at least part of the time they are ambivalent about college, but before the student riots of the 1960s educators never thought it either right or necessary to pay any attention to student feelings. But when students rebelling against the Vietnam war and the draft discovered they could disrupt a campus completely, administrators had to act on some student complaints. Few understood that the protests had tapped the basic discontent with college itself, a discontent that did not go away when the riots subsided. 7

Today students protest individually rather than in concert. They turn inward and withdraw from active participation. They drop out to travel to India or to feed themselves on subsistence farms. Some refuse to go to college at all. Most, of course, have neither the funds nor the self-confidence for constructive articulation of their discontent. They simply hang around college unhappily and reluctantly. 8

All across the country, I have been overwhelmed by the prevailing sadness on American campuses. Too many young people speak little, and then only in drowned voices. Sometimes the mood surfaces as diffidence, wariness, or coolness, but whatever its form, it looks like a defense mechanism, and that rings a bell. This is the way it used to be with women, and just as society had systematically damaged women by insisting that their proper place was in the home, so we may be systematically damaging 18-year-olds by insisting that their proper place is in college. 9

Campus watchers everywhere know what I mean when I say students are sad, but they don't agree on the reason for it. During the Vietnam war some ascribed the sadness to the draft; now others blame affluence, or say it has something to do with permissive upbringing. 10

Not satisfied with any of these explanations, I looked for some answers with the journalistic tools of my trade—scholarly studies, economic analyses, the historical record, the opinions of the especially knowledgeable, conversations with parents, professors, college administrators, and employers, all of whom spoke as alumni too. Mostly I learned from my interviews with hundreds of young people on and off campuses all over the country. 11

My unnerving conclusion is that students are sad because they are not needed. Somewhere between the nursery and the employment office, they become unwanted adults. No one has anything in particular against them. But no one knows what to do with them 12 either. We already have too many people in the world of the 1970s, and there is no room for so many newly minted 18-year-olds. So we temporarily get them out of the way by sending them to college where in fact only a few belong.

To make it more palatable, we fool ourselves into believing that 13 we are sending them there for their own best interests, and that it's good for them, like spinach. Some, of course, learn to like it, but most wind up preferring green peas.

Educators admit as much. Nevitt Sanford, distinguished student 14 of higher education, says students feel they are "capitulating to a kind of voluntary servitude." Some of them talk about their time in college as if it were a sentence to be served. I listened to a 1970 Mount Holyoke graduate: "For two years I was really interested in science, but in my junior and senior years I just kept saying, 'I've done two years; I'm going to finish.' When I got out I made up my mind that I wasn't going to school anymore because so many of my courses had been bullshit."

But bad as it is, college is often preferable to a far worse fate. It 15 is better than the drudgery of an uninspiring nine-to-five job, and better than doing nothing when no jobs are available. For some young people, it is a graceful way to get away from home and become independent without losing the financial support of their parents. And sometimes it is the only alternative to an intolerable home situation.

It is difficult to assess how many students are in college reluc- 16 tantly. The conservative Carnegie Commission estimates from 5 to 30 percent. Sol Linowitz, who was once chairman of a special committee on campus tension of the American Council on Education, found that "a significant number were not happy with their college experience because they felt they were there only in order to get the 'ticket to the big show' rather than to spend the years as productively as they otherwise could."

Older alumni will identify with Richard Baloga, a policeman's 17 son, who stayed in school even though he "hated it" because he thought it would do him some good. But fewer students each year feel this way. Daniel Yankelovich has surveyed undergraduate attitudes for a number of years, and reported in 1971 that 74 percent thought education was "very important." But just two years earlier, 80 percent thought so.

The doubters don't mind speaking up. Leon Lefkowitz, chairman 18 of the department of social studies at Central High School in Valley Stream, New York, interviewed 300 college students at random, and reports that 200 of them didn't think that the education they were getting was worth the effort. "In two years I'll pick up a diploma," said one student, "and I can honestly say it was a waste of my father's bread."

Nowadays, says one sociologist, you don't have to have a reason 19 for going to college; it's an institution. His definition of an institution is an arrangement everyone accepts without question; the burden of proof is not on why you go, but why anyone thinks there might be a reason for not going. The implication is that an 18-year-old is too young and confused to know what he wants to do, and that he should listen to those who know best and go to college.

I don't agree. I believe that college has to be judged not on what 20 other people think is good for students, but on how good it feels to the students themselves.

I believe that people have an inside view of what's good for them. 21 If a child doesn't want to go to school some morning, better let him stay at home, at least until you find out why. Maybe he knows something you don't. It's the same with college. If high-school graduates don't want to go, or if they don't want to go right away, they may perceive more clearly than their elders that college is not for them. It is no longer obvious that adolescents are best off studying a core curriculum that was constructed when all educated men could agree on what made them educated, or that professors, advisors, or parents can be of any particular help to young people in choosing a major or a career. High-school graduates see college graduates driving cabs, and decide it's not worth going. College students find no intellectual stimulation in their studies and drop out.

If students believe that college isn't necessarily good for them, 22 you can't expect them to stay on for the general good of mankind. They don't go to school to beat the Russians to Jupiter, improve the national defense, increase the GNP, or create a new market for the arts—to mention some of the benefits taxpayers are supposed to get for supporting higher education.

Nor should we expect to bring about social equality by putting 23 all young people through four years of academic rigor. At best, it's a roundabout and expensive way to narrow the gap between the highest and lowest in our society anyway. At worst, it is unconsciously elitist. Equalizing opportunity through universal higher education subjects the whole population to the intellectual mode natural only to a few. It violates the fundamental egalitarian principle of respect for the differences between people.

Of course, most parents aren't thinking of the "higher" good at 24 all. They send their children to college because they are convinced young people benefit financially from those four years of higher education. But if money is the only goal, college is the dumbest investment you can make. I say this because a young banker in Poughkeepsie, New York, Stephen G. Necel, used a computer to compare college as an investment with other investments available in 1974 and college did not come out on top.

For the sake of argument, the two of us invented a young man 25 whose rich uncle gave him, in cold cash, the cost of a four-year education at any college he chose, but the young man didn't have to spend the money on college. After bales of computer paper, we had our mythical student write to his uncle: "Since you said I could spend the money foolishly if I wished, I am going to blow it all on Princeton."

The much respected financial columnist Sylvia Porter echoed the 26 common assumption when she said last year, "A college education is among the very best investments you can make in your entire life." But the truth is not quite so rosy, even if we assume that the Census Bureau is correct when it says that as of 1972, a man who completed four years of college would expect to earn $199,000 more between the ages of 22 and 64 than a man who had only a high-school diploma.

If a 1972 Princeton-bound high-school graduate had put the 27 $34,181 that his four years of college would have cost him into a savings bank at 7.5 percent interest compounded daily, he would have at age 64 a total of $1,129,200, or $528,200 more than the earnings of a male college graduate, and more than five times as much as the $199,000 extra the more educated man could expect to earn between 22 and 64.

The big advantage of getting your college money in cash now is 28 that you can invest it in something that has a higher return than a diploma. For instance, a Princeton-bound high-school graduate of 1972 who liked fooling around with cars could have banked his $34,181, and gone to work at the local garage at close to $1,000 more per year than the average high-school graduate. Meanwhile, as he was learning to be an expert auto mechanic, his money would be ticking away in the bank. When he became 28, he would have earned $7,199 less on his job from age 22 to 28 than his college-educated friend, but he would have had $73,113 in his passbook—enough to buy out his boss, go into the used-car business, or acquire his own new-car dealership. If successful in business, he could expect to make more than the average college graduate. And if he had the brains to get into Princeton, he would be just as likely to make money without the four years spent on campus. Unfortunately, few college-bound high-school graduates get the opportunity to bank such a large sum of money, and then wait for it to make them rich. And few parents are sophisticated enough to understand that in financial returns alone, their children would be better off with the money than with the education.

COLLABORATIVE ACTIVITY

Have students, working in groups, decide how else they could spend the money they are now spending on college. Be sure they consider how much of this money would be theirs to spend. In class discussion, consider how their spending might affect their future lives.

Rates of return and dollar signs on education are fascinating brain 29
teasers, but obviously there is a certain unreality to the game. Quite
aside from the noneconomic benefits of college, and these should
loom larger once the dollars are cleared away, there are grave difficulties in assigning a dollar value to college at all.

In fact there is no real evidence that the higher income of college 30
graduates is due to college. College may simply attract people who
are slated to earn more money anyway; those with higher IQs, better
family backgrounds, a more enterprising temperament. No one who
has wrestled with the problem is prepared to attribute all of the higher
income to the impact of college itself.

Christopher Jencks, author of *Inequality*, a book that assesses the 31
effect of family and schooling in America, believes that education in
general accounts for less than half of the difference in income in the
American population. "The biggest single source of income differences," writes Jencks, "seems to be the fact that men from high-status
families have higher incomes than men from low-status families even
when they enter the same occupations, have the same amount of
education, and have the same test scores."

Jacob Mincer of the National Bureau of Economic Research and 32
Columbia University states flatly that of "20 to 30 percent of students
at any level, the additional schooling has been a waste, at least in
terms of earnings." College fails to work its income-raising magic for
almost a third of those who go. More than half of those people in
1972 who earned $15,000 or more reached that comfortable bracket
without the benefit of a college diploma. Jencks says that financial
success in the U.S. depends a good deal on luck, and the most sophisticated regression analyses have yet to demonstrate otherwise.

But most of today's students don't go to college to earn more 33
money anyway. In 1968, when jobs were easy to get, Daniel Yankelovich made his first nationwide survey of students. Sixty-five percent of them said they "would welcome less emphasis on money."
By 1973, when jobs were scarce, that figure jumped to 80 percent.

The young are not alone. Americans today are all looking less to 34
the pay of a job than to the work itself. They want "interesting" work
that permits them "to make a contribution," "express themselves"
and "use their special abilities," and they think college will help them
find it.

Jerry Darring of Indianapolis knows what it is to make a dollar. 35
He worked with his father in the family plumbing business, on the
line at Chevrolet, and in the Chrysler foundry. He quit these jobs to
enter Wright State University in Dayton, Ohio, because "in a job like

that a person only has time to work, and after that he's so tired that he can't do anything else but come home and go to sleep."

Jerry came to college to find work "helping people." And he is 36 perfectly willing to spend the dollars he earns at dull, well-paid work to prepare for lower-paid work that offers the reward of service to others.

Jerry's case is not unusual. No one works for money alone. In 37 order to deal with the nonmonetary rewards of work, economists have coined the concept of "psychic income" which according to one economic dictionary means "income that is reckoned in terms of pleasure, satisfaction, or general feelings of euphoria."

Psychic income is primarily what college students mean when 38 they talk about getting a good job. During the most affluent years of the late 1960s and early 1970s college students told their placement officers that they wanted to be researchers, college professors, artists, city planners, social workers, poets, book publishers, archeologists, ballet dancers, or authors.

The psychic income of these and other occupations popular with 39 students is so high that these jobs can be filled without offering high salaries. According to one study, 93 percent of urban university professors would choose the same vocation again if they had the chance, compared with only 16 percent of unskilled auto workers. Even though the monetary gap between college professor and auto worker is now surprisingly small, the difference in psychic income is enormous.

But colleges fail to warn students that jobs of these kinds are hard 40 to come by, even for qualified applicants, and they rarely accept the responsibility of helping students choose a career that will lead to a job. When a young person says he is interested in helping people, his counselor tells him to become a psychologist. But jobs in psychology are scarce. The Department of Labor, for instance, estimates there will be 4,300 new jobs for psychologists in 1975 while colleges are expected to turn out 58,430 B.A.s in psychology that year.

Of 30 psych majors who reported back to Vassar what they were 41 doing a year after graduation in 1972, only five had jobs in which they could possibly use their courses in psychology, and two of these were working for Vassar.

The outlook isn't much better for students majoring in other 42 psychic-pay disciplines: sociology, English, journalism, anthropology, forestry, education. Whatever college graduates want to do, most of them are going to wind up doing what there is to do.

John Shingleton, director of placement at Michigan State Univer- 43 sity, accuses the academic community of outright hypocrisy. "Educators have never said, 'Go to college and get a good job,' but this has been implied, and now students expect it. . . . If we care what happens to students after college, then let's get involved with what should be one of the basic purposes of education: career preparation."

In the 1970s, some of the more practical professors began to see 44 that jobs for graduates meant jobs for professors too. Meanwhile, students themselves reacted to the shrinking job market, and a "new vocationalism" exploded on campus. The press welcomed the change as a return to the ethic of achievement and service. Students were still idealistic, the reporters wrote, but they now saw that they could best make the world better by healing the sick as physicians or righting individual wrongs as lawyers.

But there are no guarantees in these professions either. The Amer- 45 ican Enterprise Institute estimated in 1971 that there would be more than the target ratio of 100 doctors for every 100,000 people in the population by 1980. And the odds are little better for would-be lawyers. Law schools are already graduating twice as many new lawyers every year as the Department of Labor thinks will be needed, and the oversupply is growing every year.

And it's not at all apparent that what is actually learned in a 46 "professional" education is necessary for success. Teachers, engineers and others I talked to said they find that on the job they rarely use what they learned in school. In order to see how well college prepared engineers and scientists for actual paid work in their fields, The Carnegie Commission queried all the employees with degrees in these fields in two large firms. Only one in five said the work they were doing bore a "very close relationship" to their college studies, while almost a third saw "very little relationship at all." An overwhelming majority could think of many people who were doing their same work, but had majored in different fields.

Majors in nontechnical fields report even less relationship 47 between their studies and their jobs. Charles Lawrence, a communications major in college and now the producer of "Kennedy & Co.," the Chicago morning television show, says, "You have to learn all that stuff and you never use it again. I learned my job doing it." Others employed as architects, nurses, teachers and other members of the so-called learned professions report the same thing.

Most college administrators admit that they don't prepare their 48 graduates for the job market. "I just wish I had the guts to tell parents that when you get out of this place you aren't prepared to do anything," the academic head of a famous liberal-arts college told us. Fortunately, for him, most people believe that you don't have to defend a liberal-arts education on those grounds. A liberal-arts education is supposed to provide you with a value system, a standard, a set of ideas, not a job. "Like Christianity, the liberal arts are seldom practiced and would probably be hated by the majority of the populace if they were," said one defender.

The analogy is apt. The fact is, of course, that the liberal arts are 49 a religion in every sense of that term. When people talk about them, their language becomes elevated, metaphorical, extravagant, theoretical and reverent. And faith in personal salvation by the liberal arts is professed in a creed intoned on ceremonial occasions such as commencements.

If the liberal arts are a religious faith, the professors are its priests. 50 But disseminating ideas in a four-year college curriculum is slow and most expensive. If you want to learn about Milton, Camus, or even Margaret Mead you can find them in paperback books, the public library, and even on television.

And when most people talk about the value of a college education, 51 they are not talking about great books. When at Harvard commencement, the president welcomes the new graduates into "the fellowship of educated men and women," what he could be saying is, "Here is a piece of paper that is a passport to jobs, power and instant prestige." As Glenn Bassett, a personnel specialist at G.E. says, "In some parts of G.E., a college degree appears completely irrelevant to selection to, say, a manager's job. In most, however, it is a ticket of admission."

But now that we have doubled the number of young people 52 attending college, a diploma cannot guarantee even that. The most charitable conclusion we can reach is that college probably has very little, if any, effect on people and things at all. Today, the false premises are easy to see:

First, college doesn't make people intelligent, ambitious, happy, 53 or liberal. It's the other way around. Intelligent, ambitious, happy, liberal people are attracted to higher education in the first place.

Second, college can't claim much credit for the learning experi- 54 ences that really change students while they are there. Jobs, friends, history, and most of all the sheer passage of time, have as big an impact as anything even indirectly related to the campus.

Third, colleges have changed so radically that a freshman entering 55 in the fall of 1974 can't be sure to gain even the limited value research studies assigned to colleges in the '60s. The sheer size of undergraduate campuses of the 1970s makes college even less stimulating now than it was 10 years ago. Today even motivated students are disappointed with their college courses and professors.

Finally, a college diploma no longer opens as many vocational 56 doors. Employers are beginning to realize that when they pay extra for someone with a diploma, they are paying only for an empty credential. The fact is that most of the work for which employers now expect college training is now or has been capably done in the past by people without higher educations.

College, then, may be a good place for those few young people 57 who are really drawn to academic work, who would rather read than eat, but it has become too expensive, in money, time, and intellectual effort, to serve as a holding pen for large numbers of our young. We ought to make it possible for those reluctant, unhappy students to find alternative ways of growing up, and more realistic preparation for the years ahead.

RESPONDING TO READING

1. Bird's essay was written in 1975. Do her points still apply? Are your reasons for attending college similar to or different from the ones she describes? Explain.   **2.** Does the school you now attend sell college "like soap" (paragraph 6)? What is your opinion of this kind of self-promotion? Do you agree that colleges should avoid self-promotion? Can you think of any alternatives to self-promotion?   **3.** What criteria, other than financial, do *you* use to determine the worth of a college education? Are problems created when words like *worth*, *return*, and *value* are applied to a college degree?

Gryphon

CHARLES BAXTER

Charles Baxter (1947–   ), born in Minneapolis, is a fiction writer and professor of English who now teaches at the University of Michigan. Baxter's novel, *First Light*, was published in 1987. *Harmony of the World* (1984), *Through the Safety Net* (1985) and *Relative Stranger* (1990) are collections of his short stories. "Gryphon," a story from *Through the Safety Net*, looks through the eyes of a fourth grader to tell a tale of a substitute teacher with an eccentric and often unbalanced imagination.

On Wednesday afternoon, between the geography lesson on 1 ancient Egypt's hand-operated irrigation system and an art project that involved drawing a model city next to a mountain, our fourth-grade teacher, Mr. Hibler, developed a cough. This cough began with a series of muffled throat clearings and progressed to propulsive noises contained within Mr. Hibler's closed mouth. "Listen to him," Carol Peterson whispered to me. "He's gonna blow up." Mr. Hibler's laughter—dazed and infrequent—sounded a bit like his cough, but as we worked on our model cities we would look up, thinking he was enjoying a joke, and see Mr. Hibler's face turning red, his cheeks puffed out. This was not laughter. Twice he bent over, and his loose tie, like a plumb line, hung down straight from his neck as he exploded himself into a Kleenex. He would excuse himself, then go on coughing. "I'll bet you a dime," Carol Peterson whispered, "we get a substitute tomorrow."

Carol sat at the desk in front of mine and was a bad person— when she thought no one was looking she would blow her nose on notebook paper, then crumble it up and throw it into the waste-basket—but at times of crisis she spoke the truth. I knew I'd lose the dime. 2

"No deal," I said. 3

When Mr. Hibler stood us up in formation at the door just prior to the final bell, he was almost incapable of speech. "I'm sorry, boys and girls," he said. "I seem to be coming down with something." 4

"I hope you feel better tomorrow, Mr. Hibler," Bobby Kryza-nowicz, the faultless brown-noser said, and I heard Carol Peterson's evil giggle. Then Mr. Hibler opened the door and we walked out to the buses, a clique of us starting noisily to hawk and cough as soon as we thought we were a few feet beyond Mr. Hibler's earshot. 5

Five Oaks being a rural community, and in Michigan, the supply of substitute teachers was limited to the town's unemployed com-munity college graduates, a pool of about four mothers. These ladies fluttered, provided easeful class days, and nervously covered material we had mastered weeks earlier. Therefore it was a surprise when a woman we had never seen came into the class the next day, carrying a purple purse, a checkerboard lunchbox, and a few books. She put the books on one side of Mr. Hibler's desk and the lunchbox on the other, next to the Voice of Music phonograph. Three of us in the back of the room were playing with Heever, the chameleon that lived in the terrarium and on one of the plastic drapes, when she walked in. 6

She clapped her hands at us. "Little boys," she said, "why are you bent over together like that?" She didn't wait for us to answer. "Are you tormenting an animal? Put it back. Please sit down at your desks. I want no cabals this time of the day." We just stared at her. "Boys," she repeated, "I asked you to sit down." 7

I put the chameleon in his terrarium and felt my way to my desk, never taking my eyes off the woman. With white and green chalk, she had started to draw a tree on the left side of the blackboard. She didn't look usual. Furthermore, her tree was outsized, dispropor-tionate, for some reason. 8

"This room needs a tree," she said, with one line drawing the suggestion of a leaf. "A large, leafy, shady, deciduous . . . oak." 9

ADDITIONAL QUESTIONS FOR RESPONDING TO READING

1. How do the children react to Miss Ferenczi initially? How do their reactions change?
2. Miss Ferenczi uses the lecture method of teaching, a method often disparaged by modern education specialists. Is her use of this strategy successful? Why or why not?
3. Children are highly impressionable. Does Miss Ferenczi take advantage of the children's naiveté? Does she contribute to their devel-opment or exploit their innocence? Explain.
4. Which of the "facts" Miss Ferenczi tells her students are true? Which are incorrect? Which are partially accurate?

Her fine, light hair had been done up in what I would learn years 10 later was called a chignon, and she wore gold-rimmed glasses whose lenses seemed to have the faintest blue tint. Harold Knardahl, who sat across from me, whispered "Mars," and I nodded slowly, savoring the imminent weirdness of the day. The substitute drew another branch with an extravagant arm gesture, then turned around and said, "Good morning. I don't believe I said good morning to all you yet."

Facing us, she was no special age—an adult is an adult—but her 11 face had two prominent lines, descending vertically from the sides of her mouth to her chin. I knew where I had seen those lines before: *Pinocchio.* They were marionette lines. "You may stare at me," she said to us, as a few more kids from the last bus came into the room, their eyes fixed on her, "for a few more seconds, until the bell rings. Then I will permit no more staring. Looking I will permit. Staring, no. It is impolite to stare, and a sign of bad breeding. You cannot make a social effort while staring."

Harold Knardahl did not glance at me, or nudge, but I heard him 12 whisper "Mars" again, trying to get more mileage out of his single joke with the kids who had just come in.

When everyone was seated, the substitute teacher finished her 13 tree, put down her chalk fastidiously on the phonograph, brushed her hands, and faced us. "Good morning," she said. "I am Miss Ferenczi, your teacher for the day. I am fairly new to your community, and I don't believe any of you know me. I will therefore start by telling you a story about myself."

While we settled back, she launched into her tale. She said her 14 grandfather had been a Hungarian prince; her mother had been born in some place called Flanders, had been a pianist, and had played concerts for people Miss Ferenczi referred to as "crowned heads." She gave us a knowing look. "Grieg," she said, "the Norwegian master, wrote a concerto for piano that was," she paused, "my mother's triumph at her debut concert in London." Her eyes searched the ceiling. Our eyes followed. Nothing up there but ceiling tile. "For reasons that I shall not go into, my family's fortunes took us to Detroit, then north to dreadful Saginaw, and now here I am in Five Oaks, as your substitute teacher, for today, Thursday, October the eleventh. I believe it will be a good day: All the forecasts coincide. We shall start with your reading lesson. Take out your reading book. I believe it is called *Broad Horizons,* or something along those lines."

Jeannie Vermeesch raised her hand. Miss Ferenczi nodded at her. 15 "Mr. Hibler always starts the day with the Pledge of Allegiance," Jeannie whined.

"Oh, does he? In that case," Miss Ferenczi said, "you must know 16
it *very* well by now, and we certainly need not spend our time on it.
No, no allegiance pledging on the premises today, by my reckoning.
Not with so much sunlight coming into the room. A pledge does not
suit my mood." She glanced at her watch. "Time *is* flying. Take out
Broad Horizons."

She disappointed us by giving us an ordinary lesson, complete 17
with vocabulary word drills, comprehension questions, and recitation. She didn't seem to care for the material, however. She sighed
every few minutes and rubbed her glasses with a frilly perfumed
handkerchief that she withdrew, magician style, from her left sleeve.

After reading we moved on to arithmetic. It was my favorite time 18
of the morning, when the lazy autumn sunlight dazzled its way
through ribbons of clouds past the windows on the east side of the
classroom, and crept across the linoleum floor. On the playground
the first group of children, the kindergartners, were running on the
quack grass just beyond the monkey bars. We were doing multipli-
cation tables. Miss Ferenczi had made John Wazny stand up at his
desk in the front row. He was supposed to go through the tables of
six. From where I was sitting, I could smell the Vitalis soaked into
John's plastered hair. He was doing fine until he came to six times
eleven and six times twelve. "Six times eleven," he said, "is sixty-
eight. Six times twelve is . . ." He put his fingers to his head, quickly
and secretly sniffed his fingertips, and said, "seventy-two." Then he
sat down.

"Fine," Miss Ferenczi said. "Well now. That was very good." 19

"Miss Ferenczi!" One of the Eddy twins was waving her hand 20
desperately in the air. "Miss Ferenczi! Miss Ferenczi!"

"Yes?" 21

"John said that six times eleven is sixty-eight and you said he 22
was right!"

"*Did* I?" She gazed at the glass with a jolly look breaking across 23
her marionette's face. "Did I say that? Well, what *is* six times eleven?"

"It's sixty-six!" 24

She nodded. "Yes. So it is. But, and I know some people will not 25
entirely agree with me, at some times it is sixty-eight."

"When? When is it sixty-eight?" 26

We were all waiting. 27

"In higher mathematics, which you children do not yet under- 28
stand, six times eleven can be considered to be sixty-eight." She
laughed through her nose. "In higher mathematics numbers are . . .
more fluid. The only thing a number does is contain a certain amount

COLLABORATIVE ACTIVITY

Ask students, working in groups, to contrast
Miss Ferenczi's brand of education with Mr. Hibler's. Which one is more effective? Why? Ask
students whether Baxter is setting up a false
duality. That is, should education consist of elements from both brands of education?

of something. Think of water. A cup is not the only way to measure a certain amount of water, is it?" We were staring, shaking our heads. "You could use saucepans or thimbles. In either case, the water *would be the same*. Perhaps," she started again, "it would be better for you to think that six times eleven is sixty-eight only when I am in the room."

"Why is it sixty-eight," Mark Poole asked, "when you're in the 29 room?"

"Because it's more interesting that way," she said, smiling very 30 rapidly behind her blue-tinted glasses. "Besides, I'm your substitute teacher, am I not?" We all nodded. "Well, then, think of six times eleven equals sixty-eight as a substitute fact."

"A substitute fact?" 31

"Yes." Then she looked at us carefully. "Do you think," she 32 asked, "that anyone is going to be hurt by a substitute fact?"

We looked back at her. 33

"Will the plants on the windowsill be hurt?" We glanced at them. 34 There were sensitive plants thriving in a green plastic tray, and several wilted ferns in small clay pots. "Your dogs and cats, or your moms and dads?" She waited. "So," she concluded, "what's the problem?"

"But it's wrong," Janice Weber said, "isn't it?" 35

"What's your name, young lady?" 36

"Janice Weber." 37

"And you think it's wrong, Janice?" 38

"I was just asking." 39

"Well, all right. You were just asking. I think we've spent enough 40 time on this matter by now, don't you, class? You are free to think what you like. When your teacher, Mr. Hibler, returns, six times eleven will be sixty-six again, you can rest assured. And it will be that for the rest of your lives in Five Oaks. Too bad, eh?" She raised her eyebrows and glinted herself at us. "But for now, it wasn't. So much for that. Let us go to your assigned problems for today, as painstakingly outlined, I see, in Mr. Hibler's lesson plan. Take out a sheet of paper and write your names in the upper left-hand corner."

For the next half hour we did the rest of our arithmetic problems. 41 We handed them in and went on to spelling, my worst subject. Spelling always came before lunch. We were taking spelling dictation and looking at the clock. "Thorough," Miss Ferenczi said. "Boundary." She walked in the aisles between the desks, holding the spelling book open and looking down at our papers. "Balcony." I clutched my pencil. Somehow, the way she said those words, they seemed foreign, Hungarian, mis-voweled and mis-consonanted. I stared down at what I had spelled. *Balconie*. I turned my pencil upside down and erased my mistake. *Balconey.* That looked better, but still incorrect. I cursed the world of spelling and tried erasing it again and saw the paper beginning to wear away. *Balkony.* Suddenly I felt a hand on my shoulder.

"I don't like that word either," Miss Ferenczi whispered, bent 42 over, her mouth near my ear. "It's ugly. My feeling is, if you don't like a word, you don't have to use it." She straightened up, leaving behind a slight odor of Clorets.

At lunchtime we went out to get our trays of sloppy joes, peaches 43 in heavy syrup, coconut cookies, and milk, and brought them back to the classroom, where Miss Ferenczi was sitting at the desk, eating a brown sticky thing she had unwrapped from tightly rubber-banded wax paper. "Miss Ferenczi," I said, raising my hand. "You don't have to eat with us. You can eat with the other teachers. There's a teachers' lounge," I ended up, "next to the principal's office."

"No, thank you," she said. "I prefer it here." 44

"We've got a room monitor," I said. "Mrs. Eddy." I pointed to 45 where Mrs. Eddy, Joyce and Judy's mother, sat silently at the back of the room, doing her knitting.

"That's fine," Miss Ferenczi said. "But I shall continue to eat here, 46 with you children. I prefer it," she repeated.

"How come?" Wayne Razmer asked without raising his hand. 46

"I talked with the other teachers before class this morning," Miss 48 Ferenczi said, biting into her brown food. "There was a great rattling of the words for the fewness of ideas. I didn't care for their brand of hilarity. I don't like ditto machine jokes."

"Oh," Wayne said. 49

"What's that you're eating?" Maxine Sylvester asked, twitching 50 her nose. "Is it food?"

"It most certainly *is* food. It's a stuffed fig. I had to drive almost 51 down to Detroit to get it. I also bought some smoked sturgeon. And this," she said, lifting some green leaves out of her lunchbox, "is raw spinach, cleaned this morning before I came out here to the Garfield-Murry school."

"Why're you eating raw spinach?" Maxine asked. 52

"It's good for you," Miss Ferenczi said. "More stimulating than 53 soda pop or smelling salts." I bit into my sloppy joe and stared blankly out the window. An almost invisible moon was faintly silvered in the daytime autumn sky. "As far as food is concerned," Miss Ferenczi was saying, "you have to shuffle the pack. Mix it up. Too many people eat . . . well, never mind."

"Miss Ferenczi," Carol Peterson said, "what are we going to do 54 this afternoon?"

"Well," she said, looking down at Mr. Hibler's lesson plan, "I 55 see that your teacher, Mr. Hibler, has you scheduled for a unit on the Egyptians." Carol groaned. "Yessss," Miss Ferenczi continued, "that is what we will do: the Egyptians. A remarkable people. Almost as remarkable as the Americans. But not quite." She lowered her head, did her quick smile, and went back to eating her spinach.

After noon recess we came back into the classroom and saw that 56 Miss Ferenczi had drawn a pyramid on the blackboard, close to her oak tree. Some of us who had been playing baseball were messing around in the back of the room, dropping the bats and the gloves into the playground box, and I think that Ray Schontzeler had just slugged me when I heard Miss Ferenczi's high-pitched voice quavering with emotion. "Boys," she said, "come to order right this minute and take your seats. I do not wish to waste a minute of class time. Take out your geography books." We trudged to our desks and, still sweating, pulled out *Distant Lands and Their People*. "Turn to page forty-two." She waited for thirty seconds, then looked over at Kelly Munger. "Young man," she said, "why are you still fossicking in your desk?"

Kelly looked as if his foot had been stepped on. "Why am I what?" 57

"Why are you . . . burrowing in your desk like that?" 58

"I'm lookin' for the book, Miss Ferenczi." 59

Bobby Kryzanowicz, the faultless brown-noser who sat in the first 60 row by choice, softly said, "His name is Kelly Munger. He can't ever find his stuff. He always does that."

"I don't care what his name is, especially after lunch," Miss Ferenczi said. *"Where is your book?"* 61

"I just found it." Kelly was peering into his desk and with both 62 hands pulled at the book, shoveling along in front of it several pencils and crayons, which fell into his lap and then to the floor.

"I hate a mess," Miss Ferenczi said. "I hate a mess in a desk or 63 a mind. It's . . . unsanitary. You wouldn't want your house at home to look like your desk at school, now, would you?" She didn't wait for an answer. "I should think not. A house at home should be as neat as human hands can make it. What were we talking about? Egypt. Page forty-two. I note from Mr. Hibler's lesson plan that you have been discussing the modes of Egyptian irrigation. Interesting, in my view, but not so interesting as what we are about to cover. The pyramids and Egyptian slave labor. A plus on one side, a minus on the other." We had our books open to page forty-two, where there was a picture of a pyramid, but Miss Ferenczi wasn't looking at the book. Instead, she was staring at some object just outside the window.

"Pyramids," Miss Ferenczi said, still looking past the window. 64 "I want you to think about the pyramids. And what was inside. The bodies of the pharaohs, of course, and their attendant treasures. Scrolls. Perhaps," Miss Ferenczi said, with something gleeful but unsmiling in her face, "these scrolls were novels for the pharaohs, helping them to pass the time in their long voyage through the centuries. But then, I am joking." I was looking at the lines on Miss Ferenczi's face. "Pyramids," Miss Ferenczi went on, "were the repositories of special cosmic powers. The nature of a pyramid is to guide cosmic energy forces into a concentrated point. The Egyptians knew that; we have generally forgotten it. Did you know," she asked, walking to the side of the room so that she was standing by the coat closet, "that George Washington had Egyptian blood, from his grandmother? Certain features of the Constitution of the United States are notable for their Egyptian ideas."

Without glancing down at the book, she began to talk about the 65 movement of souls in Egyptian religion. She said that when people die, their souls return to Earth in the form of carpenter ants or walnut trees, depending on how they behaved—"well or ill"—in life. She said that the Egyptians believed that people act the way they do because of magnetism produced by tidal forces in the solar system, forces produced by the sun and by its "planetary ally," Jupiter. Jupiter, she said, was a planet, as we had been told, but had "certain properties of stars." She was speaking very fast. She said that the Egyptians were great explorers and conquerors. She said that the greatest of all the conquerors, Genghis Khan, had had forty horses and forty young women killed on the site of his grave. We listened. No one tried to stop her. "I myself have been in Egypt," she said, "and have witnessed much dust and many brutalities." She said that an old man in Egypt who worked for a circus had personally shown her an animal in a cage, a monster, half bird and half lion. She said that this monster was called a gryphon and that she had heard about them but never seen them until she traveled to the outskirts of Cairo. She said that Egyptian astronomers had discovered the planet Saturn, but had not seen its rings. She said that the Egyptians were the first to discover that dogs, when they are ill, will not drink from rivers, but wait for rain, and hold their jaws open to catch it.

"She lies." 66

We were on the school bus home. I was sitting next to Carl White- 67 side, who had bad breath and a huge collection of marbles. We were arguing. Carl thought she was lying. I said she wasn't, probably.

"I didn't believe that stuff about the bird," Carl said, "and what 68 she told us about the pyramids? I didn't believe that either. She didn't know what she was talking about."

"Oh yeah?" I had liked her. She was strange. I thought I could 69 nail him. "If she was lying," I said, "what'd she say that was a lie?"

"Six times eleven isn't sixty-eight. It isn't ever. It's sixty-six, I 70 know for a fact."

"She said so. She admitted it. What else did she lie about?" 71

"I don't know," he said. "Stuff." 72

"What stuff?" 73

"Well." He swung his legs back and forth. "You ever see an 74 animal that was half lion and half bird?" He crossed his arms. "It sounded real fakey to me."

"It could happen," I said. I had to improvise, to outrage him. "I 75 read in this newspaper my mom bought in the IGA about this scientist, this mad scientist in the Swiss Alps, and he's been putting genes and chromosomes and stuff together in test tubes, and he combined a human being and a hamster." I waited, for effect. "It's called a humster."

"You never." Carl was staring at me, his mouth open, his terrible 76 bad breath making its way toward me. "What newspaper was it?"

"The *National Enquirer*," I said, "that they sell next to the cash 77 registers." When I saw his look of recognition, I knew I had bested him. "And this mad scientist," I said, "his name was, um, Dr. Frankenbush." I realized belatedly that this name was a mistake and waited for Carl to notice its resemblance to the name of the other famous mad master to permutations, but he only sat there.

"A man and a hamster?" He was staring at me, squinting, his 78 mouth opening in distaste. "Jeez. What'd it look like?"

When the bus reached my stop, I took off down our dirt road 79 and ran up through the back yard, kicking the tire swing for good luck. I dropped my books on the back steps so I could hug and kiss our dog, Mr. Selby. Then I hurried inside. I could smell Brussels sprouts cooking, my unfavorite vegetable. My mother was washing other vegetables in the kitchen sink, and my baby brother was hollering in his yellow playpen on the kitchen floor.

"Hi, Mom," I said, hopping around the playpen to kiss her, 80 "Guess what?"

"I have no idea." 81

"We had this substitute today, Miss Ferenczi, and I'd never seen 82 her before, and she had all these stories and ideas and stuff."

"Well. That's good." My mother looked out the window behind 83 the sink, her eyes on the pine woods west of our house. Her face and hairstyle always reminded other people of Betty Crocker, whose picture was framed inside a gigantic spoon on the side of the Bisquick box; to me, though, my mother's face just looked white. "Listen, Tommy," she said, "go upstairs and pick your clothes off the bathroom floor, then go outside to the shed and put the shovel and ax away that your father left outside this morning."

"She said that six times eleven was sometimes sixty-eight!" I said. 84 "And she said she once saw a monster that was half lion and half bird." I waited. "In Egypt, she said."

"Did you hear me?" my mother asked, raising her arm to wipe 85 her forehead with the back of her hand. "You have chores to do."

"I know," I said. "I was just telling you about the substitute." 86

"It's very interesting," my mother said, quickly glancing down 87 at me, "and we can talk about it later when your father gets home. But right now you have some work to do."

"Okay, Mom." I took a cookie out of the jar on the counter and 88 was about to go outside when I had a thought. I ran into the living room, pulled out a dictionary next to the TV stand, and opened it to the G's. *Gryphon:* "variant of griffin." *Griffin:* "a fabulous beast with the head and wings of an eagle and the body of a lion." Fabulous was right. I shouted with triumph and ran outside to put my father's tools back in their place.

Miss Ferenczi was back the next day, slightly altered. She had 89 pulled her hair down and twisted it into pigtails, with red rubber bands holding them tight one inch from the ends. She was wearing a green blouse and pink scarf, making her difficult to look at for a full class day. This time there was no pretense of doing a reading lesson or moving on to arithmetic. As soon as the bell rang, she simply began to talk.

She talked for forty minutes straight. There seemed to be less 90 connection between her ideas, but the ideas themselves were, as the dictionary would say, fabulous. She said she had heard of a huge jewel, in what she called the Antipodes, that was so brilliant that when the light shone into it at a certain angle it would blind whoever was looking at its center. She said that the biggest diamond in the world was cursed and had killed everyone who owned it, and that by a trick of fate it was called the Hope diamond. Diamonds are magic, she said, and this is why women wear them on their fingers, as a sign of the magic of womanhood. Men have strength, Miss Ferenczi said, but no true magic. That is why men fall in love with women but women do not fall in love with men; they just love being loved. George Washington had died because of a mistake he made about a diamond. Washington was not the first *true* President, but she did not say who was. In some places in the world, she said, men and women still live in the trees and eat monkeys for breakfast. Their doctors are magicians. At the bottom of the sea are creatures thin as pancakes which have never been studied by scientists because when you take them up to the air, the fish explode.

There was not a sound in the classroom, except for Miss Ferenczi's voice, and Donna DeShano's coughing. No one even went to the bathroom. 91

Beethoven, she said, had not been deaf; it was a trick to make himself famous, and it worked. As she talked, Miss Ferenczi's pigtails swung back and forth. There are trees in the world, she said, that eat meat: their leaves are sticky and close up on bugs like hands. She lifted her hands and brought them together, palm to palm. Venus, which most people think is the next closest planet to the sun, is not always closer, and, besides, it is the planet of greatest mystery because of its thick cloud cover. "I know what lies underneath those clouds," Miss Ferenczi said, and waited. After the silence, she said, "Angels. Angels live under those clouds." She said that angels were not invisible to everyone and were in fact smarter than most people. They did not dress in robes as was often claimed but instead wore formal evening clothes, as if they were about to attend a concert. Often angels *do* attend concerts and sit in the aisles where, she said, most people pay no attention to them. She said the most terrible angel had the shape of the Sphinx. "There is no running away from that one," she said. She said that unquenchable fires burn just under the surface of the earth in Ohio, and that the baby Mozart fainted dead away in his cradle when he first heard the sound of a trumpet. She said that someone named Narzim al Harrardim was the greatest writer who ever lived. She said that planets control behavior, and anyone conceived during a solar eclipse would be born with webbed feet. 92

"I know you children like to hear these things," she said, "these secrets, and that is why I am telling you all this." We nodded. It was better than doing comprehension questions for the readings in *Broad Horizons*. 93

"I will tell you one more story," she said, "and then we will have to do arithmetic." She leaned over, and her voice grew soft. "There is no death," she said. "You must never be afraid. Never. That which is, cannot die. It will change into different earthly and unearthly elements, but I know this as sure as I stand here in front of you, and I swear it: you must not be afraid. I have seen this truth with these eyes. I know it because in a dream God kissed me. Here." And she 94 pointed with her right index finger to the side of her head, below the mouth, where the vertical lines were carved into her skin.

Absent-mindedly we all did our arithmetic problems. At recess 95 the class was out on the playground, but no one was playing. We were all standing in small groups, talking about Miss Ferenczi. We didn't know if she was crazy, or what. I looked out beyond the playground, at the rusted cars piled in a small heap behind a clump of sumac, and I wanted to see shapes there, approaching me.

96

On the way home, Carl sat next to me again. He didn't say much, and I didn't either. At last he turned to me. "You know what she said about the leaves that close up on bugs?"

"Huh?" 97

"The leaves," Carl insisted. "The meat-eating plants. I know it's 98 true. I saw it on television. The leaves have this icky glue that the plants have got smeared all over them and the insects can't get off 'cause they're stuck. I saw it." He seemed demoralized. "She's tellin' the truth."

"Yeah." 99

"You think she's seen all those angels?" 100

I shrugged. 101

"I don't think she has," Carl informed me. "I think she made 102 that part up."

"There's a tree," I suddenly said. I was looking out the window 103 at the farms along County Road H. I knew every barn, every broken windmill, every fence, every anhydrous ammonia tank, by heart. "There's a tree that's . . . that I've seen . . ."

"Don't you try to do it," Carl said. "You'll just sound like a jerk." 104

I kissed my mother. She was standing in front of the stove. "How 105 was your day?" she asked.

"Fine." 106

"Did you have Miss Ferenczi again?" 107

"Yeah." 108

"Well?" 109

"She was fine. Mom," I asked, "can I go to my room?" 110

"No," she said, "not until you've gone out to the vegetable garden 111 and picked me a few tomatoes." She glanced at the sky. "I think it's going to rain. Skedaddle and do it now. Then you come back inside and watch your brother for a few minutes while I go upstairs. I need to clean up before dinner." She looked down at me. "You're looking a little pale, Tommy." She touched the back of her hand to my forehead and I felt her diamond ring against my skin. "Do you feel all right?"

"I'm fine," I said, and went out to pick the tomatoes. 112

Coughing mutedly, Mr. Hibler was back the next day, slipping 113 lozenges into his mouth when his back was turned at forty-five minute intervals and asking us how much of the prepared lesson plan Miss Ferenczi had followed. Edith Atwater took the responsibility for the class of explaining to Mr. Hibler that the substitute hadn't always done exactly what he would have done, but we had worked hard even though she talked a lot. About what? he asked. All kinds of things, Edith said. I sort of forgot. To our relief, Mr. Hibler seemed not at all interested in what Miss Ferenczi had said to fill the day. He probably thought it was woman's talk; unserious and not suited for school. It was enough that he had a pile of arithmetic problems from us to correct.

For the next month, the sumac turned a distracting red in the 114 field, and the sun traveled toward the southern sky, so that its rays reached Mr. Hibler's Halloween display on the bulletin board in the back of the room, fading the scarecrow with a pumpkin head from orange to tan. Every three days I measured how much farther the sun had moved toward the southern horizon by making small marks with my black Crayola on the north wall, ant-sized marks only I knew were there, inching west.

And then in early December, four days after the first permanent 115 snowfall, she appeared again in our classroom. The minute she came in the door, I felt my heart begin to pound. Once again, she was different: this time, her hair hung straight down and seemed hardly to have been combed. She hadn't brought her lunchbox with her, but she was carrying what seemed to be a small box. She greeted all of us and talked about the weather. Donna DeShano had to remind her to take her overcoat off.

When the bell to start the day finally rang, Miss Ferenczi looked 116 out at all of us and said, "Children, I have enjoyed your company in the past, and today I am going to reward you." She held up the small box. "Do you know what this is?" She waited. "Of course you don't. It is a tarot pack."

Edith Atwater raised her hand. "What's a tarot pack, Miss Fer- 117 enczi?"

"It is used to tell fortunes," she said. "And that is what I shall do 118 this morning. I shall tell your fortunes, as I have been taught to do."

"What's fortune?" Bobby Kryzanowicz asked. 119

"The future, young man. I shall tell you what your future will 120 be. I can't do your whole future, of course. I shall have to limit myself to the five-card system, the wands, cups, swords, pentacles, and the higher arcanes. Now who wants to be first?''

There was a long silence. Then Carol Peterson raised her hand.   121

''All right,'' Miss Ferenczi said. She divided the pack into five   122 smaller packs and walked back to Carol's desk, in front of mine. ''Pick one card from each of these packs,'' she said. I saw that Carol had a four of cups, a six of swords, but I couldn't see the other cards. Miss Ferenczi studied the cards on Carol's desk for a minute. ''Not bad,'' she said. ''I do not see much higher education. Probably an early marriage. Many children. There's something bleak and dreary here, but I can't tell what. Perhaps just the tasks of a housewife life. I think you'll do very well, for the most part.'' She smiled at Carol, a smile with a certain lack of interest. ''Who wants to be next?''

Carl Whiteside raised his hand slowly.   123

''Yes,'' Miss Ferenczi said, ''let's do a boy.'' She walked over to   124 where Carl sat. After he picked his five cards, she gazed at them for a long time. ''Travel,'' she said. ''Much distant travel. You might go into the Army. Not too much romantic interest here. A late marriage, if at all. Squabbles. But the Sun is in your major arcana, here, yes, that's a very good card.'' She giggled. ''Maybe a good life.''

Next I raised my hand, and she told me my future. She did the   125 same with Bobby Kryzanowicz. Kelly Munger, Edith Atwater, and Kim Foor. Then she came to Wayne Razmer. He picked his five cards, and I could see that the Death card was one of them.

''What's your name?'' Miss Ferenczi asked.   126

''Wayne.''   127

''Well, Wayne,'' she said, you will undergo a *great* metamor-   128 phosis, the greatest, before you become an adult. Your earthly element will leap away, into thin air, you sweet boy. This card, this nine of swords here, tells of suffering and desolation. And this ten of wands, well, that's certainly a heavy load.''

''What about this one?'' Wayne pointed to the Death card.   129

''That one? That one means you will die soon, my dear.'' She   130 gathered up the cards. We were all looking at Wayne. ''But do not fear,'' she said. ''It's not really death, so much as change.'' She put the cards on Mr. Hibler's desk. ''And now, let's do some arithmetic.''

At lunchtime Wayne went to Mr. Faegre, the principal, and told   131 him what Miss Ferenczi had done. During the noon recess, we saw Miss Ferenczi drive out of the parking lot in her green Rambler. I stood under the slide, listening to the other kids coasting down and landing in the little depressive bowl at the bottom. I was kicking stones and tugging at my hair right up to the moment when I saw Wayne come out to the playground. He smiled, the dead fool, and with the fingers of his right hand he was showing everyone how he had told on Miss Ferenczi.

I made my way toward Wayne, pushing myself past two girls 132 from another class. He was watching me with his little pinhead eyes.

"You told," I shouted at him. "She was just kidding." 133

"She shouldn't have," he shouted back. "We were supposed to 134 be doing arithmetic."

"She just scared you," I said. "You're a chicken. You're a chicken, 135 Wayne. You are. Scared of a little card," I singsonged.

Wayne fell at me, his two fists hammering down on my nose. I 136 gave him a good one in the stomach and then I tried for his head. Aiming my fist, I saw that he was crying. I slugged him.

"She was right," I yelled. "She was always right! She told the 137 truth!" Other kids were whooping. "You were just scared, that's all!"

And then large hands pulled at us, and it was my turn to speak 138 to Mr. Faegre.

In the afternoon Miss Ferenczi was gone, and my nose was stuffed 139 with cotton clotted with blood, and my lip had swelled, and our class had been combined with Mrs. Mantei's sixth-grade class for a crowded afternoon science unit on insect life in ditches and swamps. I knew where Mrs. Mantei lived: she had a new house trailer just down the road from us, at the Clearwater Park. She was no mystery. Somehow she and Mr. Bodine, the other fourth-grade teacher, had managed to fit forty-five desks into the room. Kelly Munger asked if Miss Ferenczi had been arrested, and Mrs. Mantei said no, of course not. All that afternoon, until the buses came to pick us up, we learned about field crickets and two-striped grasshoppers, water bugs, cicadas, mosquitoes, flies, and moths. We learned about insects' hard outer shell, the exoskeleton, and the usual parts of the mouth, including the labrum, mandible, maxilla, and glossa. We learned about compound eyes and the four-stage metamorphosis from egg to larva to pupa to adult. We learned something, but not much, about mating. Mrs. Mantei drew, very skillfully, the internal anatomy of the grasshopper on the blackboard. We learned about the dance of the honeybee, directing other bees in the hive to pollen. We found out about which insects were pests to man, and which were not. On lined white pieces of paper we made lists of insects we might actually see, then a list of insects too small to be clearly visible, such as fleas; Mrs. Mantei said that our assignment would be to memorize these lists for the next day, when Mr. Hibler would certainly return and test us on our knowledge.

WRITING SUGGESTIONS

1. Write a sequel to "Gryphon." For example, you could show the students rebelling against Mr. Hibler and petitioning for the return of Miss Ferenczi.
2. Write an essay about an unusual teacher who had a great influence on your life.

RESPONDING TO READING

1. What connotations does *substitute teacher* have to you? In what ways is Miss Ferenczi like and unlike your idea of a substitute?   **2.** As the story goes on, Miss Ferenczi's remarks become increasingly unorthodox. Is she simply eccentric, or even unstable, or do you think that she has a purpose in mind?   **3.** Have you ever had a teacher who undercut and challenged your ideas? How did you react to this challenge? Do you think teachers like Miss Ferenczi are necessary or dangerous to education?

Baca Grande

JIM SAGEL

Jim Sagel (1947–   ) is a teacher, poet, fiction writer, and journalist who writes about the people of the Española Valley in northern New Mexico. Sagel is best known for his book of stories *Tunomas Honey* (*Only You, Honey*) (1981). Two of his other books are *Foreplay and French Fries: Poems* (1981) and *Sabelotodo Entiendelonada and Other Stories* (1988). In "Baca Grande," Sagel examines the confrontation between old and new values.

Una vaca se topó con un ratón
y le dice: "Tú—¿tan chiquito
y con bigote?" Y le responde
el ratón: "Y tú tan grandota—
¿y sin brassiere?"[1]

It was nearly a miracle
James Baca remembered anyone at all
from the old hometown gang
having been two years at Yale
   no less   5
and halfway through law school
at the University of California at Irvine

They hardly recognized him either
in his three-piece grey business suit

---

[1] A cow met a rat and said, "You—so small and with a moustache?" The rat replied: "And you so big and without a bra?"

TEACHING STRATEGY

Ask students how essential it is that Baca be Hispanic. Could the same poem have been written about a person from another ethnic group?

COLLABORATIVE ACTIVITY

In groups examine the specific words used to describe Baca, his future, and his "rise." Do these words have positive or negative connotations?

and surfer-swirl haircut   10
with just the menacing hint
of a tightly trimmed Zapata[2] moustache
    for cultural balance
and relevance

He had come to deliver the keynote address   15
to the graduating class of 80
at his old alma mater
and show off his well-trained lips
which laboriously parted
    each Kennedyish "R"   20
and drilled the first person pronoun
through the microphone
like an oil bit
with the slick, elegantly honed phrases
that slid so smoothly   25
off his meticulously bleached
    tongue

He talked Big Bucks
with astronautish fervor and if he
    the former bootstrapless James A. Baca   30
could dazzle the ass
off the universe
then even you
    yes you

Joey Martínez toying with your yellow   35
    tassle
and staring dumbly into space
could emulate Mr. Baca someday
    possibly
well   40
there was of course
such a thing
as being an outrageously successful
gas station attendant too
    let us never forget   45

---

[2]Emiliano Zapata (1879–1919), a Mexican revolutionary who attempted to seize land by force and redistribute it to the poor. [Eds.]

it doesn't really matter what you do
so long as you excel
   James said
never believing a word
of it   50
for he had already risen
   as high as they go

Wasn't nobody else
from this deprived environment
who'd ever jumped   55
   straight out of college
into the Governor's office
and maybe one day
he'd sit in that big chair
   himself   60
and when he did
he'd forget this damned town
and all the petty little people
in it
once and for all   65

That much he promised himself

RESPONDING TO READING

1. In what ways has James Baca changed since he was at his old high school? What is the speaker's definition of being "educated"? What is yours?   **2.** What message does Baca bring back to his neighborhood? How does the poem's speaker react to it? Does the poem's speaker imply that Baca should not have gone to Yale? Do you agree?   **3.** In what ways have you changed since you began college? Are these changes positive or negative? Do you think you could have started college and remained the same?

When I Heard the Learn'd Astronomer

WALT WHITMAN

Walt Whitman (1819–1892) was an eccentric and bold character who wrote radical poetry about sexuality, technology, and nature to unsettle "all the settled laws." He first published his best-known work, *Leaves of Grass*, in 1855 with no author's name on the title page. Whitman was also a journalist who reported on the Civil War

ADDITIONAL QUESTIONS FOR RESPONDING TO READING

1. What effect does the repetition of "When I" in the first four lines produce?
2. Why is the night air "mystical"?
3. In what way is the silence of the stars "perfect"?

TEACHING STRATEGY

Compare this poem to Twain's "Reading the River" (page 98). In many ways both Twain and Whitman express the same, or at least similar, sentiments toward education. Ask students if they think one writer is more hostile to education than the other. Then ask them to explain the differences between their attitudes.

COLLABORATIVE ACTIVITIES

1. Assign groups to look for examples of alliteration, varying line lengths, lists, and repetition. What effect is produced by each strategy?
2. Have each group of students summarize each segment of the poem in a single sentence. Compare the contrasting ideas as they are expressed in prose and in the poem.

WRITING SUGGESTION

Write an essay in which you describe how education changed your view of something. Be specific when describing your original and your changed viewpoints.

ANSWERS TO RESPONDING TO READING

1. The first segment expresses the scientific approach; the second, the romantic, imaginative approach.
2. The speaker devalues formal education and emphasizes the possibilities of spontaneous, individual responses to life.
3. Answers will vary.

and an essayist who commented on American society and democracy. He wrote about and for working-class Americans, but his work appealed mostly to intellectuals. In the poem "When I Heard the Learn'd Astronomer," Whitman unites two of his favorite and seemingly incompatible themes: science and nature.

When I heard the learn'd astronomer,
When the proofs, the figures, were ranged in columns before me,
When I was shown the charts and diagrams, to add, divide, and measure them,
When I sitting heard the astronomer where he lectured with much applause in the lecture-room,
How soon unaccountable I became tired and sick,   5
Till rising and gliding out I wander'd off by myself,
In the mystical moist night-air, and from time to time,
Look'd up in perfect silence at the stars.

RESPONDING TO READING

1. This poem is divided into two 4-line segments. What ideas are expressed in each segment? How are the ideas opposed?   **2.** What attitudes toward education are inherent in the poem? Do you agree with the speaker's sentiments?   **3.** Can you think of any courses you have taken or books you have read that have changed the way you look at the world? Were these changes positive or negative? Explain.

WRITING: THINKING AND LEARNING

1. In "My Built-in Doubter" Isaac Asimov demonstrates how skepticism is necessary for a scientist—and, for that matter, for any thinker. Write an essay in which you discuss a time when you should have been skeptical but were not.

2. Recent books, such as E. D. Hirsch's *Cultural Literacy* (1987) and Allan Bloom's *The Closing of the American Mind* (1987), have stressed the need for a shared body of knowledge. What information do you believe should constitute this body of knowledge? Why?

3. One question that is never resolved in "Gryphon" by Charles Baxter is whether Miss Ferenczi is a good or bad teacher. Imagine you are the principal of the school in which Miss Ferenczi taught. Write an evaluation of her performance.

4. Both Maya Angelou in "Graduation" and Shelby Steele in "The Recoloring of Campus Life" believe race affects the educational experience. In what ways do your high school and college experiences support or contradict their views?

5. Write an essay in which you discuss the steps that should be taken to make a college education a more positive and meaningful experience.

6. Write an essay analyzing your own high school education. In what ways was it strong? In what ways was it weak? What suggestions can you offer to improve it?

7. In "Thinking as a Hobby" William Golding describes three types of thinkers. Write an essay in which you explain what kind of thinker you are. Use examples from your own experience.

8. In "The Recoloring of Campus Life" Shelby Steele says, "On our campuses . . . all that remains unresolved between blacks and whites, all the old wounds and shame that have never been addressed, present themselves for attention—and present our youth with pressures they cannot always handle" (paragraph 7). Write an essay in which you discuss the racial situation on your campus. Do you, like Steele, think it presents students "with pressures they cannot always handle"?

9. Write an essay in which you consider which elements of formal and informal education are most valuable. Base your essay on your own experiences as well as on your reading in this chapter.

3

THE POWER OF WORDS

CONFRONTING THE ISSUES

Many students do not understand that words have the power to convey attitudes and value judgments as well as meanings. For example, describing an executive as *pushy* implies that he or she is inappropriately aggressive. Describing that same executive as *assertive* or *forceful* implies that his or her personality traits are praiseworthy.

In order to dispel the mistaken impression that words with similar meanings are interchangeable, do the following in-class exercise. Duplicate a page or two from either *Webster's* or *Roget's Thesaurus* and ask students to consider the synonyms that are listed. For example, the following synonyms are listed in one thesaurus under the entry *crisis: juncture, contingency, crossroads, emergency, exigency, pass, pinch, strait, turning point,* and *zero hour.* After some discussion it should become clear that these words all have differences in denotation and connotation. Adding each of them to the following sentence should further illustrate this point: *Declining enrollment and decreasing tuition revenue have caused a financial _____ in many colleges.* Clearly, most of these "synonyms" do not convey exactly the same meaning as *crisis.*

You can go on to point out that writers are especially aware of the subtle differences that exist between words. The poet Louis Zukofsky called language the "finer mathematics," and writer Dorothy Parker called wisecracking "calisthenics with words." Once students are sensitized to the importance writers place on words, they can begin to understand the struggle that goes on in every selection in this book to find the one word that has just the right shade of meaning to convey the writer's ideas and feelings.

During the years he spent in prison, political activist Malcolm X became increasingly frustrated by his inability to express himself in writing, so he began the tedious and often frustrating task of copying words from the dictionary—page by page. The eventual result was that for the first time in his life he could pick up a book and read it with understanding. "Anyone who has read a great deal," he says, "can imagine the new world that opened." Most of us are not as fortunate as Malcolm X because we do not fully realize the power of words.

But language is vitally important. In fact, when we consider the potential power of words, the dictionary definition, or *denotation*, of a word is no more than the tip of the iceberg; the bulk of the word's meaning lies somewhere beneath the surface. Often a word's *connotations*—the associations that surround it—are powerful and subtle. As a result, language can be quite confusing—and even harmful. This potential for danger makes accurate word choice all the more important, and it is one reason why members of some minority groups have preferences for certain designations over others.

To one extent or another all the writers in this chapter are concerned with the power of words to convey ideas, influence how we think, and shape our actions. In "A Homemade Education" Malcolm X describes how his education began with the study of words, and in "Politics and the English Language" George Orwell illustrates how inexact words can muddle thinking and, as a result, undermine an entire culture. In "Aria" Richard Rodriguez makes the point that even though English alienated him from his family, he had to learn it if he was to enter into the mainstream of American culture. In "Sexism in English: A 1990s Update," Alleen Pace Nilsen shows how a study of the words in a dictionary reveals deep-seated biases against women. These and other selections in this chapter examine both the nature and the value of language.

PREPARING TO READ AND WRITE

As you read and prepare to write about the selections in this chapter, you may consider the following questions:

- Does the selection deal primarily with written or spoken language?

- Does the writer place more emphasis on the connotations or the denotations of words?

- How much emphasis does the writer place on clear, exact expression?

- Does the writer make any distinctions between the use of language by males and by females? Do you consider these distinctions valid?

- Does the writer discuss language in the context of a particular culture? Does he or she see language as a unifying or a divisive factor?

- Does the writer believe that people are shaped by language or that language is shaped by people?

- Does the writer see language as a political or a social tool? In what sense?

- Does the writer make assumptions about the status of individuals on the basis of their use of particular words? Do these assumptions seem justified?

- Does the writer make a reasonable case for the importance of words, or does his or her case seem overstated?

- In what ways are your ideas about the power of words similar to or different from the writer's?

A Homemade Education

MALCOLM X

Writer, lecturer, and political activist Malcolm X (1925–1965) was born Malcolm Little in Omaha, Nebraska. His father, a Baptist minister, supported the back-to-Africa movement of the 1920s. Because of these activities the family was threatened by the Klu Klux Klan and forced to move several times. Eventually, his father was murdered, and his mother was committed to a mental institution. Malcolm X quit high school, preferring the street world of criminals and drug addicts. While he served time in prison from 1946 to 1952, he read books and studied the Black Muslim religion, finally becoming an articulate advocate of black separatism. Malcolm X later split with Elijah Muhammad, the Black Muslim leader, rejecting the notion that whites were evil and working for worldwide African-American unity and equality. For his defection, Malcolm X was assassinated. Some of his writings are *The Autobiography of Malcolm X* (1965), *Malcolm X Talks to Young People* (1969), and *Malcolm X on Afro-American Unity* (1970). "A Homemade Education" is from Malcolm X's autobiography.

It was because of my letters that I happened to stumble upon starting to acquire some kind of a homemade education. 1

I became increasingly frustrated at not being able to express what I wanted to convey in letters that I wrote, especially those to Mr. Elijah Muhammad. In the street, I had been the most articulate hustler out there—I had commanded attention when I said something. But now, trying to write simple English, I not only wasn't articulate, I wasn't even functional. How would I sound writing in slang, the way I would *say* it, something such as, "Look, daddy, let me pull your coat about a cat, Elijah Muhammad—" 2

Many who today hear me somewhere in person, or on television, or those who read something I've said, will think I went to school far beyond the eighth grade. This impression is due entirely to my prison studies. 3

It had really begun back in the Charlestown Prison, when Bimbi[1] first made me feel envy of his stock of knowledge. Bimbi had always taken charge of any conversations he was in, and I had tried to emulate him. But every book I picked up had few sentences which didn't contain anywhere from one to nearly all of the words that might as well have been in Chinese. When I just skipped those words, of course, I really ended up with little idea of what the book said. So I 4

---

[1]A fellow inmate. [Eds.]

had come to the Norfolk Prison Colony still going through only book-reading motions. Pretty soon, I would have quit even these motions, unless I had received the motivation that I did.

I saw that the best thing I could do was get hold of a dictionary— to study, to learn some words. I was lucky enough to reason also that I should try to improve my penmanship. It was sad. I couldn't even write in a straight line. It was both ideas together that moved me to request a dictionary along with some tablets and pencils from the Norfolk Prison Colony school. 5

I spent two days just riffling uncertainly through the dictionary's pages. I'd never realized so many words existed! I didn't know *which* words I needed to learn. Finally, just to start some kind of action, I began copying. 6

In my slow, painstaking, ragged handwriting, I copied into my tablet everything printed on that first page, down to the punctuation marks. 7

I believe it took me a day. Then, aloud, I read back, to myself, everything I'd written on the tablet. Over and over, aloud, to myself, I read my own handwriting. 8

I woke up the next morning, thinking about those words— immensely proud to realize that not only had I written so much at one time, but I'd written words that I never knew were in the world. More-over, with a little effort, I also could remember what many of these words meant. I reviewed the words whose meanings I didn't remember. Funny thing, from the dictionary first page right now, that "aardvark" springs to my mind. The dictionary had a picture of it, a long-tailed, long-eared, burrowing African mammal, which lives off termites caught by sticking out its tongue as an anteater does for ants. 9

I was so fascinated that I went on—I copied the dictionary's next page. And the same experience came when I studied that. With every succeeding page, I also learned of people and places and events from history. Actually the dictionary is like a miniature encyclopedia. Finally the dictionary's A section had filled a whole tablet—and I went on into the B's. That was the way I started copying what even-tually became the entire dictionary. It went a lot faster after so much practice helped me to pick up handwriting speed. Between what I wrote in my tablet, and writing letters, during the rest of my time in prison I would guess I wrote a million words. 10

I suppose it was inevitable that as my word-base broadened, I could for the first time pick up a book and read and now begin to understand what the book was saying. Anyone who has read a great deal can imagine the new world that opened. Let me tell you some-thing: from then until I left that prison, in every free moment I had, if I was not reading in the library, I was reading on my bunk. You 11

ADDITIONAL QUESTIONS FOR RESPONDING TO READING

1. What specifically did Malcolm X learn as he taught himself to read?
2. Why does Malcolm X provide the extensive example of the British exploitation of China?
3. What motivated Malcolm X to begin his prison studies?
4. What words did Malcolm X copy from the dictionary? Do they give you any insight into his character? His aspirations?

TEACHING STRATEGIES

1. Discuss the problems caused by Malcolm X's inability to express himself in a language other than slang. Do style and level of diction really matter as long as one is able to get a message across?
2. Poll students on the following questions: How often do you use a dictionary? For what purposes? Has reading this essay affected the way you view the dictionary?
3. Ask students how much African-American history was presented to them in the course of their education. Do African-Americans have reason to object to the way American history is taught? Do other groups also have reason to complain?
4. Discuss the subjective nature of history. Make clear that human beings record it and that the details preserved depend entirely on what the person recording it perceives as important.
5. Discuss the following with your students:
Paragraph 24: What conclusion is made "clear"? What is Malcolm X implying?
Paragraph 27, line 9: To what or to whom is Malcolm X referring?
Paragraph 38: Have students heard the phrase "new world order" before? What does Malcolm X mean when he uses it?
Paragraphs 42–43: Ask students whether they agree with the reasoning of this digression.

couldn't have gotten me out of books with a wedge. Between Mr. Muhammad's teachings, my correspondence, my visitors—usually Ella and Reginald[2]—and my reading of books, months passed without my even thinking about being imprisoned. In fact, up to then, I never had been so truly free in my life.

The Norfolk Prison Colony's library was in the school building. 12 A variety of classes was taught there by instructors who came from such places as Harvard and Boston universities. The weekly debates between inmate teams were also held in the school building. You would be astonished to know how worked up convict debaters and audiences would get over subjects like "Should Babies Be Fed Milk?"

Available on the prison library's shelves were books on just about 13 every general subject. Much of the big private collection that Parkhurst[3] had willed to the prison was still in crates and boxes in the back of the library—thousands of old books. Some of them looked ancient: covers faded; old-time parchment-looking binding. Parkhurst, I've mentioned, seemed to have been principally interested in history and religion. He had the money and the special interest to have a lot of books that you wouldn't have in general circulation. Any college library would have been lucky to get that collection.

As you can imagine, especially in a prison where there was heavy 14 emphasis on rehabilitation, an inmate was smiled upon if he demonstrated an unusually intense interest in books. There was a sizable number of well-read inmates, especially the popular debaters. Some were said by many to be practically walking encyclopedias. They were almost celebrities. No university would ask any student to devour literature as I did when this new world opened to me, of being able to read and *understand*.

I read more in my room than in the library itself. An inmate who 15 was known to read a lot could check out more than the permitted maximum number of books. I preferred reading in the total isolation of my own room.

When I had progressed to really serious reading, every night at 16 about ten P.M. I would be outraged with the "lights out." It always seemed to catch me right in the middle of something engrossing.

Fortunately, right outside my door was a corridor light that cast 17 a glow into my room. The glow was enough to read by, once my eyes adjusted to it. So when "lights out" came, I would sit on the floor where I could continue reading in that glow.

At one-hour intervals the night guards paced past every room. 18

---

[2]Ella was his half sister and Reginald was his brother. [Eds.]
[3]A philanthropist who willed his library to the prison. [Eds.]

Each time I heard the approaching footsteps, I jumped into bed and feigned sleep. And as soon as the guard passed, I got back out of bed onto the floor area of that light-glow, where I would read for another fifty-eight minutes—until the guard approached again. That went on until three or four every morning. Three or four hours of sleep a night was enough for me. Often in the years in the streets I had slept less than that.

The teachings of Mr. Muhammad stressed how history had been "whitened"—when white men had written history books, the black man simply had been left out. Mr. Muhammad couldn't have said anything that would have struck me much harder. I had never forgotten how when my class, me and all of those whites, had studied seventh-grade United States history back in Mason,[4] the history of the Negro had been covered in one paragraph, and the teacher had gotten a big laugh with his joke, "Negroes' feet are so big that when they walk, they leave a hole in the ground." 19

This is one reason why Mr. Muhammad's teachings spread so swiftly all over the United States, among *all* Negroes, whether or not they became followers of Mr. Muhammad. The teachings ring true—to every Negro. You can hardly show me a black adult in America—or a white one, for that matter—who knows from the history books anything like the truth about the black man's role. In my own case, once I heard of the "glorious history of the black man," I took special pains to hunt in the library for books that would inform me on details about black history. 20

I can remember accurately the very first set of books that really impressed me. I have since bought that set of books and I have it at home for my children to read as they grow up. It's called *Wonders of the World*. It's full of pictures of archeological finds, statues that depict, usually, non-European people. 21

I found books like Will Durant's *Story of Civilization*. I read H. G. Wells' *Outline of History*. *Souls of Black Folk* by W. E. B. Du Bois gave me a glimpse into the black people's history before they came to this country. Carter G. Woodson's *Negro History* opened my eyes about black empires before the black slave was brought to the United States, and the early Negro struggles for freedom. 22

J. A. Rogers' three volumes of *Sex and Race* told about race-mixing before Christ's time; about Aesop being a black man who told fables; about Egypt's Pharaohs; about the great Coptic Christian Empires; 23

---

[4]The junior high school that Malcolm X attended. [Eds.]

about Ethiopia, the earth's oldest continuous black civilization, as China is the oldest continuous civilization.

Mr. Muhammad's teaching about how the white man had been   24 created led me to *Findings in Genetics* by Gregor Mendel.[5] (The dictionary's G section was where I had learned what "genetics" meant.) I really studied this book by the Austrian monk. Reading it over and over, especially certain sections, helped me to understand that if you started with a black man, a white man could be produced; but starting with a white man, you never could produce a black man—because the white chromosome is recessive. And since no one disputes that there was but one Original Man, the conclusion is clear.

During the last year or so, in the *New York Times*, Arnold Toynbee[6]   25 used the word "bleached" in describing the white man. (His words were: "White [i.e. bleached] human beings of North European origin. . . .") Toynbee also referred to the European geographic area as only a peninsula of Asia. He said there is no such thing as Europe. And if you look at the globe, you will see for yourself that America is only an extension of Asia. (But at the same time Toynbee is among those who have helped to bleach history. He has written that Africa was the only continent that produced no history. He won't write that again. Every day now, the truth is coming to light.)

I never will forget how shocked I was when I began reading about   26 slavery's total horror. It made such an impact upon me that it later became one of my favorite subjects when I became a minister of Mr. Muhammad's. The world's most monstrous crime, the sin and the blood on the white man's hands, are almost impossible to believe. Books like the one by Frederick Olmstead[7] opened my eyes to the horrors suffered when the slave was landed in the United States. The European woman, Fannie Kimball, who had married a Southern white slaveowner, described how human beings were degraded. Of course I read *Uncle Tom's Cabin*. In fact, I believe that's the only novel I have ever read since I started serious reading.

Parkhurst's collection also contained some bound pamphlets of   27 the Abolitionist Anti-Slavery Society of New England. I read descriptions of atrocities, saw those illustrations of black slave women tied up and flogged with whips; of black mothers watching their babies being dragged off, never to be seen by their mothers again; of dogs after slaves, and of the fugitive slave catchers, evil white men with

---

[5] Austrian monk (1822–84) acknowledged as the father of modern genetics. [Eds.]
[6] English historian (1889–1975). [Eds.]
[7] American landscape architect and writer (1822–1903) who first achieved fame for his accounts of the South in the early 1850s. [Eds.]

whips and clubs and chains and guns. I read about the slave preacher Nat Turner, who put the fear of God into the white slavemaster. Nat Turner wasn't going around preaching pie-in-the-sky and "non-violent" freedom for the black man. There in Virginia one night in 1831, Nat and seven other slaves started out at his master's home and through the night they went from one plantation "big house" to the next, killing, until by the next morning 57 white people were dead and Nat had about 70 slaves following him. White people, terrified for their lives, fled from their homes, locked themselves up in public buildings, hid in the woods, and some even left the state. A small army of soldiers took two months to catch and hang Nat Turner. Somewhere I have read where Nat Turner's example is said to have inspired John Brown to invade Virginia and attack Harper's Ferry nearly thirty years later, with thirteen white men and five Negroes.

I read Herodotus, "the father of History," or, rather, I read about 28 him. And I read the histories of various nations, which opened my eyes gradually, then wider and wider, to how the whole world's white men had indeed acted like devils, pillaging and raping and bleeding and draining the whole world's non-white people. I remember, for instance, books such as Will Durant's *The Story of Oriental Civilization*, and Mahatma Gandhi's accounts of the struggle to drive the British out of India.

Book after book showed me how the white man had brought 29 upon the world's black, brown, red, and yellow peoples every variety of the sufferings of exploitation. I saw how since the sixteenth century, the so-called "Christian trader" white man began to ply the seas in his lust for Asian and African empires, and plunder, and power. I read, I saw, how the white man never has gone among the non-white peoples bearing the Cross in the true manner and spirit of Christ's teachings—meek, humble, and Christlike.

I perceived, as I read, how the collective white man had been 30 actually nothing but a piratical opportunist who used Faustian machinations to make his own Christianity his initial wedge in criminal conquests. First, always "religiously," he branded "heathen" and "pagan" labels upon ancient non-white cultures and civilizations. The stage thus set, he then turned upon his non-white victims his weapons of war.

I read how, entering India—half a *billion* deeply religious brown 31 people—the British white man, by 1759, through promises, trickery and manipulations, controlled much of India through Great Britain's East India Company. The parasitical British administration kept tentacling out to half of the subcontinent. In 1857, some of the desperate people of India finally mutinied—and, excepting the African slave

COLLABORATIVE ACTIVITY

In recent years, some parents have tried to remove their children from the public schools and educate them at home. Stage a debate on the superiority of this kind of "homemade education" over an institutionalized one. Students should support their arguments with evidence from Malcolm X's essay as well as from their personal experience.

trade, nowhere has history recorded any more unnecessary bestial and ruthless human carnage than the British suppression of the non-white Indian people.

Over 115 million African blacks—close to the 1930s population of the United States—were murdered or enslaved during the slave trade. And I read how when the slave market was glutted, the cannibalistic white powers of Europe next carved up, as their colonies, the richest areas of the black continent. And Europe's chancelleries for the next century played a chess game of naked exploitation and power from Cape Horn to Cairo. [32]

Ten guards and the warden couldn't have torn me out of those books. Not even Elijah Muhammad could have been more eloquent than those books were in providing indisputable proof that the collective white man had acted like a devil in virtually every contact he had with the world's collective non-white man. I listen today to the radio, and watch television, and read the headlines about the collective white man's fear and tension concerning China. When the white man professes ignorance about why the Chinese hate him so, my mind can't help flashing back to what I read, there in prison, about how the blood forebears of this same white man raped China at a time when China was trusting and helpless. Those original white "Christian traders" sent into China millions of pounds of opium. By 1839, so many of the Chinese were addicts that China's desperate government destroyed twenty thousand chests of opium. The first Opium War was promptly declared by the white man. Imagine! Declaring *war* upon someone who objects to being narcotized! The Chinese were severely beaten, with Chinese-invented gunpowder. [33]

The Treaty of Nanking made China pay the British white man for the destroyed opium: forced open China's major ports to British trade; forced China to abandon Hong Kong; fixed China's import tariffs so low that cheap British articles soon flooded in, maiming China's industrial development. [34]

After a second Opium War, the Tientsin Treaties legalized the ravaging opium trade, legalized a British-French-American control of China's customs. China tried delaying that Treaty's ratification; Peking was looted and burned. [35]

"Kill the foreign white devils!" was the 1901 Chinese war cry in the Boxer Rebellion. Losing again, this time the Chinese were driven from Peking's choicest areas. The vicious, arrogant white man put up the famous signs, "Chinese and dogs not allowed." [36]

Red China after World War II closed its doors to the Western white world. Massive Chinese agricultural, scientific, and industrial efforts are described in a book that *Life* magazine recently published. Some observers inside Red China have reported that the world never [37] has known such a hate-white campaign as is now going on in this non-white country where, present birthrates continuing, in fifty more years Chinese will be half the earth's population. And it seems that some Chinese chickens will soon come home to roost, with China's recent successful nuclear tests.

38 Let us face reality. We can see in the United Nations a new world order being shaped, along color lines—an alliance among the non-white nations. America's U.N. Ambassador Adlai Stevenson complained not long ago that in the United Nations "a skin game" was being played. He was right. He was facing reality. A "skin game" *is* being played. But Ambassador Stevenson sounded like Jesse James accusing the marshal of carrying a gun. Because who in the world's history ever has played a worse "skin game" than the white man?

39 Mr. Muhammad, to whom I was writing daily, had no idea of what a new world had opened up to me through my efforts to document his teachings in books.

40 When I discovered philosophy, I tried to touch all the landmarks of philosophical development. Gradually, I read most of the old philosophers, Occidental and Oriental. The Oriental philosophers were the ones I came to prefer; finally, my impression was that most Occidental philosophy had largely been borrowed from the Oriental thinkers. Socrates, for instance, traveled in Egypt. Some sources even say that Socrates was initiated into some of the Egyptian mysteries. Obviously Socrates got some of his wisdom among the East's wise men.

41 I have often reflected upon the new vistas that reading opened to me. I knew right there in prison that reading had changed forever the course of my life. As I see it today, the ability to read awoke inside me some long dormant craving to be mentally alive. I certainly wasn't seeking any degree, the way a college confers a status symbol upon its students. My homemade education gave me, with every additional book that I read, a little bit more sensitivity to the deafness, dumbness, and blindness that was afflicting the black race in America. Not long ago, an English writer telephoned me from London, asking questions. One was, "What's your alma mater?" I told him, "Books." You will never catch me with a free fifteen minutes in which I'm not studying something I feel might be able to help the black man.

42 Yesterday I spoke in London, and both ways on the plane across the Atlantic I was studying a document about how the United Nations proposes to insure the human rights of the oppressed minorities of the world. The American black man is the world's most shameful case of minority oppression. What makes the black man think of himself as only an internal United States issue is just a catch-phrase, two words, "civil rights." How is the black man going to get "civil rights" before first he wins his *human* rights? If the American black

WRITING SUGGESTIONS

1. Using the information you generated during your collaborative learning activity, write an essay in which you argue for or against the superiority of a "homemade education."
2. In addition to learning facts in college, you also learn a number of specialized vocabularies. Write an essay describing the specialized vocabularies you have learned in two or three of your classes. In what way have these vocabularies enabled you to express new ideas?

man will start thinking about his *human* rights, and then start thinking of himself as part of one of the world's great peoples, he will see he has a case for the United Nations.

I can't think of a better case! Four hundred years of black blood and sweat invested here in America, and the white man still has the black man begging for what every immigrant fresh off the ship can take for granted the minute he walks down the gangplank. 43

But I'm digressing. I told the Englishman that my alma mater was books, a good library. Every time I catch a plane, I have with me a book that I want to read—and that's a lot of books these days. If I weren't out here every day battling the white man, I could spend the rest of my life reading, just satisfying my curiosity—because you can hardly mention anything I'm not curious about. I don't think anybody ever got more out of going to prison than I did. In fact, prison enabled me to study far more intensively than I would have if my life had gone differently and I had attended some college. I imagine that one of the biggest troubles with colleges is there are too many distractions, too much panty-raiding, fraternities, and boola-boola and all of that. Where else but in a prison could I have attacked my ignorance by being able to study intensely sometimes as much as fifteen hours a day? 44

RESPONDING TO READING

1. Have you, like Malcolm X, ever wanted to express an idea but not been able to because you could not find the exact words? In what way was your experience similar to and different from the one described by Malcolm X?   **2.** Malcolm X realized that to spread his message he would have to develop an idiom different from the one he used when speaking to his friends. Is there a difference between the way you speak to your friends and the way you speak at school or at work? What factors determine what kind of language is appropriate?   **3.** Malcolm X began his education by copying words from the dictionary and learning their definitions. What are the advantages and the disadvantages of this strategy?

Politics and the English Language

GEORGE ORWELL

George Orwell's (see also p. 61) "Politics and the English Language," published in his collection *Shooting an Elephant and Other Stories*, makes a plea for clear thinking and writing. Even in this essay on language, Orwell's political voice is strong. He believes that people can change society by changing the way they use language. His six rules for writing good English (paragraph 19) are still sound advice for beginning writers.

Most people who bother with the matter at all would admit that the English language is in a bad way, but it is generally assumed that we cannot by conscious action do anything about it. Our civilization is decadent and our language—so the argument runs—must inevitably share in the general collapse. It follows that any struggle against the abuse of language is a sentimental archaism, like preferring candles to electric light or hansom cabs to airplanes. Underneath this lies the half-conscious belief that language is a natural growth and not an instrument which we shape for our own purposes.

Now, it is clear that the decline of a language must ultimately have political and economic causes: it is not due simply to the bad influence of this or that individual writer. But an effect can become a cause, reinforcing the original cause and producing the same effect in an intensified form, and so on indefinitely. A man may take to drink because he feels himself to be a failure, and then fail all the more completely because he drinks. It is rather the same thing that is happening to the English language. It becomes ugly and inaccurate because our thoughts are foolish, but the slovenliness of our language makes it easier for us to have foolish thoughts. The point is that the process is reversible. Modern English, especially written English, is full of bad habits which spread by imitation and which can be avoided if one is willing to take the necessary trouble. If one gets rid of these habits one can think more clearly, and to think clearly is a necessary first step towards political regeneration: so that the fight against bad English is not frivolous and is not the exclusive concern of professional writers. I will come back to this presently, and I hope that by that time the meaning of what I have said here will have become clearer. Meanwhile, here are five specimens of the English language as it is now habitually written.

These five passages have not been picked out because they are especially bad—I could have quoted far worse if I had chosen—but because they illustrate various of the mental vices from which we now suffer. They are a little below the average, but are fairly repre-

BACKGROUND ON READING

Begin by discussing the abuses of language to which Orwell was reacting in this essay. Nazi Germany had developed a propaganda machine that manipulated language to achieve its ends. Then, after World War II, the Soviet Union had lowered the "Iron Curtain," behind which it too manipulated language in order to maintain control. Orwell deplored this misuse of language and also the general devaluation of language he perceived in most Western countries.

FOR OPENERS

1. Discuss recently coined political phrases, such as *new world order, a thousand points of light, politically correct,* and *litmus test.* Point out the ambiguity of these phrases and question their purposes.
2. Ask students to supply connotations and denotations for the following labels: *gay, liberal, conservative,* and *feminist.*

sentative samples. I number them so that I can refer back to them when necessary:

"(1) I am not, indeed, sure whether it is not true to say that the Milton who once seemed not unlike a seventeenth-century Shelley had not become, out of an experience ever more bitter in each year, more alien (*sic*) to the founder of that Jesuit sect which nothing could induce him to tolerate."

Professor Harold Laski (Essay in *Freedom of Expression*).

"(2) Above all, we cannot play ducks and drakes with a native battery of idioms which prescribes such egregious collocations of vocables as the Basic *put up with* for *tolerate* or *put at a loss* for *bewilder*."

Professor Lancelot Hogben (*Interglossa*).

"(3) On the one side we have the free personality: by definition it is not neurotic, for it has neither conflict nor dream. Its desires, such as they are, are transparent, for they are just what institutional approval keeps in the forefront of consciousness; another institutional pattern would alter their number and intensity; there is little in them that is natural, irreducible, or culturally dangerous. But *on the other side*, the social bond itself is nothing but the mutual reflection of these self-secure integrities. Recall the definition of love. Is not this the very picture of a small academic? Where is there a place in this hall of mirrors for either personality or fraternity?"

Essay on psychology in *Politics* (New York).

"(4) All the 'best people' from the gentlemen's clubs, and all the frantic fascist captains, united in common hatred of Socialism and bestial horror of the rising tide of the mass revolutionary movement, have turned to acts of provocation, to foul incendiarism, to medieval legends of poisoned wells, to legalize their own destruction of proletarian organizations, and rouse the agitated petty-bourgeoisie to chauvinistic fervor on behalf of the fight against the revolutionary way out of the crisis."

Communist pamphlet.

"(5) If a new spirit *is* to be infused into this old country, there is one thorny and contentious reform which must be tackled, and that is the humanization and galvanization of the B.B.C. Timidity here will bespeak cancer and atrophy of the soul. The heart of Britain may be sound and of strong beat, for instance, but the British lion's roar at present is like that of Bottom in Shakespeare's *Midsummer Night's Dream*—as gentle as any sucking dove. A virile new Britain cannot continue indefinitely to be traduced in the eyes or rather ears, of the world by the effete languors of Langham Place, brazenly masquerading as 'standard English'. When the Voice of Britain is heard at nine o'clock, better far and infinitely less ludicrous to hear aitches honestly dropped than the present priggish, inflated, inhibited, school-ma'amish arch braying of blameless bashful mewing maidens!"

Letter in *Tribune*.

Each of these passages has faults of its own, but, quite apart from avoidable ugliness, two qualities are common to all of them. The first is staleness of imagery: the other is lack of precision. The writer either has a meaning and cannot express it, or he inadvertently says something else, or he is almost indifferent as to whether his words mean anything or not. This mixture of vagueness and sheer incompetence is the most marked characteristic of modern English prose, and especially of any kind of political writing. As soon as certain topics are raised, the concrete melts into the abstract and no one seems able to think of turns of speech that are not hackneyed: prose consists less and less of *words* chosen for the sake of their meaning, and more and more of *phrases* tacked together like the sections of a prefabricated hen-house. I list below, with notes and examples, various of the tricks by means of which the work of prose-construction is habitually dodged:

Dying Metaphors

A newly invented metaphor assists thought by evoking a visual image, while on the other hand a metaphor which is technically "dead" (e.g. *iron resolution*) has in effect reverted to being an ordinary word and can generally be used without loss of vividness. But in between these two classes there is a huge dump of worn-out metaphors which have lost all evocative power and are merely used because they save people the trouble of inventing phrases for themselves. Examples are: *Ring the changes on, take up the cudgels for, toe the line, ride roughshod over, stand shoulder to shoulder with, play into the hands of, no axe to grind, grist to the mill, fishing in troubled waters, on the order of the day, Achilles' heel, swan song, hotbed.* Many of these are used without knowledge of their meaning (what is a "rift," for instance),[1] and incompatible metaphors are frequently mixed, a sure sign that the writer is not interested in what he is saying. Some metaphors now current have been twisted out of their original meaning without those who use them even being aware of the fact. For example, *toe the line* is sometimes written *tow the line*. Another example is *the hammer and the anvil*, now always used with the implication that the anvil gets the worst of it. In real life it is always the anvil that breaks the hammer, never the other way about: a writer

---

[1]Originally *rift* referred to a geological fault or fissure. Now it is commonly used to indicate a breach or estrangement. [Eds.]

ADDITIONAL QUESTIONS FOR RESPONDING TO READING

1. Which comes first: language or thought? According to the Sapir-Whorf hypothesis, a linguistic theory, the way we use language in terms of grammatical structure and word choice influences the way we think. Does the distinction between language and thought seem reasonable to you? What social and political implications does this theory have?
2. Why did Orwell title his essay "Politics and the English Language"? What connections does he draw between the two?
3. Do you think Orwell is inventing a problem, or are his complaints justifiable? Explain your answer.

TEACHING STRATEGY
Discuss the following with your students:
Paragraph 2: What cause-and-effect relationship does Orwell discuss here? Explain the reasoning behind his analysis and decide whether you agree.
Paragraph 4: To what "certain topics" does Orwell refer?
Paragraph 5: An interesting phenomenon some composition teachers have lately observed is the distortion of worn-out phrases by student writers who have heard the phrases widely used but have never seen them in print: for example, *take for granite* instead of *take for granted* and *It's a doggie dog world* instead of *It's a dog-eat-dog world.* Note the difference in meanings between the phrases. Are such distortions cause for amusement, or do they have serious implications?
Paragraph 6: This is a good opportunity to discuss the problems of the passive voice. For example, what is the difference between the following two phrases: *Taxes must be raised* and *We must raise taxes*? The active-voice phrase has a human subject. The passive-voice phrase does not; therefore, it allows the speaker to avoid responsibility for an action or for what is being said.
Paragraph 7: Emphasize that here Orwell attacks pretentious diction, not the varied, creative vocabulary necessary for effective communication.
Paragraph 8: Return to the "For Openers" discussion; reintroduce the terms and apply them in the context of this passage.
Paragraph 10: Why do you think Orwell chose a verse from Ecclesiastes for his parody? Could another kind of quotation have served as well?

who stopped to think what he was saying would be aware of this, and would avoid perverting the original phrase.

Operators or Verbal False Limbs

These save the trouble of picking out appropriate verbs and nouns, and at the same time pad each sentence with extra syllables which give it an appearance of symmetry. Characteristic phrases are: *render inoperative, militate against, make contact with, be subjected to, give rise to, give grounds for, have the effect of, play a leading part (role) in, make itself felt, take effect, exhibit a tendency to, serve the purpose of, etc., etc.* The keynote is the elimination of simple verbs. Instead of being a single word, such as *break, stop, spoil, mend, kill,* a verb becomes a *phrase,* made up of a noun or adjective tacked on to some general-purposes verb such as *prove, serve, form, play, render.* In addition, the passive voice is wherever possible used in preference to the active, and noun constructions are used instead of gerunds (*by examination of* instead of *by examining*). The range of verbs is further cut down by means of the *-ize* and *de-* formation, and the banal statements are given an appearance of profundity by means of the *not un-* formation. Simple conjunctions and prepositions are replaced by such phrases as *with respect to, having regard to, the fact that, by dint of, in view of, in the interests of, on the hypothesis that*; and the ends of sentences are saved from anticlimax by such resounding commonplaces as *greatly to be desired, cannot be left out of account, a development to be expected in the near future, deserving of serious consideration, brought to a satisfactory conclusion,* and so on and so forth.

6

Pretentious Diction

Words like *phenomenon, element, individual* (as noun), *objective, categorical, effective, virtual, basic, primary, promote, constitute, exhibit, exploit, utilize, eliminate, liquidate,* are used to dress up simple statements and give an air of scientific impartiality to biased judgments. Adjectives like *epoch-making, epic, historic, unforgettable, triumphant, age-old, inevitable, inexorable, veritable,* are used to dignify the sordid processes of international politics, while writing that aims at glorifying war usually takes on an archaic color, its characteristic words being: *realm, throne, chariot, mailed fist, trident, sword, shield, buckler, banner, jackboot, clarion.* Foreign words and expressions such as *cul de sac, ancien régime, deus ex machina, mutatis mutandis, status quo, gleichschaltung, weltanschauung,* are used to give an air of culture and elegance.

7

Except for the useful abbreviations *i.e.*, *e.g.*, and *etc.*, there is no real need for any of the hundreds of foreign phrases now current in English. Bad writers, and especially scientific, political and sociological writers, are nearly always haunted by the notion that Latin or Greek words are grander than Saxon ones, and unnecessary words like *expedite, ameliorate, predict, extraneous, deracinated, clandestine, subaqueous* and hundreds of others constantly gain ground from their Anglo-Saxon opposite numbers.[2] The jargon peculiar to Marxist writing (*hyena, hangman, cannibal, petty bourgeois, these gentry, lacquey, flunkey, mad dog, White Guard*, etc.) consists largely of words and phrases translated from Russian, German or French; but the normal way of coining a new word is to use a Latin or Greek root with the appropriate affix and, where necessary, the *-ize* formation. It is often easier to make up words of this kind (*deregionalize, impermissible, extramarital, nonfragmentatory* and so forth) than to think up the English words that will cover one's meaning. The result, in general, is an increase in slovenliness and vagueness.

Meaningless Words

In certain kinds of writing, particularly in art criticism and literary   8
criticism, it is normal to come across long passages which are almost completely lacking in meaning.[3] Words like *romantic, plastic, values, human, dead, sentimental, natural, vitality*, as used in art criticism, are strictly meaningless in the sense that they not only do not point to any discoverable object, but are hardly ever expected to do so by the reader. When one critic writes, "The outstanding feature of Mr. X's work is its living quality", while another writes, "The immediately striking thing about Mr. X's work is its peculiar deadness", the reader accepts this as a simple difference of opinion. If words like *black* and *white* were involved, instead of the jargon words *dead* and *living*, he would see at once that language was being used in an improper way. Many political words are similarly abused. The word *Fascism* has now no meaning except in so far as it signifies "something not desirable."

---

[2]An interesting illustration of this is the way in which the English flower names which were in use till very recently are being ousted by Greek ones, *snapdragon* becoming *antirrhinum, forget-me-not* becoming *myosotis*, etc. It is hard to see any practical reason for this change of fashion: it is probably due to an instinctive turning-away from the more homely word and a vague feeling that the Greek word is scientific.

[3]Example: "Comfort's catholicity of perception and image, strangely Whitmanesque in range, almost the exact opposite in aesthetic compulsion, continues to evoke that trembling atmospheric accumulative hinting at a cruel, an inexorably serene timelessness. . . . Wrey Gardiner scores by aiming at simple bull's-eyes with precision. Only they are not so simple, and through this contended sadness - runs more than the surface bittersweet of resignation" (*Poetry Quarterly*).

The words *democracy, socialism, freedom, patriotic, realistic, justice,* have each of them several different meanings which cannot be reconciled with one another. In the case of a word like *democracy,* not only is there no agreed definition, but the attempt to make one is resisted from all sides. It is almost universally felt that when we call a country democratic we are praising it: consequently the defenders of every kind of régime claim that it is a democracy, and fear that they might have to stop using the word if it were tied down to any one meaning. Words of this kind are often used in a consciously dishonest way. That is, the person who uses them has his own private definition, but allows his hearer to think he means something quite different. Statements like *Marshal Pétain was a true patriot, The Soviet Press is the freest in the world, The Catholic Church is opposed to persecution,* are almost always made with intent to deceive. Other words used in variable meanings, in most cases more or less dishonestly, are: *class, totalitarian, science, progressive, reactionary, bourgeois, equality.*

Now that I have made this catalogue of swindles and perversions,   9
let me give another example of the kind of writing that they lead to. This time it must of its nature be an imaginary one. I am going to translate a passage of good English into modern English of the worst sort. Here is a well-known verse from *Ecclesiastes*:

"I returned and saw under the sun, that the race is not to the swift, nor the battle to the strong, neither yet bread to the wise, nor yet riches to men of understanding, nor yet favor to men of skill; but time and chance happeneth to them all."

Here it is in modern English: 10

"Objective consideration of contemporary phenomena compels the conclusion that success or failure in competitive activities exhibits no tendency to be commensurate with innate capacity, but that a considerable element of the unpredictable must invariably be taken into account."

This is a parody, but not a very gross one. Exhibit (3), above, for   11
instance, contains several patches of the same kind of English. It will be seen that I have not made a full translation. The beginning and ending of the sentence follow the original meaning fairly closely, but in the middle the concrete illustrations—race, battle, bread—dissolve into the vague phrase "success or failure in competitive activities." This had to be so, because no modern writer of the kind I am discussing—no one capable of using phrases like "objective consideration of contemporary phenomena"—would ever tabulate his thoughts in that precise and detailed way. The whole tendency of modern prose is away from concreteness. Now analyze these two sentences a little more closely. The first contains forty-nine words but only sixty syl-

WRITING SUGGESTION

Write a translation of a Bible passage or a well-known fable or fairy tale in a style similar to Orwell's translation in paragraph 10.

lables, and all its words are those of everyday life. The second contains thirty-eight words of ninety syllables: eighteen of its words are from Latin roots, and one from Greek. The first sentence contains six vivid images, and only one phrase ("time and chance") that could be called vague. The second contains not a single fresh, arresting phrase, and in spite of its ninety syllables it gives only a shortened version of the meaning contained in the first. Yet without a doubt it is the second kind of sentence that is gaining ground in modern English. I do not want to exaggerate. This kind of writing is not yet universal, and outcrops of simplicity will occur here and there in the worst-written page. Still, if you or I were told to write a few lines on the uncertainty of human fortunes, we should probably come much nearer to my imaginary sentence than to the one from *Ecclesiastes*.

As I have tried to show, modern writing at its worst does not 12 consist in picking out words for the sake of their meaning and inventing images in order to make the meaning clearer. It consists in gumming together long strips of words which have already been set in order by someone else, and making the results presentable by sheer humbug. The attraction of this way of writing is that it is easy. It is easier—even quicker, once you have the habit—to say *In my opinion it is a not unjustifiable assumption that* than to say *I think*. If you use ready-made phrases, you not only don't have to hunt about for words; you also don't have to bother with the rhythms of your sentences, since these phrases are generally so arranged as to be more or less euphonious. When you are composing in a hurry—when you are dictating to a stenographer, for instance, or making a public speech—it is natural to fall into a pretentious, Latinized style. Tags like a *consideration which we should do well to bear in mind* or *a conclusion to which all of us would readily assent* will save many a sentence from coming down with a bump. By using stale metaphors, similes and idioms, you save much mental effort, at the cost of leaving your meaning vague, not only for your reader but for yourself. This is the significance of mixed metaphors. The sole aim of a metaphor is to call up a visual image. When these images clash—as in *The Fascist octopus has sung its swan song, the jackboot is thrown into the melting pot*—it can't be taken as certain that the writer is not seeing a mental image of the objects he is naming; in other words he is not really thinking. Look again at the examples I gave at the beginning of this essay. Professor Laski (1) uses five negatives in fifty-three words. One of these is superfluous, making nonsense of the whole passage, and in addition there is the slip *alien* for *akin*, making further nonsense, and several avoidable pieces of clumsiness which increase the general vagueness. Professor Hogben (2) plays ducks and drakes with a battery which is able to write prescriptions, and, while disapproving of the everyday phrase *put up with*, is unwilling to look *egregious* up in the dictionary and see what it means. (3), if one takes an uncharitable attitude towards it, is simply meaningless: probably one could work out its intended meaning by reading the whole of the article in which it occurs. In (4), the writer knows more or less what he wants to say, but an accumulation of stale phrases chokes him like tea leaves blocking a sink. In (5), words and meaning have almost parted company. People who write in this manner usually have a general emotional meaning—they dislike one thing and want to express solidarity with another—but they are not interested in the detail of what they are saying. A scrupulous writer, in every sentence that he writes, will ask himself at least four questions, thus: What am I trying to say? What words will express it? What image or idiom will make it clearer? Is this image fresh enough to have an effect? And he will probably ask himself two more: Could I put it more shortly? Have I said anything that is avoidably ugly? But you are not obliged to go to all this trouble. You can shirk it by simply throwing your mind open and letting the ready-made phrases come crowding in. They will construct your sentences for you—even think your thoughts for you, to a certain extent—and at need they will perform the important service of partially concealing your meaning even from yourself. It is at this point that the special connection between politics and the debasement of language becomes clear.

In our time it is broadly true that political writing is bad writing. 13 Where it is not true, it will generally be found that the writer is some kind of rebel, expressing his private opinions and not a "party line." Orthodoxy, of whatever color, seems to demand a lifeless, imitative style. The political dialects to be found in pamphlets, leading articles, manifestos, White Papers and the speeches of under-secretaries do, of course, vary from party to party, but they are all alike in that one almost never finds in them a fresh, vivid, home-made turn of speech. When one watches some tired hack on the platform mechanically repeating the familiar phrases—*bestial atrocities, iron heel, bloodstained tyranny, free peoples of the world, stand shoulder to shoulder*—one often has a curious feeling that one is not watching a live human being but some kind of dummy: a feeling which suddenly becomes stronger at moments when the light catches the speaker's spectacles and turns them into blank discs which seem to have no eyes behind them. And this is not altogether fanciful. A speaker who uses that kind of phraseology has gone some distance towards turning himself into a machine. The appropriate noises are coming out of his larynx, but his brain is not involved as it would be if he were choosing his words for himself. If the speech he is making is one that he is accustomed to make over and over again, he may be almost unconscious of what he is saying, as one is when one utters the responses in church. And this reduced state of consciousness, if not indispensable, is at any rate favorable to political conformity.

In our time, political speech and writing are largely the defence 14 of the indefensible. Things like the continuance of British rule in India, the Russian purges and deportations, the dropping of the atom bombs on Japan, can indeed be defended, but only by arguments which are too brutal for most people to face, and which do not square with the professed aims of political parties. Thus political language has to consist largely of euphemism, question-begging and sheer cloudy vagueness. Defenceless villages are bombarded from the air, the inhabitants driven out into the countryside, the cattle machine-gunned, the huts set on fire with incendiary bullets: this is called *pacification*. Millions of peasants are robbed of their farms and sent trudging along the roads with no more than they can carry: this is called *transfer of population* or *rectification of frontiers*. People are imprisoned for years without trial, or shot in the back of the neck or sent to die of scurvy in Arctic lumber camps: this is called *elimination of unreliable elements*. Such phraseology is needed if one wants to name things without calling up mental pictures of them. Consider for instance some comfortable English professor defending Russian totalitarianism. He cannot say outright, "I believe in killing off your opponents when you can get good results by doing so." Probably, therefore, he will say something like this:

"While freely conceding that the Soviet régime exhibits certain 15 features which the humanitarian may be inclined to deplore, we must, I think, agree that a certain curtailment of the right to political opposition is an unavoidable concomitant of transitional periods, and that the rigors which the Russian people have been called upon to undergo have been amply justified in the sphere of concrete achievement."

The inflated style is itself a kind of euphemism. A mass of Latin 16 words falls upon the facts like soft snow, blurring the outlines and covering up all the details. The great enemy of clear language is insincerity. When there is a gap between one's real and one's declared aims, one turns as it were instinctively to long words and exhausted idioms, like a cuttlefish squirting out ink. In our age there is no such thing as "keeping out of politics." All issues are political issues, and politics itself is a mass of lies, evasions, folly, hatred and schizophrenia. When the general atmosphere is bad, language must suffer. I should expect to find—this is a guess which I have not sufficient knowledge to verify—that the German, Russian and Italian languages have all deteriorated in the last ten to fifteen years, as a result of dictatorship.

But if thought corrupts language, language can also corrupt 17 thought. A bad usage can spread by tradition and imitation, even among people who should and do know better. The debased language that I have been discussing is in some ways very convenient. Phrases like *a not unjustifiable assumption, leaves much to be desired, would serve no good purpose, a consideration which we should do well to bear in mind*, are a continuous temptation, a packet of aspirins always at one's elbow. Look back through this essay, and for certain you will find that I have again and again committed the very faults I am protesting against. By this morning's post I have received a pamphlet dealing with conditions in Germany. The author tells me that he "felt impelled" to write it. I open it at random, and here is almost the first sentence that I see: "(The Allies) have an opportunity not only of achieving a radical transformation of Germany's social and political structure in such a way as to avoid a nationalistic reaction in Germany itself, but at the same time of laying the foundations of a cooperative and unified Europe." You see, he "feels impelled" to write—feels, presumably, that he has something new to say—and yet his words, like cavalry horses answering the bugle, group themselves automatically into the familiar dreary pattern. This invasion of one's mind by ready-made phrases (*lay the foundations, achieve a radical transformation*) can only be prevented if one is constantly on guard against them, and every such phrase anaesthetizes a portion of one's brain.

I said earlier that the decadence of our language is probably 18 curable. Those who deny this would argue, if they produced an argument at all, that language merely reflects existing social conditions, and that we cannot influence its development by any direct tinkering with words and constructions. So far as the general tone or spirit of a language goes, this may be true, but it is not true in detail. Silly words and expressions have often disappeared, not through any evolutionary process but owing to the conscious action of a minority. Two recent examples were *explore every avenue* and *leave no stone unturned*, which were killed by the jeers of a few journalists. There is a long list of flyblown metaphors which could similarly be got rid of if enough people would interest themselves in the job; and it should also be possible to laugh the *not un-* formation out of existence,[4] to reduce the amount of Latin and Greek in the average sentence, to drive out foreign phrases and strayed scientific words, and, in general, to make pretentiousness unfashionable. But all these are minor points. The defence of the English language implies more than this, and perhaps it is best to start by saying what it does *not* imply.

---

[4]One can cure oneself of the *not un-*formation by memorizing this sentence: *A not unblack dog was chasing a not unsmall rabbit across a not ungreen field.*

To begin with it has nothing to do with archaism, with the sal- 19
vaging of obsolete words and turns of speech, or with the setting up
of a "standard English" which must never be departed from. On the
contrary, it is especially concerned with the scrapping of every word
or idiom which has outworn its usefulness. It has nothing to do with
correct grammar and syntax, which are of no importance so long as
one makes one's meaning clear, or with the avoidance of American-
isms, or with having what is called a "good prose style." On the other
hand it is not concerned with fake simplicity and the attempt to make
written English colloquial. Nor does it even imply in every case preferring the Saxon word to the Latin one, though it does imply using
the fewest and shortest words that will cover one's meaning. What
is above all needed is to let the meaning choose the word, and not
the other way about. In prose, the worst thing one can do with words
is to surrender to them. When you think of a concrete object, you
think wordlessly, and then, if you want to describe the thing you
have been visualizing you probably hunt about till you find the exact
words that seem to fit. When you think of something abstract you
are more inclined to use words from the start, and unless you make
a conscious effort to prevent it, the existing dialect will come rushing
in and do the job for you, at the expense of blurring or even changing
your meaning. Probably it is better to put off using words as long as
possible and get one's meaning as clear as one can through pictures
or sensations. Afterwards one can choose—not simply accept—the
phrases that will best cover the meaning, and then switch round and
decide what impression one's words are likely to make on another
person. This last effort of the mind cuts out all stale or mixed images,
all prefabricated phrases, needless repetitions, and humbug and
vagueness generally. But one can often be in doubt about the effect
of a word or a phrase, and one needs rules that one can rely on when
instinct fails. I think the following rules will cover most cases:

(i) Never use a metaphor, simile or other figure of speech which you
    are used to seeing in print.

(ii) Never use a long word where a short one will do.

(iii) If it is possible to cut a word out, always cut it out.

(iv) Never use the passive where you can use the active.

(v) Never use a foreign phrase, a scientific word or a jargon word if
    you can think of an everyday English equivalent.

(vi) Break any of these rules sooner than say anything outright bar-
    barous.

These rules sound elementary, and so they are, but they demand 20
a deep change of attitude in anyone who has grown used to writing

in the style now fashionable. One could keep all of them and still write bad English, but one could not write the kind of stuff that I quoted in those five specimens at the beginning of this article.

I have not here been considering the literary use of language, but merely language as an instrument for expressing and not for concealing or preventing thought. Stuart Chase[5] and others have come near to claiming that all abstract words are meaningless, and have used this as a pretext for advocating a kind of political quietism. Since you don't know what Fascism is, how can you struggle against Fascism? One need not swallow such absurdities as this, but one ought to recognize that the present political chaos is connected with the decay of language, and that one can probably bring about some improvement by starting at the verbal end. If you simplify your English, you are freed from the worst follies of orthodoxy. You cannot speak any of the necessary dialects, and when you make a stupid remark its stupidity will be obvious, even to yourself. Political language—and with variations this is true of all political parties, from Conservatives to Anarchists—is designed to make lies sound truthful and murder respectable, and to give an appearance of solidity to pure wind. One cannot change this all in a moment, but one can at least change one's own habits, and from time to time one can even, if one jeers loudly enough, send some worn-out and useless phrase—some *jackboot, Achilles' heel, hotbed, melting pot, acid test, veritable inferno* or other lump of verbal refuse—into the dustbin where it belongs.

RESPONDING TO READING

1. Look through a newspaper or magazine and pick out some examples of dying metaphors. Do you agree with Orwell that they undermine clear thought and expression? Why or why not? **2.** What does Orwell mean in paragraph 14 when he says, "In our time, political speech and writing are largely a defence of the indefensible"? Do you believe his statement applies to current times as well? Find several present-day examples of political language that support your conclusion. **3.** What biases does Orwell seem to have? Do these biases have a positive or negative effect on your reactions to his essay?

ANSWERS TO RESPONDING TO READING

1. Answers will vary.
2. Politicians and governments use vague, inexact language to justify, but not to explain, their actions.
3. The main focus of Orwell's criticism falls on Germany, Italy, and the Soviet Union, all of which were under totalitarianism at the time his essay was written (1946). Orwell seems to have a bias against anyone who tampers with his mother tongue. His attitude toward language seems informed by his English public school education. These elitist biases make him seem snobbish.

---

[5]Author known for his advocacy of clear writing and clear thinking. See his essay "Gobbledygook" on p. 257. [Eds.]

Aria[1]

RICHARD RODRIGUEZ

Writer and journalist Richard Rodriguez (1944–   ) was born in San Francisco, the son of Mexican-American immigrants. A graduate of Stanford University who also holds a graduate degree in English Renaissance Literature, Rodriguez believes that preserving Spanish culture and language in schools creates "socially disadvantaged" children who do not fully belong in American society. The following essay, from the autobiographical collection *Hunger of Memory: The Education of Richard Rodriguez* (1982), first appeared in *The American Scholar* in 1981.

1   Supporters of bilingual education today imply that students like me miss a great deal by not being taught in their family's language. What they seem not to recognize is that, as a socially disadvantaged child, I considered Spanish to be a private language. What I needed to learn in school was that I had the right—and the obligation—to speak the public language of *los gringos*.[2] The odd truth is that my first-grade classmates could have become bilingual, in the conventional sense of that word, more easily than I. Had they been taught (as upper-middle-class children are often taught early) a second language like Spanish or French, they could have regarded it simply as that: another public language. In my case such bilingualism could not have been so quickly achieved. What I did not believe was that I could speak a single public language.

2   Without question, it would have pleased me to hear my teachers address me in Spanish when I entered the classroom. I would have felt much less afraid. I would have trusted them and responded with ease. But I would have delayed—for how long postponed?—having to learn the language of public society, I would have evaded—and for how long could I have afforded to delay?—learning the great lesson of school, that I had a public identity.

3   Fortunately, my teachers were unsentimental about their responsibility. What they understood was that I needed to speak a public language. So their voices would search me out, asking me questions. Each time I'd hear them, I'd look up in surprise to see a nun's face frowning at me. I'd mumble, not really meaning to answer. The nun would persist, "Richard, stand up. Don't look at the floor. Speak up. Speak to the entire class, not just to me!" But I couldn't believe that the English language was mine to use. (In part, I did not want to

---

[1]Solo vocal piece with instrumental accompaniment or melody. [Eds.]
[2]Foreigners, especially Americans and English. [Eds.]

BACKGROUND ON READING

Explain the concept of bilingual education. Students will not be aware of the debate that rages around this issue. Let them know that Rodriguez's opinions have made him the focus of some negative criticism from the Hispanic community. Also introduce the idea of the United States as a melting pot, and ask students whether they think this idea is dated.

FOR OPENERS

What do you assume is the opinion of various ethnic groups in America toward bilingual education? Toward cultural education? What and where do you think children should learn about their ethnicity and heritage?

ADDITIONAL QUESTIONS FOR RESPONDING TO READING

1. How much do you know about the culture of your ethnic group? Where did you gain this knowledge? Do you wish you knew more?
2. Can Rodriguez be accused of trying to deny his culture? How do you think he would respond to this charge? (Read "The Fear of Losing a Culture" in Chapter 6 before you answer this question.)

TEACHING STRATEGY

Discuss the following with your students:
Paragraph 4: Note the differences between public and private language.
Paragraph 8: Why did Rodriguez feel that his parents' switch to speaking English "pushed [him] away"?
Paragraph 11: How did Rodriguez's transformation originate? What seems to have been the ultimate goal, and why is this important? What were the specific drawbacks of his achievement?
Paragraph 20: What is the main point of Rodriguez's argument?

believe it.) I continued to mumble. I resisted the teacher's demands. (Did I somehow suspect that once I learned public language my pleasing family life would be changed?) Silent, waiting for the bell to sound, I remained dazed, diffident, afraid.

Because I wrongly imagined that English was intrinsically a public language and Spanish an intrinsically private one, I easily noted the difference between classroom language and the language of home. At school, words were directed to a general audience of listeners. ("Boys and girls.") Words were meaningfully ordered. And the point was not self-expression alone but to make oneself understood by many others. The teacher quizzed: "Boys and girls, why do we use that word in this sentence? Could we think of a better word to use there? Would the sentence change its meaning if the words were differently arranged? And wasn't there a better way of saying much the same thing?" (I couldn't say. I wouldn't try to say.) 4

Three months. Five. Half a year passed. Unsmiling, ever watchful, my teachers noted my silence. They began to connect my behavior with the difficult progress my older sister and brother were making. Until one Saturday morning three nuns arrived at the house to talk to our parents. Stiffly, they sat on the blue living room sofa. From the doorway of another room, spying the visitors, I noted the incongruity—the clash of two worlds, the faces and voices of school intruding upon the familiar setting of home. I overheard one voice gently wondering, "Do your children speak only Spanish at home, Mrs. Rodriguez?" While another voice added, "That Richard especially seems so timid and shy." 5

That Rich-heard! 6

With great tact the visitors continued, "Is it possible for you and your husband to encourage your children to practice their English when they are home?" Of course, my parents complied. What would they not do for their children's well-being? And how could they have questioned the Church's authority which those women represented? In an instant, they agreed to give up the language (the sounds) that had revealed and accentuated our family's closeness. The moment after the visitors left, the change was observed, "*Ahora*, speak to us en inglés,[3] my father and mother united to tell us. 7

At first, it seemed a kind of game. After dinner each night, the family gathered to practice "our" English. (It was still then *inglés*, a language foreign to us, so we felt drawn as strangers to it.) Laughing, we would try to define words we could not pronounce. We played with strange English sounds, often overanglicizing our pronuncia- 8

---

[3]"Now, speak to us in English." [Eds.]

tions. And we filled the smiling gaps of our sentences with familiar Spanish sounds. But that was cheating, somebody shouted. Everyone laughed. In school, meanwhile, like my brother and sister, I was required to attend a daily tutoring session. I needed a full year of special attention. I also needed my teachers to keep my attention from straying in class by calling out, *Rich-heard*—their English voices slowly prying loose my ties to my other name, its three notes, *Ri-car-do*. Most of all I needed to hear my mother and father speak to me in a moment of seriousness in broken—suddenly heartbreaking—English. The scene was inevitable: One Saturday morning I entered the kitchen where my parents were talking in Spanish. I did not realize that they were talking in Spanish however until, at the moment they saw me, I heard their voices change to speak English. Those *gringo* sounds they uttered startled me. Pushed me away. In that moment of trivial misunderstanding and profound insight, I felt my throat twisted by unsounded grief. I turned quickly and left the room. But I had no place to escape to with Spanish. (The spell was broken.) My brother and sisters were speaking English in another part of the house.

Again and again in the days following, increasingly angry, I was obliged to hear my mother and father: "Speak to us *en inglés*" (*Speak.*) Only then did I determine to learn classroom English. Weeks after, it happened: One day in school I raised my hand to volunteer an answer. I spoke out in a loud voice. And I did not think it remarkable when the entire class understood. That day, I moved very far from the disadvantaged child I had been only days earlier. The belief, that calming assurance that I belonged in public, had at last taken hold. 9

Shortly after, I stopped hearing the high and loud sounds of *los gringos*. A more and more confident speaker of English, I didn't trouble to listen to *how* strangers sounded, speaking to me. And there simply were too many English-speaking people in my day for me to hear American accents anymore. Conversations quickened. Listening to persons who sounded eccentrically pitched voices, I usually noted their sounds for an initial few seconds before I concentrated on *what* they were saying. Conversations became content-full. Transparent. Hearing someone's *tone* of voice—angry or questioning or sarcastic or happy or sad—I didn't distinguish it from the words it expressed. Sound and word were thus tightly wedded. At the end of a day, I was often bemused, always relieved, to realize how "silent," though crowded with words, my day in public had been. (This public silence measured and quickened the change in my life.) 10

At last, seven years old, I came to believe what had been tech- nically true since my birth: I was an American citizen. 11

But the special feeling of closeness at home was diminished by then. Gone was the desperate, urgent, intense feeling of being at 12 home, rare was the experience of feeling myself individualized by family intimates. We remained a loving family, but one greatly changed. No longer so close; no longer bound tight by the pleasing and troubling knowledge of our public separateness. Neither my older brother nor sister rushed home after school anymore. Nor did I. When I arrived home there would often be neighborhood kids in the house. Or the house would be empty of sounds.

Following the dramatic Americanization of their children, even 13 my parents grew more publicly confident. Especially my mother. She learned the names of all the people on our block. And she decided we needed to have a telephone installed in the house. My father continued to use the word *gringo*. But it was no longer charged with the old bitterness or distrust. (Stripped of any emotional content, the word simply became a name for those Americans not of Hispanic descent.) Hearing him, sometimes, I wasn't sure if he was pronouncing the Spanish word *gringo* or saying gringo in English.

Matching the silence I started hearing in public was a new quiet 14 at home. The family's quiet was partly due to the fact that, as we children learned more and more English, we shared fewer and fewer words with our parents. Sentences needed to be spoken slowly when a child addressed his mother or father. (Often the parent wouldn't understand.) The child would need to repeat himself. (Still the parent misunderstood.) The young voice, frustrated, would end up saying, "Never mind"—the subject was closed. Dinners would be noisy with the clinking of knives and forks against dishes. My mother would smile softly between her remarks; my father at the other end of the table would chew and chew at his food, while he stared over the heads of his children.

My *mother!* My *father!* After English became my primary language, 15 I no longer knew what words to use in addressing my parents. The old Spanish words (those tender accents of sound) I had used earlier— *mamá* and *papá*—I couldn't use anymore. They would have been too painful reminders of how much had changed in my life. On the other hand, the words I heard neighborhood kids call their parents seemed equally unsatisfactory. *Mother* and *Father*; *Ma, Papa, Pa, Dad, Pop* (how I hated the all American sound of that last word especially)—all these terms I felt were unsuitable, not really terms of address for my parents. As a result, I never used them at home. Whenever I'd speak to my parents, I would try to get their attention with eye contact alone. In public conversations, I'd refer to "my parents" or "my mother and father."

My mother and father, for their part, responded differently, as 16 their children spoke to them less. She grew restless, seemed troubled and anxious at the scarcity of words exchanged in the house. It was she who would question me about my day when I came home from school. She smiled at small talk. She pried at the edges of my sentences to get me to say something more. (What?) She'd join conversations she overheard, but her intrusions often stopped her children's talking. By contrast, my father seemed reconciled to the new quiet. Though his English improved somewhat, he retired into silence. At dinner he spoke very little. One night his children and even his wife help-lessly giggled at his garbled English pronunciation of the Catholic Grace before Meals. Thereafter he made his wife recite the prayer at the start of each meal, even on formal occasions, when there were guests in the house. Hers became the public voice of the family. On official business, it was she, not my father, one would usually hear on the phone or in stores, talking to strangers. His children grew so accustomed to his silence that, years later, they would speak routinely of his shyness. (My mother would often try to explain: Both his par-ents died when he was eight. He was raised by an uncle who treated him like little more than a menial servant. He was never encouraged to speak. He grew up alone. A man of few words.) But my father was not shy, I realized, when I'd watch him speaking Spanish with relatives. Using Spanish, he was quickly effusive. Especially when talking with other men, his voice would spark, flicker, flare alive with sounds. In Spanish, he expressed ideas and feelings he rarely revealed in English. With firm Spanish sounds, he conveyed confidence and authority English would never allow him.

The silence at home, however, was finally more than a literal 17 silence. Fewer words passed between parent and child, but more profound was the silence that resulted from my inattention to sounds. At about the time I no longer bothered to listen with care to the sounds of English in public, I grew careless about listening to the sounds family members made when they spoke. Most of the time I heard someone speaking at home and didn't distinguish his sounds from the words people uttered in public. I didn't even pay much attention to my parents' accented and ungrammatical speech. At least not at home. Only when I was with them in public would I grow alert to their accents. Though, even then, their sounds caused me less and less concern. For I was increasingly confident of my own public identity.

I would have been happier about my public success had I not 18 sometimes recalled what it had been like earlier, when my family had conveyed its intimacy through a set of conveniently private sounds. Sometimes in public, hearing a stranger, I'd hark back to my past. A Mexican farmworker approached me downtown to ask directions to

COLLABORATIVE ACTIVITY

Ask students, working in small groups, to discuss the private and public aspects of family life. Ask them in what sense they, like Rodriguez, speak a private language. Then ask them to dis-cuss how their private language differs from their public language.

somewhere, "*¿Hijito . . .?*"[4] he said. And his voice summoned deep longing. Another time, standing beside my mother in the visiting room of a Carmelite convent, before the dense screen which rendered the nuns shadowy figures, I heard several Spanish-speaking nuns— their busy, singsong overlapping voices—assure us that yes, yes, we were remembered, all our family was remembered in their prayers. (Their voices echoed faraway family sounds.) Another day, a dark-faced old woman—her hand light on my shoulder—steadied herself against me as she boarded a bus. She murmured something I couldn't quite comprehend. Her Spanish voice came near, like the face of a never-before-seen relative in the instant before I was kissed. Her voice, like so many of the Spanish voices I'd hear in public, recalled the golden age of my youth. Hearing Spanish then, I continued to be a careful, if sad, listener to sounds. Hearing a Spanish-speaking family walking behind me, I turned to look. I smiled for an instant, before my glance found the Hispanic-looking faces of strangers in the crowd going by.

WRITING SUGGESTIONS

1. Write an essay in which you discuss to what degree new immigrants should assimilate into United States society. For example, should the public school system be responsible for helping them to maintain their ethnic identities?
2. Write an essay describing the private language that your family uses at home.

Today I hear bilingual educators say that children lose a degree 19 of "individuality" by becoming assimilated into public society. (Bilingual schooling was popularized in the seventies, that decade when middle-class ethnics began to resist the process of assimilation—the American melting pot.) But the bilingualists simplistically scorn the value and necessity of assimilation. They do not seem to realize that there are *two* ways a person is individualized. So they do not realize that while one suffers a diminished sense of *private* individuality by becoming assimilated into public society, such assimilation makes possible the achievement of *public* individuality.

The bilingualists insist that a student should be reminded of his 20 difference from others in mass society, his heritage. But they equate mere separateness with individuality. The fact is that only in private— with intimates—is separateness from the crowd a prerequisite for individuality. (An intimate draws me apart, tells me that I am unique, unlike all others.) In public, by contrast, full individuality is achieved, paradoxically, by those who are able to consider themselves members of the crowd. Thus it happened for me: Only when I was able to think of myself as an American, no longer an alien in *gringo* society, could I seek the rights and opportunities necessary for full public individuality. The social and political advantages I enjoy as a man result from the day that I came to believe that my name, indeed, is *Rich-heard Road-ree-guess.* It is true that my public society today is often

---

[4]"Little boy . . . .?" [Eds.]

impersonal. (My public society is usually mass society). Yet despite the anonymity of the crowd and despite the fact that the individuality I achieve in public is often tenuous—because it depends on my being one in a crowd—I celebrate the day I acquired my new name. Those middle-class ethnics who scorn assimilation seem to me filled with decadent self-pity, obsessed by the burden of public life. Dangerously, they romanticize public separateness and they trivialize the dilemma of the socially disadvantaged.

My awkward childhood does not prove the necessity of bilingual education. My story discloses instead an essential myth of child-hood—inevitable pain. If I rehearse here the changes in my private life after my Americanization, it is finally to emphasize the public gain. The loss implies the gain: The house I returned to each afternoon was quiet. Intimate sounds no longer rushed to the door to greet me. There were other noises inside. The telephone rang. Neighborhood kids ran past the door of the bedroom where I was reading my school-books—covered with shopping-bag paper. Once I learned public lan-guage, it would never again be easy for me to hear intimate family voices. More and more of my day was spent hearing words. But that may only be a way of saying that the day I raised my hand in class and spoke loudly to an entire roomful of faces, my childhood started to end. 21

RESPONDING TO READING

1. Richard Rodriguez has been criticized by those who favor teaching Spanish-speaking children in both Spanish and English. Do you agree with Rodriguez's contention that Spanish-speaking children should be taught only in English?   **2.** Do you agree with Rodriguez when he says that, by empha-sizing the separateness of Spanish language and culture, those who favor bilingual education "romanticize public separateness and they trivialize the dilemma of the socially disadvantaged" (paragraph 20)?   **3.** Many of Rod-riguez's critics have accused him of being too middle class. Why is this a criticism? How do you feel about this criticism?

ANSWERS TO RESPONDING
TO READING
1. Answers will vary.
2. Answers will vary.
3. This is a criticism because identifying oneself with one class and its values impedes one's ability to empathize with other classes and their values. However, there is no evidence that Rodriguez's views represent those of a specific class. Rodriguez is reported to have responded to this criticism by saying that only someone who has achieved middle-class status can use the term *middle class* in a derogatory way.

The Language of Prejudice

GORDON ALLPORT

Gordon Allport (1897–1967) gained fame as a social psychologist interested in personality theory, expressive behavior, and religion. Also respected as an international authority on racial prejudice, Allport was the editor of the *Journal of Abnormal and Social Psychology* from 1937 to 1949. He has said that individuals act "not so much because of universal primordial drives, but rather as a result of individual characteristics developed over a lifetime." Among his books are *Personality: A Psychological Interpretation* (1937, a standard text in the field for a time), *The Psychology of Rumor* (1947), and *Writing for the Lord: 33 Meditations on God and Man* (1978). In the following selection from *The Nature of Prejudice* (1954), Allport examines the link between prejudice and language.

FOR OPENERS

Discuss "categories" of people we know by their labels. Avoid ethnic slurs or political identifications; instead, focus on terms like *handicapped*, *mother*, *jock*, *bookworm*, or *tomboy*. Tell students to attach connotations to the words and then analyze the origins of those connotations.

1   Without words we should scarcely be able to form categories at all. A dog perhaps forms rudimentary generalizations, such as small-boys-are-to-be avoided—but this concept runs its course on the conditioned reflex level, and does not become the object of thought as such. In order to hold a generalization in mind for reflection and recall, for identification and for action, we need to fix it in words. Without words our world would be, as William James said, an "empirical sand-heap."

Nouns That Cut Slices

2   In the empirical world of human beings there are some two and a half billion grains of sand corresponding to our category "the human race." We cannot possibly deal with so many separate entities in our thought, nor can we individualize even among the hundreds whom we encounter in our daily round. We must group them, form clusters. We welcome, therefore, the names that help us to perform the clustering.

3   The most important property of a noun is that it brings many grains of sand into a single pail, disregarding the fact that the same grains might have fitted just as appropriately into another pail. To state the matter technically, a noun *abstracts* from a concrete reality some one feature and assembles different concrete realities only with respect to this one feature. The very act of classifying forces us to overlook all other features, many of which might offer a sounder basis than the rubric we select. Irving Lee gives the following example:

> I knew a man who had lost the use of both eyes. He was called a "blind man." He could also be called an expert typist, a conscientious

ADDITIONAL QUESTIONS FOR RESPONDING TO READING

1. Keep this question in mind as you begin to read: Which comes first, language or thought?
2. Define *empirical*. How does this word operate in this essay?
3. In what ways do the labels we use reinforce or undercut our prejudices?

worker, a good student, a careful listener, a man who wanted a job. But he couldn't get a job in the department store order room where employees sat and typed orders which came over the telephone. The personnel man was impatient to get the interview over. "But you're a blind man," he kept saying, and one could almost feel his silent assumption that somehow the incapacity in one aspect made the man incapable in every other. So blinded by the label was the interviewer that he could not be persuaded to look beyond it.

Some labels, such as "blind man," are exceedingly salient and powerful. They tend to prevent alternative classification, or even cross-classification. Ethnic labels are often of this type, particularly if they refer to some highly visible feature, e.g., Negro, Oriental. They resemble the labels that point to some outstanding incapacity—*feeble-minded, cripple, blind man*. Let us call such symbols "labels of primary potency." These symbols act like shrieking sirens, deafening us to all finer discriminations that we might otherwise perceive. Even though the blindness of one man and the darkness of pigmentation of another may be defining attributes for some purposes, they are irrelevant and "noisy" for others.

Most people are unaware of this basic law of language—that every label applied to a given person refers properly only to one aspect of his nature. You may correctly say that a certain man is *human, a philanthropist, a Chinese, a physician, an athlete*. A given person may be all of these; but the chances are that *Chinese* stands out in your mind as the symbol of primary potency. Yet neither this nor any other classificatory label can refer to the whole of a man's nature. (Only his proper name can do so.)

Thus each label we use, especially those of primary potency, distracts our attention from concrete reality. The living, breathing, complex individual—the ultimate unit of human nature—is lost to sight. As in the figure,[1] the label magnifies one attribute out of all proportion to its true significance, and masks other important attributes of the individual.

A category, once formed with the aid of a symbol of primary potency, tends to attract more attributes than it should. The category labeled *Chinese* comes to signify not only ethnic membership but also reticence, impassivity, poverty, treachery. To be sure, . . . there may be genuine ethnic-linked traits, making for a certain *probability* that the member of an ethnic stock may have these attributes. But our cognitive process is not cautious. The labeled category, as we have seen, includes indiscriminately the defining attribute, probable attributes, and wholly fanciful, nonexistent attributes.

---

[1]Not reprinted here. [Eds.]

TEACHING STRATEGY

Discuss the following with your students:

Paragraph 1: Explain James's phrase. Imagine perceptions without language. How might human beings behave?

Paragraph 4: Although Allport concedes that "labels of primary potency" may sometimes be useful, some people may argue that such labels (particularly those referring to race) are *never* appropriate. What do you think?

Paragraph 6: What does Allport believe to be the primary flaw of such labels?

Paragraph 28: Can you think of other periods in America during which "differentiated thinking" was "at a low ebb"? Did this kind of thinking occur during the Persian Gulf War?

Paragraph 29: Representative Martin's diatribe resembles President Bush's characterization of Massachusetts Governor Michael Dukakis as a "card-carrying member of the ACLU" during the 1988 presidential debates.

Paragraph 36: How might we liberate ourselves from monopolistic categories?

Even proper names—which ought to invite us to look at the   8
individual person—may act like symbols of primary potency, especially if they arouse ethnic associations. Mr. Greenberg is a person,
but since his name is Jewish, it activates in the hearer his entire
category of Jews-as-a-whole. An ingenious experiment performed by
Razran shows this point clearly, and at the same time demonstrates
how a proper name, acting like an ethnic symbol, may bring with it
an avalanche of stereotypes.

> Thirty photographs of college girls were shown on a screen to 150
> students. The subjects rated the girls on a scale from one to five for
> *beauty, intelligence, character, ambition, general likability*. Two months
> later the same subjects were asked to rate the same photographs
> (and fifteen additional ones introduced to complicate the memory
> factor). This time five of the original photographs were given Jewish
> surnames (Cohen, Kantor, etc.), five Italian (Valenti, etc.), and five
> Irish (O'Brien, etc.); and the remaining girls were given names
> chosen from the signers of the Declaration of Independence and
> from the Social Register (Davis, Adams, Clark, etc.).
>
> When Jewish names were attached to photographs there
> occurred the following changes in ratings:
>
> > decrease in liking
> >
> > decrease in character
> >
> > decrease in beauty
> >
> > increase in intelligence
> >
> > increase in ambition
>
> For those photographs given Italian names there occurred:
>
> > decrease in liking
> >
> > decrease in character
> >
> > decrease in beauty
> >
> > decrease in intelligence
>
> Thus a mere proper name leads to prejudgments of personal attri-
> butes. The individual is fitted to the prejudice ethnic category, and
> not judged in his own right.
>
> While the Irish names also brought about depreciated judgment,
> the depreciation was not as great as in the case of the Jews and
> Italians. The falling of likability of the "Jewish girls" was twice as
> great as for "Italians" and five times as great as for "Irish." We note,
> however, that the "Jewish" photographs caused higher ratings in
> *intelligence* and in *ambition*. Not all stereotypes of out-groups are
> unfavorable.

The anthropologist, Margaret Mead, has suggested that labels of   9
primary potency lose some of their force when they are changed from
nouns into adjectives. To speak of a Negro soldier, a Catholic teacher,
or a Jewish artist calls attention to the fact that some other group

classifications are just as legitimate as the racial or religious. If George Johnson is spoken of not only as a Negro but also as a *soldier*, we have at least two attributes to know him by, and two are more accurate than one. To depict him truly as an individual, of course, we should have to name many more attributes. It is a useful suggestion that we designate ethnic and religious membership where possible with *adjectives* rather than *nouns*.

Emotionally Toned Labels

Many categories have two kinds of labels—one less emotional 10 and one more emotional. Ask yourself how you feel, and what thoughts you have, when you read the words *school teacher*, and then *school marm*. Certainly the second phrase calls up something more strict, more ridiculous, more disagreeable than the former. Here are four innocent letters: *m-a-r-m*. But they make us shudder a bit, laugh a bit, and scorn a bit. They call up an image of a spare, humorless, irritable old maid. They do not tell us that she is an individual human being with sorrows and troubles of her own. They force her instantly into a rejective category.

In the ethnic sphere even plain labels such as *Negro, Italian, Jew,* 11 *Catholic, Irish-American, French-Canadian* may have emotional tone for a reason that we shall soon explain. But they all have their higher key equivalents: *nigger, wop, kike, papist, harp, canuck*. When these labels are employed we can be almost certain that the speaker *intends* not only to characterize the person's membership, but also to disparage and reject him.

Quite apart from the insulting intent that lies behind the use of 12 certain labels, there is also an inherent ("physiognomic") handicap in many terms designating ethnic membership. For example, the proper names characteristic of certain ethnic memberships strike us as absurd. (We compare them, of course, with what is familiar and therefore "right.") Chinese names are short and silly; Polish names intrinsically difficult and outlandish. Unfamiliar dialects strike us as ludicrous. Foreign dress (which, of course, is a visual ethnic symbol) seems unnecessarily queer.

But of all these "physiognomic" handicaps the reference to color, 13 clearly implied in certain symbols, is the greatest. The word *Negro* comes from the Latin *niger* meaning black. In point of fact, no Negro has a black complexion, but by comparison with other blonder stocks, he has come to be known as a "black man." Unfortunately *black* in the English language is a word having a preponderance of sinister connotations: *the outlook is black, blackball, blackguard, black-hearted, black death, blacklist, blackmail, Black Hand.* In his novel *Moby Dick,* Herman Melville considers at length the remarkably morbid connotations of black and the remarkably virtuous connotations of white.

Nor is the ominous flavor of black confined to the English language. A cross-cultural study reveals that the semantic significance of black is more or less universally the same. Among certain Siberian tribes, members of a privileged clan call themselves "white bones," and refer to all others as "black bones." Even among Uganda Negroes there is some evidence for a white god at the apex of the theocratic hierarchy; certain it is that a white cloth, signifying purity, is used to ward off evil spirits and disease. 14

There is thus an implied value-judgment in the very concept of *white race* and *black race.* One might also study the numerous unpleasant connotations of *yellow,* and their possible bearing on our conception of the people of the Orient. 15

Such reasoning should not be carried too far, since there are undoubtedly, in various contexts, pleasant associations with both black and yellow. Black velvet is agreeable, so too are chocolate and coffee. Yellow tulips are well liked; the sun and moon are radiantly yellow. Yet it is true that "color" words are used with chauvinistic overtones more than most people realize. There is certainly condescension indicated in many familiar phrases: *dark as a nigger's pocket, darktown strutters, white hope* (a term originated when a white contender was sought against the Negro heavyweight champion, Jack Johnson), *the white man's burden, the yellow peril, black boy.* Scores of everyday phrases are stamped with the flavor of prejudice, whether the user knows it or not. 16

We spoke of the fact that even the most proper and sedate labels for minority groups sometimes seem to exude a negative flavor. In many contexts and situations the very terms *French-Canadian, Mexican,* or *Jew,* correct and nonmalicious though they are, sound a bit opprobrious. The reason is that they are labels of social deviants. Especially in a culture where uniformity is prized, the name of *any* deviant carries with it *ipso facto* a negative value-judgment. Words like *insane, alcoholic, pervert* are presumably neutral designations of a human condition, but they are more: they are finger-pointing at a deviance. Minority groups are deviants, and for this reason, from the very outset, the most innocent labels in many situations imply a shading of disrepute. When we wish to highlight the deviance and denigrate it still further we use words of a higher emotional key: crackpot, soak, pansy, greaser, Okie, nigger, harp, kike. 17

Members of minority groups are often understandably sensitive to names given them. Not only do they object to deliberately insulting epithets, but sometimes see evil intent where none exists. Often the 18

COLLABORATIVE ACTIVITY

Ask students to list labels that they feel others might apply to them; these labels can characterize them by college major, ethnic group, or familial and other social roles. Students should then anonymously exchange lists and, with the lists they obtain, attempt to identify the person who compiled the list solely on the basis of the labels. Discuss the results of the exercise with the class, focusing on the inaccuracy of stereotypes.

word *Negro* is spelled with a small *n*, occasionally as a studied insult, more often from ignorance. (The term is not cognate with *white*, which is not capitalized, but rather with *Caucasian*, which is.) Terms like *mulatto* or *octoroon* cause hard feeling because of the condescension with which they have often been used in the past. Sex differentiations are objectionable, since they seem doubly to emphasize ethnic difference: why speak of *Jewess* and not of *Protestantess*, or of *Negress* and not of *whitess*? Similar overemphasis is implied in the terms like Chinamen or Scotchman; why not American man? Grounds for misunderstanding lie in the fact that minority group members are sensitive to such shadings, while majority members may employ them unthinkingly.

The Communist Label

Until we label an out-group it does not clearly exist in our minds.   19
Take the curiously vague situation that we often meet when a person wishes to locate responsibility on the shoulders of some out-group whose nature he cannot specify. In such a case he usually employs the pronoun "they" without an antecedent. "Why don't they make these sidewalks wider?" "I hear they are going to build a factory in this town and hire a lot of foreigners." "I won't pay this tax bill; they can just whistle for their money." If asked "who?" the speaker is likely to grow confused and embarrassed. The common use of the orphaned pronoun *they* teaches us that people often want and need to designate out-groups (usually for the purpose of venting hostility) even when they have no clear conception of the out-group in question. And so long as the target of wrath remains vague and ill-defined specific prejudice cannot crystallize around it. To have enemies we need labels.

Until relatively recently—strange as it may seem—there was no   20
agreed-upon symbol for *communist*. The word, of course, existed but it had no special emotional connotation, and did not designate a public enemy. Even when, after World War I, there was a growing feeling of economic and social menace in this country, there was no agreement as to the actual source of the menace.

A content analysis of the Boston *Herald* for the year 1920 turned   21
up the following list of labels. Each was used in a content implying some threat. Hysteria had overspread the country, as it did after World War II. Someone must be responsible for the postwar malaise, rising prices, uncertainty. There must be a villain. But in 1920 the villain was impartially designated by reporters and editorial writers with the following symbols:

alien, agitator, anarchist, apostle of bomb and torch. Bolshevik, communist, communist laborite, conspirator, emissary of false promise, extremist, foreigner, hyphenated-American, incendiary, IWW, parlor anarchist, parlor pink, parlor socialist, plotter, radical, red, revolutionary, Russian agitator, socialist, Soviet, syndicalist, traitor, undesirable.

From this excited array we note that the *need* for an enemy   22
(someone to serve as a focus for discontent and jitters) was considerably more apparent than the precise *identity* of the enemy. At any rate, there was no clearly agreed upon label. Perhaps partly for this reason the hysteria abated. Since no clear category of "communism" existed there was no true focus for the hostility.

But following World War II this collection of vaguely interchange-   23
able labels became fewer in number and more commonly agreed upon. The out-group menace came to be designated almost always as *communist* or *red*. In 1920 the threat, lacking a clear label, was vague; after 1945 both symbol and thing became more definite. Not that people knew precisely what they meant when they said "communist," but with the aid of the term they were at least able to point consistently to *something* that inspired fear. The term developed the power of signifying menace and led to various repressive measures against anyone to whom the label was rightly or wrongly attached.

Logically, the label should apply to specifiable defining attributes,   24
such as members of the Communist Party, or people whose allegiance is with the Russian system, or followers, historically, of Karl Marx. But the label came in for far more extensive use.

What seems to have happened is approximately as follows.   25
Having suffered through a period of war and being acutely aware of devastating revolutions abroad, it is natural that most people should be upset, dreading to lose their possessions, annoyed by high taxes, seeing customary moral and religious values threatened, and dreading worse disasters to come. Seeking an explanation for this unrest, a single identifiable enemy is wanted. It is not enough to designate "Russia" or some other distant land. Nor is it satisfactory to fix blame on "changing social conditions." What is needed is a human agent near at hand: someone in Washington, someone in our schools, in our factories, in our neighborhood. If we *feel* an immediate threat, we reason, there must be a near-lying danger. It is, we conclude, communism, not only in Russia but also in America, at our doorstep, in our government, in our churches, in our colleges, in our neighborhood.

Are we saying that hostility toward communism is prejudice? Not   26
necessarily. There are certainly phases of the dispute wherein realistic social conflict is involved. American values (e.g., respect for the

person) and totalitarian values as represented in Soviet practice are intrinsically at odds. A realistic opposition in some form will occur. Prejudice enters only when the defining attributes of "communist" grow imprecise, when anyone who favors any form of social change is called a communist. People who fear social change are the ones most likely to affix the label to any persons or practices that seem to them threatening.

For them the category is undifferentiated. It includes books, 27 movies, preachers, teachers who utter what for them are uncongenial thoughts. If evil befalls—perhaps forest fires or a factory explosion— it is due to communist saboteurs. The category becomes monopolistic, covering almost anything that is uncongenial. On the floor of the House of Representatives in 1946, Representative Rankin called James Roosevelt a communist. Congressman Outland replied with psychological acumen, "Apparently everyone who disagrees with Mr. Rankin is a communist."

When differentiated thinking is at a low ebb—as it is in times of 28 social crises—there is a magnification of two-valued logic. Things are perceived as either inside or outside a moral order. What is outside is likely to be called "communist." Correspondingly—and here is where damage is done—whatever is called "communist" (however erroneously) is immediately cast outside the moral order.

This associative mechanism places enormous power in the hands 29 of a demagogue. For several years Senator McCarthy managed to discredit many citizens who thought differently from himself by the simple device of calling them communist. Few people were able to see through this trick and many reputations were ruined. But the famous senator has no monopoly on the device. As reported in the Boston *Herald* on November 1, 1946, Representative Joseph Martin, Republican leader in the House, ended his election campaign against his Democratic opponent by saying, "The people will vote tomorrow between chaos, confusion, bankruptcy, state socialism or communism, and the preservation of our American life, with all its freedom and its opportunities." Such an array of emotional labels placed his opponent outside the accepted moral order. Martin was re-elected. . . .

Not everyone, of course, is taken in, Demagogy, when it goes 30 too far, meets with ridicule. Elizabeth Dilling's book, *The Red Network*, was so exaggerated in its two-valued logic that it was shrugged off by many people with a smile. One reader remarked, "Apparently if you step off the sidewalk with your left foot you're a communist." But it is not easy in times of social strain and hysteria to keep one's balance, and to resist the tendency of a verbal symbol to manufacture large and fanciful categories of prejudiced thinking.

Verbal Realism and Symbol Phobia

Most individuals rebel at being labeled, especially if the label is 31
uncomplimentary. Very few are willing to be called "fascistic,"
"socialistic," or "anti-Semitic." Unsavory labels may apply to others;
but not to us.

An illustration of the craving that people have to attach favorable 32
symbols to themselves is seen in the community where white people
banded together to force out a Negro family that had moved in. They
called themselves "Neighborly Endeavor" and chose as their motto
the Golden Rule. One of the first acts of this symbol-sanctified band
was to sue the man who sold property to Negroes. They then flooded
the house which another Negro couple planned to occupy. Such were
the acts performed under the banner of the Golden Rule.

Studies made by Stagner and Hartmann show that a person's 33
political attitudes may in fact entitle him to be called a fascist or a
socialist, and yet he will emphatically repudiate the unsavory label,
and fail to endorse any movement or candidate that overtly accepts
them. In short, there is a *symbol phobia* that corresponds to *symbol
realism*. We are more inclined to the former when we ourselves are
concerned, though we are much less critical when epithets of "fascist," "communist," "blind man," "school marm" are applied to
others.

When symbols provoke strong emotions they are sometimes 34
regarded no longer as symbols, but as actual things. The expressions
"son of a bitch" and "liar" are in our culture frequently regarded as
"fighting words." Softer and more subtle expressions of contempt
may be accepted. But in these particular cases, the epithet itself must
be "taken back." We certainly do not change our opponent's attitude
by making him take back a word, but it seems somehow important
that the word itself be eradicated.

Such verbal realism may reach extreme length. 35

> The City Council of Cambridge, Massachusetts, unanimously passed
> a resolution (December, 1939) making it illegal "to possess, harbor,
> sequester, introduce or transport, within the city limits, any book,
> map, magazine, newspaper, pamphlet, handbill or circular con-
> taining the words Lenin or Leningrad."

Such naiveté in confusing language with reality is hard to comprehend
unless we recall that word-magic plays an appreciable part in human
thinking. The following examples, like the one preceding, are taken
from Hayakawa.[2]

---

[2]S.I. Hayakawa (1906–   ) is an American linguist. [Eds.]

WRITING SUGGESTION

Write an essay about a time you discovered
that the label you applied to a person or group
did not apply. What led you to your conclusion?
What effect did your discovery have on you?

The Malagsy soldier must eschew kidneys, because in the Malagasy language the word for kidney is the same as that for "shot"; so shot he would certainly be if he ate a kidney.

In May, 1937, a state senator of New York bitterly opposed a bill for the control of syphilis because "the innocence of children might be corrupted by a widespread use of the term. . . . This particular word creates a shudder in every decent woman and decent man."

This tendency to reify words underscores the close cohesion that 36 exists between category and symbol. Just the mention of "communist," "Negro," "Jew," "England," "Democrats," will send some people into a panic of fear or a frenzy of anger. Who can say whether it is the word or the thing that annoys them? The label is an intrinsic part of any monopolistic category. Hence to liberate a person from ethnic or political prejudice it is necessary at the same time to liberate him from *word fetishism*. This fact is well known to students of general semantics, who tell us that prejudice is due in large part to verbal realism and to symbol phobia. Therefore any program for the reduction of prejudice must include a large measure of semantic therapy.

RESPONDING TO READING

1. How do you react to Allport's contention in paragraph 4 that certain labels are exceedingly powerful? What does he mean? What particular labels have the power he describes?   **2.** What does Allport mean when he says in paragraph 9 that we should "designate ethnic and religious membership . . . with *adjectives* rather than *nouns*"? Do you think that doing this would make a difference?   **3.** In 1990 many of the Communist bloc countries asserted their independence from the Soviet Union. Some political analysts believe that by doing so they all but ended the cold war and the Soviet Union's threat to the West. In what way do you think these events have affected the *communist* label Allport discusses in paragraph 23?

ANSWERS TO RESPONDING
TO READING

1. Labels such as *feebleminded*, *cripple*, and *blind man* are "labels of primary potency" that focus on one characteristic at the expense of all others. You might tell students that the term *handicapped*, which replaced *crippled*, is now in disfavor among many persons with disabilities. Why do students believe this is so?
2. Allport employs Margaret Mead's observation that adjectives serve to modify, not to define. Therefore, they must be used with another word, and there is a greater likelihood that the two-word label will be more accurate than a noun.
3. In the West the "communist" label is likely to be perceived with less fear.

Remember My Name

TREY ELLIS

Trey Ellis (1962–   ) is a novelist, essayist, and journalist. He has published one novel to date, *Platitudes* (1988), a comic story about the struggles of a writer in New York. This novel, in which Ellis comments on the different styles in African-American literary tradition, has been praised for its realistic adolescent dialogue; the style is varied and experimental, and includes survey charts, menus, lyrics, and TV and film dialogue. In the following essay, Ellis takes issue with the term *African-American*.

I'm a Colored Spade,
A Nigra,
A Black Nigger,
A Jungle Bunny,
Jigaboo, Coon,
Pickaninny, Mau Mau,
Uncle Tom, Aunt Jemima,
Little Black Sambo,
Cotton Pickin' Swamp Guinea,
Junk Man, Shoeshine Boy, Elevator Operator,
Table Cleaner at Horn & Hardart,
Slave voodoo zombie,
Ubangi-lipped flat-nosed tap-dancer,
Resident of Harlem,
And President of the United States of Love

—"Colored Spade" from the musical *Hair*

FOR OPENERS

Why have various ethnic groups begun to identify themselves with hyphenated labels (Nationality-American)? Do you see this phenomenon as positive or negative?

ADDITIONAL QUESTIONS FOR RESPONDING TO READING

1. Does the designation *African-American* seem to carry less power than the term *black*? Why or why not?
2. Should people have the right to apply labels of their own choosing to themselves?

To Jesse Jackson and many other African-American leaders whom I greatly admire, I have to ask why this, why now. Like the debate in Israel today over how much Jewish blood makes you Jewish, this current black semantic brouhaha[1] is a waste of time. While Israel should be worrying day and night about peacemaking, and while blacks (Blacks, Afro-Americans, African-Americans) should be worrying about the daily litany of our worsening, horror-story statistics (infant mortality, college dropout, murder, crack-addiction rates, you name it), up pops this nonissue to sap energy that we cannot spare. This is a topic to take up Sunday afternoon over barbecue, reward for a week of wrestling with real problems.

African-American is merely a more specific, more formal, and less powerful synonym for *black*. *Afro-American*, like *Italo-American*, is simply a more wieldy, slightly less formal version of its longer brother.

The change from *colored* to *black* was an important linguistic battle for our self-determination; our own Russian revolution into good Soviets. While the terms *black* and *African-American* both predate this century, *black* was the one my parents fought for from the wrong end of a fire hose. Why throw it away? It is equal in importance and weight (and, while we're at it, number of letters) to *white* and graphically demonstrates how divided we still are. African-American, though more specific, relegates us to just another hyphenate satellite around WASP[2] America. Yet no matter what you call it or how you

---

[1]Uproar. [Eds.]
[2]*WASP* (White Anglo Saxon Protestant) often implies the ruling elite. [Eds.]

capitalize it, today's world is not divided between African-American and white, but still, unfortunately, between black and white.

Black unifies all people of African descent across national borders. Africans themselves are blacks. Whether Senegalese, Brazilian, Jamaican, Haitian, or Alabaman, *black* integrates us all. In England, Africans and Afro-Caribbeans call themselves *blacks*. Aboriginal Australians are black and call themselves just that. Many Polynesians are black, and there are even black Mexicans called *morenos* (blacks).

Before the '60s, *black* meant something very different to black people: *If you're white you're all right, if you're yellow you're mellow, if you're brown stick around, if you're black stay back*. Unlike Brazil's encyclopedia of skin-tone and hair-texture gradations, *black* unified the rainbow coalition of African-Americans. After the term was coined here, whether yellow or chocolate or pitch, we all rallied around the very word that had been a shameful insult for decades.

In 1878, Ferdinand Lee Barnett spearheaded the drive to capitalize *Negro*. "This breach of orthography," he wrote in his Chicago newspaper *The Conservator*, "is the white man's mark of disrespect." After *black* arose, many also insisted on capitalizing it—never mind that *white* is lowercase. I say if capitalization brings respect, why not go all the way to *BLACK*. Then how about a respect-commanding exclamation point: *BLACK!* And for Spanish speaking blacks, maybe . . . ¡*BLACK!* That's certainly far easier tongue-wagging than *African-Hispanic (Latino?)-American*.

> . . .blood, darky, Tar Baby, Kaffir, shine. . .

The argument for *African-American* over *black* is that all other American ethnic groups are hyphenate Americans, the first word a tribute to the country of their ancestors. And I'm ashamed we don't involve ourselves in overthrowing South Africa as much as American Jews have supported Israel. I wish we would revel in our African roots at least as fervently as Italian-Americans celebrate themselves on Columbus Day and Irish-Americans on St. Paddy's. I wish more of us would call ourselves simply *Africans* the way Italian-Americans and Irish-Americans often speak of themselves as simply *Italians* or *Irish*. It's not only because our forced immigration came so long ago that too many of us stopped identifying with the continent. Tarzan taught us to despise it and the African within us. The only non-Native Americans (a much more correct term than Columbus's "Indians") who've been living in America as long as blacks are WASPs. While they, for the most part, don't align themselves too often with the United Kingdom, neither are they ashamed of their homeland. Although I appreciate the motivation of this new African-American semantic movement, I just feel they jumped on this easy target

TEACHING STRATEGY

Discuss the following with your students:

Paragraph 1: Note Ellis's analogy between African-Americans and Jews. Is this analogy valid? What other situations are analogous to the ones he describes?

Paragraph 3: Discuss Ellis's argumentative technique. In this paragraph he explores the superiority and advantages of the term *black*. What are these advantages? What shortcomings does he see as inherent in the term African-American?

Paragraph 3: Explain what Ellis means when he says that his parents fought for the term *black* "from the wrong end of a fire hose."

Paragraph 7: How does the conclusion of this paragraph affect you? Why?

Paragraph 13: Refer students to Malcolm X's discovery of the subjective nature of history and the truth of race in world development ("A Homemade Education," page 194).

COLLABORATIVE ACTIVITIES

1. Divide the class into groups. Ask them to consider Ellis's technique of listing offensive racial labels between the sections of the essay. How effective is this technique? In what way does it reinforce Ellis's ideas?
2. Ask groups to discuss the connotations of the different terms in the lines from *Hair* that open the essay. In class discussion, consider why Ellis opens with these lines.

because solutions to our hard problems are so painful. Yet, no amount of all-night copy editing is going to colorblind this world.

> . . .*Moor, blackamoor, Jim Crow, spook*. . .

Bringing our long hyphenate out of the classrooms and into the streets could only happen in this post-*Cosby* world where blacks are more accepted than ever. *Middle-class* blacks, that is. But no matter how successfully we are beginning to assimilate, for now our place as "Minority No. 1" is unshakable. Like the Jews in Europe, we've always been distinctly separated from the mainstream. (Maybe that's why black and Jewish women were the only female humans ever queerly suffixed like tigresses and lionesses as "Negress" and "Jewess.") Our "otherness" is the other by which all other "others" are judged.   8

Though the strongest proponents of *African-American* are pan-Africanists and Black (or, I guess, now *African-American*) Nationalists, ironically, the term is the most assimilationist we have ever known. An African-American is one American of many who happens to have African forebears. A black American is a breed apart. Unfortunately, the world hasn't yet earned the new, politically-correct term.   9

> . . .*quadroon, meriney, red bone, high yellow*. . .

The importance of the term's rise now is its coincidence with the rise in the number of mulattoes. (Spanish for *young mule*, half mare, half jackass. If anyone needs nicer terminology, it's them.) *African-American* is clearly the only correct choice when describing the black component of a mixed-race person's ancestry. And if the world were fair these people could claim allegiance to all their hyphenates. However, in America, racism forces them black. *African-American* for them is a positive step in learning how to successfully straddle the fence. In fact, mixed-race Americans are just now beginning to organize themselves as a self-sustaining group. South Africa solved this identity problem by calling them *coloured*. Yet for a little while longer at least, yellow is black, too. As comedian Chris Rock said about one mixed-race black actress, "You're black—go try and marry a fucking Kennedy and see how black you really are."   10

> . . .*Mammy, porch monkey, home, homeboy, George*. . .

Naming black people has preoccupied Americans since we were shoveled off the boats. Check Roget's[3]—we have more synonyms than any other ethnic group, most of them unflattering. America first   11

---

[3]*Roget's Thesaurus* is a reference book that lists words and their synonyms. [Eds.]

called us what the Spanish and Portuguese slave traders had dubbed us, *negro*, their word for black. According to Stanford University professor Sylvia Winter, royal West African slave-trading collaborators were so desperate to distance themselves from the common *negros* that they arbitrarily dubbed themselves yet another Portuguese word for black, *prietos*. Today in Brazil, among the dozens of degrees of blackness, *negros* are the black-skinned Afro-Brazilians (don't even think about the ugly sounding *African-Brazilian* for that gorgeous girl from Ipanema), while *prietos* are brown-skinned and *mulatos* are yellow.

None too much explanation is needed for the *negro*-derived word   12
nigger when it bubbles out of the mouth of nonblacks. But the truncated *nigga* becomes pityingly affectionate when uttered black to black (though I personally have never been able to bring myself to let it fly, and am not here advocating its replacing *black* in newspaper headlines).

. . .*spearchucker, schwartze, Leroy, Smokey.* . .

Colored was no improvement. With it the dominant culture was   13
branding us a burned or sooted or shadowy mutation. But little Lucy, the Australopithecus[4] unearthed in Kenya's Rift Valley, proved brown skin was the norm and pink the spin-off. Imperialism has always created its own truths. The Great Works[5] debate in America's universities is but another vestige of this Eurocentric myopia.

People of color, a 1980s term to encompass the entire Third World, I like a lot because it suggests an empowered superset, instead of a disenfranchised subset. In the world as a whole, *people of color* are the thundering majority.

. . .*mouli, buck, Ethiopian, brother, sistah.* . .

Some days I'm black, others I'm Afro- or African-American. I'm   14
a black writer, so more than anything, my label depends on the rhythm of the sentence. Of course, despite this reductivist semantics, the world knows few whites as white as milk, few blacks as black as pitch, and, depending on the season, everyone is, to a certain degree, colored.

Fine. Newspaper headlines *should* be more specific and formal   15

WRITING SUGGESTION

Write an essay in which you agree or disagree with Ellis's position, supporting your thesis with examples drawn from personal experience.

---

[4]An extinct African ape-like creature that is thought to be a remote ancestor of human beings. As a result of its discovery, scientists believe that human beings are a much older species than previously suspected. [Eds.]

[5]For years, many academics and literary critics have contended that the great works of literature were written only by white European and American males. Now, however, many scholars believe (as Ellis does) that the canon of literature should be expanded to include works by women, non-Western writers, and members of minority groups. [Eds.]

and read "African-American leaders irate over *Mississippi Burning's* gross misrepresentations." But when somebody tries to tell me what to call myself in all uses just because they came to some decision at a cocktail party to which I wasn't even invited, my mama raised me to tell them to kiss my black ass. In many cases, *African-American* just won't do.

RESPONDING TO READING

1. Do you agree with Ellis's contention in paragraph 2 that "*African-American* is merely a more specific, more formal, and less powerful synonym for *black*"? Does it, as Ellis contends, relegate "black Americans to just another hyphenate satellite around WASP America"?   **2.** In what way do the terms *black, African-American,* and *people of color* illustrate the power of words to convey attitudes and to influence thought?   **3.** Do you believe that the term *African-American* should replace the term *black*? Why or why not?

You Are What You Say

ROBIN LAKOFF

Linguistics professor Robin Lakoff (1942–   ) was born in Brooklyn and teaches at the University of California at Berkeley. Her books include *Face Value: The Politics of Beauty* (1984), written with Raquel L. Sherr, and *When Talk Is Not Cheap: Or, How to Find the Right Therapist When You Don't Know Where to Begin* (1985), written with Mandy Aftel. *Language and Woman's Place* (1975) is Lakoff's nonscientific analysis of her personal observations and interpretations of language use. In her essay "You Are What You Say," published in *Ms.* in 1974, Lakoff argues that women are socially limited by the language they have been taught to speak and that, for women, "it's time to speak up."

"Women's language" is that pleasant (dainty?), euphemistic   1 never-aggressive way of talking we learned as little girls. Cultural bias was built into the language we were allowed to speak, the subjects we were allowed to speak about, and the ways we were spoken of. Having learned our linguistic lesson well, we go out in the world, only to discover that we are communicative cripples—damned if we do, and damned if we don't.

If we refuse to talk "like a lady," we are ridiculed and criticized   2 for being unfeminine. ("She thinks like a man," is, at best, a left-handed compliment.) If we do learn all the fuzzy-headed, unassertive language of our sex, we are ridiculed for being unable to think clearly, unable to take part in a serious discussion, and therefore unfit to hold a position of power.

It doesn't take much of this for a woman to begin feeling she 3 deserves such treatment because of inadequacies in her own intelligence and education.

"Women's language" shows up in all levels of English. For 4 example, women are encouraged and allowed to make far more precise discriminations in naming colors than men do. Words like *mauve, beige, ecru, aquamarine, lavender,* and so on, are unremarkable in a woman's active vocabulary, but largely absent from that of most men. I know of no evidence suggesting that women actually *see* a wider range of colors than men do. It is simply that fine discriminations of this sort are relevant to women's vocabularies, but not to men's; to men, who control most of the interesting affairs of the world, such distinctions are trivial—irrelevant.

In the area of syntax, we find similar gender-related peculiarities 5 of speech. There is one construction, in particular, that women use conversationally far more than men: the tag question. A tag is midway between an outright statement and a yes-no question; it is less assertive than the former, but more confident than the latter.

A *flat statement* indicates confidence in the speaker's knowledge 6 and is fairly certain to be believed; a *question* indicates a lack of knowledge on some point and implies that the gap in the speaker's knowledge can and will be remedied by an answer. For example, if, at a Little League game, I have had my glasses off, I can legitimately ask someone else: "Was the player out at third?" A *tag question*, being intermediate between statement and question, is used when the speaker is stating a claim, but lacks full confidence in the truth of that claim. So if I say, "Is Joan here?" I will probably not be surprised if my respondent answers "no"; but if I say, "Joan is here, isn't she?" instead, chances are I am already biased in favor of a positive answer, wanting only confirmation. I still want a response, but I have enough knowledge (or think I have) to predict that response. A tag question, then, might be thought of as a statement that doesn't demand to be believed by anyone but the speaker, a way of giving leeway, of not forcing the addressee to go along with the views of the speaker.

Another common use of the tag question is in small talk when 7 the speaker is trying to elicit conversation: "Sure is hot here, isn't it?"

But in discussing personal feelings or opinions, only the speaker 8 normally has any way of knowing the correct answer. Sentences such as "I have a headache, don't I?" are clearly ridiculous. But there are other examples where it is the speaker's opinions, rather than per-

ADDITIONAL QUESTION FOR RESPONDING TO READING

According to some feminists, English is a patriarchal language and therefore an inadequate mode of expression for women because it cannot accurately address their perceptions and experiences. Ask students to respond to this view.

ceptions, for which corroboration is sought, as in "The situation in Southeast Asia is terrible, isn't it?"

While there are, of course, other possible interpretations of a   9
sentence like this, one possibility is that the speaker has a particular answer in mind—"yes" or "no"—but is reluctant to state it baldly. This sort of tag question is much more apt to be used by women than by men in conversation. Why is this the case?

The tag question allows a speaker to avoid commitment, and   10
thereby avoid conflict with the addressee. The problem is that, by so doing, speakers may also give the impression of not really being sure of themselves, or looking to the addressee for confirmation of their views. This uncertainty is reinforced in more subliminal ways, too. There is a peculiar sentence-intonation pattern, used almost exclusively by women, as far as I know, which changes a declarative answer into a question. The effect of using the rising inflection typical of a yes-no question is to imply that the speaker is seeking confirmation, even though the speaker is clearly the only one who has the requisite information, which is why the question was put to her in the first place:

(Q) When will dinner be ready?
(A) Oh . . . around six o'clock . . . ?

It is as though the second speaker were saying, "Six o'clock—if that's okay with you, if you agree." The person being addressed is put in the position of having to provide confirmation. One likely consequence of this sort of speech pattern in a woman is that, often unbeknownst to herself, the speaker builds a reputation of tentativeness, and others will refrain from taking her seriously or trusting her with any real responsibilities, since she "can't make up her mind," and "isn't sure of herself."

Such idiosyncrasies may explain why women's language sounds   11
much more "polite" than men's. It is polite to leave a decision open, not impose your mind, or views, or claims, on anyone else. So a tag question is a kind of polite statement, in that it does not force agreement or belief on the addressee. In the same way a request is a polite command, in that it does not force obedience on the addressee, but rather suggests something be done as a favor to the speaker. A clearly stated order implies a threat of certain consequences if it is not followed, and—even more impolite—implies that the speaker is in a superior position and able to enforce the order. By couching wishes in the form of a request, on the other hand, a speaker implies that if the request is not carried out, only the speaker will suffer; noncompliance cannot harm the addressee. So the deci-

TEACHING STRATEGY

Discuss the following with your students:

Paragraph   1: Explain Lakoff's charge "damned if we do, and damned if we don't."

Paragraph 2: Why does Lakoff call the phrase *she thinks like a man* a "left-handed compliment"?

Paragraph 10: Why is the "tag question" and rising inflection an important linguistic event to explore?

Paragraph 14: Note that many public buildings and eating establishments label restrooms *men* and *ladies.* Ask students if they think *ladies* should be replaced with the more neutral *women.*

Paragraph 16: Remind students of Margaret Mead's suggestion that labels of primary potency are likely to be more accurate when used as adjectives ("The Language of Prejudice," paragraph 9, page 222). Would Lakoff agree? What distinction must we make in answering this question?

Paragraph 25: Gauge students' reactions to Lakoff's evidence for the English "double standard" she perceives. Do students generally agree or disagree?

sion is really left up to the addressee. The distinction becomes clear in these examples:

> Close the door.
> Please close the door.
> Will you close the door?
> Will you please close the door?
> Won't you close the door?

In the same ways as words and speech patterns used *by* women undermine her image, those used to *describe* women make matters even worse. Often a word may be used of both men and women (and perhaps of things as well); but when it is applied to women, it assumes a special meaning that, by implication rather than outright assertion, is derogatory to women as a group.   12

The use of euphemisms has this effect. A euphemism is a substitute for a word that has acquired a bad connotation by association with something unpleasant or embarrassing. But almost as soon as the new word comes into common usage, it takes on the same old bad connotations, since feelings about the things or people referred to are not altered by a change of name; thus new euphemisms must be constantly found.   13

There is one euphemism for *woman* still very much alive. The word, of course, is *lady*. *Lady* has a masculine counterpart, namely *gentleman*, occasionally shortened to *gent*. But for some reason *lady* is very much commoner than *gent(leman)*.   14

The decision to use *lady* rather than *woman*, or vice versa, may considerably alter the sense of a sentence, as the following examples show: 15

> (a) A woman (lady) I know is a dean at Berkeley.
> (b) A woman (lady) I know makes amazing things out of shoelaces and old boxes.

The use of *lady* in (a) imparts a frivolous, or nonserious, tone to the sentence: the matter under discussion is not one of great moment. Similarly, in (b), using *lady* here would suggest that the speaker considered the "amazing things" not to be serious art, but merely a hobby or an aberration. If *woman* is used, she might be a serious sculptor. To say *lady doctor* is very condescending, since no one ever says *gentleman doctor* or even *man doctor*. For example, mention in the San Francisco *Chronicle* of January 31, 1972, of Madalyn Murray O'Hair as the *lady atheist* reduces her position to that of scatterbrained eccentric. Even *woman atheist* is scarcely defensible: sex is irrelevant to her philosophical position.   16

Many women argue that, on the other hand, *lady* carries with it   17

COLLABORATIVE ACTIVITY

Divide students into groups. Have them make lists of words that are gender specific, such as *actress* and *mailman*. Then ask them to think of a corresponding term for each word on their list that is gender neutral, such as *actor* and *letter carrier*. Ask the class to discuss the advantages and disadvantages of the gender-neutral terms.

overtones recalling the age of chivalry: conferring exalted stature on the person so referred to. This makes the term seem polite at first, but we must also remember that these implications are perilous: they suggest that a "lady" is helpless, and cannot do things by herself.

Lady can also be used to infer frivolousness, as in titles of organizations. Those that have a serious purpose (not merely that of enabling "the ladies" to spend time with one another) cannot use the word *lady* in their titles, but less serious ones may. Compare the *Ladies' Auxiliary* of a men's group, or the *Thursday Evening Ladies' Browning and Garden Society* with *Ladies' Liberation* or *Ladies' Strike for Peace*. 18

What is curious about this split is that *lady* is in origin a euphemism—a substitute that puts a better face on something people find uncomfortable—for *woman*. What kind of euphemism is it that subtly denigrates the people to whom it refers? Perhaps *lady* functions as a euphemism for *woman* because it does not contain the sexual implications present in *woman*: it is not "embarrassing" in that way. If this is so, we may expect that, in the future, *lady* will replace woman as the primary word for the human female, since *woman* will have become too blatantly sexual. That this distinction is already made in some contexts at least is shown in the following examples, where you can try replacing *woman* with *lady*: 19

(a) She's only twelve; but she's already a woman.
(b) After ten years in jail, Harry wanted to find a woman.
(c) She's my woman, see, so don't mess around with her.

Another common substitute for *woman* is *girl*. One seldom hears a man past the age of adolescence referred to as a boy, save in expressions like "going out with the boys," which are meant to suggest an air of adolescent frivolity and irresponsibility. But women of all ages are "girls": one can have a man—not a boy—Friday, but only a girl—never a woman or even a lady—Friday; women have girlfriends, but men do not—in a nonsexual sense—have boyfriends. It may be that this use of *girl* is euphemistic in the same way the use of *lady* is: in stressing the idea of immaturity, it removes the sexual connotations lurking in *woman*. *Girl* brings to mind irresponsibility: you don't send a girl to do a woman's errand (or even, for that matter, a boy's errand). She is a person who is both too immature and too far from real life to be entrusted with responsibilities or with decisions of any serious or important nature. 20

Now let's take a pair of words which, in terms of the possible relationships in an earlier society, were simple male-female equivalents, analogous to *bull:cow*. Suppose we find that, for independent reasons, society has changed in such a way that the original meanings now are irrelevant. Yet the words have not been discarded, but have 21 acquired new meanings, metaphorically related to their original senses. But suppose these new metaphorical uses are no longer parallel to each other. By seeing where the parallelism breaks down, we discover something about the different roles played by men and women in this culture. One good example of such a divergence through time is found in the pair, *master:mistress*. Once used with reference to one's power over servants, these words have become unusable today in their original master-servant sense as the relationship has become less prevalent in our society. But the words are still common.

Unless used with reference to animals, *master* now generally refers 22 to a man who has acquired consummate ability in some field, normally nonsexual. But its feminine counterpart cannot be used this way. It is practically restricted to its sexual sense of "paramour." We start out with two terms, both roughly paraphrasable as "one who has power over another." But the masculine form, once one person is no longer able to have absolute power over another, becomes usable metaphorically in the sense of "having power over *something*." *Master* requires as its object only the name of some activity, something inanimate and abstract. But *mistress* requires a masculine noun in the possessive to precede it. One cannot say: "Rhonda is a mistress." One must be *someone's* mistress. A man is defined by what he does, a woman by her sexuality, that is, in terms of one particular aspect of her relationship to men. It is one thing to be an *old master* like Hans Holbein, and another to be an *old mistress*.

The same is true of the words *spinster* and *bachelor*—gender words 23 for "one who is not married." The resemblance ends with the definition. While *bachelor* is a neuter term, often used as a compliment, *spinster* normally is used pejoratively, with connotations of prissiness, fussiness, and so on. To be a bachelor implies that one has the choice of marrying or not, and this is what makes the idea of a bachelor existence attractive, in the popular literature. He has been pursued and has successfully eluded his pursuers. But a spinster is one who has not been pursued, or at least not seriously. She is old, unwanted goods. The metaphorical connotations of *bachelor* generally suggest sexual freedom; of *spinster*, puritanism or celibacy.

These examples could be multiplied. It is generally considered a 24 *faux pas*, in society, to congratulate a woman on her engagement, while it is correct to congratulate her fiancé. Why is this? The reason seems to be that it is impolite to remind people of things that may be uncomfortable to them. To congratulate a woman on her engagement is really to say, "Thank goodness! You had a close call!" For the man, on the other hand, there was no such danger. His choosing to marry is viewed as a good thing, but not something essential.

WRITING SUGGESTION

Do you agree or disagree with Lakoff's thesis? Using your own observations as support, write an essay in which you argue your position.

The linguistic double standard holds throughout the life of the   25
relationship. After marriage, bachelor and spinster become man and
wife, not man and woman. The woman whose husband dies remains
"John's widow"; John, however, is never "Mary's widower."

Finally, why is it that salesclerks and others are so quick to call   26
women customers "dear," "honey," and other terms of endearment
they really have no business using? A male customer would never
put up with it. But women, like children, are supposed to enjoy these
endearments, rather than being offended by them.

In more ways than one, it's time to speak up.   27

RESPONDING TO READING

1. What do you think of Lakoff's assertion in paragraph 1 that there is a
"women's language"? Could you argue that, by identifying a special category
of language for women, Lakoff does more harm than good? Explain.   **2.** Is
there a "men's language"? Give examples of words and expressions that are
the opposite of what Lakoff sees as "dainty," "euphemistic," and "never-
aggressive."   **3.** Are "men's language" and "women's language"
mutually exclusive, or do they overlap? What are the social consequences of
a man using "women's language"—or vice versa?

Sexism in English: A 1990s Update

ALLEEN PACE NILSEN

Alleen Pace Nilsen (1936–   ) is an educator and essayist who has
contributed to many journals and has taught English at Arizona State
University and other schools. In 1967, Nilsen lived in Afghanistan,
where for two years she observed the subordinate position of women
in that society. When she returned to the United States, she began
to study American English for its cultural biases toward men and
women. She says of that project, "As I worked my way through the
dictionary, I concentrated on the way that particular usages, metaphors, slang terms, and definitions reveal society's attitude towards
males and females." Currently interested in what teenagers read,
Nilsen has coauthored *Literature for Today's Young Adults* (1988). The
following essay is an updated version of some of Nilsen's findings
from her dictionary study.

Twenty years ago I embarked on a study of the sexism inherent   1
in American English. I had just returned to Ann Arbor, Michigan,

after living for two years (1967–69) in Kabul, Afghanistan, where I had begun to look critically at the role society assigned to women. The Afghan version of the *chaderi* prescribed for Moslem women was particularly confining. Afghan jokes and folklore were blatantly sexist, such as this proverb: "If you see an old man, sit down and take a lesson; if you see an old woman, throw a stone."

But it wasn't only the native culture that made me question women's roles, it was also the American community.

Most of the American women were like myself—wives and mothers whose husbands were either career diplomats, employees of USAID, or college professors who had been recruited to work on various contract teams. We were suddenly bereft of our traditional roles: some of us became alcoholics, others got very good at bridge, while still others searched desperately for ways to contribute either to our families or to the Afghans. The local economy provided few jobs for women and certainly none for foreigners; we were isolated from former friends and the social goals we had grown up with.

When I returned in the fall of 1969 to the University of Michigan in Ann Arbor, I was surprised to find that many other women were also questioning the expectations they had grown up with. In the spring of 1970, a women's conference was announced. I hired a baby-sitter and attended, but I returned home more troubled than ever. The militancy of these women frightened me. Since I wasn't ready for a revolution, I decided I would have my own feminist movement. I would study the English language and see what it could tell me about sexism. I started reading a desk dictionary and making notecards on every entry that seemed to tell something about male and female. I soon had a dog-eared dictionary, along with a collection of notecards filling two shoe boxes.

Ironically, I started reading the dictionary because I wanted to avoid getting involved in social issues, but what happened was that my notecards brought me right back to looking at society. Language and society are as intertwined as a chicken and an egg. The language a culture uses is telltale evidence of the values and beliefs of that culture. And because there is a lag in how fast a language changes— new words can easily be introduced, but it takes a long time for old words and usages to disappear—a careful look at English will reveal the attitudes that our ancestors held and that we as a culture are therefore predisposed to hold. My notecards revealed three main points. Friends have offered the opinion that I didn't need to read the dictionary to learn such obvious facts. Nevertheless, it was interesting to have linguistic evidence of sociological observations.

2

3

4

5

ADDITIONAL QUESTION FOR RESPONDING TO READING

What do you know about the treatment of women in the Near East? How do you view such treatment? How does Nilsen's encounter with this culture affect her perception of her own culture?

Women Are Sexy; Men Are Successful

First, in American culture a woman is valued for the attractiveness and sexiness of her body, while a man is valued for his physical strength and accomplishments. A woman is sexy. A man is successful. 6

A persuasive piece of evidence supporting this view are the eponyms—words that have come from someone's name—found in English. I had a two-and-a-half-inch stack of cards taken from men's names but less than a half-inch stack from women's names, and most of those came from Greek mythology. In the words that came into American English since we separated from Britain, there are many eponyms based on the names of famous American men: *Bartlett pear, boysenberry, diesel engine, Franklin stove, Ferris wheel, Gatling gun, mason jar, sideburns, sousaphone, Schick test,* and *Winchester rifle.* The only common eponyms taken from American women's names are *Alice blue* (after Alice Roosevelt Longworth), *bloomers* (after Amelia Jenks Bloomer), and *Mae West jacket* (after the buxom actress). Two out of the three feminine eponyms relate closely to a woman's physical anatomy, while the masculine eponyms (except for *sideburns* after General Burnsides) have nothing to do with the namesake's body but, instead, honor the man for an accomplishment of some kind. 7

Although in Greek mythology women played a bigger role than they did in the biblical stories of the Judeo-Christian cultures and so the names of goddesses are accepted parts of the language in such place names as *Pomona* from the goddess of fruit and *Athens* from Athena and in such common words as *cereal* from Ceres, *psychology* from Psyche, and *arachnoid* from Arachne, the same tendency to think of women in relation to sexuality is seen in the eponyms *aphrodisiac* from Aphrodite, the Greek name for the goddess of love and beauty, and *venereal disease* from Venue, the Roman name for Aphrodite. 8

Another interesting word from Greek mythology is *Amazon.* According to Greek folk etymology, the *a* means "without" as in *atypical* or *amoral,* while *mazon* comes from *mazos* meaning "breast" as still seen in *mastectomy.* In the Greek legend, Amazon women cut off their right breasts so that they could better shoot their bows. Apparently, the storytellers had a feeling that for women to play the active, "masculine" role the Amazons adopted for themselves, they had to trade in part of their femininity. 9

This preoccupation with women's breasts is not limited to ancient stories. As a volunteer for the University of Wisconsin's *Dictionary of American Regional English (DARE),* I read a western trapper's diary from the 1930s. I was to make notes of any unusual usages or language patterns. My most interesting finding was that the trapper referred to a range of mountains as *The Teats,* a metaphor based on the sim- 10 ilarity between the shapes of mountains and women's breasts. Because today we use the French wording, *The Grand Tetons*, the metaphor isn't as obvious, but I wrote to mapmakers and found the following listings: *Nippletop* and *Little Nipple Top* near Mount Marcy in the Adirondacks; *Nipple Mountain* in Archuleta County, Colorado; *Nipple Peak* in Coke County, Texas; *Nipple Butte* in Pennington, South Dakota; *Squaw Peak* in Placer County, California (and many other locations); *Maiden's Peak* and *Squaw Tit* (they're the same mountain) in the Cascade Range in Oregon; *Mary's Nipple* near Salt Lake City, Utah; and *Jane Russell Peaks* near Stark, New Hampshire.

Except for the movie star Jane Russell, the women being referred 11 to are anonymous—it's only a sexual part of their body that is mentioned. When topographical features are named after men, it's probably not going to be to draw attention to a sexual part of their bodies but instead to honor individuals for an accomplishment. For example, no one thinks of a part of the male body when hearing a reference to Pike's Peak, Colorado, or Jackson Hole, Wyoming.

Going back to what I learned from my dictionary cards, I was 12 surprised to realize how many pairs of words we have in which the feminine word has acquired sexual connotations while the masculine word retains a serious businesslike aura. For example, a *callboy* is the person who calls actors when it is time for them to go on stage, but a *callgirl* is a prostitute. Compare *sir* and *madam*. *Sir* is a term of respect, while *madam* has acquired the specialized meaning of a brothel manager. Something similar has happened to *master* and *mistress*. Would you rather have a painting by an *old master* or an *old mistress*?

It's because the word *woman* had sexual connotations, as in "She's 13 his woman," that people began avoiding its use, hence such terminology as *ladies' room*, *lady of the house*, and *girls' school* or *school for young ladies*. Feminists, who ask that people use the term *woman* rather than *girl* or *lady*, are rejecting the idea that *woman* is primarily a sexual term. They have been at least partially successful in that today *woman* is commonly used to communicate gender without intending implications about sexuality.

I found two hundred pairs of words with masculine and feminine 14 forms, e.g., *heir-heiress*, *hero-heroine*, *steward-stewardess*, *usher-usherette*. In nearly all such pairs, the masculine word is considered the base, with some kind of a feminine suffix being added. The masculine form is the one from which compounds are made, e.g., from *king-queen* comes *kingdom* but not *queendom*, from *sportsman-sportslady* comes *sportmanship* but not *sportsladyship*. There is one—and only one— semantic area in which the masculine word is not the base or more powerful word. This is in the area dealing with sex and marriage. When someone refers to a *virgin*, a listener will probably think of a

COLLABORATIVE ACTIVITY

Ask members of student groups to recall their upbringing and socialization as children with reference to sex roles. Ask them to list behaviors that were encouraged and those that were explicitly or implicitly discouraged. Direct them to look especially for subtleties (room decor, clothing, toys). Groups should present their findings and conclusions to the class.

female, unless the speaker specifies *male* or uses a masculine pronoun. The same is true for *prostitute*.

In relation to marriage, there is much linguistic evidence showing 15 that weddings are more important to women than to men. A woman cherishes the wedding and is considered a bride for a whole year, but a man is referred to as a groom only on the day of the wedding. The word *bride* appears in *bridal attendant, bridal gown, bridesmaid, bridal shower*, and even *bridegroom. Groom* comes from the Middle English *grom*, meaning "man," and in the sense is seldom used outside of the wedding. With most pairs of male/female words, people habitually put the masculine word first, *Mr. and Mrs., his and hers, boys and girls, men and women, kings and queens, brothers and sisters, guys and dolls,* and *host and hostess*, but it is the *bride and groom* who are talked about, not the *groom and bride*.

The importance of marriage to a woman is also shown by the fact 16 that when a marriage ends in death, the woman gets the title of *widow*. A man gets the derived title of *widower*. This term is not used in other phrases or contexts, but *widow* is seen in *widowhood, widow's peak*, and *widow's walk*. A *widow* in a card game is an extra hand of cards, while in typesetting it is an extra line of type.

How changing cultural ideas bring changes to language is clearly 17 visible in this semantic area. The feminist movement has caused the differences between the sexes to be downplayed, and since I did my dictionary study two decades ago, the word *singles* has largely replaced such sex specific and value-laden terms as *bachelor, old maid, spinster, divorcee, widow*, and *widower*. And in 1970 I wrote that when a man is called *a professional* he is thought to be a doctor or a lawyer, but when people hear a woman referred to as *a professional* they are likely to think of a prostitute. That's not as true today because so many women have become doctors and lawyers that it's no longer incongruous to think of women in those professional roles.

Another change that has taken place is in wedding announce- 18 ments. They used to be sent out from the bride's parents and did not even give the name of the groom's parents. Today, most couples choose to list either all or none of the parents' names. Also it is now much more likely that both the bride and groom's picture will be in the newspaper, while a decade ago only the bride's picture was published on the "Women's" or the "Society" page. Even the traditional wording of the wedding ceremony is being changed. Many officials now pronounce the couple "husband and wife" instead of the old "man and wife," and they ask the bride if she promises "to love, honor, and cherish," instead of "to love, honor, and obey."

Women Are Passive; Men Are Active

The wording of the wedding ceremony also relates to the second 19
point that my cards showed, which is that women are expected to
play a passive or weak role while men play an active or strong role.
In the traditional ceremony, the official asks, "Who gives the bride
away?" and the father answers, "I do." Some fathers answer, "Her
mother and I do," but that doesn't solve the problem inherent in the
question. The idea that a bride is something to be handed over from
one man to another bothers people because it goes back to the days
when a man's servants, his children, and his wife were all considered
to be his property. They were known by his name because they
belonged to him, and he was responsible for their actions and their
debts.

The grammar used in talking or writing about weddings as well 20
as other sexual relationships shows the expectation of men playing
the active role. Men *wed* women while women *become* brides of men.
A man *possesses* a woman; he *deflowers* her; he *performs*; he *scores*; he
takes away her virginity. Although a woman can *seduce* a man, she
cannot offer him her virginity. When talking about virginity, the only
way to make the woman the actor in the sentence is to say that "She
lost her virginity," but people lose things by accident rather than by
purposeful actions, and so she's only the grammatical, not the real-
life, actor.

The reason that women tried to bring the term *Ms.* into the lan- 21
guage to replace *Miss* and *Mrs.* relates to this point. Married women
resent being identified only under their husband's names. For
example, when Susan Glascoe did something newsworthy, she would
be identified in the newspaper only as Mrs. John Glascoe. The dictionary cards showed what appeared to be an attitude on the part of
the editors that it was almost indecent to let a respectable woman's
name march unaccompanied across the pages of a dictionary. Women
were listed with male names whether or not the male contributed to
the woman's reason for being in the dictionary or in his own right
was as famous as the woman. For example, Charlotte Brontë was
identified as Mrs. Arthur B. Nicholls, Amelia Earhart as Mrs. George
Palmer Putnam, Helen Hayes as Mrs. Charles MacArthur, Jenny Lind
as Mme. Otto Goldschmit, Cornelia Otis Skinner as the daughter of
Otis, Harriet Beecher Stowe as the sister of Henry Ward Beecher, and
Edith Sitwell as the sister of Osbert and Sacheverell.[1] A very small

---

[1]Charlotte Brontë (1816–55), author of *Jane Eyre*; Amelia Earhart (1898–1937), first woman to
fly over the Atlantic; Helen Hayes (1900–   ), actress; Jenny Lind (1820–87), Swedish soprano
known as the "Swedish nightingale"; Cornelia Otis Skinner (1901–79), actress and writer; Harriet

number of women got into the dictionary without the benefit of a masculine escort. They were rebels and crusaders: temperance leaders Frances Elizabeth Caroline Willard and Carry Nation, women's rights leaders Carrie Chapman Catt and Elizabeth Cady Stanton, birth control educator Margaret Sanger, religious leader Mary Baker Eddy, and slaves Harriet Tubman and Phillis Wheatley.

Etiquette books used to teach that if a woman had *Mrs.* in front 22 of her name, then the husband's name should follow because *Mrs.* is an abbreviated form of *Mistress* and a woman couldn't be a mistress of herself. As with many arguments about "correct" language usage, this isn't very logical because *Miss* is also an abbreviation of *Mistress.* Feminists hoped to simplify matters by introducing *Ms.* as an alternative to both *Mrs.* and *Miss*, but what happened is that *Ms.* largely replaced *Miss*, to become a catch-all business title for women. Many married women still prefer the title *Mrs.*, and some resent being addressed with the term *Ms.* As one frustrated newspaper reporter complained, "Before I can write about a woman, I have to know not only her marital status but also her political philosophy." The result of such complications may contribute to the demise of titles, which are already being ignored by many computer programmers who find it more efficient to simply use names, for example in a business letter: "Dear Joan Garcia," instead of "Dear Mrs. Joan Garcia," "Dear Ms. Garcia," or "Dear Mrs. Louis Garcia."

The titles given to royalty provide an example of how males can 23 be disadvantaged by the assumption that they are always to play the more powerful role. In British royalty, when a male holds a title, his wife is automatically given the feminine equivalent. But the reverse is not true. For example, a *count* is a high political officer with a *countess* being his wife. The same is true for a *duke* and a *duchess* and a *king* and a *queen.* But when a female holds the royal title, the man she marries does not automatically acquire the matching title. For example, Queen Elizabeth's husband has the title of *prince* rather than *king*, but if Prince Charles should become king while he is still married to Lady or Princess Diana, she will be known as the queen. The reasoning appears to be that since masculine words are stronger, they are reserved for true heirs and withheld from males coming into the royal family by marriage. If Prince Phillip were called *King Phillip*, it would be much easier for British subjects to forget where the true power lies.

The names that people give their children show the hopes and 24 dreams they have for them, and when we look at the differences

---

Beecher Stowe (1811–96), author of *Uncle Tom's Cabin*; and Edith Sitwell (1877–1964), English poet and critic. [Eds.]

between male and female names in a culture, we can see the cumulative expectations of that culture. In our culture girls often have names taken from small, aesthetically pleasing items, e.g., *Ruby, Jewel,* and *Pearl. Esther* and *Stella* mean "star," *Ada* means "ornament," and *Vanessa* means "butterfly." Boys are more likely to be given names with meanings of power and strength, e.g., *Neil* means "champion," *Martin* is from Mars, the God of War, *Raymond* means "wise protection," *Harold* means "chief of the army," *Ira* means "vigilant," *Rex* means "king," and *Richard* means "strong king."

We see similar differences in food metaphors. Food is a passive 25 substance just sitting there waiting to be eaten. Many people have recognized this and so no longer feel comfortable describing women as "delectable morsels." However, when I was a teenager, it was considered a compliment to refer to a girl (we didn't call anyone a *woman* until she was middle-aged) as a *cute tomato, a peach,* a *dish,* a *cookie, honey, sugar,* or *sweetie-pie.* When being affectionate, women will occasionally call a man *honey* or *sweetie,* but in general, food metaphors are used much less often with men than with women. If a man is called *a fruit,* his masculinity is being questioned. But it's perfectly acceptable to use a food metaphor if the food is heavier and more substantive than that used for women. For example pin-up pictures of women have long been known as *cheesecake,* but when Burt Reynolds posed for a nude centerfold the picture was immediately dubbed *beefcake,* c.f., *a hunk of meat.* That such sexual references to men have come into the language is another reflection of how society is beginning to lessen the differences between their attitudes toward men and women.

Something similar to the *fruit* metaphor happens with references 26 to plants. We insult a man by calling him a *pansy,* but it wasn't considered particularly insulting to talk about a girl being a *wallflower,* a *clinging vine,* or a *shrinking violet,* or to give girls such names as *Ivy, Rose, Lily, Iris, Daisy, Camellia, Heather,* and *Flora.* A plant metaphor can be used with a man if the plant is big and strong, for example, Andrew Jackson's nickname of *Old Hickory.* Also, the phrases *blooming idiots* and *budding geniuses* can be used with either sex, but notice how they are based on the most active thing a plant can do, which is to bloom or bud.

Animal metaphors also illustrate the different expectations for 27 males and females. Men are referred to as *studs, bucks,* and *wolves* while women are referred to with such metaphors as *kitten, bunny, beaver, bird, chick,* and *lamb.* In the 1950s we said that boys went *tomcatting,* but today it's just *catting around* and both boys and girls do it. When the term *foxy,* meaning that someone was sexy, first became popular it was used only for girls, but now someone of either sex can be described as *a fox*. Some animal metaphors that are used predominantly with men have negative connotations based on the size and/or strength of the animals, e.g., *beast, bullheaded, jackass, rat, loanshark,* and *vulture*. Negative metaphors used with women are based on smaller animals, e.g., *social butterfly, mousy, catty,* and *vixen*. The feminine terms connote action, but not the same kind of large scale action as with the masculine terms.

Women Are Connected with Negative Connotations; Men with Positive Connotations

The final point that my notecards illustrated was how many positive connotations are associated with the concept of masculine, while there are either trivial or negative connotations connected with the corresponding feminine concept. An example from the animal metaphors makes a good illustration. The word *shrew* taken from the name of a small but especially vicious animal was defined in my dictionary as "an ill-tempered scolding woman," but the word *shrewd* taken from the same root was defined as "marked by clever, discerning awareness" and was illustrated with the phrase "a shrewd businessman." 28

Early in life, children are conditioned to the superiority of the masculine role. As child psychologists point out, little girls have much more freedom to experiment with sex roles than do little boys. If a little girl acts like a *tomboy*, most parents have mixed feelings, being at least partially proud. But if their little boy acts like a *sissy* (derived from *sister*), they call a psychologist. It's perfectly acceptable for a little girl to sleep in the crib that was purchased for her brother, to wear his hand-me-down jeans and shirts, and to ride the bicycle that he has outgrown. But few parents would put a boy baby in a white and gold crib decorated with frills and lace, and virtually no parents would have their little boys wear his sister's hand-me-down dresses, nor would they have their son ride a girl's pink bicycle with a flower-bedecked basket. The proper names given to girls and boys show this same attitude. Girls can have "boy" names—*Cris, Craig, Jo, Kelly, Shawn, Teri, Toni,* and *Sam*—but it doesn't work the other way around. A couple of generations ago, *Beverley, Frances, Hazel, Marion,* and *Shirley* were common boys' names. As parents gave these names to more and more girls, they fell into disuse for males, and some older men who have these names prefer to go by their initials or by such abbreviated forms as *Haze* or *Shirl*. 28

When a little girl is told to *be a lady*, she is being told to sit with   30
her knees together and to be quiet and dainty. But when a little boy
is told to *be a man* he is being told to be noble, strong, and virtuous—
to have all the qualities that the speaker looks on as desirable. The
concept of manliness has such positive connotations that it used to
be a compliment to call someone a *he-man*, to say that he was doubly
a man. Today many people are more ambivalent about this term and
respond to it much as they do to the word *macho*. But calling someone
a *manly man* or a *virile man* is nearly always meant as a compliment.
Virile comes from the Indo-European *vir* meaning "man," which is
also the basis for *virtuous*. Contrast the positive connotations of both
virile and *virtuous* with the negative connotations of *hysterical*. The
Greeks took this latter word from their name for *uterus* (as still seen
in *hysterectomy*). They thought that women were the only ones who
experienced uncontrolled emotional outbursts, and so the condition
must have something to do with a part of the body that only women
have.

Differences in the connotations between positive male and neg-   31
ative female connotations can be seen in several pairs of words that
differ denotatively only in the matter of sex. *Bachelor* as compared to
spinster or *old maid* has such positive connotations that women try to
adopt them by using the term *bachelor-girl* or *bachelorette*. *Old maid* is
so negative that it's the basis for metaphors: pretentious and fussy
old men are called *old maids*, as are the leftover kernels of unpopped
popcorn, and the last card in a popular children's game.

Patron and *matron* (Middle English for *father* and *mother* have such   32
different levels of prestige that women try to borrow the more positive
masculine connotations with the word *patroness*, literally "female
father." Such a peculiar term came about because of the high prestige
attached to *patron* in such phrases as *a patron of the arts* or *a patron
saint*. *Matron* is more apt to be used in talking about a woman in
charge of a jail or a public restroom.

When men are doing jobs that women often do, we apparently   33
try to pay the men extra by giving them fancy titles, for example, a
male cook is more likely to be called a *chef* while a male seamstress
will get the title of *tailor*. The armed forces have a special problem in
that they recruit under such slogans as "The Marine Corps builds
men!" and "Join the Army! Become a Man." Once the recruits are
enlisted, they find themselves doing much of the work that has been
traditionally thought of as "women's work." The solution to getting
the work done and not insulting anyone's masculinity was to change
the titles as shown below:

waitress	orderly
nurse	medic or corpsman
secretary	clerk-typist
assistant	adjutant
dishwasher or	KP (kitchen police)
kitchen helper	

Compare *brave* and *squaw*. Early settlers in America truly admired   34
Indian men and hence named them with a word that carried connotations of youth, vigor, and courage. But they used the Algonquin's
name for "woman" and over the years it developed almost opposite
connotations to those of *brave*. *Wizard* and *witch* contrast almost as
much. The masculine *wizard* implies skill and wisdom combined with
magic, while the feminine *witch* implies evil intentions combined with
magic. Part of the unattractiveness of both *witch* and *squaw* is that
they have been used so often to refer to old women, something with
which our culture is particularly uncomfortable, just as the Afghans
were. Imagine my surprise when I ran across the phrases *grandfatherly
advice* and *old wives' tales* and realized that the underlying implication
is the same as the Afghan proverb about old men being worth listening
to while old women talk only foolishness.

Other terms that show how negative we view old women as   35
compared to young women are *old nag* as compared to *filly*, *old crow*
or *old bat* as compared to *bird*, and of being *catty* as compared to being
kittenish. There is no matching set of metaphors for men. The chicken
metaphor tells the whole story of a woman's life. In her youth she is
a *chick*. Then she marries and begins *feathering her nest*. Soon she begins
feeling *cooped up*, so she goes to *hen parties* where she *cackles* with her
friends. Then she has her *brood*, begins to *henpeck* her husband, and
finally turns into an *old biddy*.

I embarked on my study of the dictionary not with the intention   36
of prescribing language change but simply to see what the language
would tell me about sexism. Nevertheless I have been both surprised
and pleased as I've watched the changes that have occurred over the
past two decades. I'm one of those linguists who believes that new
language customs will cause a new generation of speakers to grow
up with different expectations. This is why I'm happy about people's
efforts to use inclusive language, to say *he or she* or *they* when speaking
about individuals whose names they do not know. I'm glad that
leading publishers have developed guidelines to help writers use
language that is fair to both sexes, and I'm glad that most newspapers
and magazines list women by their own names instead of only by
their husbands' names and that educated and thoughtful people no
longer begin their business letters with "Dear Sir" or "Gentlemen,"

but instead use a memo form or begin with such salutations as "Dear Colleagues," "Dear Reader," or "Dear Committee Members." I'm also glad that such words as *poetess, authoress, conductress,* and *aviatrix* now sound quaint and old-fashioned and that *chairman* is giving way to *chair* or *head, mailman* to *mail carrier, clergyman* to *clergy,* and *stewardess* to *flight attendant.* I was also pleased when the National Oceanic and Atmospheric Administration bowed to feminist complaints and in the late 1970s began to alternate men's and women's names for hurricanes. However, I wasn't so pleased to discover that the change did not immediately erase sexist thoughts from everyone's mind, as shown by a headline about Hurricane David in a 1979 New York tabloid, "David Rapes Virgin Islands." More recently a similar metaphor appeared in a headline in the *Arizona Republic* about Hurricane Charlie, "Charlie Quits Carolinas, Flirts with Virginia."

What these incidents show is that sexism is not something existing 37 independently in American English or in the particular dictionary that I happened to read. Rather, it exists in people's minds. Language is like an X-ray in providing visible evidence of invisible thoughts. The best thing about people being interested in and discussing sexist language is that as they make conscious decisions about what pronouns they will use, what jokes they will tell or laugh at, how they will write their names, or how they will begin their letters, they are forced to think about the underlying issue of sexism. This is good because as a problem that begins in people's assumptions and expectations, it's a problem that will be solved only when a great many people have given it a great deal of thought.

RESPONDING TO READING

1. What point is Nilsen making about the culture in which she lives? Does your experience support her conclusions?   **2.** Does Nilsen use enough examples to illustrate her claims? What others can you think of? In what way do her examples—and your own—illustrate the power of language to define and, in some cases, to cloud thought?   **3.** Many of the connotations of the words Nilsen discusses are hundreds of years old and found in languages other than English. Given the widespread and long-standing linguistic bias against women, do you think the attempts by feminists such as Nilsen to change this situation can succeed?

Notes on Punctuation

LEWIS THOMAS

Lewis Thomas (1913–   ), born in Flushing, New York, is a doctor, researcher, and teacher who has been affiliated with Johns Hopkins University, New York University, and the Memorial Sloan-Kettering Cancer Center. Thomas began writing a column called "Notes of a Biology Watcher" for the *New England Journal of Medicine* in 1971 and gained popularity with new readers when some of these columns were collected in *Lives of a Cell* (1974), which won the National Book Award. Other collections of his essays are *The Medusa and the Snail: More Notes of a Biology Watcher* (1979) and *Late Night Thoughts on Listening to Mahler's Ninth Symphony* (1983). Thomas is known for his optimistic views of relationships in the natural world, and he combines scientific observation with sometimes lyrical prose. "Notes on Punctuation" first appeared in the *New England Journal of Medicine* in 1979.

BACKGROUND ON READING

It will most likely come as a surprise to many students that punctuation conventions have not been fixed forever. You might tell them that writers began using punctuation in about the third century B.C. At this time, punctuation appeared either above the line or on the line. Punctuation marks signalled a place for the reader to take a breath and were not, as our punctuation marks are, dependent on style, syntax, or meaning. By the seventeenth century punctuation began to resemble the system with which we are familiar.

FOR OPENERS

Why do we have punctuation rules? Can you recall any of these rules changing during your years as a student?

1   There are no precise rules about punctuation (Fowler[1] lays out some general advice (as best he can under the complex circumstances of English prose (he points out, for example, that we possess only four stops (the comma, the semicolon, the colon and the period (the question mark and exclamation point are not, strictly speaking, stops; they are indicators of tone (oddly enough, the Greeks employed the semicolon for their question mark (it produces a strange sensation to read a Greek sentence which is a straightforward question: Why weepest thou; (instead of Why weepest thou? (and, of course, there are parentheses (which are surely a kind of punctuation making this whole much more complicated by having to count up the left-handed parentheses in order to be sure of closing with the right number (but if the parentheses were left out, with nothing to work with but the stops, we would have considerably more flexibility in the deploying of layers of meaning than if we tried to separate all the clauses by physical barriers (and in the latter case, while we might have more precision and exactitude for our meaning, we would lose the essential flavor of language, which is its wonderful ambiguity)))))))))))).

2   The commas are the most useful and usable of all the stops. It is highly important to put them in place as you go along. If you try to come back after doing a paragraph and stick them in the various spots that tempt you you will discover that they tend to swarm like minnows into all sorts of crevices whose existence you hadn't realized and before you know it the whole long sentence becomes immobilized

---

[1]H.W. Fowler (1858–1933), author of *Modern English Usage* (1926, revised in 1965 by Sir Ernest Gowers). Thomas cites him as an authority on English usage. [Eds.]

and lashed up squirming in commas. Better to use them sparingly, and with affection, precisely when the need for each one arises, nicely, by itself.

I have grown fond of semicolons in recent years. The semicolon tells you that there is still some question about the preceding full sentence; something needs to be added; it reminds you sometimes of the Greek usage. It is almost always a greater pleasure to come across a semicolon than a period. The period tells you that that is that; if you didn't get all the meaning you wanted or expected, anyway you got all the writer intended to parcel out and now you have to move along. But with a semicolon there you get a pleasant little feeling of expectancy; there is more to come; read on; it will get clearer.

Colons are a lot less attractive, for several reasons: firstly, they give you the feeling of being rather ordered around, or at least having your nose pointed in a direction you might not be inclined to take if left to yourself, and, secondly, you suspect you're in for one of those sentences that will be labeling the points to be made: firstly, secondly and so forth, with the implication that you haven't sense enough to keep track of a sequence of notions without having them numbered. Also, many writers use this system loosely and incompletely, starting out with number one and number two as though counting off on their fingers but then going on and on without the succession of labels you've been led to expect, leaving you floundering about searching for the ninthly or seventeenthly that out to be there but isn't.

Exclamation points are the most irritating of all. Look! they say, look at what I just said! How amazing is my thought! It is like being forced to watch someone else's small child jumping up and down crazily in the center of the living room shouting to attract attention. If a sentence really has something of importance to say, something quite remarkable, it doesn't need a mark to point it out. And if it is really, after all, a banal sentence needing more zing, the exclamation point simply emphasizes its banality!

Quotation marks should be used honestly and sparingly, when there is a genuine quotation at hand, and it is necessary to be very rigorous about the words enclosed by the marks. If something is to be quoted, the *exact* words must be used. If part of it must be left out because of space limitations, it is good manners to insert three dots to indicate the omission, but it is unethical to do this if it means connecting two thoughts which the original author did not intend to have tied together. Above all, quotation marks should not be used for ideas that you'd like to disown, things in the air so to speak. Nor should they be put in place around clichés; if you want to use a cliché you must take full responsibility for it yourself and not try to job it off on anon., or on society. The most objectionable misuse of quo-

3

4

5

6

ADDITIONAL QUESTIONS FOR RESPONDING TO READING

1. What tone does Thomas use in this essay? Is his strategy appropriate for his purpose?
2. How does Thomas link his discussions of the different punctuation marks? How successful are his transitions?
3. Elsewhere in his writing Thomas addresses the importance of the earth and his reverence for the role of the scientist in maintaining simplicity. In what way, if any, does this essay reinforce these ideas?

TEACHING STRATEGY

Discuss the following with your students:

Paragraph 1: Thomas says that "the essential flavor of language" is its "wonderful ambiguity." Is he saying that ambiguous language is desirable? If so, what does he mean?

Paragraph 2: Why does Thomas neglect to place a comma between the "you you" in the second sentence? Note the variations in sentence length and style in this paragraph. How do these stylistic techniques contribute to the overall effect of the essay?

Paragraph 6: What main point is Thomas making in his discussion of question marks?

COLLABORATIVE ACTIVITY

Assign individual groups different passages from "The Lesson" (page 266) and "Modern Secrets" (page 274). Ask them to explain the punctuation using a grammar book's explanations and then using Thomas's essay.

WRITING SUGGESTION

Write a letter to Thomas in which you humorously critique his essay on punctuation. You could, for example, praise his efforts to liberate punctuation from the tyranny of handbooks or criticize him for attempting to subvert society by attacking punctuation rules.

ANSWERS TO RESPONDING TO READING

1. Students will probably find Thomas's treatment of punctuation quite subtle. With some help they may realize that his treatment sheds light on punctuation conventions by dealing with their use and value and their effect on the reader's perceptions. He does not consider them as rules mechanically applied to written discourse.

2. He does so, but only implicitly. Punctuation leads readers to follow a writer's intention; it is a mechanical device writers employ to achieve certain effects.

3. Answers will vary. Some students might not "get" what Thomas is up to. You might have to explain that not only is Thomas playing with language, but he is also undercutting the fixed, dry rules that characterize most handbook treatments of punctuation.

tation marks, but one which illustrates the dangers of misuse in ordinary prose, is seen in advertising, especially in advertisements for small restaurants, for example "just around the corner," or "a good place to eat." No single, identifiable, citable person ever really said, for the record, "just around the corner," much less "a good place to eat," least likely of all for restaurants of the type that use this type of prose.

The dash is a handy device, informal and essentially playful, 7 telling you that you're about to take off on a different tack but still in some way connected with the present course—only you have to remember that the dash is there, and either put a second dash at the end of the notion to let the reader know that he's back on course, or else end the sentence, as here, with a period.

The greatest danger in punctuation is for poetry. Here it is nec- 8 essary to be as economical and parsimonious with comms and periods as with the words themselves, and any marks that seem to carry their own subtle meanings, like dashes and little rows of periods, even semicolons and question marks, should be left out altogether rather than inserted to clog up the thing with ambiguity. A single exclamation point in a poem, no matter what else the poem has to say, is enough to destroy the whole work.

The things I like best in T. S. Eliot's poetry, especially in the *Four* 9 *Quartets*,[2] are the semicolons. You cannot hear them, but they are there, laying out the connections between the images and the ideas. Sometimes you get a glimpse of a semicolon coming, a few lines farther on, and it is like climbing a steep path through woods and seeing a wooden bench just at a bend in the road ahead, a place where you can expect to sit for a moment, catching your breath.

Commas can't do this sort of thing; they can only tell you how 10 the different parts of a complicated thought are to be fitted together, but you can't sit, not even take a breath, just because of a comma.

RESPONDING TO READING

1. In what ways are Thomas's comments on punctuation different from those you might find in a handbook of English usage? Are his more or less useful? Explain. **2.** Does Thomas make a connection between punctuation and the power of words? Do you think there is one? **3.** What is your initial reaction to Thomas's essay? Does your reaction change when you realize his purpose?

---

[2]Thomas Stearns Eliot (1888–1965) is a major figure in English poetry. His works include "The Love Song of J. Alfred Prufrock," *The Waste Land*, and the *Four Quartets*, a long poem in four parts that deals with the interplay of Christian faith and modern experience. [Eds.]

Gobbledygook

STUART CHASE

An advisor to President Franklin D. Roosevelt during the Depression, Stuart Chase (1888–1985) is believed to have coined the term *New Deal*. Although his background was in economics and social science, Chase became known for his book about language, *The Power of Words* (1954), and for his work helping government officials write "plain" English. Throughout his long career, Chase had an interest in social problems. As he explained, "My interests, changing with time and history, veer farther than ever away from ideologies. These always seemed less important to me than practical measures to abolish poverty." He also wrote *The Tragedy of Waste* (1925), *Mexico: A Study of Two Americas* (1931), and *Money to Grow On* (1964). In "Gobbledygook," his classic essay on writing clearly, Chase points out the marks of pretentious language and offers practical advice on "reducing the gobble."

Said Franklin Roosevelt, in one of his early presidential speeches: "I see one-third of a nation ill-housed, ill-clad, ill-nourished." Translated into standard bureaucratic prose his statement would read: 1

> It is evident that a substantial number of persons within the Continental boundaries of the United States have inadequate financial resources with which to purchase the products of agricultural communities and industrial establishments. It would appear that for a considerable segment of the population, possibly as much as 33.3333 of the total, there are inadequate housing facilities, and an equally significant proportion is deprived of the proper types of clothing and nutriment.

This rousing satire on gobbledygook—or talk among the bureaucrats—is adapted from a report[1] prepared by the Federal Security Agency[2] is an attempt to break out of the verbal squirrel cage. "Gobbledygook" was coined by an exasperated Congressman, Maury Maverick of Texas, and means using two, or three, or ten words in the place of one, or using a five-syllable word where a single syllable would suffice. Maverick was censuring the forbidding prose of executive departments in Washington, but the term has now spread to windy and pretentious language in general. 2

"Gobbledygook" itself is a good example of the way a language grows. There was no word for the event before Maverick's invention; one had to say: "You know, that terrible, involved, polysyllabic lan- 3

[1]This and succeeding quotations from F.S.A. report by special permission of the author, Milton Hall.
[2]This became the Department of Health, Education, and Welfare, later divided into the Department of Education and the Department of Health and Human Services. [Eds.]

FOR OPENERS

Bring in several examples of contemporary gobbledygook from newspapers or magazines. Distribute copies to the class and discuss the effect of the language use on readers.

ADDITIONAL QUESTION FOR RESPONDING TO READING

What need does gobbledygook serve?

guage those government people use down in Washington." Now one word takes the place of a dozen.

A British member of Parliament, A. P. Herbert, also exasperated 4
with bureaucratic jargon, translated Nelson's[3] immortal phrase, "England expects every man to do his duty":

> England anticipates that, as regards the current emergency, personnel will face up to the issues, and exercise appropriately the functions allocated to their respective occupational groups.

A New Zealand official made the following report after surveying 5
a plot of ground for an athletic field:[4]

> It is obvious from the difference in elevation with relation to the short depth of the property that the contour is such as to preclude any reasonable development potential for active recreation.

Seems the plot was too steep.

An office manager sent this memo to his chief. 6

> Verbal contact with Mr. Blank regarding the attached notification of promotion has elicited the attached representation intimating that he prefers to decline the assignment.

Seems Mr. Blank didn't want the job.

> A doctor testified at an English trial that one of the parties was suffering from "circumorbital haematoma."

Seems the party had a black eye.

> In August 1952 the U.S. Department of Agriculture put out a pamphlet entitled: "Cultural and Pathogenic Variability in Single-Condial and Hyphaltip Isolates of Hemlin-Thosporium Turcicum Pass."

Seems it was about corn leaf disease.

On reaching the top of the Finsteraarhorn in 1845, M. Dollfus- 7
Ausset, when he got his breath, exclaimed:

> The soul communes in the infinite with those icy peaks which seem to have their roots in the bowels of eternity.

Seems he enjoyed the view.

A governmental department announced: 8

> Voucherable expenditures necessary to provide adequate dental treatment required as adjunct to medical treatment being rendered a pay patient in in-patient status may be incurred as required at the expense of the Public Health Service.

---

[3]Horatio Nelson (1758–1805) was a British admiral who defeated the French fleet at the Battle of Trafalgar. [Eds.]

[4]This item and the next two are from the piece on gobbledygook by W.E. Farbstein, *New York Times*, March 29, 1953.

Seems you can charge your dentist bill to the Public Health Service. Or can you?

Legal Talk

Gobbledygook not only flourishes in government bureaus but grows wild and lush in the law, the universities, and sometimes among the literati. Mr. Micawber[5] was a master of gobbledygook, which he hoped would improve his fortunes. It is almost always found in offices too big for face-to-face talk. Gobbledygook can be defined as squandering words, packing a message with excess baggage and so introducing semantic "noise." Or it can be scrambling words in a message so that meaning does not come through. The directions on cans, bottles, and packages for putting the contents to use are often a good illustration. Gobbledygook must not be confused with double talk, however, for the intentions of the sender are usually honest.   9

I offer you a round fruit and say, "Have an orange." Not so an expert in legal phraseology, as parodied by editors of *Labor*:   10

> I hereby give and convey to you, all and singular, my estate and interests, right, title, claim and advantages of and in said orange, together with all rind, juice, pulp, and pits, and all rights and advantages therein . . . anything hereinbefore or hereinafter or in any other deed or deeds, instrument or instruments of whatever nature or kind whatsoever, to the contrary, in any wise, notwithstanding.

The state of Ohio, after five years of work, has redrafted its legal code in modern English, eliminating 4,500 sections and doubtless a blizzard of "whereases" and "hereinafters." Legal terms of necessity must be closely tied to their referents, but the early solons tried to do this the hard way, by adding synonyms. They hoped to trap the physical event in a net of words, but instead they created a mumbo-jumbo beyond the power of the layman, and even many a lawyer, to translate. Legal talk is studded with tautologies,[6] such as "cease and desist," "give and convey," "irrelevant, incompetent, and immaterial." Furthermore, legal jargon is a dead language; it is not spoken and it is not growing. An official of one of the big insurance companies calls their branch of it "bafflegab." Here is a sample from his collection.[7]   11

> One-half to his mother, if living, if not to his father, and one-half to his mother-in-law, if living, if not to his mother, if living, if not

---

[5]A character in Dickens's *David Copperfield*. [Eds.]
[6]Needless repetitions of ideas, statements, or words. [Eds.]
[7]Interview with Clifford B. Reeves by Sylvia F. Porter, New York *Evening Post*, March 14, 1952.

to his father. Thereafter payment is to be made in a single sum to his brothers. On the one-half payable to his mother, if living, if not to his father, he does not bring in his mother-in-law as the next payee to receive, although on the one-half to his mother-in-law, he does bring in the mother or father.

You apply for an insurance policy, pass the tests, and instead of 12 a straightforward "here is your policy," you receive something like this:

> This policy is issued in consideration of the application therefor, copy of which application is attached hereto and made part hereof, and of the payment for said insurance on the life of the above-named insured.

Academic Talk

The pedagogues may be less repetitious than the lawyers, but 13 many use even longer words. It is a symbol of their calling to prefer Greek and Latin derivatives to Anglo-Saxon. Thus instead of saying: "I like short clear words," many a professor would think it more seemly to say: "I prefer an abbreviated phraseology, distinguished for its lucidity." Your professor is sometimes right, the longer word may carry the meaning better—but not because it is long. Allen Upward in his book *The New Word* warmly advocates Anglo-Saxon English as against what he calls "Mediterranean" English, with its polysyllables built up like a skyscraper.

Professional pedagogy, still alternating between the Middle Ages 14 and modern science, can produce what Henshaw Ward[8] once called the most repellent prose known to man. It takes an iron will to read as much as a page of it. Here is a sample of what is known in some quarters as "pedageese":

> Realization has grown that the curriculum or the experiences of learners change and improve only as those who are most directly involved examine their goals, improve their understandings and increase their skill in performing the tasks necessary to reach newly defined goals. This places the focus upon teacher, lay citizen and learner as partners in curricular improvement and as the individuals who must change, if there is to be curriculum change.

I think there is an idea concealed here somewhere. I think it 15 means: "If we are going to change the curriculum, teacher, parent, and student must all help." The reader is invited to get out his

---

[8]A writer of the 1930s and '40s who wrote scientific essays for general audiences. [Eds.]

semantic decoder and check on my translation. Observe there is no technical language in this gem of pedageese, beyond possibly the word "curriculum." It is just a simple idea heavily ververbalized.

In another kind of academic talk the author may display his 16 learning to conceal a lack of ideas. A bright instructor, for instance, in need of prestige may select a common sense proposition for the subject of a learned monograph—say, "Modern cities are hard to live in" and adorn it with imposing polysyllables: "Urban existence in the perpendicular declivities of megalopolis. . ." etc. He coins some new terms to transfix the reader—"mega-decibel" or "strato-cosmop-olis"—and works them vigorously. He is careful to add a page or two of differential equations to show the "scatter." And then he publishes, with 147 footnotes and a bibliography to knock your eye out. If the authorities are dozing, it can be worth an associate pro-fessorship.

While we are on the campus, however, we must not forget that 17 the technical language of the natural sciences and some terms in the social sciences, forbidding as they may sound to the layman, are quite necessary. Without them, specialists could not communicate what they find. Trouble arises when experts expect the uninitiated to under-stand the words; when they tell the jury, for instance, that the defen-dant is suffering from "circumorbital haematoma."

Here are two authentic quotations. Which was written by a dis-18 tinguished modern author, and which by a patient in a mental hos-pital? You will find the answer at the end of this essay.

> **1.** Have just been to supper. Did not knowing what the wood-chuck sent me here. How when the blue blue blue on the said anyone can do it that tries. Such is the presidential candidate.
>
> **2.** No history of a family to close with those and close. Never shall he be alone to be alone to be alone to be alone to be alone to lend a hand and leave it left and wasted.

Reducing the Gobble

As government and business offices grow larger, the need for 19 doing something about gobbledygook increases. Fortunately the big-gest office in the world is working hard to reduce it. The Federal Security Agency in Washington, with nearly 100 million clients on its books, began analyzing its communication lines some years ago, with gratifying results. Surveys find trouble in three main areas: corre-spondence with clients about their social security problems, office memos, official reports.

Clarity and brevity, as well as common humanity, are urgently 20 needed in this vast establishment which deals with disability, old age, and unemployment. The surveys found instead many cases of long-windedness, foggy meanings, clichés, and singsong phrases, and gross neglect of the reader's point of view. Rather than talking to a real person, the writer was talking to himself. "We often write like a man walking on stilts."

Here is a typical case of long-windedness: 21

> *Gobbledygook as found:* "We are wondering if sufficient time has passed so that you are in a position to indicate whether favorable action may now be taken on our recommendation for the reclassification of Mrs. Blank, junior clerk-stenographer, CAF 2, to assistant clerk-stenographer, CAF 3?" *Suggested improvement:* "Have you yet been able to act on our recommendation to reclassify Mrs. Blank?"

Another case: 22

> Although the Central Efficiency Rating Committee recognizes that there are many desirable changes that could be made in the present efficiency rating system in order to make it more realistic and more workable than it now is, this committee is of the opinion that no further change should be made in the present system during the current year. Because of conditions prevailing throughout the country and the resultant turnover in personnel, and difficulty in administering the Federal programs, further mechanical improvement in the present rating system would require staff retraining and other administrative expense which would seem best withheld until the official termination of hostilities, and until restoration of regular operation.

The F.S.A. invites us to squeeze the gobbledygook out of this statement. Here is my attempt:

> The Central Efficiency Rating Committee recognizes that desirable changes could be made in the present system. We believe, however, that no change should be attempted until the war is over.

This cuts the statement from 111 to 30 words, about one-quarter 23 of the original, but perhaps the reader can do still better. What of importance have I left out?

Sometimes in a book which I am reading for information—not 24 for literary pleasure—I run a pencil through the surplus words. Often I can cut a section to half its length with an improvement in clarity. Magazines like *The Reader's Digest* have reduced this process to an art. Are long-windedness and obscurity a cultural lag from the days when writing was reserved for priests and cloistered scholars? The more words and the deeper the mystery, the greater their prestige and the firmer the hold on their jobs. And the better the candidate's chance today to have his doctoral thesis accepted.

The F.S.A. surveys found that a great deal of writing was obscure 25

WRITING SUGGESTION

Construct an argument in which you contend that bureaucratic and specialized language is sometimes useful and even necessary. Use examples like Chase's to explain your position.

although not necessarily prolix.[9] Here is a letter sent to more than 100,000 inquirers, a classic example of murky prose. To clarify it, one needs to *add* words, not cut them:

> In order to be fully insured, an individual must have earned $50 or more in covered employment for as many quarters of coverage as half the calendar quarters elapsing between 1936 and the quarter in which he reaches age 65 or dies, whichever first occurs.

Probably no one without the technical jargon of the office could translate this: nevertheless, it was sent out to drive clients mad for seven years. One poor fellow wrote back: "I am no longer in covered employment. I have an outside job now."

Many words and phrases in officialese seem to come out automatically, as if from lower centers of the brain. In this standardized prose people never *get jobs,* they "secure employment"; *before* and *after* become "prior to" and "subsequent to"; one does not *do,* one "performs"; nobody *knows* a thing, he is "fully cognizant"; one never *says,* he "indicates." A great favorite at present is "implement."   26

Some charming boners occur in this talking-in-one's-sleep. For instance: 27

> The problem of extending coverage to all employees, regardless of size, is not as simple as surface appearances indicate.
> Though the proportions of all males and females in ages 16–45 are essentially the same. . . .
> Dairy cattle, usually and commonly embraced in dairying. . . .

In its manual to employees, the F.S.A. suggests the following: 28

Instead of	Use
give consideration to	consider
make inquiry regarding	inquire
is of the opinion	believes
comes into conflict with	conflicts
information which is of a confidential nature	confidential information

Professional or office gobbledygook often arises from using the passive rather than the active voice. Instead of looking you in the eye, as it were, and writing "This act requires. . ." the office worker looks out of the window and writes: "It is required by this statute that. . . ." When the bureau chief says, "We expect Congress to cut your budget," the message is only too clear; but usually he says, "It is expected that the departmental budget estimates will be reduced by Congress."   29

---

[9]Wordy. [Eds.]

Gobbled: "All letters prepared for the signature of the Administrator will be single spaced."

Ungobbled: "Single space for all letters for the Administrator." (Thus cutting 13 words to 7.)

Only People Can Read

The F.S.A. surveys pick up the point that human communication 30 involves a listener as well as a speaker. Only people can read, though a lot of writing seems to be addressed to beings in outer space. To whom are you talking? The sender of the officialese message often forgets the chap on the other end of the line.

A woman with two small children wrote the F.S.A. asking what 31 she should do about payments, as her husband had lost his memory. "If he never gets able to work," she said, "and stays in an institution would I be able to draw any benefits? . . . I don't know how I am going to live and raise my children since he is disable to work. Please give me some information. . . ."

To this human appeal, she received a shattering blast of gob- 32 bledygook, beginning, "State unemployment compensation laws do not provide any benefits for sick or disabled individuals . . . in order to qualify an individual must have a certain number of quarters of coverage . . ." etc., etc. Certainly if the writer had been thinking about the poor woman he would not have dragged in unessential material about old-age insurance. If he had pictured a mother without means to care for her children, he would have told her where she might get help—from the local office which handles aid to dependent children, for instance.

Gobbledygook of this kind would largely evaporate if we thought 33 of our messages as two way—in the above case, if we pictured ourselves talking on the doorstep of a shabby house to a woman with two children tugging at her skirts, who in her distress does not know which way to turn.

Results of the Survey

The F.S.A. survey showed that office documents could be cut 20 34 to 50 percent, with an improvement in clarity and a great saving to taxpayers in paper and payrolls.

A handbook was prepared and distributed by key officials.[10] They 35
read it, thought about it, and presently began calling section meetings
to discuss gobbledygook. More booklets were ordered, and the local
output of documents began to improve. A Correspondence Review
Section was established as a kind of laboratory to test murky messages. A supervisor could send up samples for analysis and suggestions. The handbook is now used for training new members; and
many employees keep it on their desks along with the dictionary. . . .

The handbook makes clear the enormous amount of gobbledy- 36
gook which automatically spreads in any large office, together with
ways and means to keep it under control. I would guess that at least
half of all the words circulating around the bureaus of the world are
"irrelevant, incompetent, and immaterial"—to use a favorite legalism;
or are just plain "unnecessary"—to ungobble it.

My favorite story of removing the gobble from gobbledygook 37
concerns the Bureau of Standards at Washington. I have told it before
but perhaps the reader will forgive the repetition. A New York
plumber wrote the Bureau that he had found hydrochloric acid fine
for cleaning drains, and was it harmless? Washington replied: "The
efficacy of hydrochloric acid is indisputable, but the chlorine residue
is incompatible with metallic permanence."

The plumber wrote back that he was mighty glad the Bureau agreed 38
with him. The Bureau replied with a note of alarm: "We cannot assume
responsibility for the production of toxic and noxious residues with
hydrochloric acid, and suggest that you use an alternate procedure."
The plumber was happy to learn that the Bureau still agreed with him.

Whereupon Washington exploded: "Don't use hydrochloric acid; 39
it eats hell out of the pipes!"[11]

RESPONDING TO READING

1. A study of what Stuart Chase calls gobbledygook concluded that many
employees of large corporations use it on purpose, to remain anonymous
and to avoid taking responsibility for their actions. What do you think Chase
would say about this finding? What is your reaction to this tactic?   **2.** How
prevalent is gobbledygook in your textbooks? Find some examples. Is this
kind of language a barrier to learning, or are you so used to it that it is no
longer an obstacle?   **3.** Do you ever use gobbledygook in your own
writing? If so, find several examples. What purpose does it serve?

---

[10]By Milton Hall.
[11]The second quotation (paragraph 18) comes from Gertrude Stein's *Lucy Church Amiably.*

**ANSWERS TO RESPONDING
TO READING**

1. He would not be surprised at all; see paragraphs 16 and 29.
2. Such language is definitely a barrier because
   it gets in the way of clear communication and
   precise thinking, both of which are necessary
   for learning.
3. Many students will admit they do, most likely
   to lengthen a paper, to sound more intelligent, or to dance around ideas that they do
   not completely understand.

The Lesson

TONI CADE BAMBARA

Originally trained as a dancer and actor, Toni Cade Bambara (1939–   ) has taught African-American literature in universities all over the United States. In her essay "What It Is I Think I'm Doing Anyhow," she says, "Through writing, I attempt to celebrate the tradition of resistance, attempt to tap Black potential, and try to join the chorus of voices that argues that exploitation and misery are neither inevitable nor necessary." Bambara writes fiction and nonfiction, and her stories are often marked by colloquial dialogue and street talk. The following short story is from Bambara's collection *Gorilla, My Love.*

FOR OPENERS

Ask students to respond to Bambara's quotation in the headnote. What do they think of her purposes for writing? Who are those who argue that exploitation and misery are inevitable and necessary?

Back in the days when everyone was old and stupid or young 1 and foolish and me and Sugar were the only ones just right, this lady moved on our block with nappy hair and proper speech and no makeup. And quite naturally we laughed at her, laughed the way we did at the junk man who went about his business like he was some big-time president and his sorry-ass horse his secretary. And we kinda hated her too, hated the way we did the winos who cluttered up our parks and pissed on our handball walls and stank up our hallways and stairs so you couldn't halfway play hide-and-seek without a goddamn gas mask. Miss Moore was her name. The only woman on the block with no first name. And she was black as hell, cept for her feet, which were fish-white and spooky. And she was always planning these boring-ass things for us to do, us being my cousin, mostly, who lived on the block cause we all moved North the same time and to the same apartment then spread out gradual to breathe. And our parents would yank our heads into some kinda shape and crisp up our clothes so we'd be presentable for travel with Miss Moore, who always looked like she was going to church, though she never did. Which is just one of things the grown-ups talked about when they talked behind her back like a dog. But when she came calling with some sachet she'd sewed up or some gingerbread she'd made or some book, why then they'd all be too embarrassed to turn her down and we'd get handed over all spruced up. She'd been to college and said it was only right that she should take responsibility for the young ones' education, and she not even related by marriage or blood. So they'd go for it. Specially Aunt Gretchen. She was the main gofer in the family. You got some ole dumb shit foolishness you want somebody to go for, you send for Aunt Gretchen. She been screwed into the go-along for so long, it's a blood-deep natural thing with her. Which is how she got saddled with me and Sugar and Junior in the first place while our mothers were in a la-de-da apartment up the block having a good ole time.

So this one day Miss Moore rounds us all up at the mailbox and it's puredee hot and she's knockin herself out about arithmetic. And school suppose to let up in summer I heard, but she don't never let up. And the starch in my pinafore scratching the shit outta me and I'm really hating this nappy-head bitch and her goddamn college degree. I'd much rather go to the pool or to the show where it's cool. So me and Sugar leaning on the mailbox being surly, which is a Miss Moore word. And Flyboy checking out what everybody brought for lunch. And Fat Butt already wasting his peanut-butter-and-jelly sandwich like the pig he is. And Junebug punchin on Q.T.'s arm for potato chips. And Rosie Giraffe shifting from one hip to the other waiting for somebody to step on her foot or ask her if she from Georgia so she can kick ass, perferably Mercedes'. And Miss Moore asking us do we know what money is, like we a bunch of retards. I mean real money, she say, like it's only poker chips or monopoly papers we lay on the grocer. So right away I'm tired of this and say no. And would much rather snatch Sugar and go to the Sunset and terrorize the West Indian kids and take their hair ribbons and their money too. And Miss Moore files that remark away for next week's lesson on brotherhood, I can tell. And finally I say we oughta get to the subway cause it's cooler and besides we might meet some cute boys. Sugar done swiped her mama's lipstick, so we ready.

So we heading down the street and she's boring us silly about what things cost and what our parents make and how much goes for rent and how money ain't divided up right in this country. And then she gets to the part about we all poor and live in the slums, which I don't feature. And I'm ready to speak on that, but she steps out in the street and hails two cabs just like that. Then she hustles half the crew in with her and hands me a five-dollar bill and tells me to calculate 10 percent tip for the driver. And we're off. Me and Sugar and Junebug and Flyboy hangin out the window and hollering to everybody, putting lipstick on each other cause Flyboy a faggot anyway, and making farts with our sweaty armpits. But I'm mostly trying to figure how to spend this money. But they all fascinated with the meter ticking and Junebug starts laying bets as to how much it'll read when Flyboy can't hold his breath no more. Then Sugar lays bets as to how much it'll be when we get there. So I'm stuck. Don't nobody want to go for my plan, which is to jump out at the next light and run off to the first bar-b-que we can find. Then the driver tells us to get the hell out cause we there already. And the meter reads eighty-five cents. And I'm stalling to figure out the tip and Sugar say give him a dime. And I decide he don't need it

2

3

ADDITIONAL QUESTIONS FOR RESPONDING TO READING

1. Pay very close attention to Sylvia's dialogue and actions throughout the story. What does the language add to the story? What do we gradually discover about Sylvia?

2. What function does Sugar serve in the story?

bad as I do, so later for him. But then he tries to take off with Junebug foot still in the door so we talk about his mama something ferocious. Then we check out that we on Fifth Avenue and everybody dressed up in stockings. One lady in a fur coat, hot as it is. White folks crazy.

"This is the place," Miss Moore say, presenting it to us in the 4 voice she uses at the museum. "Let's look in the windows before we go in."

"Can we steal?" Sugar asks very serious like she's getting the 5 ground rules squared away before she plays. "I beg your pardon," says Miss Moore, and we fall out. So she leads us around the windows of the toy store and me and Sugar screamin, "This is mine, that's mine, I gotta have that, that was made for me, I was born for that," till Big Butt drowns us out.

"Hey, I'm goin to buy that there." 6

"That there? You don't even know what it is, stupid." 7

"I do so," he say punchin on Rosie Giraffe. "It's a microscope." 8

"Watcha gonna do with a microscope, fool?" 9

"Look at things." 10

"Like what, Ronald?" ask Miss Moore. And Big Butt ain't got the 11 first notion. So here go Miss Moore gabbing about the thousands of bacteria in a drop of water and the somethinorother in a speck of blood and the million and one living things in the air around us is invisible to the naked eye. And what she say that for? Junebug go to town on that "naked" and we rolling. Then Miss Moore ask what it cost. So we all jam into the window smudgin it up and the price tag say $300. So then she ask how long'd take for Big Butt and Junebug to save up their allowances. "Too long," I say. "Yeh," adds Sugar, "outgrown it by that time." And Miss Moore say no, you never outgrow learning instruments. "Why, even medical students and interns and," blah, blah, blah. And we ready to choke Big Butt for bringing it up in the first damn place.

"This here costs four hundred eighty dollars," say Rosie Giraffe. 12 So we pile up all over her to see what she pointin out. My eyes tell me it's a chunk of glass cracked with something heavy, and different-color inks dripped into the splits, then the whole thing put into a oven or something. But the $480 it don't make sense.

"That's a paperweight made of semi-precious stones fused 13 together under tremendous pressure," she explains slowly, with her hands doing the mining and all the factory work.

"So what's a paperweight?" asks Rosie Giraffe. 14

"To weigh paper with, dumbbell," say Flyboy, the wise man from 15 the East.

"Not exactly," say Miss Moore, which is what she say when you 16

TEACHING STRATEGY

Discuss the following with your students:
Paragraph 1: Who is Miss Moore? Why does she spend her time with the neighborhood children? What does Sylvia think of her?
Paragraph 40: Why is Sylvia reluctant to enter the toy store?
Paragraph 44: What is the significance of Sylvia's reasoning about costs?
Paragraph 51: Explain what Sylvia means when she says, "And somethin weird is goin on, I can feel it in my chest."

warm or way off too. "It's to weigh paper down so it won't scatter and make your desk untidy." So right away me and Sugar curtsy to each other and then to Mercedes who is more the tidy type.

"We don't keep paper on top of the desk in my class," say 17 Junebug, figuring Miss Moore crazy or lyin one.

"At home, then," she say. "Don't you have a calendar and a pencil 18 case and a blotter and a letter-opener on your desk at home where you do your homework?" And she know damn well what our homes look like cause she nosys around in them every chance she gets.

"I don't even have a desk," say Junebug. "Do we?"   19

"No. And I don't get no homework neither," say Big Butt.   20

"And I don't even have a home," say Flyboy like he do at school 21 to keep the white folks off his back and sorry for him. Send this poor kid to camp posters, is his specialty.

"I do," says Mercedes. "I have a box of stationery on my desk 22 and a picture of my cat. My godmother bought the stationery and the desk. There's a big rose on each sheet and the envelopes smell like roses."

"Who wants to know about your smelly-ass stationery," say Rosie 23 Giraffe fore I can get my two cents in.

"It's important to have a work area all your own so that . . ."   24

"Will you look at this sailboat, please," say Flyboy, cuttin her off 25 and pointin to the thing like it was his. So once again we tumble all over each other to gaze at this magnificent thing in the toy store which is just big enough to maybe sail two kittens across the pond if you strap them to the posts tight. We all start reciting the price tag like we in assembly. "Handcrafted sailboat of fiberglass at one thousand one hundred ninety-five dollars."

"Unbelievable," I hear myself say and am really stunned. I read 26 it again for myself just in case the group recitation put me in a trance. Same thing. For some reason this pisses me off. We look at Miss Moore and she lookin at us, waiting for I dunno what.

Who'd pay all that when you can buy a sailboat set for a quarter 27 at Pop's, a tube of glue for a dime, and a ball of string for eight cents? "It must have a motor and a whole lot else besides," I say. "My sailboat cost me about fifty cents."

"But will it take water?" say Mercedes with her smart ass.   28

"Took mine to Alley Pond Park once," say Flyboy. "String broke. 29 Lost it. Pity."

"Sailed mine in Central Park and it keeled over and sank. Had 30 to ask my father for another dollar."

"And you got the strap," laugh Big Butt. "The jerk didn't even 31 have a string on it. My old man wailed on his behind."

Little Q.T. was staring hard at the sailboat and you could see he 32 wanted it bad. But he too little and somebody'd just take it from him. So what the hell. "This boat for kids, Miss Moore?"

"Parents silly to buy something like that just to get all broke up," 33 say Rosie Giraffe.

"That much money it should last forever," I figure.   34

"My father'd buy it for me if I wanted it."   35

"Your father, my ass," say Rosie Giraffe getting a chance to finally 36 push Mercedes.

"Must be rich people shop here," say Q.T.   37

"You are a very bright boy," say Flyboy. "What was your first 38 clue?" And he rap him on the head with the back of his knuckles, since Q.T. the only one he could get away with. Though Q.T. liable to come up behind you years later and get his licks in when you half expect it.

"What I want to know," I says to Miss Moore though I never talk 39 to her, I wouldn't give the bitch that satisfaction, "is how much a real boat costs? I figure a thousand'd get you a yacht any day."

"Why don't you check that out," she says, "and report back to 40 the group?" Which really pains my ass. If you gonna mess up a perfectly good swim day least you could do is have some answers. "Let's go in," she say like she got something up her sleeve. Only she don't lead the way. So me and Sugar turn the corner to where the entrance is, but when we get there I kinda hang back. Not that I'm scared, what's there to be afraid of, just a toy store. But I feel funny, shame. But what I got to be shamed about? Got as much right to go in as anybody. But somehow I can't seem to get hold of the door, so I step away for Sugar to lead. But she hangs back too. And I look at her and she looks at me and this is ridiculous. I mean, damn, I have never ever been shy about doing nothing or going nowhere. But then Mercedes steps up and then Rosie Giraffe and Big Butt crowd in behind and shove, and next thing we all stuffed into the doorway with only Mercedes squeezing past us, smoothing out her jumper and walking right down the aisle. Then the rest of us tumble in like a glued-together jigsaw done all wrong. And people lookin at us. And it's like the time me and Sugar crashed into the Catholic church on a dare. But once we got in there and everything so hushed and holy and the candles and the bowin and the handkerchiefs on all the drooping heads, I just couldn't go through with the plan. Which was for me to run up to the altar and do a tap dance while Sugar played the nose flute and messed around in the holy water. And Sugar kept givin me the elbow. Then later teased me so bad I tied her up in the shower and turned it on and locked her in. And she'd be there till this day if Aunt Gretchen hadn't finally figured I was lyin about the boarder takin a shower.

Same thing in the store. We all walkin on tiptoe and hardly 41
touchin the games and puzzles and things. And I watched Miss Moore
who is steady watchin us like she waitin for a sign. Like Mama
Drewery watches the sky and sniffs the air and takes note of just how
much slant is in the bird formation. Then me and Sugar bump smack
into each other, so busy gazing at the toys, 'specially the sailboat. But
we don't laugh and go into our fat-lady bump-stomach routine. We
just stare at that price tag. Then Sugar run a finger over the whole
boat. And I'm jealous and want to hit her. Maybe not her, but I sure
want to punch somebody in the mouth.

"Watcha bring us here for, Miss Moore?" 42

"You sound angry, Sylvia. Are you mad about something?" Givin 43
me one of them grins like she tellin a grown-up joke that never turns
out to be funny. And she's lookin very closely at me like maybe she
plannin to do my portrait from memory. I'm mad, but I won't give
her that satisfaction. So I slouch around the store bein very bored
and say, "Let's go."

Me and Sugar at the back of the train watchin the tracks whizzin 44
by large then small then gettin gobbled up in the dark. I'm thinkin
about this tricky toy I saw in the store. A clown that somersaults on
a bar then does chin-ups just cause you yank lightly at his leg. Cost
$35. I could see me askin my mother for a $35 birthday clown. "You
wanna who that costs what?" she'd say, cocking her head to the side
to get a better view of the hole in my head. Thirty-five dollars could
buy new bunk beds for Junior and Gretchen's boy. Thirty-five dollars
and the whole household could visit Grandaddy Nelson in the
country. Thirty-five dollars would pay for the rent and the piano bill
too. Who are these people that spend that much for performing
clowns and $1,000 for toy sailboats? What kinda work they do and
how they live and how come we ain't in on it? Where we are is who
we are, Miss Moore always pointin out. But it don't necessarily have
to be that way, she always adds then waits for somebody to say that
poor people have to wake up and demand their share of the pie and
don't none of us know what kind of pie she talkin about in the first
damn place. But she ain't so smart cause I still got her four dollars
from the taxi and she ain't gettin it. Messin up my day with this shit.
Sugar nudges me in my pocket and winks.

Miss Moore lines us up in front of the mailbox where we started 45
from, seem like years ago, and I got a headache for thinkin so hard.
And we lean all over each other so we can hold up under the draggy-
ass lecture she always finishes us off with at the end before we thank
her for borin us to tears. But she just looks at us like she readin tea
leaves. Finally she say, "Well, what did you think of F.A.O.
Schwarz?"

COLLABORATIVE ACTIVITY

Divide the class into two groups. Have one side argue that Sylvia learned something from Miss Moore. Have the other argue that she did not.

WRITING SUGGESTIONS

1. Write an essay in which you discuss whether Sylvia has learned anything as a result of her experience. Be specific and use examples from the story to support your points.
2. Write an essay about a person, who like Miss Moore, made a contribution to your informal education.

ANSWERS TO RESPONDING TO READING

1. The narrator speaks in colloquial language, whereas Miss Moore uses formal language. The difference indicates age, education level, and perhaps social class. This contrast in diction level suggests that Sylvia and Miss Moore come from different worlds. Miss Moore, however, attempts to bridge the gap by serving as an example of success.
2. Even though Sylvia thinks she has the upper hand, Miss Moore's lesson has changed her, whether she wants to admit it or not.
3. Answers will vary, but her colloquial diction does make Sylvia more real, a legitimate speaking voice that reveals a distinct personality. Even so, Sylvia's diction will most likely separate her from some students, who, like Miss Moore, must attempt to bridge the gap.

Rosie Giraffe mumbles, "White folks crazy." 46

"I'd like to go there again when I get my birthday money," says 47 Mercedes, and we shove her out the pack so she has to lean on the mailbox by herself.

"I'd like a shower. Tiring day," say Flyboy. 48

Then Sugar surprises me by sayin, "You know, Miss Moore, I 49 don't think all of us here put together eat in a year what that sailboat costs." And Miss Moore lights up like somebody goosed her. "And?" she say, urging Sugar on. Only I'm standin on her foot so she don't continue.

"Imagine for a minute what kind of society it is in which some 50 people can spend on a toy what it would cost to feed a family of six or seven. What do you think?"

"I think," say Sugar pushing me off her feet like she never done 51 before, cause I whip her ass in a minute, "that this is not much of a democracy if you ask me. Equal chance to pursue happiness means an equal crack at the dough, don't it?" Miss Moore is besides herself and I am disgusted with Sugar's treachery. So I stand on her foot one more time to see if she'll shove me. She shuts up, and Miss Moore looks at me, sorrowfully I'm thinkin. And somethin weird is goin on, I can feel it in my chest.

"Anybody else learn anything today?" lookin dead at me. I walk 52 away and Sugar has to run to catch up and don't even seem to notice when I shrug her arm off my shoulder.

"Well, we got four dollars anyway," she says. 53

"Uh hunh." 54

"We could go to Hascombs and get half a chocolate layer and 55 then go to the Sunset and still have plenty money for potato chips and ice-cream sodas."

"Uh hunh." 56

"Race you to Hascombs," she say. 57

We start down the block and she gets ahead which is O.K. by 58 me cause I'm going to the West End and then over to the Drive to think this day through. She can run if she want to and even run faster. But ain't nobody gonna beat me at nuthin.

RESPONDING TO READING

1. How does the narrator's level of diction differ from Miss Moore's? What does this difference suggest about their relative positions in society? About the terms of their relationship?   **2.** Who do you think has the upper hand in this story, the narrator or Miss Moore? Why?   **3.** How do you respond to the narrator? Does her level of diction play any part in shaping this response?

Jabberwocky

LEWIS CARROLL

The Reverend Charles Lutwidge Dodgson (1832–1898) took the pen name Lewis Carroll for his nonsense writing for children. Author of the classic *Alice in Wonderland* (1865), Carroll was born into a clergyman's family in Cheshire, England; he studied and later lectured in math at Oxford University. In his preface to his *Curiosa Mathematica, Part I* (1888), he praised pure mathematics for "the absolute certainty of its results." Throughout his life, he was both fascinated and dismayed by language and its potential for ambiguity. His books range from *The Formulae of Plane Trigonometry* (1861) to *Phantasmagoria and Other Poems* (1868) to *Eight or Nine Wise Words About Letter-Writing* (1890). "Jabberwocky" is the epitome of the nonsense poem, with its nonwords created for their sound as well as their sense. It appears in the first chapter of *Through the Looking Glass, and What Alice Found There* (1872).

'Twas brillig, and the slithy toves
　Did gyre and gimble in the wabe;
All mimsy were the borogoves,
　And the mome raths outgrabe.

"Beware the Jabberwock, my son!　　　　　5
　The jaws that bite, the claws that catch!
Beware the Jubjub bird, and shun
　The frumious Bandersnatch!"

He took his vorpal sword in hand;
　Long time the manxome foe he sought—　　10
So rested he by the Tumtum tree,
　And stood awhile in thought.

And, as in uffish thought he stood,
　The Jabberwock, with eyes of flame,
Came whiffling through the tulgey wood,　　15
　And burbled as it came!

One, two! One, two! And through and through
　The vorpal blade went snicker-snack!
He left it dead, and with its head
　He went galumphing back.　　　　　　　20

FOR OPENERS

Explain to students how we may decode words in English by studying their position in a sentence, their relationship to other words, and their characteristic forms. For example, we expect adjectives to precede the words they modify. Carroll relies on this characteristic of language in "Jabberwocky." His use of characteristic adjective and adverb endings further helps readers decipher some nonsense words grammatically. Because of their form and position, certain words—*uffish*, for example—appear to have a grammatical function as well as a hint of meaning. In addition, his use of actual English function words—articles, prepositions, and conjunctions—provides clues to a word's meaning. After this explanation, ask students to try to guess which words in the poem are coinages. (Do not use a dictionary at this point.)

TEACHING STRATEGIES

1. In *Through the Looking Glass*, Humpty Dumpty explains to Alice what some of the words in "Jabberwocky" mean. Many of these are portmanteau words, those in which the sounds and meanings of two words are "packed up" in one (*portmanteau* is the French word for a large two-sided suitcase.):

   slithy: lithe and slimy

   mimsy: flimsy and miserable

   burble: bleat and murmur and warble

   vorpal: voracious and purple

   galumphing: galloping and triumph

   Ask students to examine these and other unfamiliar words and to see whether they can divide them up as in the examples above.
2. Define *onomatopoeia*, in which the pronunciation of a word mimics meaning or sound. Ask students to identify examples in the poem.
3. Point out that some of the unfamiliar words in the poem do appear in the dictionary: *chortled, gyre, rath, whiffling,* and *callooh.*

COLLABORATIVE ACTIVITY

Break the class into four groups. Have each group agree on a version of the story that the poem appears to tell. Compare versions in class discussion.

WRITING SUGGESTION

Rewrite the poem, substituting words that you know for the unfamiliar nonsense words. Make sure you convey the sense of the story you developed during your collaborative work.

ANSWERS TO RESPONDING TO READING

1. Answers will vary.
2. Review the information in points 1 and 3 under "Teaching Strategies." This is a good opportunity to introduce students to the *Oxford English Dictionary* in the library. After going over what an unabridged dictionary is and how to use one, turn the students loose and see what they find.
3. Even though Carroll uses unfamiliar words and nonsense words, he conveys the flexibility and beauty of the English language. Carroll, like Lewis Thomas, makes his point most effectively by showing, rather than telling, the power of language.

BACKGROUND ON READING

Discuss with students what is lost and what is gained when a person emigrates to America. Remind them that immigrants usually feel a sense of loss as well as a sense of gain, especially if they do not know how to speak English. You might refer students to Richard Rodriguez's "Aria" (page 222) or "The Fear of Losing a Culture" (page 495). Encourage students to talk about their own roots, and ask any new immigrants to discuss the advantages and disadvantages of being raised in a bilingual household.

FOR OPENERS

Ask students to explain the poem's title. What does Lim mean by "modern"? By "secrets"?

COLLABORATIVE ACTIVITY

Have small groups of students make lists of the advantages and disadvantages of identifying with an ethnic group.

"And hast thou slain the Jabberwock?
  Come to my arms, my beamish boy!
O frabjous day! Callooh! Callay!"
  He chortled in his joy.

'Twas brillig, and the slithy toves   25
  Did gyre and gimble in the wabe;
All mimsy were the borogoves,
  And the mome raths outgrabe.

RESPONDING TO READING

1. Speaking of "Jabberwocky" in *Through the Looking Glass*, Alice says, "It seems very pretty . . . but it's *rather* hard to understand! Somehow it seems to fill my head with ideas—only I don't exactly know what they are!" What ideas does "Jabberwocky" suggest to you? Do you have better luck interpreting the poem than Alice does?   **2.** Throughout the poem Lewis Carroll uses words—some real words, some coined—that imitate sounds. Which unfamiliar words are real, and which are made up? Check them in a dictionary.   **3.** What point about the power of words do you think Carroll is trying to make? Why do you think he chooses to make it in this way? Could he have made his point more effectively in a different way?

Modern Secrets

SHIRLEY GEOK–LIN LIM

Poet Shirley Geok-Lin Lim (1944–   ), with coeditor Mayumi Tsutakawa, published *The Forbidden Stitch: An Asian-American Woman's Anthology* (1989). The stitch in the title refers to a particular embroidery knot that symbolizes the writing that was long forbidden to Asian-American women. This unusual collection includes stories, poems, and art. In "Modern Secrets," which appears in Lim's 1980 volume *Crossing the Peninsula & Other Poems*, she describes in symbolic images the blending of old and new cultures.

Last night I dreamt in Chinese.
Eating Yankee shredded wheat,
I told it in English terms
To a friend who spoke
In monosyllables,

All of which I understood:
The dream shrunk
To its fiction.
I knew its end
Many years ago.   10
The sallow child
Eating from a rice-bowl
Hides in the cupboard
With the tea-leaves and china.

RESPONDING TO READING

1. Why is it significant that the speaker says she dreamed in Chinese? What does this remark tell you about the speaker?   **2.** What does the poem say about being Chinese-American? In what way does language connect you to your ethnic roots?   **3.** The poem ends with the image of a child hiding in a cupboard. Can you identify with this child?

WRITING SUGGESTIONS

1. Write an essay in which you discuss the value of your ethnic group to you. Feel free to discuss both advantages and disadvantages.
2. Is it possible to be a hyphenated American (that is, to maintain a balance between two cultures), or must one be either Chinese or American?

ANSWERS TO RESPONDING TO READING

1. Dreaming is a state that brings out subconscious thoughts not normally acknowledged. The fact that the speaker dreams in Chinese also shows that no matter how assimilated she may be, a part of her will always be Chinese.
2. On one level, being Chinese-American is something to be hidden, placed on a shelf; her adjustment is depicted in the contrast between the child eating rice and the fact that she is now eating "Yankee" shredded wheat.
3. Answers will vary.

WRITING: THE POWER OF WORDS

1. According to George Orwell, good writing is simple, direct, and clear. His essay concerns the cleaning up of language: the elimination of dead metaphors, obsolete language, pretentious words, and complicated phrasing. Write an essay in which you discuss whether Orwell follows his own advice in "Politics and the English Language."

2. How do people's spoken and written language affect your response to them? Considering friends as well as public figures, write an essay in which you define and illustrate the criteria by which you evaluate the communication skills of others.

3. In his essay, Stuart Chase comments that gobbledygook is found in offices "too big for face-to-face talk"; in this way he associates gobbledygook with the dehumanizing quality of large organizations. Find some examples of gobbledygook in your university—in catalog course descriptions or policy statements, for example—and analyze them using Chase's essay as a guide. In your essay, consider why such language is used and what its likely effect will be on readers.

4. Which of the writers in this chapter do you see as a model for the writer you would like to be? Write an essay in which you support your choice. In addition, comment on how the writer's words lend power to his or her ideas.

5. Both Malcolm X in "A Homemade Education" and Richard Rodriguez in "Aria" talk about how education changed their use of language. Write an essay discussing the effect that education has had on your spoken and written language. What do you think you gained and lost by learning more about language?

6. In "You Are What You Say" Robin Lakoff says that women are handicapped by the language they have been conditioned to speak. Write an essay in which you discuss whether or not you agree with her contention. Use examples from newspapers or magazines as well as your own observations to support your assertions.

7. In "Aria" Richard Rodriguez distinguishes between private and public language. For him the private language is Spanish and the public one is English. Write an essay in which you define and discuss the private and public languages in your family.

8. In "Notes on Punctuation" Lewis Thomas says, "The greatest danger in punctuation is for poetry. Here it is necessary to be as economical and parsimonious with commas and periods as with the words themselves" (paragraph 8). He goes on to say, "A single exclamation point in a poem, no matter what else the poem has to say, is enough to destroy the whole work." Do you think Thomas overstates the importance of punctuation in poetry? Select one poem in this text and write an essay in which you examine its use of punctuation.

9. In "The Language of Prejudice" Gordon Allport warns against using labels. He suggests in paragraph 9 that, instead of using nouns to refer to people, we should use adjectives that convey a sense of a person as an individual. How do you think Allport's ideas apply to Alleen Pace Nilsen's comments in "Sexism in English: A 1990s Update."

10. Choose a textbook, newspaper, or magazine, and analyze its language in terms of its use of labels, gobbledygook, and sexism.

4

ACROSS THE GENERATIONS

CONFRONTING THE ISSUES

Before you assign any of the reading selections in this chapter, ask your students to make a chronological list of what they consider the major milestones of their lives—the "bests," "worsts," "firsts," "lasts," and "onlys." Then ask students to conduct an interview (in person or by telephone) with one of their parents. In this interview, parents should do just what the students have previously done: They should trace their children's lives from birth to the present, identifying significant milestones.

After the interview, each student should compare the two lists and write a paragraph or two accounting for any discrepancies between them. In class, encourage students to generalize about the differences between the way they see their own lives and the way their parents see them. For example, are their parents more or less likely than the students to remember negative milestones? Which years do parents (and students) recall most vividly? Most favorably? Are there any events that students see as positive and parents as negative, or vice versa?

Finally, introduce to your class the idea that many of this chapter's selections depend on memory and on subjective views of parents or other family members. Students will most likely realize by now that such readings cannot present a "true" or "complete" picture of a family member's life or of relationships within families because there is no single, complete "truth." As they read the selections in this chapter, then, they should be concerned not just with facts but with subtleties: motivations, emotional reactions, and differing or changing points of view.

In essays, stories, and poems, writers reconsider the past, trying to understand it, to come to terms with it, to recapture it, or to recreate it. In each selection in this chapter a narrator—sometimes the writer, sometimes the writer's fictional creation—concentrates on seeing across the barriers imposed by time. In some cases memories appear in sharp focus; in others, details are blurred, confused, or even partially invented. Many writers focus on parents or other family members, trying to do what N. Scott Momaday describes as seeing "in reality what [his grandmother] had seen more perfectly in the mind's eye." In some selections—for example, Tillie Olsen's "I Stand Here Ironing," Joan Didion's "On Going Home," and E. B. White's "Once More to the Lake"—the narrator speaks in part from a parent's perspective, but in most selections the narrator speaks as an adult looking back at his or her childhood. In nearly every case the narrators struggle to close generational gaps, to replay events, to see through the eyes of others—and thus to understand themselves more fully.

Certain selections in this chapter share more specific parallels. For instance, some writers—such as Walker and Olsen—set two generations in clear opposition; others—such as White and Bradley—trace family ties across two or more generations. Several authors—such as Howe and Soto—write about parents' attitudes toward work, examining how a child is affected by that work (and, by implication, commenting on the American work ethic and even the American Dream). Others—such as Carver and Sanders—struggle with painful recollections of their parents' weaknesses and with their own difficulties as children and as adults in coming to terms with them. A central concern shared by many of the selections, regardless of the author's age, sex, or ethnic background, is the ambivalence that children feel toward their parents and that parents feel toward their children.

PREPARING TO READ AND WRITE

As you read and prepare to write about the selections in this chapter, consider the following questions:

- Is the narrator focusing on himself or herself, on a relationship between two people, or on family dynamics?

- Do you think the narrator's perspective is subjective or objective? On what evidence do you base your conclusion?

- Is the selection about the experiences and emotions of the narrator as an adult or as a child? Does the narrator seem to have more insight now than when the recounted events occurred? What has the narrator learned—and how?

- Are family members seen from a distance or close up? Is the picture clear and distinct or hazy and blurred? How reliable is the writer's memory? Why might essayists choose to "fictionalize" their memoirs?

- What outside social, political, economic, or cultural forces influence the way the family functions and the way the writer views the family? To what degree is the selection about a specific historical time, a place, or a culture rather than about an individual?

- Does one family member seem to have a disproportionately large influence over others in the family? If so, is this influence positive or negative?

- Is the characterization of the selection's subject favorable, unfavorable, neutral, or ambivalent?

- Is the narrator honest with himself or herself? With readers? How can you tell?

- Is the selection's purpose observation, exploration, self-discovery, explanation, rationalization, or something else?

- Do some works speak more specifically and directly than others to your own experiences with family members? Is this because your sex or ethnic background corresponds to that of the writer, or are there other reasons?

- What strengths and weaknesses do adult children see in their parents? Are their perceptions accurate? How can you tell? Do their observations apply to families in general, or are they culture specific, or even idiosyncratic?

On Going Home

JOAN DIDION

Joan Didion (see also p. 54) is a master of the personal essay. She claims in "Why I Write" that she is not an intellectual, that she does not think in abstractions; rather, she says, she writes "entirely to find out what I'm thinking, what I'm looking at, what I see and what it means." Her prose is specific and tangible. As she states in "On Keeping a Notebook", "It is a good idea . . . to keep in touch"; in the following essay, Didion reconnects with home.

FOR OPENERS

Didion writes in paragraph 3 that she and her mother are "veterans of a guerilla war" neither ever understood. What is a guerilla war? How is it unlike conventional combat? Why is a parent-child relationship like a guerilla war?

ADDITIONAL QUESTIONS FOR RESPONDING TO READING

1. In what different ways does Didion use the word *home* in the essay? Do the various meanings seem paradoxical? Do they apply to your life?
2. What implications does Didion make here about the search for a personal identity? Does her reunion with her family facilitate this search?
3. In light of all the conflicts Didion associates with "home," why does she want to offer a "home" to her daughter?
4. According to Didion, is it possible to come to some full understanding about who we are or where we come from? Do you agree with her implications?

I am home for my daughter's first birthday. By "home" I do not 1 mean the house in Los Angeles where my husband and I and the baby live, but the place where my family is, in the Central Valley of California. It is a vital although troublesome distinction. My husband likes my family but is uneasy in their house, because once there I fall into their ways, which are difficult, oblique, deliberately inarticulate, not my husband's ways. We live in dusty houses ("D-U-S-T," he once wrote with his finger on surfaces all over the house, but no one noticed it) filled with mementos quite without value to him (what could the Canton dessert plates mean to him? how could he have known about the assay scales,[1] why should he care if he did know?), and we appear to talk exclusively about people we know who have been committed to mental hospitals, about people we know who have been booked on drunk-driving charges, and about property, particularly about property, land, price per acre and C-2 zoning and assessments and freeway access. My brother does not understand my husband's inability to perceive the advantage in the rather common real-estate transaction known as "sale-leaseback," and my husband in turn does not understand why so many of the people he hears about in my father's house have recently been committed to mental hospitals or booked on drunk-driving charges. Nor does he understand that when we talk about sale-leasebacks and right-of-way condemnations we are talking in code about the things we like best, the yellow fields and the cottonwoods and the rivers rising and falling and the mountain roads closing when the heavy snow comes in. We miss each other's points, have another drink and regard the fire. My brother refers to my husband, in his presence, as "Joan's husband." Marriage is the classic betrayal.

Or perhaps it is not any more. Sometimes I think that those of 2 us who are now in our thirties were born into the last generation to carry the burden of "home," to find in family life the source of all

---

[1]Scales used to weigh ore. [Eds.]

tension and drama. I had by all objective accounts a "normal" and a "happy" family situation, and yet I was almost thirty years old before I could talk to my family on the telephone without crying after I had hung up. We did not fight. Nothing was wrong. And yet some nameless anxiety colored the emotional charges between me and the place that I came from. The question of whether or not you could go home again was a very real part of the sentimental and largely literary baggage with which we left home in the fifties; I suspect that it is irrelevant to the children born of the fragmentation after World War II. A few weeks ago in a San Francisco bar I saw a pretty young girl on crystal take off her clothes and dance for the cash prize in an "amateur-topless" contest. There was no particular sense of moment about this, none of the effect of romantic degradation, of "dark journey," for which my generation strived so assiduously. What sense could that girl possibly make of, say, *Long Day's Journey into Night*?[2] Who is beside the point?

That I am trapped in this particular irrelevancy is never more 3 apparent to me than when I am home. Paralyzed by the neurotic lassitude engendered by meeting one's past at every turn, around every corner, inside every cupboard, I go aimlessly from room to room. I decide to meet it head-on and clean out a drawer, and I spread the contents on the bed. A bathing suit I wore the summer I was seventeen. A letter of rejection from *The Nation*, an aerial photograph of the site for a shopping center my father did not build in 1954. Three teacups hand-painted with cabbage roses and signed "E.M.," my grandmother's initials. There is no final solution for letters of rejection from *The Nation* and teacups hand-painted in 1900. Nor is there any answer to snapshots of one's grandfather as a young man on skis, surveying around Donner Pass in the year 1910. I smooth out the snapshot and look into his face, and do and do not see my own. I close the drawer, and have another cup of coffee with my mother. We get along very well, veterans of a guerrilla war we never understood.

Days pass. I see no one. I come to dread my husband's evening 4 call, not only because he is full of news of what by now seems to me our remote life in Los Angeles, people he has seen, letters which require attention, but because he asks what I have been doing, suggests uneasily that I get out, drive to San Francisco or Berkeley. Instead I drive across the river to a family graveyard. It has been vandalized since my last visit and the monuments are broken, over-

TEACHING STRATEGY

Point out to your students how Didion balances abstract concepts with specific terms. Have your students suggest their own interpretations of such generalizations as "Marriage is the classic betrayal" (paragraph 1) and their own views on the question of whether you can ever go home again (paragraphs 2 and 3).

---

[2]Semi-autobiographical play by American dramatist Eugene O'Neill (1888–1953) written in 1941 and published after his death. The play is about a troubled family. The mother is a drug addict and one son is an alcoholic. [Eds.]

WRITING SUGGESTION

What solutions or answers does Didion seem to be looking for when she returns home? What solutions do you find yourself looking for when you revisit family? Write an essay in which you describe such a visit and tell what you found.

**ANSWERS TO RESPONDING
TO READING**

1. Family life for Didion is full of painful surprises. Her visit with her family pushes her back into behavior she thought she had left behind. It erases mature identity and draws her into old tensions and ambivalences. She must admit that her past and her adult identity are interwoven.

2. Didion may be more tolerant of older family members because she realizes that, in spite of its tensions, family life involved many memorable family experiences that she will be unable to offer her daughter.

3. Didion suggests that a sense of family is unavailable to children born after World War II. This is even more true for children born today, whose families may not even sit down to meals together and who all seem to be on different schedules. Family will no longer be central because of the social changes that have occurred—for example, the increased mobility that separates family members and the rising numbers of single-parent families and "nontraditional" households.

turned in the dry grass. Because I once saw a rattlesnake in the grass I stay in the car and listen to a country-and-Western station. Later I drive with my father to a ranch he has in the foothills. The man who runs his cattle on it asks us to the roundup, a week from Sunday, and although I know that I will be in Los Angeles I say, in the oblique way my family talks, that I will come. Once home I mention the broken monuments in the graveyard. My mother shrugs.

I go to visit my great-aunts. A few of them think now that I am 5 my cousin, or their daughter who died young. We recall an anecdote about a relative last seen in 1948, and they ask if I still like living in New York City. I have lived in Los Angeles for three years, but I say that I do. The baby is offered a horehound drop, and I am slipped a dollar bill "to buy a treat." Questions trail off, answers are abandoned, the baby plays with the dust motes in a shaft of afternoon sun.

It is time for the baby's birthday party: a white cake, strawberry-6 marshmallow ice cream, a bottle of champagne saved from another party. In the evening, after she has gone to sleep, I kneel beside the crib and touch her face, where it is pressed against the slats, with mine. She is an open and trusting child, unprepared for and unaccustomed to the ambushes of family life, and perhaps it is just as well that I can offer her little of that life. I would like to give her more. I would like to promise her that she will grow up with a sense of her cousins and of rivers and of her great-grandmother's teacups, would like to pledge her a picnic on a river with fried chicken and her hair uncombed, would like to give her *home* for her birthday, but we live differently now and I can promise her nothing like that. I give her a xylophone and a sundress from Madeira, and promise to tell her a funny story.

RESPONDING TO READING

1. Didion characterizes family life as full of "ambushes" (paragraph 6). What does she mean? How does this characterization apply to her life as she describes it? Is it true of your life?   **2.** How do you think the fact that it is her daughter's first birthday shapes Didion's attitude toward older family members in this essay?   **3.** Didion believes that her generation may be the last "to carry the burden of 'home,' to find in family life the source of all tension and drama" (paragraph 2). What implications does her idea have for children born in this decade? Does your own experience support her generalizations?

Indelible Marks: Growing Up in a Chinese Laundry

JOYCE HOWE

Joyce Howe (1958–   ), a journalist and book critic who frequently writes on issues relating to Asian-Americans, grew up in New York where her father was a laundryman. In 1983 she published the following essay in *The Village Voice* about her memories of the laundry. She no longer lives in New York, but she visits regularly and continues to pass by the building in which she grew up and where her late father worked.

1   It is a Sunday afternoon, and I am in a friend's East Village apartment, watching him sort laundry. He and his roommate throw a month's worth of dirty wash into large white drawstring bags and stretched-out pillowcases for the short trek down Second Avenue to a laundry where for four dollars the owner will wash 15 pounds.

2   The sheets, underwear, socks, towels, polos, and T's are bundled up into their bags, but the long-sleeved cotton shirts—the young professional uniforms—are set aside. The next day, these will be brought around the corner to the Chinese laundry, to the featureless man behind the counter, Mr. Lee or Mr. Chan, whose English is bad, who irons out the creases, and promises they will be ready next Wednesday.

3   "Oh, you're going to the Chinks!" laughs a visitor from the Upper West Side, whom I have just met. My face reddens. "In Riverdale, that's how we said we were going to the Chinese laundry," he says. I laugh. As the daughter of a former Chinese laundryman, I figure I have learned how.

4   My older sisters and I grew up in the back of laundries. In 1964, when I was six years old, we moved from my father's first laundry on Amsterdam Avenue to his last, in Jackson Heights. All of us lived in the rear rooms of the business just as the nearly 8000 mostly lone laundrymen in New York did at the turn of the century. A single long curtain divided the workplace from home.

5   I grew up with the sight of my stocky father wringing the milky, handmixed starch solution, that turned even the limpest collar stiff, from a clean shirt into a pail. Or my father was bent low over the "hong-chong," an ironing bed, built waist-high along the laundry wall from planks and boards and covered with a felt pad and muslin hammered in with tacks. (The "hong-chong" was traditionally used for storage too; a sheet of cloth hung down from it, hiding boxes of tickets, starch, and other tools.) In his right hand, the old heavy wood-

handled electric iron glided across the front of a customer's button-down shirt or smoothed the corner of a cotton handkerchief.

My father preferred the dull smooth-bottomed irons with their own metal plates to the modern chrome steam irons, and he wet the wrinkled cloth with spray from two triggered hoses hanging overhead. As children, my sisters and I had terrific water-gun fights with those hoses. 6

My father, now 66, ran a laundry for almost 30 years. Born in Albany in 1916, he learned the business from his father, a former farmer from Canton who, with his wife, had sailed to America that same year. His father (my Goong, or paternal grandfather) had come to Albany with the same hopes of a prosperous life that all immigrants bring. Still, I know very little about him, and very little about my father's youth. What I, the youngest of four daughters, know comes only from an old gilt-framed photograph sitting on my parents' dresser and from those occasions, perhaps fewer than 10, when I have asked questions and my father has answered. 7

The black-and-white photograph is a formal portrait of my grand-parents and their three children—my father and his two younger sisters—taken sometime in the late 1920s. Goong sits tall; his thin body is hidden in a dark, American suit, a bow tie tight at this throat. There is a gentle look about his mouth, the barest smile on a long face which I like to think was kind. My father does not look like him at all. In the photo, he stands as an adolescent, in short pants and suit jacket, to the right of my seated grandmother; her bound feet are not noticeable. It is she whom my father resembles—the same broad forehead and nose, the full lips and heavy brows, the face set tight, betraying nothing. 8

What *do* I know? I know that my father, who raised his children as agnostics, was once an altar boy in an Albany Catholic church, and that after finishing the eighth grade he left school to work full time in his ailing father's store. I know that neighborhood children ran in and out of that store, calling Goong and my father names, like "Chink" or "Chinaman." Even now, when I bring up discrimination, he remembers the name-calling. He is insistent that such things no longer happen, certain that things are now better. He has told me that when he was 18, Goong sent him off to China with a family friend, a laundryman from nearby Mechanicsville, for Chinese education. While there, according to his father's wishes, he met and married the friend's youngest daughter, my mother. Goong died during the year or so my father was away. A short time later, my grandmother died. 9

My father sailed back to the U.S. alone. He sold his father's laundry. After service in the army, he apprenticed with an uncle in Manhattan. This bachelor uncle, who'd arrived in New York years 10

TEACHING STRATEGY

Note the ironies in the essay:

- The past continues into the present in the sense that her friend will take his shirts to a Chinese laundry much like the one from which Howe "escaped."
- Even though her father's life was rooted in the emigrant Chinese experience, he actually was born in America, was American in most of his habits, and could not read or write Chinese.
- The daughters trained to work in the store were too highly educated to take over the work there.

before, was debilitated by an old opium habit begun long ago to relieve the tedium of his work day.

My mother, because of strict immigration laws forbidding the 11 entry of Chinese females into the country, was still in Canton. The pretty young wife, whom he hardly knew, wrote letters to my father, describing how she and my oldest sister, who was born after he left, fled their rural village to escape the invading Japanese—how for days, they stayed with whoever would take them in. In each letter she asked for money, and my father always sent it. His literacy in Chinese was limited, so his uncle read my mother's letters aloud, translating my father's prompt responses into delicate Chinese script.

After his uncle's death (my father blames it on the opium), the 12 laundry at 966 Amsterdam Avenue, on whose plate-glass window was painted the name "Jim Lee Laundry" in red for luck, was left to him. In 1949 my mother and oldest sister, then 12 years old, arrived in New York. My sister later married a young Chinese immigrant and for $4500, they soon bought their own laundry, 20 blocks south of my father's. They are still there, and the laundry is one of the few remaining in the area.

In Queens, on the block where we moved, my father was known 13 as the man who ran the Chinese laundry, like Ernie who ran the deli, Benny the upholsterer, and the butcher a few doors down. To all of his customers he was Joe. And they—middle-aged housewives, young bachelors and students, mainly white—were known to him by a first name or by the unique indelible "mark" on their collars and hems. (This "mark," consisting of one or more characters, was written on each item for the duration of a customer's patronage; if he switched laundries, the new establishment usually did not bother changing it.) With all of them, as tickets, laundry bills, and change passed from hand to hand over the wide counter, my father exchanged comments: "Too much of this rain, huh?", "Yeah, the Mets looked lousy last night," or "How's the wife and the kids?"

Saturday was his busiest day. It was not only the day more cus- 14 tomers came in and out, but it was also one of the three days on which the long and tedious job of laundry-sorting was done. The entire floor of the store became a dumping ground for soiled clothes. My father divided the laundry into piles: 10 to 15 sheets and pillowcases were bundled up into one sheet and the ticket stubs of the customers whose laundry made up the bundle were then stapled together and put aside for later identification. "Wet items," such as towels, underwear, and socks were separated into two categories— light and dark; shirts were separated into four categories—colored, white, starch, and no starch. Each pile of "wet items" and shirts was then placed in a laundry bag with its respective tag.

The bags and bundles were picked up Sunday morning by the 15
truck drivers, who had names like Rocky and Louie, from the wholesale laundry or "wet wash" contracted by my father. ("Hand laundry"
has been a misnomer since the late 1930s and '40s, when a whole
new industry of Chinese-operated wholesale laundries and pressing
concerns sprang up and contracted to do the actual washing and
pressing for laundrymen.) Every Sunday, we were awakened from
our sleep by the sound of the drivers' keys turning in the front door's
locks.

When the "wet wash" drivers returned Monday with the previous 16
day's load, the sheets and pillowcases, or "flat pieces," were wrapped
in a heavy brown paper which my mother later would use for table-
cloths. The shirts returned in the same bags they went out in. My
father pulled out the bag of shirts to be starched and hand-ironed,
leaving the rest for the shirt-press truck to pick up that night. On
Tuesday night, they returned—clean, pressed, folded—in large
square cardboard boxes, each shirt ringed in its own pale blue paper
band.

For a short time, we had our own automatic dryer to take care of 17
the damp "wet items" when they returned. After it broke down,
irreparably, the dryer retired, and was left to hold stacks of comic
books and board games. My sisters and I took turns making pilgrimages to the local laundromat, our metal shopping cart bent from the
weight of the load. We wheeled those three blocks three times a week.
On my turn, I always hoped that no one I knew would see me as I
struggled with two hands to keep laundry and cart intact when
maneuvering the high curbs. Even then, the irony of going from the
laundry to the laundromat was not lost.

Of course, there were days when the system was off, when the 18
shirt press might return its load late, or when my father didn't feel
well enough to wrap every package. On those days, we were all
expected to help. We made sure that the promise my father had made
to customers on Saturday that their shirts would be ready by
Wednesday was kept. Behind the tan curtain drawn across our plate-
glass window every evening at seven and the door's pulled venetian
blind, we settled into a tableau. My family formed a late-night
assembly line, each member taking his place amid the shelves, boxes,
white cones of string, rolls of wrapping paper, and the familiar fragrance of newly laundered cloth.

There were those customers who took an interest in my father's 19
life and in his children, who gave my sisters and me candy, and asked
how we were doing in school. Without offering any of his own, my
father heard their problems, while making sure it was only a little
starch they wanted or that their shirts should be hung rather than
folded.

I was always glad when these customers came in. In my child's 20
eyes, their interest somehow legitimized us. My sisters and I, who
often wished our father ran a candy store instead, were not just seen
as three faceless Chinese daughters with braids, dutifully making
change, delivering laundry or cleaning up. We became individuals,
known by our first names, with other concerns.

Hearing my father converse with the customers reassured me that 21
not everyone saw his life revolving entirely around his livelihood.
His identity was not solely that of the role of Chinese laundryman.
He had interests in the outside world. He read the *Daily News* and
the *Post*. He bet on the harness races with Benny the upholsterer,
who drove him to the track. During the baseball season, he sat in the
back, on the orange vinyl couch discarded from a friend's take-out
restaurant, and watched the day games on TV, getting up at the sound
of the front door's chimes as someone came in.

I needed the reassurance of others. It seemed as if it would be 22
easier, on those endless forms handed out in school, to fill in "candy
store owner" in the space for "father's occupation." Instead of
"Chinese laundryman," my sisters taught me to write "Chinese
laundry proprietor," as if the latter were somehow more respectable.
No one else we knew at school lived behind a store.

Shouldn't our American-born father—who drank beer with his 23
rice at dinner, who took us to James Bond movies and amusement
parks, to LaGuardia airport to watch the planes take off—be something more than another laundryman? He wasn't an immigrant like
his father, another Chinaman who came to find gold but found the
washing industry instead.

My father retired when he was 60. I was a sophomore away at 24
college; my family had bought a three-family brick house three years
before. His average weekly income of $400 (considered "good busi-
ness" for a hand laundry) had gradually plummeted to a low of $175
as the racial and economic face of our Jackson Heights neighborhood
changed from middle-class whites to lower-income Hispanics. When
his rent ($200 when he moved in 14 years earlier) threatened to double,
my father let the laundry go.

There would have been no one to pass it on to. No only son to 25
try and make a go of it. His younger children—who had spent hours
after school and during weekends learning to sort laundry, count
change quickly, and securely tie string—were all too grown, all too
educated.

According to the New York Chinatown History Project, which 26
has put together a traveling exhibit on the history of Chinese laundry
workers in the United States, only an estimated 1000 hand laundries
remain in the New York metropolitan area. The city's Department of
Consumer Affairs, which licenses all "establishments which take in

COLLABORATIVE ACTIVITY

Each group should trace one of the following
recurring motifs in the essay:

- The theme of identity
- The contrast between the children's world
  and the world of their parents
- The significance of family "portraits" in the
  essay

In class discussion, ask students whether the
recurrence of these motifs makes Howe's experiences seem like or unlike their own.

WRITING SUGGESTIONS

1. Have you changed your attitude toward the kind of work your parents did or do? Write an essay about how your feelings about their occupations changed as you grew older.

2. What "indelible marks" have your parents left on you? Write an essay in which you discuss their influences on you, focusing either on your feelings about your ethnic heritage or on your attitudes toward work.

ANSWERS TO RESPONDING TO READING

1. Howe implies that it is difficult to separate an individual from his or her occupation. In her father's case, she suggests, the associations generated by his occupation are not likely to be positive ones. Although customers exchange small talk with him, they see him as almost invisible, interchangeable with other Chinese laundrymen. In some sense, this is how she herself sees him, but she eventually sees beyond the label.

2. The biographical information enables Howe to see her father's life as shaped by social and cultural events. This in turn makes her more tolerant of his status than she might otherwise be.

3. The act of writing this essay demonstrates Howe's acceptance of her father.

laundry" (except for dry cleaners) every two years, reports that as of September 13, there were only 305 licensed hand laundries in New York.

When my father retired, he referred his remaining customers to 27 another laundry, owned by friends, two blocks away. His laundry and former home have since become in turn, a dry cleaner, a dress shop, a bodega, and another dress shop named "Fuego." On the few times I've driven by, I've looked carefully for its latest occupant, catching a quick glimpse of an iron gate instead.

I have a favorite photo of my father. It is in color. Taken two or 28 three years ago in the garden that he and my mother tend behind the family house, my shirt-sleeved father is kneeling among the leafy green cabbage, tomato plants, and other vegetables growing in straight rows. His fine white hair is combed back from the broad forehead, black-rimmed spectacles frame his eyes. Looking straight at the camera, he is smiling.

I showed it once to my friend, laughing proudly, "Doesn't he 29 look like a Russian dissident intellectual here?" But of course, he is not. The man in the photograph is my father. He used to run a Chinese laundry.

RESPONDING TO READING

1. Howe writes, "In Queens, on the block where we moved, my father was known as the man who ran the Chinese laundry." What assumptions about her father's occupation are implicit in Howe's essay? How is the perception of her father by outsiders similar to and different from her own? How have outsiders' views shaped your view of your family?   **2.** Howe provides a good deal of background information about her father's family. What purpose does this information serve in the essay? How might similar biographical or historical information help you understand your parents?   **3.** Does Howe admire her father? Is she disappointed in him? Or does she simply accept him for what he is? Explain your conclusion.

One Last Time

GARY SOTO

Gary Soto (1952–   ) was raised in the San Joaquin valley of California, where he worked for a time as a migrant laborer. He studied geography in college but then turned to poetry, often using his childhood locale in poems about poverty and desolation among Mexican-Americans. His style is lean and simple, and his characters struggle to rise above their difficult situations. In 1985, Soto won the American Book Award for his autobiographical prose work *Living Up the Street: Narrative Recollections*. In an unpublished interview about this book, Soto says, "I would rather show and not tell about certain levels of poverty, of childhood; I made a conscious effort not to tell anything but just present the stories and let the reader come up with assumptions." The following essay about picking grapes for a raisin company is from *Living Up the Street*.

Yesterday I saw the movie *Gandhi* and recognized a few of the people—not in the theater but in the film. I saw my relatives, dusty and thin as sparrows, returning from the fields with hoes balanced on their shoulders. The workers were squinting, eyes small and veined, and were using their hands to say what there was to say to those in the audience with popcorn and Cokes. I didn't have anything, though. I sat thinking of my family and their years in the fields, beginning with Grandmother who came to the United States after the Mexican revolution to settle in Fresno where she met her husband and bore children, many of them. She worked in the fields around Fresno, picking grapes, oranges, plums, peaches, and cotton, dragging a large white sack like a sled. She worked in the packing houses, Bonner and Sun-Maid Raisin, where she stood at a conveyor belt passing her hand over streams of raisins to pluck out leaves and pebbles. For over twenty years she worked at a machine that boxed raisins until she retired at sixty-five.

Grandfather worked in the fields, as did his children. Mother also found herself out there when she separated from Father for three weeks. I remember her coming home, dusty and so tired that she had to rest on the porch before she trudged inside to wash and start dinner. I didn't understand the complaints about her ankles or the small of her back, even though I had been in the grape fields watching her work. With my brother and sister I ran in and out of the rows; we enjoyed ourselves and pretended not to hear Mother scolding us to sit down and behave ourselves. A few years later, however, I caught on when I went to pick grapes rather than play in the rows.

Mother and I got up before dawn and ate quick bowls of cereal. She drove in silence while I rambled on how everything was now solved, how I was going to make enough money to end our misery and even buy her a beautiful copper tea pot, the one I had shown her in Long's Drugs. When we arrived I was frisky and ready to go, self-consciously aware of my grape knife dangling at my wrist. I almost ran to the row the foreman had pointed out, but I returned to help Mother with the grape pans and jug of water. She told me to settle down and reminded me not to lose my knife. I walked at her side and listened to her explain how to cut grapes; bent down, hands

1   **FOR OPENERS**

Based on what Soto tells us, is this really the "one last time"?

2

3

on knees, I watched her demonstrate by cutting a few bunches into my pan. She stood over me as I tried it myself, tugging at a bunch of grapes that pulled loose like beads from a necklace. "Cut the stem all the way," she told me as last advice before she walked away, her shoes sinking in the loose dirt, to begin work on her own row.

I cut another bunch, then another, fighting the snap and whip 4 of vines. After ten minutes of groping for grapes, my first pan brimmed with bunches. I poured them on the paper tray, which was bordered by a wooden frame that kept the grapes from rolling off, and they spilled like jewels from a pirate's chest. The tray was only half filled, so I hurried to jump under the vines and begin groping, cutting, and tugging at the grapes again. I emptied the pan, raked the grapes with my hands to make them look like they filled the tray, and jumped back under the vine on my knees. I tried to cut faster because Mother, in the next row, was slowly moving ahead. I peeked into her row and saw five trays gleaming in the early morning. I cut, pulled hard, and stopped to gather the grapes that missed the pan; already bored, I spat on a few to wash them before tossing them like popcorn into my mouth.

So it went. Two pans equaled one tray—or six cents. By lunchtime 5 I had a trail of thirty-seven trays behind me while mother had sixty or more. We met about halfway from our last trays, and I sat down with a grunt, knees wet from kneeling on dropped grapes. I washed my hands with the water from the jug, drying them on the inside of my shirt sleeve before I opened the paper bag for the first sandwich, which I gave to Mother. I dipped my hand in again to unwrap a sandwich without looking at it. I took a first bite and chewed it slowly for the tang of mustard. Eating in silence I looked straight ahead at the vines, and only when we were finished with cookies did we talk.

"Are you tired?" she asked. 6

"No, but I got a sliver from the frame," I told her. I showed her 7 the web of skin between my thumb and index finger. She wrinkled her forehead but said it was nothing.

"How many trays did you do?" 8

I looked straight ahead, not answering at first. I recounted in my 9 mind the whole morning of bend, cut, pour again and again, before answering a feeble "thirty-seven." No elaboration, no detail. Without looking at me she told me how she had done field work in Texas and Michigan as a child. But I had a difficult time listening to her stories. I played with my grape knife, stabbing it into the ground, but stopped when Mother reminded me that I had better not lose it. I left the knife sticking up like a small, leafless plant. She then talked about school, the junior high I would be going to that fall, and then about Rick and Debra, how sorry they would be that they hadn't come out to pick grapes because they'd have no new clothes for the school year. She

ADDITIONAL QUESTIONS FOR RESPONDING TO READING

1. What triggers Soto's memory? What is the specific association between the Indians in the film and the people Soto remembers?
2. What warning does Soto's mother repeatedly offer? Have you received warnings from your parents that you took more seriously when you matured?
3. What things seem to be valued by the youth Soto describes? What things does he himself seem to have thought were worth working for? Are these typical teenage values?
4. What does Soto mean in paragraph 10 by "boredom was a terror almost as awful as the work itself?" Is he exaggerating?

stopped talking when she peeked at her watch, a bandless one she kept in her pocket. She got up with an "*Ay, Dios,*" and told me that we'd work until three, leaving me cutting figures in the sand with my knife and dreading the return to work.

Finally I rose and walked slowly back to where I had left off, again 10 kneeling under the vine and fixing the pan under bunches of grapes. By that time, 11:30, the sun was over my shoulder and made me squint and think of the pool at the Y.M.C.A. where I was a summer member. I saw myself diving face first into the water and loving it. I saw myself gleaming like something new, at the edge of the pool. I had to daydream and keep my mind busy because boredom was a terror almost as awful as the work itself. My mind went dumb with stupid things, and I had to keep it moving with dreams of baseball and would-be girlfriends. I even sang, however softly, to keep my mind moving, my hands moving.

I worked less hurriedly and with less vision. I no longer saw that 11 copper pot sitting squat on our stove or Mother waiting for it to whistle. The wardrobe that I imagined, crisp and bright in the closet, numbered only one pair of jeans and two shirts because, in half a day, six cents times thirty-seven trays was two dollars and twenty-two cents. It became clear to me. If I worked eight hours, I might make four dollars. I'd take this, even gladly, and walk downtown to look into store windows on the mall and long for the bright madras shirts from Walter Smith or Coffee's, but settling for two imitation ones from Penney's.

That first day I laid down seventy-three trays while Mother had 12 a hundred and twenty behind her. On the back of an old envelope, she wrote out our numbers and hours. We washed at the pump behind the farm house and walked slowly to our car for the drive back to town in the afternoon heat. That evening after dinner I sat in a lawn chair listening to music from a transistor radio while Rick and David King played catch. I joined them in a game of pickle, but there was little joy in trying to avoid their tags because I couldn't get the fields out of my mind: I saw myself dropping on my knees under a vine to tug at a branch that wouldn't come off. In bed, when I closed my eyes, I saw the fields, yellow with kicked up dust, and a crooked trail of trays rotting behind me.

The next day I woke tired and started picking tired. The grapes 13 rained into the pan, slowly filling like a belly, until I had my first tray and started my second. So it went all day, and the next, and all through the following week, so that by the end of thirteen days the foreman counted out, in tens mostly, my pay of fifty-three dollars. Mother earned one hundred and forty-eight dollars. She wrote this on her envelope, with a message I didn't bother to ask her about.

The next day I walked with my friend Scott to the downtown 14

TEACHING STRATEGY

In a set of autobiographical notes, "Comments addressed to Juan Rodriguez, May 1977," Soto writes: "I write because there is pain in my life, our family, and those living in the San Joaquin Valley. . . . I write because those I work and live among can't write. I only have to think of the black factory worker I worked with in L.A., or that toothless farm laborer I hoed beside in the fields outside Fresno . . . they're everything." Ask your students to comment on this statement as it relates to what they have read. Does it provide further insight into the emotional quality of the piece?

mall where we drooled over the clothes behind fancy windows, bought popcorn, and sat at a tier of outdoor fountains to talk about girls. Finally we went into Penney's for more popcorn, which we ate walking around, before we returned home without buying anything. It wasn't until a few days before school that I let my fifty-three dollars slip quietly from my hands, buying a pair of pants, two shirts, and a maroon T-shirt, the kind that was in style. At home I tried them on while Rick looked on enviously; later, the day before school started, I tried them on again wondering not so much if they were worth it as who would see me first in those clothes.

Along with my brother and sister I picked grapes until I was 15 fifteen, before giving up and saying that I'd rather wear old clothes than stoop like a Mexican. Mother thought I was being stuck-up, even stupid, because there would be no clothes for me in the fall. I told her I didn't care, but when Rick and Debra rose at five in the morning, I lay awake in bed feeling that perhaps I had made a mistake but unwilling to change my mind. That fall Mother bought me two pairs of socks, a packet of colored T-shirts, and underwear. The T-shirts would help, I thought, but who would see that I had new underwear and socks? I wore a new T-shirt on the first day of school, then an old shirt on Tuesday, than another T-shirt on Wednesday, and on Thursday an old Nehru shirt that was embarrasingly out of style. On Friday I changed into the corduroy pants my brother had handed down to me and slipped into my last new T-shirt. I worked like a magician, blinding my classmates, who were all clothes conscious and small-time social climbers, by arranging my wardrobe to make it seem larger than it really was. But by spring I had to do something— my blue jeans were almost silver and my shoes had lost their form, puddling like black ice around my feet. That spring of my sixteenth year, Rick and I decided to take a labor bus to chop cotton. In his old Volkswagen, which was more noise than power, we drove on a Saturday morning to West Fresno—or Chinatown as some call it— parked, walked slowly toward a bus, and stood gawking at the winos, toothy blacks, Okies, *Tejanos*[1] with gold teeth, whores, Mexican families, and labor contractors shouting "Cotton" or "Beets," the work of spring.

We boarded the "Cotton" bus without looking at the contractor 16 who stood almost blocking the entrance because he didn't want winos. We boarded scared and then were more scared because two blacks in the rear were drunk and arguing loudly about what was better, a two-barrel or four-barrel Ford carburetor. We sat far from

[1]Texans. [Eds.]

them, looking straight ahead, and only glanced briefly at the others who boarded, almost all of them broken and poorly dressed in loudly mismatched clothes. Finally when the contractor banged his palm against the side of the bus, the young man at the wheel, smiling and talking in Spanish, started the engine, idled it for a moment while he adjusted the mirrors, and started off in slow chugs. Except for the windshield there was no glass in the windows, so as soon as we were on the rural roads outside Fresno, the dust and sand began to be sucked into the bus, whipping about like irate wasps as the gravel ticked about us. We closed our eyes, clotted up our mouths that wanted to open with embarrassed laughter because we couldn't believe we were on that bus with those people and the dust attacking us for no reason.

When we arrived at a field we followed the others to a pickup 17 where we each took a hoe and marched to stand before a row. Rick and I, self-conscious and unsure, looked around at the others who leaned on their hoes or squatted in front of the rows, almost all talking in Spanish, joking, lighting cigarettes—all waiting for the foreman's whistle to begin work. Mother had explained how to chop cotton by showing us with a broom in the backyard.

"Like this," she said, her broom swishing down weeds. "Leave 18 one plant and cut four—and cut them! Don't leave them standing or the foreman will get mad."

The foreman whistled and we started up the row stealing glances 19 at other workers to see if we were doing it right. But after awhile we worked like we knew what we were doing, neither of us hurrying or falling behind. But slowly the clot of men, women, and kids began to spread and loosen. Even Rick pulled away. I didn't hurry, though. I cut smoothly and cleanly as I walked at a slow pace, in a sort of funeral march. My eyes measured each space of cotton plants before I cut. If I missed the plants, I swished again. I worked intently, seldom looking up, so when I did I was amazed to see the sun, like a broken orange coin, in the east. It looked blurry, unbelievable, like something not of this world. I looked around in amazement, scanning the eastern horizon that was a taut line jutted with an occasional mountain. The horizon was beautiful, like a snapshot of the moon, in the early light of morning, in the quiet of no cars and few people.

The foreman trudged in boots in my direction, stepping awk- 20 wardly over the plants, to inspect the work. No one around me looked up. We all worked steadily while we waited for him to leave. When he did leave, with a feeble complaint addressed to no one in particular, we looked up smiling under straw hats and bandanas.

By 11:00, our lunch time, my ankles were hurting from walking 21 on clods the size of hardballs. My arms ached and my face was dusted by a wind that was perpetual, always busy whipping about. But the work was not bad, I thought. It was better, so much better, than picking grapes, especially with the hourly wage of a dollar twenty-five instead of piece work. Rick and I walked sorely toward the bus where we washed and drank water. Instead of eating in the bus or in the shade of the bus, we kept to ourselves by walking down to the irrigation canal that ran the length of the field, to open our lunch of sandwiches and crackers. We laughed at the crackers, which seemed like a cruel joke from our Mother, because we were working under the sun and the last thing we wanted was a salty dessert. We ate them anyway and drank more water before we returned to the field, both of us limping in exaggeration. Working side by side, we talked and laughed at our predicament because our Mother had warned us year after year that if we didn't get on track in school we'd have to work in the fields and then we would see. We mimicked Mother's whining voice and smirked at her smoky view of the future in which we'd be trapped by marriage and screaming kids. We'd eat beans and then we'd see.

Rick pulled slowly away to the rhythm of his hoe falling faster 22 and smoother. It was better that way, to work alone. I could hum made-up songs or songs from the radio and think to myself about school and friends. At the time I was doing badly in my classes, mainly because of a difficult stepfather, but also because I didn't care anymore. All through junior high and into my first year of high school there were those who said I would never do anything, be anyone. They said I'd work like a donkey and marry the first Mexican girl that came along. I was reminded so often, verbally and in the way I was treated at home, that I began to believe that chopping cotton might be a lifetime job for me. If not chopping cotton, then I might get lucky and find myself in a car wash or restaurant or junkyard. But it was clear; I'd work, and work hard.

I cleared my mind by humming and looking about. The sun was 23 directly above with a few soft blades of clouds against a sky that seemed bluer and more beautiful than our sky in the city. Occasionally the breeze flurried and picked up dust so that I had to cover my eyes and screw up my face. The workers were hunched, brown as the clods under our feet, and spread across the field that ran without end—fields that were owned by corporations, not families.

I hoed trying to keep my mind busy with scenes from school and 24 pretend girlfriends until finally my brain turned off and my thinking went fuzzy with boredom. I looked about, no longer mesmerized by the beauty of the landscape, no longer wondering if the winos in the fields could hold out for eight hours, no longer dreaming of the clothes I'd buy with my pay. My eyes followed my chopping as the plants, thin as their shadows, fell with each strike. I worked slowly with ankles and arms hurting, neck stiff, and eyes stinging from the dust and the sun that glanced off the field like a mirror.

By quitting time, 3:00, there was such an excruciating pain in my 25 ankles that I walked as if I were wearing snowshoes. Rick laughed at me and I laughed too, embarrassed that most of the men were walking normally and I was among the first timers who had to get used to this work. "And what about you, wino," I came back at Rick. His eyes were meshed red and his long hippie hair was flecked with dust and gnats and bits of leaves. We placed our hoes in the back of a pickup and stood in line for our pay, which was twelve fifty. I was amazed at the pay, which was the most I had ever earned in one day, and thought that I'd come back the next day, Sunday. This was too good.

Instead of joining the others in the labor bus, we jumped in the 26 back of a pickup when the driver said we'd get to town sooner and were welcome to join him. We scrambled into the truck bed to be joined by a heavy-set and laughing *Tejano* whose head was shaped like an egg, particularly so because the bandana he wore ended in a point on the top of his head. He laughed almost demonically as the pickup roared up the dirt path, a gray cape of dust rising behind us. On the highway, with the wind in our faces, we squinted at the fields as if we were looking for someone. The *Tejano* had quit laughing but was smiling broadly, occasionally chortling tunes he never finished. I was scared of him, though Rick, two years older and five inches taller, wasn't. If the *Tejano* looked at him, Rick stared back for a second or two before he looked away to the fields.

I felt like a soldier coming home from war when we rattled into 27 Chinatown. People leaning against car hoods stared, their necks following us, owl-like; prostitutes chewed gum more ferociously and showed us their teeth; Chinese grocers stopped brooming their storefronts to raise their cadaverous faces at us. We stopped in front of the Chi Chi Club where Mexican music blared from the juke box and cue balls cracked like dull ice. The *Tejano*, who was dirty as we were, stepped awkwardly over the side rail, dusted himself off with his bandana, and sauntered into the club.

Rick and I jumped from the back, thanked the driver who said 28 *de nada* and popped his clutch, so that the pickup jerked and coughed blue smoke. We returned smiling to our car, happy with the money we had made and pleased that we had, in a small way, proved ourselves to be tough; that we worked as well as other men and earned the same pay.

We returned the next day and the next week until the season was 29 over and there was nothing to do. I told myself that I wouldn't pick

WRITING SUGGESTION

Write an essay about the most difficult job you have ever had. In what ways were its challenges similar to or different from those of Soto's job? What motivated you to continue to work despite these difficulties?

grapes that summer, saying all through June and July that it was for Mexicans, not me. When August came around and I still had not found a summer job, I ate my words, sharpened my knife, and joined Mother, Rick, and Debra for one last time.

RESPONDING TO READING

1. Work brings Soto closer to an understanding of his family. How? Do you think his reaction to work is unusual, or do you believe others might share his response? Have you had a similar reaction?   **2.** In the essay's opening lines Soto says that he recognizes his relatives in the characters he sees in the film *Gandhi*. What does he mean? Do you recognize any of your own relatives in the essay "One Last Time?"   **3.** Why would Soto at age fifteen "rather wear old clothes than stoop like a Mexican" (paragraph 15)? Does the adult Soto understand the reasons for this sentiment? Does he share it? What does this comment reveal about the society in which Soto lived?

Once More to the Lake

E. B. WHITE

One of the America's best-loved essayists, E. B. White (1899–1986) enjoyed an almost idyllic childhood in Mt. Vernon, New York, graduated from college in 1921, and embarked on a career writing for newspapers. Soon he was writing essays for *The New Yorker* and *Harper's Magazine* with his characteristic wit and insight into people and nature. White wrote the children's classic *Charlotte's Web* (1952); in 1959 he expanded Will Strunk's grammar book, which White had used as his student, into the now classic *The Elements of Style*; and he published essays in the collections *One Man's Meat* (1944) and *Essays of E. B. White* (1977). In his nostalgic "Once More to the Lake," White revisits the lake in Maine where he vacationed as a boy with his family and explores the themes of time and change.

One summer, along about 1904, my father rented a camp on a   1
lake in Maine and took us all there for the month of August. We all got ringworm from some kittens and had to rub Pond's Extract on our arms and legs night and morning, and my father rolled over in a canoe with all his clothes on; but outside of that the vacation was a success and from then on none of us ever thought there was any place in the world like that lake in Maine. We returned summer after summer—always on August 1st for one month. I have since become a salt-water man, but sometimes in summer there are days when the

restlessness of the tides and the fearful cold of the sea water and the incessant wind which blows across the afternoon and into the evening make me wish for the placidity of a lake in the woods. A few weeks ago this feeling got so strong I bought myself a couple of bass hooks and a spinner and returned to the lake where we used to go, for a week's fishing and to revisit old haunts.

I took along my son, who had never had any fresh water up his nose and who had seen lily pads only from train windows. On the journey over to the lake I began to wonder what it would be like. I wondered how time would have marred this unique, this holy spot—the coves and streams, the hills that the sun set behind, the camps and the paths behind the camps. I was sure the tarred road would have found it out and I wondered in what other ways it would be desolated. It is strange how much you can remember about places like that once you allow your mind to return into the grooves which lead back. You remember one thing, and that suddenly reminds you of another thing. I guess I remembered clearest of all the early mornings, when the lake was cool and motionless, remembered how the bedroom smelled of the lumber it was made of and of the wet woods whose scent entered through the screen. The partitions in the camp were thin and did not extend clear to the top of the rooms, and as I was always the first up I would dress softly so as not to wake the others, and sneak out into the sweet outdoors and start out in the canoe, keeping close along the shore in the long shadows of the pines. I remembered being very careful never to rub my paddle against the gunwale for fear of disturbing the stillness of the cathedral.

The lake had never been what you would call a wild lake. There were cottages sprinkled around the shores, and it was in farming country although the shores of the lake were quite heavily wooded. Some of the cottages were owned by nearby farmers, and you would live at the shore and eat your meals at the farmhouse. That's what our family did. But although it wasn't wild, it was a fairly large and undisturbed lake and there were places in it which, to a child at least, seemed infinitely remote and primeval.

I was right about the tar: it led to within half a mile of the shore. But when I got back there, with my boy, and we settled into a camp near a farmhouse and into the kind of summertime I had known, I could tell that it was going to be pretty much the same as it had been before—I knew it, lying in bed the first morning, smelling the bedroom, and hearing the boy sneak quietly out and go off along the shore in a boat. I began to sustain the illusion that he was I, and therefore, by simple transposition, that I was my father. This sensation persisted, kept cropping up all the time we were there. It was not an entirely new feeling, but in this setting it grew much stronger.

2

3

4

ADDITIONAL QUESTIONS FOR RESPONDING TO READING

1. In what ways is this an essay about the links between generations? In what ways is it also about the gaps between generations?
2. What aspects of the lake seem disappointing when White revisits them?
3. White's essay takes us backward and forward in time. What stylistic techniques does he use to signal shifts in time to readers?

TEACHING STRATEGY

Part of the vividness of White's essay derives from the clarity with which he evokes particular details. Have your students make note of especially strong images, and ask them to talk about what makes these images so evocative.

I seemed to be living a dual existence. I would be in the middle of some simple act, I would be picking up a bait box or laying down a table fork, or I would be saying something, and suddenly it would be not I but my father who was saying the words or making the gesture. It gave me a creepy sensation.

We went fishing the first morning. I felt the same damp moss covering the worms in the bait can, and saw the dragonfly alight on the tip of my rod as it hovered a few inches from the surface of the water. It was the arrival of this fly that convinced me beyond any doubt that everything was as it always had been, that the years were a mirage and there had been no years. The small waves were the same, chucking the rowboat under the chin as we fished at anchor, and the boat was the same boat, the same color green and the ribs broken in the same places, and under the floor-boards the same fresh-water leavings and débris—the dead helgramite,[1] the wisps of moss, the rusty discarded fishhook, the dried blood from yesterday's catch. We stared silently at the tips of our rods, at the dragonflies that came and went. I lowered the tip of mine into the water, tentatively, pensively dislodging the fly, which darted two feet away, poised, darted two feet back, and came to rest again a little farther up the rod. There had been no years between the ducking of this dragonfly and the other one—the one that was part of memory. I looked at the boy, who was silently watching his fly, and it was my hands that held his rod, my eyes watching. I felt dizzy and didn't know which rod I was at the end of.

We caught two bass, hauling them in briskly as though they were mackerel, pulling them over the side of the boat in a businesslike manner without any landing net, and stunning them with a blow on the back of the head. When we got back for a swim before lunch, the lake was exactly where we had left it, the same number of inches from the dock, and there was only the merest suggestion of a breeze. This seemed an utterly enchanted sea, this lake you could leave to its own devices for a few hours and come back to, and find that it had not stirred, this constant and trustworthy body of water. In the shallows, the dark, water-soaked sticks and twigs, smooth and old, were undulating in clusters on the bottom against the clean ribbed sand, and the track of the mussel was plain. A school of minnows swam by, each minnow with its small individual shadow, doubling the attendance, so clear and sharp in the sunlight. Some of the other campers were in swimming, along the shore, one of them with a cake of soap, and the water felt thin and clear and unsubstantial. Over the

---

[1]The nymph of the May-fly, used as bait. [Eds.]

years there had been this person with the cake of soap, this cultist, and here he was. There had been no years.

Up to the farmhouse to dinner through the teeming, dusty field, the road under our sneakers was only a two-track road. The middle track was missing, the one with the marks of the hooves and the splotches of dried, flaky manure. There had always been three tracks to choose from in choosing which track to walk in; now the choice was narrowed down to two. For a moment I missed terribly the middle alternative. But the way led past the tennis court, and something about the way it lay there in the sun reassured me; the tape had loosened along the backline, the alleys were green with plantains and other weeds, and the net (installed in June and removed in September) sagged in the dry noon, and the whole place steamed with midday heat and hunger and emptiness. There was a choice of pie for dessert, and one was blueberry and one was apple, and the waitresses were the same country girls, there having been no passage of time, only the illusion of it as in a dropped curtain—the waitresses were still fifteen; their hair had been washed, that was the only difference—they had been to the movies and seen the pretty girls with the clean hair.

Summertime, oh summertime, pattern of life indelible, the fadeproof lake, the woods unshatterable, the pasture with the sweetfern and the juniper forever and ever, summer without end; this was the background, and the life along the shore was the design, the cottagers with their innocent and tranquil design, their tiny docks with the flagpole and the American flag floating against the white clouds in the blue sky, the little paths over the roots of the trees leading from camp to camp and the paths leading back to the outhouses and the can of lime for sprinkling, and at the souvenir counters at the store the miniature birch-bark canoes and the post cards that showed things looking a little better than they looked. This was the American family at play, escaping the city heat, wondering whether the newcomers in the camp at the head of the cove were "common" or "nice," wondering whether it was true that the people who drove up for Sunday dinner at the farmhouse were turned away because there wasn't enough chicken.

It seemed to me, as I kept remembering all this, that those times and those summers had been infinitely precious and worth saving. There had been jollity and peace and goodness. The arriving (at the beginning of August) had been so big a business in itself, at the railway station the farm wagon drawn up, the first smell of the pine-laden air, the first glimpse of the smiling farmer, and the great importance of the trunks and your father's enormous authority in such matters, and the feel of the wagon under you for the long ten-mile haul, and

7

8

9

COLLABORATIVE ACTIVITY

Ask students to work in groups to list the specific images White uses to describe the lake. Assign one group to list sounds associated with the spot, two or three groups to identify visual images, and one group to compile a list of tactile or other images.

at the top of the last long hill catching the first view of the lake after eleven months of not seeing this cherished body of water. The shouts and cries of the other campers when they saw you, and the trunks to be unpacked, to give up their rich burden. (Arriving was less exciting nowadays, when you sneaked up in your car and parked it under a tree near the camp and took out the bags and in five minutes it was all over, no fuss, no loud wonderful fuss about trunks.)

Peace and goodness and jollity. The only thing that was wrong   10 now, really, was the sound of the place, an unfamiliar nervous sound of the outboard motors. This was the note that jarred, the one thing that would sometimes break the illusion and set the years moving. In those other summertimes all motors were inboard; and when they were at a little distance, the noise they made was a sedative, an ingredient of summer sleep. They were one-cylinder and two-cylinder engines, and some were make-and-break and some were jump-spark,[2] but they all made a sleepy sound across the lake. The one-lungers throbbed and fluttered, and the twin-cylinder ones purred and purred, and that was a quiet sound too. But now the campers all had outboards. In the daytime, in the hot mornings, these motors made a petulant, irritable sound; at night, in the still evening when the afterglow lit the water, they whined about one's ears like mosquitoes. My boy loved our rented outboard, and his great desire was to achieve singlehanded mastery over it, and authority, and he soon learned the trick of choking it a little (but not too much), and the adjustment of the needle valve. Watching him I would remember the things you could do with the old one-cylinder engine with the heavy flywheel, how you could have it eating out of your hand if you got really close to it spiritually. Motor boats in those days didn't have clutches, and you would make a landing by shutting off the motor at the proper time and coasting in with a dead rudder. But there was a way of reversing them, if you learned the trick, by cutting the switch and putting it on again exactly on the final dying revolution of the flywheel, so that it would kick back against compression and begin reversing. Approaching a dock in a strong following breeze, it was difficult to slow up sufficiently by the ordinary coasting method, and if a boy felt he had complete mastery over his motor, he was tempted to keep it running beyond its time and then reverse it a few feet from the dock. It took a cool nerve, because if you threw the switch a twentieth of a second too soon you would catch the flywheel when it still had speed enough to go up past center, and the boat would leap ahead, charging bull-fashion at the dock.

---

[2]Methods of ignition timing. [Eds.]

We had a good week at the camp. The bass were biting well and   11
the sun shone endlessly, day after day. We would be tired at night
and lie down in the accumulated heat of the little bedrooms after the
long hot day and the breeze would stir almost imperceptibly outside
and the smell of the swamp drift in through the rusty screens. Sleep
would come easily and in the morning the red squirrel would be on
the roof, tapping out his gay routine. I kept remembering everything,
lying in bed in the mornings—the small steamboat that had a long
rounded stern like the lip of a Ubangi, and how quietly she ran on
the moonlight sails, when the older boys played their mandolins and
the girls sang and we ate doughnuts dipped in sugar, and how sweet
the music was on the water in the shining night, and what it had felt
like to think about girls then. After breakfast we would go up to the
store and the things were in the same place—the minnows in a bottle,
the plugs and spinners disarranged and pawed over by the youngsters
from the boys' camp, the fig newtons and the Beeman's gum. Outside,
the road was tarred and cars stood in front of the store. Inside, all
was just as it had always been, except there was more Coca-Cola and
not so much Moxie and root beer and birch beer and sarsaparilla. We
would walk out with a bottle of pop apiece and sometimes the pop
would backfire up our noses and hurt. We explored the streams,
quietly, where the turtles slid off the sunny logs and dug their way
into the soft bottom; and we lay on the town wharf and fed worms
to the tame bass. Everywhere we went I had trouble making out which
was I, the one walking at my side, the one walking in my pants.

One afternoon while we were there at that lake a thunderstorm   12
came up. It was like the revival of an old melodrama that I had seen
long ago with childish awe. The second-act climax of the drama of
the electrical disturbance over a lake in America had not changed in
any important respect. This was the big scene, still the big scene. The
whole thing was so familiar, the first feeling of oppression and heat
and a general air around camp of not wanting to go very far away.
In midafternoon (it was all the same) a curious darkening of the sky,
and a lull in everything that had made life tick; and then the way the
boats suddenly swung the other way at their moorings with the
coming of a breeze out of the new quarter, and the premonitory
rumble. Then the kettle drum, then the snare, then the bass drum
and cymbals, then crackling light against the dark, and the gods
grinning and licking their chops in the hills. Afterward the calm, the
rain steadily rustling in the calm lake, the return of light and hope
and spirits, and the campers running out in joy and relief to go
swimming in the rain, their bright cries perpetuating the deathless
joke about how they were getting simply drenched, and the children
screaming with delight at the new sensation of bathing in the rain,

WRITING SUGGESTION

Write about an experience you had that seemed to erase (or to reinforce) the differences between generations.

**ANSWERS TO RESPONDING
TO READING**

1. White claims that, in all significant respects, the lake has not changed. The essay focuses on his return to the lake as an adult and on the way the passage of time seems to have been a mirage.
2. In focusing primarily on a return visit to a particular place, White also manages to convey the mysterious nature of time and the relationship between fathers and sons.
3. Although one might need to be a parent to share White's particular reexperiencing of himself in his son, many of us recall the youthful sense that things will never change. As we mature, we realize that summer is not "without end" and that there have indeed been (and will continue to be) profound changes in our lives.

FOR OPENERS

Students are likely to be repulsed by the brutality and cruelty described and may even object to having had to read it. You might want to open with a discussion of whether any of the unpleasant details could be omitted. Ask students what effect such omissions would have on the essay. Would they, for example, make the essay less forceful?

and the joke about getting drenched linking the generations in a strong indestructible chain. And the comedian who waded in carrying an umbrella.

When the others went swimming my son said he was going in 13 too. He pulled his dripping trunks from the line where they had hung all through the shower, and wrung them out. Languidly, and with no thought of going in, I watched him, his hard little body, skinny and bare, saw him wince slightly as he pulled up around his vitals the small, soggy, icy garment. As he buckled the swollen belt suddenly my groin felt the chill of death.

RESPONDING TO READING

1. How is White's "holy spot" different when he visits it with his son? Is the essay primarily about his visits as a child or about his return? Is there a place that has the same kind of special significance for you or your family?   **2.** Does this essay focus primarily on a time, a place, or a relationship? Explain.   **3.** Why does White feel "the chill of death" (paragraph 13) as he watches his son? Do you think White is just being morbid, or is he making a valid point about his own mortality? Do you think you have to be a parent to share White's sentiments? Explain.

No Name Woman

MAXINE HONG KINGSTON

Maxine Hong Kingston (1940–   ), a native of California, is a nonfiction writer who has also taught English in high school and at the University of Hawaii. She also contributes to *Ms.*, *The New Yorker*, *American Heritage*, and other publications. Her most recent work is the novel *Tripmaster Monkey: His Fake Book* (1989). In her autobiography, *The Woman Warrior: Memoirs of a Girlhood Among Ghosts* (1976), and in *China Men* (1980) Kingston explores her Chinese ancestry. She said of *The Woman Warrior* in a 1983 interview, "One of the themes in *Warrior* was: what is it that's a story and what is it that's life? . . . Sometimes the boundaries are very clear, and sometimes they interlace and we live out stories." In the following selection from *The Woman Warrior*, Kingston tells the story of her aunt in China, who disgraced her family and suffered neglect and despair.

"You must not tell anyone," my mother said, "what I am about 1 to tell you. In China your father had a sister who killed herself. She jumped into the family well. We say that your father has all brothers because it is as if she had never been born.

"In 1924 just a few days after our village celebrated seventeen hurry-up weddings—to make sure that every young man who went 'out on the road' would responsibly come home—your father and his brothers and your grandfather and his brothers and your aunt's new husband sailed for America, the Gold Mountain. It was your grandfather's last trip. Those lucky enough to get contracts waved good-bye from the decks. They fed and guarded the stowaways and helped them off in Cuba, New York, Bali, Hawaii. 'We'll meet in California next year,' they said. All of them sent money home.

"I remember looking at your aunt one day when she and I were dressing; I had not noticed before that she had such a protruding melon of a stomach. But I did not think, 'She's pregnant,' until she began to look like other pregnant women, her shirt pulling and the white tops of her black pants showing. She could not have been pregnant, you see, because her husband had been gone for years. No one said anything. We did not discuss it. In early summer she was ready to have the child, long after the time when it could have been possible.

"The village had also been counting. On the night the baby was to be born the villagers raided our house. Some were crying. Like a great saw, teeth strung with lights, files of people walked zigzag across our land, tearing the rice. Their lanterns doubled in the disturbed black water, which drained away through the broken bunds. As the villagers closed in, we could see that some of them, probably men and women we knew well, wore white masks. The people with long hair hung it over their faces. Women with short hair made it stand up on end. Some had tied white bands around their foreheads, arms, and legs.

"At first they threw mud and rocks at the house. Then they threw eggs and began slaughtering our stock. We could hear the animals scream their deaths—the roosters, the pigs, a last great roar from the ox. Familiar wild heads flared in our night windows; the villagers encircled us. Some of the faces stopped to peer at us, their eyes rushing like searchlights. The hands flattened against the panes, framed heads, and left red prints.

"The villagers broke in the front and the back doors at the same time, even though we had not locked the doors against them. Their knives dripped with the blood of our animals. They smeared blood on the doors and walls. One woman swung a chicken, whose throat she had slit, splattering blood in red arcs about her. We stood together in the middle of our house, in the family hall with the pictures and tables of the ancestors around us, and looked straight ahead.

"At the time the house had only two wings. When the men came back, we would build two more to enclose our courtyard and a third one to begin a second courtyard. The villagers pushed through both

2

3

4

5

6

7

ADDITIONAL QUESTIONS FOR RESPONDING TO READING

1. Kingston's mother used the aunt's story as a warning to her daughters. Does the lesson appear to have had the desired effect? Does Kingston imply that it was a valuable lesson? Is Kingston's interpretation of the story different from her mother's? Explain.
2. In what ways is this essay about not speaking? What does this silence suggest about the power that is invested in words?
3. Does Kingston appear to judge harshly any of the parties involved in the aunt's story?

wings, even your grandparents' rooms, to find your aunt's, which was also mine until the men returned. From this room a new wing for one of the younger families would grow. They ripped up her clothes and shoes and broke her combs, grinding them underfoot. They tore her work from the loom. They scattered the cooking fire and rolled the new weaving in it. We could hear them in the kitchen breaking our bowls and banging the pots. They overturned the great waist-high earthenware jugs; duck eggs, pickled fruits, vegetables burst out and mixed in acrid torrents. The old woman from the next field swept a broom through the air and loosed the spirits-of-the-broom over our heads. 'Pig.' 'Ghost.' 'Pig,' they sobbed and scolded while they ruined our house.

"When they left, they took sugar and oranges to bless themselves. 8 They cut pieces from the dead animals. Some of them took bowls that were not broken and clothes that were not torn. Afterward we swept up the rice and sewed it back up into sacks. But the smells from the spilled preserves lasted. Your aunt gave birth in the pigsty that night. The next morning when I went for the water, I found her and the baby plugging up the family well.

"Don't let your father know that I told you. He denies her. Now 9 that you have started to menstruate, what happened to her could happen to you. Don't humiliate us. You wouldn't like to be forgotten as if you had never been born. The villagers are watchful."

Whenever she had to warn us about life, my mother told stories 10 that ran like this one, a story to grow up on. She tested our strength to establish realities. Those in the emigrant generations who could not reassert brute survival died young and far from home. Those of us in the first American generations have had to figure out how the invisible world the emigrants built around our childhoods fit in solid America.

The emigrants confused the gods by diverting their curses, mis- 11 leading them with crooked streets and false names. They must try to confuse their offspring as well, who, I suppose, threaten them in similar ways—always trying to get things straight, always trying to name the unspeakable. The Chinese I know hide their names; sojourners take new names when their lives change and guard their real names with silence.

Chinese-Americans, when you try to understand what things in 12 you are Chinese, how do you separate what is peculiar to childhood, to poverty, insanities, one family, your mother who marked your growing with stories, from what is Chinese? What is Chinese tradition and what is the movies?

If I want to learn what clothes my aunt wore, whether flashy or 13 ordinary, I would have to begin, "Remember Father's drowned-in-the-well sister?" I cannot ask that. My mother has told me once and for all the useful parts. She will add nothing unless powered by Necessity, a riverbank that guides her life. She plants vegetable gardens rather than lawns; she carries the odd-shaped tomatoes home from the fields and eats food left for the gods.

Whenever we did frivolous things, we used up energy; we flew   14
high kites. We children came up off the ground over the melting cones our parents brought home from work and the American movie on New Year's Day—*Oh, You Beautiful Doll* with Betty Grable one year, and *She Wore a Yellow Ribbon* with John Wayne another year. After the one carnival ride each, we paid in guilt; our tired father counted his change on the dark walk home.

Adultery is extravagance. Could people who hatch their own   15
chicks and eat the embryos and the heads for delicacies and boil the feet in vinegar for party food, leaving only the gravel, eating even the gizzard lining—could such people engender a prodigal aunt? To be a woman, to have a daughter in starvation time was a waste enough. My aunt could not have been the lone romantic who gave up everything for sex. Women in the old China did not choose. Some man had commanded her to lie with him and be his secret evil. I wonder whether he masked himself when he joined the raid on her family.

Perhaps she encountered him in the fields or on the mountain   16
where the daughters-in-law collected fuel. Or perhaps he first noticed her in the marketplace. He was not a stranger because the village housed no strangers. She had to have dealings with him other than sex. Perhaps he worked an adjoining field, or he sold her the cloth for the dress she sewed and wore. His demand must have surprised, then terrified her. She obeyed him; she always did as she was told.

When the family found a young man in the next village to be her   17
husband, she stood tractably beside the best rooster, his proxy, and promised before they met that she would be his forever. She was lucky that he was her age and she would be the first wife, an advantage secure now. The night she first saw him, he had sex with her. Then he left for America. She had almost forgotten what he looked like. When she tried to envision him, she only saw the black and white face in the group photograph the men had had taken before leaving.

The other man was not, after all, much different from her hus-   18
band. They both gave orders: she followed. "If you tell your family, I'll beat you. I'll kill you. Be here again next week." No one talked sex, ever. And she might have separated the rapes from the rest of living if only she did not have to buy her oil from him or gather wood in the same forest. I want her fear to have lasted just as long as rape

TEACHING STRATEGY

Kingston's story weaves the "real" and the supernatural together just as it intertwines the Chinese past and Kingston's memories of her American girlhood. How does Kingston accomplish this interweaving of "fact" and fantasy? What transitional devices does she use to link them? What tone and mood are established through this effect?

COLLABORATIVE ACTIVITY

Assign students, working in groups, to brainstorm about who was most guilty of causing pain to Kingston's aunt and who, if anyone, could have saved her reputation (or her life).

lasted so that the fear could have been contained. No drawn-out fear. But women at sex hazarded birth and hence lifetimes. The fear did not stop but permeated everywhere. She told the man, "I think I'm pregnant." He organized the raid against her.

On nights when my mother and father talked about their life back 19 home, sometimes they mentioned an "outcast table" whose business they still seemed to be settling, their voices tight. In a commensal[1] tradition, where food is precious, the powerful older people made wrongdoers eat alone. Instead of letting them start separate new lives like the Japanese, who could become samurais and geishas, the Chinese family, faces averted but eyes glowering sideways, hung on to the offenders and fed them leftovers. My aunt must have lived in the same house as my parents and eaten at an outcast table. My mother spoke about the raid as if she had seen it, when she and my aunt, a daughter-in-law to a different household, should not have been living together at all. Daughters-in-law lived with their husbands' parents, not their own; a synonym for marriage in Chinese is "taking a daughter-in-law." Her husband's parents could have sold her, mortgaged her, stoned her. But they had sent her back to her own mother and father, a mysterious act hinting at disgraces not told me. Perhaps they had thrown her out to deflect the avengers.

She was the only daughter; her four brothers went with her father, 20 husband, and uncles "out on the road" and for some years became western men. When the goods were divided among the family, three of the brothers took land, and the youngest, my father, chose an education. After my grandparents gave their daughter away to her husband's family, they had dispensed all the adventure and all the property. They expected her alone to keep the traditional ways, which her brothers, now among the barbarians, could fumble without detection. The heavy, deep-rooted women were to maintain the past against the flood, safe for returning. But the rare urge west had fixed upon our family, and so my aunt crossed boundaries not delineated in space.

The work of preservation demands that the feelings playing about 21 in one's guts not be turned into action. Just watch their passing like cherry blossoms. But perhaps my aunt, my forerunner, caught in a slow life, let dreams grow and fade and after some months or years went toward what persisted. Fear at the enormities of the forbidden kept her desires delicate, wire and bone. She looked at a man because she liked the way the hair was tucked behind his ears, or she liked the question-mark line of a long turso curving at the shoulder and straight at the hip. For warm eyes or a soft voice or a slow walk—

---

[1]Eating at the same table; sharing meals as table companions. [Eds.]

that's all—a few hairs, a line, a brightness, a sound, a pace, she gave up family. She offered us up for a charm that vanished with tiredness, a pigtail that didn't toss when the wind died. Why, the wrong lighting could erase the dearest thing about him.

It could very well have been, however, that my aunt did not take 22 subtle enjoyment of her friend, but, a wild woman, kept rollicking company. Imagining her free with sex doesn't fit, though. I don't know any women like that, or men either. Unless I see her life branching into mine, she gives me no ancestral help.

To sustain her being in love, she often worked at herself in the 23 mirror, guessing at the colors and shapes that would interest him, changing them frequently in order to hit on the right combination. She wanted him to look back.

On a farm near the sea, a woman who tended her appearance 24 reaped a reputation for eccentricity. All the married women blunt-cut their hair in flaps about their ears or pulled it back in tight buns. No nonsense. Neither style blew easily into heart-catching tangles. And at their weddings they displayed themselves in their long hair for the last time. "It brushed the backs of my knees," my mother tells me. "It was braided, and even so, it brushed the backs of my knees."

At the mirror my aunt combed individuality into her bob. A bun 25 could have been contrived to escape into black streamers blowing in the wind or in quiet wisps about her face, but only the older women in our picture album wear buns. She brushed her hair back from her forehead, tucking the flaps behind her ears. She looped a piece of thread, knotted into a circle between her index fingers and thumbs, and ran the double strand across her forehead. When she closed her fingers as if she were making a pair of shadow geese bite, the string twisted together catching the little hairs. Then she pulled the thread away from her skin, ripping the hairs out neatly, her eyes watering from the needles of pain. Opening her fingers, she cleaned the thread, then rolled it along her hairline and the tops of her eyebrows. My mother did the same to me and my sisters and herself. I used to believe that the expression "caught by the short hairs" meant a captive held with a depilatory string. It especially hurt at the temples, but my mother said we were lucky we didn't have to have our feet bound when we were seven. Sisters used to sit on their beds and cry together, she said, as their mothers or their slave removed the bandages for a few minutes each night and let the blood gush back into their veins. I hope that the man my aunt loved appreciated a smooth brow, that he wasn't just a tits-and-ass man.

Once my aunt found a freckle on her chin, at a spot that the 26 almanac said predestined her for unhappiness. She dug it out with a hot needle and washed the wound with peroxide.

More attention to her looks than these pullings of hairs and pick- 27
ings at spots would have caused gossip among the villagers. They
owned work clothes and good clothes, and they wore good clothes
for feasting the new seasons. But since a woman combing her hair
hexes beginnings, my aunt rarely found an occasion to look her best.
Women looked like great sea snails—the corded wood, babies, and
laundry they carried were the whorls on their backs. The Chinese did
not admire a bent back; goddesses and warriors stood straight. Still
there must have been a marvelous freeing of beauty when a worker
laid down her burden and stretched and arched.

Such commonplace loveliness, however, was not enough for my 28
aunt. She dreamed of a lover for the fifteen days of New Year's, the
time for families to exchange visits, money, and food. She plied her
secret comb. And sure enough she cursed the year, the family, the
village, and herself.

Even as her hair lured her imminent lover, many other men 29
looked at her. Uncles, cousins, nephews, brothers would have looked,
too, had they been home between journeys. Perhaps they had already
been restraining their curiosity, and they left, fearful that their
glances, like a field of nesting birds, might be startled and caught.
Poverty hurt, and that was their first reason for leaving. But another,
final reason for leaving the crowded house was the never-said.

She may have been unusually beloved, the precious only 30
daughter, spoiled and mirror gazing because of the affection the
family lavished on her. When her husband left, they welcomed the
chance to take her back from the in-laws; she could live like the little
daughter for just a while longer. There are stories that my grandfather
was different from other people, "crazy ever since the little Jap bay-
oneted him in the head." He used to put his naked penis on the
dinner table, laughing. And one day he brought home a baby girl,
wrapped up inside his brown western-style greatcoat. He had traded
one of his sons, probably my father, the youngest, for her. My grandmother made him trade back. When he finally got a daughter of his
own, he doted on her. They must have all loved her, except perhaps
my father, the only brother who never went back to China, having
once been traded for a girl.

Brothers and sisters, newly men and women, had to efface their 31
sexual color and present plain miens.[2] Disturbing hair and eyes, a
smile like no other, threatened the ideal of five generations living
under one roof. To focus blurs, people shouted face to face and yelled
from room to room. The immigrants I know have loud voices, un-
modulated to American tones even after years away from the village

---

[2]Appearances. [Eds.]

where they called their friendships out across the fields. I have not been able to stop my mother's screams in public libraries or over telephones. Walking erect (knees straight, toes pointed forward, not pigeon-toed, which is Chinese-feminine) and speaking in an inaudible voice, I have tried to turn myself American-feminine. Chinese communication was loud, public. Only sick people had to whisper. But at the dinner table, where the family members came nearest one another, no one could talk, not the outcasts nor any eaters. Every word that falls from the mouth is a coin lost. Silently they gave and accepted food with both hands. A preoccupied child who took his bowl with one hand got a sideways glare. A complete moment of total attention is due everyone alike. Children and lovers have no singularity here, but my aunt used a secret voice, a separate attentiveness.

She kept the man's name to herself throughout her labor and 32 dying; she did not accuse him that he be punished with her. To save her inseminator's name she gave silent birth.

He may have been somebody in her own household, but inter- 33 course with a man outside the family would have been no less abhorrent. All the village were kinsmen, and the titles shouted in loud country voices never let kinship be forgotten. Any man within visiting distance would have been neutralized as a lover—"brother," "younger brother," "older brother"—one hundred and fifteen relationship titles. Parents researched birth charts probably not so much to assure good fortune as to circumvent incest in a population that has but one hundred surnames. Everybody has eight million relatives. How useless then sexual mannerisms, how dangerous.

As if it came from an atavism[3] deeper than fear, I used to add 34 "brother" silently to boys' names. It hexed the boys, who would or would not ask me to dance, and made them less scary and as familiar and deserving of benevolence as girls.

But, of course, I hexed myself also—no dates. I should have stood 35 up, both arms waving, and shouted out across libraries, "Hey, you! Love me back." I had no idea, though, how to make attraction selective, how to control its direction and magnitude. If I made myself American-pretty so that the five or six Chinese boys in the class fell in love with me, everyone else—the Caucasian, Negro, and Japanese boys—would too. Sisterliness, dignified and honorable, made much more sense.

Attraction eludes control so stubbornly that whole societies 36 designed to organize relationships among people cannot keep order, not even when they bind people to one another from childhood and

---

[3]The reappearance of a characteristic after a long absence. [Eds.]

raise them together. Among the very poor and the wealthy, brothers married their adopted sisters, like doves. Our family allowed some romance, paying adult brides' prices and providing dowries so that their sons and daughters could marry strangers. Marriage promises to turn strangers into friendly relatives—a nation of siblings.

In the village structure, spirits shimmered among the live crea- 37
tures, balanced and held in equilibrium by time and land. But one human being flaring up into violence could open up a black hole, a maelstrom that pulled in the sky. The frightened villagers, who depended on one another to maintain the real, went to my aunt to show her a personal, physical representation of the break she had made in the "roundness." Misallying couples snapped off the future, which was to be embodied in true offspring. The villagers punished her for acting as if she could have a private life, secret and apart from them.

If my aunt had betrayed the family at a time of large grain yields 38
and peace, when many boys were born, and wings were being built on many houses, perhaps she might have escaped such severe punishment. But the men—hungry, greedy, tired of planting in dry soil, cuckolded—and had to leave the village in order to send food-money home. There were ghost plagues, bandit plagues, wars with the Japanese, floods. My Chinese brother and sister had died of an unknown sickness. Adultery, perhaps only a mistake during good times, became a crime when the village needed food.

The round moon cakes and round doorways, the round tables of 39
graduated size that fit one roundness inside another, round windows and rice bowls—these talismans had lost their power to warn this family of the law: a family must be whole, faithfully keeping the descent line by having sons to feed the old and the dead, who in turn look after the family. The villagers came to show my aunt and her lover-in-hiding a broken house. The villagers were speeding up the circling of events because she was too shortsighted to see that her infidelity had already harmed the village, that waves of consequences would return unpredictably, sometimes in disguise, as now, to hurt her. This roundness had to be made coin-sized so that she would see its circumference: punish her at the birth of her baby. Awaken her to the inexorable. People who refused fatalism because they could invent small resources insisted on culpability. Deny accidents and wrest fault from the stars.

After the villagers left, their lanterns now scattering in various 40
directions toward home, the family broke their silence and cursed her. "Aiaa, we're going to die. Death is coming. Death is coming. Look what you've done. You've killed us. Ghost! Dead ghost! Ghost! You've never been born." She ran out into the fields, far enough from

the house so that she could no longer hear their voices, and pressed herself against the earth, her own land no more. When she felt the birth coming, she thought that she had been hurt. Her body seized together. "They've hurt me too much," she thought. "This is gall, and it will kill me." With forehead and knees against the earth, her body convulsed and then relaxed. She turned on her back, lay on the ground. The black well of sky and stars went out and out and out forever; her body and her complexity seemed to disappear. She was one of the stars, a bright dot in blackness, without home, without a companion, in eternal cold and silence. And agoraphobia rose in her, speeding higher and higher, bigger and bigger; she would not be able to contain it; there would be no end to fear.

Flayed, unprotected against space, she felt pain return, focusing 41 her body. This pain chilled her—a cold, steady kind of surface pain. Inside, spasmodically, the other pain, the pain of the child, heated her. For hours she lay on the ground, alternately body and space. Sometimes a vision of normal comfort obliterated reality: she saw the family in the evening gambling at the dinner table, the young people massaging their elders' backs. She saw them congratulating one another, high joy on the mornings the rice shoots came up. When these pictures burst, the stars drew yet further apart. Black space opened.

She got to her feet to fight better and remembered that old-fash- 42 ioned women gave birth in their pigsties to fool the jealous, pain-dealing gods, who do not snatch piglets. Before the next spasms could stop her, she ran to the pigsty, each step a rushing out into emptiness. She climbed over the fence and knelt in the dirt. It was good to have a fence enclosing her, a tribal person alone.

Laboring, this woman who had carried her child as a foreign 43 growth that sickened her every day, expelled it at last. She reached down to touch the hot, wet, moving mass, surely smaller than anything human, and could feel that it was human after all—fingers, toes, nails, nose. She pulled it up on to her belly, and it lay curled there, butt in the air, feet precisely tucked one under the other. She opened her loose shirt and buttoned the child inside. After resting, it squirmed and thrashed and she pushed it up to her breast. It turned its head this way and that until it found her nipple. There, it made little snuffling noises. She clenched her teeth at its preciousness, lovely as a young calf, a piglet, a little dog.

She may have gone to the pigsty as a last act of responsibility: 44 she would protect this child as she had protected its father. It would look after her soul, leaving supplies on her grave. But how would this tiny child without family find her grave when there would be no marker for her anywhere, neither in the earth nor the family hall? No one would give her a family hall name. She had taken the child with her into the wastes. At its birth the two of them had felt the same raw pain of separation, a wound that only the family pressing tight could close. A child with no descent line would not soften her life but only trail after her, ghost-like, begging her to give it purpose. At dawn the villagers on their way to the fields would stand around the fence and look.

Full of milk, the little ghost slept. When it awoke, she hardened her breasts against the milk that crying loosens. Toward morning she picked up the baby and walked to the well. 45

Carrying the baby to the well shows loving. Otherwise abandon it. Turn its face into the mud. Mothers who love their children take them along. It was probably a girl; there is some hope of forgiveness for boys. 46

"Don't tell anyone you had an aunt. Your father does not want to hear her name. She has never been born." I have believed that sex was unspeakable and words so strong and fathers so frail that "aunt" would do my father mysterious harm. I have thought that my family, having settled among immigrants who had also been their neighbors in the ancestral land, needed to clean their name, and a wrong word would incite the kinspeople even here. But there is more to this silence: they want me to participate in her punishment. And I have. 47

In the twenty years since I heard this story I have not asked for details nor said my aunt's name; I do not know it. People who can comfort the dead can also chase after them to hurt them further—a reverse ancestor worship. The real punishment was not the raid swiftly inflicted by the villagers, but the family's deliberately forgetting her. Her betrayal so maddened them, they saw to it that she would suffer forever, even after death. Always hungry, always needing, she would have to beg food from other ghosts, snatch and steal it from those whose living descendants give them gifts. She would have to fight the ghosts massed at crossroads for the buns a few thoughtful citizens leave to decoy her away from village and home so that the ancestral spirits could feast unharassed. At peace, they could act like gods, not ghosts, their descent lines providing them with paper suits and dresses, spirit money, paper houses, paper automobiles, chicken, meat, and rice into eternity—essences delivered up in smoke and flames, steam and incense rising from each rice bowl. In an attempt to make the Chinese care for people outside the family, Chairman Mao encourages us now to give our paper replicas to the spirits of outstanding soldiers and workers, no matter whose ancestors they may be. My aunt remains forever hungry. Goods are not distributed evenly among the dead. 48

WRITING SUGGESTIONS

1. Kingston claims to be surrounded by an "invisible world." Are you conscious of having an invisible world of ancestors? Write an essay in which you describe your invisible world or the reasons why you might not have one.

2. Write a case study of Kingston's aunt from the point of view of a Western observer. Present her situation, and offer recommendations about how her problems could have been alleviated. Try to use an objective, "scientific" tone.

My aunt haunts me—her ghost drawn to me because now, after 49 fifty years of neglect, I alone devote pages of paper to her, though not origamied into houses and clothes. I do not think she always means me well. I am telling on her, and she was a spite suicide, drowning herself in the drinking water. The Chinese are always very frightened of the drowned one, whose weeping ghost, wet hair hanging and skin bloated, waits silently by the water to pull down a substitute.

RESPONDING TO READING

1. In paragraph 48 Kingston says of her aunt, "The real punishment was not the raid swiftly inflicted by the villagers, but the family's deliberately forgetting her." How does Kingston's essay attempt to make up for this punishment?   **2.** How accurate do you imagine Kingston's facts are? Why? Does strict accuracy matter in this essay? Why or why not?   **3.** Kingston never met her aunt. In what sense is this essay nevertheless about her relationship with her aunt (and with other family members, both known and unknown)? Is there a family member other than your parents who has had a profound effect on your life? In what way is this relationship like and unlike the one Kingston has with her aunt?

The Way to Rainy Mountain

N. SCOTT MOMADAY

N. Scott Momaday (1934–   ) is a poet, novelist, and nonfiction writer who won the Pulitzer Prize for his novel *House Made of Dawn* (1968). Critic Baine Kerr in *Southwest Review* describes this book as an attempt to "transliterate Indian culture, myth, and sensibility into an alien art form without loss." Momaday grew up on a reservation in New Mexico and now teaches at the University of Arizona. He is also an artist, as well as a Kiowa tribal dancer and member of the Gourd Dance Society of the Kiowa Tribe. Momaday's work chronicles Native American experience and portrays Indian culture as strongly identified with the land. He published his autobiographical essays in *The Way to Rainy Mountain* (1969), from which the following selection is taken. Here, Momaday describes Kiowa culture through the stories and legends his grandfather told him.

A single knoll rises out of the plain in Oklahoma, north and west of the Wichita Range. For my people, the Kiowas, it is an old landmark, and they gave it the name Rainy Mountain. The hardest weather in the world is there. Winter brings blizzards, hot tornadic

ADDITIONAL QUESTIONS FOR
RESPONDING TO READING

1. What do Momaday's images of enclosure suggest about the Kiowa people? What aspects of life and nature do the people seem to cherish?
2. Momaday writes that his grandmother "must have known from birth the affliction of defeat." What does he mean? Does he expect readers to take this observation literally?

winds arise in the spring, and in summer the prairie is an anvil's edge. The grass turns brittle and brown, and it cracks beneath your feet. There are green belts along the rivers and creeks, linear groves of hickory and pecan, willow and witch hazel. At a distance in July or August the steaming foliage seems almost to writhe in fire. Great green and yellow grasshoppers are everywhere in the tall grass, popping up like corn to sting the flesh, and tortoises crawl about on the red earth, going nowhere in the plenty of time. Loneliness is an aspect of the land. All things in the plain are isolate; there is no confusion of objects in the eye, but *one* hill or *one* tree or *one* man. To look upon that landscape in the early morning, with the sun at your back, is to lose the sense of proportion. Your imagination comes to life, and this, you think, is where Creation was begun.

I returned to Rainy Mountain in July. My grandmother had died 2 in the spring, and I wanted to be at her grave. She had lived to be very old and at last infirm. Her only living daughter was with her when she died, and I was told that in death her face was that of a child.

I like to think of her as a child. When she was born, the Kiowas 3 were living the last great moment of their history. For more than a hundred years they had controlled the open range from the Smoky Hill River to the Red, from the headwaters of the Canadian to the fork of the Arkansas and Cimarron. In alliance with the Comanches, they had ruled the whole of the southern Plains. War was their sacred business, and they were among the finest horsemen the world has ever known. But warfare for the Kiowas was preeminently a matter of disposition rather than of survival, and they never understood the grim, unrelenting advance of the U.S. Cavalry. When at last, divided and ill-provisioned, they were driven onto the Staked Plains in the cold rains of autumn, they fell into panic. In Palo Duro Canyon they abandoned their crucial stores to pillage and had nothing then but their lives. In order to save themselves, they surrendered to the soldiers at Fort Sill and were imprisoned in the old stone corral that now stands as a military museum. My grandmother was spared the humiliation of those high gray walls by eight or ten years, but she must have known from birth the affliction of defeat, the dark brooding of old warriors.

Her name was Aho, and she belonged to the last culture to evolve 4 in North America. Her forebears came down from the high country in western Montana nearly three centuries ago. They were a mountain people, a mysterious tribe of hunters whose language has never been positively classified in any major group. In the late seventeenth century they began a long migration to the south and east. It was a journey toward the dawn, and it led to a golden age. Along the way the Kiowas were befriended by the Crows, who gave them the culture and religion of the Plains. They acquired horses, and their ancient nomadic spirit was suddenly free of the ground. They acquired Taime, the sacred Sun Dance doll, from that moment the object and symbol of their worship, and so shared in the divinity of the sun. Not least, they acquired the sense of destiny, therefore courage and pride. When they entered upon the southern Plains they had been transformed. No longer were they slaves to the simple necessity of survival; they were a lordly and dangerous society of fighters and thieves, hunters and priests of the sun. According to their origin myth, they entered the world through a hollow log. From one point of view, their migration was the fruit of an old prophecy, for indeed they emerged from a sunless world.

Although my grandmother lived out her long life in the shadaw 5 of Rainy Mountain, the immense landscape of the continental interior lay like memory in her blood. She could tell of the Crows, whom she had never seen, and of the Black Hills, where she had never been. I wanted to see in reality what she had seen more perfectly in the mind's eye, and traveled fifteen hundred miles to begin my pilgrimage.

Yellowstone, it seemed to me, was the top of the world, a region 6 of deep lakes and dark timber, canyons and waterfalls. But, beautiful as it is, one might have the sense of confinement there. The skyline in all directions is close at hand, the high wall of the woods and deep cleavages of shade. There is a perfect freedom in the mountains, but it belongs to the eagle and the elk, the badger and the bear. The Kiowas reckoned their stature by the distance they could see, and they were bent and blind in the wilderness.

Descending eastward, the highland meadows are a stairway to 7 the plain. In July the inland slope of the Rockies is luxuriant with flax and buckwheat, stonecrop and larkspur. The earth unfolds and the limit of the land recedes. Clusters of trees, and animals grazing far in the distance, cause the vision to reach away and wonder to build upon the mind. The sun follows a longer course in the day, and the sky is immense beyond all comparison. The great billowing clouds that sail upon it are shadows that move upon the grain like water, dividing light. Farther down, in the land of the Crows and Blackfeet, the plain is yellow. Sweet clover takes hold of the hills and bends upon itself to cover and seal the soil. There the Kiowas paused on their way; they had come to the place where they must change their lives. The sun is at home on the plains. Precisely there does it have the certain character of a god. When the Kiowas came to the land of the Crows, they could see the dark lees of the hills at dawn across the Bighorn River, the profusion of light on the grain shelves, the oldest deity ranging after the solstices. Not yet would they veer southward to the caldron of the land that lay below; they must wean their blood from the northern winter and hold the mountains a while longer in their view. They bore Tai-me in procession to the east.

A dark mist lay over the Black Hills, and the land was like iron. At the top of a ridge I caught sight of Devil's Tower upthrust against the gray sky as if in the birth of time the core of the earth had broken through its crust and the motion of the world was begun. There are things in nature that engender an awful quiet in the heart of man; Devil's Tower is one of them. Two centuries ago, because they could not do otherwise, the Kiowas made a legend at the base of the rock. My grandmother said:

8

> Eight children were there at play, seven sisters and their brother. Suddenly the boy was struck dumb; he trembled and began to run upon his hands and feet. His fingers became claws, and his body was covered with fur. Directly there was a bear where the boy had been. The sisters were terrified; they ran, and the bear after them. They came to the stump of a great tree, and the tree spoke to them. It bade them climb upon it, and as they did so it began to rise into the air. The bear came to kill them, but they were just beyond its reach. It reared against the tree and scored the bark all around with its claws. The seven sisters were borne into the sky, and they became the stars of the Big Dipper.

From that moment, and so long as the legend lives, the Kiowas have kinsmen in the night sky. Whatever they were in the mountains, they could be no more. However tenuous their well-being, however much they had suffered and would suffer again, they had found a way out of the wilderness.

My grandmother had a reverence for the sun, a holy regard that now is all but gone out of mankind. There was a wariness in her, and an ancient awe. She was a Christian in her later years, but she had come a long way about, and she never forgot her birthright. As a child she had been to the Sun Dances; she had taken part in those annual rites, and by them she had learned the restoration of her people in the presence of Tai-me. She was about seven when the last Kiowa Sun Dance was held in 1887 on the Washita River above Rainy Mountain Creek. The buffalo were gone. In order to consummate the ancient sacrifice—to impale the head of a buffalo bull upon the medicine tree—a delegation of old men journeyed into Texas, there to beg and barter for an animal from the Goodnight herd. She was ten when the Kiowas came together for the last time as a living Sun Dance culture. They could find no buffalo; they had to hang an old hide from the sacred tree. Before the dance could begin, a company of soldiers rode out from Fort Sill under orders to disperse the tribe. Forbidden without cause the essential act of their faith, having seen

TEACHING STRATEGY

Consider the strategies Momaday uses to make his grandmother a mythical, larger-than-life figure. Do these strategies make her more or less human? Why do you think he uses these strategies?

the wild herds slaughtered and left to rot upon the ground, the Kiowas backed away forever from the medicine tree. That was July 20, 1890, at the great bend of the Washita. My grandmother was there. Without bitterness, and for as long as she lived, she bore a vision of deicide.[1]

Now that I can have her only in memory, I see my grandmother   10 in the several postures that were peculiar to her: standing at the wood stove on a winter morning and turning meat in a great iron skillet; sitting at the south window, bent above her beadwork, and afterwards, when her vision failed, looking down for a long time into the fold of her hands; going out upon a cane, very slowly as she did when the weight of age came upon her; praying. I remember her most often at prayer. She made long, rambling prayers out of suffering and hope, having seen many things. I was never sure that I had the right to hear, so exclusive were they of all mere custom and company. The last time I saw her she prayed standing by the side of her bed at night, naked to the waist, the light of a kerosene lamp moving upon her dark skin. Her long, black hair, always drawn and braided in the day, lay upon her shoulders and against her breasts like a shawl. I do not speak Kiowa, and I never understood her prayers, but there was something inherently sad in the sound, some merest hesitation upon the syllables of sorrow. She began in a high and descending pitch, exhausting her breath to silence; then again and again—and always the same intensity of effort, of something that is, and is not, like urgency in the human voice. Transported so in the dancing light among the shadows of her room, she seemed beyond the reach of time. But that was illusion; I think I knew then that I should not see her again.

Houses are like sentinels in the plain, old keepers of the weather   11 watch. There, in a very little while, wood takes on the appearance of great age. All colors wear soon away in the wind and rain, and then the wood is burned gray and the grain appears and the nails turn red with rust. The windowpanes are black and opaque; you imagine there is nothing within, and indeed there are many ghosts, bones given up to the land. They stand here and there against the sky, and you approach them for a longer time than you expect. They belong in the distance; it is their domain.

Once there was a lot of sound in my grandmother's house, a lot   12 of coming and going, feasting and talk. The summers there were full of excitement and reunion. The Kiowas are a summer people; they abide the cold and keep to themselves, but when the season turns and the land becomes warm and vital they cannot hold still; an old

---

[1]The killing of a god. [Eds.]

COLLABORATIVE ACTIVITY

Ask students, working in groups, to identify instances in which Momaday describes his sense of awe in viewing certain features of the landscape. Then assign each group to experiment with rewriting a different one of these descriptive passages in plainer, more objective language. As a class, compare the two versions of each description and discuss the advantages and disadvantages of each.

WRITING SUGGESTION

Through his grandmother, Momaday is connected to his people's history. Write an essay in which you discuss how your grandparents connect you to your ethnic and cultural heritage.

love of going returns upon them. The aged visitors who came to my grandmother's house when I was a child were made of lean and leather, and they bore themselves upright. The wore great black hats and bright ample shirts that shook in the wind. They rubbed fat upon their hair and wound their braids with strips of colored cloth. Some of them painted their faces and carried the scars of old and cherished enmities. They were an old council of warloads, come to remind and be reminded of who they were. Their wives and daughters served them well. The women might indulge themselves; gossip was at once the mark and compensation of their servitude. They made loud and elaborate talk among themselves, full of jest and gesture, fright and false alarm. They went abroad in fringed and flowered shawls, bright beadwork and German silver. They were at home in the kitchen, and they prepared meals that were banquets.

There were frequent prayer meetings, and great nocturnal feasts. 13 When I was a child I played with my cousins outside, where the lamplight fell upon the ground and the singing of the old people rose up around us and carried away into the darkness. There were a lot of good things to eat, a lot of laughter and surprise. And afterwards, when the quiet returned, I lay down with my grandmother and could hear the frogs away by the river and feel the motion of the air.

Now there is funeral silence in the rooms, the endless wake of 14 some final word. The walls have closed in upon my grandmother's house. When I returned to it in mourning, I saw for the first time in my life how small it was. It was late at night, and there was a white moon, nearly full. I sat for a long time on the stone steps by the kitchen door. From there I could see out across the land; I could see the long row of trees by the creek, the low light upon the rolling plains, and the stars of the Big Dipper. Once I looked at the moon and caught sight of a strange thing. A cricket had perched upon the handrail, only a few inches away from me. My line of vision was such that the creature filled the moon like a fossil. It had gone there, I thought, to live and die, for there, of all places, was its small definition made whole and eternal. A warm wind rose up and purled[2] like the longing within me.

The next morning I awoke at dawn and went out on the dirt road 15 to Rainy Mountain. It was already hot, and the grasshoppers began to fill the air. Still, it was early in the morning, and the birds sang out of the shadows. The long yellow grass on the mountain shone in the bright light, and a scissortail hied above the land. There, where it ought to be, at the end of a long and legendary way, was my

---

[2]Flowed; rippled. [Eds.]

grandmother's grave. Here and there on the dark stones were ancestral names. Looking back once, I saw the mountain and came away.

RESPONDING TO READING

1. Does Momaday portray his grandmother as an individual or as a symbol meant to stand for some larger idea? Explain.   **2.** What is Momaday's purpose in placing his grandmother in a very specific historical, geographical, and ethnic context? Does the background he provides make his grandmother's life easier or harder for you to understand?   **3.** This essay focuses on Momaday's grandmother herself, not on his own relationship with her. In what sense is it about the author himself as well as about his grandmother?

Beauty: When the Other Dancer Is the Self

ALICE WALKER

Like the essay "Saving the Life That Is Your Own" (p. 68), this selection is also from the collection *In Search of Our Mothers' Gardens*. In the essay that follows, Alice Walker traces the changes she experienced in her self-image after losing the sight in her right eye in a childhood accident. Only years later, through her daughter's eyes, she was able to see that there was a special beauty about her damaged eye.

It is a bright summer day in 1947. My father, a fat, funny man   1
with beautiful eyes and a subversive wit, is trying to decide which of his eight children he will take with him to the county fair. My mother, of course, will not go. She is knocked out from getting most of us ready: I hold my neck stiff against the pressure of her knuckles as she hastily completes the braiding and then beribboning of my hair.

My father is the driver for the rich old white lady up the road.   2
Her name is Miss Mey. She owns all the land for miles around, as well as the house in which we live. All I remember about her is that she once offered to pay my mother thirty-five cents for cleaning her house, raking up piles of her magnolia leaves, and washing her family's clothes, and that my mother—she of no money, eight children, and a chronic earache—refused it. But I do not think of this in 1947. I am two and a half years old. I want to go everywhere my daddy goes. I am excited at the prospect of riding in a car. Someone has told me fairs are fun. That there is room in the car for only three of

ANSWERS TO RESPONDING TO READING

1. For the most part the reader does not learn much about Momaday's grandmother as an individual; instead, we see her life as a parallel to the history of the Kiowa people. The memories Momaday recounts seem to make the grandmother a symbol of the once powerful, but now dying, culture.
2. Whereas we do not know Momaday's grandmother as an individual, her historical and cultural background enables us to understand more about the Kiowa people. We come to know something of their pleasures, hardships, struggles, and defeats.
3. Momaday's journey is as much an imaginative, or a spiritual, excursion as it is a physical one. In writing about his grandmother, Momaday reasserts his own identity.

FOR OPENERS

Walker's accident transformed her life in many ways. How might her fear of blindness have affected her development as a writer? (You might mention to your students that some great writers, such as Homer and Milton, found that blindness paradoxically led them to new insights.)

ADDITIONAL QUESTIONS FOR
RESPONDING TO READING

1. What is the effect of Walker's recounting her
   memories in the present tense? What does
   this form of narration suggest about her
   ability to resolve her childhood pain?
2. Notice those words around which Walker has
   placed quotation marks. What is suggested
   by the following: "beautiful," "on the ranch,"
   not "real" guns, "cute," and "accident"?
3. What strategies does Walker use to break her
   essay into sections? Why does she do so?

us doesn't faze me at all. Whirling happily in my starchy frock, showing off my biscuit-polished patent-leather shoes and lavender socks, tossing my head in a way that makes my ribbons bounce, I stand, hands on hips, before my father. "Take me, Daddy," I say with assurance; "I'm the prettiest!"

Later, it does not surprise me to find myself in Miss Mey's shiny 3 black car, sharing the back seat with the other lucky ones. Does not surprise me that I thoroughly enjoy the fair. At home that night I tell the unlucky ones all I can remember about the merry-go-round, the man who eats live chickens, and the teddy bears, until they say: that's enough, baby Alice. Shut up now, and go to sleep.

It is Easter Sunday, 1950. I am dressed in a green, flocked, scal- 4 loped-hem dress (handmade by my adoring sister, Ruth) that has its own smooth satin petticoat and tiny hot-pink roses tucked into each scallop. My shoes, new T-strap patent leather, again highly biscuit-polished. I am six years old and have learned one of the longest Easter speeches to be heard that day, totally unlike the speech I said when I was two: "Easter lilies/pure and white/blossom in/the morning light." When I rise to give my speech I do so on a great wave of love and pride and expectation. People in the church stop rustling their new crinolines. They seem to hold their breath. I can tell they admire my dress, but it is my spirit, bordering on sassiness (womanishness), they secretly applaud.

"That girl's a little *mess*," they whisper to each other, pleased. 5

Naturally I say my speech without stammer or pause, unlike those 6 who stutter, stammer, or, worst of all, forget. This is before the word "beautiful" exists in people's vocabulary, but "Oh, isn't she the *cutest* thing!" frequently floats my way. "And got so much sense!" they gratefully add . . . for which thoughtful addition I thank them to this day.

It was great fun being cute. But then, one day, it ended. 7

I am eight years old and a tomboy. I have a cowboy hat, cowboy 8 boots, checkered shirt and pants, all red. My playmates are my brothers, two and four years older than I. Their colors are black and green, the only difference in the way we are dressed. On Saturday nights we all go to the picture show, even my mother; Westerns are her favorite kind of movie. Back home, "on the ranch," we pretend we are Tom Mix, Hopalong Cassidy, Lash LaRue (we've even named one of our dogs Lash LaRue); we chase each other for hours rustling cattle, being outlaws, delivering damsels from distress. Then my parents decide to buy my brothers guns. These are not "real" guns. They shoot "BBs," copper pellets my brothers say will kill birds. Because

I am a girl, I do not get a gun. Instantly I am relegated to the position of Indian. Now there appears a great distance between us. They shoot and shoot at everything with their new guns. I try to keep up with my bow and arrows.

One day while I am standing on top of our makeshift "garage"— 9 pieces of tin nailed across some poles—holding my bow and arrow and looking out toward the fields, I feel an incredible blow in my right eye. I look down just in time to see my brother lower his gun.

Both brothers rush to my side. My eye stings, and I cover it with 10 my hand. "If you tell," they say, "we will get a whipping. You don't want that to happen, do you?" I do not. "Here is a piece of wire," says the older brother, picking it up from the roof; "say you stepped on one end of it and the other flew up and hit you." The pain is beginning to start. "Yes," I say, "Yes, I will say that is what happened." If I do not say this is what happened, I know my brothers will find ways to make me wish I had. But now I will say anything that gets me to my mother.

Confronted by our parents we stick to the lie agreed upon. They 11 place me on a bench on the porch and I close my left eye while they examine the right. There is a tree growing from underneath the porch that climbs past the railing to the roof. It is the last thing my right eye sees. I watch as its trunk, its branches, and then its leaves are blotted out by the rising blood.

I am in shock. First there is intense fever, which my father tries 12 to break using lily leaves bound around my head. Then there are chills: my mother tries to get me to eat soup. Eventually, I do not know how, my parents learn what has happened. A week after the "accident" they take me to see a doctor. "Why did you wait so long to come?" he asks, looking into my eye and shaking his head. "Eyes are sympathetic," he says. "If one is blind, the other will likely become blind too."

This comment of the doctor's terrifies me. But it is really how I 13 look that bothers me most. Where the BB pellet struck there is a glob of whitish scar tissue, a hideous cataract, on my eye. Now when I stare at people—a favorite pastime, up to now—they will stare back. Not at the "cute" little girl, but at her scar. For six years I do not stare at anyone, because I do not raise my head.

Years later, in the throes of a mid-life crisis, I ask my mother and 14 sister whether I changed after the "accident." "No," they say, puzzled. "What do you mean?"

What do I mean?   15

I am eight, and, for the first time, doing poorly in school, where 16 I have been something of a whiz since I was four. We have just moved to the place where the "accident" occurred. We do not know any of

the people around us because this is a different county. The only time
I see the friends I knew is when we go back to our old church. The
new school is the former state penitentiary. It is a large stone building,
cold and drafty, crammed to overflowing with boisterous, ill-disci-
plined children. On the third floor there is a huge circular imprint of
some partition that has been torn out.

"What used to be here?" I ask a sullen girl next to me on our way 17
past it to lunch.

"The electric chair," says she.   18

At night I have nightmares about the electric chair, and about all 19
the people reputedly "fried" in it. I am afraid of the school, where
all the students seem to be budding criminals.

"What's the matter with your eye?" they ask, critically.   20

When I don't answer (I cannot decide whether it was an "acci- 21
dent" or not), they shove me, insist on a fight.

My brother, the one who created the story about the wire, comes 22
to my rescue. But then brags so much about "protecting" me, I become
sick.

After months of torture at the school, my parents decide to send 23
me back to our old community, to my old school. I live with my
grandparents and the teacher they board. But there is no room for
Phoebe, my cat. By the time my grandparents decide there *is* room,
and I ask for my cat, she cannot be found. Miss Yarborough, the
boarding teacher, takes me under her wing, and begins to teach me
to play the piano. But soon she marries an African—a "prince," she
says—and is whisked away to his continent.

At my old school there is at least one teacher who loves me. She 24
is the teacher who "knew me before I was born" and bought my first
baby clothes. It is she who makes life bearable. It is her presence that
finally helps me turn on the one child at the school who continually
calls me "one-eyed bitch." One day I simply grab him by his coat
and beat him until I am satisfied. It is my teacher who tells me my
mother is ill.

My mother is lying in bed in the middle of the day, something I 25
have never seen. She is in too much pain to speak. She has an abscess
in her ear. I stand looking down on her, knowing that if she dies, I
cannot live. She is being treated with warm oils and hot bricks held
against her cheek. Finally a doctor comes. But I must go back to my
grandparents' house. The weeks pass but I am hardly aware of it. All
I know is that my mother might die, my father is not so jolly, my
brothers still have their guns, and I am the one sent away from home.

"You did not change," they say.   26

Did I imagine the anguish of never looking up?   27

I am twelve. When relatives come to visit I hide in my room. My   28
cousin Brenda, just my age, whose father works in the post office
and whose mother is a nurse, comes to find me. "Hello," she says.
And then she asks, looking at my recent school picture, which I did
not want taken, and on which the "glob," as I think of it, is clearly
visible, "You still can't see out of that eye?"

"No," I say, and flop back on the bed over my book.   29

That night, as I do almost every night, I abuse my eye. I rant and   30
rave at it, in front of the mirror. I plead with it to clear up before
morning. I tell it I hate and despise it. I do not pray for sight. I pray
for beauty.

"You did not change," they say.   31

I am fourteen and baby-sitting for my brother Bill, who lives in   32
Boston. He is my favorite brother and there is a strong bond between
us. Understanding my feelings of shame and ugliness he and his wife
take me to a local hospital, where the "glob" is removed by a doctor
named O. Henry. There is still a small bluish crater where the scar
tissue was, but the ugly white stuff is gone. Almost immediately I
become a different person from the girl who does not raise her head.
Or so I think. Now that I've raised my head I win the boyfriend of
my dreams. Now that I've raised my head I have plenty of friends.
Now that I've raised my head classwork comes from my lips as fault-
lessly as Easter speeches did, and I leave high school as valedictorian,
most popular student, and *queen*, hardly believing my luck. Ironically,
the girl who was voted most beautiful in our class (and was) was later
shot twice through the chest by a male companion, using a "real"
gun, while she was pregnant. But that's another story in itself. Or
is it?

"You did not change," they say.   33

It is now thirty years since the "accident." A beautiful journalist   34
comes to visit and to interview me. She is going to write a cover story
for her magazine that focuses on my latest book. "Decide how you
want to look on the cover," she says. "Glamorous, or whatever."

Never mind "glamorous," it is the "whatever" that I hear. Sud-   35
denly all I can think of is whether I will get enough sleep the night
before the photography session: if I don't, my eye will be tired and
wander, as blind eyes will.

At night in bed with my lover I think up reasons why I should   36
not appear on the cover of a magazine. "My meanest critics will say
I've sold out," I say. "My family will now realize I write scandalous
books."

"But what's the real reason you don't want to do this?" he asks.   37

TEACHING STRATEGY

Walker frequently understates emotional
reactions. Ask your students to identify instances
in which they believe she is understating such
reactions. Why do they believe she uses this flat,
relatively unemotional tone to recount particularly painful experiences?

COLLABORATIVE ACTIVITY

Ask students, working in groups, to experiment with recasting Walker's narrative into a screenplay. Assign a different section of the essay to each group, and have them create appropriate dialogue, descriptions of costumes and scenery, and so forth.

"Because in all probability," I say in a rush, "my eye won't be straight." 38

"It will be straight enough," he says. Then, "Besides, I thought you'd made your peace with that." 39

And I suddenly remember that I have. 40

I remember: 41

I am talking to my brother Jimmy, asking if he remembers anything unusual about the day I was shot. He does not know I consider that day the last time my father, with his sweet home remedy of cool lily leaves, chose me, and that I suffered and raged inside because of this. "Well," he says, "all I remember is standing by the side of the highway with Daddy, trying to flag down a car. A white man stopped, but when Daddy said he needed somebody to take his little girl to the doctor, he drove off." 42

I remember: 43

I am in the desert for the first time. I fall totally in love with it. I am so overwhelmed by its beauty, I confront for the first time, consciously, the meaning of the doctor's words years ago: "Eyes are sympathetic. If one is blind, the other will likely become blind too." I realize I have dashed about the world madly, looking at this, looking at that, storing up images against the fading of the light. *But I might have missed seeing the desert!* The shock of that possibility—and gratitude for over twenty-five years of sight—sends me literally to my knees. Poem after poem comes—which is perhaps how poets pray. 44

On Sight

I am so thankful I have seen
The Desert
And the creatures in the desert
And the desert Itself.

The desert has its own moon   5
Which I have seen
With my own eye.
There is no flag on it.

Trees of the desert have arms
All of which are always up   10
That is because the moon is up
The sun is up
Also the sky
The stars
Clouds   15
None with flags.

If there were flags, I doubt
the trees would point.
Would you?

But mostly, I remember this: 45

I am twenty-seven, and my baby daughter is almost three. Since   46
her birth I have worried about her discovery that her mother's eyes
are different from other people's. Will she be embarrassed? I think.
What will she say? Every day she watches a television program called
"Big Blue Marble." It begins with a picture of the earth as it appears
from the moon. It is bluish, a little battered-looking, but full of light,
with whitish clouds swirling around it. Every time I see it I weep with
love, as if it is a picture of Grandma's house. One day when I am
putting Rebecca down for her nap, she suddenly focues on my eye.
Something inside me cringes, gets ready to try to protect myself. All
children are cruel about physical differences, I know from experience,
and that they don't always mean to be is another matter. I assume
Rebecca will be the same.

But no-o-o-o. She studies my face intently as we stand, her inside   47
and me outside her crib. She even holds my face maternally between
her dimpled little hands. Then, looking every bit as serious and law-
yerlike as her father, she says, as if it may just possibly have slipped
my attention: "Mommy, there's a *world* in your eye." (As in, "Don't
be alarmed, or do anything crazy.") And then, gently, but with great
interest: "Mommy, where did you get that world in your eye?"

For the most part, the pain left then. (So what, if my brothers   48
grew up to buy even more powerful pellet guns for their sons and
to carry real guns themselves. So what, if a young "Morehouse man"[1]
once nearly fell off the steps of Trevor Arnett Library because he
thought my eyes were blue.) Crying and laughing I ran to the bathroom, while Rebecca mumbled and sang herself off to sleep. Yes
indeed, I realized, looking into the mirror. There was a world in my
eye. And I saw that it was possible to love it: that in fact, for all it
had taught me of shame and anger and inner vision, I *did* love it.
Even to see it drifting out of orbit in boredom, or rolling up out of
fatigue, not to mention floating back at attention in excitement
(bearing witness, a friend has called it), deeply suitable to my personality, and even characteristic of me.

That night I dream I am dancing to Stevie Wonder's song   49
"Always" (the name of the song is really "As," but I hear it as
"Always"). As I dance, whirling and joyous, happier than I've ever

WRITING SUGGESTION

Walker's accident affected her development
in unforeseen ways. Write about an experience
whose full consequences you did not comprehend until some time later.

---

[1]A student at Morehouse College, a historically black college in Atlanta, Georgia. [Eds.]

been in my life, another bright-faced dancer joins me. We dance and kiss each other and hold each other through the night. The other dancer has obviously come through all right, as I have done. She is beautiful, whole and free. And she is also me.

RESPONDING TO READING

1. How does the narrator's physical appearance affect the way she was treated by her parents? How does the essay's title shed light on this subject? Do you think your physical appearance has ever affected your parents' attitude toward you? Explain.   **2.** At several points in the essay Walker repeats the words her relatives used to reassure her: "You did not change." Why does she repeat this phrase? What does it reveal about the underlying problems she faced as a child?   **3.** Who, if anyone, does Walker blame for the childhood problems she describes? For example, what part do race and gender play in Walker's trauma? Does the adult writer seem to forgive those at fault? Whom do you blame?

My Father's Life

RAYMOND CARVER

Raymond Carver (1939–1988) was a fiction and poetry writer who grew up in a working-class family in the Pacific Northwest. Influenced by his father's storytelling, he began writing stories himself as a boy. Collections of Carver's stories include *Will You Please Be Quiet, Please?* (1976), *What We Talk About When We Talk About Love* (1981), and *Cathedral* (1984). Carver's stories, usually about desperate people struggling for daily survival, often have enigmatic endings. In "My Father's Life," which originally appeared in *Esquire* in 1984, Carver tells how his father first struggled financially during the Great Depression and later suffered from psychological depression.

My dad's name was Clevie Raymond Carver. His family called him Raymond and friends called him C. R. I was named Raymond Clevie Carver Jr. I hated the "Junior" part. When I was little my dad called me Frog, which was okay. But later, like everybody else in the family, he began calling me Junior. He went on calling me this until I was thirteen or fourteen and announced that I wouldn't answer to that name any longer. So he began calling me Doc. From then until his death, on June 17, 1967, he called me Doc, or else Son.

When he died, my mother telephoned my wife with the news. I was away from my family at the time, between lives, trying to enroll in the School of Library Science at the University of Iowa. When my wife answered the phone, my mother blurted out. "Raymond's dead!" For a moment, my wife thought my mother was telling her that I was dead. Then my mother made it clear *which* Raymond she was talking about and my wife said, "Thank God. I thought you meant *my* Raymond."

My dad walked, hitched rides, and rode in empty boxcars when 3 he went from Arkansas to Washington State in 1934, looking for work. I don't know whether he was pursuing a dream when he went out to Washington. I doubt it. I don't think he dreamed much. I believe he was simply looking for steady work at decent pay. Steady work was meaningful work. He picked apples for a time and then landed a construction laborer's job on the Grand Coulee Dam. After he'd put aside a little money, he bought a car and drove back to Arkansas to help his folks, my grandparents, pack up for the move west. He said later that they were about to starve down there, and this wasn't meant as a figure of speech. It was during that short while in Arkansas, in a town called Leola, that my mother met my dad on the sidewalk as he came out of a tavern.

"He was drunk," she said. "I don't know why I let him talk to 4 me. His eyes were glittery. I wish I'd had a crystal ball." They'd met once, a year or so before, at a dance. He'd had girlfriends before her, my mother told me. "Your dad always had a girlfriend, even after we married. He was my first and last. I never had another man. But I didn't miss anything."

They were married by a justice of the peace on the day they left 5 for Washington, this big, tall country girl and a farmhand-turned-construction worker. My mother spent her wedding night with my dad and his folks, all of them camped beside the road in Arkansas.

In Omak, Washington, my dad and mother lived in a little place 6 not much bigger than a cabin. My grandparents lived next door. My dad was still working on the dam, and later, with the huge turbines producing electricity and the water backed up for a hundred miles into Canada, he stood in the crowd and heard Franklin D. Roosevelt when he spoke at the construction site. "He never mentioned those guys who died building that dam," my dad said. Some of his friends had died there, men from Arkansas, Oklahoma, and Missouri.

He then took a job in a sawmill in Clatskanie, Oregon, a little 7 town alongside the Columbia River. I was born there, and my mother has a picture of my dad standing in front of the gate to the mill, proudly holding me up to face the camera. My bonnet is on crooked and about to come untied. His hat is pushed back on his forehead, and he's wearing a big grin. Was he going in to work or just finishing his shift? It doesn't matter. In either case, he had a job and a family. These were his salad days.

ADDITIONAL QUESTIONS FOR RESPONDING TO READING

1. What might be the significance of the names and dates that are so precisely recounted to us in the first section? How does Carver's emphasis on these details lead to an understanding of his theme or themes?
2. What definitions of "work" does Carver present? How does his view of "work" seem to differ from his father's? Which definition is closer to your own?
3. Analyze paragraph 4, in which Carver's mother discusses her relationship to her husband. Can you paraphrase this complex of emotions? What does she seem to have felt for the man to whom she was married?
4. What aspects of Carver's father's life seem surprising to you? How does this lack of predictability seem to have affected the narrator?

TEACHING STRATEGIES

1. Is the father presented as an individual or a symbol? Although the essay's last line suggests that to Carver he is an individual, students may see him as something else as well. If he is a symbol, what does he represent?
2. Students will need to establish the distinction between the mature narrator's attitude toward his father and his probable feelings as a boy. What does the narrator understand that he seems not to have understood before? You may want to try taking some guesses as to Carver's possible motives in writing the piece.

In 1941 we moved to Yakima, Washington, where my dad went 8 to work as a saw filer, a skilled trade he'd learned in Clatskanie. When war broke out, he was given a deferment because his work was considered necessary to the war effort. Finished lumber was in demand by the armed services, and he kept his saws so sharp they could shave the hair off your arm.

After my dad had moved us to Yakima, he moved his folks into 9 the same neighborhood. By the mid-1940s the rest of my dad's family—his brother, his sister, and her husband, as well as uncles, cousins, nephews, and most of their extended family and friends— had come out from Arkansas. All because my dad came out first. The men went to work at Boise Cascade, where my dad worked, and the women packed apples in the canneries. And in just a little while, it seemed—according to my mother—everybody was better off than my dad. "Your dad couldn't keep money," my mother said. "Money burned a hole in his pocket. He was always doing for others."

The first house I clearly remember living in, at 1515 South Fif- 10 teenth Street, in Yakima, had an outdoor toilet. On Halloween night, or just any night, for the hell of it, neighbor kids, kids in their early teens, would carry our toilet away and leave it next to the road. My dad would have to get somebody to help him bring it home. Or these kids would take the toilet and stand it in somebody else's backyard. Once they actually set it on fire. But ours wasn't the only house that had an outdoor toilet. When I was old enough to know what I was doing, I threw rocks at the other toilets when I'd see someone go inside. This was called bombing the toilets. After a while, though, everyone went to indoor plumbing until, suddenly, our toilet was the last outdoor one in the neighborhood. I remember the shame I felt when my third-grade teacher, Mr. Wise, drove me home from school one day. I asked him to stop at the house just before ours, claiming I lived there.

I can recall what happened one night when my dad came home 11 late to find that my mother had locked all the doors on him from the inside. He was drunk, and we could feel the house shudder as he rattled the door. When he'd managed to force open a window, she hit him between the eyes with a colander and knocked him out. We could see him down there on the grass. For years afterward, I used to pick up this colander—it was as heavy as a rolling pin—and imagine what it would feel like to be hit in the head with something like that.

It was during this period that I remember my dad taking me into 12 the bedroom, sitting me down on the bed, and telling me that I might have to go live with my Aunt LaVon for a while. I couldn't understand what I'd done that meant I'd have to go away from home to live. But this, too—whatever prompted it—must have blown over, more or less, anyway, because we stayed together, and I didn't have to go live with her or anyone else.

I remember my mother pouring his whiskey down the sink. Sometimes she'd pour it all out and sometimes, if she was afraid of getting caught, she'd only pour half of it out and then add water to the rest. I tasted some of his whiskey once myself. It was terrible stuff, and I don't see how anybody could drink it.   13

After a long time without one, we finally got a car, in 1949 or 1950, a 1938 Ford. But it threw a rod the first week we had it, and my dad had to have the motor rebuilt.   14

"We drove the oldest car in town," my mother said. "We could have had a Cadillac for all he spent on car repairs." One time she found someone else's tube of lipstick on the floorboard, along with a lacy handkerchief. "See this?" she said to me. "Some floozy left this in the car."   15

Once I saw her take a pan of warm water into the bedroom where my dad was sleeping. She took his hand from under the covers and held it in the water. I stood in the doorway and watched. I wanted to know what was going on. This would make him talk in his sleep, she told me. There were things she needed to know, things she was sure he was keeping from her.   16

Every year or so, when I was little, we would take the North Coast Limited across the Cascade Range from Yakima to Seattle and stay in the Vance Hotel and eat, I remember, at a place called the Dinner Bell Cafe. Once we went to Ivar's Acres of Clams and drank glasses of warm clam broth.   17

In 1956, the year I was to graduate from high school, my dad quit his job at the mill in Yakima and took a job in Chester, a little sawmill town in northern California. The reasons given at the time for his taking the job had to do with a higher hourly wage and the vague promise that he might, in a few years' time, succeed to the job of head filer in this new mill. But I think, in the main, that my dad had grown restless and simply wanted to try his luck elsewhere. Things had gotten a little too predictable for him in Yakima. Also, the year before, there had been the deaths, within six months of each other, of both his parents.   18

But just a few days after graduation, when my mother and I were packed to move to Chester, my dad penciled a letter to say he'd been sick for a while. He didn't want us to worry, he said, but he'd cut himself on a saw. Maybe he'd got a tiny sliver of steel in his blood. Anyway, something had happened and he'd had to miss work, he   19 said. In the same mail was an unsigned postcard from somebody down there telling my mother that my dad was about to die and that he was drinking "raw whiskey."

When we arrived in Chester, my dad was living in a trailer that 20 belonged to the company. I didn't recognize him immediately. I guess for a moment I didn't want to recognize him. He was skinny and pale and looked bewildered. His pants wouldn't stay up. He didn't look like my dad. My mother began to cry. My dad put his arm around her and patted her shoulder vaguely, like he didn't know what this was all about, either. The three of us took up life together in the trailer, and we looked after him as best we could. But my dad was sick, and he couldn't get any better. I worked with him in the mill that summer and part of the fall. We'd get up in the mornings and eat eggs and toast while we listened to the radio, and then go out the door with our lunch pails. We'd pass through the gate together at eight in the morning, and I wouldn't see him again until quitting time. In November I went back to Yakima to be closer to my girlfriend, the girl I'd made up my mind I was going to marry.

He worked at the mill in Chester until the following February, 21 when he collapsed on the job and was taken to the hospital. My mother asked if I would come down there and help. I caught a bus from Yakima to Chester, intending to drive them back to Yakima. But now, in addition to being physically sick, my dad was in the midst of a nervous breakdown, though none of us knew to call it that at the time. During the entire trip back to Yakima, he didn't speak, not even when asked a direct question. ("How do you feel, Raymond?" "You okay, Dad?") He'd communicate if he communicated at all, by moving his head or by turning his palms up as if to say he didn't know or care. The only time he said anything on the trip, and for nearly a month afterward, was when I was speeding down a gravel road in Oregon and the car muffler came loose. "You were going too fast," he said.

Back in Yakima a doctor saw to it that my dad went to a psychi- 22 atrist. My mother and dad had to go on relief, as it was called, and the county paid fo the psychiatrist. The psychiatrist asked my dad. "Who is the President?" He'd had a question put to him that he could answer. "Ike," my dad said. Nevertheless, they put him on the fifth floor of Valley Memorial Hospital and began giving him electroshock treatments. I was married by then and about to start my own family. My dad was still locked up when my wife went into this same hospital, just one floor down, to have our first baby. After she had delivered, I went upstairs to give my dad the news. They let me in through a steel door and showed me where I could find him. He was sitting on a couch with a blanket over his lap. *Hey*, I thought. *What in hell is happening to my dad?* I sat down next to him and told him he was a grandfather. He waited a minute and then he said, "I feel like a grandfather." That's all he said. He didn't smile or move. He was in a big room with a lot of other people. Then I hugged him, and he began to cry.

Somehow he got out of there. But now came the years when he 23 couldn't work and just sat around the house trying to figure what next and what he'd done wrong in his life that he'd wound up like this. My mother went from job to crummy job. Much later she referred to that time he was in the hospital, and those years just afterward, as "when Raymond was sick." The word *sick* was never the same for me again.

In 1964, through the help of a friend, he was lucky enough to 24 be hired on at a mill in Klamath, California. He moved down there by himself to see if he could hack it. He lived not far from the mill, in a one-room cabin not much different from the place he and my mother had started out living in when they went west. He scrawled letters to my mother, and if I called she'd read them aloud to me over the phone. In the letters, he said it was touch and go. Every day that he went to work, he felt like it was the most important day of his life. But every day, he told her, made the next day that much easier. He said for her to tell me he said hello. If he couldn't sleep at night, he said, he thought about me and the good times we used to have. Finally, after a couple of months, he regained some of his confidence. He could do the work and didn't think he had to worry that he'd let anybody down ever again. When he was sure, he sent for my mother.

He'd been off from work for six years and had lost everything in 25 that time—home, car, furniture, and appliances, including the big freezer that had been my mother's pride and joy. He'd lost his good name too—Raymond Carver was someone who couldn't pay his bills—and his self-respect was gone. He'd even lost his virility. My mother told my wife, "All during that time Raymond was sick we slept together in the same bed, but we didn't have relations. He wanted to a few times, but nothing happened. I didn't miss it, but I think he wanted to, you know."

During those years I was trying to raise my own family and earn 26 a living. But, one thing and another, we found ourselves having to move a lot. I couldn't keep track of what was going down in my dad's life. But I did have a chance one Christmas to tell him I wanted to be a writer. I might as well have told him I wanted to become a plastic surgeon. "What are you going to write about?" he wanted to know. Then, as if to help me out, he said, "Write about stuff you know about. Write about some of those fishing trips we took." I said I would,

COLLABORATIVE ACTIVITY

Ask students to work in groups to analyze the way in which Carver conveys an emotional attitude by showing rather than telling. Assign a different section of the essay to each group. In class discussion, consider these questions: Why does Carver choose to include the sorts of details he does? What is the cumulative effect of these details?

but I knew I wouldn't. "Send me what you write," he said. I said I'd do that, but then I didn't. I wasn't writing anything about fishing, and I didn't think he'd particularly care about, or even necessarily understand, what I was writing in those days. Besides, he wasn't a reader. Not the sort, anyway, I imagined I was writing for.

Then he died. I was a long way off, in Iowa City, with things still 27 to say to him. I didn't have the chance to tell him goodbye, or that I thought he was doing great at his new job. That I was proud of him for making a comeback.

My mother said he came in from work that night and ate a big 28 supper. Then he sat at the table by himself and finished what was left of a bottle of whiskey, a bottle she found hidden in the bottom of the garbage under some coffee grounds a day or so later. Then he got up and went to bed, where my mother joined him a little later. But in the night she had to get up and make a bed for herself on the couch. "He was snoring so loud I couldn't sleep," she said. The next morning when she looked in on him, he was on his back with his mouth open, his cheeks caved in. *Graylooking*, she said. She knew he was dead—she didn't need a doctor to tell her that. But she called one anyway, and then she called my wife.

Among the pictures my mother kept of my dad and herself during 29 those early days in Washington was a photograph of him standing in front of a car, holding a beer and a stringer of fish. In the photograph he is wearing his hat back on his forehead and has this awkward grin on his face. I asked her for it and she gave it to me, along with some others. I put it up on my wall, and each time we moved, I took the picture along and put it up on another wall. I looked at it carefully from time to time, trying to figure out some things about my dad, and maybe myself in the process. But I couldn't. My dad just kept moving further and further away from me and back into time. Finally, in the course of another move, I lost the photograph. It was then that I tried to recall it, and at the same time make an attempt to say something about my dad, and how I thought that in some important ways we might be alike. I wrote the poem when I was living in an apartment house in an urban area south of San Francisco, at a time when I found myself, like my dad, having trouble with alcohol. The poem was a way of trying to connect up with him.

Photograph of My Father in His Twenty-Second Year

October. Here in this dank, unfamiliar kitchen
I study my father's embarrassed young man's face.
Sheepish grin, he holds in one hand a string
of spiny yellow perch, in the other
a bottle of Carlsberg beer.   5

In jeans and flannel shirt, he leans
against the front fender of a 1934 Ford.
He would like to pose brave and hearty for his posterity,
wear his old hat cocked over his ear.
All his life my father wanted to be bold.   10

But the eyes give him away, and the hands
that limply offer the string of dead perch
and the bottle of beer. Father, I love you,
yet how can I say thank you, I who can't hold my liquor either
and don't even know the places to fish.   15

The poem is true in its particulars, except that my dad died in   30
June and not October, as the first word of the poem says. I wanted
a word with more than one syllable to it to make it linger a little. But
more than that, I wanted a month appropriate to what I felt at the
time I wrote the poem—a month of short days and failing light, smoke
in the air, things perishing. June was summer nights and days, grad-
uations, my wedding anniversary, the birthday of one of my children.
June wasn't a month your father died in.

After the service at the funeral home, after we had moved outside,   31
a woman I didn't know came over to me and said, "He's happier
where he is now." I stared at this woman until she moved away. I
still remember the little knob of a hat she was wearing. Then one of
my dad's cousins—I didn't know the man's name—reached out and
took my hand, "We all miss him," he said, and I knew he wasn't
saying it just to be polite.

I began to weep for the first time since receiving the news. I hadn't   32
been able to before. I hadn't had the time, for one thing. Now, suddenly, I couldn't stop. I held my wife and wept while she said and
did what she could do to comfort me there in the middle of that
summer afternoon.

I listened to people say consoling things to my mother, and I was   33
glad that my dad's family had turned up, had come to where he was.
I thought I'd remember everything that was said and done that day
and maybe find a way to tell it sometime. But I didn't. I forgot it all,
or nearly. What I do remember is that I heard our name used a lot
that afternoon, my dad's name and mine. But I knew they were talking
about my dad. *Raymond*, these people kept saying in their beautiful
voices out of my childhood. *Raymond*.

RESPONDING TO READING

1. Why does Carver include details about his father's work history? His
drinking? His mental illness? The photograph?   **2.** What aspects of your
father's life do you find hard to understand? Why?   **3.** Is any information

3. Carver uses the poetic form to express an emotional attitude toward his father from his mature perspective. In the poem he comments on his father's youth, confusion, and vulnerability. Carver conveys a sense that, in spite of whatever conflicts may have arisen between the two "Raymonds," the poet finds himself finally unable to criticize his father's "weakness." The poet seems to have come to a similar understanding of life's hardships.

provided by the poem in paragraph 29 that is not provided by the essay itself? Does the poem express any of your own emotional reactions toward your father? Explain.

Under the Influence
SCOTT RUSSELL SANDERS

Scott Russell Sanders (1945–   ), born in Memphis, writes fiction, science fiction, children's stories, essays, and historical novels. As a political activist, Sanders has worked against nuclear weapons and the militarization of the United States, and for environmental protection. Sanders has said of his writing, "In all of my work, regardless of period or style, I am concerned with the way in which human beings come to terms with the practical problems of living on a small planet, in nature and in communities." Some of his books are *Wilderness Plots: Tales About the Settlement of the American Land* (1983), *Fetching the Dead: Stories* (1984), *Hear the Wind Blow: American Folksongs Retold* (1985), and *The Paradise of Bombs* (1988). In "Under the Influence," he tells of the problems of children of alcoholics, who often inherit the "griefs" of their parents.

1   My father drank. He drank as a gut-punched boxer gasps for breath, as a starving dog gobbles food—compulsively, secretly, in pain and trembling. I use the past tense not because he ever quit drinking but because he quit living. That is how the story ends for my father, age sixty-four, heart bursting, body cooling, slumped and forsaken on the linoleum of my brother's trailer. The story continues for my brother, my sister, my mother, and me, and will continue as long as memory holds.

2   In the perennial present of memory, I slip into the garage or barn to see my father tipping back the flat green bottles of wine, the brown cylinders of whiskey, the cans of beer disguised in paper bags. His Adam's apple bobs, the liquid gurgles, he wipes the sandy-haired back of a hand over his lips, and then, his bloodshot gaze bumping into me, he stashes the bottle or can inside his jacket, under the workbench, between two bales of hay, and we both pretend the moment has not occurred.

3   "What's up, buddy?" he says, thick-tongued and edgy.

4   "Sky's up," I answer, playing along.

5   "And don't forget prices," he grumbles. "Prices are always up. And taxes."

6   In memory, his white 1951 Pontiac with the stripes down the hood and the Indian head on the snout lurches to a stop in the

driveway; or it is the 1956 Ford station wagon, or the 1963 Rambler shaped like a toad, or the sleek 1969 Bonneville that will do 120 miles per hour on straightaways; or it is the robin's-egg-blue pickup, new in 1980, battered in 1981, the year of his death. He climbs out, grinning dangerously, unsteady on his legs, and we children interrupt our game of catch, our building of snow forts, our picking of plums, to watch in silence as he weaves past us into the house, where he drops into his overstuffed chair and falls asleep. Shaking her head, our mother stubs out a cigarette he has left smoldering in the ashtray. All evening, until our bedtimes, we tiptoe past him, as past a snoring dragon. Then we curl fearfully in our sheets, listening. Eventually he wakes with a grunt, Mother slings accusations at him, he snarls back, she yells, he growls, their voices clashing. Before long, she retreats to their bedroom, sobbing—not from the blows of fists, for he never strikes her, but from the force of his words.

Left alone, our father prowls the house, thumping into furniture, 7 rummaging in the kitchen, slamming doors, turning the pages of the newspaper with a savage crackle, muttering back at the late-night drivel from television. The roof might fly off, the walls might buckle from the pressure of his rage. Whatever my brother and sister and mother may be thinking on their own rumpled pillows, I lie there hating him, loving him, fearing him, knowing I have failed him. I tell myself he drinks to ease the ache that gnaws at his belly, an ache I must have caused by disappointing him somehow, a murderous ache I should be able to relieve by doing all my chores, earning A's in school, winning baseball games, fixing the broken washer and the burst pipes, bringing in the money to fill his empty wallet. He would not hide the green bottles in his toolbox, would not sneak off to the barn with a lump under his coat, would not fall asleep in the daylight, would not roar and fume, would not drink himself to death, if only I were perfect.

I am forty-four, and I know full well now that my father was an 8 alcoholic, a man consumed by disease rather than by disappointment. What had seemed to me a private grief is in fact, of course, a public scourge. In the United States alone, some ten or fifteen million people share his ailment, and behind the doors they slam in fury or disgrace, countless other children tremble. I comfort myself with such knowledge, holding it against the throb of memory like an ice pack against a bruise. Other people have keener sources of grief: poverty, racism, rape, war. I do not wish to compete to determine who has suffered most. I am only trying to understand the corrosive mixture of helplessness, responsibility, and shame that I learned to feel as the son of an alcoholic. I realize now that I did not cause my father's illness, nor could I have cured it. Yet for all this grown-up knowledge, I am

ADDITIONAL QUESTIONS FOR
RESPONDING TO READING

1. Does Sanders perceive himself as a victim? Was he helpless as a child? Is he helpless as an adult?
2. Is it possible to feel both hatred and love at the same time? Does Sanders demonstrate any love for his father?
3. What do you take to be Sanders's thesis? Is it explicitly stated or implied? How is the main idea supported in the essay?

still ten years old, my own son's age, and as that boy I struggle in guilt and confusion to save my father from pain.

Consider a few of our synonyms for *drunk*: tipsy, tight, pickled, soused, and plowed; stoned and stewed, lubricated and inebriated, juiced and sluiced; three sheets to the wind, in your cups, out of your mind, under the table; lit up, tanked up, wiped out; besotted, blotto, bombed, and buzzed; plastered, polluted, putrefied; loaded or looped, boozy, woozy, fuddled, or smashed; crocked and shit-faced, corked and pissed, snockered and sloshed. 9

It is a mostly humorous lexicon, as the lore that deals with drunks—in jokes and cartoons, in plays, films, and television skits—is largely comic. Aunt Matilda nips elderberry wine from the sideboard and burps politely during supper. Uncle Fred slouches to the table glassy-eyed, wearing a lampshade for a hat and murmuring, "Candy is dandy, but liquor is quicker." Inspired by cocktails, Mrs. Somebody recounts the events of her day in a fuzzy dialect, while Mr. Somebody nibbles her ear and croons a bawdy song. On the sofa with Boyfriend, Daughter Somebody giggles, licking gin from her lips, and loosens the bows in her hair. Junior knocks back some brews with his chums at the Leopard Lounge and stumbles home to the wrong house, wonders foggily why he cannot locate his pajamas, and crawls naked into bed with the ugliest girl in school. The family dog slurps from a neglected martini and wobbles to the nursery, where he vomits in Baby's shoe. 10

It is all great fun. But if in the audience you notice a few laughing faces turn grim when the drunk lurches onstage, don't be surprised, for these are the children of alcoholics. Over the grinning mask of Dionysus, the leering face of Bacchus, these children cannot help seeing the bloated features of their own parents. Instead of laughing, they wince, they mourn. Instead of celebrating the drunk as one freed from constraints, they pity him as one enslaved. They refuse to believe *in vino veritas*,[1] having seen their befuddled parents skid away from truth toward folly and oblivion. And so these children bite their lips until the lush staggers into the wings. 11

My father, when drunk, was neither funny nor honest; he was pathetic, frightening; deceitful. There seemed to be a leak in him somewhere, and he poured in booze to keep from draining dry. Like a torture victim who refuses to squeal, he would never admit that he had touched a drop, not even in his last year, when he seemed to be dissolving in alcohol before our very eyes. I never knew him to lie 12

---

[1]In wine, truth. [Eds.]

about anything, ever, except about this one ruinous fact. Drowsy, clumsy, unable to fix a bicycle tire, balance a grocery sack, or walk across a room, he was stripped of his true self by drink. In a matter of minutes, the contents of a bottle could transform a brave man into a coward, a buddy into a bully, a gifted athlete and skilled carpenter and shrewd businessman into a bumbler. No dictionary of synonyms for *drunk* would soften the anguish of watching our prince turn into a frog.

Father's drinking became the family secret. While growing up, we children never breathed a word of it beyond the four walls of our house. To this day, my brother and sister rarely mention it, and then only when I press them. I did not confess the ugly, bewildering fact to my wife until his wavering and slurred speech forced me to. Recently, on the seventh anniversary of my father's death, I asked my mother if she ever spoke of his drinking to friends. "No, no, never," she replied hastily. "I couldn't bear for anyone to know." | 13

The secret bores under the skin, gets in the blood, into the bone, and stays there. Long after you have supposedly been cured of malaria, the fever can flare up, the tremors can shake you. So it is with the fevers of shame. You swallow the bitter quinine[2] of knowledge, and you learn to feel pity and compassion toward the drinker. Yet the shame lingers and, because of it, anger. | 14

For a long stretch of my childhood we lived on a military reservation in Ohio, an arsenal where bombs were stored underground in bunkers and vintage airplanes burst into flames and unstable artillery shells boomed nightly at the dump. We had the feeling, as children, that we played within a minefield, where a heedless footfall could trigger an explosion. When Father was drinking, the house, too, became a minefield. The least bump could set off either parent. | 15

The more he drank, the more obsessed Mother became with stopping him. She hunted for bottles, counted the cash in his wallet, sniffed at his breath. Without meaning to snoop, we children blundered left and right into damning evidence. On afternoons when he came home from work sober, we flung ourselves at him for hugs and felt against our ribs the telltale lump in his coat. In the barn we tumbled on the hay and heard beneath our sneakers the crunch of broken glass. We tugged open a drawer in his workbench, looking for screwdrivers or crescent wrenches, and spied a gleaming six-pack among the tools. Playing tag, we darted around the house just in time to see him sway on the rear stoop and heave a finished bottle | 16

---

[2]A bitter substance, derived from the bark of the cinchona tree, used to treat malaria. [Eds.]

TEACHING STRATEGIES

1. Sanders manipulates his tenses for a purpose. Discuss the transitions from past to present to future tense. Point out to your students the power Sanders achieves by reinvoking his childhood memories in the present tense.

2. Sanders's prose is rich in figurative language. Define literary devices such as *allusion, imagery, simile,* and *metaphor,* and ask students to find examples in Sanders's essay.

COLLABORATIVE ACTIVITY

Distribute copies of Theodore Roethke's "My Papa's Waltz," a portion of which Sanders quotes in paragraph 17, and assign groups to consider similarities between the poem's father and the essay's and to consider what Sanders accomplishes with his use of a stanza from this poem. When the groups have finished their work, discuss the poem's connection to the essay with the class.

into the woods. In his good-night kiss we smelled the cloying sweetness of Clorets, the mints he chewed to camouflage his dragon's breath.

I can summon up that kiss right now by recalling Theodore 17 Roethke's lines about his own father:

> The whiskey on your breath
> Could make a small boy dizzy;
> But I hung on like death:
> Such waltzing was not easy.

Such waltzing was hard, terribly hard, for with a boy's scrawny arms I was trying to hold my tipsy father upright.

For years, the chief source of those incriminating bottles and cans 18 was a grimy store a mile from us, a cinderblock place called Sly's, with two gas pumps outside and a mangy dog asleep in the window. Inside, on rusty metal shelves or in wheezing coolers, you could find pop and Popsicles, cigarettes, potato chips, canned soup, raunchy postcards, fishing gear, Twinkies, wine, and beer. When Father drove anywhere on errands, Mother would send us along as guards, warning us not to let him out of our sight. And so with one or more of us on board, Father would cruise up to Sly's, pump a dollar's worth of gas or plump the tires with air, and then, telling us to wait in the car, he would head for the doorway.

Dutiful and panicky, we cried, "Let us go with you!" 19

"No," he answered. "I'll be back in two shakes." 20

"Please!" 21

"No!" he roared. "Don't you budge or I'll jerk a knot in your 22 tails!"

So we stayed put, kicking the seats, while he ducked inside. 23 Often, when he had parked the car at a careless angle, we gazed in through the window and saw Mr. Sly fetching down from the shelf behind the cash register two green pints of Gallo wine. Father swigged one of them right there at the counter, stuffed the other in his pocket, and then out he came, a bulge in his coat, a flustered look on his reddened face.

Because the mom and pop who ran the dump were neighbors of 24 ours, living just down the tar-blistered road, I hated them all the more for poisoning my father. I wanted to sneak in their store and smash the bottles and set fire to the place. I also hated the Gallo brothers, Ernest and Julio, whose jovial faces beamed from the labels of their wine, labels I would find, torn and curled, when I burned the trash. I noted the Gallo brothers' address in California and studied the road atlas to see how far that was from Ohio, because I meant to go out there and tell Ernest and Julio what they were doing to my father, and then, if they showed no mercy, I would kill them.

While growing up on the back roads and in the country schools   25
and cramped Methodist churches of Ohio and Tennessee, I never
heard the word *alcoholic*, never happened across it in books or magazines. In the nearby towns, there were no addiction-treatment programs, no community mental-health centers, no Alcoholics
Anonymous chapters, no therapists. Left alone with our grievous
secret, we had no way of understanding Father's drinking except as
an act of will, a deliberate folly or cruelty, a moral weakness, a sin.
He drank because he chose to, pure and simple. Why our father, so
playful and competent and kind when sober, would choose to ruin
himself and punish his family we could not fathom.

Our neighborhood was high on the Bible, and the Bible was hard   26
on drunkards. "Woe to those who are heroes at drinking wine and
valiant men in mixing strong drink," wrote Isaiah. "The priest and
the prophet reel with strong drink, they are confused with wine, they
err in vision, they stumble in giving judgment. For all tables are full
of vomit, no place is without filthiness." We children had seen those
fouled tables at the local truck stop where the notorious boozers hung
out, our father occasionally among them. "Wine and new wine take
away the understanding," declared the prophet Hosea. We had also
seen evidence of that in our father, who could multiply seven-digit
numbers in his head when sober but when drunk could not help us
with fourth-grade math. Proverbs warned: "Do not look at wine when
it is red, when it sparkles in the cup and goes down smoothly. At
the last it bites like a serpent and stings like an adder. Your eyes will
see strange things, and your mind utter perverse things." Woe, woe.

Dismayingly often, these biblical drunkards stirred up trouble for   27
their own kids. Noah made fresh wine after the flood, drank too
much of it, fell asleep without any clothes on, and was glimpsed in
the buff by his son Ham, whom Noah promptly cursed. In one passage—it was so shocking we had to read it under our blankets with
flashlights—the patriarch Lot fell down drunk and slept with his
daughters. The sins of the fathers set their children's teeth on edge.

Our ministers were fond of quoting St. Paul's pronouncement   28
that drunkards would not inherit the kingdom of God. These grave
preachers assured us that the wine referred to in the Last Supper was
in fact grape juice. Bible and sermons and hymns combined to give
us the impression that Moses should have brought down from the
mountain another stone tablet, bearing the Eleventh Commandment:
Thou shalt not drink.

The scariest and most illuminating Bible story apropos of drun-   29
kards was the one about the lunatic and the swine. We knew it by
heart: When Jesus climbed out of his boat one day, this lunatic came
charging up from the graveyard, stark naked and filthy, frothing at
the mouth, so violent that he broke the strongest chains. Nobody

would go near him. Night and day for years, this madman had been wailing among the tombs and bruising himself with stones. Jesus took one look at him and said, "Come out of the man, you unclean spirits!" for he could see that the lunatic was possessed by demons. Meanwhile, some hogs were conveniently rooting nearby. "If we have to come out," begged the demons, "at least let us go into those swine." Jesus agreed, the unclean spirits entered the hogs, and the hogs raced straight off a cliff and plunged into a lake. Hearing the story in Sunday school, my friends thought mainly of the pigs. (How big a splash did they make? Who paid for the lost pork?) But I thought of the redeemed lunatic, who bathed himself and put on clothes and calmly sat at the feet of Jesus, restored—so the Bible said—to "his right mind."

When drunk, our father was clearly in his wrong mind. He became a stranger, as fearful to us as any graveyard lunatic, not quite frothing at the mouth but fierce enough, quick-tempered, explosive; or else he grew maudlin and weepy, which frightened us nearly as much. In my boyhood despair, I reasoned that maybe he wasn't to blame for turning into an ogre: Maybe, like the lunatic, he was possessed by demons. 30

If my father was indeed possessed, who would exorcise him? If he was a sinner, who would save him? If he was ill, who would cure him? If he suffered, who would ease his pain? Not ministers or doctors, for we could not bring ourselves to confide in them; not the neighbors, for we pretended they had never seen him drunk; not Mother, who fussed and pleaded but could not budge him; not my brother and sister, who were only kids. That left me. It did not matter that I, too, was only a child, and a bewildered one at that. I could not excuse myself. 31

On first reading a description of delirium tremens[3]—in a book on alcoholism I smuggled from a university library—I thought immediately of the frothing lunatic and the frenzied swine. When I read stories or watched films about grisly metamorphoses—Dr. Jekyll becoming Mr. Hyde,[4] the mild husband changing into a werewolf, the kindly neighbor inhabited by a brutal alien—I could not help but see my own father's mutation from sober to drunk. Even today, knowing better, I am attracted by the demonic theory of drink, for when I recall my father's transformation, the emergence of his ugly second self, I find it easy to believe in being possessed by unclean 32

---

[3]Acute delirium caused by alcohol poisoning. [Eds.]
[4]Characters in *The Strange Case of Dr. Jekyll and Mr. Hyde* (1886) by Robert Louis Stevenson (1850–94). [Eds.]

spirits. We never knew which version of Father would come home from work, the true or the tainted, nor could we guess how far down the slope toward cruelty he would slide.

How far a man *could* slide we gauged by observing our back-road 33 neighbors—the out-of-work miners who had dragged their families to our corner of Ohio from the desolate hollows of Appalachia, the tightfisted farmers, the surly mechanics, the balked and broken men. There was, for example, whiskey-soaked Mr. Jenkins, who beat his wife and kids so hard we could hear their screams from the road. There was Mr. Lavo the wino, who fell asleep smoking time and again, until one night his disgusted wife bundled up the children and went outside and left him in his easy chair to burn; he awoke on his own, staggered out coughing into the yard, and pounded her flat while the children looked on and the shack turned to ash. There was the truck driver, Mr. Sampson, who tripped over his son's tricycle one night while drunk and got mad, jumped into his semi, and drove away, shifting through the dozen gears, and never came back. We saw the bruised children of these fathers clump onto our school bus, we saw the abandoned children huddle in the pews at church, we saw the stunned and battered mothers begging for help at our doors.

Our own father never beat us, and I don't think he beat Mother, 34 but he threatened often. The Old Testament Yahweh[5] was not more terrible in His rage. Eyes blazing, voice booming, Father would pull out his belt and swear to give us a whipping, but he never followed through, never needed to, because we could imagine it so vividly. He shoved us, pawed us with the back of his hand, not to injure, just to clear a space. I can see him grabbing Mother by the hair as she cowers on a chair during a nightly quarrel. He twists her neck back until she gapes up at him, and then he lifts over her skull a glass quart bottle of milk, the milk spilling down his forearm, and he yells at her, "Say just one more word, one goddamn word, and I'll shut you up!" I fear she will prick him with her sharp tongue, but she is terrified into silence, and so am I, and the leaking bottle quivers in the air, and milk seeps through the red hair of my father's uplifted arm, and the entire scene is there to this moment, the head jerked back, the club raised.

When the drink made him weepy, Father would pack, kiss each 35 of us children on the head, and announce from the front door that he was moving out. "Where to?" we demanded, fearful each time that he would leave for good, as Mr. Simpson had roared away for good in his diesel truck. "Someplace where I won't get hounded every

---

[5]God; usually translated as "Lord" in the English Bible. [Eds.]

minute," Father would answer, his jaw quivering. He stabbed a look at Mother, who might say, "Don't run into the ditch before you get there," or "Good riddance," and then he would slink away. Mother watched him go with arms crossed over her chest, her face closed like the lid on a box of snakes. We children bawled. Where could he go? To the truck stop, that den of iniquity? To one of those dark, ratty flophouses in town? Would he wind up sleeping under a railroad bridge or on a park bench or in a cardboard box, mummied in rags like the bums we had seen on our trips to Cleveland and Chicago? We bawled and bawled, wondering if he would ever come back.

He always did come back, a day or a week later, but each time 36 there was a sliver less of him.

In Kafka's *Metamorphosis*,[6] opens famously with Gregor Samsa 37 waking up from uneasy dreams to find himself transformed into an insect, Gregor's family keep reassuring themselves that things will be just fine again "when he comes back to us." Each time alcohol transformed our father we held out the same hope, that he would really and truly come back to us, our authentic father, the tender and playful and competent man, and then all things would be fine. We had grounds for such hope. After his tearful departures and chap-fallen returns, he would sometimes go weeks, even months, without drinking. Those were glad times. Every day without the furtive glint of bottles, every meal without a fight, every bedtime without sobs encouraged us to believe that such bliss might go on forever.

Mother was fooled by such a hope all during the forty-odd years 38 she knew Greeley Ray Sanders. Soon after she met him in a Chicago delicatessen on the eve of World War II and fell for his butter-melting Mississippi drawl and his wavy red hair, she learned that he drank heavily. But then so did a lot of men. She would soon coax or scold him into breaking the nasty habit. She would point out to him how ugly and foolish it was, this bleary drinking, and then he would quit. He refused to quit during their engagement, however, still refused during the first years of marriage, refused until my older sister came along. The shock of fatherhood sobered him, and he remained sober through my birth at the end of the war and right on through until we moved in 1951 to the Ohio arsenal. The arsenal had more than its share of alcoholics, drug addicts, and other varieties of escape artists. There I turned six and started school and woke into a child's flickering awareness, just in time to see my father begin sneaking swigs in the garage.

---

[6]A 1915 novella by Franz Kafka (1883–1924). [Eds.]

He sobered up again for most of a year at the height of the Korean   39
War, to celebrate the birth of my brother. But aside from that dry
spell, his only breaks from drinking before I graduated from high
school were just long enough to raise and then dash our hopes. Then
during the fall of my senior year—the time of the Cuban Missile
Crisis,[7] when it seemed that the nightly explosions at the munitions
dump and the nightly rages in our household might spread to engulf
the globe—Father collapsed. His liver, kidneys, and heart all conked
out. The doctors saved him, but only by a hair. He stayed in the
hospital for weeks, going through a withdrawal so terrible that Mother
would not let us visit him. If he wanted to kill himself, the doctors
solemnly warned him, all he had to do was hit the bottle again. One
binge would finish him.

Father must have believed them, for he stayed dry the next fifteen   40
years. It was an answer to prayer, Mother said, it was a miracle. I
believe it was a reflex of fear, which he sustained over the years
through courage and pride. He knew a man could die from drink,
for his brother Roscoe had. We children never laid eyes on doomed
Uncle Roscoe, but in the stories Mother told us he became a fairy-
tale figure, like a boy who took the wrong turn in the woods and was
gobbled up by the wolf.

The fifteen-year dry spell came to an end with Father's retirement   41
in the spring of 1978. Like many men, he gave up his identity along
with his job. One day he was a boss at the factory, with a brass plate
on his door and a reputation to uphold; the next day he was a nobody
at home. He and Mother were leaving Ontario, the last of the many
places to which his job had carried them, and they were moving to
a new house in Mississippi, his childhood stomping ground. As a
boy in Mississippi, Father sold Coca-Cola during dances while the
moonshiners peddled their brew in the parking lot; as a young blade,
he fought in bars and in the ring, winning a state Golden Gloves
championship; he gambled at poker, hunted pheasant, raced motor-
cycles and cars, played semiprofessional baseball, and, along with all
his buddies—in the Black Cat Saloon, behind the cotton gin, in the
woods—he drank hard. It was a perilous youth to dream of
recovering.

After his final day of work, Mother drove on ahead with a car   42
full of begonias and violets, while Father stayed behind to oversee
the packing. When the van was loaded, the sweaty movers broke
open a six-pack and offered him a beer.

[7]1962. [Eds.]

"Let's drink to retirement!" they crowed. "Let's drink to freedom! 43
to fishing! hunting! loafing! Let's drink to a guy who's going home!"

At least I imagine some such words, for that is all I can do, 44
imagine, and I see Father's hand trembling in midair as he thinks
about the fifteen sober years and about the doctors' warning, and he
tells himself, *Goddamnit, I am a free man*, and *Why can't a free man drink
one beer after a lifetime of hard work?* and I see his arm reaching, his
fingers closing, the can tilting to his lips. I even supply a label for the
beer, a swaggering brand that promises on television to deliver the
essence of life. I watch the amber liquid pour down his throat, the
alcohol steal into his blood, the key turn in his brain.

Soon after my parents moved back to Father's treacherous 45
stomping ground, my wife and I visited them in Mississippi with our
four-year-old daughter. Mother had been too distraught to warn me
about the return of the demons. So when I climbed out of the car
that bright July morning and saw my father napping in the hammock,
I felt uneasy, and when he lurched upright and blinked his bloodshot
eyes and greeted us in a syrupy voice, I was hurled back into
childhood.

"What's the matter with Papaw?" our daughter asked.   46

"Nothing," I said. "Nothing!"   47

Like a child again, I pretended not to see him in his stupor, and 48
behind my phony smile I grieved. On that visit and on the few that
remained before his death, once again I found bottles in the workbench, bottles in the woods. Again his hands shook too much for
him to run a saw, to make his precious miniature furniture, to drive
straight down back roads. Again he wound up in the ditch, in the
hospital, in jail, in the treatment center. Again he shouted and wept.
Again he lied. "I never touched a drop," he swore. "Your mother's
making it up."

I no longer fancied I could reason with the men whose names I 49
found on the bottles—Jim Bean, Jack Daniel's—but I was able now
to recall the cold statistics about alcoholism: ten million victims, fifteen
million, twenty. And yet, in spite of my age, I reacted in the same
blind way as I had in childhood, by vainly seeking to erase through
my efforts whatever drove him to drink. I worked on their place
twelve and sixteen hours a day, in the swelter of Mississippi summers,
digging ditches, running electrical wires, planting trees, mowing
grass, building sheds, as though what nagged at him was some list
of chores, as though by taking his worries upon my shoulders I could
redeem him. I was flung back into boyhood, acting as though my
father would not drink himself to death if only I were perfect.

I failed of perfection; he succeeded in dying. To the end, he 50
considered himself not sick but sinful. "Do you want to kill yourself?"
I asked him. "Why not?" he answered. "Why the hell not? What's there
to save?" To the end, he would not speak about his feelings, would not
or could not give a name to the beast that was devouring him.

In silence, he went rushing off the cliff. Unlike the biblical swine, 51
however, he left behind a few of the demons to haunt his children.
Life with him and the loss of him twisted us into shapes that will be
familiar to other sons and daughters of alcoholics. My brother became
a rebel, my sister retreated into shyness, I played the stalwart and
dutiful son who would hold the family together. If my father was
unstable, I would be a rock. If he squandered money on drink, I
would pinch every penny. If he wept when drunk—and only when
drunk—I would not let myself weep at all. If he roared at the Little
League umpire for calling my pitches balls, I would throw nothing
but strikes. Watching him flounder and rage, I came to dread the loss
of control. I would go through life without making anyone mad. I
vowed never to put in my mouth or veins any chemical that would
banish my everyday self. I would never make a scene, never lash out
at the ones I loved, never hurt a soul. Through hard work, relentless
work, I would achieve something dazzling—in the classroom, on the
basketball court, in the science lab, in the pages of books—and my
achievement would distract the world's eyes from his humiliation. I
would become a worthy sacrifice, and the smoke of my burning would
please God.

It is far easier to recognize these twists in my character than to 52
undo them. Work has become an addiction for me, as drink was an
addiction for my father. Knowing this, my daughter gave me a placard
for the wall: WORKAHOLIC. The labor is endless and futile, for I
can no more redeem myself through work than I could redeem my
father. I still panic in the face of other people's anger, because his
drunken temper was so terrible. I shrink from causing sadness or
disappointment even to strangers, as though I were still concealing
the family shame. I still notice every twitch of emotion in those faces
around me, having learned as a child to read the weather in faces,
and I blame myself for their least pang of unhappiness or anger. In
certain moods I blame myself for everything. Guilt burns like acid in
my veins.

I am moved to write these pages now because my own son, at 53
the age of ten, is taking on himself the griefs of the world, and in
particular the griefs of his father. He tells me that when I am gripped
by sadness, he feels responsible; he feels there must be something

WRITING SUGGESTION

Reread paragraphs 9–10, in which Sanders
discusses the public image of alcoholism. Then
write an essay in which you discuss how advertising, television programs, films, and popular
sports and media personalities shape (and distort) our view of what it really means to be
"under the influence." Give specific examples
to support your thesis.

he can do to spring me from depression, to fix my life. And that crushing sense of responsibility is exactly what I felt at the age of ten in the face of my father's drinking. My son wonders if I, too, am possessed. I write, therefore, to drag into the light what eats at me— the fear, the guilt, the shame—so that my own children may be spared.

I still shy away from nightclubs, from bars, from parties where 54 the solvent is alcohol. My friends puzzle over this, but it is no more peculiar than for a man to shy away from the lions' den after seeing his father torn apart. I took my own first drink at the age of twenty-one, half a glass of burgundy. I knew the odds of my becoming an alcoholic were four times higher than for the children of nonalcoholic fathers. So I sipped warily.

I still do—once a week, perhaps, a glass of wine, a can of beer, 55 nothing stronger, nothing more. I listen for the turning of a key in my brain.

RESPONDING TO READING

1. What could Sanders have done as a child to "make things better?" What could he have done as an adult? What does he know now that he did not know as a child?   **2.** Sanders reveals a variety of conflicting emotions about his father. Where does he reveal anger? Guilt? Frustration? Disgust? Fear? Have you ever realized the fallibility of one of your parents? With what emotions did you struggle?   **3.** At least part of Sanders's purpose in this essay is to sort out his feelings toward his father; he also seems to want his readers to understand his father's illness and how it affected him. What other goals do you think he hopes to achieve? How does the essay's title reveal the author's purposes?

Harvest Home

DAVID BRADLEY

Pennsylvania-born David Bradley (1950–   ) is an editor, teacher, novelist, lecturer, and reviewer. His two novels, *South Street* (1975) and *The Chaneysville Incident* (1981), have established him as an author concerned with racism, history, and the meaning of community. Bradley's mother once told him a story about thirteen runaway slaves who chose death rather than a return to slavery and were buried in unmarked graves. This story he used as the basis for *The Chaneysville Incident*, a novel blending fact with fiction which won the 1982 PEN/Faulkner Prize. In the following essay, Bradley traces his family's history, which unfolds mostly in western Pennsylvania, up to the time Bradley himself becomes "clan chief."

Thanksgiving 1988. In the house my father built my mother and
I sit down to dine. A snowy cloth and ivory china give wintry background to browns of turkey and stuffing and gravy, mild yellow of
parched corn, mellow orange of candied yams. Amidst those
autumnal shades cranberry sauce flares red like flame in fallen leaves,
and steam rises like scentless smoke. Head up, eyes open, I chant
prefabricated grace (Father, we thank Thee for this our daily bread
which we are about to partake of . . .) and long for the extempora-
neous artistry of my father, now almost a decade dead. His blessings—couched in archaic diction ("Harvest Home," he called this
holiday) and set in meter measured as a tolling bell—were grounded
in a childhood in which daily bread was hoped for, not expected; his
grace had gravity, unlike this airy ditty I now mutter.

Still, it seems there is even in this doggerel dogma (. . . May it
nourish our souls and bodies . . .) an echo of his voice. Hope flutters
in me, rises as I come to the end (. . . in Jesus' name and for His
sake . . .), then hangs, gliding in the silence, as I pause and listen.
My mother sits, head bowed, patient and unsurprised; for nine years
I have paused so, just short of "amen." What I wait for she has never
asked. And I have never before said.

Once there were more of us. For once we were a mighty clan,
complete with house and lineage. As we are dark (and sometimes
comely), outsiders might expect us to trace that lineage to Africa, but
we have benign contempt for those who pin their pride to ancestries
dotted by the Middle Passage[1] or *griot*[2]-given claims to Guinean
thrones. For what is Africa (spicy groves, cinnamon trees, or ancient
dusky rivers?) to a clan that knows, as we know, the precise when
and where of our origin: on March 10, 1836, in Seaford, Delaware.
Then and there a justice of the peace named Harry L-something (the
paper is browned, the ink faded, and ornate script all but undeci-
pherable) certified that a "Col. man by the name of Peter Bradley"
was henceforth a freedman. This Peter was our progenitor.

Outsiders might wonder that we do not fix our origin in 1815,
the year of Peter's birth. The reason: the slave laws—what oxymoron
that!—decreed that a bondsman had right to neither property nor
person. Peter could not own a family, for he did not own himself.
But on March 10, Peter's master gave Peter to Peter for Peter's
birthday; this not only made him, legally, his own man but entitled
him to purchase a (black) woman. He could have owned her, and

FOR OPENERS

Ask students to take a few minutes to outline
a family tree, filling in as many branches as they
can. How far back can most students go? (Most
will probably not be able to go beyond their
grandparents. Their limited knowledge of their
ancestors will effectively contrast with Bradley's
detailed family portrait.) Some points to note:
Bradley's family has probably been in the United
States longer than most white students' families;
tracing family history is difficult and challenging;
knowledge of family history can strengthen a
family's sense of unity.

---

[1]Best known of the so-called "triangular trade" routes (shipping patterns with three destinations) of colonial commerce. In the African slave trade, rum was sent to Africa in exchange for
slaves, who were brought (via the Middle Passage) to the West Indies or to the American South
to be sold. [Eds.]

[2]African tribal storyteller. [Eds.]

any children he fathered on her. But he did not. Peter wed a free woman; thus the two sons he sired were free from the moment of their birth. But Peter, by that time, was not. For after being given by his master to himself he gave himself to his Master, and became a minister of the gospel.

Such service became a clan tradition. Both Peter's sons became 5 ministers, licensed by the African Methodist Episcopal Zion Church, the first denomination organized by American blacks who chafed at the unequal opportunity offered by the Methodist Episcopal Church. One son was "M.A."—we do not know his full name, or date of birth. The other was Daniel Francis, born in 1852. Through him our line descends.

Daniel Francis became a minister at the age of nineteen. Although 6 we know nothing of his early assignments, we are sure that they were plentiful, for Zion Methodists followed the dictate of John Wesley[3] that ministers should never stand long in any pulpit, lest they become too powerful. And we know that the Presiding Bishop eventually sent him to Williamsport, Pennsylvania, where he met Cora Alice Brewer. Though in those rigid times, Daniel Francis, at forty-four, would have been called a confirmed bachelor and Cora Alica, at twenty-seven, old enough to be called a spinster, love blossomed into marriage in 1896. The first fruit of the union was a man-child, John, born in 1898. A daughter, Gladys, followed in 1900. More sons, David and Andrew, were born in 1905 and 1906, after the family left Williamsport for Sewickley, Pennsylvania, outside Pittsburgh.

The house came in 1911, when Daniel Francis, who had been 7 reassigned at least five times since Williamsport, was sent to a church called Mt. Pisgah, in the town of Bedford, in the south-central part of Pennsylvania. As Mt. Pisgah had no parsonage, Daniel Francis went ahead of the family to find a place to live. On the train he met a man called Bixler, who offered to sell him an eleven-acre homestead two miles west of Bedford, near the hamlet of Wolfsburg. The price was steep (seven hundred and fifty dollars), the terms usurious (one hundred dollars down, one hundred per year plus annual interest and a widow's dower), but Daniel Francis found both price and terms acceptable, perhaps because there were no other terms at all. And so, in the spring of 1912, our clan took up residence in our first permanent home.

But Daniel Francis did not see the Wolfsburg property as just a 8 home. In early 1915 he announced plans to create what the local weekly, the *Bedford Gazette*, called a "an attractive summer resort for

---

[3]British founder of Methodism (1703–91). [Eds.]

those of his race who will gather here from Pittsburgh and Western Pennsylvania." His future plans called for the building of a "large tabernacle for divine services, lectures and entertainments" and in time a normal school for the education of black craftsmen modeled on Tuskegee Institute—Booker T. Washington,[4] Daniel Francis told the *Gazette*, had promised to come to Wolfsburg to speak. Although Booker T. Washington never did appear, a camp meeting was held in August on a sylvan portion of the homestead (christened "Green Brier Grove" in printed advertisements) and the next year a loan from the Bedford County Trust Company liberated the deed from Bixler's clutches and brought Daniel Francis's dream closer to reality. But Zion Methodists, like Wesley, feared empire-building pastors; later that year the bishop kicked Daniel Francis upstairs, appointing him Presiding Elder, the spiritual and financial manager of a group of churches in Pennsylvania and eastern Ohio.

But though the promotion killed a dream, it established our clan's mark of achievement: a successful son is he who follows in his father's footsteps and goes a step further. And though it forced us once again to wander, we never forgot the homestead. Somehow we made mortgage payments. By 1921 the homestead was ours, free and clear. A year later we returned to it. It was not, however, a joyful repatriation. On October 15, 1922, Daniel Francis died of "diabetes mellitus." His first son, John, now at twenty-one our chieftain, paid one hundred dollars for a funeral and secured a permit of removal. We escorted the body of Daniel Francis back to Wolfsburg, he to be buried in Mt. Ross, the local Negro cemetery, we to live.

The homestead did not long save us from wandering. Bedford, which to Daniel Francis seemed prosperous enough to support even black ambitions, soon proved capable of supporting few ambitions at all. White youths who wished to do more than sell hats to each other had to leave, if only to get higher education. Black youths, regardless of ambition, were virtually exiled; Bedford had no place for blacks skilled with pens rather than push brooms, and its small black community offered opportunity for exogamy.[5] Some blacks made do. Bradleys do not make do.

And so we dispersed. Gladys married a man named Caldwell and settled in Cleveland, Ohio. David finished high school, won a scholarship, and went South to college. Andrew, after graduation, attached himself to the local Democratic party—a quixotic alliance, as Bedford blacks were fewer and less powerful than Bedford Democrats—and then went east to Harrisburg, the capital. John, who supported the

9

10

11

ADDITIONAL QUESTIONS FOR RESPONDING TO READING

1. What would you say is the *tone* of Bradley's essay? What elements contribute to the creation of this mood?
2. What humor do you find in "Harvest Home"?
3. What important lesson about truth does Bradley learn from his father? From his Uncle John? Are these lessons contradictory? How might you imagine these lessons influenced Bradley in his decision to become a writer?
4. To whom is the story relevant? That is, is it strictly about the Bradleys, or does it have importance for other African-American families? For families of other racial heritages?
5. Why does Bradley call "slave laws" an oxymoron (paragraph 4)?

---

[4]Black educator (1856–1915), founder of Tuskegee Institute in Alabama. [Eds.]
[5]Custom of marrying outside the tribe, clan, family, or other social unit. [Eds.]

clan until Andrew's graduation, married and settled in Sewickley, and fathered three daughters. But though we dispersed, the homestead remained—a haven in time of trouble, a gathering place for feasts, a totem signifying that, though we were wanderers, we were not Gypsies.

That is what it signified to outsiders. And so it was that in 1956, 12 our clan's one hundred and twentieth year, the *Gazette*, by then a daily, found our clan of local interest. "The rise of the Bradley family from the enforced degradation of slavery to dignity and high achievement is not unparalleled in the history of the American Negro," wrote reporter Gene Farkas. "But it is certainly one of the more outstanding examples of hard-won Negro accomplishment in the nation and the state. In the annals of Bedford County, the story of the Bradley family is without precedent . . . for it was from these hills and valleys, from the one-room schoolhouse at Wolfsburg and the old Bedford High School . . . that the Bradley boys emerged to eminence and respect."

Cosmopolitans and outsiders would have said that it was Andrew 13 who had risen highest; in 1954, he became State Budget Secretary and the first black to sit in the Pennsylvania Governor's Cabinet. But local interest, and perhaps a sense of our clan's traditions—he even used the phrase "the footsteps of his father"—caused Farkas to give more space to David, who in 1948 had been elected an AME Zion General Officer—a step beyond Daniel Francis's final rank of Presiding Elder. Though his new duties called for travel, he was free to fix his base where he chose; David purchased land adjacent to the homestead and built what Farkas called "a modern stone bungalow," in which he housed both his own family and Cora Alice, who spent her days in the spartan familiarity of the homestead but at night enjoyed the sybaritic comforts of indoor plumbing and central heating.

Farkas did a good job for an outsider. Although he did not spe- 14 cifically mention another of David's contributions to the clan, that he alone of the third generation sired a son to carry on the name, the photographs that accompanied the story did depict the lad, David Jr., then six. And though Farkas did give short shrift to John, not mentioning the names of his wife and children (as he did with David and Andrew) and referring to his occupation with a euphemism (". . . he has worked for a private family for 25 or 30 years"), in this he only reflected the values of outsiders; men who hold advanced degrees and cabinet posts are commonly deemed more noteworthy than those who held rakes in "private" service. Farkas cannot be blamed for this affront to our dignity. How was he to know that the man so slighted was the chief among us? For the tale as Farkas told it was the tale as we told it to him. Sadly, it was the tale as we were telling it to our children. Except at Harvest Home.

Even when I was too young to comprehend a calendar I knew   15
Harvest Home was coming; I could tell by the smell of my grandmother, Cora Alice. Usually she spent her days in the old homestead
crocheting, reading the *Gazette*, and listening in on the party line. But
the week before Harvest Home she abandoned leisure, stoked up her
big Majestic coal stove, and got busy baking: tangy gingerbread,
golden pound cakes, and pies of pumpkin, sweet potato, and mince.
In the evening she would come back to the house my father built
perfumed with molasses and mace, and I would crawl into her lap
and lick surreptitiously at the vestiges of brown sugar that clung to
her upper arms. The night before the feast she would not return at
all. That would be my signal; I would sneak to my window to keep
watch on the homestead a hundred yards away. At last I would see
a sweep of headlights. I would press my ear against the gelid glass
and listen. The sounds of car doors slammed, greetings shouted,
would not satisfy me—I would stand, shivering, until I heard an odd
and mighty booming. Then I would know the clan was gathered.

The next afternoon would find us in the rear chamber of the   16
homestead, arrayed around a dark Victorian table with saurian legs
and dragon feet. To an outsider the order of our seating might have
seemed to loosely reflect Fifties customs—most of the children placed
at a separate table and all the men at the main table, while the women
served. In fact, it reflected our deep reverence for name and blood.
The segregated children had the blood—they were of the fifth generation—but had it through their mothers; none had the name. The
women who served—including Cora Alice herself, who, although
she presided over the gathering, did so from the sideboard—had the
name by marriage. The only woman at table not of the blood was my
Uncle Andrew's wife, Gussie, who made it clear she waited on no
one. She also smoked and drank in public. (My grandmother had
declared her mad; she was left alone.) My cousins—the women of
our fourth generation—although they'd lost the name through marriage, had the blood and so had seats. Their husbands had seats only
as a courtesy to the chief of a related clan—once a husband tried to
displace his wife; Cora Alice took away his plate. The men of the
third generation had both blood and name, and so had seats of honor.
And I too had a seat of honor: a creaky chair, made tall with cushions,
set at the table's foot. For I was David, son of David, the only male
of the fourth generation, the only hope for the continuation of the
name.

I, of course, did not then understand why I alone among the   17
children had a seat at the table. But I was glad I did. For when all
closed eyes and bowed heads to listen to my father bless our gathering
in fervent baritone extempore, I could raise my head and look down

the table, a virtual continent of sustenance—Great Lakes of gravy, Great Plains of yams, tectonic plates of turkey slices thrust upward by the bulk of the bird itself, which rose like Rushmore. But in the place of the visage of Washington or Lincoln this Rushmore was crowned by a huge dark head with massive jowls, pebbly with beard, a broad flat nose, a gently sloping forehead, grizzled brows: the visage of our clan chief, my Uncle John.

18 Uncle John was titanic. Below his head was a neck thick with muscle and a broad chest, powerful and deep, on which his huge hands prayerfully rested, the fingers like a logjam. When the food was duly blessed the jam burst. For Uncle John did not eat—he fed. His plate—actually a spare meat platter—was filled and refilled with turkey, potatoes, and stuffing all drenched with tureens of gravy, and garnished with enough corn on the cob to fill a field—once I counted a dozen ears lying ravished by his plate, and always I watched his trench work with apprehension, convinced that one day he would explode.

19 He made all the noise of an explosion. He did not talk—he roared. He roared with jokes—always corny and often in poor taste—and aphorisms—"You can live forever if you don't quit breathin!"—and responses to conversational gambits—once Uncle Andrew twitted him about his shabby clothing. "Rags to riches! I ain't rich yet!" Uncle John roared, off and on for the next twenty years. Mostly, though, he roared with a laugh as big as he was, so concussive it subsumed all ordinary vibrations. Halfway between a boom and a cackle, Uncle John's laugh was like a bushel of corn husks rustling in a hundred-gallon drum. It was not precisely a pleasant sound, but to me it was a Siren song[6]—or perhaps the call of the wild.

20 When I was small I would leave my place as soon as I could to go and stand beside him. He would be busy devouring dessert—quarters of pie, one each of pumpkin, sweet potato, mince—like Cronus[7] consuming his children, but would catch me up in the crook of his arm and balance me effortlessly on his knee, where I would sit in greatest contentment, remarkably unoffended by his smell—sweat, smoke, and bay rum (which he used for no good reason, since he rarely shaved). When I grew too big for that I would simply stand beside him while he finished eating. Then we would go to kill his car. He didn't call it that, of course. He termed it "blowing out the pipes" and claimed that without it the car—a spavined station

---

[6] In Greek mythology, the Sirens were a group of sea nymphs whose sweet songs lured sailors to destruction on the rocks surrounding their island. [Eds.]

[7] In Greek mythology, Cronus was a Titan who ruled the universe until he was dethroned by his son Zeus. [Eds.]

wagon—would never climb the mountains between Bedford and Sewickley. But to me, at six or seven, it seemed like bloody murder.

From the back of the wagon he would take a quart jar of kero- 21 sene—he called it "coal oil"—and give it to me to hold while he started the engine, raised the hood, and removed the air cleaner. Then he would take the jar and begin to pour the coal oil into the unsuspecting intake manifold. The engine would pause in shock, then sputter, bark, and bellow at the same time, while from the tail pipe issued gouts of greasy black smoke. Meanwhile Uncle John poured more coal oil into the carburetor, his expression like that of a father administering foul-tasting medicine to an ailing child. When the jar was empty he would leap behind the wheel and pump the throttle; the engine would scream and thrash madly on its mounts, while the smoke from the tail pipe would take on bile-green overtones and show tiny flicks of flame. After a while Uncle John—at some clue known to him alone—would stop pumping. The engine would rattle, almost stop. Then the kerosene would clear through the cylinders; the grateful engine would settle into a smooth, fast idle, and Uncle John would smile.

Years later I marveled at all of this, not because the car survived 22 it, but because we did. For it took no mechanical genius to see that we had toyed with tragedy, that that abused engine could easily have exploded, covering us with burning fuel, shredding us with shrapnel, generally blowing us to Kingdom Come. And I marveled that, even had I known that then—which I of course did not—it would have made no difference. Because then—and now—those dangerous pyrotechnics seemed a fitting prerequisite for what followed. For when the smoke showed clean and white I would sit beside Uncle John as he gently blipped the throttle—helping, he said, the pistons settle down—and recounted chronicles of the clan.

Clan history was nothing new—I heard it every day. But what I 23 heard daily were parables, intended to indoctrinate me with the values and courage that had let us rise up from slavery. At Harvest Home, Uncle John told a different story—unpretentious, earthy, human as an unlimed outhouse. Cora Alice told me about Daniel Francis, after the barn was struck by lightning, burning his hands in the steaming ashes as he searched for nails with which to rebuild. Uncle John told me about my grandfather misjudging the dosage when he wormed the mule. David told me about the Christmas Eve when he, knowing his family was too poor for presents, asked for nothing and cried himself to sleep—but woke to find a hand-carved train, three walnuts, and one incredible orange. Uncle John told me about the time my father had the back of his pants gored by a roving bull. My grandmother and father told me of the glory of my people. Uncle John told me that we *were* people. This was vital. For it was something we were forgetting.

On Harvest Home 1957 I was drummed out of my clan. My crime was lying—a peccadillo,[8] outsiders might say, especially as all children tell lies occasionally, some frequently. But I lied almost constantly, even when there was nothing to be gained. My father said I'd rather crawl up Fib Alley than march down Truth Street; this drove him crazy. For he believed a sterling reputation was some shield against the sanctions society—both American and Bedford County—could bring to bear on a Negro male. He was proud that we were held in high repute and feared what would happen to me—to all of us—were our name to lose its luster because of my lying. He announced that he would break me of it.   24

But he did not realize how good a liar I'd become—so good I took him in. For a while I told him many obvious lies, let him catch and punish me. Then I tapered off. Catching me less often, he assumed I was lying less. But on that morning he discovered . . . well, I don't recall exactly what he discovered; some silken web of half-truths I had been spinning out for weeks. He confronted me, hard evidence in his hands, hot fury in his face.   25

Corporal punishment was not his way. His cat-o'-ninetails was a Calibanian tongue wetted with Prosperian vocabulary,[9] his lashes sad scenarios starring the local sheriff. That morning he seemed so angry I expected J. Edgar Hoover[10] to make a cameo appearance; I could not imagine what salt he would rub into the wounds—I doubt the uusal "thou shalt never amount to anything if thou keepest this up" would suffice. But he was too angry for anything like the usual treatment; he simply looked at me coldly and in a frighteningly quiet voice said, "Bradleys don't lie."   26

That statement rocked me. For I knew—at least I thought I knew—that it was true. My grandmother did not lie. My father surely did not lie. In the Church he had a reputation for truthfulness—and was in some quarters hated for it. His historical writing was marred by a concern for literal truth; he wouldn't say that two and two were four unless he had a picture of both twos and did the arithmetic three times. And God knows he preached what he saw as truth, and practiced what he preached. So I believed him when he said Bradleys did not lie. But I also knew that I did lie.   27

---

[8]A small sin or fault. [Eds.]

[9]In William Shakespeare's *The Tempest*, Caliban is the son of a devil and a witch; Prospero is a magician. Caliban symbolizes Prospero's control of the so-called lower elements, earth and water. [Eds.]

[10](1895–1972); director of the FBI 1924–72. [Eds.]

On any other day the conclusion of the syllogism—that I was not 28 a Bradley—would have disturbed me. But that day was Harvest Home. I sat in my favored place, accepting accolades and choicest bits of feast food—the heel of the bread, the drumstick of the turkey— that all thought were my due, as sole heir to the name, but I knowing in my heart I had no right to them. I could barely eat.

Later, in the car, I only half listened to Uncle John's chronicle, 29 wondering if I could ever explain to him that I had no right to listen at all. But in the midst of my dilemma I detected a variation from an earlier telling. "Wait," I said. "That's not what you said before."

"No," he said easily. "But don't it work out better that way?" 30

"Well, yeah," I said—and it did work out it better—"but it's not 31 the truth."

"Oh yeah," he said. "The truth. Well, truth is funny. Because 32 you never know it all. So you end up makin' things up to fill in the blanks. Everybody does that. But some folks always makes things up that's make folks sound good, make things sound clean and pretty. Trouble is, the truth usually turns out to be whatever makes the most sense. And if you think you got the whole truth, if it don't make sense, you better make a few things up. And even if you're wrong, it makes a better story." He paused, looked at me. I can't imagine what was on my face—amazement, probably, to hear the head of my clan drumming me back into it as firmly as I'd been drummed out. "Now don't you dare ever tell your daddy I said that," he admonished. And then he sent his laughter rustling and booming around the car.

It is interesting to speculate what would have happened if the 33 *Gazette* had done a follow-up on The Bradley Family Twelve Years Later. By 1968 Andrew had served a second term in the cabinet and served there no longer only because the Democrats had lost the State-house—he remained a force in the Party, and had had influence with both the Kennedy and Johnson administrations. He had also followed in at least one of Daniel Francis's footsteps, becoming a trustee of Lincoln University, an institution originally dedicated to the education of blacks. David, meanwhile, retraced his father's footsteps even as he stepped beyond; still a General Officer, he was rumored to be a strong candidate for Bishop, the highest office in the Church, and also preached at Mt. Pisgah, which was now too small to pay its own pastor. David Jr. seemed poised to follow. A senior in high school, he had been admitted to the University of Pennsylvania and awarded several national scholarships. Occasionally he too occupied the pulpit of Mt. Pisgah. Such facts could have led a reporter to believe the Bradley family was still upward bound, might even have caused him or her to see a rising track in tragedy; though Cora Alice had died in 1960, her funeral was resplendent with dignitaries: two ministers and a Presiding Elder of the AME Zion Church, and—the Democrats were then still in power—several state cabinet secretaries and the governor himself. Had such a story been done—it wasn't—the reporter might have written that, after a hundred and thirty-two years of freedom, the Bradleys continued to rise.

To say that, though, the reporter would have had to ignore clip- 34 pings from the *Gazette* itself—a 1962 story describing the destruction of the Bradley homestead by a fire, photo of the ravished house, its windows like blackened eyes, its clapboard siding stripped away, revealing underlying logs. But to be fair, few reporters would have seen the fire as metaphor. Fewer still would have explored the implications of the fire's aftermath: that for months the house stood unrepaired; that the eventual repairs were minimal; that they were financed by a note cosigned by only David and Andrew; that money to repay the loan was to come from rental of the homestead—to whites. And none, probably, would have understood that the *Gazette's* account of Cora Alice's funeral reiterated an ancient insult. For although the second paragraph noted the careers of David and Andrew, the clan's chief was not mentioned until the final paragraph, and in passing: "She is survived by another son, John Bradley of Sewickley."

I was only nine when my grandmother died, and so recall little 35 of the pomp and circumstance that surrounded her death. I do recall the lavish spread of ham and turkey and covered dishes brought by neighbors to assuage our grief. I recall that Uncle John ate little. And I recall that at the end of the day I stood beside him on my father's lawn while he looked sadly at the homestead. "I guess that's that," he said, and turned away.

And I do recall my grandmother's final Harvest Home. I 36 remember overhearing my elders in council. The only items on the agenda were her failing health and her refusal to give up her days in the homestead. It was moved and seconded that Uncle Andrew take her to Harrisburg to see a specialist. During discussion the opinion was stated (loudly) that no doctor could cure the fact that my grandmother was ninety years old, but the countermotion ("Let her live the way she wants until she dies") was ruled out of order. The motion carried on a two-to-one vote. Council was adjourned, *sine die*.[11] I remember the meal itself—the mood: heavy, the food: dry, the

---

[11]Latin, "without date" (that is, indefinitely adjourned). [Eds.]

laughter: absent without leave. And I remember how quiet Uncle John was as he watched my father and Uncle Andrew get my grandmother settled in Uncle Andrew's Chrysler. Mostly I remember how, after my grandmother was driven away, Uncle John went to work with coal oil and a vengeance; I can still hear the sounds he tortured from the engine, the fan belt screaming, the valve lifters chattering like dry bones, the exhaust bellowing like nothing known to man.

Mostly I recall the burning of the house. For if our homestead was once a totem, was it not a totem still? Was not the burning a harbinger of greater doom? For months I would go, sometimes in the dead of night, and circle the hulk of our homestead like a satellite in orbit, pulled down and thrown up simultaneously. In daylight I would peer into the now exposed basement, full of detritus, alive with rats, in darkness sniff the scorched and rotten timber, seeking a message in the rubble and the stench. And when the house was lost to me—repaired and occupied by people my grandmother would have dismissed as poor white trash—I sought a message in the keepsakes of our clan—chipped photographs, browned bills and deeds, yellowed newspaper clippings. When I combined those mementos with my memories I found discrepancies. And when I thought about what made most sense I found a devastating truth: Bradleys did lie. 37

Most of our lies were common cover-ups of minor moral failures. Others drove to the heart of our history—it seemed doubtful, for example, that Booker T. Washington had ever heard of Daniel Francis. But no lie was as destructive as the one we'd told about my Uncle John. 38

There are many ways to say it. Then, when clichés were new to me and irony was *terra incognita*,[12] I would have said that Uncle John was our black sheep. Now I say he was the nigger in our woodpile, proof that through Bradley blood flowed in dreamers, power brokers, and preachers, it also flowed in a hewer of wood, a drawer of water, a man content to work in service all his life. This embarrassed us, especially as he was not the least among us; he was the first. And so, while we did not deny him, we denied him his place. We allowed outsiders to see him as a minor footnote to our grand history. And then, made bold by headlines and column inches, tokens Society respects, we had forgotten the rules by which a clan exists and survives. Our junior elders—my father and Uncle Andrew—had rebelled against our rightful leader. This, I decided, was the message of the burned boards and beams of the house of Bradley. Our house had fallen because we had fallen away. 39

---

[12]Foreign territory; unknown land. [Eds.]

I did not want to fall away. For the years between the burning 40 and my graduation were hard, lonely, desperate years. I needed my people. I needed my clan. I needed my chief. And though I despaired that we had fallen too far from our ways, I hoped that we had not.

I hoped hardest when those years were ending, when to the world 41 outside I seemed poised to take my clan to greater heights. I feared those heights. And so, on the night of my commencement, as my class assembled for its final march, I stood quietly despairing. They chattered about parties and graduation gifts. I wanted only one gift: the presence of my chief. I doubted I would get it. I had sent him an invitation, but Uncle John was almost seventy and Sewickley was more than a hundred mountainous miles away. To make it worse, a violent thunderstorm was raging. Only a fool would make the trip.

But as we marched up to the auditorium door I saw him standing 42 outside the hall, his threadbare coat and tattered sweater soaked with rain, his eyes searching for me in the line of robed seniors. "Who's *that*?" one of my classmates whispered. "My Uncle John," I said. In that moment he saw me. And even in the auditorium they heard, over the pounding of the processional, his booming, rustling laugh.

On Wednesday, September 26, 1979, the *Gazette* recounted the 43 tale of Bradley clan much as it had in 1956 as part of the page-one obituary of the Reverend David H. Bradley. The burial at Mt. Ross Cemetery would be private, but, later, friends would be received at the Louis Geisel Funeral Home. Memorial services set for the next day, the *Gazette* anticipated, would be appropriately impressive; two AME Zion bishops—mentioned by name—were scheduled to appear. Among the surviving family was listed "John, of Sewickley."

Uncle John was too ill to attend the burial or memorial service, 44 but I prevailed upon the husband of some cousin I did not recall to drive him to the wake, even though his legs were too weak to carry him inside. And so I saw him for the last time when I sat beside him in the car.

He seemed small, shrunken. He joked, but feebly, and when I 45 teased him about the new clothes he was wearing he said, "Rags to riches! Guess I'm gettin' there," but with no force behind it. And he did not even try to laugh. That depressed me, to be honest, more than my father's death, for it told me that my uncle's death would not be long in coming. The death of a father causes grief; the death of a chief causes fear. I was especially fearful. For when he died the chieftainship would descend to me. I was not ready. I was not worthy. And so I sat beside him and cast about for something that would conjure up his laughter.

Inside, I told him, there were two wakes, in adjacent rooms. In 46
our room there was no casket—we'd buried my father that morning.
But in the other, in a grand, flower-bedecked coffin lined with crin-
oline, a rail-thin ancient white lady was laid out. Bedford being a
small town, many visitors paid respects in both rooms. Seeing this,
the undertaker, to make things more convenient, had opened the
doors between the rooms. This caused no problem—until some of
my father's ministerial colleagues arrived. Although ignorant of the
specific arrangements, they knew just what to do on such sad occasions. Gliding as if on casters, they went to my mother and murmured
comfort, then came to give me that two-fisted handshake of condo-
lence before moving on to their next target: the deceased. When they
saw no casket they did not panic—they said more comforting words
while shaking their heads in sadness, their eyes covertly scanning.
Eventually they locked onto the casket in the other room and launched
themselves in that direction.

"I should have let them go," I told Uncle John. "But I just couldn't. 47
So I said, 'Gentlemen, please don't go over there. Because if you do
you're going to think he suffered a lot more than he did.' " I laughed,
hoping that he would laugh too. But his reaction was but a polite
chuckle. "Damn," I said. "I should have let them go."

He looked at me and smiled. "Well, don't let it bother you, son. 48
Next time you tell it, you will." And then he did laugh. Not long,
but long enough. Not loud, but loud enough.

He died nine months later. I did not attend the funeral. It would 49
have been too quiet. Oh, there would have been sound aplenty—
slow hymns, generous lies, even laughter—of a sort. But it would
not have been his laughter, a laugh that could shake the earth. And
hearing other laughter would have made me know that he and his
laugh were gone.

I will never be made to know that, I've decided. I have the right 50
to that decision, for I am clan chief now. I do not have all the wisdom
that a chief needs, but I have come to understand some things. I
understand that the hypocrisy and hubris that brought our house to
ruin were inevitable dangers. For any fool could see that black people
in America could not rise on wings of doves. To even think of rising
we should have quills of iron, rachises[13] of steel. Of course, we do
not have such mighty wings. And so we stiffen our pinfeathers with
myths, flap madly, and sometimes gain a certain height.

---

[13]Spines. [Eds.]

This my clan did. We told ourselves good stories, said we were 51 destined for the skies and launched forth. It worked. We rose. But as we rose we learned that flight is a risky and temporary thing, that there are powerful downdrafts in American air. Our solution was simple: don't look down. That worked too. But it brought us to another danger; we lost contact with the ground.

We were not wrong to dream of rising. Nor were we wrong to 52 keep our eyes fixed ever upward—we did not make the air so treacherous. We were wrong because we ceased to listen for the echoes from below. This, I have decided, we will do no longer. We will rise no further until we do. And so I pause and listen, each year at Harvest Home, as now I pause and listen, while the steam rises from the cooling feast food and hangs accusing in the air. My mother grows impatient; I hear her chair creak with shifting weight. And it comes to me that I could lie about this. Could say I heard laughter booming, or heard, at least, an ancient echo. But truth makes a better story. And so I say, "Amen."

RESPONDING TO READING

1. What emotions do you associate with the idea of the harvest? Of home? Of Thanksgiving? How does Bradley use his knowledge of his readers' associations to his advantage?   **2.** Bradley refers to his family as a "clan" and to nonfamily members as "outsiders"; he also uses the pronoun *we* throughout his essay, even when he speaks of events that preceded his birth. How does this language provide insight into his possible motivations for writing this essay? How does this language affect your reaction to his essay?   **3.** In paragraph 3 Bradley says, "Once there were more of us. For once we were a mighty clan, complete with house and lineage." In paragraph 51 he says, "As we rose we learned that flight is a risky and temporary thing, that there are powerful downdrafts in American air." How do these two statements reveal Bradley's ambivalence about his family history? How is his attitude toward his extended family similar to or different from your attitude toward yours?

Everyday Use

ALICE WALKER

The writings of Alice Walker (see also p. 68) focus on racism and sexism, especially that which confronts African-American women. Her short stories, essays, and poetry are collected in *In Love and Trouble: Stories of Black Women* (1973), *You Can't Keep a Good Woman Down* (1981), and *Living by the Word: Selected Writings* (1988). In

"Everyday Use," from *In Love and Trouble*, Walker tells of a reunion between a family and a daughter who had left her rural home.

For your grandmama

I will wait for her in the yard that Maggie and I made so clean 1
and wavy yesterday afternoon. A yard like this is more comfortable than most people know. It is not just a yard. It is like an extended living room. When the hard clay is swept clean as a floor and the fine sand around the edges lined with tiny, irregular grooves anyone can come and sit and look up into the elm tree and wait for the breezes that never come inside the house.

Maggie will be nervous until after her sister goes: she will stand 2
hopelessly in corners homely and ashamed of the burn scars down her arms and legs, eyeing her sister with a mixture of envy and awe. She thinks her sister has held life always in the palm of one hand, that "no" is a word the world never learned to say to her.

You've no doubt seen those TV shows where the child who has 3
"made it" is confronted, as a surprise, by her own mother and father, tottering in weakly from backstage. (A pleasant surprise, of course: What would they do if parent and child came on the show only to curse out and insult each other?) On TV mother and child embrace and smile into each other's faces. Sometimes the mother and father weep, the child wraps them in her arms and leans across the table to tell how she would not have made it without their help. I have seen these programs.

Sometimes I dream a dream in which Dee and I are suddenly 4
brought together on a TV program of this sort. Out of a dark and soft-seated limousine I am ushered into a bright room filled with many people. There I meet a smiling, gray, sporty man like Johnny Carson who shakes my hand and tells me what a fine girl I have. Then we are on the stage and Dee is embracing me with tears in her eyes. She pins on my dress a large orchid, even though she has told me once that she thinks orchids are tacky flowers.

In real life I am a large, big-boned woman with rough, man- 5
working hands. In the winter I wear flannel nightgowns to bed and overalls during the day. I can kill and clean a hog as mercilessly as a man. My fat keeps me hot in zero weather. I can work outside all day, breaking ice to get water for washing. I can eat pork liver cooked over the open fire minutes after it comes steaming from the hog. One winter I knocked a bull calf straight in the brain between the eyes with a sledge hammer and had the meat hung up to chill before nightfall. But of course all this does not show on television. I am the way my daughter would want me to be: a hundred pounds lighter,

FOR OPENERS

What is the effect of Walker's dedication, "For your grandmama"?

ADDITIONAL QUESTIONS FOR RESPONDING TO READING

1. What elements of the narrative contribute to the sense that the narrator is personally addressing the reader? Is this strategy effective?
2. What sorts of long-held angers and grudges does Dee seem to harbor? Does the mother seem to have any of her own?
3. What are the two views of "heritage" under dispute in Walker's story? Are they contradictory, or is one more valid than the other?

my skin like an uncooked barley pancake. My hair glistens in the hot bright lights. Johnny Carson has much to do to keep up with my quick and witty tongue.

But that is a mistake. I know even before I wake up. Who ever   6
knew a Johnson with a quick tongue? Who can even imagine me looking a strange white man in the eye? It seems to me I have talked to them always with one foot raised in flight, with my head turned in whichever way is farthest from them. Dee, though. She would always look anyone in the eye. Hesitation was no part of her nature.

"How do I look, Mama?" Maggie says, showing just enough of   7
her thin body enveloped in pink skirt and red blouse for me to know she's there, almost hidden by the door.

"Come out into the yard," I say.   8

Have you ever seen a lame animal, perhaps a dog run over by   9
some careless person rich enough to own a car, sidle up to someone who is ignorant enough to be kind to him? That is the way my Maggie walks. She has been like this, chin on chest, eyes on ground, feet in shuffle, ever since the fire that burned the other house to the ground.

Dee is lighter than Maggie, with nicer hair and a fuller figure.   10
She's a woman now, though sometimes I forget. How long ago was it that the other house burned? Ten, twelve years? Sometimes I can still hear the flames and feel Maggie's arms sticking to me, her hair smoking and her dress falling off her in little black papery flakes. Her eyes seemed stretched open, blazed open by the flames reflected in them. And Dee. I see her standing off under the sweet gum tree she used to dig gum out of; a look of concentration on her face as she watched the last dingy gray board of the house fall in toward the red-hot brick chimney. Why don't you do a dance around the ashes? I'd wanted to ask her. She had hated the house that much.

I used to think she hated Maggie, too. But that was before we   11
raised the money, the church and me, to send her to Augusta to school. She used to read to us without pity; forcing words, lies, other folks' habits, whole lives upon us two, sitting trapped and ignorant underneath her voice. She washed us in a river of make-believe, burned us with a lot of knowledge we didn't necessarily need to know. Pressed us to her with the serious way she read, to shove us away at just the moment, like dimwits, we seemed about to understand.

Dee wanted nice things. A yellow organdy dress to wear to her   12
graduation from high school; black pumps to match a green suit she'd made from an old suit somebody gave me. She was determined to stare down any disaster in her efforts. Her eyelids would not flicker for minutes at a time. Often I fought off the temptation to shake her. At sixteen she had a style of her own: and knew what style was.

I never had an education myself. After second grade the school 13
was closed down. Don't ask me why: in 1927 colored asked fewer
questions than they do now. Sometimes Maggie reads to me. She
stumbles along good-naturedly but can't see well. She knows she is
not bright. Like good looks and money, quickness passed her by. She
will marry John Thomas (who has mossy teeth in an earnest face)
and then I'll be free to sit here and I guess just sing church songs to
myself. Although I never was a good singer. Never could carry a
tune. I was always better at a man's job. I used to love to milk till I
was hoofed in the side in '49. Cows are soothing and slow and don't
bother you, unless you try to milk them the wrong way.

I have deliberately turned my back on the house. It is three rooms, 14
just like the one that burned, except the roof is tin; they don't make
shingle roofs any more. There are no real windows, just some holes
cut in the sides, like the portholes in a ship, but not round and not
square, with rawhide holding the shutters up on the outside. This
house is in a pasture, too, like the other one. No doubt when Dee
sees it she will want to tear it down. She wrote me once that no matter
where we "choose" to live, she will manage to come see us. But she
will never bring her friends. Maggie and I thought about this and
Maggie asked me, "Mama, when did Dee ever *have* any friends?"

She had a few. Furtive boys in pink shirts hanging about on 15
washday after school. Nervous girls who never laughed. Impressed
with her they worshiped the well-turned phrase, the cute shape, the
scalding humor that erupted like bubbles in lye. She read to them.

When she was courting Jimmy T she didn't have much time to 16
pay to us, but turned all her faultfinding power on him. He *flew* to
marry a cheap gal from a family of ignorant flashy people. She hardly
had time to recompose herself.

When she comes I will meet—but there they are! 17

Maggie attempts to make a dash for the house, in her shuffling 18
way, but I stay her with my hand. "Come back here," I say. And she
stops and tries to dig a well in the sand with her toe.

It is hard to see them clearly through the strong sun. But even 19
the first glimpse of leg out of the car tells me it is Dee. Her feet were
always neat-looking, as if God himself had shaped them with a certain
style. From the other side of the car comes a short, stocky man. Hair
is all over his head a foot long and hanging from his chin like a kinky
mule tail. I hear Maggie suck in her breath. "Uhnnnh," is what it
sounds like. Like when you see the wriggling end of a snake just in
front of your foot on the road. "Uhnnnh."

Dee next. A dress down to the ground, in this hot weather. A 20
dress so loud it hurts my eyes. There are yellows and oranges enough

TEACHING STRATEGIES

1. Discuss how Walker's portraits of the three women are strong and clearly defined. Your students may not notice that Maggie is presented solely through her movements and gestures, whereas Dee is presented largely through descriptions of her appearance. We know the mother through her thoughts and feelings, so her actions may seem most comprehensible.

2. The story offers many opportunities to discuss literary devices, such as point of view, characterization, irony, and hyperbole.

to throw back the light of the sun. I feel my whole face warming from the heat waves it throws out. Earrings, too, gold and hanging down to her shoulders. Bracelets dangling and making noises when she moves her arm up to shake the folds of the dress out of her armpits. The dress is loose and flows, and as she walks closer, I like it. I hear Maggie go "Uhnnnh" again. It is her sister's hair. It stands straight up like the wool on a sheep. It is black as night and around the edges are two long pigtails that rope about like small lizards disappearing behind her ears.

"Wa-su-zo-Tean-o!" she says, coming on in that gliding way the 21 dress makes her move. The short stocky fellow with the hair to his navel is all grinning and he follows up with "Asalamalakim, my mother and sister!" He moves to hug Maggie but she falls back, right up against the back of my chair. I feel her trembling there and when I look up I see the perspiration falling off her chin.

"Don't get up," says Dee. Since I am stout it takes something of 22 a push. You can see me trying to move a second or two before I make it. She turns, showing white heels through her sandals, and goes back to the car. Out she peeks next with a Polaroid. She stoops down quickly and lines up picture after picture of me sitting there in front of the house with Maggie cowering behind me. She never takes a shot without making sure the house is included. When a cow comes nibbling around the edge of the yard she snaps it and me and Maggie *and* the house. Then she puts the Polaroid in the back seat of the car, and comes up and kisses me on the forehead.

Meanwhile Asalamalakim is going through the motions with Mag- 23 gie's hand. Maggie's hand is as limp as a fish, and probably as cold, despite the sweat, and she keeps trying to pull it back. It looks like Asalamalakim wants to shake hands but wants to do it fancy. Or maybe he don't know how people shake hands. Anyhow, he soon gives up on Maggie.

"Well," I say. "Dee." 24

"No, Mama," she says. "Not 'Dee,' Wangero Leewanika 25 Kemanjo!"

"What happened to 'Dee'?" I wanted to know. 26

"She's dead," Wangero said. "I couldn't bear it any longer being 27 named after the people who oppress me."

"You know as well as me you was named after your aunt Dicie," 28 I said. Dicie is my sister. She named Dee. We called her "Big Dee" after Dee was born.

"But who was *she* named after?" asked Wangero. 29

"I guess after Grandma Dee," I said. 30

"And who was she named after?" asked Wangero. 31

"Her mother," I said, and saw Wangero was getting tired. "That's 32 about as far back as I can trace it," I said. Though, in fact, I probably could have carried it back beyond the Civil War through the branches.

"Well," said Asalamalakim, "there you are." 33

"Uhnnnh," I heard Maggie say. 34

"There I was not," I said, "before 'Dicie' cropped up in our family, 35 so why should I try to trace it that far back?"

He just stood there grinning, looking down on me like somebody 36 inspecting a Model A car. Every once in a while he and Wangero sent eye signals over my head.

"How do you pronounce this name?" I asked. 37

"You don't have to call me by it if you don't want to," said 38 Wangero.

"Why shouldn't I?" I asked. "If that's what you want us to call 39 you, we'll call you."

"I know it might sound awkward at first," said Wangero. 40

"I'll get used to it," I said. "Ream it out again." 41

Well, soon we got the name out of the way. Asalamalakim had 42 a name twice as long and three times as hard. After I tripped over it two or three times he told me to just call him Hakim-a-barber. I wanted to ask him was he a barber, but I didn't really think he was, so I didn't ask.

"You must belong to those beef-cattle peoples down the road," 43 I said. They said "Asalamalakim" when they met you, too, but they didn't shake hands. Always too busy: feeding the cattle, fixing the fences, putting up salt-lick shelters, throwing down hay. When the white folks poisoned some of the herd the men stayed up all night with rifles in their hands. I walked a mile and a half just to see the sight.

Hakim-a-barber said, "I accept some of their doctrines, but 44 farming and raising cattle is not my style." (They didn't tell me, and I didn't ask, whether Wangero [Dee] had really gone and married him.)

We sat down to eat and right away he said he didn't eat collards 45 and pork was unclean. Wangero, though, went on through the chit-lins and corn bread, the greens and everything else. She talked a blue streak over the sweet potatoes. Everything delighted her. Even the fact that we still used the benches her daddy made for the table when we couldn't afford to buy chairs.

"Oh, Mama!" she cried. Then turned to Hakim-a-barber. "I never 46 knew how lovely these benches are. You can feel the rump prints," she said, running her hands underneath her and along the bench. Then she gave a sigh and her hand closed over Grandma Dee's butter

COLLABORATIVE ACTIVITY

Divide the class into three groups, and make each group responsible for analyzing one of the three major characters. What sorts of details does Walker select to describe each? What makes each characterization appropriate?

dish. "That's it!" she said. "I knew there was something I wanted to ask you if I could have." She jumped up from the table and went over in the corner where the churn stood, the milk in it clabber by now. She looked at the churn and looked at it.

"This churn top is what I need," she said. "Didn't Uncle Buddy 47 whittle it out of a tree you all used to have?"

"Yes," I said. 48

"Uh huh," she said happily. "And I want the dasher, too." 49

"Uncle Buddy whittle that, too?" asked the barber. 50

Dee (Wangero) looked up at me. 51

"Aunt Dee's first husband whittled the dash," said Maggie so 52 low you almost couldn't hear her. "His name was Henry, but they called him Stash."

"Maggie's brain is like an elephant's," Wangero said, laughing. 53 "I can use the churn top as a centerpiece for the alcove table," she said, sliding a plate over the churn, "and I'll think of something artistic to do with the dasher."

When she finished wrapping the dasher the handle stuck out. I 54 took it for a moment in my hands. You didn't even have to look close to see where hands pushing the dasher up and down to make butter had left a kind of sink in the wood. In fact, there were a lot of small sinks; you could see where thumbs and fingers had sunk into the wood. It was beautiful light yellow wood, from a tree that grew in the yard where Big Dee and Stash had lived.

After dinner Dee (Wangero) went to the trunk at the foot of my 55 bed and started rifling through it. Maggie hung back in the kitchen over the dishpan. Out came Wangero with two quilts. They had been pieced by Grandma Dee and then Big Dee and me had hung them on the quilt frames on the front porch and quilted them. One was in the Lone Star pattern. The other was Walk Around the Mountain. In both of them were scraps of dresses Grandma Dee had worn fifty and more years ago. Bits and pieces of Grandpa Jarrell's paisley shirts. And one teeny faded blue piece, about the piece of a penny matchbox, that was from Great Grandpa Ezra's uniform that he wore in the Civil War.

"Mama," Wangero said sweet as a bird. "Can I have these old 56 quilts?"

I heard something fall in the kitchen, and a minute later the 57 kitchen door slammed.

"Why don't you take one or two of the others?" I asked. "These 58 old things was just done by me and Big Dee from some tops your grandma pieced before she died."

"No," said Wangero. "I don't want those. They are stitched 59 around the borders by machine."

"That's make them last better," I said. 60

"That's not the point," said Wangero. "These are all pieces of 61 dresses Grandma used to wear. She did all this stitching by hand. Imagine!" She held the quilts securely in her arms, stroking them.

"Some of the pieces, like those lavender ones, come from old 62 clothes her mother handed down to her," I said, moving up to touch the quilts. Dee (Wangero) moved back just enough so that I couldn't reach the quilts. They already belonged to her.

"Imagine!" she breathed again, clutching them closely to her 63 bosom.

"The truth is," I said, "I promised to give them quilts to Maggie, 64 for when she marries John Thomas."

She gasped like a bee had stung her.   65

"Maggie can't appreciate these quilts!" she said. "She'd probably 66 be backward enough to put them to everyday use."

"I reckon she would," I said. "God knows I been saving 'em for 67 long enough with nobody using 'em. I hope she will!" I didn't want to bring up how I had offered Dee (Wangero) a quilt when she went away to college. Then she had told me they were old-fashioned, out of style.

"But they're *priceless*!" she was saying now, furiously; for she has 68 a temper. "Maggie would put them on the bed and in five years they'd be in rags. Less than that!"

"She can always make some more," I said. "Maggie knows how 69 to quilt."

Dee (Wangero) looked at me with hatred. "You just will not 70 understand. The point is these quilts, *these* quilts!"

"Well," I said, stumped. "What would *you* do with them?"   71

"Hang them," she said. As if that was the only thing you *could* 72 do with quilts.

Maggie by now was standing in the door. I could almost hear the 73 sound her feet made as they scraped over each other.

"She can have them, Mama," she said, like somebody used to 74 never winning anything, or having anything reserved for her. "I can 'member Grandma Dee without the quilts."

I looked at her hard. She had filled her bottom lip with check- 75 erberry snuff and it gave her face a kind of dopey, hangdog look. It was Grandma Dee and Big Dee who taught her how to quilt herself. She stood there with her scarred hands hidden in the folds of her skirt. She looked at her sister with something like fear but she wasn't mad at her. This was Maggie's portion. This was the way she knew God to work.

When I looked at her like that something hit me in the top of my 76 head and ran down to the soles of my feet. Just like when I'm in church and the spirit of God touches me and I get happy and shout. I did something I never had done before: hugged Maggie to me, then

WRITING SUGGESTION

Write an essay in which you analyze the relationship between Dee and her mother. Do the two women love each other? Are they alike in any way?

ANSWERS TO RESPONDING TO READING

1. Answers will vary. Readers might identify with the mother because we are allowed to share many of her thoughts and dreams. Many young readers, however, may identify with the narrator's daughters—either rebellious Dee or shy, reclusive Maggie.
2. Students might be asked to analyze their own values here. What is it about those objects or traditions that makes them particularly valuable? Is it the object itself that is valued? Or does it suggest other associations?
3. Although Dee's particular version of youthful rebellion might be most typical of the African-American experience, from a broader perspective the generational conflict Walker portrays seems to be a fairly typical one.

dragged her on into the room, snatched the quilts out of Miss Wangero's hands and dumped them into Maggie's lap. Maggie just sat there on my bed with her mouth open.

"Take one or two of the others," I said to Dee.   77

But she turned without a word and went out to Hakim-a-barber.   78

"You just don't understand," she said, as Maggie and I came out   79
to the car.

"What don't I understand?" I wanted to know.   80

"Your heritage," she said. And then she turned to Maggie, kissed   81
her, and said, "You ought to try to make something of yourself, too, Maggie. It's really a new day for us. But from the way you and Mama still live you'd never know it."

She put on some sunglasses that hid everything above the tip of   82
her nose and her chin.

Maggie smiled; maybe at the sunglasses. But a real smile, not   83
scared. After we watched the car dust settle I asked Maggie to bring me a dip of snuff. And then the two of us sat there just enjoying, until it was time to go in the house and go to bed.

RESPONDING TO READING

1. With whom do you most identify—Dee (Wangero), Maggie, or their mother? Why?   **2.** What family objects and traditions are most important to you? Why? How do your feelings about these things affect your response to the story?   **3.** Do you think the conflicts between Dee and her mother are typical, or does the change in Dee seem extreme? Use your own experience to explain your conclusion.

I Stand Here Ironing

TILLIE OLSEN

Fiction writer, essayist, and teacher, Tillie Olsen (1913–   ) tells compassionate stories of the lives of working-class people. Her best-known story collection is *Tell Me a Riddle* (1961). Born of Russian immigrant parents and raised in Nebraska, she completed the eleventh grade and considers public libraries her college. She raised four children while working and trying to write. Her only novel, *Yonnonido: From the Thirties* (1974), was started when she was nineteen and was finished years later. In her essay collection *Silences* (1978), Olsen writes about how women struggle—against social class, racism, and sexism—to have creative lives. In the following story she writes of the struggles of a single mother in "the pre-relief, pre-WPA world of the Depression."

I stand here ironing, and what you asked me moves tormented back and forth with the iron.

"I wish you would manage the time to come in and talk with me about your daughter. I'm sure you can help me understand her. She's a youngster who needs help and whom I'm deeply interested in helping."

"Who needs help." . . . Even if I came, what good would it do? You think because I am her mother I have a key, or that in some way you could use me as a key? She has lived for nineteen years. There is all that life that has happened outside of me, beyond me.

And when is there time to remember, to sift, to weigh, to estimate, to total? I will start and there will be an interruption and I will have to gather it all together again. Or I will become engulfed with all I did or did not do, with what should have been and what cannot be helped.

She was a beautiful baby. The first and only one of our five that was beautiful at birth. You do not guess how new and uneasy her tenancy in her now-loveliness. You did not know her all those years she was thought homely, or see her poring over her baby pictures, making me tell her over and over how beautiful she had been—and would be, I would tell her—and was now, to the seeing eye. But the seeing eyes were few or nonexistent. Including mine.

I nursed her. They feel that's important nowadays. I nursed all the children, but with her, with all the fierce rigidity of first motherhood. I did like the books then said. Though her cries battered me to trembling and my breasts ached with swollenness, I waited till the clock decreed.

Why do I put that first? I do not even know if it matters, or if it explains anything.

She was a beautiful baby. She blew shining bubbles of sound. She loved motion, loved light, loved color and music and textures. She would lie on the floor in her blue overalls patting the surface so hard in ecstasy her hands and feet would blur. She was a miracle to me, but when she was eight months old I had to leave her daytimes with the woman downstairs to whom she was no miracle at all, for I worked or looked for work and for Emily's father, who "could no longer endure" (he wrote in his good-bye note) "sharing want with us."

I was nineteen, it was the pre-relief, pre-WPA[1] world of the Depression. I would start running as soon as I got off the streetcar,

[1]Works Progress Administration. Part of Franklin Delano Roosevelt's New Deal, the WPA was a program created in 1935 to provide jobs for the unemployed. [Eds.]

FOR OPENERS

To whom is this story being told? Who is the narrator's most important audience?

ADDITIONAL QUESTIONS FOR RESPONDING TO READING

1. Are this story's issues limited to the particular time and place in which it is set? (You might remind students that single-parent families are even more common today and that despite the increased availability of social services, problems remain. For example, good, inexpensive child care is available to only a fraction of those who need it.) Is there anything modern about the story?
2. Do you see the conclusion as hopeful or pessimistic? What is your attitude toward the conclusion?
3. Is Emily's "gift" an appropriate one for her to have developed? Why or why not?
4. Is there any correspondence between the narrator's physical activity (ironing) and her mental activity (interior monologue)?

running up the stairs, the place smelling sour, and awake or asleep to startle awake, when she saw me she would break into a clogged weeping that could not be comforted, a weeping I can hear yet.

After a while I found a job hashing at night so I could be with 10 her days, and it was better. But it came to where I had to bring her to his family and leave her.

It took a long time to raise the money for her fare back. Then she 11 got chicken pox and I had to wait longer. When she finally came, I hardly knew her, walking quick and nervous like her father, looking like her father, thin, and dressed in a shoddy red that yellowed her skin and glared at the pockmarks. All the baby loveliness gone.

She was two. Old enough for nursery school they said, and I did 12 not know then what I know now—the fatigue of the long day, and the lacerations of group life in the kinds of nurseries that are only parking places for children.

Except that it would have made no difference if I had known. It 13 was the only place there was. It was the only way we could be together, the only way I could hold a job.

And even without knowing, I knew. I knew the teacher that was 14 evil because all these years it has curdled into my memory, the little boy hunched in the corner, her rasp, "why aren't you outside, because Alvin hits you? that's no reason, go out, scaredy." I knew Emily hated it even if she did not clutch and implore "don't go Mommy" like the other children, mornings.

She always had a reason why we should stay home. Momma, 15 you look sick, Momma. I feel sick. Momma, the teachers aren't there today, they're sick. Momma, we can't go, there was a fire there last night. Momma, it's a holiday today, no school, they told me.

But never a direct protest, never rebellion. I think of our others 16 in their three-, four-year-oldness—the explosions, the tempers, the denunciations, the demands—and I feel suddenly ill. I put the iron down. What in me demanded that goodness in her? And what was the cost, the cost to her of such goodness?

The old man living in the back once said in his gentle way: "You 17 should smile at Emily more when you look at her." What *was* in my face when I looked at her? I loved her. There were all the acts of love.

It was only with the others I remembered what he said, and it 18 was the face of joy, and not of care or tightness or worry I turned to them—too late for Emily. She does not smile easily, let alone almost always as her brothers and sisters do. Her face is closed and sombre, but when she wants, how fluid. You must have seen it in her pantomimes, you spoke of her rare gift for comedy on the stage that rouses a laughter out of the audience so dear they applaud and applaud and do not want to let her go.

Where does it come from, that comedy? There was none of it in 19
her when she came back to me that second time, after I had had to
send her away again. She had a new daddy now to learn to love, and
I think perhaps it was a better time.

Except when we left her alone nights, telling ourselves she was 20
old enough.

"Can't you go some other time, Mommy, like tomorrow?" she 21
would ask. "Will it be just a little while you'll be gone? Do you
promise?"

The time we came back, the front door open, the clock on the 22
floor in the hall. She rigid awake. "It wasn't just a little while. I didn't
cry. Three times I called you, just three times, and then I ran downstairs to open the door so you could come faster. The clock talked
loud. I threw it away, it scared me what it talked."

She said the clock talked loud again that night I went to the 23
hospital to have Susan. She was delirious with the fever that comes
before red measles, but she was fully conscious all the week I was
gone and the week after we were home when she could not come
near the new baby or me.

She did not get well. She stayed skeleton thin, not wanting to 24
eat, and night after night she had nightmares. She would call for me,
and I would rouse from exhaustion to sleepily call back: "You're all
right, darling, go to sleep, it's just a dream," and if she still called,
in a sterner voice, "now go to sleep, Emily, there's nothing to hurt
you." Twice, only twice, when I had to get up for Susan anyhow, I
went in to sit with her.

Now when it is too late (as if she would let me hold and comfort 25
her like I do the others) I get up and go to her at once at her moan
or restless stirring. "Are you awake, Emily? Can I get you something?" And the answer is always the same. "No, I'm all right, go
back to sleep, Mother."

They persuaded me at the clinic to send her away to a convalescent 26
home in the country where "she can have the kind of food and care
you can't manage for her, and you'll be free to concentrate on the
new baby." They still send children to that place. I see pictures on
the society page of sleek young women planning affairs to raise money
for it, or dancing at the affairs, or decorating Easter eggs or filling
Christmas stockings for the children.

They never have a picture of the children so I do not know if the 27
girls still wear those gigantic red bows and the ravaged looks on the
every other Sunday when parents can come to visit "unless otherwise
notified"—as we were notified the first six weeks.

Oh it is a handsome place, green lawns and tall trees and fluted 28
flower beds. High up on the balconies of each cottage the children

TEACHING STRATEGIES

1. Many students are unable to sympathize with
the mother's story, finding her tone "whiny"
and her belated excuses inadequate. To balance such responses, ask your students to
consider what possible alternatives the
mother really had, and what alternatives a
young single parent with limited financial
resources has today. Some—perhaps
many—will say that things are better today.
Remind them that in 1991 in New Jersey, a
young single mother was arrested—and later
released—when her young daughter was
found locked in her car trunk while the mother
was at work. The mother, who had left toys
and food with her child, said she could find
no affordable day care.

2. Evaluate the effectiveness of such descriptive
phrases as "the lacerations of group life" and
"curdled" into memory, or the effect of the
tightly compacted verbs in paragraph 4.

stand, the girls in their red bows and white dresses, the boys in white suits and gigantic red ties. The parents stand below shrieking up to be heard and the children shriek down to be heard, and between them the invisible wall "Not To Be Contaminated by Parental Germs or Physical Affection."

There was a tiny girl who always stood hand in hand with Emily. 29 Her parents never came. One visit she was gone. "They moved her to Rose Cottage," Emily shouted in explanation. "They don't like you to love anybody here."

She wrote once a week, the labored writings of a seven-year-old. 30 "I am fine. How is the baby. If I write my letter nicly I will have a star. Love." There never was a star. We wrote every other day, letters she could never hold or keep but only hear read—once. "We simply do not have room for children to keep any personal possessions, they patiently explained when we pieced one Sunday's shrieking together to plead how much it would mean to Emily, who loved so to keep things, to be allowed to keep her letters and cards.

Each visit she looked frailer. "She isn't eating," they told us. 31

(They had runny eggs for breakfast or mush with lumps, Emily 32 said later, I'd hold it in my mouth and not swallow. Nothing ever tasted good, just when they had chicken.)

It took us eight months to get her released home, and only the 33 fact that she gained back so little or her seven lost pounds convinced the social worker.

I used to try to hold and love her after she came back, but her 34 body would stay stiff, and after a while she'd push away. She ate little. Food sickened her, and I think much of life too. Oh she had physical lightness and brightness, twinkling by on skates, bouncing like a ball up and down up and down over the jump rope, skimming over the hill; but these were momentary.

She fretted about her appearance, thin and dark and foreign- 35 looking at a time when every little girl was supposed to look or thought she should look like a chubby blonde replica of Shirley Temple. The doorbell sometimes rang for her, but no one seemed to come and play in the house or be a best friend. Maybe because we moved so much.

There was a boy she loved painfully through two school semes- 36 ters. Months later she told me how she had taken pennies from my purse to buy him candy. "Licorice was his favorite and I brought him some every day, but he still liked Jennifer better'n me. Why, Mommy?" The kind of question for which there is no answer.

School was a worry to her. She was not glib or quick in a world 37 where glibness and quickness were easily confused with ability to learn. To her overworked and exasperated teachers she was an over-

conscientious "slow learner" who kept trying to catch up and was
absent entirely too often.

I let her be absent, though sometimes the illness was imaginary.   38
How different from my now-strictness about attendance with the
others. I wasn't working. We had a new baby, I was home anyhow.
Sometimes, after Susan grew old enough, I would keep her home
from school, too, to have them all together.

Mostly Emily had asthma, and her breathing, harsh and labored,   39
would fill the house with a curiously tranquil sound. I would bring
the two old dresser mirrors and her boxes of collections to her bed.
She would select beads and single earrings, bottle tops and shells,
dried flowers and pebbles, old postcards and scraps, all sorts of odd-
ments; then she and Susan would play Kingdom, setting up landscapes and furniture, peopling them with action.

Those were the only times of peaceful companionship between   40
her and Susan. I have edged away from it, that poisonous feeling
between them, that terrible balancing of hurts and needs I had to do
between the two, and did so badly, those earlier years.

Oh there are conflicts between the others too, each one human,   41
needing, demanding, hurting, taking—but only between Emily and
Susan, no, Emily toward Susan that corroding resentment. It seems
so obvious on the surface, yet it is not obvious. Susan, the second
child, Susan, golden- and curly-haired and chubby, quick and articulate and assured, everything in appearance and manner Emily was
not; Susan, not able to resist Emily's precious things, losing or sometimes clumsily breaking them; Susan telling jokes and riddles to company for applause while Emily sat silent (to say to me later; that was
my riddle, Mother, I told it to Susan); Susan, who for all the five years'
difference in age was just a year behind Emily in developing physically.

I am glad for that slow physical development that widened the   42
difference between her and her contemporaries, though she suffered
over it. She was too vulnerable for that terrible world of youthful
competition, of preening and parading, of constant measuring of
yourself against every other, of envy, "If I had that copper hair," "If
I had that skin. . . ." She tormented herself enough about not looking
like the others, there was enough of the unsureness, the having to
be conscious of words before you speak, the constant caring—what
are they thinking of me? without having it all magnified by the merciless physical drives.

Ronnie is calling. He is wet and I change him. It is rare there is   43
such a cry now. That time of motherhood is almost behind me when
the ear is not one's own but must always be racked and listening for
the child cry, the child call. We sit for a while and I hold him, looking

COLLABORATIVE ACTIVITIES

1. Ask students, working in groups, to select the
details in the story that convey information
about the mother and about Emily. For which
character do we feel greater sympathy? Why?
2. Have student groups list Emily's grievances.
Which are her mother's fault? Which could
not have been helped?

out over the city spread in charcoal with its soft aisles of light. "*Shoogily*," he breathes and curls closer. I carry him back to bed, asleep. *Shoogily*. A funny word, a family word, inherited from Emily, invented by her to say: *comfort*.

In this and other ways she leaves her seal, I say aloud. And startle   44
at me saying it. What do I mean? What did I start to gather together, to try and make coherent? I was at the terrible, growing years. War years. I do not remember them well. I was working, there were four smaller ones now, there was not time for her. She had to help be a mother, and housekeeper, and shopper. She had to set her seal. Mornings of crisis and near hysteria trying to get lunches packed, hair combed, coats and shoes found, everyone to school or Child Care on time, the baby ready for transportation. And always the paper scribbled on by a smaller one, the book looked at by Susan then mislaid, the homework not done. Running out to that huge school where she was one, she was lost, she was a drop; suffering over her unpreparedness, stammering and unsure in her classes.

There was so little time left at night after the kids were bedded   45
down. She would struggle over books, always eating (it was in those years she developed her enormous appetite that is legendary in our family) and I would be ironing, or preparing food for the next day, or writing V-mail to Bill, or tending the baby. Sometimes, to make me laugh, or out of her despair, she would imitate happenings or types at school.

I think I said once: "Why don't you do something like this in the   46
school amateur show?" One morning she phoned me at work, hardly understandable through the weeping: "Mother, I did it. I won, I won; they gave me first prize; they clapped and clapped and wouldn't let me go."

Now suddenly she was Somebody, and as imprisoned in her   47
difference as she had been in anonymity.

She began to be asked to perform at other high schools, even in   48
colleges, then at city and statewide affairs. The first one we went to, I only recognized her that first moment when thin, shy, she almost drowned herself into the curtains. Then: Was this Emily? The control, the command, the convulsing and deadly drowning, the spell, then the roaring, stamping audience, unwilling to let this rare and precious laughter out of their lives.

Afterwards: You ought to do something about her with a gift like   49
that—but without money or knowing how, what does one do? We have left it all to her, and the gift has as often eddied inside, clogged and clotted, as been used and growing.

She is coming. She runs up the stairs two at a time with her light   50
graceful step, and I know she is happy tonight. Whatever it was that occasioned your call did not happen today.

"Aren't you ever going to finish the ironing, Mother? Whistler 51 painted his mother in a rocker. I'd have to paint mine standing over an ironing board." This is one of her communicative nights and she tells me everything and nothing as she fixes herself a plate of food out of the icebox.

She is so lovely. Why did you want me to come in at all? Why 52 were you concerned? She will find her way.

She starts up the stairs to bed. "Don't get me up with the rest in 53 the morning." "But I thought you were having midterms." "Oh, those," she comes back in, kisses me, and says quite lightly, "in a couple of years when we'll be all atom-dead they won't matter a bit."

She has said it before. She *believes* it. But because I have been 54 dredging the past, and all that compounds a human being is so heavy and meaningful in me, I cannot endure it tonight.

I will never total it all. I will never come in to say: She was a child 55 seldom smiled at. Her father left me before she was a year old. I had to work her first six years when there was work, or I sent her home and to his relatives. There were years she had care she hated. She was dark and thin and foreign-looking in a world where the prestige went to blondeness and curly hair and dimples, she was slow where glibness was prized. She was a child of anxious, not proud, love. We were poor and could not afford for her the soil of easy growth. I was a younger mother, I was a distracted mother. There were the other children pushing up, demanding. Her younger sister seemed all that she was not. There were years she did not want me to touch her. She kept too much in herself, her life was such she had to keep too much in herself. My wisdom came too late. She has much to her and probably little will come of it. She is a child of her age, of depression, of war, of fear.

RESPONDING TO READING

1. Olsen's narrator gives historical background in paragraph 9 and social background in paragraph 55. Does such background explain her relationship with Emily?   **2.** In light of your own relationships with your parents, do you believe the central explanation offered by Emily's mother for what she sees as her shortcomings as a parent—"My wisdom came too late"—is justified?   **3.** Do you think Emily understands her mother's struggle? Has she survived unharmed, or has her childhood had a negative effect on her?

WRITING SUGGESTION

Write a letter from Emily to her mother—or to her long-absent father. In this letter, present her version of events and express her attitudes toward her parents and siblings.

ANSWERS TO RESPONDING
TO READING

1. Details of historical and social background help to explain the mother's relationship with her daughter. (For additional background about the Depression era, students can read Studs Terkel's "Hard Times" in Chapter 9.)
2. Answers will vary.
3. Like her mother, Emily has learned survival techniques. She has not emerged from childhood unscathed, but she has learned to cope with the pressures to which she may be subjected.

FOR OPENERS

"What did I know, what did I know?" What does the poet know now that he did not know as a child?

ADDITIONAL QUESTIONS FOR RESPONDING TO READING

1. How could you paraphrase the complex of emotions the poet has come to recognize in his father?
2. How would you define the particular kind of love the father felt for his son?

COLLABORATIVE ACTIVITY

Ask your students to read Raymond Carver's poem "Photograph of My Father in His Twenty-Second Year" (included in his essay "My Father's Life," which appears earlier in this chapter). Then assign students, working in groups, to identify similarities and differences in the two speakers' attitudes toward their fathers. (If your students have read Theodore Roethke's "My Papa's Waltz" in conjunction with Scott Russell Sanders's "Under the Influence," page 336, they can include this poem in the exercise as well.)

WRITING SUGGESTION

Rewrite "Those Winter Sundays" in the form of a eulogy to be delivered by the son at his father's funeral. You may use language from the poem, but you should also blend in invented details that will characterize the father and present his struggle in specific terms.

ANSWERS TO RESPONDING TO READING

1. The father has warmed the house and polished his son's shoes. But the son seems to have feared the "chronic anger" of his father's pent-up and unexpressed frustrations. Words that reveal the poet's understanding of his father's hardships include "Sundays too"; "cracked hands that ached"; "splintering"; "breaking"; "indifferently"; and "austere and lonely."
2. Answers will vary.
3. The mature speaker seems to feel some remorse for his own youthful blindness.

Those Winter Sundays

ROBERT HAYDEN

Robert Hayden (1913–1980) published his first book of poems, *Heart-Shaped in the Dust*, in 1940. He taught at Fiske University and the University of Michigan and served as a consultant in poetry to the Library of Congress. His belief that racism is best understood through historical causes is evident in his poems about the slave rebellions. Some of his many works include *A Ballad of Remembrance* (1962), *Words in Mourning Time* (1970), *American Journal* (1978), and *Complete Poems* (1985). Hayden once said that "writing poetry is one way of coming to grips with both inner and external realities." "Those Winter Sundays" is from the 1975 collection *Angle of Ascent, New and Selected Poems*.

Sundays too my father got up early
and put his clothes on in the blueblack cold,
then with cracked hands that ached
from labor in the weekday weather made
banked fires blaze. No one ever thanked him.   5

I'd wake and hear the cold splintering, breaking,
When the rooms were warm, he'd call,
and slowly I would rise and dress,
fearing the chronic angers of that house,

Speaking indifferently to him,   10
who had driven out the cold
and polished my good shoes as well.
What did I know, what did I know
of love's austere and lonely offices?

RESPONDING TO READING

1. Other than having "driven out the cold," what has the father done for his son? To what might the "chronic angers" (line 9) refer? What words in this poem reveal the speaker's understanding of the physical and emotional hardships his father faced?   **2.** What do you know now about your parents' responsibilities and sacrifices that you did not know as a child?   **3.** What does line 13's repetition of "What did I know, what did I know" reveal about the speaker's attitude toward his father?

Heritage

LINDA HOGAN

Linda Hogan (1947–   ), born in Oklahoma, now lives in Colorado, where she works as a teacher and writer. She is active in the Native American movement, especially in the promotion of Native American women's literature. Hogan's collections of poetry include *Calling Myself Home* (1979), *Daughters, I Love You* (1981), *Eclipse* (1983), and *Seeing Through the Sun* (1985). Her short fiction is collected in *That Horse* (1985) and *The Big Woman* (1987), and her first novel, *Mean Spirit*, was published in 1991. In "Heritage," from *Calling Myself Home*, Hogan connects her physical appearance and character traits with those of her family.

From my mother, the antique mirror
where I watch my face take on her lines.
She left me the smell of baking bread
to warm fine hairs in my nostrils,
she left the large white breasts that weigh down   5
my body.

From my father I take his brown eyes,
the plague of locusts that leveled our crops,
they flew in formation like buzzards.

From my uncle the whittled wood   10
that rattles like bones
and is white
and smells like all our old houses
that are no longer there. He was the man
who sang old chants to me, the words   15
my father was told not to remember.

From my grandfather who never spoke
I learned to fear silence.
I learned to kill a snake
when you're begging for rain.   20

And grandmother, blue-eyed woman
whose skin was brown,
she used snuff.
When her coffee can full of black saliva
spilled on me   25
it was like the brown cloud of grasshoppers

FOR OPENERS

What does the speaker mean to suggest in the poem's last two lines?

ADDITIONAL QUESTIONS FOR RESPONDING TO READING

1. What physical characteristics has the speaker inherited from her parents and grandparents? What else has she inherited?
2. How does the image of the "antique mirror" (line 1) express the poem's theme or themes? What other images convey these themes?

COLLABORATIVE ACTIVITY

Ask students to work in groups to identify the images that have positive and negative associations for them. In class discussion, consider these questions: Do all groups classify images in the same way? Does Hogan's speaker share readers' reactions? Is the speaker's attitude toward her heritage essentially positive, negative, or ambivalent?

WRITING SUGGESTION

What do you consider to be your heritage? Write an essay in which you discuss the positive and negative attributes you have inherited from your parents and your culture.

that leveled her fields.
It was the brown stain
that covered my white shirt,
my whiteness a shame.   30
That sweet black liquid like the food
she chewed up and spit into my father's mouth
when he was an infant.
It was the brown earth of Oklahoma
stained with oil.   35
She said tobacco would purge your body of poisons.
It has more medicine than stones and knives
against your enemies.

That tobacco is the dark night that covers me.
She said it is wise to eat the flesh of deer   40
so you will be swift and travel over many miles.
She told me how our tribe has always followed a stick
that pointed west
that pointed east.

From my family I have learned the secrets   45
of never having a home.

ANSWERS TO RESPONDING TO READING

1. Answers will vary.
2. The poem expresses unspoken lessons the speaker has learned. These are not practical lessons but learned attitudes toward life and the world.
3. The speaker is confused about her heritage. On the one hand, her heritage has made her fearful, suspicious, and ashamed: She has learned to fear words and chants that should not be uttered, to fear silences and pestilences, and to feel shame for growing away from her people. On the other hand, she also feels a sense of pride and identification with a group of people who no longer have any home to claim.

RESPONDING TO READING

1. What traits, abilities, values, habits, or fears have you inherited from your parents? What do you think you will pass on to your children?   **2.** What important lessons has the speaker learned? Are these lessons primarily practical or theoretical? Explain.   **3.** What is the speaker's heritage? Is it something she is proud of? Ashamed of? Afraid of? Confused about? Do you have conflicting feelings toward your own heritage? Explain.

WRITING: ACROSS THE GENERATIONS

1. When Joan Didion looks at a snapshot of her grandfather as a young man on skis, she examines his face and says, "I . . . do and do not see my own" (paragraph 3). What does she mean? Write an essay in which you discuss in what respects this sentiment is true for one or two other writers represented in this chapter—for instance, for Raymond Carver, Gary Soto, or Scott Russell Sanders. If you like, you may also discuss in what sense is it true for you.

2. What role does setting play in essays about family? For example, how is the concept of home defined? How important is the geographical location? The landscape? Discuss the development of setting in two or three of the essays in this chapter; or, consider the role of setting in shaping your own memories about your family.

3. Consider the impotence, inadequacy, and guilt expressed by the narrator of Tillie Olsen's story "I Stand Here Ironing." Which of the parents portrayed in this chapter's selections might have experienced similar feelings of regret and guilt? Focusing on two of this chapter's selections, write an essay in which you consider the reasons for each parent's feelings and explain whether you believe such feelings are justified in each case.

4. Several of the writers represented in this chapter—for example, Kingston, Momaday, and Carver—present fairly detailed biographical sketches of their subjects. Using these essays as guides, write a detailed biographical sketch of a member of your family. Make certain that the essay conveys a clear sense of the person's importance to you.

5. Scott Russell Sanders says, "For all this grown-up knowledge, I am still ten years old, . . . and as that boy I struggle in guilt and confusion to save my father from pain" (paragraph 8). In what sense do you share this dual perspective toward your own parents?

6. In many of the selections in this chapter, central figures are portrayed as outsiders, even outcasts. Sometimes these people have chosen isolation themselves, sometimes they have been set apart by their behavior, and sometimes they have been ostracized by the society or by their own family. Analyze the factors that might have led various individuals portrayed in this chapter to be isolated.

7. David Bradley says that for his family "a successful son is he who follows in his father's footsteps and goes a step further" (paragraph 9). Does this statement apply to your own family? Write an essay in which you discuss how and why.

8. Some writers—for example, Alice Walker and Scott Russell Sanders—seem to have good reason to feel anger toward their parents. Are there negative events or situations in your own life for which you blame your parents? Identify several such events, and explain in an essay why you believe your anger is justified.

5
ATTITUDES ABOUT GENDER

CONFRONTING THE ISSUES

Present the class with each of the following scenarios, one at a time. In each case, ask students how they themselves would react to the scenario, how they think most males would react, and how they believe most females would react. In class discussion, try to account for the differences in male and female responses as well as the differences in the behavior expected by the two genders.

- At a sporting event, someone insults your date.
- A tire of your car blows out on a busy highway. No other passengers are in the car.
- You miss the last bus home. You live a mile away, and it is 11 P.M.
- An unusually beautiful woman walks by. You are alone.
- An unusually beautiful woman walks by. You are with several friends.
- An unusually handsome man walks by. You are alone.
- An unusually handsome man walks by. You are with several friends.
- A male teacher is having trouble moving a large piece of audiovisual equipment.
- Your dentist places a reassuring hand on your arm.
- Your best friend stops by with his or her new baby.
- You are told by a recruiter that the job for which you are applying has traditionally gone to a man because it calls for supervision of an all-male staff.
- You go with a male friend to see a sentimental film that really moves you emotionally.
- Alone at a fraternity party, you suddenly feel ill. You really don't know anyone at the party, but a fraternity brother tells you you can lie down and rest in his room until you feel better.
- You see a young teenager harassing an elderly man.
- You have always been interested in the health professions, but you do not feel you can invest the time or money required for medical school. You learn you have been awarded a full-tuition scholarship to a four-year baccalaureate program in nursing.
- You are given tickets to the Superbowl and to the hottest new musical on Broadway. The only catch is that both are for the same day.
- You read in your college newspaper that a student you know has filed rape charges

Until 1920, the struggle for women's rights in the United States centered on winning the right to vote. The next wave of feminism, developing alongside the civil rights movement in the 1960s and continuing today, has focused on practical issues like equal pay for equal work but also on subtler (though no less important) issues, such as changing stereotyped attitudes toward both sexes and restructuring the traditional nuclear family. Attitudes about gender have changed dramatically over the last twenty-five years, and they continue to change. For some, of course, the changes have produced confusion and anger as well as liberation. However, many men and women—uncomfortable with the demands of confining sex roles and unhappy with the expectations those roles create—yearn for less rigidity, for an escape from stereotypes into the flexibility and freedom of a society where roles are not defined almost exclusively by gender.

Is such a society possible—or even desirable? Certainly people differ in their responses to this question. In fact, none of the problems discussed in this chapter have easy solutions; consequently, the readings tend to raise questions rather than supply answers. For example, when Barbara Lazear Ascher considers the relationship between gender and power, she raises the larger question of what constitutes power. When Judy Brady and Noel Perrin mourn the limitations of their roles, readers may wonder whether these writers would prefer to be constrained by the limitations of a different gender. When we read Virginia Woolf's speculations about Shakespeare's sister alongside more contemporary selections, we may ask how much society has really changed since Woolf wrote her essay. And when we read any of the selections, we may find ourselves asking what it actually means to "be a man" or to "be a woman."

Most of all, in confronting the issues associated with our society's attitudes toward gender, we question the validity of the dangerously limiting stereotypes of men and women. Unfortunately, many people tend to see men and women in terms of outdated and unrealistic stereotypes: Men are strong, tough, and brave, and women are soft, weak, and in need of protection. Men understand mathematics and science and have a natural aptitude for mechanical tasks. They also have the drive, the aggressiveness, the competitive edge, and the power to succeed. They are never sentimental, and they never cry. Women are better at small, repetitive tasks than at bold, decisive actions. They enjoy—and are good at—domestic activities and have a natural aptitude for nurturing. They may like their jobs, but they will leave them without hesitation to devote themselves to husband and children.

As we read the preceding list of stereotypes, some of us may react neutrally (or even favorably) and others with annoyance; how we react tells us something about our society and something about ourselves. But as a number of the writers in this section observe, stereotypes are not just inaccurate; they also limit the way people think, the opportunities to which they have access, the roles they choose to fill—and, ultimately, the positions they occupy in society.

PREPARING TO READ AND WRITE

As you read and prepare to write about the selections in this chapter, consider the following questions:

- Is the writer male or female? Does the writer's gender really matter? Is the writer's focus on females, on males, or on both sexes?

- When was the selection written? How does its date of publication affect its content? How does the date affect your assessment of the work?

- How fair-minded or balanced does the selection seem?

- Does the writer discuss gender as a sexual, political, economic, or social issue?

- What does the work suggest are the specific advantages or disadvantages of being male? Of being female?

- Does the selection support the status quo, or does it suggest that change is necessary? Possible? Inevitable?

- Does the selection recommend specific changes? What are they? How optimistic is it about the likelihood of change?

- Is your interpretation of the problem the same as the interpretation presented in the selection? Are your ideas about possible solutions similar to those presented?

- Does the work express the view that men and women are fundamentally different? If so, does it suggest that these differences can be overcome, or at least lessened?

- Are gender differences seen as the result of environment or of heredity?

against another student, whom you also know.
- A teacher praises a literary work that portrays women in a negative—even insulting—manner.

How do students' responses differ? How do students explain such differences? Are they solely the result of social conditioning? Are the responses of male students always different from those of female students? On what points do they agree?

On Power

BARBARA LAZEAR ASCHER

Barbara Lazear Ascher (1946–   ) is an attorney, an essayist and former contributor to the *New York Times* column called "Hers." Ascher is interested in how women often struggle to reconcile their feminist ideals with the traditional roles of nurturing. In 1989, Ascher published *The Habit of Loving*, which deals with marriage, childbirth, aging, and other subjects. In the following excerpt from this book, Ascher takes a look at power and at some of the inequalities she and other women encountered as lawyers.

FOR OPENERS

Review with the class the Cinderella story, in which a prince saves a girl from a poor and miserable life by marrying her. How is Ascher's story like and unlike Cinderella's? You may also discuss the idea of what has been called the "Prince Charming fantasy": the desire to be carried off and rescued. Is this a fantasy only women have, or do men also dream of being saved? How do men's and women's rescue fantasies differ? Who (or what) is the rescuer in each case?

1   When I graduated from law school, I was hired by what is known in the business as a Prestigious New York Law Firm. I felt privileged to be associated with talent and money and respectability, to be in a place that promised me four weeks vacation, my own secretary, an office with a window, and, above all, a shot at power. I would not have preferred working for a single practitioner who struggled to pay rent on his windowless, one-room office in the Bronx.

2   There's a lot to be said for the accouterments of power. Those who asked where I worked immediately assumed, upon being told the name of the firm, that I must have been at the top of my class, an editor of the Law Review and a clerk for a federal judge. I was none of these, but being where the power is frees you from having to explain yourself.

3   The "outsider's" version of the "insider" is always distorted by the mental glass through which they observe. The outsider tends to think that once inside the power structure the voyage is over, destination reached. No more struggle or strain. But in fact, once you have "arrived," you discover that there are power structures within the power. You may share office space and a central switchboard, but that doesn't mean you are at the controls.

4   In my firm, the partners (male) took the young associates (also male), resplendent in their red suspenders and newly sported cigars, to lunch, to Dallas, Los Angeles, and Atlanta to meet the clients. The "girl" associates were sent to the library to do research. Actually, they were sent to the library to stay out of trouble.

5   Soon the clients with whom the associates dined were calling them for advice. These associates were learning how to practice law. Those of us hidden away in the stacks were learning how to be invisible.

6   A friend at a similar Prestigious New York Law Firm told me that she had tried and failed to enlist the cooperation of the one woman partner. "I suggested that we, the women associates and she, have

monthly luncheons to discuss some of the problems we faced. After all, she'd been one of us." But she was no longer "one of us" and feared that if her partners perceived her as an ally of women associates, they might forget that she was, first and foremost, one of "them." She knew that hanging out with weak sisters was no way to safeguard her tentative grasp of success.

Eight years later, when my friend became a partner, she learned   7
that the woman she had approached for help was powerless within the partnership. She was, in the eyes of the men, their token "girl" partner, and power, like beauty, is in the eye of the beholder. She was a lady and that's how she was perceived. How could her mother have known as she trained her daughter for power in the drawing room that what she would want was power in the boardroom?

However, even if hers was a token acceptance, she had entered   8
that heady realm, she was feted around town as "the first woman partner" and she proceeded to follow a pattern not unusual for women who achieve some semblance of power. She refused to reach behind to pull other women along. It was too risky. She might fall backwards. I blush to recall that when, in fourth grade I was the only girl on the boys' baseball team, I joined in their systematic "girl trashing." I enthusiastically participated in disparaging conversations about people who were "just girls." Who threw like girls. Who giggled like girls. Who couldn't whistle through their fingers, burp on command or slide into home plate. Then, all I knew was that my power depended on keeping·other girls out. Now, I know about identification with the aggressor.

Not that it makes much difference. There are uncanny similarities   9
between being the only girl on a fourth grade baseball team and the only woman in bigger boys' games. Take, for instance, the response of Harvard Business School's tenured, female professors when their former colleague, Barbara Bund Jackson, filed suit against the school for its refusal to grant her tenure. Nonsense, these women replied to Jackson's charge of a sexist "institutional bias." Not so, they said of her contention that the school sets "impossible standards for female faculty members." Why shouldn't they? Why should Harvard deviate from the accepted wisdom that a man can occasionally goof off and still be perceived as powerful? It's kind of cute, we say. Oh, look, he's got nice human touches, an ability to have fun. How boyish. How charming. Not so for a woman. She who goofs off is a goof-off.

Tenured Harvard professor Regina E. Herzlinger's response to   10
Jackson's claim of discrimination was, "I don't feel there is . . . friction caused by the fact that there are few women on the faculty . . . I don't think there is discrimination on the basis of sex." Of course there isn't friction for those "few women." And Regina'd better keep quiet

ADDITIONAL QUESTIONS FOR RESPONDING TO READING

1. Ascher says she never asked her friend Linda to play baseball with them "even though she ran like the wind and threw overhand" (paragraph 10). Is baseball a useful analogy for Ascher's analysis of the power structure? Explain.
2. According to Ascher, what must a man do to acquire power? What must a woman do? How do their actions differ? Is her analysis accurate? Explain.
3. Ascher says that "power, who has it and who doesn't, is not limited to the realm of male/female strife (paragraph 11)." Think of some other examples. For instance, do students have power?
4. Ascher says the imbalance of power does not make "mature sense" (paragraph 22). What does she mean?
5. Why, according to Ascher, does a woman who wants power in a male-dominated environment have to separate herself from "the girls"?
6. Does it anger you that Ascher, a middle-class doctor's wife, voluntarily gave up something many other women (and men) desperately want?

TEACHING STRATEGIES

1. Discuss hierarchy and its relationship to power. Who defines the power structure? Given our historical and social conditioning, can we imagine a kind of power that does not depend on subordination of particular groups of people?
2. Olga Broumas's poem "Cinderella" echoes Ascher's theme in precise poetic language. Reading it to the class may help provoke discussion (*Beginning with O*, vol. 72 of the Yale Series of Younger Poets, Yale University Press, 1977). Anne Sexton also has written a poem entitled "Cinderella," and it is frequently anthologized. This too would be a good poem to read aloud.

if she thinks otherwise. Boys don't like girls who turn around and say, "But what about the other girls?" I certainly never invited my friend Linda to play baseball with us, even though she ran like the wind and threw overhand.

But power, who has it and who doesn't, is not limited to the 11 realm of male/female strife. My husband, a physician in practice for many years, volunteers his time, one day a week at a hospital often described with the same breathless reverence as my law firm. This is the place to which ailing shahs and wealthy dowagers come to be healed. The full time attendings (those with the power) don't like the voluntary attendings (those without the power), and occasionally rise up to divest them of responsibility. How, you might ask, when wise and seasoned physicians are willing to give their time, free of charge, to teach students and treat patients, could there be a complaint? The volunteers are not part of the power structure. And power's particular drive is to grab more for itself, an act which invariably involves stripping others of any.

Recently, some of the voluntary attendings went to the head 12 of their department and informed him, "You make us feel like second-class citizens." He listened, nodded, and assured: "You are second-class citizens."

Irrational, you say? Of course. But whoever thought that the 13 power drive made sense?

In fifth grade, secret clubs were the order of the day. The purpose 14 was, first of all, the secret. A secret name. Secret rules. Secret members. Secret meeting places. The purpose was to exclude, which is the first step in establishing a power base. The second is to create fear in those excluded. Those of us who assembled the group of meanest and most popular children had the run of the playground. We were a force to contend with.

Recently, when I went to choose a puppy from a litter, I was told, 15 "Don't get the Alpha dog, whatever you do!" It seems that, like their ancestors the wolves, each litter has a leader. He or she is the power in the pack, and once the Alpha dog comes to live with your family, you become the pack.

What does the Alpha dog get for his trouble? A certain haugh- 16 tiness. A certain swagger. What did the Alpha attorneys in my firm get for their power? A certain haughtiness. A certain swagger. And an occasional invitation to the Piping Rock Country Club.

So who cares? We all did. We who sat in the library working on 17 Blue Sky Memos, something my twelve-year-old daughter could have done, given the careful and patronizing instructions we received. We were enraged at being excluded from Making It Big. What we didn't know at the time is that the ones who Make It Big are always watching their backs, but then girls rarely have the opportunity to learn these finer points.

Power sanctions self-centeredness. (It could be argued that that's 18 why girls don't have it—"They're so giving.") It returns you, full circle, to the delicious years of being an infant and toddler when, it seemed, you were the center of the universe. But what is missing at thirty-five, forty, or fifty years of age is the innocence of the infant, the two- or three-year-old. It is a dangerous absence. Self-interest plus muscle power and experience combine to create a being more pervasively harmful than the sandbox bully.

Take, for instance, Manhattan real estate developers. They are 19 currently a favorite target of the less powerful, and are, in some instances, a legitimate target. There are those who use their amassed fortunes to gain political sway by contributing to the campaign funds of elected officials. The elected officials then turn deaf ears to the complaints of less powerful constituents dispossessed from low rent buildings razed to make room for luxury high rises complete with Jacuzzis in every bath.

Donald Trump's song of himself is on the best-seller lists. *Vanity* 20 *Fair* featured a breathlessly infatuated profile of his wife. Why? Because if you can't be powerful, the next best thing is to fancy yourself on intimate terms with those who are. There is a hunger to know how they make their deals, shop for their children's Christmas presents, stay fresh and alert from five A.M. until Peter Duchin's orchestra plays its last charity ball waltz at midnight. All this, and not a wrinkle in the brow to show for it.

People read about power for the same reason that little girls read 21 *Cinderella*, they want to believe that someday a prince will come to deliver a subject into sovereignty.

One might ask whether adulation of those who are flagrantly self- 22 involved makes any sense when there are thousands of dispossessed sleeping in Grand Central and Pennsylvania Station. It certainly doesn't make mature sense.

But then power is not necessarily in mature hands. It is most 23 often achieved, and clung to by those whose passion for it is fueled by childlike greed and self-interest. What they find, once they have it, is that being the proud possessor of power bears an uncanny similarity to being the two-year-old with the biggest plastic pail and shovel on the beach. It's a life of nervous guardianship.

I left the law because I wasn't motivated to engage in the struggle 24 required to move myself from library to the light of day and lunches with clients. The struggle would have required molding myself in the partners' images, a hard concept for them to visualize since I was female and they were male. It would have been necessary to

COLLABORATIVE ACTIVITY

In small groups, study Ascher's argument. Assign each group one of the following topics for discussion:

1. What is the "outsider's" view of power? Compare it with the "insider's" view. Is one view more accurate than the other?
2. Why, according to Ascher, does female acquisition of power mean cutting oneself off from "weaker sisters"?
3. Examine Ascher's examples of powerful people and her opposition to Donald Trump and Regina Herzlinger. According to Ascher, how is power tantalizing?
4. Compare the images of Ascher's male and female associates. Are they stereotypes? Can someone like Ascher, who does not occupy a position of power, really understand the nature of power?

Follow up with full class discussion.

WRITING SUGGESTIONS

1. Who is the most powerful person you know? How did this person gain power? How does he or she maintain it? Write an essay in which you define power by describing this person.
2. Ascher's analysis of power grew out of personal experience. Analyze a power structure with which you are familiar—for example, one you see in the dynamics of your school, workplace, or family—by looking at its strengths and weaknesses. Do Ascher's criticisms apply?

ANSWERS TO RESPONDING TO READING

1. To Ascher, power means not only having a prestigious career and earning a lot of money, but also being an "insider." Power is "tantalizing," and it separates one from identification with the powerless "outsiders." Its "particular drive is to grab more for itself, an act which invariably involves stripping others of any" (paragraph 11). Ultimately, the powerful life is one of "nervous guardianship." Answers will vary.
2. Answers will vary. Ascher suggests that the first step in establishing a power base is "to exclude"; the next is "to create fear in those excluded." As a woman lawyer, her power depended on "keeping other girls out" and on her "identification with the aggressor."
3. Answers will vary. It might be interesting to review what "partners' image" means for Ascher; it involves "self-interest plus muscle power and experience" combining to "create a being more pervasively harmful than the sandbox bully."

BACKGROUND ON READING

The Men We Carry in Our Minds" is from *The Paradise of Bombs*, a collection of personal narratives concerning "the culture of violence" in America. Tracing the history of his writing, Sanders told *Contemporary Authors*, "When I began writing in my late twenties, I wanted to ask, through literature, many of the fundamental questions that scientists ask. In particular, I wanted to understand our place in nature, trace the sources of our violence, and speculate about the future evolution of our species" (*Contemporary Authors*, New Revision Series, vol. 15).

remember when to speak and when to keep my mouth shut. I would have had to create an asexual aura. I would have had to work very, very hard.

I left the law because that wasn't the power that interested me. 25 Which is not to say that power itself doesn't interest me. I remember the full glory of being the only girl on the boy's baseball team. I remember the total sense of worthlessness that resulted when I grew breasts and the guys banished me from the pitcher's mound to the powerless world of hopscotch. Power is as tantalizing as a hypnotist's swinging pendulum. Power promises that you will never again be stuck with "the girls." Ask Regina Herzlinger. She knows.

RESPONDING TO READING

1. How does Ascher define power? Do you agree with her definition? Does she have a realistic or idealistic image of power? According to Ascher's definition, do you have power? Explain.   **2.** In your experience, who are the most (and least) powerful people in a society? How does one gain (and maintain) power?   **3.** In paragraph 24 Ascher explains, "I left the law because I wasn't motivated to engage in the struggle required to move myself from library to the light of day and lunches with clients"—that is, because she did not want to remake herself "in the partners' image." Do you think Ascher is rationalizing? Could you argue that her decision to leave the law helps confirm her male bosses' opinion of women?

The Men We Carry in Our Minds

SCOTT RUSSELL SANDERS

Scott Russell Sanders (see also p. 336) examines the issue of how men see women and women see men in "The Men We Carry in our Minds," from his 1988 book, *The Paradise of Bombs*. With honest and vivid descriptions, he remembers the toll that hard work took on the laborers he knew when he was growing up, men whose faces were "creased like the leather of old work gloves" and who had "finicky backs and guts weak from hernias." Sanders admits that the way he perceived adult sexual roles as a child made him "slow to understand the deep grievances of women" but says that now he feels like an "ally."

"This must be a hard time for women," I say to my friend Anneke.   1 "They have so many paths to choose from, and so many voices calling them."

"I think it's a lot harder for men," she replies.   2

"How do you figure that?"   3

"The women I know feel excited, innocent, like crusaders in a   4
just cause. The men I know are eaten up with guilt."

We are sitting at the kitchen table drinking sassafras tea, our   5
hands wrapped around the mugs because this April morning is cool
and drizzly. "Like a Dutch morning," Anneke told me earlier. She is
Dutch herself, a writer and midwife and peacemaker, with the round
face and sad eyes of a woman in a Vermeer[1] painting who might be
waiting for the rain to stop, for a door to open. She leans over to sniff
a sprig of lilac, pale lavender, that rises from a vase of cobalt blue.

"Women feel such pressure to be everything, do everything," I   6
say. "Career, kids, art, politics. Have their babies and get back to the
office a week later. It's as if they're trying to overcome a million years'
worth of evolution in one lifetime."

"But we help one another. We don't try to lumber on alone, like   7
so many wounded grizzly bears, the way men do." Anneke sips her
tea. I gave her the mug with owls on it, for wisdom. "And we have
this deep-down sense that we're in the *right*—we've been held back,
passed over, used—while men feel they're in the wrong. Men are
the ones who've been discredited, who have to search their souls."

I search my soul. I discover guilty feelings aplenty—toward the   8
poor, the Vietnamese, Native Americans, the whales, an endless list
of debts—a guilt in each case that is as bright and unambiguous as
a neon sign. But toward women I feel something more confused, a
snarl of shame, envy, wary tenderness, and amazement. This muddle
troubles me. To hide my unease I say, "You're right, it's tough being
a man these days."

"Don't laugh." Anneke frowns at me, mournful-eyed, through   9
the sassafras steam. "I wouldn't be a man for anything. It's much
easier being the victim. All the victim has to do is break free. The
persecutor has to live with his past."

How deep is that past? I find myself wondering after Anneke has   10
left. How much of an inheritance do I have to throw off? Is it just the
beliefs I breathed in as a child? Do I have to scour memory back
through father and grandfather? Through St. Paul? Beyond
Stonehenge[2] and into the twilit caves? I'm convinced the past we
must contend with is deeper even than speech. When I think back
on my childhood, on how I learned to see men and women, I have
a sense of ancient, dizzying depths. The back roads of Tennessee and
Ohio where I grew up were probably closer, in their sexual patterns,

---

[1]Dutch painter Jan Vermeer (1632–75). [Eds.]
[2]Prehistoric ceremonial ruin near Salisbury, England, begun c. 1900 B.C., consisting of circular
formations of stone slabs. It was built by the Druids, who used it as a calendar. [Eds.]

TEACHING STRATEGY

Sanders carefully establishes a context in which he identifies with women and their struggles. He claims to be another of the victims of the real "persecutors." With the class, examine how he conveys this attitude. Some of his strategies include the following:

- Overtly sympathetic comments about women
- Expression of ambiguity rather than guilt about women
- Identification with people in lower socioeconomic groups
- Separation of himself from the men who run the world
- Identification with women's desire for power
- Portrayal of men as prisoners of their destiny

to the campsites of Stone Age hunters than to the genderless cities of the future into which we are rushing.

The first men, besides my father, I remember seeing were black 11 convicts and white guards, in the cottonfield across the road from our farm on the outskirts of Memphis. I must have been three or four. The prisoners wore dingy gray-and-black zebra suits, heavy as canvas, sodden with sweat. Hatless, stooped, they chopped weeds in the fierce heat, row after row, breathing the acrid dust of boll-weevil poison. The overseers wore dazzling white shirts and broad shadowy hats. The oiled barrels of their shotguns flashed in the sunlight. Their faces in memory are utterly blank. Of course those men, white and black, have become for me an emblem of racial hatred. But they have also come to stand for the twin poles of my early vision of manhood—the brute toiling animal and the boss.

When I was a boy, the men I knew labored with their bodies. 12 They were marginal farmers, just scraping by, or welders, steelworkers, carpenters; they swept floors, dug ditches, mined coal, or drove trucks, their forearms ropy with muscle; they trained horses, stoked furnaces, built tires, stood on assembly lines wrestling parts onto cars and refrigerators. They got up before light, worked all day long whatever the weather, and when they came home at night they looked as though somebody had been whipping them. In the evenings and on weekends they worked on their own places, tilling gardens that were lumpy with clay, fixing broken-down cars, hammering on houses that were always too drafty, too leaky, too small.

The bodies of the men I knew were twisted and maimed in ways 13 visible and invisible. The nails of their hands were black and split, the hands tattooed with scars. Some had lost fingers. Heavy lifting had given many of them finicky backs and guts weak from hernias. Racing against conveyor belts had given them ulcers. Their ankles and knees ached from years of standing on concrete. Anyone who had worked for long around machines was hard of hearing. They squinted, and the skin of their faces was creased like the leather of old work gloves. There were times, studying them, when I dreaded growing up. Most of them coughed, from dust or cigarettes, and most of them drank cheap wine or whiskey, so their eyes looked bloodshot and bruised. The fathers of my friends always seemed older than the mothers. Men wore out sooner. Only women lived into old age.

As a boy I also knew another sort of men, who did not sweat 14 and break down like mules. They were soldiers, and so far as I could tell they scarcely worked at all. During my early school years we lived on a military base, an arsenal in Ohio, and every day I saw GIs in the guardshacks, on the stoops of barracks, at the wheels of olive drab Chevrolets. The chief fact of their lives was boredom. Long after

I left the Arsenal I came to recognize the sour smell the soldiers gave off as that of souls in limbo. They were all waiting—for wars, for transfers, for leaves, for promotions, for the end of their hitch—like so many braves waiting for the hunt to begin. Unlike the warriors of older tribes, however, they would have no say about when the battle would start or how it would be waged. Their waiting was broken only when they practiced for war. They fired guns at targets, drove tanks across the churned-up fields of the military reservation, set off bombs in the wrecks of old fighter planes. I knew this was all play. But I also felt certain that when the hour for killing arrived, they would kill. When the real shooting started, many of them would die. This was what soldiers were *for*, just as a hammer was for driving nails.

15   Warriors and toilers: those seemed, in my boyhood vision, to be the chief destinies for men. They weren't the only destinies, as I learned from having a few male teachers, from reading books, and from watching television. But the men on television—the politicians, the astronauts, the generals, the savvy lawyers, the philosophical doctors, the bosses who gave orders to both soldiers and laborers—seemed as remove and unreal to me as the figures in tapestries. I could no more imagine growing up to become one of these cool, potent creatures than I could imagine becoming a prince.

16   A nearer and more hopeful example was that of my father, who had escaped from a red-dirt farm to a tire factory, and from the assembly line to the front office. Eventually he dressed in a white shirt and tie. He carried himself as if he had been born to work with his mind. But his body, remembering the earlier years of slogging work, began to give out on him in his fifties, and it quit on him entirely before he turned sixty-five. Even such a partial escape from man's fate as he had accomplished did not seem possible for most of the boys I knew. They joined the Army, stood in line for jobs in the smoky plants, helped build highways. They were bound to work as their fathers had worked, killing themselves or preparing to kill others.

17   A scholarship enabled me not only to attend college, a rare enough feat in my circle, but even to study in a university meant for the children of the rich. Here I met for the first time young men who had assumed from birth that they would lead lives of comfort and power. And for the first time I met women who told me that men were guilty of having kept all the joys and privileges of the earth for themselves. I was baffled. What privileges? What joys? I thought about the maimed, dismal lives of most of the men back home. What had they stolen from their wives and daughters? The right to go five days a week, twelve months a year, for thirty or forty years to a steel mill

COLLABORATIVE ACTIVITY

Ask students, working in groups, to discuss their male relatives' occupational roles. Do they see them as "warriors and toilers" or as something else? In class discussion, try to identify other categories into which working men can be classified.

or a coal mine? The right to drop bombs and die in war? The right to feel every leak in the roof, every gap in the fence, every cough in the engine, as a wound they must mend? The right to feel, when the lay-off comes or the plant shuts down, not only afraid but ashamed?

I was slow to understand the deep grievances of women. This 18 was because, as a boy, I had envied them. Before college, the only people I had ever known who were interested in art or music or literature, the only ones who read books, the only ones who ever seemed to enjoy a sense of ease and grace were the mothers and daughters. Like the menfolk, they fretted about money, they scrimped and made-do. But, when the pay stopped coming in, they were not the ones who had failed. Nor did they have to go to war, and that seemed to me a blessed fact. By comparison with the narrow, ironclad days of fathers, there was an expansiveness, I thought, in the days of mothers. They went to see neighbors, to shop in town, to run errands at school, at the library, at church. No doubt, had I looked harder at their lives, I would have envied them less. It was not my fate to become a woman, so it was easier for me to see the graces. Few of them held jobs outside the home, and those who did filled thankless roles as clerks and waitresses. I didn't see, then, what a prison a house could be, since houses seemed to me brighter, handsomer places than any factory. I did not realize—because such things were never spoken of—how often women suffered from men's bullying. I did learn about the wretchedness of abandoned wives, single mothers, widows; but I also learned about the wretchedness of lone men. Even then I could see how exhausting it was for a mother to cater all day to the needs of young children. But if I had been asked, as a boy, to choose between tending a baby and tending a machine, I think I would have chosen the baby. (Having now tended both, I know I would choose the baby.)

So I was baffled when the women at college accused me and my 19 sex of having cornered the world's pleasures. I think something like my bafflement has been felt by other boys (and by girls as well) who grew up in dirt-poor farm country, in mining country, in black ghettos, in Hispanic barrios, in the shadows of factories, in Third World nations—any place where the fate of men is as grim and bleak as the fate of women. Toilers and warriors. I realize now how ancient these identities are, how deep the tug they exert on men, the undertow of a thousand generations. The miseries I saw, as a boy, in the lives of nearly all men I continue to see in the lives of many— the body-breaking toil, the tedium, the call to be tough, the humiliating powerlessness, the battle for a living and for territory.

When the women I met at college thought about the joys and 20 privileges of men, they did not carry in their minds the sort of men

WRITING SUGGESTIONS

1. Sanders says he has ambiguous feelings about women. How would you describe your feelings toward the relative power of the opposite sex? Relate personal experiences to illustrate your points.

2. Compare and contrast Sanders's view of power with that of Barbara Lazear Ascher's view (previous selection). What differences may be attributed to the writers' respective genders?

I had known in my childhood. They thought of their fathers, who were bankers, physicians, architects, stockbrokers, the big wheels of the big cities. These fathers rode the train to work or drove cars that cost more than any of my childhood houses. They were attended from morning to night by female helpers, wives and nurses and secretaries. They were never laid off, never short of cash at month's end, never lined up for welfare. These fathers made decisions that mattered. They ran the world.

The daughters of such men wanted to share in this power, this 21 glory. So did I. They yearned for a say over their future, for jobs worthy of their abilities, for the right to live at peace, unmolested, whole. Yes, I thought, yes yes. The difference between me and these daughters was that they saw me, because of my sex, as destined from birth to become like their fathers, and therefore as an enemy to their desires. But I knew better. I wasn't an enemy, in fact or in feeling. I was an ally. If I had known, then, how to tell them so, would they have believed me? Would they now?

RESPONDING TO READING

1. Do you agree with Sanders that it is harder to be a woman today than a man? Or do you agree with his friend Anneke, who takes the opposite view? Explain your conclusion. Does your reasoning differ from theirs? If so, how?   **2.** What does Anneke mean when she says, "All the victim has to do is break free. The persecutor has to live with his past" (paragraph 9)? Is it fair to use the word *persecutor* in this context? Does your own experience suggest that Anneke is exaggerating the situation or defining it accurately?   **3.** What do the men Sanders carries in his mind—his father, the convicts and guards, farmers, blue-collar workers, and soldiers—have in common? How have they shaped his attitude toward gender? How are they like and unlike the men you carry in your mind?

If Shakespeare Had a Sister

VIRGINIA WOOLF

English novelist, essayist, and critic Virginia Woolf (1882–1941) was educated at home in her father's extensive library and grew up among literary people such as Henry James and James Russell Lowell. She became a member of the famous Bloomsbury group, which promoted excellence in literature and art and resisted Victorian traditions. Woolf is known for her experimental, stream-of-consciousness writing in such novels as *Mrs. Dalloway* (1925), *To the*

Lighthouse (1927), and *The Waves* (1931) and for her clear and uncomplicated essay style. She once wrote, "If one wishes to better the world, one must, paradoxically enough, withdraw and spend more time fashioning one's sentences to perfection in solitude." "If Shakespeare Had a Sister," which examines the difficulties all creative women face, is from the collection *A Room of One's Own* (1929).

BACKGROUND ON READING

For Woolf, life and fiction are vitally connected. According to her theory of history, "Once a thing's done, no one ever knows how it happened." This idea underlies the purpose of her experiments in fiction, which challenge conventions and the idea that the writer should merely reflect reality. To Woolf, paradoxically, greater truth might be found in fictional recreations (*DLB*, vol. 36)—for example, Judith Shakespeare.

FOR OPENERS

Discuss the idea of a literary canon and the possible historical reasons that a work has been included or excluded. Do we blindly accept the canon? (You may want to refer to the "Confronting the Issues" section of Chapter 2, "Thinking and Learning.")

It was disappointing not to have brought back in the evening some important statement, some authentic fact. Women are poorer than men because—this or that. Perhaps now it would be better to give up seeking for the truth, and receiving on one's head an avalanche of opinion hot as lava, discolored as dish-water. It would be better to draw the curtains; to shut out distractions; to light the lamp; to narrow the enquiry and to ask the historian, who records not opinions but facts, to describe under what conditions women lived, not throughout the ages, but in England, say in the time of Elizabeth.[1] 1

For it is a perennial puzzle why no woman wrote a word of that extraordinary literature when every other man, it seemed, was capable of song or sonnet. What were the conditions in which women lived, I asked myself; for fiction, imaginative work that is, is not dropped like a pebble upon the ground, as science may be; fiction is like a spider's web, attached ever so lightly perhaps, but still attached to life at all four corners. Often the attachment is scarcely perceptible; Shakespeare's plays, for instance, seem to hang there complete by themselves. But when the web is pulled askew, hooked up at the edge, torn in the middle, one remembers that these webs are not spun in midair by incorporeal creatures, but are the work of suffering human beings, and are attached to grossly material things, like health and money and the houses we live in. 2

I went, therefore, to the shelf where the histories stand and took down one of the latest, Professor Trevelyan's *History of England*. Once more I looked up Women, found "position of," and turned to the pages indicated. "Wife-beating," I read, "was a recognized right of man, and was practised without shame by high as well as low. . . . Similarly," the historian goes on, "the daughter who refused to marry the gentleman of her parents' choice was liable to be locked up, beaten and flung about the room, without any shock being inflicted on public opinion. Marriage was not an affair of personal affection, but of family avarice, particularly in the 'chivalrous' upper classes. . . . Betrothal often took place while one or both of the parties was in the cradle, and marriage when they were scarcely out of the nurses' charge." That was about 1470, soon after Chaucer's time. The next reference 3

[1]Queen Elizabeth I of England reigned from 1558 to 1603. [Eds.]

to the position of women is some two hundred years later, in the time of the Stuarts. "It was still the exception for women of the upper and middle class to choose their own husbands, and when the husband had been assigned, he was lord and master, so far at least as law and custom could make him. Yet even so," Professor Trevelyan concludes, "neither Shakespeare's women nor those of authentic seventeenth-century memoirs, like the Verneys and the Hutchinsons, seem wanting in personality and character." Certainly, if we consider it, Cleopatra must have had a way with her; Lady Macbeth, one would suppose, had a will of her own; Rosalind, one might conclude, was an attractive girl. Professor Trevelyan is speaking no more than the truth when he remarks that Shakespeare's women do not seem wanting in personality and character. Not being a historian, one might go even further and say that women have burnt like beacons in all the works of all the poets from the beginning of time—Clytemnestra, Antigone, Cleopatra, Lady Macbeth, Phèdre, Cressida, Rosalind, Desdemona, the Duchess of Malfi, among the dramatists; then among the prose writers: Millamant, Clarissa, Becky Sharp, Anna Karenina, Emma Bovary, Madame de Guermantes—the names flock to mind, nor do they recall women "lacking in personality and character." Indeed, if woman had no existence save in the fiction written by men, one would imagine her a person of the utmost importance; very various; heroic and mean; splendid and sordid; infinitely beautiful and hideous in the extreme; as great as a man, some think even greater. But this is woman in fiction. In fact, as Professor Trevelyan points out, she was locked up, beaten and flung about the room.

A very queer, composite being thus emerges. Imaginatively she   4
is of the highest importance; practically she is completely insignificant. She pervades poetry from cover to cover; she is all but absent from history. She dominates the lives of kings and conquerors in fiction; in fact she was the slave of any boy whose parents forced a ring upon her finger. Some of the most inspired words, some of the most profound thoughts in literature fall from her lips; in real life she could hardly read, could scarcely spell, and was the property of her husband.

It was certainly an odd monster that one made up by reading the   5
historians first and the poets afterwards—a worm winged like an eagle; the spirit of life and beauty in a kitchen chopping up suet. But these monsters, however amusing to the imagination, have no existence in fact. What one must do to bring her to life was to think poetically and prosaically at one and the same moment, thus keeping in touch with fact—that she is Mrs. Martin, aged thirty-six, dressed in blue, wearing a black hat and brown shoes; but not losing sight of fiction either—that she is a vessel in which all sorts of spirits and

ADDITIONAL QUESTIONS FOR RESPONDING TO READING

1. To what does Woolf attribute her belief that Shakespeare "got his work expressed completely" (paragraph 17)? How does she relate this achievement to the books she says are missing from the shelves?

2. What does Woolf mean when she says that a woman needs "a room of her own" (paragraph 12)?

3. Historically, what frustrations have gifted women had to face?

4. What do Woolf's uses of sarcasm ("cats do not go to heaven," paragraph 6) and unusual juxtapositions ("a worm winged like an eagle," paragraph 5) add to her essay?

TEACHING STRATEGIES

1. Because many of Woolf's allusions are likely to puzzle students, you may want to prepare a handout explaining the more difficult ones.
2. Women writers have encountered more difficulty than men in being able to write and in getting published. Bring to class an older literature anthology and a very recent one, or photocopy the two tables of contents. Note the differences. Is there still inequality in representation by women authors as compared with men? Discuss cultural causes. Is inequality of representation in any way justified today? Is it justified in the older anthology? Do equal numbers alone constitute equal treatment? Remind students that to be canonized a work must have been written. Woolf asks an even more fundamental question: Under the circumstances she describes, how could women write at all? Identify and discuss the arguments she presents to explain the relative literary "silence" of women. In our culture, is it still difficult for women to write and publish their work? Why or why not?

COLLABORATIVE ACTIVITY

Assign groups the task of researching women writers whose work has only recently been incorporated into the canon—for example, Kate Chopin or Woolf herself. Have each group give a short presentation on a writer's life and tell the story of her revival from obscurity.

forces are coursing and flashing perpetually. The moment, however, that one tries this method with the Elizabethan woman, one branch of illumination fails; one is held up by the scarcity of facts. One knows nothing detailed, nothing perfectly true and substantial about her. History scarcely mentions her. And I turned to Professor Trevelyan again to see what history meant to him. I found by looking at his chapter headings that it meant—

"The Manor Court and the Methods of Open-field Agriculture ... The Cistercians and Sheep-farming ... The Crusades ... The University ... The House of Commons ... The Hundred Years' War ... The Wars of the Roses ... The Renaissance Scholars ... The Dissolution of the Monasteries ... Agrarian and Religious Strife ... The Origin of English Seapower ... The Armada ..." and so on. Occasionally an individual woman is mentioned, an Elizabeth, or a Mary; a queen or a great lady. But by no possible means could middle-class women with nothing but brains and character at their command have taken part in any one of the great movements which, brought together, constitute the historian's view of the past. Nor shall we find her in any collection of anecdotes. Aubrey[2] hardly mentions her. She never writes her own life and scarcely keeps a diary; there are only a handful of her letters in existence. She left no plays or poems by which we can judge her. What one wants, I thought—and why does not some brilliant student at Newnham or Girton[3] supply it?—is a mass of information; at what age did she marry; how many children had she as a rule; what was her house like; had she a room to herself; did she do the cooking; would she be likely to have a servant? All these facts lie somewhere, presumably, in parish registers and account books; the life of the average Elizabethan woman must be scattered about somewhere, could one collect it and make a book of it. It would be ambitious beyond my daring, I thought, looking about the shelves for books that were not there, to suggest to the students of those famous colleges that they should re-write history, though I own that it often seems a little queer as it is, unreal, lop-sided; but why should they not add a supplement to history? calling it, of course, by some inconspicuous name so that women might figure there without impropriety? For one often catches a glimpse of them in the lives of the great, whisking away into the background, concealing, I sometimes think a wink, a laugh, perhaps a tear. And, after all, we have lives enough of Jane Austen; it scarcely seems necessary to consider again

6

---

[2]John Aubrey (1626–97), English antiquary and folklorist who wrote biographical sketches of celebrated persons of his time, which were collected in *Brief Lives* (1813). [Eds.]

[3]Girton and Newnham Colleges, colleges of Cambridge University founded in the 1870s, were the first to admit women. The essays in *A Room of One's Own* were adapted from lectures Woolf gave there in 1928. [Eds.]

the influence of the tragedies of Joanna Baillie[4] upon the poetry of Edgar Allan Poe; as for myself, I should not mind if the homes and haunts of Mary Russell Mitford[5] were closed to the public for a century at least. But what I find deplorable, I continued, looking about the bookshelves again, is that nothing is known about women before the eighteenth century. I have no model in my mind to turn about this way and that. Here I am asking why women did not write poetry in the Elizabethan age, and I am not sure how they were educated; whether they were taught to write; whether they had sitting-rooms to themselves; how many women had children before they were twenty-one; what, in short, they did from eight in the morning till eight at night. They had no money evidently; according to Professor Trevelyan they were married whether they liked it or not before they were out of the nursery, at fifteen or sixteen very likely. It would have been extremely odd, even upon this showing, had one of them suddenly written the plays of Shakespeare, I concluded, and I thought of that old gentleman, who is dead now, but was a bishop, I think, who declared that it was impossible for any woman, past, present, or to come, to have the genius of Shakespeare. He wrote to the papers about it. He also told a lady who applied to him for information that cats do not as a matter of fact go to heaven, though they have, he added, souls of a sort. How much thinking those old gentlemen used to save one! How the borders of ignorance shrank back at their approach! Cats do not go to heaven. Women cannot write the plays of Shakespeare.

Be that as it may, I could not help thinking, as I looked at the works of Shakespeare on the shelf, that the bishop was right at least in this; it would have been impossible, completely and entirely, for any woman to have written the plays of Shakespeare in the age of Shakespeare. Let me imagine, since facts are so hard to come by, what would have happened had Shakespeare had a wonderfully gifted sister, called Judith, let us say. Shakespeare himself went, very probably—his mother was an heiress—to the grammar school, where he may have learned Latin—Ovid, Virgil and Horace—and the elements of grammar and logic. He was, it is well known, a wild boy who poached rabbits, perhaps shot a deer, and had, rather sooner than he should have done, to marry a woman in the neighborhood, who bore him a child rather quicker than was right. That escapade sent him to seek his fortune in London. He had, it seemed, a taste for the theatre; he began by holding horses at the stage door. Very soon he got work in the theatre, became a successful actor, and lived

7

---

[4]Scottish dramatist and poet (1762–1851). [Eds.]
[5]English writer (1787–1855), author of *Our Village*, sketches of rural life. [Eds.]

at the hub of the universe, meeting everybody, knowing everybody, practising his art on the boards, exercising his wits in the streets, and even getting access to the palace of the queen. Meanwhile his extraordinarily gifted sister, let us suppose, remained at home. She was as adventurous, as imaginative, as agog to see the world as he was. But she was not sent to school. She had no chance of learning grammar and logic, let alone of reading Horace and Virgil. She picked up a book now and then, one of her brother's perhaps, and read a few pages. But then her parents came in and told her to mend the stockings or mind the stew and not moon about with books and papers. They would have spoken sharply but kindly, for they were substantial people who knew the conditions of life for a woman and loved their daughter—indeed, more likely than not she was the apple of her father's eye. Perhaps she scribbled some pages up in an apple loft on the sly, but was careful to hide them or set fire to them. Soon, however, before she was out of her teens, she was to be betrothed to the son of a neighboring wool-stapler. She cried out that marriage was hateful to her, and for that she was severely beaten by her father. Then he ceased to scold her. He begged her instead not to hurt him, not to shame him in this matter of her marriage. He would give her a chain of beads or a fine petticoat, he said; and there were tears in his eyes. How could she disobey him? How could she break his heart? The force of her own gift alone drove her to it. She made up a small parcel of her belongings, let herself down by a rope one summer's night and took the road to London. She was not seventeen. The birds that sang in the hedge were not more musical than she was. She had the quickest fancy, a gift like her brother's, for the tune of words. Like him, she had a taste for the theatre. She stood at the stage door; she wanted to act, she said. Men laughed in her face. The manager—a fat, loose-lipped man—guffawed. He bellowed something about poodles dancing and women acting—no woman, he said, could possibly be an actress. He hinted—you can imagine what. She could get no training in her craft. Could she even seek her dinner in a tavern or roam the streets at midnight? Yet her genius was for fiction and lusted to feed abundantly upon the lives of men and women and the study of their ways. At last—for she was very young, oddly like Shakespeare the poet in her face, with the same grey eyes and rounded brows—at last Nick Greene the actor-manager took pity on her; she found herself with child by that gentleman and so—who shall measure the heat and violence of the poet's heart when caught and tangled in a woman's body?—killed herself one winter's night and lies buried at some cross-roads where the omnibuses now stop outside the Elephant and Castle.[6]

°A London pub. [Eds.]

That, more or less, is how the story would run, I think, if a woman   8
in Shakespeare's day had had Shakespeare's genius. But for my part,
I agree with the deceased bishop, if such he was—it is unthinkable
that any woman in Shakespeare's day should have had Shakespeare's
genius. For genius like Shakespeare's is not born among laboring,
uneducated, servile people. It was not born in England among the
Saxons and the Britons. It is not born today among the working
classes. How, then, could it have been born among women whose
work began, according to Professor Trevelyan, almost before they
were out of the nursery, who were forced to it by their parents and
held to it by all the power of law and custom? Yet genius of a sort
must have existed among women as it must have existed among the
working classes. Now and again an Emily Brontë or a Robert Burns
blazes out and proves its presence. But certainly it never got itself on
to paper. When, however, one reads of a witch being ducked, of a
woman possessed by devils, of a wise woman selling herbs, or even
of a very remarkable man who had a mother, then I think we are on
the track of a lost novelist, a suppressed poet, of some mute and
inglorious Jane Austen, some Emily Brontë who dashed her brains
out on the moor or mopped and mowed about the highways crazed
with the torture that her gift had put her to. Indeed, I would venture
to guess that Anon,[7] who wrote so many poems without signing them,
was often a woman. It was a woman Edward Fitzgerald,[8] I think,
suggested who made the ballads and the folk-songs, crooning them
to her children, beguiling her spinning with them, or the length of
the winter's night.

This may be true or it may be false—who can say?—but what is   9
true in it, so it seemed to me, reviewing the story of Shakespeare's
sister as I had made it, is that any woman born with a great gift in
the sixteenth century would certainly have gone crazed, shot herself,
or ended her days in some lonely cottage outside the village, half
witch, half wizard, feared and mocked at. For it needs little skill in
psychology to be sure that a highly gifted girl who had tried to use
her gift for poetry would have been so thwarted and hindered by
other people, so tortured and pulled asunder by her own contrary
instincts, that she must have lost her health and sanity to a certainty.
No girl could have walked to London and stood at a stage door and
forced her way into the presence of actor-managers without doing
herself a violence and suffering an anguish which may have been
irrational—for chastity may be a fetish invented by certain societies
for unknown reasons—but were none the less inevitable. Chastity
had then, it has even now, a religious importance in a woman's life,

---

[7]Anonymous. [Eds.]
[8]English poet (1809–83) and translator of the *Rubáiyát of Omar Khayyám* (1859). [Eds.]

and has so wrapped itself round with nerves and instincts that to cut it free and bring it to the light of day demands courage of the rarest. To have lived a free life in London in the sixteenth century would have meant for a woman who was poet and playwright a nervous stress and dilemma which might well have killed her. Had she survived, whatever she had written would have been twisted and deformed, issuing from a strained and morbid imagination. And undoubtedly, I thought, looking at the shelf where there are no plays by women, her work would have gone unsigned. That refuge she would have sought certainly. It was the relic of the sense of chastity that dictated anonymity to women even so late as the nineteenth century. Currer Bell, George Eliot, George Sand,[9] all the victims of inner strife as their writings prove, sought ineffectively to veil themselves by using the name of a man. Thus they did homage to the convention, which if not implanted by the other sex was liberally encouraged by them (the chief glory of a woman is not to be talked of, said Pericles,[10] himself a much-talked-of man), that publicity in women is detestable. Anonymity runs in their blood. The desire to be veiled still possesses them. They are not even now as concerned about the health of their fame as men are, and, speaking generally, will pass a tombstone or a signpost without feeling an irresistible desire to cut their names on it, as Alf, Bert or Chas. must do in obedience to their instinct, which murmurs if it sees a fine woman go by, or even a dog, Ce chien est à moi.[11] And, of course, it may not be a dog, I thought, remembering Parliament Square, the Sieges Allee and other avenues; it may be a piece of land or a man with curly black hair. It is one of the great advantages of being a woman that one can pass even a very fine negress without wishing to make an Englishwoman of her.

That woman, then, who was born with a gift of poetry in the 10 sixteenth century, was an unhappy woman, a woman at strife against herself. All the conditions of her life, all her own instincts, were hostile to the state of mind which is needed to set free whatever is in the brain. But what is the state of mind that is most propitious to the act of creation, I asked. Can one come by any notion of the state that furthers and makes possible that strange activity? Here I opened the volume containing the Tragedies of Shakespeare. What was Shakespeare's state of mind, for instance, when he wrote *Lear* and *Antony and Cleopatra*? It was certainly the state of mind most favorable to

---

[9]Pen names for English novelists Charlotte Brontë (1816–55) and Mary Ann Evans (1819–80) and French novelist Armandine Dupin (1804–76). [Eds.]

[10]Athenian statesman, orator, and general (495?–429 BC). [Eds.]

[11]"This dog is mine." [Eds.]

poetry that there has ever existed. But Shakespeare himself said nothing about it. We only know casually and by chance that he "never blotted a line." Nothing indeed was ever said by the artist himself about his state of mind until the eighteenth century perhaps. Rousseau[12] perhaps began it. At any rate, by the nineteenth century self-consciousness had developed so far that it was the habit for men of letters to describe their minds in confessions and autobiographies. Their lives also were written, and their letters were printed after their deaths. Thus, though we do not know what Shakespeare went through when he wrote *Lear*, we do know what Carlyle went through when he wrote the *French Revolution*; what Flaubert went through when he wrote *Madame Bovary*; what Keats was going through when he tried to write poetry against the coming of death and the indifference of the world.

And one gathers from this enormous modern literature of confession and self-analysis that to write a work of genius is almost always a feat of prodigious difficulty. Everything is against the likelihood that it will come from the writer's mind whole and entire. Generally material circumstances are against it. Dogs will bark; people will interrupt; money must be made; health will break down. Further, accentuating all these difficulties and making them harder to bear is the world's notorious indifference. It does not ask people to write poems and novels and histories; it does not need them. It does not care whether Flaubert finds the right word or whether Carlyle scrupulously verifies this or that fact. Naturally, it will not pay for what it does not want. And so the writer, Keats, Flaubert, Carlyle, suffers, especially in the creative years of youth, every form of distraction and discouragement. A curse, a cry of agony rises from those books of analysis and confession. "Mighty poets in their misery dead"—that is the burden of their song. If anything comes through in spite of all this, it is a miracle, and probably no book is born entire and uncrippled as it was conceived.   11

But for women, I thought, looking at the empty shelves, these difficulties were infinitely more formidable. In the first place, to have a room of her own, let alone a quiet room or a sound-proof room, was out of the question, unless her parents were exceptionally rich or very noble, even up to the beginning of the nineteenth century. Since her pin money, which depended on the good will of her father, was only enough to keep her clothed, she was debarred from such alleviations as came even to Keats or Tennyson or Carlyle, all poor men, from a walking tour, a little journey to France, from the separate   12

---

[12]Jean-Jacques Rousseau (1712–78), French philosopher whose posthumously published *Confessions* are considered his masterpiece. [Eds.]

lodging which, even if it were miserable enough, sheltered them from the claims and tyrannies of their families. Such material difficulties were formidable; but much worse were the immaterial. The indifference of the world which Keats and Flaubert and other men of genius have found so hard to bear was in her case not indifference but hostility. The world did not say to her as it said to them, Write if you choose; it makes no difference to me. The world said with a guffaw, Write? What's the good of your writing? Here the psychologists of Newnham and Girton might come to our help, I thought, looking again at the blank spaces on the shelves. For surely it is time that the effect of discouragement upon the mind of the artist should be measured, as I have seen a dairy company measure the effect of ordinary milk and Grade A milk upon the body of the rat. They sat two rats in cages side by side, and of the two one was furtive, timid and small, and the other was glossy, bold and big. Now what food do we feed women as artists upon? I asked, remembering, I suppose, that dinner of prunes and custard. To answer that question I had only to open the evening paper and to read that Lord Birkenhead[13] is of opinion— but really I am not going to trouble to copy out Lord Birkenhead's opinion upon the writing of women. What Dean Inge says I will leave in peace. The Harley Street specialist may be allowed to rouse the echoes of Harley Street with his vociferations without raising a hair on my head. I will quote, however, Mr. Oscar Browning, because Mr. Oscar Browning was a great figure in Cambridge at one time, and used to examine the students at Girton and Newnham. Mr. Oscar Browning was wont to declare "that the impression left on his mind, after looking over any set of examination papers, was that, irrespective of the marks he might give, the best woman was intellectually the inferior of the worst man." After saying that Mr. Browning went back to his rooms—and it is this sequel that endears him and makes him a human figure of some bulk and majesty—he went back to his rooms and found a stable-boy lying on the sofa—"a mere skeleton, his cheeks were cavernous and sallow, his teeth were black, and he did not appear to have the full use of his limbs. . . . 'That's Arthur' [said Mr. Browning]. 'He's a dear boy really and most high-minded.' " The two pictures always seem to me to complete each other. And happily in this age of biography the two pictures often do complete each other, so that we are able to interpret the opinions of great men not only by what they say, but by what they do.

But though this is possible now, such opinions coming from the 13 lips of important people must have been formidable enough even fifty

---

[13]English lawyer, orator, and statesman (1872–1930). [Eds.]

years ago. Let us suppose that a father from the highest motives did not wish his daughter to leave home and become a writer, painter or scholar. "See what Mr. Oscar Browning says," he would say; and there was not only Mr. Oscar Browning; there was the *Saturday Review*; there was Mr. Greg—the "essentials of a woman's being," said Mr. Greg emphatically, "are that *they are supported by, and they minister to, men*"—there was an enormous body of masculine opinion to the effect that nothing could be expected of women intellectually. Even if her father did not read out loud these opinions, any girl could read them for herself; and the reading, even in the nineteenth century, must have lowered her vitality, and told profoundly upon her work. There would always have been that assertion—you cannot do this, you are incapable of doing that—to protest against, to overcome. Probably for a novelist this germ is no longer of much effect; for there have been women novelists of merit. But for painters it must still have some sting in it; and for musicians, I imagine, is even now active and poisonous in the extreme. The woman composer stands where the actress stood in the time of Shakespeare. Nick Greene, I thought, remembering the story I had made about Shakespeare's sister, said that a woman acting put him in mind of a dog dancing. Johnson[14] repeated the phrase two hundred years later of women preaching. And here, I said, opening a book about music, we have the very words used again in this year of grace, 1928, of women who try to write music. "Of Mlle. Germaine Taillesferre one can only repeat Dr. Johnson's dictum concerning a woman preacher, transposed into terms of music. "Sir, a woman's composing is like a dog's walking on his hind legs. It is not done well, but you are surprised to find it done at all.' " So accurately does history repeat itself.

Thus, I concluded, shutting Mr. Oscar Browning's life and pushing away the rest, it is fairly evident that even in the nineteenth century a woman was not encouraged to be an artist. On the contrary, she was snubbed, slapped, lectured and exhorted. Her mind must have been strained and her vitality lowered by the need of opposing this, of disproving that. For here again we come within range of that very interesting and obscure masculine complex which has had so much influence upon the woman's movement; that deep-seated desire, not so much that *she* shall be inferior as that *he* shall be superior, which plants him wherever one looks, not only in front of the arts, but barring the way to politics too, even when the risk to himself seems infinitesimal and the suppliant humble and devoted. Even Lady Bessborough, I remembered, with all her passion for politics,

[14]Samuel Johnson (1709–84), English lexicographer, critic, and author. [Eds.]

must humbly bow herself and write to Lord Granville Leveson-Gower: ". . . notwithstanding all my violence in politics and talking so much on that subject, I perfectly agree with you that no woman has any business to meddle with that or any other serious business, farther than giving her opinion (if she is ask'd)." And so she goes on to spend her enthusiasm where it meets with no obstacle whatsoever upon that immensely important subject, Lord Granville's maiden speech in the House of Commons. The spectacle is certainly a strange one, I thought. The history of men's opposition to women's emancipation is more interesting perhaps than the story of that emancipation itself. An amusing book might be made of it if some young student at Girton or Newnham would collect examples and deduce a theory—but she would need thick gloves on her hands, and bars to protect her of solid gold.

But what is amusing now, I recollected, shutting Lady Bessborough, had to be taken in desperate earnest once. Opinions that one now pastes in a book labelled cock-a-doodle-dum and keeps for reading to select audiences on summer nights once drew tears, I can assure you. Among your grandmothers and great-grandmothers there were many that wept their eyes out. Florence Nightingale shrieked aloud in her agony. Moreover, it is all very well for you, who have got yourselves to college and enjoy sitting-rooms—or is it only bed-sitting-rooms?—of your own to say that genius should disregard such opinions; that genius should be above caring what is said of it. Unfortunately, it is precisely the men or women of genius who mind most what is said of them. Remember Keats. Remember the words he had cut on his tombstone.[15] Think of Tennyson; think—but I need hardly multiply instances of the undeniable, if very unfortunate, fact that it is the nature of the artist to mind excessively what is said about him. Literature is strewn with the wreckage of men who have minded beyond reason the opinions of others.

And this susceptibility of theirs is doubly unfortunate, I thought, returning again to my original enquiry into what state of mind is most propitious for creative work, because the mind of an artist, in order to achieve the prodigious effort of freeing whole and entire the work that is in him, must be incandescent, like Shakespeare's mind, I conjectured, looking at the book which lay open at *Antony and Cleopatra*. There must be no obstacle in it, no foreign matter unconsumed.

For though we say that we know nothing about Shakespeare's state of mind, even as we say that, we are saying something about Shakespeare's state of mind. The reason perhaps why we know so

WRITING SUGGESTIONS

1. Woolf writes, "When . . . one reads of a witch being ducked, of a woman possessed by devils, of a wise woman selling herbs, or even of a very remarkable man who had a mother, then I think we are on the track of a lost novelist, a suppressed poet." Write an essay exploring the basis for Woolf's thesis. Do you agree? Explain.

2. Add to Woolf's story of Judith Shakespeare's life by creating a scene in which she shows her brother or father a sample of her writing.

---

[15]"Here lies one whose name was writ in water." [Eds.]

little of Shakespeare—compared with Donne or Ben Jonson or Milton—is that his grudges and spites and antipathies are hidden from us. We are not held up by some "revelation" which reminds us of the writer. All desire to protest, to preach, to proclaim an injury, to pay off a score, to make the world the witness of some hardship or grievance was fired out of him and consumed. Therefore his poetry flows from him free and unimpeded. If ever a human being got his work expressed completely, it was Shakespeare. If ever a mind was incandescent, unimpeded, I thought, turning again to the bookcase, it was Shakespeare's mind.

RESPONDING TO READING

1. Woolf asserts in paragraph 2 that "it is a perennial puzzle why no woman wrote a word of that extraordinary [Elizabethan] literature when every other man, it seemed, was capable of song or sonnet." Does this situation remain a puzzle to Woolf, and to you, or does she present the solution in her essay? Explain.   **2.** In paragraph 3 Woolf contrasts the woman in fiction written by men—"heroic and mean; splendid and sordid; infinitely beautiful and hideous in the extreme; as great as a man, some think even greater"—with actual women, who were "locked up, beaten and flung about the room." How can you account for this discrepancy? Do you believe this discrepancy persists today?   **3.** Does the stark contrast developed in paragraph 7 between Shakespeare and his sister—their parents' (and society's) expectations for them, their upbringing, their education, their search for employment—have any validity in your own life? In the lives of people you know?

ANSWERS TO RESPONDING TO READING

1. Woolf presents a solution to the puzzle, citing evidence that material circumstances and the world's hostility prevented women from writing. In moral terms, the situation remains a puzzle.
2. Little is known about the real Elizabethan woman, except that she was considered the property of men. An argument for the discrepancy between fictional and real women lies in men's ambivalence and guilt about their treatment of women. Students' responses will vary.
3. Answers will vary. Encourage specific illustrations.

Women's Brains

STEPHEN JAY GOULD

Writer and lecturer Stephen Jay Gould (1941–   ) is a paleontologist and professor whose speciality is snails. He explains in an interview for the *Contemporary Authors* series, "Snails suit my own interest because I'm concerned with the relationship between growth and evolution, and snails preserve in their shell the record of their growth from babyhood to adult." Gould is especially skilled at writing about science—particularly about evolution and biological determinism—for the layperson. He publishes a column in *Natural History* magazine and has collected his essays in *Ever Since Darwin* (1977), *The Panda's Thumb: More Reflections in Natural History* (1980), *An Urchin in the Storm* (1987), and *Bully for Brontosaurus* (1991). "Women's Brains," which gives a historical account of how scientists have used data about brain size, is typical of Gould's informal and informative style.

BACKGROUND ON AUTHOR

Gould is known for his clear explanations of difficult scientific concepts. His books on evolution and biological determinism are "simultaneously entertaining and teaching," according to James Gorman in the *New York Times Book Review*. As a paleontologist, he studies fossil records; as a humanist, he studies culture, believing that science is "not a heartless pursuit of objective information" but a "creative human activity" (quoted in *Contemporary Authors*, New Revision Series, vol. 10).

BACKGROUND ON READING

"Women's Brains" appears in *The Panda's Thumb: More Reflections on Natural History*, a collection of essays on evolutionary theory. In general, Gould observes in his work that culture has always influenced scientific exploration. In *The Mismeasure of Man*, he debunks the work of scientists who have attempted to prove that human intelligence may be measured objectively. He begins in the mid 1800s, with the hypothesis that intelligence is related to skull size, and concludes with an evaluation of relatively recent arguments for the inferiority of blacks. Gould discovered through analysis of scientific records that data were distorted to support the scientists' assumptions. Gould also challenges the IQ test developed by the French psychologist Alfred Binet in 1905, which he says was used unfairly as biased evidence of ethnic inferiority, particularly in newly arrived immigrants.

FOR OPENERS

Discuss the concept of culturally biased (and gender-biased) intelligence tests: tests that do not take into consideration the different ways men and women (or people from other cultural backgrounds) view the world. Should IQ tests—or, for that matter, the SATs—take gender and cultural background into account?

In the prelude to *Middlemarch*, George Eliot lamented the unfulfilled lives of talented women: 1

> Some have felt that these blundering lives are due to the inconvenient indefiniteness with which the Supreme Power has fashioned the natures of women: if there were one level of feminine incompetence as strict as the ability to count three and no more, the social lot of women might be treated with scientific certitude.

Eliot goes on to discount the idea of innate limitation, but while she wrote in 1872, the leaders of European anthropometry were trying to measure "with scientific certitude" the inferiority of women. Anthropometry, or measurement of the human body, is not so fashionable a field these days, but it dominated the human sciences for much of the nineteenth century and remained popular until intelligence testing replaced skull measurement as a favored device for making invidious comparisons among races, classes, and sexes. Craniometry, or measurement of the skull, commanded the most attention and respect. Its unquestioned leader, Paul Broca (1824–80), professor of clinical surgery at the Faculty of Medicine in Paris, gathered a school of disciples and imitators around himself. Their work, so meticulous and apparently irrefutable, exerted great influence and won high esteem as a jewel of nineteenth-century science. 2

Broca's work seemed particularly invulnerable to refutation. Had he not measured with the most scrupulous care and accuracy? (Indeed, he had. I have the greatest respect for Broca's meticulous procedure. His numbers are sound. But science is an inferential exercise, not a catalog of facts. Numbers, by themselves, specify nothing. All depends upon what you do with them.) Broca depicted himself as an apostle of objectivity, a man who bowed before facts and cast aside superstition and sentimentality. He declared that "there is no faith, however respectable, no interest, however legitimate, which must not accommodate itself to the progress of human knowledge and bend before truth." Women, like it or not, had smaller brains than men and, therefore, could not equal them in intelligence. This fact, Broca argued, may reinforce a common prejudice in male society, but it is also a scientific truth. L. Manouvrier, a black sheep in Broca's fold, rejected the inferiority of women and wrote with feeling about the burden imposed upon them by Broca's numbers: 3

> Women displayed their talents and their diplomas. They also invoked philosophical authorities. But they were opposed by *numbers* unknown to Condorcet[1] or to John Stuart Mill.[2] These numbers fell

---

[1]Jean Antoine, Marquis de Condorcet (1743–94), one of a group of French writers, known as Les Philosophes, who examined religious, philosophical, and ethical issues. [Eds.]
[2]English economist, philosopher, and political theorist (1806–73). [Eds.]

upon poor women like a sledge hammer, and they were accompanied by commentaries and sarcasms more ferocious than the most misogynist imprecations of certain church fathers. The theologians had asked if women had a soul. Several centuries later, some scientists were ready to refuse them a human intelligence.

Broca's argument rested upon two sets of data: the larger brains of men in modern societies, and a supposed increase in male superiority through time. His most extensive data came from autopsies performed personally in four Parisian hospitals. For 292 male brains, he calculated an average weight of 1,325 grams; 140 female brains averaged 1,144 grams for a difference of 181 grams, or 14 percent of the male weight. Broca understood, of course, that part of this difference could be attributed to the greater height of males. Yet he made no attempt to measure the effect of size alone and actually stated that it cannot account for the entire difference because we know, a priori, that women are not as intelligent as men (a premise that the data were supposed to test, not rest upon):

> We might ask if the small size of the female brain depends exclusively upon the small size of her body. Tiedemann has proposed this explanation. But we must not forget that women are, on the average, a little less intelligent than men, a difference which we should not exaggerate but which is, nonetheless, real. We are therefore permitted to suppose that the relatively small size of the female brain depends in part upon her physical inferiority and in part upon her intellectual inferiority.

In 1873, the year after Eliot published *Middlemarch*, Broca measured the cranial capacities of prehistoric skulls from L'Homme Mort cave. Here he found a difference of only 99.5 cubic centimeters between males and females, while modern populations range from 129.5 to 220.7. Topinard, Broca's chief disciple, explained the increasing discrepancy through time as a result of differing evolutionary pressures upon dominant men and passive women:

> The man who fights for two or more in the struggle for existence, who has all the responsibility and the cares of tomorrow, who is constantly active in combating the environment and human rivals, needs more brain than the woman whom he must protect and nourish, the sedentary woman, lacking any interior occupations, whose role is to raise children, love, and be passive.

In 1879, Gustave Le Bon, chief misogynist of Broca's school, used these data to publish what must be the most vicious attack upon women in modern scientific literature (no one can top Aristotle).[3] I

---

[3]In his philosophical writings, Aristotle (384–322 B.C.) notes that women are (among other things) "more dispirited, more despondent, more imprudent, and more given to falsehood" than men and also that they are "more envious, more querulous, more slanderous, and more contentious." [Eds.]

4

5

6

ADDITIONAL QUESTIONS FOR RESPONDING TO READING

1. Gould concludes that "setting a biological value upon groups" is "irrelevant and highly injurious" (paragraph 16). What does he mean?
2. How does Gould resolve the apparent differences among competing scientific theories that try to prove the superiority of one sex over another?

TEACHING STRATEGY

Gould's essay is useful for analyzing argument at two levels: (1) the nineteenth-century argument embedded in the essay, and (2) Gould's use of that argument to make his own point. Although the scientists Gould quotes now sound dated, even ridiculous, at one time they were very influential. Analyze their statements and note the kinds of logical fallacies they reveal.

COLLABORATIVE ACTIVITY

Ask students, working in groups, to consider whether they see evidence that attitudes like LeBon's still prevail today. For example, do they believe math and science teachers have similar expectations for their male and female students. In class discussion, compare students' responses.

do not claim his views were representative of Broca's school, but they were published in France's most respected anthropological journal. Le Bon concluded:

> In the most intelligent races, as among the Parisians, there are a large number of women whose brains are closer in size to those of gorillas than to the most developed male brains. This inferiority is so obvious that no one can contest it for a moment; only its degree is worth discussion. All psychologists who have studied the intelligence of women, as well as poets and novelists, recognize today that they represent the most inferior forms of human evolution and that they are closer to children and savages than to an adult, civilized man. They excel in fickleness, inconstancy, absence of thought and logic, and incapacity to reason. Without doubt there exist some distinguished women, very superior to the average man, but they are as exceptional as the birth of any monstrosity, as, for example, of a gorilla with two heads; consequently, we may neglect them entirely.

Nor did Le Bon shrink from the social implications of his views. 7 He was horrified by the proposal of some American reformers to grant women higher education on the same basis as men:

> A desire to give them the same education, and, as a consequence, to propose the same goals for them, is a dangerous chimera. . . . The day when, misunderstanding the inferior occupations which nature has given her, women leave the home and take part in our battles; on this day a social revolution will begin, and everything that maintains the sacred ties of the family will disappear.

Sound familiar?[4]

I have reexamined Broca's data, the basis for all this derivative 8 pronouncement, and I find his numbers sound but his interpretation ill-founded, to say the least. The data supporting his claim for increased difference through time can be easily dismissed. Broca based his contention on the samples from L'Homme Mort alone— only seven male and six female skulls in all. Never have so little data yielded such far ranging conclusions.

In 1888, Topinard published Broca's more extensive data on the 9 Parisian hospitals. Since Broca recorded height and age as well as brain size, we may use modern statistics to remove their effect. Brain weight decreases with age, and Broca's women were, on average, considerably older than his men. Brain weight increases with height, and his average man was almost half a foot taller than his average woman. I used multiple regression, a technique that allowed me to

---

[4]When I wrote this essay, I assumed that Le Bon was a marginal, if colorful, figure. I have since learned that he was a leading scientist, one of the founders of social psychology, and best known for a seminal study on crowd behavior, still cited today (*La psychologie des foules*, 1895), and for his work on unconscious motivation.

assess simultaneously the influence of height and age upon brain size. In an analysis of the data for women, I found that, at average male height and age, a woman's brain would weigh 1,212 grams. Correction for height and age reduces Broca's measured difference of 181 grams by more than a third, to 113 grams.

I don't know what to make of this remaining difference because 10 I cannot assess other factors known to influence brain size in a major way. Cause of death has an important effect: degenerative disease often entails a substantial diminution of brain size. (This effect is separate from the decrease attributed to age alone.) Eugene Schreider, also working with Broca's data, found that men killed in accidents had brains weighing, on average, 60 grams more than men dying of infectious diseases. The best modern data I can find (from American hospitals) records a full 100-gram difference between death by degenerative arteriosclerosis and by violence or accident. Since so many of Broca's subjects were very elderly women, we may assume that lengthy degenerative disease was more common among them than among the men.

More importantly, modern students of brain size still have not 11 agreed on a proper measure for eliminating the powerful effect of body size. Height is partly adequate, but men and women of the same height do not share the same body build. Weight is even worse than height, because most of its variation reflects nutrition rather than intrinsic size—fat versus skinny exerts little influence upon the brain. Manouvrier took up this subject in the 1880s and argued that muscular mass and force should be used. He tried to measure this elusive property in various ways and found a marked difference in favor of men, even in men and women of the same height. When he corrected for what he called "sexual mass," women actually came out slightly ahead in brain size.

Thus, the corrected 113-gram difference is surely too large; the 12 true figure is probably close to zero and may as well favor women as men. And 113 grams, by the way, is exactly the average difference between a 5 foot 4 inch and a 6 foot 4 inch male in Broca's data. We would not (especially us short folks) want to ascribe greater intelligence to tall men. In short, who knows what to do with Broca's data? They certainly don't permit any confident claim that men have bigger brains than women.

To appreciate the social role of Broca and his school, we must 13 recognize that his statements about the brains of women do not reflect an isolated prejudice toward a single disadvantaged group. They must be weighed in the context of a general theory that supported contemporary social distinctions as biologically ordained. Women, blacks, and poor people suffered the same disparagement, but women bore

WRITING SUGGESTION

Write a letter to Le Bon from a woman who is a contemporary of his. Using nonscientific language and information, argue against his theory. Be sure to use a reasonable tone.

the brunt of Broca's argument because he had easier access to data on women's brains. Women were singularly denigrated but they also stood as surrogates for other disenfranchised groups. As one of Broca's disciples wrote in 1881: "Men of the black races have a brain scarcely heavier than that of white women." This juxtaposition extended into many other realms of anthropological argument, particularly to claims that, anatomically and emotionally, both women and blacks were like white children—and that white children, by the theory of recapitulation, represented an ancestral (primitive) adult stage of human evolution. I do not regard as empty rhetoric the claim that women's battles are for all of us.

Maria Montessori did not confine her activities to educational 14 reform for young children. She lectured on anthropology for several years at the University of Rome, and wrote an influential book entitled *Pedagogical Anthropology* (English edition, 1913). Montessori was no egalitarian. She supported most of Broca's work and the theory of innate criminality proposed by her compatriot Cesare Lombroso. She measured the circumference of children's heads in her schools and inferred that the best prospects had bigger brains. But she had no use for Broca's conclusions about women. She discussed Manouvrier's work at length and made much of his tentative claim that women, after proper correction of the data, had slightly larger brains than men. Women, she concluded, were intellectually superior, but men had prevailed heretofore by dint of physical force. Since technology has abolished force as an instrument of power, the era of women may soon be upon us: "In such an epoch there will really be superior human beings, there will really be men strong in morality and in sentiment. Perhaps in this way the reign of women is approaching, when the enigma of her anthropological superiority will be deciphered. Woman was always the custodian of human sentiment, morality and honor."

This represents one possible antidote to "scientific" claims for the 15 constitutional inferiority of certain groups. One may affirm the validity of biological distinctions but argue that the data have been misinterpreted by prejudiced men with a stake in the outcome, and that disadvantaged groups are truly superior. In recent years, Elaine Morgan has followed this strategy in her *Descent of Woman*, a speculative reconstruction of human prehistory from the woman's point of view—and as farcical as more famous tall tales by and for men.

I prefer another strategy. Montessori and Morgan followed Broca's philosophy to reach a more congenial conclusion. I would rather label the whole enterprise of setting a biological value upon groups for what it is: irrelevant and highly injurious. George Eliot well appreciated the special tragedy that biological labeling imposed upon members of disadvantaged groups. She expressed it for people like herself—women of extraordinary talent. I would apply it more widely—not only to those whose dreams are flouted but also to those who never realize that they may dream—but I cannot match her prose. In conclusion, then, the rest of Eliot's prelude to *Middlemarch*:

> The limits of variation are really much wider than anyone would imagine from the sameness of women's coiffure and the favorite love stories in prose and verse. Here and there a cygnet is reared uneasily among the ducklings in the brown pond, and never finds the living stream in fellowship with its own oary-footed kind. Here and there is born a Saint Theresa,[5] foundress of nothing, whose loving heart-beats and sobs after an unattained goodness tremble off and are dispersed among hindrances instead of centering in some long-rec-ognizable deed.

RESPONDING TO READING

1. Although this essay is solidly grounded in scientific research and quotes researchers extensively, Gould uses the first person, contractions, and other characteristics of informal style. How does this level of diction affect your response to Gould's ideas?   **2.** In paragraph 6 Gould describes the remarks of Gustave Le Bon as "what must be the most vicious attack upon women in modern scientific literature." What shocks or angers you most about Le Bon's theory as Gould presents it?   **3.** In his analysis of the larger implications of Broca's theories, Gould comments, "Women were singularly denigrated but they also stood as surrogates for other disenfranchised groups" (paragraph 13). What does he mean? What application, if any, does this statement have to inequities that you see in modern society?

The Androgynous Man

NOEL PERRIN

Nonfiction writer Noel Perrin (1927–   ) is a Dartmouth College professor of English who contributes regularly to *The New Yorker*. Perrin has written a variety of books, including *A Passport Secretly Green* (1961), *Dr. Bowdler's Legacy: A History of Expurgated Books in England and America* (1969), and *Vermont in All Weathers* (1973). His essay "The Androgynous Man" is a lighthearted discussion of gender roles in which Perrin claims he is "a fairly good natural mother."

---

[5]One of the principal saints of the Catholic Church (1515–82). [Eds.]

FOR OPENERS

1. Ask students to find and bring to class examples of the kind of quiz that Perrin answered on the train (they can be found in many magazines). Discuss the ways in which these devices reinforce gender distinctions.
2. Define *androgyny*: having the characteristics or nature of "both male and female" (*Webster's New Collegiate Dictionary*). Give examples of androgynous appearance and behavior in everyday life.

ADDITIONAL QUESTIONS FOR RESPONDING TO READING

1. What mistake does Perrin claim feminists have made? Do you agree or disagree?
2. Perrin says that "red-blooded Americans" (males) do not have a range of choice (paragraphs 7–8). What does he mean? How does he express sympathy for the "he-man"? Why do "androgynes" have more options?
3. To what purpose does Perrin assert that God is androgynous?
4. Analyze the kinds of illustrations of masculinity and femininity Perrin uses as support. Are they effective? Why or why not?

The summer I was 16, I took a train from New York to Steamboat 1 Springs, Colo., where I was going to be assistant horse wrangler at a camp. The trip took three days, and since I was much too shy to talk to strangers, I had quite a lot of time for reading. I read all of *Gone With the Wind*. I read all the interesting articles in a couple of magazines I had, and then I went back and read all the dull stuff. I also took all the quizzes, a thing of which magazines were even fuller then than now.

The one that held my undivided attention was called "How Mas- 2 culine/Feminine Are You?" It consisted of a large number of inkblots. The reader was supposed to decide which of four objects each blot most resembled. The choices might be a cloud, a steam engine, a caterpillar and a sofa.

When I finished the test, I was shocked to find that I was barely 3 masculine at all. On a scale of 1 to 10, I was about 1.2. Me, the horse wrangler? (And not just wrangler, either. That summer, I had to skin a couple of horses that died—the camp owner wanted the hides.)

The results of that test were so terrifying to me that for the first 4 time in my life I did a piece of original analysis. Having unlimited time on the train, I looked at the "masculine" answers over and over, trying to find what it was that distinguished real men from people like me—and eventually I discovered two very simple patterns. It was "masculine" to think the blots looked like man-made objects, and "feminine" to think they looked like natural objects. It was masculine to think they looked like things capable of causing harm, and feminine to think of innocent things.

Even at 16, I had the sense to see that the compilers of the test 5 were using rather limited criteria—maleness and femaleness are both more complicated than *that*—and I breathed a huge sigh of relief. I wasn't necessarily a wimp, after all.

That the test did reveal something other than the superficiality 6 of its makers I realized only many years later. What it revealed was that there is a large class of men and women both, to which I belong, who are essentially androgynous. That doesn't mean we're gay, or low in the appropriate hormones, or uncomfortable performing the jobs traditionally assigned our sexes. (A few years after that summer, I was leading troops in combat and, unfashionable as it now is to admit this, having a very good time. War is exciting. What a pity the 20th century went and spoiled it with high-tech weapons.)

What it does mean to be spiritually androgynous is a kind of 7 freedom. Men who are all-male, or he-man, or 100 percent red-blooded Americans, have a little biological set that causes them to be attracted to physical power, and probably also to dominance. Maybe even to watching football. I don't say this to criticize them. Completely masculine men are quite often wonderful people: good husbands, good (though sometimes overwhelming) fathers, good members of society. Furthermore, they are often so unself-consciously at ease in the world that other men seek to imitate them. They just aren't as free as us androgynes. They pretty nearly have to be what they are; we have a range of choices open.

The sad part is that many of us never discover that. Men who 8 are not 100 percent red-blooded Americans—say, those who are only 75 percent red-blooded—often fail to notice their freedom. They are too busy trying to copy the he-men ever to realize that men, like women, come in a wide variety of acceptable types. Why this frantic imitation? My answer is mere speculation, but not casual. I have speculated on this for a long time.

Partly they're just envious of the he-man's unconscious ease. 9 Mostly they're terrified of finding that there may be something wrong with them deep down, some weakness at the heart. To avoid discovering that, they spend their lives acting out the role that the he-man naturally lives. Sad.

One thing that men owe to the women's movement is that this 10 kind of failure is less common than it used to be. In releasing themselves from the single ideal of the dependent woman, women have more or less incidentally released a lot of men from the single ideal of the dominant male. The one mistake the feminists have made, I think, is in supposing that *all* men need this release, or that the world would be a better place if all men achieved it. It wouldn't. It would just be duller.

So far I have been pretty vague about just what the freedom of 11 the androgynous man is. Obviously it varies with the case. In the case I know best, my own, I can be quite specific. It has freed me most as a parent. I am, among other things, a fairly good natural mother. I like the nurturing role. It makes me feel good to see a child eat—and it turns me to mush to see a 4-year-old holding a glass with both small hands, in order to drink. I even enjoyed sewing patches on the knees of my daughter Amy's Dr. Dentons when she was at the crawling stage. All that pleasure I would have lost if I had made myself stick to the notion of the paternal role that I started with.

Or take a smaller and rather ridiculous example. I feel free to kiss 12 cats. Until recently it never occurred to me that I would want to, though my daughters have been doing it all their lives. But my elder daughter is now 22, and in London. Of course, I get to look after her cat while she is gone. He's a big, handsome farm cat named Petrushka, very unsentimental, though used from kittenhood to being kissed on the top of the head by Elizabeth. I've gotten very fond of

TEACHING STRATEGIES

1. Introduce the distinction between sex (biological) and gender (cultural). Discuss the ways in which culture establishes gender difference. How does Perrin's essay reflect those cultural assumptions about gender?
2. Ask students whether they find Perrin's tone offensive. Does he seem to be trivializing the issue?

COLLABORATIVE ACTIVITY

Instruct small groups to brainstorm on the connotations of the terms *masculine* and *feminine*. Follow up with class discussion about why students make these associations.

WRITING SUGGESTION

Write an essay that explains Perrin's concept of androgyny. Take a position on his view—stating whether it is idealistic, realistic, or a mixture of both—and support your position.

ANSWERS TO RESPONDING TO READING

1. While Perrin asserts his "femininity," he also demonstrates a need to undercut that image, to establish a balance. He does not want to be seen as a "wimp."
2. A mother might observe that the examples of "nurturing" that Perrin offers are stereotypical and actually do not involve direct contact with the child. Although many men might agree with Perrin that such examples show that he is indeed "a fairly good natural mother," many others (and many women) will see his argument as self-congratulatory.
3. Answers will vary. Some students may find Perrin's approach appealing, whereas others may find his assumptions about gender to be stereotypical.

him (he's the adventurous kind of cat who likes to climb hills with you), and one night I simply felt like kissing him on the top of the head, and did. Why did no one tell me sooner how silky cat fur is?

Then there's my relation to cars. I am completely unembarrassed 13 to my inability to diagnose even minor problems in whatever object I happen to be driving, and don't have to make some insider's remark to mechanics to try to establish that I, too, am a "Man With His Machine."

The same ease extends to household maintenance. I do it, of 14 course. Service people are expensive. But for the last decade my house has functioned better than it used to because I've had the aid of a volume called "Home Repairs Any Woman Can Do," which is pitched just right for people at my technical level. As a youth, I'd as soon have touched such a book as I would have become a transvestite. Even though common sense says there is really nothing sexual whatsoever about fixing sinks.

Or take public emotion. All my life I have easily been moved by 15 certain kinds of voices. The actress Siobhan McKenna's, to take a notable case. Give her an emotional scene in a play, and within 10 words my eyes are full of tears. In boyhood, my great dread was that someone might notice. I struggled manfully, you might say, to suppress this weakness. Now, of course, I don't see it as a weakness at all, but as a kind of fulfillment. I even suspect that the true he-men feel the same way, or one kind of them does, at least, and it's only the poor imitators who have to struggle to repress themselves.

Let me come back to the inkblots, with their assumption that 16 masculine equates with machinery and science, and feminine with art and nature. I have no idea whether the right pronoun for God is He, She or It. But this I'm pretty sure of. If God could somehow be induced to take that test, God would not come out macho, and not feminismo, either, but right in the middle. Fellow androgynes, it's a nice thought.

RESPONDING TO READING

1. Despite his claim that he is "spiritually androgynous" (paragraph 7), Perrin goes out of his way to mention some of his "he-man" exploits. For instance, he tells readers that he worked as a horse wrangler, skinned horses, and led troops in combat. What do you think motivates him to mention such activities?   **2.** How do you suppose a mother might respond to Perrin's claims for himself as a parent in paragraph 11? How do you imagine most men would assess Perrin on the basis of the examples he cites in paragraphs 13–15? Do you think most women would be likely to respond differently?

Why?   **3.** In what way do Perrin's lighthearted tone and purely domestic examples affect your reaction to his essay? Do these elements strengthen his case or trivialize the issues of gender identification and sex-role stereotypes? Explain.

Why I Want a Wife

JUDY BRADY

Judy Brady (1937–   ) studied painting in college and wanted to pursue painting as a career. Instead, she has said, she was discouraged from an art career in higher education by her male teachers, and so she married and had a family. First a housewife, Brady began to write articles on social issues and became involved in the feminist movement. Her popular essay "Why I Want a Wife" appeared in the preview issue of *Ms.* in 1972.

1   I belong to that classification of people known as wives. I am A Wife. And, not altogether incidentally, I am a mother.

2   Not too long ago a male friend of mine appeared on the scene fresh from a recent divorce. He had one child, who is, of course, with his ex-wife. He is looking for another wife. As I thought about him while I was ironing one evening, it suddenly occurred to me that I, too, would like to have a wife. Why do I want a wife?

3   I would like to go back to school so that I can become economically independent, support myself, and, if need be, support those dependent upon me. I want a wife who will work and send me to school. And while I am going to school I want a wife to take care of my children. I want a wife to keep track of the children's doctor and dentist appointments. And to keep track of mine, too. I want a wife to make sure my children eat properly and are kept clean. I want a wife who will wash the children's clothes and keep them mended. I want a wife who is a good nurturant attendant to my children, who arranges for their schooling, makes sure that they have an adequate social life with their peers, takes them to the park, the zoo, etc. I want a wife who takes care of the children when they are sick, a wife who arranges to be around when the children need special care, because, of course, I cannot miss classes at school. My wife must arrange to lose time at work and not lose the job. It may mean a small cut in my wife's income from time to time, but I guess I can tolerate that. Needless to say, my wife will arrange and pay for the care of the children while my wife is working.

FOR OPENERS

1. Ask students to freewrite about their ideal spouse.
2. Brainstorm to generate a list of family tasks and roles. Are they gender related? Which are associated with men, and which with women? Why?

ADDITIONAL QUESTIONS FOR RESPONDING TO READING

1. What attitude toward children is revealed in this essay?
2. What is the purpose of the repetition of "I want a wife . . ."?
3. What evidence of Brady's socioeconomic background can be found in the essay? In what ways, if any, would the essay be different if written from the perspective of a very wealthy—or a very poor—woman?
4. Does Brady seem to have a political agenda? Is she simply criticizing male and female roles in marriage, or does she have another purpose in mind?

TEACHING STRATEGIES

1. This essay frequently provokes strong reactions from students. Use it to talk about tone, irony, and persuasion, with particular focus on audience.
2. Consider the organization of Brady's argument. First, she discusses the wife's routine tasks, then the "ideal" of wifely subservience, and then the double standard between the sexes.
3. If possible, bring in a copy of *Ms.* magazine, Spring 1972 (the issue in which Brady's article first appeared). Briefly discuss some of the other articles. How does Brady's piece fit in with the others?

COLLABORATIVE ACTIVITY

Assign groups the task of drafting responses to Brady's essay from different perspectives: (1) the divorced man seeking a wife, (2) the husband, (3) one of the children, (4) a working mother, and (5) an older wife. Have them present the results in class as a basis for discussion.

I want a wife who will take care of *my* physical needs. I want a 4
wife who will keep my house clean. A wife who will pick up after me. I want a wife who will keep my clothes clean, ironed, mended, replaced when need be, and who will see to it that my personal things are kept in their proper place so that I can find what I need the minute I need it. I want a wife who cooks the meals, a wife who is a *good* cook. I want a wife who will plan the menus, do the necessary grocery shopping, prepare the meals, serve them pleasantly, and then do the cleaning up while I do my studying. I want a wife who will care for me when I am sick and sympathize with my pain and loss of time from school. I want a wife to go along when our family takes a vacation so that someone can continue to care for me and my children when I need a rest and change of scene.

I want a wife who will not bother me with rambling complaints 5
about a wife's duties. But I want a wife who will listen to me when I feel the need to explain a rather difficult point I have come across in my course of studies. And I want a wife who will type my papers for me when I have written them.

I want a wife who will take care of the details of my social life. 6
When my wife and I are invited out by friends, I want a wife who will take care of the babysitting arrangements. When I meet people at school that I like and want to entertain, I want a wife who will have the house clean, will prepare a special meal, serve it to me and my friends, and not interrupt when I talk about the things that interest me and my friends. I want a wife who will have arranged that the children are fed and ready for bed before my guests arrive so that the children do not bother us. I want a wife who takes care of the needs of my guests so that they feel comfortable, who makes sure that they have an ashtray, that they are passed the hors d'oeuvres, that they are offered a second helping of the food, that their wine glasses are replenished when necessary, that their coffee is served to them as they like it. And I want a wife who knows that sometimes I need a night out by myself.

I want a wife who is sensitive to my sexual needs, a wife who 7
makes love passionately and eagerly when I feel like it, a wife who makes sure that I am satisfied. And, of course, I want a wife who will not demand sexual attention when I am not in the mood for it. I want a wife who assumes the complete responsibility for birth control, because I do not want more children. I want a wife who will remain sexually faithful to me so that I do not have to clutter up my intellectual life with jealousies. And I want a wife who understands that *my* sexual needs may entail more than strict adherence to monogamy. I must, after all, be able to relate to people as fully as possible.

If, by chance, I find another person more suitable as a wife than the wife I already have, I want the liberty to replace my present wife with another one. Naturally, I will expect a fresh, new life; my wife will take the children and be solely responsible for them so that I am left free. 8

When I am through with school and have a job, I want my wife to quit working and remain at home so that my wife can more fully and completely take care of a wife's duties. 9

My God, who *wouldn't* want a wife? 10

RESPONDING TO READING

1. What is your definition of a wife? How closely does it conform to Brady's? Do you know any women who satisfy Brady's criteria?   **2.** This essay, written over 20 years ago, has been anthologized many times. To what do you attribute its continued popularity? Is the essay dated?   **3.** What is your emotional response to Brady's grievances? Are you sympathetic? Saddened? Impatient? How do you imagine a middle-class husband would respond? How might a working-class wife react? How might a single parent react? Why?

Fighting Back

STANTON L. WORMLEY, JR.

Stanton L. Wormley, Jr. (1951–   ), who holds a B.A. in Spanish from Howard University and a Master's in forensic science from George Washington University, has held various administrative positions at Howard and at the University of Southern Maine in Portland. Now a freelance writer based in Maine, Wormley has published technical writing pieces, video scripts for industrial training films, science articles, and three articles about a Washington, D.C., family in *American Negro Biography*. In addition, he has published a number of articles about shooting and firearms, subjects on which he says he plans to concentrate in the future. In the following essay Wormley talks about the lessons to be learned from fighting back—and from not fighting back—especially for members of minority groups who feel "disenfranchised and often victimized by discrimination and poverty."

In the spring of 1970, I was an 18-year-old army private at Fort Jackson, S.C. I had been in the Army for less than six months and was still making the difficult transition from life as an only child in an upper-middle-class black family. One rite of passage was particularly intense: on a cool April night, a drunken white soldier whom I barely knew attacked me as I lay sleeping. 1

ADDITIONAL QUESTIONS FOR
RESPONDING TO READING

1. What distinction does Wormley make between "fighting back" and self-defense?
2. What does Wormley mean by his "sadness" in the knowledge that he has learned to fight back? Do you find it sad? Explain.
3. What relationship does Wormley see between his race and the desire to fight back? Do you agree with his analysis?

TEACHING STRATEGIES

1. Note that Wormley's argument depends on the ways in which he defines certain words and concepts, such as *fighting back, self-defense, retribution,* and *justification.* Discuss the associations he makes with each of these words, and examine how they help organize his argument.
2. Show students how the essay approaches its thesis inductively—that is, how it raises questions in the introduction that are answered only by the conclusion.

COLLABORATIVE ACTIVITY

Ask groups to bring in clippings from newspapers and magazines that describe incidents of "fighting back" in self-defense. Have each group present one incident and ask the class to consider whether the response was justified in each case.

My recollection of the incident is, in some details, still hazy. Like the seven other men in the squad bay, I was asleep in my bunk. I half-remember some vigorous off-key singing, the ceiling light going on and someone roughly shaking my foot. I sat up, drowsily irritated at being disturbed. Everything happened very quickly then: a voice began shouting, an arm tightened around my neck and a fist pounded the top of my head. I was still somewhat asleep and confused. Why was this happening to me? It didn't occur to me to fight. I simply covered my head as best I could. There was a hubbub, arms reaching in to separate us and then the sight of the man above me, struggling against the others holding him back, his face red with fury. By then I was fully awake, and I saw the strained tendons in the man's neck, the wormlike vein pulsing at his temple, the spittle that sprayed as he screamed obscenities at me. I wasn't hurt, at least not physically, and all I could do was stare, bewildered. I never did discover what had provoked him. 2

Afterward, I was angrily confronted by a young black streetwise soldier named Morris. He eyed me with unconcealed contempt. "What the hell's wrong with you, man?" he demanded. "Why didn't you fight back? I would've killed that mother." I had no answer for him. How could I have made him understand the sheltered world of my childhood, in which violence was deplored and careful deliberation encouraged. I was brought up to *think*, not just react. 3

Nevertheless, that question—*Why didn't I fight back?*—haunted me long after the incident had been forgotten by everyone else. Was I less of a man for not having beaten my attacker to a bloody pulp? Morris—and undoubtedly others—certainly thought so. And so, perhaps, would the majority of American men. The ability and the will to fight back are integral parts of our society's conception of manhood. It goes beyond mere self-defense, I think, for there is a subtle but significant difference between self-defense and fighting back. Self-defense is essentially passive; it involves no rancor, pride or ego. Running away from danger is what martial-arts instructors sometimes recommend as the appropriate response, the best self-defense strategy. Fighting back, on the other hand, is active and defiant. It involves the adoption of an attitude that one's retribution is morally justified—or even, at times, morally obligatory. 4

And we American men buy that attitude—especially those of us who are members of minority groups. For us, largely disenfranchised and often victimized by discrimination and poverty, fighting back is a statement of individual potency and self-determination. It is the very antithesis of victimization: it is a sign of empowerment. The symbolic consequences of fighting back—or failing to do so—reflect upon the group as a whole. To Morris, I had disgraced the entire black American population. 5

I suppose that there are still situations in which immediate, violent 6
retaliation is necessary. Sometimes it seems that fighting back is the
only way to command respect in the world. Women are now learning
that unfortunate lesson, as did blacks and other minorities in recent
decades. I can't help feeling, however, that when one gains the ability
to fight back one loses something as well. What that something is, I
can't easily define: a degree of compassion, perhaps, or tolerance or
empathy. It is a quality I hope is possessed by the men in Washington
and Moscow who have the power to dispense the ultimate retribution.

Once in a great while, past events are repeated, granting people 7
a chance either to redeem themselves or to relive their mistakes. Two
years ago, in a small roadside diner in Virginia, a man—again white,
again drunk—chanced to make a derogatory remark to me. I was
sitting with my back to him and ignored it. Thinking I had not heard
him, he drew close to repeat his taunt, grabbing my shoulder. I suppose I could have moved away, shaken his hand off or complained
to the manager. But the accumulated frustrations of years of ignoring
such remarks—plus the memory of the incident at Fort Jackson, dictated otherwise. Before I knew what was happening, I was up out of
my chair. I hit the man hard in the stomach and he sank to one knee
with a moan. Grasping his collar, I almost hit again, but it was obvious
that he had had enough. He looked up at me, gasping, his face
contorted with pain and fear. The man was perhaps 50, of average
size, with a fleshy, florid face surmounted by close-cropped gray
bristle. I noted that he had bad teeth, a fact that gave me a moment
of spiteful satisfaction. Suddenly sober, he stammered something
unintelligible—it might have been an apology—and I let him go.

As I walked away, I was filled with a feeling of exultation. I had 8
not stopped to wonder why; I had not been checked by compassion
or sympathy. I had retaliated and it had felt good. But later, my
exhilaration passed, leaving a strange sensation of hollowness. I felt
vaguely embarrassed, even ashamed. In my mind I was still confident
I had acted rightly, but my heart was no longer sure. I remembered
my fury, and the quiet way the people in the diner had watched me
stalk angrily away. I remembered, too, the abject grimace on the man's
face, partly from the pain of the blow and partly in anticipation of a
second; and I realized that there was a trace of sadness in the knowledge that I, too, had learned to fight back.

RESPONDING TO READING

1. Have you ever been in a situation where you could have fought back and
did not? Why did you choose not to fight? Did you regret your decision?
Why or why not?   **2.** In many ways Wormley's initial situation is similar
to that of a woman: When first attacked, his instinctive response is to protect

woman who fights back may place more value on the less familiar feeling of empowerment.

3. As an African-American, Wormley experiences a particular kind of attack, one incited by racism. He is chastised by Morris for letting down his race. For those "largely disenfranchised and often victimized by discrimination and poverty, fighting back is a statement of individual potency and self-determination"; it is the "antithesis of victimization," a "sign of empowerment." As an only child, Wormley might have been overprotected; he also would not have learned from siblings how to fight back. As a member of an upper-middle-class family, he probably did not grow up in a neighborhood where fighting was common.

BACKGROUND ON AUTHOR

Steinem dates her involvement in the women's movement to a Redstockings meeting she attended in 1968 to gather material for a magazine column. She was cofounder of the Women's Action Alliance and the National Women's Political Caucus. In 1970, she was one of the strategists for the Women's Strike for Equality, one of the first strong national demonstrations in support of the women's movement. Steinem is the granddaughter of Pauline Steinem, an early feminist who was president of a suffrage group and representative to the 1908 international Council of Women.

FOR OPENERS

1. Have students freewrite on their definition of the word *feminism*. Follow up with a discussion. If possible, bring in the premier issue of *Ms.* and examine the issues that most concerned feminists at the time. Which aspects of feminism as articulated by Steinem, then and now, are important to students? Which are not?

2. Identify the issues that are now provoking debate and activism on your campus. Discuss how they would be characterized according to Steinem's ideas about activism.

himself; it simply does not occur to him to fight back. Later he says, "When one gains the ability to fight back one loses something as well" (paragraph 6). Do you think most women would agree with him? Do you agree?   **3.** Is the fact that Wormley is black of any special significance in this essay? Is the fact that he is an only child? That he comes from an upper-middle-class family? Does any of this information influence your expectations about how Wormley might respond to a physical challenge? If so, how?

The Good News Is: These Are Not the Best Years of Your Life
GLORIA STEINEM

Feminist writer, editor, speaker, and political activist Gloria Steinem (1934–   ) was born in Toledo, Ohio. After graduation from college, she won a fellowship to study in India. Later, she became active in the women's movement as an organizer and speaker, worked as a journalist, and founded *Ms.* magazine in 1971. Steinem came to national prominence with her essay "I Was a Playboy Bunny," a humorous and sarcastic exposé of the harassment she suffered on the job. Her essays are collected in *Outrageous Acts and Everyday Rebellions* (1983). In "The Good New Is: These Are Not the Best Years of Your Life," first published in *Ms.* in 1979, Steinem asserts that women, unlike men, grow "more radical with age."

If you had asked me a decade or more ago, I certainly would have said the campus was the first place to look for the feminist or any other revolution. I also would have assumed that student-age women, like student-age men, were much more likely to be activist and open to change than their parents. After all, campus revolts have a long and well-publicized tradition, from the students of medieval France, whose "heresy" was suggesting that the university be separate from the church, through the anticolonial student riots of British India; from students who led the cultural revolution of the People's Republic of China, to campus demonstrations against the Shah of Iran. Even in this country, with far less tradition of student activism, the populist movement to end the war in Vietnam was symbolized by campus protests and mistrust of anyone over thirty.

It has taken me many years of traveling as a feminist speaker and organizer to understand that I was wrong about women; at least, about women acting on their own behalf. In activism, as in so many other things, I had been educated to assume that men's cultural pattern was the natural or the only one. If student years were the peak time of rebellion and openness to change for men, then the same must be true for women. In fact, a decade of listening to every kind of women's group—from brown-bag lunchtime lectures organized by office workers to all-night rap sessions at campus women's centers; from housewives' self-help groups to campus rallies—has convinced me that the reverse is more often true. Women may be the one group that grows more radical with age. Though some students are big exceptions to this rule, women in general don't begin to challenge the politics of our own lives until later.

Looking back, I realize that this pattern has been true for my life, too. My college years were full of uncertainties and the personal conservatism that comes from trying to win approval and fit into the proper grown-up and womanly role whether that means finding a well-to-do man to be supported by or a male radical to support. Nonetheless, I went right on assuming that brave exploring youth and cowardly conservative old age were the norms for everybody, and that I must be just an isolated and guilty accident. Though every generalization based on female culture has many exceptions, and should never be used as a crutch or excuse, I think we might be less hard on ourselves and each other as students, feel better about our potential for change as we grow older—and educate reporters who announce feminism's demise because its red-hot center is not on campus—if we figured out that for most of us as women, the traditional college period is an unrealistic and cautious time. Consider a few of the reasons.

As students, women are probably treated with more equality than we ever will be again. For one thing, we're consumers. The school is only too glad to get the tuitions we pay, or that our families or government grants pay on our behalf. With population rates declining because of women's increased power over childbearing, that money is even more vital to a school's existence. Yet more than most consumers, we're too transient to have much power as a group. If our families are paying our tuition, we may have even less power.

As young women, whether students or not, we're still in the stage most valued by male-dominant cultures: We have our full potential as workers, wives, sex partners, and childbearers.

That means we haven't yet experienced the life events that are most radicalizing for women: entering the paid-labor force and discovering how women are treated there; marrying and finding out that it is not yet an equal partnership; having children and discovering who is responsible for them and who is not; and aging, still a greater penalty for women than for men.

Furthermore, new ambitions nourished by the rebirth of feminism may make young women feel and behave a little like a classical immi-

3

4

5

6

7

ADDITIONAL QUESTIONS FOR RESPONDING TO READING

1. Find passages that suggest Steinem's intended audience. Would her argument be persuasive to this group? To women from other socioeconomic groups? To young professional men? To older men? Explain.

2. How does Steinem establish her authority to speak on the subject?

3. Why, according to Steinem, are the traditional college years an "unrealistic and cautious" time for young women (paragraph 3)? Do you agree? Explain. Do Steinem's points reinforce or undercut the need for all-female colleges?

TEACHING STRATEGIES

1. Identify and summarize with the class the points of Steinem's argument. Which are most—and least—persuasive? Why?
2. Point out Steinem's strong identification with her intended audience, women. Does she make any concessions to men who might be reading the essay?
3. Steinem varies her paragraph length considerably. Observe the effect of longer paragraphs as compared with shorter ones. (For example, her last sentence is emphasized by being set apart).

grant group. We are determined to prove ourselves, to achieve academic excellence, and to prepare for interesting and successful careers. More noses are kept to more grindstones in an effort to demonstrate newfound abilities, and perhaps to allay suspicions that women still have to have more and better credentials than men. This doesn't leave much time for activism. Indeed, we may not yet know that it is necessary.

In addition, the very progress into previously all-male careers that 8 may be revolutionary for women is seen as conservative and conformist by outside critics. Assuming male radicalism to be the measure of change, they interpret any concern with careers as evidence of "campus conservatism." In fact, "dropping out" may be a departure for men, but "dropping in" is a new thing for women. Progress lies in the direction we have not been.

Like most groups of the newly arrived or awakened, our faith in 9 education and paper degrees also has yet to be shaken. For instance, the percentage of women enrolled in colleges and universities has been increasing at the same time that the percentage of men has been decreasing. Among students entering college in 1978, women *outnumbered* men for the first time. This hope of excelling at the existing game is probably reinforced by the greater cultural pressure on females to be "good girls" and observe somebody else's rules.

Though we may know intellectually that we need to have new 10 games with new rules, we probably haven't quite absorbed such facts as the high unemployment rate among female Ph.D.s; the lower average salary among women college graduates of all races than among counterpart males who graduated from high school or less; the middle-management ceiling against which even those eagerly hired new business-school graduates seem to bump their heads after five or ten years; and the barrier-breaking women in nontraditional fields who become the first fired when recession hits. Sadly enough, we may have to personally experience some of these reality checks before we accept the idea that lawsuits, activism, and group pressure will have to accompany our individual excellence and crisp new degrees.

Then there is the female guilt trip, student edition. If we're not 11 sailing along as planned, it must be *our* fault. If our mothers didn't "do anything" with their educations, it must have been *their* fault. If we can't study as hard as we think we must (because women still have to be better prepared than men), and have a substantial personal and sexual life at the same time (because women are supposed to care more about relationships than men do), then we feel inadequate, as if each of us were individually at fault for a problem that is actually culture-wide.

I've yet to be on a campus where most women weren't worrying 12
about some aspect of combining marriage, children, and a career. I've
yet to find one where many men were worrying about the same thing.
Yet women will go right on suffering from the double-role problem
and terminal guilt until men are encouraged, pressured, or otherwise
forced, individually and collectively, to integrate themselves into the
"women's work" of raising children and homemaking. Until then,
and until there are changed job patterns to allow equal parenthood,
children will go right on growing up with the belief that only women
can be loving and nurturing, and only men can be intellectual or
active outside the home. Each half of the world will go on limiting
the full range of its human talent.

Finally, there is the intimate political training that hits women in 13
the teens and early twenties: the countless ways we are still brain-
washed into assuming that women are dependent on men for our
basic identities, both in our work and our personal lives, much more
than vice versa. After all, if we're going to enter a marriage system
that's still legally designed for a person and a half, submit to an
economy in which women still average about fifty-nine cents on the
dollar earned by men, and work mainly as support staff and assistants, or co-directors and vice-presidents at best, then we have to be
convinced that we are not whole people on our own.

In order to make sure that we will see ourselves as half-people, 14
and thus be addicted to getting our identity from serving others,
society tries hard to convert us as young women into "man junkies";
that is, into people who are addicted to regular shots of male-approval
and presence, both professionally and personally. We need a man
standing next to us, actually and figuratively, whether it's at work,
on Saturday night, or throughout life. (If only men realized how little
it matters *which* man is standing there, they would understand that
this addiction depersonalizes them, too.) Given the danger to a male-
dominant system if young women stop internalizing this political
message of derived identity, it's no wonder that those who try to kick
the addiction—and, worse yet, to help other women do the same—
are likely to be regarded as odd or dangerous by everyone from
parents to peers.

With all that pressure combined with little experience, it's no 15
wonder that younger women are often less able to support each other.
Even young women who espouse feminist goals as individuals may
refrain from identifying themselves as "feminist": it's okay to want
equal pay for yourself (just one small reform) but it's not okay to
want equal pay for women as a group (an economic revolution). Some
retreat into individualized career obsessions as a way of avoiding this
dangerous discovery of shared experience with women as a group.

COLLABORATIVE ACTIVITY

Have groups gather information about and
report on campus services and activities that
reflect feminist concerns. Topics may include
the following: women's studies, rape awareness
programs, sexual harassment guidelines, discussions of equal employment opportunities for
women, scholarships especially for women, or
women's athletics programs. Follow up with a
discussion. Which of the services and activities
are still associated with feminism, and which
have been incorporated into the "establishment"? Discuss the possible reasons for this distinction.

Others retreat into the safe middle ground of "I'm not a feminist but. . . ." Still others become politically active, but only on issues that are taken seriously by their male counterparts.

The same lesson about the personal conservatism of younger 16 women is taught by the history of feminism. If I hadn't been conned into believing the masculine stereotype of youth as the "natural" time for freedom and rebellion, a time of "sowing wild oats" that actually is made possible by the assurance of power and security later on, I could have figured out the female pattern of activism by looking at women's movements of the past.

In this country, for instance, the nineteenth-century wave of fem- 17 inism was started by older women who had been through the radicalizing experience of getting married and becoming the legal chattel of their husbands (or the equally radicalizing experience of *not* getting married and being treated as spinsters). Most of them had also worked in the antislavery movement and learned from the political parallels between race and sex. In other countries, that wave was also led by women who were past the point of maximum pressure toward marriageability and conservatism.

Looking at the first decade of this second wave, it's clear that the 18 early feminist activist and consciousness-raising groups of the 1960s were organized by women who had experienced the civil rights movement, or homemakers who had discovered that raising kids and cooking didn't occupy all their talents. While most campuses of the late sixties were still circulating the names of illegal abortionists privately (after all, abortion could damage our marriage value), slightly older women were holding press conferences and speak-outs about the reality of abortions (including their own, even though that often meant confessing to an illegal act) and demanding reform or repeal of antichoice laws. Though rape had been a quiet epidemic on campus for generations, younger women victims were still understandably fearful of speaking up, and campuses encouraged silence in order to retain their reputation for safety with tuition-paying parents. It took many off-campus speak-outs, demonstrations against laws of evidence and police procedures, and testimonies in state legislatures before most student groups began to make demands on campus and local cops for greater rape protection. In fact, "date rape"—the common campus phenomenon of a young woman being raped by someone she knows, perhaps even by several students in a fraternity house—is just now being exposed. Marital rape, a more difficult legal issue, was taken up several years ago. As for battered women and the attendant exposé of husbands and lovers as more statistically dangerous than unknown muggers in the street, that issue still seems to be thought of as a largely noncampus concern, yet at many of the colleges and universities where I've spoken, there has been at least one case within current student memory of a young woman beaten or murdered by a jealous lover.

This cultural pattern of youthful conservatism makes the growing number of older women going back to school very important. They are life examples and pragmatic activists who radicalize women young enough to be their daughters. Now that the median female undergraduate age in this country is twenty-seven because so many older women have returned, the campus is becoming a major place for cross-generational connections. 19

None of this should denigrate the courageous efforts of young women, especially women on campus, and the many changes they've pioneered. On the contrary, they should be seen as even more remarkable for surviving the conservative pressures, recognizing societal problems they haven't yet fully experienced, and organizing successfully in the midst of a transient student population. Every women's history course, rape hot line, or campus newspaper that is finally covering *all* the news; every feminist professor whose job has been created or tenure saved by student pressure, or male administrator whose consciousness has been permanently changed; every counselor who's stopped guiding women one way and men another; every lawsuit that's been fueled by student energies against unequal athletic funds or graduate school requirements: all those accomplishments are even more impressive when seen against the backdrop of the female pattern of activism. 20

Finally, it would help to remember that a feminist revolution rarely resembles a masculine-style one—just as a young woman's most radical act toward her mother (that is, connecting as women in order to help each other get some power) doesn't look much like a young man's most radical act toward his father (that is, breaking the father-son connection in order to separate identities or take over existing power). 21

It's those father-son conflicts at a generational, national level that have often provided the conventional definition of revolution; yet they've gone on for centuries without basically changing the role of the female half of the world. They have also failed to reduce the level of violence in society, since both fathers and sons have included some degree of aggressiveness and superiority to women in their definition of masculinity, thus preserving the anthropological model of dominance. 22

Furthermore, what current leaders and theoreticians define as revolution is usually little more than taking over the army and the radio stations. Women have much more in mind than that. We have to uproot the sexual caste system that is the most pervasive power 23

WRITING SUGGESTIONS

1. Write an essay in which you discuss the "female cultural pattern" and the ways in which it differs from the "male cultural pattern."
2. Using personal experience and observation, assess the general climate for women today on campus, in the business world, or in the family. Has this climate changed appreciably over the years? Explain.
3. Does the word *feminism* evoke positive or negative associations for you? Write an essay analyzing your personal feelings.

structure in society, and that means transforming the patriarchal values of those who run the institutions, whether they are politically the "right" or the "left," the fathers or the sons. This cultural part of the change goes very deep, and is often seen as too intimate, and perhaps too threatening, to be considered as either serious or possible. Only conflicts among men are "serious." Only a takeover of existing institutions is "possible."

That's why the definition of "political," on campus as elsewhere, 24 tends to be limited to who's running for president, who's demonstrating against corporate investments in South Africa, or which is the "moral" side of some conventional revolution, preferably one that is thousands of miles away.

As important as such activities are, they are also the most com- 25 fortable ones when we're young. They provide a sense of virtue without much disruption in the power structure of our daily lives. Even when the most consistent energies on campus are actually concentrated around feminist issues, they may be treated as apolitical and invisible. Asked "What's happening on campus?" a student may reply, "The antinuke movement," even though that resulted in one demonstration of two hours, while student antirape squads have been patrolling the campus every night for two years and women's studies have begun to transform the very textbooks we read.

No wonder reporters and sociologists looking for revolution on 26 campus often miss the depth of feminist change and activity that is really there. Women students themselves may dismiss it as not political and not serious. Certainly, it rarely comes in the masculine sixties style of bombing buildings or burning draft cards. In fact, it goes much deeper than protesting a temporary symptom—say, the draft— and challenges the right of one group to dominate another, which is the disease itself.

Young women have a big task of resisting pressures and chal- 27 lenging definitions. Their increasing success is a miracle of foresight and courage that should make us all proud. But they should know that they, too, may grow more radical with age.

One day, an army of gray-haired women may quietly take over 28 the earth.

ANSWERS TO RESPONDING TO READING

1. Answers will vary.
2. Answers will vary. Some female students may dismiss the idea of an addiction to men. Others may observe a recent conservative trend that makes Steinem's observation more

RESPONDING TO READING

1. On the basis of your own experience, do you agree with Steinem that "women may be the one group that grows more radical with age" (paragraph 2)? Explain.   **2.** Does the "female guilt trip, student edition" defined by Steinem in paragraph 11 accurately represent the feelings of the female college students you know? Is the picture of young women as "man junkies" (paragraph 14) a valid one? If not, do you attribute these discrepancies to the time that has passed since the essay was written, or to other factors?   **3.** What does Steinem mean when she says, "One day, an army of gray-haired women may quietly take over the earth" (paragraph 28)? Do you think she intends readers to take her comment literally? Do you think the scenario she suggests is desirable? Necessary? Likely?

applicable today than it would have been five years ago.

3. The key to Steinem's statement is "quietly"; it follows her discussion of the idea that women's revolutions (unlike men's) occur with little bombast or attention. She suggests that as women mature and are confronted with radicalizing circumstances, their numbers and influence will grow.

Pornography

MARGARET ATWOOD

Margaret Atwood (1939–   ) is a Canadian poet, novelist, critic, and teacher who first received public attention with her poems in *Double Persephone* (1961). She voices feminist concerns and creates characters who are intelligent women in search of themselves. Her novel *The Handmaid's Tale* (1986) has won acclaim as a futuristic satire that one critic considers to be "in the honorable tradition of *Brave New World* and other warnings of dystopia." Atwood's articles and short fiction have appeared in Canadian and American literary magazines. In "Pornography," Atwood asks important questions about what pornography is and what harm it does.

When I was in Finland a few years ago for an international writers' conference, I had occasion to say a few paragraphs in public on the subject of pornography. The context was a discussion of political repression, and I was suggesting the possibility of a link between the two. The immediate result was that a male journalist took several large bites out of me. Prudery and pornography are two halves of the same coin, said he, and I was clearly a prude. What could you expect from an Anglo-Canadian? Afterward, a couple of pleasant Scandinavian men asked me what I had been so worked up about. All "pornography" means, they said, is graphic depictions of whores, and what was the harm in that?

Not until then did it strike me that the male journalist and I had two entirely different things in mind. By "pornography," he meant naked bodies and sex. I, on the other hand, had recently been doing the research for my novel *Bodily Harm*, and was still in a state of shock from some of the material I had seen, including the Ontario Board of Film Censors' "outtakes." By "pornography," I meant women getting their nipples snipped off with garden shears, having meat hooks stuck into their vaginas, being disemboweled; little girls being raped; men (yes, there are some men) being smashed to a pulp and forcibly sodomized. The cutting edge of pornography, as far as I could see,

BACKGROUND ON AUTHOR

According to the *Dictionary of Literary Biography*, Atwood is one of Canada's most public literary figures; she "has made her reputation as much by being versatile as by being controversial" (*DLB*, vol. 53, p. 18). A familiar theme in Atwood's work is metamorphosis, an interest that she links with her childhood reading of *Grimm's Fairy Tales* and Native American legends.

1   **BACKGROUND ON READING**

Atwood's feminism has been considered one of the most controversial elements of her writing. In some of her work, she uses myths, such as Bluebeard, Dracula, and comic book material, "to project and examine certain images of men *and women*." Critics have occasionally expressed uneasiness over some of her images, especially given her straightforward style: "If I love you / is that a fact or a weapon?" (*DLB*, vol 53, p. 24).

2   **FOR OPENERS**

1. Read aloud some of Atwood's poetry (for example, "You Fit Into Me") or a few passages from her fiction (perhaps from *The Handmaid's Tale*).
2. Atwood says that *pornography* is one of those words, like *Marxism* and *feminism*, for which the meaning has become too broad. Ask your students for a definition of pornography.

ADDITIONAL QUESTIONS FOR RESPONDING TO READING

1. Many of the images of pornography that Atwood uses are intended to be unsettling. What is her purpose in presenting these images?
2. According to Atwood, how is pornography addictive?
3. In what ways is pornography an "educational tool" and "propaganda device"?
4. Do you think pornography should be protected by the First Amendment to the Constitution?

TEACHING STRATEGIES

1. Identify the two opposing camps in the emotional debate around pornography, as described by Atwood. Which groups fall on which side? Analyze their possible motives.
2. Discuss Atwood's use of the question as a stylistic device and tool of argument.
3. Examine Atwood's "three other models for looking at pornography" (paragraph 11).

was no longer simple old copulation, hanging from the chandelier or otherwise: it was death, messy, explicit and highly sadistic. I explained this to the nice Scandinavian men. "Oh, but that's just the United States," they said. "Everyone knows they're sick." In their country, they said, violent "pornography" of that kind was not permitted on television or in movies; indeed, excessive violence of any kind was not permitted. They had drawn a clear line between erotica, which earlier studies had shown did not incite men to more aggressive and brutal behavior toward women, and violence, which later studies indicated did.

Some time after that I was in Saskatchewan, where, because of 3 the scenes in *Bodily Harm*, I found myself on an open-line radio show answering questions about "pornography." Almost no one who phoned in was in favor of it, but again they weren't talking about the same stuff I was, because they hadn't seen it. Some of them were all set to stamp out bathing suits and negligees, and, if possible, any depictions of the female body whatsoever. God, it was implied, did not approve of female bodies, and sex of any kind, including that practised by bumblebees, should be shoved back into the dark, where it belonged. I had more than a suspicion that *Lady Chatterley's Lover*,[1] Margaret Laurence's *The Diviners*,[2] and indeed most books by most serious modern authors would have ended up as confetti if left in the hands of these callers.

For me, these two experiences illustrate the two poles of the 4 emotionally heated debate that is now thundering around this issue. They also underline the desirability and even the necessity of defining the terms. "Pornography" is now one of those catchalls, like "Marxism" and "feminism," that have become so broad they can mean almost anything, ranging from certain verses in the Bible, ads for skin lotion and sex texts for children to the contents of Penthouse, Naughty '90s postcards and films with titles containing the word *Nazi* that show vicious scenes of torture and killing. It's easy to say that sensible people can tell the difference. Unfortunately, opinions on what constitutes a sensible person vary.

But even sensible people tend to lose their cool when they start 5 talking about this subject. They soon stop talking and start yelling, and the name-calling begins. Those in favor of censorship (which may include groups not noticeably in agreement on other issues, such as some feminists and religious fundamentalists) accuse the others of

---

[1]Novel by English writer D. H. Lawrence (1885–1930), subject of a famous 1961 obscenity trial. An expurgated edition was published in 1928, and an unabridged version was published in Paris in 1929. The full version was not published in England until 1960. [Eds.]
[2]Controversial 1974 novel by Canadian novelist (1926–87) includes explicit accounts of a sexual encounter and an abortion. [Eds.]

exploiting women through the use of degrading images, contributing to the corruption of children, and adding to the general climate of violence and threat in which both women and children live in this society; or, though they may not give much of a hoot about actual women and children, they invoke moral standards and God's supposed aversion to "filth," "smut" and deviated *preversion*, which may mean ankles.

The camp in favor of total "freedom of expression" often comes out howling as loud as the Romans would have if told they could no longer have innocent fun watching the lions eat up Christians. It too may include segments of the population who are not natural bedfellows: those who proclaim their God-given right to freedom, including the freedom to tote guns, drive when drunk, drool over chicken porn and get off on videotapes of women being raped and beaten, may be waving the same anticensorship banner as responsible liberals who fear the return of Mrs. Grundy,[3] or gay groups for whom sexual emancipation involves the concept of "sexual theatre." *Whatever turns you on* is a handy motto, as is *A man's home is his castle* (and if it includes a dungeon with beautiful maidens strung up in chains and bleeding from every pore, that's his business).

Meanwhile, theoreticians theorize and speculators speculate. Is today's pornography yet another indication of the hatred of the body, the deep mind-body split, which is supposed to pervade Western Christian society? Is it a backlash against the women's movement by men who are threatened by uppity female behavior in real life, so like to fantasize about women done up like outsize parcels, being turned into hamburger, kneeling at their feet in slavelike adoration or sucking off guns? Is it a sign of collective impotence, of a generation of men who can't relate to real women at all but have to make do with bits of celluloid and paper? Is the current flood just a result of smart marketing and aggressive promotion by the money men in what has now become a multibillion-dollar industry? If they were selling movies about men getting their testicles stuck full of knitting needles by women with swastikas on their sleeves, would they do as well, or is this penchant somehow peculiarly male? If so, why? Is pornography a power trip rather than a sex one? Some say that those ropes, chains, muzzles and other restraining devices are an argument for the immense power female sexuality still wields in the male imagination: you don't put these things on dogs unless you're afraid of them. Others, more literary, wonder about the shift from the 19th-century Magic Women or Femme Fatale image to the lollipop-licker,

6

7

---

[3]Character in *Speed the Plow*, a 1798 comic play by Thomas Morton (1764?–1838); symbol of conventional propriety. [Eds.]

airhead or turkey-carcass treatment of women in porn today. The proporners don't care much about theory: they merely demand product. The anti-porners don't care about it in the final analysis either: there's dirt on the street, and they want it cleaned up, now.

It seems to me that this conversation, with its *You're-a-prude/* 8 *You're-a-pervert* dialectic, will never get anywhere as long as we continue to think of this material as just "entertainment." Possibly we're deluded by the packaging, the format: magazine, book, movie, theatrical presentation. We're used to thinking of these things as part of the "entertainment industry," and we're used to thinking of ourselves as free adult people who ought to be able to see any kind of "entertainment" we want to. That was what the First Choice pay-TV debate was all about. After all, it's only entertainment, right? Entertainment means fun, and only a killjoy would be antifun. What's the harm?

This is obviously the central question: *What's the harm?* If there 9 isn't any real harm to any real people, then the antiporners can tsk-tsk and/or throw up as much as they like, but they can't rightfully expect more legal controls or sanctions. However, the no-harm position is far from being proven.

(For instance, there's a clear-cut case for banning—as the federal 10 government has proposed—movies, photos and videos that depict children engaging in sex with adults: real children are used to make the movies, and hardly anybody thinks this is ethical. The possibilities for coercion are too great.)

To shift the viewpoint, I'd like to suggest three other models for 11 looking at "pornography"—and here I mean the violent kind.

Those who find the idea of regulating pornographic materials 12 repugnant because they think it's Fascist or Communist or otherwise not in accordance with the principles of an open democratic society should consider that Canada has made it illegal to disseminate material that may lead to hatred toward any group because of race or religion. I suggest that if pornography of the violent kind depicted these acts being done predominantly to Chinese, to blacks, to Catholics, it would be off the market immediately, under the present laws. Why is hate literature illegal? Because whoever made the law thought that such material might incite real people to do real awful things to other real people. The human brain is to a certain extent a computer: garbage in, garbage out. We only hear about the extreme cases (like that of American multimurderer Ted Bundy) in which pornography has contributed to the death and/or mutilation of women and/or men. Although pornography is not the only factor involved in the creation of such deviance, it certainly has upped the ante by suggesting both a variety of techniques and the social acceptability of such actions. Nobody knows yet what effect this stuff is having on the less psychotic.

Studies have shown that a large part of the market for all kinds   13
of porn, soft and hard, is drawn from the 16-to-21-year-old population
of young men. Boys used to learn about sex on the street, or (in Italy,
according to Fellini movies) from friendly whores, or, in more genteel
surroundings, from girls, their parents, or, once upon a time, in
school, more or less. Now porn has been added, and sex education
in the schools is rapidly being phased out. The buck has been passed,
and boys are being taught that all women secretly like to be raped
and that real men get high on scooping out women's digestive tracts.

Boys learn their concept of masculinity from other men: is this   14
what most men want them to be learning? If word gets around that
rapists are "normal" and even admirable men, will boys feel that in
order to be normal, admirable and masculine they will have to be
rapists? Human beings are enormously flexible, and how they turn
out depends a lot on how they're educated, by the society in which
they're immersed as well as by their teachers. In a society that advertises and glorifies rape or even implicitly condones it, more women
get raped. It becomes socially acceptable. And at a time when men
and the traditional male role have taken a lot of flak and men are
confused and casting around for an acceptable way of being male
(and, in some cases, not getting much comfort from women on that
score), this must be at times a pleasing thought.

It would be naïve to think of violent pornography as just harmless   15
entertainment. It's also an educational tool and a powerful propaganda device. What happens when boy educated on porn meets girl
brought up on Harlequin romances? The clash of expectations can be
heard around the block. She wants him to get down on his knees
with a ring, he wants her to get down on all fours with a ring in her
nose. Can this marriage be saved?

Pornography has certain things in common with such addictive   16
substances as alcohol and drugs: for some, though by no means for
all, it induces chemical changes in the body, which the user finds
exciting and pleasurable. It also appears to attract a "hard core" of
habitual users and a penumbra of those who use it occasionally but
aren't dependent on it in any way. There are also significant numbers
of men who aren't much interested in it, not because they're under-
sexed but because real life is satisfying their needs, which may not
require as many appliances as those of users.

For the "hard core," pornography may function as alcohol does   17
for the alcoholic: tolerance develops, and a little is no longer enough.
This may account for the short viewing time and fast turnover in porn
theatres. Mary Brown, chairwoman of the Ontario Board of Film Censors, estimates that for every one mainstream movie requesting
entrance to Ontario, there is one porno flick. Not only the quantity
consumed but the quality of explicitness must escalate, which may

COLLABORATIVE ACTIVITY

Set up a debate on the pornography issue.
Instruct groups to prepare arguments representing different perspectives for full class discussion.

account for the growing violence: once the big deal was breasts, then it was genitals, then copulation, then that was no longer enough and the hard users had to have more. The ultimate kick is death, and after that, as the Marquis de Sade[4] so boringly demonstrated, multiple death.

The existence of alcoholism has not led us to ban social drinking. 18 On the other hand, we do have laws about drinking and driving, excessive drunkenness and other abuses of alcohol that may result in injury or death to others.

This leads us back to the key question: what's the harm? Nobody 19 knows, but this society should find out fast, before the saturation point is reached. The Scandinavian studies that showed a connection between depictions of sexual violence and increased impulse toward it on the part of male viewers would be a starting point, but many more questions remain to be raised as well as answered. What, for instance, is the crucial difference between men who are users and men who are not? Does using affect a man's relationship with actual women, and, if so, adversely? Is there a clear line between erotica and violent pornography, or are they on an escalating continuum? Is this a "men versus women" issue, with all men secretly siding with the proporners and all women secretly siding against? (I think not; there *are* lots of men who don't think that running their true love through the Cuisinart is the best way they can think of to spend a Saturday night, and they're just as nauseated by films of someone else doing it as women are.) Is pornography merely an expression of the sexual confusion of this age or an active contributor to it?

Nobody wants to go back to the age of official repression, when 20 even piano legs were referred to as "limbs" and had to wear panta-loons to be decent. Neither do we want to end up in George Orwell's *1984*, in which pornography is turned out by the State to keep the proles in a state of torpor, sex itself is considered dirty and the approved practise is only for reproduction. But Rome under the emperors isn't such a good model either.

If all men and women respected each other, if sex were considered 21 joyful and life-enhancing instead of a wallow in germ-filled glop, if everyone were in love all the time, if, in other words, many people's lives were more satisfactory for them than they appear to be now, pornography might just go away on its own. But since this is obviously not happening, we as a society are going to have to make some informed and responsible decisions about how to deal with it.

---

[4]French libertine (1740–1814) and man of letters from whose name the term *sadism* is derived. [Eds.]

WRITING SUGGESTIONS

1. Atwood says pornography is not just harmless "entertainment." Write an essay agreeing or taking issue with her position.
2. Write an essay in which you develop the parallel Atwood draws in paragraphs 16–18 between pornography and addictive substances.
3. Use one of the questions raised by Atwood in paragraphs 7 or 19 as a starting point for an argument about whether or not pornography should be censored. Write a letter to a member of Congress in which you present your position.

RESPONDING TO READING

1. According to Atwood, what constitutes pornography? Are her views consistent with your own? Do you agree with her distinctions between acceptable and unacceptable pornography? Why or why not?   **2.** Do you think Atwood is too pessimistic about the abilities of consumers of pornography to resist what she sees as its harmful effects, or do you think her reaction to the potential dangers is realistic? Do you think she is being unfair to men?   **3.** Do you think pornography is a "woman's issue"? Why or why not? Is Atwood advocating censorship? Is her position consistent with other positions feminists have taken, such as freedom of choice?

In Search of Our Mothers' Gardens

ALICE WALKER

This selection, first published in *Ms.* magazine in 1974, is the title essay in the 1983 collection *In Search of Our Mothers' Gardens*. As a feminist, Alice Walker (see also p. 68) calls on African-American women to transcend their heritage as "the mule of the world" and "identify with our lives the living creativity some of our great-grandmothers were not allowed to know." Walker urges her readers to look close to themselves, as she looks to the stories of her mother's life, for "the truest answer to the question that really matters."

I described her own nature and temperament. Told how they needed a larger life for their expression. . . . I pointed out that in lieu of proper channels, her emotions had overflowed into paths that dissipated them. I talked, beautifully I thought, about an art that would be born, an art that would open the way for women the likes of her. I asked her to hope, and build up an inner life against the coming of that day. . . . I sang, with a strange quiver in my voice, a promise song.
—JEAN TOOMER, "Avey," *Cane*

The poet speaking to a prostitute who falls asleep while he's talking—   1

When the poet Jean Toomer walked through the South in the early twenties, he discovered a curious thing: black women whose spirituality was so intense, so deep, so *unconscious*, that they were themselves unaware of the richness they held. They stumbled blindly through their lives: creatures so abused and mutilated in body, so dimmed and confused by pain, that they considered themselves unworthy even of hope. In the selfless abstractions their bodies became to the men who used them, they became more than "sexual objects," more even than mere women: they became "Saints." Instead

ADDITIONAL QUESTIONS FOR
RESPONDING TO READING

1. Why does Walker refer to African-American
   women as "the mule[s] of the world"? Identify
   other images that she evokes of creative
   African-American women.
2. What is the significance of Walker's mention
   of a quilt on display at the Smithsonian? (If
   your class has read Walker's "Everyday Use"
   in Chapter 4, you might ask them to compare
   her use of the quilt in the two works.)

TEACHING STRATEGIES

1. Identify and discuss Walker's thesis. What is
   she saying about gender and race?
2. Walker's essay is a good starting point for a
   discussion of style because of her use of
   poetic language in nonfiction. Examine the
   language and make lists of images, figures of
   speech, parallel structures, poetic rhythms,
   examples of alliteration and assonance, and
   so on. Discuss the effectiveness of her style.
   Paraphrase a passage of Walker's prose into
   plain, unadorned language; note the effect of
   the style change. What is lost?

of being perceived as whole persons, their bodies became shrines: what was thought to be their minds became temples suitable for worship. These crazy Saints stared out at the world, wildly, like lunatics—or quietly, like suicides; and the "God" that was in their gaze was as mute as a great stone.

Who were these Saints? These crazy, loony, pitiful women? 2

Some of them, without a doubt, were our mothers and grand- 3 mothers.

In the still heat of the post-Reconstruction South, this is how they 4 seemed to Jean Toomer: exquisite butterflies trapped in an evil honey, toiling away their lives in an era, a century, that did not acknowledge them, except as "the *mule* of the world." They dreamed dreams that no one knew—not even themselves, in any coherent fashion—and saw visions no one could understand. They wandered or sat about the countryside crooning lullabies to ghosts, and drawing the mother of Christ in charcoal on courthouse walls.

They forced their minds to desert their bodies and their striving 5 spirits sought to rise, like frail whirlwinds from the hard red clay. And when those frail whirlwinds fell, in scattered particles, upon the ground, no one mourned. Instead, men lit candles to celebrate the emptiness that remained, as people do who enter a beautiful but vacant space to resurrect a God.

Our mothers and grandmothers, some of them: moving to music 6 not yet written. And they waited.

They waited for a day when the unknown thing that was in them 7 would be made known; but guessed, somehow in their darkness, that on the day of their revelation they would be long dead. Therefore to Toomer they walked, and even ran, in slow motion. For they were going nowhere immediate, and the future was not yet within their grasp. And men took our mothers and grandmothers, "but got no pleasure from it." So complex was their passion and their calm.

To Toomer, they lay vacant and fallow as autumn fields, with 8 harvest time never in sight: and he saw them enter loveless marriages, without joy; and become prostitutes, without resistance; and become mothers of children, without fulfillment.

For these grandmothers and mothers of ours were not Saints, but 9 Artists; driven to a numb and bleeding madness by the springs of creativity in them for which there was no release. They were Creators, who lived lives of spiritual waste, because they were so rich in spirituality—which is the basis of Art—that the strain of enduring their unused and unwanted talent drove them insane. Throwing away this spirituality was their pathetic attempt to lighten the soul to a weight their work-worn, sexually abused bodies could bear.

What did it mean for a black woman to be an artist in our grand- 10 mothers' time? In our great-grandmothers' day? It is a question with an answer cruel enough to stop the blood.

Did you have a genius of a great-great-grandmother who died under 11 some ignorant and depraved white overseer's lash? Or was she required to bake biscuits for a lazy backwater tramp, when she cried out in her soul to paint watercolors of sunsets, or the rain falling on the green and peaceful pasturelands? Or was her body broken and forced to bear children (who were more often than not sold away from her)—eight, ten, fifteen, twenty children—when her one joy was the thought of modeling heroic figures of rebellion, in stone or clay?

How was the creativity of the black woman kept alive, year after 12 year and century after century, when for most of the years black people have been in America, it was a punishable crime for a black person to read or write? And the freedom to paint, to sculpt, to expand the mind with action did not exist. Consider, if you can bear to imagine it, what might have been the result if singing, too, had been forbidden by law. Listen to the voices of Bessie Smith, Billie Holiday, Nina Simone, Roberta Flack, and Aretha Franklin, among others, and imagine those voices muzzled for life. Then you may begin to comprehend the lives of our "crazy," "Sainted" mothers and grandmothers. The agony of the lives of women who might have been Poets, Novelists, Essayists, and Short-Story Writers (over a period of centuries), who died with their real gifts stifled within them.

And, if this were the end of the story, we would have cause to 13 cry out in my paraphrase of Okot p'Bitek's great poem:

> O, my clanswomen
> Let us all cry together!
> Come,
> Let us mourn the death of our mother,
> The death of a Queen   5
> The ash that was produced
> By a great fire!
> O, this homestead is utterly dead
> Close the gates
> With *lacari* thorns,   10
> For our mother
> The creator of the Stool is lost!
> And all the young women
> Have perished in the wilderness!

But this is not the end of the story, for all the young women— 14 our mothers and grandmothers, *ourselves*—have not perished in the wilderness. And if we ask ourselves why, and search for and find the answer, we will know beyond all efforts to erase it from our minds, just exactly who, and of what, we black American women are.

COLLABORATIVE ACTIVITY

Have groups bring in and present to the class passages from Walker's fiction and poetry in which she explores ideas relevant to "In Search of Our Mothers' Gardens" (suggestions: passages from her novel *The Color Purple* and her collection of poems *Horses Make a Landscape Look More Beautiful*).

One example, perhaps the most pathetic, most misunderstood   15
one, can provide a backdrop for our mothers' work: Phillis Wheatley,[1]
a slave in the 1700s.

Virginia Woolf, in her book *A Room of One's Own*[2], wrote that in   16
order for a woman to write fiction she must have two things, certainly:
a room of her own (with key and lock) and enough money to support
herself.

What then are we to make of Phillis Wheatley, a slave, who owned   17
not even herself? This sickly, frail black girl who required a servant
of her own at times—her health was so precarious—and who, had
she been white, would have been easily considered the intellectual
superior of all the women and most of the men in the society of
her day.

Virginia Woolf wrote further, speaking of course not of our Phillis,   18
that "any woman born with a great gift in the sixteenth century [insert
"eighteenth century," insert "black woman," insert "born or made a
slave"] would certainly have gone crazed, shot herself, or ended her
days in some lonely cottage outside the village, half witch, half wizard
[insert "Saint"], feared and mocked at. For it needs little skill and
psychology to be sure that a highly gifted girl who had tried to use
her gift for poetry would have been so thwarted and hindered by
contrary instincts [add "chains, guns, the lash, the ownership of one's
body by someone else, submission to an alien religion"], that she
must have lost her health and sanity to a certainty."

The key words, as they relate to Phillis, are "contrary instincts."   19
For when we read the poetry of Phillis Wheatley—and when we read
the novels of Nella Larsen[3] or the oddly false-sounding autobiography
of that freest of all black women writers, Zora Hurston[4]—evidence
of "contrary instincts" is everywhere. Her loyalties were completely
divided, as was, without question, her mind.

But how could this be otherwise? Captured at seven, a slave of   20
wealthy, doting whites who instilled in her the "savagery" of the
Africa they "rescued" her from . . . one wonders if she was even able
to remember her homeland as she had known it, or as it really was.

Yet, because she did try to use her gift for poetry in a world that   21
made her a slave, she was "so thwarted and hindered by . . . contrary
instincts, that she . . . lost her health. . . ." In the last years of brief
life, burdened not only with the need to express her gift but also with
a penniless, friendless "freedom" and several small children for

---

[1] Poet (1753?–84) whose work was well-known among American intellectuals. [Eds.]
[2] English essayist and novelist (1882–1941). See p. 395. [Eds.]
[3] Award-winning novelist (1891–1964) associated with the Harlem Renaissance. [Eds.]
[4] Folklorist and novelist (1903–60), also associated with the Harlem Renaissance. [Eds.]

whom she was forced to do strenuous work to feed, she lost her health, certainly. Suffering from malnutrition and neglect and who knows what mental agonies, Phillis Wheatley died.

So torn by "contrary instincts" was black, kidnapped, enslaved 22 Phillis that her description of "the Goddess"—as she poetically called the Liberty she did not have—is ironically, cruelly humorous. And, in fact, has held Phillis up to ridicule for more than a century. It is usually read prior to hanging Phillis's memory as that of a fool. She wrote:

> The Goddess comes, she moves divinely fair,
> Olive and laurel binds her *golden* hair.
> Wherever shines this native of the skies,
> Unnumber'd charms and recent graces rise. [My italics]

It is obvious that Phillis, the slave, combed the "Goddess's" hair 23 every morning; prior, perhaps, to bringing in the milk, or fixing her mistress's lunch. She took her imagery from the one thing she saw elevated above all others.

With the benefit of hindsight we ask, "How could she?"   24

But at last, Phillis, we understand. No more snickering when 25 your stiff, struggling, ambivalent lines are forced on us. We know now that you were not an idiot or a traitor; only a sickly little black girl, snatched from your home and country and made a slave; a woman who still struggled to sing the song that was your gift, although in a land of barbarians who praised you for your bewildered tongue. It is not so much what you sang, as that you kept alive, in so many of our ancestors, *the notion of song*.

Black women are called, in the folklore that so aptly identifies 26 one's status in society, "the *mule* of the world," because we have been handed the burdens that everyone else—*everyone* else—refused to carry. We have also been called "Matriarchs," "Superwomen," and "Mean and Evil Bitches." Not to mention "Castraters" and "Sapphire's Mama." When we have pleaded for understanding, our character has been distorted; when we have asked for simple caring, we have been handed empty inspirational appellations, then stuck in the farthest corner. When we have asked for love, we have been given children. In short, even our plainer gifts, our labors of fidelity and love, have been knocked down our throats. To be an artist and a black woman, even today, lowers our status in many respects, rather than raises it: and yet, artists we will be.

Therefore we must fearlessly pull out of ourselves and look at 27 and identify with our lives the living creativity some of our great-grandmothers were not allowed to know. I stress *some* of them because it is well known that the majority of our great-grandmothers knew, even without "knowing" it, the reality of their spirituality, even if they didn't recognize it beyond what happened in the singing at church—and they never had any intention of giving it up.

How they did it—those millions of black women who were not   28
Phillis Wheatley, or Lucy Terry[5] or Frances Harper[6] or Zora Hurston or Nella Larsen or Bessie Smith[7]; or Elizabeth Catlett,[8] or Katherine Dunham,[9] either—brings me to the title of this essay, "In Search of Our Mothers' Gardens," which is a personal account that is yet shared, in its theme and its meaning, by all of us. I found, while thinking about the far-reaching world of the creative black woman, that often the truest answer to a question that really matters can be found very close.

In the late 1920s my mother ran away from home to marry my   29
father. Marriage, if not running away, was expected of seventeen-year-old girls. By the time she was twenty, she had two children and was pregnant with a third. Five children later, I was born. And this is how I came to know my mother: she seemed a large, soft, loving-eyed woman who was rarely impatient in our home. Her quick, violent temper was on view only a few times a year, when she battled with the white landlord who had the misfortune to suggest to her that her children did not need to go to school.

She made all the clothes we wore, even my brothers' overalls.   30
She made all the towels and sheets we used. She spent the summers canning vegetables and fruits. She spent the winter evenings making quilts enough to cover all our beds.

During the "working" day, she labored beside—not behind—my   31
father in the fields. Her day began before sunup, and did not end until late at night. There was never a moment for her to sit down, undisturbed, to unravel her own private thoughts; never a time free from interruption—by work or the noisy inquiries of her many children. And yet, it is to my mother—and all our mothers who were not famous—that I went in search of the secret of what has fed that muzzled and often mutilated, but vibrant, creative spirit that the black woman has inherited, and that pops out in wild and unlikely places to this day.

---

[5]Poet (1730–1821) and former slave. [Eds.]
[6]Poet and abolitionist (1825–1911). [Eds.]
[7]American blues singer (1898?–1937). [Eds.]
[8]Sculptor and painter (b. 1919). [Eds.]
[9]Dancer and choreographer (1910–   ). [Eds.]

But when, you will ask, did my overworked mother have time 32
to know or care about feeding the creative spirit?

The answer is so simple that many of us have spent years dis- 33
covering it. We have constantly looked high, when we should have
looked high—and low.

For example: in the Smithsonian Institution in Washington, D.C., 34
there hangs a quilt unlike any other in the world. In fanciful, inspired,
and yet simple and identifiable figures, it portrays the story of the
Crucifixion. It is considered rare, beyond price. Though it follows no
known pattern of quilt-making, and though it is made of bits and
pieces of worthless rags, it is obviously the work of a person of powerful imagination and deep spiritual feeling. Below this quilt I saw a
note that says it was made by "an anonymous Black woman in Alabama, a hundred years ago."

If we could locate this "anonymous" black woman from Alabama, 35
she would turn out to be one of our grandmothers—an artist who
left her mark in the only materials she could afford, and in the only
medium her position in society allowed her to use.

As Virginia Woolf wrote further, in *A Room of One's Own:* 36

> Yet genius of a sort must have existed among women as it must
> have existed among the working class. [Change this to "slaves" and
> "the wives and daughters of sharecroppers."] Now and again an
> Emily Brontë or a Robert Burns [change this to "a Zora Hurston or
> a Richard Wright"] blazes out and proves its presence. But certainly
> it never got itself on to paper. When, however, one reads of a witch
> being ducked, of a woman possessed by devils [or "Sainthood"], of
> a wise woman selling herbs [our root workers], or even a very
> remarkable man who had a mother, then I think we are on the track
> of a lost novelist, a suppressed poet, of some mute and inglorious
> Jane Austen. . . . Indeed, I would venture to guess that Anon, who
> wrote so many poems without signing them, was often a
> woman. . . .

And so our mothers and grandmothers have, more often than 37
not anonymously, handed on the creative spark, the seed of the flower
they themselves never hoped to see: or like a sealed letter they could
not plainly read.

And so it is, certainly, with my own mother. Unlike "Ma" 38
Rainey's[10] songs, which retained their creator's name even while
blasting forth from Bessie Smith's mouth, no song or poem will bear
my mother's name. Yet so many of the stories that I write, that we
all write, are my mother's stories. Only recently did I fully realize
this: that through years of listening to my mother's stories of her life,

---

[10]"Mother of the Blues" (1886–1939). [Eds.]

I have absorbed not only the stories themselves, but something of the manner in which she spoke, something of the urgency that involves the knowledge that her stories—like her life—must be recorded. It is probably for this reason that so much of what I have written is about characters whose counterparts in real life are so much older than I am.

But the telling of these stories, which came from my mother's lips 39 as naturally as breathing, was not the only way my mother showed herself as an artist. For stories, too, were subject to being distracted, to dying without conclusion. Dinners must be started, and cotton must be gathered before the big rains. The artist that was and is my mother showed itself to me only after many years. This is what I finally noticed:

Like Mem, a character in *The Third Life of Grange Copeland*,[11] my 40 mother adorned with flowers whatever shabby house we were forced to live in. And not just your typical straggly country stand of zinnias, either. She planted ambitious gardens—and still does—with over fifty different varieties of plants that bloom profusely from early March until late November. Before she left home for the fields, she watered her flowers, chopped up the grass, and laid out new beds. When she returned from the fields she might divide clumps of bulbs, dig a cold pit, uproot and replant roses, or prune branches from her taller bushes or trees—until night came and it was too dark to see.

Whatever she planted grew as if by magic, and her fame as a 41 grower of flowers spread over three counties. Because of her creativity with her flowers, even my memories of poverty are seen through a screen of blooms—sunflowers, petunias, roses, dahlias, forsythia, spirea, delphiniums, verbena . . . and on and on.

And I remember people coming to my mother's yard to be given 42 cuttings from her flowers; I hear again the praise showered on her because whatever rocky soil she landed on, she turned into a garden. A garden so brilliant with colors, so original in its design, so magnificent with life and creativity, that to this day people drive by our house in Georgia—perfect strangers and imperfect strangers—and ask to stand or walk among my mother's art.

I notice that it is only when my mother is working in her flowers 43 that she is radiant, almost to the point of being invisible—except as Creator: hand and eye. She is involved in work her soul must have. Ordering the universe in the image of her personal conception of Beauty.

Her face, as she prepares the Art that is her gift, is a legacy of 44 respect she leaves to me, for all that illuminates and cherishes life.

[11]Novel (1970) by Walker. [Eds.]

She has handed down respect for the possibilities—and the will to grasp them.

For her, so hindered and intruded upon in so many ways, being 45 an artist has still been a daily part of her life. This ability to hold on, even in very simple ways, is work black women have done for a very long time.

This poem is not enough, but it is something, for the woman who 46 literally covered the holes in our walls with sunflowers:

> They were women then
> My mama's generation
> Husky of voice—Stout of
> Step
> With fists as well as   5
> Hands
> How they battered down
> Doors
> And ironed
> Starched white   10
> Shirts
> How they led
> Armies
> Headragged Generals
> Across mined   15
> Fields
> Booby-trapped
> Kitchens
> To discover books
> Desks   20
> A place for us
> How they knew what we
> *Must* know
> Without knowing a page
> Of it   25
> Themselves.

Guided by my heritage of a love of beauty and a respect for 47 strength—in search of my mother's garden, I found my own.

And perhaps in Africa over two hundred years ago, there was 48 just such a mother; perhaps she painted vivid and daring decorations in oranges and yellows and greens on the walls of her hut; perhaps she sang—in a voice like Roberta Flack's—*sweetly* over the compounds of her village; perhaps she wove the most stunning mats or told the most ingenious stories of all the village storytellers. Perhaps she was herself a poet—though only her daughter's name is signed to the poems that we know.

Perhaps Phillis Wheatley's mother was also an artist. 49

Perhaps in more than Phillis Wheatley's biological life is her moth- 50 er's signature made clear.

WRITING SUGGESTION

1. What do Phillis Wheatley and the fictional Judith Shakespeare (from Woolf's essay, page 395) have in common? How is their experience different? Write an essay in which you compare and contrast the two women.

ANSWERS TO RESPONDING TO READING

1. Although Wheatley's circumstances made it impossible for her to fully develop her gift, she expressed what she could in the only way she knew how. She kept alive the idea that she had something to express, a creative spark. Walker says that black women artists must "look at and identify with [their] lives the living creativity some of [their] great-grandmothers were not allowed to know."

2. Walker clearly limits her discussion to the lineage of the mother, from which she says her own gift comes. She sees African-American women as "the mule[s] of the world," who carry the most weight but are the least personally fulfilled. Walker finds the source of her creativity close to home, in the metaphor of her mother's "ambitious" gardens. The problems facing African-American male artists, Walker would probably argue, are very different.

3. Walker speaks both literally and figuratively. She absorbed her mother's stories themselves and also "the manner in which she spoke, something of the urgency that involves the knowledge that her stories—like her life—must be recorded." The garden is a metaphor for creativity; it is where she orders the "universe in the image of her personal conception of Beauty." With the garden, she hands down "respect for the possibilities—and the will to grasp them." Personal experiences will vary.

BACKGROUND ON AUTHOR

Mailer includes among his influences E. M. Forster, James Farrell, John Dos Passos, John Steinbeck, F. Scott Fitzgerald, Thomas Wolfe, and Ernest Hemingway (whom he admires the most). Prolific and controversial, Mailer has resisted identification with literary movements; his style has been associated with New Journalism, "a blend of factual and dramatic, usually highly subjective reporting, which is often unsympathetic to traditional attitudes" (*Contemporary Literary Criticism*, vol. 28, p. 25). In 1970, he was attacked by leading feminists, who denounced him as "the principal voice of male chauvinism on the American literary scene." Mailer counterattacked with *The Prisoner of Sex* (1971), in which he comically "reexplores his relationship with women . . . and sets forth his own ideas on the sex game and his own sexuality" (*CLC*, vol. 28, p. 287).

RESPONDING TO READING

1. Walker says of poet Phillis Wheatley, "It is not so much what you sang, as that you kept alive, in so many of our ancestors, *the notion of song*" (paragraph 25). What does she mean? Do you think it is enough just to keep alive the idea of song—that is, to have "handed on the creative spark" (paragraph 37)? Does Walker? Is there a contemporary writer or recording artist who does for you what Wheatley does for Walker? **2.** How much of what Walker says about African-American women's struggles do you suppose applies also to African-American men? Why do you think Walker does not discuss the problems facing black male artists? Is this omission a weakness in her essay? **3.** When Walker says, "So many of the stories that I write, that we all write, are my mother's stories" (paragraph 38), does she expect to be taken literally or figuratively? Is the image of her mother's garden meant to be taken literally or figuratively—or both? Can you think of any stories that are your mother's stories?

The Language of Men

NORMAN MAILER

Norman Mailer (1923–   ) won a fiction award from *Story* magazine while he was studying engineering in college. After serving in World War II, Mailer wrote *The Naked and the Dead* (1948), the story of an American invasion of a Japanese-held island, which established his literary reputation. Mailer is a prolific and controversial writer who is influenced by an awareness of and concern for American culture. Among his novels are *The Deer Park* (1955) and *The American Dream* (1965). His nonfiction—for which he has won two Pulitzer Prizes—includes *The Armies of the Night* (1968), about the 1967 march on the Pentagon to protest the Vietnam War; *Of a Fire on the Moon* (1970), about the space program; *Marilyn* (1973), a biography of Marilyn Monroe; and *The Executioner's Song: A True Life Novel* (1979), about a convicted murderer. "The Language of Men," first published in 1953, is the story of an army cook who struggles to gain the respect of his fellow soldiers without resorting to physical force.

In the beginning, Sanford Carter was ashamed of becoming an 1 Army cook. This was not from snobbery, at least not from snobbery of the most direct sort. During the two and a half years Carter had been in the Army he had come to hate cooks more and more. They existed for him as a symbol of all that was corrupt, overbearing, stupid, and privileged in Army life. The image which came to mind was a fat cook with an enormous sandwich in one hand, and a bottle of beer in the other, sweat pouring down a porcine face, foot on a flour barrel, shouting at the K.P.'s, "Hurry up, you men, I ain't got all day." More than once in those two and a half years, driven to exasperation, Carter had been on the verge of throwing his food into a cook's face as he passed on the serving line. His anger often derived from nothing: the set of a pair of fat lips, the casual heavy thump of the serving spoon into his plate, or the resentful conviction that the cook was not serving him enough. Since life in the Army was in most aspects a marriage, this rage over apparently harmless details was not a sign of unbalance. Every soldier found some particular habit of the Army spouse impossible to support.

Yet Sanford Carter became a cook and, to elaborate the irony, did 2
better as a cook than he had done as anything else. In a few months he rose from a Private to a first cook with the rank of Sergeant, Technician. After the fact, it was easy to understand. He had suffered through all his Army career from an excess of eagerness. He had cared too much, he had wanted to do well, and so he had often been tense at moments when he would better have been relaxed. He was very young, twenty-one, had lived the comparatively gentle life of a middle-class boy, and needed some success in the Army to prove to himself that he was not completely worthless.

In succession, he had failed as a surveyor in Field Artillery, a 3
clerk in an Infantry headquarters, a telephone wireman, and finally a rifleman. When the war ended, and his regiment went to Japan, Carter was still a rifleman; he had been a rifleman for eight months. What was more to the point, he had been in the platoon as long as any of its members; the skilled hard-bitten nucleus of veterans who had run his squad had gone home one by one, and it seemed to him that through seniority he was entitled to at least a corporal's rating. Through seniority he was so entitled, but on no other ground. Whenever responsibility had been handed to him, he had discharged it miserably, tensely, overconscientiously. He had always asked too many questions, he had worried the task too severely, he had conveyed his nervousness to the men he was supposed to lead. Since he was also sensitive enough and proud enough never to curry favor with the noncoms in the platoons, he was in no position to sit in on their occasional discussions about who was to succeed them. In a vacuum of ignorance, he had allowed himself to dream that he would be given a squad to lead, and his hurt was sharp when the squad was given to a replacement who had joined the platoon months after him.

The war was over, Carter had a bride in the States (he had lived 4
with her for only two months), he was lonely, he was obsessed with going home. As one week dragged into the next, and the regiment,

BACKGROUND ON READING

After Mailer's graduation in 1943 from Harvard, he joined the army and was sent to the Pacific. Private Mailer became, by his own admission, "the third lousiest GI in the platoon of twelve." Less interested in becoming a good soldier than in writing the definitive American novel of World War II, he went ashore with U.S. infantry in the invasion of Luzon and volunteered as a rifleman with a platoon fighting in the Philippines. Mailer wrote his first novel (*The Naked and the Dead*) about war because he believed that an individual's real nature could only be revealed in a crisis. Mailer's basic theme is the conflict between individual will and external, societal power.

FOR OPENERS

Discuss differences between "the language of men" and "the language of women." Is there *literally* a language of men (or of women)?

the company, and his own platoon continued the same sort of training
which they had been doing ever since he had entered the Army, he
thought he would snap. There were months to wait until he would
be discharged and meanwhile it was intolerable to him to be taught
for the fifth time the nomenclature of the machine gun, to stand a
retreat parade three evenings a week. He wanted some niche where
he could lick his wounds, some Army job with so many hours of
work and so many hours of complete freedom, where he could be
alone by himself. He hated the Army, the huge Army which had
proved to him that he was good at no work, and incapable of succeeding at anything. He wrote long, aching letters to his wife, he
talked less and less to the men around him and he was close to violent
attacks of anger during the most casual phases of training—during
close-order drill or cleaning his rifle for inspection. He knew that if
he did not find his niche it was possible that he would crack.

   So he took an opening in the kitchen. It promised him nothing   5
except a day of work, and a day of leisure which would be completely
at his disposal. He found that he liked it. He was given at first the
job of baking the bread for the company, and every other night he
worked till early in the morning, kneading and shaping his fifty-
pound mix of dough. At two or three he would be done, and for his
work there would be the tangible reward of fifty loaves of bread, all
fresh from the oven, all clean and smelling of fertile accomplished
creativity. He had the rare and therefore intensely satisfying emotion
of seeing at the end of an Army chore the product of his labor.

   A month after he became a cook the regiment was disbanded,   6
and those men who did not have enough points to go home were
sent to other outfits. Carter ended at an ordnance company in another
Japanese city. He had by now given up all thought of getting a non-
com's rating before he was discharged, and was merely content to
work each alternate day. He took his work for granted and so he
succeeded at it. He had begun as a baker in the new company kitchen;
before long he was the first cook. It all happened quickly. One cook
went home on points, another caught a skin disease, a third was
transferred from the kitchen after contracting a venereal infection.
On the shift which Carter worked there were left only himself and a
man who was illiterate. Carter was put nominally in charge, and was
soon actively in charge. He looked up each menu in an Army recipe
book, collected the items, combined them in the order indicated, and
after the proper time had elapsed, took them from the stove. His
product tasted neither better nor worse than the product of all other
Army cooks. But the mess sergeant was impressed. Carter had filled
a gap. The next time ratings were given out Carter jumped at a bound
from Private to Sergeant T/4.

On the surface he was happy; beneath the surface he was over-   7
joyed. It took him several weeks to realize how grateful and delighted
he felt. The promotion coincided with his assignment to a detachment
working in a small seaport up the coast. Carter arrived there to discover that he was in charge of cooking for thirty men, and would act
as mess sergeant. There was another cook, and there were four permanent Japanese K.P.'s, all of them good workers. He still cooked
every other day, but there was always time between meals to take a
break of at least an hour and often two; he shared a room with the
other cook and lived in comparative privacy for the first time in several
years; the seaport was beautiful; there was only one officer, and he
left the men alone; supplies were plentiful due to a clerical error which
assigned rations for forty men rather than thirty; and in general everything was fine. The niche had become a sinecure.

This was the happiest period of Carter's life in the Army. He came   8
to like his Japanese K.P.'s. He studied their language, he visited their
homes, he gave them gifts of food from time to time. They worshiped
him because he was kind to them and generous, because he never
shouted, because his good humor bubbled over into games, and made
the work of the kitchen seem pleasant. All the while he grew in
confidence. He was not a big man, but his body filled out from the
heavy work; he was likely to sing a great deal, he cracked jokes with
the men on the chow line. The kitchen became his property, it became
his domain, and since it was a warm room, filled with sunlight, he
came to take pleasure in the very sight of it. Before long his good
humor expanded into a series of efforts to improve the food. He began
to take little pains and make little extra efforts which would have
been impossible if he had been obliged to cook for more than thirty
men. In the morning he would serve the men fresh eggs scrambled
or fried to their desire in fresh butter. Instead of cooking sixty eggs
in one large pot he cooked two eggs at a time in a frying pan, turning
them to the taste of each soldier. He baked like a housewife satisfying
her young husband; at lunch and dinner there was pie or cake, and
often both. He went to great lengths. He taught the K.P.'s how to
make the toast come out right. He traded excess food for spices in
Japanese stores. He rubbed paprika and garlic on the chickens. He
even made pastries to cover such staples as corn beef hash and meat
and vegetable stew.

It all seemed to be wasted. In the beginning the men might have   9
noticed these improvements, but after a period they took them for
granted. It did not matter how he worked to satisfy them; they
trudged through the chow line with their heads down, nodding coolly
at him, and they ate without comment. He would hang around the
tables after the meal, noticing how much they consumed, and what

COLLABORATIVE ACTIVITY

In groups, have students discuss prevalent
stereotypes of men and the ways in which they
are reinforced in groups and relationships. Have
each group present a hypothetical case history.

they discarded; he would wait for compliments, but the soldiers seemed indifferent. They seemed to eat without tasting the food. In their faces he saw mirrored the distaste with which he had once stared at cooks.

The honeymoon was ended. The pleasure he took in the kitchen 10 and himself curdled. He became aware again of his painful desire to please people, to discharge responsibility, to be a man. When he had been a child, tears had come into his eyes at a cross word, and he had lived in an atmosphere where his smallest accomplishment was warmly praised. He was the sort of young man, he often thought bitterly, who was accustomed to the attention and the protection of women. He would have thrown away all he possessed—the love of his wife, the love of his mother, the benefits of his education, the assured financial security of entering his father's business—if he had been able just once to dig a ditch as well as the most ignorant farmer.

Instead, he was back in the painful unprotected days of his first 11 entrance into the Army. Once again the most casual actions became the most painful, the events which were most to be taken for granted grew into the most significant, and the feeding of the men at each meal turned progressively more unbearable.

So Sanford Carter came full circle. If he had once hated the cooks, 12 he now hated the troops. At mealtimes his face soured into the belligerent scowl with which he had once believed cooks to be born. And to himself he muttered the age-old laments of the housewife: how little they appreciated what he did.

Finally there was an explosion. He was approached one day by 13 Corporal Taylor, and he had come to hate Taylor, because Taylor was the natural leader of the detachment and kept the other men endlessly amused with his jokes. Taylor had the ability to present himself as inefficient, shiftless, and incapable, in such a manner as to convey that really the opposite was true. He had the lightest touch, he had the greatest facility, he could charm a geisha in two minutes and obtain anything he wanted from a supply sergeant in five. Carter envied him, envied his grace, his charmed indifference; then grew to hate him.

Taylor teased Carter about the cooking, and he had the knack of 14 knowing where to put the knife. "Hey, Carter," he would shout across the mess hall while breakfast was being served, "you turned my eggs twice, and I asked for them raw." The men would shout with laughter. Somehow Taylor had succeeded in conveying all of the situation, or so it seemed to Carter, insinuating everything, how Carter worked and how it meant nothing, how Carter labored to gain their affection and earned their contempt. Carter would scowl, Carter would answer in a rough voice, "Next time I'll crack them over your head." "You crack 'em, I'll eat 'em," Taylor would pipe back, "but just don't put your fingers in 'em." And there would be another laugh. He hated the sight of Taylor.

It was Taylor who came to him to get the salad oil. About twenty 15 of the soldiers were going to have a fish fry at the geisha house; they had bought the fish at the local market, but they could not buy oil, so Taylor was sent as the deputy to Carter. He was charming to Carter, he complimented him on the meal, he clapped him on the back, he dissolved Carter to warmth, to private delight in the attention, and the thought that he had misjudged Taylor. Then Taylor asked for the oil.

Carter was sick with anger. Twenty men out of the thirty in the 16 detachment were going on the fish fry. It meant only that Carter was considered one of the ten undesirables. It was something he had known, but the proof of knowledge is always more painful than the acquisition of it. If he had been alone his eyes would have clouded. And he was outraged at Taylor's deception. He could imagine Taylor saying ten minutes later, "You should have seen the grease job I gave to Carter. I'm dumb, but man, he's dumber."

Carter was close enough to giving him the oil. He had a sense of 17 what it would mean to refuse Taylor, he was on the very edge of mild acquiescence. But he also had a sense of how he would despise himself afterward.

"No," he said abruptly, his teeth gritted, "you can't have it." 18

"What do you mean we can't have it?" 19

"I won't give it to you." Carter could almost feel the rage which 20 Taylor generated at being refused.

"You won't give away a lousy five gallons of oil to a bunch of 21 G.I.'s having a party?"

"I'm sick and tired," Carter began. 22

"So am I." Taylor walked away. 23

Carter knew he would pay for it. He left the K.P.'s and went to 24 change his sweat-soaked work shirt, and as he passed the large dormitory in which most of the detachment slept he could hear Taylor's high-pitched voice. Carter did not bother to take off his shirt. He returned instead to the kitchen, and listened to the sound of men going back and forth through the hall and of a man shouting with rage. That was Hobbs, a Southerner, a big man with a big bellowing voice.

There was a formal knock on the kitchen door. Taylor came in. 25 His face was pale and his eyes showed a cold satisfaction. "Carter," he said, "the men want to see you in the big room."

Carter heard his voice answer huskily. "If they want to see me," 26 they can come into the kitchen."

He knew he would conduct himself with more courage in his own 27
kitchen than anywhere else. "I'll be here for a while."

Taylor closed the door, and Carter picked up a writing board to 28
which was clamped the menu for the following day. Then he made
a pretense of examining the food supplies in the pantry closet. It was
his habit to check the stocks before deciding what to serve the next
day, but on this night his eyes ranged thoughtlessly over the canned
goods. In a corner were seven five-gallon tins of salad oil, easily
enough cooking oil to last a month. Carter came out of the pantry
and shut the door behind him.

He kept his head down and pretended to be writing the menu 29
when the soldiers came in. Somehow there were even more of them
than he had expected. Out of the twenty men who were going to the
party, all but two or three had crowded through the door.

Carter took his time, looked up slowly. "You men want to see 30
me?" he asked flatly.

They were angry. For the first time in his life he faced the hostile 31
expressions of many men. It was the most painful and anxious
moment he had ever known.

"Taylor says you won't give us the oil," someone burst out.   32

"That's right, I won't," said Carter. He tapped his pencil against 33
the scratchboard, tapping it slowly and, he hoped, with an appearance
of calm.

"What a stink deal," said Porfirio, a little Cuban whom Carter 34
had always considered his friend.

Hobbs, the big Southerner, stared down at Carter. "Would you 35
mind telling the men why you've decided not to give us the oil?" he
asked quietly.

" 'Cause I'm blowed if I'm going to cater to you men. I've catered 36
enough," Carter said. His voice was close to cracking with the outrage
he had suppressed for so long, and he knew that if he continued he
might cry. "I'm the acting mess sergeant," he said as coldly as he
could, "and I decide what goes out of this kitchen." He stared at each
one in turn, trying to stare them down, feeling mired in the rut of
his own failure. They would never have dared this approach to
another mess sergeant.

"What crud," someone muttered.   37

"You won't give a lousy five-gallon can of oil for a G.I. party," 38
Hobbs said more loudly.

"I won't. That's definite. You men can get out of here."   39

"Why, you lousy little snot," Hobbs burst out, "how many five- 40
gallon cans of oil have you sold on the black market?"

"I've never sold any." Carter might have been slapped with the 41
flat of a sword. He told himself bitterly, numbly, that this was the
reward he received for being perhaps the single honest cook in the

whole United States Army. And he even had time to wonder at the obscure prejudice which had kept him from selling food for his own profit.

"Man, I've seen you take it out," Hobbs exclaimed. "I've seen 42
you take it to the market."

"I took food to trade for spices," Carter said hotly. 43

There was an ugly snicker from the men. 44

"I don't mind if a cook sells," Hobbs said, "every man has his 45
own deal in this Army. But a cook ought to give a little food to a G.I.
if he wants it."

"Tell him," someone said. 46

"It's bull," Taylor screeched. "I've seen Carter take butter, eggs, 47
every damn thing to the market."

Their faces were red, they circled him. 48

"I never sold a thing," Carter said doggedly. 49

"And I'm telling you," Hobbs said, "that you're a two-bit crook. 50
You been raiding that kitchen, and that's why you don't give to us
now."

Carter knew there was only one way he could possibly answer 51
if he hoped to live among these men again. "That's a goddam lie,"
Carter said to Hobbs. He laid down the scratchboard, he flipped his
pencil slowly and deliberately to one corner of the room, and with
his heart aching he lunged toward Hobbs. He had no hope of beating
him. He merely intended to fight until he was pounded unconscious,
advancing the pain and bruises he would collect as collateral for his
self-respect.

To his indescribable relief Porfirio darted between them, held 52
them apart with the pleased ferocity of a small man breaking up a
fight. "Now, stop this! Now, stop this!" he cried out.

Carter allowed himself to be pushed back, and he knew that 53
he had gained a point. He even glimpsed a solution with some
honor.

He shrugged violently to free himself from Porfirio. He was in a 54
rage, and yet it was a rage he could have ended at any instant. "All
right, you men," he swore, "I'll give you the oil, but now that we're
at it, I'm going to tell you a thing or two." His face red, his body
perspiring, he was in the pantry and out again with a five-gallon tin.
"Here," he said, "you better have a good fish fry, 'cause it's the last
good meal you're going to have for quite a while. I'm sick of trying
to please you. You think I have to work—" he was about to say, my
fingers to the bone—"well, I don't. From now on, you'll see what
chow in the Army is supposed to be like." He was almost hysterical.
"Take that oil. Have your fish fry." The fact that they wanted to cook
for themselves was the greatest insult of all. "Tomorrow I'll give you
real Army cooking."

WRITING SUGGESTIONS

1. Carter is obsessed with "becoming a man." Analyze the ways in which the men in Mailer's story mark their territory and reinforce their sense of identity within a group.
2. Women are absent from Mailer's story, except in a brief mention of Carter's wife in paragraph 4. What do you suppose his relationship with his wife is like? Write a story in which they interact, or a letter to her from Carter.

His voice was so intense that they backed away from him. "Get 55 out of this kitchen," he said. "None of you has any business here."

They filed out quietly, and they looked a little sheepish. 56

Carter felt weary, he felt ashamed of himself, he knew he had 57 not meant what he said. But half an hour later, when he left the kitchen and passed the large dormitory, he heard shouts of raucous laughter, and he heard his name mentioned and then more laughter.

He slept badly that night, he was awake at four, he was in the 58 kitchen by five, and stood there white-faced and nervous, waiting for the K.P.'s to arrive. Breakfast that morning landed on the men like a lead bomb. Carter rummaged in the back of the pantry and found a tin of dehydrated eggs covered with dust, memento of a time when fresh eggs were never on the ration list. The K.P.'s looked at him in amazement as he stirred the lumpy powder into a pan of water. While it was still half-dissolved he put it on the fire. While it was still wet, he took it off. The coffee was cold, the toast was burned, the oatmeal stuck to the pot. The men dipped forks into their food, took cautious sips of their coffee, and spoke in whispers. Sullenness drifted like vapors through the kitchen.

At noontime Carter opened cans of meat and vegetable stew. He 59 dumped them into a pan and heated them slightly. He served the stew with burned string beans and dehydrated potatoes which tasted like straw. For dessert the men had a single lukewarm canned peach and cold coffee.

So the meals continued. For three days Carter cooked slop, and 60 suffered even more than the men. When mealtime came he left the chow line to the K.P.'s and sat in his room, perspiring with shame, determined not to yield and sick with the determination.

Carter won. On the fourth day a delegation of men came to see 61 him. They told him that indeed they had appreciated his cooking in the past, they told him that they were sorry they had hurt his feelings, they listened to his remonstrances, they listened to his grievances, and with delight Carter forgave them. That night, for supper, the detachment celebrated. There was roast chicken with stuffing, lemon meringue pie and chocolate cake. The coffee burned their lips. More than half the men made it a point to compliment Carter on the meal.

In the weeks which followed the compliments diminished, but 62 they never stopped completely. Carter became ashamed at last. He realized the men were trying to humor him, and he wished to tell them it was no longer necessary.

Harmony settled over the kitchen. Carter even became friends 63 with Hobbs, the big Southerner. Hobbs approached him one day, and in the manner of a farmer talked obliquely for an hour. He spoke about his father, he spoke about his girl friends, he alluded indirectly to the night they had almost fought, and finally with the courtesy of a Southerner he said to Carter, "You know, I'm sorry about shooting off my mouth. You were right to want to fight me, and if you're still mad I'll fight you to give you satisfaction, although I just as soon would not."

"No, I don't want to fight with you now," Carter said warmly. 64 They smiled at each other. They were friends.

Carter knew he had gained Hobbs' respect. Hobbs respected him 65 because he had been willing to fight. That made sense to a man like Hobbs. Carter liked him so much at this moment that he wished the friendship to be more intimate.

"You know," he said to Hobbs, "it's a funny thing. You know I 66 really never did sell anything on the black market. Not that I'm proud of it, but I just didn't."

Hobbs frowned. He seemed to be saying that Carter did not have 67 to lie. "I don't hold it against a man," Hobbs said, "if he makes a little money in something that's his own proper work. Hell, I sell gas from the motor pool. It's just I also give gas if one of the G.I.'s wants to take the jeep out for a joy ride, kind of."

"No, but I never did sell anything." Carter had to explain. "If I 68 ever had sold on the black market, I would have given the salad oil without question."

Hobbs frowned again, and Carter realized he still did not believe 69 him. Carter did not want to lose the friendship which was forming. He thought he could save it only by some further admission. "You know," he said again, "remember when Porfirio broke up our fight? I was awful glad when I didn't have to fight you." Carter laughed, expecting Hobbs to laugh with him, but a shadow passed across Hobbs' face.

"Funny way of putting it," Hobbs said. 70

He was always friendly thereafter, but Carter knew that Hobbs 71 would never consider him a friend. Carter thought about it often, and began to wonder about the things which made him different. He was no longer so worried about becoming a man; he felt that to an extent he had become one. But in his heart he wondered if he would ever learn the language of men.

RESPONDING TO READING

1. The army "had proved to [Carter] that he was good at no work, and incapable of succeeding at anything" (paragraph 4). Why is this fact, and the string of Carter's failures summarized in paragraph 3, important to the story? How does his history of failure prepare you for the events that follow?   **2.** Which of Carter's behavior and personality traits do you asso-

scientiously." He falls into a job that he comes to enjoy, but he impresses the sergeant merely because he fills a gap.

2. Carter is excessively eager and overconscientious, cares too much, wants approval, and is tense when he should be relaxed—characteristics that Mailer seems to associate with women.

The narrator tells us in paragraph 8 that Carter is happy as a cook and that life in the army is in many ways a marriage. The kitchen becomes Carter's life: he bakes "like a housewife satisfying her young husband," but the men are indifferent; the honeymoon is over. In paragraphs 58–61 Carter stops being the nurturing wife; to punish his men for their behavior he serves them cold, dehydrated, badly prepared "slop." When a delegation of men comes to apologize and tell him "that indeed they had appreciated his cooking," he again prepares meals with love, thus reverting to his earlier posture.

Carter may "become a man" in stereotypical and surface ways, but he worries that he will never learn "the language of men."

3. Carter's alternative is to back down, which would further alienate him from the men. Mailer implies that because backing down is not a typical male response to this kind of situation, Carter's action would be misunderstood. The idea that violence is the stereotypical response is part of Mailer's point.

BACKGROUND ON READING

Munro uses the techniques of photographic realism, and her work has been compared to that of two American writers she admires, James Agee and Eudora Welty. Students might observe her careful description of details that appeal to the senses and the absence of elaborate figurative language, which makes her occasional use of simile more striking. Most of Munro's stories are told from the perspective of a child or adolescent, especially a young girl "who feels herself to be different from those around her, usually because she is a secretly developing artist in an environment alien and hostile to art." She creates convincing portraits of men but seldom writes from a male point of view (*The Oxford Companion to Canadian Literature*, ed. William Toye, pp. 536–537).

Typical of Munro's work is the "manipulation of logical perspectives." She describes family expectations that reinforce traditional gender roles and details "the process by which a girl comes not to rebel against them but to question the freedom from them that she had thought she possessed" (*Literary History of Canada*, 2nd ed., vol. 3, p. 271).

ciate with women? How does his behavior and the men's response to it in paragraphs 8 and 9 and paragraphs 58–61 mimic a stereotypical male-female relationship? At the end of the story he believes he has "to an extent" become a man (paragraph 71). Does your experience suggest that he is right? What does "becoming a man" mean to Carter? What do you think it means?   **3.** The story's narrator tells us that Carter sees physical force as his only possible response: "Carter knew there was only one way he could possibly answer if he hoped to live among these men again" (paragraph 51). Do you think Carter has any other alternative? Do you believe that resorting to physical force can be a solution, or do you see it simply as the stereotypical male way to resolve a problem?

Boys and Girls

ALICE MUNRO

Alice Munro (1931–   ) won the Canadian Governor General's Literary Award for her story collection *Dance of Happy Shades* (1968), from which the following story is taken. Her other story collections are *Something I've Been Meaning to Tell You* (1974) and *Friend of My Youth* (1990), and she has also written a novel, *Lives of Girls and Women* (1971). Munro writes about the farmers and townspeople in southwest Ontario, and she details Canadian small town life. In "Boys and Girls," Munro's narrator recalls key events of her childhood as the daughter of a fox farmer—events that teach her a harsh lesson about the limitations of conventional gender roles.

My father was a fox farmer. That is, he raised silver foxes, in 1 pens; and in the fall and early winter, when their fur was prime, he killed them and skinned them and sold their pelts to the Hudson's Bay Company or the Montreal Fur Traders. These companies supplied us with heroic calendars to hang, one on each side of the kitchen door. Against a background of cold blue sky and black pine forests and treacherous northern rivers, plumed adventurers planted the flags of England or of France; magnificent savages bent their backs to the portage.

For several weeks before Christmas, my father worked after 2 supper in the cellar of our house. The cellar was whitewashed, and lit by a hundred-watt bulb over the worktable. My brother Laird and I sat on the top step and watched. My father removed the pelt inside-out from the body of the fox, which looked surprisingly small, mean and rat-like, deprived of its arrogant weight of fur. The naked, slippery bodies were collected in a sack and buried at the dump. One time the hired man, Henry Bailey, had taken a swipe at me with this sack, saying, "Christmas present!" My mother thought that was not funny. In fact she disliked the whole pelting operation—that was what the killing, skinning, and preparation of the furs was called—and wished it did not have to take place in the house. There was the smell. After the pelt had been stretched inside-out on a long board my father scraped away delicately, removing the little clotted webs of blood vessels, the bubbles of fat; the smell of blood and animal fat, with the strong primitive odour of the fox itself, penetrated all parts of the house. I found it reassuringly seasonal, like the smell of oranges and pine needles.

Henry Bailey suffered from bronchial troubles. He would cough and cough until his narrow face turned scarlet, and his light blue, derisive eyes filled up with tears; then he took the lid off the stove, and, standing well back, shot out a great clot of phlegm—hsss—straight into the heart of the flames. We admired him for this performance and for his ability to make his stomach growl at will, and for his laughter, which was full of high whistlings and gurglings and involved the whole faulty machinery of his chest. It was sometimes hard to tell what he was laughing at, and always possible that it might be us.

After we had been sent to bed we could still smell fox and still hear Henry's laugh, but these things, reminders of the warm, safe, brightly lit downstairs world, seemed lost and diminished, floating on the stale cold air upstairs. We were afraid at night in the winter. We were not afraid of *outside* though this was the time of year when snowdrifts curled around our house like sleeping whales and the wind harassed us all night, coming up from the buried fields, the frozen swamp, with its old bugbear chorus of threats and misery. We were afraid of *inside*, the room where we slept. At this time the upstairs of our house was not finished. A brick chimney went up one wall. In the middle of the floor was a square hole, with a wooden railing around it; that was where the stairs came up. On the other side of the stairwell were the things that nobody had any use for any more—a soldiery roll of linoleum, standing on end, a wicker baby carriage, a fern basket, china jugs and basins with cracks in them, a picture of the Battle of Balaclava,[1] very sad to look at. I had told Laird, as soon as he was old enough to understand such things, that bats and skeletons lived over there; whenever a man escaped from the county jail, twenty miles away, I imagined that he had somehow let himself in the window and was hiding behind the linoleum. But we had rules to keep us safe. When the light was on, we were safe as long as we

3

4

[1]Devastating Crimean War battle, fought on October 25, 1854, in which the British "Light Brigade" charged Russian positions. About half the soldiers were killed or wounded. [Eds.]

FOR OPENERS

1. Define the initiation story, in which a character has an experience that in some way ushers him or her into maturity. (Remind students that such stories do not have to focus on children.)
2. Ask students at what point they realized that the narrator was female.
3. Why is the story called "Boys and Girls"?

ADDITIONAL QUESTIONS FOR RESPONDING TO READING

1. Laird takes a step toward identifying with his father. Identify passages that demonstrate his initiation.
2. Why does the narrator resent her mother's presence at the barn?
3. What indications are there that the narrator's attitude is changing?
4. The narrator says that by calling her "only a girl," her father "absolved and dismissed [her] for good." What does she mean?
5. Why does the narrator identify with Flora?

TEACHING STRATEGIES

1. The story proceeds by shifting back and forth from the outdoors, the world of the father and masculinity, to the indoors, the world of the mother and femininity. Discuss the associations that the narrator has with each world and the ways in which her feelings develop in the story. How does the narrator's movement from outside to inside advance the theme?
2. Point out that the father's work involves killing, whereas the mother's work involves preserving. Ask if there is anything significant in this.
3. Learning can involve loss as well as gain. Discuss this idea in relation to "Boys and Girls" and Mark Twain's "Reading the River" (Chapter 2).

did not step off the square of worn carpet which defined our bedroom-space; when the light was off no place was safe but the beds themselves. I had to turn out the light kneeling on the end of my bed, and stretching as far as I could to reach the cord.

In the dark we lay on our beds, our narrow life rafts, and fixed   5
our eyes on the faint light coming up the stairwell, and sang songs. Laird sang "Jingle Bells," which he would sing any time, whether it was Christmas or not, and I sang "Danny Boy." I loved the sound of my own voice, frail and supplicating, rising in the dark. We could make out the tall frosted shapes of the windows now, gloomy and white. When I came to the part, *When I am dead, as dead I well may be*—a fit of shivering caused not by the cold sheets but by pleasurable emotion almost silenced me. *You'll kneel and say, an Ave there above me*—What was an Ave? Every day I forgot to find out.

Laird went straight from singing to sleep. I could hear his long,   6
satisfied, bubbly breaths. Now for the time that remained to me, the most perfectly private and perhaps the best time of the whole day, I arranged myself tightly under the covers and went on with one of the stories I was telling myself from night to night. These stories were about myself, when I had grown a little older; they took place in a world that was recognizably mine, yet one that presented opportunities for courage, boldness and self-sacrifice, as mine never did. I rescued people from a bombed building (it discouraged me that the real war had gone on so far away from Jubilee). I shot two rabid wolves who were menacing the schoolyard (the teachers cowered terrified at my back). I rode a fine horse spiritedly down the main street of Jubilee, acknowledging the towns-people's gratitude for some yet-to-be-worked-out piece of heroism (nobody ever rode a horse there, except King Billy in the Orangemen's Day parade). There was always riding and shooting in these stories, though I had only been on a horse twice—bareback because we did not own a saddle—and the second time I had slid right around and dropped under the horse's feet; it had stepped placidly over me. I really was learning to shoot, but I could not hit anything yet, not even tin cans on fence posts.

Alive, the foxes inhabited a world my father made for them. It   7
was surrounded by a high guard fence, like a medieval town, with a gate that was padlocked at night. Along the streets of this town were ranged large, sturdy pens. Each of them had a real door that a man could go through, a wooden ramp along the wire, for the foxes to run up and down on, and a kennel—something like a clothes chest with airholes—where they slept and stayed in winter and had their young. There were feeding and watering dishes attached to the wire

in such a way that they could be emptied and cleaned from the outside. The dishes were made of old tin cans, and the ramps and kennels of odds and ends of old lumber. Everything was tidy and ingenious; my father was tirelessly inventive and his favourite book in the world was Robinson Crusoe. He had fitted a tin drum on a wheelbarrow, for bringing water down to the pens. This was my job in summer, when the foxes had to have water twice a day. Between nine and ten o'clock in the morning, and again after supper, I filled the drum at the pump and trundled it down through the barnyard to the pens, where I parked it, and filled my watering can and went along the streets. Laird came too, with his little cream and green gardening can, filled too full and knocking against his legs and slopping water on his canvas shoes. I had the real watering can, my father's, though I could only carry it three-quarters full.

The foxes all had names, which were printed on a tin plate and hung beside their doors. They were not named when they were born, but when they survived the first year's pelting and were added to the breeding stock. Those my father had named were called names like Prince, Bob, Wally and Betty. Those I had named were called Star or Turk, or Maureen or Diana. Laird named one Maud after a hired girl we had when he was little, one Harold after a boy at school, and one Mexico, he did not say why.   8

Naming them did not make pets out of them, or anything like it. Nobody but my father ever went into the pens, and he had twice had blood-poisoning from bites. When I was bringing them their water they prowled up and down on the paths they had made inside their pens, barking seldom—they saved that for nighttime, when they might get up a chorus of community frenzy—but always watching me, their eyes burning, clear gold, in their pointed, malevolent faces. They were beautiful for their delicate legs and heavy, aristocratic tails and the bright fur sprinkled on dark down their backs—which gave them their name—but especially for their faces, drawn exquisitely sharp in pure hostility, and their golden eyes.   9

Besides carrying water I helped my father when he cut the long grass, and the lamb's quarter and flowering money-musk, that grew between the pens. He cut with the scythe and I raked into piles. Then he took a pitchfork and threw fresh-cut grass all over the top of the pens, to keep the foxes cooler and shade their coats, which were browned by too much sun. My father did not talk to me unless it was about the job we were doing. In this he was quite different from my mother, who, if she was feeling cheerful, would tell me all sorts of things—the name of a dog she had had when she was a little girl, the names of boys she had gone out with later on when she was grown up, and what certain dresses of hers had looked like—she   10 could not imagine now what had become of them. Whatever thoughts and stories my father had were private, and I was shy of him and would never ask him questions. Nevertheless I worked willingly under his eyes, and with a feeling of pride. One time a feed salesman came down into the pens to talk to him and my father said, "Like to have you meet my new hired man." I turned away and raked furiously, red in the face with pleasure.

"Could of fooled me," said the salesman. "I thought it was only 11 a girl."

After the grass was cut, it seemed suddenly much later in the 12 year. I walked on stubble in the earlier evening, aware of the red-dening skies, the entering silences, of fall. When I wheeled the tank out of the gate and put the padlock on, it was almost dark. One night at this time I saw my mother and father standing talking on the little rise of ground we called the gangway, in front of the barn. My father had just come from the meathouse; he had his stiff bloody apron on, and a pail of cut-up meat in his hand.

It was an odd thing to see my mother down at the barn. She did 13 not often come out of the house unless it was to do something—hang out the wash or dig potatoes in the garden. She looked out of place, with her bare lumpy legs, not touched by the sun, her apron still on and damp across the stomach from the supper dishes. Her hair was tied up in a kerchief, wisps of it falling out. She would tie her hair up like this in the morning, saying she did not have time to do it properly, and it would stay tied up all day. It was true, too; she really did not have time. These days our back porch was piled with baskets of peaches and grapes and pears, bought in town, and onions and tomatoes and cucumbers grown at home, all waiting to be made into jelly and jam and preserves, pickles and chili sauce. In the kitchen there was a fire in the stove all day, jars clinked in boiling water, sometimes a cheesecloth bag was strung on a pole between two chairs, straining blue-black grape pulp for jelly. I was given jobs to do and I would sit at the table peeling peaches that had been soaked in the hot water, or cutting up onions, my eyes smarting and streaming. As soon as I was done I ran out of the house, trying to get out of earshot before my mother thought of what she wanted me to do next. I hated the hot dark kitchen in summer, the green blinds and the flypapers, the same old oilcloth table and wavy mirror and bumpy linoleum. My mother was too tired and preoccupied to talk to me, she had no heart to tell about the Normal School Graduation Dance; sweat trickled over her face and she was always counting under her breath, pointing at jars, dumping cups of sugar. It seemed to me that work in the house was endless, dreary and peculiarly depressing; work done out of doors, and in my father's service, was ritualistically important.

I wheeled the tank up to the barn, where it was kept, and I heard 14
my mother saying, "Wait till Laird gets a little bigger, then you'll
have a real help."

What my father said I did not hear. I was pleased by the way he 15
stood listening, politely as he would to a salesman or a stranger, but
with an air of wanting to get on with his real work. I felt my mother
had no business down here and I wanted him to feel the same way.
What did she mean about Laird? He was no help to anybody. Where
was he now? Swinging himself sick on the swing, going around in
circles, or trying to catch caterpillars. He never once stayed with me
till I was finished.

"And then I can use her more in the house," I heard my mother 16
say. She had a dead-quiet, regretful way of talking about me that
always made me uneasy. "I just get my back turned and she runs
off. It's not like I had a girl in the family at all."

I went and sat on a feedbag in the corner of the barn, not wanting 17
to appear when this conversation was going on. My mother, I felt,
was not to be trusted. She was kinder than my father and more easily
fooled, but you could not depend on her, and the real reasons for
the things she said and did were not to be known. She loved me,
and she sat up late at night making a dress of the difficult style I
wanted, for me to wear when school started, but she was also my
enemy. She was always plotting. She was plotting now to get me to
stay in the house more, although she knew I hated it (*because* she
knew I hated it) and keep me from working for my father. It seemed
to me she would do this simply out of perversity, and to try her
power. It did not occur to me that she could be lonely, or jealous.
No grown-up could be; they were too fortunate. I sat and kicked my
heels monotonously against a feedbag, raising dust, and did not come
out till she was gone.

At any rate, I did not expect my father to pay any attention to 18
what she said. Who could imagine Laird doing my work—Laird
remembering the padlock and cleaning out the watering-dishes with
a leaf on the end of a stick, or even wheeling the tank without it
tumbling over? It showed how little my mother knew about the way
things really were.

I have forgotten to say what the foxes were fed. My father's bloody 19
apron reminded me. They were fed horsemeat. At this time most
farmers still kept horses, and when a horse got too old to work, or
broke a leg or got down and would not get up, as they sometimes
did, the owner would call my father, and he and Henry went out to
the farm in the truck. Usually they shot and butchered the horse
there, paying the farmer from five to twelve dollars. If they had

already too much meat on hand, they would bring the horse back alive, and keep it for a few days or weeks in our stable, until the meat was needed. After the war the farmers were buying tractors and gradually getting rid of horses altogether, so it sometimes happened that we got a good healthy horse, that there was just no use for any more. If this happened in the winter we might keep the horse in our stable till spring, for we had plenty of hay and if there was a lot of snow—and the plow did not always get our road cleared—it was convenient to be able to go to town with a horse and cutter.

The winter I was eleven years old we had two horses in the stable. 20 We did not know what names they had had before, so we called them Mack and Flora. Mack was an old black workhorse, sooty and indifferent. Flora was a sorrel mare, a driver. We took them both out in the cutter. Mack was slow and easy to handle. Flora was given to fits of violent alarm, veering at cars and even at other horses, but we loved her speed and high-stepping, her general air of gallantry and abandon. On Saturdays we went down to the stable and as soon as we opened the door on its cosy, animal-smelling darkness Flora threw up her head, rolled her eyes, whinnied despairingly and pulled herself through a crisis of nerves on the spot. It was not safe to go into her stall; she would kick.

This winter also I began to hear a great deal more on the theme 21 my mother had sounded when she had been talking in front of the barn. I no longer felt safe. It seemed that in the minds of the people around me there was a steady undercurrent of thought, not to be deflected, on this one subject. The word *girl* had formerly seemed to me innocent and unburdened, like the word *child*; now it appeared that it was no such thing. A girl was not, as I had supposed, simply what I was; it was what I had to become. It was a definition, always touched with emphasis, with reproach and disappointment. Also it was a joke on me. Once Laird and I were fighting, and for the first time ever I had to use all my strength against him; even so, he caught and pinned my arm for a moment, really hurting me. Henry saw this, and laughed, saying, "Oh, that there Laird's gonna show you, one of these days!" Laird was getting a lot bigger. But I was getting bigger too.

My grandmother came to stay with us for a few weeks and I heard 22 other things. "Girls don't slam doors like that." "Girls keep their knees together when they sit down." And worse still, when I asked some questions, "That's none of girls' business." I continued to slam the doors and sit as awkwardly as possible, thinking that by such measures I kept myself free.

When spring came, the horses were let out in the barnyard. Mack 23 stood against the barn wall trying to scratch his neck and haunches, but Flora trotted up and down and reared at the fences, clattering her hooves against the rails. Snow drifts dwindled quickly, revealing the hard grey and brown earth, the familiar rise and fall of the ground, plain and bare after the fantastic landscape of winter. There was a great feeling of opening-out, of release. We just wore rubbers now, over our shoes; our feet felt ridiculously light. One Saturday we went out to the stable and found all the doors open, letting in the unaccustomed sunlight and fresh air. Henry was there, just idling around looking at his collection of calendars which were tacked up behind the stalls in a part of the stable my mother had probably never seen.

"Come to say goodbye to your old friend Mack?" Henry said. 24 "Here, you give him a taste of oats." He poured some oats into Laird's cupped hands and Laird went to feed Mack. Mack's teeth were in bad shape. He ate very slowly, patiently shifting the oats around in his mouth, trying to find a stump of a molar to grind it on. "Poor old Mack," said Henry mournfully. "When a horse's teeth's gone, he's gone. That's about the way."

"Are you going to shoot him today?" I said. Mack and Flora had 25 been in the stable so long I had almost forgotten they were going to be shot.

Henry didn't answer me. Instead he started to sing in a high, 26 trembly, mocking-sorrowful voice, *Oh, there's no more work, for poor Uncle Ned, he's gone where the good darkies go.* Mack's thick, blackish tongue worked diligently at Laird's hand. I went out before the song was ended and sat down on the gangway.

I had never seen them shoot a horse, but I knew where it was 27 done. Last summer Laird and I had come upon a horse's entrails before they were buried. We had thought it was a big black snake, coiled up in the sun. That was around in the field that ran up beside the barn. I thought that if we went inside the barn, and found a wide crack or a knothole to look through, we would be able to see them do it. It was not something I wanted to see; just the same, if a thing really happened, it was better to see it, and know.

My father came down from the house, carrying the gun.   28

"What are you doing here?" he said.   29

"Nothing."   30

"Go on up and play around the house."   31

He sent Laird out of the stable. I said to Laird, "Do you want to 32 see them shoot Mack?" and without waiting for an answer led him around to the front door of the barn, opened it carefully, and went in. "Be quiet or they'll hear us," I said. We could hear Henry and my father talking in the stable, then the heavy, shuffling steps of Mack being backed out of his stall.

In the loft it was cold and dark. Thin, crisscrossed beams of sun- 33 light fell through the cracks. The hay was low. It was a rolling country, hills and hollows, slipping under our feet. About four feet up was a beam going around the walls. We piled hay up in one corner and I boosted Laird up and hoisted myself. The beam was not very wide; we crept along it with our hands flat on the barn walls. There were plenty of knotholes, and I found one that gave me the view I wanted— a corner of the barnyard, the gate, part of the field. Laird did not have a knothole and began to complain.

I showed him a widened crack between two boards. "Be quiet 34 and wait. If they hear you you'll get us in trouble."

My father came in sight carrying the gun. Henry was leading 35 Mack by the halter. He dropped it and took out his cigarette papers and tobacco; he rolled cigarettes for my father and himself. While this was going on Mack nosed around in the old, dead grass along the fence. Then my father opened the gate and they took Mack through. Henry led Mack away from the path to a patch of ground and they talked together, not loud enough for us to hear. Mack again began searching for a mouthful of fresh grass, which was not to be found. My father walked away in a straight line, and stopped short at a distance which seemed to suit him. Henry was walking away from Mack too, but sideways, still negligently holding on to the halter. My father raised the gun and Mack looked up as if he had noticed something and my father shot him.

Mack did not collapse at once but swayed, lurched sideways and 36 fell, first on his side; then he rolled over on his back, and amazingly, kicked his legs for a few seconds in the air. At this Henry laughed, as if Mack had done a trick for him. Laird, who had drawn a long, groaning breath of surprise when the shot was fired, said out loud, "He's not dead." And it seemed to me it might be true. But his legs stopped, he rolled on his side again, his muscles quivered and sank. The two men walked over and looked at him in a businesslike way; they bent down and examined his forehead where the bullet had gone in, and now I saw his blood on the brown grass.

"Now they just skin him and cut him up," I said. "Let's go." My 37 legs were a little shaky and I jumped gratefully down into the hay. "Now you've seen how they shoot a horse," I said in a congratulatory way, as if I had seen it many times before. "Let's see if any barn cat's had kittens in the hay." Laird jumped. He seemed young and obedient again. Suddenly I remembered how, when he was little, I had brought him into the barn and told him to climb the ladder to the top beam. That was in the spring, too, when the hay was low. I had done it out of a need for excitement, a desire for something to happen so that I could tell about it. He was wearing a little bulky brown and white checked coat, made down from one of mine. He went all the way up, just as I told him, and sat down on the top beam with the hay far below him on one side, and the barn floor and some old machinery on the other. Then I ran screaming to my father, "Laird's up on the top beam!" My father came, my mother came, my father went up the ladder talking very quietly and brought Laird down under his arm, at which my mother leaned against the ladder and began to cry. They said to me, "Why weren't you watching him?" but nobody ever knew the truth. Laird did not know enough to tell. But whenever I saw the brown and white checked coat hanging in the closet, or at the bottom of the rag bag, which was where it ended up, I felt a weight in my stomach, the sadness of unexorcized guilt.

I looked at Laird who did not even remember this, and I did not 38 like the look on his thin, winter-pale face. His expression was not frightened or upset, but remote, concentrating. "Listen," I said, in an unusually bright and friendly voice, "you aren't going to tell, are you?"

"No," he said absently. 39

"Promise." 40

"Promise," he said. I grabbed the hand behind his back to make 41 sure he was not crossing his fingers. Even so, he might have a nightmare; it might come out that way. I decided I had better work hard to get all thoughts of what he had seen out of his mind—which, it seemed to me, could not hold very many things at a time. I got some money I had saved and that afternoon we went into Jubilee and saw a show, with Judy Canova, at which we both laughed a great deal. After that I thought it would be all right.

Two weeks later I knew they were going to shoot Flora. I knew 42 from the night before, when I heard my mother ask if the hay was holding out all right, and my father said, "Well, after to-morrow there'll just be the cow, and we should be able to put her out to grass in another week." So I knew it was Flora's turn in the morning.

This time I didn't think of watching it. That was something to 43 see just one time. I had not thought about it very often since, but sometimes when I was busy, working at school, or standing in front of the mirror combing my hair and wondering if I would be pretty when I grew up, the whole scene would flash into my mind: I would see the easy, practised way my father raised the gun, and hear Henry laughing when Mack kicked his legs in the air. I did not have any great feeling of horror and opposition, such as a city child might have had; I was too used to seeing the death of animals as a necessity by which we lived. Yet I felt a little ashamed, and there was a new wariness, a sense of holding-off, in my attitude to my father and his work.

It was a fine day, and we were going around the yard picking up 44 tree branches that had been torn off in winter storms. This was something we had been told to do, and also we wanted to use them to make a teepee. We heard Flora whinny, and then my father's voice and Henry's shouting, and we ran down to the barnyard to see what was going on.

The stable door was open. Henry had just brought Flora out, and 45 she had broken away from him. She was running free in the barnyard, from one end to the other. We climbed up on the fence. It was exciting to see her running, whinnying, going up on her hind legs, prancing and threatening like a horse in a Western movie, an unbroken ranch horse, though she was just an old driver, an old sorrel mare. My father and Henry ran after her and tried to grab the dangling halter. They tried to work her into a corner, and they had almost succeeded when she made a run between them, wild-eyed, and disappeared around the corner of the barn. We heard the rails clatter down as she got over the fence, and Henry yelled, "She's into the field now!"

That meant she was in the long L-shaped field that ran up by the 46 house. If she got around the center, heading towards the lane, the gate was open; the truck had been driven into the field this morning. My father shouted to me, because I was on the other side of the fence, nearest the lane, "Go shut the gate!"

I could run very fast. I ran across the garden, past the tree where 47 our swing was hung, and jumped across a ditch into the lane. There was the open gate. She had not got out, I could not see her up on the road; she must have run to the other end of the field. The gate was heavy. I lifted it out of the gravel and carried it across the roadway. I had it half-way across when she came in sight, galloping straight towards me. There was just time to get the chain on. Laird came scrambling through the ditch to help me.

Instead of shutting the gate, I opened it as wide as I could. I did 48 not make any decision to do this, it was just what I did. Flora never slowed down; she galloped straight past me, and Laird jumped up and down, yelling, "Shut it, shut it!" even after it was too late. My father and Henry appeared in the field a moment too late to see what I had done. They only saw Flora heading for the township road. They would think I had not got there in time.

They did not waste any time asking about it. They went back 49 to the barn and got the gun and the knives they used, and put these in the truck; then they turned the truck around and came bouncing up the field toward us. Laird called to them, "Let me go too, let me go too!" and Henry stopped the truck and they took him in. I shut the gate after they were all gone.

I supposed Laird would tell. I wondered what would happen to 50 me. I had never disobeyed my father before, and I could not understand why I had done it. Flora would not really get away. They would catch up with her in the truck. Or if they did not catch her this morning somebody would see her and telephone us this afternoon or tomorrow. There was no wild country here for her to run to, only farms. What was more, my father had paid for her, we needed the meat to feed the foxes, we needed the foxes to make our living. All I had done was make more work for my father who worked hard enough already. And when my father found out about it he was not going to trust me any more; he would know that I was not entirely on his side. I was on Flora's side, and that made me no use to anybody, not even to her. Just the same, I did not regret it; when she came running at me and I held the gate open, that was the only thing I could do.

I went back to the house, and my mother said, "What's all the 51 commotion?" I told her that Flora had kicked down the fence and got away. "Your poor father," she said, "now he'll have to go chasing over the countryside. Well, there isn't any use planning dinner before one." She put up the ironing board. I wanted to tell her, but thought better of it and went upstairs and sat on my bed.

Lately I had been trying to make my part of the room fancy, 52 spreading the bed with old lace curtains, and fixing myself a dressing-table with some leftovers of cretonne for a skirt. I planned to put up some kind of barricade between my bed and Laird's, to keep my section separate from his. In the sunlight, the lace curtains were just dusty rags. We did not sing at night any more. One night when I was singing Laird said, "You sound silly," and I went right on but the next night I did not start. There was not so much need to anyway, we were no longer afraid. We knew it was just old furniture over there, old jumble and confusion. We did not keep to the rules. I still stayed awake after Laird was asleep and told myself stories, but even in these stories something different was happening, mysterious alterations took place. A story might start off in the old way, with a spectacular danger, a fire or wild animals, and for a while I might rescue people; then things would change around, and instead, somebody would be rescuing me. It might be a boy from our class at school, or even Mr. Campbell, our teacher, who tickled girls under the arms. And at this point the story concerned itself at great length with what I looked like—how long my hair was, and what kind of dress I had on; by the time I had these details worked out the real excitement of the story was lost.

It was later than one o'clock when the truck came back. The 53 tarpaulin was over the back, which meant there was meat in it. My mother had to heat dinner up all over again. Henry and my father had changed from their bloody overalls into ordinary working overalls in the barn, and they washed their arms and necks and faces at the sink, and splashed water on their hair and combed it. Laird lifted his arm to show off a streak of blood. "We shot old Flora," he said, "and

COLLABORATIVE ACTIVITY

Assign different groups of students to identify passages in the story that deal with one of the following: the narrator's attitude toward animals, her attitude toward her mother, her attitude toward herself, and her attitude toward her gender. Ask each group to trace changes in a particular attitude throughout the story.

WRITING SUGGESTIONS

1. Write a narrative describing personal experiences that led to your identification as "girl" or "boy."
2. What does it mean to be "only a girl" or "only a boy"? Write an essay in which you give examples that explain these concepts.

ANSWERS TO RESPONDING TO READING

1. The narrator realizes that she will have to adopt certain attitudes and behavior to meet the culture's expectations of what it means to be a girl. Personal responses will vary.
2. The narrator tells herself stories in which she is the rescuer. She later "rescues" Flora, but it is a futile act: the horse will be shot anyway, and her action earns not cheers but her father's disapproval. In her later stories, the narrator is the one rescued. In moving from rescuer to rescued, hero to victim, she adopts the culturally feminine role.
3. Answers will vary. The narrator may be suggesting that girls' experience involves more intense confusion over identity, but both the narrator and her brother, like their parents, are locked into very limited roles. In this sense, neither can expect to have an easy life.

cut her up in fifty pieces."

"Well I don't want to hear about it," my mother said. "And don't 54 come to my table like that."

My father made him go and wash the blood off. 55

We sat down and my father said grace and Henry pasted his 56 chewing-gum on the end of his fork, the way he always did; when he took it off he would have us admire the pattern. We began to pass the bowls of steaming, overcooked vegetables. Laird looked across the table at me and said proudly, distinctly, "Anyway it was her fault Flora got away."

"What?" my father said. 57

"She could of shut the gate and she didn't. She just open' it up 58 and Flora run out."

"Is that right?" my father said. 59

Everybody at the table was looking at me. I nodded, swallowing 60 food with great difficulty. To my shame, tears flooded my eyes.

My father made a curt sound of disgust. "What did you do that 61 for?"

I did not answer. I put down my fork and waited to be sent from 62 the table, still not looking up.

But this did not happen. For some time nobody said anything, 63 then Laird said matter-of-factly, "She's crying."

"Never mind," my father said. He spoke with resignation, even 64 good humor, the words which absolved and dismissed me for good. "She's only a girl," he said.

I didn't protest that, even in my heart. Maybe it was true. 65

RESPONDING TO READING

1. What does the narrator mean when she says, "A girl was not, as I had supposed, simply what I was; it was what I had to become" (paragraph 21)? Have you ever had a similar realization? If so, what prompted it?   **2.** Early in the story, the narrator makes up stories about herself in a world "that presented opportunities for courage, boldness and self-sacrifice" (paragraph 6), and she portrays herself as a rescuer. Why do you think she has these rescue fantasies? When she opens the gate to allow Flora to escape, is she successfully acting out her fantasies? What do you think actually motivates her?   **3.** Who in this story will have an easier life, the narrator or her brother? Why? Who do you believe has an easier life in the United States today, men or women? Why?

The Secretary Chant

MARGE PIERCY

Poet and novelist Marge Piercy (1934–   ) was born and educated in Michigan. Since 1969, she has been active in the women's movement, which, Piercy says, "has been a great energy source (as well as energy sink!) and healer of the psyche for me." Piercy has written several novels, including *Woman on the Edge of Time* (1976) and *Gone to Soldiers* (1988). Her poetry is collected in *Living in the Open* (1981), *The Moon Is Always Female* (1981), and *Circles on the Water* (1988). Piercy wants her poems to be useful; she hopes, as she explains in *Circles on the Water*, "that readers will find poems that speak to and for them." "The Secretary Chant" is from this collection.

My hips are a desk.
From my ears hang
chains of paper clips.
Rubber bands form my hair.
My breasts are wells of mimeograph ink.   5
My feet bear casters.
Buzz. Click.
My head is a badly organized file.
My head is a switchboard
where crossed lines crackle.   10
Press my fingers
and in my eyes appear
credit and debit.
Zing. Tinkle.
My navel is a reject button.   15
From my mouth issue canceled reams.
Swollen, heavy, rectangular
I am about to be delivered
of a baby
Xerox machine.   20
File me under W
because I wonce
was
a woman.

BACKGROUND ON AUTHOR

Piercy first became politically active in the 1960s as a civil rights activist and organizer for Students for a Democratic Society (SDS). She shifted her attention to the women's movement in 1969, having become discouraged by what she saw as the male power structure and the subservient roles for women in the antiwar movement. Although politics have always been important to her, however, she insists that "it is as absurd to reduce poems to political statements as it is to deny they have a political dimension" (quoted in *Contemporary Authors*, New Revision Series, vol. 13, p. 409).

FOR OPENERS

Discuss students' associations with the word *secretary*. What images comes to mind? Do we inevitably think of secretaries as female? If students have seen the 1980 film *9 to 5,* in which female employees take revenge on their odious male boss, you might discuss its treatment of secretaries.

ADDITIONAL QUESTIONS FOR RESPONDING TO READING

1. Why does Piercy repeat the *w* in the last four lines?
2. What effect does Piercy's use of onomatopoeia produce in lines 7 and 14?
3. What is the significance of giving birth to a Xerox machine? Why would Piercy choose this object?
4. Has the recent increase in secretaries' wages changed their status? Does it change your reaction to the poem? To secretaries?

TEACHING STRATEGY

Discuss the ugly and dehumanizing images in the poem, and speculate on the significance of each choice. Notice that no strong "I" appears in the poem. The two times the pronoun is used, it is weak: "I am about to be delivered . . ." (not "I am giving birth . . ."); "I wonce was a woman" (but not any more).

WRITING SUGGESTIONS

1. Write an essay about ways in which employment can limit and dehumanize the worker. Use personal experience, if possible.
2. Write a letter of resignation from the poem's speaker to her boss.

ANSWERS TO RESPONDING TO READING

1. The objects mentioned are accurate in that they are familiar in a secretary's world, but the merging of woman with object creates a strange and unsettling hyperbolic effect.
2. Many of the references in the poem are specifically female (breasts, birth), but workers who are underpaid and powerless, defined solely by their functions, may well identify with the theme.
3. The speaker's tone seems angry, but also a little resigned. She may be speaking to her boss or to the world in general. Opinions will vary.

RESPONDING TO READING

1. Is this poem strictly *hyperbole*—intentional exaggeration for effect—or is it in any way an accurate characterization? Do the grotesque figures of speech shock or alienate you? Why or why not?   **2.** To what extent, if any, does Piercy's dehumanizing characterization of the secretary apply to workers—male as well as female—in other subordinate positions?   **3.** How would you characterize the speaker's attitude toward her audience? For instance, is she angry? Frightened? Defiant? Who is this audience? Does the fact that there is a shortage of qualified secretaries and that some can earn very high salaries affect your response to the poem?

WRITING: ATTITUDES ABOUT GENDER

1.   Virginia Woolf observes that "any woman born with a great gift in the sixteenth century would certainly have gone crazed, shot herself, or ended her days in some lonely cottage outside the village, half witch, half wizard, feared and mocked at" (paragraph 9). Write an essay in which you discuss how this statement applies to gifted women of your own generation and of your parents' generation. You may consider the essays by Ascher, Brady, and Steinem and the story "Boys and Girls" as you plan your response.

2.   List all the stereotypes of women—and of men—identified in the selections you read in this chapter. Then, write an essay in which you identify those that have had the most negative effects on your life and explain why. Do you consider these stereotypes to be annoying or even dangerous?

3.   Stephen Jay Gould says, "I do not regard as empty rhetoric the claim that women's battles are for all of us" (paragraph 13). Do you agree with Gould? Use examples from your own experience to support your points.

4.   Write an essay in which you identify the burdens society places on men—or on women—through its expectations, based solely on gender, that they will behave in a certain fashion. Referring to the selections in this chapter as well as to your own experience, explain how such expectations limit members of both sexes.

5.   In her discussion of pornography in paragraph 7 Margaret Atwood asks, "Is it a sign of collective impotence, of a generation of men who can't relate to real women at all but have to make do with bits of celluloid and paper?" Drawing from the chapter's reading selections or your own life, write an essay in which you consider possible reasons for the popularity of the kind of violent, sadistic pornography Atwood describes.

6.   Compare and contrast Alice Walker's description of what it meant "for a black woman to be an artist in our grandmothers' time" (paragraph 10) to Virginia Woolf's discussion of Shakespeare's imaginary sister and her contemporaries. (Note that Walker comments on Woolf's work in paragraphs 16–18 and 36.) Or, compare and contrast Walker's description with your own grandmothers'—or mother's—experiences.

7.   Several of the selections in this chapter draw distinctions, implicitly or explicitly, between "men's work" and "women's work." Write an essay in which you consider the extent to which such distinctions exist today and how they have affected your professional goals.

8.   Assuming there really is a language of men—and a language of women—define these languages. In your essay, consider whether these languages consist only of words, or of gestures, facial expressions, postures, and even behavior patterns as well. You may also consider whether such languages are necessary and what function, if any, they serve.

9.   Write an essay in which you define the role parents play in promoting—or challenging—gender stereotypes. In your discussion, focus on your own parents' roles in shaping your gender identity. (If you like, you may also refer to "The Men We Carry in Our Minds," "In Search of Our Mothers' Gardens," or "Boys and Girls.")

10. Commenting on her story "Boys and Girls," Alice Munro said, "What it says is something like this: it is permissible to have fine feelings, impractical sympathies, if you are a girl, because what you say or do does not finally count. On the other hand, if you are a boy, certain feelings are not permissible at all. So taking on these roles, whichever you get, is a hard and damaging thing." Write an essay in which you examine how Munro's statement applies to your own life as a child and as an adult.

6

STRANGERS IN THE VILLAGE

CONFRONTING THE ISSUES

An individual may be isolated from a society by race, class, language, gender, nationality, age, personality, or some other specific factor. In many cases, the isolated individual is also someone who does not share the social norms—the ideas about accepted standards of conduct—of a social group or culture. William Graham Sumner (1840–1910), one of the founders of sociology in the United States, divided these norms into *folkways* and *mores*.

Folkways are accepted standards of behavior passed down from one generation to another. They include familiar, routine (and sometimes trivial) customs such as shaking hands as a greeting or making a comment when someone sneezes. Folkways vary, sometimes quite significantly, from culture to culture.

Mores are shared moral and ethical attitudes that establish the behavior necessary for maintaining the social order. Examples of mores include coming to the aid of an accident victim, being honest in business dealings, and accepting the authority of the law.

Twentieth-century sociologist Robert Merton, building on Sumner's ideas, divided norms into *positive norms*—things we *should* do, such as report a crime, and things we *must* do, such as support our minor children—and *negative norms*—things we *should not* do, such as cheat on an exam, or *must not* do, such as commit murder.

In "Stranger in the Village" James Baldwin confronts his separateness from the predominantly white culture he inhabits, acknowledging that the Europeans he lives among see him "quite rightly, not only as a stranger in their village but as a suspect latecomer, bearing no credentials, to everything they have—however unconsciously—inherited." They approach him, he says, not as a human being but as "an exotic rarity." The village in which Baldwin feels so alone and so conspicuous extends far beyond the geographical boundaries of a small town in Switzerland. For his readers as well as for himself, this village may be a past, a heritage, a culture, a country, a society, a town, a family, or even a state of mind. The stranger in this village can be anyone who feels excluded.

Occasionally such isolation is voluntary: An individual may reject a particular environment for a short time or leave it behind forever. Some of the narrators, fictional characters, and poetic voices we hear in this chapter are estranged from their world because of their lifestyles, ideas, or behavior. Many more are outsiders because people or social forces keep them outside; they are isolated by misunderstanding, by prejudice, and by their own powerlessness.

The selections in this chapter are connected by their common focus on what it means to be an outsider, but the reasons for this alienation differ. Joan Didion and George Orwell are observers of another country, and this observer status accounts in part for their sense of alienation. Martin Luther King, Jr., is an outsider within his own society's dominant culture, rejected by many of his fellow citizens. Philip Roth, like the child in Liliana Heker's "The Stolen Party," is an outsider because of cultural and class differences that make him feel alienated from those around him.

The perspective from which each story is told also varies: Jamaica Kincaid sees the tourists who visit her country as outsiders; Willa Cather writes of the emotional estrangement of an adolescent boy; Roth and King write poignantly and powerfully of their own alienation. Outsiders also have different attitudes toward their exclusion: Some despair in their isolation, some define it as irrelevant, and others relish their separateness. Even so, the fundamental questions raised in each selection remain the same: How does being a stranger in the village affect the stranger—and how does it affect the village?

PREPARING TO READ AND WRITE

As you read and prepare to write about the selections in this chapter, consider the following questions:

- From whom or what is the outsider estranged? Home and family? The past? Mainstream society? Something else?

- What specific factors account for the outsider's isolation? For example, do emotional, social, economic, religious, cultural, class, behavioral, aesthetic, or generational differences set him or her apart from others in the society?

- How does the outsider react to his or her isolation? For example, is the outsider sad? Angry? Bitter? Confused? Resigned?

- Does the outsider's behavior change in response to his or her estrangement?

- Does the outsider seem to understand the forces that alienate him or her? How can you tell?

- Does the outsider want to change his or her status? What steps, if any, could the outsider take to win acceptance?

- What is the outsider's attitude toward the group of which he or she is not (or cannot be) a part?

- What (or whom), if anything, does the outsider blame for his or her status?

- Where does the outsider feel most comfortable? In what situations does the outsider feel most alone? Most conspicuous? Most threatened?

- Is the outsider presented as an individual or as a representative— for example, of a race, a culture, or a nation?

Laws are norms that have been formally adopted as the rules that will govern a society's behavior. (Many negative norms are forbidden by law.)

A society's norms stem from its *values*, shared beliefs about what the society considers to be important. For example, individualism, democracy, the work ethic, achievement and success, and equality are some of the values that characterize American society.

After introducing students to these concepts, explain that shared value systems increase the cohesiveness of a "village" and make it impervious to "strangers." The outsiders in this chapter may therefore be seen as isolated because they do not share the social norms of the dominant culture. Ask your students to analyze reading selections in this chapter with the concept of social norms in mind. Are the outsiders' norms different from those of the larger society? If so, why? How can we tell? How do these differences help to explain—and promote—their isolation?

BACKGROUND ON READING

Students will need background about the early years of the civil rights movement (and King's role in it) as well as about the August 28, 1963, march on Washington at which he gave this speech. If possible, show a videotape of King delivering the speech, or play a recording.

FOR OPENERS

King's style is sermonic; he embellishes his writings and orations with extended figures of speech and uses repetition, balance, and parallelism to create stylistic interest. Ask students to identify one example of each stylistic device, and remind them to look for others as they review the selection.

ADDITIONAL QUESTIONS FOR RESPONDING TO READING

1. How much do you know about specific events that occurred within the civil rights movement?
2. Why might it be important for us to recall the early years of our nation's civil rights movement?

I Have a Dream

MARTIN LUTHER KING, JR.

One of the greatest civil rights leaders and orators of this century, Martin Luther King, Jr. (1929–1968), was also a Baptist minister and winner of the 1964 Nobel Peace Prize. He was born in Atlanta, Georgia, and earned degrees from four institutions. Influenced by Thoreau and Gandhi, King altered the spirit of African-American protest in the United States by advocating nonviolent civil disobedience to achieve racial equality. King's books include *Letter From Birmingham Jail* (1963) and *Where Do We Go from Here: Chaos or Community?* (1967). King was assassinated on April 4, 1968. He delivered the following speech from the steps of the Lincoln Memorial during the March on Washington on August 28, 1963.

1 I am happy to join with you today in what will go down in history as the greatest demonstration for freedom in the history of our nation.

2 Fivescore years ago, a great American, in whose symbolic shadow we stand today, signed the Emancipation Proclamation. This momentous decree came as a great beacon light of hope to millions of Negro slaves who had been seared in the flames of withering injustice. It came as a joyous daybreak to end the long night of their captivity.

3 But one hundred years later, the Negro still is not free; one hundred years later, the life of the Negro is still sadly crippled by the manacles of segregation and the chains of discrimination; one hundred years later, the Negro lives on a lonely island of poverty in the midst of a vast ocean of material prosperity; one hundred years later, the Negro is still languishing in the corners of American society and finds himself in exile in his own land.

4 So we've come here today to dramatize a shameful condition. In a sense we've come to our nation's capital to cash a check. When the architects of our republic wrote the magnificent words of the Constitution and the Declaration of Independence, they were signing a promissory note to which every American was to fall heir. This note was the promise that all men, yes, black men as well as white men, would be guaranteed the unalienable rights of life, liberty, and the pursuit of happiness.

5 It is obvious today that America has defaulted on this promissory note in so far as her citizens of color are concerned. Instead of honoring this sacred obligation, America has given the Negro people a bad check; a check which has come back marked "insufficient funds." We refuse to believe that there are insufficient funds in the great vaults of opportunity of this nation. And so we've come to cash this check, a check that will give us upon demand the riches of freedom and the security of justice.

We have also come to this hallowed spot to remind America of the fierce urgency of now. This is no time to engage in the luxury of cooling off or to take the tranquilizing drug of gradualism. Now is the time to make real the promises of democracy; now is the time to rise from the dark and desolate valley of segregation to the sunlit path of racial justice; now is the time to lift our nation from the quicksands of racial injustice to the solid rock of brotherhood; now is the time to make justice a reality for all God's children. It would be fatal for the nation to overlook the urgency of the moment. This sweltering summer of the Negro's legitimate discontent will not pass until there is an invigorating autumn of freedom and equality.

Nineteen sixty-three is not an end, but a beginning. And those who hope that the Negro needed to blow off steam and will now be content, will have a rude awakening if the nation returns to business as usual.

There will be neither rest nor tranquility in America until the Negro is granted his citizenship rights. The whirlwinds of revolt will continue to shake the foundations of our nation until the bright day of justice emerges.

But there is something that I must say to my people who stand on the warm threshold which leads into the palace of justice. In the process of gaining our rightful place we must not be guilty of wrongful deeds.

Let us not seek to satisfy our thirst for freedom by drinking from the cup of bitterness and hatred. We must forever conduct our struggle on the high plane of dignity and discipline. We must not allow our creative protest to degenerate into physical violence. Again and again we must rise to the majestic heights of meeting physical force with soul force.

The marvelous new militancy which has engulfed the Negro community must not lead us to a distrust of all white people, for many of our white brothers, as evidenced by their presence here today, have come to realize that their destiny is tied up with our destiny and they have come to realize that their freedom is inextricably bound to our freedom. This offense we share mounted to storm the battlements of injustice must be carried forth by a biracial army. We cannot walk alone.

And as we walk, we must make the pledge that we shall always march ahead. We cannot turn back. There are those who are asking the devotees of civil rights, "When will you be satisfied?" We can never be satisfied as long as the Negro is the victim of the unspeakable horrors of police brutality.

We can never be satisfied as long as our bodies, heavy with fatigue of travel, cannot gain lodging in the motels of the highways and the

6

7

8

9

10

11

12

13

TEACHING STRATEGY

Discuss the following with your students:
Paragraph 2: What familiar speech do the opening words of this paragraph echo? Why did King use these words? Note also the allusion to the Emancipation Proclamation.
Paragraph 3: Note the repetition of words and patterns. Note also that the paragraph is all one sentence. You might take this opportunity to explain the difference between a sentence that is simply long and one that is a run-on (and to explain the use of the semicolon).
Paragraphs 4 & 5: What metaphor does King employ here? Why is it appropriate and effective?
Paragraphs 7 & 8: Might hostile listeners interpret the tone of this portion of the speech as threatening? How does King go on to address the possibility of such an interpretation?
Paragraphs 10 & 11: Of what importance are the warnings King addresses to his African-American followers? What is his purpose?
Paragraph 14: Why does King distinguish between the treatment of African-Americans in the North and their treatment in the South? What, if any, are the differences?
Paragraph 35: Here King employs a rhetorical technique called "distribution," a dividing of a whole into its parts. What purpose does this strategy serve here?

hotels of the cities. We cannot be satisfied as long as the Negro's basic mobility is from a smaller ghetto to a larger one.

14   We can never be satisfied as long as our children are stripped of their selfhood and robbed of their dignity by signs stating "for whites only." We cannot be satisfied as long as a Negro in Mississippi cannot vote and a Negro in New York believes he has nothing for which to vote. No, we are not satisfied, and we will not be satisfied until justice rolls down like waters and righteousness like a mighty stream.

15   I am not unmindful that some of you have come here out of excessive trials and tribulation. Some of you have come fresh from narrow jail cells. Some of you have come from areas where your quest for freedom left you battered by the storms of persecution and staggered by the winds of police brutality. You have been the veterans of creative suffering. Continue to work with the faith that unearned suffering is redemptive.

16   Go back to Mississippi; go back to Alabama; go back to South Carolina; go back to Georgia; go back to Louisiana; go back to the slums and ghettos of the northern cities, knowing that somehow this situation can, and will be changed. Let us not wallow in the valley of despair.

17   So I say to you, my friends, that even though we must face the difficulties of today and tomorrow, I still have a dream. It is a dream deeply rooted in the American dream that one day this nation will rise up and live out the true meaning of its creed—we hold these truths to be self-evident, that all men are created equal.

18   I have a dream that one day on the red hills of Georgia, sons of former slaves and sons of former slave-owners will be able to sit down together at the table of brotherhood.

19   I have a dream that one day, even the state of Mississippi, a state sweltering with the heat of injustice, sweltering with the heat of oppression, will be transformed into an oasis of freedom and justice.

20   I have a dream my four little children will one day live in a nation where they will not be judged by the color of their skin but by content of their character. I have a dream today!

21   I have a dream that one day, down in Alabama, with its vicious racists, with its governor having his lips dripping with the words of interposition and nullification, that one day, right there in Alabama, little black boys and black girls will be able to join hands with little white boys and white girls as sisters and brothers. I have a dream today!

22   I have a dream that one day every valley shall be exalted, every hill and mountain shall be made low, the rough places shall be made plain, and the crooked places shall be made straight and the glory of the Lord will be revealed and all flesh shall see it together.

This is our hope. This is the faith that I go back to the South with. 23

With this faith we will be able to hew out of the mountain of 24 despair a stone of hope. With this faith we will be able to transform the jangling discords of our nation into a beautiful symphony of brotherhood.

With this faith we will be able to work together, to pray together, 25 to struggle together, to go to jail together, to stand up for freedom together, knowing that we will be free one day. This will be the day when all of God's children will be able to sing with new meaning— "my country 'tis of thee; sweet land of liberty; of thee I sing; land where my fathers died, land of the pilgrim's pride; from every mountain side, let freedom ring"—and if America is to be a great nation, this must become true.

So let freedom ring from the prodigious hilltops of New Hamp- 26 shire.

Let freedom ring from the mighty mountains of New York. 27

Let freedom ring from the heightening Alleghenies of Pennsyl- 28 vania.

Let freedom ring from the snow-capped Rockies of Colorado. 29

Let freedom ring from the curvaceous slopes of California. 30

But not only that. 31

Let freedom ring from Stone Mountain of Georgia. 32

Let freedom ring from Lookout Mountain of Tennessee. 33

Let freedom ring from every hill and molehill of Mississippi, from 34 every mountainside, let freedom ring.

And when we allow freedom to ring, when we let it ring from 35 every village and hamlet, from every state and city, we will be able to speed up that day when all of God's children—black men and white men, Jews and Gentiles, Catholics and Protestants—will be able to join hands and to sing in the words of the old Negro spiritual, "Free at last, free at last; thank God Almighty, we are free at last."

RESPONDING TO READING

1. Speaking as a representative of his black fellow citizens, King tells his audience that African-Americans find themselves "in exile in [their] own land" (paragraph 3). Do you believe this is true for members of minority groups today? Why or why not?   **2.** What specific privileges does King believe African-Americans are denied? What other, more subtle barriers does he imply also exist? Do such barriers still exist today, nearly thirty years later? Or has King's dream come true, at least in part?   **3.** What do you think King means when he says, "It would be fatal for the nation to overlook the urgency of the moment" (paragraph 6)? Does your knowledge of the racial climate in the United States today lead you to agree or disagree with King's statement?

WRITING SUGGESTION

What dream do you have for yourself, your family, your ethnic group, your community, or your country? Write a speech that expresses your hopes, if possible addressing your comments to a group that you believe holds you back.

ANSWERS TO RESPONDING TO READING

1. Answers will vary. You might also ask students whether this statement applies to all minority groups and to discuss *why* these minorities are exiled.
2. Segregation and discrimination were rampant at the time of this speech. In the South (before the 1964 Voting Rights Act) many African-Americans were still prevented from voting, and throughout the country there was racially motivated police brutality. As a result, African-Americans could not even begin to achieve upward economic mobility. Despite the very real gains that African-Americans have made, King's dream has not been fully realized.
3. He is calling for immediate attention to the discontent of those angered by the injustice and prepared to act upon their anger.

Being Prohibited

DORIS LESSING

British novelist Doris Lessing (1919–   ) was born in Persia (now Iran) to expatriate English parents. The family soon moved to Rhodesia (now Zimbabwe) and Lessing's early stories were clearly influenced by the racial injustice she was exposed to in Africa. She left for England in 1949 and became a political activist, and in 1962 she published *The Golden Notebook*, a novel about changing political and sexual attitudes. She is also known for the novels *The Grass Is Singing* (1950), *The Habit of Loving* (1957), the five-volume series *Children of Violence* (1952–1969), the science fiction series *Canopus in Argos: Archives* (1979–1982), and *The Good Terrorist* (1985). The following essay, about an outsider's view of apartheid, is from Lessing's 1976 collection, *A Small Personal Voice*.

BACKGROUND ON WRITER

Lessing attended a convent school in her early years, and in her teens she rebelled against her parents' concept of a "proper" British education and quit school. For a time in her later life, she worked as an organizer for the British Communist party.

FOR OPENERS

Ask students what they know about apartheid. (You may, if you like, refer them to Joseph Lelyveld's "The Laws," page 662, for background.) Why would a government treat a race in this manner? Can we explain the source as simple prejudice? As fear? Although some positive changes are occurring presently in South Africa, for many years the American government has chosen to ignore the human rights violations committed there against the black majority. (You might find it appropriate here to discuss U.S. policy toward South Africa.)

ADDITIONAL QUESTIONS FOR RESPONDING TO READING

What experiences with racial prejudice can your recall? How did these affect your view of the society in which you live?

The border is Mafeking, a little dorp[1] with nothing interesting about it but its name. The train waits (or used to wait) interminably on the empty tracks, while immigration and customs officials made their leisurely way through the coaches, and pale gritty dust settled over everything. Looking out, one saw the long stretch of windows, with the two, three, or four white faces at each; then at the extreme end, the single coach for "natives" packed tight with black humans; and, in between, two or three Indians or Colored people on sufferance in the European coaches.

Outside, on the scintillating dust by the tracks, a crowd of ragged black children begged for *bonsellas*. One threw sandwich crusts or bits of spoiled fruit and watched them dive and fight to retrieve them from the dirt.

I was sixteen. I was not, as one says, politically conscious; nor did I know the score. I knew no more, in fact, than on which side my bread was buttered. But I already felt uneasy about being a member of the Herrenvolk.[2] When the immigration official reached me, I had written on the form; *Nationality*, British, *Race*, European; and it was the first time in my life I had had to claim myself as a member of one race and disown the others. I remember distinctly that I had to suppress an impulse opposite *Race*: Human. Of course I *was* very young.

The immigration man had the sarcastic surliness which characterises the Afrikaans[3] official, and he looked suspiciously at my form for a long time before saying that I was in the wrong part of the train.

---

[1] Village. [Eds.]
[2] Master race. [Eds.]
[3] Descendents of the Dutch settlers of South Africa. [Eds.]

I did not understand him. (I forgot to mention that where the form asked, Where were you born?, I had written, Persia.)

"Asiatics," said he, "have to go to the back of the train; and anyway you are prohibited from entry unless you have documents proving you conform to the immigration quota for Asians." 5

"But," I said, "I am not an Asiatic." 6

The compartment had five other females in it; skirts were visibly being drawn aside. To prove my bona fides I should, of course, have exclaimed with outraged indignation at any such idea. 7

"You were born in Persia?" 8

"Yes." 9

"Then you are an Asiatic. You know the penalties for filling in the form wrongly?" 10

This particular little imbroglio involved my being taken off the train, escorted to an office, and kept under watch while they telephoned Pretoria for a ruling. 11

When next I entered the Union[4] it was 1939. Sophistication had set in in the interval, and it took me no more than five minutes to persuade the official that one could be born in a country without being its citizen. The next two times there was no trouble at all, although my political views had in the meantime become nothing less than inflammatory: in a word, I had learned to disapprove of the colour bar. 12

This time, two weeks ago, what happened was as follows: one gets off the plane and sits for about fifteen minutes in a waiting room while they check the plane list with a list, or lists, of their own. They called my name first, and took me to an office which had two tables in it. At one sat a young man being pleasant to the genuine South African citizens. At the one where they made me sit was a man I could have sworn I had seen before. He proceeded to go through my form item by item, as follows: "You *say*, Mrs. Lessing, that, etc. . . ." From time to time he let out a disbelieving laugh and exchanged ironical looks with a fellow official who was standing by. Sure enough, when he reached that point on my form when he had to say: "You *claim* that you are British; you *say* you were born in Persia," I merely said "*Yes*," and sat still while he gave me a long, exasperated stare. Then he let out an angry exclamation in Afrikaans and went next door to telephone Pretoria.[5] Ten minutes later I was informed I must leave at once. A plane was waiting and I must enter it immediately. 13

TEACHING STRATEGY

Discuss the following with your students:

Paragraphs 1 & 2: What does the description of the town and people accomplish?

Paragraph 3: Why is information about the writer important here? For what does it prepare the reader? Specifically, what does the last sentence mean?

Paragraph 11: Instead of *imbroglio*, why didn't Lessing use a word like *confusion* or *misunderstanding*?" Why doesn't Lessing reveal the outcome of this dispute?

Paragraph 13: Explain the questioner's manner. Why the emphasis on *claim* and *say*?

Paragraph 16: Explain Lessing's uneasiness at the incident's conclusion. Why should the reason for "these attentions" matter to her?

COLLABORATIVE ACTIVITY

Assign groups to do out-of-class research on South Africa's policies toward blacks. Possible topics might include the history of specific laws regarding housing, employment, marriage, voting, identification, and education.

WRITING SUGGESTION

In protest against South Africa's apartheid laws, many individuals and groups outside South Africa have taken economic, social, and political action. For example, entertainers have refused to perform there, investors have refused to buy stocks in South African companies (or those that do business with South Africa), and consumers have refused to buy products manufactured by companies with ties to South Africa. Do you believe such actions are fair? Effective? Write a position paper in which you explain your views.

---

[4]The Union (later Republic) of South Africa. [Eds.]
[5]Administrative capital of the Republic of South Africa. [Eds.]

I did so with dignity. Since then I have been unable to make up 14 my mind whether I should have made a scene or not. I never have believed in the efficacy of dignity.

On the plane I wanted to sit near the window but was made to 15 sit by myself and away from the window. I regretted infinitely that I had no accomplices hidden in the long grass by the airstrip, but, alas, I had not thought of it beforehand.

It was some time before it came home to me what an honor had 16 been paid me. But now I am uneasy about the whole thing: suppose that I owe these attentions, not to my political views, but to the accident of my birthplace?

RESPONDING TO READING

1. Lessing characterizes herself as an outsider in the land in which she grew up. What sets her apart from the immigration officials she encounters? From what other groups is she different? What does she mean when she says she had been paid an "honor" (paragraph 16)? **2.** Lessing specifies her nationality as British and her race as European. How would you describe your own national, racial, religious, and ethnic identity? Do other members of your family describe themselves in the same way? **3.** How do the many labels that identify groups by race and nationality—*natives, Indians, Coloured people, British, Asiatic, European*—establish Lessing's awareness of her outsider status? How does she feel the label *Herrenvolk* (paragraph 3) sets her apart? Do you think such labels inevitably set people apart from other groups? Do they serve any positive purpose?

**ANSWERS TO RESPONDING
TO READING**

1. She was born in Persia, a fact that immediately creates suspicion of her true nationality; the officials assume her to be Asian, not British. She is, in fact, British, not a member of the races oppressed by Afrikaaners. She "belongs" to neither group. Her use of the word *honour* is ironic.
2. Answers will vary.
3. Note Lessing's ironic reference to her age and attitude, which implies that the young have no need for such distinctions; only adults feel compelled to dehumanize one another. Her discomfort reflects an unwillingness to enjoy privileges at the expense of others.

FOR OPENERS

Ask students to reminisce about their childhood. Can they recall any prejudices held against them by their peers on the basis of race, class, or religion? Do they remember having any prejudice against members of their peer group? Where was such prejudice learned?

Safe at Home

PHILIP ROTH

One of the dominant voices in modern American literature, Philip Roth (1933–   ) is a novelist and short story writer who grew up during World War II in a neighborhood of Jewish immigrants who inspired many of Roth's plots and characters. Roth once said that his fiction "is about people in trouble." He is known for sarcasm, wit, black humor, colloquial American speech, and stinging political satire. A film was made of the title story in his collection *Goodbye, Columbus and Five Short Stories* (1959). Some of his other works include *Portnoy's Complaint* (1969), *Our Gang,* (1971), *The Great American Novel* (1973), *My Life as a Man* (1974), *The Ghost Writer* (1979), *The Counterlife* (1986), and *Patrimony* (1990). "Safe at Home," a reminiscence of Roth's childhood, is from *The Facts: A Novelist's Autobiography* (1988).

The greatest menace while I was growing up came from abroad, from the Germans and the Japanese, our enemies because we were American. I still remember my terror as a nine-year-old when, running in from playing on the street after school, I saw the banner headline CORREGIDOR FALLS on the evening paper in our doorway and understood that the United States actually could lose the war it had entered only months before. At home the biggest threat came from the Americans who opposed or resisted us—or condescended to us or rigorously excluded us—because we were Jews. Though I knew that we were tolerated and accepted as well—in publicized individual cases, even specially esteemed—and though I never doubted that this country was mine (and New Jersey and Newark as well), I was not unaware of the power to intimidate that emanated from the highest and lowest reaches of gentile America.

At the top were the gentile executives who ran my father's company, the Metropolitan Life, from the home office at Number One Madison Avenue (the first Manhattan street address I ever knew). When I was a small boy, my father, then in his early thirties, was still a new Metropolitan agent, working a six-day week, including most evenings, and grateful for the steady, if modest, living this job provided, even during the Depression; a family shoe store he'd opened after marrying my mother had gone bankrupt some years before, and in between he'd had to take a variety of low-paying, unpromising jobs. He proudly explained to his sons that the Metropolitan was "the largest financial institution in the world" and that as an agent he provided Metropolitan Life policyholders with "an umbrella for a rainy day." The company put out dozens of pamphlets to educate its policyholders about health and disease; I collected a new batch off the racks in the waiting room on Saturday mornings when he took me along with him to the narrow downtown street where the Essex district office of Newark occupied nearly a whole floor of a commercial office building. I read up on "Tuberculosis," "Pregnancy," and "Diabetes," while he labored over his ledger entries and his paperwork. Sometimes at his desk, impressing myself by sitting in his swivel chair, I practiced my penmanship on Metropolitan stationery; in one corner of the paper was my father's name and in the other a picture of the home-office tower, topped with the beacon that he described to me, in the Metropolitan's own phrase, as the light that never failed.

In our apartment a framed replica of the Declaration of Independence hung above the telephone table on the hallway wall—it had been awarded by the Metropolitan to the men of my father's district for a successful year in the field, and seeing it there daily during my

ADDITIONAL QUESTIONS FOR RESPONDING TO READING

1. What are the long-lasting effects of childhood experiences? Do you believe it is necessarily true that traumatic episodes damage the developing personality? Explain your answer.
2. What was young Roth's attitude concerning his "Jewishness"? How did he differ from his parents in that respect?
3. What is "the feeling" that existed among Roth and his childhood friends?

TEACHING STRATEGY

Discuss the following with your students:

Paragraph 1: Differentiate between "the greatest menace" and "the biggest threat" that Roth identifies.

Paragraph 3: What does the replica of the Declaration of Independence represent for Roth? Ask students if his faith in its ideas is realistic.

Paragraph 4: How did young Roth view Mr. Peterfreund? Explain Roth's two-pronged explanation of the man's character.

Paragraph 5: Identify the "highest and lowest reaches" to which Roth refers; what does the phrase imply about his situation?

Paragraph 6: What is ironic about the "race riots" at Bradley Beach? Explain the gentile children's hatred.

Paragraph 7: Why does Roth use the word *apocryphal* rather than *invented*? What purpose does the question concluding this paragraph serve?

Paragraphs 8 & 9: At this point readers begin to see that the childhood memory is more than an isolated incident. In what way does it serve a greater purpose in the essay as a whole?

Paragraph 13: Why does Roth choose to run rather than fight? What do you think about this behavior? (You might refer students to Stanton L. Wormley, Jr., "Fighting Back," page 419, for an additional perspective.)

WRITING SUGGESTION

Were your parents or teachers prejudiced against certain groups? If so, how did they exhibit this prejudice? Write an essay in which you discuss how their biases affected your childhood outlook.

first school years forged an association between the venerated champions of equality who signed that cherished document and our benefactors, the corporate fathers at Number One Madison Avenue, where the reigning president was, fortuitously, a Mr. Lincoln. If that wasn't enough, the home-office executive whom my father would trek from New Jersey to see when his star began to rise slightly in the company was the superintendent of agencies, a Mr. Wright, whose good opinion my father valued inordinately all his life and whose height and imposing good looks he admired nearly as much as he did the man's easygoing diplomacy. As my father's son I felt no less respectful toward these awesomely named gentiles than he did, but I, like him, knew that they had to be the very officials who openly and guiltlessly conspired to prevent more than a few token Jews from assuming positions of anything approaching importance within the largest financial institution in the world.

One reason my father so admired the Jewish manager of his own district, Sam Peterfreund—aside, of course, from the devotion that Peterfreund inspired by recognizing my father's drive early on and making him an assistant manager—was that Peterfreund had climbed to the leadership of such a large, productive office despite the company's deep-rooted reluctance to allow a Jew to rise too high. When Mr. Peterfreund was to make one of his rare visits for dinner, the green felt protective pads came out of the hall closet and were laid by my brother and me on the dining room table, it was spread with a fresh linen cloth and linen napkins, water goblets appeared, and we ate off "the good dishes" in the dining room, where there hung a large oil painting of a floral arrangement, copied skillfully from the Louvre by my mother's brother, Mickey; on the sideboard were framed photographic portraits of the two dead men for whom I'd been named, my mother's father, Philip, and my father's younger brother, Milton. We ate in the dining room only on religious holidays, on special family occasions, and when Mr. Peterfreund came—and we all called him Mr. Peterfreund, even when he wasn't there; my father also addressed him directly as "Boss." "Want a drink, Boss?" Before dinner we sat unnaturally, like guests in our own living room, while Mr. Peterfreund sipped his schnapps and I was encouraged to listen to his wisdom. The esteem he inspired was a tribute to a gentile-sanctioned Jew managing a big Metropolitan office as much as to an immediate supervisor whose goodwill determined my father's occupational well-being and our family fate. A large, bald-headed man with a gold chain across his vest and a slightly mysterious German accent, whose family lived (in high style, I imagined) in New York (*and* on Long Island) while (no less glamorously to me) he slept during the week in a Newark hotel, the Boss was our family's Bernard Baruch.[1]

Opposition more frightening than corporate discrimination came from the lowest reaches of the gentile world, from the gangs of *lumpen*[2] kids who, one summer, swarmed out of Neptune, a ramshackle little town on the Jersey shore, and stampeded along the boardwalk into Bradley Beach, hollering "Kikes! Dirty Jews!" and beating up whoever hadn't run for cover. Bradley Beach, a couple of miles south of Asbury Park on the mid-Jersey coast, was the very modest little vacation resort where we and hundreds of other lower-middle-class Jews from humid, mosquito-ridden north Jersey cities rented rooms or shared small bungalows for several weeks during the summer. It was paradise for me, even though we lived three in a room, and four when my father drove down the old Cheesequake highway to see us on weekends or to stay for his two-week vacation. In all of my intensely secure and protected childhood, I don't believe I ever felt more exuberantly snug than I did in those mildly anarchic rooming houses, where—inevitably with more strain than valor—some ten or twelve women tried to share the shelves of a single large icebox, and to cook side by side, in a crowded communal kitchen, for children, visiting husbands, and elderly parents. Meals were eaten in the unruly, kibbutzlike atmosphere—so unlike the ambiance in my own orderly home—of the underventilated dining room.

The hot, unhomelike, homey hubbub of the Bradley Beach rooming house was somberly contrasted, in the early forties, by reminders all along the shore that the country was fighting in an enormous war: bleak, barbwired Coast Guard bunkers dotted the beaches, and scores of lonely, very young sailors played the amusement machines in the arcades at Asbury Park; the lights were blacked out along the boardwalk at night and the blackout shades on the rooming-house windows made it stifling indoors after dinner; there was even tarry refuse, alleged to be from torpedoed ships, that washed up and littered the beach—I sometimes had fears of wading gleefully with my friends into the surf and bumping against the body of someone killed at sea. Also—and most peculiarly, since we were all supposed to be pulling together to beat the Axis Powers—there were these "race riots," as we children called the hostile nighttime invasions by the boys from Neptune: violence directed against the Jews by youngsters who, as everyone said, could only have learned their hatred from what they heard at home.

[1]American financier (1870–1965). [Ed.]
[2]Literally, "rag." [Eds.]

Though the riots occurred just twice, for much of one July and   7
August it was deemed unwise for a Jewish child to venture out after
supper alone, or even with friends, though nighttime freedom in
shorts and sandals was one of Bradley's greatest pleasures for a ten-
year-old on vacation from homework and the school year's bedtime
hours. The morning after the first riot, a story spread among the kids
collecting Popsicle sticks and playing ring-a-lievo on the LaReine
Avenue beach; it was about somebody (whom nobody seemed to
know personally) who had been caught before he could get away:
the anti-Semites had held him down and pulled his face back and
forth across the splintery surface of the boardwalk's weathered
planks. This particular horrific detail, whether apocryphal or not—
and it needn't necessarily have been—impressed upon me how barbaric was this irrational hatred of families who, as anyone could see,
were simply finding in Bradley Beach a little inexpensive relief from
the city heat, people just trying to have a quiet good time, bothering
no one, except occasionally each other, as when one of the women
purportedly expropriated from the icebox, for her family's corn on
the cob, somebody else's quarter of a pound of salt butter. If that was
as much harm as any of us could do, why make a bloody pulp of a
Jewish child's face?

The home-office gentiles in executive positions at Number One   8
Madison Avenue were hardly comparable to the kids swarming into
Bradley screaming "Kike!"; and yet when I thought about it, I saw
that they were no more reasonable or fair: they too were against Jews
for no good reason. Small wonder that at twelve, when I was advised
to begin to think seriously about what I would do when I grew up,
I decided to oppose the injustices wreaked by the violent and the
privileged by becoming a lawyer for the underdog.

When I entered high school, the menace shifted to School   9
Stadium, then the only large football grounds in Newark, situated on
alien Bloomfield Avenue, a forty-minute bus ride from Weequahic
High. On Saturdays in the fall, four of the city's seven high schools
would meet in a doubleheader, as many as two thousand kids pouring
in for the first game, which began around noon, and then emptying
en masse into the surrounding streets when the second game had
ended in the falling shadows. It was inevitable after a hard-fought
game that intense school rivalries would culminate in a brawl somewhere in the stands and that, in an industrial city of strongly divergent
ethnic backgrounds and subtle, though pronounced, class gradations,
fights would break out among volatile teenagers from four very different neighborhoods. Yet the violence provoked by the presence of
a Weequahic crowd—particularly after a rare Weequahic victory—
was unlike any other.

I remember being in the stands with my friends in my sophomore   10
year, rooting uninhibitedly for the "Indians," as our Weequahic teams
were known in the Newark sports pages; after never having beaten
Barringer High in the fourteen years of Weequahic's existence, our
team was leading them 6–0 in the waning minutes of the Columbus
Day game. The Barringer backfield was Berry, Peloso, Short, and
Thompson; in the Weequahic backfield were Weissman, Weiss, Gold,
and fullback Fred Rosenberg, who'd led a sustained march down the
field at the end of the first half and then, on a two-yard plunge, had
scored what Fred, now a PR consultant in New Jersey, recently wrote
to tell me was "one of the only touchdowns notched by the Indians
that entire season, on a run that probably was one of the longer runs
from scrimmage in 1947."

As the miraculous game was nearing its end—as Barringer, tied   11
with Central for first place in the City League, was about to be upset
by the weakest high school team in Newark—I suddenly noticed that
the rival fans on the other side of the stadium bowl had begun to
stream down the aisles, making their way around the far ends of the
stadium toward us. Instead of waiting for the referee's final whistle,
I bolted for an exit and, along with nearly everyone else who understood what was happening, ran down the stadium ramp in the direction of the buses waiting to take us back to our neighborhood. Though
there were a number of policemen around, it was easy to see that
once the rampage was under way, unless you were clinging to a cop
with both arms and both legs, his protection wouldn't be much help;
should you be caught on your own by a gang from one of the other
three schools waiting to get their hands on a Weequahic Jew—our
school was almost entirely Jewish—it was unlikely that you'd emerge
from the stadium without serious injury.

The nearest bus was already almost full when I made it on board;   12
as soon as the last few kids shoved their way in, the uniformed Public
Service driver, fearful for his own safety as a transporter of Weequahic
kids, drew the front door shut. By then there were easily ten of fifteen
of the enemy, aged twelve to twenty, surrounding the bus and hammering their fists against its sides. Fred Rosenberg contends that
"every able-bodied man from north Newark, his brother, and their
offspring got into the act." When one of them, having worked his
hands through a crevice under the window beside my seat, started
forcing the window up with his fingers, I grabbed it from the top and
brought it down as hard as I could. He howled and somebody took
a swing at the window with a baseball bat, breaking the frame but
miraculously not the glass. Before the others could join together to
tear back the door, board the bus, and go straight for me—who would
have been hard put to explain that the reprisal had been uncharac-

teristic and intended only in self-defense—the driver had pulled out from the curb and we were safely away from the postgame pogrom, which, for our adversaries, constituted perhaps the most enjoyable part of the day's entertainment.

That evening I fled again, not only because I was a fourteen-year-old weighing only a little over a hundred pounds but because I was never to be one of the few who stayed behind for a fight but always among the many whose impulse is to run to avoid it. A boy in our neighborhood might be expected to protect himself in a schoolyard confrontation with another boy his age and size, but no stigma attached to taking flight from a violent melee—by and large it was considered both shameful and stupid for a bright Jewish child to get caught up in something so dangerous to his physical safety, and so repugnant to Jewish instincts. The collective memory of Polish and Russian pogroms[3] had fostered in most of our families the idea that our worth as human beings, even perhaps our distinction as a people, was embodied in the *incapacity* to perpetrate the sort of bloodletting visited upon our ancestors.

For a while during my adolescence I studiously followed prize-fighting, could recite the names and weights of all the champions and contenders, and even subscribed briefly to *Ring,* Nat Fleischer's colorful boxing magazine. As kids my brother and I have been taken by our father to the local boxing arena, where invariably we all had a good time. From my father and his friends I heard about the prowess of Benny Leonard, Barney Ross, Max Baer, and the clownishly nicknamed Slapsie Maxie Rosenbloom. And yet Jewish boxers and boxing aficionados remained, like boxing itself, "sport" in the bizarre sense, a strange deviation from the norm and interesting largely for that reason: in the world whose values first formed me, unrestrained physical aggression was considered contemptible everywhere else. I could no more smash a nose with a fist than fire a pistol into someone's heart. And what imposed this restraint, if not on Slapsie Maxie Rosenbloom, then on me, was my being Jewish. In my scheme of things, Slapsie Maxie was a more miraculous Jewish phenomenon by far than Dr. Albert Einstein.

The evening following our escape from School Stadium the ritual victory bonfire was held on the dirt playing field on Chancellor Avenue, across from Syd's, a popular Weequahic hangout where my brother and I each did part-time stints selling hot dogs and french fries. I'd virtually evolved as a boy on that playing field; it was two blocks from my house and bordered on the grade school—"Chan-

13

14

15

---

[3]Organized massacres of Jews conducted by the Czar's army during the late nineteenth and early twentieth century in Russia. [Eds.]

cellor Avenue''—that I'd attended for eight years, which itself stood next to Weequahic High. It was the field where I'd played pickup football and baseball, where my brother had competed in school track meets, where I'd shagged flies for hours with anybody who would fungo the ball out to me, where my friends and I hung around on Sunday mornings, watching with amusement as the local fathers— the plumbers, the electricians, the produce merchants—kibitzed their way through their weekly softball game. If ever I had been called on to express my love for my neighborhood in a single reverential act, I couldn't have done better than to get down on my hands and knees and kiss the ground behind home plate.

Yet upon this, the sacred heart of my inviolate homeland, our   16 stadium attackers launched a nighttime raid, the conclusion to the violence begun that afternoon, their mopping-up exercise. A few hours after the big fire had been lit, as we happily sauntered around the dark field, joking among ourselves and looking for girls to impress, while in the distance the cartwheeling cheerleaders led the chant of the crowd encircling the fire—"And when you're up against Weequahic/you're upside down!"—the cars pulled up swiftly on Chancellor Avenue, and the same guys who'd been pounding on the sides of my bus (or so I quickly assumed) were racing onto the field, some of them waving baseball bats. The field was set into the slope of the Chancellor Avenue hill; I ran through the dark to the nearest wall, jumped some six feet down into Hobson Street, and then just kept going, through alleyways, between garages, and over backyard fences, until I'd made it safely home in less than five minutes. One of my Leslie Street friends, the football team water boy, who'd been standing in the full glare of the fire wearing his Weequahic varsity jacket, was not so quick or lucky; his assailants—identified in the neighborhood the next day as "Italians"—picked him up and threw him bodily toward the flames. He landed just at the fire's edge and, though he wasn't burned, spent days in the hospital recovering from internal injuries.

But this was a unique calamity. Our lower-middle-class neigh-   17 borhood of houses and shops—a few square miles of tree-lined streets at the corner of the city bordering on residential Hillside and semi-industrial Irvington—was as safe and peaceful a haven for me as his rural community would have been for an Indiana farm boy. Ordinarily nobody more disquieting ever appeared there than the bearded old Jew who sometimes tapped on our door around dinnertime; to me an unnerving specter from the harsh and distant European past, he stood silently in the dim hallway while I went to get a quarter to drop into his collection can for the Jewish National Fund (a name that never sank all the way in: the only nation for Jews, as I saw it, was the

democracy to which I was so loyally—and lyrically—bound, regardless of the unjust bias of the so-called best and the violent hatred of
some of the worst). Shapiro, the immigrant tailor who also did dry
cleaning, had two thumbs on one hand, and that made bringing our
clothes to him a little eerie for me when I was still small. And there
was LeRoy "the moron," a somewhat gruesome but innocuous neighborhood dimwit who gave me the creeps when he sat down on the
front stoop to listen to a bunch of us talking after school. On our
street he was rarely teased but just sat looking at us stupidly with his
hollow eyes and rhythmically tapping one foot—and that was about
as frightening as things ever got.

A typical memory is of five or six of us energetically traversing 18
the whole length of the neighborhood Friday nights on our way back
from a double feature at the Roosevelt Theater. We would stop off at
the Watson Bagel Company on Clinton Place to buy, for a few pennies
each, a load of the first warm bagels out of the oven—and this was
four decades before the bagel became a breakfast staple at Burger
King. Devouring three and four apiece, we'd circuitously walk one
another home, howling with laughter at our jokes and imitating our
favorite baritones. When the weather was good we'd sometimes wind
up back of Chancellor Avenue School, on the wooden bleachers along
the sidelines of the asphalt playground adjacent to the big dirt playing
field. Stretched on our backs in the open night air, we were as carefree
as any kids anywhere in postwar America, and certainly we felt ourselves no less American. Discussions about Jewishness and being
Jewish, which I was to hear so often among intellectual Jews once I
was an adult in Chicago and New York, were altogether unknown;
we talked about being misunderstood by our families, about movies
and radio programs and sex and sports, we even argued about politics, though this was rare since our fathers were all ardent New
Dealers and there was no disagreement among us about the sanctity
of F.D.R. and the Democratic Party. About being Jewish there was
nothing more to say than there was about having two arms and two
legs. It would have seemed to us strange *not* to be Jewish—stranger
still, to hear someone announce that he wished he weren't a Jew or
that he intended not to be in the future.

Yet, simultaneously, this intense adolescent camaraderie was the 19
primary means by which we were deepening our *Americanness*. Our
parents were, with few exceptions, the first-generation offspring of
poor turn-of-the-century immigrants from Galicia[4] and Polish Russia,
raised in predominantly Yiddish[5]speaking Newark households where

---

[4]Region of southeastern Poland, including the cities of Kraków and Lvov. [Eds.]
[5]Language derived from German dialects and written in Hebrew characters. [Eds.]

religious Orthodoxy was only just beginning to be seriously eroded by American life. However unaccented and American-sounding their speech, however secularized their own beliefs, and adept and convincing their American style of lower-middle-class existence, they were influenced still by their childhood training and by strong parental ties to what often seemed to us antiquated, socially useless old-country mores and perceptions.

My larger boyhood society cohered around the most inherently American phenomenon at hand—the game of baseball, whose mystique was encapsulated in three relatively inexpensive fetishes that you could have always at your side in your room, not only while you did your homework but in bed with you while you slept if you were a worshiper as primitive as I was at ten and eleven: they were a ball, a bat, and a glove. The solace that my Orthodox grandfather doubtless took in the familiar leathery odor of the flesh-worn straps of the old phylacteries[6] in which he wrapped himself each morning, I derived from the smell of my mitt, which I ritualistically donned every day to work a little on my pocket. I was an average playground player, and the mitt's enchantment had to do less with foolish dreams of becoming a major leaguer, or even a high school star, than with the bestowal of membership in a great secular nationalistic church from which nobody had ever seemed to suggest that Jews should be excluded. (The blacks were another story, until 1947.)[7] The softball and hardball teams we organized and reorganized obsessively throughout our grade-school years—teams we called by unarguably native names like the Seabees and the Mohawks and described as "social and athletic clubs"—aside from the opportunity they afforded to compete against one another in a game we loved, also operated as secret societies that separated us from the faint, residual foreignness still clinging to some of our parents' attitudes and that validated our own spotless credentials as American kids. Paradoxically, our remotely recent old-country Jewish origins may well have been a source of our especially intense devotion to a sport that, unlike boxing or even football, had nothing to do with the menace of brute force unleashed against flesh and bones.

The Weequahic neighborhood for over two decades now has been part of the vast black Newark slum. Visiting my father in Elizabeth, I'll occasionally take a roundabout route off the parkway into my old Newark and, to give myself an emotional workout, drive through the

20

21

---

[6]Small leather boxes containing strips of parchment inscribed with quotations from the Hebrew scriptures, used in morning prayers. [Eds.]

[7]In 1947, professional baseball signed its first black player: Jackie Robinson of the Brooklyn Dodgers. [Eds.]

streets still entirely familiar to me despite the boarded-up shops and badly decaying houses, and the knowledge that my white face is not at all welcome. Recently, snaking back and forth in my car along the one-way streets of the Weequahic section, I began to imagine house plaques commemorating the achievements of the boys who'd once lived there, markers of the kind you see in London and Paris on the residences of the historically renowned. What I inscribed on those plaques, along with my friends' names and their years of birth and of local residence, wasn't the professional status they had attained in later life but the position each had played on those neighborhood teams of ours in the 1940s. I thought that if you knew that in this four-family Hobson Street house there once lived the third baseman Seymour Feldman and that down a few doors had lived Ronnie Rubin, who in his boyhood had been our catcher, you'd understand how and where the Feldman and the Rubin families had been naturalized irrevocably by their young sons.

In 1982, while I was visiting my widowered father in Miami Beach   22 during his first season there on his own, I got him one night to walk over with me to Meyer Lansky's [8] old base of operations, the Hotel Singapore on Collins Avenue; earlier in the day he'd told me that wintering at the Singapore were some of the last of his generation from our neighborhood—the ones, he mordantly added, "still aboveground." Among the faces I recognized in the lobby, where the elderly residents met to socialize each evening after dinner, was the mother of one of the boys who also used to play ball incessantly "up the field" and who hung around on the playground bleachers after dark back when we were Seabees together. As we sat talking at the edge of a gin-rummy game, she suddenly took hold of my hand and, smiling at me with deeply emotional eyes—with that special heart-filled look that *all* our mothers had—she said, "Phil, the feeling there was among you boys—I've never seen anything like it again." I told her, altogether truthfully, that I haven't either.

RESPONDING TO READING

1. In what respects does Roth see himself, as a child and as an adolescent, as different from his non-Jewish counterparts? In what ways do you think adult Jews feel different from non-Jews? Do you think such differentness is likely to increase or decrease as members of minority groups become adults?   **2.** Roth sees himself "opposed," "resisted," "condescended to," and "rigorously excluded" by a powerful non-Jewish elite. Still, he finds the gentile children who call him names even more frightening than these pow-

---

[8]Reputed underworld crime figure during the 1930s. [Eds.]

erful adults. Why? Do you agree with his assessment?   **3.** When Roth speaks of being "safe at home," what does he mean by "safe"? By "home"? What does being "safe at home" mean to you?

How It Feels to Be Colored Me

ZORA NEALE HURSTON

Folklorist and writer Zora Neale Hurston (1901–1969) grew up in Eatonville, Florida, the first incorporated African-American community in the United States, and Hurston herself was the first African-American woman admitted to Barnard College. There she developed an interest in anthropology, and she studied with Columbia University's famous anthropologist, Franz Boas. *Mules and Men* (1935) is her book of folklore about voodoo among southern blacks. During the Harlem Renaissance of the 1920s and 1930s, Hurston wrote stories celebrating the hope and joy of African-American life, music, and stories. Her most notable novel is *Their Eyes Were Watching God* (1937). The essay below, which features Hurston's strong personal voice, is from the collection *I Love Myself When I Am Laughing* (1979), edited by Alice Walker.

I am colored but I offer nothing in the way of extenuating circumstances except the fact that I am the only Negro in the United States whose grandfather on the mother's side was *not* an Indian chief.

I remember the very day that I became colored. Up to my thirteenth year I lived in the little Negro town of Eatonville, Florida. It is exclusively a colored town. The only white people I knew passed through the town going to or coming from Orlando. The native whites rode dusty horses, the Northern tourists chugged down the sandy village road in automobiles. The town knew the Southerners and never stopped cane chewing[1] when they passed. But the Northerners were something else again. They were peered at cautiously from behind curtains by the timid. The more venturesome would come out on the porch to watch them go past and got just as much pleasure out of the tourists as the tourists got out of the village.

The front porch might seem a daring place for the rest of the town, but it was a gallery seat for me. My favorite place was atop the gate-post. Proscenium[2] box for a born first-nighter. Not only did I

---

[1]Chewing sugar cane. [Eds.]
[2]In the ancient Greek theater, the stage; in the modern theater, the area between the curtain and the orchestra. [Eds.]

FOR OPENERS

Ask students to describe their reactions to the title of this essay. What connotations does the word *colored* have?

ADDITIONAL QUESTIONS FOR RESPONDING TO READING

1. Exactly when did you become aware of your own racial or ethnic identity?
2. What message is Hurston sending to other members of her race? What flaws in attitudes does she perceive among them? What is her solution?
3. How does Hurston respond when she is confronted by discrimination? Do you agree with her actions?

enjoy the show, but I didn't mind the actors knowing that I liked it. I usually spoke to them in passing. I'd wave at them and when they returned my salute, I would say something like this: "Howdy-do-well-I-thank-you-where-you-goin'?" Usually automobile or the horse paused at this, and after a queer exchange of compliments, I would probably "go a piece of the way" with them, as we say in farthest Florida. If one of my family happened to come to the front in time to see me, of course negotiations would be rudely broken off. But even so, it is clear that I was the first "welcome-to-our-state" Floridian, and I hope the Miami Chamber of Commerce will please take notice.

During this period, white people differed from colored to me only 4 in that they rode through town and never lived there. They liked to hear me "speak pieces" and sing and wanted to see me dance the parse-me-la, and gave me generously of their small silver for doing these things, which seemed strange to me for I wanted to do them so much that I needed bribing to stop. Only they didn't know it. The colored people gave no dimes. They deplored any joyful tendencies in me, but I was their Zora nevertheless. I belonged to them, to the nearby hotels, to the county—everybody's Zora.

But changes came in the family when I was thirteen, and I was 5 sent to school in Jacksonville. I left Eatonville, the town of the oleanders,[3] as Zora. When I disembarked from the river-boat at Jacksonville, she was no more. It seemed that I had suffered a sea change. I was not Zora of Orange County any more, I was now a little colored girl. I found it out in certain ways. In my heart as well as in the mirror, I became a fast brown—warranted not to rub nor run.

But I am not tragically colored. There is no great sorrow dammed 6 up in my soul, nor lurking behind my eyes. I do not mind at all. I do not belong to the sobbing school of Negrohood who hold that nature somehow has given them a lowdown dirty deal and whose feelings are all hurt about it. Even in the helter-skelter skirmish that is my life, I have seen that the world is to the strong regardless of a little pigmentation more or less. No, I do not weep at the world—I am too busy sharpening my oyster knife.[4]

Someone is always at my elbow reminding me that I am the 7 granddaughter of slaves. It fails to register depression with me. Slavery is sixty years in the past. The operation was successful and the patient is doing well, thank you. The terrible struggle[5] that made me an American out of a potential slave said "On the line!" The

---

[3]Tropical flowers. [Eds.]
[4]Reference is to the expression "The world is my oyster." [Eds.]
[5]The Civil War. [Eds.]

Reconstruction[6] said "Get set!"; and the generation before said "Go!" I am off to a flying start and I must not halt in the stretch to look behind and weep. Slavery is the price I paid for civilization, and the choice was not with me. It is a bully adventure and worth all that I have paid through my ancestors for it. No one on earth ever had a greater chance for glory. The world to be won and nothing to be lost. It is thrilling to think—to know that for any act of mine, I shall get twice as much praise or twice as much blame. It is quite exciting to hold the center of the national stage, with the spectators not knowing whether to laugh or to weep.

The position of my white neighbor is much more difficult. No   8 brown specter pulls up a chair beside me when I sit down to eat. No dark ghost thrusts its leg against mine in bed. The game of keeping what one has is never so exciting as the game of getting.

I do not always feel colored. Even now I often achieve the uncon-   9 scious Zora of Eatonville before the Hegira.[7] I feel most colored when I am thrown against a sharp white background.

For instance at Barnard.[8] "Beside the waters of the Hudson" I   10 feel my race. Among the thousand white persons, I am a dark rock surged upon, and overswept, but through it all, I remain myself. When covered by the waters, I am; and the ebb but reveals me again.

Sometimes it is the other way around. A white person is set down   11 in our midst, but the contrast is just as sharp for me. For instance, when I sit in the drafty basement that is The New World Cabaret with a white person, my color comes. We enter chatting about any little nothing that we have in common and are seated by the jazz waiters. In the abrupt way that jazz orchestras have, this one plunges into a number. It loses no time in circumlocutions, but gets right down to business. It constricts the thorax and splits the heart with its tempo and narcotic harmonies. This orchestra grows rambunctious, rears on its hind legs and attacks the tonal veil with primitive fury, rending it, clawing it until it breaks through to the jungle beyond. I follow those heathen—follow them exultingly. I dance wildly inside myself; I yell within, I whoop; I shake my assegai[9] above my head, I hurl it true to the mark *yeeeeooww!* I am in the jungle and living in the jungle way. My face is painted red and yellow and my body is painted blue. My pulse is throbbing like a war drum. I want to slaughter some-thing—give paid, give death to what, I do not know. But the piece

---

[6]The period immediately following the Civil War. [Eds.]
[7]The flight of Mohammed from Mecca in A.D. 622; here, an escape from a dangerous situation. [Eds.]
[8]Women's college in New York City. [Eds.]
[9]South American hunting spear. [Eds.]

ends. The men of the orchestra wipe their lips and rest their fingers. I creep back slowly to the veneer we call civilization with the last tone and find the white friend sitting motionless in his seat, smoking calmly.

"Good music they have here," he remarks, drumming the table with his fingertips. 12

Music. The great blobs of purpose and red emotion have not touched him. He has only heard what I felt. He is far away and I see him but dimly across the ocean and the continent that have fallen between us. He is so pale with his whiteness then and I am so colored. 13

At certain times I have no race, I am *me*. When I set my hat at a certain angle and saunter down Seventh Avenue, Harlem City, feeling as snooty as the lions in front of the Forty-Second Street Library, for instance. So far as my feelings are concerned, Peggy Hopkins Joyce[10] on the Boule Mich with her gorgeous raiment, stately carriage, knees knocking together in a most aristocratic manner, has nothing on me. The cosmic Zora emerges. I belong to no race nor time. I am the eternal feminine with its string of beads. 14

I have no separate feeling about being an American citizen and colored. I am merely a fragment of the Great Soul that surges within the boundaries. My country, right or wrong. 15

Sometimes, I feel discriminated against, but it does not make me angry. It merely astonishes me. How *can* any deny themselves the pleasure of my company? It's beyond me. 16

But in the main, I feel like a brown bag of miscellany propped against a wall. Against a wall in company with other bags, white, red and yellow. Pour out the contents, and there is discovered a jumble of small things priceless and worthless. A first-water diamond, an empty spool, bits of broken glass, lengths of string, a key to a door long since crumbled away, a rusty knife-blade, old shoes saved for a road that never was and never will be, a nail bent under the weight of things too heavy for any nail, a dried flower or two still a little fragrant. In your hand is the brown bag. On the ground before you is the jumble it held—so much like the jumble in the bags, could they be emptied, that all might be dumped in a single heap and the bags refilled without altering the contents of any greatly. A bit of colored glass more or less would not matter. Perhaps that is how the Great Stuffer of Bags filled them in the first place—who knows? 17

WRITING SUGGESTION

Develop question 3 in "Responding to Reading" into a full-length essay: Examine both sides of the question, and support your conclusion with specific details.

---

[10]American known for setting trends in beauty and fashion in the nineteen-twenties. The Boule Mich (also Boul' Mich) is a street on Paris's Left Bank. [Eds.]

RESPONDING TO READING

1. How, according to Hurston, does it feel to be "colored"? How do her feelings about her color change as she grows older? Why do they change? What feelings about yourself did you have that changed as you grew older?   **2.** In what sense does Hurston see herself as fundamentally different from the whites she encounters? Does she see this difference as a problem? Does her reaction surprise you?   **3.** When Hurston says, "At certain times I have no race, I am *me* (paragraph 14), does she mean she feels assimilated into the larger society, or does she mean something else? Do you think it is possible to be only yourself and not a member of a racial or ethnic group? Explain.

The Fear of Losing a Culture

RICHARD RODRIGUEZ

Richard Rodriguez (see also p. 215) has strong opinions about language and culture; he says in a *People* magazine interview: "I refuse to accept my generation's romanticism about discovering 'roots.' The trouble with that is it somehow holds children accountable for maintaining their culture, and freezes them into thinking of themselves as Mexicans or as Chinese or as blacks." In "The Fear of Losing a Culture," written in 1988, Rodriguez defines Hispanic-American culture, which stands "where the past meets the future," and argues that this culture has something essential to offer America.

What is culture?

The immigrant shrugs. Latin American immigrants come to the United States with only the things they need in mind—not abstractions like culture. Money. They need dollars. They need food. Maybe they need to get out of the way of bullets.

Most of us who concern ourselves with Hispanic-American culture, as painters, musicians, writers—or as sons and daughters—are the children of immigrants. We have grown up on this side of the border, in the land of Elvis Presley and Thomas Edison; our lives are prescribed by the mall, by the DMV and the Chinese restaurant. Our imagination yet vascillate between and Edenic Latin America (the blue door)—which nevertheless betrayed our parents—and the repellent plate glass of a real American city—which has been good to us.

Hispanic-American culture is where the past meets the future. Hispanic-American culture is not an Hispanic milestone only, not simply a celebration at the crossroads. America transforms into plea-

ANSWERS TO RESPONDING TO READING

1, 2. She does not view her "differentness" as a detriment to achievement; rather, she accepts white society's attitudes about her race as a challenge. As she matures, she becomes aware of some racial differences in attitudes and preferences, primarily cultural, but she prefers to identify herself as a part of an all-encompassing race.

3. Hurston suggests that there are times when race is irrelevant.

FOR OPENERS

How many different ethnic groups can you identify in the United States? What specific aspects of their culture set them apart from other groups?

ADDITIONAL QUESTIONS FOR RESPONDING TO READING

1. What are the advantages and disadvantages of trying to preserve an ethnic identity in the United States?
2. What is the "Hispanic-American predicament"? According to Rodriguez, what is the origin of Hispanic-American anxiety?
3. What are the differences between Latin American and North American world views? How do these differences affect the Hispanic-American?

TEACHING STRATEGY

Discuss the following with your students:

Paragraph 3: What paradox does Rodriguez identify in the attitudes toward ethnicity of Hispanic-American immigrants' children? What source(s) does he identify?

Paragraph 16: What is the United States's present response to the influx of alternative culture? How does Rodriguez account for this response?

Conclusion (paragraph 20): To whom is this message addressed? Is the message a prediction of things to come? Do you perceive it as a negative or a positive prediction? What response do you suppose Rodriguez expects?

sure what America cannot avoid. Is it any coincidence that at a time when Americans are troubled by the encroachment of the Mexican desert, Americans discover a chic in cactus, in the decorator colors of the Southwest? In sand?

Hispanic-American culture of the sort that is now showing (the teen movie, the rock songs) may exist in an hourglass; may in fact be irrelevant to the epic. The U.S. Border Patrol works through the night to arrest the flow of illegal immigrants over the border, even as Americans wait in line to get into "La Bamba." Even as Americans vote to declare, once and for all, that English shall be the official language of the United States, Madonna starts recording in Spanish. 5

But then so is Bill Cosby's show irrelevant to the 10 o'clock news, where families huddle together in fear on porches, pointing at the body of the slain boy bagged in tarpoline. Which is not to say that Bill Cosby or Michael Jackson are irrelevant to the future or without neo-Platonic[1] influence. Like players within the play, they prefigure, they resolve. They make black and white audiences aware of a bond that may not yet exist. 6

Before a national TV audience, Rita Moreno tells Geraldo Rivera that her dream as an actress is to play a character rather like herself: "I speak English perfectly well . . . I'm not dying from poverty . . . I want to play *that* kind of Hispanic woman, which is to say, an American citizen." This is an actress talking, these are show-biz pieties. But Moreno expresses as well the general Hispanic-American predicament. Hispanics want to belong to America without betraying the past. 7

Hispanics fear losing ground in any negotiation with the American city. We come from an expansive, an intimate culture that has been judged second-rate by the United States of America. For reasons of pride, therefore, as much as of affection, we are reluctant to give up our past. Hispanics often express a fear of "losing" culture. Our fame in the United States has been our resistance to assimilation. 8

The symbol of Hispanic culture has been the tongue of flame—Spanish. But the remarkable legacy Hispanics carry from Latin America is not language—an inflatable skin—but breath itself, capacity of soul, an inclination to live. The genius of Latin America is the habit of synthesis. 9

We assimilate. Just over the border there is the example of Mexico, the country from which the majority of U.S. Hispanics come. Mexico 10

---

[1] A philosophical and religious system developed in the third century A.D., based on doctrines of Plato and other Greek philosophers, and incorporating elements of Oriental mysticism and some Christian and Judaic ideas. [Eds.]

is mestizo—Indian and Spanish. Within a single family, Mexicans are light-skinned and dark. It is impossible for the Mexican to say, in the scheme of things, where the Indian begins and the Spaniard surrenders.

In culture as in blood, Latin America was formed by a rape that became a marriage. Due to the absorbing generosity of the Indian, European culture took on new soil. What Latin America knows is that people create one another as they marry. In the music of Latin America you will hear the litany of bloodlines—the African drum, the German accordian, the cry from the minaret.

The United States stands as the opposing New World experiment. In North America the Indian and the European stood apace. Whereas Latin America was formed by a medieval Catholic dream of one world—of meltdown conversion—the United States was built up from Protestant individualism. The American melting pot washes away only embarrassment; it is the necessary initiation into public life. The American faith is that our national strength derives from separateness, from "diversity." The glamour of the United States is a carnival promise: You can lose weight, get rich as Rockefeller, tough up your roots, get a divorce.

Immigrants still come for the promise. But the United States wavers in its faith. As long as there was space enough, sky enough, as long as economic success validated individualism, loneliness was not too high a price to pay. (The cabin on the prairie or the Sony Walkman.)

As we near the end of the American century, two alternative cultures beckon the American imagination—both highly communal cultures—the Asian and the Latin American. The United States is a literal culture. Americans devour what we might otherwise fear to become. Sushi will make us corporate warriors. Combination Plate #3, smothered in mestizo gravy, will burn a hole in our hearts.

Latin America offers passion. Latin America has a life—I mean *life*—big clouds, unambiguous themes, death, birth, faith, that the United States, for all its quality of life, seems without now. Latin America offers communal riches: an undistressed leisure, a kitchen table, even a full sorrow. Such is the solitude of America, such is the urgency of American need, Americans reach right past a fledgling, homegrown Hispanic-American culture for the real thing—the darker bottle of Mexican beer; the denser novel of a Latin American master.

For a long time, Hispanics in the United States withheld from the United States our Latin American gift. We denied the value of assimilation. But as our presence is judged less foreign in America, we will produce a more generous art, less timid, less parochial. Carlos San-

11

12

13

14

15

16

COLLABORATIVE ACTIVITIES

1. Assign groups different aspects of popular culture for examination, and instruct them to look for Asian, Hispanic, African, and Native American influences in items such as bestseller lists, record charts, clothing styles, television shows, and food. Then, as a class, discuss the influence of various ethnic groups on American culture. To what degree has each group's culture been assimilated into American culture?

2. Is there such a thing as American culture? Have students work in groups to identify characteristics of this culture. Then, discuss the groups' findings and encourage the class to try to define and illustrate "American culture."

WRITING SUGGESTION

In paragraph 1 Rodriguez asks, "What is culture?" Write an essay in which you answer his question, developing your definitions with examples drawn from your own cultural background.

tana, Luis Valdez, Linda Ronstadt[2]—Hispanic Americans do not have a "pure" Latin American art to offer. Expect bastard themes, expect ironies, comic conclusions. For we live on this side of the border, where Kraft manufactures bricks of "Mexican style" Velveeta, and where Jack in the Box serves "Fajita Pita."

The flame-red Chevy floats a song down the Pan American Highway: 17 *From a rolled-down window, the grizzled voice of Willie Nelson rises in disembodied harmony with the voice of Julio Iglesias. Gabby Hayes and Cisco are thus resolved.*

Expect marriage. We will change America even as we will be 18 changed. We will disappear with you into a new miscegenation.[3]

Along the border, real conflicts remain. But the ancient tear sep- 19 arating Europe from itself—the Catholic Mediterranean from the Protestant north—may yet heal itself in the New World. For generations, Latin America has been the place—the bed—of a confluence of so many races and cultures that Protestant North America shuddered to imagine it.

Imagine it. 20

ANSWERS TO RESPONDING TO READING

1. Rodriguez considers as central the ability to synthesize aspects of past histories and cultures that have exerted a strong influence, including bloodlines, music, literature, and world views.
2. He sees assimilation as a positive development, an opportunity for Hispanics to give the United States what he calls their "Latin American gift."
3. Answers will vary.

RESPONDING TO READING

1. What characteristics does Rodriguez consider to be central to a definition of his culture? Do you think non-Hispanics are likely to characterize that culture as Rodriguez does? Why or Why not? **2.** Rodriguez believes assimilation is inevitable. Do you? Does he see assimilation as a positive or negative development? What are your feelings on this issue? **3.** Do you believe it is possible for Hispanic Americans—or members of other ethnic minorities—to retain their culture *and* assimilate into American Society?

[2]Carlos Santana (1947–), guitarist and founder of the rock band Santana; Luis Valdez (1940–), playwright focusing on Chicano experience; Linda Ronstadt (1946–), popular singer. [Eds.]
[3]Interbreeding between races. [Eds.]

Stranger in the Village

JAMES BALDWIN

James Baldwin (1924–1987), born in Harlem, had a long career as a novelist, essayist, and civil rights activist. In 1938, Baldwin became a storefront preacher, an experience that served as the basis for his first novel, *Go Tell It on the Mountain* (1953). Later, fellow writer Richard Wright helped Baldwin obtain a fellowship to write essays, some of which are collected in *Notes of a Native Son* (1955). Baldwin lived for a time in Paris, returned to the United States in 1957, and became involved in the civil rights movement. His writings depict the injustices—social, economic, and political—that African-Americans suffer in the United States. Baldwin writes in the introduction to *Notes of a Native Son*, from which the essay that follows is taken, "I love America more than any other country in the world, and, exactly for this reason, I insist on the right to criticize her perpetually."

From all available evidence no black man had ever set foot in this 1
tiny Swiss village before I came. I was told before arriving that I would probably be a "sight" for the village; I took this to mean that people of my complexion were rarely seen in Switzerland, and also that city people are always something of a "sight" outside of the city. It did not occur to me—possibly because I am an American—that there could be people anywhere who had never seen a Negro.

It is a fact that cannot be explained on the basis of the inacces- 2
sibility of the village. The village is very high, but it is only four hours from Milan and three hours from Lausanne. It is true that it is virtually unknown. Few people making plans for a holiday would elect to come here. On the other hand, the villagers are able, presumably, to come and go as they please—which they do: to another town at the foot of the mountain, with a population of approximately five thousand, the nearest place to see a movie or go to the bank. In the village there is no movie house, no bank, no library, no theater; very few radios, one jeep, one station wagon; and at the moment, one typewriter, mine, an invention which the woman next door to me here had never seen. There are about six hundred people living here, all Catholic— I conclude this from the fact that the Catholic church is open all year round, whereas the Protestant chapel, set off on a hill a little removed from the village, is open only in the summertime when the tourists arrive. There are four or five hotels, all closed now, and four or five *bistros*, of which, however, only two do any business during the winter. These two do not do a great deal, for life in the village seems to end around nine or ten o'clock. There are a few stores, butcher, baker, *épicerie*,[1] a hardware store, and a money-changer—who cannot

---

[1]Grocery store. [Eds.]

change travelers' checks, but must send them down to the bank, an operation which takes two or three days. There is something called the *Ballet Haus*, closed in the winter and used for God knows what, certainly not ballet, during the summer. There seems to be only one schoolhouse in the village, and this for the quite young children; I suppose this to mean that their older brothers and sisters at some point descend from these mountains in order to complete their education—possibly, again, to the town just below. The landscape is absolutely forbidding, mountains towering on all four sides, ice and snow as far as the eye can reach. In this white wilderness, men and women and children move all day, carrying washing, wood, buckets of milk or water, sometimes skiing on Sunday afternoons. All week long boys and young men are to be seen shoveling snow off the rooftops, or dragging wood down from the forest in sleds.

The village's only real attraction, which explains the tourist season, is the hot spring water. A disquietingly high proportion of these tourists are cripples, or semi-cripples, who come year after year—from other parts of Switzerland, usually—to take the waters. This lends the village, at the height of the season, a rather terrifying air of sanctity, as though it were a lesser Lourdes.[2] There is often something beautiful, there is always something awful, in the spectacle of a person who has lost one of his faculties, a faculty he never questioned until it was gone, and who struggles to recover it. Yet people remain people, on crutches or indeed on deathbeds; and wherever I passed, the first summer I was here, among the native villagers or among the lame, a wind passed with me—of astonishment, curiosity, amusement, and outrage. That first summer I stayed two weeks and never intended to return. But I did return in the winter, to work; the village offers, obviously, no distractions whatever and has the further advantage of being extremely cheap. Now it is winter again, a year later, and I am here again. Everyone in the village knows my name, though they scarcely ever use it, knows that I come from America—though, this, apparently, they will never really believe: black men come from Africa—and everyone knows that I am the friend of the son of a woman who was born here, and that I am staying in their chalet. But I remain as much a stranger today as I was the first day I arrived, and the children shout *Neger! Neger!*[3] as I walk along the streets.

It must be admitted that in the beginning I was far too shocked to have any real reaction. In so far as I reacted at all, I reacted by

3

4

---

[2]A town in southwestern France, site of a shrine to the Virgin Mary (Our Lady of Lourdes). [Eds.]
[3]Negro. [Eds.]

trying to be pleasant—it being a great part of the American Negro's education (long before he goes to school) that he must make people "like" him. This smile-and-the-world-smiles-with-you routine worked about as well in this situation as it had in the situation for which it was designed, which is to say that it did not work at all. No one, after all, can be liked whose human weight and complexity cannot be, or has not been, admitted. My smile was simply another unheard-of phenomenon which allowed them to see my teeth—they did not, really, see my smile and I began to think that, should I take to snarling, no one would notice any difference. All of the physical characteristics of the Negro which had caused me, in America, a very different and almost forgotten pain were nothing less than miraculous—or infernal—in the eyes of the village people. Some thought my hair was the color of tar, that it had the texture of wire, or the texture of cotton. It was jocularly suggested that I might let it all grow long and make myself a winter coat. If I sat in the sun for more than five minutes some daring creature was certain to come along and gingerly put his fingers on my hair, as though he were afraid of an electric shock, or put his hand on my hand, astonished that the color did not rub off. In all of this, in which it must be conceded there was the charm of genuine wonder and in which there were certainly no element of intentional unkindness, there was yet no suggestion that I was human: I was simply a living wonder.

I knew that they did not mean to be unkind, and I know it now; 5
it is necessary, nevertheless, for me to repeat this to myself each time that I walk out of the chalet. The children who shout *Neger!* have no way of knowing the echoes this sound raises in me. They are brimming with good humor and the more daring swell with pride when I stop to speak with them. Just the same, there are days when I cannot pause and smile, when I have no heart to play with them; when, indeed, I mutter sourly to myself, exactly as I muttered on the streets of a city these children have never seen, when I was no bigger than these children are now: *Your* mother was a *nigger.* Joyce[4] is right about history being a nightmare—but it may be the nightmare from which no one *can* awaken. People are trapped in history and history is trapped in them.

There is a custom in the village—I am told it is repeated in many 6
villages—of "buying" African natives for the purpose of converting them to Christianity. There stands in the church all year round a small box with a slot for money, decorated with a black figurine, and into this box the villagers drop their francs. During the *carnaval* which

---

[4]James Joyce (1882–1941), Irish novelist. The allusion is to his 1922 novel *Ulysses:* "History, Stephen, [the protagonist] said, is a nightmare from which I am trying to awake." [Eds.]

COLLABORATIVE ACTIVITY

Ask your students, working in groups, to list characteristics that they believe identify an individual as an outsider on your college campus. In class discussion, consider the validity of their judgments.

precedes Lent, two village children have their faces blackened—out of which bloodless darkness their blue eyes shine like ice—and fantastic horsehair wigs are placed on their blond heads; thus disguised, they solicit among the villagers for money for the missionaries in Africa. Between the box in the church and the blackened children, the village "bought" last year six or eight African natives. This was reported to me with pride by the wife of one of the *bistro* owners and I was careful to express astonishment and pleasure at the solicitude shown by the village for the souls of black folks. The *bistro* owner's wife beamed with a pleasure far more genuine than my own and seemed to feel that I might now breathe more easily concerning the souls of at least six of my kinsmen.

I tried not to think of these so lately baptized kinsmen, of the price paid for them, or the peculiar price they themselves would pay, and said nothing about my father, who having taken his own conversion too literally never, at bottom, forgave the white world (which he described as heathen) for having saddled him with a Christ in whom, to judge at least from their treatment of him, they themselves no longer believed. I thought of white men arriving for the first time in an African village, strangers there, as I am a stranger here, and tried to imagine the astounded populace touching their hair and marveling at the color of their skin. But there is a great difference between being the first white man to be seen by Africans and being the first black man to be seen by whites. The white man takes the astonishment as tribute, for he arrives to conquer and to convert the natives, whose inferiority in relation to himself is not even to be questioned; whereas I, without a thought of conquest, find myself among a people whose culture controls me, has even, in a sense, created me, people who have cost me more in anguish and rage than they will ever know, who yet do not even know of my existence. The astonishment with which I might have greeted them, should they have stumbled into my African village a few hundred years ago, might have rejoiced their hearts. But the astonishment with which they greet me today can only poison mine. 7

And this is so despite everything I may do to feel differently, despite my friendly conversations with the *bistro* owner's wife, despite their three-year-old son who has at last become my friend, despite the *saluts* and *bonsoirs*[5] which I exchange with people as I walk, despite the fact that I know that no individual can be taken to task for what history is doing, or has done. I say that the culture of these people controls me—but they can scarcely be held responsible for European culture. America comes out of Europe, but these people 8

---

[5]"Hellos" and "good evenings." [Eds.]

have never seen America, nor have most of them seen more of Europe than the hamlet at the foot of their mountain. Yet they move with an authority which I shall never have; and they regard me, quite rightly, not only as a stranger in their village but as a suspect latecomer, bearing no credentials, to everything they have—however unconsciously—inherited.

For this village, even were it incomparably more remote and 9 incredibly more primitive, is the West, the West onto which I have been so strangely grafted. These people cannot be, from the point of view of power, strangers anywhere in the world; they have made the modern world, in effect, even if they do not know it. The most illiterate among them is related, in a way that I am not, to Dante, Shakespeare, Michelangelo, Aeschylus, Da Vinci, Rembrandt, and Racine; the cathedral at Chartres says something to them which it cannot say to me, as indeed would New York's Empire State Building, should anyone here ever see it. Out of their hymns and dances come Beethoven and Bach. Go back a few centuries and they are in their full glory—but I am in Africa, watching the conquerors arrive.

The rage of the disesteemed is personally fruitless, but it is also 10 absolutely inevitable; this rage, so generally discounted, so little understood even among the people whose daily bread it is, is one of the things that make history. Rage can only with difficulty, and never entirely, be brought under the domination of the intelligence and is therefore not susceptible to any arguments whatever. This is a fact which ordinary representatives of the *Herrenvolk*,[6] having never felt this rage and being unable to imagine, quite fail to understand. Also, rage cannot be hidden, it can only be dissembled. This dissembling deludes the thoughtless, and strengthens rage and adds, to rage, contempt. There are, no doubt, as many ways of coping with the resulting complex of tensions as there are black men in the world, but no black man can hope ever to be entirely liberated from this internal warfare—rage, dissembling, and contempt having inevitably accompanied his first realization of the power of white men. What is crucial here is that, since white men represent in the black man's world so heavy a weight, white men have for black men a reality which is far from being reciprocal; and hence all black men have toward all white men an attitude which is designed, really, either to rob the white man of the jewel of his naïveté, or else to make it cost him dear.

The black man insists, by whatever means he finds at his disposal, 11 that the white man cease to regard him as an exotic rarity and recognize him as a human being. This is a very charged and difficult

---

[6]Master race. [Eds.]

moment, for there is a great deal of will power involved in the white man's naïveté. Most people are not naturally reflective any more than they are naturally malicious, and the white man prefers to keep the black man at a certain human remove because it is easier for him thus to preserve his simplicity and avoid being called to account for crimes committed by his forefathers, or his neighbors. He is inescapably aware, nevertheless, that he is in a better position in the world than black men are, nor can he quite put to death the suspicion that he is hated by black men therefore. He does not wish to be hated, neither does he wish to change places, and at this point in his uneasiness he can scarcely avoid having recourse to those legends which white men have created about black men, the most usual effect of which is that the white man finds himself enmeshed, so to speak, in his own language which describes hell, as well as the attributes which lead one to hell, as being as black as night.

Every legend, moreover, contains its residuum of truth, and the root function of language is to control the universe by describing it. It is of quite considerable significance that black men remain, in the imagination, and in overwhelming numbers in fact, beyond the disciplines of salvation; and this despite the fact that the West has been "buying" African natives for centuries. There is, I should hazard, an instantaneous necessity to be divorced from this so visibly unsaved stranger, in whose heart, moreover, one cannot guess what dreams of vengeance are being nourished; and, at the same time, there are few things on earth more attractive than the idea of the unspeakable liberty which is allowed the unredeemed. When, beneath the black mask, a human being begins to make himself felt one cannot escape a certain awful wonder as to what kind of human being it is. What one's imagination makes of other people is dictated, of course, by the laws of one's own personality and it is one of the ironies of black-white relations that, by means of what the white man imagines the black man to be, the black man is enabled to know who the white man is. 12

I have said, for example, that I am as much a stranger in this village today as I was the first summer I arrived, but this is not quite true. The villagers wonder less about the texture of my hair than they did then, and wonder rather more about me. And the fact that their wonder now exists on another level is reflected in their attitudes and in their eyes. There are the children who make those delightful, hilarious, sometimes astonishingly grave overtures of friendship in the unpredictable fashion of children; other children, having been taught that the devil is a black man, scream in genuine anguish as I approach. Some of the older women never pass without a friendly greeting, never pass, indeed, if it seems that they will be able to engage me in 13 conversation; other women look down or look away or rather con-temptuously smirk. Some of the men drink with me and suggest that I learn how to ski—partly, I gather, because they cannot imagine what I would look like on skis—and want to know if I am married, and ask questions about my *métier*.[7] But some of the men have accused *le sale nègre*[8]—behind my back—of stealing wood and there is already in the eyes of some of them that peculiar, intent, paranoiac male-volence which one sometimes surprises in the eyes of American white men when, out walking with their Sunday girl, they see a Negro male approach.

There is a dreadful abyss between the streets of this village and   14 the streets of the city in which I was born, between the children who shout *Neger!* today and those who shouted *Nigger!* yesterday—the abyss is experience, the American experience. The syllable hurled behind me today expresses, above all, wonder: I am a stranger here. But I am not a stranger in America and the same syllable riding on the American air expresses the war my presence has occasioned in the American soul.

For this village brings home to me this fact: that there was a day,   15 and not really a very distant day, when Americans were scarcely Americans at all but discontented Europeans, facing a great uncon-quered continent and strolling, say, into a marketplace and seeing black men for the first time. The shock this spectacle afforded is suggested, surely, by the promptness with which they decided that these black men were not really men but cattle. It is true that the necessity on the part of the settlers of the New World of reconciling their moral assumptions with the fact—and the necessity—of slavery enhanced immensely the charm of this idea, and it is also true that this idea expresses, with a truly American bluntness, the attitude which to varying extents all masters have had toward all slaves.

But between all former slaves and slave-owners and the drama   16 which begins for Americans over three hundred years ago at James-town,[9] there are at least two differences to be observed. The American Negro slave could not suppose, for one thing, as slaves in past epochs had supposed and often done, that he would ever be able to wrest the power from his master's hands. This was a supposition which the modern era, which was to bring about such vast changes in the aims and dimensions of power, put to death; it only begins, in unprec-edented fashion, and with dreadful implications, to be resurrected today. But even had this supposition persisted with undiminished

---

[7]Trade; line of work. [Eds.]
[8]The dirty Negro. [Eds.]
[9]First successful English settlement in North America (1607) [Eds.]

force, the American Negro slave could not have used it to lend his condition dignity, for the reason that this supposition rests on another: that the slave in exile yet remains related to his past, has some means—if only in memory— of revering and sustaining the forms of his former life, is able, in short, to maintain his identity.

This was not the case with the American Negro slave. He is unique 17 among the black men of the world in that his past was taken from him, almost literally, at one blow. One wonders what on earth the first slave found to say to the first dark child he bore. I am told that there are Haitians able to trace their ancestry back to African kings, but any American Negro wishing to go back so far will find his journey through time abruptly arrested by the signature on the bill of sale which served as the entrance paper for his ancestor. At the time—to say nothing of the circumstances—of the enslavement of the captive black man who was to become the American Negro, there was not the remotest possibility that he would ever take power from his master's hands. There was no reason to suppose that his situation would ever change, nor was there, shortly, anything to indicate that his situation had ever been different. It was his necessity, in the words of E. Franklin Frazier,[10] to find a "motive for living under American culture or die." The identity of the American Negro comes out of this extreme situation, and the evolution of this identity was a source of the most intolerable anxiety in the minds and the lives of his masters.

For the history of the American Negro is unique also in this: that 18 the question of his humanity, and of his rights therefore as a human being, became a burning one for several generations of Americans, so burning a question that it ultimately became one of those used to divide the nation. It is out of this argument that the venom of the epithet *Nigger!* is derived. It is an argument which Europe has never had, and hence Europe quite sincerely fails to understand how or why the argument arose in the first place, why its effects are frequently disastrous and always so unpredictable, why it refuses until today to be entirely settled. Europe's black possessions remained— and do remain—in Europe's colonies, at which remove they represented no threat whatever to European identity. If they posed any problem at all for the European conscience it was a problem which remained comfortably abstract: in effect, the black man, as a *man* did not exist for Europe. But in America, even as a slave, he was an inescapable part of the general social fabric and no American could escape having an attitude toward him. Americans attempt until today to make an abstraction of the Negro, but the very nature of these

---

[10]Sociologist (1894–1962) specializing in studies of the African-American community, in particular the effects of racial prejudice. [Eds.]

abstractions reveals the tremendous effects the presence of the Negro has had on the American character.

When one considers the history of the Negro in America it is of 19 the greatest importance to recognize that the moral beliefs of a person, or a people, are never really as tenuous as life—which is not moral— very often causes them to appear; these create for them a frame of reference and a necessary hope, the hope being that when life has done its worst they will be enabled to rise above themselves and to triumph over life. Life would scarcely be bearable if this hope did not exist. Again, even when the worst has been said, to betray a belief is not by any means to have put oneself beyond its power; the betrayal of a belief is not the same thing as ceasing to believe. If this were not so there would be no moral standards in the world at all. Yet one must also recognize that morality is based on ideas and that all ideas are dangerous—dangerous because ideas can only lead to action and where the action leads no man can say. And dangerous in this respect: that confronted with the impossibility of remaining faithful to one's beliefs, and the equal impossibility of becoming free of them, one can be driven to the most inhuman excesses. The ideas on which American beliefs are based are not, though Americans often seem to think so, ideas which originated in America. They came out of Europe. And the establishment of democracy on the American continent was scarcely as radical a break with the past as was the necessity, which Americans faced, of broadening this concept to include black men.

This was, literally, a hard necessity. It was impossible, for one 20 thing, for Americans to abandon their beliefs, not only because these beliefs alone seemed able to justify the sacrifices they had endured and the blood that they had spilled, but also because these beliefs afforded them their only bulwark against a moral chaos as absolute as the physical chaos of the continent it was their destiny to conquer. But in the situation in which Americans found themselves, these beliefs threatened an idea which, whether or not one likes to think so, is the very warp and woof[11] of the heritage of the West, the idea of white supremacy.

Americans have made themselves notorious by the shrillness and 21 the brutality with which they have insisted on this idea, but they did not invent it; and it has escaped the world's notice that those very excesses of which Americans have been guilty imply a certain, unprecedented uneasiness over the idea's life and power, if not, indeed, the idea's validity. The idea of white supremacy rests simply on the fact that white men are the creators of civilization (the present civilization,

---

[11]Base; foundation; underlying structure. [Eds.]

which is the only one that matters; all previous civilizations are simply "contributions" to our own) and are therefore civilization's guardians and defenders. Thus it was impossible for Americans to accept the black man as one of themselves, for to do so was to jeopardize their status as white men. But not so to accept him was to deny his human reality, his human weight and complexity, and the strain of denying the overwhelmingly undeniable forced Americans into rationalizations so fantastic that they approached the pathological.

At the root of the American Negro problem is the necessity of the American white man to find a way of living with the Negro in order to be able to live with himself. And the history of this problem can be reduced to the means used by Americans—lynch law and law, segregation and legal acceptance, terrorization and concession—either to come to terms with this necessity, or to find a way around it, or (most usually) to find a way of doing both these things at once. The resulting spectacle, at once foolish and dreadful, led someone to make the quite accurate observation that "the Negro-in-America is a form of insanity which overtakes white men." 22

In this long battle, a battle by no means finished, the unforeseeable effects of which will be felt by many future generations, the white man's motive was the protection of his identity; the black man was motivated by the need to establish an identity. And despite the terrorization which the Negro in America endured and endures sporadically until today, despite the cruel and totally inescapable ambivalence of his status in his country, the battle for his identity has long ago been won. He is not a visitor to the West, but a citizen there, an American; as American as the Americans who despise him, the Americans who fear him, the Americans who love him—the Americans who became less than themselves, or rose to be greater than themselves by virtue of the fact that the challenge he represented was inescapable. He is perhaps the only black man in the world whose relationship to white men is more terrible, more subtle, and more meaningful than the relationship of bitter possessed to uncertain possessors. His survival depended, and his development depends, on his ability to turn his peculiar status in the Western world to his own advantage and, it may be, to the very great advantage of that world. It remains for him to fashion out of his experience that which will give him sustenance, and a voice. 23

The cathedral at Chartres, I have said, says something to the people of this village which it cannot say to me; but it is important to understand that this cathedral says something to me which it cannot say to them. Perhaps they are struck by the power of the spires, the glory of the windows; but they have known God, after all, longer than I have known him, and in a different way, and I am terrified by the slippery bottomless well to be found in the crypt, 24 down which heretics were hurled to death, and by the obscene, inescapable gargoyles jutting out of the stone and seeming to say that God and the devil can never be divorced. I doubt that the villagers think of the devil when they face a cathedral because they have never been identified with the devil. But I must accept the status which myth, if nothing else, gives me in the West before I can hope to change the myth.

Yet, if the American Negro has arrived at his identity by virtue 25 of the absoluteness of his estrangement from his past, American white men still nourish the illusion that there is some means of recovering the European innocence, of returning to a state in which black men do not exist. This is one of the greatest errors Americans can make. The identity they fought so hard to protect has, by virtue of that battle, undergone a change: Americans are as unlike any other white people in the world as it is possible to be. I do not think, for example, that it is too much to suggest that the American vision of the world—which allows so little reality, generally speaking, for any of the darker forces in human life, which tends until today to paint moral issues in glaring black and white—owes a great deal to the battle waged by Americans to maintain between themselves and black men a human separation which could not be bridged. It is only now beginning to be borne in on us—very faintly, it must be admitted, very slowly, and very much against our will—that this vision of the world is dangerously inaccurate, and perfectly useless. For it protects our moral high-mindedness at the terrible expense of weakening our grasp of reality. People who shut their eyes to reality simply invite their own destruction, and anyone who insists on remaining in a state of innocence long after that innocence is dead turns himself into a monster.

The time has come to realize that the interracial drama acted out 26 on the American continent has not only created a new black man, it has created a new white man, too. No road whatever will lead Americans back to the simplicity of this European village where white men still have the luxury of looking on me as a stranger. I am not, really, a stranger any longer for any American alive. One of the things that distinguishes Americans from other people is that no other people has ever been so deeply involved in the lives of black men, and vice versa. This fact faced, with all its implications, it can be seen that the history of the American Negro problem is not merely shameful, it is also something of an achievement. For even when the worst has been said, it must also be added that the perpetual challenge posed by this problem was always, somehow, perpetually met. It is precisely this black-white experience which may prove of indispensable value to us in the world we face today. This world is white no longer, and it will never be white again.

WRITING SUGGESTIONS

1. Compare Malcolm X's discussion of American history and its results in "A Homemade Education" (Chapter 3) to Baldwin's. What similar conclusions do they come to? Do you find any important differences in their views?

2. How might Zora Neale Hurston ("How It Feels to Be Colored Me", page 491) respond to Baldwin's essay?

RESPONDING TO READING

1. How does Baldwin's detailed description of the "tiny Swiss village" provide an appropriate introduction to the true subject of his essay? Have you ever felt like a stranger in the village?   **2.** What besides color does Baldwin believe has set blacks like himself apart in their own society? What historical forces have contributed to the problem? Does he believe these historical forces can be overcome? Do you?   **3.** In paragraph 7 Baldwin discusses the great difference between being the first white to be seen by Africans and being the first black to be seen by whites. Do you think his interpretation of this difference is accurate?

A Small Place

JAMAICA KINCAID

Jamaica Kincaid (1949–   ), born Elaine Potter Richardson in Antigua, West Indies, and now a resident of Bennington, Vermont, writes short stories and novels. Her story collection *At the Bottom of the River* (1983) and her novel *Annie John* (1985) focus on life in Antigua; *Lucy* (1990), her latest book, is about an island girl who comes to the mainland and struggles to become an artist. In a *Boston Globe* interview, Kincaid says of her homeland, "When I'm in the place where I'm from, I can't really think . . . I just absorb it, take it all in. Then I come back and take it out and unpack it and walk through it." The following excerpt is from *A Small Place* (1988), an essay in book form.

If you go to Antigua as a tourist, this is what you will see. If you 1
come by aeroplane, you will land at the V. C. Bird International Airport. Vere Cornwall (V. C.) Bird is the Prime Minister of Antigua. You may be the sort of tourist who would wonder why a Prime Minister would want an airport named after him—why not a school, why not a hospital, why not some great public monument? You are a tourist and you have not yet seen a school in Antigua, you have not yet seen the hospital in Antigua, you have not yet seen a public monument in Antigua. As your plane descends to land, you might say, What a beautiful island Antigua is—more beautiful than any of the other islands you have seen, and they were very beautiful, in their way, but they were much too green, much too lush with vegetation, which indicated to you, the tourist, that they got quite a bit of rainfall, and rain is the very thing that you, just now, do not want, for you are thinking of the hard and cold and long days you spent

working in North America (or, worse, Europe), earning some money so that you could stay in this place (Antigua) where the sun always shines and where the climate is deliciously hot and dry for the four to ten days you are going to be staying there; and since you are on your holiday, since you are a tourist, the thought of what it might be like for someone who had to live day in, day out in a place that suffers constantly from drought, and so has to watch carefully every drop of fresh water used (while at the same time surrounded by a sea and an ocean—the Caribbean Sea on one side, the Atlantic Ocean on the other), must never cross your mind.

You disembark from your plane. You go through customs. Since 2 you are a tourist, a North American or European—to be frank, white—and not an Antiguan black returning to Antigua from Europe or North America with cardboard boxes of much needed cheap clothes and food for relatives, you move through customs swiftly, you move through customs with ease. Your bags are not searched. You emerge from customs into the hot, clean air: immediately you feel cleansed, immediately you feel blessed (which is to say special); you feel free. You see a man, a taxi driver; you ask him to take you to your destination; he quotes you a price. You immediately think that the price is in the local currency, for you are a tourist and you are familiar with these things (rates of exchange) and you feel even more free, for things seem so cheap, but then your driver ends by saying, "In U.S. currency." You may say, "Hmmmm, do you have a formal sheet that lists official prices and destinations?" Your driver obeys the law and shows you the sheet, and he apologizes for the incredible mistake he has made in quoting you a price off the top of his head which is so vastly different (favoring him) from the one listed. You are driven to your hotel by this taxi driver in his taxi, a brand-new Japanese-made vehicle. The road on which you are travelling is a very bad road, very much in need of repair. You are feeling wonderful, so you say, "Oh what a marvellous change these bad roads are from the splendid highways I am used to in North America." (Or, worse, Europe.) Your driver is reckless; he is a dangerous man who drives in the middle of the road when he thinks no other cars are coming in the opposite direction, passes other cars on blind curves that run uphill, drives at sixty miles an hour on narrow, curving roads when the road sign, a rusting, beat-up thing left over from colonial days, says 40 MPH. This might frighten you (you are on your holiday; you are a tourist); this might excite you (you are on your holiday; you are a tourist), though if you are from New York and take taxis you are used to this style of driving: most of the taxi drivers in New York are from places in the world like this. You are looking out the window (because you want to get your money's worth); you notice that all the cars you see are

ADDITIONAL QUESTIONS FOR RESPONDING TO READING

1. What roles does the tourist play for the country that she or he visits? For the inhabitants of the country?
2. How are the lives of Antiguans fundamentally different from the lives of tourists? Why should this matter to us as Americans?
3. How does Kincaid's tone affect you? What does it reveal about her attitude toward her readers? Does she, for instance, see her readers as people like herself or as "tourists"?
4. What does it really mean to be a tourist? Is it possible to be a tourist in your own neighborhood or city?

brand-new, or almost brand-new, and that they are all Japanese-made. There are no American cars in Antigua—no new ones, at any rate; none that were manufactured in the last ten years. You continue to look at the cars and say to yourself, Why, they look brand-new, but they have an awful sound, like an old car—a very old, dilapidated car. How to account for that? Well, possibly it's because they use leaded gasoline in these brand-new cars whose engines were built to use non-leaded gasoline, but you musn't ask the person driving the car if this is so, because he or she has never heard of unleaded gasoline. You look closely at the car; you see that it's a model of a Japanese car that you might hesitate to buy; it's a model that's very expensive; it's a model that's quite impractical for a person who has to work as hard as you do and who watches every penny you earn so that you can afford this holiday you are on. How do they afford such a car? And do they live in a luxurious house to match such a car? Well, no. You will be surprised, then, to see that most likely the person driving this brand-new car filled with the wrong gas lives in a house that, in comparison, is far beneath the status of the car; and if you were to ask why you would be told that the banks are encouraged by the government to make loans available for cars, but loans for houses not so easily available; and if you ask again why, you will be told that the two main car dealerships in Antigua are owned in part or outright by ministers in government. Oh, but you are on holiday and the sight of these brand-new cars driven by people who may or may not have really passed their driving test (there was once a scandal about driving licenses for sale) would not really stir up these thoughts in you. You pass a building sitting in a sea of dust and you think, It's some latrines for people just passing by, but when you look again you see the building has written on it PIGOTT'S SCHOOL. You pass the hospital, the Holberton Hospital, and how wrong you are not to think about this, for though you are a tourist on your holiday, what if your heart should miss a few beats? What if a blood vessel in your neck should break? What if one of those people driving those brand-new cars filled with the wrong gas fails to pass safely while going uphill on a curve and you are in the car going in the opposite direction? Will you be comforted to know that the hospital is staffed with doctors that no actual Antiguan trusts; that Antiguans always say about the doctors, "I don't want them near me"; that Antiguans refer to them not as doctors but as "the three men" (there are three of them); that when the Minister of Health himself doesn't feel well he takes the first plane to New York to see a real doctor; that if any one of the ministers in government needs medical care he flies to New York to get it?

It's a good thing that you brought your own books with you, for 3 you couldn't just go to the library and borrow some. Antigua used to have a splendid library, but in The Earthquake (everyone talks about it that way—The Earthquake; we Antiguans, for I am one, have a great sense of things, and the more meaningful the thing, the more meaningless we make it) the library building was damaged. This was in 1974, and soon after that a sign was placed on the front of the building saying, THIS BUILDING WAS DAMAGED IN THE EARTHQUAKE OF 1974. REPAIRS ARE PENDING. The sign hangs there, and hangs there more than a decade later, with its unfulfilled promise of repair, and you might see this as a sort of quaintness on the part of these islanders, these people descended from slaves—what a strange, unusual perception of time they have. REPAIRS ARE PENDING, and here it is many years later, but perhaps in a world that is twelve miles long and nine miles wide (the size of Antigua) twelve years and twelve minutes and twelve days are all the same. The library is one of those splendid old buildings from colonial times, and the sign telling of the repairs is a splendid old sign from colonial times. Not very long after The Earthquake Antigua got its independence from Britain, making Antigua a state in its own right, and Antiguans are so proud of this that each year, to mark the day, they go to church and thank God, a British God, for this. But you should not think of the confusion that must lie in all that and you must not think of the damaged library. You have brought your own books with you, and among them is one of those new books about economic history, one of those books explaining how the West (meaning Europe and North America after its conquest and settlement by Europeans) got rich: the West got rich not from the free (free—in this case meaning got-for-nothing) and then undervalued labour, for generations, of the people like me you see walking around you in Antigua but from the ingenuity of small shopkeepers in Sheffield and Yorkshire and Lancashire, or wherever; and what a great part the invention of the wristwatch played in it, for there was nothing noble-minded men could not do when they discovered they could slap time on their wrists just like that (isn't that the last straw; for not only did we have to suffer the unspeakableness of slavery, but the satisfaction to be had from "We made you bastards rich" is taken away, too), and so you needn't let that slightly funny feeling you have from time to time about exploitation, oppression, domination develop into full-fledged unease, discomfort; you could ruin your holiday. They are not responsible for what you have; you owe them nothing; in fact, you did them a big favor, and you can provide one hundred examples. For here you are now, passing by Government House. And here you are now, passing by the Prime Minister's Office and the Parliament Building, and overlooking these, with a splendid view of St. John's Harbour, the American Embassy. If it were not for you, they would not have Government

House, and Prime Minister's Office, and Parliament Building and embassy of powerful country. Now you are passing a mansion, an extraordinary house painted the color of old cow dung, with more aerials and antennas attached to it than you will see even at the American Embassy. The people who live in this house are a merchant family who came to Antigua from the Middle East less than twenty years ago. When this family first came to Antigua, they sold dry goods door to door from suitcases they carried on their backs. Now they own a lot of Antigua; they regularly lend money to the government, they build enormous (for Antigua), ugly (for Antigua), concrete buildings in Antigua's capital, St. John's, which the government then rents for huge sums of money; a member of their family is the Antiguan Ambassador to Syria; Antiguans hate them. Not far from this mansion is another mansion, the home of a drug smuggler. Everybody knows he's a drug smuggler, and if just as you were driving by he stepped out of his door your driver might point him out to you as the notorious person that he is, for this drug smuggler is so rich people say he buys cars in tens—ten of this one, ten of that one—and that he bought a house (another mansion) near Five Islands, contents included, with cash he carried in a suitcase: three hundred and fifty thousand American dollars, and, to the surprise of the seller of the house, lots of American dollars were left over. Overlooking the drug smuggler's mansion is yet another mansion, and leading up to it is the best paved road in all of Antigua—even better than the road that was paved for the Queen's visit in 1985 (when the Queen came, all the roads that she would travel on were paved anew, so that the Queen might have been left with the impression that riding in a car in Antigua was a pleasant experience). In this mansion lives a woman sophisticated people in Antigua call Evita. She is a notorious woman. She's young and beautiful and the girlfriend of somebody very high up in the government. Evita is notorious because her relationship with this high government official has made her the owner of boutiques and property and given her a say in cabinet meetings, and all sorts of other privileges such a relationship would bring a beautiful young woman.

Oh, but by now you are tired of all this looking, and you want to reach your destination—your hotel, your room. You long to refresh yourself; you long to eat some nice lobster, some nice local food. You take a bath, you brush your teeth. You get dressed again; as you get dressed, you look out the window. That water—have you ever seen anything like it? Far out, to the horizon, the colour of the water is navy-blue; nearer, the water is the colour of the North American sky. From there to the shore, the water is pale, silvery, clear, so clear that you can see its pinkish-white sand bottom. Oh, what beauty! Oh, what beauty! You have never seen anything like this. You are so excited. You breathe shallow. You breathe deep. You see a beautiful boy skimming the water, godlike, on a Windsurfer. You see an incredibly unattractive, fat, pastrylike-fleshed woman enjoying a walk on the beautiful sand, with a man, an incredibly unattractive, fat, pastrylike-fleshed man; you see the pleasure they're taking in their surroundings. Still standing, looking out the window, you see yourself lying on the beach, enjoying the amazing sun (a sun so powerful and yet so beautiful, the way it is always overhead as if on permanent guard, ready to stamp out any cloud that dares to darken and so empty rain on you and ruin your holiday; a sun that is your personal friend). You see yourself taking a walk on that beach, you see yourself meeting new people (only they are new in a very limited way, for they are people just like you). You see yourself eating some delicious, locally grown food. You see yourself, you see yourself . . . You must not wonder what exactly happened to the contents of your lavatory when you flushed it. You must not wonder where your bathwater went when you pulled out the stopper. You must not wonder what happened when you brushed your teeth. Oh, it might all end up in the water you are thinking of taking a swim in; the contents of your lavatory might, just might, graze gently against your ankle as you wade carefree in the water, for you see, in Antigua, there is no proper sewage-disposal system. But the Caribbean Sea is very big and the Atlantic Ocean is even bigger; it would amaze even you to know the number of black slaves this ocean has swallowed up. When you sit down to eat your delicious meal, it's better that you don't know that most of what you are eating came off a plane from Miami. And before it got on a plane in Miami, who knows where it came from? A good guess is that it came from a place like Antigua first, where it was grown dirt-cheap, went to Miami, and came back. There is a world of something in this, but I can't go into it right now.

The thing you have always suspected about yourself the minute   5
you become a tourist is true: A tourist is an ugly human being. You are not an ugly person all the time; you are not an ugly person ordinarily; you are not an ugly person day to day. From day to day, you are a nice person. From day to day, all the people who are supposed to love you on the whole do. From day to day, as you walk down a busy street in the large and modern and prosperous city in which you work and live, dismayed, puzzled (a cliché, but only a cliché can explain you) at how alone you feel in this crowd, how awful it is to go unnoticed, how awful it is to go unloved, even as you are surrounded by more people than you could possibly get to know in a lifetime that lasted for millennia, and then out of the corner of your eye you see someone looking at you and absolute pleasure is written

TEACHING STRATEGIES

1. Remind students that the author's narrative style and tone will profoundly influence their perceptions.
2. Instruct students to question the use of parentheses throughout the essay.
3. Discuss the following aspects of the essay:

Paragraph 1: Explain the fast-paced repetition of the phrase "you have not yet seen . . . in Antigua." What effect does this have on the tone of the passage?

Paragraph 4: When Kincaid interprets the tourist's thoughts, what effect does her interpretation have on readers? How do we begin to view this person, and why is this view important?

Paragraph 4, middle: Note the repetition of "You see yourself," followed by an ellipsis that marks a sudden change in tone. What does Kincaid then reveal? (A contrast between the idyllic and reality.)

Paragraph 5: Essentially, why is a tourist an "ugly human being"? Do you agree with Kincaid here?

all over that person's face, and then you realize that you are not as revolting a presence as you think you are (for that look just told you so). And so, ordinarily, you are a nice person, an attractive person, a person capable of drawing to yourself the affection of other people (people just like you), a person at home in your own skin (sort of; I mean, in a way; I mean, your dismay and puzzlement are natural to you, because people like you just seem to be like that, and so many of the things people like you find admirable about yourselves—the things you think about, the things you think really define you—seem rooted in these feelings): a person at home in your own house (and all its nice house things), with its nice back yard (and its nice back-yard things), at home on your street, your church, in community activities, your job, at home with your family, your relatives, your friends—you are a whole person. But one day, when you are sitting somewhere, alone in that crowd, and that awful feeling of displacedness comes over you, and really, as an ordinary person you are not well equipped to look too far inward and set yourself aright, because being ordinary is already so taxing, and being ordinary takes all you have out of you, and though the words "I must get away" do not actually pass across your lips, you make a leap from being that nice blob just sitting like a boob in your amniotic sac of the modern experience to being a person visiting heaps of death and ruin and feeling alive and inspired at the sight of it; to being a person lying on some faraway beach, your stilled body stinking and glistening in the sand, looking like something first forgotten, then remembered, then not important enough to go back for; to being a person marvelling at the harmony (ordinarily, what you would say is the backwardness) and the union these other people (and they are other people) have with nature. And you look at the things they can do with a piece of ordinary cloth, the things they fashion out of cheap, vulgarly colored (to you) twine, the way they squat down over a hole they have made in the ground, the hole itself is something to marvel at, and since you are being an ugly person, this ugly but joyful thought will swell inside you: their ancestors were not clever in the way yours were and not ruthless in the way yours were, for then would it not be you who would be in harmony with nature and backwards in that charming way? An ugly thing, that is what you are when you become a tourist, an ugly, empty thing, a stupid thing, a piece of rubbish pausing here and there to gaze at this and taste that, and it will never occur to you that the people who inhabit the place in which you have just paused cannot stand you, that behind their closed doors they laugh at your strangeness (you do not look the way they look); the physical sight of you does not please them; you have bad manners (it is their custom to eat their food with their hands; you try eating their way, you look silly; you try eating the way you always eat, you look silly); they do not like the way you speak (you have an accent); they collapse helpless from laughter, mimicking the way they imagine you must look as you carry out some everyday bodily function. They do not like you. *They do not like me!* That thought never actually occurs to you. Still, you feel a little uneasy. Still, you feel a little foolish. Still, you feel a little out of place. But the banality of your own life is very real to you; it drove you to this extreme, spending your days and nights in the company of people who despise you, people you do not like really, people you would not want to have as your actual neighbour. And so you must devote yourself to puzzling out how much of what you are told is really, really true (Is ground-up bottle glass in peanut sauce really a delicacy around here, or will it do just what you think ground-up bottle glass will do? Is this rare, multicolored, snout-mouthed fish really an aphrodisiac, or will it cause you to fall asleep permanently?). Oh, the hard work all of this is, and is it any wonder, then, that on your return home you feel the need for a long rest, so that you can recover from your life as a tourist?

That the native does not like the tourist is not hard to explain. 6 For every native of every place is a potential tourist, and every tourist is a native of somewhere. Every native everywhere lives a life of overwhelming and crushing banality and boredom and desperation and depression, and every deed, good and bad, is an attempt to forget this. Every native would like to find a way out, every native would like a rest, every native would like a tour. But some natives—most natives in the world—cannot go anywhere. They are too poor. They are too poor to go anywhere. They are too poor to escape the reality of their lives; and they are too poor to live properly in the place where they live, which is the very place you, the tourist, want to go—so when the natives see you, the tourist, they envy you, they envy your ability to leave your own banality and boredom, they envy your ability to turn their own banality and boredom into a source of pleasure for yourself.

RESPONDING TO READING

1. How would you characterize Kincaid's attitude toward the tourists who visit Antigua? Does her essay convince you that this attitude is justified?   **2.** In what sense does Kincaid portray herself and her fellow Antiguans as outsiders in their own country? Do you think the word *tourist* is meant to be taken figuratively as well as literally? Have you ever felt like a tourist?   **3.** Why do you think Kincaid chooses to speak directly to her readers ("You are a tourist. . .") instead of using third person throughout? What effect does this strategy have on you?

WRITING SUGGESTION

Write a travel brochure for Antigua. Make sure your tone is positive and inviting, and remember to minimize or ignore negative aspects of island life.

ANSWERS TO RESPONDING TO READING

1. Kincaid sees tourists as ignorant, selfish pleasure seekers looking only for self-fulfillment; she also characterizes them as believing themselves to be racially superior, as in the archetypal master-servant relationship.
2. The natives suffer from a lack of basic necessities because the government's attention to the tourist trade supercedes its concern for the welfare of its citizens; the comfort of the rich white visitors is the government's first priority. The entire economy is therefore dependent on the whims of foreigners.
3. This stylistic device keeps readers at a distance (and at times makes Kincaid's essay read like an attack on readers).

The Arab World

EDWARD T. HALL

Edward T. Hall (1914–   ) was born in Missouri. Trained as an anthropologist, he has taught at several colleges and universities in the United States, and his field research has taken him to Micronesia, the American Southwest, and Europe. Hall's essays about culture and society have been collected in such books as *The Silent Language* (1959), *The Man Power Potential in Our Ethnic Groups* (1967), and *Beyond Culture* (1976). In "The Arab World," excerpted from *The Hidden Dimension* (1966), Hall explores cultural differences between the ways Arabs and Americans perceive the world.

In spite of over two thousand years of contact, Westerners and Arabs still do not understand each other. Proxemic[1] research reveals some insights into this difficulty. Americans in the Middle East are immediately struck by two conflicting sensations. In public they are compressed and overwhelmed by smells, crowding, and high noise levels; in Arab homes Americans are apt to rattle around, feeling exposed and often somewhat inadequate because of too much space! (The Arab houses and apartments of the middle and upper classes which Americans stationed abroad commonly occupy are much larger than the dwellings such Americans usually inhabit.) Both the high sensory stimulation which is experienced in public places and the basic insecurity which comes from being in a dwelling that is too large provide Americans with an introduction to the sensory world of the Arab.

Behavior in Public

Pushing and shoving in public places is characteristic of Middle Eastern culture. Yet it is not entirely what Americans think it is (being pushy and rude) but stems from a different set of assumptions concerning not only the relations between people but how one experiences the body as well. Paradoxically, Arabs consider northern Europeans and Americans pushy, too. This was very puzzling to me when I started investigating these two views. How could Americans who stand aside and avoid touching be considered pushy? I used to ask Arabs to explain this paradox. None of my subjects was able to tell me specifically what particulars of American behavior were

[1]Proxemics is the study of human beings' and animals' spatial requirements and the effects of population density on behavior, communication, and social relationships. [Eds.]

responsible, yet they all agreed that the impression was widespread among Arabs. After repeated unsuccessful attempts to gain insight into the cognitive world of the Arab on this particular point, I filed it away as a question that only time would answer. When the answer came, it was because of a seemingly inconsequential annoyance.

While waiting for a friend in a Washington, D.C., hotel lobby and wanting to be both visible and alone, I had seated myself in a solitary chair outside the normal stream of traffic. In such a setting most Americans follow a rule, which is all the more binding because we seldom think about it, that can be stated as follows: as soon as a person stops or is seated in a public place, there balloons around him a small sphere of privacy which is considered inviolate. The size of the sphere varies with the degree of crowding, the age, sex, and the importance of the person, as well as the general surroundings. Anyone who enters this zone and stays there is intruding. In fact, a stranger who intrudes, even for a specific purpose, acknowledges the fact that he has intruded by beginning his request with "Pardon me, but can you tell me . . . ?"

To continue, as I waited in the deserted lobby, a stranger walked up to where I was sitting and stood close enough so that not only could I easily touch him but I could even hear him breathing. In addition, the dark mass of his body filled the peripheral field of vision on my left side. If the lobby had been crowded with people, I would have understood his behavior, but in an empty lobby his presence made me exceedingly uncomfortable. Feeling annoyed by this intrusion, I moved my body in such a way as to communicate annoyance. Strangely enough, instead of moving away, my actions seemed only to encourage him, because he moved even closer. In spite of the temptation to escape the annoyance, I put aside thoughts of abandoning my post, thinking, "To hell with it. Why should I move? I was here first and I'm not going to let this fellow drive me out even if he is a boor." Fortunately, a group of people soon arrived whom my tormentor immediately joined. Their mannerisms explained his behavior, for I knew from both speech and gestures that they were Arabs. I had not been able to make this crucial identification by looking at my subject when he was alone because he wasn't talking and he was wearing American clothes.

In describing the scene later to an Arab colleague, two contrasting patterns emerged. My concept and my feelings about my own circle of privacy in a "public" place immediately struck my Arab friend as strange and puzzling. He said, "After all, it's a public place, isn't it?" Pursuing this line of inquiry, I found that an Arab thought I had no rights whatsoever by virtue of occupying a given spot; neither my place nor my body was inviolate! For the Arab, there is no such thing

3

4

5

TEACHING STRATEGY

Discuss the following with your students:

Paragraph 2: How do Arabs view Americans' public behavior? Why is Hall confused by this view?

Paragraph 4: What purpose does the incident Hall describes serve in the essay?

Paragraph 6: What is the primary difference between Arabs' and Americans' concept of the right to space while one is in motion?

Paragraph 8: How does Hall account for the Arabs' lack of concern for "a private zone outside the body"?

Paragraph 14: This obsession with smell would no doubt strike Westerners as strangely humorous; however, what in Hall's discussion helps us to make sense of this phenomenon?

Paragraph 20: How do Americans commonly respond when altercations arise in public? Why do Americans hate to become involved?

Paragraph 23: How would you construct a typical American hierarchy of loyalties? Would it be different from the Arabs'? If so, how?

COLLABORATIVE ACTIVITY

Begin by introducing students to the ongoing conflict between Korean merchants and African-American customers in some New York City neighborhoods. Explain how these conflicts are in part related to proxemics: when Korean cashiers put money down on the counter instead of handing it to the customers and when they avoid smiles and eye contact, African-Americans are insulted. Koreans explain that their actions are consistent with their cultural norms, but customers feel they are being treated rudely.

Divide students into small groups, and have two students in each group take the parts of cashier and customer while the remaining students act as spectator and secretary. How can the two sides avoid hurt feelings? Anger? Physical violence? Discuss the groups' findings with the whole class.

as an intrusion in public. Public means public. With this insight, a great range of Arab behavior that had been puzzling, annoying, and sometimes even frightening began to make sense. I learned, for example, that if *A* is standing on a street corner and *B* wants his spot, *B* is within his rights if he does what he can to make *A* uncomfortable enough to move. In Beirut only the hardy sit in the last row in a movie theater, because there are usually standees who want seats and who push and shove and make such a nuisance that most people give up and leave. Seen in this light, the Arab who "intruded" on my space in the hotel lobby had apparently selected it for the very reason I had: it was a good place to watch two doors and the elevator. My show of annoyance, instead of driving him away, had only encouraged him. He thought he was about to get me to move.

Another silent source of friction between Americans and Arabs   6
is in an area that Americans treat very informally—the manners and rights of the road. In general, in the United States we tend to defer to the vehicle that is bigger, more powerful, faster, and heavily laden. While a pedestrian walking along a road may feel annoyed he will not think it unusual to step aside for a fast-moving automobile. He knows that because he is moving he does not have the right to the space around him that he has when he is standing still (as I was in the hotel lobby). It appears that the reverse is true with the Arabs who apparently *take on rights to space as they move.* For someone else to move into a space an Arab is also moving into is a violation of his rights. It is infuriating to an Arab to have someone else cut in front of him on the highway. It is the American's cavalier treatment of moving space that makes the Arab call him aggressive and pushy.

Concepts of Privacy

The experience described above and many others suggested to me   7
that Arabs might actually have a wholly contrasting set of assumptions concerning the body and the rights associated with it. Certainly the Arab tendency to shove and push each other in public and to feel and pinch women in public conveyances would not be tolerated by Westerners. It appeared to me that they must not have any concept of a private zone outside the body. This proved to be precisely the case.

In the Western world, the person is synonymous with an indi-   8
vidual inside a skin. And in northern Europe generally, the skin and even the clothes may be inviolate. You need permission to touch either if you are a stranger. This rule applies in some parts of France, where the mere touching of another person during an argument used to be

legally defined as assault. For the Arab the location of the person in relation to the body is quite different. The person exists somewhere down inside the body. The ego is not completely hidden, however, because it can be reached very easily with an insult. It is protected from touch but not from words. The dissociation of the body and the ego may explain why the public amputation of a thief's hand is tolerated as standard punishment in Saudi Arabia. It also sheds light on why an Arab employer living in a modern apartment can provide his servant with a room that is a boxlike cubicle approximately 5 by 10 by 4 feet in size that is not only hung from the ceiling to conserve floor space but has an opening so that the servant can be spied on.

As one might suspect, deep orientations toward the self such as the one just described are also reflected in the language. This was brought to my attention one afternoon when an Arab colleague who is the author of an Arab-English dictionary arrived in my office and threw himself into a chair in a state of obvious exhaustion. When I asked him what had been going on, he said: "I have spent the entire afternoon trying to find the Arab equivalent of the English word 'rape'. There is no such word in Arabic. All my sources, both written and spoken, can come up with no more than an approximation, such as 'He took her against her will.' There is nothing in Arabic approaching your meaning as it is expressed in that one word." 9

Differing concepts of the placement of the ego in relation to the body are not easily grasped. Once an idea like this is accepted, however, it is possible to understand many other facets of Arab life that would otherwise be difficult to explain. One of these is the high population density of Arab cities like Cairo, Beirut, and Damascus. According to the animal studies described in the earlier chapters the Arabs should be living in a perpetual behavioral sink. While it is probable that Arabs are suffering from population pressures, it is also just as possible that continued pressure from the desert has resulted in a cultural adaptation to high density which takes the form described above. Tucking the ego down inside the body shell not only would permit higher population densities but would explain why it is that Arab communications are stepped up as much as they are when compared to northern European communication patterns. Not only is the sheer noise level much higher, but the piercing look of the eyes, the touch of the hands, and the mutual bathing in the warm moist breath during conversation represent stepped-up sensory inputs to a level which many Europeans find unbearably intense. 10

The Arab dream is for lots of space in the home, which unfortunately many Arabs cannot afford. Yet when he has space, it is very different from what one finds in most American homes. Arab spaces inside their upper middle-class homes are tremendous by our stan- 11 dards. They avoid partitions because Arabs *do not like to be alone.* The form of the home is such as to hold the family together inside a single protective shell, because Arabs are deeply involved with each other. Their personalities are intermingled and take nourishment from each other like the roots and soil. If one is not with people and actively involved in some way, one is deprived of life. An old Arab saying reflects this value: "Paradise without people should not be entered because it is Hell." Therefore, Arabs in the United States often feel socially and sensorially deprived and long to be back where there is human warmth and contact.

Since there is no physical privacy as we know it in the Arab family, not even a word for privacy, one could expect that the Arabs might use some other means to be alone. Their way to be alone is to stop talking. Like the English, the Arab who shuts himself off in this way is not indicating that anything is wrong or that he is withdrawing, only that he wants to be alone with his own thoughts or does not want to be intruded upon. One subject said that her father would come and go for days at a time without saying a word, and no one in the family thought anything of it. Yet for this very reason, an Arab exchange student visiting a Kansas farm failed to pick up the cue that his American hosts were mad at him when they gave him the "silent treatment." He only discovered something was wrong when they took him to town and tried forcibly to put him on a bus to Washington, D.C., the headquarters of the exchange program responsible for his presence in the U.S. 12

Arab Personal Distances

Like everyone else in the world, Arabs are unable to formulate specific rules for their informal behavior patterns. In fact, they often deny that there are any such rules, and they are made anxious by suggestions that such is the case. Therefore, in order to determine how the Arab sets distances, I investigated the use of each sense separately. Gradually, definite and distinctive behavioral patterns began to emerge. 13

Olfaction occupies a prominent place in the Arab life. Not only is it one of the distance-setting mechanisms, but it is a vital part of a complex system of behavior. Arabs consistently breathe on people when they talk. However, this habit is more than a matter of different manners. To the Arab good smells are pleasing and a way of being involved with each other. To smell one's friend is not only nice but desirable, for to deny him your breath is to act ashamed. Americans, on the other hand, trained as they are not to breathe in people's faces, 14 automatically communicate shame in trying to be polite. Who would expect that when our highest diplomats are putting on their best manners they are also communicating shame? Yet this is what occurs constantly, because diplomacy is not only "eyeball to eyeball" but breath to breath.

By stressing olfaction, Arabs do not try to eliminate all the body's odors, only to enhance them and use them in building human relationships. Nor are they self-conscious about telling others when they don't like the way they smell. A man leaving his house in the morning may be told by his uncle, "Habib, your stomach is sour and your breath doesn't smell too good. Better not talk too close to people today." Smell is even considered in the choice of a mate. When couples are being matched for marriage, the man's go-between will sometimes ask to smell the girl, who may be turned down if she doesn't "smell nice." Arabs recognize that smell and disposition may be linked.

In a word, the olfactory boundary performs two roles in Arab life. It enfolds those who want to relate and separates those who don't. The Arab finds it essential to stay inside the olfactory zone as a means of keeping tab on changes in emotion. What is more, he may feel crowded as soon as he smells something unpleasant. While not much is known about "olfactory crowding," this may prove to be as significant as any other variable in the crowding complex because it is tied directly to the body chemistry and hence to the state of health and emotions . . . . It is not surprising, therefore, that the olfactory boundary constitutes for the Arabs an informal distance-setting mechanism in contrast to the visual mechanisms of the Westerner.

Facing and Not Facing

One of my earliest discoveries in the field of intercultural communication was that the position of the bodies of people in conversation varies with the culture. Even so, it used to puzzle me that a special Arab friend seemed unable to walk and talk at the same time. After years in the United States, he could not bring himself to stroll along, facing forward while talking. Our progress would be arrested while he edged ahead, cutting slightly in front of me and turning sideways so we could see each other. Once in this position, he would stop. His behavior was explained when I learned that for Arabs to view the other person peripherally is regarded as impolite, and to sit or stand back-to-back is considered very rude. You must be involved when interacting with Arabs who are friends.

One mistaken American notion is that Arabs conduct all conver- 18
sations at close distances. This is not the case at all. On social occasions, they may sit on opposite sides of the room and talk across the
room to each other. They are, however, apt to take offense when
Americans use what are to them ambiguous distances, such as the
four- to seven-foot social-consultative distance. They frequently complain that Americans are cold or aloof or "don't care." This was what
an elderly Arab diplomat in an American hospital thought when the
American nurses used "professional" distance. He had the feeling
that he was being ignored, that they might not take good care of him.
Another Arab subject remarked, referring to American behavior,
"What's the matter? Do I smell bad? Or are they afraid of me?"

Arabs who interact with Americans report experiencing a certain 19
flatness traceable in part to a very different use of the eyes in private
and in public as well as between friends and strangers. Even though
it is rude for a guest to walk around the Arab home eying things,
Arabs look at each other in ways which seem hostile or challenging
to the American. One Arab informant said that he was in constant
hot water with Americans because of the way he looked at them
without the slightest intention of offending. In fact, he had on several
occasions barely avoided fights with American men who apparently
thought their masculinity was being challenged because of the way
he was looking at them. As noted earlier, Arabs look each other in
the eye when talking with an intensity that makes most Americans
highly uncomfortable.

Involvement

As the reader must gather by now, Arabs are involved with each 20
other on many different levels simultaneously. Privacy in a public
place is foreign to them. Business transactions in the bazaar, for
example, are not just between buyer and seller, but are participated
in by everyone. Anyone who is standing around may join in. If a
grownup sees a boy breaking a window, he must stop him even if
he doesn't know him. Involvement and participation are expressed
in other ways as well. If two men are fighting, the crowd must intervene. On the political level, *to fail to intervene* when trouble is brewing
is to take sides, which is what our State Department always seems
to be doing. Given the fact that few people in the world today are
even remotely aware of the cultural mold that forms their thoughts,
it is normal for Arabs to view *our* behavior as though it stemmed from
their own hidden set of assumptions.

Feelings About Enclosed Spaces

In the course of my interviews with Arabs the term "tomb" kept 21 cropping up in conjunction with enclosed space. In a word, Arabs don't mind being crowded by people but hate to be hemmed in by walls. They show a much greater overt sensitivity to architectural crowding than we do. Enclosed space must meet at least three requirements that I know of if it is to satisfy the Arabs: there must be plenty of unobstructed space in which to move around (possibly as much as a thousand square feet); very high ceilings—so high in fact that they do not normally impinge on the visual field; and, in addition, there must be an unobstructed view. It was spaces such as these in which the Americans referred to earlier felt so uncomfortable. One sees the Arab's need for a view expressed in many ways, even negatively, for to cut off a neighbor's view is one of the most effective ways of spiting him. In Beirut one can see what is known locally as the "spite house." It is nothing more than a thick, four-story wall, built at the end of a long fight between neighbors, on a narrow strip of land for the express purpose of denying a view of the Mediterranean to any house built on the land behind. According to one of my informants, there is also a house on a small plot of land between Beirut and Damascus which is completely surrounded by a neighbor's wall built high enough to cut off the view from all windows.

Boundaries

Proxemic patterns tell us other things about Arab culture. For 22 example, the whole concept of the boundary as an abstraction is almost impossible to pin down. In one sense, there are no boundaries. "Edges" of town, yes, but permanent boundaries out in the country (hidden lines), no. In the course of my work with Arab subjects I had a difficult time translating our concept of a boundary into terms which could be equated with theirs. In order to clarify the distinctions between the two very different definitions, I thought it might be helpful to pinpoint acts which constituted trespass. To date, I have been unable to discover anything even remotely resembling our own legal concept of trespass.

Arab behavior in regard to their own real estate is apparently an 23 extension of, and therefore consistent with, their approach to the body. My subjects simply failed to respond whenever trespass was mentioned. They didn't seem to understand what I meant by this term. This may be explained by the fact that they organize relation-

WRITING SUGGESTION

Study the proxemics of your family or peer group, paying special attention to the roles of public and private space. Write an essay in which you present your conclusions.

ANSWERS TO RESPONDING TO READING

1. The Arab world—like the Western world—is a state of mind as well as a physical place. The concept of boundaries is alien to Arabs; rather, they establish relationships based on connections among people. Westerners, however, establish boundaries to ensure that their space is not encroached upon.
2. Failure to see differences between one's own basic assumptions and those of others leads to inevitable misunderstandings, and—as we can see from the contrast between Arab and American views in Hall's essay—to conflicts as well.
3. The source of misunderstandings is stubborn ethnocentrism on the part of all parties involved. This obstacle will be extremely difficult to overcome.

BACKGROUND ON READING

What do students know about Central America and U.S. foreign policy there? The instructor should present some background before discussing the essay.

FOR OPENERS

The following essay's descriptions may shock students' sensibilities. It may be necessary to remind them that the essay is an eye-witness account and that the writer's purpose is to reveal the truth of what she sees. Note that the writer does not offer judgments or analysis.

ships with each other according to closed systems rather than spatially. For thousands of years Moslems, Marinites, Druses, and Jews have lived in their own villages, each with strong kin affiliations. Their hierarchy of loyalties is: first to one's self, then to kinsman, townsman, or tribesman, co-religionist and/or countryman. Anyone not in these categories is a stranger. Strangers and enemies are very closely linked, if not synonymous, in Arab thought. Trespass in this context is a matter of who you are, rather than a piece of land or a space with a boundary that can be denied to anyone and everyone, friend and foe alike.

In summary, proxemic patterns differ. By examining them it is 24 possible to reveal cultural frames that determine the structure of a given people's perceptual world. Perceiving the world differently leads to differential definitions of what constitutes crowded living, different interpersonal relations, and a different approach to both local and international politics. . . .

RESPONDING TO READING

1. Is the Arab world Hall describes a physical place? Is the Western world a physical place? What characteristics define the boundaries of these two worlds? **2.** In paragraph 13 Hall says, "Like everyone else in the world, Arabs are unable to formulate specific rules for their informal behavior patterns. In fact, they often deny that there are any rules." What implications do you think this statement has for the future of relationships among individuals in culturally diverse societies? **3.** Does Hall's essay encourage you to be optimistic or pessimistic about the ability of different cultures to coexist in a single society—for example, about the possibility of peace in the Middle East?

Salvador

JOAN DIDION

With her book *Salvador*, published in 1983, Joan Didion (see also p. 54) expanded on the journalistic personal essay form. In the excerpt that follows, she captures people, places, and feelings with her reportorial eye. Didion had long been interested in Central America and had spent two weeks in El Salvador when she wrote these stark and sometimes brutal descriptions.

The three-year-old El Salvador International Airport is glassy and 1 white and splendidly isolated, conceived during the waning of the

Molina "National Transformation" as convenient less to the capital (San Salvador is forty miles away, until recently a drive of several hours) than to a central hallucination of the Molina and Romero[1] regimes, the projected beach resorts, the Hyatt, the Pacific Paradise, tennis, golf, water-skiing, condos, *Costa del Sol*; the visionary invention of a tourist industry in yet another republic where the leading natural cause of death is gastrointestinal infection. In the general absence of tourists these hotels have since been abandoned, ghost resorts on the empty Pacific beaches, and to land at this airport built to service them is to plunge directly into a state in which no ground is solid, no depth of field reliable, no perception so definite that it might not dissolve into its reverse.

The only logic is that of acquiescence. Immigration is negotiated in a thicket of automatic weapons, but by whose authority the weapons are brandished (Army or National Guard or National Police or Customs Police or Treasury Police or one of a continuing proliferation of other shadowy and overlapping forces) is a blurred point. Eye contact is avoided. Documents are scrutinized upside down. Once clear of the airport, on the new highway that slices through green hills rendered phosphorescent by the cloud cover of the tropical rainy season, one sees mainly underfed cattle and mongrel dogs and armored vehicles, vans and trucks and Cherokee Chiefs fitted with reinforced steel and bulletproof Plexiglas an inch thick. Such vehicles are a fixed feature of local life, and are popularly associated with disappearance and death. There was the Cherokee Chief seen following the Dutch television crew killed in Chalatenango province in March of 1982. There was the red Toyota three-quarter-ton pickup sighted near the van driven by the four American-Catholic workers on the night they were killed in 1980. There were, in the late spring and summer of 1982, the three Toyota panel trucks, one yellow, one blue, and one green, none bearing plates, reported present at each of the mass detentions (a "detention" is another fixed feature of local life, and often precedes a "disappearance") in the Amatepec district of San Salvador. These are the details—the models and the colors of armored vehicles, the makes and calibers of weapons, the particular methods of dismemberment and decapitation used in particular instances—on which the visitor to Salvador learns immediately to concentrate, to the exclusion of past or future concerns, as in a prolonged amnesiac fugue.

2

---

[1]Former presidents of El Salvador, Arturo Armando Molina (1972–77) and Carlos Humberto Romero (1972–79). [Eds.]

ADDITIONAL QUESTIONS FOR RESPONDING TO READING

1. Does Didion reveal any political biases in her essay? If so, what are they?
2. Why has the United States neglected to investigate the deaths of Americans?

TEACHING STRATEGY

Discuss the following with your students:

Paragraph 1: How does Didion's comment on tourism echo Jamaica Kincaid's ("A Small Place," page 510)?

Paragraph 2: To what conclusions is Didion's discussion of auto sightings meant to lead the reader?

Paragraph 5: Why do the discrepancies between agencies exist?

Paragraph 7: Who are the death squads?

Paragraph 12: Explain "the exact mechanism of terror" as Didion comes to understand it.

Terror is the given of the place. Black-and-white police cars cruise in pairs, each with the barrel of a rifle extruding from an open window. Roadblocks materialize at random, soldiers fanning out from trucks and taking positions, fingers always on triggers, safeties clicking on and off. Aim is taken as if to pass the time. Every morning *El Diario de Hoy* and *La Prensa Gráfica* carry cautionary stories. *"Una madre y sus dos hijos fueron asesinados con arma cortante (corvo) por ocho sujetos desconocidos el lunes en la noche"*: A mother and her two sons hacked to death in their beds by eight *desconocidos,* unknown men. The same morning's paper: the unidentified body of a young man, strangled, found on the shoulder of a road. Same morning, different story: the unidentified bodies of three young men, found on another road, their faces partially destroyed by bayonets, one face carved to represent a cross.

It is largely from these reports in the newspapers that the United States embassy compiles its body counts, which are transmitted to Washington in a weekly dispatch referred to by embassy people as "the grim-gram." These counts are presented in a kind of tortured code that fails to obscure what is taken for granted in El Salvador, that government forces do most of the killing. In a January 15 1982 memo to Washington, for example, the embassy issued a "guarded" breakdown on its count of 6,909 "reported" political murders between September 16 1980 and September 15 1981. Of these 6,909, according to the memo, 922 were "believed committed by security forces," 952 "believed committed by leftist terrorists," 136 "believed committed by rightist terrorists," and 4,889 "committed by unknown assailants," the famous *desconocidos* favored by those San Salvador newspapers still publishing. (The figures actually add up not to 6,909 but to 6,899, leaving ten in a kind of official limbo.) The memo continued:

> "The uncertainty involved here can be seen in the fact that responsibility cannot be fixed in the majority of cases. We note, however, that it is generally believed in El Salvador that a large number of the unexplained killings are carried out by the security forces, officially or unofficially. The Embassy is aware of dramatic claims that have been made by one interest group or another in which the security forces figure as the primary agents of murder here. El Salvador's tangled web of attack and vengeance, traditional criminal violence and political mayhem make this an impossible charge to sustain. In saying this, however, we make no attempt to lighten the responsibility for the deaths of many hundreds, and perhaps thousands, which can be attributed to the security forces. . . ."

The body count kept by what is generally referred to in San Salvador as "the Human Rights Commission" is higher than the embassy's, and documented periodically by a photographer who goes out looking for bodies. These bodies he photographs are often broken

3

4

5

into unnatural positions, and the faces to which the bodies are attached (when they are attached) are equally unnatural, sometimes unrecognizable as human faces, obliterated by acid or beaten to a mash of misplaced ears and teeth or slashed ear to ear and invaded by insects. *"Encontrado en Antiguo Cuscatlán el día 25 de Marzo 1982: camison de dormir celeste,"* the typed caption reads on one photograph: found in Antiguo Cuscatlán March 25 1982 wearing a sky-blue night-shirt. The captions are laconic. Found in Soyapango May 21 1982. Found in Mejicanos June 11 1982. Found at El Playón May 30, 1982, white shirt, purple pants, black shoes.

The photograph accompanying that last caption shows a body with no eyes, because the vultures got to it before the photographer did. There is a special kind of practical information that the visitor to El Salvador acquires immediately, the way visitors to other places acquire information about the currency rates, the hours for the museums. In El Salvador one learns that vultures go first for the soft tissue, for the eyes, the exposed genitalia, the open mouth. One learns that an open mouth can be used to make a specific point, can be stuffed with something emblematic; stuffed, say, with a penis, or if the point has to do with land title, stuffed with some of the dirt in question. One learns that hair deteriorates less rapidly than flesh, and that a skull surrounded by a perfect corona of hair is a not uncommon sight in the body dumps.

All forensic photographs induce in the viewer a certain protective numbness, but dissociation is more difficult here. In the first place these are not, technically, "forensic" photographs, since the evidence they document will never be presented in a court of law. In the second place the disfigurement is too routine. The locations are too near, the dates too recent. There is the presence of the relatives of the disappeared: the women who sit every day in this cramped office on the grounds of the archdiocese, waiting to look at the spiral-bound photo albums in which the photographs are kept. These albums have plastic covers bearing soft-focus color photographs of young Americans in dating situation (strolling through autumn foliage on one album, recumbent in a field of daisies on another), and the women, looking for the bodies of their husbands and brothers and sisters and children, pass them from hand to hand without comment or expression.

> "One of the more shadowy elements of the violent scene here [is] the death squad: Existence of these groups has long been disputed, but not by many Salvadorans. . . . Who constitutes the death squads is yet another difficult question. We do not believe that these squads exist as permanent formations but rather as ad hoc vigilante groups that coalesce according to perceived need. Membership is also uncertain, but in addition to civilians we believe that both on- and

off-duty members of the security forces are participants. This was unofficially confirmed by right-wing spokesman Maj. Roberto D'Aubuisson who stated in an interview in early 1981 that security force members utilize the guise of the death squad when a potentially embarrassing or odious task needs to be performed."

> —From the confidential but later declassified January 15, 1982
> memo previously cited, drafted for the State Department by
> the political section at the embassy in San Salvador.

The dead and pieces of the dead turn up in El Salvador everywhere, every day, as taken for granted as in a nightmare, or a horror movie. Vultures of course suggest the presence of a body. A knot of children on the street suggests the presence of a body. Bodies turn up in the brush of vacant lots, in the garbage thrown down ravines in the richest districts, in public rest rooms, in bus stations. Some are dropped in Lake Ilopango, a few miles east of the city, and wash up near the lakeside cottages and clubs frequented by what remains in San Salvador of the sporting bourgeoisie. Some still turn up in El Playón, the lunar lava field of rotting human flesh visible at one time or another on every television screen in America but characterized in June of 1982 in the *El Salvador News Gazette*, an English-language weekly edited by an American named Mario Rosenthal, as an "uncorroborated story . . . dredged up from the files of leftist propaganda." Others turn up at Puerta del Diablo, above Parque Balboa, a national *Turicentro* described as recently as the April-July 1982 issue of *Aboard TACA*, the magazine provided passengers on the national airline of El Salvador, as "offering excellent subjects for color photography."   8

I drove up to Puerta del Diablo one morning in June of 1982, past the Casa Presidencial and the camouflaged watch towers and heavy concentrations of troops and arms south of town, on up a narrow road narrowed further by landslides and deep crevices in the roadbed, a drive so insistently premonitory that after a while I began to hope that I would pass Puerta del Diablo without knowing it, just miss it, write it off, turn around and go back. There was however no way of missing it. Puerta del Diablo is a "view site" in an older and distinctly literary tradition, nature as lesson, an immense cleft rock through which half of El Salvador seems framed, a site so romantic and "mystical," so theatrically sacrificial in aspect, that it might be a cosmic parody of nineteenth-century landscape painting. The place presents itself as pathetic fallacy:[2] the sky "broods," the stones "weep," a constant seepage of water weighting the ferns and moss. The foliage is thick and slick with moisture. The only sound is a steady buzz, I believe of cicadas.   9

---

[2]Attributing human abilities and feelings to natural objects. [Eds.]

Body dumps are seen in El Salvador as a kind of visitors' must- 10
do, difficult but worth the detour. "Of course you have seen El
Playón," an aide to President Alvaro Magaña said to me one day,
and proceeded to discuss the site geologically, as evidence of the
country's geothermal resources. He made no mention of the bodies.
I was unsure if he was sounding me out or simply found the geothermal aspect of overriding interest. One difference between El
Playón and Puerta del Diablo is that most bodies at El Playón appear
to have been killed somewhere else, and then dumped; at Puerta del
Diablo the executions are believed to occur in place, at the top, and
the bodies thrown over. Sometimes reporters will speak of wanting
to spend the night at Puerta del Diablo, in order to document the
actual execution, but at the time I was in Salvador no one had.

The aftermath, the daylight aspect, is well documented. "Nothing 11
fresh today, I hear," an embassy officer said when I mentioned that
I had visited Puerta del Diablo. "Were there any on top?" someone
else asked. "There were supposed to have been three on top yesterday." The point about whether or not there had been any on top
was that usually it was necessary to go down to see bodies. The way
down is hard. Slabs of stone, slippery with moss, are set into the
vertiginous cliff, and it is down this cliff that one begins the descent
to the bodies, or what is left of the bodies, pecked and maggoty masses
of flesh, bone, hair. On some days there have been helicopters circling, tracking those making the descent. Other days there have been
militia at the top, in the clearing where the road seems to run out,
but on the morning I was there the only people on top were a man
and a woman and three small children, who played in the wet grass
while the woman started and stopped a Toyota pickup. She appeared
to be learning how to drive. She drove forward and then back toward
the edge, apparently following the man's signals, over and over again.

We did not speak, and it was only later, down the mountain and 12
back in the land of the provisionally living, that it occurred to me that
there was a definite question about why a man and a woman might
choose a well-known body dump for a driving lesson. This was one
of a number of occasions, during the two weeks my husband and I
spent in El Salvador, on which I came to understand, in a way I had
not understood before, the exact mechanism of terror.

Whenever I had nothing better to do in San Salvador I would 13
walk up in the leafy stillness of the San Benito and Escalón districts,
where the hush at midday is broken only by the occasional crackle
of a walkie-talkie, the click of metal moving on a weapon. I recall a
day in San Benito when I opened my bag to check an address, and
heard the clicking of metal on metal all up and down the street. On

the whole no one walks up here, and pools of blossoms lie undis-turbed on the sidewalks. Most of the houses in San Benito are more recent than those in Escalón, less idiosyncratic and probably smarter, but the most striking architectural features in both districts are not the houses but their walls, walls built upon walls, walls stripped of the usual copa de oro[3] and bougainvillea, walls that reflect successive generations of violence: the original stone, the additional five or six or ten feet of brick, and finally the barbed wire, sometimes concertina, sometimes electrified; walls with watch towers, gun ports, closed-circuit television cameras, walls now reaching twenty and thirty feet.

San Benito and Escalón appear on the embassy security maps as   14 districts of relatively few "incidents," but they remain districts in which a certain oppressive uneasiness prevails. In the first place there are always "incidents"—detentions and deaths and disappearances—in the *barrancas*, the ravines lined with shanties that fall down behind the houses with the walls and the guards and the walkie-talkies; one day in Escalón I was introduced to a woman who kept the lean-to that served as a grocery in a *barranca* just above the Hotel Sheraton. She was sticking prices on bars of Camay and Johnson's baby soap, stopping occasionally to sell a plastic bag or two filled with crushed ice and Coca-Cola, and all the while she talked in a low voice about her fear, about her eighteen-year-old son, about the boys who had been taken out and shot on successive nights recently in a neighboring *barranca*.

In the second place there is, in Escalón, the presence of the Sher-   15 aton itself, a hotel that has figured rather too prominently in certain local stories involving the disappearance and death of Americans. The Sheraton always seems brighter and more mildly festive than either the Camino Real or the Presidente, with children in the pool and flowers and pretty women in pastel dresses, but there are usually several bullet-proofed Cherokee Chiefs in the parking area, and the men drinking in the lobby often carry the little zippered purses that in San Salvador suggest not passports or credit cards but Browning 9-mm pistols.

It was at the Sheraton that one of the few American *desaparecidos*,[4]   16 a young free-lance writer named John Sullivan, was last seen in December of 1980. It was also at the Sheraton, after eleven on the evening of January 3 1981, that the two American advisers on agrarian reform, Michael Hammer and Mark Pearlman, were killed, along with the Salvadoran director of the Institute for Agrarian Transformation, José Rodolfo Viera. The three were drinking coffee in a dining room

---

[3]Cupflower (in Spanish, literally cup of gold). [Eds.]
[4]Missing (that is, abducted) persons. [Eds.]

of the lobby, and whoever killed them used an Ingram MAC-10, without sound suppressor, and then walked out through the lobby, unapprehended. The Sheraton has even turned up in the investigation into the December 1980 deaths of the four American churchwomen, Sisters Ita Ford and Maura Clarke, the two Maryknoll nuns; Sister Dorothy Kazel, the Ursuline nun; and Jean Donovan, the lay volunteer. In *Justice in El Salvador: A Case Study*, prepared and released in July of 1982 in New York by the Lawyers' Committee for International Human Rights, there appears this note:

> "On December 19, 1980, the [Duarte government's] Special Investigative Commission reported that 'a red Toyota ¾-ton pickup was seen leaving (the crime scene) at about 11:00 P.M. on December 2' and that 'a red splotch on the burned van' of the churchwomen was being checked to determine whether the paint splotch 'could be the result of a collision between that van and the red Toyota pickup.' By February 1981, the Maryknoll Sisters' Office of Social Concerns, which has been actively monitoring the investigation, received word from a source which it considered reliable that the FBI had matched the red splotch on the burned van with a red Toyota pickup belonging to the Sheraton hotel in San Salvador. . . . Subsequent to the FBI's alleged matching of the paint splotch and a Sheraton truck, the State Department has claimed, in a communication with the families of the churchwomen, that 'the FBI could not determine the source of the paint scraping.' "

There is also mention in this study of a young Salvadoran businessman named Hans Christ (his father was a German who arrived in El Salvador at the end of World War II), a part owner of the Sheraton. Hans Christ lives now in Miami, and that his name should have even come up in the Maryknoll investigation made many people uncomfortable, because it was Hans Christ, along with his brother-in-law, Ricardo Sol Meza, who, in April of 1981, was first charged with the murders of Michael Hammer and Mark Pearlman and José Rodolfo Viera at the Sheraton. These charges were later dropped, and were followed by a series of other charges, arrests, releases, expressions of "dismay" and "incredulity" from the American embassy, and even, in the fall of 1982, confessions to the killings from two former National Guard corporals, who testified that Hans Christ had led them through the lobby and pointed out the victims. Hans Christ and Ricardo Sol Meza have said that the dropped case against them was a government frame-up, and that they were only having drinks at the Sheraton the night of the killings, with a National Guard intelligence officer. It was logical for Hans Christ and Ricardo Sol Meza to have drinks at the Sheraton because they both had interests in the hotel, and Ricardo Sol Meza had just opened a roller disco, since closed, off the lobby into which the killers walked that night. The killers were described by witnesses as well dressed, their faces covered. The room from which they walked was at the time I was in San Salvador no longer a restaurant, but the marks left by the bullets were still visible, on the wall facing the door.

Whenever I had occasion to visit the Sheraton I was apprehensive, 18 and this apprehension came to color the entire Escalón district for me, even its lower reaches, where there were people and movies and restaurants. I recall being struck by it on the canopied porch of a restaurant near the Mexican embassy, on an evening when rain or sabotage or habit had blacked out the city and I became abruptly aware, in the light cast by a passing car, of two human shadows, silhouettes illuminated by the headlights and then invisible again. One shadow sat behind the smoked glass windows of a Cherokee Chief parked at the curb in front of the restaurant; the other crouched between the pumps at the Esso station next door, carrying a rifle. It seemed to me unencouraging that my husband and I were the only people seated on the porch. In the absence of the headlights the candle on our table provided the only light, and I fought the impulse to blow it out. We continued talking carefully. Nothing came of this, but I did not forget the sensation of having been in a single instant demoralized, undone, humiliated by fear, which is what I meant when I said that I came to understand in El Salvador the mechanism of terror.

RESPONDING TO READING

1. Didion devotes a good deal of attention to physical description. What mood do her descriptions create? What emotions do the descriptions make you feel? How do these emotions serve Didion's purpose? **2.** Is Didion an outsider in El Salvador because she is an American? Because she is a woman? Because she is a reporter? Or do other factors contribute to her feelings of differentness? **3.** Do you believe it is possible for someone to witness the horror of which Didion writes and remain a detached, neutral observer? Is Didion really the "visitor" she claims to be?

Marrakech

GEORGE ORWELL

George Orwell (see also p. 61) was a staunch opponent of totalitarianism and imperialism. In "Marrakech" from *Such, Such Were the Days* (1953), he describes the cruel poverty of the people of Morocco under colonial rule, where "it is always difficult to believe that you are walking among human beings." With a reporter's eye, he observes injustices and, as an outsider, he wonders uneasily when the brown-skinned army will "turn their guns in the other direction."

As the corpse went past the flies left the restaurant table in a
cloud and rushed after it, but they came back a few minutes later.

The little crowd of mourners—all men and boys, no women—
threaded their way across the market-place between the piles of pome-
granates and the taxis and the camels, wailing a short chant over and
over again. What really appeals to the flies is that the corpses here
are never put into coffins, they are merely wrapped in a piece of rag
and carried on a rough wooden bier on the shoulders of four friends.
When the friends get to the burying-ground they hack an oblong hole
a foot or two deep, dump the body in it and fling over it a little of
the dried-up, lumpy earth, which is like broken brick. No gravestone,
no name, no identifying mark of any kind. The burying-ground is
merely a huge waste of hummocky earth, like a derelict building-lot.
After a month or two no one can even be certain where his own
relatives are buried.

When you walk through a town like this—two hundred thousand
inhabitants, of whom at least twenty thousand own literally nothing
except the rags they stand up in—when you see how people live,
and still more how easily they die, it is always difficult to believe that
you are walking among human beings. All colonial empires are in
reality founded upon that fact. The people have brown faces—
besides, there are so many of them! Are they really the same flesh
as yourself? Do they even have names? Or are they merely a kind of
undifferentiated brown stuff, about as individual as bees or coral
insects? They rise out of the earth, they sweat and starve for a few
years, and then they sink back into the nameless mounds of the
graveyard and nobody notices that they are gone. And even the
graves themselves soon fade back into the soil. Sometimes, out for a
walk, as you break your way through the prickly pear, you notice
that it is rather bumpy underfoot, and only a certain regularity in the
bumps tells you that you are walking over skeletons.

I was feeding one of the gazelles in the public gardens.

Gazelles are almost the only animals that look good to eat when
they are still alive, in fact, one can hardly look at their hindquarters
without thinking of mint sauce. The gazelle I was feeding seemed to
know that this thought was in my mind, for though it took the piece
of bread I was holding out it obviously did not like me. It nibbled
rapidly at the bread, then lowered its head and tried to butt me, then
took another nibble and then butted again. Probably its idea was that
if it could drive me away the bread would somehow remain hanging
in mid-air.

An Arab navvy[1] working on the path nearby lowered his heavy
hoe and sidled towards us. He looked from the gazelle to the bread

---

[1]Laborer. [Eds.]

FOR OPENERS

What do students know about living conditions in Third World countries? What do they
know about colonialism?

**ADDITIONAL QUESTIONS FOR
RESPONDING TO READING**

1. Who is responsible for the living conditions
of Third World people?
2. What makes it difficult for Orwell to believe
he is "walking among human beings"? Do
you find his reaction understandable? Offensive? (Be sure your students understand the
basic assumptions of the British colonial
system, with its arrogant "White man's
burden" perspective toward natives.)

TEACHING STRATEGY

Discuss the following with your students:

Paragraph 1: Do you find this opening effective? (It certainly attracts attention, but do students find that it makes them want to read on or that it repels them?)

Paragraph 5: What analogy does Orwell create by including the description of the gazelle?

Paragraph 11: From Orwell's tone in the description of the Jewish neighborhood, what can you detect about his attitude? What is your reaction to this attitude?

Paragraph 12: What does Orwell mean to imply in his reference to Hitler?

Paragraph 17: Why is it so easy for Westerners to overlook the natives?

Paragraph 21: "But what is strange"—This transition implies that the conditions of the natives in the two preceding paragraphs are not anomalous. Why? Do you agree?

Paragraph 22: Why does Orwell feel such sympathy for the donkey and not for the people? (You might point out the similarity between this reaction and his sympathy for the elephant in "Shooting an Elephant," page 1008.)

Paragraph 27: Do you believe Orwell's statement that "every white man there has this thought stowed somewhere or other in his mind"? Defend your answer.

and from the bread to the gazelle, with a sort of quiet amazement, as though he had never seen anything quite like this before. Finally he said shyly in French:

"*I could eat some of that bread.*" 7

I tore off a piece and he stowed it gratefully in some secret place under his rags. This man is an employee of the Municipality. 8

When you go through the Jewish quarters you gather some idea 9 of what the medieval ghettoes were probably like. Under their Moorish rulers the Jews were only allowed to own land in certain restricted areas, and after centuries of this kind of treatment they have ceased to bother about overcrowding. Many of the streets are a good deal less than six feet wide, the houses are completely windowless, and sore-eyed children cluster everywhere in unbelievable numbers, like clouds of flies. Down the center of the street there is generally running a little river of urine.

In the bazaar huge families of Jews, all dressed in the long black 10 robe and little black skull-cap, are working in dark fly-infested booths that look like caves. A carpenter sits cross-legged at a prehistoric lathe, turning chair-legs at lightning speed. He works the lathe with a bow in his right hand and guides the chisel with his left foot, and thanks to a lifetime of sitting in this position his left leg is warped out of shape. At his side his grandson, aged six, is already starting on the simpler parts of the job.

I was just passing the coppersmiths' booths when somebody 11 noticed that I was lighting a cigarette. Instantly, from the dark holes all round, there was a frenzied rush of Jews, many of them old grandfathers with flowing grey beards, all clamoring for a cigarette. Even a blind man somewhere at the back of one of the booths heard a rumor of cigarettes and came crawling out, groping in the air with his hand. In about a minute I had used up the whole packet. None of these people, I suppose, works less than twelve hours a day, and every one of them looks on a cigarette as a more or less impossible luxury.

As the Jews live in self-contained communities they follow the 12 same trades as the Arabs, except for agriculture. Fruit-sellers, potters, silversmiths, blacksmiths, butchers, leather-workers, tailors, water-carriers, beggars, porters—whichever way you look you see nothing but Jews. As a matter of fact there are thirteen thousand of them, all living in the space of a few acres. A good job Hitler isn't here. Perhaps he is on his way, however. You hear the usual dark rumors about the Jews, not only from the Arabs but from the poorer Europeans.

"Yes, *mon vieux*, they took my job away from me and gave it to 13 a Jew. The Jews! They're the real rulers of this country, you know. They've got all the money. They control the banks, finance—everything."

"But," I said, "isn't it a fact that the average Jew is a laborer 14 working for about a penny an hour?"

"Ah, that's only for show! They're all moneylenders really. 15 They're cunning, the Jews."

In just the same way, a couple of hundred years ago, poor old 16 women used to be burned for witchcraft when they could not even work enough magic to get themselves a square meal.

All people who work with their hands are partly invisible, and 17 the more important the work they do, the less visible they are. Still, a white skin is always fairly conspicuous. In northern Europe, when you see a laborer ploughing a field, you probably give him a second glance. In a hot country, anywhere south of Gibraltar or east of Suez, the chances are that you don't even see him. I have noticed this again and again. In a tropical landscape one's eye takes in everything except the human beings. It takes in the dried-up soil, the prickly pear, the palm-tree and the distant mountain, but it always misses the peasant hoeing at his patch. He is the same color as the earth, and a great deal less interesting to look at.

It is only because of this that the starved countries of Asia and 18 Africa are accepted as tourist resorts. No one would think of running cheap trips to the Distressed Areas. But where the human beings have brown skins their poverty is simply not noticed. What does Morocco mean to a Frenchman? An orange-grove or a job in government service. Or to an Englishman? Camels, castles, palm-trees, Foreign Legionnaires, brass trays and bandits. One could probably live here for years without noticing that for nine-tenths of the people the reality of life is an endless, back-breaking struggle to wring a little food out of an eroded soil.

Most of Morocco is so desolate that no wild animal bigger than 19 a hare can live on it. Huge areas which were once covered with forest have turned into a treeless waste where the soil is exactly like broken-up brick. Nevertheless a good deal of it is cultivated, with frightful labor. Everything is done by hand. Long lines of women, bent double like inverted capital Ls, work their way slowly across the fields, tearing up the prickly weeds with their hands, and the peasant gathering lucerne for fodder pulls it up stalk by stalk instead of reaping it, thus saving an inch or two on each stalk. The plough is a wretched wooden thing, so frail that one can easily carry it on one's shoulder, and fitted underneath with a rough iron spike which stirs the soil to a depth of about four inches. This is as much as the strength of the animals is equal to. It is usual to plough with a cow and a donkey yoked together. Two donkeys would not be quite strong enough, but on the other hand two cows would cost a little more to feed. The peasants possess no harrows, they merely plough the soil several times over in different directions, finally leaving it in rough furrows, after which the whole field has to be shaped with hoes into small oblong patches, to conserve water. Except for a day or two after the rare rainstorms there is never enough water. Along the edges of the fields channels are hacked out to a depth of thirty or forty feet to get at the tiny trickles which run through the subsoil.

Every afternoon a file of very old women passes down the road   20 outside my house, each carrying a load of firewood. All of them are mummified with age and the sun, and all of them are tiny. It seems to be generally the case in primitive communities that the women, when they get beyond a certain age, shrink to the size of children. One day a poor old creature who could not have been more than four feet tall crept past me under a vast load of wood. I stopped her and put a five-sou piece (a little more than a farthing) into her hand. She answered with a shrill wail, almost a scream, which was partly gratitude but mainly surprise. I suppose that from her point of view, by taking any notice of her, I seemed almost to be violating a law of nature. She accepted her status as an old woman, that is to say as a beast of burden. When a family is travelling it is quite usual to see a father and a grown-up son riding ahead on donkeys, and an old woman following on foot, carrying the baggage.

But what is strange about these people is their invisibility. For   21 several weeks, always at about the same time of day, the file of old women had hobbled past the house with their firewood, and though they had registered themselves on my eyeballs I cannot truly say that I had seen them. Firewood was passing—that was how I saw it. It was only that one day I happened to be walking behind them, and the curious up-and-down motion of a load of wood drew my attention to the human being underneath it. Then for the first time I noticed the poor old earth-colored bodies, bodies reduced to bones and leathery skin, bent double under the crushing weight. Yet I suppose I had not been five minutes on Moroccan soil before I noticed the overloading of the donkeys and was infuriated by it. There is no question that the donkeys are damnably treated. The Moroccan donkey is hardly bigger than a St. Bernard dog, it carries a load which in the British army would be considered too much for a fifteen-hands mule, and very often its pack-saddle is not taken off its back for weeks together. But what is peculiarly pitiful is that it is the most willing creature on earth, it follows its master like a dog and does not need either bridle or halter. After a dozen years of devoted work it suddenly drops dead, whereupon its master tips it into the ditch and the village dogs have torn its guts out before it is cold.

This kind of thing makes one's blood boil, whereas—on the   22 whole—the plight of the human beings does not. I am not commenting, merely pointing to a fact. People with brown skins are next door to invisible. Anyone can be sorry for the donkey with its galled back, but it is generally owing to some kind of accident if one even notices the old woman under her load of sticks.

As the storks flew northward the Negroes were marching south-ward—a long, dusty column, infantry, screw-gun batteries and then more infantry, four or five thousand men in all, winding up the road with a clumping of boots and a clatter of iron wheels.

They were Senegalese, the blackest Negroes in Africa, so black that sometimes it is difficult to see whereabouts on their necks the hair begins. Their splendid bodies were hidden in reach-me-down khaki uniforms, their feet squashed into boots that looked like blocks of wood, and every tin hat seemed to be a couple of sizes too small. It was very hot and the men had marched a long way. They slumped under the weight of their packs and the curiously sensitive black faces were glistening with sweat.

As they went past a tall, very young Negro turned and caught my eye. But the look he gave me was not in the least the kind of look you might expect. Not hostile, not contemptuous, not sullen, not even inquisitive. It was the shy, wide-eyed Negro look, which actually is a look of profound respect. I saw how it was. This wretched boy, who is a French citizen and has therefore been dragged from the forest to scrub floors and catch syphilis in garrison towns, actually has feelings of reverence before a white skin. He has been taught that the white race are his masters, and he still believes it.

But there is one thought which every white man (and in this connection it doesn't matter twopence if he calls himself a Socialist) thinks when he sees a black army marching past. "How much longer can we go on kidding these people? How long before they turn their guns in the other direction?"

It was curious, really. Every white man there has this thought stowed somewhere or other in his mind. I had it, so had the other onlookers, so had the officers on their sweating chargers and the white NCOs marching in the ranks. It was a kind of secret which we all knew and were too clever to tell; only the Negroes didn't know it. And really it was almost like watching a flock of cattle to see the long column, a mile or two miles of armed men, flowing peacefully up the road, while the great white birds drifted over them in the opposite direction, glittering like scraps of paper.

RESPONDING TO READING

1. As a white man in Morocco, Orwell is very much aware that he is an outsider. In what way does colonialism set Orwell apart from the Moroccans? Does he believe his estrangement from them is logical, even inevitable? Do

23
24
25
26
27

WRITING SUGGESTION

Reread the last five paragraphs of Orwell's essay. Then write a brief speech, letter, or essay, written from the point of view of a Senegalese soldier, in which you examine the fairness and accuracy of Orwell's characterization of blacks' attitudes toward whites.

ANSWERS TO RESPONDING TO READING

1. He is privileged economically; he has no idea what the lives of the natives are really like; he is merely a "detached" observer. He is

aware of his status, which makes him uncomfortable in his role. He knows that he is living the lie of cultural superiority. The unequal relationship that was established from the beginning is logical, in terms of human behavior, and yet it is also immoral.

2. His characterizations illustrate the way an imperialist occupation dehumanizes natives in the eyes of the conquerors and how terrible it is for one human being to fail to recognize the humanity of those who are different. Students' views about whether or not Orwell is a racist will vary.

3. Were he to recognize the natives and their intolerable living conditions, he would be obliged to feel something for them—perhaps sadness, perhaps outrage, perhaps guilt for the role he plays in perpetuating their misery.

BACKGROUND ON READING

After graduating from the University of Nebraska, Cather lived for ten years in Pittsburgh, where Paul's neighborhood is located.

BACKGROUND ON WRITER

Cather's family moved from Virginia to Red Cloud, Nebraska when she was nine years old. At an early age she identified with displaced Scandinavian and Eastern European immigrant settlers who lived in the Midwest, where they struggled to forge lives for themselves against many obstacles. Cather also chose to dress in men's clothing for much of her life, thus consciously establishing herself as an outsider.

FOR OPENERS

Have you ever met someone you would call a rebel? What was this person rebelling against? Did you sympathize with this person, or did you view him or her as misguided?

you agree? **2.** Throughout this essay Orwell describes the native inhabitants of Morocco in very unappealing, almost nonhuman, terms. Do his negative characterizations lead you to conclude that he is a racist, or do they lead you to another conclusion? **3.** What explanation does Orwell give for his tendency to not *see* Moroccans? Are there any groups that are "invisible" to you? Why are they invisible?

Paul's Case

WILLA CATHER

Novelist and short story writer Willa Cather (1876–1947) was raised in Nebraska when it was still a pioneer territory. Most of her early writing is based on her childhood memories of the prairie and her respect for the people who settled the American West, especially strong pioneer women. Cather is known for her stark and beautiful depictions of the midwestern and southwestern landscapes in such novels as *O Pioneers!* (1913), *Song of the Lark* (1915), *My Antonia* (1918), and *Death Comes for the Archbishop* (1927). She said that she tried in her writing to provide "suggestion rather than enumeration." Cather also wrote *The Professor's House* (1925), *My Mortal Enemy* (1926), and *Shadows on the Rock* (1931). In 1922, she won the Pulitzer Prize for *One of Our Own*. "Paul's Case" published in 1905, is her best-known story.

It was Paul's afternoon to appear before the faculty of the Pittsburgh High School to account for his various misdemeanors. He had been suspended a week ago, and his father had called at the Principal's office and confessed his perplexity about his son. Paul entered the faculty room suave and smiling. His clothes were a trifle outgrown, and the tan velvet on the collar of his open overcoat was frayed and worn; but for all that there was something of the dandy about him, and he wore an opal pin in his neatly knotted black four-in-hand, and a red carnation in his buttonhole. This latter adornment the faculty somehow felt was not properly significant of the contrite spirit befitting a boy under the ban of suspension. 1

Paul was tall for his age and very thin, with high, cramped shoulders and a narrow chest. His eyes were remarkable for a certain hysterical brilliancy, and he continually used them in a conscious, theatrical sort of way, peculiarly offensive in a boy. The pupils were abnormally large, as though he were addicted to belladonna, but there was a glassy glitter about them which that drug does not produce. 2

When questioned by the Principal as to why he was there, Paul stated, politely enough, that he wanted to come back to school. This was a lie, but Paul was quite accustomed to lying; found it, indeed, 3 indispensable for overcoming friction. His teachers were asked to state their respective charges against him, which they did with such a rancor and aggrievedness as evinced that this was not a usual case. Disorder and impertinence were among the offenses named, yet each of his instructors felt that it was scarcely possible to put into words the real cause of the trouble, which lay in a sort of hysterically defiant manner of the boy's; in the contempt which they all knew he felt for them, and which he seemingly made not the least effort to conceal. Once, when he had been making a synopsis of a paragraph at the blackboard, his English teacher had stepped to his side and attempted to guide his hand. Paul had started back with a shudder and thrust his hands violently behind him. The astonished woman could scarcely have been more hurt and embarrassed had he struck at her. The insult was so involuntary and definitely personal as to be unforgettable. In one way and another, he had made all his teachers, men and women alike, conscious of the same feeling of physical aversion. In one class he habitually sat with his hand shading his eyes; in another he always looked out of the window during the recitation; in another he made a running commentary on the lecture, with humorous intent.

His teachers felt this afternoon that his whole attitude was symbolized by his shrug and his flippantly red carnation flower, and they fell upon him without mercy, his English teacher leading the pack. He stood through it smiling, his pale lips parted over his white teeth. (His lips were continually twitching, and he had a habit of raising his eyebrows that was contemptuous and irritating to the last degree.) Older boys than Paul had broken down and shed tears under that ordeal, but his set smile did not once desert him, and his only sign of discomfort was the nervous trembling of the fingers that toyed with the buttons of his overcoat, and an occasional jerking of the other hand which held his hat. Paul was always smiling, always glancing about him, seeming to feel that people might be watching him and trying to detect something. This conscious expression, since it was as far as possible from boyish mirthfulness, was usually attributed to insolence or "smartness."   4

As the inquisition proceeded, one of his instructors repeated an impertinent remark of the boy's, and the Principal asked him whether he thought that a courteous speech to make to a woman. Paul shrugged his shoulders slightly and his eyebrows twitched.   5

"I don't know," he replied. "I didn't mean to be polite or impolite, either. I guess it's a sort of way I have, of saying things regardless."   6

The Principal asked him whether he didn't think that a way it would be well to get rid of it. Paul grinned and said he guessed so. When he was told that he could go, he bowed gracefully and went out. His bow was like a repetition of the scandalous red carnation.   7

His teachers were in despair, and his drawing master voiced the   8

ADDITIONAL QUESTION FOR RESPONDING TO READING

Do you recall adolescence as a particularly anxious or unsettled time? Do you think it was so for your friends? What is it about adolescence that might encourage restlessness or dissatisfaction?

TEACHING STRATEGY

After the class has finished reading the story, arrange a talk show panel with the following panelists:

Paul—who has fortunately survived the suicide attempt

Paul's father—who has decided to institutionalize his son

English teacher—who agrees with Paul's father

Drawing master—who feels sympathetic toward Paul

Expert psychiatrist—who has his or her own opinions on the case

Choose students who you feel best suit the above roles and allow each a brief preparation period while the rest of the class, working in groups, generates audience questions; the instructor, as the talk show host, should guide discussion toward some basic conclusions about the nature of Paul's discontentment and anxiety, the role Paul's father plays in his son's view of reality, and basic flaws in Paul's entire personality.

feeling of them all when he declared there was something about the boy which none of them understood. He added "I don't really believe that smile of his comes altogether from insolence; there's something sort of haunted about it. The boy is not strong, for one thing. There is something wrong about the fellow."

The drawing master had come to realize that, in looking at Paul, one saw only his white teeth and the forced animation of his eyes. One warm afternoon the boy had gone to sleep at his drawing board, and his master had noted with amazement what a white, blue-veined face it was; drawn and wrinkled like an old man's about the eyes, the lips twitching even in his sleep. 9

His teachers left the building dissatisfied and unhappy; humiliated to have felt so vindictive toward a mere boy, to have uttered this feeling in cutting terms, and to have set each other on, as it were, in the gruesome game of intemperate reproach. One of them remembered having seen a miserable street cat set at bay by a ring of tormentors. 10

As for Paul, he ran down the hill whistling the Soldiers' Chorus from *Faust*,[1] looking wildly behind him now and then to see whether some of his teachers were not there to witness his light-heartedness. As it was now late in the afternoon and Paul was on duty that evening as usher at Carnegie Hall,[2] he decided that he would not go home to supper. 11

When he reached the concert hall the doors were not yet open. It was chilly outside, and he decided to go up into the picture gallery— always deserted at this hour—where there were some of Raffaëlli's[3] gay studies of Paris streets and an airy blue Venetian scene or two that always exhilarated him. He was delighted to find no one in the gallery but the old guard, who sat in the corner, a newspaper on his knee, a black patch over one eye and the other closed. Paul possessed himself of the place and walked confidently up and down, whistling under his breath. After a while he sat down before a blue Rico[4] and lost himself. When he bethought him to look at his watch, it was after seven o'clock, and he rose with a start and ran downstairs, making a face at Augustus Caesar, peering out from the cast-room, and an evil gesture at the Venus of Milo[5] as he passed her on the stairway. 12

When Paul reached the ushers' dressing-room half a dozen boys were there already, and he began excitedly to tumble into his uniform. 13

---

[1]Opera by Charles Gounod (1818–93). [Eds.]

[2]In Pittsburgh. [Eds.]

[3]Jean-François Rafaëlli (1850–1924), impressionist painter known for scenes of Parisian life. [Eds.]

[4]Martin Rico (1833–1908), Spanish painter known for his landscapes. [Eds.]

[5]Copies of the famous statues of Augustus Caesar in the Vatican Museum and the Venus de Milo in the Louvre. [Eds.]

It was one of the few that at all approached fitting, and Paul thought it very becoming—though he knew the tight, straight coat accentuated his narrow chest, about which he was exceedingly sensitive. He was always excited while he dressed, twanging all over to the tuning of the strings and preliminary flourishes of the horns in the music-room; but tonight he seemed quite beside himself, and he teased and plagued the boys until, telling him that he was crazy, they put him down on the floor and sat on him.

Somewhat calmed by his suppression, Paul dashed out to the front of the house to seat the early comers. He was a model usher. Gracious and smiling he ran up and down the aisles. Nothing was too much trouble for him; he carried messages and brought programs as though it were his greatest pleasure in life, and all the people in his section thought him a charming boy, feeling that he remembered and admired them. As the house filled, he grew more and more vivacious and animated, and the color came to his cheeks and lips. It was very much as though this were a great reception and Paul were the host. Just as the musicians came out to take their places, his English teacher arrived with checks for the seat which a prominent manufacturer had taken for the season. She betrayed some embarrassment when she handed Paul the tickets, and a *hauteur* which subsequently made her feel very foolish. Paul was startled for a moment and had the feeling of wanting to put her out; what business had she here among all these fine people and gay colors? He looked her over and decided that she was not appropriately dressed and must be a fool to sit downstairs in such togs. The tickets had probably been sent her out of kindness, he reflected, as he put down a seat for her, and she had about as much right to sit there as he had. 14

When the symphony began Paul sank into one of the rear seats with a long sigh of relief, and lost himself as he had done before the Rico. It was not that symphonies, as such, meant anything in particular to Paul, but the first sigh of the instruments seemed to free some hilarious spirit within him; something that struggled there like the Genius in the bottle found by the Arab fisherman.[6] He felt a sudden zest for life; the lights danced before his eyes and the concert hall blazed into unimaginable splendor. When the soprano soloist came on, Paul forgot even the nastiness of his teacher's being there, and gave himself up to the peculiar intoxication such personages always had for him. The soloist chanced to be a German woman, by no means in her first youth, and the mother of many children; but she wore a satin gown and a tiara, and she had that indefinable air of achieve- 15

---

[6]A reference to the tale of "The Fisherman and the Jinni" from *The Arabian Nights*. [Eds.]

COLLABORATIVE ACTIVITY

Rent the film version of *Paul's Case*, which was produced for PBS's American Short Story series, and show it to the class. During the next class period, divide students into groups and have them brainstorm about similarities and differences between the film and the short story. In class discussion, focus on the relationships between Paul and the other characters.

ment, the world-shine upon her, which always blinded Paul to any possible defects.

After a concert was over, Paul was often irritable and wretched 16 until he got to sleep—and tonight he was even more than usually restless. He had the feeling of not being able to let down; of its being impossible to give up this delicious excitement which was the only thing that could be called living at all. During the last number he withdrew and, after hastily changing his clothes in the dressing-room, slipped out to the side door where the singer's carriage stood. Here he began pacing rapidly up and down the walk, waiting to see her come out.

Over yonder the Schenley, in its vacant stretch, loomed big and 17 square through the fine rain, the windows of its twelve stories glowing like those of a lighted cardboard house under a Christmas tree. All the actors and singers of any importance stayed there when they were in the city, and a number of the big manufacturers of the place lived there in the winter. Paul had often hung about the hotel, watching the people go in and out, longing to enter and leave schoolmasters and dull care behind him forever.

At last the singer came out, accompanied by the conductor, who 18 helped her into her carriage and closed the door with a cordial *auf Wiedersehen*,[7]—which set Paul to wondering whether she were not an old sweetheart of his. Paul followed the carriage over to the hotel, walking so rapidly as not to be far from the entrance when the singer alighted and disappeared behind the swinging glass doors which were opened by a Negro in a tall hat and a long coat. In the moment that the door was ajar, it seemed to Paul that he, too, entered. He seemed to feel himself go after her up the steps, into the warm, lighted building, into an exotic, a tropical world of shiny, glistening surfaces and basking ease. He reflected upon the mysterious dishes that were brought into the dining-room, the green bottles in buckets of ice, as he had seen them in the supper party pictures of the Sunday supplement. A quick gust of wind brought the rain down with sudden vehemence, and Paul was startled to find that he was still outside in the slush of the gravel driveway; that his boots were letting in the water and his scanty overcoat was clinging wet about him; that the lights in front of the concert hall were out, and that the rain was driving in sheets between him and the orange glow of the windows above him. There it was, what he wanted—tangibly before him, like the fairy world of Christmas pantomime; as the rain beat in his face, Paul wondered whether he were destined always to shiver in the black night outside, looking up at it.

---

[7]Good-bye. [Eds.]

He turned and walked reluctantly toward the car tracks. The end   19
had to come some time; his father in his night-clothes at the top of
the stairs, explanations that did not explain, hastily improvised fic-
tions that were forever tripping him up, his upstairs room and its
horrible yellow wallpaper, the creaking bureau with the greasy plush
collar-box, and over his painted wooden bed the pictures of George
Washington and John Calvin,[8] and the framed motto, "Feed my
Lambs,"[9] which had been worked in red worsted by his mother,
whom Paul could not remember.

Half an hour later, Paul alighted from the Negley Avenue car and   20
went slowly down one of the side streets off the main thoroughfare.
It was a highly respectable street, where all the houses were exactly
alike, and where business men of moderate means begot and reared
large families of children, all of whom went to Sabbath-school and
learned the shorter catechism, and were interested in arithmetic; all
of whom were as exactly alike as their homes, and of a piece with
the monotony in which they lived. Paul never went up Cordelia Street
without a shudder of loathing. His home was next to the house of
the Cumberland minister. He approached it tonight with the nerveless
sense of defeat, the hopeless feeling of sinking back forever into
ugliness and commonness that he had always had when he came
home. The moment he turned into Cordelia Street he felt the waters
close above his head. After each of these orgies of living, he experienced all the physical depression which follows a debauch; the loathing of respectable beds, of common food, of those permeated by
kitchen odors; a shuddering repulsion for the flavorless, colorless
mass of everyday existence; a morbid desire for cool things and soft
lights and fresh flowers.

The nearer he approached the house, the more absolutely unequal   21
Paul felt to the sight of it all; his ugly sleeping chamber, the cold
bathroom with the grimy zinc tub, the cracked mirror, the dripping
spiggots; his father, at the top of the stairs, his hairy legs sticking out
from his nightshirt, his feet thrust into carpet slippers. He was so
much later than usual that there would certainly be inquiries and
reproaches. Paul stopped short before the door. He felt that he could
not be accosted by his father tonight; that he could not toss again on
that miserable bed. He would not go in. He would tell his father that
he had no car fare, and it was raining so hard he had gone home
with one of the boys and stayed all night.

---

[8]French theologian and religious reformer (1509–64) whose doctrines stressed the supremacy
of the Scriptures in the revelation of truth and the sinfulness of human beings, who could be saved
only through God's grace. [Eds.]
[9]See John 21:15–17. [Eds.]

Meanwhile, he was wet and cold. He went around to the back 22
of the house and tried one of the basement windows, found it open,
raised it cautiously, and scrambled down the cellar wall to the floor.
There he stood, holding his breath, terrified by the noise he had made;
but the floor above him was silent, and there was no creak on the
stairs. He found a soap-box, and carried it over to the soft ring of
light that streamed from the furnace door, and sat down. He was
horribly afraid of rats, so he did not try to sleep, but sat looking
distrustfully at the dark, still terrified lest he might have awakened
his father. In such reactions, after one of the experiences which made
days and nights out of the dreary blanks of the calendar, when his
senses were deadened, Paul's head was always singularly clear. Suppose his father had heard him getting in at the window and had come
down and shot him for a burglar? Then, again, suppose his father
had come down, pistol in hand, and he had cried out in time to save
himself, and his father had been horrified to think how nearly he had
killed him? Then, again, suppose a day should come when his father
would remember that night, and wish there had been no warning
cry to stay his hand? With this last supposition Paul entertained himself until daybreak.

The following Sunday was fine; the sodden November chill was 23
broken by the last flash of autumnal summer. In the morning Paul
had to go to church and Sabbath-school, as always. On seasonable
Sunday afternoons the burghers[10] of Cordelia Street usually sat out
on their front "stoops," and talked to their neighbors on the next
stoop, or called to those across the street in neighborly fashion. The
men sat placidly on gay cushions placed upon the steps that led down
to the sidewalk, while the women, in their Sunday "waists," sat in
rockers on the cramped porches, pretending to be greatly at their
ease. The children played in the streets; there were so many of them
that the place resembled the recreation grounds of a kindergarten.
The men on the steps—all in their shirt sleeves, their vests unbuttoned—sat with their legs well apart, their stomachs comfortably
protruding, and talked of the prices of things, or told anecdotes of
the sagacity of their various chiefs and overlords. They occasionally
looked over the multitude of squabbling children, listened affectionately to their high-pitched, nasal voices, smiling to see their own
proclivities reproduced in their offspring, and interspersed their legends of the iron kings with remarks about their sons's progress at
school, their grades in arithmetic, and the amounts they had saved
in their toy banks. On this last Sunday of November, Paul sat all the
afternoon on the lowest step of his "stoop," staring into the street,

---

[10]Solid citizens. [Eds.]

while his sisters, in their rockers, were talking to the minister's daughters next door about how many shirtwaists they had made in the last week, and how many waffles someone had eaten in the last church supper. When the weather was warm, and his father was in a particularly jovial frame of mind, the girls made lemonade, which was always brought out in a red-glass pitcher, ornamented with forget-me-nots in blue enamel. This the girls thought very fine, and the neighbors joked about the suspicious color of the pitcher.

Today Paul's father, on the top step, was talking to a young man 24
who shifted a restless baby from knee to knee. He happened to be the young man who was daily held up to Paul as a model, and after whom it was his father's dearest hope that he would pattern. This young man was of a ruddy complexion, with a compressed, red mouth, and faded, near-sighted eyes, over which he wore thick spectacles, with gold bows that curved about his ears. He was clerk to one of the magnates of a great steel corporation, and was looked upon in Cordelia Street as a young man with a future. There was a story that, come five years ago—he was now barely twenty-six—he had been a trifle 'dissipated,' but in order to curb his appetites and save the loss of time and strength that a sowing of wild oats might have entailed, he had taken his chief's advice, oft reiterated to his employees, and at twenty-one had married the first woman whom he could persuade to share his fortunes. She happened to be an angular school mistress, much older than he, who also wore thick glasses, and who had now borne him four children, all near-sighted, like herself.

The young man was relating how his chief, now cruising in the 25
Mediterranean, kept in touch with all the details of the business, arranging his office hours on his yacht just as though he were at home, and "knocking off work enough to keep two stenographers busy." His father told, in turn, the plan his corporation was considering, of putting in an electric railway plant at Cairo. Paul snapped his teeth; he had an awful apprehension that they might spoil it all before he got there. Yet he rather liked to hear these legends of the iron kings, that were told and retold on Sundays and holidays; these stories of palaces in Venice, yachts on the Mediterranean, and high play at Monte Carlo appealed to his fancy, and he was interested in the triumphs of cash boys[11] who had become famous, though he had no mind for the cash-boy stage.

After supper was over, and he had helped to dry the dishes, Paul 26
nervously asked his father whether he could go to George's to get

---

[11]*The Cash Boy* is one of the popular "rags to riches" novels by American writer Horatio Alger (1832–99). [Eds.]

some help in his geometry, and still more nervously asked for car fare. This latter request he had to repeat, as his father, on principle, did not like to hear requests for money, whether much or little. He asked Paul whether he could not go to some boy who lived nearer, and told him that he ought not to leave his school work until Sunday; but he gave him the dime. He was not a poor man, but he had a worthy ambition to come up in the world. His only reason for allowing Paul to usher was that he thought a boy ought to be earning a little.

Paul bounded upstairs, scrubbed the greasy odor of the dishwater 27 from his hands with the ill-smelling soap he hated, and then shook over his fingers a few drops of violet water from the bottle he kept hidden in his drawer. He left the house with his geometry conspicuously under his arm, and the moment he got out of Cordelia Street and boarded a downtown car, he shook off the lethargy of two deadening days, and began to live again.

The leading juvenile of the permanent stock company which 28 played at one of the downtown theaters was an acquaintance of Paul's, and the boy had been invited to drop in at the Sunday night rehearsals whenever he could. For more than a year Paul had spent every available moment loitering about Charley Edwards's dressing-room. He had won a place among Edwards's following not only because the young actor, who could not afford to employ a dresser, often found him useful, but because he recognized in Paul something akin to what churchmen term "vocation."

It was at the theater and at Carnegie Hall that Paul really lived; 29 the rest was but a sleep and a forgetting. This was Paul's fairy tale, and it had for him all the allurement of a secret love. The moment he inhaled the gassy, painty, dusty odor behind the scenes, he breathed like a prisoner set free, and felt within him the possibility of doing or saying splendid, brilliant things. The moment the cracked orchestra beat out the overture from *Martha*, or jerked at the serenade from *Rigoletto*, all stupid and ugly things slid from him, and his senses were deliciously, yet delicately fired.

Perhaps it was because, in Paul's world, the natural nearly always 30 wore the guise of ugliness, that a certain element of artificiality seemed to him necessary in beauty. Perhaps it was because his experience of life elsewhere was so full of Sabbath-school picnics, petty economies, wholesome advice as to how to succeed in life, and the unescapable odors of cooking, that he found this existence so alluring, these smartly-clad men and women so attractive, that he was so moved by these starry apple orchards that bloomed perennially under the lime-light.

It would be difficult to put it strongly enough how convincingly 31 the stage entrance of that theater was for Paul the actual portal of

Romance. Certainly none of the company ever suspected it, least of all Charley Edwards. It was very like the old stories that used to float about London of fabulously rich Jews, who had subterranean halls, with palms, and fountains, and soft lamps and richly apparelled women who never saw the disenchanting light of London day. So, in the midst of that smoke-palled city, enamored of figures and grimy toil, Paul had his secret temple, his wishing-carpet, his bit of blue-and-white Mediterranean shore bathed in perpetual sunshine.

32 Several of Paul's teachers had a theory that his imagination had been perverted by garish fiction; but the truth was, he scarcely ever read at all. The books at home were not such as would either tempt or corrupt a youthful mind, and as for reading the novels that some of his friends urged upon him—well, he got what he wanted much more quickly from music; any sort of music, from an orchestra to a barrel organ. He needed only the spark, the indescribable thrill that made his imagination master of his senses, and he could make plots and pictures enough of his own. It was equally true that he was not stage-struck—not, at any rate, in the usual acceptation of that expression. He had no desire to become an actor, any more than he had to become a musician. He felt no necessity to do any of these things; what he wanted was to see, to be in the atmosphere, float on the wave of it, to be carried out, blue league after blue league, away from everything.

33 After a night behind the scenes, Paul found the school-room more than ever repulsive; the bare floors and naked walls; the prosy men who never wore frock coats, or violets in their buttonholes; the women with their dull gowns, shrill voices, and pitiful seriousness about prepositions that govern the dative. He could not bear to have the other pupils think, for a moment, that he took these people seriously; he must convey to them that he considered it all trivial, and was there only by way of a joke, anyway. He had autograph pictures of all the members of the stock company which he showed to classmates, telling them the most incredible stories of his familiarity with these people, of his acquaintance with the soloists who came to Carnegie Hall, his suppers with them and the flowers he sent them. When these stories lost their effect, and his audience grew listless, he would bid all the boys good-by, announcing that he was going to travel for a while; going to Naples, to California, to Egypt. Then, next Monday, he would slip back, conscious and nervously smiling; his sister was ill, and he would have to defer his voyage until spring.

34 Matters went steadily worse with Paul at school. In the itch to let his instructors know how heartily he despised them, and how thoroughly he was appreciated elsewhere, he mentioned once or twice that he had no time to fool with theorems; adding—with a twitch

of the eyebrows and a touch of that nervous bravado which so perplexed them—that he was helping the people down at the stock company; they were old friends of his.

The upshot of the matter was, that the Principal went to Paul's 35 father, and Paul was taken out of school and put to work. The manager at Carnegie Hall was told to get another usher in his stead; the doorkeeper at the theater was warned not to admit him to the house; and Charley Edwards remorsefully promised the boy's father not to see him again.

The members of the stock company were vastly amused when 36 some of Paul's stories reached them—especially the women. They were hard-working women, most of them supporting indolent husbands or brothers, and they laughed rather bitterly at having stirred the boy to such fervid and florid inventions. They agreed with the faculty and with his father, that Paul's was a bad case.

The east-bound train was plowing through a January snowstorm; 37 the dull dawn was beginning to show gray when the engine whistled a mile out of Newark. Paul started up from the seat where he had lain curled in uneasy slumber, rubbed the breath-misted window glass with his hand, and peered out. The snow was whirling in curling eddies above the white bottom lands, and the drifts lay already deep in the fields and along the fences, while here and there the long dead grass and dried weed stalks protruded black above it. Lights shone from the scattered houses, and a gang of laborers who stood beside the track waved their lanterns.

Paul had slept very little, and he felt grimy and uncomfortable. 38 He had made the all-night journey in a day coach because he was afraid if he took a Pullman he might be seen by some Pittsburgh business man who had noticed him in Denny & Carson's office. When the whistle woke him, he clutched quickly at his breast pocket, glancing about him with an uncertain smile. But the little, clay-bespattered Italians were still sleeping, the slatternly women across the aisle were in open-mouthed oblivion, and even the crumby, crying babies were for the nonce[12] stilled. Paul settled back to struggle with his impatience as best he could.

When he arrived at the Jersey City station, he hurried through 39 his breakfast, manifestly ill at ease and keeping a sharp eye about him. After he reached the Twenty-third Street Station, he consulted a cabman, and had himself driven to a men's furnishing establishment which was just opening for the day. He spent upward of two hours

---

[12]For the time being. [Eds.]

there, buying with endless reconsidering and great care. His new street suit he put on in the fitting-room; the frock coat and dress clothes he had bundled into the cab with his new shirts. Then he drove to a hatter's and a shoe house. His next errand was at Tiffany's, where he selected silver-mounted brushes and a scarf-pin. He would not wait to have his silver marked, he said. Lastly, he stopped at a trunk shop on Broadway, and had his purchases packed into various traveling bags.

It was a little after one o'clock when he drove up to the Waldorf, 40 and, after settling with the cabman, went into the office. He registered from Washington; said his mother and father had been abroad, and that he had come down to await the arrival of their steamer. He told his story plausibly and had no trouble, since he offered to pay for them in advance, in engaging his rooms; a sleeping-room, sitting room and bath.

Not once, but a hundred times Paul had planned this entry into 41 New York. He had gone over every detail of it with Charley Edwards, and in his scrap book at home there were pages of description about New York hotels, cut from the Sunday papers.

When he was shown to his sitting room on the eighth floor, he 42 saw at a glance that everything was as it should be; there was but one detail in his mental picture that the place did not realize, so he rang for the bell boy and sent him down for flowers. He moved about nervously until the boy returned, putting away his new linen and fingering it delightedly as he did so. When the flowers came, he put them hastily into water, and then tumbled into a hot bath. Presently he came out of his white bathroom, resplendent in his new silk under-wear, and playing with the tassels of his red robe. The snow was whirling so fiercely outside his windows that he could scarcely see across the street; but within, the air was deliciously soft and fragrant. He put the violets and jonquils on the tabouret beside the couch, and threw himself down with a long sigh, covering himself with a Roman blanket. He was thoroughly tired; he had been in such haste, he had stood up to such a strain, covered so much ground in the last twenty-four hours, that he wanted to think how it had all come about. Lulled by the sound of the wind, the warm air, and the cool fragrance of the flowers, he sank into deep, drowsy retrospection.

It had been wonderfully simple; when they had shut him out of 43 the theater and concert hall, when they had taken away his bone, the whole thing was virtually determined. The rest was a mere matter of opportunity. The only thing that at all surprised him was his own courage—for he realized well enough that he had always been tor-mented by fear, a sort of apprehensive dread that, of late years, as the meshes of the lies he had told closed about him, had been pulling the muscles of his body tighter and tighter. Until now, he could not remember a time when he had not been dreading something. Even when he was a little boy, it was always there—behind him, or before, or on either side. There had always been the shadowed corner, the dark place into which he dared not look, but from which something seemed always to be watching him—and Paul had done things that were not pretty to watch, he knew.

But now he had a curious sense of relief, as though he had at 44 last thrown down the gauntlet to the thing in the corner.

Yet it was but a day since he had been sulking in the traces; but 45 yesterday afternoon that he had been sent to the bank with Denny & Carston's deposit, as usual—but this time he was instructed to leave the book to be balanced. There was above two thousand dollars in checks, and nearly a thousand in the bank notes which he had taken from the book and quietly transferred to his pocket. At the bank he had made out a new deposit slip. His nerves had been steady enough to permit of his returning to the office, where he had finished his work and asked for a full day's holiday tomorrow, Saturday, giving a perfectly reasonable pretext. The bank book, he knew, would not be returned before Monday or Tuesday, and his father would be out of town for the next week. From the time he slipped the bank notes into his pocket until he boarded the night train for New York, he had not known a moment's hesitation.

How astonishingly easy it had all been; here he was, the thing 46 done; and this time there would be no awakening, no figure at the top of the stairs. He watched the snowflakes whirling by his window until he fell asleep.

When he awoke, it was four o'clock in the afternoon. He bounded 47 up with a start; one of his precious days gone already! He spent nearly an hour in dressing, watching every stage of his toilet carefully in the mirror. Everything was quite perfect; he was exactly the kind of boy he had always wanted to be.

When he went downstairs, Paul took a carriage and drove up 48 Fifth avenue toward the Park. The snow had somewhat abated; carriages and tradesmen's wagons were hurrying soundlessly to and fro in the winter twilight; boys in woolen mufflers were shoveling off the doorsteps; the avenue stages made fine spots of color against the white street. Here and there on the corners whole flower gardens blooming behind glass windows, against which the snow flakes stuck and melted; violets, roses, carnations, lilies of the valley—somehow vastly more lovely and alluring that they blossomed thus unnaturally in the snow. The Park itself was a wonderful stage winter-piece.

When he returned, the pause of the twilight had ceased, and the 49 tune of the streets had changed. The snow was falling faster, lights streamed from the hotels that reared their many stories fearlessly up into the storm, defying the raging Atlantic winds. A long, black stream of carriages poured down the avenue, intersected here and there by other streams, tending horizontally. There were a score of cabs about the entrance of his hotel, and his driver had to wait. Boys in livery were running in and out of the awning stretched across the sidewalk, up and down the red velvet carpet laid from the door to the street. Above, about, within it all, was the rumble and roar, the hurry and toss of thousands of human beings as hot for pleasure as himself, and on every side of him towered the glaring affirmation of the omnipotence of wealth.

The boy set his teeth and drew his shoulders together in a spasm 50 of realization; the plot of all dramas, the text of all romances, the nerve-stuff of all sensations was whirling about him like the snowflakes. He burnt like a faggot in a tempest.

When Paul came down to dinner, the music of the orchestra 51 floated up the elevator shaft to greet him. As he stepped into the thronged corridor, he sank back into one of the chairs against the wall to get his breath. The lights, the chatter, the perfumes, the bewildering medly of color—he had, for a moment, the feeling of not being able to stand it. But only for a moment; these were his own people, he told himself. He went slowly about the corridors, through the writing-rooms, smoking-rooms, reception-rooms, as though he were exploring the chambers of an enchanted palace, built and peopled for him alone.

When he reached the dining room he sat down at a table near a 52 window. The flowers, the white linen, the many-colored wine glasses, the gay toilettes of the women, the low popping of corks, the undulating repetitions of the *Blue Danube*[13] from the orchestra, all flooded Paul's dream with bewildering radiance. When the roseate tinge of his champagne was added—that cold, precious, bubbling stuff that creamed and foamed in his glass—Paul wondered that there were honest men in the world at all. This was what all the world was fighting for, he reflected; this was what all the struggle was about. He doubted the reality of his past. Had he ever known a place called Cordelia Street, a place where fagged-looking business men boarded the early car? Mere rivets in a machine they seemed to Paul—sickening men, with combings of children's hair always hanging to their coats, and the smell of cooking in their clothes. Cordelia Street—Ah, that belonged to another time and country! Had he not always been thus, had he not sat here night after night, from as far back as he

---

[13]Waltz composed by Johann Strauss (1825–99). [Eds.]

could remember, looking pensively over just such shimmering textures, and slowly twirling the stem of a glass like this one between his thumb and middle finger? He rather thought he had.

He was not in the least abashed or lonely. He had no special   53
desire to meet or to know any of these people; all he demanded was the right to look on and conjecture, to watch the pageant. The mere stage properties were all he contended for. Nor was he lonely later in the evening, in his loge[14] at the Opera. He was entirely rid of his nervous misgivings, of his forced aggressiveness, of the imperative desire to show himself different from his surroundings. He felt now that his surroundings explained him. Nobody questioned the purple; he had only to wear it passively. He had only to glance down at his dress coat to reassure himself that here it would be impossible for anyone to humiliate him.

He found it hard to leave his beautiful sitting room to go to bed   54
that night, and sat long watching the raging storm from his turret window. When he went to sleep, it was with the lights turned on in his bedroom; partly because of his old timidity, and partly so that, if he should wake in the night there would be no wretched moment of doubt, no horrible suspicion of yellow wall-paper, or of Washington and Calvin above his bed.

On Sunday morning the city was practically snow-bound. Paul   55
breakfasted late, and in the afternoon he fell in with a wild San Francisco boy, a freshman at Yale, who said he had run down for a "little flyer" over Sunday. The young man offered to show Paul the night side of the town, and the two boys went off together after dinner, not returning to the hotel until seven o'clock the next morning. They had started out in the confiding warmth of a champagne friendship, but their parting in the elevator was singularly cool. The freshman pulled himself together to make his train, and Paul went to bed. He woke at two o'clock in the afternoon, very thirsty and dizzy, and rang for ice water, coffee, and the Pittsburgh papers.

On the part of the hotel management, Paul excited no suspicion.   56
There was this to be said for him, that he wore his spoils with dignity and in no way made himself conspicuous. His chief greediness lay in his ears and eyes, and his excesses were not offensive ones. His dearest pleasures were the gray winter twilights in his sitting room; his quiet enjoyment of his flowers, his clothes, his wide divan, his cigarette and his sense of power. He could not remember a time when he had felt so at peace with himself. The mere release from the necessity of petty lying, lying every day and every day, restored his self-respect. He had never lied for pleasure, even at school; but to make

---

[14]Box. [Eds.]

himself noticed and admired, to assert his difference from other Cordelia Street boys; and he felt a good deal more manly, more honest, even, now that he had no need for boastful pretensions, now that he could, as his actor friends used to say, "dress the part." It was characteristic that remorse did not occur to him. His golden days went by without a shadow, and he made each as perfect as he could.

On the eighth day after his arrival in New York, he found the 57 whole affair exploited in the Pittsburgh papers, exploited with a wealth of detail which indicated that local news of a sensational nature was at a low ebb. The firm of Denny & Carson announced that the boy's father had refunded the full amount of his theft, and that they had no intention of prosecuting. The Cumberland minister had been interviewed, and expressed his hope of yet reclaiming the motherless lad, and Paul's Sabbath-school teacher declared that she would spare no effort to that end. The rumor had reached Pittsburgh that the boy had been seen in a New York hotel, and his father had gone East to find him and bring him home.

Paul had just come in to dress for dinner; he sank into a chair, 58 weak in the knees, and clasped his head in his hands. It was to be worse than jail, even; the tepid waters of Cordelia Street were to close over him finally and forever. The gray monotony stretched before him in hopeless, unrelieved years; Sabbath-school, Young People's Meeting, the yellow-papered room, the damp dish-towels; it all rushed back upon him with sickening vividness. He had the old feeling that the orchestra had suddenly stopped, the sinking sensation that the play was over. The sweat broke out on his face, and he sprang to his feet, looked about him with his white, conscious smile, and winked at himself in the mirror. With something of the childish belief in miracles with which he had so often gone to class, all his lessons unlearned, Paul dressed and dashed whistling down the corridor to the elevator.

He had no sooner entered the dining room and caught the mea- 59 sure of the music, than his remembrance was lightened by his old elastic power of claiming the moment, mounting with it, and finding it all sufficient. The glare and glitter about him, the mere scenic accessories had again, and for the last time, their old potency. He would show himself that he was game, he would finish the thing splendidly. He doubted, more than ever, the existence of Cordelia Street, and for the first time he drank his wine recklessly. Was he not, after all, one of these fortunate beings? Was he not still himself, and in his own place? He drummed a nervous accompaniment to the music and looked about him, telling himself over and over that it had paid.

He reflected drowsily, to the swell of the violin and the chill 60 sweetness of his wine, that he might have done it more wisely. He might have caught an outbound steamer and been well out of their clutches before now. But the other side of the world had seemed too far away and too uncertain then; he could not have waited for it; his need had been too sharp. If he had to choose over again, he would do the same thing tomorrow. He looked affectionately about the dining room, now gilded with a soft mist. Ah, it had paid indeed!

Paul was awakened the next morning by a painful throbbing in 61 his head and feet. He had thrown himself across the bed without undressing, and had slept with his shoes on. His limbs and hands were lead heavy, and his tongue and throat were parched. There came upon him one of those fateful attacks of clear-headedness that never occurred except when he was physically exhausted and his nerves hung loose. He lay still and closed his eyes and let the tide of realities wash over him.

His father was in New York; "stopping at some joint or other," 62 he told himself. The memory of successive summers on the front stoop fell upon him like a weight of black water. He had not a hundred dollars left, and he knew now, more than ever, that money was everything, the wall that stood between all he loathed and all he wanted. The thing was winding itself up; he had thought of that on his first glorious day in New York, and had even provided a way to snap the thread. It lay on his dressing-table now; he had got it out last night when he came blindly up from dinner,—but the shiny metal hurt his eyes, and he disliked the look of it, anyway.

He rose and moved about with a painful effort, succumbing now 63 and again to attacks of nausea. It was the old depression exaggerated; all the world had become Cordelia Street. Yet somehow he was not afraid of anything, was absolutely calm; perhaps because he had looked into the dark corner at last, and knew. It was bad enough, what he saw there; but somehow not so bad as his long fear of it had been. He saw everything clearly now. He had a feeling that he had made the best of it, that he had lived the sort of life he was meant to live, and for half an hour sat staring at the revolver. But he told himself that was not the way, so he went downstairs and took a cab to the ferry.

When Paul arrived at Newark, he got off the train and took 64 another cab, directing the driver to follow the Pennsylvania tracks out of the town. The snow lay heavy on the roadways and had drifted deep in the open fields. Only here and there the dead grass or dried weed stalks projected, singularly black, above it. Once well into the country, Paul dismissed the carriage and walked, floundering along the tracks, his mind a medley of irrelevant things. He seemed to hold in his brain an actual picture of everything he had seen that morning. He remembered every feature of both his drivers, the toothless old woman from whom he had bought the red flowers in his coat, the agent from whom he had got his ticket, and all of his fellow-passengers on the ferry. His mind, unable to cope with vital matters near at hand, worked feverishly and deftly at sorting and grouping these images. They made for him a part of the ugliness of the world, of the ache in his head, and the bitter burning on his tongue. He stooped and put a handful of snow into his mouth as he walked, but that, too, seemed hot. When he reached a little hillside, where the tracks ran through a cut some twenty feet below him, he stopped and sat down.

The carnations in his coat were drooping with the cold, he noticed; all their red glory over. It occurred to him that all the flowers he had seen in the show windows that first night must have gone the same way, long before this. It was only one splendid breath they had, in spite of their brave mockery at the winter outside the glass. It was a losing game in the end, it seemed, this revolt against the homilies[15] by which the world is run. Paul took one of the blossoms carefully from his coat and scooped a little hole in the snow, where he covered it up. Then he dozed a while, from his weak condition, seeming insensible to the cold.

The sound of an approaching train woke him, and he started to his feet, remembering only his resolution, and afraid lest he should be too late. He stood watching the approaching locomotive, his teeth chattering, his lips drawn away from them in a frightened smile; once or twice he glanced nervously sidewise, as though he were being watched. When the right moment came, he jumped. As he fell, the folly of his haste occurred to him with merciless clearness, the vastness of what he had left undone. There flashed through his brain, clearer than ever before, the blue of Adriatic water, the yellow of Algerian sands.

He felt something strike his chest,—his body was being thrown swiftly through the air, on and on, immeasurably far and fast, while his limbs gently relaxed. Then, because the picture-making mechanism was crushed, the disturbing visions flashed into black, and Paul dropped back into the immense design of things.

65

66

67

WRITING SUGGESTION

Write a suicide note that Paul might have written. Addressing the note to his father, explain his motivations for his suicide and for the actions leading up to it.

RESPONDING TO READING

1. What traits isolate Paul from home, family, and friends? Is it within his power to overcome the forces that set him apart? If it is, why does he choose not to do so?   **2.** Do you feel sorry for Paul, or do you believe he gets what he deserves? Why?   **3.** "Paul's Case" was written in 1905. What

ANSWERS TO RESPONDING TO READING

1. His love of beauty and romance isolates him; he despises the reality of "common" existence. He could act like his peers (even if he does not share their values), but he is not willing to expend the effort to fit in. He wants what he desires to come to him easily.

---

[15]Sermons; tedious moralizing lectures. [Eds.]

FOR OPENERS

When do children become aware of differences between themselves and other children? What impact do you suppose this realization has on their view of themselves and their place in society?

ADDITIONAL QUESTION FOR RESPONDING TO READING

Try to recall any realizations about people's differences (class, race, gender, and religious differences) you noticed as a child. As far as you can tell, how great a role did these realizations play in shaping your present attitudes?

kinds of antisocial feelings or behavior might isolate an adolescent from his or her family today? What behavior might alienate an adolescent from his or her peers? Is differentness as devastating for a contemporary adolescent as it is for Paul?

The Stolen Party

LILIANA HEKER

Considered one of Argentina's best writers since the 1960s, Liliana Heker (1943–   ) has published a collection of short stories called *Los Que Vieron la Zarza* (1966) (*Those Who Behold the Burning Bush*). She is also editor of the literary magazine, *El Ornitorrinco* (*The Platypus*), which has continued to publish despite Argentina's repressive government. Heker has said about the role of the writer in a tortured society, "To be heard, we must shout from within." In the following story, written in 1982 and collected in *Other Fires: Short Fiction by Latin American Women* (1986), Heker tells of a young girl's painful discovery of class differences at a birthday party.

As soon as she arrived she went straight to the kitchen to see if 1
the monkey was there. It was: what a relief! She wouldn't have liked to admit that her mother had been right. *Monkeys at a birthday?* her mother had sneered. *Get away with you, believing any nonsense you're told!* She was cross, but not because of the monkey, the girl thought; it's just because of the party.

"I don't like you going," she told her. "It's a rich people's party." 2

"Rich people go to Heaven too," said the girl, who studied reli- 3
gion at school.

"Get away with Heaven," said the mother. "The problem with 4
you, young lady, is that you like to fart higher than your ass."

The girl didn't approve of the way her mother spoke. She was 5
barely nine, and one of the best in her class.

"I'm going because I've been invited," she said. "And I've been 6
invited because Luciana is my friend. So there."

"Ah yes, your friend," her mother grumbled. She paused. 7
"Listen, Rosaura," she said at last. "That one's not your friend. You know what you are to them? The maid's daughter, that's what."

Rosaura blinked hard: she wasn't going to cry. Then she yelled: 8
"Shut up! You know nothing about being friends!"

Every afternoon she used to go to Luciana's house and they would 9
both finish their homework while Rosaura's mother did the cleaning.

They had their tea in the kitchen and they told each other secrets. Rosaura loved everything in the big house, and she also loved the people who lived there.

"I'm going because it will be the most lovely party in the whole world, Luciana told me it would. There will be a magician, and he will bring a monkey and everything."   10

The mother swung around to take a good look at her child, and pompously put her hands on her hips.   11

"Monkeys at a birthday?" she said. "Get away with you, believing any nonsense you're told!"   12

Rosaura was deeply offended. She thought it unfair of her mother to accuse other people of being liars simply because they were rich. Rosaura too wanted to be rich, of course. If one day she managed to live in a beautiful palace, would her mother stop loving her? She felt very sad. She wanted to go to that party more than anything else in the world.   13

"I'll die if I don't go," she whispered, almost without moving her lips.   14

And she wasn't sure whether she had been heard, but on the morning of the party she discovered that her mother had starched her Christmas dress. And in the afternoon, after washing her hair, her mother rinsed it in apple vinegar so that it would be all nice and shiny. Before going out, Rosaura admired herself in the mirror, with her white dress and glossy hair, and thought she looked terribly pretty.   15

Señora Ines also seemed to notice. As soon as she saw her, she said: 16

"How lovely you look today, Rosaura."   17

Rosaura gave her starched skirt a slight toss with her hands and walked into the party with a firm step. She said hello to Luciana and asked about the monkey. Luciana put on a secretive look and whispered into Rosaura's ear: "He's in the kitchen. But don't tell anyone, because it's a surprise."   18

Rosaura wanted to make sure. Carefully she entered the kitchen and there she saw it: deep in thought, inside its cage. It looked so funny that the girl stood there for a while, watching it, and later, every so often, she would slip out of the party unseen and go and admire it. Rosaura was the only one allowed into the kitchen. Señora Ines had said: "You yes, but not the others, they're much too boisterous, they might break something." Rosaura had never broken anything. She even managed the jug of orange juice, carrying it from the kitchen into the dining room. She held it carefully and didn't spill a single drop. And Señora Ines had said: "Are you sure you can manage   19

TEACHING STRATEGY

Discuss the following with your students:
Paragraphs 10–13: Explain the conflict between the beliefs of the mother and the daughter. Who is right, in your opinion? Who is more realistic?
Paragraph 15: Why does Rosaura's mother allow her to attend the party after all?
Paragraph 32: Why does Rosaura omit "And proud of it"?
Paragraph 39: What are you beginning to suspect about Rosaura's presence at the party?
Paragraphs 72–73: Explain Rosaura's reaction; explain her mother's. To what does "an infinitely delicate balance" refer?

a jug as big as that?" Of course she could manage. She wasn't a butterfingers, like the others. Like that blonde girl with the bow in her hair. As soon as she saw Rosaura, the girl with the bow had said:

"And you? Who are you?" 20

"I'm a friend of Luciana," said Rosaura. 21

"No," said the girl with the bow, "you are not a friend of Luciana 22 because I'm her cousin and I know all her friends. And I don't know you."

"So what," said Rosaura. "I come here every afternoon with my 23 mother and we do our homework together."

"You and your mother do your homework together?" asked the 24 girl, laughing.

"I and Luciana do our homework together," said Rosaura, very 25 seriously.

The girl with the bow shrugged her shoulders. 26

"That's not being friends," she said. "Do you go to school 27 together?"

"No." 28

"So where do you know her from?" said the girl, getting impa- 29 tient.

Rosaura remembered her mother's words perfectly. She took a 30 deep breath.

"I'm the daughter of the employee," she said. 31

Her mother had said very clearly: "If someone asks, you say 32 you're the daughter of the employee; that's all." She also told her to add: "And proud of it." But Rosaura thought that never in her life would she dare say something of the sort.

"What employee?" said the girl with the bow. "Employee in a 33 shop?"

"No," said Rosaura angrily. "My mother doesn't sell anything in 34 any shop, so there."

"So how come she's an employee?" said the girl with the bow. 35

Just then Señora Ines arrived saying *shh shh*, and asked Rosaura 36 if she wouldn't mind helping serve out the hotdogs, as she knew the house so much better than the others.

"See?" said Rosaura to the girl with the bow, and when no one 37 was looking she kicked her in the shin.

Apart from the girl with the bow, all the others were delightful. 38 The one she liked best was Luciana, with her golden birthday crown; and then the boys. Rosaura won the sack race, and nobody managed to catch her when they played tag. When they split into two teams to play charades, all the boys wanted her for their side. Rosaura felt she had never been so happy in all her life.

COLLABORATIVE ACTIVITY

Ask students working in groups, to discuss a time when they became aware of class differences between themselves and others. In class discussion, focus on how these experiences are alike and different.

But the best was still to come. The best came after Luciana blew   39
out the candles. First the cake. Señora Ines had asked her to help
pass the cake around, and Rosaura had enjoyed the task immensely,
because everyone called out to her, shouting "Me, me!" Rosaura
remembered a story in which there was a queen who had the power
of life or death over her subjects. She had always loved that, having
the power of life or death. To Luciana and the boys she gave the
largest pieces, and to the girl with the bow she gave a slice so thin
one could see through it.

After the cake came the magician, tall and bony, with a fine red   40
cape. A true magician: he could untie handkerchiefs by blowing on
them and make a chain with links that had no openings. He could
guess what cards were pulled out from a pack, and the monkey was
his assistant. He called the monkey "partner." "Let's see here,
partner," he would say, "turn over a card." And, "Don't run away,
partner: time to work now."

The final trick was wonderful. One of the children had to hold   41
the monkey in his arms and the magician said he would make him
disappear.

"What, the boy?" they all shouted.   42

"No, the monkey!" shouted back the magician.   43

Rosaura thought that this was truly the most amusing party in   44
the whole world.

The magician asked a small fat boy to come and help, but the   45
small fat boy got frightened almost at once and dropped the monkey
on the floor. The magician picked him up carefully, whispered something in his ear, and the monkey nodded almost as if he understood.

"You mustn't be so unmanly, my friend," the magician said to   46
the fat boy.

"What's unmanly?" said the fat boy.   47

The magician turned around as if to look for spies.   48

"A sissy," said the magician. "Go sit down."   49

Then he stared at all the faces, one by one. Rosaura felt her heart   50
tremble.

"You, with the Spanish eyes," said the magician. And everyone   51
saw that he was pointing at her.

She wasn't afraid. Neither holding the monkey, nor when the   52
magician made him vanish; not even when, at the end, the magician
flung his red cape over Rosaura's head and uttered a few magic words
. . . and the monkey reappeared, chattering happily, in her arms.
The children clapped furiously. And before Rosaura returned to her
seat, the magician said:

"Thank you very much, my little countess."   53

WRITING SUGGESTION

Write a letter from Rosaura to Señora Ines in which she returns the money and explains her reasons for doing so.

She was so pleased with the compliment that a while later, when 54 her mother came to fetch her, that was the first thing she told her.

"I helped the magician and he said to me, 'Thank you very much, 55 my little countess!'"

It was strange because up to then Rosaura had thought that she 56 was angry with her mother. All along Rosaura had imagined that she would say to her: "See that the monkey wasn't a lie?" But instead she was so thrilled that she told her mother all about the wonderful magician.

Her mother tapped her on the head and said: "So now we're a 57 countess!"

But one could see that she was beaming. 58

And now they both stood in the entrance, because a moment ago 59 Señora Ines, smiling, had said: "Please wait here a second."

Her mother suddenly seemed worried. 60

"What is it?" she asked Rosaura. 61

"What is what?" said Rosaura. "It's nothing; she just wants to 62 get the presents for those who are leaving, see?"

She pointed at the fat boy and at a girl with pigtails who were 63 also waiting there, next to their mothers. And she explained about the presents. She knew, because she had been watching those who left before her. When one of the girls was about to leave, Señora Ines would give her a bracelet. When a boy left, Señora Ines gave him a yo-yo. Rosaura preferred the yo-yo because it sparkled, but she didn't mention that to her mother. Her mother might have said: "So why don't you ask for one, you blockhead?" That's what her mother was like. Rosaura didn't feel like explaining that she'd be horribly ashamed to be the odd one out. Instead she said:

"I was the best-behaved at the party." 64

And she said no more because Señora Ines came out into the hall 65 with two bags, one pink and one blue.

First she went up to the fat boy, gave him a yo-yo out of the blue 66 bag, and the fat boy left with his mother. Then she went up to the girl and gave her a bracelet out of the pink bag, and the girl with the pigtails left as well.

Finally she came up to Rosaura and her mother. She had a big 67 smile on her face and Rosaura liked that. Señora Ines looked down at her, then looked up at her mother, and then said something that made Rosaura proud:

"What a marvelous daughter you have, Herminia." 68

For an instant, Rosaura thought that she'd give her two presents: 69 the bracelet and the yo-yo. Señora Ines bent down as if about to look for something. Rosaura also leaned forward, stretching out her arm. But she never completed the movement.

Señora Ines didn't look in the pink bag. Nor did she look in the 70 blue bag. Instead she rummaged in her purse. In her hand appeared two bills.

"You really and truly earned this," she said handing them over. 71 "Thank you for all your help, my pet."

Rosaura felt her arms stiffen, stick close to her body, and then 72 she noticed her mother's hand on her shoulder. Instinctively, she pressed herself against her mother's body. That was all. Except her eyes. Rosaura's eyes had a cold, clear look that fixed itself on Señora Ines's face.

Señora Ines, motionless, stood there with her hand outstretched. 73 As if she didn't dare draw it back. As if the slightest change might shatter an infinitely delicate balance.

RESPONDING TO READING

1. Why does Rosaura not realize that she is different from Luciana? Do you think Luciana is aware of their differences? Why does Rosaura's mother not warn her daughter of the dangers of her assumptions? Do you think she should have done so?   **2.** In what way is the society in which Rosaura and Luciana live different from or similar to your own?   **3.** Did you expect this story to have a happy ending? Did any personal experiences influence your expectations?

ANSWERS TO RESPONDING TO READING

1. Luciana treats Rosaura as an equal in friendship; she does not yet appear to be aware of their differences. Rosaura's mother obviously does not want to hurt her daughter. She does drop hints, however, and Rosaura's response is defiant. To warn her daughter of the dangers of her assumptions would suggest to the child that she must accept her limitations, not question or challenge them.
2. Answers may vary, but students should find many similarities.
3. Although some foreshadowing of the outcome occurs within the course of the party, some students will probably have expected a happy ending, as the story might have had in a movie or television program.

Telephone Conversation

WOLE SOYINKA

Nobel Prize-winning playwright, poet, and novelist Wole Soyinka (1934–   ), was born in Ake, Nigeria, a member of the Yoruba tribe. Most of Soyinka's writing is a record of twentieth-century political turmoil in Africa. He has said that in African tradition an artist "has always functioned as the record of the mores and experience of his culture." Soyinka's first novel, *The Interpreters* (1965), is about life in Nigeria before independence. *The Man Died: Prison Notes of Wole Soyinka* (1972) is his memoir of the time in the 1960s when he was wrongly imprisoned. Other titles are *Myth, Literature and the African World* (essays, 1976), *Ogun Ahibimen* (poems, 1976), *The Years of Childhood* (autobiography, 1981), and *Requiem for a Futurologist* (play, 1985). The following poem about prejudice appears in *Modern Poetry from Africa*.

The price seemed reasonable, location
Indifferent. The landlady swore she lived

FOR OPENERS

Notice the characterization of the woman whom neither the speaker nor the reader can see. Ask students to describe her.

TEACHING STRATEGY

Focus on the following specifics in the poem:

Line 7: "Pressurized good-breeding"
Line 9: "Caught I was, foully."
Lines 14–15: What is the setting? How can you tell?
Lines 21–22: "clinical . . . light / Impersonality"
Lines 24–25: "spectroscopic / Flight of fancy"
Lines 35–36: What is it that the woman refuses to see?

WRITING SUGGESTION

Rewrite this poem as a short story, changing the setting to the United States.

Off premises. Nothing remained
But self-confession. 'Madam,' I warned,
'I hate a wasted journey—I am African.'   5
Silence. Silenced transmission of
Pressurized good-breeding. Voice, when it came,
Lipstick coated, long gold-rolled
Cigarette-holder pipped. Caught I was, foully.
'HOW DARK?' . . . I had not misheard. . . . 'ARE YOU
    LIGHT   10
OR VERY DARK?' Button B. Button A. Stench
Of rancid breath of public hide-and-speak.
Red booth. Red pillar-box.[1] Red double-tiered
Omnibus[2] squelching tar. It *was* real! Shamed   15
By ill-mannered silence, surrender
Pushed dumbfoundment to beg simplification.
Considerate she was, varying the emphasis—
'ARE YOU DARK? OR VERY LIGHT?' Revelation came.
'You mean—like plain or milk chocolate?'   20
Her assent was clinical, crushing in its light
Impersonality. Rapidly, wave-length adjusted,
I chose. 'West African sepia'—and as afterthought,
'Down in my passport.' Silence for spectroscopic
Flight of fancy, till truthfulness clanged her accent   25
Hard on the mouthpiece. 'WHAT'S THAT?' conceding
'DON'T KNOW WHAT THAT IS.' 'Like brunette.'
'THAT'S DARK, ISN'T IT?' 'Not altogether.
Facially, I am brunette, but madam, you should see
The rest of me. Palm of my hand, soles of my feet   30
Are a peroxide blonde. Friction, caused—
Foolishly madam—by sitting down, has turned
My bottom raven black—One moment madam!'—sensing
Her receiver rearing on the thunderclap
About my ears—'Madam,' I pleaded, 'wouldn't you   35
    rather
See for yourself?'

**ANSWERS TO RESPONDING
TO READING**

1. "Nothing remained / But self-confession": The speaker is aware of his position; he has probably been rejected before.
2. He continues to call her "madam," and he is patient in explaining his color. He adopts this tone because his purpose is to rent the apartment. His reasonable tone causes us to feel sympathy for him and to feel anger at the woman's ignorance.

RESPONDING TO READING

1. Soyinka, a Nigerian, creates a speaker who is subject to racial discrimination because of his skin color. What details in the poem make clear his exclusion from the social mainstream?   **2.** Despite the tense situation, the speaker in the poem remains very polite. Give examples of his polite language.

---

[1]Mail box. [Eds.]
[2]Bus. [Eds.]

Why do you think the speaker uses this tone? How does this tone affect your attitude toward the speaker? **3.** Some readers of the poem have reacted by suggesting that the speaker should have given up his quest for the apartment. Would you have given up? Why or why not?

3. There is always the hope that once someone knows you as a person, outside appearances will cease to matter.

WRITING: STRANGERS IN THE VILLAGE

1. When Philip Roth writes of "the power to intimidate that emanated from the highest and lowest reaches of gentile America" (paragraph 1), he identifies a basic conflict that applies not only to Jews but also to many other groups excluded from the largely white, male, upper-class mainstream. Could you argue that the existence and dominance of this powerful class makes outsiders out of many—or even most—Americans?

2. To what extent can a person's differentness be the very force that drives his or her life? Consider Zora Neale Hurston, Paul in "Paul's Case," and any other writer or character—or person you know—whose separateness is a source of strength or power.

3. Richard Rodriguez writes, "Hispanics want to belong to America without betraying the past" (paragraph 3). Using examples from readings in this chapter, write an essay in which you consider whether or not this is possible for your own ethnic group, or for any other group of ethnic "outsiders."

4. Roth, Hurston, and Rodriguez identify strongly with a culture that is set apart from the mainstream United States society. Compare and contrast their views about assimilation into that culture. Then, consider whose view is most like your own.

5. Study an ethnic group or culture other than your own and, like Edward T. Hall, describe it. Make sure you tell how the culture is like and unlike the culture with which you are familiar.

6. Rodriguez closes his essay by stating, "For generations, Latin America has been the place—the bed—of a confluence of so many races and cultures that Protestant North America shuddered to imagine it. Imagine it." Write an essay in which you explain what Rodriguez means and explore the possible effects on North America of the shift of perspective he would have us imagine.

7. In explaining why natives dislike tourists, Kincaid says, "An ugly thing, that is what you are when you become a tourist, an ugly, empty thing, a stupid thing, a piece of rubbish pausing here and there to gaze at this and taste that" (paragraph 5). Consider how one of the following writers is like or unlike Kincaid's tourist: Baldwin in the Swiss village; Didion in El Salvador; Lessing in South Africa; Orwell in Marrakech.

8. Baldwin believes that the people who inhabit the Swiss village represent the West and therefore they "cannot be, from the point of view of power, strangers anywhere in the world; they have made the modern world, in effect, even if they do not know it" (paragraph 9). Do you agree that being a white person of European descent guarantees one a certain insider status? Why or why not?

7

THE CULTURE OF SPORT

CONFRONTING THE ISSUES

Since ancient times athletic competition has expressed some of our highest ideals. In ancient Greece, the Olympics brought individuals, groups, and even nations together in friendly rivalry. Wars were suspended so athletes could complete in the Olympics, and the modern Olympic games have been held since 1896 (except for 1916 and 1940 and 1944, when they were suspended because of World War I and World War II). It is ironic, then, that internal disputes threaten to undermine the visionary spirit of the Olympics. Currently, the greatest source of conflict involves athletes taking steroids to enhance their performance. For years, steroids have been a routine part of training for athletes in many countries. The issue came to a head during the 1988 Olympics when Ben Jonson, a Canadian runner, was stripped of his gold medal when tests showed that he had been taking steroids. During the debate that ensued, a number of athletes contended that in the highly competitive world of the Olympics, performance-enhancing drugs are absolutely necessary. Without such artificial aids, they insisted, athletes could not consistently set the records that both governments and the public have come to expect. Others pointed out that taking steroids involves certain risks and that without careful medical supervision steroids can cause serious physical problems. Most important, they argued that international cooperation and understanding—not excessive competition and nationalism—should be the goal of the Olympics.

After introducing the contrast between the ideal of the Olympic games (a pure, abstract idea of international cooperation and sportsmanship) and its reality (bitter rivalries and intense pressure to win, exemplified by the use of steroids), ask students if they think Olympic athletes should be allowed to take steroids. If they are administered by a physician and the status of the athlete is monitored by a doctor, what is the problem? Ask them what they think of a proposal that has been seriously put forward to have two levels of athletes in the Olympics: those that do not take steroids and those that do.

Then, ask students to consider the place of the Olympics in world culture and what the legitimization of steroids would do to that position. Finally, ask them if the expectations and standards of behavior should be different for professional athletes. Do they see anything wrong with a football player, for example, taking steroids to achieve the bulk he needs to be a lineman?

IN the 1980s and 1990s, sports and sports figures have been elevated to unprecedented heights. It is not unusual to read about baseball players signing contracts that equal the national debt of some small countries. High school athletes are wooed by coaches and college administrators with the enthusiasm formerly reserved for Nobel Prize winners or distinguished writers. Television networks pay tens of millions of dollars for the rights to broadcast National Football League games. And manufacturers of athletic shoes routinely pay certain coaches large sums just to have teams wear their newest line of footwear. Some observers have predicted that the runaway inflation in the ranks of American sports cannot go on forever and that, like the inflation that preceded the stock market crash of 1929, it signals approaching disaster. Even so, the national obsession with sports does not seem to be lessening: Professional baseball and football revenues continue to set records in many cities, and so does spending on athletic gear and clothing.

Our nation's obsession with sports reveals a lot about our national character, and many of the writers in this chapter implicitly address the distinctly American passion for certain sports. Others use sports as a metaphor for various aspects of American society, exploring, for example, its mythical qualities (Murray Ross), its violent tendencies (John McMurtry, Norman Cousins), its sexism (Marie Hart), and its racism (Roy Campanella II). In the world of professional sports, as in the society at large, competition, business acumen, courage, determination, and toughness matter a great deal, as the writers in this chapter are well aware. Even for those, such as Doris Kearns Goodwin and Stephen Jay Gould, who simply present their emotional and intellectual reactions, the meaning and power of sports go far beyond the games themselves.

As these and other writers attempt to demonstrate, many sports have become much more than entertainment. In some mysterious way they embody aspects of the national character.

PREPARING TO READ AND WRITE

As you read and prepare to write about the selections in this chapter, consider the following questions:

- Does the writer discuss sports in general or one particular sport?
- Is the writer's view of sports positive or negative?
- Does the writer give an objective picture of a sport, or does he or she present personal reactions?

- What values does the writer think are inherent in a sport?
- Does the writer believe that social issues have affected sports in any way?
- Does the writer address the issue of social class?
- Does the writer address issues related to race or gender?
- What lessons does the writer think an individual can learn from sports? Do these lessons also apply to life?
- What preconceived ideas does the writer think readers have about a particular sport? Does the writer challenge these ideas or reinforce them?
- Judging from your personal experience, do you think the writer presents an accurate picture of sports? Or, does the writer tend to idealize sports and sports figures?

Sport: Women Sit in the Back of the Bus

MARIE HART

Essayist Marie Hart (1932–   ) writes about what she knows, women and sports. She has been a high school physical education teacher and a professor of physical education and kinesiology. In addition to contributing to books, journals, and periodicals, she is the author of *Sex Discrimination in Physical Education and Athletics Programs in California Higher Education* (1974). In the following 1971 essay, Hart talks about the difficulty women athletes have trying to be "womanly" and yet be accepted as skilled professionals in the "male territory" of sports.

Other things being equal, the man who has had the most experience in outdoor sports should be the best aviator. By the same token, women should be barred . . . women have not the background of games of strength and skill that most men have. Their powers of correlation are correspondingly limited and their ability to cope with sudden emergency is inadequate.

—*Outing Magazine*, November 1912

The roles of woman and successful female athlete are almost incompatible in the United States. The woman who wishes to participate in sports and remain "womanly" faces great stress. By choosing sport she usually places herself outside the social mainstream.

Today's new movements offer little support. What does Women's Lib have to say about freeing the woman athlete? Not much. If woman is to be more than mother, secretary and Miss America, we must reward her for sports achievement instead of stigmatizing her for it.

But the struggle focuses on other areas, such as dance. "Dance is a field for women, and male homosexuals," said *Women: A Journal of Liberation*, which described dance as one of the few ways to escape "Amerika's sick sexuality." And we seem to see sport as a field for men, and female homosexuals. Certainly, for a woman, sport intensifies sex-role problems. In most other parts of the Western world women coexist with men in sport as accepted and respected partners. Not in the United States. A female athlete meets more oppression than most other women in the American way of life.

Norms

Being female in this culture does not necessarily mean that one is perceived or accepted as feminine. Every culture has its social norms and sex roles. In the United States these seem to be especially rigid and narrow; women in sport do not fit our particular concept of femininity and those who persist in sport suffer for it.

Why has it been so difficult for women to remain "womanly" and yet be athletes, especially in games that require great physical skill? Games of physical skill are mostly associated with achievement and aggressiveness, which seem to make them the exclusive province of males. Women are more traditionally associated with obedience training and routine responsibility training and with games of strategy and games of chance. Conditioning begins early—in elementary school a girl feels pressure to select some games and avoid others if she is to be a "real" girl. If she is told often enough at 11 or 12 that sports are not ladylike, she may at that point make a choice between being a lady and being an athlete. This forced choice may create deep conflict that persists into adulthood. Sport is male territory; therefore participation of female intruders is a peripheral, noncentral aspect of sport. The sexually separate (and unequal) facilities and organizations in sport in the United States illustrate the subordination of women athletes.

Conflict

As a girl becomes more and more proficient in sport, her level of personal investment increases and the long hours of practice and limited associations may isolate her socially. Personal conflict and stress increase as it becomes necessary for her to convince others of her femininity. This tension and conflict may increase still more if a girl chooses a sport that most regard as exclusive male territory.

Chi Cheng, a student at California State Polytechnic College at Pomona who holds several world track records for women, was quoted as saying, "The public sees women competing and immediately thinks they must be manly—but at night, we're just like other women."

Why would a woman need to comment about herself in this way and how does this awareness of stigma affect her daily life? For Chi Cheng, one solution is "to give a lot of public appearances—where I can show off my femininity."

Hair

Numerous discussions with college groups over the past few years have convinced me that our society imposes a great burden on women who commit themselves to sport, as participants or as teachers. Sev-

TEACHING STRATEGY

List on the board (with help from the class) all the characteristics associated with male and female athletes. Examine the adjectives used. Ask students to characterize the differences between the adjectives used to describe female athletes and those used to describe male athletes. Is there any gender bias?

COLLABORATIVE ACTIVITIES

1. Divide the class into groups by gender. Ask male students to list all the "male" sports and then list all the "female" sports. Ask the female students to do the same. Ask the class to discuss the differences between the lists compiled by the two groups of students. What, if anything, do these differences show about how males and females view each other?

2. Divide the class into three groups—one group all male, another all female, and a third composed equally of both sexes. Ask each group to define femininity and masculinity and to present its findings to the class.

eral married women students majoring in physical education confided at one discussion group that they had wanted to cut their hair but felt that they couldn't: They simply didn't want the stereotyped image. Even when general hair styles are short, women in sport are judged by a standard other than fashion. And if the married woman experiences anxiety over such things, one can imagine the struggle of the single woman.

10 When young women do enjoy sport, what activities are really open to them? In a 1963 study, 200 first- and second-year college women from four southern California schools strongly recommended that girls not participate in track and field activities. The sports they did recommend were tennis, swimming, ice skating, diving, bowling, skiing and golf, all of which have aesthetic social and fashion aspects. Physical strength and skill may be components of some but are not their primary identifications.

11 In startling contrast is the black woman athlete. In the black community, it seems, a woman can be strong and competent in sport and still not deny her womanliness. She can even win respect and status; Wilma Rudolph[1] is an example.

Tomboy

12 Sport standards are male and the woman in sport is compared with men—not with other women. It starts early: *Wow, what a beautiful throw. You've got an arm like a guy. Look at that girl run; she could beat lots of boys.* Father comments, *Yes, she loves sports. She's our little tomboy.* It would seem strange to say of a small boy, *Oh, yes, he is our little marygirl.* (We have ways of getting messages to boys who don't fit the role, but we haven't integrated them into our language so securely.)

13 These comments carry the message of expected cultural behavior. When the girl has the message clearly she loses games to a boy on purpose. She knows that she may win the game and lose the boy.

14 Male performance standards and the attending social behavior have resulted in even more serious problems. In international sports events a woman must now pass a sex test of cells collected from inside of the cheek. In a normal woman, about 20 cells in every hundred contain Barr bodies (collections of chromatins). At the 1968 Olympic

---

[1]Wilma Rudolph (1940–   ), runner in 1956 and 1960 Olympics who set women's world records in the 100 meter, 200 meter, and 400 meter relays. In 1960 she was the first woman to win both sprint gold medals. [Eds.]

games, women whose tests showed Barr bodies in fewer than 10 cells in every hundred were barred from competition. Marion Lay, a Canadian swimmer, said that at those Olympics a long line of women awaiting the test in Mexico erupted in reactions that ranged from tension-releasing jokes to severe stress and upset. Some athletes suggested that if the doctor were good-looking enough, one might skip the test and prove her femininity by seducing him. Many were baffled, feeling that their honesty was in question along with their femininity.

There is also the problem of the use by some women performers   15
of "steroid" drugs, male sex-hormone derivatives that tend to increase muscle size. There have been strong and continued warnings against the use of steroids by men because of their dangerous effects, but little has been published about the negative effects of male steroids on women. They are known to increase muscle size, to change fat distribution and also to produce secondary male characteristics such as increased face and body hair and lowered voice.

Why would a woman take such a drug? Because the values are   16
on male records and performance and she will attempt to come as close to this goal as possible.

Bar

Social attitudes that limit sport choices for women have a long   17
history. Here's an editorial from a 1912 issue of *Outing Magazine:*

"Other things being equal, the man who has had the most experience in outdoor sports should be the best aviator. By the same token, women should be barred . . . Women have not the background of games of strength and skill that most men have. Their powers of correlation are correspondingly limited and their ability to cope with sudden emergency is inadequate."

In 1936 the editor of *Sportsman*, a magazine for the wealthy, com-   18
mented of the Olympic Games that he was ". . . fed up to the ears with women as track and field competitors." He continued, "a woman's charms shrink to something less than zero" and urged the organizers to "keep them where they were competent. As swimmers and divers, girls are as beautiful and adroit as they are ineffective and unpleasing on the track."

More recent publications such as *Sports Illustrated* have not been   19
as openly negative; but they sustain sexual bias by limiting their coverage of women in sport. The emphasis in periodicals is still largely on women as attractive objects rather than as skilled and effective athletes.

WRITING SUGGESTIONS

1. Marie Hart's thesis is that women in sports usually place themselves outside the social mainstream. What evidence within the essay supports this claim? Do your own experiences support this thesis?

2. Do today's female athletes provide role models that help women overcome the problems Hart discusses? *Should* they? Write an essay explaining your position.

3. Should female sportswriters be allowed into the locker rooms of male athletes? Should any reporters be permitted to interview athletes in locker rooms? Write a newspaper editorial expressing your views.

Muscles

Operating alongside sex bias to scare girls from sport have been such misunderstandings as the muscle myth—the fear that athletics will produce bulging muscles which imply masculinity. The fact, well documented by the exercise physiologists, Carl E. Klafs and Daniel D. Arnheim, is that "excessive development (muscle) is not a concomitant of athletic competition." They further report: "Contrary to lay opinion, participation in sports does not masculinize women. . . ." Some girl and women athletes are indeed muscular. Klafs and Arnheim explain: "Girls whose physiques reflect considerable masculinity are stronger per unit of weight than girls who are low in masculinity and boys who display considerable femininity of build. Those who are of masculine type often do enter sports and are usually quite successful because of the mechanical advantages possessed by the masculine structure. However, such types are the exception, and by far the greater majority of participants possess a feminine body build." 20

Opening

Myths die hard, but they do die. Today, gradually, women *have* begun to enter sport with more social acceptance and individual pride. In 1952, researchers from the Finnish Institute of Occupational Health who conducted an intensive study of the athletes participating in the Olympics in Helsinki predicted that "women are able to shake off civil disabilities which millennia of prejudice and ignorance have imposed upon them." The researchers found that the participation of women in sport was a significant indicator of the health and living standards of a country. 21

Simone de Beauvoir[2] wrote in *The Second Sex* ". . . In sports the end in view is not success independent of physical equipment; it is rather the attainment of perfection within the limitations of each physical type; the featherweight boxing champion is as much of a champion as is the heavyweight; the woman skiing champion is not the inferior of the faster male champion; they belong to two different classes. It is precisely the female athletes who, being positively interested in their own game, feel themselves least handicapped in comparison with the male." 22

---

[2]French novelist (1908–86). Her influential book *The Second Sex* (1949) is a major work of feminist critical thought. [Eds.]

Americans seem to be still unable to apply to the woman in sport   23
this view of "attainment of perfection within the limitations of each."

The experiencing of one's body in sport must not be denied to   24
anyone in the name of an earlier century's image of femininity—a
binding, limiting, belittling image. This is the age of the woman in
space, and she demands her female space and identity in sport.

RESPONDING TO READING

1. Judging from your experience, do you think things have improved significantly since Hart wrote her essay in 1971? For example, are girls still told "at 11 or 12 that sports are not ladylike" (paragraph 5)? Is it true, as Hart says in paragraph 19, that sports publications emphasize female athletes as attractive objects rather than as skilled professionals?   **2.** In paragraph 11 Hart states that there is a difference between black and white women athletes but offers little support for her assertion. Do your own experiences or observations support or contradict Hart's claim? Should she have accounted for the differences she says exist? How important is this omission?   **3.** How do you explain the great popularity of women's tennis and golf? In light of your answer, how do you explain the inability of women's basketball to achieve the same popular following as men's basketball?

The Black and White Truth about Basketball

JEFF GREENFIELD

Political commentator and media critic Jeff Greenfield (1943–   ) once worked as a legislative aid for Senator Robert Kennedy and has made his career in the media about which he writes. His books include *Television: The First Fifty Years* (1977) and *The Real Campaign: The Media and the Battle for the White House* (1982). The latter work is controversial because of Greenfield's argument that the media made no difference in the outcome of the 1980 presidential race, a position that challenges the accepted opinion. He is also the author of *The World's Greatest Team: A Portrait of the Boston Celtics, 1957–1969* (1976). In the 1984 revised version of "The Black and White Truth About Basketball," Greenfield again challenges his readers by asserting that the two races have inherently different styles on the court.

The dominance of black athletes over professional basketball is   1
beyond dispute. Two thirds of the players are black, and the number
would be greater were it not for the continuing practice of picking

**ADDITIONAL QUESTIONS FOR
RESPONDING TO READING**

1. Based on personal observation, can you
name a sport in which whites perform better
than blacks? Are the differences racial, cultural, or environmental?
2. Is it a racist statement to say that blacks are
better than whites at basketball? Why or why
not?
3. In his essay Greenfield characterizes the
Celtics as a "white" team and defines the
quick forward as a "white" position. Are
Greenfield's characterizations justified? Do
you think he is setting up a false duality?

white bench warmers for the sake of balance. The Most Valuable
Player award of the National Basketball Association has gone to blacks
for twenty-three of the last twenty-five years. The NBA was the first
pro sports league of any stature to hire a black coach (Bill Russell of
the Celtics) and the first black general manager (Wayne Embry of the
Bucks). What discrimination remains—lack of opportunity for lucrative benefits such as speaking engagements and product endorse-
ments—has more to do with society than with basketball.

This dominance reflects a natural inheritance; basketball is a pas- 2
time of the urban poor. The current generation of black athletes are
heirs to a tradition half a century old: In a neighborhood without the
money for bats, gloves, hockey sticks, tennis rackets, or shoulder
pads, basketball is accessible. "Once it was the game of the Irish and
Italian Catholics in Rockaway and the Jews on Fordham Road in the
Bronx," writes David Wolf in his brilliant book, *Foul!* "It was recreation, status, and a way out." But now the ethnic names are changed;
instead of Red Holzmans, Red Auerbachs, and McGuire brothers,
there are Julius Ervings and Darryl Dawkinses and Kareem Abdul-
Jabbars. And professional basketball is a sport with a national television contract and million-dollar salaries.

But the mark on basketball of today's players can be measured 3
by more than money or visibility. It is a question of style. For there
is a clear difference between "black" and "white" styles of play that
is as clear as the difference between 155th Street at Eighth Avenue
and Crystal City, Missouri. Most simply (remembering we are talking
about culture, not chromosomes), "black" basketball is the use of
superb athletic skill to adapt to the limits of space imposed by the
game. "White" ball is the pulverization of that space by sheer intensity.

It takes a conscious effort to realize how constricted the space is 4
on a basketball court. Place a regulation court (ninety-four by fifty
feet) on a football field, and it will reach from the back of the end
zone to the twenty-one-yard line; its width will cover less than a third
of the field. On a baseball diamond, a basketball court will reach from
home plate to just beyond first base. Compared to its principal indoor
rival, ice hockey, basketball covers about one-fourth the playing area.
And during the normal flow of the game, most of the action takes
place on about the third of the court nearest the basket. It is in this
dollhouse space that ten men, each of them half a foot taller than the
average man, come together to battle each other.

There is, thus, no room; basketball is a struggle for the edge: the 5
half step with which to cut around the defender for a lay-up, the half
second of freedom with which to release a jump shot, the instant a

head turns allowing a pass to a teammate breaking for the basket. It is an arena for the subtlest of skills: the head fake, the shoulder fake, the shift of body weight to the right and the sudden cut to the left. Deception is crucial to success; and to young men who have learned early and painfully that life is a battle for survival, basketball is one of the few games in which the weapon of deception is a legitimate rule and not the source of trouble.

If there is, then, the need to compete in a crowd, to battle for the 6 edge, then the surest strategy is to develop the *unexpected*; to develop a shot that is simply and fundamentally different from the usual methods of putting the ball in the basket. Drive to the hoop, but go under it and come up the other side; hold the ball at waist level and shoot from there instead of bringing the ball up to eye level; leap into the air and fall away from the basket instead of toward it. All these tactics take maximum advantage of the crowding on a court; they also stamp uniqueness on young men who may feel it nowhere else.

"For many young men in the slums," David Wolf writes, "the 7 school yard is the only place they can feel true pride in what they do, where they can move free of inhibitions and where they can, by being spectacular, rise for the moment against the drabness and anonymity of their lives. Thus, when a player develops extraordinary 'school yard' moves and shots . . . [they] become his measure as a man."

So the moves that begin as tactics for scoring soon become calling 8 cards. You don't just lay the ball in for an uncontested basket; you take the ball in both hands, leap as high as you can, and slam the ball through the hoop. When you jump in the air, fake a shot, bring the ball back to your body, and throw up a shot, all without coming back down, you have proven your worth in uncontestable fashion.

This liquid grace is an integral part of "black" ball, almost exclu- 9 sively the province of the playground player. Some white stars like Bob Cousy, Billy Cunningham, Doug Collins, and Paul Westphal had it: the body control, the moves to the basket, the free-ranging mobility. They also had the surface ease that is integral to the "black" style; an incorporation of the ethic of mean streets—to "make it" is not just to have wealth, but to have it without strain. Whatever the muscles and organs are doing, the face of the "black" star almost never shows it. George Gervin of the San Antonio Spurs can drive to the basket with two men on him, pull up, turn around, and hit a basket without the least flicker of emotion. The Knicks' former great Walt Frazier, flamboyant in dress, cars, and companions, displayed nothing but a quickly raised fist after scoring a particularly important basket. (Interestingly, the black coaches in the NBA exhibit far less emotion on the

TEACHING STRATEGY

This essay claims that environment rather than heredity determines competence in basketball. List on the board all the characteristics of a good basketball player, and attribute each trait to either heredity or environment.

COLLABORATIVE ACTIVITY

Divide the class into groups to examine different portions of Greenfield's essay for racial bias. Have each group make a presentation that explains whether the essay is racist or not, supporting its claim with examples from the text. Ask the groups to speculate on what Greenfield does *not* say and why.

bench than their white counterparts; Al Attles and K. C. Jones are statuelike compared with Jack Ramsey or Dick Motta or Kevin Loughery.)

If there is a single trait that characterizes "black" ball it is leaping 10 agility. Bob Cousy, ex-Celtic great and former pro coach, says that "when coaches get together, one is sure to say, 'I've got the one black kid in the country who can't jump.' When coaches see a white boy who can jump or who moves with extraordinary quickness, they say, 'He should have been born black, he's that good.' "

Don Nelson, former Celtic and coach of the Milwaukee Bucks, 11 recalls that in 1970, Dave Cowens, then a relatively unknown Florida State graduate, prepared for his rookie season by playing in the Rucker League, an outdoor Harlem competition that pits pros against playground stars and college kids. So ferocious was Cowens' leaping power, Nelson says, that "when the summer was over, everyone wanted to know who the white son of a bitch was who could jump so high." That's another way to overcome a crowd around the basket—just go over it.

Speed, mobility, quickness, acceleration, "the moves"—all of 12 these are catch-phrases that surround the "black" playground style of play. So does the most racially tinged of attributes, "rhythm." Yet rhythm is what the black stars themselves talk about; feeling the flow of the game, finding the tempo of the dribble, the step, the shot. It is an instinctive quality, one that has led to difficulty between systematic coaches and free-form players. "Cats from the street have their own rhythm when they play," said college dropout Bill Spivey, onetime New York highschool star. "It's not a matter of somebody setting you up and you shooting. You *feel* the shot. When a coach holds you back, you lose the feel and it isn't fun anymore."

Connie Hawkins, the legendary Brooklyn playground star, said 13 of Laker coach Bill Sharman's methodical style of teaching, "He's systematic to the point where it begins to be a little too much. It's such an action-reaction type of game that when you have to do everything the same way, I think you lose something."

There is another kind of basketball that has grown up in America. 14 It is not played on asphalt playgrounds with a crowd of kids competing for the court; it is played on macadam[1] driveways by one boy with a ball and a backboard nailed over the garage; it is played in Midwestern gyms and on southern dirt courts. It is a mechanical, precise development of skills (when Don Nelson was an Iowa farm boy his incentive to make his shots was that an errant rebound would

---

[1]Blacktop; asphalt. [Eds.]

land in the middle of chicken droppings), without frills, without flow, but with effectiveness. It is "white" basketball: jagged, sweaty, stumbling, intense. A "black" player overcomes an obstacle with finesse and body control; a "white" player reacts by outrunning or outpowering the obstacle.

By this definition, the Boston Celtics are a classically "white" team. The Celtics almost never use a player with dazzling moves; that would probably make Red Auerbach swallow his cigar. Instead, the Celtics wear you down with execution, with constant running, with the same play run again and again. The rebound triggers the fast break, with everyone racing downcourt; the ball goes to Larry Bird, who pulls up and takes the jump shot, or who fakes the shot and passes off to the man following, the "trailer," who has the momentum to go inside for a relatively easy shot.

Perhaps the most classically "white" position is that of the quick forward, one without great moves to the basket, without highly developed shots, without the height and mobility for rebounding effectiveness. What does he do? He runs. He runs from the opening jump to the last horn. He runs up and down the court, from base line to base line, back and forth under the basket, looking for the opening, for the pass, for the chance to take a quick step and the high-percentage shot. To watch San Antonio's Mark Olberding, a player without speed or moves, is to wonder what he is doing in the NBA—until you see him swing free and throw up a shot that, without demanding any apparent skill, somehow goes in the basket more frequently than the shots of any of his teammates. To watch Kurt Rambis of the Los Angeles Lakers, an ungainly collection of arms, legs, and elbows, thumping up and down the court at half-speed is to wonder whether the NBA has begun a hire-the-handicapped program—until you see Rambis muscling aside an opponent to grab a rebound, or watch him trail the fast-break to steer an errant shot into the basket. And to have watched Boston Celtic immortal John Havlicek is to have seen "white" ball at its best.

Havlicek stands in dramatic contrast to Julius Erving of the Philadelphia 76ers. Erving has the capacity to make legends come true; leaping from the foul line and slam-dunking the ball on his way down; going up for a lay-up, pulling the ball to his body and throwing under and up the other side of the rim, defying gravity and probability with moves and jumps. Havlicek looked like the living embodiment of his small-town Ohio background. He would bring the ball downcourt, weaving left, then right, looking for the path. He would swing the ball to a teammate, cut behind a pick, take the pass and release the shot in a flicker of time. It looked plain, unvarnished. But there are not half a dozen players in the league who can see such possibilities for a free shot, then get that shot off as quickly and efficiently as Havlicek.

To former pro Jim McMillian, a black with "white" attributes,   18
himself a quick forward, "it's a matter of environment. Julius Erving grew up in a different environment from Havlicek—John came from a very small town in Ohio. There everything was done the easy way, the shortest distance between two points. It's nothing fancy, very few times will he go one-on-one; he hits the lay-up, hits the jump shot, makes the free throw, and after the game you look up and you say, 'How did he hurt us that much?' "

"White" ball, then, is the basketball of patience and method.   19
"Black" ball is the basketball of electric self-expression. One player has all the time in the world to perfect his skills, the other a need to prove himself. These are slippery categories, because a poor boy who is black can play "white" and a white boy of middle-class parents can play "black." Jamaal Wilkes and Paul Westphal are athletes who seem to defy these categories. And what makes basketball the most intriguing of sports is how these styles do not necessarily clash; how the punishing intensity of "white" players and the dazzling moves of the "blacks" can fit together, a fusion of cultures that seems more and more difficult in the world beyond the out-of-bounds line.

RESPONDING TO READING

1. Greenfield's main point is that blacks and whites have different styles on the basketball court. Do your observations support this idea?   **2.** Some readers have reacted negatively to Greenfield's essay, accusing him of racial stereotyping. Do you think this is a valid reaction? Explain.   **3.** During the 1970s, many basketball team owners thought that white fans would not support a team that was predominantly black, so they tried to limit the number of black players on their teams. Twenty years later, with African-American players dominating the game, basketball still attracts white fans. In light of this information, could you say that Greenfield is writing about a nonissue?

Roy Campanella

ROY CAMPANELLA II

Roy Campanella II (1948–   ) an honors graduate of Harvard with an MBA from Columbia, is the son of the famous baseball player Roy Campanella (1921–   ), who was voted Most Valuable Player in the National League three times and was voted into the Baseball Hall of Fame in 1969. Campanella senior's career was cut short in

---

WRITING SUGGESTION

Write an essay in which you discuss whether there is any danger in classifying success on the basis of race, gender, or creed. If such factors exist, should they be discussed?

ANSWERS TO RESPONDING TO READING

1. Students should give specific examples and list implied reasons for the differences.
2. When answering this question, students should consider whether any intelligent discussion of racial differences is possible or even desirable in contemporary society.
3. This issue continues to fascinate sports enthusiasts, and because sports play a major role in American culture, the question will not be forgotten. Greenfield is not writing about a nonissue, but he may be trying to accomplish the impossible.

1958 when a car accident left him paralyzed. Roy Campanella II is a filmmaker whose directing credits include numerous television movies, episodes, commercials, and documentary films. He is also an associate editor of *Black Film Review.* In the following essay Campanella talks about the racism his father had to overcome to play baseball in the major leagues during the 1950s.

A Sunday doubleheader in St. Paul, Minnesota, a memorable   1
Father's Day, June 20, 1948. My father was catching for the local Dodger farm team. He hit two home runs, and just after six P.M. my birth was announced to the crowd at the ballpark. Later that week my father received the other good news he had been waiting for: Branch Rickey wanted him to join the Dodgers in Brooklyn. It has always seemed appropriate that my birth coincided with the advancement of my father into the major leagues.

The youngest of four children, Roy Campanella was born in Phil-   2
adelphia in 1921. His father, John Campanella, the popular owner of a fruit and vegetable market, was white, a first-generation Italian American. His parents came from Palermo in Sicily, where the rhythm of peasant life is affected by the sounds emanating from church bell towers. *Campanella* means "little bell" in Italian; *campanilismo* symbolizes the spirit of the rural peasantry in Italy. John married Ida Mercer, a lovely, intelligent black woman. They met considerable resistance because of their integrated marriage, but the question of color never posed a conflict in their household.

By the time he was fifteen, Dad was playing in a tough sandlot   3
league, more than holding his own against men in their twenties. That same year, 1936, he was recruited by the Baltimore Elite Giants of the Negro National League. This meant being on the road for as much as two months at a time and occasionally catching as many as four games a day. While he had power and natural ability, he greatly benefited from the instruction of a mentor, "Biz" Mackey, the seasoned manager and catcher of the Giants. Mackey provided the insights Dad would need to develop defensively. He also taught him "the art of enlightened conversation," or how to break a batter's concentration by initiating light chatter.

During the winters Dad played in such places as Cuba, Puerto   4
Rico, Mexico, Panama, and Venezuela, where he also was a manager. He was as popular in the winter-baseball circuit as in the Negro Leagues. But here, too, he had difficulties with a color caste system. When I was eight, he told me of having once stood in line at the post office in Panama, where there were separate queues for white, brown, and black people. He told me many other stories of degrading scenes of white racism, taking place in America and Latin America, before and after he joined the Dodgers, to prepare me for manhood and give

FOR OPENERS

Does a sports celebrity have an obligation to present a socially acceptable public image? Define such an image, and give positive and negative recent examples.

ADDITIONAL QUESTIONS FOR RESPONDING TO READING

1. Was Roy Campanella a courageous man? Give specific examples to support your claim.
2. Roy Campanella is never described in negative terms in the essay by his son. Does this factor affect your acceptance of the essay's thesis?
3. Do you think that Roy Campanella responded appropriately to the racial incidents described in the essay? What other options did he have?

TEACHING STRATEGY

Point out this biographical narrative's subtle messages:
Paragraph 4: "Living well is the best revenge."
Paragraphs 6 & 7: Blacks can be respected for intelligence and leadership abilities as well as for athletic prowess.
Paragraph 10: "Compete against yourself."
Paragraph 15: Hard work breeds happiness.
Paragraph 21: Courage takes many forms.

me a context for understanding his approach to life. Most of my father's fans may not understand that his ability to see beyond the bitterness and disillusionment, which can result from facing years of prejudice, is based on deep religious convictions and the intelligent, pragmatic conclusion that "living well is the best revenge."

After nine years with the Giants, my father spent time in the 5 Dodgers' farm system with Nashua, Montreal, and St. Paul. He was already twenty-six when he joined Brooklyn. Though he detested the racism that had prevented African Americans from playing in big leagues until 1947, he was not angry knowing that a player of his caliber should have started in the majors five years earlier. Instead he embraced this opportunity. He wanted to carry the torch for Josh Gibson, whom he idolized, and other Negro League stars who would never get his chance. Also, he just loved the game too much to be bitter—his life was and is baseball.

He was the first black catcher in the majors. Branch Rickey knew 6 that the bigotry Jackie Robinson faced as a black infielder from fans and opponents could be worse for my father, because a catcher was responsible for "calling the shots." A former catcher himself, Rickey simply advised that he use his natural leadership skills, immense knowledge, and intuitive sense of the game to develop highly individualized relationships with the Dodger hurlers. He pointed out that if race came between him and a pitcher, their relationship could rapidly deteriorate. My father agreed. This did not mean he would become a "yes" man who would accept their racial slurs. A passive approach would have undermined his authority and eliminated the essential element of mutual respect. As it turned out, my father's sanguine personality was perfectly suited to Rickey's proposed strategy. White pitchers like Carl Erskine, Johnny Podres, Clem Labine and Ed Roebuck developed close, trusting relationships with him. Of course, the same could be said about black pitchers such as Don Newcombe and Joe Black.

Rickey came to call him "the perfect receiver." He had a quick, 7 analytical mind that contributed to the team's defensive strategy, an encyclopedic knowledge of hitters' strengths and weaknesses, excellent fielding ability, and was a master at handling pitchers. "He took charge of his pitchers," attested Rickey. "He assumed authority."

As a hitter, my father always had power but worked hard to bat 8 over .300 in his three MVP seasons. He learned by studying other hitters. He particularly admired Joe DiMaggio because of his consistency, Ted Williams because of his concentration, and Henry Aaron because he proved a ball could be driven if you use your wrists. As in everything he did on the field, my father took great pleasure in hitting. He was proud of his many homers with the Dodgers, including 41 in 1953, then a record for major league catchers. But he spoke with more excitement about his homers in exhibition games in the South in 1946–47. He felt a sense of triumph in having homered off white pitchers in segregated ballparks where black fans were forced to sit in the unshaded bleachers.

Dad always had a sense for the dramatic. On October 2, 1953, he was scheduled to be the featured guest on the premiere of Edward R. Murrow's *Person to Person*.[1] That afternoon, the Dodgers played the Yankees in the second game of the World Series. The Dodgers' PR man joked it would be great if he had a good game before appearing on national TV in prime time. So he homered in the bottom of the eighth to win the game, 3–2.   9

He made everything look easy. He was just in that circle of greatness where talent coincides with opportunity and dreams come true. While proud of his achievements, he *never* boasted or infringed on others. He had a distinct sense of dignity and humility. He was at peace with himself. Which isn't to say he didn't get depressed if he got injured or disappointed if he had a bad game. He always wanted to do better. He'd advise me, "There is no need to compete with other people. The important thing is to try to be better each time you have a chance at something. Compete against yourself."   10

As a youngster I spent a lot of time at wonderful Ebbets Field. I'd sit in a box seat near the Dodger dugout. Even during important games, my father was never too busy to acknowledge me and ask if I was hungry or thirsty, and being very protective, to remind me not to eat too many hot dogs or go running around the stadium, which I did anyway. Until I was about five or six I'd cheer wildly any time he hit the ball, even if he made an out. I distinctly remember one time when he grounded out to second and I jumped up and applauded. He turned to go back to the dugout and I said, "Good try, Dad!" He smiled and said, "Not good enough." The fans around me laughed, and that was the first time I realized there were other people in the park watching my father, that it wasn't just a private thing the two of us shared.   11

Even as a young boy I could tell he was one of the best players. I remember when Willie Mays, a close family friend, took a big lead off first and my dad noticed him leaning and picked him off from a squatting position. I was as startled as Mays. "It's all in the wrist," Dad explained to me, like a magician revealing his secrets. I remember his hitting home runs. I also remember his getting triples because   12

COLLABORATIVE ACTIVITY

In a *New York Times* op-ed piece (4/23/91), essayist Joseph Epstein, editor of *The American Scholar*, makes a distinction between *heroes*, those admired for their achievements and noble qualities, and *role models*, those whose behavior is imitated by others. His point is that, contrary to what present-day society teaches, heroes are more important than role models because heroism, he says, "is about real possibilities. In heroes one sees what humans are capable of achieving; that heroes don't happen to be in the least like you doesn't make what they have done any the less impressive." After dividing your students into groups, ask them to list those individuals they consider heroes and those they consider role models. Then have them discuss their findings. Finally, see if the class can reach a consensus about whether or not Epstein's distinction is valid—and if so, whether heroes or role models are more important to contemporary society.

---

[1]American news broadcaster (1908–65) noted for his famous radio broadcasts from London during the Battle of Britain. He later produced and broadcast the popular *See It Now* and *Person to Person* television programs during the 1950s. [Eds.].

fielders underestimated his speed. He was much faster than you'd think when you saw his hefty, squat physique. In the stands, I shared my father's enthusiasm on the field and I also felt excitement and a sense of danger. Once a baserunner rounded third, and I could tell by the way he was charging home plate that he intended to spike my father. Dad moved gracefully to the right, planted one leg, and while tagging him out, kicked him in the ass (so hard that the strap on his shin guard broke) and sent him flying. He did it all in one motion and it was so beautiful.

Sitting so close, I could also hear the racist remarks coming from 13 the opposing dugout that were directed at my father, Jackie Robinson, and the other black Dodgers. Eddie Stanky, when he managed the Cardinals, was particularly abusive and encouraged his players to emulate him. Casey Stengel is so beloved that it may surprise some people that he was particularly insulting to blacks; he was a racist who used the word "nigger" as if he thought it were appropriate.

Many strangers commonly assume it was wonderful growing up 14 Roy Campanella's son. They are right but for the wrong reasons. While I am very proud of my father's accomplishments and cherish our father-son relationship, living on borrowed importance has never brought me any pleasure. As a youngster I would occasionally ask my friends to introduce me as just "Roy" when meeting other children. I learned to accept the extra attention and curiosity because it was usually given out of respect for my dad, but it was difficult to adjust to the persistent name-association game I was forced to play with the general public. "Are you related to . . . ? Is your father really . . . ? I felt so bad when he had his accident. Is your father still alive? I'm from Brooklyn and I loved watching your father play. Let me shake your hand, it's an honor. . . . Didn't you want to follow in your father's footsteps?" In retrospect, had I not been an "all-star" Little Leaguer, playing baseball as a youngster could have been a miserable peer-pressure experience. Also, it's fortunate that I knew at an early age that I wanted to be a filmmaker and my parents encouraged me to pursue my dreams. "Do what you love most," Dad advised, "and make sure you can earn a living at it."

My father and at times our entire family have been under a micro- 15 scope of media and public attention. In the mid-fifties, when we'd go to restaurants or out shopping, my father would constantly be approached by sports fans and well-wishers seeking autographs. On weekends a steady stream of onlookers would cruise by our home in Glen Cove, Long Island, pointing at our house. Inside was a closeknit family. I was the first child of my father's marriage to my mother, and his first son; both my parents had children from prior marriages. My father had two daughters, Joyce and Beverly, who lived with their mother in Philadelphia but visited often, and my mother had a son, David, who was five years older than me and lived with us. My brother Tony was born two years after me, and in 1953, my parents had a daughter, Ruthe, whom we affectionately nicknamed Princess. My father owned a liquor store and every year a photo of a different child would be on the calendar he gave to his customers—I used to think it strange that people all over Harlem had my picture hanging on their walls. In the mid-sixties, my father would adopt Joni and John, the children of his third wife, Roxie.

My parents were loving but also strict. They placed a high value 16 on discipline. My father never read Tolstoy but his philosophy certainly reflects the saying "The only true happiness comes from honest hard word and sacrifice." Although we had a housekeeper, the kids were expected to participate in all of the domestic chores. But it wasn't always work. The boys often played catch with my father. And we enjoyed his hobbies, like his extensive collection of electric trains and his passion for fishing. Some of our happiest weekends were spent on our yacht, fishing in the Long Island Sound.

My parents were adamant that their kids get a good education 17 and continually encouraged us to go further than what was being taught in school. As a youngster with a voracious appetite for the written word, I developed a passion for Ernest Hemingway.[2] Before reaching my midteens I had read all his work. (I was struck that Hemingway's definition of courage as "grace under pressure" seemed an accurate description of how my father handled tough situations on and off the field.) Years later, my father revealed that when the Dodgers were in Cuba in the late forties, he and Jackie Robinson were the only Dodgers not invited by Hemingway to the author's home. An oversight? Papa Hemingway specifically requested that the Dodgers not bring any black ballplayers. As my father explained, he had not spoken of this encounter when I was a teenager because he didn't want to discourage me from reading, Hemingway or any other authors.

"Celebrity is a mask that eats into the face," observed John 18 Updike. My father would reply, "Only if you let it." My father's "public mask" is an honest but selective representation of his private self. Nothing about him in public is artificial, especially the kindness he displayed in the 1950s to children at Ebbets Field and at such places as the Harlem YMCA. In public and during press conferences, Dad always expressed himself in terms that could easily be grasped by the

---

[2]American novelist and short story writer (1899–1951) who won the Nobel Prize in literature in 1954. [Eds.]

public. He is a complex man but knows it doesn't make sense approaching an interview as if it were a therapy session. Even so, the press has on many occasions taken his comments out of context and even worse, invented thoughts he never expressed. Jules Tygiel, in his much praised *The Great Baseball Experiment*, states that "when young black Dodgers would complain about discrimination, Campanella would call them aside and explain, 'You're in the big leagues now. It's nice up here. You're getting an opportunity to show what you can do; don't louse it up for everybody else.'" In fact, my father never tried to stop other blacks from complaining about discrimination. His good-natured, optimistic approach to life never meant that in public or private he was an apologist for discrimination. There were numerous examples of his standing up to racists on and off the field. In a minor league game a white player, Sal Yvars, deliberately threw dirt in my father's face as he squatted behind the plate. My dad's response was immediate and forceful: "Try that again and I'll beat you to a pulp." Tygiel even mentions an ugly incident in 1953 when Lew Burdette, who was notorious for throwing beanballs at black players, twice knocked down my father and then yelled, "Nigger, get up and hit." My father got up and charged the mound.

My father was unfairly characterized by some sportswriters as [19] being less committed to civil rights than Jackie Robinson. But the fundamental difference between them was style and not substance. In the early fifties, we lived in the same neighborhood, St. Alban's, Queens, and they would drive to work together. There were no great debates. They both detested racism and wanted to see the full benefits of democracy extended to all Americans of African descent. Both resented being treated as second-class citizens, but they expressed their resentment in different ways. For instance, after an exhibition game in Miami, they approached a cab to take them to the Lord Calvert, the impressive black hotel where we stayed. They were rejected by a white driver. "Jackie wanted to stay there arguing with the fool," my father recalls, "and I told him it didn't make sense because he wasn't listening to us." Besides, my father didn't want to do business with the driver. The driver never changed his mind and Jackie finally agreed with my father that they should call a private car. Both Robinson and my dad hated such racial terrorism, and that is what segregation and apartheid really are, but neither could change things that moment outside a ballpark in Miami. Whether hot or cool, no African American was going to ride in that racist's cab.

Both men were inspiring role models to American youth and [20] authentic heroes to African Americans. So it is a disservice for sportswriters such as Tygiel and Lowell Reidenbaugh to stereotype Robinson a "militant" and my father a "conservative." Such labels are easily revealed as false when the actions of both men are examined in relation to the political persecution of Paul Robeson by the House Un-American Activities Committee.[3] Branch Rickey urged both Robinson and my father to testify against Robeson at a committee hearing. Robinson agreed—a decision he would always regret—and my dad declined. Years later, Paul Robeson, Jr., would tell me with touching sincerity how deeply his father appreciated my dad's refusal to denounce him.

My father always saw himself as a baseball player and not a social   21 crusader. But he was deeply committed to the civil rights movement led by Martin Luther King. He and Robinson knew Dr. King because they stayed at his home in Atlanta when the KKK threatened to kill them if they played in an integrated Dodger exhibition game.

In 1959, about a year after my father's tragic auto accident that   22 left him a quadriplegic, our family traveled to the West Coast to attend "Roy Campanella Night" at the Los Angeles Coliseum. Dodger owner Walter O'Malley had organized a spectacular tribute exhibition game that was attended by 94,000 adoring fans. We all cried when everyone lit matches to honor my father and the entire coliseum was like a huge birthday cake. The applause was thunderous. It was a beautiful, touching evening. But our trip was marred by the Jim Crow[4] treatment we received at the Sheraton Hotel in Los Angeles. The management informed my parents that no blacks were permitted to use the pool facilities. My parents were livid. After unsuccessfully protesting to the hotel manager, my dad complained to O'Malley. The Dodgers subsequently withdrew all business from the hotel. My father's style may not have been combative, but it was not passive. He initiated change. I was ten years old at the time and was filled with such anger and resentment—I wanted to inform on the hotel to the 94,000 fans who had been so nice to my father and, I was sure, would have been appalled by what had happened. My father told me, "Regardless of what you've accomplished, regardless of how much education you have, there are some people who will still treat you as a second-class citizen just because of race. But I hope you never let anyone convince you that things should be like that." And I never have.

Many of the roads I have taken return to the lessons of my father.   23 His life has certainly been an example of turning adversity into a valuable lesson for self-development. Dad is a firm believer in will-

---

[3]Robeson (1898–1976) was an actor, singer, and outspoken critic of American racial bigotry. Because of his pro-Soviet statements, the State Department revoked his passport in 1950. In 1958 the Supreme Court upheld his right to travel abroad. [Eds.]

[4]Jim Crow laws were statutes enacted in the 1880s by Southern states to legalize segregation between blacks and whites. The name "Jim Crow" is thought to be derived from a character in a popular minstrel show. [Eds.]

power. He is a wellspring of courage and conviction. He is a true competitor and spirited team player. He is the quintessential athlete.

In the late sixties, I read *Zen and the Art of Archery*. It told how 24 Zen archers are able to repeatedly achieve bull's eyes while blindfolded and in total darkness. They use bows that are unusually difficult to pull and require not just strength but a powerful skill that eludes most archers. I discovered a surprising similarity between my father, as a ballplayer, and these Zen archers. My father had the same distinctive power. He was in perfect harmony with the game of baseball.

RESPONDING TO READING

1. Campanella sees his father as a hero. Do you? Do you think Campanella paints a realistic or an idealized portrait? Explain.   **2.** How much does Campanella assume his audience knows about the racism his father faced in professional baseball? Does Campanella's account of this racism shock you? Why or why not?   **3.** In paragraph 2 Campanella says that his father, who had an Italian father and an African-American mother, was considered black, not Italian. Why do you think this is so? Is this misconception an example of racism?

Fathers, Daughters, and the Magic of Baseball

DORIS KEARNS GOODWIN

Doris Kearns Goodwin (1943–   ) served as special assistant and consultant to President Lyndon B. Johnson and now teaches courses in government and politics at Harvard University. She is also a television political analyst and a member of the Women's Political Caucus of Massachusetts. Goodwin is known for two highly praised biographies, *Lyndon Johnson and the American Dream* (1976) and *The Fitzgeralds and the Kennedys: An American Saga* (1987). In the following essay, first published in the *Boston Globe* in 1986, Goodwin remembers how as a child she loved baseball, "a game that has defied the ravages of modern life."

The game of baseball has always been linked in my mind with 1 the mystic texture of childhood, with the sounds and smells of summer nights and with the memories of my father.

My love for baseball was born the first day my father took me to 2 Ebbets Field in Brooklyn. Riding in the trolley car, he seemed as excited as I was. He never stopped talking; now describing for me the street in Brooklyn where he had grown up, now recalling the first game he had been taken to by his own father, now recapturing for me his favorite memories from the Dodgers of his youth—the Dodgers of Casey Stengel, Zach Wheat, and Jimmy Johnston.

In the evenings, when my dad came home from work, we would sit together on our porch and relive the events of that afternoon's game, which I had so carefully preserved in the large, red scorebook I'd been given for my seventh birthday. I can still remember how proud I was to have mastered all those strange and wonderful symbols that permitted me to recapture, in miniature form, the every movement of Jackie Robinson and Pee Wee Reese, Duke Snider and Gil Hodges. But the real power of that scorebook lay in the responsibility it entailed. For all through my childhood, my father kept from me the knowledge that the daily papers printed daily box scores, allowing me to believe that without my personal renderings of all those games he missed while he was at work, he would be unable to follow our team in the only proper way a team should be followed—day by day, inning by inning. In other words, without me, his love for baseball would be forever incomplete.

To be sure, there were risks involved in making a commitment as boundless as mine. For me, as for all too many Brooklyn fans, the presiding memory of "the boys of summer" was the memory of the final playoff game in 1951 against the Giants. Going into the ninth, the Dodgers held a 4–1 lead. Then came two singles and a double, placing the winning run at the plate with Bobby Thomson at bat. As manager Dressen replaced pitcher Carl Erskine with Ralph Branca, my older sister, with maddening foresight, predicted the forever famous Thomas homer. This prediction left me so angry, imagining that with her words she had somehow brought it about, that I would not speak to her for days.

So the seasons of my childhood passed until that miserable summer when the Dodgers were taken away to Los Angeles by the unforgivable O'Malley, leaving all our rash hopes and dreams of glory behind. And then came a summer of still deeper sadness when my father died. Suddenly my feelings for baseball seemed an aspect of my departing youth, along with my childhood freckles and my favorite childhood haunts, to be left behind when I went away to college and never came back.

Then one September day, having settled into teaching at Harvard, I agreed, half reluctantly, to go to Fenway Park. There it was again: the cozy ballfield scaled to human dimensions so that every word of encouragement and every scornful yell could be heard on the field; the fervent crowd that could, with equal passion, curse a player for today's failures after cheering his heroics the day before; the team

3

4

5

6

COLLABORATIVE ACTIVITY

Divide the class into several groups composed of both males and females. Assign a different sport to each class group—baseball, football, basketball, boxing, and so forth—and ask students to describe the elements in each sport that appeal to the mythic imagination. What metaphors for life does each sport suggest?

WRITING SUGGESTIONS

1. Goodwin finds "something deeply satisfying in the knowledge" of baseball's relative permanence. Write an essay in which you determine whether her enthusiasm for the sport is based on appreciation of the sport's technical aspects or on other factors. Give examples.
2. What famous sports figure would you like to meet and why? What does that sports figure represent to you?

that always seemed to break your heart in the last week of the season. It took only a matter of minutes before I found myself directing all my old intensities toward my new team—the Boston Red Sox.

I am often teased by my women friends about my obsession, but 7 just as often, in the most unexpected places—in academic conferences, in literary discussions, at the most elegant dinner parties—I find other women just as crazily committed to baseball as I am, and the discovery creates an instant bond between us. All at once, we are deep in conversation, mingling together the past and the present, as if the history of the Red Sox had been our history too.

There we stand, one moment recollecting the unparalleled per- 8 formance of Carl Yazstremski in '67, the next sharing ideas on how the present lineup should be changed; one moment recapturing the splendid career of "the Splendid Splinter," the next complaining about the manager's decision to pull the pitcher the night before. And then, invariably, comes the most vivid memory of all, the frozen image of Carlton Fisk as he rounded first in the sixth game of the '75 World Series, an image as intense in its evocation of triumph as the image of Dodger pitcher Ralph Branca weeping in the dugout is in its portrayal of heartache.

There is another, more personal memory associated with Carlton 9 Fisk, for he was, after all the years I had followed baseball, the first player I actually met in person. Apparently he had read the biography I had written on Lyndon Johnson and wanted to meet me. Yet when the meeting took place, I found myself reduced to the shyness of childhood. There I was, a professor at Harvard, accustomed to speaking with presidents of the United States, and yet, standing beside this young man in a baseball uniform, I was speechless.

Finally, Fisk said that it might have been an awesome experience 10 to work with a man of such immense power as President Johnson— and with that, I was at last able to stammer out, with a laugh, "Not as awesome as the thought that I am really standing here talking with you."

Perhaps I have circled back to my childhood, but if this is so, I 11 am certain that my journey through time is connected in some fundamental way to the fact that I am now a parent myself, anxious to share with my three sons the same ritual I once shared with my father.

For in this linkage between the generations rests the magic of 12 baseball, a game that has defied the ravages of modern life, a game that is still played today by the same basic rules and at the same pace as it was played 100 years ago. There is something deeply satisfying in the knowledge of this continuity.

And there is something else as well that I have experienced sitting 13 in Fenway Park with my small boys on a warm summer's day. If I close my eyes against the sun, all at once I am back at Ebbets Field, a young girl once more in the presence of my father, watching the players of my youth on the grassy field below. There is magic in this moment, for when I open my eyes and see my sons in the place where my father once sat, I feel an invisible bond between our three generations, an anchor of loyalty linking my sons to the grandfather whose face they never saw, but whose person they have already come to know through this most timeless of all sports, the game of baseball.

RESPONDING TO READING

1. In what sense is baseball "magic" to Goodwin? Is there a sport or other pursuit that plays a similar role in your life?   **2.** What ideas does Goodwin assume her readers have about women and baseball? Do you think she reinforces or undercuts these ideas?   **3.** Does your own experience suggest that Goodwin might be exaggerating the importance of baseball in the lives of women? Explain.

Dusty Rhodes

STEPHEN JAY GOULD

In the essay that follows, Stephan Jay Gould (see also p. 407) chooses as his subject a sports figure who is not a hero in the conventional sense. Instead, he writes about Dusty Rhodes, "a strictly average ballplayer who had a moment of glory."

Circumstance is the great leveler. In a world of too much predictability, where records by season and career belong only to the greatest players, any competent person in uniform may produce an unforgettable feat of the moment. A journeyman pitcher, Don Larsen, hurled a perfect game in the World Series of 1956. Does Bill Wambsganss, with his unusual name and strictly average play as an infielder, ever evoke any memory beyond the unassisted triple play that fortuitously fell his way in the fifth inning of the fifth game of the 1920 World Series?

All ship's carpenters are named "Chips," all radio engineers "Sparks." By a similar custom, anyone named Rhodes will end up with the nickname "Dusty." James Lamar (Dusty) Rhodes, an alcoholic utility outfielder from Mathews, Alabama, made me the happiest boy in New York when he won the 1954 World Series for the New

ANSWERS TO RESPONDING TO READING

1. Baseball's magic for Goodwin is linked to its symbolic value as an emblem of permanence, linked to her memories of the past and hopes for the future as a parent.
2. Goodwin assumes that most women will not understand her enthusiasm for baseball (paragraph 7). Her own enthusiasm would most likely undercut any stereotypical ideas her readers might have about women and baseball. Some purists might observe that she does not seem to appreciate the technical side of the game, but then neither do many fans, regardless of whether they are male or female.
3. Goodwin is probably exaggerating baseball's importance to enhance her thesis that baseball has an importance beyond its sports value.

FOR OPENERS

Do you have a sports fantasy in which you help the team win a crucial game? Have you ever dreamed of glory? You might ask students to read "Ex-Basketball Player" (page 639) to see another dimension of this question.

ADDITIONAL QUESTIONS FOR RESPONDING TO READING

1. Do we value sports because we can project ourselves in the role of the hero?
2. Do you, like Gould, have a sports hero who is neither a superstar nor a role model?
3. Analyze the structure of Gould's essay. Is the organization of the essay effective? Why or why not?

1

2

York Giants, all by himself. (I will admit that a few other events of note occurred during these four short days—Mays's legendary catch off Vic Wertz among others—but no man, and certainly not a perpetually inebriated pinch hitter, has ever so dominated our favorite days of October.)

The 1954 Cleveland Indians were probably the greatest team of my lifetime. They compiled the best record of the modern era, 111–43 for an incredible winning percentage of .721. (I just turned forty-eight, and no other team on my watch has come close to breaking .700. The 1939 Yankees, another of our century's greatest clubs, squeaked by the barrier at .702 when I was minus two. People forget the ironic fact that the Yankees, who won the American League pennant in every other year between 1949–1958, actually compiled their best record of the decade by coming in second to the Indians at 103–51 in 1954). With a pitching staff of Bob Lemon, Early Wynn, and Mike Garcia (not to mention an aging, but still able, Bob Feller), Cleveland was an overwhelming favorite to slaughter my beloved Giants with dispatch.

The Giants won that World Series in the greatest surprise of modern history (matched only, perhaps, by the 1969 Mets, whose victory, or so George Burns tells us, was the only verifiable miracle since the parting of the Red Sea). Those two Series, 1954 and 1969, have two other interesting elements in common, but in each case the 1954 Giants provide the cleaner and more memorable case. One, both the Giants and the Mets were overwhelming underdogs, yet both won commandingly with four straight victories. But the 1969 Series lasted five games, because Baltimore beat Tom Seaver in the first contest; the Giants put the Indians away in four—clean, simple, and minimal. Two, both victories were sparked by the most unlikely utility ballplayer. Al Weis (remember Big Al?) won the Mets' first game with a two-out single in the ninth, then tied the last game with an improbable homer. Dusty Rhodes fared even better. He won, tied, or assured victory in each of the first three games. By then, the Indians were so discouraged that they pretty much lay down and died for the finale.

If Leo Durocher, the Giants' manager, had been able to call the shots, Rhodes wouldn't have been on the team at all. In fact, Durocher told Giants' boss Horace Stoneham that he would quit as manager unless Rhodes were traded. Durocher had two objections to Rhodes: he couldn't field, and he couldn't stay sober. Stoneham agreed and put Rhodes on the block, but no other team even nibbled. As Durocher said, "Everybody else had heard about Mr. Rhodes, too. Any club could have claimed him for a dollar bill. Thank the Lord none did." Durocher was appeased by Stoneham's honest effort, and even more

3

4

5

by Rhodes's stellar performance as a pinch hitter in 1954, when he batted .333, in that role at 15 for 45.

Rhodes won the first game of the 1954 Series with a three-run homer in the tenth (after Willie Mays had saved the game with his legendary catch off Vic Wertz). It wasn't the most commanding home run in the history of baseball, but they all have the same effect whether Carlton Fisk grazes the left-field foul pole in Fenway Park or Mantle hits one nearly into orbit. I loved the old Polo Grounds, but it had a bizarre shape, with a cavernous center field and short fences down the lines to compensate. The right-field corner sat at a major league minimal distance of 258 feet from home plate. Dusty just managed to nudge one over the right fielder's outstretched glove—an out anywhere else. 6

In game two, Durocher called upon Rhodes earlier. Wynn held a 1–0 lead in the fifth, but the Giants had two on and nobody out. Rhodes, pinch-hitting for Monte Irvin, dumped a single to center, tying the score. In the seventh, he added an insurance run and silenced the grousing about his "cheapie" of the day before by blasting a massive homer that was still rising when it hit the upper facade, 350 feet from home. 7

Durocher, on a roll, inserted Rhodes as an even-earlier pinch hitter in game three. He came in with the bases loaded in the third inning and knocked in two more runs, including the ultimate game-winner, with a single. 8

All this happened long ago, but my memories of joy and vindication could not be more clear or immediate. I had taken all manner of abuse, mostly from Dodger fans, for my optimism about the Giants. I had also bet every cent I owned (about four bucks) at very favorable odds. I ended up with about fifteen dollars and felt like the richest kid in New York. I'd have bought Dusty a double bourbon, but we never met, and I was underage. 9

Dusty Rhodes was a great and colorful character, but a strictly average ballplayer who had a moment of glory. You will find him in record books for a few other items—he once hit three homers in a single game, two pinch-hit homers in a single inning, and has the most extrabase hits in a doubleheader. But he was no star during his seven-year career, all with the Giants. People tend to focus on great moments and forget averages. They then falsely extrapolate the moment to the totality. Thus, many fans think that Dusty was a great pinch hitter throughout his career. Not so. As Bill James points out, Dusty's career pinch-hitting average is .186. He could do no wrong in 1954, but his pinch-hitting averages in his other six years were .111, .172, .250, .179, .152, and .188. 10

COLLABORATIVE ACTIVITY

Break the class into groups to make lists of specific activities other than sports (such as religious rituals or artistic pursuits) in which an ordinary person can achieve "an act of transcendence" (paragraph 11). How are these activities like and unlike sports?

WRITING SUGGESTION

How important are the personal lives of sports figures? Write an essay in which you analyze how Rhodes's drinking affects your perception of him. Must sports figures be held up as perfect examples, or can they have personal flaws? (You may consider examples of "flawed" sports figures, such as Pete Rose, in your essay.)

ANSWERS TO RESPONDING TO READING

1. Gould means that any person can have a moment of glory. Rhodes's moment gives a romantic importance to his life. Baseball provides a medium for these kinds of transcendent moments.
2. Rhodes serves as a metaphor for Gould's democratic concept of baseball as a dream factory.
3. Answers will vary. Most students will probably mention the superstars. They should also be encouraged to think of those who just play the game, who have a sense of professionalism, and who do their best, knowing they will never be one of the greats.

Who cares? Our joys and our heroes come in many modes and on many time scales. We treasure the consistency of a Ted Williams, the resiliency of a Pete Rose. But we hold special affection for the journeyman fortunate enough to taste greatness in an indelible moment of legitimate glory. We love DiMaggio because he was a paragon. We love Dusty Rhodes because he was a man like us. And his few days of majesty nurture a special hope that no ordinary man can deny. Any of us might get one chance for an act of transcendence—an opportunity to bake the greatest cake ever, to offer just the right advice or support, even to save a life. And when that opportunity comes, we do not want to succeed because we bought the lucky ticket in a lottery. Whatever the humdrum quality of our daily life, we yearn to know that, at some crucial moment, our special skills may be exactly right and specially suited for the task required. Dusty Rhodes is a symbol of that hope, that ever-present possibility. 11

Last I heard, Dusty Rhodes, still fighting the demon rum, was working on a tugboat in New York harbor. The past can set a cruel standard but can also provide solace. I only hope that Dusty Rhodes, the agent, continues to feel even half the pleasure that I, a mere observer, experience whenever my thoughts turn to the Polo Grounds and the early autumn of 1954. 12

RESPONDING TO READING

1. In paragraph 1 Gould says, "Circumstance is the great leveler." What does he mean? In what way does this statement apply to Dusty Rhodes? To baseball? **2.** Rhodes is an unlikely subject for an essay on baseball. Neither a superstar nor a role model, he was, as Gould says in paragraph 10, "a strictly average ballplayer." Why, then, does Gould write about him? Do you think Rhodes is a worthy subject for an essay about a sport known for its "greats"? **3.** What sports figures do you most admire? With which do you most identify? Is there a difference between the two categories? If so, how do you explain the difference?

Football Red and Baseball Green

MURRAY ROSS

Murray Ross (1942–   ), born in Pasadena, California, currently lives in Colorado Springs, where he is director of the theater program at the University of Colorado and artistic director of Theatreworks, the resident theater group. Although Ross's attention is far more often directed toward the classes he teaches and the plays he directs,

"Football Red and Baseball Green" reveals him to be an astute observer of these sports and their place in American life. Originally published in the *Chicago Review* in 1971, when Ross was still a graduate student, "Football Red and Baseball Green" appears here in a revised and updated version.

Every Superbowl played in the 1980s rates among the top television draws of the decade—pro football's championship game is right up there on the charts with blockbusters like *Star Wars*, *Batman*, and the *Rockys*. This revelation is one way of indicating just how popular spectator sports are in this country. Americans, or American men anyway, seem to care about the games they watch as much as the Elizabethans[1] cared about their plays, and I suspect for some of the same reasons. There is, in sport, some of the rudimentary drama found in popular theater: familiar plots, type characters, heroic and comic action spiced with new and unpredictable variations. And common to watching both activities is the sense of participation in a shared tradition and in shared fantasies. If sport exploits these fantasies without significantly transcending them, it seems no less satisfying for all that.

It is my guess that sport spectating involves something more than the vicarious pleasures of identifying with athletic prowess. I suspect that each sport contains a fundamental myth which it elaborates for its fans, and that our pleasure in watching such games derives in part from belonging briefly to the mythical world which the game and its players bring to life.[2] I am especially interested in baseball and football because they are so popular and so uniquely *American*; they began here and unlike basketball they have not been widely exported. Thus whatever can be said, mythically, about these games would seem to apply to our culture.

Baseball's myth may be the easier to identify since we have a greater historical perspective on the game. It was an instant success during the Industrialization, and most probably it was a reaction to the squalor, the faster pace, and the dreariness of the new conditions. Baseball was old-fashioned right from the start; it seems conceived in nostalgia, in the resuscitation of the Jeffersonian dream.[3] It established an artificial rural environment, one removed from the toil of an urban life, which spectators could be admitted to and temporarily

FOR OPENERS

Ask the class which sport is America's pasttime and why. Which most represents the true nature of American sports? Of American culture?

ADDITIONAL QUESTIONS FOR RESPONDING TO READING

1. Do you feel a sport can have any meaning beyond entertainment? If so, how?
2. Does a person's attraction to a certain sport say something about his or her personality? Give examples for several different sports.

---

[1]People who lived during the reign of Elizabeth I (1553–1603). The Elizabethan era was a time of great political and social unrest, but it also saw the flowering of English art and literature. [Eds.]

[2]A myth is a story, usually associated with religious beliefs, that reflects the basic values and tenets of a people. [Eds.]

[3]Thomas Jefferson—author of the Declaration of Independence and third President of the United States—envisioned the United States as a nation of small farmers who could avoid the evils of European city life. [Eds.]

breathe in. Baseball is a *pastoral* sport,[4] and I think the game can be best understood as this kind of art. For baseball does what all good pastoral does—it creates an atmosphere in which everything exists in harmony.

Consider, for instance, the spatial organization of the game. A 4 kind of controlled openness is created by having everything fan out from home plate, and the crowd sees the game through an arranged perspective that is rarely violated. Visually this means that the game is always seen as a constant, rather calm whole, and that the players and the playing field are viewed in relationship to each other. Each player has a certain position, a special area to tend, and the game often seems to be as much a dialogue between the fielders and the field as it is a contest between the players themselves: Will that ball get through the hole? Can that outfielder run under that fly? As a moral genre, pastoral asserts the virtue of communion with nature. As a competitive game, baseball asserts that the team which best relates to the playing field (by hitting the ball in the right places) will win.

Having established its landscape, pastoral art operates to elimi- 5 nate any reference to that bigger, more disturbing, more real world it has left behind. All games are to some extent insulated from the outside by having their own rules, but baseball has a circular structure as well which furthers its comfortable feeling of self-sufficiency. By this I mean that every motion of extention is also one of return—a ball hit outside is a *home* run, a full circle. Home—familiar, peaceful, secure—it is the beginning and end. You must go out but you must come back; only the completed movement is registered.

Time is a serious threat to any form of pastoral. The genre poses 6 a timeless world of perpetual spring, and it does its best to silence the ticking of clocks which remind us that in time the green world fades into winter. One's sense of time is directly related to what happens in it, and baseball is so structured as to stretch out and ritualize whatever action it contains. Dramatic moments are few, and they are almost always isolated by the routine texture of normal play. It is certainly a game of climax and drama, but it is perhaps more a game of repeated and predictable action: the foul balls, the walks, the pitcher fussing around on the mound, the lazy fly ball to center field. This is, I think, as it should be, for baseball exists as an alternative to a world of too much action, struggle, and change. It is a merciful release from a more grinding and insistent tempo, and its time, as

TEACHING STRATEGY

Ask students to provide some technical terms from baseball and football. Analyze the language to see if the class can arrive at conclusions about the two sports that support or contradict Ross's. You may note, for example, that baseball terms, such as *bunt* and *sacrifice*, are quite benign compared with football terms, such as *blitz* and *bomb*.

---

[4]Refers to a work of literature (usually a poem) that celebrates rural life. [Eds.]

William Carlos Williams suggests, makes a virtue out of idleness simply by providing it:

> The crowd at the ball game
> is moved uniformly
> by a spirit of uselessness
> Which delights them. . . .

Within this expanded and idle time the baseball fan is at liberty   7
to become a ceremonial participant and a lover of style. Because the action is normalized, how something is done becomes as important as the action itself. Thus baseball's most delicate and detailed aspects are often, to the spectator, the most interesting. The pitcher's windup, the anticipatory crouch of the infielders, the quick waggle of the bat as it poises for the pitch—these subtle miniature movements are as meaningful as the home runs and the strikeouts. It somehow matters in baseball that all the tiny rituals are observed: The shortstop must kick the dirt and the umpire must brush the plate with his pocket broom. In a sense baseball is largely a continuous series of small gestures, and I think it characteristic that the game's most treasured moment came when Babe Ruth pointed to where he subsequently hit a home run.

Baseball is a game where the little things mean a lot, and this,   8
together with its clean serenity, its open space, and its ritualized action is enough to place it in a world of yesterday. Baseball evokes for us a past which may never have been ours, but which we believe was, and certainly that is enough. In the Second World War, supposedly, we fought for "Baseball, Mom, and Apple Pie," and considering what baseball means, that phrase is a good one. We fought then for the right to believe in a green world of tranquility and uninterrupted contentment, where the little things would count. But now the possibilities of such a world are more remote, and it seems that while the entertainment of such a dream has an enduring appeal, it is no longer sufficient for our fantasies. I think this may be why baseball is no longer our preeminent national pastime, and why its myth is being replaced by another more appropriate to the new realities (and fantasies) of our time.

Football, especially professional football, is the embodiment of a   9
newer myth, one which in many respects is opposed to baseball's. The fundamental difference is that football is not a pastoral game; it is a heroic one. Football wants to convert men into gods; it suggests that magnificence and glory are as desirable as happiness. Football is designed, therefore, to impress its audience rather differently than baseball.

COLLABORATIVE ACTIVITY

Assign class members to attend a sporting event in small groups and analyze that event's appeal in a class presentation.

As a pastoral game, baseball attempts to close the gap between 10
the players and the crowd. It creates the illusion, for instance, that
with a lot of hard work, a little luck, and possibly some extra talent,
the average spectator might well be playing, not watching. For most
of us can do a few of the things the ball players do: catch a pop-up,
field a ground ball, and maybe get a hit once in a while. As a heroic
game, football is not concerned with a shared community of near-
equals. It seeks almost the opposite relationship between its spectators
and players, one which stresses the distance between them. We are
not allowed to identify directly with the likes of Jim Brown, the legendary running back for the Cleveland Browns, any more than we
are with Zeus, because to do so would undercut his stature as something more than human. Pittsburgh's Mean Joe Green, in a classic
commercial from the seventies, walks off the battlefield like Achilles,
clouded by combat. A little boy offers him a Coke, reluctantly accepted
but enthusiastically drunk, and Green tosses the boy his jersey afterwards—the token of a generous god. Football encourages us to see
its players much as the little boy sees Mean Joe: We look up to them
with something approaching awe. For most of us could not begin to
imagine ourselves playing their game without risking imminent
humiliation. The players are all much bigger and much faster and
much stronger than we are, and even as fans we have trouble enough
just figuring out what's going on. In baseball what happens is what
meets the eye, but in football each play means eleven men acting
against eleven other men: It's too much for a single set of eyes to
follow. We now are provided with several television commentators
to explain the action to us, with the help of the ubiquitous slow-
motion instant replay. Even the coaches need their spotters in the
stands and their long postgame film analyses to arrive at something
like full comprehension of the game they direct and manage.

If football is distanced from its fans by its intricacy and its "super- 11
human" play, it nonetheless remains an intense spectacle. Baseball,
as I have implied, dissolves time and urgency in a green expanse,
thereby creating a luxurious and peaceful sense of leisure. As is appropriate to a heroic enterprise, football reverses this procedure and
converts space into time. The game is ideally played in an oval
stadium, not in a "park," and the difference is the elimination of
perspective. This makes football a perfect television game, because
even at first hand it offers a flat, perpetually moving foreground
(wherever the ball is). The eye in baseball viewing opens up; in football
it zeroes in. There is no democratic vista in football, and spectators
are not asked to relax, but to concentrate. You are encouraged to
watch the drama, not a medley of ubiquitous gestures, and you are
constantly reminded that this event is taking place in time. The third

element in baseball is the field; in football this element is the clock. Traditionally heroes do reckon with time, and football players are no exceptions. Time in football is wound up inexorably until it reaches the breaking point in the last minutes of a close game. More often than not it is the clock which emerges as the real enemy, and it is the sense of time running out that regularly produces a pitch of tension uncommon in baseball.

A further reason for football's intensity is that the game is played   12
like a war. The idea is to win by going through, around, or over the opposing team and the battle lines, quite literally, are drawn on every play. Violence is somewhere at the heart of the game, and the combat quality is reflected in football's army language ("blitz," "trap," "zone," "bomb," "trenches," etc.). Coaches often sound like generals when they discuss their strategy. Woody Hayes, the former coach of Ohio State, explained his quarterback option play as if it had been conceived in the Pentagon: "You know," he said, "the most effective kind of warfare is siege. You have to attack on broad fronts. And that's all the option is—attacking on a broad front. You know General Sherman ran an option through the South."

Football like war is an arena for action, and like war football leaves   13
little room for personal style. It seems to be a game which projects "character" more than personality, and for the most part football heroes, publicly, are a rather similar lot. They tend to become personifications rather than individuals, and, with certain exceptions, they are easily read emblematically as embodiments of heroic qualities such as "strength," "confidence," "grace," etc.—clichés really, but forceful enough when represented by the play of a Lawrence Taylor, a Joe Montana, or a Jim Rice. Perhaps this simplification of personality results in part from the heroes' total identification with their mission, to the extent that they become more characterized by what they do than by what they intrinsically "are." At any rate football does not make as many allowances for the idiosyncrasies that baseball actually seems to encourage, and as a result there have been few football players as uniquely crazy or human as, say, Casey Stengel or Dizzy Dean.

A further reason for the underdeveloped qualities of football per-   14
sonalities, and one which gets us to the heart of the game's modernity, is that football is very much a game of modern technology. Football's action is largely interaction, and the game's complexity requires that its players mold themselves into a perfectly coordinated unit. The smoothness and precision of play execution are insatiable preoccupations, and most coaches believe that the team which makes the fewest mistakes will be the team that wins. Individual identity thus comes to be associated with the team or unit that one plays for to a

much greater extent than in baseball. Darryl Strawberry is mostly Darryl Strawberry, but Dan Hampton is mostly a Chicago Bear. The latter metaphor is a precise one, since football heroes stand out not only because of purely individual acts, but also because they epitomize the action and style of the groups they are connected to. Ideally a football team should be what Camelot was supposed to have been, a group of men who function as equal parts of a larger whole, dependent on each other for total meaning.

The humanized machine as hero is something very new in sport, 15 for in baseball anything approaching a machine has always been suspect. The famous Yankee teams of the fifties were almost flawlessly perfect, yet they never were especially popular. Their admirers took pains to romanticize their precision into something more natural than plain mechanics—Joe DiMaggio, for instance, became the "Yankee Clipper." Even so, most people seemed to want the Brooklyn Dodgers (the "bums") to thrash them in the World Series. One of the most memorable triumphs in recent decades—the victory of the Amazin' Mets in 1969—was memorable precisely because it was the triumph of a random collection of inspired rejects over the superbly skilled, fully integrated, and almost homogenized Baltimore Orioles. In baseball, machinery seems tantamount to villainy, whereas in football this smooth perfection is part of the unexpected integration a championship team must attain.

It is not surprising, really, that we should have a game which 16 asserts the heroic function of a mechanized group, since we have become a country where collective identity is a reality. Yet football's collective pattern is only one aspect of the way in which it seems to echo our contemporary environment. The game, like our society, can be thought of as a cluster of people living under great tension in a state of perpetual flux. The potential for sudden disaster or triumph is as great in football as it is in our own age, and although there is something ludicrous in equating interceptions with assassinations and long passes with moonshots, there is also something valid and appealing in the analogies. It seems to me that football does successfully reflect those salient and common conditions which affect us all, and it does so with the end of making us feel better about them and our lot. For one thing, it makes us feel that something can be released and connected in all this chaos; out of the accumulated pile of bodies something can emerge—a runner breaks into the clear or a pass finds its way to a receiver. To the spectator, plays such as these are human and dazzling. They suggest to the audience what it has hoped for (and been told) all along, that technology is still a tool and not a master. Fans get living proof of this every time a long pass is completed; they appreciate that it is the result of careful planning, perfect integration, and an effective "pattern," but they see too that it is human and that what counts as well is man, his desire, his natural skill, and his "grace under pressure." Football metaphysically yokes heroic action and technology by violence to suggest that they are mutually supportive. It's a doubtful proposition, but given how we live, it has its attractions.

Football, like the space program, is a game in the grand manner. 17
Homer would have chronicled it; Beowulf would have played full-back. Baseball's roots are at least as deep; it's a variation of the Satyr play, it's a feast of fools. But today their mythic resonance has been eroded by commercial success. Like so much else in America, their character has been modified by money.

More and more, both baseball and football are being played 18
indoors on rugs in multipurpose spaces. It doesn't make good business sense to play outside where it might rain and snow and do terrible things; it isn't really prudent to play on a natural field that can be destroyed in a single afternoon; and why build a whole stadium or park that's good for only one game? The fans in these stadiums are constantly diverted by huge whiz-bang scoreboards that dominate and describe the action, while the fans at home are constantly being reminded by at least three lively sportscasters of the other games, the other sports, and the other shows that are coming up later on the same stations. Both pro football and pro baseball now play vastly extended seasons, so that the World Series now takes place on chilly October nights and football is well under way before the summer ends. From my point of view all this is regrettable, because these changes tend to remove the games from their intangible but palpable mythic contexts. No longer clearly set in nature, no longer given the chance to breathe and steep in their own special atmospheres, both baseball and football risk becoming demythologized. As fans we seem to participate a little less in mythic ritual these days, while being subjected even more to the statistics, the hype, and the salary disputes that proceed from a jazzed-up, inflated, yet somehow flattened sporting world—a world that looks too much like the one we live in all the time.

Still, there is much to be thankful for, and every season seems to 19
bring its own contribution to mythic lore. Some people will think this nonsense, and I must admit there are good reasons for finding both games simply varieties of decadence.

In its preoccupation with mechanization, and in its open display 20
of violence, football is the more obvious target for social moralists, but I wonder if this is finally more "corrupt" than the seductive picture of sanctuary and tranquility that baseball has so artfully drawn for us. Almost all sport is vulnerable to such criticism because it is not

strictly ethical in intent, and for this reason there will always be room for puritans like the Elizabethan John Stubbes who howled at the "wanton fruits which these cursed pastimes bring forth." As a long-time dedicated fan of almost anything athletic, I confess myself out of sympathy with most of this; which is to say, I guess, that I am vulnerable to those fantasies which these games support, and that I find happiness in the company of people who feel as I do.

A final note. It is interesting that the heroic and pastoral conventions which underlie our most popular sports are almost classically opposed. The contrasts are familiar: city versus country, aspirations versus contentment, activity versus peace, and so on. Judging from the rise of professional football, we seem to be slowly relinquishing that unfettered rural vision of ourselves that baseball so beautifully mirrors, and we have come to cast ourselves in a genre more reflective of a nation confronted by constant and unavoidable challenges. Right now, like the Elizabethans, we seem to share both heroic and pastoral yearnings, and we reach out to both. Perhaps these divided needs account in part for the enormous attention we as a nation now give to spectator sports. For sport provides one place where we can have our football and our baseball too. 21

RESPONDING TO READING

1. Do you think that Ross's main idea, which he states in paragraph 2, is farfetched? Do you agree that the fundamental myth in each sport is what accounts for its appeal? What myths could be associated with popular sports like ice hockey and basketball?   **2.** In paragraph 2 Ross characterizes baseball and football as "uniquely *American*." Do you agree? What qualifies a sport as "American"? What sports fit your definition?   **3.** What does baseball (or football) mean to you as a spectator? Do you think Ross misses the true meaning of these sports in his complex analysis? Explain.

Kill 'Em! Crush 'Em! Eat 'Em Raw!

JOHN McMURTRY

John McMurtry (1939–   ), a professor of philosophy, now teaches at the University of Guelph in Canada. He was a linebacker for his college football team and then played for the Calgary Stampeders in the Canadian Football League. In the following selection, published in 1971 in *Macleans*, a Canadian news magazine, McMurtry compares football to war and takes issue with the violence of the sport.

A few months ago my neck got a hard crick in it. I couldn't turn my head; to look left or right I'd have to turn my whole body. But I'd had cricks in my neck since I started playing grade-school football and hockey, so I just ignored it. Then I began to notice that when I reached for any sort of large book (which I do pretty often as a philosophy teacher at the University of Guelph) I had trouble lifting it with one hand. I was losing the strength in my left arm, and I had such a steady pain in my back I often had to stretch out on the floor of the room I was in to relieve the pressure.

A few weeks later I mentioned to my brother, an orthopedic surgeon, that I'd lost the power in my arm since my neck began to hurt. Twenty-four hours later I was in a Toronto hospital not sure whether I might end up with a wasted upper limb. Apparently the steady pounding I had received playing college and professional football in the late fifties and early sixties had driven my head into my backbone so that the discs had crumpled together at the neck—"acute herniation"—and had cut the nerves to my left arm like a pinched telephone wire (without nerve stimulation, of course, the muscles atrophy, leaving the arm crippled). So I spent my Christmas holidays in the hospital in heavy traction and much of the next three months with my neck in a brace. Today most of the pain has gone, and I've recovered most of the strength in my arm. But from time to time I still have to don the brace, and surgery remains a possibility.

Not much of this will surprise anyone who knows football. It is a sport in which body wreckage is one of the leading conventions. A few days after I went into hospital for that crick in my neck, another brother, an outstanding football player in college, was undergoing spinal surgery in the same hospital two floors above me. In his case it was a lower, more massive herniation, which every now and again buckled him so that he was unable to lift himself off his back for days at a time. By the time he entered the hospital for surgery he had already spent several months in bed. The operation was successful, but, as in all such cases, it will take him a year to recover fully.

These aren't isolated experiences. Just about anybody who has ever played football for any length of time, in high school, college or one of the professional leagues, has suffered for it later physically.

Indeed, it is arguable that body shattering is the very *point* of football, as killing and maiming are of war. (In the United States, for example, the game results in 15 to 20 deaths a year and about 50,000 major operations on knees alone.) To grasp some of the more conspicuous similarities between football and war, it is instructive to listen to the imperatives most frequently issued to the players by their coaches, teammates and fans. "Hurt 'em!" "Level 'em!" "Kill 'em!" "Take 'em apart!" Or watch for the plays that are most enthusiastically

FOR OPENERS

This essay compares football to war and questions the rationale of a sport that brings out the worst in spectators. Do students see such an analogy as justified? Does their own experience as spectators or participants confirm McMurtry's thesis?

ADDITIONAL QUESTIONS FOR RESPONDING TO READING

1. Compare and contrast the positive and negative aspects of football to arrive at a conclusion about its social value.
2. In what ways do the fans at a baseball game behave differently from the fans at a football game? How can you account for the differences?
3. Do spectators experience catharsis—an emotional release—when they watch a football game? Explain why or why not. Give examples.

TEACHING STRATEGY

Examine McMurtry's attitudes toward football, society, and injuries, citing specific examples from the essay. Ask the class to discuss whether they think there is any value in watching a violent sport. Remind them that the Elizabethans loved to watch extremely violent tragedies, some of which, like *Hamlet* and *Macbeth*, are considered great works of drama. Is there a difference?

applauded by the fans. Where someone is "smeared," "knocked silly," "creamed," "nailed," "broken in two," or even "crucified." (One of my coaches when I played corner linebacker with the Calgary Stampeders in 1961 elaborated, often very inventively, on this language of destruction: admonishing us to "unjoin" the opponent, "make 'im remember you" and "stomp 'im like a bug.") Just as in hockey, where a fight will bring fans to their feet more often than a skillful play, so in football the mouth waters most of all for the really crippling block or tackle. For the kill. Thus the good teams are "hungry," the best players are "mean," and "casualties" are as much a part of the game as they are of a war.

The family resemblance between football and war is, indeed, striking. Their languages are similar: "field general," "long bomb," "blitz," "take a shot," "front line," "pursuit," "good hit," "the draft" and so on. Their principles and practices are alike: mass hysteria, the art of intimidation, absolute command and total obedience, territorial aggression, censorship, inflated insignia and propaganda, blackboard maneuvers and strategies, drills, uniforms, formations, marching bands and training camps. And the virtues they celebrate are almost identical: hyper-aggressiveness, coolness under fire and suicidal bravery. All this has been implicitly recognized by such jock-loving Americans as media stars General Patton and President Nixon, who have talked about war as a football game. Patton wanted to make his Second World War tank men look like football players. And Nixon, as we know, was fond of comparing attacks on Vietnam to football plays and drawing coachly diagrams on a blackboard for TV war fans. 6

One difference between war and football, though, is that there is little or no protest against football. Perhaps the most extraordinary thing about the game is that the systematic infliction of injuries excites in people not concern, as would be the case if they were sustained at, say, a rock festival, but a collective rejoicing and euphoria. Players and fans alike revel in the spectacle of a combatant felled into semi-consciousness, "blindsided," "clotheslined" or "decapitated." I can remember, in fact, being chided by a coach in pro ball for not "getting my hat" injuriously into a player who was already lying helpless on the ground. (On another occasion, after the Stampeders had traded the celebrated Joe Kapp to BC, we were playing the Lions in Vancouver and Kapp was forced on one play to run with the ball. He was coming "down the chute," his bad knee wobbling uncertainly, so I simply dropped on him like a blanket. After I returned to the bench I was reproved for not exploiting the opportunity to unhinge his bad knee.) 7

After every game, of course, the papers are full of reports on the day's injuries, a sort of post-battle "body count," and the respective 8 teams go to work with doctors and trainers, tape, whirlpool baths, cortisone and morphine to patch and deaden the wounds before the next game. Then the whole drama is reenacted—injured athletes held together by adhesive, braces and drugs—and the days following it are filled with even more feverish activity to put on the show yet again at the end of the next week. (I remember being so taped up in college that I earned the nickname "mummy.") The team that survives this merry-go-round spectacle of skilled masochism with the fewest incapacitating injuries usually wins. It is a sort of victory by ordeal: "We hurt them more than they hurt us."

My own initiation into this brutal circus was typical. I loved the   9
game from the moment I could run with a ball. Played shoeless on a green open field with no one keeping score and in a spirit of reckless abandon and laughter, it's a very different sport. Almost no one gets hurt and it's rugged, open and exciting (it still is for me). But then, like everything else, it starts to be regulated and institutionalized by adult authorities. And the fun is over.

So it was as I began the long march through organized football.   10
Now there was a coach and elders to make it clear by their behavior that beating other people was the only thing to celebrate and that trying to shake someone up every play was the only thing to be really proud of. Now there were severe rule enforcers, audiences, formally recorded victors and losers, and heavy equipment to permit crippling bodily moves and collisions (according to one American survey, more than 80% of all football injuries occur to fully equipped players). And now there was the official "given" that the only way to keep playing was to wear suffocating armor, to play to defeat, to follow orders silently and to renounce spontaneity for joyless drill. The game had been, in short, ruined. But because I loved to play and play skillfully, I stayed. And progressively and inexorably, as I moved through high school, college and pro leagues, my body was dismantled. Piece by piece.

I started off with torn ligaments in my knee at 13. Then, as the   11
organization and the competition increased, the injuries came faster and harder. Broken nose (three times), broken jaw (fractured in the first half and dismissed as a "bad wisdom tooth," so I played with it for the rest of the game), ripped knee ligaments again. Torn ligaments in one ankle and a fracture in the other (which I remember feeling relieved about because it meant I could honorably stop drill-blocking a 270-pound defensive end). Repeated rib fractures and cartilage tears (usually carried, again, through the remainder of the game). More dislocations of the left shoulder than I can remember (the last one I played with because, as the Calgary Stampeder doctor said, it "couldn't be damaged any more"). Occasional broken or dislocated

COLLABORATIVE ACTIVITY

Divide the class into three groups. One group will argue for the value of football, the other against, and the third group will judge who wins the debate.

fingers and toes. Chronically hurt lower back (I still can't lift with it or change a tire without worrying about folding). Separated right shoulder (as with many other injuries, like badly bruised hips and legs, needled with morphine for the games). And so on. The last pro game I played—against the Winnipeg Blue Bombers in the Western finals in 1961—I had a recently dislocated left shoulder, a more recently wrenched right shoulder and a chronic pain center in one leg. I was so tied up with soreness I couldn't drive my car to the airport. But it never occurred to me or anyone else that I miss a play as a corner linebacker.

By the end of my football career, I had learned that physical 12 injury—giving it and taking it—is the real currency of the sport. And that in the final analysis the "winner" is the man who can hit to kill even if only half his limbs are working. In brief, a warrior game with a warrior ethos into which (like almost everyone else I played with) my original boyish enthusiasm had been relentlessly taunted and conditioned.

In thinking back on how all this happened, though, I can pick 13 out no villains. As with the social system as a whole, the game has a life of its own. Everyone grows up inside it, accepts it and fulfills its dictates as obediently as helots.[1] Far from ever questioning the principles of the activity, people simply concentrate on executing these principles more aggressively than anybody around them. The result is a group of people who, as the leagues become of a higher and higher class, are progressively insensitive to the possibility that things could be otherwise. Thus, in football, anyone who might question the wisdom or enjoyment of putting on heavy equipment on a hot day and running full speed at someone else with the intention of knocking him senseless would be regarded simply as not really a devoted athlete and probably "chicken." The choice is made straightforward. Either you, too, do your very utmost to efficiently smash and be smashed, or you admit incompetence or cowardice and quit. Since neither of these admissions is very pleasant, people generally keep any doubts they have to themselves and carry on.

Of course, it would be a mistake to suppose that there is more 14 blind acceptance of brutal practices in organized football than elsewhere. On the contrary, a recent Harvard study has approvingly argued that football's characteristics of "impersonal acceptance of inflicted injury," an overriding "organization goal," the "ability to turn oneself on and off" and being, above all, "out to win" are of "inestimable value" to big corporations. Clearly, our sort of football

---

[1]A member of any group deprived of rights or privileges. [Eds.]

is no sicker than the rest of our society. Even its organized destruction of physical well-being is not anomalous. A very large part of our wealth, work and time is, after all, spent in systematically destroying and harming human life. Manufacturing, selling and using weapons that tear opponents to pieces. Making ever bigger and faster predator-named cars with which to kill and injure one another by the million every year. And devoting our very lives to outgunning one another for power in an ever more destructive rat race. Yet all these practices are accepted without question by most people, even zealously defended and honored. Competitive, organized injuring is integral to our way of life, and football is simply one of the more intelligible mirrors of the whole process: a sort of colorful morality play showing us how exciting and rewarding it is to Smash Thy Neighbor.

Now it is fashionable to rationalize our collaboration in all this by 15 arguing that, well, man *likes* to fight and injure his fellows and such games as football should be encouraged to discharge this original-sin urge into less harmful channels than, say, war. Public-show football, this line goes, plays the same sort of cathartic role as Aristotle said stage tragedy does: without real blood (or not much), it releases players and audience from unhealthy feelings stored up inside them.

As an ex-player in the seasonal coast-to-coast drama, I see little 16 to recommend such a view. What organized football did to me was make me *suppress* my natural urges and re-express them in an alien-ating, vicious form. Spontaneous desires for free bodily exuberance and fraternization with competitors were shamed and forced under ("If it ain't hurtin' it ain't helpin' ") and in their place were demanded armored mechanical moves and cool hatred of all opposition. Endless authoritarian drill and dressing-room harangues (ever wonder why competing teams can't prepare for a game in the same dressing room?) were the kinds of mechanisms employed to reconstruct joyful energies into mean and alien shapes. I am quite certain that everyone else around me was being similarly forced into this heavily equipped mil-itary precision and angry antagonism, because there was always a mutinous attitude about full-dress practices, and everybody (the pros included) had to concentrate incredibly hard for days to whip them-selves into just one hour's hostility a week against another club. The players never speak of these things, of course, because everyone is so anxious to appear tough.

The claim that men like seriously to battle one another to some 17 sort of finish is a myth. It only endures because it wears one of the oldest and most propagandized of masks—the romantic combatant. I sometimes wonder whether the violence all around us doesn't depend for its survival on the existence and preservation of this tough-guy disguise.

WRITING SUGGESTIONS

1. Do you agree with McMurtry when he says that football endures because its violence is dressed up in the image of the "romantic combatant" (paragraph 17)? What do you think is football's greatest attraction?
2. One of McMurtry's main points is that the forces that control organized football have ruined our enjoyment of the sport. Summarize his reasons and agree or disagree.
3. Compare McMurtry's analysis of football's relationship to society with Ross's analysis (p. 596).

ANSWERS TO RESPONDING TO READING

1. McMurtry is attempting to establish his credentials as an expert capable of discussing this subject. Some students might argue, however, that McMurtry's academic stance distances him from the game and from those who enjoy it. In this sense McMurtry could be undercutting his credibility with some readers by announcing in the first paragraph that he is a philosophy professor.
2. McMurtry assumes that readers generally like football but have not examined its unspoken social implications.
3. McMurtry sees football as a metaphor for America's love of "violent self-assertion" (paragraph 18).

As for the effect of organized football on the spectator, the fan is not released from supposed feelings of violent aggression by watching his athletic heroes perform it so much as encouraged in the view that people-smashing is an admirable mode of self-expression. The most savage attackers, after all, are, by general agreement, the most efficient and worthy players of all (the biggest applause I ever received as a football player occurred when I ran over people or slammed them so hard they couldn't get up). Such circumstances can hardly be said to lessen the spectators' martial tendencies. Indeed it seems likely that the whole show just further develops and titillates the North American addiction for violent self-assertion. . . . Perhaps, as well, it helps explain why the greater the zeal of U.S. political leaders as football fans (Johnson, Nixon, Agnew), the more enthusiastic the commitment to hard-line politics. At any rate there seems to be a strong correlation between people who relish tough football and people who relish intimidating and beating the hell out of commies, hippies, protest marchers and other opposition groups. 18

Watching well-advertised strong men knock other people round, make them hurt, is in the end like other tastes. It does not weaken with feeding and variation in form. It grows. 19

I got out of football in 1962. I had asked to be traded after Calgary had offered me a $25-a-week-plus-commissions off-season job as a clothing-store salesman. ("Dear Mr. Finks:" I wrote. [Jim Finks was then the Stampeders' general manager.] "Somehow I do not think the dialectical subtleties of Hegel, Marx and Plato would be suitably oriented amidst the environmental stimuli of jockey shorts and herringbone suits. I hope you make a profitable sale or trade of my contract to the East.") So the Stampeders traded me to Montreal. In a preseason intersquad game with the Alouettes I ripped the cartilages in my ribs on the hardest block I'd ever thrown. I had trouble breathing and I had to shuffle-walk with my torso on a tilt. The doctor in the local hospital said three weeks rest, the coach said scrimmage in two days. Three days later I was back home reading philosophy. 20

RESPONDING TO READING

1. Why does McMurtry mention in paragraph 1 that he is a philosophy professor? What effect do you think he wants this information to have on readers? What effect does it have on you?   **2.** What attitude does McMurtry assume his readers have toward football? Do you have such an attitude? How do you react to his statement in paragraph 6 that football is like war? Can you think of an analogy that is more accurate?   **3.** What parallels does McMurtry see between American culture and football? Do your own observations support this analogy, or do you think McMurtry overstates his case?

Who Killed Benny Paret?

NORMAN COUSINS

Norman Cousins (1912–1990) was an editor, essayist, diplomat, and professor of medical humanities. Most of his writing is about political and social issues. Cousins was active in support of nuclear disarmament, and his best-known work is *Modern Man Is Obsolete* (1945), a response to the bombing of Hiroshima. More recently, Cousins drew attention with his book *Anatomy of an Illness* (1979), in which he chronicles his battle against cancer with his own method of diet and positive emotions. He wrote about medicine and illness in *Healing and Belief* (1982), *The Healing Heart* (1983), and *Head First, the Biology of Hope* (1989). "Who Killed Benny Paret?," in which Cousins assigns blame for a boxer's death in the ring, appeared in the *Saturday Review* in 1962.

Sometime about 1935 or 1936 I had an interview with Mike Jacobs, the prizefight promoter. I was a fledgling reporter at that time; my beat was education but during the vacation season I found myself on varied assignments, all the way from ship news to sports reporting. In this way I found myself sitting opposite the most powerful figure in the boxing world.   1

There was nothing spectacular in Mr. Jacobs' manner or appearance; but when he spoke about prize fights, he was no longer a bland little man but a colossus who sounded the way Napoleon must have sounded when he reviewed a battle. You knew you were listening to Number One. His saying something made it true.   2

We discussed what to him was the only important element in successful promoting—how to please the crowd. So far as he was concerned, there was no mystery to it. You put killers in the ring and the people filled your arena. You hire boxing artists—men who are adroit at feinting, parrying, weaving, jabbing, and dancing, but who don't pack dynamite in their fists—and you wind up counting your empty seats. So you searched for the killers and sluggers and maulers—fellows who could hit with the force of a baseball bat.   3

I asked Mr. Jacobs if he was speaking literally when he said people came out to see the killer.   4

"They don't come out to see a tea party," he said evenly. "They come out to see the knockout. They come out to see a man hurt. If they think anything else, they're kidding themselves."   5

Recently, a young man by the name of Benny Paret was killed in the ring. The killing was seen by millions; it was on television. In the twelfth round, he was hit hard in the head several times, went down, was counted out, and never came out of the coma.   6

The Paret fight produced a flurry of investigations. Governor Rockefeller was shocked by what happened and appointed a com-   7

FOR OPENERS

What do you like about boxing? The skill of the boxers? The drama? The violence? What do you dislike?

ADDITIONAL QUESTIONS FOR RESPONDING TO READING

1. Who was the greatest boxer of all time? Why?
2. Is an occasional death in the boxing ring an acceptable occurrence, or should society reexamine its acceptance of boxing?
3. Other sports, such as skydiving, auto racing, and skiing, have more deaths than boxing. Why do you think boxing routinely gets more criticism? What about the sport seems to attract all the negative attention?

TEACHING STRATEGY

At a 1979 concert by The Who in Cincinnati, eleven fans were trampled to death. In 1991 in Salt Lake City, three teenage fans were trampled and suffocated. The blame was placed on festival seating—standing-room-only space in which fans, whipped into a frenzy by the music, struggle to get to the front. Without this wildness and potential for danger, many fans would not want to attend rock concerts. In other words, rock fans do not come for the artistry of the musicians any more than boxing fans come for the "dodging and weaving." Ask students if they think this is a valid analogy. If so, should festival seating be outlawed nationwide, as it is already in some cities? Should heavy metal concerts be outlawed or restricted in some manner? Whose fault are the concert deaths?

COLLABORATIVE ACTIVITY

Have students brainstorm in groups to decide what other factors could have caused Paret's death. Ask them whether they think Cousins is sidestepping the issue by blaming Paret's death on society.

WRITING SUGGESTIONS

1. In paragraph 6, why does Cousins use the passive voice to discuss Paret's death?
2. Are there other socially accepted activities that merit reexamination because of the violence associated with them? Select one and briefly describe the problem in an essay.
3. Cousins says, "No crowd was ever brought to its feet screaming and cheering at the sight of two men beautifully dodging and weaving out of each other's jabs. The time the crowd comes alive is when a man is hit hard over the heart or the head" (paragraph 9). Do you agree? What do you think is the attraction of the knockout?

mittee to assess the responsibility. The New York State Boxing Commission decided to find out what was wrong. The District Attorney's office expressed its concern. One question that was solemnly studied in all three probes concerned the action of the referee. Did he act in time to stop the fight? Another question had to do with the role of the examining doctors who certified the physical fitness of the fighters before the bout. Still another question involved Mr. Paret's manager; did he rush his boy into the fight without adequate time to recuperate from the previous one?

In short, the investigators looked into every possible cause except 8 the real one. Benny Paret was killed because the human fist delivers enough impact, when directed against the head, to produce a massive hemorrhage in the brain. The human brain is the most delicate and complex mechanism in all creation. It has a lacework of millions of highly fragile nerve connections. Nature attempts to protect this exquisitely intricate machinery by encasing it in a hard shell. Fortunately, the shell is thick enough to withstand a great deal of pounding. Nature, however, can protect man against everything except man himself. Not every blow to the head will kill a man—but there is always the risk of concussion and damage to the brain. A prizefighter may be able to survive even repeated brain concussions and go on fighting, but the damage to his brain may be permanent.

In any event, it is futile to investigate the referee's role and seek 9 to determine whether he should have intervened to stop the fight earlier. That is not where the primary responsibility lies. The primary responsibility lies with the people who pay to see a man hurt. The referee who stops a fight too soon from the crowd's viewpoint can expect to be booed. The crowd wants the knockout; it wants to see a man stretched out on the canvas. This is the supreme moment in boxing. It is nonsense to talk about prizefighting as a test of boxing skills. No crowd was ever brought to its feet screaming and cheering at the sight of two men beautifully dodging and weaving out of each other's jabs. The time the crowd comes alive is when a man is hit hard over the heart or the head, when his mouthpiece flies out, when the blood squirts out of his nose or eyes, when he wobbles under the attack and his pursuer continues to smash at him with pole-ax[1] impact.

Don't blame it on the referee. Don't even blame it on the fight 10 managers. Put the blame where it belongs—on the prevailing mores that regard prizefighting as a perfectly proper enterprise and vehicle of entertainment. No one doubts that many people enjoy prizefighting and will miss it if it should be thrown out. And that is precisely the point.

---

[1]A battle axe with a small handle. [Eds.]

RESPONDING TO READING

1. Supporters of boxing have traditionally dismissed its critics as "do-gooders" who do not understand the skill or beauty of the sport. Cousins obviously disagrees. With whom do you side? Why? **2.** Cousins is very critical of boxing, but he offers no solutions to the problems he identifies. Should boxing be banned? Or can you offer other, less drastic suggestions that might make boxing more humane? **3.** Boxing has always attracted poor young men who wanted to use their fists to fight their way out of poverty. Does Cousins's failure to examine the racial and class dimensions of boxing weaken his case? How might he have brought these aspects into his essay?

On Boxing

JOYCE CAROL OATES

One of the most prolific contemporary American writers, Joyce Carol Oates (1938–   ) was born in Lockport, New York, and received degrees from Syracuse University and from the University of Wisconsin. Her first collection of fiction, *By the North Gate*, was published in 1963. Since then she has published over two dozen books. Oates's writing reflects her concern with violence in contemporary society and the hostility of modern culture toward the individual. She often mixes realism with the supernatural in her fiction. Her many novels include *A Garden of Earthly Delights* (1967), *Them* (1969), *Childwold* (1976), *Bellefleur* (1980), and *American Appetites* (1989). In the following essay, which was first published in the *New York Times Magazine* in 1985, Oates responds to people who ask her how she can enjoy "so brutal a sport" as boxing.

They are young welterweight boxers so evenly matched they might be twins—though one has a redhead's pallor and the other is a dusky-skinned Hispanic. Circling each other in the ring, they try jabs, tentative left hooks, right crosses that dissolve in midair or turn into harmless slaps. The Madison Square Garden crowd is derisive, impatient. "Those two! What'd they do, wake up this morning and decide they were boxers?" a man behind me says contemptuously. (He's dark, nattily dressed, with a neatly trimmed mustache and tinted glasses. A sophisticated fight fan. Two hours later he will be crying. "Tommy! Tommy! Tommy!" over and over in a paroxysm of grief as, on the giant closed-circuit television screen, middleweight champion Marvelous Marvin Hagler batters his challenger, Thomas Hearns, into insensibility.)

The young boxers must be conscious of the jeers and boos in this great cavernous space reaching up into the $20 seats in the balconies amid the constant milling of people in the aisles, the smell of hotdogs, beer, cigarette and cigar smoke, hair oil. But they are locked desperately together, circling, jabbing, slapping, clinching, now a flurry of light blows, clumsy footwork, another sweaty stumbling despairing clinch into the ropes that provokes a fresh wave of derision. Why are they here in the Garden of all places, each fighting what looks like his first professional fight? What are they doing? Neither is angry at the other. When the bell sounds at the end of the sixth and final round, the crowd boos a little louder. The Hispanic boy, silky yellow shorts, damp, frizzy, floating hair, strides about his corner of the ring with his gloved hand aloft—not in defiance of the boos, which increase in response to his gesture, or even in acknowledgment of them. It's just something he has seen older boxers do. He seems to be saying "I'm here, I made it, I did it." When the decision is announced as a draw, the crowd's derision increases in volume. "Get out of the ring!" "Go home!" Contemptuous male laughter follows the boys in their robes, towels about their heads, sweating, breathless. Why had they thought they were boxers?

How can you enjoy so brutal a sport, people ask. Or don't ask.   3

And it's too complicated to answer. In any case, I don't "enjoy"   4
boxing, and never have; it isn't invariably "brutal"; I don't think of it as a sport.

Nor do I think of it in writerly terms as a metaphor for something   5
else. (For *what* else?) No one whose interest in boxing began in childhood—as mine did as an offshoot of my father's interest—is likely to suppose it is a symbol of something beyond itself, though I can entertain the proposition that life is a metaphor for boxing—for one of those bouts that go on and on, round following round, small victories, small defeats, nothing determined, again the bell and again the bell and you and your opponent so evenly matched it's clear your opponent *is* you and why are the two of you jabbing and punching at each other on an elevated platform enclosed by ropes as in a pen beneath hot crude all-exposing lights in the presence of an indifferent crowd: that sort of writerly metaphor. But if you have seen 500 boxing matches, you have seen 500 boxing matches, and their common denominator, which surely exists, is not of primary interest to you. "If the Host[1] is only a symbol," the Catholic writer Flannery O'Connor said, "I'd say the hell with it."

---

[1]The wafer or bread, symbolizing the body of Christ, used during the sacrament of communion. [Eds.]

ADDITIONAL QUESTIONS FOR RESPONDING TO READING

1. Can anyone who has not boxed criticize boxing? Explain.
2. Do any sports exist that are more directly physical than boxing? Discuss.
3. Is boxing more entertainment or sport? Why?
4. Why does Oates quote Yeats in her essay?

Each boxing match is a story, a highly condensed, highly dramatic   6
story—even when nothing much happens: then failure is the story.
There are two principal characters in the story, overseen by a shadowy
third. When the bell rings no one knows what will happen. Much is
speculated, nothing known. The boxers bring to the fight everything
that is themselves, and everything will be exposed: including secrets
about themselves they never knew. There are boxers possessed of
such remarkable intuition, such prescience, one would think they had
fought this particular fight before. There are boxers who perform
brilliantly, but mechanically, who cannot improvise in midfight; there
are boxers performing at the height of their skill who cannot quite
comprehend that it won't be enough; to my knowledge there was
only one boxer who possessed an extraordinary and disquieting
awareness, not only of his opponent's every move or anticipated
move, but of the audience's keenest shifts in mood as well—
Muhammad Ali, of course.

In the ring, death is always a possibility, which is why I prefer   7
to see films or tapes of fights already past—already crystallized into
art. In fact, death is a statistically rare possibility of which no one
likes to think—like your possible death tomorrow morning in an
automobile crash, or in next month's airplane crash, or in a freak
accident involving a fall on the stairs—a skull fracture, subarachnoid
hemorrhage.

A boxing match is a play without words, which doesn't mean   8
that it has no text or no language, only that the text is improvised in
action, the language a dialogue between the boxers in a joint response
to the mysterious will of the crowd, which is always that the fight be
a worthy one so that the crude paraphernalia of the setting—the ring,
the lights, the onlookers themselves—be obliterated. To go from an
ordinary preliminary match to a "Fight of the Century"—like those
between Joe Louis and Billy Conn, Muhammad Ali and Joe Frazier,
most recently Marvin Hagler and Thomas Hearns—is to go from
listening or half-listening to a guitar being idly plucked to hearing
Bach's "Well-Tempered Clavier" being perfectly played, and that too
is part of the story. So much is happening so swiftly and so subtly
you cannot absorb it except to know that something memorable is
happening and it is happening in a place beyond words.

The fighters in the ring are time-bound—is anything so excru-   9
ciatingly long as a fiercely contested three-minute round?—but the
fight itself is timeless. By way of films and tapes, it has become history,
art. If boxing is a sport, it is the most tragic of all sports because,
more than any human activity, it consumes the very excellence it
displays: Its very drama is this consumption. To expend oneself in
fighting the greatest fight of one's life is to begin immediately the

TEACHING STRATEGY

   Isolate each of Oates's metaphors about boxing and discuss its effectiveness.

downward turn that next time may be a plunge, a sudden incomprehensible fall. *I am the greatest*, Muhammad Ali says. *I am the greatest*, Marvin Hagler says. You always think you're going to win, Jack Dempsey wryly observed in his old age, otherwise you can't fight at all. The punishment—to the body, the brain, the spirit—a man must endure to become a great boxer is inconceivable to most of us whose idea of personal risk is largely ego related or emotional. But the punishment, as it begins to show in even a young and vigorous boxer, is closely assessed by his rivals. After junior-welterweight champion Aaron Pryor won a lackluster fight on points a few months ago, a younger boxer in his weight division, interviewed at ringside, said: "My mouth is watering."

So the experience of seeing great fighters of the past—and great 10 sporting events are always *past*—is radically different from having seen them when they were reigning champions. Jack Johnson, Jack Dempsey, Joe Louis, Sugar Ray Robinson, Willie Pep, Rocky Marciano, Muhammad Ali—as spectators we know not only how a fight ends but how a career ends. Boxing is always particulars, second by incalculable second, but in the abstract it suggests these haunting lines by Yeats:

> Everything that man esteems
> Endures a moment or a day.
> Love's pleasure drives his love away,
> The painter's brush consumes his dreams;
> The herald's cry, the soldier's tread   5
> Exhaust his glory and his might:
> Whatever flames upon the night
> Man's own resinous heart has fed.
>
> —from "The Resurrection"

The referee, the third character in the story, usually appears to 11 be a mere observer, even an intruder, a near-ghostly presence as fluid in motion and quick-footed as the boxers themselves (he is frequently a former boxer). But so central to the drama of boxing is the referee that the spectacle of two men fighting each other unsupervised in an elevated ring would appear hellish, obscene—life rather than art. The referee is our intermediary in the fight. He is our moral conscience, extracted from us as spectators so that, for the duration of the fight, "conscience" is not a factor in our experience, nor is it a factor in the boxers' behavior.

Though the referee's role is a highly demanding one, and it has 12 been estimated that there are perhaps no more than a dozen really skilled referees in the world, it seems to be necessary in the intense dramatic action of the fight that the referee have no dramatic identity. Referees' names are quickly forgotten, even as they are announced over the microphone preceding a fight. Yet, paradoxically, the ref-

COLLABORATIVE ACTIVITY

Divide the class into small groups and ask each to decide which is the most violent sport. Ask them to consider violence in the stands and on the field or court, violence among players and among fans, and violence that is sanctioned by the sport's rules as well as violence that is incidental to the sport. Have each group come to a decision, and then try to have the class as a whole reach a consensus.

eree's position is one of crucial significance. The referee cannot control what happens in the ring, but he can frequently control, to a degree, *that* it happens: He is responsible for the fight, if not for the individual fighter's performance. It is the referee solely who holds the power of life and death at certain times; whose decision to terminate a fight, or to allow it to continue, determines a man's fate. (One should recall that a well-aimed punch with a boxer's full weight behind it can have an astonishing impact—a blow that must be absorbed by the brain in its jelly sac.)

In a recent heavyweight fight in Buffalo, 220-pound Tim With-   13 erspoon repeatedly struck his 260-pound opponent James Broad, caught in the ropes, while the referee looked on without acting— though a number of spectators called for the fight to be stopped. In the infamous Benny Paret-Emile Griffith fight of March 24, 1962, the referee Ruby Goldstein was said to have stood paralyzed as Paret, trapped in the ropes, suffered as many as 18 powerful blows to the head before he fell. (He died 10 days later.) Boxers are trained not to quit; if they are knocked down they will try to get up to continue the fight, even if they can hardly defend themselves. The primary rule of the ring—to defend oneself at all times—is both a parody and a distillation of life.

Boxing is a purely masculine world. (Though there are female   14 boxers—the most famous is the black champion Lady Tyger Trimiar with her shaved head and tiger-striped attire—women's role in the sport is extremely marginal.) The vocabulary of boxing is attuned to a quintessentially masculine sensibility in which the role of patriarch/ protector can only be assured if there is physical strength underlying it. First comes this strength—"primitive," perhaps; then comes civilization. It should be kept in mind that "boxing" and "fighting," though always combined in the greatest of boxers, can be entirely different and even unrelated activities. If boxing can be, in the lighter weights especially, a highly complex and refined skill belonging solely to civilization, fighting seems to belong to something predating civilization, the instant not merely to defend oneself—for when has the masculine ego ever been assuaged by so minimal a gesture?—but to attack another and to force him into absolute submission. Hence the electrifying effect upon a typical fight crowd when fighting emerges suddenly out of boxing—the excitement when a boxer's face begins to bleed. The flash of red is the visible sign of the fight's authenticity in the eyes of many spectators, and boxers are right to be proud—if they are—of their facial scars.

To the untrained eye, boxers in the ring usually appear to be   15 angry. But, of course, this is "work" to them; emotion has no part in it, or should not. Yet in an important sense—in a symbolic sense—

the boxers *are* angry, and boxing is fundamentally about anger. It is the only sport in which anger is accommodated, ennobled. Why are boxers angry? Because, for the most part, they belong to the disenfranchised of our society, to impoverished ghetto neighborhoods in which anger is an appropriate response. ("It's hard being black. You ever been black? I was black once—when I was poor," Larry Holmes has said.) Today, when most boxers—most good boxers—are black or Hispanic, white men begin to look anemic in the ring. Yet after decades of remarkable black boxers—from Jack Johnson to Joe Louis to Muhammad Ali—heavyweight champion Larry Holmes was the object of racist slurs and insults when he defended his title against the overpromoted white challenger Gerry Cooney a few years ago.

Liberals who have no personal or class reason to feel anger tend 16 to disparage, if not condemn, such anger in others. Liberalism is also unfairly harsh in its criticism of all that predates civilization—or "liberalism" itself—without comprehending that civilization is a concept, an idea, perhaps at times hardly more than a fiction, attendant upon, and always subordinate to, physical strength: missiles, nuclear warheads. The terrible and tragic silence dramatized in the boxing ring is the silence of nature before language, when the physical *was* language, a means of communication swift and unmistakable.

The phrase "killer instinct" is said to have been coined in reference 17 to Jack Dempsey in his famous early fights against Jess Willard, Georges Carpentier, Luis Firpo ("The Wild Bull of the Pampas") and any number of other boxers, less renowned, whom he savagely beat. The ninth of 11 children born to an impoverished Mormon sharecropper and itinerant railroad worker, Dempsey seems to have been, as a young boxer in his prime, the very embodiment of angry hunger; and if he remains the most spectacular heavyweight champion in history, it is partly because he fought when rules governing boxing were somewhat casual by present-day standards. Where aggression must be learned, even cultivated, in some champion boxers (Tunney, Louis, Marciano, Patterson, for example), Dempsey's aggression was direct and natural: Once in the ring he seems to have wanted to kill his opponent.

Dempsey's first title fight in 1919, against the aging champion 18 Jess Willard, was called "pugilistic murder" by some sportswriters and is said to have been one of boxing's all-time blood baths. Today, this famous fight—which brought the nearly unknown 24-year-old Dempsey to national prominence—would certainly have been stopped in the first minute of the first round. Badly out of condition, heavier than Dempsey by almost 60 pounds, the 37-year-old Willard had virtually no defense against the challenger. By the end of the fight, Willard's jaw was broken, his cheekbone split, nose smashed, six teeth broken off at the gum, an eye was battered shut, much further damage was done to his body. Both boxers were covered in Willard's blood. Years later Dempsey's estranged manager Kearns confessed—perhaps falsely—that he had "loaded" Dempsey's gloves—treated his hand tape with a talcum substance that turned concrete-hard when wet.

For the most part, boxing matches today are scrupulously mon- 19 itored by referees and ring physicians. The devastating knockout blow is frequently the one never thrown. In a recent televised junior-middleweight bout between Don Curry and James Green, the referee stopped the fight because Green seemed momentarily disabled: His logic was that Green had dropped his gloves and was therefore in a position to be hurt. (Green and his furious trainer protested the decision but the referee's word is final: No fight, stopped, can be resumed.) The drama of the ring begins to shift subtly as more and more frequently one sees a referee intervene to embrace a weakened or defenseless man in a gesture of paternal solicitude that in itself carries much theatrical power—a gesture not so dramatic as the killing blow but one that suggests that the ethics of the ring are moving toward those that prevail beyond it. As if fighter-brothers whose mysterious animosity has somehow brought them to battle are saved by their father. . . .

In the final moment of the Hagler-Hearns fight, the dazed 20 Hearns—on his feet but clearly not fully conscious, gamely prepared to take Hagler's next assault—was saved by the referee from what might well have been serious injury, if not death, considering the ferocity of Hagler's fighting and the personal anger he seems to have brought to it that night. This 8-minute fight, generally believed to be one of the great fights in boxing history, ends with Hearns in the referee's protective embrace—an image that is haunting, in itself profoundly mysterious, as if an indefinable human drama had been spontaneously created for us, brilliantly improvised, performed one time and one time only, yet permanently ingrained upon our consciousness.

Years ago in the early 1950s, when my father first took me to a 21 Golden Gloves boxing tournament in Buffalo, I asked him why the boys wanted to fight one another, why they were willing to get hurt. My father said, "Boxers don't feel pain quite the way we do."

Gene Tunney's single defeat in an 11-year career was to a flam- 22 boyant and dangerous fighter named Harry Greb ("The Human Windmill") who seems to have been, judging from boxing literature, the dirtiest fighter in history. Low blows, butting, fouls, holding and hitting, using his laces on an opponent's eyes—Greb was famous for his lack of interest in the rules. He was world middleweight champion for three years but a presence in the boxing world for a long time. After the first of his several fights with Greb, the 24-year-old Tunney had to spend a week in bed, he was so badly hurt; he'd lost two quarts of blood during the 15-round fight. But as Tunney said years afterward: "Greb gave me a terrible whipping. He broke my nose, maybe with a butt. He cut my eyes and ears, perhaps with his laces. . . . My jaw was swollen from the right temple down the cheek, along under the chin and part way up the other side. The referee, the ring itself, was full of blood. . . . But it was in that first fight, in which I lost my American light-heavyweight title, that I knew I had found a way to beat Harry eventually. I was fortunate, really. If boxing in those days had been afflicted with the commission doctors we have today—who are always poking their noses into the ring and examining superficial wounds—the first fight with Greb would have been stopped before I learned how to beat him. It's possible, even probable, that if this had happened I would never have been heard of again."

Tommy Loughran, the light-heavyweight champion from 1927 to   23
1929, was a master boxer greatly admired by other boxers. He approached boxing literally as a science—as Tunney did—studying his opponents' styles and mapping out ring strategy for each fight. He rigged up mirrors in his basement so that he could see himself as he worked out—for, as Loughran realized, no boxer ever sees himself quite as he appears to his opponent. But the secret of Loughran's career was that he had a right hand that broke so easily he could use it only once in each fight: It had to be the knockout punch or nothing. "I'd get one shot, then the agony of the thing would hurt me if the guy got up. Anybody I ever hit with a left hook, I knocked flat on his face, but I would never take a chance for fear if my left hand goes, I'm done for."

Both Tunney and Loughran, it is instructive to note, retired from   24
boxing before they were forced to retire. Tunney was a highly successful businessman and Loughran a successful sugar broker on the Wall Street commodities market—just to suggest that boxers are not invariably illiterate, stupid, or punch-drunk.

One of the perhaps not entirely acknowledged reasons for the   25
attraction of serious writers to boxing (from Swift, Pope, Johnson to Hazlitt, Lord Byron, Hemingway, and our own Normal Mailer, George Plimpton, Wilfrid Sheed, Daniel Halpern et al.) is the sport's systematic cultivation of pain in the interests of a project, a life-goal: the willed transposing of the sensation called "pain" (whether physical or psychological) into its opposite. If this is masochism—and I doubt that it is, or that it is simply—it is also intelligence, cunning, strategy. It is the active welcoming of that which most living beings

try to avoid and to flee. It is the active subsuming of the present moment in terms of the future. Pain now but control (and therefore pleasure) later.

Still, it is the rigorous training period leading up to the public   26
appearance that demands the most discipline. In this, too, the writer senses some kinship, however oblique and one-sided, with the professional boxer. The brief public spectacle of the boxing match (which could last as little as 60 seconds), like the publication of the writer's book, is but the final, visible stage in a long, arduous, fanatic, and sometimes quixotic, subordination of the self. It was Rocky Marciano who seems to have trained with the most monastic devotion, secluding himself from his wife and family for as long as three months before a fight. Quite apart from the grueling physical training of this period and the constant preoccupation with diet and weight, Marciano concentrated on only the upcoming fight, the opening bell, his opponent. Every minute of the boxer's life was planned for one purpose. In the training camp the name of the opponent was never mentioned and Marciano's associates were careful about conversation in his presence: They talked very little about boxing.

In the final month, Marciano would not write a letter. The last   27
10 days before a fight he saw no mail, took no telephone calls, met no new acquaintances. The week before the fight he would not shake hands with anyone. Or go for a ride in a car. No new foods! No envisioning the morning after the fight! All that was not *the fight* was taboo: When Marciano worked out punching the bag he saw his opponent before him, when he jogged early in the morning he saw his opponent close beside him. What could be a more powerful image of discipline—madness?—than this absolute subordination of the self, this celibacy of the fighter-in-training? Instead of focusing his energies and fantasies upon Woman, the boxer focuses them upon the Opponent.

No sport is more physical, more direct, than boxing. No sport   28
appears more powerfully homoerotic: the confrontation in the ring—the disrobing—the sweaty, heated combat that is part dance, courtship, coupling—the frequent urgent pursuit by one boxer of the other in the fight's natural and violent movement toward the "knockout." Surely boxing derives much of its appeal from this mimicry of a species of erotic love in which one man overcomes the other in an exhibition of superior strength.

Most fights, however fought, lead to an embrace between the   29
boxers after the final bell—a gesture of mutual respect and apparent affection that appears to the onlooker to be more than perfunctory. Rocky Graziano, often derided for being a slugger rather than a "classic" boxer, sometimes kissed his opponents out of gratitude for

the fight. Does the boxing match, one almost wonders, lead irresistibly to this moment: the public embrace of two men who otherwise, in public or in private, could not approach each other with such passion? Are men privileged to embrace with love only after having fought? A woman is struck by the tenderness men will express for boxers who have been hurt, even if it is only by way of commentary on photographs: the startling picture of Ray (Boom Boom) Mancini after his second losing fight with Livingstone Bramble, for instance, when Mancini's face was hideously battered (photographs in *Sports Illustrated* and elsewhere were gory, near-pornographic); the much-reprinted photograph of the defeated Thomas Hearns being carried to his corner in the arms of an enormous black man in formal attire—the "Hit Man" from Detroit now helpless, only semiconscious, looking precisely like a black Christ taken from the cross. These are powerful, haunting, unsettling images, cruelly beautiful, very much bound up with the primitive appeal of the sport.

Yet to suggest that men might love one another directly without the violent ritual of combat is to misread man's greatest passion—for war, not peace. Love, if there is to be love, comes second.   30

Boxing is, after all, about lying. It is about cultivating a double personality. As José Torres, the ex-light-heavyweight champion who is now the New York State Boxing Commissioner, says: "We fighters understand lies. What's a feint? What's a left hook off the jab? What's an opening? What's thinking one thing and doing another. . . ?"   31

There is nothing fundamentally playful about boxing, nothing that seems to belong to daylight, to pleasure. At its moments of greatest intensity it seems to contain so complete and so powerful an image of life—life's beauty, vulnerability, despair, incalculable and often reckless courage—that boxing *is* life, and hardly a mere game. During a superior boxing match we are deeply moved by the body's communion with itself by way of another's flesh. The body's dialogue with its shadow-self—or Death. Baseball, football, basketball—these quintessentially American pastimes are recognizably sports because they involve play: They are games. One *plays* football; one doesn't *play* boxing.   32

Observing team sports, teams of adult men, one sees how men are children in the most felicitous sense of the word. But boxing in its elemental ferocity cannot be assimilated into childhood—though very young men box, even professionally, and numerous world champions began boxing when they were hardly more than children. Spectators at public games derive much of their pleasure from reliving the communal emotions of childhood, but spectators at boxing matches relive the murderous infancy of the race. Hence the notorious cruelty   33 of boxing crowds and the excitement when a man begins to bleed. ("When I see blood," says Marvin Hagler, "I become a bull." He means his own.)

The boxing ring comes to seem an altar of sorts, one of those ³⁴ legendary magical spaces where the laws of a nation are suspended: Inside the ropes, during an officially regulated three-minute round, a man may be killed at his opponent's hands but he cannot be legally murdered. Boxing inhabits a sacred space predating civilization; or, to use D. H. Lawrence's phrase,[2] before God was love. If it suggests a savage ceremony or a rite of atonement, it also suggests the futility of such rites. For what atonement is the fight waged, if it must shortly be waged again. . . ?

All this is to speak of the paradox of boxing—its obsessive appeal ³⁵ for many who find in it not only a spectacle involving sensational feats of physical skill but an emotional experience impossible to convey in words; an art form, as I have suggested, with no natural analogue in the arts. And of course this accounts, too, for the extreme revulsion it arouses in many people. ("Brutal," "disgusting," "barbaric," "inhuman," "a terrible, terrible sport"—typical comments on the subject.)

In December 1984, the American Medical Association passed a ³⁶ resolution calling for the abolition of boxing on the principle that it is the only sport in which the *objective* is to cause injury. This is not surprising. Humanitarians have always wanted to reform boxing— or abolish it altogether. The 1896 heavyweight title match between Ruby Robert Fitzsimmons and Peter Maher was outlawed in many parts of the United States, so canny promoters staged it across the Mexican border 400 miles from El Paso. (Some 300 people made the arduous journey to see what must have been one of the most disappointing bouts in boxing history—Fitzsimmons knocked out his opponent in a mere 95 seconds.)

During the prime of Jack Dempsey's career in the 1920s, boxing ³⁷ was illegal in many states, like alcohol, and like alcohol, seems to have aroused a hysterical public enthusiasm. Photographs of jammed outdoor arenas taken in the 1920s with boxing rings like postage-sized altars at their centers, the boxers themselves scarcely visible, testify to the extraordinary emotional appeal boxing had at that time, even as reform movements were lobbying against it. When Jack Johnson won the heavyweight title in 1908 (he had to pursue the white champion Tommy Burns all the way to Australia to confront him), the special "danger" of boxing was also that it might expose and humiliate

---

[2]D. H. Lawrence (1885–1930), English novelist. [Eds.]

WRITING SUGGESTIONS

1. One argument in favor of boxing is that it has a symbolic significance beyond the two individuals battling in the ring. For example, when Joe Lewis knocked out Max Schmeling, his victory was seen as the triumph of a black man over a German, who was supposedly ethnically superior. Does contemporary boxing have any symbolic significance? If so, does this significance mitigate the obvious violence of the sport?

2. What is it about sport that encourages fights among players? Why is it that stockbrokers, for example, do not regularly get into fights at work? Comparing the work environment, attire, and backgrounds of white-collar workers with those of athletes, write an essay that answers this question.

white men in the ring. After Johnson's victory over the "White Hope" contender Jim Jeffries, there were race riots and lynchings throughout the United States; even films of some of Johnson's fights were outlawed in many states. And because boxing has become a sport in which black and Hispanic men have lately excelled, it is particularly vulnerable to attack by white middle-class reformers, who seem uninterested in lobbying against equally dangerous but "establishment" sports like football, auto racing, and thoroughbred horse racing.

There is something peculiarly American in the fact that, while 38 boxing is our most controversial sport, it is also the sport that pays its top athletes the most money. In spite of the controversy, boxing has never been healthier financially. The three highest paid athletes in the world in both 1983 and 1984 were boxers; a boxer with a long career like heavyweight champion Larry Holmes—48 fights in 13 years as a professional—can expect to earn somewhere beyond $50 million. (Holmes said that after retirement what he would miss most about boxing is his million-dollar checks.) Dempsey, who said that a man fights for one thing only—money—made somewhere beyond $3,500,000 in the ring in his long and varied career. Now $1.5 million is a fairly common figure for a single fight. Thomas Hearns made at least $7 million in his fight with Hagler while Hagler made at least $7.5 million. For the first of his highly publicized matches with Roberto Duran in 1980—which he lost on a decision—the popular black welterweight champion Sugar Ray Leonard received a staggering $10 million to Duran's $1.3 million. And none of these figures takes into account various subsidiary earnings (from television commercials, for instance) which in Leonard's case are probably as high as his income was from boxing.

Money has drawn any number of retired boxers back into the 39 ring, very often with tragic results. The most notorious example is perhaps Joe Louis, who, owing huge sums in back taxes, continued boxing well beyond the point at which he could perform capably. After a career of 17 years he was stopped by Rocky Marciano—who was said to have felt as upset by his victory as Louis by the defeat. (Louis then went on to a degrading second career as a professional wrestler. This, too, ended abruptly when 300-pound Rocky Lee stepped on the 42-year-old Louis's chest and damaged his heart.) Ezzard Charles, Jersey Joe Walcott, Joe Frazier, Muhammad Ali—each continued fighting when he was no longer in condition to defend himself against young heavyweight boxers on the way up. Of all heavyweight champions, only Rocky Marciano, to whom fame and money were not of paramount significance, was prudent enough to retire before he was defeated. In any case, the prodigious sums of money a few boxers earn do not account for the sums the public is willing to pay them.

Though boxing has long been popular in many countries and under many forms of government, its popularity in the United States since the days of John L. Sullivan has a good deal to do with what is felt as the spirit of the individual—his "physical" spirit—in conflict with the constrictions of the state. The rise of boxing in the 1920s in particular might well be seen as a consequence of the diminution of the individual vis-à-vis society; the gradual attrition of personal freedom, will, and strength—whether "masculine" or otherwise. In the Eastern bloc of nations, totalitarianism is a function of the state; in the Western bloc it has come to seem a function of technology, or history—"fate." The individual exists in his physical supremacy, but does the individual matter? 40

In the magical space of the boxing ring so disquieting a question has no claim. There, as in no other public arena, the individual as a unique physical being asserts himself; there, for a dramatic if fleeting period of time, the great world with its moral and political complexities, its terrifying impersonality, simply ceases to exist. Men fighting one another with only their fists and their cunning are all contemporaries, all brothers, belonging to no historical time. "He can run, but he can't hide"—so said Joe Louis before his famous fight with young Billy Conn in 1941. In the brightly lighted ring, man is *in extremis*, performing an atavistic rite or agon[3] for the mysterious solace of those who can participate only vicariously in such drama: the drama of life in the flesh. Boxing has become America's tragic theater. 41

RESPONDING TO READING

1. What is Oates's opinion of boxing? How is it different from the stereotypical female view? Does she seem to feel the need to justify her unconventional position? Explain.   **2.** In paragraphs 15 and 16 Oates notes that the spectators who are not among the disenfranchised of society have trouble understanding the basic human instincts that go hand in hand with boxing— for example, the anger of the combatants. Do you think she is correct? Explain.   **3.** What relationship does Oates see between boxing and American culture? What would Oates's response be to those who would do away with boxing? In what way does your own view of boxing correspond to or differ from the one presented by Oates?

---

[3]*Atavistic* means "primitive"; an *agon* is a struggle or contest. [Eds.]

ANSWERS TO RESPONDING TO READING

1. Oates admires boxing and feels compelled to understand her admiration in terms of her nature as a writer. Her view is probably different from the stereotypical female view because of her father's influence and because she has found a certain literary truth in boxing.
2. Although Oates is generalizing for emotional effect, her sentiments are probably accurate. Middle-class spectators see boxing as a performance, not as a way of making a better life. In this sense spectators are removed from one source of the intensity that characterizes the best boxing matches.
3. Oates sees boxing as America's "tragic theater" and would condemn those trying to end boxing because they do not understand it.

The Eighty-Yard Run

IRWIN SHAW

Irwin Shaw (1913–1984) was a prolific novelist and playwright who dealt with social themes and the common experiences of ordinary people. His best-selling novels include *The Young Lions* (1948) and *Evening in Byzantium* (1973) and his plays include *Bury the Dead* (1936) and *The Assassin* (1945). Shaw, considered a modern master of the short story, used his storytelling talent in many genres, even writing scripts for the "Dick Tracy" radio shows from 1934 to 1936. His collected stories were published in 1957 under the title *Tip on a Dead Jockey*. Written in 1940, the following story, "The Eighty-Yard Run," is about values, responsibilities, and a moment of glory.

FOR OPENERS

What do students make of the protagonist's name—Christian Darling?

ADDITIONAL QUESTIONS FOR RESPONDING TO READING

1. Why can't Darling reexperience the same happiness he found during his eighty-yard run?
2. According to Darling, why does he have extramarital affairs? Do you believe his explanations? Why do you think he has these affairs?
3. Why doesn't Darling want his wife to call him "Baby"? What does his request indicate about him? About their relationship?
4. After reading the story, what values would you say it seems to celebrate?

The pass was high and wide and he jumped for it, feeling it slap flatly against his hands, as he shook his hips to throw off the halfback who was diving at him. The center floated by, his hands desperately brushing Darling's knee as Darling picked his feet up high and delicately ran over a blocker and an opposing linesman in a jumble on the ground near the scrimmage line. He had ten yards in the clear and picked up speed, breathing easily, feeling his thigh pads rising and falling against his legs, listening to the sound of cleats behind him, pulling away from them, watching the other backs heading him off toward the sideline, the whole picture, the men closing in on him, the blockers fighting for position, the ground he had to cross, all suddenly clear in his head, for the first time in his life not a meaningless confusion of men, sounds, speed. He smiled a little to himself as he ran, holding the ball lightly in front of him with his two hands, his knees pumping high, his hips twisting in the almost girlish run of a back in a broken field. The first halfback came at him and he fed him his leg, then swung at the last moment, took the shock of the man's shoulder without breaking stride, ran right through him, his cleats biting securely into the turf. There was only the safety man now, coming warily at him, his arms crooked, hands spread. Darling tucked the ball in, spurted at him, driving hard, hurling himself along, all two hundred pounds bunched into controlled attack. He was sure he was going to get past the safety man. Without thought, his arms and legs working beautifully together, he headed right for the safety man, stiff-armed him, feeling blood spurt instantaneously from the man's nose onto his hand, seeing his face go awry, head turned, mouth pulled to one side. He pivoted away, keeping the arm locked, dropping the safety man as he ran easily toward the goal line, with the drumming of cleats diminishing behind him.

How long ago? It was autumn then, and the ground was getting hard because the nights were cold and leaves from the maples around the stadium blew across the practice fields in gusts of wind, and the girls were beginning to put polo coats over their sweaters when they came to watch practice in the afternoons. . . . Fifteen years. Darling walked slowly over the same ground in the spring twilight, in his neat shoes, a man of thirty-five dressed in a double-breasted suit, ten pounds heavier in the fifteen years, but not fat, with the years between 1925 and 1940 showing in his face.

The coach was smiling quietly to himself and the assistant coaches were looking at each other with pleasure the way they always did when one of the second stringers suddenly did something fine, bringing credit to them, making their $2,000 a year a tiny bit more secure.

Darling, trotted back, smiling, breathing deeply but easily, feeling wonderful, not tired, though this was the tail end of practice and he'd run eighty yards. The sweat poured off his face and soaked his jersey and he liked the feeling, the warm moistness lubricating his skin like oil. Off in a corner of the field some players were punting and the smack of leather against the ball came pleasantly through the afternoon air. The freshmen were running signals on the next field and the quarterback's sharp voice, the pound of the eleven pairs of cleats, the ''Dig, now *dig!*'' of the coaches, the laughter of the players all somehow made him feel happy as he trotted back to midfield listening to the applause and shouts of the students along the side-lines, knowing that after that run the coach would have to start him Saturday against Illinois.

Fifteen years, Darling thought, remembering the shower after the workout, the hot water steaming off his skin and the deep soapsuds and all the young voices singing with the water streaming down and towels going and managers running in and out and the sharp sweet smell of oil of wintergreen and everybody clapping him on the back as he dressed and Packard, the captain, who took being captain very seriously, coming over to him and shaking his hand and saying, ''Darling, you're going to go places in the next two years.''

The assistant manager fussed over him, wiping a cut on his leg with alcohol and iodine, the little sting making him realize suddenly how fresh and whole and solid his body felt. The manager slapped a piece of adhesive over the cut, and Darling noticed the sharp clean white of the tape against the ruddiness of the skin, fresh from the shower.

He dressed slowly, the softness of his shirt and the soft warmth of his wool socks and his flannel trousers a reward against his skin after the harsh pressure of the shoulder harness and thigh and hip

2

3

4 **TEACHING STRATEGY**

One approach to this story is to present Darling as someone trapped in his past, unable to change. Analyze the story, noting the moments when the world begins to change while Darling cannot match that change. One way to see the boy and girl at the story's end is as a symbol of Darling's paralysis.

5

6

7

pads. He drank three glasses of cold water, the liquid reaching down coldly inside of him, soothing the harsh dry places in his throat and belly left by the sweat and running and shouting of practice.

Fifteen years.   8

The sun had gone down and the sky was green behind the   9
stadium and he laughed quietly to himself as he looked at the stadium, rearing above the trees, and knew that on Saturday when the 70,000 voices roared as the team came running out onto the field, part of that enormous salute would be for him. He walked slowly, listening to the gravel crunch satisfactorily under his shoes in the still twilight, feeling his clothes swing lightly against his skin, breathing the thin evening air, feeling the wind more softly in his damp hair, wonderfully cool behind his ears and at the nape of his neck.

Louise was waiting for him at the road, in her car. The top was   10
down and he noticed all over again, as he always did when he saw her, how pretty she was, the rough blond hair and the large, inquiring eyes and the bright mouth, smiling now.

She threw the door open. "Were you good today?" she asked.   11

"Pretty good," he said. He climbed in, sank luxuriously into the   12
soft leather, stretched his legs far out. He smiled, thinking of the eighty yards. "Pretty damn good."

She looked at him seriously for a moment, then scrambled   13
around, like a little girl, kneeling on the seat next to him, grabbed him, her hands along his ears, and kissed him as he sprawled, head back, on the seat cushion. She let go of him, but kept her head close to his, over his. Darling reached up slowly and rubbed the back of his hand against her cheek, lit softly by a street lamp a hundred feet away. They looked at each other, smiling.

Louise drove down to the lake and they sat there silently,   14
watching the moon rise behind the hills on the other side. Finally he reached over, pulled her gently to him, kissed her. Her lips grew soft, her body sank into his, tears formed slowly in her eyes. He knew, for the first time, that he could do whatever he wanted with her.

"Tonight," he said. "I'll call for you at seven-thirty. Can you get   15
out?"

She looked at him. She was smiling, but the tears were still full   16
in her eyes. "All right," she said. "I'll get out. How about you? Won't the coach raise hell?"

Darling grinned. "I got the coach in the palm of my hand," he   17
said. "Can you wait till seven-thirty?"

She grinned back at him. "No," she said.   18

They kissed and she started the car and they went back to town   19
for dinner. He sang on the way home.

Christian Darling, thirty-five years old, sat on the frail spring   20
grass, greener now than it ever would be again on the practice field,
looked thoughtfully up at the stadium, a deserted ruin in the twilight.
He had started on the first team that Saturday and every Saturday
after that for the next two years, but it had never been as satisfactory
as it should have been. He never had broken away, the longest run
he'd ever made was thirty-five yards, and that in a game that was
already won, and then that kid had come up from the third team,
Diederich, a blank-faced German kid from Wisconsin, who ran like
a bull, ripping lines to pieces Saturday after Saturday, plowing
through, never getting hurt, never changing his expression, scoring
more points, gaining more ground than all the rest of the team put
together, making everybody's All-American, carrying the ball three
times out of four, keeping everybody else out of the headlines. Darling
was a good blocker and he spent his Saturday afternoons working
on the big Swedes and Polacks who played tackle and end for Michigan, Illinois, Purdue, hurling into huge pile-ups, bobbing his head
wildly to elude the great raw hands swinging like meat-cleavers
at him as he went charging in to open up holes for Diederich coming
through like a locomotive behind him. Still, it wasn't so bad. Everybody liked him and he did his job and he was pointed out
on the campus and boys always felt important when they introduced
their girls to him at their proms, and Louise loved him and watched
him faithfully in the games, even in the mud, when your own mother
wouldn't know you, and drove him around in her car keeping
the top down because she was proud of him and wanted to show
everybody that she was Christian Darling's girl. She bought
him crazy presents because her father was rich, watches, pipes, humi-
dors,[1] an icebox for beer for his room, curtains, wallets, a fifty-dollar
dictionary.

"You'll spend every cent your old man owns," Darling protested   21
once when she showed up at his rooms with seven different packages
in her arms and tossed them onto the couch.

"Kiss me," Louise said, "and shut up."   22

"Do you want to break your poor old man?"   23

"I don't mind. I want to buy you presents."   24

"Why?"   25

"It makes me feel good. Kiss me. I don't know why. Did you   26
know that you're an important figure?"

"Yes," Darling said gravely.   27

---

[1]A case for storing cigars in which the air is kept properly humidified. [Eds.]

"When I was waiting for you at the library yesterday two girls   28
saw you coming and one of them said to the other, 'That's Christian
Darling. He's an important figure.' "

"You're a liar."   29

"I'm in love with an important figure."   30

"Still, why the hell did you give me a forty-five pound dic-   31
tionary?"

"I wanted to make sure," Louise said, "that you had a token of   32
my esteem. I want to smother you in tokens of my esteem."

Fifteen years ago.   33

They'd married when they got out of college. There'd been other   34
women for him, but all casual and secret, more for curiosity's sake,
and vanity, women who'd thrown themselves at him and flattered
him, a pretty mother at a summer camp for boys, an old girl from
his home town who'd suddenly blossomed into a coquette, a friend
of Louise's who had dogged him grimly for six months and had taken
advantage of the two weeks that Louise went home when her mother
died. Perhaps Louise had known, but she'd kept quiet, loving him
completely, filling his rooms with presents, religiously watching him
battling with the big Swedes and Polacks on the line of scrimmage
on Saturday afternoons, making plans for marrying him and living
with him in New York and going with him there to the night clubs,
the theaters, the good restaurants, being proud of him in advance,
tall, white-teethed, smiling, large, yet moving lightly, with an athlete's grace, dressed in evening clothes, approvingly eyed by mag-
nificently dressed and famous women in theater lobbies, with Louise
adoringly at his side.

Her father, who manufactured inks, set up a New York office for   35
Darling to manage and presented him with three hundred accounts,
and they lived on Beekman Place with a view of the river with fifteen
thousand dollars a year between them, because everybody was
buying everything in those days, including ink. They saw all the
shows and went to all the speakeasies and spent their fifteen thousand
dollars a year and in the afternoons Louise went to the art galleries
and the matinees of the more serious plays that Darling didn't like
to sit through and Darling slept with a girl who danced in the chorus
of *Rosalie* and with the wife of a man who owned three copper mines.
Darling played squash three times a week and remained as solid as
a stone barn and Louise never took her eyes off him when they were
in the same room together, watching him with a secret, miser's smile,
with a trick of coming over to him in the middle of a crowded room
and saying gravely, in a low voice, "You're the handsomest man I've
ever seen in my whole life. Want a drink?"

Nineteen twenty-nine came to Darling and to his wife and father-   36
in-law, the maker of inks, just as it came to everyone else. The father-

in-law waited until 1933 and then blew his brains out and when Darling went to Chicago to see what the books of the firm looked like he found out all that was left were debts and three or four gallons of unbought ink.

"Please, Christian," Louise said, sitting in their neat Beekman   37
Place apartment, with a view of the river and prints of paintings by Dufy and Braque and Picasso on the wall, "please, why do you want to start drinking at two o'clock in the afternoon?"

"I have nothing else to do," Darling said, putting down his glass,   38
emptied of its fourth drink. "Please pass the whisky."

Louise filled his glass. "Come take a walk with me," she said.   39
"We'll walk along the river."

"I don't want to walk along the river," Darling said, squinting   40
intensely at the prints of paintings by Dufy, Braque and Picasso.

"We'll walk along Fifth Avenue."   41

"I don't want to walk along Fifth Avenue."   42

"Maybe," Louise said gently, "you'd like to come with me to   43
some art galleries. There's an exhibition by a man named Klee. . . ."

"I don't want to go to any art galleries. I want to sit here and   44
drink Scotch whisky," Darling said. "Who the hell hung these god-damn pictures up on the wall?"

"I did," Louise said.   45

"I hate them."   46

"I'll take them down," Louise said.   47

"Leave them there. It gives me something to do in the afternoon.   48
I can hate them." Darling took a long swallow. "Is that the way people paint these days?"

"Yes, Christian. Please don't drink any more."   49

"Do you like painting like that?"   50

"Yes, dear."   51

"Really?"   52

"Really."   53

Darling looked carefully at the prints once more. "Little Louise   54
Tucker. The middle-western beauty. I like pictures with horses in them. Why should you like pictures like that?"

"I just happen to have gone to a lot of galleries in the last few   55
years. . . ."

"Is that what you do in the afternoon?"   56

"That's what I do in the afternoon," Louise said.   57

"I drink in the afternoon."   58

Louise kissed him lightly on the top of his head as he sat there   59
squinting at the pictures on the wall, the glass of whisky held firmly in his hand. She put on her coat and went out without saying another word. When she came back in the early evening, she had a job on a woman's fashion magazine.

They moved downtown and Louise went to work every morning 60
and Darling sat home and drank and Louise paid the bills as they
came up. She made believe she was going to quit work as soon as
Darling found a job, even though she was taking over more responsibility day by day at the magazine, interviewing authors, picking
painters for the illustrations and covers, getting actresses to pose for
pictures, going out for drinks with the right people, making a thousand new friends whom she loyally introduced to Darling.

"I don't like your hat," Darling said, once, when she came in in 61
the evening and kissed him, her breath rich with Martinis.

"What's the matter with my hat, Baby?" she asked, running her 62
fingers through her hair. "Everybody says it's very smart."

"It's too damned smart," he said. "It's not for you. It's for a rich, 63
sophisticated woman of thirty-five with admirers."

Louise laughed. "I'm practicing to be a rich, sophisticated woman 64
of thirty-five with admirers," she said. He stared soberly at her.
"Now, don't look so grim, Baby. It's still the same simple little wife
under the hat." She took the hat off, threw it into a corner, sat on
his lap. "See? Homebody Number One."

"Your breath could run a train," Darling said, not wanting to be 65
mean, but talking out of boredom, and sudden shock at seeing his
wife curiously a stranger in a new hat, with a new expression in her
eyes under the little brim, secret, confident, knowing.

Louise tucked her head under his chin so he couldn't smell her 66
breath. "I had to take an author out for cocktails," she said. "He's a
boy from the Ozark Mountains and he drinks like a fish. He's a
Communist."

"What the hell is a Communist from the Ozarks doing writing 67
for a woman's fashion magazine?"

Louise chuckled. "The magazine business is getting all mixed up 68
these days. The publishers want to have a foot in every camp. And
anyway, you can't find an author under seventy these days who isn't
a Communist."

"I don't think I like you to associate with all those people, Louise," 69
Darling said. "Drinking with them."

"He's a very nice, gentle boy," Louise said. "He reads Ernest 70
Dowson."

"Who's Ernest Dowson?" 71

Louise patted his arm, stood up, fixed her hair. "He's an English 72
poet."

Darling felt that somehow he had disappointed her. "Am I sup- 73
posed to know who Ernest Dowson is?"

"No, dear. I'd better go in and take a bath." 74

After she had gone, Darling went over to the corner where the 75
hat was lying and picked it up. It was nothing, a scrap of straw, a

red flower, a veil, meaningless on his big hand, but on his wife's head a signal of something . . . big city, smart and knowing women drinking and dining with men other than their husbands, conversation about things a normal man wouldn't know much about. Frenchmen who painted as though they used their elbows instead of brushes, composers who wrote whole symphonies without a single melody in them, writers who knew all about politics and women who knew all about writers, the movement of the proletariat, Marx, somehow mixed up with five-dollar dinners and the best-looking women in America and fairies who made them laugh and half-sentences immediately understood and secretly hilarious and wives who called their husbands "Baby." He put the hat down, a scrap of straw and a red flower, and a little veil. He drank some whisky straight and went into the bathroom where his wife was lying deep in her bath, singing to herself and smiling from time to time like a little girl, paddling the water gently with her hands, sending up a slight spicy fragrance from the bath salts she used.

He stood over her, looking down at her. She smiled up at him,   76 her eyes half closed, her body pink and shimmering in the water, scented water. All over again, with all the old suddenness, he was hit deep inside him with the knowledge of how beautiful she was, how much he needed her.

"I came in here," he said, "to tell you I wish you wouldn't call   77 me 'Baby.' "

She looked up at him from the bath, her eyes quickly full of   78 sorrow, half-understanding what he meant. He knelt and put his arms around her, his sleeves plunged heedlessly in the water, his shirt and jacket soaking wet as he clutched her wordlessly, holding her crazily tight, crushing her breath from her, kissing her desperately, searchingly, regretfully.

He got jobs after that, selling real estate and automobiles,   79 but somehow, although he had a desk with his name on a wooden wedge on it, and he went to the office religiously at nine each morning, he never managed to sell anything and he never made any money.

Louise was made assistant editor, and the house was always full   80 of strange men and women who talked fast and got angry on abstract subjects like mural painting, novelists, labor unions. Negro short-story writers drank Louise's liquor, and a lot of Jews, and big solemn men with scarred faces and knotted hands who talked slowly but clearly about picket lines and battles with guns and leadpipe at mine-shaftheads and in front of factory gates. And Louise moved among them all, confidently, knowing what they were talking about just as though she were a man. She knew everybody, condescended to no one, devoured books that Darling had never heard of, walked along the streets of the city, excited, at home, soaking in all the million tides of New York without fear, with constant wonder.

Her friends liked Darling and sometimes he found a man who wanted to get off in the corner and talk about the new boy who played fullback for Princeton, and the decline of the double wing-back, or even the state of the stock market, but for the most part he sat on the edge of things, solid and quiet in the high storm of words. "The dialectics of the situation . . . The theater has been given over to expert jugglers . . . Picasso? What man has a right to paint old bones and collect ten thousand dollars for them? . . . I stand firmly behind Trotsky . . . Poe was the last American critic. When he died they put lilies on the grave of American criticism. I don't say this because they panned my last book, but . . ." 81

Once in a while he caught Louise looking soberly and consideringly at him through the cigarette smoke and the noise and he avoided her eyes and found an excuse to get up and go into the kitchen for more ice or to open another bottle. 82

"Come on," Cathal Flaherty was saying, standing at the door with a girl, "you've got to come down and see this. It's down on Fourteenth Street, in the old Civic Repertory, and you can only see it on Sunday nights and I guarantee you'll come out of the theater singing." Flaherty was a big young Irishman with a broken nose who was the lawyer for a longshoreman's union, and he had been hanging around the house for six months on and off, roaring and shutting everybody else up when he got in an argument. "It's a new play, *Waiting for Lefty*; it's about taxi-drivers." 83

"Odets," the girl with Flaherty said. "It's by a guy named Odets." 84

"I never heard of him," Darling said. 85

"He's a new one," the girl said. 86

"It's like watching a bombardment," Flaherty said. "I saw it last Saturday night. You've got to see it." 87

"Come on, Baby," Louise said to Darling, excitement in her eyes already. "We've been sitting in the Sunday *Times* all day, this'll be a great change." 88

"I see enough taxi-drivers every day," Darling said, not because he meant that, but because he didn't like to be around Flaherty, who said things that made Louise laugh a lot and whose judgment she accepted on almost every subject. "Let's go to the movies." 89

"You've never seen anything like this before," Flaherty said. "He wrote this play with a baseball bat." 90

"Come on," Louise coaxed, "I bet it's wonderful." 91

"He has long hair," the girl with Flaherty said. "Odets. I met him at a party. He's an actor. He didn't say a goddam thing all night." 92

"I don't feel like going down to Fourteenth Street," Darling said, wishing Flaherty and his girl would get out. "It's gloomy." 93

"Oh, hell!" Louise said loudly. She looked coolly at Darling, as   94
though she'd just been introduced to him and was making up her
mind about him, and not very favorably. He saw her looking at him,
knowing there was something new and dangerous in her face and
he wanted to say something, but Flaherty was there and his damned
girl, and anyway, he didn't know what to say.

"I'm going," Louise said, getting her coat. "I don't think Four-   95
teenth Street is gloomy."

"I'm telling you," Flaherty was saying, helping her on with her   96
coat, "it's the Battle of Gettysburg, in Brooklynese."

"Nobody could get a word out of him," Flaherty's girl was saying   97
as they went through the door. "He just sat there all night."

The door closed. Louise hadn't said good night to him. Darling   98
walked around the room four times, then sprawled out on the sofa,
on top of the Sunday *Times*. He lay there for five minutes looking at
the ceiling, thinking of Flaherty walking down the street talking in
that booming voice between the girls, holding their arms.

Louise had looked wonderful. She'd washed her hair in the after-   99
noon and it had been very soft and light and clung close to her head
as she stood there angrily putting her coat on. Louise was getting
prettier every year, partly because she knew by now how pretty she
was, and made the most of it.

"Nuts," Darling said, standing up. "Oh, nuts."   100

He put on his coat and went down to the nearest bar and had   101
five drinks off by himself in a corner before his money ran out.

The years since then had been foggy and downhill. Louise had   102
been nice to him, and in a way, loving and kind, and they'd fought
only once, when he said he was going to vote for Landon. ("Oh,
Christ," she'd said, "doesn't *anything* happen inside your head? Don't
you read the papers? The penniless Republican!") She'd been sorry
later and apologized for hurting him, but apologized as she might to
a child. He'd tried hard, had gone grimly to the art galleries, the
concert halls, the bookshops, trying to gain on the trail of his wife,
but it was no use. He was bored, and none of what he saw or heard
or dutifully read made much sense to him and finally he gave it up.
He had thought, many nights as he ate dinner alone, knowing that
Louise would come home late and drop silently into bed without
explanation, of getting a divorce, but he knew the loneliness, the
hopelessness, of not seeing her again would be too much to take. So
he was good, completely devoted, ready at all times to go any place
with her, do anything she wanted. He even got a small job, in a
broker's office and paid his own way, bought his own liquor.

Then he'd been offered a job of going from college to college as   103
a tailor's representative. "We want a man," Mr. Rosenberg had said,
"who as soon as you look at him, you say, 'There's a university

man.' " Rosenberg had looked approvingly at Darling's broad shoulders and well-kept waist, at his carefully brushed hair and his honest, wrinkle-less face. "Frankly, Mr. Darling, I am willing to make you a proposition. I have inquired about you, you are favorably known on your old campus, I understand you were in the backfield with Alfred Diederich."

Darling nodded. "Whatever happened to him?" 104

"He is walking around in a cast for seven years now. An iron 105 brace. He played professional football and they broke his neck for him."

Darling smiled. That, at least, had turned out well. 106

"Our suits are an easy product to sell, Mr. Darling," Rosenberg 107 said. "We have a handsome, custom-made garment. What has Brooks Brothers got that we haven't got? A name. No more."

"I can make fifty-sixty dollars a week," Darling said to Louise 108 that night. "And expenses. I can save some money and then come back to New York and really get started here."

"Yes, Baby," Louise said. 109

"As it is," Darling said carefully, "I can make it back here once 110 a month, and holidays and the summer. We can see each other often."

"Yes, Baby." He looked at her face, lovelier now at thirty-five 111 than it had ever been before, but fogged over now as it had been for five years with a kind of patient, kindly, remote boredom.

"What do you say?" he asked. "Should I take it?" Deep within 112 him he hoped fiercely, longingly, for her to say "No, Baby, you stay right here," but she said, as he knew she'd say, "I think you'd better take it."

He nodded. He had to get up and stand with his back to her, 113 looking out the window, because there were things plain on his face that she had never seen in the fifteen years she'd known him. "Fifty dollars is a lot of money," he said. "I never thought I'd ever see fifty dollars again." He laughed. Louise laughed, too.

Christian Darling sat on the frail green grass of the practice field. 114 The shadow of the stadium had reached out and covered him. In the distance the lights of the university shone a little mistily in the light haze of evening. Fifteen years. Flaherty even now was calling for his wife, buying her a drink, filling whatever bar they were in with that voice of his and that easy laugh. Darling half-closed his eyes, almost saw the boy fifteen years ago reach for the pass, slip the halfback, go skittering lightly down the field, his knees high and fast and graceful, smiling to himself because he knew he was going to get past the safety man. That was the high point, Darling thought, fifteen years ago, on an autumn afternoon, twenty years old and far from death, with the air coming easily into his lungs, and a deep feeling inside him that he could do anything, knock over anybody, outrun whatever had to be outrun. And the shower after and the three glasses of water and the cool night air on his damp head and Louise sitting hatless in the open car with a smile and the first kiss she ever really meant. The high point, an eighty-yard run in the practice, and a girl's kiss and everything after that a decline. Darling laughed. He had practiced the wrong thing, perhaps. He hadn't practiced for 1929 and New York City and a girl who would turn into a woman. Somewhere, he thought, there must have been a point where she moved up to me, was even with me for a moment, when I could have held her hand, if I'd known, held tight, gone with her. Well, he'd never known. Here he was on a playing field that was fifteen years away and his wife was in another city having dinner with another and better man, speaking with him a different, new language, a language nobody had ever taught him.

Darling stood up, smiled a little, because if he didn't smile he 115 knew the tears would come. He looked around him. This was the spot. O'Connor's pass had come sliding out just to here . . . the high point. Darling put up his hands, felt all over again the flat slap of the ball. He shook his hips to throw off the halfback, cut back inside the center, picked his knees high as he ran gracefully over two men jumbled on the ground at the line of scrimmage, ran easily, gaining speed, for ten yards, holding the ball lightly in his two hands, swung away from the halfback diving at him, ran, swinging his hips in the almost girlish manner of a back in a broken field, tore into the safety man, his shoes drumming heavily on the turf, stiff-armed, elbow locked, pivoted, raced lightly and exultantly for the goal line.

It was only after he had sped over the goal line and slowed to a 116 trot that he saw the boy and girl sitting together on the turf, looking at him wonderingly.

He stopped short, dropping his arms. "I . . ." he said, gasping 117 a little, though his condition was fine and the run hadn't winded him. "I—once played here."

The boy and the girl said nothing. Darling laughed embarrassedly, 118 looked hard at them sitting there, close to each other, shrugged, turned and went toward his hotel, the sweat breaking out on his face and running down into his collar.

RESPONDING TO READING

1. Do you think the narrator likes one of the Darlings more than the other? With which character do you sympathize? Explain.   **2.** What is the significance of the eighty-yard run? What generalization is the narrator making

2. The eighty-yard run signifies the unrecoverable happiness of Darling's youth. The narrator generalizes that football players and the game itself are adolescent and dangerous because they offer a simplistic vision of life.

3. Louise holds Marxist political views, whereas Darling's views are much more conservative. Football represents a simple philosophy with clear rules, a clarity of vision that mirrors Christian Darling's own political views. The story could be effective if it were about a different sport—as long as that sport was one in which participants try to move in one direction while preventing others from moving in the opposite direction.

about football and about the kind of person who plays the game? On the basis of your experience, do you think his characterization is accurate? **3.** Until the stock market crash wipes out her father's business, Louise seems content to let her husband support her. After this event, however, she takes responsibility for herself and her life. In the process she forms a definite set of political views. What are they? In what way do her views differ from those of her husband? In what way does the game of football mirror Christian's political views? Would the story be equally effective if Christian had played a different sport? Explain.

Rainbow

ROBERT HUFF

Poet Robert Huff (1924–   ) contributes to many anthologies and has also been a professor of English and a poet-in-residence at Western Washington University since 1967. Time and place are important in his poems, which draw from the landscape of the Lake Michigan shores, the forests on the Northwest, and the waterways of Puget Sound. Huff says of his use of detail: "I believe that place (not regionalism) is important to poetry. I am often stimulated by specific reactions to individual detail to recall similarities of appearance from an earlier experience in a different place." In the poem "Rainbow," Huff uses individual details to recall a poignant lesson about hunting that a father teaches his young daughter.

FOR OPENERS

At what moment in your life did you first understand the reality of death?

ADDITIONAL QUESTIONS FOR RESPONDING TO READING

1. What happens in this poem on a literal level? Why can the poem's meaning not be fully understood at this level?
2. In what ways do the father's and his child's views of the bird differ? What is the significance of these two views?

TEACHING STRATEGY

Discuss the function of the rainbow image in the poem, focusing on its importance as a symbol of romantic innocence and beauty and its function as a contrast to the reality of death.

WRITING SUGGESTION

Write a letter from the father to his daughter explaining his views about hunting.

After the shot the driven feathers rock
In the air and are by sunlight trapped.
Their moment of descent is eloquent.
It is the rainbow echo of a bird
Whose thunder, stopped, puts in my daughter's eyes   5
A question mark. She does not see the rainbow,
And the folding bird-fall was for her too quick.
It is about the stillness of the bird
Her eyes are asking. She is three years old;
Has cut her fingers; found blood tastes of salt;   10
But she has never witnessed quiet blood,
Nor ever seen before the peace of death.
I say: "The feathers—Look!" but she is torn
And wretched and draws back. And I am glad
That I have wounded her, have winged her heart,   15
And that she goes beyond my fathering.

RESPONDING TO READING

1. Does the speaker seem to approve or disapprove of hunting? What are your feelings about hunting? Do you believe hunting is a sport?   **2.** What is the significance of the poem's title? Do you think the poem is about hunting or about something else?   **3.** Why in lines 14–15 does the speaker say that he is glad he has wounded his daughter? What does he mean? Do you agree with his sentiments? Do you think he would have said the same thing about a son?

Ex-Basketball Player

JOHN UPDIKE

John Updike (1932–   ) is a prolific novelist, essayist, critic, and poet. After graduating from college, he studied art abroad, then worked as a writer for the *New Yorker*, which continues to publish his work. Updike's novel *Rabbit, Run* (1960), about a former high school basketball player who shirks the responsibilities of adulthood, is the first in his series of four "Rabbit" novels, which concluded in 1990 with *Rabbit at Rest*. His essays and reviews are collected in *Assorted Prose* (1965), *Picked-Up Pieces* (1975), and *Hugging the Shore* (1983). "Ex-Basketball Player," first published in 1958, is a look at a high school star who never fulfilled his promise.

Pearl Avenue runs past the high-school lot,
Bends with the trolley tracks, and stops, cut off
Before it has a chance to go two blocks,
At Colonel McComsky Plaza. Berth's Garage
Is on the corner facing west, and there,
Most days, you'll find Flick Webb, who helps Berth out.   5

Flick stands tall among the idiot pumps—
Five on a side, the old bubble-head style,
Their rubber elbows hanging loose and low.
One's nostrils are two S's, and his eyes   10
An E and O. And one is squat, without
A head at all—more of a football type.

Once Flick played for the high-school team, the Wizards.
He was good: in fact, the best. In '46
He bucketed three hundred ninety points,   15

A county record still. The ball loved Flick.
I saw him rack up thirty-eight or forty
In one home game. His hands were like wild birds.

He never learned a trade, he just sells gas,
Checks oil, and changes flats. Once in a while,   20
As a gag, he dribbles an inner tube,
But most of us remember anyway.
His hands are fine and nervous on the lug wrench.
It makes no difference to the lug wrench, though.

Off work, he hangs around Mae's luncheonette.   25
Grease-gray and kind of coiled, he plays pinball,
Smokes those thin cigars, nurses lemon phosphates.
Flick seldom says a word to Mae, just nods
Beyond her face toward bright applauding tiers
Of Necco Wafers, Nibs, and Juju Beads.   30

RESPONDING TO READING

1. What comment does this poem seem to make about the lives athletes lead after they stop playing? Is this poem criticizing sports? American society? Explain.   **2.** Many athletes—Dusty Rhodes, for example—have had trouble adapting to real life after retiring from professional sports. What characteristics of professional sports make it difficult for athletes to make the transition into normal life? Can you think of some players who were able to make the transition successfully? To what do you attribute their success?   **3.** The high school star who is unable to fulfill his promise is a common character in American fiction. Do you know any former high school stars who fit this stereotype? Who defy it? Although the poem's speaker seems to see Flick as a failure, is there any indication that Flick himself is disappointed with his life?

WRITING: THE CULTURE OF SPORT

1. Write an essay about a sport in which you participated. In what ways did your involvement with the sport affect your behavior, your character, or your goals?

2. In your experience, do sports represent a set of shared interests that tie people together regardless of class, race, or education, or do they reflect all the inequalities of society that divide us as a people? Write an essay in which you explain your answer.

3. What do you think will be the future of women in sports? Are you optimistic about their increased participation as spectators, amateur and professional athletes, and sportswriters and reporters? Or do you think men will always have the edge in the world of sports? Explain your conclusions in an essay.

4. Unfortunately, racial prejudice has always been a part of professional sports in the United States. Before Jackie Robinson, African-Americans were not allowed to play professional baseball, and until recently no black quarterbacks were able to play professional football. Similar examples could be drawn from other sports. Although race relations in professional sports have improved considerably since Roy Campanella played baseball, the position of African-American athletes is still tenuous. Judging from your observations of American society, what specific problems still face African-Americans in the sports world?

5. To some writers in this chapter, athletes are noble figures who symbolize all that is best in human beings. To others, athletes are ordinary individuals who, because they live in artificial worlds, cannot face up to the realities of everyday life. Write an essay in which you present your view of athletes.

6. Many popular sports are associated with violence. Sometimes violent behavior is a built-in part of the sport, as in boxing or football. At other times, violence erupts among players or among fans. What sports do you consider most violent? To what do you attribute this violent behavior? Do you think violence in sports is harmless, or do you think it is a serious social problem? Using your own experience as a player or spectator, write an essay in which you explain your views about violence and sports.

7. Both Roy Campanella II and Doris Kearns Goodwin write about baseball. In what way are their respective views of baseball like or unlike yours?

8. Do you, like Gould, hold special affection for average athletes who have one moment of glory because they prove that people just like the rest of us can excel? Write an essay explaining your position.

9. The essays by Joyce Carol Oates and Norman Cousins can be read as a debate about boxing. Each writer discusses the issue of violence, but each draws decidedly different conclusions. In addition, each suggests a different future for the sport. Which of the two makes a better case? On the basis of your own experience, what do you think the future of boxing should be?

8

A WINDOW ON THE PRESENT

CONFRONTING THE ISSUES

In journalistic terms, a story's newsworthiness depends in part on the question of proximity—that is, on how geographically close its events are to readers. War, famine, and natural disaster are always seen as important in the abstract, but when these events occur close to home (to people near us, and, therefore, to people *like* us), their impact is much greater.

Thus readers will feel shock and compassion at news stories reporting a cholera epidemic in Peru, a devastating typhoon in Bangladesh, or the plight of displaced Kurdish refugees in Turkey and Iran. If asked to rank social problems in order of their importance, however, urban readers will probably rank a story about street crime or drugs highest, while rural readers might cite features on water pollution or farm foreclosures.

Like news stories, present-day social, political, and economic issues have greater interest and relevance for readers to whom these issues are closest and for readers whom they affect directly.

After explaining this concept of proximity and extending it to encompass emotional as well as geographical closeness, ask your students to rank in order of importance the following issues, each of which represents an ongoing problem in the United States today:

- Racial discrimination
- Teenage suicide
- Crack use
- Domestic violence
- Alcoholism
- The homeless
- Abortion rights
- Protecting the environment
- Equal rights for women
- The right to die
- Improving the education system
- Violent crime
- Access to health care
- Unemployment
- AIDS
- Bilingual education
- Rights for persons with disabilities
- Police brutality
- Teenage pregnancy
- Welfare reform
- Overcrowded jails
- Corrupt municipal governments
- Acquaintance rape
- Gay rights

Because we all have different experiences, it might be said that each of us lives in a different society—different even from that of our family members or close friends. Still, when we look out of the window on the present, many of us see the same problems: poverty and homelessness, drug abuse and violence, racial and class barriers, and deteriorating family life. This chapter presents a variety of insights into some of these problems.

Because contemporary culture in the United States is so diverse and so dynamic, it is extremely difficult to define. Sometimes, however, comparing and contrasting different viewpoints can help us get our bearings. For instance, we can gain insight into the problems of modern-day children and adolescents by reading an essay like Robert Coles's "Children of Affluence" alongside Calvin Trillin's essay "It's Just Too Late" or Joyce Carol Oates's story "Where Are You Going, Where Have You Been?" Elisabeth Kübler-Ross's analysis of our fear of death can shed light on Jessica Mitford's discussion of the funeral industry, and vice versa. Paul Fussell and Shelby Steele discuss some of the same issues in their essays on class, and both of these perspectives can help us understand a seemingly unrelated essay like Joseph Lelyveld's "The Laws," which examines a legal system that freezes individuals into a permanent underclass. Moreover, your own experiences can give you additional insights into these and other reading selections. Perhaps your own window on present-day society looks out over a landscape that is different from the ones these writers describe, and perhaps your perspective will lead you to make different connections among the selections or to draw different conclusions.

PREPARING TO READ AND WRITE

As you read the selections in this chapter and prepare to write about them, consider the following questions:

- Does the writer present a positive or negative picture of society?

- Is there a connection between the writer's own social class, race, or gender—or his or her assumptions about class, race, or gender—and the situation or problem he or she examines?

- Does the writer examine a problem from the perspective of a journalist, a social scientist, a social historian, a poet or fiction writer, or a concerned citizen? How does this perspective determine the writer's emphasis? How does it determine the selection's effect on you?

- Does the writer have a personal motive for examining his or her subject? If so, does your awareness of this motive weaken or strengthen the selection's impact on you?

- Is the writer's tone serious, humorous, ironic, or sarcastic?

- If the selection identifies a problem, does it focus on finding solutions, speculating about long-term effects, or warning about consequences?

- Does the writer focus on the need to change basic attitudes, to change habits, or to change the law?

- Is the writer optimistic or pessimistic about the possibility of change?

- Does the selection focus on a narrow segment of the society— members of a particular age or ethnic group, or residents of a particular geographical location, for example—or does it focus on the society at large?

- Do you recognize people and situations with which you are familiar, or are the issues under discussion unfamiliar to you? Are you emotionally connected to the issues, or are you relatively detached from them?

Which five of these problems do students see as most—and least—pressing? Why? Which do they believe threaten U.S. society? Which threaten their own communities? Their families? Their futures? What determines the importance of an issue? How optimistic are students about the likelihood that any of these problems will be solved? Which, if any, do they expect to disappear within ten years?

The Middle Class

PAUL FUSSELL

Paul Fussell (1924–   ), who currently teaches English at the University of Pennsylvania, writes about literature, literary theory, and military history. His experiences in the infantry in World War II gave him a deep interest in military history, and he won the National Book Award for *The Great War and Modern Memory* (1975), a study of the literature about World War I. His other books range from *Poetic Meter and Poetic Form* (1965) to *Abroad: British Literary Traveling Between the Wars* (1980) to *The Boy Scout Handbook and Other Observations* (1982). Through a careful choice of language in the following essay, excerpted from *Class: A Guide through the American Status System* (1984), Fussell looks critically at the American middle class, whose women, he says, treasure "friendliness" and whose men treasure "having a genteel occupation."

FOR OPENERS

Instruct students to freewrite to identify characteristics they feel represent the middle class in America. What possessions must a family have, for example, to achieve middle-class status? What attitudes? What level of education?

ADDITIONAL QUESTIONS FOR RESPONDING TO READING

1. According to Fussell, what are the dominant characteristics of the middle class?
2. What is "status panic"? How does the middle class respond to this phenomenon?
3. What does Fussell mean when he declares the middle class to be "rootless"?
4. Does Fussell feel hope for the younger generation of the middle class? Why or why not? Point to specific statements for evidence.

The middle class is distinguishable more by its earnestness and 1 psychic insecurity than by its middle income. I have known some very rich people who remain stubbornly middle-class, which is to say they remain terrified at what others think of them, and to avoid criticism are obsessed with doing everything right. The middle class is the place where table manners assume an awful importance and where net curtains flourish to conceal activities like hiding the salam' (a phrase no middle-class person would indulge in, surely: the fatuous *making love* is the middle-class equivalent). The middle class, always anxious about offending, is the main market for "mouthwashes," and if it disappeared the whole "deodorant" business would fall to the ground. If physicians tend to be upper-middle-class, dentists are gloomily aware that they're middle, and are said to experience frightful status anxieties when introduced socially to "physicians"— as dentists like to call them. (Physicians call themselves *doctors*, and enjoy doing this in front of dentists, as well as college professors, chiropractors, and divines.)

"Status panic": that's the affliction of the middle class, according 2 to C. Wright Mills, author of *White Collar* (1951) and *The Power Elite* (1956). Hence the middles' need to accumulate credit cards and take in *The New Yorker*, which it imagines registers upper-middle taste. Its devotion to that magazine, or its ads, is a good example of Mills's description of the middle class as the one that tends "to borrow status from higher elements." *New Yorker* advertisers have always known this about their audience, and some of their pseudo-upper-middle gestures in front of the middles are hilarious, like one recently flogging expensive stationery, here, a printed invitation card. The pretentious Anglophile spelling of the second word strikes the right opening note:

In honour of
Dr and Mrs Leonard Adam Westman,
Dr and Mrs Jeffrey Logan Brandon
request the pleasure of your company for

[at this point the higher classes might say *cocktails*, or, if thoroughly secure, *drinks*. But here, "Dr." and Mrs. Brandon are inviting you to consume specifically—]

Champagne and Caviar
on Friday, etc., etc.
Valley Hunt Club,
Stamford, Conn., etc.

The only thing missing is the brand names of the refreshments.

If the audience for that sort of thing used to seem the most deeply ³ rooted in time and place, today it seems the class that's the most rootless. Members of the middle class are not only the sort of people who buy their own heirlooms, silver, etc. They're also the people who do most of the moving long-distance (generally to very unstylish places), commanded every few years to pull up stakes by the corporations they're in bondage to. They are the geologist employed by the oil company, the computer programmer, the aeronautical engineer, the salesman assigned a new territory, and the "marketing" (formerly *sales*) manager deputed to keep an eye on him. These people and their families occupy the suburbs and developments. Their "Army and Navy," as William H. Whyte, Jr.,[1] says, is their corporate employer. IBM and DuPont hire these people from second-rate colleges and teach them that they are nothing if not members of the team. Virtually no latitude is permitted to individuality or the milder forms of eccentricity, and these employees soon learn to avoid all ideological statements, notably, as we'll see, in the furnishing of their living rooms. Terrified of losing their jobs, these people grow passive, their humanity diminished as they perceive themselves mere parts of an infinitely larger structure. And interchangeable parts, too. "The training makes our men interchangeable," an IBM executive was once heard to say.

It's little wonder that, treated like slaves most of the time, the ⁴ middle class lusts for the illusion of weight and consequence. One sign is their quest for heraldic validation ("This beautiful embossed

---

[1]American business writer (1917–   ), author of *The Organization Man* (1956) [Eds.]

certificate will show your family tree"). Another is their custom of issuing annual family newsletters announcing the most recent triumphs in the race to become "professional":

> John, who is now 22, is in his first year at the Dental School of Wayne State University.

> Caroline has a fine position as an executive secretary for a prestigious firm in Boise, Idaho.

Sometimes these letters really wring the heart, with their proud lists of new "affiliations" achieved during the past year: "This year Bob became a member of the Junior Chamber of Commerce, the Beer Can Collectors League of North America, the Alumni Council of the University of Evansville, and the Young Republicans of Vanderburgh County." (Cf. Veblen:[2] "Since conservatism is a characteristic of the wealthier and therefore more reputable portion of the community, it has acquired a certain honorific or decorative value.") Nervous lest she be considered nobody, the middle-class wife is careful to dress way up when she goes shopping. She knows by instinct what one middle-class woman told an inquiring sociologist: "You know there's class when you're in a department store and a well-dressed lady gets treated better."

"One who makes birth or wealth the sole criterion of worth": 5 that's a conventional dictionary definition of a *snob*, and the place to look for the snob is in the middle class. Worried a lot about their own taste and about whether it's working for or against them, members of the middle class try to arrest their natural tendency to sink downward by associating themselves, if ever so tenuously, with the imagined possessors of money, power, and taste. "Correctness" and doing the right thing become obsessions, prompting middle-class people to write thank-you notes after the most ordinary dinner parties, give excessively expensive or correct presents, and never allude to any place—Fort Smith, Arkansas, for example—that lacks known class. It will not surprise readers who have traveled extensively to hear that Neil Mackwood, a British authority on snobbery, finds the greatest snobs worldwide emanating from Belgium, which can also be considered world headquarters of the middle class.

The desire to belong, and to belong by some mechanical act like 6 purchasing something, is another sign of the middle class. Words like *club* and *guild* (as in Book-of-the-Month Club and Literary Guild)

---

[2]Thorstein Veblen's *The Theory of the Leisure Class* (1899) attacked the values of the wealthy. [Eds.]

extend a powerful invitation. The middle class is thus the natural target for developers' ads like this:

> You Belong
> in Park Forest!
> The moment you come to our town you know:
> You're Welcome.
> You're part of a big group. . . .

Oddity, introversion, and the love of privacy are the big enemies, a total reversal of the values of the secure upper orders. Among the middles there's a convention that erecting a fence or even a tall hedge is an affront. And there's also a convention that you may drop in on neighbors or friends without a telephone inquiry first. Being naturally innocent and well disposed and aboveboard, a member of the middle class finds it hard to believe that all are not. Being timid and conventional, no member of the middle class would expect that anyone is copulating in the afternoon instead of the evening, clearly, for busy and well-behaved corporate personnel, the correct time for it. When William H. Whyte, Jr., was poking around one suburb studying the residents, he was told by one quintessentially middle-class woman: "The street behind us is nowhere near as friendly. They knock on doors over there."

If the women treasure "friendliness," the men treasure having a   7 genteel occupation (usually more important than money), with emphasis on the word (if seldom the thing) *executive*. (As a matter of fact, an important class divide falls between those who feel veneration before the term *executive* and those who feel they want to throw up.) Having a telephone-answering machine at home is an easy way of simulating (at relatively low cost) high professional desirability, but here you wouldn't think of a facetious or eccentric text (delivered in French, for example, or in the voice of Donald Duck or Richard Nixon) asking the caller to speak his bit after the beeping sound. For the middle-class man is scared. As C. Wright Mills[3] notes, "He is always somebody's man, the corporation's, the government's, the army's. . . ." One can't be too careful. One "management adviser" told Studs Terkel:[4] "Your wife, your children have to behave properly. You've got to fit in the mold. You've got to be on guard." In *Coming*

COLLABORATIVE ACTIVITY

Stage a debate between students who feel they can arrive at a better definition of what constitutes the American middle class.

---

[3]Controversial American sociologist and social critic (1916–62) who expanded theories of Karl Marx and Max Weber; author of *The Power Elite* (1956). [Eds.]

[4]Louis ("Studs") Terkel (1912–   ), oral historian. See "Hard Times," p. 790. [Eds.]

Up for Air (1939) George Orwell, speaking for his middle-class hero, gets it right:

> There's a lot of rot talked about the sufferings of the working class. I'm not so sorry for the proles myself. . . . The prole[5] suffers physically, but he's a free man when he isn't working. But in every one of those little stucco boxes there's some poor bastard who's *never* free except when he's fast asleep.

Because he is essentially a salesman, the middle-class man 8 develops a salesman's style. Hence his optimism and his belief in the likelihood of self-improvement if you'll just hurl yourself into it. One reason musicals like *Annie* and *Man of La Mancha* make so much money is that they offer him and his wife songs, like "Tomorrow" and "The Impossible Dream," that seem to promise that all sorts of good things are on the way. A final stigma of the middle class, an emanation of its social insecurity, is its habit of laughing as its own jests. Not entirely certain what social effect he's transmitting, and yet obliged, by his role as "salesman," to promote goodwill and optimism, your middle-class man serves as his own enraptured audience. Sometimes, after uttering some would-be clever formulation in public, he will look all around to gauge the response of the audience. Favorable, he desperately hopes.

The young men of the middle class are chips off the old block. If 9 you want to know who reads John T. Molloy's[6] books, hoping to break into the upper-middle class by formulas and mechanisms, they are your answer. You can see them on airplanes especially, being forwarded from one corporate training program to another. Their shirts are implausibly white, their suits are excessively dark, their neckties resemble those worn by undertakers, and their hair is cut in the style of the 1950s. Their talk is of *the bottom line*, and for *no* they are likely to say *no way*. Often their necks don't seem long enough, and their eyes tend to be too much in motion, flicking back and forth rather than up and down. They will enter adult life as corporate trainees and, after forty-five faithful years, leave it as corporate personnel, wondering whether this is all.

RESPONDING TO READING

1. Fussell seems critical, almost contemptuous, of the middle class in this essay. What characteristics does he seem to disapprove of? Why? Do you share his contempt? Are there any indications that he himself is guilty of the behavior he criticizes? Are you?   **2.** Fussell quotes many authorities to

---

[5]Member of the Proletariat, the poorest class of working people [Eds.]
[6]American writer and clothing consultant (1937–   ), author of *Dress for Success* (1975). [Eds.]

support his points. Why does he do this? How do you react to his use of experts? Do they convince you?   **3.** Fussell uses a variety of rhetorical techniques to convey his attitude toward his subject. For example, he places certain words (such as *physicians* in paragraph 1 and *professional* in paragraph 4) in quotation marks. What attitude does this use of quotation marks suggest to you? What else conveys his attitude?

2. Fussell's quotations are provided to establish credibility and to show that others feel the same way that he does.
3. His use of quotation marks lends an ironic tone and suggests that the validity of the terms is questionable. Other terms in quotation marks—for example, "affiliations" (paragraph 4), "correctness" (paragraph 5), and "friendliness" (paragraph 7)—also contribute to the ironic, almost mocking, tone, as do words placed in italics (for example, *executive* in paragraph 7).

On Being Black and Middle Class

SHELBY STEELE

The following essay by Shelby Steele (see also p. 147) is from his book *The Content of Our Character* (1990). In this essay, Steele argues that the black middle class has gained its identity not only from "positive images gleaned from middle- and upper-class white society" but also from "negative images of lower-class blacks."

Not long ago a friend of mine, black like myself, said to me that the term "black middle class" was actually a contradiction in terms. Race, he insisted, blurred class distinctions among blacks. If you were black, you were just black and that was that. When I argued, he let his eyes roll at my naiveté. Then he went on. For us, as black professionals, it was an exercise in self-flattery, a pathetic pretension, to give meaning to such a distinction. Worse, the very idea of class threatened the unity that was vital to the black community as a whole. After all, since when had white America taken note of anything but color when it came to blacks? He then reminded me of an old Malcolm X line that had been popular in the sixties. Question: What is a black man with a Ph.D.? Answer: A nigger.

For many years I had been on my friend's side of this argument. Much of my conscious thinking on the old conundrum[1] of race and class was shaped during my high school and college years in the race-charged sixties, when the fact of my race took on an almost religious significance. Progressively, from the mid-sixties on, more and more aspects of my life found their explanation, their justification, and their motivation in race. My youthful concerns about career, romance, money, values, and even styles of dress became a subject to consultation with various oracular sources of racial wisdom. And these ranged from a figure as ennobling as Martin Luther King, Jr., to the

---

[1]A riddle in which a fanciful question is answered by a pun; a problem that has no satisfactory solution. [Eds.]

BACKGROUND ON WRITER

Many view Shelby Steele as controversial because of his stance against programs such as affirmative action, which he believes encourages African-Americans to see themselves (and others to see them) as victims. He also feels that African-Americans must become voices in the dominant culture if they are to effect change.

FOR OPENERS

Make sure your students understand the terms *class* and *race* and that they can see the difference between the two. One way to do this is to ask students to write brief, anonymous definitions, which you can collect, read aloud, and discuss.

ADDITIONAL QUESTIONS FOR RESPONDING TO READING

1. Describe the change in attitude Steele experiences. What were the causes of this change?
2. According to Steele, what is the "double bind" of the black middle class?
3. What do you think Steele hopes to accomplish with his essay?
4. How do you think middle-class African-Americans might respond to Steele's beliefs? Why do you think so?

underworld elegance of dress I found in jazz clubs on the South Side of Chicago. Everywhere there were signals, and in those days I considered myself so blessed with clarity and direction that I pitied my white classmates who found more embarrassment than guidance in the fact of *their* race. In 1968, inflated by my new power, I took a mischievous delight in calling them culturally disadvantaged.

But now, hearing my friend's comment was like hearing a priest   3
from a church I'd grown disenchanted with. I understood him, but my faith was weak. What had sustained me in the sixties sounded monotonous and off the mark in the eighties. For me, race had lost much of its juju, its singular capacity to conjure meaning. And today, when I honestly look at my life and the lives of many other middle-class blacks I know, I can see that race never fully explained our situation in American society. Black though I may be, it is impossible for me to sit in my single-family house with two cars in the driveway and a swing set in the back yard and *not* see the role class has played in my life. And how can my friend, similarly raised and similarly situated, not see it?

Yet despite my certainty I felt a sharp tug of guilt as I tried to   4
explain myself over my friend's skepticism. He is a man of many comedic facial expressions and, as I spoke, his brow lifted in extreme moral alarm as if I were uttering the unspeakable. His clear implication was that I was being elitist and possibly (dare he suggest?) anti-black—crimes for which there might well be no redemption. He pretended to fear for me. I chuckled along with him, but inwardly I did wonder at myself. Though I never doubted the validity of what I was saying, I felt guilty saying it. Why?

After he left (to retrieve his daughter from a dance lesson) I real-   5
ized that the trap I felt myself in had a tiresome familiarity and, in a sort of slow-motion epiphany, I began to see its outline. It was like the suddenly sharp vision one has at the end of a burdensome marriage when all the long-repressed incompatibilities come undeniably to light.

What became clear to me is that people like myself, my friend,   6
and middle-class blacks generally are caught in a very specific double bind that keeps two equally powerful elements of our identity at odds with each other. The middle-class values by which we were raised— the work ethic, the importance of education, the value of property ownership, of respectability, of "getting ahead," of stable family life, of initiative, of self-reliance, etc.—are, in themselves, raceless and even assimilationist. They urge us toward participation in the American mainstream, toward integration, toward a strong identification with the society—and toward the entire constellation of qualities that are implied in the word "individualism." These values are almost

rules for how to prosper in a democratic, free-enterprise society that admires and rewards individual effort. They tell us to work hard for ourselves and our families and to seek our opportunities whenever they appear, inside or outside the confines of whatever ethnic group we may belong to.

But the particular pattern of racial identification that emerged in 7
the sixties and that still prevails today urges middle-class blacks (and all blacks) in the opposite direction. This pattern asks us to see ourselves as an embattled minority, and it urges an adversarial stance toward the mainstream, an emphasis on ethnic consciousness over individualism. It is organized around an implied separatism.

The opposing thrust of these two parts of our identity results in 8
the double bind of middle-class blacks. There is no forward movement on either plane that does not constitute backward movement on the other. This was the familiar trap I felt myself in while talking with my friend. As I spoke about class, his eyes reminded me that I was betraying race. Clearly, the two indispensable parts of my identity were a threat to each other.

Of course when you think about it, class and race are both similar 9
in some ways and also naturally opposed. They are two forms of collective identity with boundaries that intersect. But whether they clash or peacefully coexist has much to do with how they are defined. Being both black and middle class becomes a double bind when class and race are defined in sharply antagonistic terms, so that one must be repressed to appease the other.

But what is the "substance" of these two identities, and how does 10
each establish itself in an individual's overall identity? It seems to me that when we identify with any collective we are basically identifying with images that tell us what it means to be a member of that collective. Identity is not the same thing as the fact of membership in a collective; it is, rather, a form of self-definition, facilitated by images of what we wish our membership in the collective to mean. In this sense, the images we identify with may reflect the aspirations of the collective more than they reflect reality, and their content can vary with shifts in those aspirations.

But the process of identification is usually dialectical. It is just as 11
necessary to say what we are *not* as it is to say what we are—so that finally identification comes about by embracing a polarity of positive and negative images. To identify as middle class, for example, I must have both positive and negative images of what being middle class entails; then I will know what I should and should not be doing in order to be middle class. The same goes for racial identity.

In the racially turbulent sixties the polarity of images that came 12
to define racial identification was very antagonistic to the polarity that

defined middle-class identification. One might say that the positive images of one lined up with the negative images of the other, so that to identify with both required either a contortionist's flexibility or a dangerous splitting of the self. The double bind of the black middle class was in place.

The black middle class has always defined its class identity by 13 means of positive images gleaned from middle- and upper-class white society, and by means of negative images of lower-class blacks. This habit goes back to the institution of slavery itself, when "house" slaves both mimicked the whites they served and held themselves above the "field" slaves. But in the sixties the old bourgeois impulse to dissociate from the lower classes (the "we-they" distinction) backfired when racial identity suddenly called for the celebration of this same black lower class. One of the qualities of a double bind is that one feels it more than sees it, and I distinctly remember the tension and strange sense of dishonesty I felt in those days as I moved back and forth like a bigamist between the demands of class and race.

Though my father was born poor, he achieved middle-class 14 standing through much hard work and sacrifice (one of his favorite words) and by identifying fully with solid middle-class values— mainly hard work, family life, property ownership, and education for his children (all four of whom have advanced degrees). In his mind these were not so much values as laws of nature. People who embodied them made up the positive images in his class polarity. The negative images came largely from the blacks he had left behind because they were "going nowhere."

No one in my family remembers how it happened, but as time 15 went on, the negative images congealed into an imaginary character named Sam, who, from the extensive service we put him to, quickly grew to mythic proportions. In our family lore he was sometimes a trickster, sometimes a boob, but always possessed of a catalogue of sly faults that gave up graphic images of everything we should not be. On sacrifice: "Sam never thinks about tomorrow. He wants it now or he doesn't care about it." On work: "Sam doesn't favor it too much." On children: "Sam likes to have them but not to raise them." On money: "Sam drinks it up and pisses it out." On fidelity: "Sam has to have two or three women." On clothes: "Sam features loud clothes. He likes to see and be seen." And so on. Sam's persona amounted to a negative instruction manual in class identity.

I don't think any of us believed Sam's faults were accurate rep- 16 resentations of lower-class black life. He was an instrument of self-definition, not of sociological accuracy. It never occurred to us that he looked very much like the white racist stereotype of blacks, or that he might have been a manifestation of our own racial self-hatred. He simply gave us a counterpoint against which to express our aspirations. If self-hatred was a factor, it was not, for us, a matter of hating lower-class blacks but of hating what we did not want to be.

Still, hate or love aside, it is fundamentally true that my middle-class identity involved a dissociation from images of lower-class black life and a corresponding identification with values and patterns of responsibility that are common to the middle class everywhere. These values sent me a clear message: be both an individual and a responsible citizen; understand that the quality of your life will approximately reflect the quality of effort you put into it; know that individual responsibility is the basis of freedom and that the limitations imposed by fate (whether fair or unfair) are no excuse for passivity. 17

Whether I live up to these values or not, I know that my acceptance of them is the result of lifelong conditioning. I know also that I share this conditioning with middle-class people of all races and that I can no more easily be free of it than I can be free of my race. Whether all this got started because the black middle class modeled itself on the white middle class is no longer relevant. For the middle-class black, conditioned by these values from birth, the sense of meaning they provide is as immutable as the color of his skin. 18

I started the sixties in high school feeling that my class-conditioning was the surest way to overcome racial barriers. My racial identity was pretty much taken for granted. After all, it was obvious to the world that I was black. Yet I ended the sixties in graduate school a little embarrassed by my class background and with an almost desperate need to be "black." The tables had turned. I knew very clearly (though I struggled to repress it) that my aspirations and my sense of how to operate in the world came from my class background, yet "being black" required certain attitudes and stances that made me feel secretly a little duplicitous. The inner compatibility of class and race I had known in 1960 was gone. 19

For blacks, the decade between 1960 and 1969 saw racial identification undergo the same sort of transformation that national identity undergoes in times of war. It became more self-conscious, more narrowly focused, more prescribed, less tolerant of opposition. It spawned an implicit party line, which tended to disallow competing forms of identity. Race-as-identity was lifted from the relative slumber it knew in the fifties and pressed into service in a social and political war against oppression. It was redefined along sharp adversarial lines and directed toward the goal of mobilizing the great mass of black Americans in this warlike effort. It was imbued with a strong moral authority, useful for denouncing those who opposed it and for cel- 20 ebrating those who honored it as a positive achievement rather than as a mere birthright.

The form of racial identification that quickly evolved to meet this 21 challenge presented blacks as a racial monolith, a singular people with a common experience of oppression. Differences within the race, no matter how ineradicable, had to be minimized. Class distinctions were one of the first such differences to be sacrificed, since they not only threatened racial unity but also seemed to stand in contradiction to the principle of equality which was the announced goal of the movement for racial progress. The discomfort I felt in 1969, the vague but relentless sense of duplicity, was the result of a historical necessity that put my race and class at odds, that was asking me to cast aside the distinction of my class and identify with a monolithic view of my race.

If the form of this racial identity was the monolith, its substance 22 was victimization. The civil rights movement and the more radical splinter groups of the late sixties were all dedicated to ending racial victimization, and the form of black identity that emerged to facilitate this goal made blackness and victimization virtually synonymous. Since it was our victimization more than any other variable that identified and unified us, moreover, it followed logically that the purest black was the poor black. It was images of him that clustered around the positive pole of the race polarity; all other blacks were, in effect, required to identify with him in order to confirm their own blackness.

Certainly there were more dimensions to the black experience 23 than victimization, but no other had the same capacity to fire the indignation needed for war. So, again out of historical necessity, victimization became the overriding focus of racial identity. But this only deepened the double bind for middle-class blacks like me. When it came to class we were accustomed to defining ourselves against lower-class blacks and identifying with at least the values of middle-class whites; when it came to race we were now being asked to identify with images of lower-class blacks and to see whites, middle class or otherwise, as victimizers. Negative lining up with positive, we were called upon to reject what we had previously embraced and to embrace what we had previously rejected. To put it still more personally, the Sam figure I had been raised to define myself against had now become the "real" black I was expected to identify with.

The fact that the poor black's new status was only passively 24 earned by the condition of his victimization, not by assertive, positive action, made little difference. Status was status apart from the means by which it was achieved, and along with it came a certain power— the power to define the terms of access to that status, to say who was black and who was not. If a lower-class black said you were not really "black"—a sellout, an Uncle Tom—the judgment was all the more devastating because it carried the authority of his status. And this judgment soon enough came to be accepted by many whites as well.

In graduate school I was once told by a white professor, "Well, 25 but . . . you're not really black. I mean, you're not disadvantaged." In his mind my lack of victim status disqualified me from the race itself. More recently I was complimented by a black student for speaking reasonably correct English, "proper" English as he put it. "But I don't know if I really want to talk like that," he went on. "Why not?" I asked. "Because then I wouldn't be black no more," he replied without a pause.

To overcome his marginal status, the middle-class black had to 26 identify with a degree of victimization that was beyond his actual experience. In college (and well beyond) we used to play a game called "nap matching." It was a game of one-upmanship, in which we sat around outdoing each other with stories of racial victimization, symbolically measured by the naps of our hair. Most of us were middle class and so had few personal stories to relate, but if we could not match naps with our own biographies, we would move on to those legendary tales of victimization that came to us from the public domain.

The single story that sat atop the pinnacle of racial victimization 27 for us was that of Emmett Till, the Northern black teenager who, on a visit to the South in 1955, was killed and grotesquely mutilated for supposedly looking at or whistling at (we were never sure which, though we argued the point endlessly) a white woman. Oh, how we probed his story, finding in his youth and Northern upbringing the quintessential embodiment of black innocence, brought down by a white evil so portentous and apocalyptic, so gnarled and hideous, that it left us with a feeling not far from awe. By telling his story and others like it, we came to *feel* the immutability of our victimization, its utter indigenousness, as a thing on this earth like dirt or sand or water.

Of course, these sessions were a ritual of group identification, a 28 means by which we, as middle-class blacks, could be at one with our race. But why were we, who had only a moderate experience of victimization (and that offset by opportunities our parents never had), so intent on assimilating or appropriating an identity that in so many ways contradicted our own? Because, I think, the sense of innocence that is always entailed in feeling victimized filled us with a corresponding feeling of entitlement, or even license, that helped us endure our vulnerability on a largely white college campus.

TEACHING STRATEGY

Discuss Steele's description of the incident between himself and the coach of the debate team. Point out the way Steele's voice analyzes, judges, and explains his reactions to the incident. Why is this passage both an important and an effective part of the essay?

In my junior year in college I rode to a debate tournament with 29 three white students and our faculty coach, an elderly English professor. The experience of being the lone black in a group of whites was so familiar to me that I thought nothing of it as our trip began. But then halfway through the trip the professor casually turned to me and, in an isn't-the-world-funny sort of tone, said that he had just refused to rent an apartment in a house he owned to a "very nice" black couple because their color would "offend" the white couple who lived downstairs. His eyebrows lifted helplessly over his hawkish nose, suggesting that he too, like me, was a victim of America's racial farce. His look assumed a kind of comradeship: he and I were above this grimy business of race, though for expediency we had occasionally to concede the world its madness.

My vulnerability in this situation came not so much from the 30 professor's blindness to his own racism as from his assumption that I would participate in it, that I would conspire with him against my own race so that he might remain comfortably blind. Why did he think I would be amenable to this? I can only guess that he assumed my middle-class identity was so complete and all-encompassing that I would see his action as nothing more than a trifling concession to the folkways of our land, that I would in fact applaud his decision not to disturb propriety. Blind to both his own racism and to me—one blindness serving the other—he could not recognize that he was asking me to betray my race in the name of my class.

His blindness made me feel vulnerable because it threatened to 31 expose my own repressed ambivalence. His comment pressured me to choose between my class identification, which had contributed to my being a college student and a member of the debating team, and my desperate desire to be "black." I could have one but not both; I was double-bound.

Because double binds are repressed there is always an element 32 of terror in them: the terror of bringing to the conscious mind the buried duplicity, self-deception, and pretense involved in serving two masters. This terror is the stuff of vulnerability, and since vulnerability is one of the least tolerable of all human feelings, we usually transform it into an emotion that seems to restore the control of which it has robbed us; most often, that emotion is anger. And so, before the professor had even finished his little story, I had become a furnace of rage. The year was 1967, and I had been primed by endless hours of nap-matching to feel, at least consciously, completely at one with the victim-focused black identity. This identity gave me the license, and the impunity, to unleash upon this professor one of those volcanic eruptions of racial indignation familiar to us from the novels of Richard Wright. Like Cross Damon in *Outsider*, who kills in perfectly righteous anger, I tried to annihilate the man. I punished him not according to the measure of his crime but according to the measure of my vulnerability, a measure set by the cumulative tension of years of repressed terror. Soon I saw that terror in *his* face, as he stared hollow-eyed at the road ahead. My white friends in the back seat, knowing no conflict between their own class and race, were astonished that someone they had taken to be so much like themselves could harbor a rage that for all the world looked murderous.

Though my rage was triggered by the professor's comment, it 33 was deepened and sustained by a complex of need, conflict, and repression in myself of which I had been wholly unaware. Out of my racial vulnerability I had developed the strong need of an identity with which to defend myself. The only such identity available was that of me as victim, him as victimizer. Once in the grip of this paradigm, I began to do far more damage to myself than he had done.

Seeing myself as a victim meant that I clung all the harder to my 34 racial identity, which, in turn, meant that I suppressed my class identity. This cut me off from all the resources my class values might have offered me. In those values, for instance, I might have found the means to a more dispassionate response, the response less of a victim attacked by a victimizer than of an individual offended by a foolish old man. As an individual I might have reported this professor to the college dean. Or I might have calmly tried to reveal his blindness to him, and possibly won a convert. (The flagrancy of his remark suggested a hidden guilt and even self-recognition on which I might have capitalized. Doesn't confession usually signal a willingness to face oneself?) Or I might have simply chuckled and then let my silence serve as an answer to his provocation. Would not my composure, in any form it might take, deflect into his own heart the arrow he'd shot at me?

Instead, my anger, itself the hair-trigger expression of a long- 35 repressed double bind, not only cut me off from the best of my own resources, it also distorted the nature of my true racial problem. The righteousness of this anger and the easy catharsis it brought buoyed the delusion of my victimization and left me as blind as the professor himself.

As a middle-class black I have often felt myself *contriving* to be 36 "black." And I have noticed this same contrivance in others—a certain stretching away from the natural flow of one's life to align oneself with a victim-focused black identity. Our particular needs are out of sync with the form of identity available to meet those needs. Middle-class blacks need to identify racially; it is better to think of ourselves as black and victimized than not black at all; so we contrive (more unconsciously than consciously) to fit ourselves into an identity that denies our class and fails to address the true source of our vulnerability.

For me this once meant spending inordinate amounts of time at 37 black faculty meetings, though these meetings had little to do with my real racial anxieties or my professional life. I was new to the university, one of two blacks in an English department of over seventy, and I felt a little isolated and vulnerable, though I did not admit it to myself. But at these meetings we discussed the problems of black faculty and students within a framework of victimization. The real vulnerability we felt was covered over by all the adversarial drama the victim/victimizer polarity inspired, and hence went unseen and unassuaged. And this, I think, explains our rather chronic ineffectiveness as a group. Since victimization was not our primary problem—the university had long ago opened its doors to us—we had to contrive to make it so, and there is not much energy in contrivance. What I got at these meetings was ultimately an object lesson in how fruitless struggle can be when it is not grounded in actual need.

At our black faculty meetings, the old equation of blackness with 38 victimization was ever present—to be black was to be a victim; therefore, not to be a victim was not to be black. As we contrived to meet the terms of this formula there was an inevitable distortion of both ourselves and the larger university. Through the prism of victimization the university seemed more impenetrable than it actually was, and we more limited in our powers. We fell prey to the victim's myopia, making the university an institution from which we could seek redress but which we could never fully join. And this mind-set often led us to look more for compensations for our supposed victimization than for opportunities we could pursue as individuals.

The discomfort and vulnerability felt by middle-class blacks in the 39 sixties, it could be argued, was a worthwhile price to pay considering the progress achieved during that time of racial confrontation. But what may have been tolerable then is intolerable now. Though changes in American society have made it an anachronism, the monolithic form of racial identification that came out of the sixties is still very much with us. It may be more loosely held, and its power to punish heretics has probably diminished, but it continues to catch middle-class blacks in a double bind, thus impeding not only their own advancement but even, I would contend, that of blacks as a group.

The victim-focused black identity encourages the individual to 40 feel that his advancement depends almost entirely on that of the group. Thus he loses sight not only of his own possibilities but of the inextricable connection between individual effort and individual advancement. This is a profound encumbrance today, when there is more opportunity for blacks than ever before, for it reimposes limitations that can have the same oppressive effect as those the society has only recently begun to remove.

It was the emphasis on mass action in the sixties that made the 41 victim-focused black identity a necessity. But in the eighties and beyond, when racial advancement will come only through a multitude of individual advancements, this form of identity inadvertently adds itself to the forces that hold us back. Hard work, education, individual initiative, stable family life, property ownership—these have always been the means by which ethnic groups have moved ahead in America. Regardless of past or present victimization, these "laws" of advancement apply absolutely to black Americans also. There is no getting around this. What we need is a form of racial identity that energizes the individual by putting him in touch with both his possibilities and his responsibilities.

It has always annoyed me to hear from the mouths of certain 42 arbiters of blackness that middle-class blacks should "reach back" and pull up those blacks less fortunate than they—as though middle-class status were an unearned and essentially passive condition in which one needed a large measure of noblesse oblige to occupy one's time. My own image is of reaching back from a moving train to lift on board those who have no tickets. A noble enough sentiment—but might it not be wiser to show them the entire structure of principles, effort, and sacrifice that puts one in a position to buy a ticket any time one likes? This, I think, is something members of the black middle class can realistically offer to other blacks. Their example is not only a testament to possibility but also a lesson in method. But they cannot lead by example until they are released from a black identity that regards that example as suspect, that sees them as "marginally" black, indeed that holds *them* back by catching them in a double bind.

To move beyond the victim-focused black identity we must learn 43 to make a difficult but crucial distinction: between actual victimization, which we must resist with every resource, and identification with the victim's status. Until we do this we will continue to wrestle more with ourselves than with the new opportunities which so many paid so dearly to win.

RESPONDING TO READING

1. Steele believes that he has achieved middle-class status in economic and educational terms. Do you think he is correct, or do you agree with his friend that the term *black middle class* is a contradiction in terms? Do you think most middle-class whites would accept Steele's status as equal to theirs?   **2.** Have you ever experienced a similar conflict between class and racial or ethnic identity? If so, what did you do to reconcile the demands of the two?   **3.** A May 30, 1990 *New York Times* article portrays Steele as a controversial figure: "To many whites and conservative blacks, Mr. Steele has given eloquent voice to painful truths that are almost always left unspoken in the nation's circumscribed public discourse on race. To many black politicians and civil rights figures, he is a turncoat, a privileged black man whose visibility and success stem from his ability to say precisely what white America most wants to hear." With whom do you agree?

The Laws

JOSEPH LELYVELD

Journalist Joseph Lelyveld (1937–   ) has been a *New York Times* correspondent in India, Pakistan, the Congo (now Zaire), and South Africa. He is currently the *Times's* Managing Editor. In 1985 he won a Pulitzer Prize for *Move Your Shadow: South Africa Black and White*, a book based on his observations of the lives of the black South Africans, their poverty and struggles. Lelyveld's writing brings the country to life and depicts the reality of everyday experience. In "The Laws," from *Move Your Shadow*, he uses irony and a controlled tone to define how apartheid works.

FOR OPENERS

1. Explore the denotative and connotative meanings of words such as *law*, *statute*, *authority*, *mandate*, *justice*, and *rights*.
2. In 1991, the South African government dismantled the foundations of apartheid by repealing the Population Registration Act, which had required all South Africans to be classified by race at birth. Even though this action has as yet had no real impact on black South Africans and other discriminatory laws remain in effect, the government requested that all foreign economic sanctions be lifted. In July 1991 President Bush lifted all sanctions against South Africa. In class discussion, summarize the most recent changes in the apartheid system, and examine their effects on the citizens of South Africa.

It's time to talk law. Where other regimes have no difficulty tyrannizing their citizens under the cloak of constitutions guaranteeing universal human rights, South Africa's white rulers have been unusually conscientious about securing statutory authority for their abuses. When a right, even a birthright, such as citizenship, is to be annulled, it is always done with a law. Most whites are uncomprehending of the argument that law is brought into disrepute when it is used to destroy habeas corpus, the presumption of innocence, equality before the law, and various other basic freedoms. Law is law. It's the principle of order and therefore of civilization, the antithesis advanced by the white man to what he knows as a matter of tribal lore, his own, to be Africa's fundamental thesis: anarchy. Excessive liberty, in his view, is what threatens civilization; law is what preserves it. The opposing view that law might preserve liberty is thus held to be a contradiction; in Africa, a promise of surrender. On this basis, it has been possible to build apartheid not simply as the sum of various kinds of segregation, or the disenfranchisement of the majority, but as a comprehensive system of racial dominance. A decade after the South African authorities announced their intention to move away from "hurtful and unnecessary discrimination," I thought I would get the feel of the basic statutes by holding them in my hands as you might if you were apprizing an eggplant or a melon. Some laws, especially those reserving the best industrial jobs for whites, had been repealed. Others, such as the Prohibition of Mixed Marriages Act, seemed destined for repeal as part of a calculated effort to lower the level of ignominy attaching to the system. I wanted to feel, literally to weigh, what remained.

What remained weighed slightly more than ten pounds when I stepped on a scale with an up-to-date volume of all the laws in South Africa that relate specifically to blacks—laws, that is, that can normally be broken only by blacks (or by persons of other racial groups only when they interfere with the state's master plan for blacks). The figure of ten pounds had to be halved immediately because the volume of 4,500 pages contained both the Afrikaans and English version of sixty-four basic statutes that regulate the lives of blacks. These then amounted to about 2,250 closely printed pages, weighing about five pounds. But the small print that followed the statutes indicated that they had given rise to some 2,000 regulations, adding two or three pounds at least. These, in turn, would have given rise to hundreds or maybe thousands of official circulars that were not in the public domain but were treated as law by the officials who regulate blacks. And that was only the racial law for blacks. There were also laws, regulations, and circulars for coloreds and Indians, running to hundreds of additional pages and another couple of pounds. And there were laws, regulations, and circulars relating to the administration of the Group Areas Act, the basic statute guaranteeing absolute resident segregation. Gathering all the materials for a precise weighing was more than I could manage; but the basic corpus of South African racial law still ran to more than 3,000 pages, and when all the regulations and circulars were added in, its dead weight was bound to be well over ten pounds. Apartheid was not wasting away. For argument's sake, there was enough of it left to give someone a concussion. And this still did not include the mass of draconian[1] security laws and the other legislation restricting political association and expression, which are certainly oppressive but not as distinctively South African.

Of course, the impact of apartheid cannot be measured in pounds. A South African Gogol[2] may contrive a way someday to measure it in "dead souls." But I could measure it only by trying to witness the system in operation, at the points where it impinges on individual

[1]Harsh; rigorous. Designating a law or code of extreme severity. [Eds.]
[2]Nicolai Gogol (1809–52), Russian novelist and dramatist whose masterpiece is the novel *Dead Souls* (1842). [Eds.]

ADDITIONAL QUESTIONS FOR RESPONDING TO READING

1. How does Lelyveld characterize the whites' view of law? Is his assessment fair? How do the whites sanction apartheid?
2. According to Lelyveld, how does South Africa's "layered, compartmentalized consciousness" affect the country's "social geography"?
3. How, according to Lelyveld, does apartheid make it possible for society to avoid thinking and talking about its needs?
4. How do recent events in South Africa affect your reaction to Lelyveld's observations?

TEACHING STRATEGIES

1. Using Lelyveld's description, chart on the board the elaborate hierarchy of South Africa's caste system.
2. Study closely Lelyveld's passages concerning law. Discuss his use of irony. Is it effective?

lives, especially in the mazelike structure of courts and official bureaus it has established to channel black laborers in and out of areas of economic opportunity while minimizing their chances of establishing permanent residence with their families. If this structure were suddenly dismantled, if whites stopped regulating black lives, there would still be migrant workers by the hundreds of thousands in South Africa and millions of impoverished blacks. There would still be wealthy suburbs, huge ranches, black townships, and squalid rural areas. But it would then be possible to think of the society as a whole and talk rationally about its needs. Apartheid ensures that the language for such a discussion hardly exists. It does so for its own cunning reasons. Once you think of the society as a whole, it is impossible not to think of the distribution of land—50,000 white farmers have twelve times as much land for cultivation and grazing as 14 million rural blacks—or of the need to relieve the pressure in those portions of the countryside that have been systematically turned into catchment areas for surplus black population.

If South Africa were viewed as one country, it might be possible 4 to recognize a glaring fact about its social geography: the existence of an almost continuous scimitar-shaped belt of black rural poverty, stretching for more than 1,000 miles from the northeastern Transvaal through the Swazi and Zulu tribal areas and down into the two "homelands" for Xhosa-speaking blacks in the eastern Cape, a belt that is inhabited by about 7 million people, amounting to nearly 30 percent of the black population. Instead, in the layered, compartmentalized consciousness that apartheid insidiously shapes, these blacks are dispersed in Venda, Gazankulu, Lebowa, KwaZulu, Transkei, and Ciskei: foreign places, hard to find on maps, another galaxy.

In apartheid's terms, it is revolutionary or at least eccentric to 5 think of this band of poverty as South Africa's problem. Apartheid thus raises the stakes, deliberately compounding mass rural poverty in order to preserve white privilege and power. It is the ultimate divide-and-rule strategy, dividing the land into racially designated areas and bogus homelands and the population into distinct racial castes and subcastes of which I can count at least eight: the whites, who are free to do anything except move into an area designated as nonwhite; the coloreds and Indians, who can move freely in the country but are barred from owning land in more than 95 percent of it; and the blacks, who are subdivided by law into six distinct impermeable or semipermeable categories.

The broad distinction between urban and rural blacks is only the 6 beginning of this process of alienation. The urban blacks come in two subcastes: the "insiders," as they are now sometimes called, and the "commuters." The insiders are conceded to have a certain immunity to arbitrary expulsion, amounting to a right of permanent residence in what is acknowledged to be South Africa. The circumstances of the urban commuters appear to be exactly the same, except that the townships in which they reside are not deemed, as a result of gerrymandering,[3] to fall within the boundaries of some homeland. Although they may be only a short bus ride from a South African city such as Pretoria, Durban, or East London, no farther than the blacks of Soweto are from Johannesburg, they are regarded by South African law as foreign or on their way to becoming foreign. But such commuters can still get "special" licenses of limited duration making them "authorized work seekers" in an urban area.

This means they are still far better off than a second group of   7
commuters who must be regarded as a separate subcaste because they commute to the industrial centers from homeland areas that remain essentially rural. These rural commuters are on a distinctly lower level of the hierarchy, but it can be argued that they are the most privileged or, rather, least abused of the four distinguishable subcastes of rural blacks. The rural commuters generally travel much longer distances to work than the urban commuters, live in officially designated "closer settlements" without such amenities as running water or electricity, rather than organized townships, and get their jobs through the state's network of labor bureaus. They generally work on annual contracts like migrant laborers, but at least they come home to their families at night and on weekends.

The migrants, the next subcaste, live in urban townships or on   8
the mines and sugar plantations in barrackslike single-sex hostels, usually for eleven months of every year; it is theoretically possible for some of them to acquire a right of urban residence after ten or fifteen years but practically impossible for them to acquire a house in which to exercise it.

Blacks who live in the white rural areas as farm laborers make up   9
the next subcaste; by tradition they receive more of their compensation in kind—sacks of mealie (corn) meal usually—than in cash, but wages are gradually coming into vogue. And finally, there are the homeland blacks, who live their whole lives in the black rural areas. Of these, a tiny elite is employed by the homeland governments as officials, teachers, or police; others are employed as menials. But overall the former tribal reserves provide gainful employment for fewer that 20 percent of the young blacks reared within their borders, only 12 percent, according to a statistic let slip by a white Cabinet minister who

---

[3]Division of state, county, or city into voting districts in such a way as to give unfair advantage to one political party. Term is derived from Elbridge Gerry (1744–1814), U.S. vice president under James Madison. [Eds.]

was trying to counter extremist arguments during a political campaign that too much was done for blacks. The rest of the homeland blacks—those who cannot become migrants themselves—are mainly dependent on the wages of migrants, or scratch out a meager existence as subsistence cultivators on exhausted soil, or are unemployed and wholly destitute. The life-threatening protein deficiency known as kwashiorkor and the starvation condition known as marasmus are endemic among children in this group. Reliable statistics are spotty, but in some black rural areas in a country that has been aptly described as the Saudi Arabia of minerals, it appears that scarcely 50 percent of the children who are alive at birth survive past the age of five.

A lopsided social structure is not peculiar to South Africa. What 10 is peculiar is the fact that it is legally mandated and rigorously imposed on the basis of race. It is impossible to change caste without an official appeals board ruling that you are a different color from what you were originally certified to be. These miraculous transformations are tabulated and announced on an annual basis. In my first year back in South Africa, 558 coloreds became whites, 15 whites became coloreds, 8 Chinese became whites, 7 whites became Chinese, 40 Indians became coloreds, 20 coloreds became Indians, 79 Africans became coloreds, and 8 coloreds became Africans. The spirit of this grotesque self-parody, which results from the deliberations of an official body known as the Race Classification Board, is obviously closer to Grand Guignol[4] than the Nuremberg Laws;[5] in other words, it's sadistic farce. "Look, man, it's all a game, it's all a big joke," I was assured once by a Cape Town colored who had managed to get himself reclassified as a white, a transformation sometimes described in Afrikaans by the term *verblankingsproses* ("whitening process").

"When you're in Rome," the man said, "what are you? A bloody 11 German? Hell, no, you're a Roman! Self-preservation is the only rule."

The legal definitions that attach to the various categories of racial 12 caste are vague, overlapping, and sometimes contradictory. A white, by one of the definitions, is "any person who in appearance obviously is or who is generally accepted as a white person, other than a person who, although in appearance obviously a white person, is generally accepted as a colored person." In other words, a rose is a rose is maybe not a rose. "A colored person," this same statute holds, is "any person who is not a member of the white group or of the black group."[6] But a colored can also be any woman "to whichever race,

---

[4]Thêatre de Grand Guignol, late nineteenth-century Parisian theatre specializing in sensational plays designed to terrify audiences with ghostly, macabre scenes. [Eds.]

[5]Passed at a 1935 Nazi Party Congress, these laws deprived German Jews of civil rights and outlawed marriage between Jews and non-Jews. [Eds.]

[6]Unless, of course, he is an Indian, who may be the same color but is legally set apart on the basis of ethnicity, most of the time, anyhow.

class or tribe she may belong" who marries a colored man, or a white man who marries a colored woman. Mixed marriages may have been illegal throughout the apartheid era—as they were, lest we forget, in a majority of American states within living memory—but even when the South African law prohibiting them is finally repealed, there will still be this other racial statute to bar mixed couples from living in white areas.

Apartheid never concerned itself with mixed marriages between 13
browns and blacks. They remained legal. It was only the white race that had to be preserved. Carel Boshoff, a theology professor at Pretoria University and son-in-law of Hendrik Verwoerd, informed me as if it were a matter of incontrovertible facts that a group could be diluted by 6 or 7 percent and still maintain its "identity." In fact, Afrikaner researchers in this esoteric field have concluded that 6.9 percent is the probable proportion of "colored blood" in their veins. Racism, it then may be deduced, is no more that 93.1 percent in their doctrine. Nevertheless, classification remains the essence of the system. No one—least of all a black—has the right to classify himself as simply a South African. Thus the single most important determinant of status and rights in South Africa remains the accident of birth. Most white South Africans would dispute this assertion, but then most white South Africans have insulated themselves from any knowledge of how the system works.

RESPONDING TO READING

1. Why do you think Lelyveld constantly emphasizes the law? How does this emphasis intensify the essay's impact on you?   **2.** Lelyveld believes that the rigid classification that is "the essence of the system" (paragraph 13) of apartheid is arbitrary, determined simply by "the accident of birth." How do you think supporters of apartheid would react to this statement?   **3.** Does Lelyveld risk losing your sympathy by writing in a calm, controlled tone? Or does this tone increase the selection's power? Explain your reaction.

Just Walk on By

BRENT STAPLES

Brent Staples (1951–   ) is an editor and writer who studied behavioral science and psychology, taught, and then turned to journalism, writing for the *Chicago Sun-Times* and the *New York Times*. He is known, too, as a book and drama critic and now contributes to *Harper's* and *Ms.* magazines. In the essay that follows, which

WRITING SUGGESTIONS

1. Write an essay in which you apply Martin Luther King's comments about just and unjust laws ("Letter from Birmingham Jail," page 1037, paragraphs 15–19) to apartheid. What would King advise black South Africans to do? Do you think such advice would alleviate their problems?
2. Write about a personal experience through which you learned about the fairness or unfairness of law.

ANSWERS TO RESPONDING TO READING

1. Lelyveld demonstrates that in South Africa the law provides statutory authority for abuses of human rights. There is a discrepancy between law and justice, and seeing this gap may provoke the reader to reevaluate basic assumptions about the purpose of law.
2. Answers will vary. Supporters of apartheid would probably downplay the classification and its inherent racism; they would emphasize the idea that law is "a principle of order and therefore of civilization" and necessary to protect the world from anarchy.
3. Lelyveld's tone heightens the irony, and because his goal is to show that apartheid is not "wasting away," he literalizes the weight of the law: it weighs over ten pounds. Reactions to his approach will vary.

appeared in *Ms.* in 1986, Staples talks personally about race and fear and tells how he learned that whistling classical melodies was a tool he could use like a "cowbell that hikers wear when they know they are in bear country."

My first victim was a woman—white, well dressed, probably in her early twenties. I came upon her late one evening on a deserted street in Hyde Park, a relatively affluent neighborhood in an otherwise mean, impoverished section of Chicago. As I swung onto the avenue behind her, there seemed to be a discreet, uninflammatory distance between us. Not so. She cast back a worried glance. To her, the youngish black man—a broad six feet two inches with a beard and billowing hair, both hands shoved into the pockets of a bulky military jacket—seemed menacingly close. After a few more quick glimpses, she picked up her pace and was soon running in earnest. Within seconds she disappeared into a cross street. 1

That was more than a decade ago. I was 22 years old, a graduate student newly arrived at the University of Chicago. It was in the echo of that terrified woman's footfalls that I first began to know the unwieldly inheritance I'd come into—the ability to alter public space in ugly ways. It was clear that she thought herself the quarry of a mugger, a rapist, or worse. Suffering a bout of insomnia, however, I was stalking sleep, not defenseless wayfarers. As a softy who is scarcely able to take a knife to a raw chicken—let alone hold it to a person's throat—I was surprised, embarrassed, and dismayed all at once. Her flight made me feel like an accomplice in tyranny. It also made it clear that I was indistinguishable from the muggers who occasionally seeped into the area from the surrounding ghetto. That first encounter, and those that followed, signified that a vast, unnerving gulf lay between nighttime pedestrians—particularly women—and me. And I soon gathered that being perceived as dangerous is a hazard in itself. I only needed to turn a corner into a dicey situation, or crowd some frightened, armed person in a foyer somewhere, or make an errant move after being pulled over by a policeman. Where fear and weapons meet—and they often do in urban America—there is always the possibility of death. 2

In that first year, my first away from my hometown, I was to become thoroughly familiar with the language of fear. At dark, shadowy intersections in Chicago, I could cross in front of a car stopped at a traffic light and elicit the *thunk, thunk, thunk, thunk* of the driver—black, white, male, or female—hammering down the door locks. On less traveled streets after dark, I grew accustomed to but never comfortable with people who crossed to the other side of the street rather than pass me. Then there were the standard unpleas- 3 antries with police, doormen, bouncers, cab drivers, and others whose business it is to screen out troublesome individuals *before* there is any nastiness.

I moved to New York nearly two years ago and I have remained 4 an avid night walker. In central Manhattan, the near-constant crowd cover minimizes tense one-on-one street encounters. Elsewhere—visiting friends in SoHo, where sidewalks are narrow and tightly spaced buildings shut out the sky—things can get very taut indeed.

Black men have a firm place in New York mugging literature. 5 Norman Podhoretz in his famed (or infamous) 1963 essay, "My Negro Problem—And Ours," recalls growing up in terror of black males; they "were tougher than we were, more ruthless," he writes—and as an adult on the Upper West Side of Manhattan, he continues, he cannot constrain his nervousness when he meets black men on certain streets. Similarly, a decade later, the essayist and novelist Edward Hoagland extols a New York where once "Negro bitterness bore down mainly on other Negroes." Where some see mere panhandlers, Hoagland sees "a mugger who is clearly screwing up his nerve to do more than just *ask* for money." But Hoagland has "the New Yorker's quick-hunch posture for broken-field maneuvering," and the bad guy swerves away.

I often witness that "hunch posture," from women after dark on 6 the warrenlike streets of Brooklyn where I live. They seem to set their faces on neutral and, with their purse straps strung across their chests bandolier style, they forge ahead as though bracing themselves against being tackled. I understand, of course, that the danger they perceive is not a hallucination. Women are particularly vulnerable to street violence, and young black males are drastically overrepresented among the perpetrators of that violence. Yet these truths are no solace against the kind of alienation that comes of being ever the suspect, against being set apart, a fearsome entity with whom pedestrians avoid making eye contact.

It is not altogether clear to me how I reached the ripe old age of 7 22 without being conscious of the lethality nighttime pedestrians attributed to me. Perhaps it was because in Chester, Pennsylvania, the small, angry industrial town where I came of age in the 1960s, I was scarcely noticeable against a backdrop of gang warfare, street knifings, and murders. I grew up one of the good boys, had perhaps a half-dozen fist fights. In retrospect, my shyness of combat has clear sources.

Many things go into the making of a young thug. One of those 8 things is the consummation of the male romance with the power to intimidate. An infant discovers that random flailings send the baby bottle flying out of the crib and crashing to the floor. Delighted, the

TEACHING STRATEGY

Point out how Staples manipulates appearance and reality. He opens with a neat twist on the word *victim*. In the first paragraph, he speaks about himself as perceived by the woman—as a threat. In the second paragraph, Staples presents his own view of himself, "a softy who is scarcely able to take a knife to a raw chicken—let alone hold it to a person's throat." Use these observations to move the class into a discussion of other words, such as *accomplice* and *suspect*, that Staples uses to contrast others' characterizations of him with his own.

COLLABORATIVE ACTIVITY

Have students work in groups to determine what traits cause a stranger to appear threatening. Encourage them to include signals that suggest deviance from social norms, such as unacceptable modes of dress, facial expressions, behavior, and grooming, rather than ethnic or racial identity. In class discussion, explore the validity of their perceptions and point out the differences in what various students find threatening. You might note, for example, that some people would be leery of young men with ponytails or earrings, features many of your students will probably *not* find threatening.

joyful babe repeats those motions again and again, seeking to duplicate the feat. Just so, I recall the points at which some of my boyhood
friends were finally seduced by the perception of themselves as tough
guys. When a mark cowered and surrendered his money without
resistance, myth and reality merged—and paid off. It is, after all, only
manly to embrace the power to frighten and intimidate. We, as men,
are not supposed to give an inch of our lane on the highway; we are
to seize the fighter's edge in work and in play and even in love; we
are to be valiant in the face of hostile forces.

Unfortunately, poor and powerless young men seem to take all   9
this nonsense literally. As a boy, I saw countless tough guys locked
away; I have since buried several, too. They were babies, really—a
teenage cousin, a brother of 22, a childhood friend in his mid-
twenties—all gone down in episodes of bravado played out in the
streets. I came to doubt the virtues of intimidation early on. I chose,
perhaps even unconsciously, to remain a shadow—timid, but a survivor.

The fearsomeness mistakenly attributed to me in public places   10
often has a perilous flavor. The most frightening of these confusions
occurred in the late 1970s and early 1980s when I worked as a journalist
in Chicago. One day, rushing into the office of a magazine I was
writing for with a deadline story in hand, I was mistaken for a burglar.
The office manager called security and, with an ad hoc posse, pursued
me through the labyrinthine halls, nearly to my editor's door. I had
no way of proving who I was. I could only move briskly toward the
company of someone who knew me.

Another time I was on assignment for a local paper and killing   11
time before an interview. I entered a jewelry store on the city's affluent
Near North Side. The proprietor excused herself and returned with
an enormous red Doberman pinscher straining at the end of a leash.
She stood, the dog extended toward me, silent to my questions, her
eyes bulging nearly out of her head. I took a cursory look around,
nodded, and bade her good night. Relatively speaking, however, I never
fared as badly as another black male journalist. He went to nearby
Waukegan, Illinois, a couple of summers ago to work on a story about
a murderer who was born there. Mistaking the reporter for the killer,
police hauled him from his car at gunpoint and but for his press credentials would probably have tried to book him. Such episodes are not
uncommon. Black men trade tales like this all the time.

In "My Negro Problem—And Ours," Podhoretz writes that the   12
hatred he feels for blacks makes itself known to him through a variety
of avenues—one being his discomfort with that "special brand of
paranoid touchiness" to which he says blacks are prone. No doubt
he is speaking here of black men. In time, I learned to smother the

rage I felt at so often being taken for a criminal. Not to do so would surely have led to madness—via that special "paranoid touchiness" that so annoyed Podhoretz at the time he wrote the essay.

I began to take precautions to make myself less threatening. I 13 move about with care, particularly late in the evening. I give a wide berth to nervous people on subway platforms during the wee hours, particularly when I have exchanged business clothes for jeans. If I happen to be entering a building behind some people who appear skittish, I may walk by, letting them clear the lobby before I return, so as not to seem to be following them. I have been calm and extremely congenial on those rare occasions when I've been pulled over by the police.

And on late-evening constitutionals along streets less traveled by, 14 I employ what has proved to be an excellent tension-reducing measure: I whistle melodies from Beethoven and Vivaldi and the more popular classical composers. Even steely New Yorkers hunching toward nighttime destinations seem to relax, and occasionally they even join in the tune. Virtually everybody seems to sense that a mugger wouldn't be warbling bright, sunny selections from Vivaldi's *Four Seasons*. It is my equivalent of the cowbell that hikers wear when they know they are in bear country.

RESPONDING TO READING

1. Staples speaks quite matter-of-factly of the fear he inspires. Does your experience support his assumption that black men have the "ability to alter public space?" Why or why not?   **2.** In paragraph 13 Staples suggests some strategies that he believes make him "less threatening." What else, if anything, could he do? Do you believe he *should* adopt such strategies? Explain your position.   **3.** Although Staples says he arouses fear in others, he also admits that he himself feels fearful. Why? Do you think he has reason to be fearful?

Children of Affluence

ROBERT COLES

Robert Coles (1929–   ) has been involved in social reform since the 1960s and is best known for his five-volume study of children and poverty, *Children of Crisis* (1967–1978), which won a Pulitzer Prize in 1973. Coles, a professor of psychiatry at the Harvard Medical School, has written about child psychology, civil rights, and literature. His books about writers include *William Carlos Williams: The Knack of Survival in America* (1975), *Walker Percy: An American Search* (1978), and *Flannery O'Connor's South* (1980). In "Children of Affluence," excerpted from *Children of Crisis*, Coles analyzes the effects of affluence on the young by presenting their words and experiences and then interpreting these in a social and psychological context.

It won't do to talk of *the* affluent in America. It won't do to say 1 that in our upper-middle-class suburbs, or among our wealthy, one observes clear-cut, consistent psychological or cultural characteristics. Even in relatively homogeneous places there are substantial differences in homelife, in values taught, hobbies encouraged, beliefs advocated or sometimes virtually instilled. But it is the obligation of a psychological observer like me, who wants to know how children make sense of a certain kind of life, to document as faithfully as possible the way a common heritage of money and power affects the assumptions of particular boys and girls.

I started my work with affluent children by seeing troubled boys 2 and girls; they were the ones I saw as a child psychiatrist *before* I began my years of "field work" in the South, then Appalachia, then the North, then the West. There are only a few hundred child psychiatrists in the United States, and often their time is claimed by those who have money. After a while, if one is not careful, the well-off and the rich come to be seen exclusively through a clinician's eye: homes full of bitterness, deceit, snobbishness, neuroses, psychoses; homes with young children in mental pain, and with older children, adolescents and young adults, who use drugs, drink, run away, rebel constantly and disruptively, become truants, delinquents, addicts, alcoholics, become compulsively promiscuous, go crazy, go wild, go to ruin.

We blame the alcoholism, insanity, meanness, apathy, drug 3 usage, despondency, and, not least, cruelty to children we see or are told exists in the ghetto or among the rural poor upon various "socioeconomic factors." All of those signs of psychological deterioration can be found among quite privileged families, too—and so we remind ourselves, perhaps, that wealth corrupts.

No—it is not that simple. Wealth does not corrupt nor does it 4 ennoble. But wealth does govern the minds of privileged children, gives them a peculiar kind of identity which they never lose, whether they grow up to be stockbrokers or communards,[1] and whether they lead healthy or unstable lives. There is, I think, a message that virtually all quite well-off American families transmit to their children—

---

[1]People who live in communes. [Eds.]

an emotional expression of those familiar, classbound prerogatives, money and power. I use the word "entitlement" to describe that message.

The word was given to me by the rather rich parents of a child I 5 began to talk with almost two decades ago, in 1959. I have watched those parents become grandparents, and have seen what they described as "the responsibilities of entitlement" handed down to a new generation. When the father, a lawyer and stockbroker from a prominent and quietly influential family, referred to the "entitlement" his children were growing up to know, he had in mind a social rather than a psychological phenomenon: the various juries or committees that select the Mardi Gras participants in New Orlean's annual parade and celebration. He knew that his daughter was "entitled" to be invited.

He wanted, however, to go beyond that social fact. He talked 6 about what he had received from his parents and what he would give to his children, "automatically, without any thought," and what they too would pass on. The father was careful to distinguish between the social entitlement and "something else," a "something else" he couldn't quite define but knew he had to try to evoke if he was to be psychologically candid: "I mean they should be responsible, and try to live up to their ideals, and not just sit around wondering which island in the Caribbean to visit this year, and where to go next summer to get away from the heat and humidity here in New Orleans."

He was worried about what a lot of money can do to a personality. 7 When his young daughter, during a Mardi Gras season, kept *assuming* she would one day become a Mardi Gras queen, he realized that his notion of "entitlement" was not quite hers. Noblesse oblige requires a gesture toward others.

He was not the only parent to express such a concern to me in 8 the course of my work. In homes where mothers and fathers profess no explicit reformist persuasions, they nevertheless worry about what happens to children who grow up surrounded by just about everything they want, virtually on demand. "When they're like that, they've gone from spoiled to spoiled rotten—and beyond, to some state I don't know how to describe."

Obviously, it is possible for parents to have a lot of money yet 9 avoid bringing up their children in such a way that they feel like members of a royal family. But even parents determined not to spoil their children often recognize what might be called the existential (as opposed to strictly psychological) aspects of their situation. A father may begin rather early on lecturing his children about the meaning

TEACHING STRATEGY

Coles's prose is direct and honest, and his explication is rendered in a clear, straightforward manner. Therefore, the essay lends itself to analysis at the paragraph level. As your students work through the essay, have them analyze transitions, topic sentences, and paragraph development.

of money; a mother may do her share by saying no, even when yes is so easy to say. And a child, by the age of five or six, has very definite notions of what is possible, even if it is not always permitted. That child, in conversation, and without embarrassment or the kind of reticence and secretiveness that come later, may reveal a substantial knowledge of economic affairs. A six-year-old girl I spoke to knew that she would, at twenty-one, inherit half a million dollars. She also knew that her father "only" gave her twenty-five cents a week, whereas some friends of hers received as much as a dollar. She was vexed; she asked her parents why they were so "strict." One friend had even used the word "stingy" for the parents. The father, in a matter-of-fact way, pointed out to the daughter that she did, after all, get "anything she really wants." Why, then, the need for an extravagant allowance? The girl was won over. But admonitions don't always modify the quite realistic appraisal children make of what they are heir to; and they don't diminish their sense of entitlement—a state of mind that pervades their view of the world.

In an Appalachian home, for instance, a boy of seven made the 10 following comment in 1963, after a mine his father owned had suffered an explosion, killing two men and injuring seriously nine others: "I heard my mother saying she felt sorry for the families of the miners. I feel sorry for them, too. I hope the men who got hurt get better. I'm sure they will. My father has called in doctors from Lexington. He wants the best doctors in all Kentucky for those miners. Daddy says it was the miners' fault; they get careless, and the next thing you know, there's an explosion. It's too bad. I guess there are a lot of kids who are praying hard for their fathers. I wish God was nice to everyone. He's been very good to us. My daddy says it's been hard work, running the mine, and another one he has. It's just as hard to run a mine as it is to go down and dig the coal! I'm glad my father is the owner, though. I wouldn't want him to get killed or hurt bad down there, way underground. Daddy has given us a good life. We have a lot of fun coming up, he says, in the next few years. We're going on some trips. Daddy deserves his vacations. He says he's happy because he can keep us happy, and he does."

Abundance is this boy's destiny, he has every reason to believe, 11 abundance and limitless possibility. He may even land on the stars. Certainly he has traveled widely in this country. He associates the seasons with travel. In winter, there is a trip south, to one or another Caribbean island. He worries, on these trips, about his two dogs, and the other animals—the guinea pigs, hamsters, rabbits, chickens. There is always someone in the house, a maid, a handyman. Still it is sad to say good-bye. Now if the family owned a plane, the animals could come along on those trips!

The boy doesn't really believe that his father will ever own a Lear 12 jet; yet he can construct a fantasy: "I had this dream. In it I was walking through the woods with Daddy, and all of a sudden there was an open field, and I looked, and I saw a hawk, and it was circling and circling. I like going hunting with Daddy, and I thought we were hunting. But when I looked at him, he didn't have his gun. Then he pointed at the hawk, and it was coming down. It landed ahead of us, and it was real strange—because the hawk turned into an airplane! I couldn't believe it. We went toward the plane, and Daddy said we could get a ride anytime we wanted, because it was ours; he'd just bought it. That's when I woke up, I think."

Four years after the boy dreamed that his father owned a plane, 13 the father got one. The boom of the 1970s in the coal fields made his father even richer. The boy was, of course, eager to go on flying trips; eager, also, to learn to fly. At thirteen, he dreamed (by day) of becoming an astronaut, or of going to the Air Force Academy and afterwards becoming a "supersonic pilot."

He would never become a commercial pilot, however; and his 14 reasons were interesting. "I've gone on a lot of commercial flights, and there are a lot of people on board, and the pilot has to be nice to everyone, and he makes all these announcements about the seat belts, and stuff like that. My dad's pilot was in the Air Force, and then he flew commercial. He was glad to get out, though. He says you have to be like a waiter; you have to answer complaints from the customers, and apologize to them, just because the ride gets bumpy. It's best to work for yourself, or work for another person, if you trust him and like him. If you go commercial, like our pilot says, you're a servant."

Many of the children I have worked with are similarly disposed; 15 they do not like large groups of people in public places—in fact, have been taught the value not only of privacy but of the quiet that goes with being relatively alone. Some of the children are afraid of those crowds, can't imagine how it would be possible to survive them. Of course, what is strange, unknown, or portrayed as unattractive, uncomfortable, or just to be avoided as a nuisance can for a given child become a source of curiosity, like an event to be experienced at all costs. An eight-year-old girl who lived on a farm well outside Boston wanted desperately to go to the city and see Santa Claus— not because she believed in him, but because she wanted to see "those crowds" she had seen on television. She got her wish, was excited at first, then became quite disappointed, and ultimately uncomfortable. She didn't like being jostled, shoved, and ignored when she protested.

A week after the girl had gone through her Boston "adventure" 16
(as she had called the trip *before* she embarked upon it), each student
in her third-grade class was asked to draw a picture in some way
connected to the Christmas season, and the girl obliged eagerly. She
drew Santa Claus standing beside a pile of packages, presents for the
many children who stood near him. They blended into one another—
a mob scene. Watching them but removed from them was one child,
bigger and on a higher level—suspended in space, it seemed, and
partially surrounded by a thin but visible line. The girl wrote on the
bottom of the drawing, "I saw Santa Claus." She made it quite clear
what she had intended to portray. "He was standing there, handing
out these gifts. They were all the same, I think, and they were plastic
squirt guns for the boys and little dolls for the girls. I felt sorry for
the kids. I asked my mother why kids wanted to push each other,
just to get that junk. My mother said a lot of people just don't know
any better. I was going to force my way up to Santa Claus and tell
him to stop being so dumb! My mother said he was probably a drunk,
trying to make a few dollars so he could spend it in a bar that evening!
I don't want to be in a store like that again. We went up to a balcony
and watched, and then we got out of the place and came home.
I told my mother that I didn't care if I ever went to Boston again. I
have two friends, and they've never been to Boston, and they don't
want to go there, except to ride through on the way to the airport."

She sounded at that moment more aloof, condescending, and 17
snobbish than she ordinarily is. She spends her time with two or three
girls who live on nearby estates. Those girls don't see each other
regularly, and each of them is quite able to be alone—in fact, rather
anxious for those times of solitude. Sometimes a day or two goes by
with no formal arrangement to play. They meet in school, and that
seems to be enough. Each girl has obligations—a horse to groom, a
stall to work on. They are quite "self-sufficient," a word they have
heard used repeatedly by their parents. Even with one's own social
circle there is no point surrendering to excessive gregariousness!

Once up on her own horse, she is (by her own description) in 18
her "own world." She has heard her mother use that expression. The
mother is not boasting, or dismissing others who live in other worlds.
The mother is describing, as does the child, a state of progressive
withdrawal from people, and the familiar routines or objects of the
environment, in favor of a mixture of reverie and disciplined activity.

Nothing seems impossible, burdensome, difficult. There are no 19
distractions, petty or boring details to attend to. And one is closer to
one's "self." The mother talks about the "self," and the child does,
too. "It is strange," the girl comments, "because you forget yourself
riding or skiing, but you also remember yourself the way you don't

when you're just sitting around watching television or reading or playing in your room."

None of the other American children I have worked with have 20 placed such a continuous and strong emphasis on the "self"—its display, its possibilities, its cultivation and development, even the repeated use of the word *self*. A ten-year-old boy who lived in Westchester County made this very clear. I met him originally because his parents were lawyers, and active in the civil rights movement. His father, a patrician Yankee, very much endorsed the students who went south in the early 1960s, and worked on behalf of integrated schools up north. The boy, however, attended private schools—a source of anguish to both father and son, who do not lend themselves to a description that suggests hypocrisy.

The boy knew that he, also, *would* be (as opposed to *wanted* to 21 be) a lawyer. He was quick to perceive and acknowledge his situation, and as he did so, he brought his "self" right into the discussion: "I don't want to tell other kids what to do. I told my father I should be going to the public schools myself. Then I could say anything. Then I could ask why we don't have black kids with us in school. But you have to try to do what's best for your own life, even if you can't speak up for the black people. When I'm grown up I'll be like my father; I'll help the black people all I can. It's this way: first you build *yourself* up. You learn all you can. Later, you can *give of yourself*. That's what Dad says: you can't help others until you've learned to help yourself. It's not that you're being selfish, if you're going to a private school and your parents have a lot of money. We had a maid here, and she wasn't right in the head. She lost her temper and told Daddy that he's a phony, and he's out for himself and no one else, and the same goes for my sister and me. Then she quit. Daddy tried to get her to talk with us, but she wouldn't. She said that's all we ever do—talk, talk. I told Daddy she was contradicting herself, because she told me a few weeks ago that I'm always doing something, and I should sit down and talk with her. But I don't know what to say to her! I think she got angry with me, because I was putting on my skis, for cross-country skiing, and she said I had too much, that was my problem. I asked her where the regular skis were, and she said she wouldn't tell me, even if she knew! It's too bad, what happened to her.

"I feel sorry for her, though. It's not fun to be a maid. The poor 22 woman doesn't look very good. She weighs too much. She's only forty, my mother thinks, but she looks as if she's sixty, and is sick. She should take better care of herself. Now she's thrown away this job, and she told my mother last year that it was the best one she'd ever had, so she's her own worst enemy. I wonder what she'll think when she looks at herself in the mirror."

This boy was no budding egotist. If anything, he was less self-centered at ten than many other children of his community and others like it. He was willing to think about those less fortunate than himself—the maid, and black people in general. True, he would often repeat uncritically his father's words, or a version of them. But he was trying to respond to his father's wishes and beliefs as well as his words. It was impossible for him, no matter how compassionate his nature, to conceive of life as others live it—the maid and, yes, millions of children his age, who don't look in the mirror very often, and may not even own one; who don't worry about how one looks, and what is said, and how one sounds, and how one smells. 23

It is important that a child's sense of entitlement be distinguished not only from the psychiatric dangers of narcissism but from the less pathological and not all that uncommon phenomenon known as being "spoiled." It is a matter of degree; "spoiled" children are self-centered all right, petulant and demanding—but not as grandiose or, alas, saddled with illusions (or delusions) as the children clinicians have in mind when using the phrase "narcissistic entitlement." The rich or quite well-to-do are all too commonly charged with producing spoiled children. Yet one sees spoiled children everywhere, among the very poor as well as the inordinately rich. 24

In one of the first wealthy families I came to know there was a girl who was described by both parents as "spoiled." At the time, I fear, I was ready to pronounce every child in New Orleans's Garden District spoiled. Were they not all living comfortable, indeed luxurious, lives, as compared to the lives of the black or working-class white children I was getting to know in other sections of that city? 25

Nevertheless, I soon began to realize that it wouldn't do to characterize without qualification one set of children as spoiled, by virtue of their social and economic background, as against another set of children who were obviously less fortunate in many respects. One meets, among the rich, restrained, disciplined, and by no means indulged children; sometimes, even, boys and girls who have learned to be remarkably self-critical, even ascetic—anything but "spoiled" in the conventional sense of the word. True, one can find a touch and more of arrogance, or at least sustained self-assurance, in those apparently spartan boys and girls who seem quite anxious to deny themselves all sorts of presumably accessible privileges if not luxuries. But one also finds in these children a consistent willingness to place serious and not always pleasant burdens on themselves—to the point where they often struck me, when I came to their homes fresh from visits with much poorer age-mates, as remarkably *less* spoiled: not so much whining or crying; fewer demands for candy or other sweets; 26

even, sometimes, a relative indifference to toys, however near at hand and expensive they may have been; a disregard of television—so often demanded by the children that I was seeing.

A New Orleans black woman said to me in 1961: "I don't know   27
how to figure out these rich white kids. They're something! I used to think, before I took a job with this family, that the only difference between a rich kid and a poor kid is that the rich kid knows he has a lot of money and he grows up and becomes spoiled rotten. That's what my mother told me; she took care of a white girl, and the girl was an only child, and her father owned a department store in McComb, Mississippi, and that girl thought she was God's special creature. My mother used to come home and tell us about the 'little princess;' but she turned out to be no good. She was so pampered, she couldn't do a thing for herself. All she knew how to do was order people around.

"It's different with these two children. I've never seen such a boy   28
and such a girl. They think they're the best ones who ever lived—like that girl in McComb—but they don't behave like her. They're never asking me to do much of anything. They even ask if they can help me! They tell me that they want to know how to do everything. The girl says she wants to learn how to run the washing machine and the dishwasher. She says she wants to learn all my secret recipes. She says she'd like to give the best parties in the Garden District when she grows up, and she'd like to be able to give them without anyone's help. She says I could serve the food, but she would like to make it. The boy says he's going to be a lawyer and a banker, so he wants to know how much everything costs. He doesn't want to waste anything. He'll see me throw something away, and he wants to know why. I only wish that my own kids were like him!

"But these children here are special, and don't they know it! That's   29
what being rich is: you know you're different from most people. These two kids act as if they're going to be tops in everything, and they're pleased as can be with themselves, because there is nothing they can't do, and there's nothing they can't get, and there's nothing they can't win, and they're always showing off what they can do, and then before you can tell them how good they are, they're telling the same thing to themselves. It's confusing! They're not spoiled one bit, but oh, they have a high opinion of themselves!"

Actually, children like the ones she speaks of don't allow them-   30
selves quite the unqualified confidence she describes, though she certainly has correctly conveyed the appearance they give. Boys and girls may seem without anxiety or self-doubt; they have been brought up, as the maid suggests, to feel important, superior, destined for a

satisfying, rewarding life—and at, say, eight or nine they already appear to know all that. Yet there are moments of hesitation, if not apprehension. An eleven-year-old boy from a prominent and quite brilliant Massachusetts family told his teachers, in an autobiographical composition about the vicissitudes of "entitlement:" "I don't always do everything right. I'd like to be able to say I don't make any mistakes, but I do, and when I do, I feel bad. My father and mother say that if you train yourself, you can be right *almost* 100 percent of the time. Even they make mistakes, though. I like to be first in sports. I like to beat my brothers at skiing. But I don't always go down the slopes as fast as I could and I sometimes fall down. Last year I broke my leg. When I get a bad cold, I feel disappointed in myself. I don't think it's right to be easy on yourself. If you are, then you slip back, and you don't get a lot of the rewards in life. If you really work for the rewards, you'll get them."

A platitude—the kind of assurance his teachers, as a matter of 31 fact, have rather often given him. In the fourth grade, for instance, the teacher had this written on the blackboard (and kept it there for weeks): "Those who want something badly enough get it, provided they are willing to wait and work." The boy considers that assertion neither banal nor unrealistic. He has been brought up to believe that such is and will be (for him) the case. He knows that others are not so lucky, but he hasn't really met those "others," and they don't cross his mind at all. What does occur to him sometimes is the need for constant exertion, lest he fail to "measure up." One "measures up" when one tries hard and succeeds. If one slackens or stumbles, one ought to be firm with oneself—but not in any self-pitying or self-excusing or self-paralyzing way. The emphasis is on a quick and efficient moment of scrutiny followed by "a fast pick-up."

Such counsel is not as callous as it may sound—or, ironically, as 32 it may well have been intended to sound. The child who hears it gets, briefly, upset; but unless he or she stops heeding what has been said, quite often "a fast pick-up" does indeed take place—an effort to redeem what has been missed or lost, or only somewhat accomplished. Again, it is a matter of feeling entitled. A child who has been told repeatedly that all he or she needs to do is try hard does not feel inclined to allow himself or herself long stretches of time for skeptical self-examination. The point is to feel *entitled*—then act upon that feeling. The boy whose composition was just quoted from used the word "entitled" in another essay he wrote, this one meant to be a description of his younger (age five) brother. The writing was not, however, without an autobiographical strain to it: "I was watching my brother from my bedroom window. He was climbing up the fence we built for our corral. He got to the top, and then he just stood there and waved and shouted. No one was there. He was talking to himself. He was very happy. Then he would fall. He would be upset for a few seconds, but he would climb right back up again. Then he would be even happier! He was entitled to be happy. It is his fence, and he has learned to climb it, and stay up, and balance himself."

RESPONDING TO READING

1. Does Coles believe that the message affluent families convey to their children—what he calls "entitlement"—is a privilege or a burden? Which do you believe it is? Why? Do you think you have this sense of entitlement? Explain.   **2.** Affluent children have very different attitudes toward their futures than their poorer counterparts. Which of your attitudes about your future have been shaped by your economic status?   **3.** Do you think the affluent children Coles describes are likely to make a valuable contribution to the world in which they live? Explain your conclusion.

It's Just Too Late

CALVIN TRILLIN

Calvin Trillin (1935–   ) is probably best known for his humorous writing about food: *American Fried* (1974), *Alice, Let's Eat* (1978), and *Third Helpings* (1983). In fact, he is a versatile writer of fiction, reportage, and political commentary. Trillin was a reporter for *Time*, a staff writer for *The New Yorker*, and a columnist for the *Nation*. *Uncivil Liberties* (1982), *With All Due Disrespect* (1985), and *If You Can't Say Something Nice* (1987) are all collections of his columns from the *Nation*. The following essay, in which Trillin looks at the tragic death of a teenage girl killed in a car chase, first appeared in Trillin's series "U.S. Journal," written for *The New Yorker* and was collected in *Killings* (1984).

Knoxsville, Tennessee
March 1979

Until she was sixteen, FaNee Cooper was what her parents sometimes called an ideal child. "You'd never have to correct her," FaNee's mother has said. In sixth grade, FaNee won a spelling contest. She played the piano and the flute. She seemed to believe what she heard every Sunday at the Beaver Dam Baptist Church about good and evil and the hereafter. FaNee was not an outgoing child. Even as a baby, she was uncomfortable when she was held and cuddled. She found it easy to tell her parents she loved them but difficult to confide in

1

ADDITIONAL QUESTIONS FOR RESPONDING TO READING

1. Why do teenagers associate themselves with specific "crowds"? Discuss how this association helps develop self-image.
2. What are the responsibilities of a parent concerning a teenager's choice of friends? Should a parent tell a teenager what friends he or she can and cannot have?
3. When teenagers seem to be preoccupied with death, should parents and teachers ignore their interest in death, viewing it as a stage or as romantic posing, or should they take some action? What kind of action is appropriate? Why are so many teenagers attracted to the concept of death?
4. Why does Leo Cooper cry when the jury finds Stevens guilty? Is the jury's decision in any way a vindication of his actions? Explain.

them. Particularly compared to her sister, Kristy, a cheerful, open little girl two and a half years younger, she was reserved and introspective. The thoughts she kept to herself, though, were apparently happy thoughts. Her eighth-grade essay on Christmas—written in a remarkably neat hand—talked of the joys of helping put together toys for her little brother, Leo, Jr., and the importance of her parents' reminder that Christmas is the birthday of Jesus. Her parents were the sort of people who might have been expected to have an ideal child. As a boy, Leo Cooper had been called "one of the greatest high-school basketball players ever developed in Knox County." He went on to play basketball at East Tennessee State, and he married the homecoming queen, JoAnn Henson. After college, Cooper became a high-school basketball coach and teacher and, eventually, an administrator. By the time FaNee turned thirteen, in 1973, he was in his third year as the principal of Gresham Junior High School, in Fountain City—a small Knox County town that had been swallowed up by Knoxville when the suburbs began to move north. A tall man, with curly black hair going on gray, Leo Cooper has an elaborate way of talking ("Unless I'm very badly mistaken, he has never related to me totally the content of his conversation") and a manner that may come from years of trying to leave errant junior-high-school students with the impression that a responsible adult is magnanimous, even humble, about invariably being in the right. His wife, a high-school art teacher, paints and does batik, and created the name FaNee because she liked the way it looked and sounded—it sounds like "Fawn*ee*" when the Coopers say it—but the impression she gives is not of artiness but of soft-spoken small-town gentility. When she found, in the course of cleaning up FaNee's room, that her ideal thirteen-year-old had been smoking cigarettes, she was, in her words, crushed. "FaNee was such a perfect child before that," JoAnn Cooper said some time later. "She was angry that we found out. She knew we knew that she had done something we didn't approve of, and then the rebellion started. I was hurt. I was very hurt. I guess it came through as disappointment."

Several months later, FaNee's grandmother died. FaNee had been devoted to her grandmother. She wrote a poem in her memory—an almost joyous poem, filled with Christian faith in the afterlife ("Please don't grieve over my happiness/Rejoice with me in the presence of the Angels of Heaven"). She also took some keepsakes from her grandmother's house, and was apparently mortified when her parents found them and explained that they would have to be returned. By then, the Coopers were aware that FaNee was going to have a difficult time as a teenager. They thought she might be self-conscious about the double affliction of glasses and braces. They thought she might be uncomfortable in the role of the principal's daughter at Gresham. In ninth grade, she entered Halls High School, where JoAnn Cooper was teaching art. FaNee was a loner at first. Then she fell in with what could only be considered a bad crowd.

Halls, a few miles to the north of Fountain City, used to be known as Halls Crossroads. It is what Knoxville people call "over the ridge"— on the side of Black Oak Ridge that has always been thought of as rural. When FaNee entered Halls High, the Coopers were already in the process of building a house on several acres of land they had bought in Halls, in a sparsely settled area along Brown Gap road. Like two or three other houses along the road, it was to be constructed basically of huge logs taken from old buildings—a house that Leo Cooper describes as being, like the name FaNee, "just a little bit different." Ten years ago, Halls Crossroads was literally a crossroads. Then some of the Knoxville expansion that had swollen Fountain City spilled over the ridge, planting subdivisions here and there on roads that still went for long stretches with nothing but an occasional house with a cow or two next to it. The increase in population did not create a town. Halls has no center. Its commercial area is a series of two or three shopping centers strung together on the Maynardville Highway, the four-lane that leads north into Union County—a place almost synonymous in east Tennessee with mountain poverty. Its restaurant is the Halls Freezo Drive-In. The gathering place for the group FaNee Cooper eventually found herself in was the Maynardville Highway Exxon station.

At Halls High School, the social poles were represented by the Jocks and the Freaks. FaNee found her friends among the Freaks. "I am truly enlighted upon irregular trains of thought aimed at strange depots of mental wards," she wrote when she was fifteen. "Yes! Crazed farms for the mental off—Oh! I walked through the halls screams & loud laughter fill my ears—Orderlys try to reason with me—but I am unreasonable! The joys of being a FREAK in a circus of imagination." The little crowd of eight or ten young people that FaNee joined has been referred to by her mother as "the Union County group." A couple of the girls were from backgrounds similar to FaNee's, but all the boys had the characteristics, if not the precise addresses, that Knoxville people associate with the poor whites of Union County. They were the sort of boys who didn't bother to finish high school, or finished it in a special program for slow learners, or get ejected from it for taking a swing at the principal.

"I guess you can say they more or less dragged us down to their level with the drugs," a girl who was in the group—a girl who can be called Marcia—said recently. "And somehow we settled for it. It seems like we had to get ourselves in the pit before we could look

TEACHING STRATEGY

Most college students, many of whom were recently in high school themselves, will have an opinion on what the parents should have done in this essay. The class may also consider the implications of FaNee's statement "It's just too late." Why would she say it? Is she right?

COLLABORATIVE ACTIVITY

Ask students to work in groups to compile lists of popular rock music lyrics that deal with death. Then have each group read its list to the class, and ask the class to consider whether lyrics such as these have any causal connection with adolescents' preoccupation with death. For example, do your students believe, as some individuals and groups do, that such lyrics encourage suicide? (You might mention that performers, such as Ozzy Osborne, have been sued—so far, unsuccessfully—for their supposed roles in teenagers' suicides.)

out." People in the group used marijuana and Valium and LSD. They sneered at the Jocks and the "prim and proper little ladies" who went with Jocks. "We set ourselves aside," Marcia now says. "We put ourselves above everyone. How we did that I don't know." In a Knox County high school, teenagers who want to get themselves in the pit need not mainline heroin. The Jocks they mean to be compared to do not merely show up regularly for classes and practice football and wear clean clothes; they watch their language and preach temperance and go to prayer meetings on Wednesday nights and talk about having a real good Christian witness. Around Knoxville, people who speak of well-behaved high-school kids often seem to use words like "perfect," or even "angels." For FaNee's group, the opposite was not difficult to figure out. "We were into wicked things, strange things," Marcia says. "It was like we were on some kind of devil trip." FaNee wrote about demons and vultures and rats. "Slithering serpents eat my sanity and bite my ass," she wrote in an essay called "The Lovely Road of Life," just after she turned sixteen, "while tornadoes derail and ever so swiftly destroy every car in my train of thought." She wrote a lot about death.

FaNee's girl friends spoke of her as "super-intelligent." Her English teacher found some of her writing profound—and disturbing. She was thought to be not just super-intelligent but super-mysterious, and even, at times, super-weird—an introverted girl who stared straight ahead with deep-brown, nearly black eyes and seemed to have thoughts she couldn't share. Nobody really knew why she had chosen to run with the Freaks—whether it was loneliness or rebellion or simple boredom. Marcia thought it might have had something to do with a feeling that her parents had settled on Kristy as their perfect child. "I guess she figured she couldn't be the best," Marcia said recently. "So she decided she might as well be the worst." 6

Toward the spring of FaNee's junior year at Halls, her problems seemed to deepen. Despite her intelligence, her grades were sliding. She was what her mother called "a mental dropout." Leo Cooper had to visit Halls twice because of minor suspensions. Once, FaNee had been caught smoking. Once, having ducked out of a required assembly, she was spotted by a favorite teacher, who turned her in. At home, she exchanged little more than short, strained formalities with Kristy, who shared their parents' opinion of FaNee's choice of friends. The Coopers had finished their house—a large house, its size accentuated by the huge old logs and a great stone fireplace and outsize "Paul Bunyan"-style furniture—but FaNee spent most of her time there in her own room, sleeping or listening to rock music through earphones. One night, there was a terrible scene when FaNee returned from a concert in a condition that Leo Cooper knew had to 7 be the result of marijuana. JoAnn Cooper, who ordinarily strikes people as too gentle to raise her voice, found herself losing her temper regularly. Finally, Leo Cooper asked a counsellor he knew, Jim Griffin, to stop in at Halls High School and have a talk with FaNee—unofficially.

Griffin—a young man with a warm, informal manner—worked   8
for the Juvenile Court of Knox County. He had a reputation for being able to reach teenagers who wouldn't talk to their parents or to school administrators. One Friday in March of 1977, he spent an hour and a half talking to FaNee Cooper. As Griffin recalls the interview, FaNee didn't seem alarmed by his presence. She seemed to him calm and controlled—Griffin thought it was something like talking to another adult—and, unlike most of the teenagers he dealt with, she looked him in the eye the entire time. Griffin, like some of FaNee's friends, found her eyes unsettling—"the coldest, most distant, but, at the same time, the most knowing eyes I'd ever seen." She expressed affection for her parents, but she didn't seem interested in exploring ways of getting along better with them. The impression she gave Griffin was that they were who they were, and she was who she was, and there didn't happen to be any connection. Several times, she made the same response to Griffin's suggestions: "It's too late."

That weekend, neither FaNee nor her parents brought up the   9
subject of Griffin's visit. Leo Cooper has spoken of the weekend as being particularly happy; a friend of FaNee's who stayed over remembers it as particularly strained. FaNee stayed home from school on Monday because of a bad headache—she often had bad headaches—but felt well enough on Monday evening to drive to the library. She was to be home at nine. When she wasn't, Mrs. Cooper began to phone her friends. Finally, around ten, Leo Cooper got into his other car and took a swing around Halls—past the teenage hangouts like the Exxon station and the Pizza Hut and the Smoky Mountain Market. Then he took a second swing. At eleven, FaNee was still not home.

She hadn't gone to the library. She had picked up two girl friends   10
and driven to the home of a third, where everyone took five Valium tablets. Then the four girls drove over to the Exxon station, where they met four boys from their crowd. After a while, the group bought some beer and some marijuana and reassembled at Charlie Stevens's trailer. Charlie Stevens was five or six years older than everyone else in the group—a skinny, slow-thinking young man with long black hair and a sparse beard. He was married and had a child, but he and his wife had separated; she was back in Union County with the baby. Stevens had remained in their trailer—parked in the yard near his mother's house, in a back-road area of Knox County dominated by

decrepit, unpainted sheds and run-down trailers and rusted-out automobiles. Stevens had picked up FaNee at home once or twice—apparently, more as a driver for the group than as a date—and the Coopers, having learned that his unsuitability extended to being married, had asked her not to see him.

In Charlie's trailer, which had no heat or electricity, the group 11 drank beer and passed around joints, keeping warm with blankets. By eleven or so, FaNee was what one of her friends has called "super-messed-up." Her speech was slurred. She was having trouble keeping her balance. She had decided not to go home. She had apparently persuaded herself that her parents intended to send her away to some sort of home for incorrigibles. "It's too late," she said to one of her friends. "It's just too late." It was decided that one of the boys, David Munsey, who was more or less the leader of the group, would drive the Coopers' car to FaNee's house, where FaNee and Charlie Stevens would pick him up in Stevens's car—a worn Pinto with four bald tires, one light, and a dragging muffler. FaNee wrote a note to her parents, and then, perhaps because her handwriting was suffering the effects of beer and marijuana and Valium, asked Stevens to rewrite it on a large piece of paper, which would be left on the seat of the Coopers' car. The Stevens version was just about the same as FaNee's, except that Stevens left out a couple of sentences about trying to work things out ("I'm willing to try") and, not having won any spelling championship himself, he misspelled a few words, like "tomorrow." The note said, "Dear Mom and Dad. Sorry I'm late. Very late. I left your car because I thought you might need it tomorrow. I love you all, but this is something I just had to do. The man talked to me privately for one and a half hours and I was really scared, so this is something I just had to do, but don't worry. I'm with a very good friend. Love you all. FaNee. P.S. Please try to understand I love you all very much, really I do. Love me if you have a chance."

At eleven-thirty or so, Leo Cooper was sitting in his living room, 12 looking out the window at his driveway—a long gravel road that runs almost four hundred feet from the house to Brown Gap Road. He saw the car that FaNee had been driving pull into the driveway. "She's home," he called to his wife, who had just left the room. Cooper walked out on the deck over the garage. The car had stopped at the end of the driveway, and the lights had gone out. He got into his other car and drove to the end of the driveway. David Munsey had already joined Charlie Stevens and FaNee, and the Pinto was just leaving, travelling at a normal rate of speed. Leo Cooper pulled out on the road behind them.

Stevens turned left on Crippen Road, a road that has a field on 13 one side and two or three small houses on the other, and there Cooper pulled his car in front of the Pinto and stopped, blocking the way.

He got out and walked toward the Pinto. Suddenly, Stevens put the car in reverse, backed into a driveway a hundred yards behind him, and sped off. Cooper jumped in his car and gave chase. Stevens raced back to Brown Gap Road, ran a stop sign there, ran another stop sign at Maynardville Highway, turned north, veered off onto the old Andersonville Pike, a nearly abandoned road that runs parallel to the highway, and then crossed back over the highway to the narrow, dark country roads on the other side. Stevens sometimes drove with his lights out. He took some of the corners by suddenly applying his hand brake to make the car swerve around in a ninety-degree turn. He was in familiar territory—he actually passed his trailer—and Cooper had difficulty keeping up. Past the trailer, Stevens swept down a hill into a sharp left turn that took him onto Foust Hollow Road, a winding, hilly road not much wider than one car.

At a fork, Cooper thought he had lost the Pinto. He started to go 14 right and then saw what seemed to be a spark from Stevens's dragging muffler off to the left, in the darkness. Cooper took the left fork, down Salem Church Road. He went down a hill and then up a long, curving hill to a crest, where he saw the Stevens car ahead. "I saw the car airborne. Up in the air," he later testified. "It was up in the air. And then it completely rolled over one more time. It started to make another flip forward, and just as it started to flip to the other side it flipped back this way, and my daughter's body came out."

Cooper slammed on his brakes and skidded to a stop up against 15 the Pinto. "Book!" Stevens shouted—the group's equivalent of "Scram!" Stevens and Munsey disappeared into the darkness. "It was dark, no one around, and so I started yelling for FaNee," Cooper had testified. "I thought it was an eternity before I could find her body, wedged under the back end of that car. . . . I tried everything I could, and saw that I couldn't get her loose. So I ran to a trailer back up to the top of the hill back up there to try to get that lady to call to get me some help, and then apparently she didn't think that I was serious. . . . I took the jack out of my car and got under, and it was dark, still couldn't see too much what was going on . . . and started prying and got her loose, and I don't know how. And then I dragged her over to the side, and, of course, at the time I felt reasonably assured that she was gone, because her head was completely—on one side just as if you had taken a sledgehammer and just hit it and bashed it in. And I did have the pleasure of one thing. I had the pleasure of listening to her breathe about the last three times she ever breathed in her life."

David Munsey did not return to the wreck that night, but Charlie 16 Stevens did. Leo Cooper was kneeling next to his daughter's body. Cooper insisted that Stevens come close enough to see FaNee. "He was kneeling down next to her," Stevens later testified. "And he said, 'Do you know what you've done? Do you really know what you've done?' Like that. And I just looked at her, and I said. 'Yes,' and just stood there. Because I couldn't say nothing." There was, of course, a legal decision to be made about who was responsible for FaNee Cooper's death. In a deposition, Stevens said he had been fleeing for his life. He testified that when Leo Cooper blocked Crippen Road, FaNee had said that her father had a gun and intended to hurt them. Stevens was bound over and eventually indicted for involuntary man-slaughter. Leo Cooper testified that when he approached the Pinto on Crippen Road, FaNee had a strange expression that he had never seen before. "It wasn't like FaNee, and I knew something was wrong," he said. "My concern was to get FaNee out of the car." The district attorney's office asked that Cooper be bound over for reckless driving, but the judge declined to do so. "Any father would have done what he did," the judge said. "I can see no criminal act on the part of Mr. Cooper."

Almost two years passed before Charlie Stevens was brought to 17 trial. Part of the problem was assuring the presence of David Munsey, who had joined the Navy but seemed inclined to assign his own leaves. In the meantime, the Coopers went to court with a civil suit—they had "uninsured-motorist coverage," which requires their insurance company to cover any defendant who has no insurance of his own—and they won a judgment. There were ways of assigning responsibility, of course, which had nothing to do with the law, civil or criminal. A lot of people in Knoxville thought that Leo Cooper had, in the words of his lawyer, "done what any daddy worth his salt would have done." There were others who believed that FaNee Cooper had lost her life because Leo Cooper had lost his temper. Leo Cooper was not among those who expressed any doubts about his actions. Unlike his wife, whose eyes filled with tears at almost any mention of FaNee, Cooper seemed able, even eager to go over the details of the accident again and again. With the help of a school-board security man, he conducted his own investigation. He drove over the route dozens of times. "I've thought about it every day, and I guess I will the rest of my life," he said as he and his lawyer and the prosecuting attorney went over the route again the day before Charlie Stevens's trial finally began. "But I can't tell any alternative for a father. I simply wanted her out of that car. I'd have done the same thing again, even at the risk of losing her."

Tennessee law permits the family of a victim to hire a special 18 prosecutor to assist the district attorney. The lawyer who acted for the Coopers in the civil case helped prosecute Charlie Stevens. Both he and the district attorney assured the jurors that the presence of a special prosecutor was not to be construed to mean that the Coopers were vindictive. Outside the courtroom, Leo Cooper said that the verdict was of no importance to him—that he felt sorry, in a way, for Charlie Stevens. But there were people in Knoxville who thought Cooper had a lot riding on the prosecution of Charlie Stevens. If Stevens was not guilty of FaNee Cooper's death—found so by twelve of his peers—who was?

At the trial, Cooper testified emotionally and remarkably graph- 19 ically about pulling FaNee out from under the car and watching her die in his arms. Charlie Stevens had shaved his beard and cut his hair, but the effort did not transform him into an impressive witness. His lawyer—trying to argue that it would have been impossible for Stevens to concoct the story about FaNee's having mentioned a gun, as the prosecution strongly implied—said, "His mind is such that if you ask him a question you can hear his mind go around, like an old mill creaking." Stevens did not deny the recklessness of his driving or the sorry condition of his car. It happened to be the only car he had available to flee in, he said, and he had fled in fear for his life.

The prosecution said that Stevens could have let FaNee out of 20 the car when her father stopped them, or could have gone to the commercial strip on the Maynardville Highway for protection. The prosecution said that Leo Cooper had done what he might have been expected to do under the circumstances—alone, late at night, his daughter in danger. The defense said precisely the same about Stevens: he had done what he might have been expected to do when being pursued by a man he had reason to be afraid of. "I don't fault Mr. Cooper for what he did, but I'm sorry he did it," the defense attorney said. "I'm sorry the girl said what she said." The jury deliberated for eighteen minutes. Charlie Stevens was found guilty. The jury recommended a sentence of from two to five years in the state penitentiary. At the announcement, Leo Cooper broke down and cried, JoAnn Cooper's eyes filled with tears; she blinked them back and continued to stare straight ahead.

In a way, the Coopers might still strike a casual visitor as an ideal 21 family—handsome parents, a bright and bubbly teenage daughter, a little boy learning the hook shot from his father, a warm house with some land around it. FaNee's presence is there, of course. A picture of her, with a small bouquet of flowers over it, hangs in the living room. One of her poems is displayed in a frame on a table. Even if Leo Cooper continues to think about that night for the rest of his life, there are questions he can never answer. Was there a way that Leo and JoAnn Cooper could have prevented FaNee from choosing the

WRITING SUGGESTIONS

1. Do our popular media—magazine stories, rock music, television movies, and so on—romanticize death? Write an essay in which you support your conclusion with specific examples from various media.

2. Why does FaNee act as she does? Write a letter from FaNee to her parents in which she explains her behavior.

path she chose? Would she still be alive if Leo Cooper had not jumped into his car and driven to the end of the driveway to investigate? Did she in fact tell Charlie Stevens that her father would hurt them—or even that her father had a gun? Did she want to get away from her family even at the risk of tearing around dark country roads in Charlie Stevens's dismal Pinto? Or did she welcome the risk? The poem of FaNee's that the Coopers have displayed is one she wrote a week before her death:

> I think I'm going to die
> And I really don't know why.
> But look in my eye
> When I tell you good-bye.
> I think I'm going to die.

RESPONDING TO READING

1. In paragraph 1 Trillin introduces FaNee Cooper as "what her parents sometimes called an ideal child." Does this characterization of FaNee provide an effective introduction to the case study the essay develops? Why or why not?   **2.** Whom do you hold responsible for FaNee's death? Do you believe anyone had the power to "save" her? If so, who? How might her slide toward death have been prevented?   **3.** Do you know anyone like FaNee? Did you feel this person's fate was inevitable? At what point in FaNee's life do you believe it really was "just too late?"

Marrying Absurd

JOAN DIDION

Some of the essays of Joan Didion (see also p. 54) are about incongruities in our culture, particularly West Coast, "Golden Land" culture. Many of these essays are collected in *Slouching Toward Bethlehem* (1968), from which "Marrying Absurd" is taken. In the following selection, Didion's skill as a reporter is apparent in her pictorial descriptions of Las Vegas, "the most extreme and allegorical of American settlements," and in her astute observations about Las Vegas marriage, which is "like craps, . . . a game to be played when the table seems hot."

To be married in Las Vegas, Clark County, Nevada, a bride must   1
swear that she is eighteen or has parental permission and a bridegroom that he is twenty-one or has parental permission. Someone must put up five dollars for the license. (On Sundays and holidays, fifteen dollars. The Clark County Courthouse issues marriage licenses

at any time of the day or night except between noon and one in the afternoon, between eight and nine in the evening, and between four and five in the morning.) Nothing else is required. The State of Nevada, alone among these United States, demands neither a premarital blood test nor a waiting period before or after the issuance of a marriage license. Driving in across the Mojave from Los Angeles, one sees the signs way out on the desert, looming up from that moonscape of rattlesnakes and mesquite, even before the Las Vegas lights appear like a mirage on the horizon: "GETTING MARRIED? Free License Information First Strip Exit." Perhaps the Las Vegas wedding industry achieved its peak operational efficiency between 9:00 P.M. and midnight of August 26, 1965, an otherwise unremarkable Thursday which happened to be, by Presidential order, the last day on which anyone could improve his draft status merely by getting married. One hundred and seventy-one couples were pronounced man and wife in the name of Clark County and the State of Nevada that night, sixty-seven of them by a single justice of the peace, Mr. James A. Brennan. Mr. Brennan did one wedding at the Dunes and the other sixty-six in his office, and charged each couple eight dollars. One bride lent her veil to six others. "I got it down from five to three minutes." Mr. Brennan said later of this feat. "I could've married them *en masse*, but they're people, not cattle. People expect more when they get married."

What people who get married in Las Vegas actually do expect— 2 what, in the largest sense, their "expectations" are—strikes one as a curious and self-contradictory business. Las Vegas is the most extreme and allegorical of American settlements, bizarre and beautiful in its venality and in its devotion to immediate gratification, a place the tone of which is set by mobsters and call girls and ladies' room attendants with amyl nitrite poppers[1] in their uniform pockets. Almost everyone notes that there is no "time" in Las Vegas, no night and no day and no past and no future (no Las Vegas casino, however, has taken the obliteration of the ordinary time sense quite so far as Harold's Club in Reno, which for a while issued, at odd intervals in the day and night, mimeographed "bulletins" carrying news from the world outside); neither is there any logical sense of where one is. One is standing on a highway in the middle of a vast hostile desert looking at an eighty-foot sign which blinks "STARDUST" or "CAESAR's PALACE." Yes, but what does that explain? This geographical implausibility reinforces the sense that what happens there has no connection with "real" life; Nevada cities like Reno and Carson are

---

[1]Drug whose potent fumes act as a stimulant. [Eds.]

ADDITIONAL QUESTIONS FOR RESPONDING TO READING

1. What is Didion's tone in this essay? Does it ever change?
2. What is incongruous about the images of the wedding signs in the midst of the desert (paragraph 1)?
3. What is the effect of the last line on the essay? What is Didion's attitude toward the sobbing bride?

TEACHING STRATEGY

Pick out examples of vivid images and incidents from the essay. How do they contribute to developing Didion's main idea? What is that idea?

ranch towns, Western towns, places behind which there is some historical imperative. But Las Vegas seems to exist only in the eye of the beholder. All of which makes it an extraordinarily stimulating and interesting place, but an odd one in which to want to wear a candle-light satin Priscilla of Boston wedding dress with Chantilly lace insets, tapered sleeves and a detachable modified train.

And yet the Las Vegas wedding business seems to appeal to 3 precisely that impulse. "Sincere and Dignified Since 1954," one wedding chapel advertises. There are nineteen such wedding chapels in Las Vegas, intensely competitive, each offering better, faster, and, by implication, more sincere services than the next: Our Photos Best Anywhere, Your Wedding on a Phonograph Record, Candlelight with Your Ceremony, Honeymoon Accommodations, Free Transportation from Your Motel to Courthouse to Chapel and Return to Motel. Religious or Civil Ceremonies. Dressing Rooms, Flowers, Rings, Announcements, Witnesses Available, and Ample Parking. All of these services, like most others in Las Vegas (sauna baths, payroll-check cashing, chinchilla coats for sale or rent) are offered twenty-four hours a day, seven days a week, presumably on the premise that marriage, like craps, is a game to be played when the table seems hot.

But what strikes one most about the Strip chapels, with their 4 wishing wells and stained-glass paper windows and their artificial bouvardia[2] is that so much of their business is by no means a matter of simple convenience, of late-night liaisons between show girls and baby Crosbys. Of course there is some of that. (One night about eleven o'clock in Las Vegas I watched a bride in an orange minidress and masses of flamecolored hair stumble from a Strip chapel on the arm of her bridegroom, who looked the part of the expendable nephew in movies like *Miami Syndicate*. "I gotta get the kids," the bride whimpered. "I gotta pick up the sitter, I gotta get to the midnight show." "What you gotta get," the bridegroom said, opening the door of a Cadillac Coupe de Ville and watching her crumple on the seat, "is sober.") But Las Vegas seems to offer something other than "convenience": it is merchandising "niceness," the facsimile of proper ritual, to children who do not know how else to find it, how to make the arrangements, how to do it "right." All day and evening long on the Strip, one sees actual wedding parties, waiting under the harsh lights at a crosswalk, standing uneasily in the parking lot of the Frontier while the photographer hired by The Little Church of the West ("Wedding Place of the Stars") certifies the occasion, takes the picture:

___

[2]Shrubs with fragrant red or white flowers. [Eds.]

COLLABORATIVE ACTIVITY

Ask student groups (some all female, some all male, and some mixed), to list expectations for the ideal wedding. What basic requirements (guests, dress, food, setting, and so forth) do the different groups have? Compare the various groups' lists and discuss any differences.

the bride in a veil and white satin pumps, the bridegroom usually in a white dinner jacket, and even an attendant or two, a sister or a best friend in hot-pink *peau de soie*,[3] a flirtation veil, a carnation nosegay. "When I Fall in Love It Will Be Forever," the organist plays, and then a few bars of Lohengrin.[4] The mother cries; the stepfather, awkward in his role, invites the chapel hostess to join them for a drink at the Sands. The hostess declines with a professional smile; she has already transferred her interest to the group waiting outside. One bride out, another in, and again the sign goes up on the chapel door: "One moment please—Wedding."

I sat next to one such wedding party in a Strip restaurant the last 5
time I was in Las Vegas. The marriage had just taken place, the bride still wore her dress, the mother her corsage. A bored waiter poured out a few swallows of pink champagne ("on the house") for everyone but the bride, who was too young to be served. "You'll need something with more kick than that," the bride's father said with heavy jocularity to his new son-in-law; the ritual jokes about the wedding night had a certain Panglossian[5] character, since the bride was clearly several months pregnant. Another round of pink champagne, this time not on the house, and the bride began to cry. "It was just as nice," she sobbed, "as I hoped and dreamed it would be."

RESPONDING TO READING

1. How are Las Vegas weddings different from traditional weddings? What exactly is so "absurd" about the kind of weddings Didion describes? In what ways are the two kinds of weddings similar? Do you think Didion is struck more by the similarities or by the differences?   **2.** In paragraphs 4 and 5 Didion narrows her focus to "actual wedding parties." Do you think her attitude toward these people is mean-spirited? Condescending? How do you react to her characterizations?   **3.** What "absurdities" have you observed in the weddings you have attended?

WRITING SUGGESTIONS

1. Assume you are a bride or a groom in one of the weddings Didion describes. Write a diary entry in which you describe your Las Vegas wedding in glowingly romantic terms. (You may invent details to embellish your description.)
2. Write an article describing a Las Vegas wedding for the bride's or groom's hometown newspaper.

ANSWERS TO RESPONDING
TO READING

1. Las Vegas weddings are conducted like package deals, which is absurd since each couple is different. Yet the similarities between the two kinds of wedding rituals and emotions probably strike Didion as much as the differences.
2. Students' responses will vary. Some will find her to be amused by the wedding parties, but others will see her as patronizing.
3. Answers will range from the uncomfortable demeanor of grooms unused to tuxedos to ostentatious displays of food, flowers, and so on.

[3]Luxury fabric; literally, silk skin. [Eds.]
[4]Wedding march composed by Richard Wagner (1813–83). [Eds.]
[5]In Voltaire's (1694–1778) *Candide* (1759), a satire on optimistic philosophy, Dr. Pangloss is a philosopher who, despite a series of unpleasant adventures, continues to have an optimistic outlook. [Eds.]

On the Fear of Death

ELISABETH KÜBLER-ROSS

Born in Zurich, Switzerland, psychologist Elisabeth Kübler-Ross (1917–   ) has made a distinguished career of her interest in dying patients and their families. She established a pioneering interdisciplinary seminar in the care of the terminally ill when she taught at the University of Chicago. Her first book on the subject was *On Death and Dying* (1969), and she has also written *Death: The Final State* (1974), *Working It Through* (1981), and *On Childhood and Death* (1985). Since 1977, Kübler-Ross has been president of a controversial therapeutic and teaching center called Shanti Nilaya (House of Peace). She argues in the following 1969 essay that we should confront death directly to reduce our fear of it.

Let me not pray to be sheltered from dangers but to be fearless in facing them.
Let me not beg for the stilling of my pain but for the heart to conquer it.
Let me not look for allies in life's battlefield but to my own strength.
Let me not crave in anxious fear to be saved but hope for the patience to win my freedom.
Grant me that I may not be a coward, feeling your mercy in my success alone; but let me find the grasp of your hand in my failure.

RABINDRANATH TAGORE,
Fruit-Gathering

Epidemics have taken a great toll of lives in past generations. Death in infancy and early childhood was frequent and there were few families who didn't lose a member of the family at an early age. Medicine has changed greatly in the last decades. Widespread vaccinations have practically eradicated many illnesses, at least in western Europe and the United States. The use of chemotherapy, especially the antibiotics, has contributed to an ever decreasing number of fatalities in infectious diseases. Better child care and education has effected a low morbidity and mortality among children. The many diseases that have taken an impressive toll among the young and middle-aged have been conquered. The number of old people is on the rise, and with this fact come the number of people with malignancies and chronic diseases associated more with old age.

Pediatricians have less work with acute and life-threatening situations as they have an ever increasing number of patients with psychosomatic disturbances and adjustment and behavior problems. Physicians have more people in their waiting rooms with emotional problems than they have ever had before, but they also have more elderly patients who not only try to live with their decreased physical abilities and limitations but who also face loneliness and isolation with all its pains and anguish. The majority of these people are not seen by a psychiatrist. Their needs have to be elicited and gratified by other professional people, for instance, chaplains and social workers. It is for them that I am trying to outline the changes that have taken place in the last few decades, changes that are ultimately responsible for the increased fear of death, the rising number of emotional problems, and the greater need for understanding of and coping with the problems of death and dying.

When we look back in time and study old cultures and people, 3 we are impressed that death has always been distasteful to man and will probably always be. From a psychiatrist's point of view this is very understandable and can perhaps best be explained by our basic knowledge that, in our unconscious, death is never possible in regard to ourselves. It is inconceivable for our unconscious to imagine an actual ending of our own life here on earth, and if this life of ours had to end, the ending is always attributed to a malicious intervention from the outside by someone else. In simple terms, in our unconscious mind we can only be killed; it is inconceivable to die of a natural cause or of old age. Therefore death in itself is associated with a bad act, a frightening happening, something that in itself calls for retribution and punishment.

One is wise to remember these fundamental facts as they are 4 essential in understanding some of the most important, otherwise unintelligible communications of our patients.

The second fact that we have to comprehend is that in our uncon- 5 scious mind we cannot distinguish between a wish and a deed. We are all aware of some of our illogical dreams in which two completely opposite statements can exist side by side—very acceptable in our dreams but unthinkable and illogical in our wakening state. Just as our unconscious mind cannot differentiate between the wish to kill somebody in anger and the act of having done so, the young child is unable to make this distinction. The child who angrily wishes his mother to drop dead for not having gratified his needs will be traumatized greatly by the actual death of his mother—even if this event is not linked closely in time with his destructive wishes. He will always take part or the whole blame for the loss of his mother. He will always say to himself—rarely to others—"I did it, I am responsible, I was bad, therefore Mommy left me." It is well to remember that the child

TEACHING STRATEGY

Assign groups the task of researching different cultures' customs and rituals related to death. Discuss these and compare them. Reading aloud the scene from Aldous Huxley's *Brave New World* in which children are indoctrinated to be unafraid of death might provoke some interesting responses.

COLLABORATIVE ACTIVITY

Have each group or pair of students write and prepare for discussion a detailed hypothetical case of a critically ill person. Discuss as a class how the patient's situation might be handled. Topics to be considered might include euthanasia, "death with dignity," hospices, life-support systems, organ donation, brain death, and so on.

will react in the same manner if he loses a parent by divorce, separation, or desertion. Death is often seen by a child as an impermanent thing and has therefore little distinction from a divorce in which he may have an opportunity to see a parent again.

Many a parent will remember remarks of their children such as, 6 "I will bury my doggy now and next spring when the flowers come up again, he will get up." Maybe it was the same wish that motivated the ancient Egyptians to supply their dead with food and goods to keep them happy and the old American Indians to bury their relatives with their belongings.

When we grow older and begin to realize that our omnipotence 7 is really not so omnipotent, that our strongest wishes are not powerful enough to make the impossible possible, the fear that we have contributed to the death of a loved one diminishes—and with it the guilt. The fear remains diminished, however, only so long as it is not challenged too strongly. Its vestiges can be seen daily in hospital corridors and in people associated with the bereaved.

A husband and wife may have been fighting for years, but when 8 the partner dies, the survivor will pull his hair, whine and cry louder and beat his chest in regret, fear and anguish, and will hence fear his own death more than before, still believing in the law of talion—an eye for an eye, a tooth for a tooth—"I am responsible for her death, I will have to die a pitiful death in retribution."

Maybe this knowledge will help us understand many of the old 9 customs and rituals which have lasted over the centuries and whose purpose is to diminish the anger of the gods or the people as the case may be, thus decreasing the anticipated punishment. I am thinking of the ashes, the torn clothes, the veil, the *Klage Weiber*[1] of the old days—they are all means to ask you to take pity on them, the mourners, and are expressions of sorrow, grief, and shame. If someone grieves, beats his chest, tears his hair, or refuses to eat, it is an attempt at self-punishment to avoid or reduce the anticipated punishment for the blame that he takes on the death of a loved one.

This grief, shame, and guilt are not very far removed from feelings 10 of anger and rage. The process of grief always includes some qualities of anger. Since none of us likes to admit anger at a deceased person, these emotions are often disguised or repressed and prolong the period of grief or show up in other ways. It is well to remember that it is not up to us to judge such feelings as bad or shameful but to understand their true meaning and origin as something very human. In order to illustrate this I will again use the example of the child—

---

[1]Wailing wives. [Eds.]

and the child in us. The five-year-old who loses his mother is both blaming himself for her disappearance and being angry at her for having deserted him and for no longer gratifying his needs. The dead person then turns into something the child loves and wants very much but also hates with equal intensity for this severe deprivation.

The ancient Hebrews regarded the body of a dead person as 11 something unclean and not to be touched. The early American Indians talked about the evil spirits and shot arrows in the air to drive the spirits away. Many other cultures have rituals to take care of the ''bad'' dead person, and they all originate in this feeling of anger which still exists in all of us, though we dislike admitting it. The tradition of the tombstone may originate in this wish to keep the bad spirits deep down in the ground, and the pebbles that many mourners put on the grave are left-over symbols of the same wish. Though we call the firing of guns at military funerals a last salute, it is the same symbolic ritual as the Indian used when he shot his spears and arrows into the skies.

I give these examples to emphasize that man has not basically 12 changed. Death is still a fearful, frightening happening, and the fear of death is a universal fear even if we think we have mastered it on many levels.

What has changed is our way of coping and dealing with death 13 and dying and our dying patients.

Having been raised in a country in Europe where science is not 14 so advanced, where modern techniques have just started to find their way into medicine, and where people still live as they did in this country half a century ago, I may have had an opportunity to study a part of the evolution of mankind in a shorter period.

I remember as a child the death of a farmer. He fell from a tree 15 and was not expected to live. He asked simply to die at home, a wish that was granted without questioning. He called his daughters into the bedroom and spoke with each one of them alone for a few moments. He arranged his affairs quietly, though he was in great pain, and distributed his belongings and his land, none of which was to be split until his wife should follow him in death. He also asked each of his children to share in the work, duties, and tasks that he had carried on until the time of the accident. He asked his friends to visit him once more, to bid good-bye to them. Although I was a small child at the time, he did not exclude me or my siblings. We were allowed to share in the preparations of the family just as we were permitted to grieve with them until he died. When he did die, he was left at home, in his own beloved home which he had built, and among his friends and neighbors who went to take a last look at him where he lay in the midst of flowers in the place he had lived in and loved so much. In that country today there is still no make-believe slumber room, no embalming, no false makeup to pretend sleep. Only the signs of very disfiguring illnesses are covered up with bandages and only infectious cases are removed from the home prior to the burial.

Why do I describe such "old-fashioned" customs? I think they 16 are an indication of our acceptance of a fatal outcome, and they help the dying patient as well as his family to accept the loss of a loved one. If a patient is allowed to terminate his life in the familiar and beloved environment, it requires less adjustment for him. His own family knows him well enough to replace a sedative with a glass of his favorite wine; or the smell of a home-cooked soup may give him the appetite to sip a few spoons of fluid which, I think is still more enjoyable than an infusion. I will not minimize the need for sedatives and infusions and realize full well from my own experience as a country doctor that they are sometimes life-saving and often unavoidable. But I also know that patience and familiar people and foods could replace many a bottle of intravenous fluids given for the simple reason that it fulfills the physiological need without involving too many people and/or individual nursing care.

The fact that children are allowed to stay at home where a fatality 17 has stricken and are included in the talk, discussions, and fears gives them the feeling that they are not alone in the grief and gives them the comfort of shared responsibility and shared mourning. It prepares them gradually and helps them view death as part of life, an experience which may help them grow and mature.

This is in great contrast to a society in which death is viewed as 18 taboo, discussion of it is regarded as morbid, and children are excluded with the presumption and pretext that it would be "too much" for them. They are then sent off to relatives, often accompanied with some unconvincing lies of "Mother has gone on a long trip" or other unbelievable stories. The child senses that something is wrong, and his distrust in adults will only multiply if other relatives add new variations of the story, avoid his questions or suspicions, shower him with gifts as a meager substitute for a loss he is not permitted to deal with. Sooner or later the child will become aware of the changed family situation and, depending on the age and personality of the child, will have an unresolved grief and regard this incident as a frightening, mysterious, in any case very traumatic experience with untrustworthy grownups, which he has no way to cope with.

It is equally unwise to tell a little child who lost her brother that 19 God loved little boys so much that he took little Johnny to heaven.

When this little girl grew up to be a woman she never solved her anger at God, which resulted in a psychotic depression when she lost her own little son three decades later.

We would think that our great emancipation, our knowledge of 20 science and of man, has given us better ways and means to prepare ourselves and our families for this inevitable happening. Instead the days are gone when a man was allowed to die in peace and dignity in his own home.

The more we are making advancements in science, the more we 21 seem to fear and deny the reality of death. How is this possible?

We use euphemisms, we make the dead look as if they were 22 asleep, we ship the children off to protect them from the anxiety and turmoil around the house if the patient is fortunate enough to die at home, we don't allow children to visit their dying parents in the hospitals, we have long and controversial discussions about whether patients should be told the truth—a question that rarely arises when the dying person is tended by the family physician who has known him from delivery to death and who knows the weaknesses and strengths of each member of the family.

I think there are many reasons for this flight away from facing 23 death calmly. One of the most important facts is that dying nowadays is more gruesome in many ways, namely, more lonely, mechanical, and dehumanized; at times it is even difficult to determine technically when the time of death has occurred.

Dying becomes lonely and impersonal because the patient is often 24 taken out of his familiar environment and rushed to an emergency room. Whoever has been very sick and has required rest and comfort especially may recall his experience of being put on a stretcher and enduring the noise of the ambulance siren and hectic rush until the hospital gates open. Only those who have lived through this may appreciate the discomfort and cold necessity of such transportation which is only the beginning of a long order—hard to endure when you are well, difficult to express in words when noise, light, pumps, and voices are all too much to put up with. It may well be that we might consider more the patient under the sheets and blankets and perhaps stop our well-meant efficiency and rush in order to hold the patient's hand, to smile, or to listen to a question. I include the trip to the hospital as the first episode in dying, as it is for many. I am putting it exaggeratedly in contrast to the sick man who is left at home—not to say that lives should not be saved if they can be saved by a hospitalization but to keep the focus on the patient's experience, his needs and his reactions.

WRITING SUGGESTION

Write a living will, giving instructions to your family about the circumstances under which you would (or would not) want your life prolonged by artificial means. Consider as many of the topics generated for the "Collaborative Activity" assignment as you wish.

When a patient is severely ill, he is often treated like a person 25 with no right to an opinion. It is often someone else who makes the decision if and when and where a patient should be hospitalized. It would take so little to remember that the sick person too has feelings, has wishes and opinions, and has—most important of all—the right to be heard.

Well, our presumed patient has now reached the emergency 26 room. He will be surrounded by busy nurses, orderlies, interns, residents, a lab technician perhaps who will take some blood, an electrocardiogram technician who takes the cardiogram. He may be moved to X-ray and he will overhear opinions of his condition and discussions and questions to members of the family. He slowly but surely is beginning to be treated like a thing. He is no longer a person. Decisions are made often without his opinion. If he tries to rebel he will be sedated and after hours of waiting and wondering whether he has the strength, he will be wheeled into the operating room or intensive treatment unit and become an object of great concern and great financial investment.

He may cry for rest, peace, and dignity, but he will get infusions, 27 transfusions, a heart machine, or tracheotomy if necessary. He may want one single person to stop for one single minute so that he can ask one single question—but he will get a dozen people around the clock, all busily preoccupied with his heart rate, pulse, electrocardiogram or pulmonary functions, his secretions or excretions but not with him as a human being. He may wish to fight it all but it is going to be a useless fight since all this is done in the fight for his life, and if they can save his life they can consider the person afterwards. Those who consider the person first may lose precious time to save his life! At least this seems to be the rationale or justification behind all this— or is it? Is the reason for this increasingly mechanical, depersonalized approach our own defensiveness? Is this approach our own way to cope with and repress the anxieties that a terminally or critically ill patient evokes in us? Is our concentration on equipment, on blood pressure, our desperate attempt to deny the impending death which is so frightening and discomforting to us that we displace all our knowledge onto machines, since they are less close to us than the suffering face of another human being which would remind us once more of our lack of omnipotence, our own limits and failures, and last but not least perhaps our own mortality?

Maybe the question has to be raised: Are we becoming less human 28 or more human? . . . [I]t is clear that whatever the answer may be, the patient is suffering more—not physically, perhaps, but emotionally. And his needs have not changed over the centuries, only our ability to gratify them.

RESPONDING TO READING

1. Despite advances in medical science over the centuries, Kübler-Ross says, death remains "a fearful, frightening happening, and the fear of death is a universal fear even if we think we have mastered it on many levels" (paragraph 12). Do you think she is correct? Do you think it is possible for a person to master his or her fear of death? If so, how?   **2.** To what extent do you agree with Kübler-Ross that we should confront the reality of death directly—for example, by being honest with children, keeping terminally ill patients at home, and allowing dying patients to determine their own treatment?   **3.** Instead of quoting medical authorities, Kübler-Ross supports her points with anecdotes. Do you find this support convincing? Would hard scientific data be more convincing? Explain.

The American Way of Death

JESSICA MITFORD

Jessica Mitford (1917–   ) was born into an affluent British family and educated at home; she later emigrated to the United States, where she became an investigative reporter. She has collected many of her articles in *Poison Pensmanship: The Gentle Art of Muckraking* (1979). For the fervor of her research and her sharp social criticism, Mitford has earned the title "Queen of the Muckrakers." She has also written *Kind and Unusual Punishment: The Prison Business* (1973) and *The American Way of Death* (1963), from which the following essay is taken. Here Mitford uses sarcasm and stark descriptions to "part the formaldehyde curtain" on the embalming industry and to criticize what she considers to be its misplaced values.

The drama begins to unfold with the arrival of the corpse at the mortuary.

Alas, poor Yorick![1] How surprised he would be to see how his counterpart of today is whisked off to a funeral parlor and is in short order sprayed, sliced, pierced, pickled, trussed, trimmed, creamed, waxed, painted, rouged and neatly dressed—transformed from a common corpse into a Beautiful Memory Picture. This process is known in the trade as embalming and restorative art, and is so universally employed in the United States and Canada that the funeral director does it routinely, without consulting corpse or kin. He regards as eccentric those few who are hardy enough to suggest that it might

---

[1]Hamlet's statement (in Act 5, scene 1) when he contemplates the skull of a court clown he had known when he was young. [Eds.]

ADDITIONAL QUESTIONS FOR RESPONDING TO READING

1. Discuss various American funeral practices and what they imply about our approach to facing the truth. Are there other American practices that help us avoid reality in a similar way? Consider our advertising, fashion, and cosmetics industries.
2. Have you ever discussed funeral arrangements with a parent or close family member? Why are such discussions so difficult?
3. What funeral arrangements do you desire for yourself? Why? How do you intend to communicate your desires?
4. How do you feel about embalming for yourself or a loved one? (Remind students that embalming is not customary in every religion. Orthodox Jews, for example, do not embalm their dead; therefore, they must be buried without delay. In other religions, such as Catholicism, however, embalming makes possible a wake and an extended mourning period before the funeral.)

be dispensed with. Yet no law requires embalming, no religious doctrine commends it, nor is it dictated by considerations of health, sanitation, or even of personal daintiness. In no part of the world but in Northern America is it widely used. The purpose of embalming is to make the corpse presentable for viewing in a suitably costly container; and here too the funeral director routinely, without first consulting the family, prepares the body for public display.

Is all this legal? The processes to which a dead body may be subjected are after all to some extent circumscribed by law. In most states, for instance, the signature of next of kin must be obtained before an autopsy may be performed, before the deceased may be cremated, before the body may be turned over to a medical school for research purposes; or such provision must be made in the decedent's will. In the case of embalming, no such permission is required nor is it ever sought. A textbook, *The Principles and Practices of Embalming*, comments on this: "There is some question regarding the legality of much that is done within the preparation room." The author points out that it would be most unusual for a responsible member of a bereaved family to instruct the mortician, in so many words, to "embalm" the body of a deceased relative. The very term "embalming" is so seldom used that the mortician must rely upon custom in the matter. The author concludes that unless the family specifies otherwise, the act of entrusting the body to the care of a funeral establishment carries with it an implied permission to go ahead and embalm. 3

Embalming is indeed a most extraordinary procedure, and one must wonder at the docility of Americans who each year pay hundreds of millions of dollars for its perpetuation, blissfully ignorant of what it is all about, what is done, how it is done. Not one in ten thousand has any idea of what actually takes place. Books on the subject are extremely hard to come by. They are not to be found in most libraries or bookshops. 4

In an era when huge television audiences watch surgical operations in the comfort of their living rooms, when, thanks to the animated cartoon, the geography of the digestive system has become familiar territory even to the nursery school set, in a land where the satisfaction of curiosity about almost all matters is a national pastime, the secrecy surrounding embalming can, surely, hardly be attributed to the inherent gruesomeness of the subject. Custom in this regard has within this century suffered a complete reversal. In the early days of American embalming, when it was performed in the home of the deceased, it was almost mandatory for some relative to stay by the embalmer's side and witness the procedure. Today, family members who might wish to be in attendance would certainly be dissuaded by 5 the funeral director. All others, except apprentices, are excluded by law from the preparation room.

A close look at what does actually take place may explain in large measure the undertaker's intractable reticence concerning a procedure that has become his major *raison d'être*.[2] Is it possible he fears that public information about embalming might lead patrons to wonder if they really want this service? If the funeral men are loath to discuss the subject outside the trade, the reader may, understandably, be equally loath to go on reading at this point. For those who have the stomach for it, let us part the formaldehyde curtain. . . .   6

The body is first laid out in the undertaker's morgue—or rather, Mr. Jones is reposing in the preparation room—to be readied to bid the world farewell.   7

The preparation room in any of the better funeral establishments has the tiled and sterile look of a surgery, and indeed the embalmer-restorative artist who does his chores there is beginning to adopt the term "dermasurgeon" (appropriately corrupted by some mortician-writers as "demi-surgeon") to describe his calling. His equipment, consisting of scalpels, scissors, augers, forceps, clamps, needles, pumps, tubes, bowls and basins, is crudely imitative of the surgeon's, as is his technique, acquired in a nine- or twelve-month post-high-school course in an embalming school. He is supplied by an advanced chemical industry with a bewildering array of fluids, sprays, pastes, oils, powders, creams, to fix or soften tissue, shrink or distend it as needed, dry it here, restore the moisture there. There are cosmetics, waxes and paints to fill and cover features, even plaster of Paris to replace entire limbs. There are ingenious aids to prop and stabilize the cadaver: a Vari-Pose Head Rest, the Edwards Arm and Hand Positioner, the Repose Block (to support the shoulders during the embalming), and the Throop Foot Positioner, which resembles an old-fashioned stocks.   8

Mr. John H. Eckels, president of the Eckels College of Mortuary Science, thus describes the first part of the embalming procedure: "In the hands of a skilled practitioner, this work may be done in a comparatively short time and without mutilating the body other than by slight incision—so slight that it scarcely would cause serious inconvenience if made upon a living person. It is necessary to remove the blood, and doing this not only helps in the disinfecting, but removes the principal cause of disfigurements due to discoloration."   9

Another textbook discusses the all-important time element: "The earlier this is done, the better, for every hour that elapses between   10

TEACHING STRATEGY

This selection offers an excellent example of how tone can convey a writer's attitude. You might examine the specific language Mitford uses to create her sarcastic tone, and how those same facts could be presented in a more positive (or at least neutral) light with different word choices. Notice too how Mitford uses many direct quotations, how she names the various technical embalming tools (such as the Vari-Pose Head Rest, the Classic Beauty Ultra Metal Casket Bier, and the Gordon Earth Dispenser), and how she makes fun of these terms and of the funeral industry's use of language in general. You might ask students to read this essay along with "The Middle Class" (page 646) and/or "Marrying Absurd" (page 690), which approach their subjects from a similar stance.

---

[2](Fr.) "Reason for being." [Eds.]

COLLABORATIVE ACTIVITY

Divide the class into small groups. Ask individual members of each group to list their religion's or ethnic group's funeral and burial rituals. Then have each group compile two lists: one of practices observed by all or most group members, and one of practices unique to one group member's religion. Discuss the similarities and differences with the class as a whole.

death and embalming will add to the problems and complications encountered. . . ." Just how soon should one get going on the embalming? The author tells us, "On the basis of such scanty information made available to this profession through its rudimentary and haphazard system of technical research, we must conclude that the best results are to be obtained if the subject is embalmed before life is completely extinct—that is, before cellular death has occurred. In the average case, this would mean within an hour after somatic death." For those who feel that there is something a little rudimentary, not to say haphazard, about this advice, a comforting thought is offered by another writer. Speaking of fears entertained in early days of premature burial, he points out, "One of the effects of embalming by chemical injection, however, has been to dispel fears of live burial." How true; once the blood is removed, chances of live burial are indeed remote.

To return to Mr. Jones, the blood is drained out through the veins and replaced by embalming fluid pumped in through the arteries. As noted in *The Principles and Practices of Embalming*, "every operator has a favorite injection and drainage point—a fact which becomes a handicap only if he fails or refuses to forsake his favorites when conditions demand it." Typical favorites are the carotid artery, femoral artery, jugular vein, subclavian vein. There are various choices of embalming fluid. If Flextone is used, it will produce a "mild, flexible rigidity. The skin retains a velvety softness, the tissues are rubbery and pliable. Ideal for women and children." It may be blended with B. and G. Products Company's Lyf-Lyk tint, which is guaranteed to reproduce "nature's own skin texture . . . the velvety appearance of living tissue." Suntone comes in three separate tints: Suntan; Special Cosmetic Tint, a pink shade "especially indicated for young female subjects;" and Regular Cosmetic Tint, moderately pink.

About three to six gallons of a dyed and perfumed solution of formaldehyde, glycerin, borax, phenol, alcohol and water is soon circulating through Mr. Jones, whose mouth has been sewn together with a "needle directed upward between the upper lip and gum and brought out through the left nostril," with the corners raised slightly "for a more pleasant expression." If he should be bucktoothed, his teeth are cleaned with Bon Ami and coated with colorless nail polish. His eyes, meanwhile, are closed with flesh-tinted eye caps and eye cement.

The next step is to have at Mr. Jones with a thing called a trocar. This is a long, hollow needle attached to a tube. It is jabbed into the abdomen, poked around the entrails and chest cavity, the contents of which are pumped out and replaced with "cavity fluid." This done, and the hole in the abdomen sewn up, Mr. Jone's face is heavily creamed (to protect the skin from burns which may be caused by leakage of the chemicals), and he is covered with a sheet and left unmolested for a while. But not for long—there is more, much more, in store for him. He has been embalmed, but not yet restored, and the best time to start the restorative work is eight to ten hours after embalming, when the tissues have become firm and dry.

The object of all this attention to the corpse, it must be remem- 14 bered, is to make it presentable for viewing in an attitude of healthy repose. "Our customs require the presentation of our dead in the semblance of normality . . . unmarred by the ravages of illness, disease or mutilation," says Mr. J. Sheridan Mayer in his *Restorative Art*. This is rather a large order since few people die in the full bloom of health, unravaged by illness and unmarked by some disfigurement. The funeral industry is equal to the challenge: "In some cases the gruesome appearance of a mutilated or disease-ridden subject may be quite discouraging. The task of restoration may seem impossible and shake the confidence of the embalmer. This is the time for intestinal fortitude and determination. Once the formative work is begun and affected tissues are cleaned or removed, all doubts of success vanish. It is surprising and gratifying to discover the results which may be obtained."

The embalmer, having allowed an appropriate interval to elapse, 15 returns to the attack, but now he brings into play the skill and equipment of sculptor and cosmetician. Is a hand missing? Casting one in plaster of Paris is a simple matter. "For replacement purposes, only a cast of the back of the hand is necessary; this is within the ability of the average operator and is quite adequate." If a lip or two, a nose or an ear should be missing, the embalmer has at hand a variety of restorative waxes with which to model replacements. Pores and skin texture are simulated by stippling with a little brush, and over this cosmetics are laid on. Head off? Decapitation cases are rather routinely handled. Ragged edges are trimmed, and head joined to torso with a series of splints, wires and sutures. It is a good idea to have a little something at the neck—a scarf or a high collar—when time for viewing comes. Swollen mouth? Cut out tissue as needed from inside the lips. If too much is removed, the surface contour can easily be restored by padding with cotton. Swollen necks and cheeks are reduced by removing tissue through vertical incisions made down each side of the neck. "When the deceased is casketed, the pillow will hide the suture incisions . . . as an extra precaution against leakage, the suture may be painted with liquid sealer."

The opposite condition is more likely to present itself—that of 16 emaciation. His hypodermic syringe now loaded with massage cream, the embalmer seeks out and fills the hollowed and sunken areas by injection. In this procedure the backs of the hands and fingers and the under-chin area should not be neglected.

Positioning the lips is a problem that recurrently challenges the [17] ingenuity of the embalmer. Closed too tightly, they tend to give a stern, even disapproving expression. Ideally, embalmers feel, the lips should give the impression of being ever so slightly parted, the upper lip protruding slightly for a more youthful appearance. This takes some engineering, however, as the lips tend to drift apart. Lip drift can sometimes be remedied by pushing one or two straight pins through the inner margin of the lower lip and then inserting them between the two front upper teeth. If Mr. Jones happens to have no teeth, the pins can just as easily be anchored in his Armstrong Face Former and Denture Replacer. Another method to maintain lip closure is to dislocate the lower jaw, which is then held in its new position by a wire run through holes which have been drilled through the upper and lower jaws at the midline. As the French are fond of saying, *il faut souffrir pour être belle.*[3]

If Mr. Jones has died of jaundice, the embalming fluid will very [18] likely turn him green. Does this deter the embalmer? Not if he has intestinal fortitude. Masking pastes and cosmetics are heavily laid on, burial garments and casket interiors are color-correlated with particular care, and Jones is displayed beneath rose-colored lights. Friends will say "How well he looks." Death by carbon monoxide, on the other hand, can be rather a good thing from the embalmer's viewpoint: "One advantage is the fact that this type of discoloration is an exaggerated form of a natural pink coloration." This is nice because the healthy glow is already present and needs but little attention.

The patching and filling completed, Mr. Jones is now shaved, [19] washed and dressed. Cream-based cosmetic, available in pink, flesh, suntan, brunette and blond, is applied to his hands and face, his hair is shampooed and combed (and, in the case of Mrs. Jones, set), his hands manicured. For the horny-handed son of toil special care must be taken; cream should be applied to remove ingrained grime, and the nails cleaned. "If he were not in the habit of having them manicured in life, trimming and shaping is advised for better appearance— never questioned by kin."

Jones is now ready for casketing (this is the present participle of [20] the verb "to casket"). In this operation his right shoulder should be depressed slightly "to turn the body a bit to the right and soften the

---

[3](Fr.) "One must suffer to be beautiful." [Eds.]

appearance of lying flat on the back." Positioning the hands is a matter of importance, and special rubber positioning blocks may be used. The hands should be cupped slightly for a more lifelike, relaxed appearance. Proper placement of the body requires a delicate sense of balance. It should lie as high as possible in the casket, yet not so high that the lid, when lowered, will hit the nose. On the other hand, we are cautioned, placing the body too low "creates the impression that the body is in a box."

Jones is next wheeled into the appointed slumber room where a few last touches may be added—his favorite pipe placed in his hand or, if he was a great reader, a book propped into position. (In the case of little Master Jones a Teddy bear may be clutched.) Here he will hold open house for a few days, visiting hours 10 A.M. to 9 P.M. 21

All now being in readiness, the funeral director calls a staff conference to make sure that each assistant knows his precise duties. Mr. Wilber Kriege writes: "This makes your staff feel that they are a part of the team, with a definite assignment that must be properly carried out if the whole plan is to succeed. You never heard of a football coach who failed to talk to his entire team before they go on the field. They have drilled on the plays they are to execute for hours and days, and yet the successful coach knows the importance of making even the bench-warming third-string substitute feel that he is important if the game is to be won." The winning of *this* game is predicated upon glass-smooth handling of the logistics. The funeral director has notified the pallbearers whose names were furnished by the family, has arranged for the presence of clergyman, organist, and soloist, has provided transportation for everybody, has organized and listed the flowers sent by friends. In *Psychology of Funeral Service* Mr. Edward A. Martin points out: "He may not always do as much as the family thinks he is doing, but it is his helpful guidance that they appreciate in knowing they are proceeding as they should. . . . The important thing is how well his services can be used to make the family believe they are giving unlimited expression to their own sentiment." 22

The religious service may be held in a church or in the chapel of the funeral home; the funeral director vastly prefers the latter arrangement, for not only is it more convenient for him but it affords him the opportunity to show off his beautiful facilities to the gathered mourners. After the clergyman has had his say, the mourners queue up to file past the casket for a last look at the deceased. The family is *never* asked whether they want an open-casket ceremony; in the absence of their instruction to the contrary, this is taken for granted. Consequently well over 90 per cent of all American funerals feature the open casket—a custom unknown in other parts of the world. 23

Foreigners are astonished by it. An English woman living in San Francisco described her reaction in a letter to the writer:

> I myself have attended only one funeral here—that of an elderly fellow worker of mine. After the service I could not understand why everyone was walking towards the coffin (sorry, I mean casket), but thought I had better follow the crowd. It shook me rigid to get there and find the casket open and poor old Oscar lying there in his brown tweed suit, wearing a suntan makeup and just the wrong shade of lipstick. If I had not been extremely fond of the old boy, I have a horrible feeling that I might have giggled. Then and there I decided that I could never face another American funeral—even dead.

24   The casket (which has been resting throughout the service on a Classic Beauty Ultra Metal Casket Bier) is now transferred by a hydraulically operated device called Porto-Lift to a balloon-tired, Glide Easy casket carriage which will wheel it to yet another conveyance, the Cadillac Funeral Coach. This may be lavender, cream, light green—anything but black. Interiors, of course, are color-correlated, "for the man who cannot stop short of perfection."

25   At graveside, the casket is lowered into the earth. This office, once the prerogative of friends of the deceased, is now performed by a patented mechanical lowering device. A "Lifetime Green" artificial grass mat is at the ready to conceal the sere earth, and overhead, to conceal the sky, is a portable Steril Chapel Tent ("resists the intense heat and humidity of summer and the terrific storms of winter . . . available in Silver Grey, Rose or Evergreen"). Now is the time for the ritual scattering of earth over the coffin, as the solemn words "earth to earth, ashes to ashes, dust to dust" are pronounced by the officiating cleric. This can today be accomplished "with a mere flick of the wrist with the Gordon Leak-Proof Earth Dispenser. No grasping of a handful of dirt, no soiled fingers. Simple, dignified, beautiful, reverent! The modern way!" The Gordon Earth Dispenser (at $5) is of nickel-plated brass construction. It is not only "attractive to the eye and long wearing;" it is also "one of the 'tools' for building better public relations" if presented as "an appropriate noncommercial gift" to the clergyman. It is shaped something like a salt-shaker.

26   Untouched by human hand, the coffin and the earth are now united.

27   It is in the function of directing the participants through this maze of gadgetry that the funeral director has assigned to himself his relatively new role of "grief therapist." He has relieved the family of every detail, he has revamped the corpse to look like a living doll, he has arranged for it to nap for a few days in a slumber room, he has put on a well-oiled performance in which the concept of *death* has played no part whatsoever—unless it was inconsiderately mentioned

---

WRITING SUGGESTIONS

1. Write a short essay, using Mitford's patronizing approach and tone, about the food available in American fast-food restaurants. Be sure to use careful description and the specific language of the industry itself, as she does.

2. Rewrite Mitford's essay in an abridged form, using the same facts but presenting them in a positive light.

by the clergyman who conducted the religious service. He has done everything in his power to make the funeral a real pleasure for everybody concerned. He and his team have given their all to score an upset victory over death.

RESPONDING TO READING

1. Throughout this essay Mitford uses a bitterly sarcastic tone to mock the language, technology, equipment, and professional standards of the funeral industry. Do you find her tone appropriate for her subject and purpose, or do you think it is unnecessarily hostile? How does this tone affect your reaction to Mitford's ideas?   **2.** Mitford is especially critical of the way the process she describes values artifice over honesty—for example, in the funeral directors' use of euphemisms for the unpleasant facts related to death and in their concern for "artistry." Do you agree with her criticism, or do you see some justification in "tidying up" unpleasant appearances and language in such sensitive situations?   **3.** In what sense, if any, could you apply this essay's criticisms of the funeral industry to other businesses or rituals in American society?

A Higher Horror of Whiteness: Cocaine's Coloring of the American Psyche

ROBERT STONE

Novelist Robert Stone (1937–   ) was once a member of the "Merry Pranksters," the counterculture group Tom Wolfe wrote about in *The Electric Kool-Aid Acid Test* (1968). Stone's *Hall of Mirrors* (1967) won the William Faulkner Foundation Award for a "notable first novel." In 1971, he was a correspondent in Vietnam; three years later, he won the National Book Award for *Dog Soldiers* (1974), an account of the Vietnam drug trade. Stone describes himself as a writer who tries to "crowd people out of their own minds and occupy their space." In the following essay, published in 1986, Stone explores—using literary terms, statistics, and personal experience— how cocaine is "intruding on the national perception rather vigorously."

One day in New York last summer I had a vision near Saint Paul's   1
Chapel of Trinity Church. I had walked a lot of the length of Manhattan, and it seemed to me that a large part of my time had been spent stepping around men who stood in the gutter snapping imag-

ANSWERS TO RESPONDING TO READING

1. Opinions will vary depending on whether readers agree with Mitford's implied criticism. Many will think, however, that her relentless hostility eventually damages her credibility. (Surely these practices could not flourish unless they filled some need.)
2. Mitford's criticism is valid and useful, but it is worthwhile to consider why families accept—in fact, need—such euphemisms. Such artifice soothes the shock of death, helps to control grief, and helps the family get through the difficult process of burying a loved one.
3. Mitford's approach could be applied to American weddings, holiday celebrations, or sporting events.

FOR OPENERS

This essay claims that America's cultural attitudes foster cocaine use. Discuss with the class the reasons for drug abuse in American society.

inary whips. Strangers had approached me trying to sell Elavil, an antidepressant. As I stood on Broadway I reflected that although I had grown to middle age seeing strange sights, I had never thought to see people selling Elavil on the street. Street Elavil, I would have exclaimed, that must be a joke!

I looked across the street from Saint Paul's and the daylight seemed strange. I had gotten used to thinking of the Wall Street area as a part of New York where people looked healthy and wholesome. But from where I stood half the men waiting for the light to change looked like Bartleby the Scrivener.[1] Everybody seemed to be listening in dread to his own heartbeat. They're all loaded, I thought. That was my vision. Everybody was loaded on cocaine.

In the morning, driving into Manhattan, the traffic had seemed particularly demonic. I'd had a peculiar exchange with a bridge toll taker who seemed to have one half of a joke I was expected to have the other half of. I didn't. Walking on Fourteenth Street, I passed a man in an imitation leopard-skin hat who was crying as though his heart would break. At Fourth Avenue I was offered the Elavil. Elavil relieves the depression attendant on the deprivation of re-refined cocaine—"crack"—which is what the men cracking the imaginary whips were selling. Moreover, I'd been reading the papers. I began to think that I was seeing stoned cops, stoned grocery shoppers, and stoned boomers. So it went, and by the time I got to lower Broadway I was concerned. I felt as though I were about to confront the primary process of hundreds of thousands of unsound minds. What I was seeing in my vision of New York as super-stoned Super City was cocaine in its role of success drug.

Not many years ago, people who didn't use cocaine didn't have to know much about it. Now, however, it's intruding on the national perception rather vigorously. The National Institute on Drug Abuse reported almost six million current users in 1985, defining a current user as one who took cocaine at least once in the course of the month preceding the survey. The same source in the same year reckoned that more than twenty-two million people had tried cocaine at least once during their lives.

So much is being heard about cocaine, principally through television, that even people who live away from the urban centers are beginning to experience it as a factor in their lives. Something of the same thing happened during the sixties, when Americans in quiet

---

ADDITIONAL QUESTIONS FOR RESPONDING TO READING

1. Should all illegal drugs be viewed as equally offensive, or should we judge them on the basis of how harmful their effects are? For example, are marijuana and cocaine equally damaging to our society? Why or why not?
2. When sentencing illegal drug users, should judges take into account the cultural, economic, and social factors that have led to the drug use, or should all responsibility for the illegal act be placed on the offender?
3. If you were capable of making American antidrug policy, what measures would you advocate for fighting America's drug problem, and why?

---

[1]Protagonist of Herman Melville's tale by the same name, published in 1856. Bartleby, former clerk in the dead letter office, is hired by a Wall Street lawyer as a copyist. A taciturn, distant figure, he withdraws from humanity; his trademark response is "I would prefer not to." [Eds.]

parts of the country began to feel they were being subjected to civil insurrection day in and day out.

One aspect that even people who don't want to know anything 6
about cocaine have been compelled to recognize is that people get unpleasantly weird under its influence. The term "dope fiend" was coined for cocaine users. You can actually seem unpleasantly weird to yourself on coke, which is one of its greatest drawbacks.

In several ways the ubiquity of cocaine and its derivative crack 7
have helped the American city to carry on its iconographic function as Vision of Hell. Over the past few years some of the street chore-ography of Manhattan has changed slightly. There seems to be less marijuana in the air. At the freight doors of garment factories and around construction sites people cluster smoking something odorless. At night in the ghettos and at the borders of ghettos, near the tunnels and at downtown intersections, an enormous ugly argument seems to be in progress. Small, contentious groups of people drift across the avenues, sometimes squaring off at each other, moving from one corner to the next, the conformations breaking up and re-forming. The purchase of illegal drugs was always a sordid process, but users and dealers (pretty much interchangeable creatures) used to attempt adherence to an idealized vision of the traffic in which smoothie dealt with smoothie in a confraternity of the hip. Crack sales tend to start with a death threat and deteriorate rapidly. The words "die" and "motherfucker" are among the most often heard. Petty race riots between white suburban buyers and minority urban sellers break out several times an hour. Every half block stand people in various states of fury, mindless exhilaration, and utter despair—all of it dreadfully authentic yet all of it essentially artificial.

On the day of my visionary walk through the city I felt beset by 8
a drug I hadn't even been in the same room with for a year. New York always seems to tremble on the brink of entropy[2]—that's why we love her even though she doesn't love us back. But that afternoon it felt as though white crystal had seeped through the plates and fouled the very frame of reference. There was an invisible whiteness deep down things, not just the glistening mounds in their little tricorn Pyramid papers tucked into compacts and under pocket handker-chiefs but, I thought, a metaphysical whiteness. It seemed a little out of place at first. I was not in California. I was among cathedrals of commerce in the midst of a city hard at work. I wondered why the sense of the drug should strike most vividly on Wall Street. It might be the shade of Bartleby, I thought, and the proximity of the harbor. The whiteness was Melvillean, like the whiteness of the Whale.

TEACHING STRATEGY

Discuss how Stone structures his argument. Note his combined use of narrative, statistics, anecdote, and literary allusion. Ask students whether this is an essay about American values that uses cocaine as a metaphor, or an essay about cocaine that tries to understand its causes.

---

[2]Randomness; disorder; chaos. [Eds.]

In the celebrated chapter on whiteness in *Moby-Dick*, Melville   9
frequently mentions the Andes—not Bolivia, as it happens, but Lima,[3]
"the strangest saddest city thou canst see. . . . There is a higher horror
in the whiteness of her woe." Higher horror seemed right. I had
found a Lima of the mind.

"But not yet," Melville writes, "have we solved the incantation   10
of this whiteness and learned why it appeals with such power to the
soul . . . and yet should be as it is, the intensifying agent in things
the most appalling to mankind . . . a dumb blankness full of meaning
in a wide landscape of snows—a colorless all-color of atheism from
which we shrink."

I was in the city to do business with some people who tend toward   11
enthusiasms, toward ardor and mild obsession. Behind every enthusiasm, every outburst of ardor, every mildly obsessive response, I
kept scouring the leprous white hand of narcosis. It's a mess when
you think everybody's high. I liked it a lot better when the weirdest
thing around was me.

We old-time pot smokers used to think we were cute with our   12
instant redefinitions and homespun minimalism. Our attention had
been caught by a sensibility a lot of us associated with black people.
We weren't as cute as we thought, but for a while we were able to
indulge the notion that a small community of minds was being nurtured through marijuana. In a very limited way, in terms of art and
music, we were right. In the early days we divided into two camps.
Some of us were elitists who thought we had the right to get high
because we were artists and musicians and consciousness was our
profession and the rest of the world, the "squares," could go to hell.
Others of us hoped the insights we got from using drugs like pot
could somehow change the world for the better. To people in the
latter camp, it was vaguely heartening when a walker in the city could
smell marijuana everywhere. The present coke-deluded cityscape is
another story.

Cocaine was never much to look at. All drugs have their coarse   13
practicalities, so in the use of narcotics and their paraphernalia, dex-
terity and savoir-faire are prized. Coke, however, is difficult to handle
gracefully. For one thing, once-refined cocaine works only in solution
with blood, mucus, or saliva, a handicap to éclat that speaks for itself.

I remember watching an elegant and beautiful woman who was   14
trying cocaine for the first time. The lady, serving herself liberally,

[3]During the winter months the city of Lima is almost constantly covered with a low mist.
[Eds.]

COLLABORATIVE ACTIVITY

Divide the class into groups, and assign each
group a particular American cultural problem
(gang warfare, latch-key children, teenage pregnancy, and so forth). Ask each group to identify
possible causes of the problem and to suggest
possible solutions.

had a minor indelicate accident. For a long time she simply sat there contentedly with her nose running, licking her lips. This woman was a person of such imposing presence that watching her get high was like watching an angel turn into an ape; she hung there at a balancing point somewhere midway along the anthropoid spectrum.

The first person I ever saw use cocaine was a poet I haven't seen for twenty-five years. It was on the Lower East Side, one night during the fifties, in an age that's as dead now as Agamemnon.[4] Coltrane's[5] "My Favorite Things" was on the record player. The poet was tall and thin and pale and self-destructive, and we all thought that was a great way to be. After he'd done up, his nose started to bleed. The bathtub was in the kitchen, and he sat down on the kitchen floor and leaned his head back against it. You had to be there.   15

Let me tell you, I honor that man. I honor him for his lonely independence and his hard outcast's road. I think he was one of the people who, in the fifties, helped to make this country a lot freer. Maybe that's the trouble. Ultimately, nothing is free, in the sense that you have to pay up somewhere along the line.   16

My friend the poet thought cocaine lived someplace around midnight that he was trying to find. He would not have expected it to become a commonplace drug. He would not have expected over 17 percent of American high school students to have tried it, even thirty years later, any more than he would have expected that one quarter of America's high school students would use marijuana. He was the wild one. In hindsight, we should have known how many of the kids to come would want to be the wild ones too.   17

A few weeks after my difficult day in the city I was sitting in my car in a New England coastal village leafing through my mail when for some reason I became aware of the car parked beside mine. In the front seat were two teenage girls whose tan summer faces seemed aglow with that combination of apparent innocence and apparent wantonness adolescence inflicts. I glanced across the space between our cars and saw that they were doing cocaine. The car windows were rolled up against the bay breeze. The drug itself was out of sight, on the car seat between them. By turns they descended to sniff. Then both of them sat upright, *bolt upright* might be the way to put it, staring straight ahead of them. They licked their fingers. The girl in the driver's seat ran her tongue over a pocket mirror. The girl beside her looked over at me, utterly untroubled by my presence; there was a six-inch length of peppermint-striped soda straw in her mouth.   18

---

[4]In Greek mythology, the King of Mycenae, leader of the Greeks against Troy. [Eds.]
[5]John Coltrane (1926–67), American jazz saxophonist and composer. [Eds.]

There are people I know who cannot remove a cigarette from its pack with someone standing behind them, who between opening the seal and lighting up perform the most elaborate pantomimes of guilty depravity. Neither of these children betrayed the slightest cautious reflex, although we couldn't have been more than a few hundred yards from the village police station. The girl with the straw between her teeth and I looked at each other for an instant and I saw something in her eyes, but I don't know what it was. It wasn't guilty pleasure or defiance or flirtatiousness. Its intellectual aspect was crazy and its emotional valence was cold.

A moment later, the driver threw the car into reverse and straight into the path of an oncoming postal truck, which fortunately braked in time. Then they were off down the road, headed wherever they thought their state of mind might make things better. One wondered where. 19

Watching their car disappear, I could still see the moment of their highs. Surfacing, they had looked frosted, their faces streaked with a cotton-candied, snotty sugary excitement, a pair of little girls having their afternoon at the fair, their carnival goodies, and all the rides in a few seconds flat. Five minutes from the parking lot, the fairy lights would be burned out. Their parents would find them testy, sarcastic, and tantrum prone. Unless, of course, they had more. 20

The destructiveness of cocaine today is a cause for concern. What form is our concern to take? 21

American politicians offer a not untypical American political response. The Democrats say they want to hang the dealers. The Republicans say they want to hang them and throw their bones to the dogs. Several individuals suggest that the military be used in these endeavors. Maybe all the partisan competition for dramatic solutions will produce results. Surely some of our politically inspired plans must work some of the time. 22

I was talking with a friend of mine who's a lawyer recently. Like many lawyers, she once used a lot of cocaine, although she doesn't anymore. She and I were discussing the satisfactions of cocaine abuse and the lack thereof, and she recounted the story of a stock-trading associate of hers who was sometimes guided in his decisions by stimulants. One day, all of his clients received telephone calls informing them that the world was coming to an end and that he was supervising their portfolios with that in mind. The world would end by water, said the financier, but the right people would turn into birds and escape. He and some of his clients were already growing feathers and wattles. 23

"Some gonna fly and some gonna die," the broker intoned darkly 24
to his startled customers.

We agreed that while this might be the kind of message you'd be 25
glad to get from your Yaqui[6] soothsayer, it hardly qualified as sound
investment strategy. (Although, God knows, the market can be that
way!)

"But sometimes," she said, "you feel this illusion of lucidity. Of 26
excellence."

I think it's more that you feel like you're *about* to feel an illusion 27
of lucidity and excellence. But lucidity and excellence are pretty hot
stuff, even in a potential state, even as illusion. Those are very contemporary goals and quite different from the electric twilight that
people were pursuing in the sixties.

"I thought of cocaine as a success drug," one addict is reported 28
saying in a recent newspaper story. Can you blame him? It certainly
looks like a success drug, all white and shiny like an artificial
Christmas morning. It glows and it shines just as success must. And
success is back! The faint sound you hear at the edges of perception
is the snap, crackle, and pop of winners winning and losers losing.

You can tell the losers by their downcast eyes bespeaking 29
unseemly scruple and self-doubt. You can tell the winners by their
winning ways and natty strut; look at them stepping out there, all
confidence and hard-edged realism. It's a new age of vim and vigor,
piss and vinegar and cocaine. If we work hard enough and live long
enough, we'll all be as young as the President.

Meanwhile, behold restored as lord of creation, pinnacle of evo- 30
lution and progress, alpha and omega[7] of the rationalized universe,
Mr. Success, together with his new partner and pal, Ms. Success.
These two have what it takes; they've got heart, they've got drive,
they've got aggression. It's a no-fault world of military options and
no draft. Hey, they got it all.

Sometimes, though, it gets scary. Some days it's hard to know 31
whether you're winning or not. You're on the go but so's the next
guy. You're moving fast but so is she. Sometimes you're afraid you'd
think awful thoughts if you had time to think. That's why you're
almost glad there isn't time. How can you be sure you're on the right
track? You might be on the wrong one. Everybody can't be a winner
or there wouldn't be a game. "Some gonna fly and some gonna die."

---

[6]Tribe of North American Indians living in Sonora, Mexico. [Eds.]
[7]Beginning and end. Alpha is the first letter of the Greek alphabet; omega is the last. [Eds.]

WRITING SUGGESTIONS

1. Write an essay about the effect that drug use has had on a family member, friend, or acquaintance.
2. How does your own school or community culture encourage (or discourage) drug use? Write a letter to the editor of your school or community newspaper in which you commend or condemn the actions of the town or institution.
3. Write a problem/solution essay suggested by the "Collaborative Activity" assignment.

Predestinarian religion[8] generated a lot of useful energy in this republic. It cast a long December shadow, a certain slant of light[9] on winter afternoons. Things were grim with everybody wondering whether he was chosen, whether he was good enough, really, truly good enough and not just faking. Finally, it stopped being useful. We got rid of it. 32

It's funny how the old due bills come up for presentation. We had Faith and not Works. Now we've got all kinds of works and no faith. And people still wonder if they've got what it takes. 33

When you're wondering if you've got what it takes, wondering whether you're on the right track and whether you're going to fly, do you sometimes want a little pick-me-up? Something upbeat and cool with nice lines, something that shines like success and snaps you to, so you can step out there feeling aggressive, like a million-dollar Mr. or Ms.? And after that, would you like to be your very own poet and see fear—yes, I said fear—in a handful of dust?[10] Have we got something for you! Something white. 34

On the New York morning of which I've spoken I beheld its whiteness. How white it really is, and what it does, was further described about 130 years ago by America's God-bestowed prophet, who delineated the great American success story with the story of two great American losers, Bartleby and Ahab.[11] From *Moby-Dick*: 35

> And when we consider that . . . theory of the natural philosophers, that all other earthly hues—every stately or lovely emblazoning—the sweet tinges of sunset skies and woods; yea, and the gilded velvets of butterflies, and the butterfly cheeks of young girls; all these are but the subtle deceits, not actually inherent in substance, but only laid on from without; and when we proceed further, and consider that the mystical cosmetic which produces every one of her hues, the great principle of light, for ever remains white or colorless in itself, and if operating without medium upon matter, would touch all objects, even tulips and roses, with it's own blank tinge—pondering all this, the palsied universe lies before us a leper; and like wilful travellers in Lapland, who refuse to wear colored and coloring glasses upon their eyes, so the wretched infidel gazes himself blind at the monumental white shroud that wraps all the prospect around him.

---

[8]Any religion supporting the doctrine that God has foreordained all things, leaving human beings helpless to change their fate. [Eds.]

[9]"There's a certain Slant of light" is the first line of a poem about death by Emily Dickinson (1830–86), American poet. [Eds.]

[10]From T. S. Eliot's *The Waste Land* (1922): "I will show you fear in a handful of dust." [Eds.]

[11]Captain Ahab, obsessed with tracking down the white whale Moby-Dick, which tore away his leg. The whale is eventually harpooned, but Ahab, caught in the line, dies. [Eds.]

All over America at this moment pleasurable surges of self-esteem 36
are fading. People are discovering that the principal thing one does
with cocaine is run out of it.

If cocaine is the great "success drug," is there a contradiction in 37
that it brings such ruin not only to the bankers and the lawyers but
to so many of the youngest, poorest Americans? I think not. The poor
and the children have always received American obsessions as
shadow and parody. They too can be relied on to "go for it."

"Just say no!" we tell them and each other when we talk about 38
crack and cocaine. It is necessary that we say this because liberation
starts from there.

But we live in a society based overwhelmingly on appetite and 39
self-regard. We train our young to be consumers and to think most
highly of their own pleasure. In this we face a contradiction that no
act of Congress can resolve.

In our debates on the subject of dealing with drug abuse, one of 40
the recurring phrases has been "the moral equivalent of war." Not
many of those who use it, I suspect, know its origin.

In 1910, the philosopher William James wrote an essay discussing 41
the absence of values, the "moral weightlessness" that seemed to
characterize modern times. James was a pacifist. Yet he conceded that
the demands of battle were capable of bringing forth virtues like
courage, loyalty, community, and mutual concern that seemed in
increasingly short supply as the new century unfolded. As a pacifist
and a moralist, James found himself in a dilemma. How, he wondered, can we nourish those virtues without having to pay the
dreadful price that war demands? We must foster courage, loyalty,
and the rest, but we must not have war. Very well, he reasoned, we
must find the *moral equivalent of war.*

Against these drugs can we ever, rhetoric aside, bring any kind 42
of real heroism to bear? When they've said no to crack, can we
someday give them something to say yes to?

RESPONDING TO READING

1. Does anything in this essay surprise or shock you? Do you find anything
in Stone's ideas about cocaine with which you disagree? How do you account
for your reactions?   **2.** Explain how each of the following affects your
reaction to the essay: Stone's view of the city as a "Vision of Hell" (paragraph 7); his characterization of himself as one of a group of "old-time pot
smokers" (paragraph 12); his sarcastic tone in paragraph 30; his breathless,
frightened tone in paragraph 31.   **3.** What does Stone gain—or lose—by
describing the cocaine problem in literary terms as well as in terms of its

**ANSWERS TO RESPONDING
TO READING**

1. Perhaps most shocking is Stone's equation
of cocaine use with American values, arguing
that cocaine's popularity flows from America's consumer mentality. He implies that our
society is responsible for the drug's prevalence. Students may have other reactions.

2. Stone's term "vision of hell" colors his
description of the city; it suggests the distorted perception of a cocaine user and reinforces his suggestion that cocaine use flows
from an unbalanced American value system,
represented by the city. When Stone characterizes himself as an "old-time pot
smoker," he suggests that the problem of
cocaine use is serious enough to frighten
someone who has advocated drug use in the
past. His sarcastic tone in paragraph 30 also
effectively reinforces his main point about the
emptiness of American values. His frightened
tone in paragraph 31 reflects the desperation
and hopelessness that is the dark side of the
cocaine user's "success story."

3. By describing the cocaine problem in literary
terms, Stone attempts to universalize it. Students will probably report that this attempt
does not work for them: they are unlikely to
understand the allusions and will probably
see the literary references as annoying distractions that make him less credible as a
social critic.

human cost? For instance, do you understand the literary allusions? Do you see the literary analyses as digressions? Does their presence reduce Stone's credibility as a social critic? Does it make you less or more likely to accept his concern?

Like a Winding Sheet

ANN PETRY

Ann Petry (1912–   ), born in Connecticut, based her novel *The Street* (1946) on her experiences in Harlem. Petry worked as a reporter for *The Amsterdam News* and *The People's Voice*, and she has written novels and children's books about race relations and a biography of Harriet Tubman. She has a understanding of and compassion for oppression, and she creates characters who are psychologically complex. The following selection was chosen for *The Best Short Stories of 1946* anthology. It is a powerful story, rich in imagery, that shows the tragic consequences for one couple of being black in America.

FOR OPENERS

Remind students that this story was written nearly fifty years ago. Ask them whether they believe it is dated or whether its issues remain relevant. If they did not know its date of publication, would they think it was a modern story?

ADDITIONAL QUESTIONS FOR RESPONDING TO READING

1. What, if anything, does this story say about men's attitudes toward women?
2. Johnson thinks of several improvements in working conditions. Why doesn't the company implement them? Does the company have a moral obligation to do so?
3. Why will Johnson hit his wife but not the two women who insult him?

He had planned to get up before Mae did and surprise her by 1 fixing breakfast. Instead he went back to sleep and she got out of bed so quietly he didn't know she wasn't there beside him until he woke up and heard the queer soft gurgle of water running out of the sink in the bathroom.

He knew he ought to get up but instead he put his arms across 2 his forehead to shut the afternoon sunlight out of his eyes, pulled his legs up close to his body, testing them to see if the ache was still in them.

Mae had finished in the bathroom. He could tell because she never 3 closed the door when she was in there and now the sweet smell of talcum powder was drifting down the hall and into the bedroom. Then he heard her coming down the hall.

"Hi, babe," she said affectionately. 4

"Hum," he grunted, and moved his arms away from his head, 5 opened one eye.

"It's a nice morning." 6

"Yeah." He rolled over and the sheet twisted around him, out- 7 lining his thighs, his chest. "You mean afternoon, don't ya?"

Mae looked at the twisted sheet and giggled. "Looks like a 8 winding sheet," she said. "A shroud—" Laughter tangled with her words and she had to pause for a moment before she could continue. "You look like a huckleberry—in a winding sheet—"

"That's no way to talk. Early in the day like this," he protested. 9

He looked at his arms silhouetted against the white of the sheets. 10 They were inky black by contrast and he had to smile in spite of

himself and he lay there smiling and savoring the sweet sound of
Mae's giggling.

"Early?" She pointed a finger at the alarm clock on the table near   11
the bed and giggled again. "It's almost four o'clock. And if you don't
spring up out of there, you're going to be late again."

"What do you mean 'again'?"   12

"Twice last week. Three times the week before. And once the   13
week before and—"

"I can't get used to sleeping in the daytime," he said fretfully.   14
He pushed his legs out from under the covers experimentally. Some
of the ache had gone out of them but they weren't really rested yet.
"It's too light for good sleeping. And all that standing beats the hell
out of my legs."

"After two years you oughta be used to it," Mae said.   15

He watched her as she fixed her hair, powdered her face, slipped   16
into a pair of blue denim overalls. She moved quickly and yet she
didn't seem to hurry.

"You look like you'd had plenty of sleep," he said lazily. He had   17
to get up but he kept putting the moment off, not wanting to move,
yet he didn't dare let his legs go completely limp because if he did
he'd go back to sleep. It was getting later and later but the thought
of putting his weight on his legs kept him lying there.

When he finally got up he had to hurry, and he gulped his break-   18
fast so fast that he wondered if his stomach could possibly use food
thrown at it at such a rate of speed. He was still wondering about it
as he and Mae were putting their coats on in the hall.

Mae paused to look at the calendar. "It's the thirteenth," she said.   19
Then a faint excitement in her voice, "Why, it's Friday the thirteenth."
She had one arm in her coat sleeve and she held it there while she
stared at the calendar. "I oughta stay home," she said. "I shouldn't
go outa the house."

"Aw, don't be a fool," he said. "Today's payday. And payday is   20
a good luck day everywhere, any way you look at it." And as she
stood hesitating he said, "Aw, come on."

And he was late for work again because they spent fifteen minutes   21
arguing before he could convince her she ought to go to work just
the same. He had to talk persuasively, urging her gently, and it took
time. But he couldn't bring himself to talk to her roughly or threaten
to strike her like a lot of men might have done. He wasn't made
that way.

So when he reached the plant he was late and he had to wait to   22
punch the time clock because the day-shift workers were streaming
out in long lines, in groups and bunches that impeded his progress.

Even now just starting his workday his legs ached. He had to   23
force himself to struggle past the outgoing workers, punch the time

TEACHING STRATEGY

Ask students to characterize this couple as
individuals. What strengths and weaknesses
does each have? How do they relate to each
other? To others?

clock, and get the little cart he pushed around all night, because he kept toying with the idea of going home and getting back in bed.

He pushed the cart out on the concrete floor, thinking that if this 24 was his plant he'd make a lot of changes in it. There were too many standing-up jobs for one thing. He'd figure out some way most of 'em could be done sitting down and he'd put a lot more benches around. And this job he had—this job that forced him to walk ten hours a night, pushing this little cart, well, he'd turn it into a sitting-down job. One of those little trucks they used around railroad stations would be good for a job like this. Guys sat on a seat and the thing moved easily, taking up little room and turning in hardly any space at all like on a dime.

He pushed the cart near the foreman. He never could remember 25 to refer to her as the forelady even in his mind. It was funny to have a white woman for a boss in a plant like this one.

She was sore about something. He could tell by the way her face 26 was red and her eyes were half-shut until they were slits. Probably been out late and didn't get enough sleep. He avoided looking at her and hurried a little, head down, as he passed her though he couldn't resist stealing a glance at her out of the corner of his eye. He saw the edge of the light-colored slacks she wore and the tip end of a big tan shoe.

"Hey, Johnson!" the woman said. 27

The machines had started full blast. The whirr and the grinding 28 made the building shake, made it impossible to hear conversations. The men and women at the machines talked to each other but looking at them from just a little distance away, they appeared to be simply moving their lips because you couldn't hear what they were saying. Yet the woman's voice cut across the machine sounds—harsh, angry.

He turned his head slowly. "Good evenin', Mrs. Scott," he said, 29 and waited.

"You're late again." 30

"That's right. My legs were bothering me." 31

The woman's face grew redder, angrier looking. "Half this shift 32 comes in late," she said. "And you're the worst one of all. You're always late. Whatsa matter with ya?"

"It's my legs," he said. "Somehow they don't ever get rested. I 33 don't seem to get used to sleeping days. And I just can't get started."

"Excuses. You guys always got excuses," her anger grew and 34 spread. "Every guy comes in here late always has an excuse. His wife's sick or his grandmother died or somebody in the family had to go to the hospital," she paused, drew a deep breath. "And the niggers is the worse. I don't care what's wrong with your legs. You get in here on time. I'm sick of you niggers—"

COLLABORATIVE ACTIVITY

In groups, look for examples of Johnson's reaction (or lack of reaction) to each stressful situation in his life. Suggest more appropriate responses. In class discussion, try to account for his behavior.

"You got the right to get mad," he interrupted softly. "You got 35 the right to cuss me four ways to Sunday but I ain't letting nobody call me a nigger."

He stepped closer to her. His fists were doubled. His lips were 36 drawn back in a thin narrow line. A vein in his forehead stood out swollen, thick.

And the woman backed away from him, not hurriedly but 37 slowly—two, three steps back.

"Aw, forget it," she said. "I didn't mean nothing by it. It slipped 38 out. It was an accident." The red of her face deepened until the small blood vessels in her cheeks were purple. "Go on and get to work," she urged. And she took three more slow backward steps.

He stood motionless for a moment and then turned away from 39 the sight of the red lipstick on her mouth that made him remember that the foreman was a woman. And he couldn't bring himself to hit a woman. He felt a curious tingling in his fingers and he looked down at his hands. They were clenched tight, hard, ready to smash some of those small purple veins in her face.

He pushed the cart ahead of him, walking slowly. When he turned 40 his head, she was staring in his direction, mopping her forehead with a dark blue handkerchief. Their eyes met and then they both looked away.

He didn't glance in her direction again but moved past the long 41 work benches, carefully collecting the finished parts, going slowly and steadily up and down, and back and forth the length of the building, and as he walked he forced himself to swallow his anger, get rid of it.

And he succeeded so that he was able to think about what had 42 happened without getting upset about it. An hour went by but the tension stayed in his hands. They were clenched and knotted on the handles of the cart as though ready to aim a blow.

And he thought he should have hit her anyway, smacked her 43 hard in the face, felt the soft flesh of her face give under the hardness of his hands. He tried to make his hands relax by offering them a description of what it would have been like to strike her because he had the queer feeling that his hands were not exactly a part of him anymore—they had developed a separate life of their own over which he had no control. So he dwelt on the pleasure his hands would have felt—both of them cracking at her, first one and then the other. If he had done that his hands would have felt good now—relaxed, rested.

And he decided that even if he'd lost his job for it, he should 44 have let her have it and it would have been a long time, maybe the rest of her life, before she called anybody else a nigger.

The only trouble was he couldn't hit a woman. A woman couldn't hit back the same way a man did. But it would have been a deeply satisfying thing to have cracked her narrow lips wide open with just one blow, beautifully timed and with all his weight in back of it. That way he would have gotten rid of all the energy and tension his anger had created in him. He kept remembering how his heart had started pumping blood so fast he had felt it tingle even in the tips of his fingers. 45

With the approach of night, fatigue nibbled at him. The corners of his mouth drooped, the frown between his eyes deepened, his shoulders sagged; but his hands stayed tight and tense. As the hours dragged by he noticed that the women workers had started to snap and snarl at each other. He couldn't hear what they said because of the sound of machines but he could see the quick lip movements that sent words tumbling from the sides of their mouths. They gestured irritably with their hands and scowled as their mouths moved. 46

Their violent jerky motions told him that it was getting close on to quitting time but somehow he felt that the night still stretched ahead of him, composed of endless hours of steady walking on his aching legs. When the whistle finally blew he went on pushing the cart, unable to believe that it had sounded. The whirring of the machines died away to a murmur and he knew then that he'd really heard the whistle. He stood still for a moment, filled with a relief that made him sigh. 47

Then he moved briskly, putting the cart in the storeroom, hurrying to take his place in the line forming before the paymaster. That was another thing he'd change, he thought. He'd have the pay envelopes handed to the people right at their benches so there wouldn't be ten or fifteen minutes lost waiting for the pay. He always got home about fifteen minutes late on payday. They did it better in the plant where Mae worked, brought the money right to them at their benches. 48

He stuck his pay envelope in his pants' pocket and followed the line of workers heading for the subway in a slow-moving stream. He glanced up at the sky. It was a nice night, the sky looked packed full to running over with stars. And he thought if he and Mae would go right to bed when they got home from work they'd catch a few hours of darkness for sleeping. But they never did. They fooled around— cooking and eating and listening to the radio and he always stayed in a big chair in the living room and went almost but not quite to sleep and when they finally got to bed it was five or six in the morning and daylight was already seeping around the edges of the sky. 49

He walked slowly, putting off the moment when he would have to plunge into the crowd hurrying toward the subway. It was a long ride to Harlem and tonight the thought of it appalled him. He paused 50 outside an all-night restaurant to kill time, so that some of the first rush of workers would be gone when he reached the subway.

The lights in the restaurant were brilliant, enticing. There was 51 life and motion inside. And as he looked through the window he thought that everything within range of his eyes gleamed—the long imitation marble counter, the tall stools, the white porcelain-topped tables and especially the big metal coffee urn right near the window. Steam issued from its top and a gas flame flickered under it—a lively, dancing, blue flame.

A lot of the workers from his shift—men and women—were 52 lining up near the coffee urn. He watched them walk to the porcelain-topped tables carrying steaming cups of coffee and he saw that just the smell of the coffee lessened the fatigue lines in their faces. After the first sip their faces softened, they smiled, they began to talk and laugh.

On a sudden impulse he shoved the door open and joined the 53 line in front of the coffee urn. The line moved slowly. And as he stood there the smell of the coffee, the sound of the laughter and the voices, helped dull the sharp ache in his legs.

He didn't pay any attention to the white girl who was serving 54 the coffee at the urn. He kept looking at the cups in the hands of the men who had been ahead of him. Each time a man stepped out of the line with one of the thick white cups the fragrant steam got in his nostrils. He saw that they walked carefully so as not to spill a single drop. There was a froth of bubbles at the top of each cup and he thought about how he would let the bubbles break against his lips before he actually took a big deep swallow.

Then it was his turn. "A cup of coffee," he said, just as he had 55 heard the others say.

The white girl looked past him, put her hands up to her head 56 and gently lifted her hair away from the back of her neck, tossing her head back a little. "No more coffee for a while," she said.

He wasn't certain he'd heard her correctly and he said "What?" 57 blankly.

"No more coffee for a while," she repeated. 58

There was silence behind him and then uneasy movement. He 59 thought someone would say something, ask why or protest, but there was only silence and then a faint shuffling sound as though the men standing behind him had simultaneously shifted their weight from one foot to the other.

He looked at the girl without saying anything. He felt his hands 60 begin to tingle and the tingling went all the way down to his finger tips so that he glanced down at them. They were clenched tight, hard, into fists. Then he looked at the girl again. What he wanted to do was hit her so hard that the scarlet lipstick on her mouth would smear and spread over her nose, her chin, out toward her cheeks, so hard that she would never toss her head again and refuse a man a cup of coffee because he was black.

He estimated the distance across the counter and reached for- 61 ward, balancing his weight on the balls of his feet, ready to let the blow go. And then his hands fell back down to his sides because he forced himself to lower them, to unclench them and make them dangle loose. The effort took his breath away because his hands fought against him. But he couldn't hit her. He couldn't even now bring himself to hit a woman, not even this one, who had refused him a cup of coffee with a toss of her head. He kept seeing the gesture with which she had lifted the length of her blond hair from the back of her neck as expressive of her contempt for him.

When he went out the door he didn't look back. If he had he 62 would have seen the flickering blue flame under the shiny coffee urn being extinguished. The line of men who had stood behind him lin-gered a moment to watch the people drinking coffee at the tables and then they left just as he had without having had the coffee they wanted so badly. The girl behind the counter poured water in the urn and swabbed it out and as she waited for the water to run out, she lifted her hair gently from the back of her neck and tossed her head before she began making a fresh lot of coffee.

But he had walked away without a backward look, his head down, 63 his hands in his pockets, raging at himself and whatever it was inside of him that had forced him to stand quiet and still when he wanted to strike out.

The subway was crowded and he had to stand. He tried grasping 64 an overhead strap and his hands were too tense to grip it. So he moved near the train door and stood there swaying back and forth with the rocking of the train. The roar of the train beat inside his head, making it ache and throb, and the pain in his legs clawed up into his groin so that he seemed to be bursting with pain and he told himself that it was due to all that anger-born energy that had piled up in him and not been used and so it had spread through him like a poison—from his feet and legs all the way up to his head.

Mae was in the house before he was. He knew she was home 65 before he put the key in the door of the apartment. The radio was going. She had it tuned up loud and she was singing along with it.

"Hello, babe," she called out, as soon as he opened the door.   66

He tried to say "hello" and it came out half grunt and half sigh.   67

"You sure sound cheerful," she said.   68

She was in the bedroom and he went and leaned against the 69 doorjamb. The denim overalls she wore to work were carefully draped

over the back of a chair by the bed. She was standing in front of the
dresser, tying the sash of a yellow housecoat around her waist and
chewing gum vigorously as she admired her reflection in the mirror
over the dresser.

"Whatsa matter?" she said. "You get bawled out by the boss or   70
somep'n?"

"Just tired," he said slowly. "For God's sake, do you have to   71
crack that gum like that?"

"You don't have to lissen to me," she said complacently. She   72
patted a curl in place near the side of her head and then lifted her
hair away from the back of her neck, ducking her head forward and
then back.

He winced away from the gesture. "What you got to be always   73
fooling with your hair for?" he protested.

"Say, what's the matter with you anyway?" She turned away   74
from the mirror to face him, put her hands on her hips. "You ain't
been in the house two minutes and you're picking on me."

He didn't answer her because her eyes were angry and he didn't   75
want to quarrel with her. They'd been married too long and got along
too well and so he walked all the way into the room and sat down
in the chair by the bed and stretched his legs out in front of him,
putting his weight on the heels of his shoes, leaning way back in the
chair, not saying anything.

"Lissen," she said sharply. "I've got to wear those overalls again   76
tomorrow. You're going to get them all wrinkled up leaning against
them like that."

He didn't move. He was too tired and his legs were throbbing   77
now that he had sat down. Besides the overalls were already wrinkled
and dirty, he thought. They couldn't help but be for she'd worn them
all week. He leaned farther back in the chair.

"Come on, get up," she ordered.   78

"Oh, what the hell," he said wearily, and got up from the chair.   79
"I'd just as soon live in a subway. There'd be just as much place to
sit down."

He saw that her sense of humor was struggling with her anger.   80
But her sense of humor won because she giggled.

"Aw, come on and eat," she said. There was a coaxing note in   81
her voice. "You're nothing but an old hungry nigger trying to act
tough and—" she paused to giggle and then continued, "You—"

He had always found her giggling pleasant and deliberately said   82
things that might amuse her and then waited, listening for the delicate
sound to emerge from her throat. This time he didn't even hear the
giggle. He didn't let her finish what she was saying. She was standing
close to him and that funny tingling started in his finger tips, went
fast up his arms and sent his fist shooting straight for her face.

WRITING SUGGESTION

Rewrite the story as a diary entry from Mae's point of view. What was her day like?

ANSWERS TO RESPONDING TO READING

1. The winding sheet (shroud) is used to wrap dead bodies, but it also suggests that both Johnson and Mae are strangling.
2. His physical responses are aggravated by his repressed emotions and lead inevitably to the outburst at the end. They help explain but not excuse his violent behavior.
3. The main emphasis seems to be on race. Johnson cannot hit the white women, but he can attack his wife, who is black.

FOR OPENERS

Try to arrange to show your class *Smooth Talk*, the film version of the story. Whether or not you have access to the film, you might want to discuss the fact that it, unlike the story, has a happy ending: Connie goes off with Arnold—and, presumably, loses her virginity—but she returns to a close and loving relationship with her family. What do students think of such an outcome? What do they think happens to Connie at the end of Oates's story?

There was the smacking sound of soft flesh being struck by a 83
hard object and it wasn't until she screamed that he realized he had
hit her in the mouth—so hard that the dark red lipstick had blurred
and spread over her full lips, reaching up toward the tip of her nose,
down toward her chin, out toward her cheeks.

The knowledge that he had struck her seeped through him slowly 84
and he was appalled but he couldn't drag his hands away from her
face. He kept striking her and he thought with horror that something
inside him was holding him, binding him to this act, wrapping and
twisting about him so that he had to continue it. He had lost all control
over his hands. And he groped for a phrase, a word, something to
describe what this thing was like that was happening to him and he
thought it was like being enmeshed in a winding sheet—that was
it—like a winding sheet. And even as the thought formed in his mind,
his hands reached for her face again and yet again.

RESPONDING TO READING

1. Why is the winding sheet an especially apt metaphor in the story? What does it suggest to you?   **2.** How do the many references to Johnson's physical discomfort—for example, his aching legs and tingling fingers—help to prepare you for the story's ending? Do these references in any way help to explain, or even excuse, his behavior?   **3.** Is this story's major emphasis on gender, race, or class? Explain your conclusion.

Where Are You Going, Where Have You Been?

JOYCE CAROL OATES

Joyce Carol Oates (see also p. 613), writer of novels, criticism, poetry, and plays, first published the story that follows in her collection *The Wheel of Love and Other Stories* (1970). In this strange and frightening tale, Oates's protagonist stays home from a family outing, leaving herself vulnerable to a dangerous seduction.

For Bob Dylan[1]

Her name was Connie. She was fifteen and she had a quick ner- 1
vous giggling habit of craning her neck to glance into mirrors, or

---

[1]Oates has said that the story was inspired in part by Dylan's song "Its All Over Now, Baby Blue." [Eds.]

checking other people's faces to make sure her own was all right. Her mother, who noticed everything and knew everything and who hadn't much reason any longer to look at her own face, always scolded Connie about it. "Stop gawking at yourself, who are you? You think you're so pretty?" she would say. Connie would raise her eyebrows at these familiar complaints and look right through her mother, into a shadowy vision of herself as she was right at that moment: she knew she was pretty and that was everything. Her mother had been pretty once too, if you could believe those old snapshots in the album, but now her looks were gone and that was why she was always after Connie.

"Why don't you keep your room clean like your sister? How've you got your hair fixed—what the hell stinks? Hair spray? You don't see your sister using that junk."

Her sister June was twenty-four and still lived at home. She was a secretary in the high school Connie attended, and if that wasn't bad enough—with her in the same building—she was so plain and chunky and steady that Connie had to hear her praised all the time by her mother and her mother's sisters. June did this, June did that, she saved money and helped clean the house and cooked and Connie couldn't do a thing, her mind was all filled with trashy daydreams. Their father was away at work most of the time and when he came home he wanted supper and he read the newspaper at supper and after supper he went to bed. He didn't bother talking much to them, but around his bent head Connie's mother kept picking at her until Connie wished her mother was dead and she herself was dead and it was all over. "She makes me want to throw up sometimes," she complained to her friends. She had a high, breathless, amused voice which made everything she said sound a little forced, whether it was sincere or not.

There was one good thing: June went places with girl friends of hers, girls who were just as plain and steady as she, and so when Connie wanted to do that her mother had no objections. The father of Connie's best girl friend drove the girls the three miles to town and left them off at a shopping plaza, so that they could walk through the stores or go to a movie, and when he came to pick them up again at eleven he never bothered to ask what they had done.

They must have been familiar sights, walking around that shopping plaza in their shorts and flat ballerina slippers that always scuffed the sidewalk, with charm bracelets jingling on their thin wrists; they would lean together to whisper and laugh secretly if someone passed by who amused or interested them. Connie had long dark blond hair that drew anyone's eye to it, and she wore part of it pulled up on her head and puffed out and the rest of it she let fall down her back. She wore a pull-over jersey blouse that looked one way when she

2

3

4

5

ADDITIONAL QUESTIONS FOR RESPONDING TO READING

1. Music is something on which Connie can depend. What else seems to offer her support?

2. At the end of the story, is there any evidence that Connie has changed or grown?

3. What might be the significance of the dedication to Bob Dylan? (Oates has said she was thinking of the song "It's All Over Now, Baby Blue" when she wrote the story.)

TEACHING STRATEGY

In discussing this story in their article "In Fairyland Without a Map: Connie's Exploration Inward in Joyce Carol Oates's 'Where Are You Going, Where Have You Been?'" critics Gretchen Schulz and R. J. R. Rockwood point to Bruno Bettleheim's insistence that fairy tales enable children to deal with their fears about coming to terms with adult sexuality and other adolescent problems. They observe that Oates has woven the motifs from several well-known fairy tales into the story, which deals in concrete terms with a girl's ambivalence about mature sexuality. Students may want to discuss Connie as innocent child and Arnold as villain and compare the story's characters, setting, and situation with those of familiar fairy tales.

was at home and another way when she was away from home. Everything about her had two sides to it, one for home and one for anywhere that was not home: her walk that could be childlike and bobbing, or languid enough to make anyone think she was hearing music in her head, her mouth which was pale and smirking most of the time, but bright and pink on these evenings out, her laugh which was cynical and drawling at home—"Ha, ha, very funny"—but high-pitched and nervous anywhere else, like the jingling of the charms on her bracelet.

Sometimes they did go shopping or to a movie, but sometimes   6 they went across the highway, ducking fast across the busy road, to a drive-in restaurant where older kids hung out. The restaurant was shaped like a big bottle, though squatter than a real bottle, and on its cap was a revolving figure of a grinning boy who held a hamburger aloft. One night in mid-summer they ran across, breathless with daring, and right away someone leaned out a car window and invited them over, but it was just a boy from high school they didn't like. It made them feel good to be able to ignore him. They went up through the maze of parked and cruising cars to the bright-lit, fly-infested restaurant, their faces pleased and expectant as if they were entering a sacred building that loomed out of the night to give them what haven and what blessing they yearned for. They sat at the counter and crossed their legs at the ankles, their thin shoulders rigid with excitement, and listened to the music that made everything so good: the music was always in the background like music at a church service, it was something to depend upon.

A boy named Eddie came in to talk with them. He sat backwards   7 on his stool, turning himself jerkily around in semi-circles and then stopping and turning again, and after a while he asked Connie if she would like something to eat. She said she did and so she tapped her friend's arm on her way out—her friend pulled her face up into a brave droll look—and Connie said she would meet her at eleven, across the way. "I just hate to leave her like that," Connie said earnestly, but the boy said that she wouldn't be alone for long. So they went out to his car and on the way Connie couldn't help but let her eyes wander over the windshields and faces all around her, her face gleaming with a joy that had nothing to do with Eddie or even this place; it might have been the music. She drew her shoulders up and sucked in her breath with the pure pleasure of being alive, and just at that moment she happened to glance at a face just a few feet from hers. It was a boy with shaggy black hair, in a convertible jalopy painted gold. He stared at her and then his lips widened into a grin. Connie slit her eyes at him and turned away, but she couldn't help glancing back and there he was still watching her. He wagged a finger and laughed and said, "Gonna get you, baby," and Connie turned away again without Eddie noticing anything.

She spent three hours with him, at the restaurant where they ate   8
hamburgers and drank Cokes in wax cups that were always sweating, and then down an alley a mile or so away, and when he left her off at five to eleven only the movie house was still open at the plaza. Her girl friend was there, talking with a boy. When Connie came up the two girls smiled at each other and Connie said, "How was the movie?" and the girl said, "*You* should know." They rode off with the girl's father, sleepy and pleased, and Connie couldn't help but look at the darkened shopping plaza with its big empty parking lot and its signs that were faded and ghostly now, and over at the drive-in restaurant where cars were still circling tirelessly. She couldn't hear the music at this distance.

Next morning June asked her how the movie was and Connie   9
said, "So-so."

She and that girl and occasionally another girl went out several   10
times a week that way, and the rest of the time Connie spent around the house—it was summer vacation—getting in her mother's way and thinking, dreaming, about the boys she met. But all the boys fell back and dissolved into a single face that was not even a face, but an idea, a feeling, mixed up with the urgent insistent pounding of the music and the humid night air of July. Connie's mother kept dragging her back to the daylight by finding things for her to do or saying, suddenly, "What's this about the Pettinger girl?"

And Connie would say nervously, "Oh, her. That dope." She   11
always drew thick clear lines between herself and such girls, and her mother was simple and kindly enough to believe her. Her mother was so simple, Connie thought, that it was maybe cruel to fool her so much. Her mother went scuffling around the house in old bedroom slippers and complained over the telephone to one sister about the other, then the other called up and the two of them complained about the third one. If June's name was mentioned her mother's tone was approving, and if Connie's name was mentioned it was disapproving. This did not really mean she disliked Connie and actually Connie thought that her mother preferred her to June because she was prettier, but the two of them kept up a pretense of exasperation, a sense that they were tugging and struggling over something of little value to either of them. Sometimes, over coffee, they were almost friends, but something would come up—some vexation that was like a fly buzzing suddenly around their heads—and their faces went hard with contempt.

One Sunday Connie got up at eleven—none of them bothered   12
with church—and washed her hair so that it could dry all day long,

in the sun. Her parents and sister were going to a barbecue at an aunt's house and Connie said no, she wasn't interested, rolling her eyes to let her mother know just what she thought of it. "Stay home alone then," her mother said sharply. Connie sat out back in a lawn chair and watched them drive away, her father quiet and bald, hunched around so that he could back the car out, her mother with a look that was still angry and not at all softened through the windshield, and in the back seat poor old June all dressed up as if she didn't know what a barbecue was, with all the running yelling kids and the flies. Connie sat with her eyes closed in the sun, dreaming and dazed with the warmth about her as if this were a kind of love, the caresses of love, and her mind slipped over onto thoughts of the boy she had been with the night before and how nice he had been, how sweet it always was, not the way someone like June would suppose but sweet, gentle, the way it was in movies and promised in songs; and when she opened her eyes she hardly knew where she was, the back yard ran off into weeds and a fence-line of trees and behind it the sky was perfectly blue and still. The asbestos "ranch house" that was now three years old startled her—it looked small. She shook her head as if to get awake.

It was too hot. She went inside the house and turned on the radio   13 to drown out the quiet. She sat on the edge of her bed, barefoot, and listened for an hour and a half to a program called XYZ Sunday Jamboree, record after record of hard, fast, shrieking songs she sang along with, interspersed by exclamations from "Bobby King:" "An' look here you girls at Napoleon's—Son and Charley want you to pay real close attention to this song coming up!"

And Connie paid close attention herself, bathed in a glow of slow-   14 pulsed joy that seemed to rise mysteriously out of the music itself and lay languidly about the airless little room, breathed in and breathed out with each gentle rise and fall of her chest.

After a while she heard a car coming up the drive. She sat up at   15 once, startled, because it couldn't be her father so soon. The gravel kept crunching all the way in from the road—the driveway was long— and Connie ran to the window. It was a car she didn't know. It was an open jalopy, painted a bright gold that caught the sunlight opaquely. Her heart began to pound and her fingers snatched at her hair, checking it, and she whispered "Christ. Christ," wondering how bad she looked. The car came to a stop at the side door and the horn sounded four short taps as if this were a signal Connie knew.

She went into the kitchen and approached the door slowly, then   16 hung out the screen door, her bare toes curling down off the step. There were two boys in the car and now she recognized the driver:

he had shaggy, shabby black hair that looked crazy as a wig and he was grinning at her.

"I ain't late, am I?" he said.   17

"Who the hell do you think you are?" Connie said.   18

"Toldja I'd be out, didn't I?"   19

"I don't even know who you are."   20

She spoke sullenly, careful to show no interest or pleasure, and   21
he spoke in a fast bright monotone. Connie looked past him to the other boy, taking her time. He had fair brown hair, with a lock that fell onto his forehead. His sideburns gave him a fierce, embarrassed look, but so far he hadn't even bothered to glance at her. Both boys wore sunglasses. The driver's glasses were metallic and mirrored everything in miniature.

"You wanta come for a ride?" he said.   22

Connie smirked and let her hair fall loose over one shoulder.   23

"Don'tcha like my car? New paint job," he said. "Hey."   24

"What?"   25

"You're cute."   26

She pretended to fidget, chasing flies away from the door.   27

"Don'tcha believe me, or what?" he said.   28

"Look, I don't even know who you are," Connie said in disgust.   29

"Hey, Ellie's got a radio, see. Mine's broke down." He lifted his   30
friend's arm and showed her the little transistor the boy was holding, and now Connie began to hear the music. It was the same program that was playing inside the house.

"Bobby King?" she said.   31

"I listen to him all the time. I think he's great."   32

"He's kind of great," Connie said reluctantly.   33

"Listen, that guy's *great*. He knows where the action is."   34

Connie blushed a little, because the glasses made it impossible   35
for her to see just what this boy was looking at. She couldn't decide if she liked him or if he was just a jerk, and so she dawdled in the doorway and wouldn't come down or go back inside. She said, "What's all that stuff painted on your car?"

"Can'tcha read it?" He opened the door very carefully, as if he   36
was afraid it might fall off. He slid out just as carefully, planting his feet firmly on the ground, the tiny metallic world in his glasses slowing down like gelatine hardening and in the midst of it Connie's bright green blouse. "This here is my name, to begin with," he said. ARNOLD FRIEND was written in tarlike black letters on the side, with a drawing of a round grinning face that reminded Connie of a pumpkin, except it wore sunglasses. "I wanta introduce myself, I'm Arnold Friend and that's my real name and I'm gonna be your friend,

honey, and inside the car's Ellie Oscar, he's kinda shy." Ellie brought his transistor radio up to his shoulder and balanced it there. "Now these numbers are a secret code, honey," Arnold Friend explained. He read off the numbers 33, 19, 17 and raised his eyebrows at her to see what she thought of that, but she didn't think much of it. The left rear fender had been smashed and around it was written, on the gleaming gold background: DONE BY CRAZY WOMAN DRIVER. Connie had to laugh at that. Arnold Friend was pleased at her laughter and looked up at her. "Around the other side's a lot more—you wanta come and see them?"

"No." 37

"Why not?" 38

"Why should I?" 39

"Don'tcha wanta see what's on the car? Don'tcha wanta go for a ride?" 40

"I don't know." 41

"Why not?" 42

"I got things to do." 43

"Like what?" 44

"Things." 45

He laughed as if she had said something funny. He slapped his thighs. He was standing in a strange way, leaning back against the car as if he were balancing himself. He wasn't tall, only an inch or so taller than she would be if she came down to him. Connie liked the way he was dressed, which was the way all of them dressed: tight faded jeans stuffed into black, scuffed boots, a belt that pulled his waist in and showed how lean he was, and a white pull-over shirt that was a little soiled and showed the hard small muscles of his arms and shoulders. He looked as if he probably did hard work, lifting and carrying things. Even his neck looked muscular. And his face was a familiar face, somehow: the jaw and chin and cheeks slightly darkened, because he hadn't shaved for a day or two, and the nose long and hawk-like, sniffing as if she were a treat he was going to gobble up and it was all a joke. 46

"Connie, you ain't telling the truth. This is your day set aside for a ride with me and you know it," he said, still laughing. The way he straightened and recovered from his fit of laughing showed that it had been all fake. 47

"How do you know what my name is?" she said suspiciously. 48

"It's Connie." 49

"Maybe and maybe not." 50

"I know my Connie," he said, wagging his finger. Now she remembered him even better, back at the restaurant, and her cheeks warmed at the thought of how she sucked in her breath just at the 51 moment she passed him—how she must have looked to him. And he had remembered her. "Ellie and I come out here especially for you," he said. "Ellie can sit in back. How about it?"

"Where?"   52

"Where what?"   53

"Where're we going?"   54

He looked at her. He took off the sunglasses and she saw how   55
pale the skin around his eyes was, like holes that were not in shadow but instead in light. His eyes were chips of broken glass that catch the light in an amiable way. He smiled. It was as if the idea of going for a ride somewhere, to some place, was a new idea to him.

"Just for a ride, Connie sweetheart."   56

"I never said my name was Connie," she said.   57

"But I know what it is. I know your name and all about you, lots   58
of things," Arnold Friend said. He had not moved yet but stood still leaning back against the side of his jalopy. "I took a special interest in you, such a pretty girl, and found out all about you like I know your parents and sister are gone somewheres and I know where and how long they're going to be gone, and I know who you were with last night, and your best girl friend's name is Betty. Right?"

He spoke in a simple lilting voice, exactly as if he were reciting   59
the words to a song. His smile assured her that everything was fine. In the car Ellie turned up the volume on his radio and did not bother to look around at them.

"Ellie can sit in the back seat," Arnold Friend said. He indicated   60
his friend with a casual jerk of his chin, as if Ellie did not count and she should not bother with him.

"How'd you find out all that stuff?" Connie said.   61

"Listen: Betty Schultz and Tony Fitch and Jimmy Pettinger and   62
Nancy Pettinger," he said, in a chant. "Raymond Stanely and Bob Hutter—"

"Do you know all those kids?"   63

"I know everybody."   64

"Look, you're kidding. You're not from around here."   65

"Sure."   66

"But—how come we never saw you before?"   67

"Sure you saw me before," he said. He looked down at his boots,   68
as if he were a little offended. "You just don't remember."

"I guess I'd remember you," Connie said.   69

"Yeah?" He looked up at this, beaming. He was pleased. He   70
began to mark time with the music from Ellie's radio, tapping his fists lightly together. Connie looked away from his smile to the car, which was painted so bright it almost hurt her eyes to look at it. She looked at that name, ARNOLD FRIEND. And up at the front fender was an

expression that was familiar—MAN THE FLYING SAUCERS. It was an expression kids had used the year before, but didn't use this year. She looked at it for a while as if the words meant something to her that she did not yet know.

"What're you thinking about? Huh?" Arnold Friend demanded. 71 "Not worried about your hair blowing around in the car, are you?"

"No."   72

"Think I maybe can't drive good?"   73

"How do I know?"   74

"You're a hard girl to handle. How come?" he said. "Don't you 75 know I'm your friend? Didn't you see me put my sign in the air when you walked by?"

"What sign?"   76

"My sign." And he drew an X in the air, leaning out toward her. 77 They were maybe ten feet apart. After his hand fell back to his side the X was still in the air, almost visible. Connie let the screen door close and stood perfectly still inside it, listening to the music from her radio and the boy's blend together. She stared at Arnold Friend. He stood there so stiffly relaxed, pretending to be relaxed, with one hand idly on the door handle as if he were keeping himself up that way and had no intention of ever moving again. She recognized most things about him, the tight jeans that showed his thighs and buttocks and the greasy leather boots and the tight shirt, and even that slippery friendly smile of his, that sleepy dreamy smile that all the boys used to get across ideas they didn't want to put into words. She recognized all this and also the singsong way he talked, slightly mocking, kidding, but serious and a little melancholy, and she recognized the way he tapped one fist against the other in homage to the perpetual music behind him. But all these things did not come together.

She said suddenly, "Hey, how old are you?"   78

His smile faded. She could see then that he wasn't a kid, he was 79 much older—thirty, maybe more. At this knowledge her heart began to pound faster.

"That's a crazy thing to ask. Can'tcha see I'm your own age?"   80

"Like hell you are."   81

"Or maybe a coupla years older, I'm eighteen."   82

"Eighteen?" she said doubtfully.   83

He grinned to reassure her and lines appeared at the corners of 84 his mouth. His teeth were big and white. He grinned so broadly his eyes became slits and she saw how thick the lashes were, thick and black as if painted with a black tarlike material. Then he seemed to become embarrassed, abruptly, and looked over his shoulder at Ellie. "*Him*, he's crazy," he said. "Ain't he a riot, he's a nut, a real character." Ellie was still listening to the music. His sunglasses told nothing about what he was thinking. He wore a bright orange shirt unbuttoned halfway to show his chest, which was a pale, bluish chest and not muscular like Arnold Friend's. His shirt collar was turned up all around and the very tips of the collar pointed out past his chin as if they were protecting him. He was pressing the transistor radio up against his ear and sat there in a kind of daze, right in the sun.

"He's kinda strange," Connie said.   85

"Hey, she says you're kinda strange! Kinda strange!" Arnold   86
Friend cried. He pounded on the car to get Ellie's attention. Ellie turned for the first time and Connie saw with shock that he wasn't a kid either—he had a fair, hairless face, cheeks reddened slightly as if the veins grew too close to the surface of his skin, the face of a forty-year-old baby. Connie felt a wave of dizziness rise in her at this sight and she stared at him as if waiting for something to change the shock of the moment, make it all right again. Ellie's lips kept shaping words, mumbling along with the words blasting in his ear.

"Maybe you two better go away," Connie said faintly.   87

"What? How come?" Arnold Friend cried. "We come out here to   88
take you for a ride. It's Sunday." He had the voice of the man on the radio now. It was the same voice, Connie thought. "Don'tcha know it's Sunday all day and honey, no matter who you were with last night today you're with Arnold Friend and don't you forget it!— Maybe you better step out here," he said, and this last was in a different voice. It was a little flatter, as if the heat was finally getting to him.

"No. I got things to do."   89

"Hey."   90

"You two better leave."   91

"We ain't leaving until you come with us."   92

"Like hell I am—"   93

"Connie, don't fool around with me. I mean, I mean, don't fool   94
around," he said, shaking his head. He laughed incredulously. He placed his sunglasses on top of his head, carefully, as if he were indeed wearing a wig, and brought the stems down behind his ears. Connie stared at him, another wave of dizziness and fear rising in her so that for a moment he wasn't even in focus but was just a blur, standing there against his gold car, and she had the idea that he had driven up the driveway all right but had come from nowhere before that and belonged nowhere and that everything about him and even about the music that was so familiar to her was only half real.

"If my father comes and sees you—"   95

"He ain't coming. He's at a barbecue."   96

"How do you know that?"   97

"Aunt Tillie's. Right now they're—uh—they're drinking. Sitting   98
around," he said vaguely, squinting as if he were staring all the way
to town and over to Aunt Tillie's backyard. Then the vision seemed
to get clear and he nodded energetically. "Yeah. Sitting around.
There's your sister in a blue dress, huh? And high heels, the poor
sad bitch—nothing like you, sweetheart! And your mother's helping
some fat woman with the corn, they're cleaning the corn—husking
the corn—"

"What fat woman?" Connie cried.   99

"How do I know what fat woman. I don't know every goddam   100
fat woman in the world!" Arnold Friend laughed.

"Oh, that's Mrs. Hornby. . . . Who invited her?" Connie said.   101
She felt a little light-headed. Her breath was coming quickly.

"She's too fat. I don't like them fat. I like them the way you are,   102
honey," he said, smiling sleepily at her. They stared at each other
for a while, through the screen door. He said softly, "Now what
you're going to do is this: you're going to come out that door. You're
going to sit up front with me and Ellie's going to sit in the back, the
hell with Ellie, right? This isn't Ellie's date. You're my date. I'm your
lover, honey."

"What? You're crazy—"

"Yes, I'm your lover. You don't know what that is but you will,"   103
he said. "I know that too. I know all about you. But look: it's real
nice and you couldn't ask for nobody better than me, or more polite.
I always keep my word. I'll tell you how it is, I'm always nice at first,
the first time. I'll hold you so tight you won't think you have to try
to get away or pretend anything because you'll know you can't. And
I'll come inside you where it's all secret and you'll give in to me and
you'll love me—"

"Shut up! You're crazy!" Connie said. She backed away from the   105
door. She put her hands against her ears as if she'd heard something
terrible, something not meant for her. "People don't talk like that,
you're crazy," she muttered. Her heart was almost too big now for
her chest and its pumping made sweat break out all over her. She
looked out to see Arnold Friend pause and then take a step toward
the porch lurching. He almost fell. But, like a clever drunken man,
he managed to catch his balance. He wobbled in his high boots and
grabbed hold of one of the porch posts.

"Honey?" he said. "You still listening?"   106

"Get the hell out of here!"   107

"Be nice, honey. Listen."   108

"I'm going to call the police—"   109

He wobbled again and out of the side of his mouth came a fast 110
spat curse, an aside not meant for her to hear. But even this "Christ!"
sounded forced. Then he began to smile again. She watched this smile
come, awkward as if he were smiling from inside a mask. His whole
face was a mask, she thought wildly, tanned down onto his throat
but then running out as if he had plastered make-up on his face but
had forgotten about his throat.

"Honey—? Listen, here's how it is. I always tell the truth and I 111
promise you this: I ain't coming in that house after you."

"You better not! I'm going to call the police if you—if you 112
don't—"

"Honey," he said, talking right through her voice, "honey, I'm 113
not coming in there but you are coming out here. You know why?"

She was panting. The kitchen looked like a place she had never 114
seen before, some room she had run inside but which wasn't good
enough, wasn't going to help her. The kitchen window had never
had a curtain, after three years, and there were dishes in the sink for
her to do—probably—and if you ran your hand across the table you'd
probably feel something sticky there.

"You listening, honey? Hey?"   115

"—going to call the police—"   116

"Soon as you touch the phone I don't need to keep my promise 117
and can come inside. You won't want that."

She rushed forward and tried to lock the door. Her fingers were 118
shaking. "But why lock it," Arnold Friend said gently, talking right
into her face. "It's just a screen door. It's just nothing." One of his
boots was at a strange angle, as if his foot wasn't in it. It pointed out
to the left, bent at the ankle. "I mean, anybody can break through a
screen door and glass and wood and iron or anything else if he needs
to, anybody at all and specially Arnold Friend. If the place got lit up
with a fire honey you'd come running out into my arms, right into
my arms and safe at home—like you knew I was your lover and'd
stopped fooling around. I don't mind a nice shy girl but I don't like
no fooling around." Part of those words were spoken with a slight
rhythmic lilt, and Connie somehow recognized them—the echo of a
song from last year, about a girl rushing into her boy friend's arms
and coming home again—

Connie stood barefoot on the linoleum floor, staring at him. 119
"What do you want?" she whispered.

"I want you," he said.   120

"What?"   121

"Seen you that night and thought, that's the one, yes sir. I never 122
needed to look any more."

"But my father's coming back. He's coming to get me. I had to 123
wash my hair first—" She spoke in a dry, rapid voice, hardly raising
it for him to hear.

"No, your daddy is not coming and yes, you had to wash your 124
hair and you washed it for me. It's nice and shining and all for me,
I thank you, sweetheart," he said, with a mock bow, but again he
almost lost his balance. He had to bend and adjust his boots. Evidently
his feet did not go all the way down; the boots must have been stuffed
with something so that he would seem taller. Connie stared out at
him and behind him Ellie in the car, who seemed to be looking off
toward Connie's right, into nothing. This Ellie said, pulling the words
out of the air one after another as if he were just discovering them,
"You want me to pull out the phone?"

"Shut your mouth and keep it shut," Arnold Friend said, his face 125
red from bending over or maybe from embarrassment because Connie
had seen his boots. "This ain't none of your business."

"What—what are you doing? What do you want?" Connie said. 126
"If I call the police they'll get you, they'll arrest you—"

"Promise was not to come in unless you touch that phone, and 127
I'll keep that promise," he said. He resumed his erect position and
tried to force his shoulders back. He sounded like a hero in a movie,
declaring something important. He spoke too loudly and it was as if
he were speaking to someone behind Connie. "I ain't made plans for
coming in that house where I don't belong but just for you to come
out to me, the way you should. Don't you know who I am?"

"You're crazy," she whispered. She backed away from the door 128
but did not want to go into another part of the house, as if this would
give him permission to come through the door. "What do you. . . .
You're crazy, you . . ."

"Huh? What're you saying, honey?" 129

Her eyes darted everywhere in the kitchen. She could not 130
remember what it was, this room.

"This is how it is, honey: you come out and we'll drive away, 131
have a nice ride. But if you don't come out we're gonna wait till your
people come home and then they're all going to get it."

"You want that telephone pulled out?" Ellie said. He held the 132
radio away from his ear and grimaced, as if without the radio the air
was too much for him.

"I toldja shut up, Ellie," Arnold Friend said, "you're deaf, get a 133
hearing aid, right? Fix yourself up. This little girl's no trouble and's
gonna be nice to me, so Ellie keep to yourself, this ain't your date—
right? Don't hem in on me. Don't hog. Don't crush. Don't bird dog.
Don't trail me," he said in a rapid meaningless voice, as if he were
running through all the expressions he'd learned but was no longer

sure which one of them was in style, then rushing on to new ones, making them up with his eyes closed, "Don't crawl under my fence, don't squeeze in my chipmunk hole, don't sniff my glue, suck my popsicle, keep your own greasy fingers on yourself!" He shaded his eyes and peered in at Connie, who was backed against the kitchen table. "Don't mind him honey he's just a creep. He's a dope. Right? I'm the boy for you and like I said you come out here nice like a lady and give me your hand, and nobody else gets hurt, I mean, your nice old bald-headed daddy and your mummy and your sister in her high heels. Because listen: why bring them in this?"

"Leave me alone," Connie whispered. 134

"Hey, you know that old woman down the road, the one with 135 the chickens and stuff—you know her?"

"She's dead!" 136

"Dead? What? You know her?" Arnold Friend said. 137

"She's dead—" 138

"Don't you like her?" 139

"She's dead—she's—she isn't here any more —" 140

"But don't you like her, I mean, you got something against her? 141 Some grudge or something?" Then his voice dipped as if he were conscious of a rudeness. He touched the sunglasses perched on top of his head as if to make sure they were still there. "Now you be a good girl."

"What are you going to do?" 142

"Just two things, or maybe three," Arnold Friend said. "But I 143 promise it won't last long and you'll like me that way you get to like people you're close to. You will. It's all over for you here, so come on out. You don't want your people in any trouble, do you?"

She turned and bumped against a chair or something, hurting 144 her leg, but she ran into the back room and picked up the telephone. Something roared in her ear, a tiny roaring, and she was so sick with fear that she could do nothing but listen to it—the telephone was clammy and very heavy and her fingers groped down to the dial but were too weak to touch it. She began to scream into the phone, into the roaring. She cried out, she cried for her mother, she felt her breath start jerking back and forth in her lungs as if it were something Arnold Friend were stabbing her with again and again with no tenderness. A noisy sorrowful wailing rose all about her and she was locked inside it the way she was locked inside the house.

After a while she could hear again. She was sitting on the floor 145 with her wet back against the wall.

Arnold Friend was saying from the door, "That's a good girl. Put 146 the phone back."

She kicked the phone away from her. 147

WRITING SUGGESTIONS

1. Write a letter from Connie to her mother in which she tries to come to terms with her ambivalent feelings about family and sexuality.

2. Write an essay in which you discuss the importance of the story's setting, including elements like the familiar teenage mall culture, the heat, Connie's isolation, and the freedom (and restlessness) generated by summer vacation. In what sense does setting force Connie to act?

3. In a short essay, explore the story's conflicts (Connie versus June, Connie versus her mother, Connie versus Arnold, Connie versus herself). Which is most important in determining the story's outcome?

"No, honey. Pick it up. Put it back right." 148

She picked it up and put it back. The dial tone stopped. 149

"That's a good girl. Now you come outside." 150

She was hollow with what had been fear, but what was now just 151 an emptiness. All that screaming had blasted it out of her. She sat, one leg cramped under her, and deep inside her brain was something like a pinpoint of light that kept going and would not let her relax. She thought, I'm not going to see my mother again. She thought, I'm not going to sleep in my bed again. Her bright green blouse was all wet.

Arnold Friend said, in a gentle-loud voice that was like a stage 152 voice, "The place where you came from ain't there any more, and where you had in mind to go is cancelled out. This place you are now—inside your daddy's house—is nothing but a cardboard box I can knock down any time. You know that and always did know it. You hear me?"

She thought, I have got to think. I have to know what to do. 153

"We'll go out to a nice field, out in the country here where it 154 smells so nice and it's sunny," Arnold Friend said. "I'll have my arms around you so you won't need to try to get away and I'll show you what love is like, what it does. The hell with this house! It looks solid all right," he said. He ran a fingernail down the screen and the noise did not make Connie shiver, as it would have the day before. "Now put your hand on your heart, honey. Feel that? That feels solid too but we know better, be nice to me, be sweet like you can because what else is there for a girl like you but to be sweet and pretty and give in?—and get away before her people come back?"

She felt her pounding heart. Her hand seemed to enclose it. She 155 thought for the first time in her life that it was nothing that was hers, that belonged to her, but just a pounding, living thing inside this body that wasn't really hers either.

"You don't want them to get hurt," Arnold Friend went on. "Now 156 get up, honey. Get up all by yourself."

She stood. 157

"Now turn this way. That's right. Come over here to me—Ellie, 158 put that away, didn't I tell you? You dope. You miserable creepy dope," Arnold Friend said. His words were not angry but only part of an incantation. The incantation was kindly. "Now come out through the kitchen to me honey and let's see a smile, try it, you're a brave sweet little girl and now they're eating corn and hotdogs cooked to bursting over an outdoor fire, and they don't know one thing about you and never did and honey you're better than them because not a one of them would have done this for you."

Connie felt the linoleum under her feet; it was cool. She brushed 159 her hair back out of her eyes. Arnold Friend let go of the post tentatively and opened his arms for her, his elbows pointing in toward each other and his wrists limp, to show that this was an embarrassed embrace and a little mocking, he didn't want to make her self-conscious.

She put out her hand against the screen. She watched herself 160 push the door slowly open as if she were safe back somewhere in the other doorway, watching this body and this head of long hair moving out into the sunlight where Arnold Friend waited.

"My sweet little blue-eyed girl," he said, in a half-sung sigh that 161 had nothing to do with her brown eyes but was taken up just the same by the vast sunlit reaches of the land behind him and on all sides of him, so much land that Connie had never seen before and did not recognize except to know that she was going to it.

RESPONDING TO READING

1. Does Connie's relationship with her mother strike you as realistic? Why or why not? Is it in any way like your own relationship with your mother? If so, how?   **2.** Why is Connie so vulnerable to Arnold? What is the nature of his appeal for her? Do you believe she is typical or atypical of fifteen-year-old girls in these respects?   **3.** Is music a positive or negative force in Connie's life? What role does music play in your life?

Dear John Wayne

LOUISE ERDRICH

Louise Erdrich (1954–   ), born in North Dakota, is the daughter of a German immigrant and a Chippewa Indian. She first gained her reputation as a writer through publication in magazines such as *The Atlantic Monthly* and *Redbook*. Erdrich has written three novels, *Love Medicine* (1984), *The Beet Queen* (1986), and *Tracks* (1988) and coauthored one, *The Crown of Columbus* (1991). In "Dear John Wayne," from *Jacklight* (1984), a collection of her poetry, Erdrich contrasts images of Native Americans on the movie screen with the images of Native American life around her.

August and the drive-in picture is packed.
We lounge on the hood of the Pontiac
surrounded by the slow-burning spirals they sell
at the window, to vanquish the hordes of mosquitoes.
Nothing works. They break through the smoke-screen for blood. 5

ADDITIONAL QUESTIONS FOR RESPONDING TO READING

1. Who is the speaker in this poem?
2. How are the present and past brought together by the images of this poem?
3. Whose face is alluded to in stanza 4? What are the characteristics of this person?
4. Why do the Indians laugh at the whites' ideas of land ownership?
5. Where is "where we want them" (line 39)? Are Native Americans today fulfilling this expectation?

TEACHING STRATEGIES

1. Point out images in the poem that contrast the reality of nature with the fiction depicted on the screen.
2. Ask students to consider the differences between the images of Indians depicted in films of the 1940s and 1950s, where they are seen as savages, and the images of more modern films, which cast them as noble and spiritual. Is the modern characterization more accurate? Is this just a case of one stereotype replacing another?

COLLABORATIVE ACTIVITY

Ask students, working in groups, to develop a plot outline and cast of characters for a movie told from a Native American viewpoint. In class discussion, consider how the films the students envision differ from past depictions of Native Americans.

WRITING SUGGESTION

Write several paragraphs describing one of the characters you created for the "Collaborative Activity" assignment. Be careful to avoid conventional stereotypes as you describe your character's personal traits and physical appearance.

Always the look-out spots the Indians first,
spread north to south, barring progress.
The Sioux, or Cheyenne, or some bunch
in spectacular columns, arranged like SAC missiles,
their feathers bristling in the meaningful sunset.   10

The drum breaks. There will be no parlance.[1]
Only the arrows whining, a death-cloud of nerves
swarming down on the settlers
who die beautifully, tumbling like dust weeds
into the history that brought us all here
together: this wide screen beneath the sign of the bear.   15

The sky fills, acres of blue squint and eye
that the crowd cheers. His face moves over us,
a thick cloud of vengeance, pitted
like the land that was once flesh. Each rut,
each scar makes a promise: *It is
not over, this fight, not as long as you resist.*   20

Everything we see belongs to us.
A few laughing Indians fall over the hood
slipping in the hot spilled butter.   25
*The eye sees a lot, John, but the heart is so blind.
How will you know what you own?*
He smiles, a horizon of teeth
the credits reel over, and then the white fields
again blowing in the true-to-life dark.   30
The dark films over everything.
We get into the car
scratching our mosquito bites, speechless and small
as people are when the movie is done.
We are back in ourselves.   35

How can we help but keep hearing his voice,
the flip side of the sound-track, still playing:
*Come on, boys, we've got them
where we want them, drunk, running.
They will give us what we want, what we need:*   40
*The heart is a strange wood inside of everything
we see, burning, doubling, splitting out of its skin.*

---

[1]Conversation. [Eds.]

RESPONDING TO READING

1. How are Native Americans characterized in the film the poem describes? Is this characterization familiar to you? Do you find it offensive?   **2.** Do you think this poem is addressed to John Wayne simply because he was featured in films like the one described, or do you think he is meant to serve as a symbol for someone—or something—else? Explain.   **3.** What are your thoughts about the portrayals of minorities and women in television and films?

WRITING: A WINDOW ON THE PRESENT

1.   What can someone do to move to a higher social class? On the basis of your own observations, how easy do you think it is to make such a move? For example, how do considerations like race and religion limit or enhance social mobility? In developing your response, consider the selections by Fussell and Steele.

2.   In "Children of Affluence" Robert Coles equates entitlement with destiny: From birth, affluent children are aware that they are special and that their lives will therefore be different from others' lives. They are "destined for a satisfying and rewarding life" (paragraph 30), and they know it. How does this idea of destiny—that is, the concept of events as inevitable and of life as following a predetermined script—square with the traditional view of the American Dream, which sees the United States as a land of unlimited possibilities? How does this idea apply to your own plans for the future?

3.   Joseph Lelyveld calls apartheid "the ultimate divide-and-rule strategy" (paragraph 5). Write an essay in which you discuss whether similar "divide-and-rule strategies" operate in the United States. What institutions do they affect? On what terms are they organized? Consider your own experience or the social stratification described in "It's Just Too Late."

4.   Do you believe the American family is deteriorating? Are the ties that connect family members weakening? If so, what forces do you hold responsible for this decline? Consider your own extended family as well as the situations presented in "It's Just Too Late" or "Where Are You Going, Where Have You Been?"

5.   In paragraph 39 Stone says that "we live in a society based overwhelmingly on appetite and self-regard. We train our young to be consumers and to think most highly of their own pleasure. In this we face a contradiction that no act of Congress can resolve." What do you think he means by this statement? In what way does it apply to your life or to the lives of people you know?

6.   As selections like "A Higher Horror of Whiteness," "It's Just Too Late," and "Like a Winding Sheet" reveal, we live in an increasingly violent society. Logically, then, we should be becoming more and more accustomed to death. Do your own observations and experiences suggest that we *are* becoming accustomed to death—especially violent death?

7. Several of the selections in this chapter suggest that some of modern-day society's problems are caused (or at least aggravated) by business interests that control private lives and turn personal problems into commodities. What role does the idea of commercialization play in essays like "Marrying Absurd" or "The American Way of Death?" Do you think business interests contribute to the deteriorating values of our society?

8. The question of power—who has it, who lacks it, who wants it—is central to many of the selections in this chapter. Considering works like "The Middle Class," "The Laws," and "Like a Winding Sheet," discuss the way the constant struggle for power affects your life.

9. In the last paragraph of his essay Stone asks, "When they've said no to crack, can we someday give them something to say yes to?" Answer his question.

9

A Sense of the Past

CONFRONTING THE ISSUES

In the April 22, 1991, issue of *U.S. News and World Report*, historian Daniel J. Boorstin writes that he believes it is important to distinguish between "history and current events"—that is, between events that are truly revolutionary and those whose long-term impact is more questionable.

On the one hand, Boorstin believes, we have "true turning points": political events of enduring importance, such as the American and French revolutions; key religious developments, such as the rise of Judaism, Christianity, Buddhism, and Islam; and revolutions in thought, such as those introduced by Copernicus, Darwin, and Freud. On the other hand, we have "questionable" turning points, events whose significance may be misinterpreted or overestimated, such as the arrival of democracy in China or the Soviet Union (and, Boorstin contends, the war in the Persian Gulf).

Not only do we tend to place unwarranted emphasis on events of temporary importance, Boorstin believes, but we also tend to underestimate the significance of many hidden turning points at the time they occur: for example, technological innovations such as television and the birth control pill.

After introducing your students to Boorstin's ideas about history, ask them to decide which historic events of their lifetimes they believe will eventually be seen as history ("true turning points") and which will be seen as merely current events. Ask them to explain their choices. Finally, ask whether all the events on which the essays in this chapter focus qualify as "history."

One of the ways we learn about the world in which we live is by studying the past: its heroes and villains, triumphs and defeats. By looking back at the past we can gain insights into how to act in particular situations, infer what results might follow from particular causes, decide whom to trust and whom not to trust, and identify emerging problems and learn what can—and cannot—be done to solve them. By studying history we can identify parallels, connections, patterns, and trends and, sometimes, recognize warnings. Occasionally, we can apply the lessons of history to our own lives and perhaps, as a result of what we learn, change our lives.

One of the more perplexing characteristics of history is that several people can treat the same subject in radically different ways. Bruce Catton, Annie Dillard, and William Manchester, for example, all focus on war, but their perspectives range from a view of war's heroes to its horrors; their tones range from detachment to emotional involvement; and the writers themselves are, respectively, historian, student of history, and participant in history.

Seeing the same events from different perspectives in this way is often illuminating. Both Gwendolyn Brooks and Alice Walker focus on the civil rights movement in the United States, but Brooks writes a poem from a reporter's perspective while Walker examines the effects of the movement on her own life, as a personal as well as a national milestone. Both Thomas Jefferson and John Hope Franklin focus on the early years of the United States, but Jefferson offers a contemporary view while Franklin looks back critically from the twentieth century, forcing readers to reassess Jefferson's statements and values. In both cases, the picture would be incomplete if only a single perspective were available.

Reading about history—paying special attention to connections between past and present and among various events in the past—gives us a picture that can be both compelling and disturbing. As the essays about war illustrate, periods of unpleasantness, stress, and disaster are often fertile ground for historians. Barbara Tuchman's "The Black Death," Studs Terkel's "Hard Times," and Gwendolyn Brooks's "The Chicago *Defender* Sends a Man to Little Rock" illustrate this tendency to focus on difficult and demanding times. But difficulty does not always mean despair, as Alice Walker shows; moreover, the periods of conflict often lead to resolution and reconciliation, as Bruce Catton explains in "Grant and Lee." Thus the study of history is much more than the study of disaster for its shock value; rather, it is an attempt to find meaning in actions.

PREPARING TO READ AND WRITE

As you read and prepare to write about the selections in this chapter, consider the following questions:

- Is the focus on history itself—its methodology, its importance, its limitations, its lessons—or on a particular historical period or event?

- On what historical period does the writer focus?

- Does the writer focus on personalities? On events? On setting?

- Does the writer draw an analogy between one particular historical period or event and another? Between a historical event and events of today?

- Could the selection be classified as social, economic, political, religious, or cultural history?

- Is the writer a participant, a witness, or a reporter?

- Does the writer attempt to present an objective account, or is he or she critical of historical events or figures? Why?

- Does the writer approach his or her subject with any preconceived ideas? If so, can these ideas be attributed to the time in which he or she lives or to a particular political ideology?

- Do the writer's ideas contradict your own ideas about history in any way? Do they contradict ideas presented to you in school? Do they challenge your assumptions? Change your ideas? Do you accept the writer's interpretation of events, or are you skeptical? Why?

- Is the writer optimistic or pessimistic about the present? About the future?

- Why does the writer treat the historical subject under discussion? To amuse? To offer a moral or lesson? To challenge commonly held beliefs or assumptions? To shock? To shame? To make a prediction about the future? To recommend change? To warn?

An Inquiry into the Persistence of Unwisdom in Government

BARBARA TUCHMAN

Historical writer and journalist Barbara Tuchman (1912–1989) won Pulitzer Prizes for two of her books, *The Guns of August* (1962) and *Stillwell and the American Experience in China, 1911–1945* (1971). Known for both her literary approach and her factual accuracy, Tuchman once said of herself, "I am a writer whose subject is history." Some of her many works are *The Proud Tower: A Portrait of the World Before the War, 1890–1914* (1966), *A Distant Mirror: The Calamitous Fourteenth Century* (1978), and a collection of essays, *Practicing History* (1981). Tuchman was awarded the American Academy of Arts and Sciences gold medal for history in 1978. The following essay looks critically at political life and asks why public servants often make unwise choices.

FOR OPENERS

Poll the class for their opinions about present and past world leaders. Discuss the qualities that cause some leaders to get high ratings while others get low ones. Be sure to encourage students to consider female leaders—Margaret Thatcher, Benazir Bhutto, Corazon Aquino—as well as males.

ADDITIONAL QUESTIONS FOR RESPONDING TO READING

1. Is Tuchman's assessment of the Russian government in paragraph 9 still valid today?
2. In paragraph 11, Tuchman gives examples of several effective leaders. What qualities does Tuchman indicate these men have in common? Can you suggest other, equally important, qualities?
3. In paragraph 15, Tuchman alludes to mistakes made during the period of American expansion. What were some of these mistakes? Could they have been avoided?
4. Is Tuchman's psychological portrait of men's tendency to equate failure with impotency accurate? Do you think a male historian would make a similar statement?
5. Does unrestricted power inevitably corrupt even the best leaders? Consider, for example, Franklin Delano Roosevelt's attempt to "pack the court" (that is, to appoint additional justices to the U.S. Supreme Court). Ask students to suggest examples from their own state and local governments.

A problem that strikes one in the study of history, regardless of period, is why man makes a poorer performance of government than of almost any other human activity. In this sphere, wisdom—meaning judgment acting on experience, common sense, available knowledge, and a decent appreciation of probability—is less operative and more frustrated than it should be. Why do men in high office so often act contrary to the way that reason points and enlightened self-interest suggests? Why does intelligent mental process so often seem to be paralyzed?

Why, to begin at the beginning, did the Trojan authorities drag that suspicious-looking wooden horse inside their gates? Why did successive ministries of George III—that "bundle of imbecility," as Dr. Johnson[1] called them collectively—insist on coercing rather than conciliating the Colonies though strongly advised otherwise by many counselors? Why did Napoleon and Hitler invade Russia? Why did the kaiser's government resume unrestricted submarine warfare in 1917 although explicitly warned that this would bring in the United States and that American belligerency would mean Germany's defeat? Why did Chiang Kai-shek[2] refuse to heed any voice of reform or alarm until he woke up to find that his country had slid from under him? Why did Lyndon Johnson, seconded by the best and the brightest, progressively involve this nation in a war both ruinous and halfhearted and from which nothing but bad for our side resulted?

---

[1] Samuel Johnson (1709–84), English lexicographer, critic, and author. [Eds.]

[2] (1887–1975); Chinese military leader and first president of the Republic of China (1928–31 and 1948–75). Removed government to Taiwan in 1949 in flight from Communists, who had risen to power on the mainland. [Eds.]

Why does the present Administration continue to avoid introducing effective measures to reduce the wasteful consumption of oil while members of OPEC follow a price policy that must bankrupt their customers? How is it possible that the Central Intelligence Agency, whose function it is to provide, at taxpayers' expense, the information necessary to conduct a realistic foreign policy, could remain unaware that discontent in a country crucial to our interests was boiling up to the point of insurrection and overthrow of the ruler upon whom our policy rested? It has been reported that the CIA was ordered *not* to investigate the opposition to the shah of Iran in order to spare him any indication that we took it seriously, but since this sounds more like the theater of the absurd than like responsible government, I cannot bring myself to believe it.

There was a king of Spain once, Philip III,[3] who is said to have died of a fever he contracted from sitting too long near a hot brazier, helplessly overheating himself because the functionary whose duty it was to remove the brazier when summoned could not be found. In the late twentieth century, it begins to appear as if mankind may be approaching a similar stage of suicidal incompetence. The Italians have been sitting in Philip III's hot seat for some time. The British trade unions, in a lunatic spectacle, seem periodically bent on dragging their country toward paralysis, apparently under the impression that they are separate from the whole. Taiwan was thrown into a state of shock by the United States' recognition of the People's Republic of China because, according to one report, in the seven years since the Shanghai Communiqué, the Kuomintang rulers of Taiwan had "refused to accept the new trend as a reality."

Wooden-headedness is a factor that plays a remarkably large role in government. Wooden-headedness consists of assessing a situation in terms of preconceived, fixed notions while ignoring or rejecting any contrary signs. It is acting according to wish while not allowing oneself to be confused by the facts.

A classic case was the French war plan of 1914, which concentrated everything on a French offensive to the Rhine, leaving the French left flank from Belgium to the Channel virtually unguarded. This strategy was based on the belief that the Germans would not use reserves in the front line and, without them, could not deploy enough manpower to extend their invasion through the French left. Reports by intelligence agents in 1913 to the effect that the Germans were indeed preparing their reserves for the front line in case of war were resolutely ignored because the governing spirits in France,

3

4

5

---

[3](1578–1621); also ruled Portugal (as Philip II). Aloof from his subjects, he spent money frivolously and allowed Spain's economic problems to worsen. [Eds.]

dreaming only of their own offensive, did not want to believe in any signals that would require them to strengthen their left at the expense of their march to the Rhine. In the event, the Germans could and did extend themselves around the French left with results that determined a long war and its fearful consequences for our century.

Wooden-headedness is also the refusal to learn from experience, a form in which fourteenth-century rulers were supreme. No matter how often and obviously devaluation of the currency disrupted the economy and angered the people, French monarchs continued to resort to it whenever they were desperate for cash until they provoked insurrection among the bourgeoisie. No matter how often a campaign that depended on living off a hostile country ran into want and even starvation, campaigns for which this fate was inevitable were regularly undertaken.

Still another form is identification of self with the state, as currently exhibited by the ayatollah Khomeini.[4] No wooden-headedness is so impenetrable as that of a religious zealot. Because he is connected with a private wire to the Almighty, no idea coming in on a lesser channel can reach him, which leaves him ill equipped to guide his country in its own best interests.

Philosophers of government ever since Plato have devoted their thinking to the major issues of ethics, sovereignty, the social contract, the rights of man, the corruption of power, the balance between freedom and order. Few—except Machiavelli,[5] who was concerned with government as it is, not as it should be—bothered with mere folly, although this has been a chronic and pervasive problem. "Know, my son," said a dying Swedish statesman in the seventeenth century, "with how little wisdom the world is governed." More recently, Woodrow Wilson warned, "In public affairs, stupidity is more dangerous than knavery."

Stupidity is not related to type of regime; monarchy, oligarchy, and democracy produce it equally. Nor is it peculiar to nation or class. The working class as represented by the Communist governments functions no more rationally or effectively in power than the aristocracy or the bourgeoisie, as has notably been demonstrated in recent history. Mao Tse-tung[6] may be admired for many things, but the Great Leap Forward, with a steel plant in every backyard, and the Cultural

---

[4]Ayatollah Ruholla Khomeini (1900?–89), Iranian Shi'ite Muslim leader who fought what he saw as corrupting western influences in Iran and led the revolution that overthrew the U.S.-backed monarchy of the Shah in 1979. [Eds.]

[5]Niccolò Machiavelli (1469–1527), Italian statesman and political theorist. In *The Prince* (1513) he argued against the relevance of morality in politics, asserting that deceit is necessary in the pursuit of political power. [Eds.]

[6]1893–1976. Father of Chinese communism; head of state 1949–59. [Eds.]

Revolution were exercises in unwisdom that greatly damaged China's progress and stability, not to mention the chairman's reputation. The record of the Russian proletariat in power can hardly be called enlightened, although after sixty years of control it must be accorded a kind of brutal success. If the majority of Russians are better off now than before, the cost in cruelty and tyranny has been no less and probably greater than under the czars.

After the French Revolution, the new order was rescued only by   10
Bonaparte's military campaigns, which brought the spoils of foreign wars to fill the treasury, and subsequently by his competence as an executive. He chose officials not on the basis of origin or ideology but on the principle of "la carrière ouverte aux talents"[7]—the said talents being intelligence, energy, industry, and obedience. That worked until the day of his own fatal mistake.[8]

I do not wish to give the impression that men in office are incap-   11
able of governing wisely and well. Occasionally, the exception appears, rising in heroic size above the rest, a tower visible down the centuries. Greece had her Pericles, who ruled with authority, moderation, sound judgment, and a certain nobility that imposes natural dominion over others. Rome had Caesar, a man of remarkable governing talents, although it must be said that a ruler who arouses opponents to resort to assassination is probably not as smart as he ought to be. Later, under Marcus Aurelius and the other Antonines, Roman citizens enjoyed good government, prosperity, and respect for about a century. Charlemagne[9] was able to impose order upon a mass of contending elements, to foster the arts of civilization no less than those of war, and to earn a prestige supreme in the Middle Ages—probably not equaled in the eyes of contemporaries until the appearance of George Washington.

Possessor of an inner strength and perseverance that enabled him   12
to prevail over a sea of obstacles, Washington was one of those critical figures but for whom history might well have taken a different course. He made possible the physical victory of American independence, while around him, in extraordinary fertility, political talent bloomed as if touched by some tropical sun. For all their flaws and quarrels, the Founding Fathers, who established our form of government, were, in the words of Arthur Schlesinger Sr., "the most remarkable generation of public men in the history of the United States or perhaps

---

[7](Fr.) Tools to those who can handle them. [Eds.]

[8]At the Battle of Waterloo (1815), Napoleon delayed his attack on the British, giving the Prussians time to arrive and join the British to defeat him. [Eds.]

[9]742–814; crowned Emperor of the Holy Roman Empire in 800. [Eds.]

of any other nation." It is worth noting the qualities Schlesinger ascribes to them: They were fearless, high-principled, deeply versed in ancient and modern political thought, astute and pragmatic, unafraid of experiment, and—this is significant—"convinced of man's power to improve his condition through the use of intelligence." That was the mark of the Age of Reason that formed them, and though the eighteenth century had a tendency to regard men as more rational than they in fact were, it evoked the best in government from these men.

For our purposes, it would be invaluable if we could know what   13 produced this burst of talent from a base of only two million inhabitants. Schlesinger suggests some contributing factors: wide diffusion of education, challenging economic opportunities, social mobility, training in self-government—all these encouraged citizens to cultivate their political aptitudes to the utmost. Also, he adds, with the Church declining in prestige and with business, science, and art not yet offering competing fields of endeavor, statecraft remained almost the only outlet for men of energy and purpose. Perhaps the need of the moment—the opportunity to create a new political system—is what brought out the best.

Not before or since, I believe, has so much careful and reasonable   14 thinking been invested in the creation of a new political system. In the French, Russian, and Chinese revolutions, too much class hatred and bloodshed were involved to allow for fair results or permanent constitutions. The American experience was unique, and the system so far has always managed to right itself under pressure. In spite of accelerating incompetence, it still works better than most. We haven't had to discard the system and try another after every crisis, as have Italy and Germany, Spain and France. The founders of the United States are a phenomenon to keep in mind to encourage our estimate of human possibilities, but their example, as a political scientist has pointed out, is "too infrequent to be taken as a basis for normal expectations."

The English are considered to have enjoyed reasonably benign   15 government during the eighteenth and nineteenth centuries, except for their Irish subjects, debtors, child laborers, and other unfortunates in various pockets of oppression. The folly that lost the American colonies reappeared now and then, notably in the treatment of the Irish and the Boers, but a social system can survive a good deal of folly when circumstances are historically favorable or when it is cushioned by large resources, as in the heyday of the British Empire, or absorbed by sheer size, as in this country during our period of expansion. Today there are no more cushions, which makes folly less affordable.

Elsewhere than in government, man has accomplished marvels: 16
invented the means in our time to leave the world and voyage to the
moon; in the past, harnessed wind and electricity, raised earthbound
stone into soaring cathedrals, woven silk brocades out of the spin-
nings of a worm, composed the music of Mozart and the dramas of
Shakespeare, classified the forms of nature, penetrated the mysteries
of genetics. Why is he so much less accomplished in government?
What frustrates, in that sphere, the operation of the intellect? Isaac
Bashevis Singer, discoursing as a Nobel laureate in mankind, offers
the opinion that God had been frugal in bestowing intellect but lavish
with passions and emotions. "He gave us," Singer says, "so many
emotions and such strong ones that every human being, even if he
is an idiot, is a millionaire in emotions."

I think Singer has made a point that applies to our inquiry. What 17
frustrates the workings of intellect is the passions and the emotions:
ambition, greed, fear, facesaving, the instinct to dominate, the needs
of the ego, the whole bundle of personal vanities and anxieties.

Reason is crushed by these forces. If the Athenians out of pride 18
and overconfidence had not set out to crush Sparta for good but had
been content with moderate victory, their ultimate fall might have
been averted. If fourteenth-century knights had not been obsessed
by the idea of glory and personal prowess, they might have defeated
the Turks at Nicopolis with incalculable consequence for all of Eastern
Europe. If the English, 200 years ago, had heeded Chatham's
knocking on the door of what he called "this sleeping and confounded
Ministry" and his urgent advice to repeal the Coercive Acts and withdraw the troops before the "inexpiable drop of blood is shed in an
impious war with a people contending in the great cause of publick
liberty" or, given a last chance, if they had heeded Edmund Burke's
celebrated plea for conciliation and his warning that it would prove
impossible to coerce a "fierce people" of their own pedigree, we might
still be a united people bridging the Atlantic, with incalculable consequence for the history of the West.[10] It did not happen that way,
because king and Parliament felt it imperative to affirm sovereignty
over arrogant colonials. The alternative choice, as in Athens and medieval Europe, was close to psychologically impossible.

In the case we know best—the American engagement in 19
Vietnam—fixed notions, preconceptions, wooden-headed thinking,

---

[10]The Coercive Acts, also known as the Intolerable Acts (1774) were laws designed to punish
the Colonists after the Boston Tea Party. Colonists' objections to these laws led to the convening
of the First Continental Congress. Chatham refers to William Pitt, First Earl of Chatham (1708–78),
British statesman and leader of the government 1756–61 and 1766–68. Edmund Burke (1729–97)
was a British statesman and philosopher. [Eds.]

and emotions accumulated into a monumental mistake and classic humiliation. The original idea was that the lesson of the failure to halt fascist aggression during the appeasement era dictated the necessity of halting the so-called aggression by North Vietnam, conceived to be the spearhead of international communism. This was applying the wrong model to the wrong facts, which would have been obvious if our policy makers had taken into consideration the history of the people on the spot instead of charging forward wearing the blinders of the cold war.

The reality of Vietnamese nationalism, of which Ho Chi Minh[11] had been the standard-bearer since long before the war, was certainly no secret. Indeed, Franklin Roosevelt had insisted that the French should not be allowed to return after the war, a policy that we instantly abandoned the moment the Japanese were out: Ignoring the Vietnamese demand for self-government, we first assisted the return of the French, and then, when incredibly, they had been put to rout by the native forces, we took their place, as if Dien Bien Phu[12] had no significance whatever. Policy founded upon error multiplies, never retreats. The pretense that North versus South Vietnam represented foreign aggression was intensified. If Asian specialists with knowledge of the situation suggested a reassessment, they were not persuasive. As a Communist aggressor, Hanoi was presumed to be a threat to the United States, yet the vital national interest at stake, which alone may have justified belligerency, was never clear enough to sustain a declaration of war.

A further, more fundamental, error confounded our policy. This was the nature of the client. In war, as any military treatise or any soldier who has seen active service will tell you, it is essential to know the nature—that is, the capabilities *and* intentions—of the enemy and no less so of an ally who is the primary belligerent. We fatally underestimated the one and foolishly overestimated the other. Placing reliance on, or hope in, South Vietnam was an advanced case of wooden-headedness. Improving on the Bourbons,[13] who forgot nothing and learned nothing, our policy makers forgot everything and learned nothing. The oldest lesson in history is the futility and, often, fatality of foreign interference to maintain in power a government unwanted or hated at home. As far back as 500 B.C., Confucius stated, "Without the confidence of the people, no government can stand," and political philosophers have echoed him down through

20

21

---

[11](1890–1969) President of Vietnam 1945–54 and of North Vietnam 1954–69. [Eds.]

[12]Site of decisive victory of Vietnamese over the French army in 1954. [Eds.]

[13]European dynastic family, branches of which were longtime rulers of France, Spain, and several independent Italian States. [Eds.]

the ages. What else was the lesson of our vain support of Chiang Kai-shek, within such recent experience? A corrupt or oppressive government may be maintained by despotic means but not for long, as the English occupiers of France learned in the fifteenth century. The human spirit protests and generates a Joan of Arc, for people will not passively endure a government that is in fact unendurable.

The deeper we became involved in Vietnam during the Johnson era, the greater grew the self-deception, the lies, the false body counts, the cheating on Tonkin Gulf,[14] the military mess, domestic dissent, and all those defensive emotions in which, as a result, our leaders became fixed. Their concern for personal ego, public image, and government status determined policy. Johnson was not going to be the first President to preside over defeat; generals could not admit failure nor civilian advisers risk their jobs by giving unpalatable advice. 22

Males, who so far in history have managed government, are obsessed with potency, which is the reason, I suspect, why it is difficult for them to admit error. I have rarely known a man who, with a smile and a shrug, could easily acknowledge being wrong. Why not? *I* can, without any damage to self-respect. I can only suppose the difference is that deep in their psyches, men somehow equate being wrong with being impotent. For a Chief of State, it is almost out of the question, and especially so for Johnson and Nixon, who both seem to me to have had shaky self-images. Johnson's showed in his deliberate coarseness and compulsion to humiliate others in crude physical ways. No self-confident man would have needed to do that. Nixon was a bundle of inferiorities and sense of persecution. I do not pretend to be a psychohistorian, but in pursuit of this inquiry, the psychological factors must be taken into account. Having no special knowledge of Johnson and Nixon, I will not pursue the question other than to say that it was our misfortune during the Vietnam period to have had two Presidents who lacked the self-confidence for a change of course, much less for a grand withdrawal. "Magnanimity in politics," said Edmund Burke, "is not seldom the truest wisdom, and a great Empire and little minds go ill together." 23

An essential component of that "truest wisdom" is the self-confidence to reassess. Congressman Morris Udall made this point in the first few days after the nuclear accident at Three Mile Island. Cautioning against a hasty decision on the future of nuclear power, he 24

---

[14] Arm of the South China Sea between Vietnam and China. In August 1964, President Lyndon Johnson, reporting that an American naval vessel had been fired upon in international waters, persuaded Congress to support an increased U.S. military presence in Southeast Asia. Many have since questioned the validity of Johnson's report. In any case, the Tonkin Gulf incident is considered the beginning of the Vietnam War. [Eds.]

said, "We have to go back and reassess. There is nothing wrong about being optimistic or making a mistake. The thing that is wrong, as in Vietnam, is *persisting* in a mistake when you see you are going down the wrong road and are caught in a bad situation."

The test comes in recognizing when persistence has become a 25 fatal error. A prince, says Machiavelli, ought always to be a great asker and a patient hearer of truth about those things of which he has inquired, and he should be angry if he finds that anyone has scruples about telling him the truth. Johnson and Nixon, as far as an outsider can tell, were not great askers; they did not want to hear the truth or to face it. Chiang Kai-shek knew virtually nothing of real conditions in his domain because he lived a headquarters life amid an entourage all of whom were afraid to be messengers of ill report. When, in World War I, a general of the headquarters staff visited for the first time the ghastly landscape of the Somme,[15] he broke into tears, saying, "If I had known we sent men to fight in that, I could not have done it." Evidently he was no great asker either.

Neither, we now know, was the shah of Iran. Like Chiang Kai- 26 shek, he was isolated from actual conditions. He was educated abroad, took his vacations abroad, and toured his country, if at all, by helicopter.

Why is it that the major clients of the United States, a country 27 founded on the principle that government derives its just powers from the consent of the governed, tend to be unpopular autocrats? A certain schizophrenia between our philosophy and our practice afflicts American policy, and this split will always make the policy based on it fall apart. On the day the shah left Iran, an article summarizing his reign said that "except for the generals, he has few friends or allies at home." How useful to us is a ruler without friends or allies at home? He is a kind of luftmensch,[16] no matter how rich or how golden a customer for American business. To attach American foreign policy to a ruler who does not have the acceptance of his countrymen is hardly intelligent. By now, it seems to me, we might have learned that. We must understand conditions—and by conditions, I mean people and history—on the spot. Wise policy can only be made on the basis of *informed*, not automatic, judgments.

When it has become evident to those associated with it that a 28 course of policy is pointed toward disaster, why does no one resign in protest or at least for the peace of his own soul? They never do. In 1917, the German chancellor Bethmann Hollweg pleaded desper-

---

[15]River that flows from northern France to the English channel; site of heavy fighting between the British and the Germans in 1916. [Eds.]
[16](Yiddish) Dreamer. [Eds.]

ately against the proposed resumption of unrestricted submarine warfare, since, by bringing in the United States, it would revive the Allies' resources, their confidence in victory, and their will to endure. When he was overruled by the military, he told a friend who found him sunk in despair that the decision meant "finis Germaniae." When the friend said simply, "You should resign," Bethmann said he could not, for that would sow dissension at home and let the world know he believed Germany would fail.

This is always the refuge. The officeholder tells himself he can   29 do more from within and that he must not reveal division at the top to the public. In fact if there is to be any hope of change in a democratic society, that is exactly what he must do. No one of major influence in Johnson's circle resigned over our Vietnam policy, although several, hoping to play it both ways, hinted their disagreement. Humphrey, waiting for the nod, never challenged the President's policy, although he campaigned afterward as an opponent of the war. Since then, I've always thought the adulation given to him misplaced.

Basically, what keeps officeholders attached to a policy they   30 believe to be wrong is nothing more nor less, I believe, than the lure of office, or Potomac fever. It is the same whether the locus is the Thames or the Rhine or, no doubt, the Nile. When Herbert Lehman ran for a second term as senator from New York after previously serving four terms as governor, his brother asked him why on earth he wanted it. "Arthur," replied the senator, "after you have once ridden behind a motorcycle escort, you are never the same again."

Here is a clue to the question of why our performance in gov-   31 ernment is worse than in other activities: because government offers power, excites that lust for power, which is subject to emotional drives—to narcissism, fantasies of omnipotence, and other sources of folly. This lust for power, according to Tacitus,[17] "is the most flagrant of all the passions" and cannot really be satisfied except by power over others. Business offers a kind of power but only to the very successful at the very top, and even they, in our day, have to play it down. Fords and Du Ponts, Hearsts and Pulitzers, nowadays are subdued, and the Rockefeller who most conspicuously wanted power sought it in government. Other activities—in sports, science, the professions, and the creative and performing arts—offer various satisfactions but not the opportunity for power. They may appeal to status seeking and, in the form of celebrity, offer crowd worship and limousines and recognition by headwaiters, but these are the trappings of power, not the essence. Of course, mistakes and stupidities

---

[17]Roman historian and orator of the late first and early second centuries A.D. [Eds.]

occur in nongovernmental activities too, but since these affect fewer people, they are less noticeable than they are in public affairs. Government remains the paramount field of unwisdom because it is there that men seek power over others—and lose it over themselves.

There are, of course, other factors that lower competence in public affairs, among them the pressure of overwork and overscheduling; bureaucracy, especially big bureaucracy; the contest for votes that gives exaggerated influence to special interests and an absurd tyranny to public opinion polls. Any hope of intelligent government would require that the persons entrusted with high office should formulate and execute policy according to their best judgment and the best knowledge available, not according to every breeze of public opinion. But reelection is on their minds, and that becomes the criterion. Moreover, given schedules broken down into fifteen-minute appointments and staffs numbering in the hundreds and briefing memos of never less than thirty pages, policy makers never have time to think. This leaves a rather important vacuum. Meanwhile, bureaucracy rolls on, impervious to any individual or cry for change, like some vast computer that when once penetrated by error goes on pumping it out forever. 32

Under the circumstances, what are the chances of improving the conduct of government? The idea of a class of professionals trained for the task has been around ever since Plato's Republic.[18] Something of the sort animates, I imagine, the new Kennedy School of Government at Harvard. According to Plato, the ruling class in a just society should be men apprenticed to the art of ruling, drawn from the rational and the wise. Since he acknowledged that in natural distribution these are few, he believed they would have to be eugenically bred and nurtured. Government, he said, was a special art in which competence, as in any other profession, could be acquired only by study of the discipline and could not be acquired otherwise. 33

Without reference to Plato, the Mandarins of China[19] were trained, if not bred, for the governing function. They had to pass through years of study and apprenticeship and weeding out by successive examinations, but they do not seem to have developed a form of government much superior to any other, and in the end, they petered out in decadence and incompetence. 34

In seventeenth-century Europe, after the devastation of the Thirty Years' War, the electors of Brandenburg, soon to be combined with 35

---

[18] In *The Republic*, one of his dialogues, Plato (c. 427–347 B.C.) describes an ideal type of state. [Eds.]

[19] Members of any of the nine ranks of public officials, each distinguished by a particular type of button worn on the cap. [Eds.]

Prussia, determined to create a strong state by means of a disciplined army and a trained civil service. Applicants for the civil positions, drawn from commoners in order to offset the nobles' control of the military, had to complete a course of study covering political theory, law and legal philosophy, economics, history, penology, and statutes. Only after passing through various stages of examination and probationary terms of office did they receive definitive appointments and tenure and opportunity for advancement. The higher civil service was a separate branch, not open to promotion from the middle and lower levels.

The Prussian system proved so effective that the state was able 36 to survive both military defeat by Napoleon in 1807 and the revolutionary surge of 1848. By then it had begun to congeal, losing many of its most progressive citizens in emigration to America; nevertheless, Prussian energies succeeded in 1871 in uniting the German states in an empire under Prussian hegemony. Its very success contained the seed of ruin, for it nourished the arrogance and power hunger that from 1914 through 1918 was to bring it down.

In England, instead of responding in reactionary panic to the 37 thunders from the Continent in 1848, as might have been expected, the authorities, with commendable enterprise, ordered an investigation of their own government practices, which were then the virtually private preserve of the propertied class. The result was a report on the need for a permanent civil service to be based on training and specialized skills and designed to provide continuity and maintenance of the long view as against transient issues and political passions. Though heavily resisted, the system was adopted in 1870. It has produced distinguished civil servants but also Burgess, Maclean, Philby, and the fourth man.[19] The history of British government in the last 100 years suggests that factors other than the quality of its civil service determine a country's fate.

In the United States, civil service was established chiefly as a 38 barrier to patronage and the pork barrel[20] rather than in search of excellence. By 1937, a presidential commission, finding the system inadequate, urged the development of a "real career service . . . requiring personnel of the highest order, competent, highly trained, loyal, skilled in their duties by reason of long experience, and assured

---

[19]Guy Burgess, Donald Maclean, and Kim Philby were diplomats who worked at the British Embassy in Washington, D.C., as espionage agents for the Soviet Union, to which they fled in 1955. A fourth man, higher up in the government, was supposed to have been part of the spy ring, but he was never identified. [Eds.]

[20]*Patronage* refers to the practice of distributing government or political positions without regard to qualifications. *Pork barrel* is a slang term denoting a government project or appropriation that benefits a specific region and a particular politician's constituents. [Eds.]

WRITING SUGGESTION

Write a proposal for changing some aspect of your local, state, or federal governmental system. You may focus on a small change or a sweeping one. In your proposal, explain both the need for the change and the benefits of your proposal.

of continuity." After much effort and some progress, that goal is still not reached, but even if it were, it would not take care of elected officials and high appointments—that is, of government at the top.

I do not know if the prognosis is hopeful or, given the underlying emotional drives, whether professionalism is the cure. In the Age of Enlightenment, John Locke[21] thought the emotions should be controlled by intellectual judgment and that it was the distinction and glory of man to be able to control them. As witnesses of the twentieth century's record, comparable to the worst in history, we have less confidence in our species. Although professionalism can help, I tend to think that fitness of character is what government chiefly requires. How that can be discovered, encouraged, and brought into office is the problem that besets us. 39

No society has yet managed to implement Plato's design. Now, with money and image-making manipulating our elective process, the chances are reduced. We are asked to choose by the packaging, yet the candidate seen in a studio-filmed spot, sincerely voicing lines from the Tele-PrompTer, is not the person who will have to meet the unrelenting problems and crucial decisions of the Oval Office. It might be a good idea if, without violating the First Amendment, we could ban all paid political commercials and require candidates (who accept federal subsidy for their campaigns) to be televised live only. 40

That is only a start. More profound change must come if we are to bring into office the kind of person our form of government needs if it is to survive the challenges of this era. Perhaps rather than educating officials according to Plato's design, we should concentrate on educating the electorate—that is, ourselves—to look for, recognize, and reward character in our representatives and to reject the ersatz.[22] 41

ANSWERS TO RESPONDING TO READING

1. Tuchman's historical examples are well chosen and highly effective. Recent events in Eastern Europe (although initially encouraging) and in Iraq seem to support Tuchman's thesis. However, the fall of the Berlin Wall and the South African government's decision to dismantle the foundations of apartheid perhaps provide some glimmer of hope for intelligent change.

2. She acknowledges exceptions to show she is a reasonable individual who anticipates readers' possible disagreements. A few more recent exceptions—such as Vaclav Havel of Czechoslovakia and Corazon Aquino of the Philippines—might make contemporary audiences more receptive to her argument.

RESPONDING TO READING

1. Tuchman characterizes government not just as unwise but also as suicidally incompetent, wooden-headed, overzealous, and just plain stupid. Do you think her examples prove her case, or is she overstating it? Do you think more recent examples of government behavior—in the United States as well as in Eastern Europe, South Africa, and Iraq—support her thesis or call it into question? **2.** Beginning with paragraph 11 Tuchman acknowledges the exceptions to her essay's thesis. Why does she do this? Can you supply additional exceptions? **3.** In paragraph 17 Tuchman blames unwisdom in government on "ambition, greed, fear, facesaving, the instinct to dominate,

---

[21]The Age of Enlightenment, also called the Age of Reason, was an eighteenth-century revolution in western thought based on the idea of human perfectibility through reason. John Locke (1632–1704), an English philosopher, wrote essays on government that advocated the concept of limited sovereignty. [Eds.]
[22]Inferior imitations. [Eds.]

the needs of the ego, the whole bundle of personal vanities and anxieties." In paragraph 23 she goes on to suggest that these weaknesses are associated with men, who are, she says, "obsessed with potency" and therefore unable to admit their mistakes. Do you believe the root of the problems Tuchman identifies is in the male ego, or do you think female heads of state behave similarly?

3. Men have traditionally held positions of power in government, but it is possible that as more women gain power they will display an equal capacity for ambition and folly. As Gloria Steinem observed in a 1970 *Time* article, "We are not more moral than men; we are only uncorrupted by power so far. When we do acquire power, we might turn out to have an equal impulse toward aggression" ("What It Would Be Like If Women Win").

Propaganda Under a Dictatorship

ALDOUS HUXLEY

British writer Aldous Huxley (1894–1963) is perhaps best known for his science fiction social satire, *Brave New World* (1932). Huxley studied science and medicine before turning to writing; in addition to novels such as *Antic Hay* (1923) and *Point Counter Point* (1928), he wrote plays, travel books, poetry, and criticism on manners and morals. Huxley was interested in the expansion of the mind and delved into mysticism, Eastern religions, and hallucinogenic drugs; it was he who coined the term *psychedelic*. *Brave New World Revisited* is Huxley's 1958 study of the dehumanization of society; in the following selection from this book, he looks at Hitler's reign and the terror of "mind-control."

At his trial after the Second World War, Hitler's Minister for Armaments, Albert Speer, delivered a long speech in which, with remarkable acuteness, he described the Nazi tyranny and analyzed its methods. "Hitler's dictatorship," he said, "differed in one fundamental point from all its predecessors in history. It was the first dictatorship in the present period of modern technical development, a dictatorship which made complete use of all technical means for the domination of its own country. Through technical devices like the radio and the loud-speaker, eighty million people were deprived of independent thought. It was thereby possible to subject them to the will of one man. . . . Earlier dictators needed highly qualified assistants even at the lowest level—men who could think and act independently. The totalitarian system in the period of modern technical development can dispense with such men; thanks to modern methods of communication, it is possible to mechanize the lower leadership. As a result of this there has arisen the new type of the uncritical recipient of orders."

In the Brave New World of my prophetic fable technology had advanced far beyond the point it had reached in Hitler's day; consequently the recipients of orders were far less critical than their Nazi

1

2

FOR OPENERS

Examine a few advertising slogans as propaganda. What are the underlying messages in each? You might begin with Nike's "Just Do It" and Burger King's "Have It Your Way," and then elicit more examples from students. Or, you can assign students to bring to class print advertisements that they believe use propaganda techniques.

counterparts, far more obedient to the order-giving elite. Moreover, they had been genetically standardized and postnatally conditioned to perform their subordinate functions, and could therefore be depended upon to behave almost as predictably as machines. As we shall see in a later chapter, this conditioning of "the lower leadership" is already going on under the Communist dictatorships. The Chinese and the Russians are not relying merely on the indirect effects of advancing technology; they are working directly on the psychophysical organisms of their lower leaders, subjecting minds and bodies to a system of ruthless and, from all accounts, highly effective conditioning. "Many a man," said Speer, "has been haunted by the nightmare that one day nations might be dominated by technical means. That nightmare was almost realized in Hitler's totalitarian system." Almost, but not quite. The Nazis did not have time—and perhaps did not have the intelligence and the necessary knowledge—to brainwash and condition their lower leadership. This, it may be, is one of the reasons why they failed.

Since Hitler's day the armory of technical devices at the disposal of the would-be dictator has been considerably enlarged. As well as the radio, the loud-speaker, the moving picture camera and the rotary press, the contemporary propagandist can make use of television to broadcast the image as well as the voice of his client, and can record both image and voice on spools of magnetic tape. Thanks to technological progress, Big Brother[1] can now be almost as omnipresent as God. Nor is it only on the technical front that the hand of the would-be dictator has been strengthened. Since Hitler's day a great deal of work has been carried out in those fields of applied psychology and neurology which are the special province of the propagandist, the indoctrinator and the brainwasher. In the past these specialists in the art of changing people's minds were empiricists. By a method of trial and error they had worked out a number of techniques and procedures, which they used very effectively without, however, knowing precisely why they were effective. Today the art of mind-control is in process of becoming a science. The practitioners of this science know what they are doing and why. They are guided in their work by theories and hypotheses solidly established on a massive foundation of experimental evidence. Thanks to the new insights and the new techniques made possible by these insights, the nightmare that was "all but realized in Hitler's totalitarian system" may soon be completely realizable.

3

ADDITIONAL QUESTIONS FOR RESPONDING TO READING

1. According to Huxley, Hitler held a low opinion of the masses. How would you characterize "the masses"? What groups constitute "the masses"?
2. What is mob rule? Can you think of examples from history when the masses ruled? Can you think of recent examples? You might ask students whether they consider acts like "wilding" to be examples of "mob rule." You might also discuss the widely publicized 1991 incident in which Los Angeles police were videotaped as they beat and kicked a handcuffed man. Do your students see any similarity between such police actions and "mob rule"?
3. In what sense is propaganda anti-intellectual?
4. Can an individual stand up against the masses and actually have an impact, or is he or she inevitably ridiculed, swallowed up, or destroyed?

---

[1]Head of the totalitarian state in George Orwell's *Nineteen Eighty-Four* (1949). [Eds.]

But before we discuss these new insights and techniques let us take a look at the nightmare that so nearly came true in Nazi Germany. What were the methods used by Hitler and Goebbels[2] for "depriving eighty million people of independent thought and subjecting them to the will of one man"? And what was the theory of human nature upon which those terrifying successful methods were based? These questions can be answered, for the most part, in Hitler's own words. And what remarkably clear and astute words they are! When he writes about such vast abstractions as Race and History and Providence, Hitler is strictly unreadable. But when he writes about the German masses and the methods he used for dominating and directing them, his style changes. Nonsense gives place to sense, bombast to a hard-boiled and cynical lucidity. In his philosophical lucubrations Hitler was either cloudily daydreaming or reproducing other people's half-baked notions. In his comments on crowds and propaganda he was writing of things he knew by firsthand experience. In the words of his ablest biographer, Mr. Alan Bullock, "Hitler was the greatest demagogue in history." Those who add, "only a demagogue," fail to appreciate the nature of political power in an age of mass politics. As he himself said, "To be a leader means to be able to move the masses." Hitler's aim was first to move the masses and then, having pried them loose from their traditional loyalties and moralities, to impose upon them (with the hypnotized consent of the majority) a new authoritarian order of his own devising. "Hitler," wrote Hermann Rauschning[3] in 1939, "has a deep respect for the Catholic church and the Jesuit order; not because of their Christian doctrine, but because of the 'machinery' they have elaborated and controlled, their hierarchical system, their extremely clever tactics, their knowledge of human nature and their wise use of human weaknesses in ruling over believers." Ecclesiasticism without Christianity, the discipline of a monastic rule, not for God's sake or in order to achieve personal salvation, but for the sake of the State and for the greater glory and power of the demagogue turned Leader—this was the goal toward which the systematic moving of the masses was to lead.

Let us see what Hitler thought of the masses he moved and how he did the moving. The first principle from which he started was a value judgment: the masses are utterly contemptible. They are incapable of abstract thinking and uninterested in any fact outside the circle of their immediate experience. Their behavior is determined, not by knowledge and reason, but by feelings and unconscious drives. It is

4   TEACHING STRATEGY

Discuss changes in American culture that have been brought about by the government or by social groups. What propaganda techniques were used to convince people to accept these changes?

5   COLLABORATIVE ACTIVITY

Have students work in groups to analyze Hitler's principles of propaganda and mind control. Then, ask them to consider the influence exerted by heavy metal or rap lyrics. Does such music try to change the way people think or act? Is it the propaganda of the 1990s?

---

[2]Joseph Goebbels, minister of propaganda under Hitler. [Eds.]
[3]Former high-ranking member of the Nazi party who, after attacking its anti-semitic stance, fled Germany in 1935. [Eds.]

in these drives and feelings that "the roots of their positive as well as their negative attitudes are implanted." To be successful a propagandist must learn how to manipulate these instincts and emotions. "The driving force which has brought about the most tremendous revolutions on this earth has never been a body of scientific teaching which has gained power over the masses, but always a devotion which has inspired them, and often a kind of hysteria which has urged them into action. Whoever wishes to win over the masses must know the key that will open the door of their hearts." . . . In post-Freudian jargon, of their unconscious.

Hitler made his strongest appeal to those members of the lower middle classes who had been ruined by the inflation of 1923, and then ruined all over again by the depression of 1929 and the following years. "The masses" of whom he speaks were these bewildered, frustrated and chronically anxious millions. To make them more mass-like, more homogeneously subhuman, he assembled them, by the thousands and the tens of thousands, in vast halls and arenas, where individuals could lose their personal identity, even their elementary humanity, and be merged with the crowd. A man or woman makes direct contact with society in two ways: as a member of some familial, professional or religious group, or as a member of a crowd. Groups are capable of being as moral and intelligent as the individuals who form them; a crowd is chaotic, has no purpose of its own and is capable of anything except intelligent action and realistic thinking. Assembled in a crowd, people lose their powers of reasoning and their capacity for moral choice. Their suggestibility is increased to the point where they cease to have any judgment or will of their own. They become very excitable, they lose all sense of individual or collective responsibility, they are subject to sudden accesses of rage, enthusiasm and panic. In a word, a man in a crowd behaves as though he had swallowed a large dose of some powerful intoxicant. He is a victim of what I have called "herd-poisoning." Like alcohol, herd-poison is an active, extraverted drug. The crowd-intoxicated individual escapes from responsibility, intelligence and morality into a kind of frantic, animal mindlessness. 6

During his long career as an agitator, Hitler had studied the effects of herd-poison and had learned how to exploit them for his own purposes. He had discovered that the orator can appeal to those "hidden forces" which motivate men's actions, much more effectively than can the writer. Reading is a private, not a collective activity. The writer speaks only to individuals, sitting by themselves in a state of normal sobriety. The orator speaks to masses of individuals, already well primed with herd-poison. They are at his mercy and, if he knows his business, he can do what he likes with them. As an orator, Hitler 7 knew his business supremely well. He was able, in his own words, "to follow the lead of the great mass in such a way that from the living emotion of his hearers the apt word which he needed would be suggested to him and in its turn this would go straight to the heart of his hearers." Otto Strasser[4] called him a "loud-speaker, proclaiming the most secret desires, the least admissible instincts, the sufferings and personal revolts of a whole nation." Twenty years before Madison Avenue embarked upon "Motivational Research," Hitler was systematically exploring and exploiting the secret fears and hopes, the cravings, anxieties and frustrations of the German masses. It is by manipulating "hidden forces" that the advertising experts induce us to buy their wares—a toothpaste, a brand of cigarettes, a political candidate. And it is by appealing to the same hidden forces—and to others too dangerous for Madison Avenue to meddle with—that Hitler induced the German masses to buy themselves a Fuehrer, an insane philosophy and the Second World War.

Unlike the masses, intellectuals have a taste for rationality and an interest in facts. Their critical habit of mind makes them resistant to the kind of propaganda that works so well on the majority. Among the masses "instinct is supreme, and from instinct comes faith. . . . While the healthy common folk instinctively close their ranks to form a community of the people" (under a Leader, it goes without saying) "intellectuals run this way and that, like hens in a poultry yard. With them one cannot make history; they cannot be used as elements composing a community." Intellectuals are the kind of people who demand evidence and are shocked by logical inconsistencies and fallacies. They regard over-simplification as the original sin of the mind and have no use for the slogans, the unqualified assertions and sweeping generalizations which are the propagandist's stock in trade. "All effective propaganda," Hitler wrote, "must be confined to a few bare necessities and then must be expressed in a few stereotyped formulas." These stereotyped formulas must be constantly repeated, for "only constant repetition will finally succeed in imprinting an idea upon the memory of a crowd." Philosophy teaches us to feel uncertain about the things that seem to us self-evident. Propaganda, on the other hand, teaches us to accept as self-evident matters about which it would be reasonable to suspend our judgment or to feel doubt. The aim of the demagogue is to create social coherence under his own leadership. But, as Bertrand Russell[5] has pointed out, "systems of dogma without empirical foundations, such as scholasticism,

8

---

[4]A leading member of the early Nazi Party who left the Party in 1930 and was then forced into exile when Hitler rose to power. [Eds.]

[5]English mathematician, philosopher and pacifist (1872–1970). [Eds.]

Marxism and fascism, have the advantage of producing a great deal of social coherence among their disciples." The demagogic propagandist must therefore be consistently dogmatic. All his statements are made without qualification. There are no grays in his picture of the world; everything is either diabolically black or celestially white. In Hitler's words, the propagandist should adopt "a systematically one-sided attitude towards every problem that has to be dealt with." He must never admit that he might be wrong or that people with a different point of view might be even partially right. Opponents should not be argued with; they should be attacked, shouted down, or, if they become too much of a nuisance, liquidated. The morally squeamish intellectual may be shocked by this kind of thing. But the masses are always convinced that "right is on the side of the active aggressor."

Such, then, was Hitler's opinion of humanity in the mass. It was a very low opinion. Was it also an incorrect opinion? The tree is known by its fruits, and a theory of human nature which inspired the kind of techniques that proved so horribly effective must contain at least an element of truth. Virtue and intelligence belong to human beings as individuals freely associating with other individuals in small groups. So do sin and stupidity. But the subhuman mindlessness to which the demagogue makes his appeal, the moral imbecility on which he relies when he goads his victims into action, are characteristic not of men and women as individuals, but of men and women in masses. Mindlessness and moral idiocy are not characteristically human attributes; they are symptoms of herd-poisoning. In all the world's higher religions, salvation and enlightenment are for individuals. The kingdom of heaven is within the mind of a person, not within the collective mindlessness of a crowd. Christ promised to be present where two or three are gathered together. He did not say anything about being present where thousands are intoxicating one another with herd-poison. Under the Nazis enormous numbers of people were compelled to spend an enormous amount of time marching in serried[6] ranks from point A to point B and back again to point A. "This keeping of the whole population on the march seemed to be a senseless waste of time and energy. Only much later," adds Hermann Rauschning, "was there revealed in it a subtle intention based on a well-judged adjustment of ends and means. Marching diverts men's thoughts. Marching kills thought. Marching makes an end of individuality. Marching is the indispensable magic stroke

9

---

[6]Pressed together in rows; in close order. [Eds.]

performed in order to accustom the people to a mechanical, quasi-ritualistic activity until it becomes second nature."

From his point of view and at the level where he had chosen to 10 do his dreadful work, Hitler was perfectly correct in his estimate of human nature. To those of us who look at men and women as individuals rather than as members of crowds, or of regimented collectives, he seems hideously wrong. In an age of accelerating over-population, of accelerating over-organization and ever more efficient means of mass communication, how can we preserve the integrity and reassert the value of the human individual? This is a question that can still be asked and perhaps effectively answered. A generation from now it may be too late to find an answer and perhaps impossible, in the stifling collective climate of that future time, even to ask the question.

WRITING SUGGESTION

Huxley explains the Nazis' use of marching as a propaganda technique for diverting thought and converting people into machines. Write a paragraph illustrating how something in our culture similarly dehumanizes us.

RESPONDING TO READING

1. Quoting Albert Speer, Huxley expresses his fear that modern nations are vulnerable to domination by technology. Do you think world events since Huxley wrote this essay in 1958 demonstrate that his apprehension is justified or that he has exaggerated the problem?   **2.** According to Huxley, Hitler's ability to control the masses depended in part on his being able to "[pry] them loose from their traditional loyalties and moralities" (paragraph 4), eventually treating them as a homogenous unit rather than as individuals. Do you think movies and television, advertising, and popular music approach their audience in a similar fashion? Do you see any danger of their undermining "traditional loyalties and moralities"?   **3.** Huxley wrote this essay only thirteen years after Hitler's death. Do you think he should have allowed more time to pass before attempting to write about such an emotionally charged subject?

ANSWERS TO RESPONDING
TO READING

1. The increased emphasis on technology in warfare and the importance of technology (especially computer technology, which was in its infancy in Huxley's time) in determining a nation's status as a world power seem to justify Huxley's fear.
2. Because of the immediacy of television and the proliferation of mass culture, changes that used to take hundreds of years now take just one generation. Many traditional ideas have been forced to adjust accordingly.
3. Thirteen years was probably enough time, since the emotional attitude toward Hitler still has not changed significantly. Huxley remains fairly objective, using Hitler's own words and actions to make his points.

The Declaration of Independence

THOMAS JEFFERSON

Thomas Jefferson (1743–1826) was a lawyer, statesman, diplomat, architect, scientist, politician, writer, education theorist, and musician. During his impressive political life, Jefferson served as governor of Virginia, member of the Continental Congress, secretary of state, vice president, and then president for two terms beginning in 1801. He collected nearly ten thousand books, and his library later became the basis of the Library of Congress. The Declaration of Indepen-

BACKGROUND ON READING

It is important to note that the First Continental Congress, meeting two years before the Second Congress adopted the Declaration, had attempted to compromise with England and had been rebuffed.

dence, drafted by Jefferson and amended by the Continental Congress, reflects Jefferson's belief in reason and the natural rights of individuals.

IN CONGRESS, JULY 4, 1776
THE UNANIMOUS DECLARATION OF THE
THIRTEEN UNITED STATES OF AMERICA

FOR OPENERS

Discuss the statement "All men are created equal." Did the founding fathers mean to exclude women?

When in the Course of human events it becomes necessary for one people to dissolve the political bands which have connected them with another, and to assume among the powers of the earth, the separate and equal station to which the Laws of Nature and of Nature's God entitle them, a decent respect to the opinions of mankind requires that they should declare the causes which impel them to the separation.   1

We hold these truths to be self-evident, that all men are created equal, that they are endowed by their Creator with certain unalienable Rights, that among these are Life, Liberty and the pursuit of Happiness. That to secure these rights, Governments are instituted among Men, deriving their just powers from the consent of the governed. That whenever any Form of Government becomes destructive of these ends, it is the Right of the People to alter or to abolish it, and to institute new Government, laying its foundation on such principles and organizing its powers in such form, as to them shall seem most likely to affect their Safety and Happiness. Prudence, indeed, will dictate that Governments long established should not be changed for light and transient causes; and accordingly all experience hath shewn that mankind are more disposed to suffer, while evils are sufferable, than to right themselves by abolishing the forms to which they are accustomed. But when a long train of abuses and usurpations, pursuing invariably the same Object evinces a design to reduce them under absolute Despotism, it is their right, it is their duty, to throw off such Government, and to provide new Guards for their future security. Such has been the patient sufferance of these Colonies; and such is now the necessity which constrains them to alter their former Systems of Government. The history of the present King of Great Britain is a history of repeated injuries and usurpations, all having in direct object the establishment of an absolute Tyranny over these States. To prove this, let Facts be submitted to a candid world.   2

ADDITIONAL QUESTIONS FOR RESPONDING TO READING

1. What grievances might some groups today have against the U.S. government? Do you see any of these grievances as justification for a group's demand for independence?
2. What complaints might the British have had against the colonies?

He has refused his Assent to Laws, the most wholesome and necessary for the public good.   3

He has forbidden his Government to pass laws of immediate and pressing importance, unless suspended in their operation till his   4

Assent should be obtained; and when so suspended, he has utterly neglected to attend to them.

He has refused to pass other Laws for the accommodation of large 5 districts of people, unless those people would relinquish the right of Representation in the Legislature, a right inestimable to them and formidable to tyrants only.

He has called together legislative bodies at places unusual, uncom- 6 fortable, and distant from the depository of their Public Records, for the sole purpose of fatiguing them into compliance with his measures.

He has dissolved Representative Houses repeatedly, for opposing 7 with manly firmness his invasions on the rights of the people.

He has refused for a long time, after such dissolutions, to cause 8 others to be elected; whereby the Legislative Powers, incapable of Annihilation, have returned to the People at large for their exercise; the State remaining in the mean time exposed to all the dangers of invasion from without, and convulsions within.

He has endeavored to prevent the population of these States; for 9 that purpose obstructing the Laws for Naturalization of Foreigners; refusing to pass others to encourage their migration hither, and raising the conditions of new Appropriations of Lands.

He has obstructed the Administration of Justice, by refusing his 10 Assent to Laws for establishing Judiciary Powers.

He has made Judges dependent on his Will alone, for the tenure 11 of their offices, and the amount and payment of their salaries.

He has erected a multitude of New Offices, and sent hither 12 swarms of Officers to harass our people, and eat out their substance.

He has kept among us, in times of peace, Standing Armies 13 without the Consent of our legislatures.

He has affected to render the Military independent of and superior 14 to the Civil Power.

He has combined with others to subject us to a jurisdiction foreign 15 to our constitution, and unacknowledged by our laws; giving his Assent to their Acts of pretended Legislation: For quartering large bodies of armed troops among us: For protecting them, by a mock Trial, from punishment for any Murders which they should commit on the Inhabitants of these States: For cutting off our Trade with all parts of the world: For imposing Taxes on us without our Consent: For depriving us in many cases, of the benefits of Trial by Jury; For transporting us beyond Seas to be tried for pretended offenses: for abolishing the free System of English Laws in a neighboring Province, establishing therein an Arbitrary government, and enlarging its Boundaries so as to render it at once an example and fit instrument for introducing the same absolute rule into these Colonies: For taking

TEACHING STRATEGY

You may use this document to introduce the concept of parallelism as a tool for adding stylistic emphasis. Have students identify parallel words, phrases, and clauses. Then, use their examples to illustrate how parallel language makes the Declaration's arguments more forceful.

COLLABORATIVE ACTIVITY

Ask students, working in groups, to read through the lists of grievances against the king, grouping the abuses into categories. Then, compare the groups' classification systems, fine-tuning them until there is agreement about which fall into each of these categories: economic, political, and human rights.

away our Charters, abolishing our most valuable Laws and altering fundamentally the Forms of our Governments: For suspending our own Legislatures, and declaring themselves invested with power to legislate for us in all cases whatsoever.

He has abdicated Government here, by declaring us out of his 16 Protection and waging War against us.

He has plundered our seas, ravaged our Coasts, burnt our towns, 17 and destroyed the lives of our people.

He is at this time transporting large Armies of foreign Mercenaries 18 to complete the works of death, desolation and tyranny, already begun with circumstances of Cruelty & Perfidy scarcely paralleled in the most barbarous ages, and totally unworthy the Head of a civilized nation.

He has constrained our fellow Citizens taken Captive on the high 19 Seas to bear Arms against their Country, to become the executioners of their friends and Brethren, or to fall themselves by their Hands.

He has excited domestic insurrections amongst us, and has endea- 20 vored to bring on the inhabitants of our frontiers, the merciless Indian Savages, whose known rule of warfare, is an undistinguished destruction of all ages, sexes, and conditions.

In every stage of these Oppressions We have Petitioned for 21 Redress in the most humble terms: Our repeated Petitions have been answered only by repeated injury. A Prince, whose character is thus marked by every act which may define a Tyrant, is unfit to be the ruler of a free people.

Nor have We been wanting in attention to our British brethren. 22 We have warned them from time to time of attempts by their legislature to extend an unwarrantable jurisdiction over us. We have reminded them of the circumstances of our emigration and settlement here. We have appealed to their native justice and magnanimity, and we have conjured them by the ties of our common kindred to disavow these usurpations, which would inevitably interrupt our connections and correspondence. They too have been deaf to the voice of justice and of consanguinity. We must, therefore, acquiesce in the necessity, which denounces our Separation, and hold them, as we hold the rest of mankind, Enemies in War, in Peace Friends.

We, THEREFORE the Representatives of the UNITED STATES OF 23 AMERICA, in General Congress, Assembled, appealing to the Supreme Judge of the world for the rectitude of our intentions, do, in the Name, and by Authority of the good People of these Colonies, solemnly publish and declare, That these United Colonies are, and of Right ought to be FREE AND INDEPENDENT STATES; that they are Absolved from all Allegiance to the British Crown, and that all political connection between them and the State of Great Britain, is and ought to

WRITING SUGGESTION

Write your own declaration of independence. What would you like to be free from? Use a structure similar to that of the Declaration: first justify yourself philosophically, then list your grievances, and then explain your next course of action.

be totally dissolved; and that as Free and Independent States, they have full Power to levy War, conclude Peace, contract Alliances, establish Commerce, and to do all other Acts and Things which Independent States may of right do. And for the support of this Declaration, with a firm reliance on the protection of Divine Providence, we mutually pledge to each other our Lives, our Fortunes, and our sacred Honor.

RESPONDING TO READING

1. The Declaration of Independence was written in the eighteenth century, a time when logic and reason were thought to be the supreme achievements of human beings. Despite the impeccable logic of its argument and its reasonable tone, however, the Declaration threatens violence, disorder, and rebellion. Do you think it is too moderate by today's standards? Do you find it too extreme?   **2.** Written over two hundred years ago, the Declaration of Independence sets forth principles that still make sense. In fact, some might argue that they make more sense than ever. Do the people of a nation have the right to redress wrongs by creating an independent nation? Should there be any restrictions on this right? How do these ideas apply to the American Civil War and the current nationalistic struggles within the Soviet Union?   **3.** What are the unspoken assumptions of the Declaration about race and gender? Would it be fair to accuse the framers of the Declaration of Independence of being both racist and sexist?

ANSWERS TO RESPONDING TO READING

1. The Declaration is certainly not too moderate, even by today's standards. Students, however, will be likely to find it quite bland because of its polite, reasonable language. It is probably not too extreme, either. (After all, it was a prelude to revolution.)
2. The seriousness of the wrongs determines the need for creating an independent nation. As a last resort, such an action makes sense. Students' ideas about whether this right should be limited in any way will vary. In the United States, the Civil War settled the issue of whether or not states could leave the Union. In the Soviet Union, struggles for independence are still under way.
3. The Declaration seems to be speaking for white men only, and in this sense its framers could perhaps be accused of racism and sexism. For their time, however, the framers expressed extremely liberal views.

The Moral Legacy of the Founding Fathers

JOHN HOPE FRANKLIN

Historian John Hope Franklin (1915–   ) has long been a leader in the study of African-American life. His important book, *From Slavery to Freedom: A History of Negro Americans* (1947), has been revised many times and is considered a correction of the many misrecordings of American history. Franklin also brought to significance the life of a nineteenth-century African-American historian in *George Washington Williams: A Biography* (1985). In the following essay, published in 1975, Franklin argues that we have so romanticized eighteenth-century American history that we refuse to see the mistakes our founding fathers made.

FOR OPENERS

Retell the story of George Washington chopping down the cherry tree and refusing to lie about it. Ask students whether they believe the event really happened. After explaining that the story was invented by Mason Weems for his biography of Washington (1808), discuss the possibility of other myths and misconceptions in our view of historical figures.

As we approach the bicentennial of the independence of the United States, it may not be inappropriate to take advantage of the   1

ADDITIONAL QUESTIONS FOR RESPONDING TO READING

1. Do we need heroes? What do we gain from them?
2. What present evils are perpetuated today for purely economic reasons, much as slavery was in the past? Consider industries that pollute the environment (toxic waste dumps), harm the body (the tobacco industry), and exploit the young (the child pornography industry). Can these be justified morally?
3. What do you think the founding fathers meant by "all men are created equal"? Who could vote in the post-Colonial United States? When did this situation change? (The Jacksonian revolution in 1828 first gave nonpropertied white men the vote; African-American males could not vote until after the Fifteenth Amendment was ratified in 1870; women could not vote until after the Nineteenth Amendment in 1920.)
4. Is Franklin too hard on the early leaders of America? (For instance, he gives them little credit for keeping slavery out of the Northwest Territory.)
5. What is paradoxical about a slave being counted as three-fifths of a person?

perspective afforded by these last two centuries. Such a perspective should enable us to understand the distance we have traveled and where we are today.

This stock-taking, as it were, seems unusually desirable, thanks to the recent crises in leadership, in confidence in our political institutions, and in the standards of public morality to which we have paid only a "nodding acquaintance" over the years. As we do so, it is well to remember that criticism does not necessarily imply hostility; and, indeed, the recognition of human weakness suggests no alienation. One thing that becomes painfully clear as we look today at the shattered careers of so many public servants, with their confusion of public service with personal gain, is that we cannot always be certain of the validity or the defensibility of the positions taken by those who claim to be our leaders.

One of the problems that we encounter as we look at our past as well as our present is that we tend to shy away from making judgments or even criticisms of those who occupy the seats of the mighty. To the uninitiated, it seems somehow inappropriate. To the seasoned or cynical politician, it is anathema.

To be sure, we ally ourselves with one political party or another— as we have done since the time of Jefferson and Hamilton—and we have railed against the politics of one party or, now and then, the conduct of party leaders.

On the whole, however, our criticisms have been superficial; and the glass houses we have occupied have, for obvious reasons, prevented our engaging in all-out strictures against our adversaries. The result has been that we have usually engaged in the most gentle rapping of the knuckles of those who have betrayed their public trust; and seldom have we called our public servants to account in a really serious way.

In the effort to create an "instant history" with which we could live and prosper, our early historians intentionally placed our early national heroes and leaders beyond the pale of criticism. From the time that Benjamin Franklin created his own hero in "Poor Richard"[1] and Mason L. Weems created the cherry tree story about George Washington, it has been virtually impossible to regard our founding fathers as normal, fallible human beings. And this distorted image of them has not only created a gross historical fallacy, but it has also rendered it utterly impossible to deal with our past in terms of the realities that existed at the time. To put it another way, our roman-

---

[1]*Poor Richard's Almanack*, written and published by Franklin between 1733 and 1758, included maxims and proverbs as well as essays full of humor and down-to-earth wisdom communicating his philosophy for achieving a useful life. [Eds.]

ticizing about the history of the late eighteenth century has prevented our recognizing the fact that the founding fathers made serious mistakes that have greatly affected the course of our national history from that time to the present.

In 1974 we observed the bicentennial of the first Continental Congress, called to protest the new trade measures invoked against the colonies by Great Britain and to protest the political and economic measures directed particularly against the colony of Massachusetts. In a sense these measures were, indeed, intolerable as the colonists were forced to house British soldiers stationed in their midst, and Quebec was given political and economic privileges that appeared to be clearly discriminatory against the thirteen colonies.   7

But were these measures imposed by the British more intolerable than those imposed or, at least, sanctioned by the colonists against their own slaves? And yet, the colonists were outraged that the mother country was denying them their own freedom—the freedom to conduct their trade as they pleased.   8

It was not that the colonists were unaware of the problem of a much more basic freedom than that for which they were fighting in London. First of all, they knew of the 1772 decision of Lord Mansfield in the Somerset case, in which slavery was outlawed in Britain on the compelling ground that human bondage was "too odious" in England without specific legislation authorizing it. Although the colonists did have the authorization to establish and maintain slavery, Lord Mansfield's strictures against slavery could not have been lost on them altogether.   9

Secondly, and even more important, the slaves themselves were already pleading for their own freedom even before the first Continental Congress met. In the first six months of 1773 several slaves in Massachusetts submitted petitions to the general court, "praying to be liberated from a State of slavery." In the following year scores of other slaves, denying that they had ever forfeited the blessings of freedom by any compact or agreement to become slaves, asked for their freedom and for some land on which each of them "could sit down quietly under his own fig tree." The legislature of the Massachusetts colony debated the subject of slavery in 1774 and 1775, but voted simply that "the matter now subside."   10

But the matter would neither die nor subside. As the colonists plunged into war with Great Britain, they were faced with the problem of what to do about Negro slavery. The problem presented itself in the form of urgent questions.   11

First, should they continue to import slaves? This was a matter of some importance to British slave-trading interests who had built fortunes out of the traffic in human beings and to colonists who feared   12

TEACHING STRATEGY

Identify Franklin's main arguments against the founding fathers. According to him, where did these individuals go wrong?

that new, raw recruits from the West Indies and Africa would be more of a problem than a blessing. Most of the colonies opposed any new importations, and the Continental Congress affirmed the prohibition in April, 1776.

Secondly, should the colonists use black soldiers in their fight 13 against Britain? Although a few were used in the early skirmishes of the war, a pattern of exclusion of blacks had developed by the time that independence was declared. In July, 1775, the policy had been set forth that recruiters were not to enlist any deserter from the British army, "nor any stroller, negro, or vagabond."

Then, late in the year the British welcomed all Negroes willing 14 to join His Majesty's troops, and promised to set them free in return. The colonists were terrified, especially with the prospect of a servile insurrection. And so the Continental Congress shortly reversed its policy and grudgingly admitted blacks into the Continental Army.

The final consideration, as the colonists fought for their own 15 freedom from Britain, was what would be the effect of their revolutionary philosophy on their own slaves. The colonists argued in the Declaration of Independence that they were oppressed; and they wanted their freedom. Thomas Jefferson, in an early draft, went so far as to accuse the king of England of imposing slavery on them; but more "practical" heads prevailed, and that provision was stricken from the Declaration.

Even so, the Declaration said "all men are created equal." "Black 16 men as well as white men?" some wondered. Every man had an inalienable right to "life, liberty, and the pursuit of happiness." "Every black man as well as every white man?" some could well have asked.

How could the colonists make distinctions in their revolutionary 17 philosophy? They either meant that *all* men were created equal or they did not mean it at all. They either meant that *every* man was entitled to life, liberty, and the pursuit of happiness, or they did not mean it at all.

To be sure, some patriots were apparently troubled by the con- 18 tradictions between their revolutionary philosophy of political freedom and the holding of human beings in bondage. Abigail Adams, the wife of John Adams, admitted that there was something strange about their fighting to achieve and enjoy a status that they daily denied to others. Patrick Henry, who had cried "Give me liberty or give me death," admitted that slavery was "repugnant to humanity"; but it must not have seemed terribly repugnant, for he continued to hold blacks in bondage. So did George Washington and Thomas Jefferson and George Mason and Edmund Randolph and many others who signed the Declaration of Independence or the federal Constitution. They simply would not or could not see how ridiculous their position was.

And where the movement to emancipate the slaves took hold, as 19 in New England and in some of the Middle Atlantic states, slavery was not economically profitable anyway. Consequently, if the patriots in those states were genuinely opposed to slavery, they could afford the luxury of speaking against it. But in both of the Continental Congresses and in the Declaration of Independence the founding fathers failed to take an unequivocal, categorical stand against slavery. Obviously, human bondage and human dignity were not as important to them as their own political and economic independence.

The founding fathers were not only compelled to live with their 20 own inconsistency but they also had to stand convicted before the very humble group which they excluded from their political and social fellowship. In 1777 a group of Massachusetts blacks told the whites of that state that every principle that impelled America to break with England "pleads stronger than a thousand arguments" against slavery. In 1779 a group of Connecticut slaves petitioned the state for their liberty, declaring that they "groaned" under the burdens and indignities they were required to bear.

In 1781, Paul Cuffe and his brother, two young enterprising 21 blacks, asked Massachusetts to excuse them from the duty of paying taxes, since they "had no influence in the election of those who tax us." And when they refused to pay their taxes, those who had shouted that England's taxation without representation was tyranny, slapped the Cuffe brothers in jail!

Thus, when the colonists emerged victorious from their war with 22 England, they had both their independence *and* their slaves. It seemed to matter so little to most of the patriots that the slaves themselves had eloquently pointed out their inconsistencies or that not a few of the patriots themselves saw and pointed out their own fallacious position. It made no difference that five thousand blacks had joined in the fight for independence, only to discover that *real* freedom did not apply to them. The agencies that forged a national policy against England—the Continental Congresses and the government under the Articles of Confederation—were incapable of forging—or unwilling to forge—a national policy in favor of human freedom.

It was not a propitious way to start a new nation, especially since 23 its professions were so different from its practices and since it presumed to be the model for other new world colonies that would, in time, seek their independence from the tyranny of Europe.

Having achieved their own independence, the patriots exhibited 24 no great anxiety to extend the blessings of liberty to those among them who did not enjoy it. They could not altogether ignore the implications of the revolutionary philosophy, however. As early as 1777 the Massachusetts legislature had under consideration a measure to prohibit "the practice of holding persons in Slavery." Three years later the new constitution of that state declared that "all men are born free and equal." Some doubtless hoped that those high sounding words would mean more in the constitution of Massachusetts than they had meant in the Declaration of Independence.

Her neighbors, however, were more equivocal, with New Hampshire, Connecticut, and Rhode Island vacillating, for one reason or another, until another decade had passed. Although Pennsylvania did abolish slavery in 1780, New York and New Jersey did no better than prepare the groundwork for gradual emancipation at a later date. 25

One may well be greatly saddened by the thought that the author of the Declaration of Independence and the commander of the Revolutionary army and so many heroes of the Revolution were slaveholders. Even more disheartening, if such is possible, is that those *same* leaders and heroes were not greatly affected by the philosophy of freedom which they espoused. At least they gave no evidence of having been greatly affected by it. 26

Nor did they show any great magnanimity of spirit, once the war was over and political independence was assured. While northerners debated the questions of how and when they would free their slaves, the institution of human bondage remained as deeply entrenched as ever—from Delaware to Georgia. The only area on which there was national agreement that slavery should be prohibited was the area east of the Mississippi River and north of the Ohio River—the Northwest Territory. The agreement to prohibit slavery in that area, where it did not really exist and where relatively few white settlers lived, posed no great problem and surely it did not reflect a ground swell for liberty. 27

Meanwhile the prohibition, it should be noted, did not apply to the area south of the Ohio River, where slaveholders were more likely to settle anyway! This clearly shows that the founding fathers were willing to "play" with the serious question of freedom, thus evincing a cynicism that was itself unworthy of statesmanship. 28

Nor is one uplifted or inspired by the attitude of the founding fathers toward the slave trade, once their independence was secured. In the decade following independence the importation of slaves into the United States actually increased over the previous decade as well as over the decade before the War for Independence began. Far from languishing, the institution of slavery was prospering and growing. In its deliberations between 1781 and 1789 the Congress of the Confederation barely touched on the question of slavery or the slave trade. There was, to be sure, some concern over the capture of slaves; and 29 the Congress gave some attention to a Quaker petition against the trade, but it took no action.

On the whole the nation did not raise a hand against it. The flurry 30 of activity in the states, which led to the prohibition of slave importations in some of them and a temporary cessation of the trade in others, had the effect of misleading many people into thinking that slavery's hold on the nation was weakening.

That this was far from the actual situation became painfully clear 31 when the delegates gathered in Philadelphia in 1787 to write a new constitution. In the discussion over the slave trade only practical and economic considerations held sway. Humane considerations simply were not present. Maryland and Virginia tended to oppose the slave trade simply because they were overstocked and were not anxious to have any large importations into their midst. South Carolina and Georgia, where the death rate in the rice swamps was high and where slaveholders needed new recruits to develop new areas, demanded an open door for slave dealers.

And who rushed to the rescue when South Carolina demanded 32 concessions on the question of the slave trade? It was Oliver Ellsworth of Connecticut, who observed that a provision in the Constitution against the slave trade would be "unjust towards South Carolina and Georgia. Let us not intermeddle," he said. "As population increases, poor laborers will be so plenty as to render slaves useless." It is impossible to conceive that such temporizing on the part of a leading colonist would have been tolerated in the late dispute with England.

Could the new national government that was designed to be 33 strong have *anything* to say regarding slavery and the slave trade in the states? Elbridge Gerry of Massachusetts answered that it could not. It only had to refrain from giving direct sanction to the system.

Perhaps this is the view that seemed to silence the venerable 34 Benjamin Franklin. The oldest and easily one of the most respected members of the Constitutional Convention, Franklin brought with him a strong resolution against the slave trade that had been entrusted to him by the Pennsylvania Abolition Society. Although he was one of the most frequent speakers at the convention, he never introduced the resolution. With faint hearts such as Gerry's and Franklin's there is little wonder that South Carolina and Georgia were able to have their own way in wording the provision that declared that the slave trade could not be prohibited for another twenty years. One need only to look at the slave importation figures between 1788 and 1808 to appreciate how much advantage was taken of this generous reprieve.

The founding fathers did no better when it came to counting 35 slaves for purposes of representation and taxation. Northerners, who regarded slaves as property, insisted that for the purpose of representation they could not be counted as people. Southern slaveholders, while cheerfully admitting that slaves were property, insisted that they were also people and should be counted as such. It is one of the remarkable ironies of the early history of this democracy that the very men who had shouted so loudly that all men were created equal could not now agree on whether or not persons of African descent were men at all.

The irony was compounded when, in the so-called major com-   36
promise of the Constitution, the delegates agreed that a slave was three-fifths of a man, meaning that five slaves were to be counted as three persons. The magic of racism can work magic with the human mind. One wonders whether Catherine Drinker Bowen had this in mind when she called her history of the Constitutional Convention *The Miracle at Philadelphia*.

If slaveholders feared possible insurrections by their slaves, they   37
were no less apprehensive about the day-to-day attrition of the institution caused by slaves running away. They wanted to be certain that the Constitution recognized slaves as property and that it offered protection to that property, especially runaways. Significantly, there was virtually no opposition to the proposal that states give up fugitive slaves to their owners. The slaveowners had already won such sweeping constitutional recognition of slavery that the fugitive slave provision may be regarded as something of an anticlimax. There was, as Roger Sherman of Connecticut pointed out, as much justification for the public seizure and surrendering of a slave as there was for the seizure of a horse. Thus, a slave, who was only three-fifths of a man, was to be regarded in this connection as no more than a horse!

And the Constitution required that slaves who ran away were   38
not to enjoy the freedom that they had won in their own private war for independence, but were to be returned to those who claimed title to them. Consequently, there was a remarkable distinction between fighting for one's political independence, which the patriots expected to win, and did, and fighting for one's freedom from slavery, which these same patriots made certain that the slaves would not win.

At the outset it was observed that we tend to shy away from   39
making criticisms or judgments of those who occupy the seats of the mighty. This is not good either for ourselves or the institutions and way of life we seek to foster. If we would deal with our past terms of the realities that existed at the time, it becomes necessary for us to deal with our early leaders in their own terms, namely, as frail, fallible human beings, and—at times—utterly indifferent to the great causes they claimed to serve.

We may admire them for many things: their courage and bravery   40
in the military struggle against Britain; their imaginative creativity in

forging a new instrument of government; and their matchless service to a cause that captured the imagination of people around the world.

It does not follow, however, that we should admire them for 41 betraying the ideals to which they gave lip service, for speaking eloquently at one moment for the brotherhood of man and in the next moment denying it to their black brothers who fought by their side in their darkest hours of peril, and for degrading the human spirit by equating five black men with three white men or equating a black man with a horse!

We are concerned here not so much for the harm that the founding 42 fathers did to the cause they claimed to serve as for the harm that their moral legacy has done to every generation of their progeny. Having created a tragically flawed revolutionary doctrine and a constitution that did *not* bestow the blessings of liberty on its posterity, the founding fathers set the stage for every succeeding generation of Americans to apologize, compromise, and temporize on those principles of liberty that were supposed to be the very foundation of our system of government and way of life.

That is why the United States was so very apprehensive when 43 Haiti and most of the other Latin American countries sought to wipe out slavery the moment they received their political independence. The consistency of those nations was alien to the view of the United States on the same question.

That is why the United States failed to recognize the existence of 44 the pioneer republics of Haiti and Liberia until this nation was in the throes of a great civil war and sought to "use" these countries for colonizing some blacks. Earlier recognition would have implied an equality in the human family that the United States was unwilling to concede.

That is why this nation tolerated and, indeed, nurtured the cul- 45 tivation of a racism that has been as insidious as it has been pervasive.

Racial segregation, discrimination, and degradation are no unan- 46 ticipated accidents in this nation's history. They stem logically and directly from the legacy that the founding fathers bestowed upon contemporary America. The denial of equality in the year of independence led directly to the denial of equality in the era of the bicentennial of independence. The so-called compromises in the Constitution of 1787 led directly to the arguments in our own time that we can compromise equality with impunity and somehow use the Constitution as an instrument to preserve privilege and to foster inequality. It has thus become easy to invoke the spirit of the founding fathers whenever we seek ideological support for the social, political, and economic inequities that have become a part of the American way.

COLLABORATIVE ACTIVITY

Ask students to work in groups to find examples of stylistic and rhetorical devices used by Franklin that are also used in the Declaration of Independence (for example, the parallel structure that introduces paragraphs 43–45). What do students conclude about the style and structure of effective arguments?

WRITING SUGGESTION

Write an editorial explaining how the principles of the American Revolution are or are not being lived up to by today's American leaders.

ANSWERS TO RESPONDING TO READING

1. The judgments and reactions of today's leaders should be subject to close scrutiny. Leaders should not be followed blindly, for they may be guilty of similar errors.
2. Franklin accuses them of not living up in full to the principles of the Declaration of Independence. It is unfair to accuse individuals in another era of having faults unless we consider the moral value system of that time. By eighteenth-century standards the founding fathers were certainly liberal—and in some respects radical.
3. Franklin's choice of words highlights the irony of his statements, thus reinforcing the hypocrisy he is trying to expose.

It would be perverse indeed to derive satisfaction from calling 47 attention to the flaws in the character and conduct of the founding fathers. And it would be irresponsible to do so merely to indulge in whimsical iconoclasm.[2] But it would be equally irresponsible in the era of the bicentennial of independence not to use the occasion to examine our past with a view to improving the human condition.

An appropriate beginning, it would seem, would be to celebrate 48 our origins for what they were—to honor the principles of independence for which so many patriots fought and died. It is equally appropriate to be outraged over the manner in which the principles of human freedom and human dignity were denied and debased by those same patriots. Their legacy to us in this regard cannot, under any circumstances, be cherished or celebrated. Rather, this legacy represents a continuing and dismaying problem that requires us all to put forth as much effort to overcome it as the founding fathers did in handing it down to us.

RESPONDING TO READING

1. In paragraph 6 Franklin contends that "our romanticizing about the history of the late eighteenth century has prevented our recognizing the fact that the founding fathers made serious mistakes that have greatly affected the course of our national history from that time to the present." What application do these words have to our attitude toward today's political leaders? What warning is Franklin implying here?   **2.** Clearly Franklin himself is not in awe of the founding fathers. With what specific criticisms does he charge them? Do these charges come as a surprise to you? Do they change your reaction to the Declaration of Independence? Is it fair to accuse the founding fathers of racism when their views were considered reasonable by most of their contemporaries?   **3.** What do you make of Franklin's word choice in the following phrases?

> "Thomas Jefferson, in an early draft, went so far as to accuse the king of England of imposing slavery on them; but more *practical* heads prevailed . . ." (paragraph 15).
>
> Slavery "must not have seemed *terribly* repugnant . . ." (paragraph 18).
>
> "Southern slaveholders, while *cheerfully* admitting that slaves were property . . ." (paragraph 35).
>
> "The *magic* of racism can work *magic* with the human mind" (paragraph 36).

Is such language appropriate in this essay? Does it make Franklin's arguments more or less convincing to you?

---

[2]Attacking established practices and institutions. [Eds.]

The French and Indian War

ANNIE DILLARD

The following selection, like *"Il Faut Travailler,"* is an excerpt from Annie Dillard's (see also p. 34) autobiography, *An American Childhood* (1987). She writes about a war that was of particular interest to her, partly because it happened "in this neck of the woods," Pittsburgh, where she grew up. Dillard remembers how she brought the war to life in her imagination—"the red-warpainted Indian tomahawked the settler woman in calico"—and how simplistic her childhood view of history was.

The French and Indian War[1] was a war of which I, for one, reading stretched out in the bedroom, couldn't get enough. The names of the places were a litany: Fort Ticonderoga on the Hudson, Fort Vincennes on the Wabash. The names of the people were a litany: the Sieur de Contrecoeur; the Marquis de Montcalm; Major Robert Rogers of the Rangers; the Seneca Chief Half-King.

How witless in comparison were the clumsy wars of Europe: on this open field at nine o'clock sharp, soldiers in heavy armor, dragged from their turnip patches in feudal obedience to Lord So-and-So, met in long ranks and heavily armored men owned or paid for by Lord So-and-So, and defeated them by knocking them over like ninepins. What was at stake? A son's ambition, or an earl's pride.

In the French and Indian War, and the Indian wars, a whole continent was at stake, and it was hard to know who to root for as I read. The Indians were the sentimental favorites, but were visibly cruel. The French excelled at Indian skills and had the endearing habit of singing in boats. But if they won, we would all speak French, which seemed affected in the woods. The Scotch-Irish settlers and the English army were very uneasy allies, but their cruelties were invisible to me, and their partisans wrote all the books that fell into my hands.

It all seemed to take place right here, here among the blossoming rhododendrons outside the sunporch windows just below our bedroom, here in the Pittsburgh forest that rose again from every vacant lot, every corner of every yard the mower missed, every dusty crack in the sidewalk, every clogged gutter on the roof—an oak tree, a sycamore, a mountain ash, a pine.

For here, on the tip of the point where the three rivers met, the French built Fort Duquesne. It linked French holdings on the Great

FOR OPENERS

Review the events of the French and Indian War. Which, if any, of Dillard's childish views are accurate?

ADDITIONAL QUESTIONS FOR RESPONDING TO READING

1. Have any historical events occurred near your home? How does it make you feel to live near "history"?
2. What events in history stimulated your imagination most as a child?

---

[1]A war fought between 1754 and 1763 in North America between England and France; France had the support of the American Indians. [Eds.]

TEACHING STRATEGY

Examine the class's views on another war. What perceptions do the students have on World War II, the Vietnam War, or the Persian Gulf War? Where did they get these ideas? From school? From their parents? From the media?

Lakes to their settlement at New Orleans. It was 1754; the forest was a wilderness. From Fort Duquesne the French set their Indian allies to raiding far-flung English-speaking settlements and homesteads. The Indians burned the farms and tortured many farm families. From Fort Duquesne the French marched out and defeated George Washington at nearby Fort Necessity. From Fort Duquesne the French marched out and defeated General Edward Braddock: Indian warriors shot from cover, which offended those British soldiers who had time to notice before they died. It was here in 1758 that General John Forbes established British hegemony over the Mississippi watershed, by driving the French from the point and building Fort Pitt.

Here our own doughty provincials in green hunting shirts fought   6
beside regiments of rangers in buckskins, actual Highlanders in kilts, pro-English Iroquois in warpaint, and British regulars in red jackets. They came marching vividly through the virgin Pittsburgh forest; they trundled up and down the nearby mountain ridges by day and slept at night on their weapons under trees. Pioneer scouts ran ahead of them and behind them; messengers snuck into their few palisaded forts, where periwigged English officers sat and rubbed their foreheads while naked Indians in the treetops outside were setting arrows on fire to burn down the roof.

Best, it was all imaginary. That the French and Indian War took   7
place in this neck of the woods merely enhanced its storied quality, as if that fact had been a particularly pleasing literary touch. This war was part of my own private consciousness, the dreamlike interior murmur of books.

Costumed enormous people, transparent, vivid, and bold as   8
decals, as tall and rippling as people in dreams, shot at each other up and down the primeval woods, race against race. Just as people in myths travel rigidly up to the sky, or are placed there by some great god's fingers, to hold still forever in the midst of their loving or battles as fixed constellations of stars, so the fighting cast of the French and Indian War moved in a colorful body—locked into position in the landscape but still loading muskets or cowering behind the log door or landing canoes on a muddy shore—into books. They were fabulous and morally neutral, like everything in history, like everything in books. They were imagination's playthings: toy soldiers, toy settlers, toy Indians. They were a part of the interior life; they were private; they were my own.

In books these wars played themselves out ceaselessly; the red-   9
warpainted Indian tomahawked the settler woman in calico, and the rangy settler in buckskin spied out the Frenchman in military braid. Whenever I opened the book, the war struck up again, like a record whose music sounded when the needle hit. The skirling of Highlan-

COLLABORATIVE ACTIVITY

Have students work in groups to compare Dillard's stereotypes of Indians with the way Native Americans are portrayed in films. (You may assign "Dear John Wayne," page 741, before they begin.)

ders' bagpipes came playing again, high and thin over the dry oak ridges. The towheaded pioneer schoolchildren were just blabbing their memorized psalms when from right outside the greased parchment window sounded the wild and fatal whoops of Indian warriors on a raid.

The wild and fatal whoops, the war whoops of the warriors, the 10 red warriors whooping on a raid. It was a delirium. The tongue diddled the brain. Private life, book life, took place where words met imagination without passing through world.

I could dream it all whenever I wanted—and how often I wanted 11 to dream it! Fiercely addicted, I dosed myself again and again with the drug of the dream.

Parents have no idea what the children are up to in their bed- 12 rooms: They are reading the same paragraphs over and over in a stupor of violent bloodshed. Their legs are limp with horror. They are reading the same paragraphs over and over, dizzy with gratification as the young lovers find each other in the French fort, as the boy avenges his father, as the sound of muskets in the woods signals the end of the siege. They could not move if the house caught fire. They hate the actual world. The actual world is a kind of tedious plane where dwells, and goes to school, the body, the boring body which houses the eyes to read the books and houses the heart the books enflame. The very boring body seems to require an inordinately big, very boring world to keep it up, a world where you have to spend far too much time, have to *do* time like a prisoner, always looking for a chance to slip away, to escape back home to books, or escape back home to any concentration—fanciful, mental, or physical—where you can lose your self at last. Although I was hungry all the time, I could not bear to hold still and eat; it was too dull a thing to do, and had no appeal either to courage or to imagination. The blinding sway of their inner lives makes children immoral. They find things good insofar as they are thrilling, insofar as they render them ever more feverish and breathless, ever more limp and senseless on the bed.

Throughout these long, wonderful wars, I saw Indian braves 13 behind every tree and parked car. They slunk around, fairly bursting with woodcraft. They led soldiers on miraculous escapes through deep woods and across lakes at night; they paddled their clever canoes noiselessly; they swam underwater without leaving bubbles; they called to each other like owls. They nocked their arrows silently on the brow of the hill and snuck up in their soft moccasins to the camp where the enemy lay sleeping under heavy guard. They shrieked, drew their osage bows, and never missed—all the while communing deeply with birds and deer.

WRITING SUGGESTION

Apply Boorstin's theory (page 748) to your own personal history or to the history of your family or community. Write an essay in which you explain which developments in your life you perceive to be turning points and which you see as not likely to be of lasting importance. Explain your distinctions.

ANSWERS TO RESPONDING TO READING

1. Dillard makes a point about the gap between a romanticized view of history and the actual events. On the one hand, her attitude illustrates how such a romanticized view can involve young children in history: Although not all her impressions were historically accurate, they nevertheless served to stimulate her imagination. On the other hand, her tone reveals that she considers her childhood perspective to have been limited.
2. Students of history should seek opposing perspectives if they expect to understand the complete picture.
3. Answers will vary.

I had been born too late. I would have made a dandy scout, although I was hungry all the time, because I had taught myself, with my friend Pin, to walk in the woods silently: without snapping a twig, which was easy, or stepping on a loud leaf, which was hard. Experience taught me a special, rolling walk for skulking in silence: you step down with your weight on the ball of your foot, and ease it to your heel. 14

The Indians who captured me would not torture me, but would exclaim at my many abilities, and teach me more, all the while feeding me handsomely. Soon I would talk to animals, become invisible, ride a horse naked and shrieking, shoot things. 15

I practiced traveling through the woods in Frick Park without leaving footprints. I practiced tracking people and animals, such as the infamous pedigreed dachshunds, by following signs. I knew the mark of Walter Milligan's blunt heel and the mark of Amy's[2] sharp one. I practiced sneaking up on Mother as she repotted a philodendron, Father as he washed the car, saying, as I hoped but doubted the Indians said, "Boo." 16

RESPONDING TO READING

1. Dillard calls the French and Indian War "a war of which I, for one, reading stretched out in the bedroom, couldn't get enough" (paragraph 1). Do her offhand, self-mocking tone and romanticized view of history alienate you? What do you think her point is? Explain your reaction to her perspective. **2.** As an adult, Dillard seems aware that her childhood view of history was a limited one; in paragraph 3, for example, she acknowledges that her sympathies lay with the Scotch-Irish and English because "their partisans wrote all the books that fell into my hands." What dangers does this statement suggest for students of history? Do you see similar limitations in your own formal study of history? **3.** In school, whom were you taught to view as the heroes of history? What qualities made them heroes? Do you still see these individuals as heroic figures? Why or why not?

---

[2]Dillard's sister. [Eds.]

Grant and Lee: A Study in Contrasts

BRUCE CATTON

Civil War historian Bruce Catton (1899–1978) first became interested in the Civil War as a boy when he listened to the stories of the Union Army veterans of his hometown in Michigan. Catton's historical writing is eloquent, lively, and accurate, and he often relates events as if he were a reporter on the scene. His *Stillness at Appomattox* won the Pulitzer Prize in 1953, and he went on to write *This Hallowed Ground* (1956) and *Gettysburg: The Final Fury* (1974). President Gerald Ford awarded Catton the Medal of Freedom for his life's accomplishments. In the essay that follows, Catton compares the two famous men and the traditions for which they stood.

When Ulysses S. Grant and Robert E. Lee met in the parlor of a modest house at Appomattox Court House, Virginia, on April 9, 1865, to work out the terms for the surrender of Lee's Army of Northern Virginia, a great chapter in American life came to a close, and a great new chapter began. 1

These men were bringing the Civil War to its virtual finish. To be sure, other armies had yet to surrender, and for a few days the fugitive Confederate government would struggle desperately and vainly, trying to find some way to go on living now that its chief support was gone. But in effect it was all over when Grant and Lee signed the papers. And the little room where they wrote out the terms was the scene of one of the poignant, dramatic contrasts in American history. 2

They were two strong men, these oddly different generals, and they represented the strengths of two conflicting currents that, through them, had come into final collision. 3

Back of Robert E. Lee was the notion that the old aristocratic concept might somehow survive and be dominant in American life. 4

Lee was tidewater Virginia, and in his background were family, culture, and tradition . . . the age of chivalry transplanted to a New World which was making its own legends and its own myths. He embodied a way of life that had come down through the age of knighthood and the English country squire. America was a land that was beginning all over again, dedicated to nothing much more complicated than the rather hazy belief that all men had equal rights and should have an equal chance in the world. In such a land Lee stood for the feeling that it was somehow of advantage to human society to have a pronounced inequality in the social structure. There should be a leisure class, backed by ownership of land; in turn, society itself should be keyed to the land as the chief source of wealth and influ- 5

ADDITIONAL QUESTIONS FOR
RESPONDING TO READING

1. Is chivalry dead? If not, give examples of
   where it still exists. Should it be dead?
2. Are your connections stronger to your region
   or to your nation? Why?

TEACHING STRATEGY

List the contrasts embodied by Lee and Grant.
What politicians or world leaders stand in similar opposition today?

ence. It would bring forth (according to this ideal) a class of men with a strong sense of obligation to the community; men who lived not to gain advantage for themselves, but to meet the solemn obligations which had been laid on them by the very fact that they were privileged. From them the country would get its leadership; to them it could look for the higher values—of thought, of conduct, of personal deportment—to give it strength and virtue.

Lee embodied the noblest elements of this aristocratic ideal. 6 Through him, the landed nobility justified itself. For four years, the Southern states had fought a desperate war to uphold the ideals for which Lee stood. In the end, it almost seemed as if the Confederacy fought for Lee; as if he himself was the Confederacy . . . the best thing that the way of life for which the Confederacy stood could ever have to offer. He had passed into legend before Appomattox. Thousands of tired, underfed, poorly clothed Confederate soldiers, long since past the simple enthusiasm of the early days of the struggle, somehow considered Lee the symbol of everything for which they had been willing to die. But they could not quite put this feeling into words. If the Lost Cause, sanctified by so much heroism and so many deaths, had a living justification, its justification was General Lee.

Grant, the son of a tanner on the Western frontier, was everything 7 Lee was not. He had come up the hard way and embodied nothing in particular except the eternal toughness and sinewy fiber of the men who grew up beyond the mountains. He was one of a body of men who owed reverence and obeisance to no one, who were self-reliant to a fault, who cared hardly anything for the past but who had a sharp eye for the future.

These frontier men were the precise opposites of the tidewater 8 aristocrats. Back of them, in the great surge that had taken people over the Alleghenies and into the opening Western country, there was a deep, implicit dissatisfaction with a past that had settled into grooves. They stood for democracy, not from any reasoned conclusion about the proper ordering of human society, but simply because they had grown up in the middle of democracy and knew how it worked. Their society might have privileges, but they would be privileges each man had won for himself. Forms and patterns meant nothing. No man was born to anything, except perhaps to a chance to show how far he could rise. Life was competition.

Yet along with this feeling had come a deep sense of belonging 9 to a national community. The Westerner who developed a farm, opened a shop, or set up in business as a trader, could hope to prosper only as his own community prospered—and his community ran from the Atlantic to the Pacific and from Canada down to Mexico. If the land was settled, with towns and highways and accessible markets, he could better himself. He saw his fate in terms of the nation's own destiny. As its horizons expanded, so did his. He had, in other words, an acute dollars-and-cents stake in the continued growth and development of his country.

And that, perhaps, is where the contrast between Grant and Lee 10 becomes most striking. The Virginia aristocrat, inevitably, saw himself in relation to his own region. He lived in a static society which could endure almost anything except change. Instinctively, his first loyalty would go to the locality in which that society existed. He would fight to the limit of endurance to defend it, because in defending it he was defending everything that gave his own life its deepest meaning.

The Westerner, on the other hand, would fight with an equal 11 tenacity for the broader concept of society. He fought so because everything he lived by was tied to growth, expansion, and a constantly widening horizon. What he lived by would survive or fall with the nation itself. He could not possibly stand by unmoved in the face of an attempt to destroy the Union. He would combat it with everything he had, because he could only see it as an effort to cut the ground out from under his feet.

So Grant and Lee were in complete contrast, representing two 12 diametrically opposed elements in American life. Grant was the modern man emerging; beyond him, ready to come on the stage, was the great age of steel and machinery, of crowded cities and a restless burgeoning vitality. Lee might have ridden down from the old age of chivalry, lance in hand, silken banner fluttering over his head. Each man was the perfect champion of his cause, drawing both his strengths and his weaknesses from the people he led.

Yet it was not all contrast, after all. Different as they were—in 13 background, in personality, in underlying aspiration—these two great soldiers had much in common. Under everything else, they were marvelous fighters. Furthermore, their fighting qualities were really very much alike.

Each man had, to begin with, the great virtue of utter tenacity 14 and fidelity. Grant fought his way down the Mississippi Valley in spite of acute personal discouragement and profound military handicaps. Lee hung on in the trenches at Petersburg after hope itself had died. In each man there was an indomitable quality . . . the born fighter's refusal to give up as long as he can still remain on his feet and lift his two fists.

Daring and resourcefulness they had, too; the ability to think 15 faster and move faster than the enemy. These were the qualities which gave Lee the dazzling campaigns of Second Manassas and Chancellorsville and won Vicksburg for Grant.

Lastly, and perhaps greatest of all, there was the ability, at the 16 end, to turn quickly from war to peace once the fighting was over. Out of the way these two men behaved at Appomattox came the

COLLABORATIVE ACTIVITY

In groups, discuss the motivations each man had for fighting. Whose reasons do you believe were stronger? Why?

WRITING SUGGESTION

Catton says that Lee symbolized the Confederacy. Is there someone or something that symbolizes America today? Write a paragraph in which you identify and explain this "symbol" of America.

ANSWERS TO RESPONDING TO READING

1. Answers will vary. Most students will probably mention some divisions based on class and race.
2. Catton admires the men's characters. Strength of character is just as important today.
3. Perhaps, but he portrays the two men as individuals as well as generals. Thus he personalizes the war and makes it real.

possibility of a peace of reconciliation. It was a possibility not wholly realized, in the years to come, but which did, in the end, help the two sections to become one nation again . . . after a war whose bitterness might have seemed to make such a reunion wholly impossible. No part of either man's life became him more than the part he played in this brief meeting in the McLean house at Appomattox. Their behavior there put all succeeding generations of Americans in their debt. Two great Americans, Grant and Lee—very different, yet under everything very much alike. Their encounter at Appomattox was one of the great moments of American history.

RESPONDING TO READING

1. Catton presents Grant and Lee as representatives of "two conflicting currents" (paragraph 3), "two diametrically opposed elements in American life" (paragraph 12). What "conflicting currents" do you see in the United States today? What leaders represent those conflicting currents? Do you think the divisions are due primarily to geography, social class, race, ethnicity, gender, education, or economics?   **2.** Catton's attitude toward the two men he profiles might be characterized as admiring. What does he admire about them? Do you also find these qualities admirable? Are the personality traits of the two men as desirable today as they were in the nineteenth century?   **3.** Do you think Catton's focus on the generals rather than on the fighting men glorifies a devastating war? Explain your conclusion.

Hard Times

STUDS TERKEL

Studs Terkel (1912–   ) has been a lawyer, actor, columnist, nonfiction writer, radio and TV broadcaster, and lecturer. He won the 1985 Pulitzer Prize for *'The Good War': An Oral History of World War II*. Terkel is famous for his use of the tape recorder and has traveled widely to get interviews. His best-known book is *Working: People Talk About What They Do All Day and How They Feel About What They Do* (1974). Terkel writes in this book and others about people from all walks of life, their passions and disappointments. He says, "I celebrate the non-celebrated . . . the average American [who] has an indigenous intelligence, a native wit." In the following essay, Terkel's introductory paragraphs precede subjective testimony from one Harry Hartman; the interview is from Terkel's *Hard Times: An Oral History of the Great Depression* (1970).

It is somewhere in the County Building. He overflows the swivel chair.   1
Heavy, slightly asthmatic, he's a year or two away from retirement. He's

been with the bailiff's office for "thirty-three and a half years"—elsewhere, a few years. He had begun in 1931.

During the Depression, "I was the only guy working in the house at the 2 *time. So the windup is they become big shots and I'm still working." But he has had compensations: "It boils down to having a front seat in the theater of life." As court bailiff, he had had in his custody, a sixteen-year-old, who had killed four people on a weekend. During the trial, "he bet me a package of cigarettes, understand, he'd get the chair. And I bet him a package of cigarettes he wouldn't. When the jury come up and found him guilty, he reached back in a nonchalant way back to me and said, 'O.K., give me the cigarettes.' I gave it to him in open court and pictures were taken:* KILLER BETS PACKAGE OF CIGARETTES. *You know what I mean, and made a big thing about it." The boy got the chair—"it was quite a shock to him."*

During the Thirties, "I was a personal custodian to the levy bailiff." 3 *Writs of replevin and levies were his world, though he occasionally took part in evictions. "Replevins is when somebody buys on a conditional sales contract and doesn't fulfill their contract. Then we come out and take the things back. 'Cause it ain't theirs till the last dollar is paid for. Levy, understand, is to go against the thing—the store, the business—collect your judgment."*

We had 'em every single day. We used to come there with trucks 4 and take the food off the table. The husband would come runnin' out of the house. We'd have to put the food on the floor, take the tables and chairs out. If they were real bad, we'd make arrangements, you understand, to leave a few things there or something. So they could get by. But it was pretty rough there for a lot of people.

Once we went to a house and there were three children. The table 5 seemed to be part of the furniture company's inventory. That and the beds and some other things. The thing that struck us funny was that these people had almost the whole thing paid for, when they went to the furniture company and bought something else. So instead of paying this and making a separate bill, the salesman said, "You take whatever you want and we'll put it on the original bill." They paid for that stuff, and then when they weren't able—when the Depression struck—to pay for the new articles they bought, everything was repossessed.

You know, like radios. You remember at that time, they used to 6 take the radio and put it in a cabinet that would cost $200 or so. The cabinet was the big thing. These people paid off the bedroom set and the dining room set. Next thing they'd want is a nice radio. The radio was put on the bill and boom! everything, the whole inventory, went.

It was a pretty rough deal. But we arranged that we left a lot of 7 things there. On the inventory, we overlooked the beds and some of the other stuff. When we got enough, we said that the mattresses

FOR OPENERS

Play a recording of or read the lyrics to a Depression era song such as "Brother, Can You Spare a Dime?" Then, discuss the lyrics. Are they still relevant today?

ADDITIONAL QUESTIONS FOR RESPONDING TO READING

1. Hartman exhibits compassion in dealing with people. Do people in positions like his today display similar feelings for others? If not, why not?
2. Why does Hartman admire the men who were "burning on the inside" but didn't break down?
3. Why do the rich and poor and men and women react so differently to misfortune?
4. Have people's attitudes toward the law today changed as Hartman suggests? Why or why not?
5. During the Depression, there was no national system of welfare or unemployment insurance such as the ones that exist today. How do you think access to welfare and unemployment benefits (and access to free legal services) would have changed things for the poor people Hartman describes?

were unsanitary and we weren't gonna take it. If we had our way, we'd see that these people—if the original bill was $500 and they paid $350—we'd figure, well, you could leave a bed for $350 and you could leave a table. Or we'd say the mattress was full of cockroaches. We'd never touch the stuff. I'd just put down: bed missing. I'd ask the guy, "Can you identify that bed as the one sold?" And I'd say to the guy, "Hey, that ain't your bed. Say your brother-in-law's got it, and he gave you this one instead." Or something like that.

8   I mean, we always had an out. It was a real human aspect. If you really wanted to help somebody, you could. By making it easier for them, you made it easier for yourself. In most cases, people had plenty of warning that if they couldn't pay it, something would have to be done. They were broke and they were holding out as long as they could. But when it came around, a lot of cases they just gave up.

9   Some of the most pitiful things were when you went into a fine home, where if they were able to sell an oil painting on the wall, it could more than pay their judgment. When you went into factories, where the guy pleaded with you, so he could have his tools, understand, and do his work at home. When you took inventory, if you let him take his stuff, you know, if there was a beef, it'd be bad. But if you let him take what he needed, he didn't care about the rest. 'Cause he'd have bread and butter to go. So you'd use your head in a lot of cases.

10   It was a question of going in like a *mensch*.[1] There was a rewarding part of it. If you treated that guy good, he appreciated it. And in the long run, we did better than any of the guys that went out on the muscle stuff. When we took inventory, it was our inventory that stood up. I could open a brand new box, say in haberdashery, for shirts. What's to stop me from marking one box "partly full?" All I had to do is take out a shirt and throw it out and I can call it "partly full."

11   We'd even go out at night to repossess cars in a different way. The attorney would want this or that car, and he'd give you an order to take it. But if we thought the guy was a nice guy and he could get some money up, understand, and he needed the car for his business, we'd tell him to park it half a block away and be sure to get hold of a lawyer, or otherwise we'd tow it in the next time. You see? We did some good.

12   At that time, they tried all their pullers, the companies, they tried to recover on their own. So they wouldn't have to file in the municipal court. They tried to save that. They had their own pullers. We put a check on them and we took all kinds of phony stars away from them. Chicken Inspector 23, you know. They tried everything. It go so,

TEACHING STRATEGY

Explain the concept of oral history—the creation of new historical documents through interviews with people (sometimes world leaders, sometimes ordinary citizens) who lived through important historical periods or events. Ask your students what historical events in their lifetimes qualify as important, and whom they think should be interviewed about those events.

---

[1](Yiddish) A person having admirable qualities, such as strength of purpose. [Eds.]

people were so mad at me—or, you know, anybody to come out. These guys would come out with their fake stars and say they were deputies. Then when we come out, they were ready to shoot us.

One of your greatest guys in town, a fella that's a big banker 13 today, when we went to his home, he met us at the head of the stairs with a rifle. And my boss at the time said, "Yeah, you'll get one of us, but we'll get you, too. Why don't you cool off, and maybe we can discuss this. We don't want this place. We knew you had the money, we knew that. Why don't you get together with the lawyer and work something out? What good would it do if you shot us? We didn't ask to come here." People would get emotionally disturbed.

One time I went to take out a radio and a young girl undressed 14 herself. And she says, "You'll have to leave. I'm in the nude." I said, "You can stay," and we took it out anyhow. All we did was throw her in the bedroom and take the thing out. But we had to have a police squad before the old lady'd let it out. Screamed and hollered and everything else. It was on the second floor and she wanted to throw it downstairs. There were many times we had sofas and divans cut up by a person in a rage.

The only way to gain entrance is if people would open the door 15 for us. Whoever wouldn't let us in, we'd try to get it another way. There are ways, if you want to get it bad enough, you can do it.

I used to work quite a bit at night. We'd go around for the cars 16 and we'd go around for places we couldn't get in in the daytime. We did whatever the job called for.

Remember your feelings when you had to go out on those jobs?

In the beginning, we were worried about it. But after you found 17 out that you could do more good and maybe ease somebody's burden—and at the same time, it was very lucrative as far as you were concerned—why then you just took it in your stride. It was just another job. It wasn't bad.

But we had places where we had to take a guy's truck and take 18 his business away, and he's gone to the drawer and reached for a gun. We'd grab him by the throat, you know what I mean, and muscle and something like that. I don't know if he reached for the gun to kill himself or to scare us or what. Anyway he went for the drawer and boom! I slammed the door on his hand and my partner got him around the neck. I opened the drawer, and there's a gun there. I said, "Whataya goin' for the gun for?" He said, "I'm going for my keys." (Laughs.) The keys were in his pocket.

We've had guys break down. We've had others that we thought 19 would, and they were the finest of the lot. No problem at all. No matter how much they were burning on the inside.

COLLABORATIVE ACTIVITY

Divide students in pairs and have them interview each other about the earliest major historical event they can remember—for example, the explosion of the space shuttle Challenger. Assign students to prepare questions in advance.

There were some miserable companies that wanted to salvage 20 *everything*. When we got a writ from them, we didn't want it. But we had to take it. Some of 'em really turned your guts. And there were others, it was a pleasure to know. All in all, we used to look at it and laugh. Take it for whatever it was. If you got so, you knew how to allay hard feelings there, and you knew how to soft soap 'em, you did all right.

Aside from the bed, the table—I suppose the humiliation . . .

We tried to keep it down. That they were sending the stuff back 21 or that they were gonna get new stuff. Frankly, their neighbors were in the same classification as they were. It was things that people knew. It was part of the hardship.

When you saw guys around the house, they'd just stand by . . . ?

Depressed . . . if you came in there and they thought they were 22 failures to their wife and children. But like everything else, they always got over it. Look, people were trying to get by as best they could, and this was our way of getting by. We might as well make it as pleasant as we possibly can. And that's what our boss wanted: less trouble. Because after all, he held a political office and he wanted good will.

The poor people took it easier and were able to much better 23 understand than the people who were in the middle or better classes.

If I walked in a house, say, where they had furniture from Smyth[2] 24 and you come into them . . . first of all on account of being ashamed of never having had things of this type . . . they were the ones who hit hardest of all. They never knew anything like this in their whole career. They'd have maybe a Spanish cabinet, with all the wormwood and that. And realize that if they could have sold that, they could have paid their bill what they owed, what the guys were closin' in on 'em for. We had men walk out of the house with tears in their eyes. And it was the woman who took over. The guys couldn't take it. Especially with cars, you know what I mean?

The poor mostly would make the best of it. They knew it was 25 gonna be taken. They knew what they were up against and they knew it was only a matter of time, you know, until somebody took it away. We had less trouble with the poor. Not, I mean, that we enjoyed going against them, 'cause if they were poor, you had to help 'em more than anybody else.

---

[2]John M. Smyth Co., one of the better furniture stores in Chicago.

It was a real rough time, but we tried to make it along with a 26 smile. Instead of being a vulture, we tried to be helpful. But they were interesting times.

Did you encounter much resistance in your work?

No. I'd say one in a hundred. 27

If you'd walk in another room and somebody all of a sudden gets 28 hot and grabs a knife and goes for one . . . I mean this can happen. But you usually get 'em when they start crying, understand. When they start crying, they're already spent. Most of all, it was surprising how they accepted their fate.

What we did then, I don't think we could do today. With the 29 way the people look at the law. And with their action and their feeling, you know what I mean. They wouldn't accept today as they did then. What we did then was different. People still respected the courts and respected the law. They didn't want to revise our laws to satisfy them. (Weary, resigned.) What am I gonna tell you?

Today you get a guy in court, you don't like what the judge says, 30 he calls him a *m f*, you know what I mean? So how can you go in a house, understand, where we had law-abiding citizens like we had in the Thirties? Today we'd possibly run into a lot of trouble. If we started these evictions, we'd move 'em out on the street, they'd move 'em right back in. Whataya gonna do then? Today I think it's different, a different type people.

Before if you wore a badge, it meant something. Today you wear 31 a badge, you better watch out, 'cause somebody'll try to take you to see if they're as good a man as you are. And we're getting older, not younger. (Laughs.)

Today it's tougher for evictions than it was in our day. Today if 32 you evict anybody, you not only have to evict the people, you have to evict about seven or eight organizations that want the people in there. And each can come up with some legal point, why they should remain without giving the landlord any rent. Now I'm not for the landlord. They bled 'em in some of these buildings, I understand. They may be perfectly right. But as far as following the law is concerned, that's something else.

RESPONDING TO READING

1. Considering the nature and degree of the hardships Harry Hartman describes, his tone is strangely matter-of-fact and understated. Does this tone make the tragic situations he presents more or less real to you? Explain. **2.** Which of the events Hartman describes can you imagine taking place today? Which do you believe could never occur? Why? **3.** This selection

WRITING SUGGESTIONS

1. Write up an oral history based on the interview conducted for the "Collaborative Activity" assignment. Reproduce both questions and answers.
2. Suppose you were an elderly person being interviewed about life back in the 1990s. Write an account of what you would say about your life at that time.

ANSWERS TO RESPONDING TO READING

1. His tone enhances the realism of the situations because he can recount events as they occurred without dramatizing or romanticizing them. (Students should be reminded that his distance in time from the events he recalls helps make such a tone possible.)
2. Repossessions are still common, especially in slow economic times, but evictions are less prevalent.
3. Oral accounts are first-person history and perhaps constitute one of the best ways to learn about the past, especially the cultural history of an era. To get the complete picture, of course, more traditional historical methods should also be used.

is *oral history*, testimony collected from witnesses to or participants in events of historical significance. Does the narrator's eyewitness account compensate for the absence of statistical data or analysis by historians? Do you think such personal reminiscences can be considered history?

Okinawa: The Bloodiest Battle of All

WILLIAM MANCHESTER

Historian William Manchester (1922–   ) writes novels, biographies, and histories about many subjects. *American Caesar* is a biography of Douglas MacArthur, and *Goodbye, Darkness* is an autobiography. Manchester was commissioned by the Kennedy family to write an official account of the death of President John F. Kennedy. The research that resulted was serialized in *Look* magazine and published as the book *The Death of a President*. The following essay about Okinawa, a battle in which Manchester participated, appeared in the *New York Times Magazine* in 1987. The essay movingly describes the lasting effects of war.

BACKGROUND ON READING

Before beginning a discussion of this essay, make sure students know the beginning and ending dates of World War II (and the dates of the U.S. involvement in the war), and remind them which countries were allied with the United States and which were our enemies.

FOR OPENERS

Discuss the quotation "Only the dead have seen the end of war" (paragraph 17). What do you think General MacArthur meant to convey with this statement? What do you think it means?

ADDITIONAL QUESTIONS FOR RESPONDING TO READING

1. What is the "common grief" shared by the survivors of Okinawa?
2. What effect did being among the surviving 20 percent of his regiment have on Manchester?
3. Manchester shifts from present to past and back several times. What effect do these shifts in time produce for the reader?
4. How does actual battle change the "myths of warfare"?
5. Does the image of man as protector and defender still exist today? Has the changing role of women in society weakened (or even destroyed) that role?

On Okinawa today, Flag Day will be observed with an extraordinary ceremony: two groups of elderly men, one Japanese, the other American will gather for a solemn rite. 1

They could scarcely have less in common. Their motives are mirror images; each group honors the memory of men who tried to slay the men honored by those opposite them. But theirs is a common grief. After forty-two years the ache is still there. They are really united by death, the one great victor in modern war. 2

They have come to Okinawa to dedicate a lovely monument in remembrance of the Americans, Japanese and Okinawans killed there in the last and bloodiest battle of the Pacific war. More than 200,000 perished in the 82-day struggle—twice the number of Japanese lost at Hiroshima and more American blood than had been shed at Gettysburg. My own regiment—I was a sergeant in the 29th Marines—lost more than 80 percent of the men who had landed on April 1, 1945. Before the battle was over, both the Japanese and American commanding generals lay in shallow graves. 3

Okinawa lies 330 miles southwest of the southernmost Japanese island of Kyushu; before the war, it was Japanese soil. Had there been no atom bombs—and at that time the most powerful Americans, in Washington and at the Pentagon, doubted that the device would 4 work—the invasion of the Nipponese homeland would have been staged from Okinawa, beginning with a landing on Kyushu to take place November 1. The six Marine divisions, storming ashore abreast, would lead the way. President Truman asked General Douglas MacArthur, whose estimates of casualties on the eve of battles had proved uncannily accurate, about Kyushu. The general predicted a million Americans would die in that first phase.

Given the assumption that nuclear weapons would contribute 5 nothing to victory, the battle of Okinawa had to be fought. No one doubted the need to bring Japan to its knees. But some Americans came to hate the things we had to do, even when convinced that doing them was absolutely necessary; they had never understood the bestial, monstrous and vile means required to reach the objective— an unconditional Japanese surrender. As for me, I could not reconcile the romanticized view of war that runs like a red streak through our literature—and the glowing aura of selfless patriotism that had led us to put our lives at forfeit—with the wet, green hell from which I had barely escaped. Today, I understand. I was there, and was twice wounded. This is the story of what I knew and when I knew it.

To our astonishment, the Marine landing on April 1 was uncon- 6 tested. The enemy had set a trap. Japanese strategy called first for kamikazes to destroy our fleet, cutting us off from supply ships; then Japanese troops would methodically annihilate the men stranded ashore using the trench-warfare tactics of World War I—cutting the Americans down as they charged heavily fortified positions. One hundred and ten thousand Japanese troops were waiting on the southern tip of the island. Intricate entrenchments, connected by tunnels, formed the enemy's defense line, which ran across the waist of Okinawa from the Pacific Ocean to the East China Sea.

By May 8, after more than five weeks of fighting, it became clear 7 that the anchor of this line was a knoll of coral and volcanic ash, which the Marines christened Sugar Loaf Hill. My role in mastering it—the crest changed hands more than eleven times—was the central experience of my youth, and of all the military bric-a-brac that I put away after the war, I cherish most the Commendation from General Lemuel C. Shepherd, Jr., U.S.M.C., our splendid division commander, citing me for "gallantry in action and extraordinary achievement," adding, "Your courage was a constant source of inspiration . . . and your conduct throughout was in keeping with the highest tradition of the United States Naval Service."

The struggle for Sugar Loaf lasted ten days; we fought under the 8 worst possible conditions—a driving rain that never seemed to slacken, day or night. (I remember wondering, in an idiotic moment—

TEACHING STRATEGY

Photocopy and distribute (or read aloud) short excerpts from other descriptions of war, including fiction, poetry, and nonfiction. Some possible selections are Wallace Terry's *Bloods* (an oral history of the Vietnam War as told by black veterans), Ron Kovic's *Born on the Fourth of July*, and Tim O'Brien's *The Things They Carried* (both also about Vietnam); Wilfred Owen's "Dulce et Decorum Est" (about World War I); and Robert Lowell's "For the Union Dead" (about an all-black Civil War regiment). What realities remain constant from one war to another?

no man in combat is really sane—whether the battle could be called off, or at least postponed, because of bad weather.)

Newsweek called Sugar Loaf "the most critical local battle of the war." *Time* described a company of Marines—270 men—assaulting the hill. They failed; fewer than 30 returned. Fletcher Pratt, the military historian, wrote that the battle was unmatched in the Pacific war for "closeness and desperation." Casualties were almost unbelievable. In the 22d and 29th Marine regiments, two out of every three men fell. The struggle for the dominance of Sugar Loaf was probably the costliest engagement in the history of the Marine Corps. But by early evening on May 18, as night thickened over the embattled armies, the 29th Marines had taken Sugar Loaf, this time for keeps.

On Okinawa today, the ceremony will be dignified, solemn, seemly. It will also be anachronistic. If the Japanese dead of 1945 were resurrected to witness it, they would be appalled by the acceptance of defeat, the humiliation of their emperor—the very idea of burying Japanese near the barbarians from across the sea and then mourning them together. Americans, meanwhile, risen from their graves, would ponder the evolution of their own society, and might wonder, What ever happened to patriotism?

When I was a child, a bracket was screwed to the sill of a front attic window; its sole purpose was to hold the family flag. At first light, on all legal holidays—including Election Day, July 4, Memorial Day and, of course, Flag Day—I would scamper up to show it. The holidays remain, but mostly they mean long weekends.

In the late 1920s, during my childhood, the whole town of Attleboro, Massachusetts, would turn out to cheer the procession on Memorial Day. The policemen always came first, wearing their number-one uniforms and keeping perfect step. Behind them was a two-man vanguard—the mayor and, at his side, my father, hero of the 5th Marines and Belleau Wood, wearing his immaculate dress blues and looking like a poster of a Marine, with one magnificent flaw: the right sleeve of his uniform was empty. He had lost the arm in the Argonne. I now think that, as I watched him pass by, my own military future was already determined.

The main body of the parade was led by five or six survivors of the Civil War, too old to march but sitting upright in open Pierce-Arrows and Packards, wearing their blue uniforms and broad-brimmed hats. Then, in perfect step, came a contingent of men in their fifties, with their blanket rolls sloping diagonally from shoulder to hip—the Spanish-American War veterans. After these—and anticipated by a great roar from the crowd—came the doughboys of World War I, some still in their late twenties. They were acclaimed in part because theirs had been the most recent conflict, but also because they had fought in the war that—we then thought—had ended all wars.

Americans still march in Memorial Day parades, but attendance is light. One war has led to another and another and yet another, and the cruel fact is that few men, however they die, are remembered beyond the lifetimes of their closest relatives and friends. In the early 1940s, one of the forces that kept us on the line, under heavy enemy fire, was the conviction that this battle was of immense historical import, and that those of us who survived it would be forever cherished in the hearts of Americans. It was rather diminishing to return in 1945 and discover that your own parents couldn't even pronounce the names of the islands you had conquered. 14

But what of those who *do* remain faithful to patriotic holidays? What are they commemorating? Very rarely are they honoring what actually happened, because only a handful know, and it's not their favorite topic of conversation. In World War II, 16 million Americans entered the armed forces. Of these, fewer than a million saw action. Logistically, it took nineteen men to back up one man in combat. All who wore uniforms are called veterans, but more than 90 percent of them are as uninformed about the killing zones as those on the home front. 15

If all Americans understood the nature of battle, they might be vulnerable to truth. But the myths of warfare are embedded deep in our ancestral memories. By the time children have reached the age of awareness, they regard uniforms, decorations and Sousa marches as exalted, and those who argue otherwise are regarded as unpatriotic. 16

General MacArthur, quoting Plato, said: "Only the dead have seen the end of war." One hopes he was wrong, for war, as it had existed for over four thousand years, is now obsolete. As late as the spring of 1945, it was possible for one man, with a rifle, to make a difference, however infinitesimal, in the struggle to defeat an enemy who had attacked us and threatened our West Coast. The bomb dropped on Hiroshima made the man ludicrous, even pitiful. Soldiering has been relegated to Sartre's theater of the absurd. The image of the man as protector and defender of the home has been destroyed (and I suggest that the seed of thought eventually led women to reexamine their own role in society). 17

Until nuclear weapons arrived, the glorifying of militarism was the nation's hidden asset. Without it, we would almost certainly have been defeated by the Japanese, probably by 1943. In 1941 American youth was isolationist and pacifist. Then war planes from Imperial Japan destroyed our fleet at Pearl Harbor on December 7, and on 18

December 8 recruiting stations were packed. Some of us later found fighting rather different from what had been advertised. Yet in combat these men risked their lives—and often lost them—in hope of winning medals. There is an old soldier's saying: "A man won't sell you his life, but he'll give it to you for a piece of colored ribbon."

Most of the men who hit the beaches came to scorn eloquence. 19 They preferred the 130-year-old "Word of Cambronne." As dusk darkened the Waterloo battlefield,[1] with the French in full retreat, the British sent word to General Pierre Cambronne, commander of the Old Guard. His position, they pointed out, was hopeless, and they suggested he capitulate. Every French textbook reports his reply as "The Old Guard dies but never surrenders." What he actually said was "*Merde*."[2]

If you mention this incident to members of the U.S. 101st Airborne 20 Division, they will immediately understand. "Nuts" was not Brigadier General Anthony C. McAuliffe's answer to the Nazi demand that he hoist a white flag over Bastogne. Instead, he quoted Cambronne.

The character of combat has always been determined by the 21 weapons available to men when their battles were fought. In the beginning they were limited to hand weapons—clubs, rocks, swords, lances. At the Battle of Camlann in 539, England's Arthur—a great warrior, not a king—led a charge that slew 930 Saxons, including their leader.

It is important to grasp the fact that those 930 men were not killed 22 by snipers, grenades or shells. The dead were bludgeoned or stabbed to death, and we have a pretty good idea how this was done. One of the facts withheld from civilians during World War II was that Kabar fighting knives, with seven-inch blades honed to such precision that you could shave with them, were issued to Marines and that we were taught to use them. You never cut downward. You drove the point of your blade into a man's lower belly and ripped upward. In the process, you yourself became soaked in the other man's gore. After that charge at Camlann, Arthur must have been half drowned in blood.

The Battle of Agincourt, fought nearly one thousand years later, 23 represented a slight technical advance: crossbows and long bows had appeared. All the same, Arthur would have recognized the battle. Like all engagements of the time, this one was short. Killing by hand

---

[1]Manchester is referring to the Battle of Waterloo (1815), in which Napoleon was defeated by the British general Wellington. [Eds.]
[2]An obscenity. [Eds.]

is hard work, and hot work. It is so exhausting that even men in peak condition collapse once the issue of triumph or defeat is settled. And Henry V's spear carriers and archers were drawn from social classes that had been undernourished for as long as anyone could remember. The duration of medieval battles could have been measured in hours, even minutes.

The Battle of Waterloo, fought exactly four hundred years later, is another matter. By 1815, the Industrial Revolution had begun cranking out appliances of death, primitive by today's standards, but revolutionary for infantrymen of that time. And Napoleon had formed mass armies, pressing every available man into service. It was a long step toward total war, and its impact was immense. Infantrymen on both sides fought with single-missile weapons—muskets or rifles—and were supported by (and were the target of) artillery firing cannonballs.   24

The fighting at Waterloo continued for three days; for a given regiment, however, it usually lasted one full day, much longer than medieval warfare. A half century later, Gettysburg lasted three days and cost 43,497 men. Then came the marathon slaughters of 1914–1918, lasting as long as ten months (Verdun) and producing hundreds of thousands of corpses lying, as F. Scott Fitzgerald wrote afterward, "like a million bloody rugs." Winston Churchill, who had been a dashing young cavalry officer when Victoria was queen, said of the new combat: "War, which was cruel and magnificent, has become cruel and squalid."   25

It may be said that the history of war is one of men packed together, getting closer and closer to the ground and then deeper and deeper into it. In the densest combat of World War I, battalion frontage—the length of the line into which the 1,000-odd men were squeezed—had been 800 yards. On Okinawa, on the Japanese fortified line, it was less than 600 yards—about 18 inches per man. We were there and deadlocked for more than a week in the relentless rain. During those weeks we lost nearly 4,000 men.   26

And now it is time to set down what this modern battlefield was like.   27

All greenery had vanished; as far as one could see, heavy shellfire had denuded the scene of shrubbery. What was left resembled a cratered moonscape. But the craters were vanishing, because the rain had transformed the earth into a thin porridge—too thin even to dig foxholes. At night you lay on a poncho as a precaution against drowning during the barrages. All night, every night, shells erupted close enough to shake the mud beneath you at the rate of five or six a minute. You could hear the cries of the dying but could do nothing.   28

Japanese infiltration was always imminent, so the order was to stay put. Any man who stood up was cut in half by machine guns manned by fellow Marines.

By day, the mud was hip deep; no vehicles could reach us. As 29 you moved up the slope of the hill, artillery and mortar shells were bursting all around you, and, if you were fortunate enough to reach the top, you encountered the Japanese defenders, almost face to face, a few feet away. To me, they looked like badly wrapped brown paper parcels someone had soaked in a tub. Their eyes seemed glazed. So, I suppose, did ours.

Japanese bayonets were fixed; ours weren't. We used the knives, 30 or, in my case, a .45 revolver and M1 carbine. The mud beneath our feet was deeply veined with blood. It was slippery. Blood is very slippery. So you skidded around, in deep shock, fighting as best you could until one side outnumbered the other. The outnumbered side would withdraw for reinforcements and then counterattack.

During those ten days I ate half a candy bar. I couldn't keep 31 anything down. Everyone had dysentery, and this brings up an aspect of war even Robert Graves, Siegfried Sassoon, Edmund Blunden and Ernest Hemingway avoided.[3] If you put more than a quarter million men in a line for three weeks, with no facilities for the disposal of human waste, you are going to confront a disgusting problem. We were fighting and sleeping in one vast cesspool. Mingled with that stench was another—the corrupt and corrupting odor of rotting human flesh.

My luck ran out on June 5, more than two weeks after we had 32 taken Sugar Loaf Hill and killed the seven thousand Japanese soldiers defending it. I had suffered a slight gunshot wound above the right knee on June 2, and had rejoined my regiment to make an amphibious landing on Oroku Peninsula behind enemy lines. The next morning several of us were standing in a stone enclosure outside some Okinawan tombs when a six-inch rocket mortar shell landed among us.

The best man in my section was blown to pieces, and the slime 33 of his viscera enveloped me. His body had cushioned the blow, saving my life; I still carry a piece of his shinbone in my chest. But I collapsed, and was left for dead. Hours later corpsmen found me still breathing, though blind and deaf, with my back and chest a junkyard of iron fragments—including, besides the piece of shinbone, four pieces of shrapnel too close to the heart to be removed. (They were not dangerous, a Navy surgeon assured me, but they still set off the metal detector at the Buffalo airport.)

---

[3]Graves, Sassoon, Blunden, and Hemingway all served in World War I and wrote about their experiences. [Eds.]

Between June and November I underwent four major operations 34
and was discharged as 100 percent disabled. But the young have
strong recuperative powers. The blindness was caused by shock, and
my vision returned. I grew new eardrums. In three years I was physically fit. The invisible wounds remain.

Most of those who were closest to me in the early 1940s had left 35
New England campuses to join the Marines, knowing it was the most
dangerous branch of the service. I remember them as bright, physically strong and inspired by an idealism and love of country they
would have been too embarrassed to acknowledge. All of us despised
the pompousness and pretentiousness of senior officers. It helped
that, almost without exception, we admired and respected our commander in chief. But despite our enormous pride in being Marines,
we saw through the scam that had lured so many of us to recruiting
stations.

Once we polled a rifle company, asking each man why he had 36
joined the Marines. A majority cited *To the Shores of Tripoli*, a marshmallow of a movie starring John Payne, Randolph Scott and Maureen
O'Hara. Throughout the film the uniform of the day was dress blues;
requests for liberty were always granted. The implication was that
combat would be a lark, and when you returned, spangled with
decorations, a Navy nurse like Maureen O'Hara would be waiting in
your sack. It was peacetime again when John Wayne appeared on
the silver screen as Sergeant Stryker in *Sands of Iwo Jima*, but that film
underscores the point; I went to see it with another ex-Marine, and
we were asked to leave the theater because we couldn't stop laughing.

After my evacuation for Okinawa, I had the enormous pleasure 37
of seeing Wayne humiliated in person at Aiea Heights Naval Hospital
in Hawaii. Only the most gravely wounded, the litter cases, were
sent there. The hospital was packed, the halls lined with beds.
Between Iwo Jima and Okinawa, the Marine Corps was being bled
white.

Each evening, Navy corpsmen would carry litters down to the 38
hospital theater so the men could watch a movie. One night they had
a surprise for us. Before the film the curtains parted and out stepped
John Wayne, wearing a cowboy outfit—ten-gallon hat, bandanna,
checkered shirt, two pistols, chaps, boots and spurs. He grinned his
aw-shucks grin, passed a hand over his face and said, "Hi ya, guys!"
He was greeted by a stony silence. Then somebody booed. Suddenly
everyone was booing.

This man was a symbol of the fake machismo we had come to 39
hate, and we weren't going to listen to him. He tried and tried to
make himself heard, but we drowned him out, and eventually he quit

COLLABORATIVE ACTIVITY

Ask students to work in groups to list images
of glory and images of defeat drawn from films
about war. (You might ask them to look again
at paragraph 36 before they begin.) In class discussion, consider these questions: What images
does a film have to stress in order to convey an
antiwar message? What images must it downplay or avoid?

and left. If you liked *Sands of Iwo Jima*, I suggest you be careful. Don't tell it to the Marines.

And so we weren't macho. Yet we never doubted the justice of 40
our cause. If we had failed—if we had lost Guadalcanal, and the Navy's pilots had lost the Battle of Midway—the Japanese would have invaded Australia and Hawaii, and California would have been in grave danger. In 1942 the possibility of an Axis victory was very real. It is possible for me to loathe war—and with reason—yet still honor the brave men, many of them boys, really, who fought with me and died beside me. I have been haunted by their loss these forty-two years, and I shall mourn them until my own death releases me. It does not seem too much to ask that they be remembered on one day each year. After all, they sacrificed their futures that you might have yours.

Yet I will not be on Okinawa for the dedication today. I would 41
enjoy being with Marines; the ceremony will be moving, and we would be solemn, remembering our youth and the beloved friends who died there.

Few, if any, of the Japanese survivors agreed to attend the cer- 42
emony. However, Edward L. Fox, chairman of the Okinawa Memorial Shrine Committee, capped almost six years' campaigning for a monument when he heard about a former Japanese naval officer, Yoshio Yazaki—a meteorologist who had belonged to a four-thousand-man force led by Rear Admiral Minoru Ota—and persuaded him to attend.

On March 31, 1945, Yazaki-san had been recalled to Tokyo, and 43
thus missed the battle of Okinawa. Ten weeks later—exactly forty-two years ago today—Admiral Ota and his men committed seppuku,[4] killing themselves rather than face surrender. Ever since than Yazaki has been tormented by the thought that his comrades have joined their ancestors and he is here, not there.

Finding Yazaki was a great stroke of luck for Fox, for whom an 44
Okinawa memorial had become an obsession. His own division commander tried to discourage him. The Japanese could hardly be expected to back a memorial on the site of their last great military defeat. But Yazaki made a solution possible.

If Yazaki can attend, why can't I? I played a role in the early stages 45
of Buzz Fox's campaign and helped write the tribute to the Marines that is engraved on the monument. But when I learned that Japanese were also participating, I quietly withdrew. There are too many graves between us, too much gore, too many memories of too many atrocities.

---

[4]Hara-kiri; ritual suicide. [Eds.]

In 1978, revisiting Guadalcanal, I encountered a Japanese businessman who had volunteered to become a kamikaze pilot in 1945 and was turned down at the last minute. Mutual friends suggested that we meet. I had expected no difficulty; neither, I think, did he. But when we confronted each other, we froze. 46

I trembled, suppressing the sudden, startling surge of primitive rage within. And I could see, from his expression, that this was difficult for him, too. Nations may make peace. It is harder for fighting men. On simultaneous impulse we both turned and walked away. 47

I set this down in neither pride nor shame. The fact is that some wounds never heal. Yazaki, unlike Fox, is dreading the ceremony. He does not expect to be shriven of his guilt. He knows he must be there but can't say why. Men are irrational, he explains, and adds that he feels very sad. 48

So do I, Yazaki-san, so do I. 49

RESPONDING TO READING

1. William Manchester is a noted historian who has written extensively on American history; here, he writes of events in which he participated. How do you imagine his role as a participant affects his presentation of events? What point is he making? Could another historian, one who did not participate in the battle, make the same point?   **2.** How does Manchester characterize the Japanese? Do you find his characterizations offensive? Is he guilty of stereotyping? Of racism? Explain your reasoning.   **3.** In paragraph 5 Manchester explains his inability to "reconcile the romanticized view of war that runs like a red streak through our literature . . . with the wet, green hell" of the battle he experienced. However, he continues, "Today I understand." What do you think he understands? Do you believe the bloody battle was worth fighting? Under what circumstances, if any, could you imagine yourself willingly participating in such a battle?

WRITING SUGGESTION

Write a story in which a veteran of the Vietnam War and a veteran of the 1991 Persian Gulf War meet to dedicate a war memorial to all American soldiers killed in battle.

ANSWERS TO RESPONDING TO READING

1. Manchester's first-person perspective legitimizes his view of war. He makes the point that the reality of war is far more terrible than monuments to its dead can suggest. Another historian could perhaps write a more objective account but probably not a more moving one, and even then his or her account would not be completely objective either.
2. Manchester characterizes the Japanese as his enemies, which they were. Taking any other viewpoint would have resulted in his not surviving the battle. Many would say that this position is not racist, just practical.
3. Manchester understands that war is not what patriotic feelings and romanticized literature suggest; it is a kind of hell. Most students would agree that the battle was necessary. Students would probably fight to defend their families and their country. (You might, however, want to examine the question of whether *any* battle is *ever* worth fighting.)

The Civil Rights Movement: What Good Was It?

ALICE WALKER

Alice Walker (see also p. 68) became involved with the civil rights movement in 1967 in Jackson, Mississippi, where she taught in the Head Start program and at Jackson State College. Returning to the South from Boston in 1973, she became convinced that the African-American middle class had lost its concern for those poorer and less fortunate than themselves. Walker writes about this change in her novel *Meridian* (1976). In the following selection, from *In Search*

In Search of Our Mothers' Gardens, Walker raises her voice as a social activist who believes the civil rights movement at least "gave us each other forever."

1   Someone said recently to an old black lady from Mississippi, whose legs had been badly mangled by local police who arrested her for "disturbing the peace," that the Civil Rights Movement was dead, and asked, since it was dead, what she thought about it. The old lady replied, hobbling out of his presence on her cane, that the Civil Rights Movement was like herself, "if it's dead, it shore ain't ready to lay down!"

2   This old lady is a legendary freedom fighter in her small town in the Delta. She has been severely mistreated for insisting on her rights as an American citizen. She has been beaten for singing Movement songs, placed in solitary confinement in prisons for talking about freedom, and placed on bread and water for praying aloud to God for her jailers' deliverance. For such a woman the Civil Rights Movement will never be over as long as her skin is black. It also will never be over for twenty million others with the same "affliction," for whom the Movement can never "lay down," no matter how it is killed by the press and made dead and buried by the white American public. As long as one black American survives, the struggle for equality with other Americans must also survive. This is a debt we owe to those blameless hostages we leave to the future, our children.

3   Still, white liberals and deserting Civil Rights sponsors are quick to justify their disaffection from the Movement by claiming that it is all over. "And since it is over," they will ask, "would someone kindly tell me what has been gained by it?" They then list statistics supposedly showing how much more advanced segregation is now than ten years ago—in schools, housing, jobs. They point to a gain in conservative politicians during the last few years. They speak of ghetto riots and of the survey that shows that most policemen are admittedly too anti-Negro to do their jobs in ghetto areas fairly and effectively. They speak of every area that has been touched by the Civil Rights Movement as somehow or other going to pieces.

4   They rarely talk, however, about human attitudes among Negroes that have undergone terrific changes just during the past seven to ten years (not to mention all those years when there was a Movement and only the Negroes knew about it). They seldom speak of changes in personal lives because of the influence of people in the Movement. They see general failure and few, if any, individual gains.

5   They do not understand what it is that keeps the Movement from "laying down" and Negroes from reverting to their former *silent* second-class status. They have apparently never stopped to wonder

why it is always the white man—on his radio and in his newspaper and on his television—who says that the Movement is dead. If a Negro were audacious enough to make such a claim, his fellows might hanker to see him shot. The Movement is dead to the white man because it no longer interests him. And it no longer interests him because he can afford to be uninterested: he does not have to live by it, with it, or for it, as Negroes must. He can take a rest from the news of beatings, killings, and arrests that reach him from North and South—if his skin is white. Negroes cannot now and will never be able to take a rest from the injustices that plague them, for they—not the white man—are the target.

Perhaps it is naïve to be thankful that the Movement "saved" a large number of individuals and gave them something to live for, even if it did not provide them with everything they wanted. (Materially, it provided them with precious little that they wanted.) When a movement awakens people to the possibilities of life, it seems unfair to frustrate them by then denying what they had thought was offered. But what was offered? What was promised? What was it all about? What good did it do? Would it have been better, as some have suggested, to leave the Negro people as they were, unawakened, unallied with one another, unhopeful about what to expect for their children in some future world?

I do not think so. If knowledge of my condition is all the freedom I get from a "freedom movement," it is better than unawareness, forgottenness, and hopelessness, the existence that is like the existence of a beast. Man only truly lives by knowing; otherwise he simply performs, copying the daily habits of others, but conceiving nothing of his creative possibilities as a man, and accepting someone else's superiority and his own misery.

When we are children, growing up in our parents' care, we await the spark from the outside world. Sometimes our parents provide it—if we are lucky—sometimes it comes from another source far from home. We sit, paralyzed, surrounded by our anxiety and dread, hoping we will not have to grow up into the narrow world and ways we see about us. We are hungry for a life that turns us on; we yearn for a knowledge of living that will save us from our innocuous lives that resemble death. We look for signs in every strange event; we search for heroes in every unknown face.

It was just six years ago that I began to be alive. I had, of course, been living before—for I am now twenty-three—but I did not really know it. And I did not know it because nobody told me that I—a pensive, yearning, typical high-school senior, but Negro—existed in the minds of others as I existed in my own. Until that time my mind was locked apart from the outer contours and complexion of my body

6

7

8

9

as if it and the body were strangers. The mind possessed both thought and spirit—I wanted to be an author or a scientist—which the color of the body denied. I had never seen myself and existed as a statistic exists, or as a phantom. In the white world I walked, less real to them than a shadow; and being young and well hidden among the slums, among people who also did not exist—either in books or in films or in the government of their own lives—I waited to be called to life. And, by a miracle, I was called.

There was a commotion in our house that night in 1960. We had 10 managed to buy our first television set. It was battered and overpriced, but my mother had gotten used to watching the afternoon soap operas at the house where she worked as maid, and nothing could satisfy her on days when she did not work but a continuation of her "stories." So she pinched pennies and bought a set.

I remained listless throughout her "stories," tales of pregnancy, 11 abortion, hypocrisy, infidelity, and alcoholism. All these men and women were white and lived in houses with servants, long staircases that they floated down, patios where liquor was served four times a day to "relax" them. But my mother, with her swollen feet eased out of her shoes, her heavy body relaxed in our only comfortable chair, watched each movement of the smartly coiffed women, heard each word, pounced upon each innuendo and inflection, and for the duration of these "stories" she saw herself as one of them. She placed herself in every scene she saw, with her braided hair turned blond, her two hundred pounds compressed into a sleek size-seven dress, her rough dark skin smooth and *white*. Her husband became "dark and handsome," talented, witty, urbane, charming. And when she turned to look at my father sitting near her in his sweat shirt with his smelly feet raised on the bed to "air," there was always a tragic look of surprise on her face. Then she would sigh and go out to the kitchen looking lost and unsure of herself. My mother, a truly great woman who raised eight children of her own and half a dozen of the neighbors' without a single complaint, was convinced that she did not exist compared to "them." She subordinated her soul to theirs and became a faithful and timid supporter of the "Beautiful White People." Once she asked me, in a moment of vicarious pride and despair, if I didn't think that "they" were "jest naturally smarter, prettier, better." My mother asked this: a woman who never got rid of any of her children, never cheated on my father, was never a hypocrite if she could help it, and never even tasted liquor. She could not even bring herself to blame "them" for making her believe what they wanted her to believe: that if she did not look like them, think like them, be sophisticated and corrupt-for-comfort's-sake like them, she was a nobody. Black was not a color on my mother; it was a shield that made her invisible.

Of course, the people who wrote the soap-opera scripts always 12 made the Negro maids in them steadfast, trusty, and wise in a home-remedial sort of way; but my mother, a maid for nearly forty years, never once identified herself with the scarcely glimpsed black servant's face beneath the ruffled cap. Like everyone else, in her daydreams at least, she thought she was free.

Six years ago, after half-heartedly watching my mother's soap 13 operas and wondering whether there wasn't something more to be asked of life, the Civil Rights Movement came into my life. Like a good omen for the future, the face of Dr. Martin Luther King, Jr., was the first black face I saw on our new television screen. And, as in a fairy tale, my soul was stirred by the meaning for me of his mission—at the time he was being rather ignominiously dumped into a police van for having led a protest march in Alabama—and I fell in love with the sober and determined face of the Movement. The singing of "We Shall Overcome"—that song betrayed by nonbelievers in it—rang for the first time in my ears. The influence that my mother's soap operas might have had on me became impossible. The life of Dr. King, seeming bigger and more miraculous than the man himself, because of all he had done and suffered, offered a pattern of strength and sincerity I felt I could trust. He had suffered much because of his simple belief in nonviolence, love, and brotherhood. Perhaps the majority of men could not be reached through these beliefs, but because Dr. King kept trying to reach them in spite of danger to himself and his family, I saw in him the hero for whom I had waited so long.

What Dr. King promised was not a ranch-style house and an acre 14 of manicured lawn for every black man, but jail and finally freedom. He did not promise two cars for every family, but the courage one day for all families everywhere to walk without shame and unafraid on their own feet. He did not say that one day it will be us chasing prospective buyers out of our prosperous well-kept neighborhoods, or in other ways exhibiting our snobbery and ignorance as all other ethnic groups before us have done; what he said was that we had a right to live anywhere in this country we chose, and a right to a meaningful well-paying job to provide us with the upkeep of our homes. He did not say we had to become carbon copies of the white American middle class; but he did say we had the right to become whatever we wanted to become.

Because of the Movement, because of an awakened faith in the 15 newness and imagination of the human spirit, because of "black and white together"—for the first time in our history in some human relationship on and off TV—because of the beatings, the arrests, the hell of battle during the past years, I have fought harder for my life and for a chance to be myself, to be something more than a shadow or a number, than I had ever done before in my life. Before, there had seemed to be no real reason for struggling beyond the effort for daily bread. Now there was a chance at that other that Jesus meant when He said we could not live by bread alone.

I have fought and kicked and fasted and prayed and cursed and cried myself to the point of existing. It has been like being born again, literally. Just "knowing" has meant everything to me. Knowing has pushed me out into the world, into college, into places, into people. 16

Part of what existence means to me is knowing the difference between what I am now and what I was then. It is being capable of looking after myself intellectually as well as financially. It is being able to tell when I am being wronged and by whom. It means being awake to protect myself and the ones I love. It means being a part of the world community, and being *alert* to which part it is that I have joined, and knowing how to change to another part if that part does not suit me. To know is to exist: to exist is to be involved, to move about, to see the world with my own eyes. This, at least, the Movement has given me. 17

The hippies and other nihilists would have me believe that it is all the same whether the people in Mississippi have a movement behind them or not. Once they have their rights, they say, they will run all over themselves trying to be just like everybody else. They will be well fed, complacent about things of the spirit, emotionless, and without that marvelous humanity and "soul" that the Movement has seen them practice time and time again. "What has the Movement done," they ask, "with the few people it has supposedly helped?" "Got them white-collar jobs, moved them into standardized ranch houses in white neighborhoods, given them nondescript gray flannel suits?" "What are those people now?" they ask. And then they answer themselves, "Nothings!" 18

I would find this reasoning—which I have heard many, many times from hippies and nonhippies alike—amusing if I did not also consider it serious. For I think it is a delusion, a cop-out, an excuse to disassociate themselves from a world in which they feel too little has been changed or gained. The real question, however, it appears to me, is not whether poor people will adopt the middle-class mentality once they are well fed; rather, it is whether they will ever be well fed enough to be able to choose whatever mentality they think will suit them. The lack of a movement did not keep my mother from *wishing* herself bourgeois in her daydreams. 19

There is widespread starvation in Mississippi. In my own state 20 of Georgia there are more hungry families than Lester Maddox[1] would like to admit—or even see fed. I went to school with children who ate red dirt. The Movement has prodded and pushed some liberal senators into pressuring the government for food so that the hungry may eat. Food stamps that were two dollars and out of the reach of many families not long ago have been reduced to fifty cents. The price is still out of the reach of some families, and the government, it seems to a lot of people, could spare enough free food to feed its own people. It angers people in the Movement that it does not; they point to the billions in wheat we send free each year to countries abroad. Their government's slowness while people are hungry, its unwillingness to believe that there are Americans starving, its stingy cutting of the price of food stamps, make many Civil Rights workers throw up their hands in disgust. But they do not give up. They do not withdraw into the world of psychedelia. They apply what pressure they can to make the government give away food to hungry people. They do not plan so far ahead in their disillusionment with society that they can see these starving families buying identical ranch-style houses and sending their snobbish children to Bryn Mawr and Yale. They take first things first and try to get them fed.

They do not consider it their business, in any case, to say what 21 kind of life the people they help must lead. How one lives is, after all, one of the rights left to the individual—when and if he has opportunity to choose. It is not the prerogative of the middle class to determine what is worthy of aspiration. There is also every possibility that the middle-class people of tomorrow will turn out ever so much better than those of today. I even know some middle-class people of today who are not *all* bad.

I think there are so few Negro hippies because middle-class 22 Negroes, although well fed, are not careless. They are required by the treacherous world they live in to be clearly aware of whoever or whatever might be trying to do them in. They are middle class in money and position, but they cannot afford to be middle class in complacency. They distrust the hippie movement because they know that it can do nothing for Negroes as a group but "love" them, which is what all paternalists claim to do. And since the only way Negroes can survive (which they cannot do, unfortunately, on love alone) is with the support of the group, they are wisely wary and stay away.

---

[1]Segregationist Governor of Georgia from 1967 to 1971 who closed a restaurant he owned rather than comply with the law and serve black patrons [Eds.]

WRITING SUGGESTION

Write a reply to Walker's essay in which you compare her hopes for the civil rights movement in the 1960s with your perception of its accomplishments and problems today.

A white writer tried recently to explain that the reason for the relatively few Negro hippies is that Negroes have built up a "supercool" that cracks under LSD and makes them have a "bad trip." What this writer doesn't guess at is that Negroes are needing drugs less than ever these days for any kind of trip. While the hippies are "tripping," Negroes are going after power, which is so much more important to their survival and their children's survival than LSD and pot. 23

Everyone would be surprised if the Israelis ignored the Arabs and took up "tripping" and pot smoking. In this country we are the Israelis. Everybody who can do so would like to forget this, of course. But for us to forget it for a minute would be fatal. "We Shall Overcome" is just a song to most Americans, *but we must do it.* Or die. 24

What good was the Civil Rights Movement? If it had just given this country Dr. King, a leader of conscience, for once in our lifetime, it would have been enough. If it had just taken black eyes off white television stories, it would have been enough. If it had fed one starving child, it would have been enough. 25

If the Civil Rights Movement is "dead," and if it gave us nothing else, it gave us each other forever. It gave some of us bread, some of us shelter, some of us knowledge and pride, all of us comfort. It gave us our children, our husbands, our brothers, our fathers, as men reborn and with a purpose for living. It broke the pattern of black servitude in this country. It shattered the phony "promise" of white soap operas that sucked away so many pitiful lives. It gave us history and men far greater than Presidents. It gave us heroes, selfless men of courage and strength, for our little boys and girls to follow. It gave us hope for tomorrow. It called us to life. 26

Because we live, it can never die. 27

ANSWERS TO RESPONDING TO READING

1. Yes. The focus is much more on economics today, though, than it was when Walker was younger.
2. Knowledge alone without any progress could prove frustrating. The 1970s and 1980s have seen a definite slowdown, and in some cases even setbacks, in the civil rights movement.
3. Typically, young people are more idealistic than older ones. And as decades go, the 1960s were very idealistic, at least at first.

RESPONDING TO READING

1. In paragraph 5 Walker says, "The Movement is dead to the white man because it no longer interests him. And it no longer interests him because he can afford to be uninterested: he does not have to live by it, with it, or for it, as Negroes must." Do you think the civil rights movement still exists today? Explain. **2.** In paragraph 7 Walker asserts that even if the only thing the civil rights movement had done was make her aware of her own status, it would have accomplished a great deal. Do you agree? **3.** Walker wrote this essay when she was twenty-three. Do you think she is naively optimistic in her claims for the value of the civil rights movement? If so, do you think her naiveté is due to her age or to the fact that the essay was written in the late 1960s?

Shiloh[1]

BOBBIE ANN MASON

Southern fiction writer Bobbie Ann Mason (1940–   ) sets most of her stories in western Kentucky, using colloquialisms and details of ordinary life to depict the region's social and physical geography in themes of loss and disappointed hopes. In her stories, love does not necessarily offer stability to the working-class and farm people about whom she writes. One critic has said that "Mason rarely says more than is necessary to convey what Hemingway called 'the real thing.'" In "Shiloh," from her collection *Shiloh and Other Stories* (1982), Mason uses history to tell a story.

1   Leroy Moffitt's wife, Norma Jean, is working on her pectorals. She lifts three-pound dumbbells to warm up, then progresses to a twenty-pound barbell. Standing with her legs apart, she reminds Leroy of Wonder Woman.

2   "I'd give anything if I could just get these muscles to where they're real hard," says Norma Jean. "Feel this arm. It's not as hard as the other one."

3   "That's 'cause you're right-handed," says Leroy, dodging as she swings the barbell in an arc.

4   "Do you think so?"

5   "Sure."

6   Leroy is a truckdriver. He injured his leg in a highway accident four months ago, and his physical therapy, which involves weights and a pulley, prompted Norma Jean to try building herself up. Now she is attending a body-building class. Leroy has been collecting temporary disability since his tractor-trailer jackknifed in Missouri, badly twisting his left leg in its socket. He has a steel pin in his hip. He will probably not be able to drive his rig again. It sits in the backyard, like a gigantic bird that has flown home to roost. Leroy has been home in Kentucky for three months, and his leg is almost healed, but the accident frightened him and he does not want to drive any more long hauls. He is not sure what to do next. In the meantime, he makes things from craft kits. He started by building a miniature log cabin from notched Popsicle sticks. He varnished it and placed it on the TV set, where it remains. It reminds him of a rustic Nativity scene. Then he tried string art (sailing ships on black velvet), a macramé

---

[1]Southwestern Tennessee site of an 1862 Civil War battle in which Union forces defeated the Confederates. Heavy casualties—about 10,000 men on each side—immobilized both sides for three weeks. [Eds.]

owl kit, a snap-together B-17 Flying Fortress, and a lamp made out of a model truck, with a light fixture screwed in the top of the cab. At first the kits were diversions, something to kill time, but now he is thinking about building a full-scale log house from a kit. It would be considerably cheaper than building a regular house, and besides, Leroy has grown to appreciate how things are put together. He has begun to realize that in all the years he was on the road he never took time to examine anything. He was always flying past scenery.

7   "They won't let you build a log cabin in any of the new subdivisions," Norma Jean tells him.

8   "They will if I tell them it's for you," he says, teasing her. Ever since they were married, he has promised Norma Jean he would build her a new home one day. They have always rented, and the house they live in is small and nondescript. It does not even feel like a home, Leroy realizes now.

9   Norma Jean works at the Rexall drugstore, and she has acquired an amazing amount of information about cosmetics. When she explains to Leroy the three stages of complexion care, involving creams, toners, and moisturizers, he thinks happily of other petroleum products—axle grease, diesel fuel. This is a connection between him and Norma Jean. Since he has been home, he has felt unusually tender about his wife and guilty over his long absences. But he can't tell what she feels about him. Norma Jean has never complained about his traveling; she has never made hurt remarks, like calling his truck a "widow-maker." He is reasonably certain she has been faithful to him, but he wishes she would celebrate his permanent home-coming more happily. Norma Jean is often startled to find Leroy at home, and he thinks she seems a little disappointed about it. Perhaps he reminds her too much of the early days of their marriage, before he went on the road. They had a child who died as an infant, years ago. They never speak about their memories of Randy, which have almost faded, but now that Leroy is home all the time, they sometimes feel awkward around each other, and Leroy wonders if one of them should mention the child. He has the feeling that they are waking up out of a dream together—that they must create a new marriage, start afresh. They are lucky they are still married. Leroy has read that for most people losing a child destroys the marriage—or else he heard this on *Donahue*. He can't always remember where he learns things anymore.

10   At Christmas, Leroy bought an electric organ for Norma Jean. She used to play the piano when she was in high school. "It don't leave you," she told him once. "It's like riding a bicycle."

11   The new instrument had so many keys and buttons that she was bewildered by it at first. She touched the keys tentatively, pushed

TEACHING STRATEGY

List the changes in Norma Jean and Leroy as the story progresses. What causes these changes? Are they positive or negative?

some buttons, then pecked out "Chopsticks." It came out in an amplified fox-trot rhythm, with marimba sounds.

"It's an orchestra!" she cried.   12

The organ had a pecan-look finish and eighteen present chords,   13
with optional flute, violin, trumpet, clarinet, and banjo accompaniments. Norma Jean mastered the organ almost immediately. At first she played Christmas songs. Then she bought *The Sixties Songbook* and learned every tune in it, adding variations to each with the rows of brightly colored buttons.

"I didn't like these old songs back then," she said. "But I have   14
this crazy feeling I missed something."

"You didn't miss a thing," said Leroy.   15

Leroy likes to lie on the couch and smoke a joint and listen to   16
Norma Jean play "Can't Take My Eyes Off You" and "I'll Be Back."
He is back again. After fifteen years on the road, he is finally settling down with the woman he loves. She is still pretty. Her skin is flawless.
Her frosted curls resemble pencil trimmings.

Now that Leroy has come home to stay, he notices how much   17
the town has changed. Subdivisions are spreading across western Kentucky like an oil slick. The sign at the edge of town says "Pop: 11,500"—only seven hundred more than it said twenty years before.
Leroy can't figure out who is living in all the new houses. The farmers who used to gather around the courthouse square on Saturday afternoons to play checkers and spit tobacco juice have gone. It has been years since Leroy has thought about the farmers, and they have disappeared without his noticing.

Leroy meets a kid named Stevie Hamilton in the parking lot at   18
the new shopping center. While they pretend to be strangers meeting over a stalled car, Stevie tosses an ounce of marijuana under the front seat of Leroy's car. Stevie is wearing orange jogging shoes and a T-shirt that says CHATTAHOOCHEE SUPER-RAT. His father is a prominent doctor who lives in one of the expensive subdivisions in a new white-columned brick house that looks like a funeral parlor. In the phone book under his name there is a separate number, with the listing "Teenagers."

"Where do you get this stuff?" asks Leroy. "From your pappy?"   19

"That's for me to know and you to find out," Stevie says. He is   20
slit-eyed and skinny.

"What else you got?"   21

"What you interested in?"   22

"Nothing special. Just wondered."   23

Leroy used to take speed on the road. Now he has to go slowly.   24
He needs to be mellow. He leans back against the car and says, "I'm

aiming to build me a log house, soon as I get time. My wife, though, I don't think she likes the idea."

"Well, let me know when you want me again," Stevie says. He 25 has a cigarette in his cupped palm, as though sheltering it from the wind. He takes a long drag, then stomps it on the asphalt and slouches away.

Stevie's father was two years ahead of Leroy in high school. Leroy 26 is thirty-four. He married Norma Jean when they were both eighteen, and their child Randy was born a few months later, but he died at the age of four months and three days. He would be about Stevie's age now. Norma Jean and Leroy were at the drive-in, watching a double feature (*Dr. Strangelove* and *Lover Come Back*), and the baby was sleeping in the back seat. When the first movie ended, the baby was dead. It was the sudden infant death syndrome. Leroy remembers handing Randy to a nurse at the emergency room, as though he were offering her a large doll as a present. A dead baby feels like a sack of flour. "It just happens sometimes," said the doctor, in what Leroy always recalls as a nonchalant tone. Leroy can hardly remember the child anymore, but he still sees vividly a scene from *Dr. Strangelove* in which the President of the United States was talking in a folksy voice on the hot line to the Soviet premier about the bomber accidentally headed toward Russia. He was in the War Room, and the world map was lit up. Leroy remembers Norma Jean standing catatonically beside him in the hospital and himself thinking: Who is this strange girl? He had forgotten who she was. Now scientists are saying that crib death is caused by a virus. Nobody knows anything, Leroy thinks. The answers are always changing.

When Leroy gets home from the shopping center, Norma Jeans' 27 mother, Mable Beasley, is there. Until this year, Leroy has not realized how much time she spends with Norma Jean. When she visits, she inspects the closets and then the plants, informing Norma Jean when a plant is droopy or yellow. Mable calls the plants "flowers," although there are never any blooms. She always notices if Norma Jean's laundry is piling up. Mable is a short, overweight woman whose tight, brown-dyed curls look more like a wig than the actual wig she sometimes wears. Today she has brought Norma Jean an off-white dust ruffle she made for the bed; Mabel works in a custom-upholstery shop.

"This is the tenth one I made this year," Mabel says. "I got started 28 and couldn't stop."

"It's real pretty," says Norma Jean. 29

"Now we can hide things under the bed," says Leroy, who gets 30 along with his mother-in-law primarily by joking with her. Mabel has never really forgiven him for disgracing her by getting Norma Jean pregnant. When the baby died, she said that fate was mocking her.

"What's that thing?" Mabel says to Leroy in a loud voice, pointing   31
to a tangle of yarn on a piece of canvas.

Leroy holds it up for Mabel to see. "It's my needlepoint." he   32
explains. "This is a *Star Trek* pillow cover."

"That's what a woman would do," says Mabel. "Great day in the   33
morning!"

"All the big football players on TV do it," he says.   34

"Why, Leroy, you're always trying to fool me. I don't believe you   35
for one minute. You don't know what to do with yourself—that's the
whole trouble. Sewing!"

"I'm aiming to build us a log house," says Leroy. "Soon as my   36
plans come."

"Like *heck* you are," says Norma Jean. She takes Leroy's need-   37
lepoint and shoves it into a drawer. "You have to find a job first.
Nobody can afford to build now anyway."

Mabel straightens her girdle and says, "I still think before you   38
get tied down y'all ought to take a little run to Shiloh."

"One of these days, Mama," Norma Jean says impatiently.   39

Mabel is talking about Shiloh, Tennessee. For the past few years,   40
she has been urging Leroy and Norma Jean to visit the Civil War
battleground there. Mabel went there on her honeymoon—the only
real trip she ever took. Her husband died of a perforated ulcer when
Norma Jean was ten, but Mabel, who was accepted into the United
Daughters of the Confederacy in 1975, is still preoccupied with going
back to Shiloh.

"I've been to kingdom come and back in that truck out yonder,"   41
Leroy says to Mabel, "but we never yet set foot in that battleground.
Ain't that something? How did I miss it?"

"It's not even that far," Mabel says.   42

After Mabel leaves, Norma Jean reads to Leroy from a list she   43
has made. "Things you could do," she announces. "You could get a
job as a guard at Union Carbide, where they'd let you set on a stool.
You could get on at the lumberyard. You could do a little carpenter
work, if you want to build so bad. You could—"

"I can't do something where I'd have to stand up all day."   44

"You ought to try standing up all day behind a cosmetics counter.   45
It's amazing that I have strong feet, coming from two parents that
never had strong feet at all." At the moment Norma Jean is holding
on to the kitchen counter, raising her knees one at a time as she talks.
She is wearing two-pound ankle weights.

"Don't worry," says Leroy. "I'll do something."   46

"You could truck calves to slaughter for somebody. You wouldn't   47
have to drive any big old truck for that."

"I'm going to build you this house," says Leroy. "I want to make   48
you a real home."

"I don't want to live in any log cabin."   49

"It's not a cabin. It's a house."   50

"I don't care. It looks like a cabin."   51

"You and me together could lift those logs. It's just like lifting   52
weights."

Norma Jean doesn't answer. Under her breath, she is counting.   53
Now she is marching through the kitchen. She is doing goose steps.

Before his accident, when Leroy came home he used to stay in   54
the house with Norma Jean, watching TV in bed and playing cards.
She would cook fried chicken, picnic ham, chocolate pie—all his favorites. Now he is home alone much of the time. In the mornings, Norma
Jean disappears, leaving a cooling place in the bed. She eats a cereal
called Body Buddies, and she leaves the bowl on the table, with the
soggy tan balls floating in a milk puddle. He sees things about Norma
Jean that he never realized before. When she chops onions, she stares
off into a corner, as if she can't bear to look. She puts on her house
slippers almost precisely at nine o'clock every evening and nudges
her jogging shoes under the couch. She saves bread heels for the
birds. Leroy watches the birds at the feeder. He notices the peculiar
way goldfinches fly past the window. They close their wings, then
fall, then spread their wings to catch and lift themselves. He wonders
if they close their eyes when they fall. Norma Jean closes her eyes
when they are in bed. She wants the lights turned out. Even then,
he is sure she closes her eyes.

He goes for long drives around town. He tends to drive a car   55
rather carelessly. Power steering and an automatic shift make a car
feel so small and inconsequential that his body is hardly involved in
the driving process. His injured leg stretches out comfortably. Once
or twice he has almost hit something, but even the prospect of an
accident seems minor in a car. He cruises the new subdivisions,
feeling like a criminal rehearsing for a robbery. Norma Jean is probably
right about a log house being inappropriate here in the new subdivisions. All the houses look grand and complicated. They depress
him.

One day when Leroy comes home from a drive he finds Norma   56
Jean in tears. She is in the kitchen making a potato and mushroom-
soup casserole, with grated-cheese topping. She is crying because her
mother caught her smoking.

"I didn't hear her coming. I was standing here puffing away pretty   57
as you please," Norma Jean says, wiping her eyes.

"I knew it would happen sooner or later," says Leroy, putting   58
his arm around her.

"She don't know the meaning of the word 'knock,' " says Norma   59
Jean. "It's a wonder she hadn't caught me years ago."

"Think of it this way," Leroy says. "What if she caught me with   60
a joint?"

"You better not let her!" Norma Jean shrieks. "I'm warning you,   61
Leroy Moffitt!"

"I'm just kidding. Here, play me a tune. That'll help you relax."   62

Norma Jean puts the casserole in the oven and sets the timer.   63
Then she plays a ragtime tune, with horns and banjo, as Leroy lights
up a joint and lies on the couch, laughing to himself about Mabel's
catching him at it. He thinks of Stevie Hamilton—a doctor's son
pushing grass. Everything is funny. The whole town seems crazy and
small. He is reminded of Virgil Mathis, a boastful policeman Leroy
used to shoot pool with. Virgil recently led a drug bust in a back room
at a bowling alley, where he seized ten thousand dollars' worth of
marijuana. The newspaper had a picture of him holding up the bags
of grass and grinning widely. Right now, Leroy can imagine Virgil
breaking down the door and arresting him with a lungful of smoke.
Virgil would probably have been alerted to the scene because of all
the racket Norma Jean is making. Now she sounds like a hard-rock
band. Norma Jean is terrific. When she switches to a Latin-rhythm
version of "Sunshine Superman," Leroy hums along. Norma Jean's
foot goes up and down, up and down.

"Well, what do you think?" Leroy says, when Norma Jean pauses   64
to search through her music.

"What do I think about what?"   65

His mind had gone blank. Then he says, "I'll sell my rig and build   66
us a house." That wasn't what he wanted to say. He wanted to know
what she thought—what she *really* thought—about them.

"Don't start in on that again," says Norma Jean. She begins   67
playing "Who'll Be the Next in Line?"

Leroy used to tell hitchhikers his whole life story—about his   68
travels, his hometown, the baby. He would end with a question:
"Well, what do you think?" It was just a rhetorical question. In time,
he had the feeling that he'd been telling the same story over and over
to the same hitchhikers. He quit talking to hitchhikers when he realized how his voice sounded—whining and self-pitying, like some
teenage-tragedy song. Now Leroy has the sudden impulse to tell
Norma Jean about himself, as if he had just met her. They have known
each other so long they have forgotten a lot about each other. They

could become reacquainted. But when the oven timer goes off and she runs to the kitchen, he forgets why he wants to do this.

The next day, Mabel drops by. It is Saturday and Norma Jean is cleaning. Leroy is studying the plans of his log house, which have finally come in the mail. He has them spread out on the table—big sheets of stiff blue paper, with diagrams and numbers printed in white. While Norma Jean runs the vacuum, Mabel drinks coffee. She sets her coffee cup on a blueprint.   69

"I'm just waiting for time to pass," she says to Leroy, drumming her fingers on the table.   70

As soon as Norma Jean switches off the vacuum, Mabel says in a loud voice, "Did you hear about the datsun dog that killed the baby?"   71

Norma Jean says, "The word is 'dachshund.' "   72

"They put the dog on trial. It chewed the baby's legs off. The mother was in the next room all the time." She raises her voice. "They thought it was neglect."   73

Norma Jean is holding her ears. Leroy manages to open the refrigerator and get some Diet Pepsi to offer Mabel. Mabel still has some coffee and she waves away the Pepsi.   74

"Datsuns are like that," Mabel says. "They're jealous dogs. They'll tear a place to pieces if you don't keep an eye on them."   75

"You better watch out what you're saying, Mabel," says Leroy.   76

"Well, facts is facts."   77

Leroy looks out the window at his rig. It is like a huge piece of furniture gathering dust in the backyard. Pretty soon it will be an antique. He hears the vacuum cleaner. Norma Jean seems to be cleaning the living room rug again.   78

Later, she says to Leroy, "She just said that about the baby because she caught me smoking. She's trying to pay me back."   79

"What are you talking about?" Leroy says, nervously shuffling blueprints.   80

"You know good and well," Norma Jean says. She is sitting in a kitchen chair with her feet up and her arms wrapped around her knees. She looks small and helpless. She says, "The very idea, her bringing up a subject like that! Saying it was neglect."   81

"She didn't mean that," Leroy says.   82

"She might not have *thought* she meant it. She always says things like that. You don't know how she goes on."   83

"But she didn't really mean it. She was just talking."   84

Leroy opens a king-sized bottle of beer and pours it into two glasses, dividing it carefully. He hands a glass to Norma Jean and   85 she takes it from him mechanically. For a long time, they sit by the kitchen window watching the birds at the feeder.

Something is happening. Norma Jean is going to night school. 86 She has graduated from her six-week body-building course and now she is taking an adult-education course in composition at Paducah Community College. She spends her evenings outlining paragraphs.

"First you have a topic sentence," she explains to Leroy. "Then 87 you divide it up. Your secondary topic has to be connected to your primary topic."

To Leroy, this sounds intimidating. "I never was any good in 88 English," he says.

"It makes a lot of sense." 89

"What are you doing this for, anyhow?" 90

She shrugs. "It's something to do." She stands up and lifts her 91 dumbbells a few times.

"Driving a rig, nobody cared about my English." 92

"I'm not criticizing your English." 93

Norma Jean used to say, "If I lose ten minutes' sleep, I just drag 94 all day." Now she stays up late, writing compositions. She got a B on her first paper—a how-to theme on soup-based casseroles. Recently Norma Jean has been cooking unusual foods—tacos, lasagna, Bombay chicken. She doesn't play the organ anymore, though her second paper was called "Why Music Is Important to Me." She sits at the kitchen table, concentrating on her outlines, while Leroy plays with his log house plans, practicing with a set of Lincoln Logs. The thought of getting a truckload of notched, numbered logs scares him, and he wants to be prepared. As he and Norma Jean work together at the kitchen table, Leroy has the hopeful thought that they are sharing something, but he knows he is a fool to think this. Norma Jean is miles away. He knows he is going to lose her. Like Mabel, he is just waiting for time to pass.

One day, Mabel is there before Norma Jean gets home from work, 95 and Leroy finds himself confiding in her. Mabel, he realizes, must know Norma Jean better than he does.

"I don't know what's got into that girl," Mabel says. "She used 96 to go to bed with the chickens. Now you say she's up all hours. Plus her a-smoking. I like to died."

"I want to make her this beautiful home," Leroy says, indicating 97 the Lincoln Logs. "I don't think she even wants it. Maybe she was happier with me gone."

"She don't know what to make of you, coming home like this." 98

"Is that it?" 99

Mabel takes the roof off his Lincoln Log cabin. "You couldn't get 100
me in a log cabin," she says. "I was raised in one. It's no picnic, let
me tell you."

"They're different now," says Leroy. 101

"I tell you what," Mabel says, smiling oddly at Leroy. 102

"What?" 103

"Take her on down to Shiloh. Y'all need to get out together, stir 104
a little. Her brain's all balled up over them books."

Leroy can see traces of Norma Jean's features in her mother's 105
face. Mabel's worn face has the texture of crinkled cotton, but suddenly she looks pretty. It occurs to Leroy that Mabel has been hinting
all along that she wants them to take her with them to Shiloh.

"Let's all go to Shiloh," he says. "You and me and her. Come 106
Sunday."

Mabel throws up her hand in protest. "Oh, no, not me. Young 107
folks want to be by theirselves."

When Norma Jean comes in with groceries, Leroy says excitedly, 108
"Your mama here's been dying to go to Shiloh for thirty-five years.
It's about time we went, don't you think?"

"I'm not going to butt in on anybody's second honeymoon," 109
Mabel says.

"Who's going on a honeymoon, for Christ's sake?" Norma Jean 110
says loudly.

"I never raised no daughter of mine to talk that-a-way," Mabel 111
says.

"You ain't seen nothing yet," says Norma Jean. She starts putting 112
away boxes and cans, slamming cabinet doors.

"There's a log cabin at Shiloh," Mabel says. "It was there during 113
the battle. There's bullet holes in it."

"When are you going to *shut up* about Shiloh, Mama?" asks 114
Norma Jean.

"I always thought Shiloh was the prettiest place, so full of his- 115
tory," Mabel goes on. "I just hoped y'all could see it once before I
die, so you could tell me about it." Later, she whispers to Leroy,
"You do what I said. A little change is what she needs."

"Your name means 'the king,' " Norma Jean says to Leroy that 116
evening. He is trying to get her to go to Shiloh, and she is reading a
book about another century.

"Well, I reckon I ought to be right proud." 117

"I guess so." 118

"Am I still king around here?" 119

Norma Jean flexes her biceps and feels them for hardness. "I'm 120
not fooling around with anybody, if that's what you mean," she says.

"Would you tell me if you were?"   121

"I don't know."   122

"What does *your* name mean?"   123

"It was Marilyn Monroe's real name."   124

"No kidding!"   125

"Norma comes from the Normans. They were invaders," she   126
says. She closes her book and looks hard at Leroy. "I'll go to Shiloh
with you if you'll stop staring at me."

On Sunday, Norma Jean packs a picnic and they go to Shiloh.   127
To Leroy's relief, Mabel says she does not want to come with them.
Norma Jean drives, and Leroy, sitting beside her, feels like some
boring hitchhiker she has picked up. He tries some conversation, but
she answers him in monosyllables. At Shiloh, she drives aimlessly
through the park, past bluffs and trails and steep ravines. Shiloh is
an immense place, and Leroy cannot see it as a battleground. It is
not what he expected. He thought it would look like a golf course.
Monuments are everywhere, showing through the thick clusters of
trees. Norma Jean passes the log cabin Mabel mentioned. It is surrounded by tourists looking for bullet holes.

"That's not the kind of log house I've got in mind," says Leroy   128
apologetically.

"I know *that*."   129

"This is a pretty place. Your mama was right."   130

"It's O.K.," says Norma Jean. "Well, we've seen it. I hope she's   131
satisfied."

They burst out laughing together.   132

At the park museum, a movie on Shiloh is shown every half hour,   133
but they decide that they don't want to see it. They buy a souvenir
Confederate flag for Mabel, and then they find a picnic spot near the
cemetery. Norma Jean has brought a picnic cooler, with pimiento
sandwiches, soft drinks, and Yodels. Leroy eats a sandwich and then
smokes a joint, hiding it behind the picnic cooler. Norma Jean has
quit smoking altogether. She is picking cake crumbs from the cello-
phane wrapper, like a fussy bird.

Leroy says, "So the boys in gray ended up in Corinth. The Union   134
soldiers zapped 'em finally. April 7, 1862."

They both know that he doesn't know any history. He is just   135
talking about some of the historical plaques they have read. He feels
awkward, like a boy on a date with an older girl. They are still just
making conversation.

"Corinth is where Mama eloped to," says Norma Jean.   136

They sit in silence and stare at the cemetery for the Union dead   137
and, beyond, at a tall cluster of trees. Campers are parked nearby,

bumper to bumper, and small children in bright clothing are cavorting and squealing. Norma Jean wads up the cake wrapper and squeezes it tightly in her hand. Without looking at Leroy, she says, "I want to leave you."

Leroy takes a bottle of Coke out of the cooler and flips off the 138 cap. He holds the bottle poised near his mouth but cannot remember to take a drink. Finally he says, "No, you don't."

"Yes, I do." 139

"I won't let you." 140

"You can't stop me." 141

"Don't do me that way." 142

Leroy knows Norma Jean will have her own way. "Didn't I 143 promise to be home from now on?" he says.

"In some ways, a woman prefers a man who wanders," says 144 Norma Jean. "That sounds crazy, I know."

"You're not crazy." 145

Leroy remembers to drink from his Coke. Then he says, "Yes, 146 you *are* crazy. You and me could start all over again. Right back at the beginning."

"We *have* started all over again," says Norma Jean. "And this is 147 how it turned out."

"What did I do wrong?" 148

"Nothing." 149

"Is this one of those women's lib things?" Leroy asks. 150

"Don't be funny." 151

The cemetery, a green slope dotted with white markers, looks 152 like a subdivision site. Leroy is trying to comprehend that his marriage is breaking up, but for some reason he is wondering about white slabs in a graveyard.

"Everything was fine till Mama caught me smoking" says Norma 153 Jean, standing up. "That set something off."

"What are you talking about?" 154

"She won't leave me alone—*you* won't leave me alone." Norma 155 Jean seems to be crying, but she is looking away from him. "I feel eighteen again. I can't face that all over again." She starts walking away. "No, it *wasn't* fine. I don't know what I'm saying. Forget it."

Leroy takes a lungful of smoke and closes his eyes as Norma 156 Jean's words sink in. He tries to focus on the fact that thirty-five hundred soldiers died on the grounds around him. He can only think of that war as a board game with plastic soldiers. Leroy almost smiles, as he compares the Confederates' daring attack on the Union camps and Virgil Mathis's raid on the bowling alley. General Grant, drunk and furious, shoved the Southerners back to Corinth, where Mabel and Jet Beasley were married years later, when Mabel was still thin and good-looking. The next day, Mabel and Jet visited the battle-ground, and then Norma Jean was born, and then she married Leroy and they had a baby, which they lost, and now Leroy and Norma Jean are here at the same battleground. Leroy knows he is leaving out a lot. He is leaving out the insides of history. History was always just names and dates to him. It occurs to him that building a house out of logs is similarly empty—too simple. And the real inner work-ings of a marriage, like most of history, have escaped him. Now he sees that building a log house is the dumbest idea he could have had. It was clumsy of him to think Norma Jean would want a log house. It was a crazy idea. He'll have to think of something else, quickly. He will wad the blueprints into tight balls and fling them into the lake. Then he'll get moving again. He opens his eyes. Norma Jean has moved away and is walking through the cemetery, following a serpentine brick path.

Leroy gets up to follow his wife, but his good leg is asleep and his bad leg still hurts him. Norma Jean is far away, walking rapidly toward the bluff by the river, and he tries to hobble toward her. Some children run past him, screaming noisily. Norma Jean has reached the bluff, and she is looking out over the Tennessee River. Now she turns toward Leroy and waves her arms. Is she beckoning to him? She seems to be doing an exercise for her chest muscles. The sky is unusually pale—the color of the dust ruffle Mabel made for their bed.

157

RESPONDING TO READING

1. Could you argue that Shiloh, in addition to representing the historical past, also represents Leroy's and Norma Jean's past? What elements of their past figure heavily in the story? What kind of history do you think is most important in the story—for example, personal or family history, national history, regional history, or marital history? What relationships do you see among these different kinds of history?   **2.** Why do Leroy and Norma Jean go to Shiloh? Do you think the brief scene at the battlefield is important enough to justify the story's title? Explain your response.   **3.** Near the end of the story, when Leroy reviews his history with Norma Jean and the history of her parents' courtship, he "knows he is leaving out a lot. He is leaving out the insides of history," and he realizes for the first time that a log house like the one he has been planning to build is empty in the same way. According to this story, what constitutes "the insides of history"? On the basis of your reactions to the other selections you have read in this chapter, do you agree or disagree?

The Bitter Word

ANDREW SUKNASKI

Canadian poet Andrew Suknaski (1942–   ) writes sensitively of the natives of North America, the values of mythology, and our common links with the earth and each other. His poetry is published in three collections, *The Zen Pilgrimage* (1972), *The Ghosts Call You Poor* (1978), and *In the Name of Narid* (1980). In "The Bitter Word," Suknaski shows two views of the treatment of Native Americans.

from fort walsh
colonel irvine brings the bitter word
to sitting bull at wood mountain
makes clear the government welcomes the teton—
yet they must not expect provisions   5
or food from canada

sitting bull proudly replies:
when did i ever ask you for provisions?
before i beg
i will cut willows for my young men to use   10
while killing mice to survive

in the spring of 1881
sitting bull gathers his remaining 1200 sioux
and treks to fort qu'appelle to make
the final request for a reservation—   15
inspector sam steele tells them
the great white mother wishes them to return
to their own country
(a rather curious view of a people
whose meaning of country changes with   20
the migrations of tatanka[1])
steele politely refuses the request
and supplies enough provisions for the return
to wood mountain

---

[1]Buffalo Tatanka Iyotake is Sitting Bull's Indian name. After years of war with the United States cavalry, as his tribe resisted the white invasion of their homeland and destruction of its natural resources, Sitting Bull and his people retreated to Canada in October 1876, refusing to return to the U.S. and be confined to a reservation. Although he was able to hold out for almost five years, the shortage of food led his followers to return to the U.S. On July 19, 1881, Sitting Bull surrendered at Fort Buford, Montana. [Eds.]

death by summer is certain
while irvine makes sure   25
provisions and seed never arrive

seeing the migrating game
sitting bull knew the tatanka
would never return   30
though his people dreamed of white tatanka rising
from the subterranean meadows other fleds to
(hideous shrieks of red river carts grating in
their ears)

he must have sensed the hunger to follow   35
which was exactly what the authorities hoped for
on both sides of the border

RESPONDING TO READING

1. Who is the speaker? What is his perspective toward the events he describes? What is his attitude toward Colonel Irvine? Toward Sam Steele? Toward Sitting Bull? Toward "the authorities . . . / on both sides of the border" (lines 36–37)? How can you tell?   **2.** What effect do Suknaski's stylistic decisions—the absence of capital letters, the absence of end punctuation, the italicized lines, and the two parenthetical comments—have on your response to the poem?   **3.** How do you think Sitting Bull and the white men differ in terms of how they view the land, boundaries, and "country"? Whose view is closer to your own?

The Chicago **Defender**[1] *Sends a Man to Little Rock, Fall, 1957*[2]

GWENDOLYN BROOKS

Gwendolyn Brooks (1917–   ) grew up on Chicago's South Side, published poetry as a child, and was encouraged by Langston Hughes and James Weldon Johnson. Brooks earned a Guggenheim fellowship for her first book, *A Street in Bronzeville* (1945). In 1949, Brooks published *Annie Allen*, a narrative verse about the passage

[1]An African-American weekly newspaper. [Eds.]
[2]After African-American students, supported by a court order, attempted to integrate Little Rock, Arkansas's Central High School, race riots resulted. [Eds.]

of an African-American girl from childhood to maturity during World War II. The next year, Brooks became the first black woman to win the Pulitzer Prize and was named Poet Laureate of Illinois. In her early work, Brooks balanced traditional forms with African-American idiom. She turned to feminist and racial issues in *In the Mecca* (1968), *Riot* (1969), *Family Pictures* (1970), and *Aloneness* (1971). She also wrote a novella, *Maud Martha* (1953) and a collection of biographical essays, *Report from Part I* (1972). In the poem that follows the speaker reports on racial conflict in Little Rock, Arkansas.

FOR OPENERS

Recall an incident from the civil rights movement (the Montgomery bus boycott, the integration of Little Rock schools). How did each side in the conflict react and why? What were the motivations and fears of each side? What do you think was the relationship between these segments of society before the crisis? If possible, arrange to show your class the section about Little Rock from the 1980s PBS series *Eyes on the Prize* or read to them from the book written to accompany the series.

In Little Rock the people bear Babes,
and comb and part their hair
And watch the want ads, put repair
To roof and latch. While wheat toast burns
A woman waters multiferns.   5

Time upholds or overturns
The many, tight, and small concerns.

In Little Rock the people sing
Sunday hymns like anything,
Through Sunday pomp and polishing.   10

And after testament and tunes,
Some soften Sunday afternoons
With lemon tea and Lorna Doones.

I forecast
And I believe   15
Come Christmas Little Rock will cleave
To Christmas tree and trifle, weave,
From laugh and tinsel, texture fast.

In Little Rock is baseball; Barcarolle.[3]
That hotness in July . . . the uniformed figures raw and   20
     implacable
And not intellectual,
Batting the hotness or clawing the suffering dust.
The Open Air Concert, on the special twilight green . . .

ADDITIONAL QUESTIONS FOR RESPONDING TO READING

1. How does the reporter characterize the people of Little Rock?
2. What change occurs in the reporter? What happens to the "hate-I-had"?
3. What is the effect of the last line of the poem? What connection is Brooks making?

---

[3]Rhythmic rowing song of Venetian gondoliers. [Eds.]

When Beethoven is brutal or whispers to ladylike air.   25
Blanket-sitters are solemn, as Johann troubles to lean
To tell them what to mean . . .
There is love, too, in Little Rock. Soft women softly
Opening themselves in kindness,
Or, pitying one's blindness,   30
Awaiting one's pleasure
In Azure
Glory with anguished rose at the root . . .
To wash away old semidiscomfitures.
They reteach purple and unsullen blue.   35
The wispy soils go. And uncertain
Half-havings have they clarified to sures.

In Little Rock they know
Not answering the telephone is a way of rejecting life,
That it is our business to be bothered, is our business   40
To cherish bores or boredom, be polite
To lies and love and many-faceted fuzziness.

I scratch my head, massage the hate-I-had.
I blink across my prim and pencilled pad.
The saga I was sent for is not down.   45
Because there is a puzzle in this town.

The biggest News I do not dare
Telegraph to the Editor's chair:
"They are like people everywhere."
The angry Editor would reply   50
In hundred harryings of Why.

And true, they are hurling spittle, rock,
Garbage and fruit in Little Rock.
And I saw coiling storm a-writhe
On bright madonnas. And a scythe   55
Of men harassing brownish girls.
(The bows and barrettes in the curls
And braids declined away from joy.)

I saw a bleeding brownish boy . . .
The lariat lynch-wise I deplored.   60
The loveliest lynchee was our Lord.

TEACHING STRATEGY

Brooks says that "there is a puzzle in this town." Ask students to set up the puzzle by plotting the way Brooks's description develops in her poem. At what point is the puzzle introduced? When is the puzzle's answer revealed?

WRITING SUGGESTION

Write an essay in which you agree or disagree with the speaker's comment in line 49 that the people of Little Rock "are like people everywhere." Support your position with references to current events and to your own experiences.

**ANSWERS TO RESPONDING
TO READING**

1. It offers a personal perspective on the situation.
2. The reporter sees things that would be invisible or obvious to the town's residents because the events are so ordinary. The reporter's being African-American makes the experience even more frightening.
3. Finding that they are ordinary people makes their prejudice even harder to understand (and ironically implies that it may be widespread). The editor was probably looking for a scapegoat for the injustice, but the reporter has found only ordinary human beings.

RESPONDING TO READING

1. What does the poem offer to you as a student of history that a discussion in a history textbook would not?   **2.** The speaker in the poem is an outsider, a reporter sent to Little Rock to report on the city's racial strife. How might what the reporter sees there differ from what the town's residents see? Does knowing that the Chicago *Defender* is a black newspaper change your answer?   **3.** The speaker says of the citizens of Little Rock, " 'They are like people everywhere' " (line 48). Why does she say this? Why does she consider this fact "the biggest News" (line 46)? Why does she say she does not dare to tell her editor this news?

WRITING: A SENSE OF THE PAST

1. Many of the essays in this chapter commemorate "hard times": war, disease, racial discrimination, economic hardship. What basic characteristics do "hard times" scenarios share? What three or four "hard times" issues of the 1990s do you see as good candidates for historical study? Explain in an essay why these issues are worthy of such study.

2. For William Manchester, "the one great victor in modern war" is death (paragraph 2). Compare his attitude toward war with your own.

3. Bruce Catton sees the Civil War as a series of conflicts or struggles between opposing forces. Choose one contemporary issue, identify the forces that are opposed in it, and try to explain why these conflicts exist.

4. Which of the writers in this chapter do you see as most and least patriotic, and why? Begin by defining your own view of *patriotism.*

5. What lessons can be learned from history? Choose one of the essays in this chapter and discuss how its perspective on historical events might encourage changes in modern-day readers' habits, expectations, goals, and priorities.

6. History is usually written by representatives of a society's dominant culture. Recently, however, other voices, formerly excluded, have begun to be heard. Explain how a nontraditional historian—for example, Dillard, Walker, Franklin, or Terkel—approaches historical events. What changes can such a historian make to correct what he or she sees as past inaccuracies or misplaced emphases?

7. In "The Chicago *Defender* Sends a Man to Little Rock, Fall, 1957" Gwendolyn Brooks writes, "Time upholds or overturns / The many, tight, and small concerns" (lines 6–7). What do you suppose she is saying about history here? Do your own experiences support her view? Explain how in an essay.

8. Interview an acquaintance or family member about his or her memories (as observer or participant) of the Depression, World War II, or the civil rights movement. Then, write an essay in which you compare this person's memories with those of Harry Hartman ("Hard Times"), William Manchester, or Alice Walker. How can you account for the similarities and differences?

9.   The Vietnam War is now part of our country's history. If this war were fought today, do you think events of the past twenty years—for example, the rise of the women's movement or the elimination of the military draft—would change the nation's response to it? If so, how? Would such events change your own response? For example, would you support this war? Would you fight? Explain your decision.

10

Science and Medicine

CONFRONTING THE ISSUES

As many of the essays in this section imply, science not only helps us understand our world but also affects the way we see it. The ability of science and technology to alter our perception was illustrated in 1991 during the Persian Gulf War, when in just over one hundred hours coalition forces decisively defeated Iraq. Most students will be familiar with this event, but they may not be aware of the staggering number of casualties that the coalition inflicted upon Iraq. What is even more disturbing is how the nature of modern warfare war insulated both soldiers and the American public from the killing that was taking place. Weapons systems, troop movements, and even entire battles were controlled through satellite links from hermetically sealed underground command centers. Field commanders used computer projections to aim, fire, and check the effectiveness of their weapons. Generals at televised press conferences showed the progress of the battle with computer-generated graphics. Throughout the course of the war, the television-viewing public saw few of the bodies, the bombed-out cities, and the fleeing refugees that are commonly associated with war. The result was that the Persian Gulf War—so vast in scope and appalling in carnage—resembled a kind of postmodern video game.

After reviewing these details, ask students whether they think that current military technology makes war more or less likely. Are weapons systems that cannot miss and that can kill from many miles away perceived as so destructive that nations will cease waging war? Or does the vast power of a modern arsenal make war even more likely? Do high-tech weapons make it possible for a small, relatively weak nation to challenge—and possibly defeat—a superpower? Finally, ask what responsibility scientists and engineers have for the weapons they help develop. Do students think scientists and engineers should refuse to develop technology that they know will be used to kill human beings?

"The greatest of all the accomplishments of twentieth-century science," says Lewis Thomas in his essay "Debating the Unknowable," "has been the discovery of human ignorance." Although it is true that modern science has split the atom, all but eradicated many diseases, landed on the moon, and cracked the DNA code, it has also more clearly defined human limitation. In 1990, with much fanfare and after a considerable delay, NASA launched the Hubble telescope into earth orbit. Costing 1.5 billion dollars, Hubble was the most expensive scientific instrument ever made and was supposed to provide an unprecedented view of the universe. It could, one scientist said wistfully, gather more in one year than astronomers had gathered over the previous five hundred. Unfortunately, this optimism faded quickly when scientists discovered they were unable to get clear pictures from the telescope. After months of painstaking work, the engineers concluded that one of the mirrors on the telescope has been ground to the wrong specifications. In other words, human error had rendered the Hubble telescope almost useless, at least until a method could be devised to repair it. As the Hubble telescope illustrates, although many of us view the pursuit of science, especially medical research, with a reverence formerly reserved for religion, it is not infallible. In fact, like the rest of human endeavor, it is filled with ambiguity and uncertainty.

Since ancient times, when technological advances were often considered curiosities or diversions for the ruling class, science has gradually come to play an important part in all our lives. Along with this change in status has come the ethical question of just how far the scientist's responsibility for his or her research extends. For example, do the creators of the atomic bomb bear the responsibility for its 1945 use against Japan? Some would say no, but others, including some of those scientists who developed the bomb, would say yes. Still others, like Jonathan Schell in "The Fate of the Earth," for example, would argue that the real responsibility for ethical decisions about the use of nuclear weapons lies with the governments that set scientific policy.

The selections in this chapter all deal in one way or another with the seemingly contradictory roles of science in society. On the one hand, scientific and medical research offer the hope of a better future; on the other, they create moral and ethical problems that lead some to question whether the benefits are always worth the cost.

PREPARING TO READ AND WRITE

As you read and prepare to write about the selections in this chapter, consider the following questions:

- On what branch of science does the selection focus?

- Is the writer a scientist? A physician? An essayist? A reporter? How does your knowledge of the writer's background affect your response to the essay?

- Is the writer's emphasis on theory or practice?

- What preconceptions do you have about science? Does the selection reinforce or contradict your preconceptions?

- Is the writer's attitude toward science and technology positive or negative?

- What background in science does the writer assume readers have? In what way does your knowledge or lack of knowledge about the scientific issue under discussion affect your reading of the selection?

- Is the selection overly complex? Does it treat scientific concepts in general terms, or does it include technical language? Could the writer have made his or her point as effectively without using complicated scientific language?

- In what way does the writer explain scientific ideas to readers who may be unfamiliar with them?

- Is the writer optimistic or pessimistic about the future?

- Is the writer's purpose to provide basic scientific education? To make readers think about a provocative idea? To warn them?

The Eureka Phenomenon

ISAAC ASIMOV

In his characteristic witty and informative style, science writer Isaac Asimov (see also p. 113) tells a story from history that illustrates how a solution to a problem can occur when "you think you are not thinking."

FOR OPENERS

Asimov believes that thinking, like breathing, is a double phenomenon, both voluntary and involuntary. He cites the story of Archimedes and others who came to important insights by using their subconscious. Ask students if they see any connection between the process of scientific discovery and the process of writing.

ADDITIONAL QUESTIONS FOR RESPONDING TO READING

1. According to Asimov, how do most scientists feel about intuition? Why do they feel the way they do? Do you agree with them?
2. How do you get your best ideas? Have you ever arrived at a solution to a problem when you were not thinking of it? Explain.
3. Whom do you think Asimov is trying to persuade in this essay? The general public? The scientific community? Explain.

In the old days, when I was writing a great deal of fiction, there would come, once in a while, moments when I was stymied. Suddenly, I would find I had written myself into a hole and could see no way out. To take care of that, I developed a technique which invariably worked. 1

It was simply this—I went to the movies. Not just any movie. I had to pick a movie which was loaded with action but which made no demands on the intellect. As I watched, I did my best to avoid any conscious thinking concerning my problem, and when I came out of the movie I knew exactly what I would have to do to put the story back on the track. 2

It never failed. 3

In fact, when I was working on my doctoral dissertation, too many years ago, I suddenly came across a flaw in my logic that I had not noticed before and that knocked out everything I had done. In utter panic, I made my way to a Bob Hope movie—and came out with the necessary change in point of view. 4

It is my belief, you see, that thinking is a double phenomenon like breathing. 5

You can control breathing my deliberate voluntary action: you can breathe deeply and quickly, or you can hold your breath altogether, regardless of the body's needs at the time. This, however, doesn't work well for very long. Your chest muscles grow tired, your body clamors for more oxygen, or less, and you relax. The automatic involuntary control of breathing takes over, adjusts it to the body's needs and unless you have some respiratory disorder, you can forget about the whole thing. 6

Well, you can think by deliberate voluntary action, too, and I don't think it is much more efficient on the whole than voluntary breath control is. You can deliberately force your mind through channels of deductions and associations in search of a solution to some problem and before long you have dug mental furrows for yourself and find yourself circling round and round the same limited pathways. If those pathways yield no solution, no amount of further conscious thought will help. 7

On the other hand, if you let go, then the thinking process comes   8
under automatic involuntary control and is more apt to take new
pathways and make erratic associations you would not think of consciously. The solution will then come while you *think* you are *not*
thinking.

The trouble is, though, that conscious thought involves no mus-   9
cular action and so there is no sensation of physical weariness that
would force you to quit. What's more, the panic of necessity tends
to force you to go on uselessly, with each added bit of useless effort
adding to the panic in a vicious cycle.

It is my feeling that it helps to relax, deliberately, by subjecting   10
your mind to material complicated enough to occupy the voluntary
faculty of thought, but superficial enough to engage the deeper involuntary one. In my case, it is an action movie; in your case, it might
be something else.

I suspect it is the involuntary faculty of thought that gives rise to   11
what we call "a flash of intuition," something that I imagine must be
merely the result of unnoticed thinking.

Perhaps the most famous flash of intuition in the history of science   12
took place in the city of Syracuse in third-century B.C. Silicy. Bear
with me and I will tell you the story—

About 250 B.C., the city of Syracuse was experiencing a kind of   13
Golden Age. It was under the protection of the rising power of Rome,
but it retained a king of its own and considerable self-government; it
was prosperous; and it had a flourishing intellectual life.

The king was Hieron II, and he had commissioned a new golden   14
crown from a goldsmith, to whom he had given an ingot of gold as
raw material. Hieron, being a practical man, had carefully weighed
the ingot and then weighed the crown he received back. The two
weights were precisely equal. Good deal!

But then he sat and thought for a while. Suppose the goldsmith   15
had subtracted a little bit of the gold, not too much, and had substi-
tuted an equal weight of the considerably less valuable copper. The
resulting alloy would still have the appearance of pure gold, but the
goldsmith would be plus a quantity of gold over and above his fee.
He would be buying gold with copper, so to speak, and Hieron would
be neatly cheated.

Hieron didn't like the thought of being cheated any more than   16
you or I would, but he didn't know how to find out for sure if he
had been. He could scarcely punish the goldsmith on mere suspicion.
What to do?

Fortunately, Hieron had an advantage few rulers in the history   17
of the world could boast. He had a relative of considerable talent.

TEACHING STRATEGY

Discuss the relationship between reasoned
thought and the Eureka phenomenon. When
should a scientist or writer stop trying to rely on
reason and let the subconscious work for him
or her?

COLLABORATIVE ACTIVITIES

1. Divide the class into groups and have each group devise a science experiment that will illustrate the principle of buoyancy.
2. Reread Asimov's explanation and list the rhetorical and stylistic techniques he uses successfully to describe buoyancy.

The relative was named Archimedes and he probably had the greatest intellect the world was to see prior to the birth of Newton.

Archimedes was called in and was posed the problem. He had 18 to determine whether the crown Hieron showed him was pure gold, or was gold to which a small but significantly quantity of copper had been added.

If we were to reconstruct Archimedes' reasoning, it might go as 19 follows. Gold was the densest known substance (at that time). Its density in modern terms is 19.3 grams per cubic centimeter. This means that a given weight of gold takes up less volume than the same weight of anything else! In fact, a given weight of pure gold takes up less volume than the same weight of *any* kind of impure gold.

The density of copper is 8.92 grams per cubic centimeter, just 20 about half that of gold. If we consider 100 grams of pure gold, for instance, it is easy to calculate it to have a volume of 5.18 cubic centimeters. But suppose that 100 grams of what looked like pure gold was really only 90 grams of gold and 10 grams of copper. The 90 grams of gold would have a volume of 4.66 cubic centimeters, while the 10 grams of copper would have a volume of 1.12 cubic centimeters; for a total value of 5.78 cubic centimeters.

The difference between 5.18 cubic centimeters and 5.78 cubic cen- 21 timeters is quite a noticeable one, and would instantly tell if the crown were of pure gold, or if it contained 10 per cent copper (with the missing 10 per cent of gold tucked neatly in the goldsmith's strongbox).

All one had to do, then, was measure the volume of the crown 22 and compare it with the volume of the same weight of pure gold.

The mathematics of the time made it easy to measure the volume 23 of many simple shapes: a cube, a sphere, a cone, a cylinder, any flattened object of simple regular shape and known thickness, and so on.

We can imagine Archimedes saying, "All that is necessary, sire, 24 is to pound that crown flat, shape it into a square of uniform thickness, and then I can have the answer for you in a moment."

Whereupon Hieron must certainly have snatched the crown away 25 and said, "No such thing. I can do that much without you; I've studied the principles of mathematics, too. This crown is a highly satisfactory work of art and I won't have it damaged. Just calculate its volume without in any way altering it."

But Greek mathematics had no way of determining the volume 26 of anything with a shape as irregular as the crown, since integral calculus had not yet been invented (and wouldn't be for two thousand years, almost). Archimedes would have had to say, "There is no known way, sire, to carry through a non-destructive determination of volume."

"Then think of one," said Hieron testily.   27

And Archimedes must have set about thinking of one, and gotten   28 nowhere. Nobody knows how long he thought, or how hard, or what hypotheses he considered and discarded, or any of the details.

What we do now is that, worn out with thinking, Archimedes   29 decided to visit the public baths and relax. I think we are quite safe in saying that Archimedes had no intention of taking his problem to the baths with him. It would be ridiculous to imagine he would, for the public baths of a Greek metropolis weren't intended for that sort of thing.

The Greek baths were a place for relaxation. Half the social aris-   30 tocracy of the town would be there and there was a great deal more to do than wash. One steamed one's self, got a massage, exercised, and engaged in general socializing. We can be sure that Archimedes intended to forget the stupid crown for a while.

One can envisage him engaging in light talk, discussing the latest   31 news from Alexandria and Carthage, the latest scandals in town, the latest funny jokes at the expense of the country-squire Romans—and then he lowered himself into a nice hot bath which some bumbling attendant had filled too full.

The water in the bath slopped over as Archimedes got in. Did   32 Archimedes notice that at once, or did he sigh, sink back, and paddle his feet awhile before noting the water-slop? I guess the latter. But, whether soon or late, he noticed, and that one fact, added to all the chains of reasoning his brain had been working on during the period of relaxation when it was unhampered by the comparative stupidities (even in Archimedes) of voluntary thought, gave Archimedes his answer in one blinding flash of insight.

Jumping out of the bath, he proceeded to run home at top speed   33 through the streets of Syracuse. He did *not* bother to put on his clothes. The thought of Archimedes running naked through Syracuse has titillated dozens of generations of youngsters who have heard this story, but I must explain that the ancient Greeks were quite lighthearted in their attitude toward nudity. They thought no more of seeing a naked man on the streets of Syracuse, than we would on the Broadway stage.

And as he ran, Archimedes shouted over and over, "I've got it!   34 I've got it!" Of course, knowing no English, he was compelled to shout it in Greek, so it came out, *"Eureka! Eureka!"*

Archimedes' solution was so simple that anyone could under-   35 stand it—once Archimedes explained it.

If an object that is not affected by water in any way, is immersed 36
in water, it is bound to displace an amount of water equal to its own
volume, since two objects cannot occupy the same space at the same
time.

Suppose, then, you had a vessel large enough to hold the crown 37
and suppose it had a small overflow spout set into the middle of its
side. And suppose further that the vessel was filled with water exactly
to the spout, so that if the water level were raised a bit higher, however
slightly, some would overflow.

Next, suppose that you carefully lower the crown into the water. 38
The water level would rise by an amount equal to the volume of the
crown, and that volume of water would pour out the overflow and
be caught in a small vessel. Next, a lump of gold, known to be pure
and exactly equal in weight to the crown, is also immersed in the
water and again the level rises and the overflow is caught in a second
vessel.

If the crown were pure gold, the overflow would be exactly the 39
same in each case, and the volume of water caught in the two small
vessels would be equal. If, however, the crown were of alloy, it would
produce a larger overflow than the pure gold would and this would
be easily noticeable.

What's more, the crown would in no way be harmed, defaced, 40
or even as much as scratched. More important, Archimedes had discovered the "principle of buoyancy."

And was the crown pure gold? I've heard that it turned out to 41
be alloy and that the goldsmith was executed, but I wouldn't swear
to it.

How often does this "Eureka phenomenon" happen? How often 42
is there this flash of deep insight during a moment of relaxation, this
triumphant cry of "I've got it! I've got it!" which must surely be a
moment of the purest ecstasy this sorry world can afford?

I wish there were some way we could tell. I suspect that in the 43
history of science it happens *often*; I suspect that very few significant
discoveries are made by the pure technique of voluntary thought; I
suspect that voluntary thought may possibly prepare the ground (if
even that), but that the final touch, the real inspiration, comes when
thinking is under involuntary control.

But the world is in a conspiracy to hide the fact. Scientists are 44
wedded to reason, to the meticulous working out of consequences
from assumptions to the careful organization of experiments designed
to check those consequences. If a certain line of experiments ends
nowhere, it is omitted from the final report. If an inspired guess turns
out to be correct, it is *not* reported as an inspired guess. Instead, a

solid line of voluntary thought is invented after the fact to lead up to the thought, and that is what is inserted in the final report.

The result is that anyone reading scientific papers would swear 45 that *nothing* took place but voluntary thought maintaining a steady clumping stride from origin to destination, and that just can't be true.

It's such a shame. Not only does it deprive science of much of 46 its glamor (how much of the dramatic story in Watson's *Double Helix*[1] do you suppose got into the final reports announcing the great discovery of the structure of DNA?[2]), but it hands over the important process of "insight," "inspiration," "revelation" to the mystic.

The scientist actually becomes ashamed of having what we might 47 call a revelation, as though to have one is to betray reason—when actually what we call revelation in a man who has devoted his life to reasoned thought, is after all merely reasoned thought that is not under voluntary control.

Only once in a while in modern times do we ever get a glimpse 48 into the workings of involuntary reasoning, and when we do, it is always fascinating. Consider, for instance, the case of Friedrich August Kekule von Stradonitz.

In Kekule's time, a century and a quarter ago, a subject of great 49 interest to chemists was the structure of organic molecules (those associated with living tissue). Inorganic molecules were generally simple in the sense that they were made up of few atoms. Water molecules, for instance, are made up of two atoms of hydrogen and one of oxygen (H_2O). Molecules of ordinary salt are made up of one atom of sodium and one of chlorine ($NaCl$), and so on.

Organic molecules, on the other hand, often contained a large 50 number of atoms. Ethyl alcohol molecules have two carbon atoms, six hydrogen atoms, and an oxygen atom (C_2H_6O); the molecule of ordinary cane sugar is $C_{12}H_{22}O_{11}$, and other molecules are even more complex.

Then, too, it is sufficient, in the case of inorganic molecules gen- 51 erally, merely to know the kinds and numbers of atoms in the molecule; in organic molecules, more is necessary. Thus, dimethyl ether has the formula C_2H_6O, just as ethyl alcohol does, and yet the two are quite different in properties. Apparently, the atoms are arranged differently within the molecules—but how to determine the arrangements?

---

[1]Francis Crick and James Watson discovered the structure of DNA in 1953 and won the Nobel Prize in Medicine and Physiology in 1962. Watson told the story of his collaboration with Crick in the best-selling *The Double Helix* (1968). [Eds.]

[2]I'll tell you, in case you're curious. None!

In 1852, an English chemist, Edward Frankland, had noticed that 52
the atoms of a particular element tended to combine with a fixed
number of other atoms. This combining number was called "valence."
Kekule in 1858 reduced this notion to a system. The carbon atom, he
decided (on the basis of plenty of chemical evidence) had a valence
of four; the hydrogen atom, a valence of one; and the oxygen atom,
a valence of two (and so on).

Why not represent the atoms as their symbols plus a number of 53
attached dashes, that number being equal to the valence. Such atoms
could then be put together as though they were so many Tinker Toy
units and "structural formulas" could be built up.

It was possible to reason out that the structural formula of ethyl 54
alcohol was

$$
\begin{array}{ccc}
H & H & \\
| & | & \\
H-C-C-O-H, \\
| & | & \\
H & H & \\
\end{array}
$$

while that of dimethyl ether was

$$
\begin{array}{ccc}
H & & H \\
| & & | \\
H-C-O-C-H. \\
| & & | \\
H & & H \\
\end{array}
$$

In each case, there were two carbon atoms, each with four dashes 55
attached; six hydrogen atoms, each with one dash attached; and an
oxygen atom with two dashes attached. The molecules were built up
of the same components, but in different arrangements.

Kekule's theory worked beautifully. It has been immensely deep- 56
ened and elaborated since his day, but you can still find structures
very much like Kekule's Tinker Toy formulas in any modern chemical
textbook. They represent oversimplifications of the true situation, but
they remain extremely useful in practice even so.

The Kekule structures were applied to many organic molecules 57
in the years after 1858 and the similarities and contrasts in the structures neatly matched similarities and contrasts in properties. The key
to the rationalization of organic chemistry had, it seemed, been found.

Yet there was one disturbing fact. The well-known chemical ben- 58
zene wouldn't fit. It was known to have a molecule made up of equal
numbers of carbon and hydrogen atoms. Its molecular weight was
known to be 78 and a single carbon-hydrogen combination had a

weight of 13. Therefore, the benzene molecule had to contain six carbon-hydrogen combinations and its formula had to be C_6H_6.

But that meant trouble. By the Kekule formulas, the hydrocarbons 59 (molecules made up of carbon and hydrogen atoms only) could easily be envisioned as chains of carbon atoms with hydrogen atoms attached. If all the valences of the carbon atoms were filled with hydrogen atoms, as in "hexane," whose molecule looks like this—

$$
\begin{array}{ccccccc}
\text{H} & \text{H} & \text{H} & \text{H} & \text{H} & \text{H} \\
| & | & | & | & | & | \\
\text{H}\!-\!\text{C}\!-\!\text{C}\!-\!\text{C}\!-\!\text{C}\!-\!\text{C}\!-\!\text{C}\!-\!\text{H} \\
| & | & | & | & | & | \\
\text{H} & \text{H} & \text{H} & \text{H} & \text{H} & \text{H}
\end{array}
$$

the compound is said to be saturated. Such saturated hydrocarbons were found to have very little tendency to react with other substances.

If some of the valences were not filled, unused bonds were added 60 to those connecting the carbon atoms. Double bonds were formed as in "hexene"—

$$
\begin{array}{ccccccc}
\text{H} & \text{H} & \text{H} & \text{H} & \text{H} & \text{H} \\
| & | & | & | & | & | \\
\text{H}\!-\!\text{C}\!-\!\text{C}\!-\!\text{C}\!=\!\text{C}\!-\!\text{C}\!-\!\text{C}\!-\!\text{H} \\
| & | & & & | & | \\
\text{H} & \text{H} & & & \text{H} & \text{H}
\end{array}
$$

Hexene is unsaturated, for that double bond has a tendency to open up and add other atoms. Hexene is chemically active.

When six carbons are present in a molecule, it takes fourteen 61 hydrogen atoms to occupy all the valence bonds and make it inert— as in hexane. In hexene, on the other hand, there are only twelve hydrogens. If there were still fewer hydrogen atoms, there would be more than one double bond; there might even be triple bonds, and the compound would be still more active than hexene.

Yet benzene, which is C_6H_6 and has eight fewer hydrogen atoms 62 than hexane, is *less* active than hexene, which has only two fewer hydrogen atoms than hexane. In fact, benzene is even less active than hexane itself. The six hydrogen atoms in the benzene molecule seem to satisfy the six carbon atoms to a greater extent than do the fourteen hydrogen atoms in hexane.

For heaven's sake, why? 63

This might seem unimportant. The Kekule formulas were so beau- 64 tifully suitable in the case of so many compounds that one might simply dismiss benzene as an exception to the general rule.

Science, however, is not English grammar. You can't just cate- 65
gorize something as an exception. If the exception doesn't fit into the
general system, then the general system must be wrong.

Or, take the more positive approach. An exception can often be 66
made to fit into a general system, provided the general system is
broadened. Such broadening generally represents a great advance
and for this reason, exceptions ought to be paid great attention.

For some seven years, Kekule faced the problem of benzene and 67
tried to puzzle out how a chain of six carbon atoms could be completely satisfied with as few as six hydrogen atoms in benzene and
yet be left unsatisfied with twelve hydrogen atoms in hexene.

Nothing came to him! 68

And then one day in 1865 (he tells the story himself) he was in 69
Ghent, Belgium, and in order to get to some destination, he boarded
a public bus. He was tired and, undoubtedly, the droning beat of the
horses' hooves on the cobblestones, lulled him. He fell into a comatose
half-sleep.

In that sleep, he seemed to see a vision of atoms attaching them- 70
selves to each other in chains that moved about. (Why not? It was
the sort of thing that constantly occupied his waking thoughts.) But
then one chain twisted in such a way that head and tail joined, forming
a ring—and Kekule woke with a start.

To himself, he must surely have shouted "Eureka," for indeed 71
he had it. The six carbon atoms of benzene formed a ring and not a
chain, so that the structural formula looked like this:

$$
\begin{array}{c}
H \\
| \\
C \\
\end{array}
$$

To be sure, there were still three double bonds, so you might 72
think the molecule had to be very active—but now there was a difference. Atoms in a ring might be expected to have different properties
from those in a chain and double bonds in one case might not have
the properties of those in the other. At least, chemists could work on
that assumption and see if it involved them in contradictions.

It didn't. The assumption worked excellently well. It turned out 73
that organic molecules could be divided into two groups: aromatic
and aliphatic. The former had the benzene ring (or certain other similar rings) as part of the structure and the latter did not. Allowing for
different properties within each group, the Kekule structures worked
very well.

For nearly seventy years, Kekule's vision held good in the hard 74
field of actual chemical techniques, guiding the chemist through the
jungle of reactions that led to the synthesis of more and more molecules. Then, in 1932, Linus Pauling applied quantum mechanics to
chemical structure with sufficient subtlety to explain just why the
benzene ring was so special and what had proven correct in practice
proved correct in theory as well.

Other cases? Certainly. 75

In 1764, the Scottish engineer James Watt was working as an 76
instrument maker for the University of Glasgow. The university gave
him a model of a Newcomen steam engine, which didn't work well,
and asked him to fix it. Watt fixed it without trouble, but even when
it worked perfectly, it didn't work well. It was far too inefficient and
consumed incredible quantities of fuel. Was there a way to improve
that?

Thought didn't help; but a peaceful, relaxed walk on a Sunday 77
afternoon did. Watt returned with the key notion in mind of using
two separate chambers, one for steam only and one for cold water
only, so that the same chamber did not have to be constantly cooled
and reheated to the infinite waste of fuel.

The Irish mathematician William Rowan Hamilton worked up a 78
theory of "quaternions" in 1843 but couldn't complete that theory until
he grasped the fact that there were conditions under which $p \times q$
was *not* equal to $q \times p$. The necessary thought came to him in a flash
one time when he was walking to town with his wife.

The German physiologist Otto Loewi was working on the mech- 79
anism of nerve action, in particular, on the chemicals produced by
nerve endings. He awoke at 3 A.M. one night in 1921 with a perfectly
clear notion of the type of experiment he would have to run to settle
a key point that was puzzling him. He wrote it down and went back
to sleep. When he woke in the morning; he found he couldn't
remember what his inspiration had been. He remembered he had
written it down, but he couldn't read his writing.

The next night, he woke again at 3 A.M. with the clear thought 80
once more in mind. This time, he didn't fool around. He got up,
dressed himself went straight to the laboratory and began work. By

WRITING SUGGESTIONS

1. Who do you think are more creative, artists or scientists? Why? What qualities or ways of thinking make a person creative?
2. Write an essay in which you discuss a time when you relied on intuition to solve a problem. If you can, differentiate intuition from the Eureka phenomenon.

5 A.M. he had proved his point and the consequences of his findings became important enough in later years so that in 1936 he received a share in the Nobel prize in medicine and physiology.

How very often this sort of thing must happen, and what a shame that scientists are so devoted to their belief in conscious thought that they so consistently obscure the actual methods by which they obtain their results. 81

RESPONDING TO READING

1. What does Asimov think is the most valuable contribution of science to society? Do you agree with him? **2.** Have you ever experienced the Eureka phenomenon? In what way was it like or unlike the phenomenon Asimov describes? **3.** What is the stereotype of science as Asimov describes it? Why do you suppose so many scientists promote this stereotype?

Nasty Little Facts

STEPHEN JAY GOULD

The following essay is a reprint of a column by Stephen Jay Gould (see also p. 407) that originally appeared in *Natural History* (1985). Here, this natural science writer shows that small facts can change what may seem to be unassailable scientific theories, and he reminds us that "science, like all of life, is filled with rich and complex ambiguity."

As a devotee of Grade B detective films, from Charlie Chan (in all his incarnations) to the *Thin Man*, I have, perforce, spent an undue amount of time passively engaged in conversations about fingerprints. Since these discussions are interminable, one might suspect that they have also been eternal in the annals of criminology. 1

In fact, Scotland Yard officially introduced fingerprints as a tool for identifying criminals in 1901 (replacing the older Bertillon system, based on complex series of body measurements and the accompanying assumption, not always vindicated, that no two people will be alike in so many ways). The chief architect and promoter of the new system was Francis Galton,[1] England's most eccentric scientific genius. 2

---

[1]English scientist (1822–1911) who made significant contributions to psychology and was the founder of biostatics, which uses statistical techniques to study large populations. [Eds.]

In his autobiography, Galton tells a story of Herbert Spencer's[2] visit to his fingerprint lab. Galton took Spencer's prints and "spoke of the failure to discover the origin of these patterns, and how the fingers of unborn children had been dissected to ascertain their earliest stages." Spencer, quick to offer certain opinions about almost anything, told Galton that he had been working the wrong way round.

> Spencer remarked . . . that I ought to consider the purpose the ridges had to fulfil, and to work backwards. Here, he said, it was obvious that the delicate mouths of the sudorific glands required the protection given to them by the ridges on either side of them, and therefrom he elaborated a consistent and ingenious hypothesis at great length. I replied that his arguments were beautiful and deserved to be true, but it happened that the mouths of the ducts did not run in the valleys between the crests, but along the crests of the ridges themselves.

Galton then ends his anecdote by giving the original source for one of the top ten among scientific quotes. Spencer, dining with T. H. Huxley[3] one night at the Athenaeum, stated that he had once written a tragedy. Huxley replied that he knew all about it. Spencer rebutted Huxley, arguing that he had never mentioned it to anyone. But Huxley insisted that he knew anyway and identified Spencer's debacle—"a beautiful theory, killed by a nasty, ugly little fact."

Some theories may be subject to such instant, brutal, and unambiguous rejection. I stated last month, for example, that no left-coiling periwinkle had ever been found among millions of snails examined. If I happen to find one during my walk on Nopsca Beach tomorrow morning, a century of well-nurtured negative evidence will collapse in an instant.

This Huxleyan vision of clean refutation buttresses one of our worst stereotypes about science. We tend to view science as a truth-seeking machine, driven by two forces that winnow error: the new discovery and the crucial experiment—prime generators of those nasty, ugly little facts. Science does, of course, seek truth; it even succeeds reasonably often, so far as we can tell. But science, like all of life, is filled with rich and complex ambiguity. The path to truth is rarely straight, marked by a gate of entry that sorts applicants by such relatively simple criteria as age and height. (When I was a kid, you could get into Yankee Stadium for half price if your head didn't reach a line prominently drawn on the entrance gate about four and

ADDITIONAL QUESTIONS FOR RESPONDING TO READING

1. The problem of the trigonians ultimately became more than a question of natural history. Summarize the political positions that the trigonians represented.
2. Identify a contemporary controversy that you believe has symbolic value similar to that of the trigonians.
3. What is the author saying about "nasty little facts"? What is their importance? Do you believe they have the power to destroy theories or not?

---

[2]English sociologist and philosopher (1820–1903) who was an early advocate of Darwin's theory of evolution and advocated the superiority of science over religion. He has been criticized for tending to look only for support for his own theories, ignoring evidence that contradicted them.
[3]English biologist (1825–95) whose ideas about philosophy and religion and advocacy of Darwinism led him to embrace agnosticism. [Eds.]

a half feet above the ground. You could scrunch down, but they checked. One nasty, ugly day, I started to pay full price, and that was that.)

Little facts rarely undo big theories all by themselves—the myth 7 of David and Goliath notwithstanding. They can refute little, highly specific theories, like my conjecture about lefty periwinkles, but they rarely slay grand and comprehensive views of nature. No single, pristine fact taught us that the earth revolves around the sun or that evolution produced the similarities among organisms. Overarching theories are much bigger than single facts, just as the army of Grenada really didn't have much chance against the combined forces of the United States (though you'd think from the consequent appeals to patriotism that some gigantic and improbable victory had been won).

Instead, little facts are assimilated into large theories. They may 8 reside there uncomfortably, bothering the honorable proponents. Large numbers of little facts may eventually combine with other social and intellectual forces to topple a grand theory. The history of ideas is a play of complex human passions interacting with an external reality only slightly less intricate. We debase the richness of both nature and our own minds if we view the great pageant of our intellectual history as a compendium of new information leading from primal superstition to final exactitude. We know that the sun is hub to our little corner of the universe, and that ties of genealogy connect all living things on our planet, because these theories assemble and explain so much otherwise disparate and unrelated information—not because Galileo trained his telescope on the moons of Jupiter or because Darwin took a ride on a Galápagos tortoise.

This essay tells the story of a pristine, unexpected little fact that 9 should have mattered, but didn't particularly. It was widely reported, discussed, and personally studied by the greatest naturalists of Europe, and then assimilated into each of several contradictory systems. Fifty years later, in 1865, a second discovery resolved the paradox generated by the first fact—and should have won, by Huxley's principle, a big and important victory for Darwin and evolution. It was welcomed, to be sure, but largely ignored. One foot soldier could not decide a battle waged on so many fronts.

Trigonia is a distinctive clam, thick shelled and triangular in shape. 10 It flourished with dinosaurs during the Mesozoic era and then became extinct in the same debacle that wiped out the ruling reptiles—one of the five greatest mass dyings in our geologic record. No trigonian had ever been found in the overlying Cenozoic strata—the entire age of mammals (about sixty million years, as we now know). *Trigonia* had therefore become a valued "guide fossil"; when you found one,

TEACHING STRATEGY

Before the class reads the essay, summarize for them the arguments of creationists and evolutionists about the importance of the trigonians. Ask students to write a paragraph supporting one view or the other. Then tell the class about the discovery of *Trigonia* in Tertiary strata. Ask the class to reevaluate their paragraphs in light of this new information.

you knew you had rocks of the earth's middle age. Everyone (who was anybody) understood this.

Then, the nasty, ugly little—and quite undeniable—fact. In 1802, 11 P. Péron, a French naturalist, found the shell of a living trigonian washed up on the beaches of southern Australia. Twenty-five years later, and following several failures, J. Quoy and J. Gaimard, naturalists aboard the *Astrolabe*, finally found a live trigonian. They had dredged for several days with definite purpose, but without success. Becalmed one night in Bass Strait and with little else to do, they tried again and brought up their single prize, a molluscan life soon snuffed and preserved in the (perhaps welcome) medium of the collector's trade—a bottle of alcohol. Quoy and Gaimard treasured their booty and wrote later:

> We were so anxious to bring back this shell with its animal that when we were, for three days, stranded on the reefs of Tonga-Tabu, it was the only object that we took from our collection. Doesn't this recall the ardent shell collector who, during seven years' war, carried constantly in his pocket an extraordinary *Phasianella*, which he had bought for twenty-five louis?

A simple story. A fact and a puzzle. *Trigonia* had not disappeared 12 in the great Cretaceous debacle, for it was hanging tough in Australia. But no fossil trigonians had been found in all the strata in between— throughout the long and well-recorded history of the age of mammals (now called the Cenozoic era). Where were they? Had they ever existed? Could such a distinctive animal die and be reborn (or re-created) later? The "Cenozoic gap" became as puzzling and portentous as the one later associated with Mr. Nixon and Ms. Woods.[4]

Trigonia occupies a specially interesting place in the history of 13 biology because its unexpected fact and consequent puzzle arose and prevailed at such an important time—at the dawn and through the greatest conceptual transition ever experienced by the profession: from creationist to evolutionary views of life. It also (or rather therefore) attracted the attention and commentary of most leaders in nineteenth-century natural history. J. B. Lamarck, most famous of pre-Darwinian evolutionists, formally described the first living trigonian. Darwin himself thought and commented about *Trigonia* for thirty years. Louis Agassiz, most able and cogent of Darwin's opponents,

---

[4]The reference is to the Watergate affair, characterized by some as the worst political scandal in United States history. After President Richard Nixon was directed to turn over taped White House conversations, investigators discovered an 18-minute gap in one tape. Nixon's secretary, Rosemary Woods, who had transcribed the tapes, was unable to explain the gap. Later many historians concluded the tape had been deliberately erased to eliminate incriminating statements. [Eds.]

COLLABORATIVE ACTIVITY

Divide the class into groups and ask them if they think people cling to theories for emotional reasons long after they have been disproved. Ask each group to list several examples. Then discuss why "nasty little facts" rarely overthrow big theories.

wrote the major technical monograph of his generation on the genus *Trigonia*.

The lesson of the living *Trigonia* can be distilled in a sentence: 14 Everyone made the best of it, incorporating favorable aspects of this new fact into his system and either ignoring or explaining away the difficulties. *Trigonia* became an illustration for everyone, not a crucial test of rival theories. Evolutionists celebrated the differences in form and distribution between ancient and modern trigonians—and ignored the Cenozoic gap. Creationists highlighted the gap and made light of the differences.

Today, we remember Lamarck best as the author of a rejected 15 evolutionary theory based on the inheritance of acquired characters (quite an unfair designation since so-called Lamarckian inheritance represents a minor part of Lamarck's own system—this, however, is another story, for another time). But his day-to-day work in post-revolutionary France involved the description of living and fossil invertebrates in his role as curator at the *Muséum d'Histoire Naturelle* in Paris. He therefore received Péron's precious shell for formal description, and he named it *Trigonia margaritacea* in 1804 (*margarita* is a Latin pearl, and the interior of a trigonian shell shines with a beautiful pearly luster). But since 1804 lay squarely between Lamarck's initial (1802) and definitive (1809) statement of his evolutionary theory, he also used his short paper on *Trigonia* to sharpen and defend his developing transmutationist views.[5]

Most fossil trigonians are ornamented with concentric ridges at 16 their anterior ends (enclosing the mouth and digestive apparatus) and radial ribs on the rear flank. A single strong rib usually separates these two areas. But all modern trigonians cover their shells entirely with radial ribs (although the embryonic shell still bears traces of the ancestral concentrics). Lamarck seized upon these differences to claim that changing environments had pressed their influence upon the shell. The shell had then altered in response and the animal within passed the favorable change to future generations by "Lamarckian" inheritance.

> They have undergone changes under the influence of circumstances that act upon them and that have themselves changed; so that fossil remains . . . of the greatest antiquity may display several differences from animals of the same type living now but nevertheless derived from them.

---

[5]Lamarck believed that animal species always developed from single to complex forms. To him *transmutation*, the changing of one thing into another, was the basic mechanism of evolution. [Eds.]

(But Lamarck had only demonstrated that the fossils looked different from the moderns. Any theory could account for this basic datum in the absence of further information—evolution by use and disuse, by natural selection, or even re-creation by God for that matter.)

Lamarck then proceeded to extract more from modern trigonians 17 to buttress other pet themes. He was, for example, a partisan at the wrong end of a great debate resolved a decade later to his disadvantage by Cuvier—does extinction occur in nature? Human rapacity, Lamarck believed, might exterminate some conspicuous beasts, but the ways of nature do not include termination without descent (Lamarck, as a transmutationist, obviously accepted the pseudoextinction that occurs when one form evolves into another). Lamarck gave the old arguments against extinction a novel twist by embedding his justification within his newfangled evolutionary views. How can extinction occur if all organisms respond creatively to changing environments and pass their favorable responses to future generations in the form of altered inheritance?

Yet Lamarck's conviction was sorely challenged by burgeoning 18 data in his own field of marine invertebrate paleontology. So many kinds of fossils are confined to rocks of early periods. Where are their descendants today? Lamarck offered the only plausible argument in a world with few remaining terrae incognitae—they live still in the unexplored depths of the sea. Since Lamarck reveals his own discomfort with such an ad hoc solution in the form of a defense too often and too zealously repeated—recall Shakespeare's "the lady doth protest too much, methinks"—we may take as genuine his delight in *Trigonia* as a real case for a generalization devoutly to be wished: "Small species, especially those that dwell in the depths of the sea, have the means to escape man; truly among these we do not find any that are really extinct." Lamarck then ends his paper by predicting that a large suite of creatures apparently extinct will soon be found at oceanic depths. We are still waiting.

Since Lamarck's argument centers upon an explanation for why 19 creatures still living yield no evidence of their continued vitality, we should not be surprised that the Cenozoic gap inspired no commentary at all. We must assume that trigonians spent the entire Cenozoic safe in the bosom of Neptune, full fathom five hundred or more, and unrecorded in a fossil archive of shallow-water sediments.

Charles Darwin, leading evolutionist of the next generation, 20 selected yet another aspect of living trigonians—their geographic distribution—to bolster a different theme dear to his view of life. Darwin's creationist opponents, as we shall see, rendered the history of life as a series of static faunas and floras separated by episodes of sudden extirpation and renewal. To confute this catastrophist credo, and to advance his own distinctive and uncompromisingly gradualist view of nature, Darwin argued that the extinction of a group should be as smooth and extended as its origin. A group should peter out, dwindle slowly, decrease steadily in numbers and geographic range—not die in full vigor during an environmental crisis. What better evidence than a family once spread throughout the world in stunning diversity but now confined to one small region and one single species. In his private essay of 1844, precursor to the *Origin of Species* (1859), Darwin wrote: "We have reason to believe that . . . the numbers of the species decrease till finally the group becomes extinct—the *Trigonia* was extinct much sooner in Europe, but now lives in the seas of Australia."

(We now regard this claim for extinction of large groups as gradual 21 dwindling in the face of competition from more successful forms—the central theme of chapter 10 in the *Origin of Species*—as among the least successful of Darwin's major arguments. Darwin may have feared that mass extinction supported the creationist view of debacle followed by divine reconstitution. But mass extinction may also clear the way for subsequent, vigorous periods of *evolution*. Again, as so often, Darwin's commitment to gradualism restricted his options for legitimate evolutionary hypotheses.)

Darwin followed Lamarck in dismissing the Cenozoic gap as an 22 artifact of our imperfect fossil record (I can, indeed, imagine no other option for an evolutionist committed to genealogical connection). But Darwin was explicit where Lamarck had been silent. Darwin also tried to accentuate the positive by arguing that the rarity of such long gaps strongly implied their artificial status. He wrote in the *Origin of Species:*

> A group does not reappear after it has once disappeared; or its existence, as long as it lasts, is continuous. I am aware that there are some apparent exceptions to this rule, but the exceptions are surprisingly few, so few that . . . the rule strictly accords with my theory.

Creationists, meanwhile, looked at *Trigonia* from the other side. 23 They treasured the Cenozoic gap and found nearly everything else puzzling. The major creationist thinkers tended to agree that life's history had been episodic—a series of stages separated by sudden, worldwide paroxysms that removed the old and set a stage for the new. But they divided into two camps on the issue of progress. Did each new episode improve upon the last; was God, in other words, learning by doing? Or had life maintained a fairly consistent complexity throughout its episodic history? Progressionists and nonprogressionists found different messages in *Trigonia*.

James Parkinson, England's leading progressionist (though he 24 switched allegiances later on), chose *Trigonia* as a premier example in his *Organic Remains of a Former World* (1811). He read the Cenozoic gap literally, extracting from it the congenial message that life's history features a series of creations not connected by ties of genealogy and physical continuity.

But *Trigonia* also presented a special problem for Parkinson. He 25 argued that each successive episode of creation had been marked "with increasing excellence in its objects," thus matching in all ways but one the Mosaic progression from chaos to Adam as described in Genesis. "So close indeed is this agreement, that the Mosaic account is thereby confirmed in every respect except as to the age of the world" (a problem then resolved by an allegorical interpretation of God's six creative "days"). Now a *Trigonia*, as some folks say about roses, is a *Trigonia* (subtleties evident to the professional eye aside). Why should a modern shell with radial ribs alone be better than a fossil representative with radials and concentrics? Why are the modern versions superior, as Parkinson's theory of progressive creation required? Parkinson was evidently troubled. In the summary statement to his three-volume work, he devoted more space to *Trigonia* than to any other genus. He clutched at the one available straw, but clearly without conviction. At least the modern trigonians are different. "*Raffiniert ist der Herrgott*" (Subtle is the Lord), as Einstein said later. We don't know why, but different must be better:

> This shell, although really of this genus, is of a different species from any shell, which has been found in a fossil state. So that none of the species of shells of this genus, which are known in a fossil state, have, in fact, been found in any stratum above the hard chalk [the Cretaceous, or last period of dinosaurs], or in our present seas.

Louis Agassiz, most able of all creationists, followed Parkinson's 26 personal route in reverse. He began as an advocate of progress in each successive creation and ended by defending the earliest of God's creatures as fully up to snuff (largely because he despised Darwinism with such passion and felt that any admission of progress would bolster the evolutionary cause). For him, therefore, the apparent lack of improvement in modern trigonians posed no problem, while the Cenozoic gap brought nothing but pleasure and confirmation. In the major pre-Darwinian work on these clams, his *Mémoire sur les trigonies* (1840), Agassiz argued explicitly that a Cenozoic gap, if conclusively affirmed, would effectively disprove evolution (quite a cogent claim, by the way):

> The absence of *Trigonia* in Tertiary [Cenozoic] strata is a very important fact for discussions of the origin and relationships of species of different epochs; for if it could one day be shown that *Trigonia* never existed throughout the entire duration of Tertiary time, it would no longer be possible to maintain the principle that species of a genus living in successive geological epochs are derived from each other.

But Agassiz well understood the discomforting uncertainty of 27 negative evidence. Find one nasty, ugly little Cenozoic trigonian tomorrow, and the entire argument collapses. So Agassiz decided to cover his rear and disclaim: No Cenozoic trigonian is dandy; but future discovery of a Cenozoic trigonian would prove nothing. God may, after all, ordain temporal continuity among a group of related, created forms.

Although his passage is an exercise in special pleading, it also 28 contains one of the most succinct and eloquent defenses ever written for the Platonic version of creationism.

> Although I now invoke this fact [the Cenozoic gap] to support my conviction that the different species of a genus are not variants of a single type . . . the discovery of a Tertiary trigonian would still not demonstrate, to my eyes, that the relationship among species of a genus is one of direct descent and successive transformation of original types. . . . I certainly do not deny that natural relationships exist among different species of a genus; on the contrary, I am convinced that species are related to each other by bonds of a higher nature than those of simple direct procreation, bonds that may be compared to the order of a system of ideas whose elements, developed at different times, form in their union an organic whole—although the elements of each time period also appear, within their limits, to be finished products.

In summary, as Darwin's revolution dawned in 1859, the sup- 29 posedly pure and simple little fact of modern trigonians stood neither as arbiter nor slayer of theories but as touted support for all major conflicting and contradictory views of life—for evolution by Lamarckian and Darwinian agencies, and for creationism in both progressionist and directionless versions. How can something so important be so undecisive? Unless Huxley's heroic vision of raw empiricism triumphant rarely describes the history of ideas or even the progress of science. Percepts do not create and drive concepts; but concepts are not intractable and immune to perceptual nudges either. Thought and observation form a wonderfully complex web of interpenetration and mutual influence—and the interaction often seems to get us somewhere useful.

The *Trigonia* story has a natural ending that should be conven- 30 tional and happy, but isn't quite. The resolution is not hard to guess, since Darwin's vision has prevailed. The elusive Cenozoic trigonian was found in Australian rocks—at just the right time, in 1865, when nascent evolutionism needed all the help it could get.

H. M. Jenkins, a minor figure in British geology, explicitly 31 defended Darwin in describing the first Cenozoic trigonians. He interpreted the happy closure of the Cenozoic gap as a clear vindication of Darwin's characteristic attitude toward the fossil record and as direct support for evolution. Darwin viewed the fossil record as riddled with imperfections—"a history of the world imperfectly kept . . . of this history we possess the last volume alone. . . . Of this volume, only here and there a short chapter has been preserved; and of each page, only here and there a few lines" (*Origin of Species*, 1859). Gaps, as the old saying goes, represent absence of evidence, not evidence of absence. Jenkins wrote, linking the newly discovered Cenozoic trigonian to this fundamental Darwinian prediction:

> Every paleontologist believes that, when a genus of animals is represented by species occurring in strata of widely different ages, it must have been perpetuated by some one or more species during the whole of the intervening period. . . . The only rational meaning that has ever been attached to this presumed general law . . . is that the perpetuation of the genus . . . has been due to "descent with modification." *Trigonia subundulata* [the formal name for the Cenozoic trigonian] is one of the links hitherto wanting; first, in explanation of the existence of the genus *Trigonia* in the Australian seas of the present day; and secondly, as showing that the great gap which before existed in its life-history was . . . simply a consequence of the imperfection of our knowledge of the geological record.

Finally, a personal confession in closing. This essay has been an exercise in self-indulgence and expiation. I put together the trigonian story at the very beginning of my professional career (when I was just barely big enough to pay full price at the stadium). I published a rather poor account in a technical journal in 1968 (frankly, it stunk). 32

I got part of the story right. I did recognize that everyone managed to slot the living trigonian into his system and that simple, single facts did not (at least in this case) undo general theories. But I got the end all wrong because the traditional, Huxleyan view still beguiled me. I told the happy ending because I read Jenkins's quote and took it at face value—as an evolutionary prediction fulfilled and an empirical vindication provided. I forgot (or hadn't yet learned) a cardinal rule of scholarly detection: Don't only weigh what you have; ask why you don't see what you ought to find. Negative evidence is important—especially when the record is sufficiently complete to indicate that an absence may be genuine. 33

I now read the Cenozoic discovery quite differently, because I have confronted what should have happened but didn't. If Darwin's vindication required a set of new, clean, pristine, unexpected facts, then why didn't the Cenozoic trigonian inspire a wave of rejoicing? Darwin had predicted it; Agassiz had invested much hope in its nonexistence. 34

Sure, Jenkins said the right things in his article; I quoted them and regarded my task as complete. But the key to the story lies elsewhere—in the nonevents. Jenkins wrote a two and a half page note 35

WRITING SUGGESTION

Write an essay in which you support or refute the idea that science can be ambiguous. Support your thesis with specific examples.

in a minor journal. No one else seemed to notice. Darwin never commented, though the *Origin of Species* still had several editions to run. *Trigonia* did not become a textbook example of evolution triumphant. Most curiously, Jenkins did not find the Cenozoic trigonian. It was unearthed by Frederick McCoy, an eminent leader of Australian science, the founder and head of the Museum of Natural History and Geology in Melbourne. He must have known what he had and what it meant. But he didn't even bother to publish his description. I should have taken my clue from the opening lines of Jenkins's paper, but I passed them by:

> The very interesting discovery of a species of *Trigonia* in the Tertiary deposits of Australia has in England remained entirely in the background, and I have been several times surprised at finding students of Tertiary paleontology, generally *au courant*[6] with the progress of their special branch of science, unacquainted with the circumstance. Its importance, in a theoretical point of view, is beyond all question, hence the deep interest always exhibited by those to whom I have spoken on the subject.

I had, in short, succumbed to the view I was questioning. I had 36 recognized that the original discovery of the living trigonian upended no theory, but I had let the Cenozoic fossil act as a Huxleyan nasty fact because Jenkins had so presented it. But when we consider what the Cenozoic trigonian did *not* provoke, we obtain a more general and consistent account of the entire affair. The living trigonian changed no theory, because it could fit (however uncomfortably) with all major views of life. The Cenozoic trigonian did not prove evolution either, because Agassiz's position of retreat was defensible (however embarrassing) and because evolution was too big a revolution to rely critically on any one datum. *Trigonia* didn't hurt, but a multitude of fish were frying, and one extra clam, however clean and pretty, didn't bring the meal to perfection (I shall anticipate a suitable recipe next month, Mr. Sokolov[7]).

Sherlock Holmes once solved a case because the dog didn't bark, 37 but would have sounded off had it been a dog. Nonevents matter, not only the new and nasty facts. Which reminds me: I must have looked at a thousand periwinkles this morning. Still no lefties. Maybe someday.

[6]Current; up-to-date. [Eds.]
[7]Raymond Sokolov, chef, food critic, and author.

RESPONDING TO READING

1. What point does Gould make about scientific theories? What does he mean when he says that his essay is about an "unexpected little fact that should have mattered, but didn't particularly" (paragraph 9)?   **2.** Does Gould's essay reinforce or undercut your ideas about the precision and objectivity of science? Explain.   **3.** Apply Gould's point about "nasty little facts" to a contemporary scientific or medical controversy. In what way, for example, do nasty little facts and "nonevents" affect the current abortion debate about when life begins?

Debating the Unknowable

LEWIS THOMAS

The following essay is from *Late Night Thoughts on Listening to Mahler's Ninth Symphony* (1983), by Lewis Thomas (see also p. 253). In this selection he asserts that we still make up stories to explain the world and that "the admission of ignorance . . . leads to progress."

The greatest of all the accomplishments of twentieth-century science has been the discovery of human ignorance. We live, as never before, in puzzlement about nature, the universe, and ourselves most of all. It is a new experience for the species. A century ago, after the turbulence caused by Darwin and Wallace had subsided and the central idea of natural selection had been grasped and accepted, we thought we knew everything essential about evolution. In the eighteenth century there were no huge puzzles; human reason was all you needed in order to figure out the universe. And for most of the earlier centuries, the Church provided both the questions and the answers, neatly packaged. Now, for the first time in human history, we are catching glimpses of our incomprehension. We can still make up stories to explain the world, as we always have, but now the stories have to be confirmed and reconfirmed by experiment. This is the scientific method, and once started on this line we cannot turn back. We are obliged to grow up in skepticism, requiring proofs for every assertion about nature, and there is no way out except to move ahead and plug away, hoping for comprehension in the future but living in a condition of intellectual instability for the long time.

It is the admission of ignorance that leads to progress, not so much because the solving of a particular puzzle leads directly to a new piece of understanding but because the puzzle—if it interests enough scientists—leads to *work*. There is a similar phenomenon in entomology known as stigmergy, a term invented by Grassé, which means "to incite to work." When three or four termites are collected together in a chamber they wander about aimlessly, but when more termites are added, they begin to build. It is the presence of other termites, in sufficient numbers at close quarters, that produces the work: they pick up each other's fecal pellets and stack them in neat columns, and when the columns are precisely the right height, the termites reach across and turn the perfect arches that form the foundation of the termitarium. No single termite knows how to do any of this, but as soon as there are enough termites gathered together they become flawless architects, sensing their distances from each other although blind, building an immensely complicated structure with its own air-conditioning and humidity control. They work their lives away in this ecosystem built by themselves. The nearest thing to a termitarium that I can think of in human behavior is the making of language, which we do by keeping *at* each other all our lives, generation after generation, changing the structure by some sort of instinct.

Very little is understood about this kind of collective behavior. It is out of fashion these days to talk of "superorganisms," but there simply aren't enough reductionist details in hand to explain away the phenomenon of termites and other social insects: some very good guesses can be made about their chemical signaling systems, but the plain fact that they exhibit something like a collective intelligence is a mystery, or anyway an unsolved problem, that might contain important implications for social life in general. This mystery is the best introduction I can think of to biological science in college. It should be taught for its strangeness, and for the ambiguity of its meaning. It should be taught to premedical students, who need lessons early in their careers about the uncertainties in science.

College students, and for that matter high school students, should be exposed very early, perhaps at the outset, to the big arguments currently going on among scientists. Big arguments stimulate their interest, and with luck engage their absorbed attention. Few things in life are as engrossing as a good fight between highly trained and skilled adversaries. But the young students are told very little about the major disagreements of the day; they may be taught something about the arguments between Darwinians and their opponents a century ago, but they do not realize that similar disputes about other matters, many of them touching profound issues for our understanding of nature, are still going on and, indeed, are an essential feature of the scientific process. There is, I fear, a reluctance on the

ADDITIONAL QUESTIONS FOR RESPONDING TO READING

1. Should students be exposed to "the big arguments going on among scientists" or taught "fundamentals"? Explain.
2. Are there some questions that scientists should not attempt to answer? Explain.
3. Why does Thomas discuss the Gaia Hypothesis? In what way does he use this example to support his main point?

part of science teachers to talk about such things, based on the belief that before students can appreciate what the arguments are about they must learn and master the "fundamentals." I would be willing to see some experiments along this line, and I have in mind several examples of contemporary doctrinal dispute in which the drift of the argument can be readily perceived without deep or elaborate knowledge of the subject.

There is, for one, the problem of animal awareness. One school 5 of ethologists devoted to the study of animal behavior has it that human beings are unique in the possession of consciousness, differing from all other creatures in being able to think things over, capitalize on past experience, and hazard informed guesses at the future. Other, "lower," animals (with possible exceptions made for chimpanzees, whales, and dolphins) cannot do such things with their minds; they live from moment to moment with brains that are programmed to respond, automatically or by conditioning, to contingencies in the environment. Behavioral psychologists believe that this automatic or conditioned response accounts for human mental activity as well, although they dislike the word "mental." On the other side are some ethologists who seem to be more generous-minded, who see no compelling reasons to doubt that animals in general are quite capable of real thinking and do quite a lot of it—thinking that isn't as dense as human thinking, that is sparser because of the lack of language and the resultant lack of metaphors to help the thought along, but thinking nonetheless.

The point about this argument is not that one side or the other 6 is in possession of a more powerful array of convincing facts; quite the opposite. There are not enough facts to sustain a genuine debate of any length; the question of animal awareness is an unsettled one. In the circumstance, I put forward the following notion about a small beetle, the mimosa girdler, which undertakes three pieces of linked, sequential behavior: finding a mimosa tree and climbing up the trunk and out to the end of a branch; cutting a longitudinal slit and laying within it five or six eggs; and crawling back on the limb and girdling it neatly down into the cambium. The third step is an eight-to-ten-hour task of hard labor, from which the beetle gains no food for itself—only the certainty that the branch will promptly die and fall to the ground in the next brisk wind, thus enabling the larvae to hatch and grow in an abundance of dead wood. I propose, in total confidence that even though I am probably wrong nobody today can prove that I am wrong, that the beetle is not doing these three things out of blind instinct, like a little machine, but is thinking its way along, just as we would think. The difference is that we possess enormous brains, crowded all the time with an infinite number of long thoughts, while

TEACHING STRATEGY

According to Thomas, isolation and moral uncertainty characterize twentieth-century intellectual thought. Discuss how moral uncertainty characterizes modern thought about such issues as surrogate motherhood, genetic engineering, and the right to die.

the beetle's brain is only a few strings of neurons connected in a modest network, capable therefore of only three *tiny* thoughts, coming into consciousness one after the other: find the right tree; get up there and lay eggs in a slit; back up and spend the day killing the branch so the eggs can hatch. End of message. I would not go so far as to anthropomorphize the mimosa tree, for I really do not believe plants have minds, but something has to be said about the tree's role in this arrangement as a beneficiary: mimosas grow for twenty-five to thirty years and then die, unless they are vigorously pruned annually, in which case they can live to be a hundred. The beetle is a piece of good luck for the tree, but nothing more: one example of pure chance working at its best in nature—what you might even wish to call good nature.

This brings me to the second example of unsettlement in biology, currently being rather delicately discussed but not yet argued over, for there is still only one orthodoxy and almost no opposition, yet. This is the matter of chance itself, and the role played by blind chance in the arrangement of living things on the planet. It is, in the orthodox view, pure luck that evolution brought us to our present condition, and things might just as well have turned out any number of other, different ways, and might go in any unpredictable way for the future. There is, of course, nothing chancy about natural selection itself: it is an accepted fact that selection will always favor the advantaged individuals whose genes succeed best in propagating themselves within a changing environment. But the creatures acted upon by natural selection are themselves there as the result of chance: mutations (probably of much more importance during the long period of exclusively microbial life starting nearly 4 billion years ago and continuing until about one billion years ago); the endless sorting and re-sorting of genes within chromosomes during replication; perhaps recombination of genes across species lines at one time or another; and almost certainly the carrying of genes by viruses from one creature to another.

The argument comes when one contemplates the whole biosphere, the conjoined life of the earth. How could it have turned out to possess such stability and coherence, resembling as it does a sort of enormous developing embryo, with nothing but chance events to determine its emergence? Lovelock and Margulis, facing this problem, have proposed the Gaia Hypothesis, which is, in brief, that the earth is itself a form of life, "a complex entity involving the Earth's biosphere, atmosphere, oceans and soil; the totality constituting a feedback or cybernetic system which seeks an optimal physical and chemical environment for life on this planet." Lovelock postulates, in addition, that "the physical and chemical condition of the surface of the Earth, of the atmosphere, and of the oceans had been and is actively made fit and comfortable by the presence of life itself."

This notion is beginning to stir up a few signs of storm, and if it 9 catches on, as I think it will, we will soon find the biological community split into fuming factions, one side saying that the evolved biosphere displays evidences of design and purpose, the other decrying such heresy. I believe that students should learn as much as they can about the argument. In an essay in *Coevolution* (Spring 1981), W. F. Doolittle has recently attacked the Gaia Hypothesis, asking, among other things, ". . . how does Gaia know if she is too cold or too hot, and how does she instruct the biosphere to behave accordingly?" This is not a deadly criticism in a world where we do not actually understand, in anything like real detail, how even Dr. Doolittle manages the stability and control of his own internal environment, including his body temperature. One thing is certain: none of us can instruct our body's systems to make the needed corrections beyond a very limited number of rather trivial tricks made possible through biofeedback techniques. If something goes wrong with my liver or my kidneys, I have no advice to offer out of my cortex. I rely on the system to fix itself; which it usually does with no help from me beyond crossing my fingers.

Another current battle involving the unknown is between socio- 10 biologists and antisociobiologists, and it is a marvel for students to behold. To observe, in open-mouthed astonishment, one group of highly intelligent, beautifully trained, knowledgeable, and imaginative scientists maintaining that all behavior, animal and human, is governed exclusively by genes, and another group of equally talented scientists asserting that all behavior is set and determined by the environment or by culture, is an educational experience that no college student should be allowed to miss. The essential lesson to be learned has nothing to do with the relative validity of the facts underlying the argument. It is the argument itself that is the education: we do not yet know enough to settle such questions.

One last example. There is an uncomfortable secret in biology, 11 not much talked about yet, but beginning to surface. It is, in a way, linked to the observations that underlie the Gaia Hypothesis. Nature abounds in instances of cooperation and collaboration, partnerships between species. There is a tendency of living things to join up whenever joining is possible: accommodation and compromise are more common results of close contact than combat and destruction. Given the opportunity and the proper circumstances, two cells from totally different species—a mouse cell and a human cell, for example—will fuse to become a single cell, and then the two nuclei will fuse into a

COLLABORATIVE ACTIVITY

Ask students, working in small groups, to summarize the scientific controversies described by Thomas and to support one side over the other. Ask them to list reasons for their opinions.

single nucleus, and then the hybrid cell will divide to produce generations of new cells containing the combined genomes of both species. Bacteria are indispensable partners in the fixation of atmospheric nitrogen by plants. The oxygen in our atmosphere is put there, almost in its entirety, by the photosynthetic chloroplasts in the cells of green plants, and these organelles are almost certainly the descendants of blue-green algae that joined up when the nucleated cells of higher plants came into existence. The mitochondria in all our own cells, and in all other nucleated cells, which enable us to use oxygen for energy, are the direct descendants of symbiotic bacteria. These are becoming accepted facts, and there is no longer an agitated argument over their probable validity; but there are no satisfactory explanations for how such amiable and useful arrangements came into being in the first place. Axelrod and Hamilton (*Science*, March 27, 1981) have recently reopened the question of cooperation in evolution with a mathematical approach based on game theory (the Prisoner's Dilemma game), which permits the hypothesis that one creature's best strategy for dealing repeatedly with another is to concede and cooperate rather than to defect and go it alone.

12   This idea can be made to fit with the mathematical justification based on kinship already accepted for explaining altruism in nature—that in a colony of social insects the sacrifice of one individual for another depends on how many of the sacrificed members' genes are matched by others and thus preserved, and that the extent of the colony's altruistic behavior can be mathematically calculated. It is, by the way, an interesting aspect of contemporary biology that true altruism—the giving away of something without return—is incompatible with dogma, even though it goes on all over the place. Nature, in this respect, keeps breaking the rules, and needs correcting by new ways of doing arithmetic.

13   The social scientists are in the hardest business of all—trying to understand how humanity works. They are caught up in debates all over town; everything they touch turns out to be one of society's nerve endings, eliciting outrage and cries of pain. Wait until they begin coming close to the bone. They surely will someday, provided they can continue to attract enough bright people—fascinated by humanity, unafraid of big numbers, and skeptical of questionnaires—and provided the government does not starve them out of business, as is now being tried in Washington. Politicians do not like pain, not even wincing, and they have some fear of what the social scientists may be thinking about thinking for the future.

14   The social scientists are themselves too modest about the history of their endeavor, tending to display only the matters under scrutiny today in economics, sociology, and psychology, for example—never

boasting, as they might, about one of the greatest of all scientific advances in our comprehension of humanity, for which they could be claiming credit. I refer to the marvelous accomplishments of the nineteenth-century comparative linguists. When the scientific method is working at its best, it succeeds in revealing the connection between things in nature that seem at first totally unrelated to each other. Long before the time when the biologists, led by Darwin and Wallace, were constructing the tree of evolution and the origin of species, the linguists were hard at work on the evolution of language. After beginning in 1786 with Sir William Jones and his inspired hunch that the remarkable similarities among Sanskrit, Greek, and Latin meant, in his words, that these three languages must "have sprung from some common source, which, perhaps, no longer exists," the new science of comparative grammar took off in 1816 with Franz Bopp's classic work "On the conjugational system of the Sanskrit language in comparison with that of the Greek, Latin, Persian and Germanic languages"—a piece of work equivalent, in its scope and in its power to explain, to the best of nineteenth-century biology. The common Indo-European ancestry of English, Germanic, Slavic, Greek, Latin, Baltic, Indic, Iranian, Hittite, and Anatolian tongues, and the meticulous scholarship connecting them was a tour de force for research—science at its best, and social science at that.

It is nice to know that a common language, perhaps 20,000 years 15 ago, had a root word for the earth which turned, much later, into the technical term for the complex polymers that make up the connective tissues of the soil: humus and what are called the humic acids. There is a strangeness, though, in the emergence from the same root of words such as "human" and "humane," and "humble." It comes as something of a shock to realize that the root for words such as "miracle" and "marvel" meant, originally, "to smile," and that from the single root *sa* were constructed, in the descendant tongues, three cognate words, "satisfied," "satiated," and "sadness." How is it possible for a species to show so much wisdom in its most collective of all behaviors—the making and constant changing of language—and at the same time be so habitually folly-prone in the building of nation-states? Modern linguistics has moved into new areas of inquiry as specialized and inaccessible for most laymen (including me) as particle physics; I cannot guess where linguistics will come out, but it is surely aimed at scientific comprehension, and its problem—human language—is as crucial to the species as any other field I can think of, including molecular genetics.

But there are some risks involved in trying to do science in the 16 humanities before its time, and useful lessons can be learned from some of the not-so-distant history of medicine. A century ago it was

WRITING SUGGESTION

Read what Thomas has to say about collective intelligence (paragraph 3). Then write an essay in which you argue for or against the idea that human beings have such a collective intelligence.

the common practice to deal with disease by analyzing what seemed to be the underlying mechanism and applying whatever treatment popped into the doctor's head. Getting sick was a hazardous enterprise in those days. The driving force in medicine was the need to *do* something, never mind what. It occurs to me now, reading in incomprehension some of the current reductionist writings in literary criticism, especially poetry criticism, that the new schools are at risk under a similar pressure. A poem is a healthy organism, really in need of no help from science, no treatment except fresh air and exercise. I thought I'd just sneak that in.

RESPONDING TO READING

1. How much does Thomas assume his readers know about science? Is he correct in your case?   **2.** Does your own experience as a student support Thomas's idea that the admission of ignorance leads to progress (paragraph 2)? Give an example.   **3.** Do you think Thomas reveals any biases in his discussions of sociobiology, social science, and literary criticism? How do his treatments of these subjects influence your own evaluation of them?

The Bird and the Machine

LOREN EISELEY

Anthropologist and philosopher Loren Eiseley (1897–1977) bridges the gap between scientists and humanists in his writing. In much of his prose, he records personal observations and then moves to broader, more objective thinking. His writing has a poetic feeling and is full of a sense of wonder at participating in, not just studying, nature. Eiseley once said that animals understand their roles, but people, "bereft of instinct, must search continually for meanings." His many books include *Darwin's Century: Evolution and the Men Who Discovered It* (1958), *All the Strange Hours: The Excavation of a Life* (1960), and *The Firmament of Time* (1960). In the following essay, from *The Immense Journey* (1957), Eiseley wonders if computers and artificial intelligence will one day replace living creatures.

I suppose their little bones have years ago been lost among the stones and winds of those high glacial pastures. I suppose their feathers blew eventually into the piles of tumbleweed beneath the straggling cattle fences and rotted there in the mountain snows, along with dead steers and all the other things that drift to an end in the corners of the wire. I do not quite know why I should be thinking of birds over the *New York Times* at breakfast, particularly the birds of

1

my youth half a continent away. It is a funny thing what the brain will do with memories and how it will treasure them and finally bring them into odd juxtapositions with other things, as though it wanted to make a design, or get some meaning out of them, whether you want it or not, or even see it.

It used to seem marvelous to me, but I read now that there are 2 machines that can do these things in a small way, machines that can crawl about like animals, and that it may not be long now until they do more things—maybe even make themselves—I saw that piece in the *Times* just now. And then they will, maybe—well, who knows— but you read about it more and more with no one making any protest, and already they can add better than we and reach up and hear things through the dark and finger the guns over the night sky.

This is the new world that I read about at breakfast. This is the 3 world that confronts me in my biological books and journals, until there are times when I sit quietly in my chair and try to hear the little purr of the cogs in my head and the tubes flaring and dying as the messages go through them and the circuits snap shut or open. This is the great age, make no mistake about it; the robot has been born somewhat appropriately along with the atom bomb, and the brain they say now is just another type of more complicated feedback system. The engineers have its basic principles worked out; it's mechanical, you know; nothing to get superstitious about; and man can always improve on nature once he gets the idea. Well, he's got it all right and that's why, I guess, that I sit here in my chair, with the article crunched in my hand, remembering those two birds and that blue mountain sunlight. There is another magazine article on my desk that reads "Machines Are Getting Smarter Every Day." I don't deny it, but I'll still stick with the birds. It's life I believe in, not machines.

Maybe you don't believe there is any difference. A skeleton is 4 all joints and pulleys, I'll admit. And when man was in his simpler stages of machine building in the eighteenth century, he quickly saw the resemblances. "What," wrote Hobbes, "is the heart but a spring, and the nerves but so many strings, and the joints but so many wheels, giving motion to the whole body?" Tinkering about in their shops it was inevitable in the end that men would see the world as a huge machine "subdivided into an infinite number of lesser machines." . . .

Then in the nineteenth century, the cell was discovered, and the 5 single machine in its turn was found to be the product of millions of infinitesimal machines—the cells. Now, finally, the cell itself dissolves away into an abstract chemical machine—and that into some intangible, inexpressible flow of energy. The secret seems to lurk all about,

ADDITIONAL QUESTIONS FOR RESPONDING TO READING

1. Can all human activities be duplicated by machines? Why or why not? Give specific examples.
2. Various parts of the human body can be described as machines (the heart as a pump, for example). Are there any functions in the human body that cannot be described mechanically?
3. At the end of the essay, does Eiseley attribute human qualities to the hawks? Describe how Eiseley feels about the female hawk remaining for her mate and the role that emotion plays in his essay's thesis.

the wheels get smaller and smaller, and they turn more rapidly, but when you try to seize it the life is gone—and so, by popular definition, some would say that life was never there in the first place. The wheels and cogs are the secret and we can make them better in time— machines that will run faster and more accurately than real mice to real cheese.

I have no doubt it can be done, though a mouse harvesting seeds 6 on an autumn thistle is to me a fine sight and more complicated, I think, in his multiform activity, than a machine "mouse" running a maze. Also, I like to think of the possible shape of the future brooding in mice, just as it brooded once in a rather ordinary mousy insectivore who became a man. It leaves a nice fine indeterminate sense of wonder that even an electronic brain hasn't got, because you know perfectly well that if the electronic brain changes, it will be because of something man has done to it. But what man will do to himself he doesn't really know. A certain scale of time and a ghostly intangible thing called change are ticking in him. Powers and potentialities like the oak in the seed, or a red and awful ruin. Either way, it's impressive; and the mouse has it, too. Or those birds, I'll never forget those birds. . . . I was young then . . . part of an expedition that had scattered its men over several hundred miles in order to carry on research more effectively. . . .

We came into that valley through the trailing mists of a spring 7 night. It was a place that looked as though it might never have known the foot of man, but our scouts had been ahead of us and we knew all about the abandoned cabin of stone that lay far up on one hillside. It had been built in the land rush of the last century and then lost to the cattlemen again as the marginal soils failed to take to the plow.

TEACHING STRATEGY

Lead a class discussion about why the author released the hawk and what that action has to do with his discussion about machine intelligence.

There were spots like this all over that country. Lost graves 8 marked by unlettered stones and old corroding rim-fire cartridge cases lying where somebody had made a stand among the boulders that rimmed the valley. They are all that remain of the range wars;[1] the men are under the stones now. I could see our cavalcade winding in and out through the mist below us: torches, the reflection of the truck lights on our collecting tins, and the far-off bumping of a loose dinosaur thigh bone in the bottom of a trailer. I stood on a rock a moment looking down and thinking what it cost in money and equipment to capture the past.

---

[1]A series of conflicts that developed in the American West during the late 1800s between farmers who wanted to fence in their land and cattle ranchers who wanted free access to the open range. [Eds.]

We had, in addition, instructions to lay hands on the present.   9
The word had come through to get them alive—birds, reptiles, anything. A zoo somewhere abroad needed restocking. It was one of
those reciprocal matters in which science involves itself. Maybe our
museum needed a stray ostrich egg and this was the pay-off. Anyhow,
my job was to help capture some birds and that was why I was there
before the trucks.

The cabin had not been occupied for years. We intended to clean   10
it out and live in it, but there were holes in the roof and the birds
had come in and were roosting in the rafters. You could depend on
it in a place like this where everything blew away, and even a bird
needed some place out of the weather and away from coyotes. A
cabin going back to nature in a wild place draws them till they come
in, listening at the eaves, I imagine, pecking softly among the shingles
till they find a hole and then suddenly the place is theirs and man is
forgotten. . . .

I got the door open softly and I had the spotlight all ready to turn   11
on and blind whatever birds there were so they couldn't see to get
out through the roof. I had a short piece of ladder to put against the
far wall where there was a shelf on which I expected to make the
biggest haul. I had all the information I needed just like any skilled
assassin. I pushed the door open, the hinges squeaking only a little.
A bird or two stirred—I could hear them—but nothing flew and there
was a faint starlight through the holes in the roof.

I padded across the floor, got the ladder up and the light ready,   12
and slithered up the ladder till my head and arms were over the shelf.
Everything was dark as pitch except for the starlight at the little place
back of the shelf near the eaves. With the light to blind them, they'd
never make it. I had them. I reached my arm carefully over in order
to be ready to seize whatever was there and I put the flash on the
edge of the shelf where it would stand by itself when I turned it on.
That way I'd be able to use both hands.

Everything worked perfectly except for one detail—I didn't know   13
what kinds of birds were there. I never thought about it at all, and
it wouldn't have mattered if I had. My orders were to get something
interesting. I snapped on the flash and sure enough there was a great
beating and feathers flying, but instead of my having them, they, or
rather he, had me. He had my hand, that is, and for a small hawk
not much bigger than my fist he was doing all right. I heard him give
one short metallic cry when the light went on and my hand descended
on the bird beside him; after that he was busy with his claws and his
beak was sunk in my thumb. In the struggle I knocked the lamp over
on the shelf, and his mate got her sight back and whisked neatly

COLLABORATIVE ACTIVITY

In small groups, discuss the moral, ethical,
and legal implications of building a thinking
machine. Should a programmer, for example,
be allowed to erase its memory? Would the
machine have certain rights? Follow with class
discussion.

through the hole in the roof and off among the stars outside. It all happened in fifteen seconds and you might think I would have fallen down the ladder, but no, I had a professional assassin's reputation to keep up, and the bird, of course, made the mistake of thinking the hand was the enemy and not the eyes behind it. He chewed my thumb up pretty effectively and lacerated my hand with his claws, but in the end I got him, having two hands to work with.

He was a sparrow hawk and a fine young male in the prime of 14 life. I was sorry not to catch the pair of them, but as I dripped blood and folded his wings carefully, holding him by the back so that he couldn't strike again, I had to admit the two of them might have been more than I could have handled under the circumstances. The little fellow had saved his mate by diverting me, and that was that. He was born to it, and made no outcry now, resting in my hand hopelessly, but peering toward me in the shadows behind the lamp with a fierce, almost indifferent glance. He neither gave nor expected mercy and something out of the high air passed from him to me, stirring a faint embarrassment.

I quit looking into that eye and managed to get my huge carcass 15 with its fist full of prey back down the ladder. I put the bird in a box too small to allow him to injure himself by struggle and walked out to welcome the arriving trucks. It had been a long day, and camp still to make in the darkness. In the morning that bird would be just another episode. He would go back with the bones in the truck to a small cage in a city where he would spend the rest of his life. And a good thing, too. I sucked my aching thumb and spat out some blood. An assassin has to get used to these things. I had a professional reputation to keep up.

In the morning, with the change that comes on suddenly in that 16 high country, the mist that had hovered below us in the valley was gone. The sky was a deep blue, and one could see for miles over the high outcroppings of stone. I was up early and brought the box in which the little hawk was imprisoned out onto the grass where I was building a cage. A wind as cool as a mountain spring ran over the grass and stirred my hair. It was a fine day to be alive. I looked up and all around and at the hole in the cabin roof out of which the other little hawk had fled. There was no sign of her anywhere that I could see.

"Probably in the next county by now," I thought cynically, but 17 before beginning work I decided I'd have a look at my last night's capture.

Secretively, I looked again all around the camp and up and down 18 and opened the box. I got him right out in my hand with his wings folded properly and I was careful not to startle him. He lay limp in my grasp and I could feel his heart pound under the feathers but he only looked beyond me and up.

I saw him look that last look away beyond me into a sky so full of light that I could not follow his gaze. The little breeze flowed over me again, and nearby a mountain aspen shook all its tiny leaves. I suppose I must have had an idea then of what I was going to do, but I never let it come up into consciousness. I just reached over and laid the hawk on the grass.

He lay there a long minute without hope, unmoving, his eyes still fixed on that blue vault above him. It must have been that he was already so far away in heart that he never felt the release from my hand. He never even stood. He just lay with his breast against the grass.

In the next second after that long minute he was gone. Like a flicker of light, he had vanished with my eyes full on him, but without actually seeing even a premonitory wing beat. He was gone straight into that towering emptiness of light and crystal that my eyes could scarcely bear to penetrate. For another long moment there was silence. I could not see him. The light was too intense. Then from far up somewhere a cry came ringing down.

I was young then and had seen little of the world, but when I heard that cry my heart turned over. It was not the cry of the hawk I had captured; for, by shifting my position against the sun, I was now seeing further up. Straight out of the sun's eye, where she must have been soaring restlessly above us for untold hours, hurtled his mate. And from far up, ringing from peak to peak of the summits over us, came a cry of such unutterable and ecstatic joy that it sounds down across the years and tingles among the cups on my quiet breakfast table.

I saw them both now. He was rising fast to meet her. They met in a great soaring gyre that turned to a whirling circle and a dance of wings. Once more, just once, their two voices, joined in a harsh wild medley of question and response, struck and echoed against the pinnacles of the valley. Then they were gone forever somewhere into those upper regions beyond the eyes of men.

I am older now, and sleep less, and have seen most of what there is to see and am not very much impressed any more, I suppose, by anything. "What Next in the Attributes of Machines?" my morning headline runs. "It Might Be the Power to Reproduce Themselves."

I lay the paper down and across my mind a phrase floats insinuatingly: "It does not seem that there is anything in the construction, constituents, or behavior of the human being which it is essentially

WRITING SUGGESTION

Are human emotions useful or harmful to the quality of life? Would people be better or worse off without emotions? Discuss your position in a brief essay.

ANSWERS TO RESPONDING
TO READING

1. Machines can functionally replace living creatures and have done so in many fields, but this essay suggests that machines can never possess or understand the motivational forces of living creatures, and therefore can never truly replace them. Although Eiseley says that machines can do many things better than living organisms can, he rejects the idea that machines will ever be superior.
2. Eiseley seeks an emotional response from his readers. Few other approaches could have suited his purpose as well; a more objective analysis would have been unable to communicate the emotion associated with the motivations of living creatures.
3. The anecdote suits the author's goal of creating antipathy to scientific progress. A more scientific example would fail to convey the essence of the human spirit.

impossible for science to duplicate and synthesize. On the other hand . . ."

All over the city the cogs in the hard, bright mechanisms have 26 begun to turn. Figures move through computers, names are spelled out, a thoughtful machine selects the fingerprints of a wanted criminal from an array of thousands. In the laboratory an electronic mouse runs swiftly through a maze toward the cheese it can neither taste nor enjoy. On the second run it does better than a living mouse.

"On the other hand . . ." Ah, my mind takes up, on the other 27 hand the machine does not bleed, ache, hang for hours in the empty sky in a torment of hope to learn the fate of another machine, nor does it cry out with joy nor dance in the air with the fierce passion of a bird. Far off, over a distance greater than space, that remote cry from the heart of heaven makes a faint buzzing among my breakfast dishes and passes on and away.

RESPONDING TO READING

1. Eiseley suggests that machines can never replace living creatures. Why not? Do you agree? Could you argue that some machines have, in part, already done so? Does Eiseley admit this?　**2.** Was your reaction to this essay largely emotional or intellectual? Why? Could Eiseley have made his point more effectively using a different kind of approach? Explain. **3.** Eiseley uses a remembered event as the center of his essay. Why do you think he did not use a more "scientific" approach? If he were writing a more technical account, what kind of information would you expect him to supply? Would you prefer such an approach? Would you find it more convincing? Why or why not?

The Summer Before Salk

CHARLES L. MEE, JR.

Charles L. Mee, Jr. (1938–　) writes popular histories, children's books, and plays. He grew up near Chicago, worked as a journalist, and was editor of *Horizon* for several years. Mee is the author of *Meeting at Potsdam* (1975), about the famous meeting between Truman, Churchill, and Stalin in 1945, and *The Ohio Gang* (1981), about Warren G. Harding. In December 1983, *Esquire* magazine devoted its fiftieth anniversary issue to fifty Americans who had made significant contributions to the world. Included was the following article by Mee about Jonas Salk, who discovered the first vaccine against polio.

The first symptom was the ache and stiffness in the lower back and neck. Then general fatigue. A vaguely upset stomach. A sense of dissociation. Fog closing in. A ringing in the ears. Dull, persistent aching in the legs. By then the doctor would have been called, the car backed out of the garage for the trip to the hospital; by then the symptoms would be vivid: fierce pain, as though the nerves in every part of the body were being probed by a dentist's device without Novocain. All this took a day, twenty-four hours.

At the hospital, nurses would command the wheelchair—crowds in the hallway backing against the walls as the group panic made its way down the hall to the examining room, where, amid a turmoil of interns, orderlies, and nurses, the head nurse would step up and pronounce instantly, with authority, "This boy has polio," and the others would draw back, no longer eager to examine the boy, as he was laid out on a cart and wheeled off to the isolation ward while all who had touched him washed their hands.

Poliomyelitis is a disease caused by a viral agent that invades the body by way of the gastrointestinal tract, where it multiplies and, on rare occasions, travels via blood and/or nervous pathways to the central nervous system, where it attacks the motor neurons of the spinal cord and part of the brain. Motor neurons are destroyed. Muscle groups are weakened or destroyed. A healthy fifteen-year-old boy of 160 pounds might lose seventy or eighty pounds in a week.

As long ago as the turn of the century doctors agreed that it was a virus, but not everyone believed that the doctors knew. One magazine article had said it was related to diet. Another article said it was related to the color of your eyes. Kids at summer camp got it, and when a boy at a camp in upstate New York got it in the summer of 1953, a health officer said no one would be let out of the camp till the polio season was over. Someone said that public gatherings had been banned altogether in the Yukon. In Montgomery, Alabama, that summer the whole city broke out; more than eighty-five people caught it. An emergency was declared, and in Tampa, Florida, a twenty-month-old boy named Gregory died of it. Five days later, his eight-year-old sister, Sandra, died of it while their mother was in the delivery room giving birth to a new baby.

The newspaper published statistics every week. As of the Fourth of July, newspapers said there were 4,680 cases in 1953—more than there had been to that date in 1952, reckoned to be the worst epidemic year in medical history, in which the final tally had been 57,628 cases. But none of the numbers were reliable; odd illnesses were added to the total, and mild cases went unreported. Nonetheless, the totals were not the most terrifying thing about polio. What was terrifying was that, like any plague, you never knew where or when it might

FOR OPENERS

One useful approach to this essay is to discuss the techniques Mee uses to create an emotional response: the revelation at the essay's end that Mee contracted polio as a child, images of polio in children's wards, and the chronological narrative that attempts to convey to the reader the contemporary horror and uncertainty of the illness.

ADDITIONAL QUESTIONS FOR RESPONDING TO READING

1. Does AIDS, like polio, have societal effects? Explain. In what ways do you think people's attitude toward AIDS victims will change if the epidemic worsens?
2. Was there a political dimension to polio? Did polio sufferers, like AIDS victims, have reason to think that they were a persecuted minority? What is the difference between these two groups?
3. Which of the five senses does Mee appeal to most in this essay? Which of the senses does he appeal to least? Why are his descriptions effective?

strike. It was more random than roulette—only it did seem to strike children disproportionately, and so it was called infantile paralysis—and it made parents crazy with anguish.

The rules were: Don't play with new friends, stick with your old friends whose germs you already have; stay away from crowded beaches and pools, especially in August; wash hands before eating; never use another person's eating utensils or toothbrush or drink out of the same Coke bottle or glass; don't bite another person's hands or fingers while playing or (for small children) put another child's toys in your mouth; don't pick up anything from the ground, especially around a beach or pool, or swallow any of the water in the pool; don't have any tooth extractions during the summer; don't get over-tired or strained; if you get a headache, tell your mother.

Nevertheless, kids caught it. In the big city hospitals, kids were stacked like cordwood in the corridors. Carts and wheelchairs congested the aisles. The dominant odor was of disinfectant. The dominant taste was of alcohol-disinfected thermometers. In the Catholic hospitals, holy medals and scapulars[1] covered the motionless arms and hands of the children. On the South Side of Chicago, a mother cried just to see the name above the door of the place where her child was taken: the Home for Destitute Crippled Children. In some places, parents were allowed to visit their children only once a week—not because of any special fact about polio, only because that was how children's wards were run in 1953. A child in bed with polio never forgot the sound made in the corridor by his mother's high-heeled shoes.

Injections of gamma globulin were prescribed for those who had not yet caught it. Certain insurance against measles, gamma globulin did not prevent catching polio, but it did seem to minimize the crippling effects. It was in short supply. Injections were given only to pregnant women and those under the age of thirty who had had a case of polio in the immediate family—or to prevent the spread of an epidemic. The precious supplies were placed under the administration of the incorruptible Office of Defense Mobilization.

In Illinois, rumors spread of bootleg gamma globulin. If you were lucky enough to qualify for a shot, you had to endure the humiliation that went with it: you had to pull down your pants and say which buttock would take the inch-long needle. To buy off your pride, the doctor gave you a free lollipop.

When the epidemic broke out in Montgomery, Alabama, the story was that 620 volunteer doctors, nurses, housewives, and military

6

7

8

9

10

---

[1]A holy badge worn over the chest. [Eds.]

TEACHING STRATEGY

A real strength of this essay is its organization. Class discussions should include an analysis of the essay's structure and the effects of that arrangement.

personnel administered sixty-seven gallons of gamma globulin (worth $625,000), thirty-three thousand inch-long needles, and thirty-three thousand lollipops. In New York, parents picketed the health department for twenty-seven hours to get it for their children. In some places people said that parents were bribing local officials for vials of gamma globulin. At the same time, an article in the June issue of *Scientific American* reported there was doubt that the stuff was worth a damn. The *New York Times* reported that one little girl came down with polio within forty-eight hours of getting a gamma globulin shot.

In the hospitals, meanwhile, children—shrouded in white gowns 11 and white sheets, nursed by women in white surgical masks, white dresses starched to the smooth brittleness of communion wafers— lay in dreadful silence, listening to the faint whispers of medical conversations on the far side of drawn white curtains, the quiet shush of soft-soled nurses' shoes, and the ever-present sound of water in a basin, the ceaseless washing of hands.

Parents stood at a distance—six feet from the bed—wearing white 12 gowns and white masks.

One boy's uncle gave him a black plastic Hopalong Cassidy bank 13 when he was in the isolation ward. After the customary two-to-three- week stay there, after the fevers passed, he was moved into the regular children's ward. On the way, the nurses discarded the con- taminated bank along with its savings.

Some children were not told what they had (lest it be too dan- 14 gerous a shock to them), and so they discovered for themselves. One boy acquired from his visitors the biggest collection of comic books he had ever had. When he dropped one, he jumped out of bed to pick it up, crumpled in a heap and found he couldn't get up off the floor again.

Some would recover almost entirely. Some would die. Some 15 would come through unable to move their legs, or unable to move arms and legs; some could move nothing but an arm, or nothing but a few fingers and their eyes. Some would leave the hospital with a cane, some with crutches, crutches and steel leg braces, or in wheel- chairs—white-faced, shrunken, with frightened eyes, light blankets over their legs. Some would remain in an iron lung—a great, eighteen- hundred-pound, casketlike contraption, like the one in which the woman in the magic show (her head and feet sticking out of either end) is sawed in half. The iron lung hissed and sighed rhythmically, performing artificial respiration by way of air pressure.

Some moaned. Some cried. Some nurtured cynicism. Some grew 16 detached. Some were swept away by ungovernable cheerfulness. Rarely did anyone scream in rage, however common the feeling. All were overpowered, all were taught respect—for the unseen powers

COLLABORATIVE ACTIVITY

Ask students, working in small groups, to dis- cuss Mee's use of point of view in different para- graphs of the story. In class discussion, note in particular how point of view helps create sym- pathy for the children and parents affected by the polio epidemic.

of nature, the smallness of human aspiration, the capacity for sudden and irrevocable change, the potential of chance.

As it happened, in the spring of 1953, Dr. Jonas Salk, an insig-   17 nificant-seeming fellow with big ears, a receding hairline, and a pale complexion, had published a paper in a scholarly journal, reporting that he had induced the formation of antibodies against three types of polio viruses. He hadn't quite fully tested it, he hastened to say, but he had tried it on 161 children and adults with no ill effects. When newspapers got hold of the story, parents phoned their family doctors. Those with medical connections tried to find a way to get to Salk. Salk became famous in an instant—and from the moment of his first announcement, such an outpouring of hope and gratitude attached to him that he came to stand, at once, as the doctor-benefactor of our times.

During the summer of 1953, reporters called him weekly for news   18 of progress. His vaccine, he explained, was a dead-virus vaccine. He devastated the virus with formaldehyde and then whipped it up into an emulsion with mineral oil to fortify it, and in this way he thought he had something that, when it was injected into a person, would stimulate a person's natural defense mechanisms to produce antibodies. However, he was not able to hurry the testing process along. In May 1953, he expanded the test to include more than seven hundred children. And not until the spring of 1954 were more than a million children inoculated in a large field trial financed by the March of Dimes, and, as the papers said, the "total conquest of polio" was in sight. Within the next half dozen years, the Salk vaccine reduced the incidence of polio by perhaps 95 percent, preventing maybe as many as three hundred thousand cases of polio in the United States.

Yet Salk's triumph did not last for long. The March of Dimes, in   19 its own need for publicity and contributions, lionized Salk mercilessly—and his fellow doctors soon got tired of his fame. He was not—and never has been since—invited to join the National Academy of Sciences. And soon enough, Salk's colleagues began to point out that Salk, after all, had made no basic scientific discovery. Many people had been working on a preventive for polio. The basic discovery had been made by three fellows at Harvard—Doctors Enders, Weller, and Robbins—who had shown that a polio virus could be grown in certain tissue cultures of primate cells. Before the Harvard finding no one had been able to make a vaccine because no one had been able to cultivate the virus in test-tube cultures. After the Harvard finding, Salk's vaccine was mere applied science. (The Harvard doctors got the Nobel; Salk did not.) Salk had just pulled together the work of others. And some of the others thought Salk had been premature in publishing his paper, that he was rushing his vaccine into the world incautiously. Then, in 1955, a batch with live virus slipped out, and 260 children came down with polio from having taken the Salk vaccine or having contact with persons who had taken it.

Meanwhile, even as Salk's vaccine was eliminating polio in the United States, it was already obsolescent. Dr. Albert Sabin, a researcher who told interviewers that work was his recreation, was coming up with a new vaccine. His vaccine used an attenuated (that is to say, live) virus with special properties to stimulate the production of antibodies, and it seemed to offer immunity for much longer than Salk's vaccine, possibly for many years. This virus retained the capacity to multiply in the intestinal tract, thus passing from someone who had received the vaccine to someone who hadn't and inoculating them as well. The Sabin vaccine could be stored indefinitely in deep-freeze units; it could be taken orally and produced cheaply. It was given extensive tests in 1958 and 1959. By 1962 it had replaced the Salk vaccine almost entirely in the United States and most of the rest of the industrialized world. Although Sabin never got the Nobel either, in the next two decades his vaccine prevented perhaps two to three million cases of polio.

But Sabin's happiness was not uncomplicated, either. Though no one likes to mention it—and it does not diminish the good of the vaccine, since the odds are only "one in six or seven million"—sometimes a Sabin inoculation would be, as one specialist in polio has said, "associated with" a case of polio: the attenuated vaccine can never be as absolutely safe as the dead-virus vaccine.

Moreover, while the Sabin vaccine has eliminated polio in most of the temperate-climate countries where it's been used, it has not done so well elsewhere: in the Third World, it turns out, polio has not been ended at all. There, uncertain conditions of refrigeration cause the Sabin vaccine to break down. For some reason, too—perhaps because people in parts of the Third World carry other viruses in their systems that interfere with the polio vaccine—some inoculations don't take. The Sabin vaccine does not work with just one dose but requires several doses, which involves massive vaccination of a community. This has been accomplished in Cuba and Brazil but the logistics are staggering in many Third World countries. Despite the inoculation programs of the past two decades, about 375,000 people come down with polio every year in the Third World: seven and a half million in the last twenty years.

Some highly refined ironies: At the moment, conditions of sanitation and hygiene are so bad in the Third World that many children come down with polio before the age of two. Fortunately, however, at that age polio comes and goes often without leaving a trace of paralysis. As physical standards of living improve, children will not

WRITING SUGGESTIONS
1. Do you feel it is possible to eliminate the political dimension of medical research? Why or why not? Use examples from this essay to support your thesis.
2. Both Sabin's and Salk's vaccines caused accidental, isolated cases of polio. Write an essay in which you discuss whether human volunteers should be used to test experimental treatments for disease. In your essay be sure to outline the arguments on both sides of this issue.

get polio at such early ages: they will get it instead when they are teenagers, when the paralytic rate is higher. So as health conditions improve in the Third World polio may well increase, increasing the need for vaccination.

Some say now that the Salk vaccine will make a comeback, that 24 it will work where the Sabin vaccine has not worked—that the Salk vaccine will hold up better under the conditions of Third World refrigeration, that there is even some indication that a more potent Salk-type vaccine might require only one or two inoculations. Recent tests by the Israeli government in the Gaza Strip seem to make a case for the Salk vaccine. A French pharmaceutical company is manufacturing a Salk-type vaccine that also vaccinates against diphtheria, tetanus, and whooping cough. It may be that Salk will become famous again.

These days, as polio continues to occur in the Third World, most 25 of those who gather at the special conferences on the disease feel that the old Salk vaccine—which has continued to be used in some of the smaller European countries—ought to be brought back on a large scale. Most of them feel not that the Salk should replace the Sabin but rather, given everyone's doubts, that both vaccines are needed, in different circumstances, or perhaps in combination.

But when the two grand old men of the fight against polio, Salk 26 and Sabin themselves, appear at these conferences, they disagree. Each man—as modest and thoughtful and impressive as he is in private—takes on a missionary zeal in public, strutting and scrapping for preeminence, each arguing for the ultimate superiority of his own vaccine. Sabin argues politics: the administration of his vaccine must be improved. Salk argues effectiveness is possible with fewer doses with his vaccine and warns of live-virus-vaccine-associated polio. At one such recent encounter, Salk tried everything, even charm and banter, to win over the audience; he and Sabin agreed on only one thing, he said with a skilled debater's smile, "that only one vaccine is necessary."

And so the two renowned old doctors go on grappling with each 27 other and with themselves, speaking not only of the progress of science and the triumph of reason but also—like those of us who got polio in the summer of 1953 and have toted around a couple of canes ever since—of the equivocalness of greatness, the elusiveness of justice, the complexity of success, the persistence of chance.

ANSWERS TO RESPONDING TO READING
1. Answers will vary, but in recent times only AIDS has created the same kind of terror created by polio.

RESPONDING TO READING

1. What diseases today create the same terror that polio did in the 1950s? How are these diseases—and people's reactions to them—like and unlike what Mee describes? Does your reaction to these diseases help you understand people's behavior toward polio? . **2.** Does the rivalry between Jonas Salk and Albert Sabin surprise you? Does it change your attitude toward scientists or scientific research? Explain.   **3.** Although polio occurs rarely in this country—chiefly among groups who, like the Amish, have refused to be inoculated—it is rampant in many Third World countries. Should Mee have placed greater emphasis on this phenomenon? How do you react to his decision not to do so?

2. Many students will express surprise at the intense rivalry between Salk and Sabin. You might point out that the same sort of rivalry existed between James D. Watson and Francis Crick (the discoverers of the structure of DNA) and Linus Pauling, who was working on a similar project.

3. Mee could have expanded his discussion of polio in the Third World to increase reader interest in his topic and make it seem more relevant to contemporary society. On the whole, however, he makes his point about Salk and the fractious nature of scientific research quite well without this added material.

India

PERRI KLASS

Perri Klass (1958–   ) is a pediatrician who attended Harvard Medical School. Some of her books are *Recombinations* (1985), a novel; *I Am Having an Adventure* (1986), a collection of short stories; and *Other Women's Children* (1990), a novel. Klass often contributes articles and reviews to such periodicals as *Mademoiselle* and the *New York Times*. The following essay is from her book about her years as a medical student, *A Not Entirely Benign Procedure* (1987). In it she recalls her experiences while working in a hospital in New Delhi, where, she says, "I found that my cultural limitations often prevented me from thinking clearly about patients."

The people look different. The examining room is crowded with children and their parents, gathered hopefully around the doctor's desk, jockeying for position. Everyone seems to believe, if the doctor gets close to *my* child everything will be okay. Several Indian medical students are also present, leaning forward to hear their professor's explanations as they watch one particular child walk across the far end of the room. I stand on my toes, straining to see over the intervening heads so I, too, can watch this patient walk. I can see her face, intent, bright dark eyes, lips pinched in concentration. She's about ten years old. I can see her sleek black head, the two long black braids pinned up in circles over her ears in the style we used to call doughnuts. All she's wearing is a long loose shirt, so her legs can be seen, as with great difficulty she wobbles across the floor. At the professor's direction, she sits down on the floor and then tries to get up again; she needs to use her arms to push her body up.

I'm confused. This patient looks like a child with absolutely classic muscular dystrophy, but muscular dystrophy is a genetic disease carried on the X chromosome, like hemophilia. It therefore almost never occurs in girls. Can this be one of those one-in-a-trillion cases?

FOR OPENERS

Discuss the moral and practical implications of sending physicians to Third World countries to learn about diseases that have been eradicated in the United States. Is there anything wrong with this kind of training? Should the physicians stay in the United States and work in areas that have severe shortages of doctors?

1

2

Or is it a more unusual form of muscle disease, one that isn't sex-linked in inheritance?

Finally the child succeeds in getting up on her feet, and her parents come forward to help her dress. They pull her over near to where I'm standing, and as they're helping with the clothing, the long shirt slides up over the child's hips. No, this isn't one of those one-in-a-trillion cases. I've been watching a ten-year-old boy with muscular dystrophy; he comes from a Sikh family, and Sikh males don't cut their hair. Adults wear turbans, but young boys often have their hair braided and pinned up in those two knots.

Recently I spent some time in India, working in the pediatric department of an important New Delhi hospital. I wanted to learn about medicine outside the United States, to work in a pediatric clinic in the Third World, and I suppose I also wanted to test my own medical education, to find out whether my newly acquired skills are in fact transferable to any place where there are human beings, with human bodies, subject to their range of ills and evils.

But it wasn't just a question of my medical knowledge. In India, I found that my cultural limitations often prevented me from thinking clearly about patients. Everyone looked different, and I was unable to pick up any clues from their appearance, their manner of speech, their clothing. This is a family of Afghan refugees. This family is from the south of India. This child is from a very poor family. This child has a Nepalese name. All the clues I use at home to help me evaluate patients, clues ranging from what neighborhood they live in to what ethnic origin their names suggest, were hidden from me in India.

The people don't just look different on the outside, of course. It might be more accurate to say *the population is different*. The gene pool, for example: there are some genetic diseases that are much more common here than there, cystic fibrosis, say, which you have to keep in mind when evaluating patients in Boston, but which would be a show-offy and highly unlikely diagnosis-out-of-a-book for a medical student to suggest in New Delhi (I know—in my innocence I suggested it).

And all of this, in the end, really reflects human diversity, though admittedly it's reflected in the strange warped mirror of the medical profession; it's hard to exult in the variety of human genetic defects, or even in the variety of human culture, when you're looking at it as a tool for examining a sick child. Still, I can accept the various implications of a world full of different people, different populations.

The diseases are different. The patient is a seven-year-old boy whose father says that over the past week and a half he has become more tired, less active, and lately he doesn't seem to understand everything going on around him. Courteously, the senior doctor turns to me,

ADDITIONAL QUESTIONS FOR
RESPONDING TO READING

1. Why does Klass take the cultural differences personally? Is she being too sensitive?
2. What does Klass want readers to learn from her experiences?
3. What do you think Klass gained from her experience? In what ways do you think her experience will help her as a physician? Could it also hurt her? Explain.

asks what my assessment is. He asks this in a tone that suggests that the diagnosis is obvious, and as a guest I'm invited to pronounce it. The diagnosis, whatever it is, is certainly not obvious to me. I can think of a couple of infections that might look like this, but no single answer. The senior doctor sees my difficulty and offers a maxim, one that I've heard many times back in Boston. Gently, slightly reprovingly, he tells me, "Common things occur commonly. There are many possibilities, of course, but I think it is safe to say that this is almost certainly tuberculous meningitis."

Tuberculous meningitis? Common things occur commonly? Somewhere in my brain (and somewhere in my lecture notes) "the complications of tuberculosis" are filed away, and yes, I suppose it can affect the central nervous system, just as I can vaguely remember that it can affect the stomach and the skeletal system. . . . To tell the truth, I've never even seen a case of straightforward tuberculosis of the lung in a small child, let alone what I would have thought of as a rare complication.

And hell, it's worse than that. I've done a fair amount of pediatrics back in Boston, but there are an awful lot of things I've never seen. When I was invited in New Delhi to give an opinion on a child's rash, I came up with quite a creative list of tropical diseases, because guess what? I had never seen a child with measles before. In the United States, children are vaccinated against measles, mumps, and rubella at the age of one year. There are occasional outbreaks of measles among college students, but the disease is now very rare in small children. ("Love this Harvard medical student. Can't recognize tuberculous meningitis. Can't recognize measles or mumps. What the hell do they teach them over there in pediatrics?")

And this, of course, is one of the main medical student reasons for going to study abroad, the chance to see diseases you wouldn't see at home. The pathology, we call it, as in "I got to see some amazing pathology while I was in India." It's embarrassing to find yourself suddenly ignorant, but it's interesting to learn all about a new range of diagnoses, symptoms, treatments, all things you might have learned from a textbook and then immediately forgotten as totally outside your own experience.

The difficult thing is that these differences don't in any way, however tortured, reflect the glory of human variation. They reflect instead the sad partitioning of the species, because they're almost all preventable diseases, and their prevalence is a product of poverty, of lack of vaccinations, of malnutrition and poor sanitation. And therefore, though it's all very educational for the medical student (and I'm by now more or less used to parasitizing my education off of human suffering), this isn't a difference to be accepted without outrage.

9

10

11

12

TEACHING STRATEGY

List all the cultural misunderstandings Klass experiences. What implied criticisms of Indian culture are inherent in Klass's misunderstandings?

COLLABORATIVE ACTIVITY

Have students discuss in small groups the cultural differences between the different ethnic groups with which they are familiar. Then, as a class, review these perceived differences and discuss how accurate they actually are.

WRITING SUGGESTION

Write an essay in which you discuss a time when you exhibited a cultural bias. Do you think your bias was justified? Did it get in the way of your understanding of the situation?

The expectations are different. The child is a seven-month-old girl 13
with diarrhea. She has been losing weight for a couple of weeks, she
won't eat or drink, she just lies there in her grandmother's arms. The
grandmother explains: one of her other grandchildren has just died
from very severe diarrhea, and this little girl's older brother died last
year, not of diarrhea but of a chest infection. . . . I look at the grandmother's face, at the faces of the baby's mother and father, who are
standing on either side of the chair where the grandmother is sitting
with the baby. All these people believe in the possibility of death,
the chance that the child will not live to grow up. They've all seen
many children die. These parents lost a boy last year, and they know
that they may lose their daughter.

The four have traveled for almost sixteen hours to come to this 14
hospital, because after the son died last year, they no longer have
faith in the village doctor. They're hopeful, they offer their sick baby
to this famous hospital. They're prepared to stay in Delhi while she's
hospitalized, the mother will sleep in the child's crib with her, the
father and grandmother may well sleep on the hospital grounds.
They've brought food, cooking pots, warm shawls because it's January and it gets cold at night. They're tough, and they're hopeful,
but they believe in the possibility of death.

Back home, in Boston, I've heard bewildered, grieving parents 15
say, essentially, "Who would have believed that in the 1980s a child
could just die like that?" Even parents with terminally ill children,
children who spend months or years getting sicker and sicker, sometimes have great difficulty accepting that all the art and machinery of
modern medicine are completely helpless. They expect every child to
live to grow up.

In India, it isn't that parents are necessarily resigned, and certainly 16
not that they love their children less. They may not want to accept
the dangers, but poor people, people living in poor villages or in
urban slums, know the possibility is there. If anything, they may be
even more terrified than American parents, just because perhaps
they're picturing the death of some other loved child, imagining this
living child going the way of that dead one.

I don't know. This is a gap I can't cross. I can laugh at my own 17
inability to interpret the signals of a different culture, and I can read
and ask questions and slowly begin to learn a little about the people
I'm trying to help care for. I can blush at my ignorance of diseases
uncommon in my home territory, study up in textbooks, and deplore
inequalities that allow preventable diseases to ravage some unfortunate populations while others are protected. But I can't draw my
lesson from this grandmother, these parents, this sick little girl. I can't
imagine their awareness, their accommodations of what they know.

I can't understand how they live with it. I can't accept their acceptance. My medical training has taken place in a world where all children are supposed to grow up, and the exceptions to this rule are rare horrible diseases, disastrous accidents. That is the attitude, the expectation I demand from patients. I'm left most disturbed not by the fact of children dying, not by the different diseases from which they die, or the differences in the medical care they receive, but by the way their parents look at me, at my profession. Perhaps it is only in this that I allow myself to take it all personally.

RESPONDING TO READING

1. Do you identify with Klass or with her patients? What reaction do you think Klass expects? Explain.   **2.** How do the reactions of Klass and the Indian patients toward disease and death differ? What factors, other than culture, might explain these differences?   **3.** What cultural biases prevent Klass from functioning effectively in India? Do you share Klass's cultural biases? Do you think she will be able to overcome her sense of differentness?

Placebos

SISSELA BOK

Swedish-born philosopher Sissela Bok (1934–   ) lectures and writes about medical ethics. Her moral arguments have a dispassionate tone, and she appeals to common values that she presumes her readers share. Bok has published *The Dilemma of Euthanasia* (1975) and *On the Ethics of Concealment and Revelation* (1983). She argues against lying and secrecy in medicine, law, and government in *Lying: Moral Choices in Public and Private Life* (1978). In the following chapter from that book, Bok explores the implications of physicians lying to patients by giving them placebos.

The common practice of prescribing placebos to unwitting patients illustrates the two miscalculations so common to minor forms of deceit: ignoring possible harm and failing to see how gestures assumed to be trivial build up into collectively undesirable practices. Placebos have been used since the beginning of medicine. They can be sugar pills, salt-water injections—in fact, any medical procedure which has no specific effect on a patient's condition, but which can have powerful psychological effects leading to relief from symptoms such as pain or depression.

1

Placebos are prescribed with great frequency. Exactly how often   2
cannot be known, the less so as physicians do not ordinarily talk
publicly about using them. At times, self-deception enters in on the
part of physicians, so that they have unwarranted faith in the powers
of what can work only as a placebo. As with salesmanship, medication
often involves unjustified belief in the excellence of what is suggested
to others. In the past, most remedies were of a kind that, unknown
to the medical profession and their patients, could have only placebic
benefits, if any.

The derivation of "placebo," from the Latin for "I shall please,"   3
gives the word a benevolent ring, somehow placing placebos beyond
moral criticism and conjuring up images of hypochondriacs whose
vague ailments are dispelled through adroit prescriptions of benefi-
cent sugar pills. Physicians often give a humorous tinge to instructions
for prescribing these substances, which helps to remove them from
serious ethical concern. One authority wrote in a pharmacological
journal that the placebo should be given a name previously unknown
to the patient and preferably Latin and polysyllabic, and added:

> [I]t is wise if it be prescribed with some assurance and emphasis for
> psychotherapeutic effect. The older physicians each had his favorite
> placebic prescriptions—one chose tincture of Condurango, another
> the Fluidextract of *Cimicifuga nigra*.

After all, health professionals argue, are not placebos far less   4
dangerous than some genuine drugs? And more likely to produce a
cure than if nothing at all is prescribed? Such a view was expressed
in a letter to *The Lancet:*

> Whenever pain can be relieved with a ml of saline, why should we
> inject an opiate? Do anxieties or discomforts that are allayed with
> starch capsules require administration of a barbiturate, diazepam,
> or propoxyphene?

Such a simplistic view conceals the real costs of placebos, both to   5
individuals and to the practice of medicine. First, the resort to placebos
may actually prevent the treatment of an underlying, undiagnosed
problem. And even if the placebo "works," the effect is often short-
lived; the symptoms may recur, or crop up in other forms. Very often,
the symptoms of which the patient complains are bound to go away
by themselves, sometimes even from the mere contact with a health
professional. In those cases, the placebo itself is unnecessary; having
recourse to it merely reinforces a tendency to depend upon pills or
treatments where none is needed.

In the aggregate, the costs of placebos are immense. Many mil-   6
lions of dollars are expended on drugs, diagnostic tests, and psy-
chotherapies of a placebic nature. Even operations can be of this

ADDITIONAL QUESTIONS FOR
RESPONDING TO READING

1. Do you believe, as Bok says, that "the entire
   institution of medicine is threatened by practices lacking in candor"? Is Bok effective in
   making her case? Why or why not?
2. Bok says that as "with salesmanship, medication often involves unjustified belief in the
   excellence of what is suggested to others."
   Discuss and explain.

nature—a hysterectomy may thus be performed, not because the condition of the patient requires such surgery, but because she goes from one doctor to another seeking to have the surgery performed, or because she is judged to have a great fear of cancer which might be alleviated by the very fact of the operation.

Even apart from financial and emotional costs and the squan- 7 dering of resources, the practice of giving placebos is wasteful of a very precious good: the trust on which so much in the medical relationship depends. The trust of those patients who find out they have been duped is lost, sometimes irretrievably. They may then lose confidence in physicians and even in bona fide medication which they may need in the future. They may obtain for themselves more harmful drugs or attach their hopes to debilitating fad cures.

The following description of a case where a placebo was pre- 8 scribed reflects a common approach:

> A seventeen-year-old girl visited her pediatrician, who had been taking care of her since infancy. She went to his office without her parents, although her mother had made the appointment for her over the telephone. She told the pediatrician that she was very healthy, but that she thought she had some emotional problems. She stated that she was having trouble sleeping at night, that she was very nervous most of the day. She was a senior in high school and claimed she was doing quite poorly in most of her subjects. She was worried about what she was going to do next year. She was somewhat overweight. This, she felt, was part of her problem. She claimed she was not very attractive to the opposite sex and could not seem to "get boys interested in me." She had a few close friends of the same sex.
>
> Her life at home was quite chaotic and stressful. There were frequent battles with her younger brother, who was fourteen, and with her parents. She claimed her parents were always "on my back." She described her mother as extremely rigid and her father as a disciplinarian, who was quite old-fashioned in his values.
>
> In all, she spent about twenty minutes talking with her pediatrician. She told him that what she thought she really needed was tranquilizers, and that that was the reason she came. She felt that this was an extremely difficult year for her, and if she could have something to calm her nerves until she got over her current crises, everything would go better.
>
> The pediatrician told her that he did not really believe in giving tranquilizers to a girl of her age. He said he thought it would be a bad precedent for her to establish. She was very insistent, however, and claimed that if he did not give her tranquilizers, she would "get them somehow." Finally, he agreed to call her pharmacy and order medication for her nerves. She accepted graciously. He suggested that she call him in a few days to let him know how things were going. He also called her parents to say that he had a talk with her and was giving her some medicine that might help her nerves.
>
> Five days later, the girl called the pediatrician back to say that

TEACHING STRATEGY

Sissela Bok assumes that readers will share her belief that the truth is always better than a lie. Poll students to find out whether or not she is correct.

the pills were really working well. She claimed that she had calmed down a great deal, that she was working things out better with her parents, and had a new outlook on life. He suggested that she keep taking them twice a day for the rest of the school year. She agreed.

A month later, the girl ran out of pills and called her pediatrician for a refill. She found that he was away on vacation. She was quite distraught at not having any medication left, so she called her uncle who was a surgeon in the next town. He called the pharmacy to renew her pills and, in speaking to the druggist, found out that they were only vitamins. He told the girl that the pills were only vitamins and that she could get them over the counter and didn't really need him to refill them. The girl became very distraught, feeling that she had been deceived and betrayed by her pediatrician. Her parents, when they heard, commented that they thought the pediatrician was "very clever."

The patients who do *not* discover the deception and are left   9
believing that a placebic remedy has worked may continue to rely on it under the wrong circumstances. This is especially true with drugs such as antibiotics, which are sometimes used as placebos and sometimes for their specific action. Many parents, for example, come to believe that they must ask for the prescription of antibiotics every time their child has a fever or a cold. The fact that so many doctors accede to such requests perpetuates the dependence of these families on medical care they do not need and weakens their ability to cope with health problems. Worst of all, those children who cannot tolerate antibiotics may have severe reactions, sometimes fatal, to such unnecessary medication.

Such deceptive practices, by their very nature, tend to escape the   10
normal restraints of accountability and can therefore spread more easily than others. There are many instances in which an innocuous-seeming practice has grown to become a large-scale and more dangerous one. Although warnings against the "entering wedge" are often rhetorical devices, they can at times express justifiable caution; especially when there are great pressures to move along the undesirable path and when the safeguards are insufficient.

In this perspective, there is much reason for concern about pla-   11
cebos. The safeguards against this practice are few or nonexistent—both because it is secretive in nature and because it is condoned but rarely carefully discussed in the medical literature. And the pressures are very great, and growing stronger, from drug companies, patients eager for cures, and busy physicians, for more medication, whether it is needed or not. Given this lack of safeguards and these strong pressures, the use of placebos can spread in a number of ways.

The clearest danger lies in the gradual shift from pharmacologi-   12
cally inert placebos to more active ones. It is not always easy to distinguish completely inert substances from somewhat active ones

COLLABORATIVE ACTIVITY

Divide the class into groups and assign each group one of the following questions to discuss and answer: (1) Is the subject of placebos important enough to merit a public debate? Why or why not? (2) Discuss what Bok says about the use of placebos with people least likely to object or to defend themselves. Do you agree? Why do these groups receive placebos? (3) Was the physician wrong to prescribe placebos to the seventeen-year-old girl described in the essay? Why or why not?

Each group should report its findings by spokesperson to the entire class.

and these in turn from more active ones. It may be hard to distinguish between a quantity of an active substance so low that it has little or no effect and quantities that have some effect. It is not always clear to doctors whether patients require an inert placebo or possibly a more active one, and there can be the temptation to resort to an active one just in case it might also have a specific effect. It is also much easier to deceive a patient with a medication that is known to be "real" and to have power. One recent textbook in medicine goes so far as to advocate the use of small doses of effective compounds as placebos rather than inert substances—because it is important for both the doctor and the patient to believe in the treatment! This shift is made easier because the dangers and side effects of active agents are not always known or considered important by the physician.

Meanwhile, the number of patients receiving placebos increases as more and more people seek and receive medical care and as their desire for instant, push-button alleviation of symptoms is stimulated by drug advertising and by rising expectations of what science can do. The use of placebos for children grows as well, and the temptations to manipulate the truth are less easily resisted once such great inroads have already been made. 13

Deception by placebo can also spread from therapy and diagnosis to experimentation. Much experimentation with placebos is honest and consented to by the experimental subjects, especially since the advent of strict rules governing such experimentation. But grievous abuses have taken place where placebos were given to unsuspecting subjects who believed they had received another substance. In 1971, for example, a number of Mexican-American women applied to a family-planning clinic for contraceptives. Some of them were given oral contraceptives and others were given placebos, or dummy pills that looked like the real thing. Without fully informed consent, the women were being used in an experiment to explore the side effects of various contraceptive pills. Some of those who were given placebos experienced a predictable side effect—they became pregnant. The investigators neither assumed financial responsibility for the babies nor indicated any concern about having bypassed the "informed consent" that is required in ethical experiments with human beings. One contented himself with the observation that if only the law had permitted it, he could have aborted the pregnant women! 14

The failure to think about the ethical problems in such a case stems at least in part from the innocent-seeming white lies so often told in giving placebos. The spread from therapy to experimentation and from harmlessness to its opposite often goes unnoticed in part *because* of the triviality believed to be connected with placebos as white lies. This lack of foresight and concern is most frequent when the 15 subjects in the experiment are least likely to object or defend themselves; as with the poor, the institutionalized, and the very young.

In view of all these ways in which placebo usage can spread, it is not enough to look at each incident of manipulation in isolation, no matter how benevolent it may be. When the costs and benefits are weighed, not only the individual consequences must be considered, but also the cumulative ones. Reports of deceptive practices inevitably leak out, and the resulting suspicion is heightened by the anxiety which threats to health always create. And so even the health professionals who do not mislead their patients are injured by those who do; the entire institution of medicine is threatened by practices lacking in candor, however harmless the results may appear in some individual cases. 16

This is not to say that all placebos must be ruled out; merely that they cannot be excused as innocuous. They should be prescribed but rarely, and only after a careful diagnosis and consideration of non-deceptive alternatives; they should be used in experimentation only after subjects have consented to their use. 17

RESPONDING TO READING

1. In her essay Bok questions methods that have been traditionally used in medical research. Do you share her concerns? Do you agree with her conclusions? Why or why not? **2.** Throughout her work Bok has consistently opposed lying in any form or for any reason. Is using placebos the same as lying? Can you think of any situation in which the use of placebos would be justified? Explain. **3.** Medical researchers frequently use double blind studies to ensure the validity of their results. In this type of study patients are divided into two groups, neither of which knows what medication it is receiving. This method eliminates the possibility of a patient's being helped by believing he or she is receiving a certain type of medication. Because double blind studies must by their very nature use placebos, it is not hard to make the case that without placebos scientific study as we know it could not proceed. How do you think Bok would respond to this argument?

The Black Death

BARBARA TUCHMAN

Barbara Tuchman (see also p. 450) was a versatile historian who wrote about the Black Death (the bubonic plague) in *A Distant Mirror: The Calamitous Fourteenth Century* (1978). In the following excerpt, Tuchman graphically describes the Black Death without sentimentality or melodrama; she uses a variety of different kinds of sources to document what happened during this plague.

In October 1347, two months after the fall of Calais, Genoese trading ships put into the harbor of Messina in Sicily with dead and dying men at the oars. The ships had come from the Black Sea port of Caffa (now Feodosiya) in the Crimea, where the Genoese maintained a trading post. The diseased sailors showed strange black swellings about the size of an egg or an apple in the armpits and groin. The swellings oozed blood and pus and were followed by spreading boils and black blotches on the skin from internal bleeding. The sick suffered severe pain and died quickly within five days of the first symptoms. As the disease spread, other symptoms of continuous fever and spitting of blood appeared instead of the swelling or buboes. These victims coughed and sweated heavily and died even more quickly, within three days or less, sometimes in 24 hours. In both types everything that issued from the body—breath, sweat, blood from the buboes and lungs, bloody urine, and blood-blackened excrement—smelled foul. Depression and despair accompanied the physical symptoms, and before the end "death is seen seated on the face."

The disease was bubonic plague, present in two forms: one that infected the bloodstream, causing the buboes and internal bleeding, and was spread by contact; and a second, more virulent pneumonic type that infected the lungs and was spread by respiratory infection. The presence of both at once caused the high mortality and speed of contagion. So lethal was the disease that cases were known of persons going to bed well and dying before they woke, of doctors catching the illness at a bedside and dying before the patient. So rapidly did it spread from one to another that to a French physician, Simon de Covino, it seemed as if one sick person "could infect the whole world." The malignity of the pestilence appeared more terrible because its victims knew no prevention and no remedy.

The physical suffering of the disease and its aspect of evil mystery were expressed in a strange Welsh lament which saw "death coming into our midst like black smoke, a plague which cuts off the young, a rootless phantom which has no mercy for fair countenance. Woe is me of the shilling in the armpit! It is seething, terrible . . . a head that gives pain and causes a loud cry . . . a painful angry knob . . . Great is its seething like a burning cinder . . . a grievous thing of ashy color." Its eruption is ugly like the "seeds of black peas, broken fragments of brittle sea-coal . . . the early ornaments of black death, cinders of the peelings of the cockle weed, a mixed multitude, a black plague like halfpence, like berries. . . ."

1

2

3

Rumors of a terrible plague supposedly arising in China and 4
spreading through Tartary (Central Asia) to India and Persia, Mes-
opotamia, Syria, Egypt, and all of Asia Minor had reached Europe in
1346. They told of a death so devastating that all of India was said to
be depopulated, whole territories covered by dead bodies, other areas
with no one left alive. As added up by Pope Clement VI at Avignon,
the total of reported dead reached 23,840,000. In the absence of a
concept of contagion, no serious alarm was felt in Europe until the
trading ships brought their black burden of pestilence into Messina
while other infected ships from the Levant carried it to Genoa and
Venice.

By January 1348 it penetrated France via Marseille, and North 5
Africa via Tunis. Shipborne along coasts and navigable rivers, it
spread westward from Marseille through the ports of Languedoc to
Spain and northward up the Rhône to Avignon, where it arrived in
March. It reached Narbonne, Montpellier, Carcassonne, and Toulouse
between February and May, and at the same time in Italy spread to
Rome and Florence and their hinterlands. Between June and August
it reached Bordeaux, Lyon, and Paris, spread to Burgundy and Nor-
mandy, and crossed the Channel from Normandy into southern
England. From Italy during the same summer it crossed the Alps into
Switzerland and reached eastward to Hungary.

In a given area the plague accomplished its kill within four to six 6
months and then faded, except in the larger cities, where, rooting
into the close-quartered population, it abated during the winter, only
to reappear in spring and rage for another six months.

In 1349 it resumed in Paris, spread to Picardy, Flanders, and the 7
Low Countries, and from England to Scotland and Ireland as well as
to Norway, where a ghost ship with a cargo of wool and a dead crew
drifted offshore until it ran aground near Bergen. From there the
plague passed into Sweden, Denmark, Prussia, Iceland, and as far as
Greenland. Leaving a strange pocket of immunity in Bohemia, and
Russia unattacked until 1351, it had passed from most of Europe by
mid-1350. Although the mortality rate was erratic, ranging from one
fifth in some places to nine tenths or almost total elimination in others,
the overall estimate of modern demographers has settled—for the
area extending from India to Iceland—around the same figure
expressed in Froissart's casual words: "a third of the world died."
His estimate, the common one at the time, was not an inspired guess
but a borrowing of St. John's figure for mortality from plague in
Revelation, the favorite guide to human affairs of the Middle Ages.

A third of Europe would have meant about 20 million deaths. No 8
one knows in truth how many died. Contemporary reports were an
awed impression, not an accurate count. In crowded Avignon, it was

said, 400 died daily; 7,000 houses emptied by death were shut up; a single graveyard received 11,000 corpses in six weeks; half the city's inhabitants reportedly died, including 9 cardinals or one third of the total, and 70 lesser prelates. Watching the endlessly passing death carts, chroniclers let normal exaggeration take wings and put the Avignon death toll at 62,000 and even at 120,000, although the city's total population was probably less than 50,000.

When graveyards filled up, bodies at Avignon were thrown into the Rhône until mass burial pits were dug for dumping the corpses. In London in such pits corpses piled up in layers until they overflowed. Everywhere reports speak of the sick dying too fast for the living to bury. Corpses were dragged out of homes and left in front of doorways. Morning light revealed new piles of bodies. In Florence the dead were gathered up by the Compagnia della Misericordia—founded in 1244 to care for the sick—whose members wore red robes and hoods masking the face except for the eyes. When their efforts failed, the dead lay putrid in the streets for days at a time. When no coffins were to be had, the bodies were laid on boards, two or three at once, to be carried to graveyards or common pits. Families dumped their own relatives into the pits, or buried them so hastily and thinly "that dogs dragged them forth and devoured their bodies."   9

Amid accumulating death and fear of contagion, people died without last rites and were buried without prayers, a prospect that terrified the last hours of the stricken. A bishop in England gave permission to laymen to make confession to each other as was done by the Apostles, "or if no man is present then even to a woman," and if no priest could be found to administer extreme unction, "then faith must suffice." Clement VI found it necessary to grant remissions of sin to all who died of the plague because so many were unattended by priests. "And no bells tolled," wrote a chronicler of Siena, "and nobody wept no matter what his loss because almost everyone expected death. . . . And people said and believed, 'this is the end of the world.' "   10

In Paris, where the plague lasted through 1349, the reported death rate was 800 a day, in Pisa 500, in Vienna 500 to 600. The total dead in Paris numbered 50,000 or half the population. Florence, weakened by the famine of 1347, lost three to four fifths of its citizens, Venice two thirds, Hamburg and Bremen, though smaller in size, about the same proportion. Cities, as centers of transportation, were more likely to be affected than villages, although once a village was infected, its death rate was equally high. At Givry, a prosperous village in Burgundy of 1,200 to 1,500 people, the parish register records 615 deaths in the space of fourteen weeks, compared to an average of thirty deaths a year in the previous decade. In three villages of Cambridge-   11

TEACHING STRATEGY

Discuss whether our advanced science and technology would make us immune from the hysteria that accompanied the bubonic plague, or whether technological advances such as television and radio would make us even more hysterical.

COLLABORATIVE ACTIVITY

Ask different groups of students to rewrite a portion of the essay in different ways—as a contemporary diary account or official report, a twentieth-century medical analysis of the disaster, or a poem, for example. Let the students present their creations and discuss how their plague accounts differ from Tuchman's and why.

shire, manorial records show a death rate of 47 percent, 57 percent, and in one case 70 percent. When the last survivors, too few to carry on, moved away, a deserted village sank back into the wilderness and disappeared from the map altogether, leaving only a grass-covered ghostly outline to show where mortals once had lived.

In enclosed places such as monasteries and prisons, the infection of one person usually meant that of all, as happened in the Franciscan convents of Carcassonne and Marseille, where every inmate without exception died. Of the 140 Dominicans at Montpellier only seven survived. Petrarch's brother Gherardo, member of a Carthusian monastery, buried the prior and 34 fellow monks one by one, sometimes three a day, until he was left alone with his dog and fled to look for a place that would take him in. Watching every comrade die, men in such places could not but wonder whether the strange peril that filled the air had not been sent to exterminate the human race. In Kilkenny, Ireland, Brother John Clyn of the Friars Minor, another monk left alone among dead men, kept a record of what had happened lest "things which should be remembered perish with time and vanish from the memory of those who come after us." Sensing "the whole world, as it were, placed within the grasp of the Evil One," and waiting for death to visit him too, he wrote, "I leave parchment to continue this work, if perchance any man survive and any of the race of Adam escape this pestilence and carry on the work which I have begun." Brother John, as noted by another hand, died of the pestilence, but he foiled oblivion.

The largest cities of Europe, with populations of about 100,000, were Paris and Florence, Venice and Genoa. At the next level, with more than 50,000, were Ghent and Bruges in Flanders, Milan, Bologna, Rome, Naples, and Palermo, and Cologne. London hovered below 50,000, the only city in England except York with more than 10,000. At the level of 20,000 to 50,000 were Bordeaux, Toulouse, Montpellier, Marseille, and Lyon in France, Barcelona, Seville, and Toledo in Spain, Siena, Pisa, and other secondary cities in Italy, and the Hanseatic trading cities of the Empire. The plague raged through them all, killing anywhere from one third to two thirds of their inhabitants. Italy, with a total population of 10 to 11 million, probably suffered the heaviest toll. Following the Florentine bankruptcies, the crop failures and workers' riots of 1346–47, the revolt of Cola di Rienzi that plunged Rome into anarchy, the plague came as the peak of successive calamities. As if the world were indeed in the grasp of the Evil One, its first appearance on the European mainland in January 1348 coincided with a fearsome earthquake that carved a path of wreckage from Naples up to Venice. Houses collapsed, church towers toppled, villages were crushed, and the destruction reached as far as

Germany and Greece. Emotional response, dulled by horrors, underwent a kind of atrophy epitomized by the chronicler who wrote, "And in these days was burying without sorrowe and wedding without friendschippe."

In Siena, where more than half of the inhabitants died of the   14
plague, work was abandoned on the great cathedral, planned to be the largest in the world, and never resumed, owing to loss of workers and master masons and "the melancholy and grief" of the survivors. The cathedral's truncated transept still stands in permanent witness to the sweep of death's scythe. Agnolo di Tura, a chronicler of Siena, recorded the fear of contagion that froze every other instinct. "Father abandoned child, wife husband, one brother another," he wrote, "for this plague seemed to strike through the breath and sight. And so they died. And no one could be found to bury the dead for money or friendship. . . . And I, Agnolo di Tura, called the Fat, buried my five children with my own hands, and so did many others likewise."

There were many to echo his account of inhumanity and few to   15
balance it, for the plague was not the kind of calamity that inspired mutual help. Its loathsomeness and deadliness did not herd people together in mutual distress, but only prompted their desire to escape each other. "Magistrates and notaries refused to come and make the wills of the dying," reported a Franciscan friar of Piazza in Sicily; what was worse, "even the priests did not come to hear their confessions." A clerk of the Archbishop of Canterbury reported the same of English priests who "turned away from the care of their benefices from fear of death." Cases of parents deserting children and children their parents were reported across Europe from Scotland to Russia. The calamity chilled the hearts of men, wrote Boccaccio in his famous account of the plague in Florence that serves an introduction to the *Decameron.* "One man shunned another . . . kinsfolk held aloof, brother was forsaken by brother, oftentimes husband by wife; nay, what is more, and scarcely to be believed, fathers and mothers were found to abandon their own children to their fate, untended, unvisited as if they had been strangers." Exaggeration and literary pessimism were common in the 14th century, but the Pope's physician, Guy de Chauliac, was a sober, careful observer who reported the same phenomenon: "A father did not visit his son, nor the son his father. Charity was dead."

Yet not entirely. In Paris, according to the chronicler Jean de   16
Venette, the nuns of the Hôtel Dieu or municipal hospital, "having no fear of death, tended the sick with all sweetness and humility." New nuns repeatedly took the places of those who died, until the majority "many times renewed by death now rest in peace with Christ as we may piously believe."

When the plague entered northern France in July 1348, it settled 17
first in Normandy and, checked by winter, gave Picardy a deceptive
interim until the next summer. Either in mourning or warning, black
flags were flown from church towers of the worst-stricken villages of
Normandy. "And in that time," wrote a monk of the abbey of Fourc-
arment, "the mortality was so great among the people of Normandy
that those of Picardy mocked them." The same unneighborly reaction
was reported of the Scots, separated by a winter's immunity from the
English. Delighted to hear of the disease that was scourging the
"southrons," they gathered forces for an invasion, "laughing at their
enemies." Before they could move, the savage mortality fell upon
them too, scattering some in death and the rest in panic to spread
the infection as they fled.

In Picardy in the summer of 1349 the pestilence penetrated the 18
castle of Coucy to kill Enguerrand's[1] mother, Catherine, and her new
husband. Whether her nine-year-old son escaped by chance or was
perhaps living elsewhere with one of his guardians is unrecorded. In
nearby Amiens, tannery workers, responding quickly to losses in the
labor force, combined to bargain for higher wages. In another place
villagers were seen dancing to drums and trumpets, and on being
asked the reason, answered that, seeing their neighbors die day by
day while their village remained immune, they believed that they
could keep the plague from entering "by the jollity that is in us. That
is why we dance." Further north in Tournai on the border of Flanders,
Gilles li Muisis, Abbot of St. Martin's, kept one of the epidemic's most
vivid accounts. The passing bells rang all day and all night, he
recorded, because sextons were anxious to obtain their fees while
they could. Filled with the sound of mourning, the city became
oppressed by fear, so that the authorities forbade the tolling of bells
and the wearing of black and restricted funeral services to two mourners. The silencing of funeral bells and of criers' announcements of
deaths was ordained by most cities. Siena imposed a fine on the
wearing of mourning clothes by all except widows.

Flight was the chief recourse of those who could afford it or 19
arrange it. The rich fled to their country places like Boccaccio's young
patricians of Florence, who settled in a pastoral palace "removed on
every side from the road" with "wells of cool water and vaults of rare
wines." The urban poor died in their burrows, "and only the stench
of their bodies informed neighbors of their death." That the poor
were more heavily afflicted than the rich was clearly remarked at the

---

[1]Throughout *A Distant Mirror*, the book from which this excerpt is taken, Tuchman traces the
impact of events on the life of a French nobleman named Enguerrand de Coucy. [Eds.]

time, in the north as in the south. A Scottish chronicler, John of Fordun, stated flatly that the pest "attacked especially the meaner sort and common people—seldom the magnates." Simon de Covino of Montpellier made the same observation. He ascribed it to the misery and want and hard lives that made the poor more susceptible, which was half the truth. Close contact and lack of sanitation was the unrecognized other half. It was noticed too that the young died in greater proportion than the old; Simon de Covino compared the disappearance of youth to the withering of flowers in the fields.

In the countryside peasants dropped dead on the roads, in the fields, in their houses. Survivors in growing helplessness fell into apathy, leaving ripe wheat uncut and livestock untended. Oxen and asses, sheep and goats, pigs and chickens ran wild and they too, according to local reports, succumbed to the pest. English sheep, bearers of the precious wool, died throughout the country. The chronicler Henry Knighton, canon of Leicester Abbey, reported 5,000 dead in one field alone, "their bodies so corrupted by the plague that neither beast nor bird would touch them," and spreading an appalling stench. In the Austrian Alps wolves came down to prey upon sheep and then, "as if alarmed by some invisible warning, turned and fled back into the wilderness." In remote Dalmatia bolder wolves descended upon a plague-stricken city and attacked human survivors. For want of herdsmen, cattle strayed from place to place and died in hedgerows and ditches. Dogs and cats fell like the rest. 20

The dearth of labor held a fearful prospect because the 14th century lived close to the annual harvest both for food and for next year's seed. "So few servants and laborers were left," wrote Knighton, "that no one knew where to turn for help." The sense of a vanishing future created a kind of dementia of despair. A Bavarian chronicler of Neuberg on the Danube recorded that "Men and women . . . wandered around as if mad" and let their cattle stray "because no one had any inclination to concern themselves about the future." Fields went uncultivated, spring seed unsown. Second growth with nature's awful energy crept back over cleared land, dikes crumbled, salt water reinvaded and soured the lowlands. With so few hands remaining to restore the work of centuries, people felt, in Walsingham's words, that "the world could never again regain its former prosperity." 21

Though the death rate was higher among the anonymous poor, the known and the great died too. King Alfonso XI of Castile was the only reigning monarch killed by the pest, but his neighbor King Pedro of Aragon lost his wife, Queen Leonora, his daughter Marie, and a niece in the space of six months. John Cantacuzene, Emperor of Byzantium, lost his son. In France the lame Queen Jeanne and her daughter-in-law Bonne de Luxemburg, wife of the Dauphin, both 22 died in 1349 in the same phase that took the life of Enguerrand's mother. Jeanne, Queen of Navarre, daughter of Louis X, was another victim. Edward III's second daughter, Joanna, who was on her way to marry Pedro, the heir of Castile, died in Bordeaux. Women appear to have been more vulnerable than men, perhaps because, being more housebound, they were more exposed to fleas. Boccaccio's mistress Fiammetta, illegitimate daughter of the King of Naples, died, as did Laura, the beloved—whether real or fictional—of Petrarch. Reaching out to us in the future, Petrarch cried, "Oh happy posterity who will not experience such abysmal woe and will look upon our testimony as a fable."

In Florence Giovanni Villani, the great historian of his time, died 23 at 68 in the midst of an unfinished sentence: ". . . *e dure questo pistolenza fino a* . . . (in the midst of this pestilence there came to an end . . .)." Siena's master painters, the brothers Ambrogio and Pietro Lorenzetti, whose names never appear after 1348, presumably perished in the plague, as did Andrea Pisano, architect and sculptor of Florence. William of Ockham and the English mystic Richard Rolle of Hampole both disappear from mention after 1349. Francisco Datini, merchant of Prato, lost both his parents and two siblings. Curious sweeps of mortality afflicted certain bodies of merchants in London. All eight wardens of the Company of Cutters, all six wardens of the Hatters, and four wardens of the Goldsmiths died before July 1350. Sir John Pulteney, master draper and four times Mayor of London, was a victim, likewise Sir John Montgomery, Governor of Calais.

Among the clergy and doctors the mortality was naturally high 24 because of the nature of their professions. Out of 24 physicians in Venice, 20 were said to have lost their lives in the plague, although, according to another account, some were believed to have fled or to have shut themselves up in their houses. At Montpellier, site of the leading medieval medical school, the physician Simon de Covino reported that, despite the great number of doctors, "hardly one of them escaped." In Avignon, Guy de Chauliac confessed that he performed his medical visits only because he dared not stay away for fear of infamy, but "I was in continual fear." He claimed to have contracted the disease but to have cured himself by his own treatment; if so, he was one of the few who recovered.

Clerical mortality varied with rank. Although the one-third toll 25 of cardinals reflects the same proportion as the whole, this was probably due to their concentration in Avignon. In England, in strange and almost sinister procession, the Archbishop of Canterbury, John Stratford, died in August 1348, his appointed successor died in May 1349, and the next appointee three months later, all three within a year. Despite such weird vagaries, prelates in general managed to sustain a higher survival rate than the lesser clergy. Among bishops the deaths have been estimated at about one in twenty. The loss of priests, even if many avoided their fearful duty of attending the dying, was about the same as among the population as a whole.

Government officials, whose loss contributed to the general 26 chaos, found, on the whole, no special shelter. In Siena four of the nine members of the governing oligarchy died, in France one third of the royal notaries, in Bristol 15 out of the 52 members of the Town Council or almost one third. Tax-collecting obviously suffered, with the result that Philip VI was unable to collect more than a fraction of the subsidy granted him by the Estates in the winter of 1347–48.

Lawlessness and debauchery accompanied the plague as they had 27 during the great plague of Athens of 430 B.C., when according to Thucydides, men grew bold in the indulgence of pleasure: "For seeing how the rich died in a moment and those who had nothing immediately inherited their property, they reflected that life and riches were alike transitory and they resolved to enjoy themselves while they could." Human behavior is timeless. When St. John had his vision of plague in Revelation, he knew from some experience or race memory that those who survived "repented not of the work of their hands. . . . Neither repented they of their murders, nor of their sorceries, nor of their fornication, nor of their thefts."

RESPONDING TO READING

1. Many passages of Tuchman's essay include graphic, unpleasant descriptions of the plague victims' symptoms. Is this kind of descriptive detail—for example, "the dead lay putrid in the streets" (paragraph 9)—necessary? Why do you think Tuchman includes it? How do you react to this kind of detail?   **2.** Which kind of supporting detail do you find most compelling in Tuchman's essay: statistics, quotations from contemporary sources, anecdotes, lists of victims, or summaries of historical sources? What do you think Tuchman would gain by adding other kinds of support, such as artists' re-creations of the scenes, quotations from modern-day historians, analysis by modern-day medical professionals, or a case study of one family?   **3.** This essay about the dead and dying is remarkably free of sentimentality. Where might another writer have become sentimental, even melodramatic? How do you think you would respond to a more emotional treatment?

A Mask on the Face of Death

RICHARD SELZER

Writer Richard Selzer (1928–   ), born in Troy, New York, is also a general surgeon and a member of the faculty at Yale University Medical School. His essays on medicine have appeared in *Harper's* and *Esquire* and are collected in *Mortal Lessons* (1977), *Confessions of a Knife* (1979), *Letters to a Young Doctor* (1982), and *Taking the World in for Repairs* (1986). *Rituals of Surgery* (1974) is a collection of his short stories. Selzer was awarded the National Magazine Award in 1975. In "Mask on the Face of Death," which appears in his 1986 collection, Selzer writes about the AIDS epidemic in Haiti, using observations he made while visiting the island.

FOR OPENERS

   What kind of AIDS education do students think is most effective? (Consider programs in the schools, advertising campaigns, and so forth.) Does the anti-AIDS education effort in the United States have a moral bias?

It is ten o'clock at night as we drive up to the Copacabana, a dilapidated brothel on the rue Dessalines in the red-light district of Port-au-Prince. My guide is a young Haitain, Jean-Bernard. Ten years before, J-B tells me, at the age of fourteen, "like every good Haitian boy" he had been brought here by his older cousins for his *rite de passage.* From the car to the entrance, we are accosted by a half dozen men and women for sex. We enter, go down a long hall that breaks upon a cavernous room with a stone floor. The cubicles of the prostitutes, I am told, are in an attached wing of the building. Save for a red-purple glow from small lights on the walls, the place is unlit. Dark shapes float by, each with a blindingly white stripe of teeth. Latin music is blaring. We take seats at the table farthest from the door. Just outside, there is the rhythmic lapping of the Caribbean Sea. About twenty men are seated at the tables or lean against the walls. Brightly dressed women, singly or in twos or threes, stroll about, now and then exchanging banter with the men. It is as though we have been deposited in act two of Bizet's *Carmen.* If this place isn't Lillas Pastia's tavern, what is it?[1]

Within minutes, three light-skinned young women arrive at our table. They are very beautiful and young and lively. Let them be Carmen, Mercedes and Frasquita.

"I want the old one," says Frasquita, ruffling my hair. The women laugh uproariously.

"Don't bother looking any further," says Mercedes. "We are the prettiest ones."

"We only want to talk," I tell her.

"Aaah, aaah," she crows. "*Massissi*. You are *massissi*." It is the contemptuous Creole term for homosexual. If we want only to talk,

---

[1]Lillas Pastia's tavern, a setting in Bizet's opera *Carmen*, is a place where gypsies and smugglers sit at tables with officers and soldiers. It is dangerous, exotic, and commonly frequented by thieves and prostitutes. [Eds.]

we must be gay. Mercedes and Carmen are slender, each weighing one hundred pounds or less. Frasquita is tall and hefty. They are dressed for work: red taffeta, purple chiffon and black sequins. Among them a thousand gold bracelets and earrings multiply every speck of light. Their bare shoulders are like animated lamps gleaming in the shadowy room. Since there is as yet no business, the women agree to sit with us. J-B orders beer and cigarettes. We pay each woman $10.

"Where are you from?" I begin.   7

"We are Dominican."   8

"Do you miss your country?"   9

"Oh, yes, we do." Six eyes go muzzy with longing. "Our country   10
is the most beautiful in the world. No country is like the Dominican. And it doesn't stink like this one."

"Then why don't you work there? Why come to Haiti?"   11

"Santo Domingo has too many whores. All beautiful, like us. All   12
light-skinned. The Haitian men like to sleep with light women."

"Why is that?"   13

"Because always, the whites have all the power and the money.   14
The black men can imagine they do, too, when they have us in bed."

Eleven o'clock. I looked around the room that is still sparsely   15
peopled with men.

"It isn't getting any busier," I say. Frasquita glances over her   16
shoulder. Her eyes drill the darkness.

"It is still early," she says.   17

"Could it be that the men are afraid of getting sick?" Frasquita is   18
offended.

"Sick! They do not get sick from us. We are healthy, strong. Every   19
week we go for a checkup. Besides, we know how to tell if we are getting sick."

"I mean sick with AIDS." The word sets off a hurricane of taffeta,   20
chiffon and gold jewelry. They are all gesticulation and fury. It is Carmen who speaks.

"AIDS!" Her lips curl about the syllable. "There is no such thing.   21
It is a false disease invented by the American government to take advantage of the poor countries. The American President hates poor people, so now he makes up AIDS to take away the little we have." The others nod vehemently.

"*Mira, mon cher.* Look, my dear," Carmen continues. "One day   22
the police came here. Believe me, they are worse than the *tonton macoutes* with their submachine guns. They rounded up one hundred and five of us and they took our blood. That was a year ago. None of us have died, you see? We are all still here. *Mira,* we sleep with all the men and we are not sick."

ADDITIONAL QUESTIONS FOR RESPONDING TO READING

1. What value judgments does Selzer make about the actions of the prostitutes, physicians, and health workers in Haiti? Do you agree with them? Explain.
2. Other than sexual habits, what behaviors is AIDS changing?
3. Does the United States bear some responsibility for the AIDS problem in Haiti as described in the essay? What is the attitude of the Haitians toward America's involvement with their AIDS epidemic?
4. What does Selzer mean when he says that the plague cannot be rendered in poetry, music, and painting today?

"But aren't there some of you who have lost weight and have 23
diarrhea?"

"One or two, maybe. But they don't eat. That is why they are 24
weak."

"Only the men die," says Mercedes. "They stop eating, so they 25
die. It is hard to kill a woman."

"Do you eat well?" 26

"Oh, yes, don't worry, we do. We eat like poor people, but we 27
eat." There is a sudden scream from Frasquita. She points to a large
rat that has emerged from beneath the table.

"My God!" she exclaims. "It is big like a pig." They burst into 28
laughter. For a moment the women fall silent. There is only the restlessness of their many bracelets. I give them each another $10.

"Are many of the men here bisexual?" 29

"Too many. They do it for money. Afterward, they come to us." 30
Carmen lights a cigarette and looks down at the small lace handkerchief she has been folding and unfolding with immense precision on
the table. All at once she turns it over as though it were the ace of
spades.

"*Mira, blanc* . . . look, white man," she says in a voice suddenly 31
full of foreboding. Her skin too seems to darken to coincide with the
tone of her voice.

"*Mira*, soon many Dominican women will die in Haiti!" 32

"Die of what?" 33

She shrugs. "It is what they do to us." 34

"Carmen," I say, "if you knew that you had AIDS, that your 35
blood was bad, would you still sleep with men?" Abruptly, she throws
back her head and laughs. It is the same laughter with which Frasquita
had greeted the rat at our feet. She stands and the others follow.

"*Méchant!* You wicked man," she says. Then, with terrible sol- 36
emnity, "You don't know anything."

"But you are killing the Haitian men," I say. 37

"As for that," she says, "everyone is killing everyone else." All 38
at once, I want to know everything about these three—their childhood, their dreams, what they do in the afternoon, what they eat for
lunch.

"Don't leave," I say. "Stay a little more." Again, I reach for my 39
wallet. But they are gone, taking all the light in the room with them—
Mercedes and Carmen to sit at another table where three men have
been waiting. Frasquita is strolling about the room. Now and then,
as if captured by the music, she breaks into a few dance steps, snapping her fingers, singing to herself.

Midnight. And the Copacabana is filling up. Now it is like any 40
other seedy nightclub where men and women go hunting. We get

up to leave. In the center a couple are dancing a *méringue*. He is the most graceful dancer I have ever watched; she, the most voluptuous. Together they seem to be riding the back of the music as it gallops to a precisely sexual beat. Closer up, I see that the man is short of breath, sweating. All at once, he collapses into a chair. The woman bends over him, coaxing, teasing, but he is through. A young man with a long polished stick blocks my way.

"I come with you?" he asks. "Very good time. You say yes? Ten   41
dollars? Five?"

I have been invited by Dr. Jean William Pape to attend the AIDS   42
clinic of which he is the director. Nothing from the outside of the low whitewashed structure would suggest it as a medical facility. Inside, it is divided into many small cubicles and a labyrinth of corridors. At nine A.M. the hallways are already full of emaciated silent men and women, some sitting on the few benches, the rest leaning against the walls. The only sounds are subdued moans of discomfort interspersed with coughs. How they eat us with their eyes as we pass.

The room where Pape and I work is perhaps ten feet by ten. It   43
contains a desk, two chairs and a narrow table that is covered with a sheet that will not be changed during the day. The patients are called in one at a time, asked how they feel and whether there is any change in their symptoms, then examined on the table. If the patient is new to the clinic, he or she is questioned about sexual activities.

A twenty-seven-year-old man whose given name is Miracle   44
enters. He is wobbly, panting, like a groggy boxer who has let down his arms and is waiting for the last punch. He is neatly dressed and wears, despite the heat, a heavy woolen cap. When he removes it, I see that his hair is thin, dull reddish and straight. It is one of the signs of AIDS in Haiti, Pape tells me. The man's skin is covered with a dry itchy rash. Throughout the interview and examination he scratches himself slowly, absentmindedly. The rash is called prurigo. It is another symptom of AIDS in Haiti. This man has had diarrhea for six months. The laboratory reports that the diarrhea is due to an organism called cryptosporidium, for which there is no treatment. The telltale rattling of the tuberculous moisture in his chest is audible without a stethoscope. He is like a leaky cistern that bubbles and froths. And, clearly, exhausted.

"Where do you live?" I ask.   45
"Kenscoff." A village in the hills above Port-au-Prince.   46
"How did you come here today?"   47
"I came on the *tap-tap*." It is the name given to the small buses   48
that swarm the city, each one extravagantly decorated with religious slogans, icons, flowers, animals, all painted in psychedelic colors. I

COLLABORATIVE ACTIVITY

Divide the class into groups and have students write a policy statement that defines the rights of AIDS victims. What rights regarding privacy, employment, medical treatment, and housing should they have? As a class, discuss the various policy statements and the differences among them.

have never seen a *tap-tap* that was not covered with passengers as well, riding outside and hanging on. The vehicles are little master-pieces of contagion, if not of AIDS then of the multitude of germs which Haitian flesh is heir to. Miracle is given a prescription for a supply of Sera, which is something like Gatorade, and told to return in a month.

"*Mangé kou bêf,*" says the doctor in farewell. "Eat like an ox." 49 What can he mean? The man has no food or money to buy any. Even had he food, he has not the appetite to eat or the ability to retain it. To each departing patient the doctor will say the same words—"*Mangé kou bêf.*" I see that it is his way of offering a hopeful goodbye.

"Will he live until his next appointment?" I ask. 50

"No." Miracle leaves to catch the *tap-tap* for Kenscoff. 51

Next is a woman of twenty-six who enters holding her right hand 52 to her forehead in a kind of permanent salute. In fact, she is shielding her eye from view. This is her third visit to the clinic. I see that she is still quite well nourished.

"Now, you'll see something beautiful, tremendous," the doctor 53 says. Once seated upon the table, she is told to lower her hand. When she does, I see that her right eye and its eyelid are replaced by a huge fungating[1] ulcerated tumor, a side product of her AIDS. As she turns her head, the cluster of lymph glands in her neck to which the tumor has spread is thrown into relief. Two years ago she received a blood transfusion at a time when the country's main blood bank was grossly contaminated with AIDS. It has since been closed down. The only blood available in Haiti is a small supply procured from the Red Cross.

"Can you give me medicine?" the woman wails. 54

"No." 55

"Can you cut it away?" 56

"No." 57

"Is there radiation therapy?" I ask. 58

"No." 59

"Chemotherapy?" The doctor looks at me in what some might 60 call weary amusement. I see that there is nothing to do. She has come here because there is nowhere else to go.

"What will she do?" 61

"Tomorrow or the next day or the day after that she will climb 62 up into the mountains to seek relief from the *houngan*, the voodoo priest, just as her slave ancestors did two hundred years ago."

Then comes a frail man in his thirties, with a strangely spiritual-63 ized face, like a child's. Pus runs from one ear onto his cheek, where

---

[1]Growing rapidly, like a fungus. [Eds.]

it has dried and caked. He has trouble remembering, he tell us. In fact, he seems confused. It is from toxoplasmosis of the brain, an effect of his AIDS. This man is bisexual. Two years ago he engaged in oral sex with foreign men for money. As I palpate the swollen glands of his neck, a mosquito flies between our faces. I swat at it, miss. Just before coming to Haiti I had read that the AIDS virus had been isolated from a certain mosquito. The doctor senses my thought.

"Not to worry," he says. "So far as we know there has never been a case transmitted by insects." 64

"Yes." I say. "I see." 65

And so it goes until the last, the thirty-sixth AIDS patient has been seen. At the end of the day I am invited to wash my hands before leaving. I go down a long hall to a sink. I turn on the faucets but there is no water. 66

"But what about *you*?" I ask the doctor. "You are at great personal risk here—the tuberculosis, the other infections, no water to wash . . ." He shrugs, smiles faintly and lifts his hands palm upward. 67

We are driving up a serpiginous[2] steep road into the barren mountains above Port-au-Prince. Even in the bright sunshine the countryside has the bloodless color of exhaustion and indifference. Our destination is the Baptist Mission Hospital, where many cases of AIDS have been reported. Along the road there are slow straggles of schoolchildren in blue uniforms who stretch out their hands as we pass and call out, "Give me something." Already a crowd of outpatients has gathered at the entrance to the mission compound. A tour of the premises reveals that in contrast to the aridity outside the gates, this is an enclave of productivity, lush with fruit trees and poinsettia. 68

The hospital is clean and smells of creosote. Of the forty beds less than a third are occupied. In one male ward of twelve beds, there are two patients. The chief physician tells us that last year he saw ten cases of AIDS each week. Lately the number has decreased to four or five. 69

"Why is that?" we want to know. 70

"Because we do not admit them to the hospital, so they have learned not to come here." 71

"Why don't you admit them?" 72

"Because we would have nothing but AIDS here then. So we send them away." 73

"But I see that you have very few patients in bed." 74

"That is also true." 75

---

[2]Creeping; winding. [Eds.]

"Where do the AIDS patients go?" 76

"Some go to the clinic in Port-au-Prince or the general hospital 77
in the city. Others go home to die or to the voodoo priest."

"Do the people with AIDS know what they have before they come 78
here?"

"Oh, yes, they know very well, and they know there is nothing 79
to be done for them."

Outside, the crowd of people is dispersing toward the gate. The 80
clinic has been canceled for the day. No one knows why. We are
conducted to the office of the reigning American pastor. He is a tall,
handsome Midwesterner with an ecclesiastical smile.

"It is voodoo that is the devil here." He warms to his subject. "It 81
is a demonic religion, a cancer on Haiti. Voodoo is worse than AIDS.
And it is one of the reasons for the epidemic. Did you know that in
order for a man to become a *houngan* he must perform anal sodomy
on another man? No, of course you didn't. And it doesn't stop there.
The *houngans* tell the men that in order to appease the spirits they
too must do the same thing. So you have ritualized homosexuality.
That's what is spreading the AIDS." The pastor tells us of a nun who
witnessed two acts of sodomy in a provincial hospital where she came
upon a man sexually assaulting a houseboy and another man
mounting a male patient in his bed.

"Fornication," he says. "It is Sodom and Gomorrah all over again, 82
so what can you expect from these people?" Outside his office we
are shown a cage of terrified, cowering monkeys to whom he coos
affectionately. It is clear that he loves them. At the car, we shake
hands.

"By the way," the pastor says, "what is your religion? Perhaps I 83
am a kinsman?"

"While I am in Haiti," I tell him, "it will be voodoo or it will be 84
nothing at all."

Abruptly, the smile breaks. It is as though a crack had suddenly 85
appeared in the face of an idol.

From the mission we go to the general hospital. In the heart of 86
Port-au-Prince, it is the exact antithesis of the immaculate facility we
have just left—filthy, crowded, hectic and staffed entirely by young
interns and residents. Though it is associated with a medical school,
I do not see any members of the faculty. We are shown around by
Jocelyne, a young intern in a scrub suit. Each bed in three large wards
is occupied. On the floor about the beds, hunkered in the posture of
the innocent poor, are family members of the patients. In the corridor
that constitutes the emergency room, someone lies on a stretcher
receiving an intravenous infusion. She is hardly more than a cadaver.

"Where are the doctors in charge?" I ask Jocelyne. She looks at 87
me questioningly.

"We are in charge." 88

"I mean your teachers, the faculty." 89

"They do not come here." 90

"What is wrong with that woman?" 91

"She has had diarrhea for three months. Now she is dehydrated." 92
I ask the woman to open her mouth. Her throat is covered with the
white plaques of thrush, a fungus infection associated with AIDS.

"How many AIDS patients do you see here?" 93

"Three or four a day. We send them home. Sometimes the families 94
abandon them, then we must admit them to the hospital. Every day,
then, a relative comes to see if the patient has died. They want to
take the body. That is important to them. But they know very well
that AIDS is contagious and they are afraid to keep them at home.
Even so, once or twice a week the truck comes to take away the
bodies. Many are children. They are buried in mass graves."

"Where do the wealthy patients go?" 95

"There is a private hospital called Canapé Vert. Or else they go 96
to Miami. Most of them, rich and poor, do not go to the hospital.
Most are never diagnosed."

"How do you know these people have AIDS?" 97

"We don't know sometimes. The blood test is inaccurate. There 98
are many false positives and false negatives. Fifteen percent of those
with the disease have negative blood tests. We go by their infections—
tuberculosis, diarrhea, fungi, herpes, skin rashes. It is not hard to
tell."

"Do they know what they have?" 99

"Yes. They understand at once and they are prepared to die." 100

"Do the patients know how AIDS is transmitted?" 101

"They know, but they do not like to talk about it. It is taboo. 102
Their memories do not seem to reach back to the true origins of their
disaster. It is understandable, is it not?"

"Whatever you write, don't hurt us any more than we have 103
already been hurt." It is a young Haitian journalist with whom I am
drinking a rum punch. He means that any further linkage of AIDS
and Haiti in the media would complete the economic destruction of
the country. The damage was done early in the epidemic when the
Centers for Disease Control in Atlanta added Haitians to the three
other high-risk groups—hemophiliacs, intravenous drug users and
homosexual and bisexual men. In fact, Haitians are no more susceptible to AIDS than anyone else. Although the CDC removed Haitians
from special scrutiny in 1985, the lucrative tourism on which so much

of the country's economy was based was crippled. Along with tourism went much of the foreign business investment. Worst of all was the injury to the national pride. Suddenly Haiti was indicated as the source of AIDS in the western hemisphere.

What caused the misunderstanding was the discovery of a large 104 number of Haitian men living in Miami with AIDS antibodies in their blood. They denied absolutely they were homosexuals. But the CDC investigators did not know that homosexuality is the strongest taboo in Haiti and that no man would ever admit to it. Bisexuality, however, is not uncommon. Many married men and heterosexually oriented males will occasionally seek out other men for sex. Further, many, if not most, Haitian men visit female prostitutes from time to time. It is not difficult to see that once the virus was set loose in Haiti, the spread would be swift through both genders.

Exactly how the virus of AIDS arrived is not known. Could it 105 have been brought home by the Cuban soldiers stationed in Angola and thence to Haiti, about fifty miles away? Could it have been passed on by the thousands of Haitians living in exile in Zaire, who later returned home or immigrated to the United States? Could it have come from the American and Canadian homosexual tourists, and, yes, even some U.S. diplomats who have traveled to the island to have sex with impoverished Haitian men all too willing to sell themselves to feed their families? Throughout the international gay community Haiti was known as a good place to go for sex.

On a private tip from an official at the Ministry of Tourism, J-B 106 and I drive to a town some fifty miles from Port-au-Prince. The hotel is owned by two Frenchmen who are out of the country, one of the staff tells us. He is a man of about thirty and clearly he is desperately ill. Tottering, short of breath, he shows us about the empty hotel. The furnishings are opulent and extreme—tiger skins on the wall, a live leopard in the garden, a bedroom containing a giant bathtub with gold faucets. Is it the heat of the day or the heat of my imagination that makes these walls echo with the painful cries of pederasty?

The hotel where we are staying is in Pétionville, the fashionable 107 suburb of Port-au-Prince. It is the height of the season but there are no tourists, only a dozen or so French and American businessmen. The swimming pool is used once or twice a day by a single person. Otherwise, the water remains undisturbed until dusk, when the fruit bats come down to drink in midswoop. The hotel keeper is an American. He is eager to set me straight on Haiti.

"What did and should attract foreign investment is a combination 108 of reliable weather, an honest and friendly populace, low wages and multilingual managers."

"What spoiled it?"   109

"Political instability and a bad American press about AIDS." He   110
pauses, then adds: "To which I hope you won't be contributing."

"What about just telling the truth?" I suggest.   111

"Look," he says, "there is no more danger of catching AIDS in   112
Haiti than in New York or Santo Domingo. It is not where you are
but what you do that counts." Agreeing, I ask if he had any idea that
much of the tourism in Haiti during the past few decades was based
on sex.

"No idea whatsoever. It was only recently that we discovered   113
that that was the case."

"How is it that you hoteliers, restaurant owners and the Ministry 114
of Tourism did not know what *tout* Haiti knew?"

"Look. All I know is that this is a middle-class, family-oriented   115
hotel. We don't allow guests to bring women, or for that matter men,
into their rooms. If they did, we'd ask them to leave immediately."

At five A.M. the next day the telephone rings in my room. A   116
creole-accented male voice.

"Is the lady still with you, sir?"   117

"There is no lady here."   118

"In your room, sir, the lady I allowed to go up with a package?"   119

"There is no lady here, I tell you."   120

At seven A.M. I stop at the front desk. The clerk is a young man. 121

"Was it you who called my room at five o'clock?"   122

"Sorry," he says with a smile. "It was a mistake, sir. I meant to 123
ring the room next door to yours." Still smiling, he holds up his
shushing finger.

Next to Dr. Pape, director of the AIDS clinic, Bernard Liautaud,   124
a dermatologist, is the most knowledgeable Haitian physician on the
subject of the epidemic. Together, the two men have published a
dozen articles on AIDS in international medical journals. In our
meeting they present me with statistics:

There are more than one thousand documented cases of AIDS in   125
Haiti, and as many as one hundred thousand carriers of the virus.

Eighty-seven percent of AIDS is now transmitted heterosexually.   126
While it is true that the virus was introduced via the bisexual community, that route has decreased to 10 percent or less.

Sixty percent of the wives or husbands of AIDS patients tested pos- 127
itive for the antibody.

Fifty percent of the prostitutes tested in the Port-au-Prince area are 128
infected.

Eighty percent of the men with AIDS have had contact with prostitutes. 129

The projected number of active cases in four years is ten thousand. 130 (Since my last visit, the Haitian Medical Association broke its silence on the epidemic by warning that one million of the country's six million people could be carriers by 1992.)

The two doctors have more to tell. "The crossing over of the 131 plague from the homosexual to the heterosexual community will follow in the United States within two years. This, despite the hesitation to say so by those who fear to sow panic among your population. In Haiti, because bisexuality is more common, there was an early crossover into the general population. The trend, inevitably, is the same in the two countries."

"What is there to do, then?" 132

"Only education, just as in America. But here the Haitians reject 133 the use of condoms. Only the men who are too sick to have sex are celibate."

"What is to be the end of it?" 134

"When enough heterosexuals of the middle and upper classes 135 die, perhaps there will be the panic necessary for the people to change their sexual lifestyles."

This evening I leave Haiti. For two weeks I have fastened myself 136 to this lovely fragile land like an ear pressed to the ground. It is a country to break a traveler's heart. It occurs to me that I have not seen a single jogger. Such a public expenditure of energy while everywhere else strength is ebbing—it would be obscene. In my final hours, I go to the Cathédral of Sainte Trinité, the inner walls of which are covered with murals by Haiti's most renowned artists. Here are all the familiar Bible stories depicted in naïveté and piety, and all in such an exuberance of color as to tax the capacity of the retina to receive it, as though all the vitality of Haiti had been turned to paint and brushed upon these walls. How to explain its efflorescence at a time when all else is lassitude and inertia? Perhaps one day the plague will be rendered in poetry, music, painting, but not now. Not now.

RESPONDING TO READING

1. Would you say that the tone of this essay is optimistic or pessimistic? Do you feel the tone is appropriate for the subject matter? **2.** In this essay, written in 1987, the author quotes a doctor as saying that within two years the situation in the United States will be the same as it is in Haiti. In fact, the spread of AIDS has actually slowed down among certain populations. In what way does this discrepancy affect your reaction to the essay? Do you think the doctor was simply mistaken or intentionally exaggerating?   **3.** If you were going to write an essay about AIDS, would you choose Haiti as the setting? What are the advantages and disadvantages of this setting? What would be the effect of using an urban area of the United States as the setting?

3. Because Haiti is a very small, self-contained society, it offers a good place to observe the effects of AIDS. An urban area of the United States would also illustrate the AIDS epidemic, but because of its size and complexity a researcher would have a difficult time gathering information and observing cultural practices.

The Fate of the Earth

JONATHAN SCHELL

Nonfiction writer Jonathan Schell (1943–   ) concerns himself with the theories about, preparations for, and consequences of nuclear war in his popular book, *The Fate of the Earth* (1982). He is a writer for *The New Yorker*, and many of his articles have become the basis for his books on American international and domestic politics, including *The Village of Ben Suc* (1967) and *The Time of Illusion* (1976). In the following excerpt from *The Fate of the Earth*, Schell describes in chilling detail the effect of dropping an atomic bomb on New York City.

One way to begin to grasp the destructive power of present-day 1 nuclear weapons is to describe the consequences of the detonation of a one-megaton bomb, which possesses eighty times the explosive power of the Hiroshima bomb, on a large city, such as New York. Burst some eighty-five hundred feet above the Empire State Building, a one-megaton bomb would gut or flatten almost every building between Battery Park and 125th Street, or within a radius of four and four-tenths miles, or in an area of sixty-one square miles, and would heavily damage buildings between the northern tip of Staten Island and the George Washington Bridge, or within a radius of about eight miles, or in an area of about two hundred square miles. A conventional explosive delivers a swift shock, like a slap, to whatever it hits, but the blast wave of a sizable nuclear weapon endures for several seconds and "can surround and destroy whole buildings" (Glasstone).[1] People, of course, would be picked up and hurled away from the blast along with the rest of the debris. Within the sixty-one square miles, the walls, roofs, and floors of any buildings that had not been flattened would be collapsed, and the people and furniture inside would be swept down onto the street. (Technically, this zone would be hit by various overpressures of at least five pounds per square inch. Overpressure is defined as the pressure in excess of normal

---

[1]Samuel Glasstone, editor with Philip Dolan of *Effects of Nuclear Weapons*. [Eds.]

atmospheric pressure.) As far away as ten miles from ground zero, pieces of glass and other sharp objects would be hurled about by the blast wave at lethal velocities. In Hiroshima, where buildings were low and, outside the center of the city, were often constructed of light materials, injuries from falling buildings were often minor. But in New York, where the buildings are tall and are constructed of heavy materials, the physical collapse of the city would certainly kill millions of people. The streets of New York are narrow ravines running between the high walls of the city's buildings. In a nuclear attack, the walls would fall and the ravines would fill up. The people in the buildings would fall to the street with the debris of the buildings, and the people in the street would be crushed by this avalanche of people and buildings. At a distance of two miles or so from ground zero, winds would reach four hundred miles an hour, and another two miles away they would reach a hundred and eighty miles an hour. Meanwhile, the fireball would be growing, until it was more than a mile wide, and rocketing upward, to a height of over six miles. For ten seconds, it would broil the city below. Anyone caught in the open within nine miles of ground zero would receive third-degree burns and would probably be killed; closer to the explosion, people would be charred and killed instantly. From Greenwich Village up to Central Park, the heat would be great enough to melt metal and glass. Readily inflammable materials, such as newspapers and dry leaves, would ignite in all five boroughs (though in only a small part of Staten Island) and west to the Passaic River, in New Jersey, within a radius of about nine and a half miles from ground zero, thereby creating an area of more than two hundred and eighty square miles in which mass fires were likely to break out.

If it were possible (as it would not be) for someone to stand at 2 Fifth Avenue and Seventy-second Street (about two miles from ground zero) without being instantly killed, he would see the following sequence of events. A dazzling white light from the fireball would illumine the scene, continuing for perhaps thirty seconds. Simultaneously, searing heat would ignite everything flammable and start to melt windows, cars, buses, lampposts, and everything else made of metal or glass. People in the street would immediately catch fire, and would shortly be reduced to heavily charred corpses. About five seconds after the light appeared, the blast wave would strike, laden with the debris of a now nonexistent midtown. Some buildings might be crushed, as though a giant fist had squeezed them on all sides, and others might be picked up off their foundations and whirled uptown with the other debris. On the far side of Central Park, the West Side skyline would fall from south to north. The four-hundred-mile-an-hour wind would blow from south to north, die down after

ADDITIONAL QUESTIONS FOR RESPONDING TO READING

1. Does the existence of nuclear weapons change the way we think about conflict? Why or why not?
2. Can the average person do anything to determine whether or not nuclear weapons are manufactured or deployed? Discuss.
3. In what way do recent events in the Soviet Union affect your response to this essay? Is nuclear war now more or less of a possibility?
4. What attitude does Schell assume his readers have about nuclear weapons?

a few seconds, and then blow in the reverse direction with diminished intensity. While these things were happening, the fireball would be burning in the sky for the ten seconds of the thermal pulse. Soon huge, thick clouds of dust and smoke would envelop the scene, and as the mushroom cloud rushed overhead (it would have a diameter of about twelve miles) the light from the sun would be blotted out, and day would turn to night. Within minutes, fires, ignited both by the thermal pulse and by broken gas mains, tanks of gas and oil, and the like, would begin to spread in the darkness, and a strong, steady wind would begin to blow in the direction of the blast. As at Hiroshima, a whirlwind might be produced, which would sweep through the ruins, and radioactive rain, generated under the meteorological conditions created by the blast, might fall. Before long, the individual fires would coalesce into a mass fire, which, depending largely on the winds, would become either a conflagration or a firestorm. In a conflagration, prevailing winds spread a wall of fire as far as there is any combustible material to sustain it; in a firestorm, a vertical updraft caused by the fire itself sucks the surrounding air in toward a central point, and the fires therefore converge in a single fire of extreme heat. A mass fire of either kind renders shelters useless by burning up all the oxygen in the air and creating toxic gases, so that anyone inside the shelters is asphyxiated, and also by heating the ground to such high temperatures that the shelters turn, in effect, into ovens, cremating the people inside them. In Dresden, several days after the firestorm raised there by Allied conventional bombing, the interiors of some bomb shelters were still so hot that when they were opened the inrushing air caused the contents to burst into flame. Only those who had fled their shelters when the bombing started had any chance of surviving. (It is difficult to predict in a particular situation which form the fires will take. In actual experience, Hiroshima suffered a firestorm and Nagasaki suffered a conflagration.)

In this vast theatre of physical effects, all the scenes of agony and 3 death that took place at Hiroshima would again take place, but now involving millions of people rather than hundreds of thousands. Like the people of Hiroshima, the people of New York would be burned, battered, crushed, and irradiated in every conceivable way. The city and its people would be mingled in a smoldering heap. And then, as the fires started, the survivors (most of whom would be on the periphery of the explosion) would be driven to abandon to the flames those family members and other people who were unable to flee, or else to die with them. Before long, while the ruins burned, the processions of injured, mute people would begin their slow progress out of the outskirts of the devastated zone. However, this time a much smaller proportion of the population than at Hiroshima would have

TEACHING STRATEGY

Discuss Schell's use of extremely detailed information as a method of persuasion. Are there any drawbacks to this method?

a chance of escaping. In general, as the size of the area of devastation increases, the possibilities for escape decrease. When the devastated area is relatively small, as it was at Hiroshima, people who are not incapacitated will have a good chance of escaping to safety before the fires coalesce into a mass fire. But when the devastated area is great, as it would be after the detonation of a megaton bomb, and fires are springing up at a distance of nine and a half miles from ground zero, and when what used to be the streets are piled high with burning rubble, and the day (if the attack occurs in the daytime) has grown impenetrably dark, there is little chance that anyone who is not on the very edge of the devastated area will be able to make his way to safety. In New York, most people would die wherever the blast found them, or not very far from there.

If instead of being burst in the air the bomb were burst on or near   4
the ground in the vicinity of the Empire State Building, the over-pressure would be very much greater near the center of the blast area but the range hit by a minimum of five pounds per square inch of overpressure would be less. The range of the thermal pulse would be about the same as that of the air burst. The fireball would be almost two miles across, and would engulf midtown Manhattan from Greenwich Village nearly to Central Park. Very little is known about what would happen to a city that was inside a fireball, but one would expect a good deal of what was there to be first pulverized and then melted or vaporized. Any human beings in the area would be reduced to smoke and ashes; they would simply disappear. A crater roughly three blocks in diameter and two hundred feet deep would open up. In addition, heavy radioactive fallout would be created as dust and debris from the city rose with the mushroom cloud and then fell back to the ground. Fallout would begin to drop almost immediately, contaminating the ground beneath the cloud with levels of radiation many times lethal doses, and quickly killing anyone who might have survived the blast wave and the thermal pulse and might now be attempting an escape; it is difficult to believe that there would be appreciable survival of the people of the city after a megaton ground burst. And for the next twenty-four hours or so more fallout would descend downwind from the blast, in a plume whose direction and length would depend on the speed and the direction of the wind that happened to be blowing at the time of the attack. If the wind was blowing at fifteen miles an hour, fallout of lethal intensity would descend in a plume about a hundred and fifty miles long and as much as fifteen miles wide. Fallout that was sublethal but could still cause serious illness would extend another hundred and fifty miles downwind. Exposure to radioactivity in human beings is measured in units called rems—an acronym for "roentgen equivalent in man." The

COLLABORATIVE ACTIVITY

Divide the class into groups and ask students to discuss their personal reactions to the essay. Did it change their position about nuclear weapons? Did it frighten them? How? Is the essay biased? What information does the essay *not* include?

roentgen is a standard measurement of gamma- and X-ray radiation, and the expression "equivalent in man" indicates that an adjustment has been made to take into account the differences in the degree of biological damage that is caused by radiation of different types. Many of the kinds of harm done to human beings by radiation—for example, the incidence of cancer and of genetic damage—depend on the dose accumulated over many years; but radiation sickness, capable of causing death, results from an "acute" dose, received in a period of anything from a few seconds to several days. Because almost ninety per cent of the so-called "infinite-time dose" of radiation from fallout—that is, the dose from a given quantity of fallout that one would receive if one lived for many thousands of years—is emitted in the first week, the one-week accumulated dose is often used as a convenient measure for calculating the immediate harm from fallout. Doses in the thousands of rems, which could be expected throughout the city, would attack the central nervous system and would bring about death within a few hours. Doses of around a thousand rems, which would be delivered some tens of miles downwind from the blast, would kill within two weeks everyone who was exposed to them. Doses of around five hundred rems, which would be delivered as far as a hundred and fifty miles downwind (given a wind speed of fifteen miles per hour), would kill half of all exposed able-bodied young adults. At this level of exposure, radiation sickness proceeds in the three stages observed at Hiroshima. The plume of lethal fallout could descend, depending on the direction of the wind, on other parts of New York State and parts of New Jersey, Pennsylvania, Delaware, Maryland, Connecticut, Massachusetts, Rhode Island, Vermont, and New Hampshire, killing additional millions of people. The circumstances in heavily contaminated areas, in which millions of people were all declining together, over a period of weeks, toward painful deaths, are ones that, like so many of the consequences of nuclear explosions, have never been experienced.

A description of the effects of a one-megaton bomb on New York 5 City gives some notion of the meaning in human terms of a megaton of nuclear explosive power, but a weapon that is more likely to be used against New York is the twenty-megaton bomb, which has one thousand six hundred times the yield of the Hiroshima bomb. The Soviet Union is estimated to have at least a hundred and thirteen twenty-megaton bombs in its nuclear arsenal, carried by Bear intercontinental bombers. In addition, some of the Soviet SS-18 missiles are capable of carrying bombs of this size, although the actual yields are not known. Since the explosive power of the twenty-megaton bombs greatly exceeds the amount necessary to destroy most military targets, it is reasonable to suppose that they are meant for use against

WRITING SUGGESTION

Schell chooses a hypothetical nuclear explosion over New York City to help the reader "grasp the destructive power of present-day nuclear weapons." Write an essay in which you use another approach—for example, an analogy or a personal anecdote—to help the reader grasp the power of nuclear weapons.

large cities. If a twenty-megaton bomb were air-burst over the Empire State Building at an altitude of thirty thousand feet, the zone gutted or flattened by the blast wave would have a radius of twelve miles and an area of more than four hundred and fifty square miles, reaching from the middle of Staten Island to the northern edge of the Bronx, the eastern edge of Queens, and well into New Jersey, and the zone of heavy damage from the blast wave (the zone hit by a minimum of two pounds of overpressure per square inch) would have a radius of twenty-one and a half miles, or an area of one thousand four hundred and fifty square miles, reaching to the southernmost tip of Staten Island, north as far as southern Rockland County, east into Nassau County, and west to Morris County, New Jersey. The fireball would be about four and a half miles in diameter and would radiate the thermal pulse for some twenty seconds. People caught in the open twenty-three miles away from ground zero, in Long Island, New Jersey, and southern New York State, would be burned to death. People hundreds of miles away who looked at the burst would be temporarily blinded and would risk permanent eye injury. (After the test of a fifteen-megaton bomb on Bikini Atoll, in the South Pacific, in March of 1954, small animals were found to have suffered retinal burns at a distance of three hundred and forty-five miles.) The mushroom cloud would be seventy miles in diameter. New York City and its suburbs would be transformed into a lifeless, flat, scorched desert in a few seconds.

If a twenty-megaton bomb were ground-burst on the Empire State Building, the range of severe blast damage would, as with the one-megaton ground blast, be reduced, but the fireball, which would be almost six miles in diameter, would cover Manhattan from Wall Street to northern Central Park and also parts of New Jersey, Brooklyn, and Queens, and everyone within it would be instantly killed, with most of them physically disappearing. Fallout would again be generated, this time covering thousands of square miles with lethal intensities of radiation. A fair portion of New York City and its incinerated population, now radioactive dust, would have risen into the mushroom cloud and would now be descending on the surrounding territory. On one of the few occasions when local fallout was generated by a test explosion in the multi-megaton range, the fifteen-megaton bomb tested on Bikini Atoll, which was exploded seven feet above the surface of a coral reef, "caused substantial contamination over an area of more than seven thousand square miles," according to Glasstone. If, as seems likely, a twenty-megaton bomb ground-burst on New York would produce at least a comparable amount of fallout, and if the wind carried the fallout onto populated areas, then this one bomb would probably doom upward of twenty million people, or almost ten per cent of the population of the United States.

RESPONDING TO READING

1. Most of this essay describes a hypothetical event, the dropping of an atomic bomb on New York City. Schell uses vivid descriptions of this event to support his argument. What point is Schell making? Does he convince you?   **2.** In a review of the book in which this essay appeared, a critic accused Schell of overstating his point and trying to influence readers with fear and intimidation. Do you agree with this criticism? Explain.   **3.** Do you think that essays such as "The Fate of the Earth" can change the way scientists and politicians as well as ordinary citizens approach science and technology? Explain.

The Yellow Wall-Paper

CHARLOTTE PERKINS GILMAN

Charlotte Perkins Gilman (1860–1935) was a social critic and feminist who wrote extensively about the need for equality in society, especially about women's need for economic independence. Born in Hartford, Connecticut, Gilman first worked as an art teacher and commercial artist. After a nervous breakdown following the birth of her daughter, and a failed marriage, she began to write on feminist issues. Her nonfiction includes *Women and Economics* (1898), *Concerning Children* (1900), and *The Man-Made World* (1911). Her novels include *Herland* (1915) and *With Her in Ourland* (1916). The short story "The Yellow Wall-Paper" (1899) describes the state of mind of a woman suffering from depression after childbirth.

It is very seldom that mere ordinary people like John and myself secure ancestral halls for the summer. 1

A colonial mansion, a hereditary estate, I would say a haunted house, and reach the height of romantic felicity—but that would be asking too much of fate! 2

Still I will proudly declare that there is something queer about it. 3

Else, why should it be let so cheaply? And why have stood so long untenanted? 4

John laughs at me, of course, but one expects that in marriage. 5

John is practical in the extreme. He has no patience with faith, an intense horror of superstition, and he scoffs openly at any talk of things not to be felt and seen and put down in figures. 6

John is a physician, and *perhaps*—(I would not say it to a living soul, of course, but this is dead paper and a great relief to my mind—) *perhaps* that is one reason I do not get well faster. 7

You see he does not believe I am sick! 8

And what can one do? 9

ADDITIONAL QUESTIONS FOR RESPONDING TO READING

1. What does the figure underneath the wall-paper represent?
2. In the story, how do men act toward women? Give examples to support your conclusion.
3. Why do you think the narrator does not challenge the men who are patronizing her? Would the women you know act the same way? Explain.

If a physician of high standing, and one's own husband, assures friends and relatives that there is really nothing the matter with one but temporary nervous depression—a slight hysterical tendency—what is one to do? 10

My brother is also a physician, and also of high standing, and he says the same thing. 11

So I take phosphates[1] or phosphites—whichever it is, and tonics, and journeys, and air, and exercise, and am absolutely forbidden to "work" until I am well again. 12

Personally, I disagree with their ideas. 13

Personally, I believe that congenial work, with excitement and change, would do me good. 14

But what is one to do? 15

I did write for a while in spite of them; but it *does* exhaust me a good deal—having to be so sly about it, or else meet with heavy opposition. 16

I sometimes fancy that in my condition if I had less opposition and more society and stimulus—but John says the very worst thing I can do is to think about my condition, and I confess it always makes me feel bad. 17

So I will let it alone and talk about the house. 18

The most beautiful place! It is quite alone, standing well back from the road, quite three miles from the village. It makes me think of English places that you read about, for there are hedges and walls and gates that lock, and lots of separate little houses for the gardeners and people. 19

There is a *delicious* garden! I never saw such a garden—large and shady, full of box-bordered paths, and lined with long grape-covered arbors with seats under them. 20

There were greenhouses, too, but they are all broken now. 21

There was some legal trouble, I believe, something about the heirs and co-heirs; anyhow, the place has been empty for years. 22

That spoils my ghostliness, I am afraid, but I don't care—there is something strange about the house—I can feel it. 23

I even said so to John one moonlight evening, but he said what I felt was a *draught*, and shut the window. 24

I get unreasonably angry with John sometimes. I'm sure I never used to be so sensitive. I think it is due to this nervous condition. 25

But John says if I feel so, I shall neglect proper self-control; so I take pains to control myself—before him, at least, and that makes me very tired. 26

---

[1]Phosphates are carbonated beverages of water, flavoring, and phosphoric acid believed to have medicinal properties. [Eds.]

I don't like our room a bit. I wanted one downstairs that opened   27
on the piazza and had roses all over the window, and such pretty
old-fashioned chintz hangings! But John would not hear of it.

He said there was only one window and not room for two beds,   28
and no near room for him if he took another.

He is very careful and loving, and hardly lets me stir without   29
special direction.

I have a schedule prescription for each hour in the day; he takes   30
all care from me, and so I feel basely ungrateful not to value it more.

He said we came here solely on my account, that I was to have   31
perfect rest and all the air I could get. "Your exercise depends on
your strength, my dear," said he, "and your food somewhat on your
appetite; but air you can absorb all the time." So we took the nursery
at the top of the house.

It is a big, airy room, the whole floor nearly, with windows that   32
look all ways, and air and sunshine galore. It was nursery first and
then playroom and gymnasium, I should judge; for the windows are
barred for little children, and there are rings and things in the walls.

The paint and paper look as if a boys' school had used it. It is   33
stripped off—the paper—in great patches all around the head of my
bed, about as far as I can reach, and in a great place on the other side
of the room low down. I never saw a worse paper in my life.

One of those sprawling flamboyant patterns committing every   34
artistic sin.

It is dull enough to confuse the eye in following, pronounced   35
enough to constantly irritate and provoke study, and when you follow
the lame uncertain curves for a little distance they suddenly commit
suicide—plunge off at outrageous angles, destroy themselves in
unheard of contradictions.

The color is repellent, almost revolting; a smouldering unclean   36
yellow, strangely faded by the slow-turning sunlight.

It is a dull yet lurid orange in some places, a sickly sulphur tint   37
in others.

No wonder the children hated it! I should hate it myself if I had   38
to live in this room long.

There comes John, and I must put this away,—he hates to have   39
me write a word.

We have been here two weeks, and I haven't felt like writing   40
before, since that first day.

I am sitting by the window now, up in this atrocious nursery,   41
and there is nothing to hinder my writing as much as I please, save
lack of strength.

John is away all day, and even some nights when his cases are   42
serious.

I am glad my case is not serious! 43

But these nervous troubles are dreadfully depressing. 44

John does not know how much I really suffer. He knows there is no *reason* to suffer, and that satisfies him. 45

Of course it is only nervousness. It does weigh on me so not to do my duty in any way! 46

I meant to be such a help to John, such a real rest and comfort, and here I am a comparative burden already! 47

Nobody would believe what an effort it is to do what little I am able,—to dress and entertain, and order things. 48

It is fortunate Mary is so good with the baby. Such a dear baby! 49

And yet I *cannot* be with him, it makes me so nervous. 50

I suppose John never was nervous in his life. He laughs at me so about this wall-paper! 51

At first he meant to repaper the room, but afterwards he said that I was letting it get the better of me, and that nothing was worse for a nervous patient than to give way to such fancies. 52

He said that after the wall-paper was changed it would be the heavy bedstead, and then the barred windows, and then that gate at the head of the stairs, and so on. 53

"You know the place is doing you good," he said, "and really, dear, I don't care to renovate the house just for a three months' rental." 54

"Then do let us go downstairs," I said, "there are such pretty rooms there." 55

Then he took me in his arms and called me a blessed little goose, and said he would go down cellar, if I wished, and have it white-washed into the bargain. 56

But he is right enough about the beds and windows and things. 57

It is an airy and comfortable room as any one need wish, and, of course, I would not be so silly as to make him uncomfortable just for a whim. 58

I'm really getting quite fond of the big room, all but that horrid paper. 59

Out of one window I can see the garden, those mysterious deep-shaded arbors, the riotous old-fashioned flowers, and bushes and gnarly trees. 60

Out of another I get a lovely view of the bay and a little private wharf belonging to the estate. There is a beautiful shaded lane that runs down there from the house. I always fancy I see people walking in these numerous paths and arbors, but John has cautioned me not to give way to fancy in the least. He says that with my imaginative power and habit of story-making, a nervous weakness like mine is sure to lead to all manner of excited fancies, and that I ought to use my will and good sense to check the tendency. So I try. 61

I think sometimes that if I were only well enough to write a little 62
it would relieve the press of ideas and rest me.

But I find I get pretty tired when I try. 63

It is so discouraging not to have any advice and companionship 64
about my work. When I get really well, John says we will ask Cousin
Henry and Julia down for a long visit; but he says he would as soon
put fireworks in my pillow-case as to let me have those stimulating
people about now.

I wish I could get well faster. 65

But I must not think about that. This paper looks to me as if it 66
knew what a vicious influence it had!

There is a recurrent spot where the pattern lolls like a broken 67
neck and two bulbous eyes stare at you upside down.

I get positively angry with the impertinence of it and the ever- 68
lastingness. Up and down and sideways they crawl, and those absurd,
unblinking eyes are everywhere. There is one place where two
breadths didn't match, and the eyes go all up and down the line, one
a little higher than the other.

I never saw so much expression in an inanimate thing before, 69
and we all know how much expression they have! I used to lie awake
as a child and get more entertainment and terror out of blank walls
and plain furniture than most children could find in a toy-store.

I remember what a kindly wink the knobs of our big, old bureau 70
used to have, and there was one chair that always seemed like a
strong friend.

I used to feel that if any of the other things looked too fierce I 71
could always hop into that chair and be safe.

The furniture in this room is no worse than inharmonious, how- 72
ever, for we had to bring it all from downstairs. I suppose when this
was used as a playroom they had to take the nursery things out, and
no wonder! I never saw such ravages as the children have made here.

The wall-paper, as I said before, is torn off in spots, and it sticketh 73
closer than a brother—they must have had perseverance as well as
hatred.

Then the floor is scratched and gouged and splintered, the plaster 74
itself is dug out here and there, and this great heavy bed which is all
we found in the room, looks as if it had been through the wars.

But I don't mind it a bit—only the paper. 75

There comes John's sister. Such a dear girl as she is, and so careful 76
of me! I must not let her find me writing.

She is a perfect and enthusiastic housekeeper, and hopes for no 77
better profession. I verily believe she thinks it is the writing which
made me sick!

But I can write when she is out, and see her a long way off from 78
these windows.

COLLABORATIVE ACTIVITY

Ask different groups of students to rewrite this story from various other characters' points of view—in the voice of John, Jennie, the narrator's brother, perhaps even the figure underneath the wallpaper. When discussing the various versions with the class, comment on the importance of first-person narrative in the story and what effect it creates.

There is one that commands the road, a lovely shaded winding 79
road, and one that just looks off over the country. A lovely country,
too, full of great elms and velvet meadows.

This wall-paper has a kind of sub-pattern in a different shade, a 80
particularly irritating one, for you can only see it in certain lights,
and not clearly then.

But in the places where it isn't faded and where the sun is just 81
so—I can see a strange, provoking, formless sort of figure, that seems
to skulk about behind that silly and conspicuous front design.

There's sister on the stairs! 82

Well, the Fourth of July is over! The people are all gone and I am 83
tired out. John thought it might do me good to see a little company,
so we just had mother and Nellie and the children down for a week.

Of course I didn't do a thing. Jennie sees to everything now. 84

But it tired me all the same. 85

John says if I don't pick up faster he shall send me to Weir Mitchell[2] 86
in the fall.

But I don't want to go there at all. I had a friend who was in his 87
hands once, and she says he is just like John and my brother, only
more so!

Besides, it is such an undertaking to go so far. 88

I don't feel as if it was worth while to turn my hand over for 89
anything, and I'm getting dreadfully fretful and querulous.

I cry at nothing, and cry most of the time. 90

Of course I don't when John is here, or anybody else, but when 91
I am alone.

And I am alone a good deal just now. John is kept in town very 92
often by serious cases, and Jennie is good and lets me alone when I
want her to.

So I walk a little in the garden or down that lovely lane, sit on 93
the porch under the roses, and lie down up here a good deal.

I'm getting really fond of the room in spite of the wall-paper. 94
Perhaps *because* of the wall-paper.

It dwells in my mind so! 95

I lie here on this great immovable bed—it is nailed down, I 96
believe—and follow that pattern about by the hour. It is as good as
gymnastics, I assure you. I start, we'll say, at the bottom, down in
the corner over there where it has not been touched, and I determine
for the thousandth time that I *will* follow that pointless pattern to
some sort of a conclusion.

---

[2]Silas Weir Mitchell (1829–1914), a Philadelphia neurologist-psychologist who introduced the
"rest cure" for nervous diseases. [Eds.]

I know a little of the principle of design, and I know this thing 97
was not arranged on any laws of radiation, or alternation, or repetition, or symmetry, or anything else that I ever heard of.

It is repeated, of course, by the breadths, but not otherwise. 98

Looked at in one way each breadth stands alone, the bloated 99
curves and flourishes—a kind of "debased Romanesque"[3]—with
delirium tremens[4] go waddling up and down in isolated columns of
fatuity.

But, on the other hand, they connect diagonally, and the 100
sprawling outlines run off in great slanting waves of optic horror, like
a lot of wallowing seaweeds in full chase.

The whole thing goes horizontally, too, at least it seems so, and 101
I exhaust myself in trying to distinguish the order of its going in that
direction.

They have used a horizontal breadth for a frieze,[5] and that adds 102
wonderfully to the confusion.

There is one end of the room where it is almost intact, and there, 103
when the crosslights fade and the low sun shines directly upon it, I
can almost fancy radiation after all,—the interminable grotesques
seem to form around a common center and rush off in headlong
plunges of equal distraction.

It makes me tired to follow it. I will take a nap I guess. 104

I don't know why I should write this. 105
I don't want to. 106
I don't feel able. 107
And I know John would think it absurd. But I *must* say what I 108
feel and think in some way—it is such a relief!

But the effort is getting to be greater than the relief. 109
Half the time now I am awfully lazy, and lie down ever so much. 110
John says I mustn't lose my strength, and has me take cod liver 111
oil and lots of tonics and things, to say nothing of ale and wine and
rare meat.

Dear John! He loves me very dearly, and hates to have me sick. 112
I tried to have a real earnest reasonable talk with him the other day,
and tell him how I wish he would let me go and make a visit to Cousin
Henry and Julia.

But he said I wasn't able to go, nor able to stand it after I got 113
there; and I did not make out a very good case for myself, for I was
crying before I had finished.

---

[3] Art characterized by solemnity, decorativeness, and symbolism. [Eds.]
[4] Mental confusion caused by alcohol poisoning and characterized by physical tremors and
hallucinations. [Eds.]
[5] A richly ornamented band. [Eds.]

It is getting to be a great effort for me to think straight. Just this 114
nervous weakness I suppose.

And dear John gathered me up in his arms, and just carried me 115
upstairs and laid me on the bed, and sat by me and read to me till it
tired my head.

He said I was his darling and his comfort and all he had, and 116
that I must take care of myself for his sake, and keep well.

He says no one but myself can help me out of it, that I must use 117
my will and self-control and not let any silly fancies run away with me.

There's one comfort, the baby is well and happy, and does not 118
have to occupy this nursery with the horrid wall-paper.

If we had not used it, that blessed child would have! What a 119
fortunate escape! Why, I wouldn't have a child of mine, an impressionable little thing, live in such a room for worlds.

I never thought of it before, but it is lucky that John kept me here 120
after all, I can stand it so much easier than a baby, you see.

Of course I never mention it to them any more—I am too wise,— 121
but I keep watch of it all the same.

There are things in that paper that nobody knows but me, or ever 122
will.

Behind that outside pattern the dim shapes get clearer every day. 123

It is always the same shape, only very numerous. 124

And it is like a woman stooping down and creeping about behind 125
that pattern. I don't like it a bit. I wonder—I begin to think—I wish
John would take me away from here!

It is so hard to talk with John about my case, because he is so 126
wise, and because he loves me so.

But I tried it last night. 127

It was moonlight. The moon shines in all around just as the sun 128
does.

I hate to see it sometimes, it creeps so slowly, and always comes 129
in by one window or another.

John was asleep and I hated to waken him, so I kept still and 130
watched the moonlight on that undulating wall-paper till I felt
creepy.

The faint figure behind seemed to shake the pattern, just as if 131
she wanted to get out.

I got up softly and went to feel and see if the paper *did* move, 132
and when I came back John was awake.

"What is it, little girl?" he said. "Don't go walking about like 133
that—you'll get cold."

I thought it was a good time to talk, so I told him that I really 134
was not gaining here, and that I wished he would take me away.

"Why, darling!" said he, "our lease will be up in three weeks, 135
and I can't see how to leave before.

"The repairs are not done at home, and I cannot possibly leave 136
town just now. Of course if you were in any danger, I could and
would, but you really are better, dear, whether you can see it or not.
I am a doctor, dear, and I know. You are gaining flesh and color,
your appetite is better, I feel really much easier about you."

"I don't weigh a bit more," said I, "nor as much; and my appetite 137
may be better in the evening when you are here, but it is worse in
the morning when you are away!"

"Bless her little heart!" said he with a big hug, "she shall be as 138
sick as she pleases! But now let's improve the shining hours by going
to sleep, and talk about it in the morning!"

"And you won't go away?" I asked gloomily. 139

"Why, how can I, dear? It is only three weeks more and then we 140
will take a nice little trip of a few days while Jennie is getting the
house ready. Really dear you are better!"

"Better in body perhaps—" I began, and stopped short, for he 141
sat up straight and looked at me with such a stern, reproachful look
that I could not say another word.

"My darling," said he, "I beg of you, for my sake and for our 142
child's sake, as well as for your own, that you will never for one
instant let that idea enter your mind! There is nothing so dangerous,
so fascinating, to a temperament like yours. It is a false and foolish
fancy. Can you not trust me as a physician when I tell you so?"

So of course I said no more on that score, and we went to sleep 143
before long. He thought I was asleep first, but I wasn't, and lay there
for hours trying to decide whether that front pattern and the back
pattern really did move together or separately.

On a pattern like this, by daylight, there is a lack of sequence, a 144
defiance of law, that is a constant irritant to a normal mind.

The color is hideous enough, and unreliable enough, and infu- 145
riating enough, but the pattern is torturing.

You think you have mastered it, but just as you get well underway 146
in following, it turns back-somersault and there you are. It slaps you
in the face, knocks you down, and tramples upon you. It is like a bad
dream.

The outside pattern is a florid arabesque, reminding one of a 147
fungus. If you can imagine a toadstool in joints, an interminable string
of toadstools, budding and sprouting in endless convolutions—why,
that is something like it.

That is, sometimes! 148

There is one marked peculiarity about this paper, a thing nobody   149
seems to notice but myself, and that is that it changes as the light
changes.

When the sun shoots in through the east window—I always   150
watch for that first long, straight ray—it changes so quickly that I
never can quite believe it.

That is why I watch it always.   151

By moonlight—the moon shines in all night when there is a   152
moon—I wouldn't know it was the same paper.

At night in any kind of light, in twilight, candlelight, lamplight,   153
and worst of all by moonlight, it becomes bars! The outside pattern
I mean, and the woman behind it is as plain as can be.

I didn't realize for a long time what the thing was that showed   154
behind, that dim sub-pattern, but now I am quite sure it is a woman.

By daylight she is subdued, quiet. I fancy it is the pattern that   155
keeps her so still. It is so puzzling. It keeps me quiet by the hour.

I lie down ever so much now. John says it is good for me, and   156
to sleep all I can.

Indeed he started the habit by making me lie down for an hour   157
after each meal.

It is a very bad habit I am convinced, for you see I don't sleep.   158

And that cultivates deceit, for I don't tell them I'm awake—O no!   159

The fact is I am getting a little afraid of John.   160

He seems very queer sometimes, and even Jennie has an inex-   161
plicable look.

It strikes me occasionally, just as a scientific hypothesis,—that   162
perhaps it is the paper!

I have watched John when he did not know I was looking, and   163
come into the room suddenly on the most innocent excuses, and I've
caught him several times *looking at the paper!* And Jennie too. I caught
Jennie with her hand on it once.

She didn't know I was in the room, and when I asked her in a   164
quiet, a very quiet voice, with the most restrained manner possible,
what she was doing with the paper—she turned around as if she had
been caught stealing, and looked quite angry—asked me why I should
frighten her so!

Then she said that the paper stained everything it touched, that   165
she had found yellow smooches on all my clothes and John's, and
she wished we would be more careful!

Did not that sound innocent? But I know she was studying that   166
pattern, and I am determined that nobody shall find it out but myself!

Life is very much more exciting now than it used to be. You see   167
I have something more to expect, to look forward to, to watch. I really
do eat better, and am more quiet than I was.

John is so pleased to see me improve! He laughed a little the other 168
day, and said I seemed to be flourishing in spite of my wall-paper.

I turned it off with a laugh. I had no intention of telling him it 169
was *because* of the wallpaper—he would make fun of me. He might
even want to take me away.

I don't want to leave now until I have found it out. There is a 170
week more, and I think that will be enough.

I'm feeling ever so much better! I don't sleep much at night, for 171
it is so interesting to watch developments; but I sleep a good deal in
the daytime.

In the daytime it is tiresome and perplexing. 172

There are always new shoots on the fungus, and new shades of 173
yellow all over it. I cannot keep count of them, though I have tried
conscientiously.

It is the strangest yellow, that wall-paper! It makes me think of 174
all the yellow things I ever saw—not beautiful ones like buttercups,
but old foul, bad yellow things.

But there is something else about that paper—the smell! I noticed 175
it the moment we came into the room, but with so much air and sun
it was not bad. Now we have had a week of fog and rain, and whether
the windows are open or not, the smell is here.

It creeps all over the house. 176

I find it hovering in the dining-room, skulking in the parlor, 177
hiding in the hall, lying in wait for me on the stairs.

It gets into my hair. 178

Even when I go to ride, if I turn my head suddenly and surprise 179
it—there is that smell!

Such a peculiar odor, too! I have spent hours in trying to analyze 180
it, to find what it smelled like.

It is not bad—at first, and very gentle, but quite the subtlest, most 181
enduring odor I ever met.

In this damp weather it is awful, I wake up in the night and find 182
it hanging over me.

It used to disturb me at first. I thought seriously of burning the 183
house—to reach the smell.

But now I am used to it. The only thing I can think of that it is 184
like is the *color* of the paper! A yellow smell.

There is a very funny mark on this wall, low down, near the 185
mopboard. A streak that runs round the room. It goes behind every
piece of furniture, except the bed, a long, straight, even *smooch*, as if
it had been rubbed over and over.

I wonder how it was done and who did it, and what they did it 186
for. Round and round and round—round and round and round!—
it makes me dizzy!

I really have discovered something at last. 187

Through watching so much at night, when it changes so, I have 188 finally found out.

The front pattern *does* move—and no wonder! The woman behind 189 shakes it!

Sometimes I think there are a great many women behind, and 190 sometimes only one, and she crawls around fast, and her crawling shakes it all over.

Then in the very bright spots she keeps still, and in the very 191 shady spots she just takes hold of the bars and shakes them hard.

And she is all the time trying to climb through. But nobody could 192 climb through that pattern—it strangles so; I think that is why it has so many heads.

They get through, and then the pattern strangles them off and 193 turns them upside down, and makes their eyes white!

If those heads were covered or taken off it would not be half so 194 bad.

I think that woman gets out in the daytime! 195

And I'll tell you why—privately—I've seen her! 196

I can see her out of every one of my windows! 197

It is the same woman, I know, for she is always creeping, and 198 most women do not creep by daylight.

I see her in that long shaded lane, creeping up and down. I see 199 her in those dark grape arbors, creeping all around the garden.

I see her on that long road under the trees, creeping along, and 200 when a carriage comes she hides under the blackberry vines.

I don't blame her a bit. It must be very humiliating to be caught 201 creeping by daylight!

I always lock the door when I creep by daylight. I can't do it at 202 night, for I know John would suspect something at once.

And John is so queer now, that I don't want to irritate him. I 203 wish he would take another room! Besides, I don't want anybody to get that women out at night but myself.

I often wonder if I could see her out of all the windows at once. 204

But, turn as fast as I can, I can only see out of one at one time. 205

And though I always see her, she *may* be able to creep faster than 206 I can turn!

I have watched her sometimes away off in the open country, 207 creeping as fast as a cloud shadow in a high wind.

If only that top pattern could be gotten off from the under one! 208 I mean to try it, little by little

I have found out another funny thing, but I shan't tell it this time! 209 It does not do to trust people too much.

There are only two more days to get this paper off, and I believe 210
John is beginning to notice. I don't like the look in his eyes.

And I heard him ask Jennie a lot of professional questions about 211
me. She had a very good report to give.

She said I slept a good deal in the daytime. 212

John knows I don't sleep very well at night, for all I'm so quiet! 213

He asked me all sorts of questions, too, and pretended to be very 214
loving and kind.

As if I couldn't see through him! 215

Still, I don't wonder he acts so, sleeping under this paper for 216
three months.

It only interests me, but I feel sure John and Jennie are secretly 217
affected by it.

Hurrah! This is the last day, but it is enough. John to stay in town 218
over night, and won't be out until this evening.

Jennie wanted to sleep with me—the sly thing! But I told her I 219
should undoubtedly rest better for a night all alone.

That was clever, for really I wasn't alone a bit! As soon as it was 220
moonlight and that poor thing began to crawl and shake the pattern,
I got up and ran to help her.

I pulled and she shook, I shook and she pulled, and before 221
morning we had peeled off yards of that paper.

A strip about as high as my head and half around the room. 222

And then when the sun came and that awful pattern began to 223
laugh at me, I declared I would finish it to-day!

We go away to-morrow, and they are moving all my furniture 224
down again to leave things as they were before.

Jennie looked at the wall in amazement, but I told her merrily 225
that I did it out of pure spite at the vicious thing.

She laughed and said she wouldn't mind doing it herself, but I 226
must not get tired.

How she betrayed herself that time! 227

But I am here, and no person touches this paper but me,—not 228
alive!

She tried to get me out of the room—it was too patent! But I said 229
it was so quiet and empty and clean now that I believed I would lie
down again and sleep all I could; and not to wake me even for
dinner—I would call when I woke.

So now she is gone, and the servants are gone, and the things 230
are gone, and there is nothing left but that great bedstead nailed
down, with the canvas mattress we found on it.

We shall sleep downstairs to-night, and take the boat home to- 231
morrow.

I quite enjoy the room, now it is bare again. 232

WRITING SUGGESTION

Write a contemporary first-person version of "The Yellow Wall-Paper." Make the setting the maternity floor of a modern hospital. In what ways would the doctor's behavior be different? How would it be the same? How would the narrator respond to the doctor?

How those children did tear about here! 233

This bedstead is fairly gnawed! 234

But I must get to work. 235

I have locked the door and thrown the key down into the front 236
path.

I don't want to go out, and I don't want to have anybody come 237
in, till John comes.

I want to astonish him. 238

I've got a rope up here that even Jennie did not find. If that woman 239
does get out, and tries to get away, I can tie her!

But I forgot I could not reach far without anything to stand on! 240

This bed will *not* move! 241

I tried to lift and push it until I was lame, and then I got so angry 242
I bit off a little piece at one corner—but it hurt my teeth.

Then I peeled off all the paper I could reach standing on the floor. 243
It sticks horribly and the pattern just enjoys it! All those strangled
heads and bulbous eyes and waddling fungus growths just shriek
with derision!

I am getting angry enough to do something desperate. To jump 244
out of the window would be admirable exercise, but the bars are too
strong even to try.

Besides I wouldn't do it. Of course not. I know well enough that 245
a step like this is improper and might be misconstrued.

I don't like to *look* out of the windows even—there are so many 246
of those creeping women, and they creep so fast.

I wonder if they all come out of that wall-paper as I did? 247

But I am securely fastened now by my well-hidden rope—you 248
don't get *me* out in the road there!

I suppose I shall have to get back behind the pattern when it 249
comes night, and that is hard!

It is so pleasant to be out in this great room and creep around as 250
I please!

I don't want to go outside. I won't, even if Jennie asks me to. 251

For outside you have to creep on the ground, and everything is 252
green instead of yellow.

But here I can creep smoothly on the floor, and my shoulder just 253
fits in that long smooch around the wall, so I cannot lose my way.

Why there's John at the door! 254

It is no use, young man, you can't open it! 255

How he does call and pound! 256

Now he's crying for an axe. 257

It would be a shame to break down that beautiful door! 258

"John dear!" said I in the gentlest voice, "the key is down by the 259
front steps, under a plaintain leaf!"

That silenced him for a few moments. 250

Then he said—very quietly indeed. "Open the door, my darling!" 261

"I can't," said I. "The key is down by the front door under a 262
plaintain leaf!"

And then I said it again, several times, very gently and slowly, 263
and said it so often that he had to go and see, and he got it of course,
and came in. He stopped short by the door.

"What is the matter?" he cried. "For God's sake, what are you 264
doing!"

I kept on creeping just the same, but I looked at him over my 265
shoulder.

"I've got out at last," said I, "in spite of you and Jane. And I've 266
pulled off most of the paper, so you can't put me back!"

Now why should that man have fainted? But he did, and right 267
across my path by the wall, so that I had to creep over him every
time!

RESPONDING TO READING

1. The narrator is suffering from postpartum depression, a condition that
commonly occurs in women who have just given birth. How much insight
does she have into her own situation? What other factors could have contributed to her depression? **2.** What is the attitude of the doctors toward
the narrator? In what ways are the doctors in the story like and unlike doctors
you have known? **3.** Why do you think the doctors discourage the narrator from writing? What other parts of her treatment strike you as odd or
misguided? In what ways do you think the doctors' ideas about gender and
disease influence their judgment?

Moon Landing

W. H. AUDEN

W. H. Auden (1907–1973) was born in York, England, and became
a naturalized American citizen in 1946. He served as an ambulance
driver in the Spanish Civil War and then traveled extensively in
Europe and Asia. His many awards include the Pulitzer Prize and
the National Book Award. Auden's well-crafted poems are noted
both for their social and moral concerns and for their wit. His *Collected
Poems* appeared in 1976. "Moon Landing" describes the urge to
pursue technology as "our lack of decorum" and hopes that, even
as we make a "mess called History," our artists will somehow
redeem us.

It's natural the Boys should whoop it up for
so huge a phallic triumph, an adventure
   it would not have occurred to women
     to think worth while, made possible only

because we like huddling in gangs and knowing   5
the exact time: yes, our sex may in fairness
   hurrah the deed, although the motives
     that primed it were somewhat less than *menschlich*.[1]

A grand gesture. But what does it period?[2]
What does it osse?[3] We were always adroiter   10
   with objects than lives, and more facile
     at courage than kindness: from the moment

the first flint was flaked this landing was merely
a matter of time. But our selves, like Adam's,
   still don't fit us exactly, modern   15
     only in this—our lack of decorum.

Homer's heroes were certainly no braver
than our Trio, but more fortunate: Hector
   was excused the insult of having
     his valor covered by television.   20

Worth *going* to see? I can well believe it.
Worth *seeing*? Mneh! I once rode through a desert
   and was not charmed: give me a watered
     lively garden, remote from blatherers

about the New, the von Brauns[4] and their ilk, where   25
on August mornings I can count the morning
   glories, where to die has a meaning,
     and no engine can shift my perspective.

Unsmudged, thank God, my Moon still queens the Heavens
as She ebbs and fulls, a Presence to glop at,   30
   Her Old Man, made of grit not protein,
     still visits my Austrian several

---

[1]Human; humane. [Eds.]
[2]Indicate. [Eds.]
[3]Prophesy. [Eds.]
[4]German engineer Wernher von Braun (1912–77) played a prominent role in rocketry, first in Nazi Germany and, after World War II, in the United States. [Eds.]

with His old detachment, and the old warnings
still have power to scare me: Hybris[5] comes to
   an ugly finish, Irreverence   *35*
   is a greater oaf than Superstition.

Our apparatniks[6] will continue making
the usual squalid mess called History:
   all we can pray for is that artists,
   chefs and saints may still appear to blithe it.   *40*

RESPONDING TO READING

1. What does the speaker mean when he says, "It's natural the Boys should whoop it up for / so huge a phallic triumph, an adventure / it would not have occurred to women / to think worth while" (lines 1–4)? Is he serious? Do you agree with these sentiments? Why or why not?   **2.** Besides being a satellite or a celestial body, what else does the moon suggest to you? Does Auden's speaker make the same or similar associations?   **3.** What does the speaker think of science and technology? Does his opinion conform to or conflict with your ideas about the space program? Do recent setbacks in the American space program have any effect on your reactions to the poem? Explain.

WRITING SUGGESTIONS

1. Write an essay arguing for or against the need for the United States to assume a greater role in space exploration.
2. Write a poem in which you celebrate or criticize the moon landing.

ANSWERS TO RESPONDING TO READING

1. The speaker denigrates the moon landing's achievement, calling it a fulfillment of male fantasy and ego.
2. Poets often consider the moon a feminine symbol. The speaker alludes to this image when he says, "my Moon still queens the Heavens." Students will probably not make these associations, but they will certainly agree that the moon has a powerful symbolic function. Help them see that their associations do not supplant, but add to, the more traditional associations that Auden presents.
3. The speaker places no faith in science and technology because of people's inability to change their basic nature. Recent setbacks in the American space program merely confirm the essentially human quality that undergirds any scientific effort.

---

[5]A varient spelling of *hubris*, meaning overwhelming pride or self-confidence; arrogance. [Eds.]
[6]Officials blindly devoted to their superiors or to authority. [Eds.]

WRITING: SCIENCE AND MEDICINE

1. Jonathan Schell in "The Fate of the Earth" warns readers of future consequences if a present trend is carried to its logical conclusion. What other trends do you think we should be warned about? Choose one such trend, and write an essay explaining why you see it as a threat.

2. A number of writers in this chapter believe that science cannot solve many of society's most pressing problems. In fact, some of them think that science may be the cause of these problems. Do you agree? Explain why or why not.

3. In his poem, Auden questions the wisdom of the 1969 moon landing. Write an essay in which you discuss whether the United States should or should not continue space exploration.

4. Since Loren Eiseley wrote "The Bird and the Machine," computers have been improved, and many scientists seriously talk about the feasibility of artificial intelligence. What human traits or abilities do you believe computers will (and will not) eventually possess? Write an essay explaining your ideas.

5. Charles L Mee, Jr., in "The Summer Before Salk," Perri Klass in "India," and Richard Selzer in "A Mask on the Face of Death" all consider the limitations of medical science. Choose a problem having to do with medical science and discuss how it presents challenges for both medical personnel and the general public.

6. Identify a technological advance that has changed your life. In what way has this development affected you—and, possibly, society as a whole?

7. Do you agree with Lewis Thomas when he says that most college and high school science courses misrepresent the true nature of science? Write an essay in which you discuss how your science courses represented the nature of science. Did they present the "big arguments," or did they present information as if it were engraved in stone?

8. In "The Yellow Wall-Paper," Charlotte Perkins Gilman describes the progression of a woman's mental illness. The problem is made worse by society's preconceptions about gender. Do you believe attitudes about gender—or race or class—still affect medical or scientific judgment? Give examples.

9.   Do you think scientists and engineers should try to prevent their work from being used in ways they consider immoral? For example, does a medical researcher who developed a certain type of laser have a moral obligation to oppose its use in the guidance system of a bomb? Write an essay in which you discuss your ideas on this subject.

11
NATURE AND THE ENVIRONMENT

CONFRONTING THE ISSUES

The interaction between human beings and the environment can often be as complicated as nature itself. Consider, for example, the battle that is currently raging in the Pacific Northwest between environmentalists and loggers. For the past several years environmentalists have been trying to discourage loggers from cutting down the old-growth forests that exist throughout the Northwest. They have tried to convince Congress to set aside millions of acres to preserve a precious natural resource and to stop loggers from destroying the only known habitat of the spotted owl, an endangered species. The loggers argue that jobs are more important than either the forest or the spotted owl. They say that successful efforts by environmentalists to restrict logging is combining with automation to cost them jobs. Eventually, they fear, environmental pressure may destroy the entire logging industry.

Recently, the debate became more complicated when the National Cancer Institute released the results of a study that showed that a new drug, taxol, has been found to reduce the size of tumors in women suffering from advanced ovarian cancer. The main source of this drug is the bark of the Pacific yew, a tree that grows in limited numbers throughout the old-growth forests in the Pacific Northwest. Because it takes the bark of six 100-year-old trees to produce enough medication to treat one patient, the environmental impact of the commercial production of taxol could be great. Although environmentalists acknowledge the benefits of the drug, they warn that a program to make large quantities of taxol could wipe out the Pacific yews. For this reason, they urge scientists to concentrate on making a synthetic version of taxol. For their part, loggers have seized upon this issue to reinforce their point that logging in the old-growth forests should not be restricted.

Ask students where they stand on this debate. Discourage them from giving easy answers to the complex problems that both the loggers and the environmentalists have defined. Is the welfare of the spotted owl worth the jobs of loggers? What about the welfare of the loggers' families, and the welfare of the thousands of other people who depend on the money that the logging industry generates? Is the possibility of saving a few lives worth the destruction of all the Pacific yews? Ask students to consider the point that environmentalists make that once a species is extinct it can never be re-created. Remind them that there is an environmental lesson to be learned from this debate. The Pacific yew, until recently considered a weed, is now quite valuable. The same may be true for the spotted owl or for the old-growth forests.

In his poem "Mother Earth: Her Whales," Gary Snyder makes a plea to preserve the environment for future generations. For Snyder nature is awe inspiring but fragile, and once damaged—by an oil spill or through overuse—it can never be wholly restored. The price we pay for not respecting nature, for turning it into "parking space for fifty thousand trucks," is the disappearance of scores of species each year, the gradual destruction of the rain forests, and ultimately the extinction of life on earth. Not all the writers in this chapter take Snyder's extreme view, but many of them, despite their differences, acknowledge his call for human beings to learn to live in harmony with the natural environment.

Over a hundred years ago essayist Henry David Thoreau, already sensing the implications of industrialization and expansionism, took up residence in the woods next to Walden Pond to reestablish his connections with the natural environment. (The irony of Thoreau's actions became obvious much later when in 1990 a developer presented a plan to the city council to clear the area around Walden Pond for residential development.) To one extent or another, *Walden*, Thoreau's account of his retreat, has influenced most of the writers in this section. All of them tend to see civilization as a destructive force. Like Thoreau, they are concerned with examining the complex, changing relationship between human beings and the environment.

Apart from its majesty, nature serves as a counterforce to the rigors of the technological culture in which many of us live. In such phenomena as grass pushing up through cracks in the pavement or the dead animals that litter the roads, nature reminds us that another, larger world exists outside our limited human sphere. It reminds us that part of the price that we pay for living in society is our estrangement from the natural environment. Of course, we are not estranged in the literal sense of the word, for we are surrounded by nature: the trees in our parks, the animals we keep as pets, and the gardens that we maintain in our yards. But these are a long way from the untamed nature that many of the authors in this section discuss—the grizzly, the wolverine, and the eagle, for example. The nature with which we have become familiar has become so domesticated that we have ceased to see it as something alien or exotic. Bears are presented as cartoon characters, tigers are pitchmen for cereal companies, and the great grasslands that once covered the middle part of the United States have been transformed into quarter-acre building lots.

Despite the gulf that seems to separate contemporary men and women from the natural environment, however, one thing remains clear: Nature continues to affect us in subtle and mysterious ways. For John McPhee in "The Grizzly" and Annie Dillard in "Sight into Insight," as well as for Gary Synder in "Mother Earth: Her Whales," nature can be refreshing and invigorating as well as fierce and mysterious. As Barry Lopez says in "Landscape and Narrative," "Each individual . . . undertakes to order his interior landscape according to the exterior landscape. To succeed in this means to achieve a balanced state of mental health." In this and other ways, we are dependent upon our natural environment, and we have a responsibility—perhaps a duty—to preserve it.

PREPARING TO READ AND WRITE

As you read and prepare to write about the selections in this chapter, consider the following questions:

- What is the writer's attitude toward the natural world?
- Is nature depicted as hostile or friendly?
- Does the writer give an objective or subjective description of nature?
- Do you think the writer is being unrealistically idealistic or romantic in his or her portrayal of nature?
- What relationship does the writer think people have with nature? What does the writer believe are the consequences of being separated from nature?
- Does the writer think people should change the way they relate to nature?
- What effect does contact with nature have on the writer?
- Is the natural environment depicted as just plants and animals, or is it something more?
- What ideas does the writer assume readers have about nature? Does the writer reinforce or challenge your ideas about nature?
- What effect does the writer think civilization has on nature? Do you agree with the writer's conclusions?

Sight into Insight

ANNIE DILLARD

Annie Dillard (see also p. 34), teacher and author, writes with intensity about nature in the Roanoke Valley of Virginia. She often begins essays and paragraphs with a careful description—for instance, of red-winged blackbirds in flight—and then uses questions and speculation to suggest a larger meaning, such as the importance of seeing. In "Sight into Insight" (1974) Dillard ponders the nature hidden in her world and realizes that she sees "only tatters of clearness through a pervading obscurity."

FOR OPENERS

The day before discussing the essay, have students spend fifteen minutes in a natural setting. Instruct them to write down everything they see (or experience through the senses).

ADDITIONAL QUESTIONS FOR RESPONDING TO READING

1. Although Dillard makes no direct reference to belief in God, she describes a "generous hand" that casts "pennies" over the world to be discovered. What sense do you get of Dillard's philosophy of nature and religion?
2. What does Dillard consider "dire poverty" (paragraph 2)? Do you agree?
3. What does Dillard mean when she says that nature "reveal[s]" as well as "conceal[s]" (paragraph 4)?
4. In paragraph 20, Dillard deliberately uses the cliché "blind as a bat." Does she make it work in this context? Explain.
5. In this essay, Dillard does not explicitly focus on protecting the environment. Is such a message implicit in her attitude toward nature? Explain.

When I was six or seven years old, growing up in Pittsburgh, I used to take a penny of my own and hide it for someone else to find. It was a curious compulsion; sadly, I've never been seized by it since. For some reason I always "hid" the penny along the same stretch of sidewalk up the street. I'd cradle it at the roots of a maple, say, or in a hole left by a chipped-off piece of sidewalk. Then I'd take a piece of chalk and, starting at either end of the block, draw huge arrows leading to the penny from both directions. After I learned to write I labeled the arrows "SURPRISE AHEAD" or "MONEY THIS WAY." I was greatly excited, during all this arrowdrawing, at the thought of the first lucky passerby who would receive in this way, regardless of merit, a free gift from the universe. But I never lurked about. I'd go straight home and not give the matter another thought, until, some months later, I would be gripped by the impulse to hide another penny. 1

There are lots of things to see, unwrapped gifts and free surprises. The world is fairly studded and strewn with pennies cast broadside from a generous hand. But—and this is the point—who gets excited by a mere penny? If you follow one arrow, if you crouch motionless on a bank to watch a tremulous ripple thrill on the water, and are rewarded by the sight of a muskrat kit paddling from its den, will you count that sight a chip of copper only, and go your rueful way? It is very dire poverty indeed for a man to be so malnourished and fatigued that he won't stoop to pick up a penny. But if you cultivate a healthy poverty and simplicity, so that finding a penny will make your day, then, since the world is in fact planted in pennies, you have with your poverty bought a lifetime of days. What you see is what you get. 2

Unfortunately, nature is very much a now-you-see-it, now-you-don't affair. A fish flashes, then dissolves in the water before my eyes like so much salt. Deer apparently ascend bodily into heaven; the brightest oriole fades into leaves. These disappearances stun me into 3 stillness and concentration; they say of nature that it conceals with a grand nonchalance, and they say of vision that it is a deliberate gift, the revelation of a dancer who for my eyes only flings away her seven veils.

For nature does reveal as well as conceal: now-you-don't-see-it, 4 now-you-do. For a week this September migrating red-winged blackbirds were feeding heavily down by Tinker Creek at the back of the house. One day I went out to investigate the racket; I walked up to a tree, an Osage orange, and a hundred birds flew away. They simply materialized out of the tree. I saw a tree, then a whisk of color, then a tree again. I walked closer and another hundred blackbirds took flight. Not a branch, not a twig budged: the birds were apparently weightless as well as invisible. Or, it was as if the leaves of the Osage orange had been freed from a spell in the form of red-winged blackbirds; they flew from the tree, caught my eye in the sky, and vanished. When I looked again at the tree, the leaves had reassembled as if nothing had happened. Finally I walked directly to the trunk of the tree and a final hundred, the real diehards, appeared, spread, and vanished. How could so many hide in the tree without my seeing them? The Osage orange, unruffled, looked just as it had looked from the house, when three hundred red-winged blackbirds cried from its crown. I looked upstream where they flew, and they were gone. Searching, I couldn't spot one. I wandered upstream to force them to play their hand, but they'd crossed the creek and scattered. One show to a customer. These appearances catch at my throat; they are the free gifts, the bright coppers at the roots of trees.

It's all a matter of keeping my eyes open. Nature is like one of 5 those line drawings that are puzzles for children: Can you find hidden in the tree a duck, a house, a boy, a bucket, a giraffe and a boot? Specialists can find the most incredibly hidden things. A book I read when I was young recommended an easy way to find caterpillars: you simply find some fresh caterpillar droppings, look up, and there's your caterpillar. More recently an author advised me to set my mind at ease about those piles of cut stems on the ground in grassy fields. Field mice make them; they cut the grass down by degrees to reach the seeds at the head. It seems that when the grass is tightly packed, as in a field of ripe grain, the blade won't topple at a single cut through the stem; instead, the cut stem simply drops vertically, held in the crush of grain. The mouse severs the bottom again and again, the stem keeps dropping an inch at a time, and finally the head is low enough for the mouse to reach the seeds. Meanwhile the mouse is positively littering the field with its little piles of cut stems into which, presumably, the author is constantly stumbling.

TEACHING STRATEGY

Discuss Dillard's capability for focusing on details. Study specific passages as examples (suggestions: Paragraphs 4, 11–13, 17–19, 31).

If I can't see these minutiae, I still try to keep my eyes open. I'm always on the lookout for ant lion traps in sandy soil, monarch pupae near milkweed, skipper larvae in locust leaves. These things are utterly common, and I've not seen one. I bang on hollow trees near water, but so far no flying squirrels have appeared. In flat country I watch every sunset in hopes of seeing the green ray. The green ray is a seldom-seen streak of light that rises from the sun like a spurting fountain at the moment of sunset; it throbs into the sky for two seconds and disappears. One more reason to keep my eyes open. A photography professor at the University of Florida just happened to see a bird die in midflight; it jerked, died, dropped, and smashed on the ground.

I squint at the wind because I read Stewart Edward White: "I have always maintained that if you looked closely enough you could see the wind—the dim, hardly-made-out, fine débris fleeing high in the air." White was an excellent observer, and devoted an entire chapter of *The Mountains* to the subject of seeing deer. "As soon as you can forget the naturally obvious and construct an artificial obvious, then you too will see deer."

But the artificial obvious is hard to see. My eyes account for less than 1 percent of the weight of my head; I'm bony and dense; I see what I expect. I just don't know what the lover knows; I can't see the artificial obvious that those in the know construct. The herpetologist asks the native, "Are there snakes in that ravine?" "No, sir." And the herpetologist comes home with, yessir, three bags full. Are there butterflies on that mountain? Are the bluets in bloom? Are there arrowheads here, or fossil ferns in the shale?

Peeping through my keyhole I see within the range of only about 30 percent of the light that comes from the sun; the rest is infrared and some little ultraviolet, perfectly apparent to many animals, but invisible to me. A nightmare network of ganglia, charged and firing without my knowledge, cuts and splices what I do see, editing it for by brain. Donald E. Carr points out that the sense impressions of one-celled animals are *not* edited for the brain: "This is philosophically interesting in a rather mournful way, since it means that only the simplest animals perceive the universe as it is."

A fog that won't burn away drifts and flows across my field of vision. When you see fog move against a backdrop of deep pines, you don't see the fog itself, but streaks of clearness floating across the air in dark shreds. So I see only tatters of clearness through a pervading obscurity. I can't distinguish the fog from the overcast sky; I can't be sure if the light is direct or reflected. Everywhere darkness and the presence of the unseen appalls. We estimate now that only one atom dances alone in every cubic meter of intergalactic space. I blink and squint. What planet or power yanks Halley's Comet out of orbit? We haven't seen it yet; it's a question of distance, density, and the pallor of reflected light. We rock, cradled in the swaddling band of darkness. Even the simple darkness of night whispers suggestions to the mind. This summer, in August, I stayed at the creek too late.

Where Tinker Creek flows under the sycamore log bridge to the 11 tear-shaped island, it is slow and shallow, fringed thinly in cattail marsh. At this spot an astonishing bloom of life supports vast breeding populations of insects, fish, reptiles, birds, and mammals. On windless summer evenings I stalk along the creek bank or straddle the sycamore log in absolute stillness, watching for muskrats. The night I stayed too late I was hunched on the log staring spellbound at spreading, reflected stains of lilac on the water. A cloud in the sky suddenly lighted as if turned on by a switch; its reflection just as suddenly materialized on the water upstream, flat and floating, so that I couldn't see the creek bottom, or life in the water under the cloud. Downstream, away from the cloud on the water, water turtles smooth as beans were gliding down with the current in a series of easy, weightless push-offs, as men bound on the moon. I didn't know whether to trace the progress of one turtle I was sure of, risking sticking my face in one of the bridge's spider webs made invisible by the gathering dark, or take a chance on seeing the carp, or scan the mudbank in hope of seeing a muskrat, or follow the last of the swallows who caught at my heart and trailed it after them like streamers as they appeared from directly below, under the log, flying upstream with their tails forked, so fast.

But shadows spread and deepened and stayed. After thousands 12 of years we're still strangers to darkness, fearful aliens in an enemy camp with our arms crossed over our chests. I stirred. A land turtle on the bank, startled, hissed the air from its lungs and withdrew to its shell. An uneasy pink here, an unfathomable blue there, gave great suggestion of lurking beings. Things were going on. I couldn't see whether that rustle I heard was a distant rattle-snake, slit-eyed, or a nearby sparrow kicking in the dry flood debris slung at the foot of a willow. Tremendous action roiled the water everywhere I looked, big action, inexplicable. A tremor welled up beside a gaping muskrat burrow in the bank and I caught my breath, but no muskrat appeared. The ripples continued to fan upstream with a steady, powerful thrust. Night was knitting an eyeless mask over my face, and I still sat transfixed. A distant airplane, a delta wing out of nightmare, made a gliding shadow on the creek's bottom that looked like a stingray cruising upstream. At once a black fin slit the pink cloud on the water, shearing it in two. The two halves merged together and seemed to dissolve before my eyes. Darkness pooled in the cleft of the creek and rose, as water collects in a well. Untamed, dreaming lights flickered over the sky. I saw hints of hulking underwater shadows, two pale splashes out of the water, and round ripples rolling close together from a blackened center.

At last I stared upstream where only the deepest violet remained 13 of the cloud, a cloud so high its underbelly still glowed, its feeble color reflected from a hidden sky lighted in turn by a sun halfway to China. And out of that violet, a sudden enormous black body arced over the water. Head and tail, if there was a head and tail, were both submerged in cloud. I saw only one ebony fling, a headlong dive to darkness; then the waters closed, and the lights went out.

I walked home in a shivering daze, up hill and down. Later I lay 14 openmouthed in bed, my arms flung wide at my sides to steady the whirling darkness. At this latitude I'm spinning 836 miles an hour round the earth's axis; I feel my sweeping fall as a breakneck arc like the dive of dolphins, and the hollow rushing of wind raises the hairs on my neck and the side of my face. In orbit around the sun I'm moving 64,800 miles an hour. The solar system as a whole, like a merry-go-round unhinged, spins, bobs, and blinks at the speed of 43,200 miles an hour along a course set east of Hercules.[1] Someone has piped, and we are dancing a tarantella[2] until the sweat pours. I open my eyes and I see dark, muscled forms curl out of water, with flapping gills and flattened eyes. I close my eyes and I see stars, deep stars giving way to deeper stars, deeper stars bowing to deepest stars at the crown of an infinite cone.

"Still," wrote Van Gogh in a letter, "a great deal of light falls on 15 everything." If we are blinded by darkness, we are also blinded by light. Sometimes here in Virginia at sunset low clouds on the southern or northern horizon are completely invisible in the lighted sky. I only know one is there because I can see its reflection in still water. The first time I discovered this mystery I looked from cloud to no-cloud in bewilderment, checking my bearings over and over, thinking maybe the ark of the covenant[3] was just passing by south of Dead Man Mountain. Only much later did I learn the explanation: polarized light from the sky is very much weakened by reflection, but the light in clouds isn't polarized. So invisible clouds pass among visible clouds, till all slide over the mountains; so a greater light extinguishes a lesser as though it didn't exist.

---

[1]A northern constellation. [Eds.]
[2]A wild, uninhibited dance with an increasing tempo. [Eds.]
[3]The sacred wooden chest of the ancient Hebrews, representative of or identified with God. [Eds.]

In the great meteor shower of August, the Perseid, I wail all day 16 for the shooting stars I miss. They're out there showering down committing hara-kiri in a flame of fatal attraction, and hissing perhaps at last into the ocean. But at dawn what looks like a blue dome clamps down over me like a lid on a pot. The stars and planets could smash and I'd never know. Only a piece of ashen moon occasionally climbs up or down the inside of the dome, and our local star without surcease explodes on our heads. We have really only that one light, one source for all power, and yet we must turn away from it by universal decree. Nobody here on the planet seems aware of this strange, powerful taboo, that we all walk about carefully averting our faces, this way and that, lest our eyes be blasted forever.

Darkness appalls and light dazzles; the scrap of visible light that 17 doesn't hurt my eyes hurts my brain. What I see sets me swaying. Size and distance and the sudden swelling of meanings confuse me, bowl me over. I straddle the sycamore log bridge over Tinker Creek in the summer. I look at the lighted creek bottom: snail tracks tunnel the mud in quavering curves. A crayfish jerks, but by the time I absorb what has happened, he's gone in a billowing smoke screen of silt. I look at the water; minnows and shiners. If I'm thinking minnows, a carp will fill my brain till I scream. I look at the water's surface: skaters, bubbles, and leaves sliding down. Suddenly, my own face, reflected, startles me witless. Those snails have been tracking my face! Finally, with a shuddering wrench of the will, I see clouds, cirrus clouds. I'm dizzy, I fall in.

This looking business is risky. Once I stood on a humped rock 18 on nearby Purgatory Mountain, watching through binoculars the great autumn hawk migration below, until I discovered that I was in danger of joining the hawks on a vertical migration of my own. I was used to binoculars, but not, apparently, to balancing on humped rocks while looking through them. I reeled. Everything advanced and receded by turns; the world was full of unexplained foreshortenings and depths. A distant huge object, a hawk the size of an elephant, turned out to be the browned bough of a nearby loblolly pine. I followed a sharp-shinned hawk against a featureless sky, rotating my head unawares as it flew, and when I lowered the glass a glimpse of my own looming shoulder sent me staggering. What prevents the men at Palomar[4] from falling, voiceless and blinded, from their tiny, vaulted chairs?

I reel in confusion: I don't understand what I see. With the naked 19 eye I can see two million light years to the Andromeda galaxy. Often

---

[4]An astronomical observatory in southern California which has the world's largest reflecting telescope. [Eds.]

I slop some creek water in a jar, and when I get home I dump it in a white china bowl. After the silt settles I return and see tracings of minute snails on the bottom, a planarian or two winding round the rim of water, roundworms shimmying, frantically, and finally, when my eyes have adjusted to these dimensions, amoebae. At first the amoebae look like *muscae volitantes*, those curled moving spots you seem to see in your eyes when you stare at a distant wall. Then I see the amoebae as drops of water congealed, bluish, translucent, like chips of sky in the bowl. At length I choose one individual and give myself over to its idea of an evening. I see it dribble a grainy foot before it on its wet, unfathomable way. Do its unedited sense impressions include the fierce focus of my eyes? Shall I take it outside and show it Andromeda, and blow its little endoplasm? I stir the water with a finger, in case it's running out of oxygen. Maybe I should get a tropical aquarium with motorized bubblers and lights, and keep this one for a pet. Yes, it would tell its fissioned descendants, the universe is two feet by five, and if you listen closely you can hear the buzzing music of the spheres.

Oh, it's mysterious, lamplit evenings here in the galaxy, one after 20 the other. It's one of those nights when I wander from window to window, looking for a sign. But I can't see. Terror and a beauty insoluble are a riband of blue woven into the fringe of garments of things both great and small. No culture explains, no bivouac offers real haven or rest. But it could be that we are not seeing something. Galileo thought comets were an optical illusion. This is fertile ground: since we are certain that they're not, we can look at what our scientists have been saying with fresh hope. What if there are *really* gleaming, castellated cities hung up-side-down over the desert sand? What limpid lakes and cool date palms have our caravans always passed untried? Until, one by one, by the blindest of leaps, we light on the road to these places, we must stumble in darkness and hunger. I turn from the window. I'm blind as a bat, sensing only from every direction the echo of my own thin cries.

I chanced on a wonderful book called *Space and Sight*, by Marius 21 Von Senden. When Western surgeons discovered how to perform safe cataract operations, they ranged across Europe and America operating on dozens of men and women of all ages who had been blinded by cataracts since birth. Von Senden collected accounts of such cases; the histories are fascinating. Many doctors had tested their patients' sense perceptions and ideas of space both before and after the operations. The vast majority of patients, of both sexes and all ages, had, in Von Senden's opinion, no idea of space whatsoever. Form, distance, and size were so many meaningless syllables. A patient "had

no idea of depth, confusing it with roundness." Before the operation
a doctor would give a blind patient a cube and a sphere; the patient
would tongue it or feel it with his hands, and name it correctly. After
the operation the doctor would show the same objects to the patient
without letting him touch them; now he had no clue whatsoever to
what he was seeing. One patient called lemonade "square" because
it pricked on his tongue as a square shape pricked on the touch of
his hands. Of another post-operative patient the doctor writes, "I
have found in her no notion of size, for example, not even within
the narrow limits which she might have encompassed with the aid
of touch. Thus when I asked her to show be how big her mother was,
she did not stretch out her hands, but set her two index fingers a few
inches apart."

For the newly sighted, vision is pure sensation unencumbered   22
by meaning. When a newly sighted girl saw photographs and paintings, she asked, " 'Why do they put those dark marks all over them?'
'Those aren't dark marks,' her mother explained, 'those are shadows.
That is one of the ways the eye knows that things have shape. If it
were not for shadows, many things would look flat.' 'Well, that's
how things do look,' Joan answered. 'Everything looks flat with dark
patches.' "

In general the newly sighted see the world as a dazzle of "color-   23
patches." They are pleased by the sensation of color, and learn quickly
to name the colors, but the rest of seeing is tormentingly difficult.
Soon after his operation a patient "generally bumps into one of these
color-patches and observes them to be substantial, since they resist
him as tactual objects do. In walking about it also strikes him—or can
if he pays attention—that he is continually passing in between the
colors he sees, that he can go past a visual object, that a part of it
then steadily disappears from view; and that in spite of this, however
he twists and turns—whether entering the room from the door, for
example, or returning back to it—he always has a visual space in front
of him. Thus he gradually comes to realize that there is also a space
behind him, which he does not see."

The mental effort involved in these reasonings proves over-   24
whelming for many patients. It oppresses them to realize that they
have been visible to people all along, perhaps unattractively so,
without their knowledge or consent. A disheartening number of them
refuse to use their new vision, continuing to go over objects with
their tongues, and lapsing into apathy and despair.

On the other hand, many newly sighted people speak well of the   25
world, and teach us how dull our vision is. To one patient, a human
hand, unrecognized, is "something bright and then holes." Shown
a bunch of grapes, a boy calls out, "It is dark, blue and shiny. . . . It

isn't smooth, it has bumps and hollows.'' A little girl visits a garden. "She is greatly astonished, and can scarcely be persuaded to answer, stands speechless in front of the tree, which she only names on taking hold of it, and then as 'the tree with the lights in it.' '' Another patient, a twenty-two-year-old girl, was dazzled by the world's brightness and kept her eyes shut for two weeks. When at the end of that time she opened her eyes again, she did not recognize any objects, but "the more she now directed her gaze upon everything about her, the more it could be seen how an expression of gratification and astonishment overspread her features; she repeatedly exclaimed: 'Oh God! How beautiful!' ''

I saw color-patches for weeks after I read this wonderful book. It 26 was summer; the peaches were ripe in the valley orchards. When I woke in the morning, color-patches wrapped round my eyes, intricately, leaving not one unfilled spot. All day long I walked among shifting color-patches that parted before me like the Red Sea and closed again in silence, transfigured, wherever I looked back. Some patches swelled and loomed, while others vanished utterly, and dark marks fitted at random over the whole dazzling sweep. But I couldn't sustain the illusion of flatness. I've been around for too long. Form is condemned to an eternal danse macabre[5] with meaning: I couldn't unpeach the peaches. Nor can I remember ever having seen without understanding; the color-patches of infancy are lost. My brain then must have been smooth as any balloon. I'm told I reached for the moon; many babies do. But the color-patches of infancy swelled as meaning filled them; they arrayed themselves in solemn ranks down distance which unrolled and stretched before me like a plain. The moon rocketed away. I live now in a world of shadows that shape and distance color, a world where space makes a kind of terrible sense. What Gnosticism[6] is this, and what physics? The fluttering patch I saw in my nursery window—silver and green and shape-shifting blue—is gone; a row of Lombardy poplars takes its place, mute, across the distant lawn. That humming oblong creature pale as light that stole along the walls of my room at night, stretching exhilaratingly around the corners, is gone, too, gone the night I ate of the bittersweet fruit,[7] put two and two together and puckered forever my brain. Martin Buber tells this tale: "Rabbi Mendel once boasted to his teacher Rabbi Elimelekh that evenings he saw the angel who rolls away the

---

[5]Dance of death. [Eds.]
[6]In this sense, mysterious or secret knowledge. [Eds.]
[7]A reference to the apple from the tree of knowledge in the Garden of Eden. Dillard is referring to an incident in her childhood in which she figured out what caused an oblong patch of light to flicker across the walls of her room. To her the incident marked the beginning of critical thought and the loss of her innocent view of the world; hence, it is bittersweet. [Eds.]

light before the darkness, and mornings the angel who rolls away the darkness before the light. 'Yes,' said Rabbi Elimelekh, 'in my youth I saw that too. Later on you don't see these things anymore.' "

Why didn't someone hand those newly sighted people paints and 27 brushes from the start, when they still didn't know what anything was? Then maybe we all could see color-patches too, the world unraveled from reason, Eden before Adam gave names. The scales would drop from my eyes; I'd see trees like men walking; I'd run down the road against all orders, hallooing and leaping.

Seeing is of course very much a matter of verbalization. Unless I 28 call my attention to what passes before my eyes, I simply won't see it. If Tinker Mountain erupted, I'd be likely to notice. But if I want to notice the lesser cataclysms of valley life, I have to maintain in my head a running description of the present. It's not that I'm observant; it's just that I talk too much. Otherwise, especially in a strange place, I'll never know what's happening. Like a blind man at the ball game, I need a radio.

When I see this way I analyze and pry. I hurl over logs and roll 29 away stones; I study the bank a square foot at a time, probing and tilting my head. Some days when a mist covers the mountains, when the muskrats won't show and the microscope's mirror shatters, I want to climb up the blank blue dome as a man would storm the inside of a circus tent, wildly, dangling, and with a steel knife claw a rent in the top, peep, and, if I must, fall.

But there is another kind of seeing that involves a letting go. 30 When I see this way I sway transfixed and emptied. The difference between the two ways of seeing is the difference between walking with and without a camera. When I walk with a camera I walk from shot to shot, reading the light on a calibrated meter. When I walk without a camera, my own shutter opens, and the moment's light prints on my own silver gut. When I see this second way I am above all an unscrupulous observer.

It was sunny one evening last summer at Tinker Creek; the sun 31 was low in the sky, upstream. I was sitting on the sycamore log bridge with the sunset at my back, watching the shiners the size of minnows who were feeding over the muddy sand in skittery schools. Again and again, one fish, then another, turned for a split second across the current and flash! the sun shot out from its silver side. I couldn't watch for it. It was always just happening somewhere else, and it drew my vision just as it disappeared: flash! like a sudden dazzle of the thinnest blade, a sparking over a dun and olive ground at chance intervals from every direction. Then I noticed white specks, some sort of pale petals, small, floating from under my feet on the creek's sur-

WRITING SUGGESTIONS

1. Write about a moment in which you "saw" something unexpected or surprising in nature. What did you learn?
2. Using one of Dillard's images as a starting point, express your personal ideas about what an individual's relationship to nature should be.

face, very slow and steady. So I blurred my eyes and gazed toward the brim of my hat and saw a new world. I saw the pale white circles roll up, roll up, like the world's turning, mute and perfect, and I saw the linear flashes, gleaming silver, like stars being born at random down a rolling scroll of time. Something broke and something opened. I filled up like a new wineskin. I breathed an air like light; I saw a light like water. I was the lip of a fountain the creek filled forever; I was ether, the leaf in the zephyr; I was flesh-flake, feather, bone.

When I see this way I see truly. As Thoreau says, I return to my 32 senses. I am the man who watches the baseball game in silence in an empty stadium. I see the game purely; I'm abstracted and dazed. When it's all over and the white suited players lope off the green field to their shadowed dugouts, I leap to my feet, I cheer and cheer.

But I can't go out and try to see this way. I'll fail, I'll go mad. All 33 I can do is try to gag the commentator, to hush the noise of useless interior babble that keeps me from seeing just as surely as a newspaper dangled before my eyes. The effort is really a discipline requiring a lifetime of dedicated struggle; it marks the literature of saints and monks of every order east and west, under every rule and no rule, discalced[8] and shod. The world's spiritual geniuses seem to discover universally that the mind's muddy river, this ceaseless flow of trivia and trash, cannot be dammed, and that trying to dam it is a waste of effort that might lead to madness. Instead you must allow the muddy river to flow unheeded in the dim channels of consciousness; you raise your sights; you look along it, mildly, acknowledging its presence without interest and gazing beyond it into the realm of the real where subjects and objects act and rest purely, without utterance. "Launch into the deep," says Jacques Ellul, "and you shall see."

The secret of seeing, then, is the pearl of great price. If I thought 34 he could teach me to find it and keep it forever I would stagger barefoot across a hundred deserts after any lunatic at all. But although the pearl may be found, it may not be sought. The literature of illumination reveals this above all: although it comes to those who wait for it, it is always, even to the most practiced and adept, a gift and a total surprise. I return from one walk knowing where the killdeer nests in the field by the creek and the hour the laurel blooms. I return from the same walk a day later scarcely knowing my own name. Litanies hum in my ears; my tongue flaps in my mouth, *Ailinon*,[9] alleluia! I cannot cause light; the most I can do is try to put myself in

---

[8]Barefoot. [Eds.]

[9]A Greek word that expresses woe or anguish. By juxtaposing it with *alleluia*, Dillard expresses two contrary emotions, mournfulness and joy. In so doing she expresses the idea that "seeing" involves both gain and loss. [Eds.]

the path of its beam. It is possible, in deep space, to sail on solar wind. Light, be it particle or wave, has force: you rig a giant sail and go. The secret of seeing is to sail on solar wind. Hone and spread your spirit till you yourself are a sail, whetted, translucent, broadside to the merest puff.

When her doctor took her bandages off and led her into the 35 garden, the girl who was no longer blind saw "the tree with the lights in it." It was for this tree I searched through the peach orchards of summer, in the forests of fall and down winter and spring for years. Then one day I was walking along Tinker Creek thinking of nothing at all and I saw the tree with the lights in it. I saw the backyard cedar where the mourning doves roost charged and transfigured, each cell buzzing with flame. I stood on the grass with the lights in it, grass that was wholly fire, utterly focused and utterly dreamed. It was less like seeing than like being for the first time seen, knocked breathless by a powerful glance. The flood of fire abated, but I'm still spending the power. Gradually the lights went out in the cedar, the colors died, the cells unflamed and disappeared. I was still ringing. I had been my whole life a bell, and never knew it until at that moment I was lifted and struck. I have since only very rarely seen the tree with the lights in it. The vision comes and goes, mostly goes, but I live for it, for the moment when the mountains open and a new light roars in spate through the crack, and the mountains slam.

RESPONDING TO READING

1. How effective is Dillard's anecdote about the penny in setting the stage for her later discussion? According to Dillard, what characteristics of human nature make us unable to see the pennies that nature scatters for us to find?   **2.** What point is Dillard making about the way most of us live our lives? About our relationship with nature? Do you agree with her?   **3.** What qualifications do you think a writer needs to write about the natural world? Does Dillard convince you that she is qualified to discuss the subjects she treats? Why or why not?

The Obligation to Endure

RACHEL CARSON

Naturalist and environmentalist Rachel Carson (1907–1964) was a specialist in marine biology. She won the National Book Award for *The Sea Around Us* (1951), which, like her other books, appeals to scientists and laypeople alike. While working as an aquatic biologist for the U.S. Fish and Wildlife Service, Carson became concerned with ecological hazards and wrote *Silent Spring* (1962), in which she

nedy's Science Advisory Committee issued a statement in agreement with the basic premise of Carson's book, warned against indiscriminate use of chemicals, and urged more stringent controls and additional research.

FOR OPENERS

Ask students to consider whether we have overreacted to the health risks of pesticides and chemicals in the environment. Do they think these substances pose more or less of a risk now than they did in 1962?

warned readers about the indiscriminate use of pesticides. This book influenced President John F. Kennedy to begin investigations into this and other environmental problems. In the selection from *Silent Spring* that follows, Carson urges us to question the use of chemical pesticides.

The history of life on earth has been a history of interaction 1 between living things and their surroundings. To a large extent, the physical form and the habits of the earth's vegetation and its animal life have been molded by the environment. Considering the whole span of earthly time, the opposite effect, in which life actually modifies its surroundings, has been relatively slight. Only within the moment of time represented by the present century has one species—man—acquired significant power to alter the nature of his world.

During the past quarter century this power has not only increased 2 to one of disturbing magnitude but it has changed in character. The most alarming of all man's assaults upon the environment is the contamination of air, earth, rivers, and sea with dangerous and even lethal materials. This pollution is for the most part irrecoverable; the chain of evil it initiates not only in the world that must support life but in living tissues is for the most part irreversible. In this now universal contamination of the environment, chemicals are the sinister and little-recognized partners of radiation in changing the very nature of the world—the very nature of its life. Strontium 90, released through nuclear explosions into the air, comes to earth in rain or drifts down in fallout, lodges in soil, enters into the grass or corn or wheat grown there, and in time takes up its abode in the bones of a human being, there to remain until his death. Similarly, chemicals sprayed on croplands or forests or gardens lie long in soil, entering into living organisms, passing from one to another in a chain of poisoning and death. Or they pass mysteriously by underground streams until they emerge and, through the alchemy of air and sunlight, combine into new forms that kill vegetation, sicken cattle, and work unknown harm on those who drink from once pure wells. As Albert Schweitzer[1] has said, "Man can hardly even recognize the devils of his own creation."

It took hundreds of millions of years to produce the life that now 3 inhabits the earth—eons of time in which that developing and evolving and diversifying life reached a state of adjustment and balance with its surroundings. The environment, rigorously shaping and directing the life it supported, contained elements that were hostile as well as supporting. Certain rocks gave out dangerous radiation;

---

[1]French theologian (1875–1965) honored for his work as a scientist, humanitarian, musician, and religious thinker. In 1952 he was awarded the Nobel Peace Prize. [Eds.]

even within the light of the sun, from which all life draws its energy, there were short-wave radiations with power to injure. Given time—time not in years but in millennia—life adjusts, and a balance has been reached. For time is the essential ingredient; but in the modern world there is no time.

The rapidity of change and the speed with which new situations 4 are created follow the impetuous and heedless pace of man rather than the deliberate pace of nature. Radiation is no longer merely the background radiation of rocks, the bombardment of cosmic rays, the ultraviolet of the sun that have existed before there was any life on earth; radiation is now the unnatural creation of man's tampering with the atom. The chemicals to which life is asked to make its adjustment are no longer merely the calcium and silica and copper and all the rest of the minerals washed out of the rocks and carried in rivers to the sea; they are the synthetic creations of man's inventive mind, brewed in his laboratories, and having no counterparts in nature.

To adjust to these chemicals would require time on the scale that 5 is nature's; it would require not merely the years of a man's life but the life of generations. And even this, were it by some miracle possible, would be futile, for the new chemicals come from our laboratories in an endless stream; almost five hundred annually find their way into actual use in the United States alone. The figure is staggering and its implications are not easily grasped—500 new chemicals to which the bodies of men and animals are required somehow to adapt each year, chemically totally outside the limits of biologic experience.

Among them are many that are used in man's war against nature. 6 Since the mid-1940s over 200 basic chemicals have been created for use in killing insects, weeds, rodents, and other organisms described in the modern vernacular as "pests"; and they are sold under several thousand different brand names.

These sprays, dusts, and aerosols are now applied almost uni- 7 versally to farms, gardens, forests, and homes—nonselective chemicals that have the power to kill every insect, the "good" and the "bad," to still the songs of birds and the leaping of fish in the streams, to coat the leaves with a deadly film, and to linger on in soil—all this though the intended target may be only a few weeds or insects. Can anyone believe it is possible to lay down such a barrage of poisons on the surface of the earth without making it unfit for all life? They should not be called "insecticides," but "biocides."

The whole process of spraying seems caught up in an endless 8 sprial. Since DDT was released for civilian use, a process of escalation has been going on in which ever more toxic materials must be found. This has happened because insects, in a triumphant vindication of Darwin's principle of the survival of the fittest, have evolved super

ADDITIONAL QUESTIONS FOR
RESPONDING TO READING
1. Why does Carson not focus on the negative health effects that have been traced to chemical poisoning?
2. Do you find Carson's statistics shocking? Convincing? Explain your reactions.
3. Are you persuaded by the authorities Carson cites? Why or why not?

TEACHING STRATEGY

Discuss whether issues such as depletion of the earth's ozone layer and destruction of the rain forests have supplanted concern about hazardous substances.

races immune to the particular insecticide used, hence a deadlier one has always to be developed—and than a deadlier one than that. It has happened also because, for reasons to be described later, destructive insects often undergo a "flare-back" or resurgence, after spraying in numbers greater than before. Thus the chemical war is never won, and all life is caught in its violent crossfile.

Along with the possibility of the extinction of mankind by nuclear war, the central problem of our age has therefore become the contamination of man's total environment with such substances of incredible potential for harm—substances that accumulate in the tissues of plants and animals and even penetrate the germ cells to shatter or alter the very material of heredity upon which the shape of the future depends.

Some would-be architects of our future look toward a time when it will be possible to alter the human germ plasm by design. But we may easily be doing so now by inadvertence, for many chemicals, like radiation, bring about gene mutations. It is ironic to think that man might determine his own future by something so seemingly trivial as the choice of an insect spray.

All this has been risked—for what? Future historians may well be amazed by our distorted sense of proportion. How could intelligent beings seek to control a few unwanted species by a method that contaminated the entire environment and brought the threat of disease and death even to their own kind? Yet this is precisely what we have done. We have done it, moreover, for reasons that collapse the moment we examine them. We are told that the enormous and expanding use of pesticides is necessary to maintain farm production. Yet is our real problem not one of *overproduction*? Our farms, despite measures to remove acreages from production and to pay farmers *not* to produce, have yielded such a staggering excess of crops that the American taxpayer in 1962 in payout out more than one billion dollars a year as the total carrying cost of the surplus-food storage program. And is the situation helped when one branch of the Agriculture Department tries to reduce production while another states, as it did in 1958, "It is believed generally that reduction of crop acreages under provisions of the Soil Bank will stimulate interest in use of chemicals to obtain maximum production on the land retained in crops."

All this is not to say there is no insect problem and no need of control. I am saying, rather, that control must be geared to realities, not to mythical situations, and that the methods employed must be such that they do not destroy us along with the insects.

The problem whose attempted solution has brought such a train of disaster in its wake is an accomplishment of our modern way of life. Long before the age of man, insects inhabited the earth—a group of extraordinarily varied and adaptable beings. Over the course of time since man's advent, a small percentage of the more than half a million species of insects have come into conflict with human welfare in two principal ways: as competitors for the food supply and as carriers of human disease.

Disease-carrying insects become important where human beings 14 are crowded together, especially under conditions where sanitation is poor, as in time of natural disaster or war or in situations of extreme poverty and deprivation. Then control of some sort becomes necessary. It is a sobering fact, however, as we shall presently see, that the method of massive chemical control has had only limited success, and also threatens to worsen the very conditions it is intended to curb.

Under primitive agricultural conditions the farmer had few insect 15 problems. These arose with the intensification of agriculture—the devotion of immense acreages to a single crop. Such a system set the stage for explosive increases in specific insect populations. Single-crop farming does not take advantage of the principles by which nature works; it is agriculture as an engineer might conceive it to be. Nature has introduced great variety into the landscape, but man has displayed a passion for simplifying it. Thus he undoes the built-in checks and balances by which nature holds the species within bounds. One important natural check is a limit on the amount of suitable habitat for each species. Obviously then, an insect that lives on wheat can build up its population to much higher levels on a farm devoted to wheat than on one in which wheat is intermingled with other crops to which the insect is not adapted.

The same thing happens in other situations. A generation or more 16 ago, the towns of large areas of the United States lined their streets with the noble elm tree. Now the beauty they hopefully created is threatened with complete destruction as disease sweeps through the elms, carried by a beetle that would have only limited chance to build up large populations and to spread from tree to tree if the elms were only occasional trees in a richly diversified planting.

Another factor in the modern insect problem is one that must be 17 viewed against a background of geologic and human history: the spreading of thousands of different kinds of organisms from their native homes to invade new territories. This worldwide migration has been studied and graphically described by the British ecologist Charles Elton in his recent book *The Ecology of Invasions*. During the Cretaceous Period, some hundred million years ago, flooding seas cut many land bridges between continents and living things found themselves confined in what Elton calls "colossal separate nature reserves." There,

COLLABORATIVE ACTIVITY

Ask groups to find out about chemicals and toxic substances in their local community. Suggestions for topics: agricultural use of pesticides and herbicides, home use of chemicals, production and dumping sites, government regulation of local facilities, and health effects of chemicals used or produced nearby. They can contact a local environmental organization or local agencies and manufacturers. Have students report about how easy it was to get information and about whether what they found out supported any of Carson's points.

isolated from others of their kind, they developed many new species. When some of the land masses were joined again, about 15 million years ago, these species began to move out into new territories—a movement that is not only still in progress but is now receiving considerable assistance from man.

The importation of plants is the primary agent in the modern 18 spread of species, for animals have almost invariably gone along with the plants, quarantine being a comparatively recent and not completely effective innovation. The United States Office of Plant Introduction alone has introduced almost 200,000 species and varieties of plants from all over the world. Nearly half of the 180 or so major insect enemies of plants in the United States are accidental imports from abroad, and most of them have come as hitchhikers on plants.

In new territory, out of reach of the restraining hand of the natural 19 enemies that kept down its numbers in its native land, an invading plant or animal is able to become enormously abundant. Thus it is no accident that our most troublesome insects are introduced species.

These invasions, both the naturally occurring and those depen- 20 dent on human assistance, are likely to continue indefinitely. Quarantine and massive chemical campaigns are only extremely expensive ways of buying time. We are faced, according to Dr. Elton, "with a life-and-death need not just to find new technological means of suppressing this plant or that animal"; instead we need the basic knowledge of animal populations and their relations to their surroundings that will "promote an even balance and damp down the explosive power of outbreaks and new invasions."

Much of the necessary knowledge is now available but we do not 21 use it. We train ecologists in our universities and even employ them in our governmental agencies but we seldom take their advice. We allow the chemical death rain to fall as though there were no alternative, whereas in fact there are many, and our ingenuity could soon discover many more if given opportunity.

Have we fallen into a mesmerized state that makes us accept as 22 inevitable that which is inferior or detrimental, as though having lost the will or the vision to demand that which is good? Such thinking, in the words of the ecologist Paul Shepard, "idealizes life with only its head out of water, inches above the limits of toleration of the corruption of its own environment . . . Why should we tolerate a diet of weak poisons, a home in insipid surroundings, a circle of acquaintances who are not quite our enemies, the noise of motors with just enough relief to prevent insanity? Who would want to live in a world which is just not quite fatal?"

Yet such a world is pressed upon us. The crusade to create a 23 chemically sterile, insect-free world seems to have engendered a fanatic zeal on the part of many specialists and most of the so-called control agencies. On every hand there is evidence that those engaged in spraying operations exercise a ruthless power. "The regulatory entomologists . . . function as prosecutor, judge and jury, tax assessor and collector and sheriff to enforce their own orders," said Connecticut entomologist Neely Turner. The most flagrant abuses go unchecked in both state and federal agencies.

It is not my contention that chemical insecticides must never be 24 used. I do contend that we have put poisonous and biologically potent chemicals indiscriminately into the hands of persons largely or wholly ignorant of their potentials for harm. We have subjected enormous numbers of people to contact with these poisons, without their consent and often without their knowledge. If the Bill of Rights contains no guarantee that a citizen shall be secure against lethal poisons distributed either by private individuals or by public officials, it is surely only because our forefathers, despite their considerable wisdom and foresight, could conceive of no such problem.

I contend, furthermore, that we have allowed these chemicals to 25 be used with little or no advance investigation of their effect on soil, water, wildlife, and man himself. Future generations are unlikely to condone our lack of prudent concern for the integrity of the natural world that supports all life.

There is still very limited awareness of the nature of the threat. 26 This is an era of specialists, each of whom sees his own problem and is unaware of or intolerant of the larger frame into which it fits. It is also an era dominated by industry, in which the right to make a dollar at whatever cost is seldom challenged. When the public protests, confronted with some obvious evidence of damaging results of pesticide applications, it is fed little tranquilizing pills of half truth. We urgently need an end to these false assurances, to the sugar coating of unpalatable facts. It is the public that is being asked to assume the risks that the insect controllers calculate. The public must decide whether it wishes to continue on the present road, and it can do so only when in full possession of the facts. In the words of Jean Rostand, "The obligation to endure gives us the right to know."

RESPONDING TO READING

1. Since this essay was written, DDT has been banned. Recently, however, some scientists have suggested that because some insects have developed resistance to safer insecticides, spraying of DDT should be reinstituted on a limited basis. Does this information strengthen or weaken Carson's position? Can you make the argument that health considerations and the need for food outweigh the environmental hazards of spraying DDT? Why or why

WRITING SUGGESTIONS

1. Write a letter from a farmer to Rachel Carson. Make sure he or she acknowledges the strength of Carson's position but also makes the point that some insecticides are necessary to run a farm profitably.
2. Do we have a "right to know" about chemicals in our environment? And, if we know, do we have a responsibility to do something about them? Explain.

ANSWERS TO RESPONDING TO READING

1. According to Carson, we should change the way we live and farm. Widespread starvation in countries in northern Africa, however, does make an absolute ban on DDT seem questionable. How, for example, can we not use DDT to prevent insects from destroying the little

food that is being produced in these countries? How can we accept the resurgence of malaria that has been reported in many Third World countries since DDT spraying was stopped?

2. Carson would point out that the chemical war is never won; destructive insects often resurge after spraying, in greater numbers. Chemical control has "only limited success, and also threatens to worsen the very conditions it is intended to curb." Carson says we have to use "knowledge of animal populations and their relations to their surroundings" to work toward balance.

3. Answers will vary. She might have described the impact of chemical use on individual people's lives or described specific examples of polluted environments. Perhaps then the sense of danger would hit closer to home.

BACKGROUND ON READING

About *Coming into the Country*, Robert Coles writes, "John McPhee's approach, justly celebrated, brings to us the dramatic terrain—a subcontinent of empty tundra, untamed rivers, forbidding mountain ranges, treacherous ice fields—and the relative handful of human beings, Eskimos and Indians, who have for generations struggled to survive the extremes of Arctic weather. He does so, in large measure, through the eyes of a number of off-beat Americans, who have left 'the lower forty-eight' . . . in search of a frontier kind of personal destiny" (*Contemporary Literary Criticism*, vol. 36, p. 298).

FOR OPENERS

Ask students to talk about their own personal encounters with the natural world. Have them make a list of specific things that they learned at the time of the experience, and then make another list of what they learned about the subject later after they thought about it. Studying the two kinds of lists should give students an idea of McPhee's method.

not? **2.** During the past few years the Mediterranean fruit fly has damaged fruit in California and Florida. In an effort to stop the damage, both states have inspected all fruit being transported across their borders and aggressively sprayed malathion, an insecticide having relatively low toxicity to plants and animals. At the present time, however, these efforts do not seem to have stopped the spread of the fruit fly. How do you think Carson would address this problem? **3.** Could Carson have made her point more forcefully by devoting more time to describing "the interaction between living things and their surroundings"—that is, by showing what we have lost, and what we have to lose? What in particular could she have described?

The Grizzly

JOHN McPHEE

A writer for *The New Yorker* for most of his career, John McPhee (1931–   ) has earned international praise for his "fact pieces" on a variety of subjects. His essays show evidence of painstaking research, with myriad details about such subjects as canoes, oranges, cooking, aeronautics, geology, and tennis. His popular books include *Oranges* (1967), *The Pine Barrens* (1968), and *Rising from the Plains* (1988). McPhee tends to look for the extraordinary in an ordinary world. "The Grizzly" is from *Coming into the Country* (1977), his book about Alaska, the last American frontier. Here McPhee creates his impression of the awesome grizzly, which first appeared to him as "a hill of fur."

We passed first through stands of fireweed, and then over ground that was wine-red with the leaves of bearberries. There were curlewberries, too, which put a deep-purple stain on the hand. We kicked at some wolf scat, old as winter. It was woolly and white and filled with the hair of a snowshoe hare. Nearby was a rich inventory of caribou pellets and, in increasing quantity as we moved downhill, blueberries—an outspreading acreage of blueberries. Fedeler stopped walking. He touched my arm. He had in an instant become even more alert than he usually was, and obviously apprehensive. His gaze followed straight on down our intended course. What he saw there I saw now. It appeared to me to be a hill of fur. "Big boar grizzly," Fedeler said in a near-whisper. The bear was about a hundred steps away, in the blueberries, grazing. The head was down, the hump high. The immensity of muscle seemed to vibrate slowly—to expand and contract, with the grazing. Not berries alone but whole bushes were going into the bear. He was big for a barren-ground grizzly. The brown bears of Arctic Alaska (or grizzlies; they are no longer thought to be different) do not grow to the size they will reach on more ample diets elsewhere. The barren-ground grizzly will rarely grow larger than six hundred pounds.

"What if he got too close?" I said.   2

Fedeler said, "We'd be in real trouble."   3

"You can't outrun them," Hession said.   4

A grizzly, no slower than a racing horse, is about half again as 5 fast as the fastest human being. Watching the great mound of weight in the blueberries, with a fifty-five-inch waist and a neck more than thirty inches around, I had difficulty imagining that he could move with such speed, but I believed it, and was without impulse to test the proposition. Fortunately, a light southerly wind was coming up the Salmon valley. On its way to us, it passed the bear. The wind was relieving, coming into our faces, for had it been moving the other way the bear would not have been placidly grazing. There is an old adage that when a pine needle drops in the forest the eagle will see it fall; the deer will hear it when it hits the ground; the bear will smell it. If the boar grizzly were to catch our scent, he might stand on his hind legs, the better to try to see. Although he could hear well and had an extraordinary sense of smell, his eyesight was not much better than what was required to see a blueberry inches away. For this reason, a grizzly stands and squints, attempting to bring the middle distance into focus, and the gesture is often misunderstood as a sign of anger and forthcoming attack. If the bear were getting ready to attack, he would be on four feet, head low, ears cocked, the hair above his hump muscle standing on end. As if that message were not clear enough, he would also chop his jaws. His teeth would make a sound that would carry like the ringing of an axe.

One could predict, but not with certainty, what a grizzly would 6 do. Odds were very great that one touch of man scent would cause him to stop his activity, pause in a moment of absorbed and alert curiosity, and then move, at a not undignified pace, in a direction other than the one from which the scent was coming. This is what would happen almost every time, but there was, to be sure, no guarantee. The forest Eskimos fear and revere the grizzly. They know that certain individual bears not only will fail to avoid a person who comes into their country but will approach and even stalk the trespasser. It is potentially inaccurate to extrapolate the behavior of any one bear from the behavior of most, since they are both intelligent and independent and will do what they choose to do according to mood, experience, whim. A grizzly that has ever been wounded by a bullet

ADDITIONAL QUESTIONS FOR RESPONDING TO READING

1. McPhee is trying to inform as well as educate the reader. Does this idea reflect his general philosophy about nature? Explain.
2. How is McPhee's attitude toward the grizzly like and unlike Annie Dillard's attitude toward the deer in "The Deer at Providencia" (Chapter 12)?

TEACHING STRATEGIES

1. In "Sight into Insight" (page 936) Annie Dillard presents images of a benign nature; the greatest fears come from within. In contrast, McPhee presents an element of nature that is potentially a real danger. What facts about the bear does McPhee relate? Under certain circumstances, the bear will kill, and this fact is outside our control. Ask students to discuss the ways in which Dillard and McPhee differ.
2. McPhee sets up a narrative frame, describes a scene, and then fills it with information he wants to relate to the reader. Ask students to consider how this method is effective for his didactic purpose.

WRITING SUGGESTIONS

1. Watch a public television documentary about a creature in the natural world. After doing so, complete two writing assignments: an informal reaction to the program's ideas, and a more formal, more critical review of its position.
2. Describe a time when you experienced fear of something in nature. What did you gain, or lose, from the experience?

ANSWERS TO RESPONDING TO READING

1. The bear is powerful, not entirely predictable, independent, and potentially dangerous—an animal to be respected, not bothered. In short, it is a force of nature not to be tamed or controlled.
2. McPhee assumes that his readers lack accurate information about the bear. Like the native Eskimos, he both fears and reveres the grizzly, and he tries to pass these attitudes on to the reader.
3. McPhee seems to suggest that nature is made up of many elements that humans must understand in order to coexist with it.

will not forget it, and will probably know that it was a human being who sent the bullet. At sight of a human, such a bear will be likely to charge. Grizzlies hide food sometimes—a caribou calf, say, under a pile of scraped-up moss—and a person the bear might otherwise ignore might suddenly not be ignored if the person were inadvertently to step into the line between the food cache and the bear. A sow grizzly with cubs, of course, will charge anything that suggests danger to the cubs, even if the cubs are nearly as big as she is. They stay with their mother two and a half years.

None of us had a gun. (None of the six of us had brought a gun 7 on the trip.) Among nonhunters who go into the terrain of the grizzly, there are several schools of thought about guns. The preferred one is: Never go without a sufficient weapon—a high-powered rifle or a shotgun and plenty of slug-loaded shells. The option is not without its own inherent peril. A professional hunter, some years ago, spotted a grizzly from the air and—with a client, who happened to be an Anchorage barber—landed on a lake about a mile from the bear. The stalking that followed was evidently conducted not only by the hunters but by the animal as well. The professional hunter was found dead from a broken neck, and had apparently died instantly, unaware of danger, for the cause of death was a single bite, delivered from behind. The barber, noted as clumsy with a rifle, had emptied his magazine, missing the bear with every shot but one, which struck the grizzly in the foot. The damage the bear did to the barber was enough to kill him several times. After the corpses were found, the bear was tracked and killed. To shoot and merely wound is worse than not to shoot at all. A bear that might have turned and gone away will possibly attack if wounded.

RESPONDING TO READING

1. What general impression of the grizzly bear is McPhee trying to create? Do you think he succeeds? Why or why not?   **2.** What attitudes toward grizzly bears does McPhee think his readers have? Do you share these attitudes? Does McPhee attempt to change his readers' minds? To what extent is he successful in changing your attitudes?   **3.** McPhee suggests that people can never understand the grizzly. Do you believe this idea can be applied to other aspects of nature? Explain.

The Brown Wasps

LOREN EISELEY

Scientist and humanist Loren Eiseley (see also p. 864) explores the mysteries of nature in his poems and essays. In "The Brown Wasps," written in 1971, he talks about change—in the world and inside people and creatures—and how we tend to "cling to a time and place."

There is a corner in the waiting room of one of the great Eastern stations where women never sit. It is always in the shadow and overhung by rows of lockers. It is, however, always frequented—not so much by genuine travelers as by the dying. It is here that a certain element of the abandoned poor seeks a refuge out of the weather, clinging for a few hours longer to the city that has fathered them. In a precisely similar manner I have seen, on a sunny day in midwinter, a few old brown wasps creep slowly over an abandoned wasp nest in a thicket. Numbed and forgetful and frost-blackened, the hum of the spring hive still resounded faintly in their sodden tissues. Then the temperature would fall and they would drop away into the white oblivion of the snow. Here in the station it is in no way different save that the city is busy in its snows. But the old ones cling to their seats as though these were symbolic and could not be given up. Now and then they sleep, their gray old heads resting with painful awkwardness on the backs of the benches.   1

Also they are not at rest. For an hour they may sleep in the gasping exhaustion of the ill-nourished and aged who have to walk in the night. Then a policeman comes by on his round and nudges them upright.   2

"You can't sleep here," he growls.   3

A strange ritual then begins. An old man is difficult to waken. After a muttered conversation the policeman presses a coin into his hand and passes fiercely along the benches prodding and gesturing toward the door. In his wake, like birds rising and settling behind the passage of a farmer through a cornfield, the men totter up, move a few paces and subside once more upon the benches.   4

One man, after a slight, apologetic lurch, does not move at all. Tubercularly thin, he sleeps on steadily. The policeman does not look back. To him, too, this has become a ritual. He will not have to notice it again officially for another hour.   5

Once in a while one of the sleepers will not awake. Like the brown wasps, he will have had his wish to die in the great droning center of the hive rather than in some lonely room. It is not so bad here with the shuffle of footsteps and the knowledge that there are others   6

BACKGROUND ON AUTHOR

Edward Weeks says of Loren Eiseley's essays, "Like Emerson, Dr. Eiseley is a philosopher whose epigrammatic sentences are clues leading to the unknown. His sentences tantalize the imagination; they lead me on, but his essays in form are elusive" (quoted in *Contemporary Literary Criticism*). In Kenneth Heuer's conclusion to *The Lost Notebooks*, he records the following anecdote and observation: "Loren's life was filled with animal-saving ventures. . . . He was always trying to return stray dogs to their masters, calling owners and waiting for them to come for their loyal friends. Soon after he died, Mabel [Eiseley] had a visitor—a lost dog who appeared unexpectedly at the back door of her house and who, when taken inside, gravely shook hands with her without being told to. Loren would have looked hard at this encounter, and it would have seemed to look hard at him."

FOR OPENERS

Ask students to freewrite about a place and time with which they have strong emotional associations.

ADDITIONAL QUESTION FOR RESPONDING TO READING

According to Eiseley, what characteristics do humans share with nature?

TEACHING STRATEGY

Call attention to Eiseley's use of analogy and illustration.

who share the bad luck of the world. There are also the whistles and the sounds of everyone, everyone in the world, starting on journeys. Amidst so many journeys somebody is bound to come out all right. Somebody.

Maybe it was on a like thought that the brown wasps fell away 7 from the old paper nest in the thicket. You hold till the last, even if it is only to a public seat in a railroad station. You want your place in the hive more than you want a room or a place where the aged can be eased gently out of the way. It is the place that matters, the place at the heart of things. It is life that you want, that bruises your gray old head with the hard chairs; a man has a right to his place.

But sometimes the place is lost in the years behind us. Or some- 8 times it is a thing of air, a kind of vaporous distortion above a heap of rubble. We cling to a time and place because without them man is lost, not only man but life. This is why the voices, real or unreal, which speak from the floating trumpets at spiritualist seances are so unnerving. They are voices out of nowhere whose only reality lies in their ability to stir the memory of a living person with some fragment of the past. Before the medium's cabinet both the dead and the living revolve endlessly about an episode, a place, an event that has already been engulfed by time.

This feeling runs deep in life; it brings stray cats running over 9 endless miles, and birds homing from the ends of the earth. It is as though all living creatures, and particularly the more intelligent, can survive only by fixing or transforming a bit of time into space or by securing a bit of space with its objects immortalized and made permanent in time. For example, I once saw, on a flower pot in my own living room, the efforts of a field mouse to build a remembered field. I have lived to see this episode repeated in a thousand guises, and since I have spent a large portion of my life in the shade of a nonexistent tree, I think I am entitled to speak for the field mouse.

One day as I cut across the field which at that time extended on 10 one side of our suburban shopping center, I found a giant slug feeding from a runnel of pink ice cream in an abandoned Dixie cup. I could see his eyes telescope and protrude in a kind of dim, uncertain ecstasy as his dark body bunched and elongated in the curve of the cup. Then, as I stood there at the edge of the concrete, contemplating the slug, I began to realize it was like standing on a shore where a different type of life creeps up and fumbles tentatively among the rocks and sea wrack. It knows its place and will only creep so far until something changes. Little by little as I stood there I began to see more of this shore that surrounds the place of man. I looked with sudden care and attention at things I had been running over thoughtlessly for years. I even waded out a short way into the grass and the wild-rose thickets to see more. A huge black-belted bee went droning by and there were some indistinct scurryings in the underbrush.

Then I came to a sign which informed me that this field was to 11 be the site of a new Wanamaker suburban store. Thousands of obscure lives were about to perish, the spores of puffballs would go smoking off to new fields, and the bodies of little white-footed mice would be crunched under the inexorable wheels of the bulldozers. Life disappears or modifies its appearances so fast that everything takes on an aspect of illusion—a momentary fizzing and boiling with smoke rings, like pouring dissident chemicals into a retort. Here man was advancing, but in a few years his plaster and bricks would be disappearing once more into the insatiable maw of the clover. Being of an archaeological cast of mind, I thought of this fact with an obscure sense of satisfaction and waded back through the rose thickets to the concrete parking lot. As I did so, a mouse scurried ahead of me, frightened of my steps if not of that ominous Wanamaker sign. I saw him vanish in the general direction of my apartment house, his little body quivering with fear in the great open sun on the blazing concrete. Blinded and confused, he was running straight away from his field. In another week scores would follow him.

I forgot the episode then and went home to the quiet of my living 12 room. It was not until a week later, letting myself into the apartment, that I realized I had a visitor. I am fond of plants and had several ferns standing on the floor in pots to avoid the noon glare by the south window.

As I snapped on the light and glanced carelessly around the room, 13 I saw a little heap of earth on the carpet and a scrabble of pebbles that had been kicked merrily over the edge of one of the flower pots. To my astonishment I discovered a full-fledged burrow delving downward among the fern roots. I waited silently. The creature who had made the burrow did not appear. I remembered the wild field then, and the fight of the mice. No house mouse, no *Mus domesticus*, had kicked up this little heap of earth or sought refuge under a fern root in a flower pot. I thought of the desperate little creature I had seen fleeing from the wild-rose thicket. Through intricacies of pipes and attics, he, or one of his fellows, had climbed to this high green solitary room. I could visualize what had occurred. He had an image in his head, a world of seed pods and quiet, of green sheltering leaves in the dim light among the weed stems. It was the only world he knew and it was gone.

Somehow in his fight he had found his way to this room with 14 drawn shades where no one would come till nightfall. And here he

COLLABORATIVE ACTIVITY

Have groups brainstorm for other analogies and illustrations, from both the human and natural worlds, that support Eiseley's thesis.

had smelled green leaves and run quickly up the flower pot to dabble his paws in common earth. He had even struggled half the afternoon to carry his burrow deeper and had failed. I examined the hole, but no whiskered twitching face appeared. He was gone. I gathered up the earth and refilled the burrow. I did not expect to find traces of him again.

Yet for three nights thereafter I came home to the darkened room 15 and my ferns to find the dirt kicked gaily about the rug and the burrow reopened, though I was never able to catch the field mouse within it. I dropped a little food about the mouth of the burrow, but it was never touched. I looked under beds or sat reading with one ear cocked for rustlings in the ferns. It was all in vain; I never saw him. Probably he ended in a trap in some other tenant's room.

But before he disappeared I had come to look hopefully for his 16 evening burrow. About my ferns there had begun to linger the insubstantial vapor of an autumn field, the distilled essence, as it were, of a mouse brain in exile from its home. It was a small dream, like our dreams, carried a long and weary journey along pipes and through spider webs, past holes over which loomed the shadows of waiting cats, and finally, desperately, into this room where he had played in the shuttered daylight for an hour among the green ferns on the floor. Every day these invisible dreams pass us on the street, or rise from beneath our feet, or look out upon us from beneath a bush.

Some years ago the old elevated railway in Philadelphia was torn 17 down and replaced by a subway system. This ancient El with its barnlike stations containing nut-vending machines and scattered food scraps had, for generations, been the the favorite feeding ground of flocks of pigeons, generally one flock to a station along the route of the El. Hundreds of pigeons were dependent upon the system. They flapped in and out of its stanchions and steel work or gathered in watchful little audiences about the feet of anyone who rattled the peanut-vending machines. They even watched people who jingled change in their hands, and prospected for food under the feet of the crowds who gathered between trains. Probably very few among the waiting people who tossed a crumb to an eager pigeon realized that this El was like a food-bearing river, and that the life which haunted its banks was dependent upon the running of the trains with their human freight.

I saw the river stop. 18

The time came when the underground tubes were ready; the 19 traffic was transferred to a realm unreachable by pigeons. It was like a great river subsiding suddenly into desert sands. For a day, for two days, pigeons continued to circle over the El or stand close to the red vending machines. They were patient birds, and surely this great river which had flowed through the lives of unnumbered generations was merely suffering from some momentary drought.

They listened for the familiar vibrations that had always heralded 20 an approaching train; they flapped hopefully about the head of an occasional workman walking along the steel runways. They passed from one empty station to another, all the while growing hungrier. Finally they flew away.

I thought I had seen the last of them about the El, but there was 21 a revival and it provided a curious instance of the memory of living things for a way of life or a locality that has long been cherished. Some weeks after the El was abandoned workmen began to tear it down. I went to work every morning by one particular station, and the time came when the demolition crews reached this spot. Acetylene torches showered passersby with sparks, pneumatic drills hammered at the base of the structure, and a blind man who, like the pigeons, had clung with his cup to a stairway leading to the change booth, was forced to give up his place.

It was then, strangely, momentarily, one morning that I witnessed 22 the return of a little band of the familiar pigeons. I even recognized one or two members of the flock that had lived around this particular station before they were dispersed into the streets. They flew bravely in and out among the sparks and the hammers and the shouting workmen. They had returned—and they had returned because the hubbub of the wreckers had convinced them that the river was about to flow once more. For several hours they flapped in and out through the empty windows, nodding their heads and watching the fall of girders with attentive little eyes. By the following morning the station was reduced to some burned-off stanchions in the street. My bird friends had gone. It was plain, however, that they retained a memory for an insubstantial structure now compounded of air and time. Even the blind man clung to it. Someone had provided him with a chair, and he sat at the same corner staring sightlessly at an invisible stairway where, so far as he was concerned, the crowds were still ascending to the trains.

I have said my life has been passed in the shade of a nonexistent 23 tree, so that such sights do not offend me. Prematurely I am one of the brown wasps and I often sit with them in the great droning hive of the station, dreaming sometimes of a certain tree. It was planted sixty years ago by a boy with a bucket and a toy spade in a little Nebraska town. That boy was myself. It was a cottonwood sapling and the boy remembered it because of some words spoken by his father and because everyone died or moved away who was supposed to wait and grow old under its shade. The boy was passed from hand to hand, but the tree for some intangible reason had taken root in his mind. It was under its branches that he sheltered; it was from this tree that his memories, which are my memories, led away into the world.

After sixty years the mood of the brown wasps grows heavier 24 upon one. During a long inward struggle I thought it would do me good to go and look upon that actual tree. I found a rational excuse in which to clothe this madness. I purchased a ticket and at the end of two thousand miles I walked another mile to an address that was still the same. The house had not been altered.

I came close to the white picket fence and reluctantly, with great 25 effort, looked down the long vista of the yard. There was nothing there to see. For sixty years that cottonwood had been growing in my mind. Season by season its seeds had been floating farther on the hot prairie winds. We had planted it lovingly there, my father and I, because he had a great hunger for soil and live things growing, and because none of these things had long been ours to protect. We had planted the little sapling and watered if faithfully, and I remembered that I had run out with my small bucket to drench its roots the day we moved away. And all the years since it had been growing in my mind, a huge tree that somehow stood for my father and the love I bore him. I took a grasp on the picket fence and forced myself to look again.

A boy with the hard bird eye of youth pedaled a tricycle slowly 26 up beside me.

"What'cha lookin' at?" he asked curiously. 27

"A tree," I said. 28

"What for?" he said. 29

"It isn't there." I said, to myself mostly, and began to walk away 30 at a pace just slow enough not to seem to be running.

"What isn't there?" the boy asked. I didn't answer. It was obvious 31 I was attached by a thread to a thing that had never been there, or certainly not for long. Something that had to be held in the air, or sustained in the mind, because it was part of my orientation in the universe and I could not survive without it. There was more than an animal's attachment to a place. There was something else, the attachment of the spirit to a grouping of events in time; it was part of our morality.

So I had come home at last, driven by a memory in the brain as 32 surely as the field mouse who had delved long ago into my flower pot or the pigeons flying forever admist the rattle of nut-vending machines. These, the burrow under the greenery in my living room and the red-bellied bowls of peanuts now hovering in midair in the minds of pigeons, were all part of an elusive world that existed

WRITING SUGGESTIONS

1. Write an essay in which you discuss an example of a time when you felt an affinity with (or an antipathy toward) an animal.
2. Do you believe Eiseley is too idealistic about the "oneness" of human beings and nature? Write an essay in which you explain your position.

nowhere and yet everywhere. I looked once at the real world about me while the persistent boy pedaled at my heels.

It was without meaning, though my feet took a remembered path. 33 In sixty years the house and street had rotted out of my mind. But the tree, the tree that no longer was, that had perished in its first season, bloomed on in my individual mind, unblemished as my father's words. "We'll plant a tree here, son, and we're not going to move any more. And when you're an old, old man you can sit under it and think how we planted it here, you and me, together."

I began to outpace the boy on the tricycle. 34

"Do you live here, Mister?" he shouted after me suspiciously. I 35 took a firm grasp on airy nothing—to be precise, on the bole of a great tree. "I do," I said. I spoke for myself, one field mouse, and several pigeons. We were all out of touch but somehow permanent. It was the world that had changed.

RESPONDING TO READING

1. Have you seen people like the ones Eiseley describes in the beginning of his essay? Do you think his analogy between people and brown wasps trivializes the plight of the people you have seen, or do you think it is effective? Explain.　**2.** Could you argue that in this essay Eiseley seems to be more concerned about nature—wasps, pigeons, and trees—than about people? Why or why not?　**3.** Many students of animal behavior say that it is a mistake for us to project human qualities onto animals because by doing so we ignore what makes them unique. Do you agree? Does Eiseley make this mistake in his essay? Or is he projecting animal qualities onto humans? Explain.

ANSWERS TO RESPONDING
TO READING
1. Answers will vary.
2. Answers will vary. One might argue that Eiseley's empathy with both people and wasps is so strong that he could hardly trivialize their plight.
3. Eiseley universalizes the experience of humans and nature in order to underscore his theme. He uses examples of human behavior to explain animal behavior and examples of animal behavior to shed light on human behavior. By doing so, he shows that both animals and humans are part of the natural world and react to the same needs.

My Wood

E. M. FORSTER

British novelist, essayist, and short story writer E. M. Forster (1879–1969) first won wide recognition with his 1924 novel, *Passage to India*. Forster also wrote biographies, literary criticism, and accounts of his travels as well as *Two Cheers for Democracy*, a 1951 collection of essays. In the following essay from his book *Abinger Harvest* (1936), Forster takes a critical look at the effect of property ownership on individuals and on society.

A few years ago I wrote a book which dealt in part with the difficulties of the English in India. Feeling that they would have had no difficulties in India themselves, the Americans read the book freely. The more they read it the better it made them feel, and a check to the author was the result. I bought a wood with the check. It is not a large wood—it contains scarcely any trees, and it is intersected, blast it, by a public footpath. Still, it is the first property that I have owned, so it is right that other people should participate in my shame, and should ask themselves, in accents that will vary in horror, this very important question: What is the effect of property upon the character? Don't let's touch economics; the effect of private ownership upon the community as a whole is another question—a more important question, perhaps, but another one. Let's keep to psychology. If you own things, what's their effect on you? What's the effect on me of my wood?

In the first place, it makes me feel heavy. Property does have this effect. Property produces men of weight, and it was man of weight who failed to get into the Kingdom of Heaven. He was not wicked, that unfortunate millionaire in the parable, he was only stout; he stuck out in front, not to mention behind, and as he wedged himself this way and that in the crystalline entrance and bruised his well-fed flanks, he saw beneath him a comparatively slim camel passing through the eye of a needle and being woven into the robe of God.[1] The Gospels all through couple stoutness and slowness. They point out what is perfectly obvious, yet seldom realized: that if you have a lot of things you cannot move about a lot, that furniture requires dusting, dusters require servants, servants require insurance stamps, and the whole tangle of them makes you think twice before you accept an invitation to dinner or go for a bath in the Jordan. Sometimes the Gospels proceed further and say with Tolstoy that property is sinful; they approach the difficult ground of asceticism here, where I cannot follow them. But as to the immediate effects of property on people, they just show straightforward logic. It produces men of weight. Men of weight cannot, by definition, move like the lightning from the East unto the West, and the ascent of a fourteen-stone bishop into a pulpit is thus the exact antithesis of the coming of the Son of Man. My wood makes me feel heavy.

In the second place, it makes me feel it ought to be larger.

The other day I heard a twig snap in it. I was annoyed at first, for I thought that someone was blackberrying, and depreciating the

---

[1]"It is easier for a camel to go through the eye of a needle, than for a rich man to enter into the Kingdom of God." Matthew 19:246 [Eds.]

value of the undergrowth. On coming nearer, I saw it was not a man who had trodden on the twig and snapped it, but a bird, and I felt pleased. My bird. The bird was not equally pleased. Ignoring the relation between us, it took fright as soon as it saw the shape of my face, and flew straight over the boundary hedge into a field, the property of Mrs. Henessy, where it sat down with a loud squawk. It had become Mrs. Henessy's bird. Something seemed grossly amiss here, something that would not have occurred had the wood been larger. I could not afford to buy Mrs. Henessy out, I dared not murder her, and limitations of this sort beset me on every side. . . .

In the third place, property makes its owner feel that he ought 5 to do something to it. Yet he isn't sure what. A restlessness comes over him, a vague sense that he has a personality to express—the same sense which, without any vagueness, leads the artist to an act of creation. Sometimes I think I will cut down such trees as remain in the wood, at other times I want to fill up the gaps between them with new trees. Both impulses are pretentious and empty. They are not honest movements toward money-making or beauty. They spring from a foolish desire to express myself and from an inability to enjoy what I have got. Creation, property, enjoyment form a sinister trinity in the human mind. Creation and enjoyment are both very, very good, yet they are often unattainable without a material basis, and at such moments property pushes itself in as a substitute, saying, "Accept me instead—I'm good enough for all three." It is not enough. It is, as Shakespeare said of lust, "The expense of spirit in a waste of shame": it is "Before, a joy proposed; behind, a dream." Yet we don't know how to shun it. It is forced on us by our economic system as the alternative to starvation. It is also forced on us by an internal defect in the soul, by the feeling that in property may lie the germs of self-development and of exquisite or heroic deeds. Our life on earth is, and ought to be, material and carnal. But we have not yet learned to manage our materialism and carnality properly; they are still entangled with the desire for ownership, where (in the words of Dante) "Possession is one with loss."

And this brings us to our fourth and final point: the blackberries. 6

Blackberries are not plentiful in this meagre grove, but they are 7 easily seen from the public footpath which traverses it, and all too easily gathered. Foxgloves, too—people will pull up the foxgloves, and ladies of an educational tendency even grub for toadstools to show them on the Monday in class. Other ladies, less educated, roll down the bracken in the arms of their gentlemen friends. There is paper, there are tins. Pray, does my wood belong to me or doesn't it? And, if it does, should I not own it best by allowing no one else to walk there? There is a wood near Lyme Regis, also cursed by a

TEACHING STRATEGY

Outline the list of effects that Forster says ownership has on human character. Discuss his use of humor here to make his point.

COLLABORATIVE ACTIVITY

Break students into groups and ask them to consider the alternatives to private property. How would they feel about living in a communal situation such as a kibbutz in Israel or a commune in the United States during the 1960s?

WRITING SUGGESTIONS

1. A bird that is on Forster's property flies onto his neighbor's land. He faces a dilemma: whose bird is it? Write an essay in which you discuss to what extent we can "own" nature, and what this ownership implies.
2. Has something you owned ever become a burden to you? Write an essay in which you explain how and why. In addition, tell what, if anything, you did to ease that burden.

public footpath, where the owner has not hesitated on this point. He had built high stone walls each side of the path, and has spanned it by bridges, so that the public circulate like termites while he gorges on the blackberries unseen. He really does own his wood, this able chap. And perhaps I shall come to this in time. I shall wall in and fence out until I really taste the sweets of property. Enormously stout, endlessly avaricious, pseudo-creative, intensely selfish, I shall weave upon my forehead the quadruple crown of possession until those nasty Bolshies[2] come and take it off again and thrust me aside into the outer darkness.

RESPONDING TO READING

1. In this essay Forster shows how an ordinary place can have special significance. What ordinary place has this kind of significance for you? What does it teach you about yourself? About nature and the environment? **2.** Would you say that owning the wood has positive or negative effects on Forster? Explain. **3.** What general point is Forster implying about private property and ownership? Do you think he overstates his case? How valid are his conclusions?

Why Smaller Refrigerators Can Preserve the Human Race

APPLETREE RODDEN

Appletree Rodden has danced with the Staatstheatre Ballet Company and was at one time a biochemical researcher at Stanford University. His essay here, first published in *Harper's* in 1975, asks us to consider whether "bigger and more" necessarily means better when it comes to technology.

Once, long ago, people had special little boxes called refrigerators in which milk, meat, and eggs could be kept cool. The grandchildren of these simple devices are large enough to store whole cows, and they reach temperatures comparable to those at the South Pole. Their operating costs increase each year, and they are so complicated that few home handymen attempt to repair them on their own.

1

---

[2]Bolsheviks. Advocates of a proletarian dictatorship in Russia by the Soviets. Forster uses the word in a general sense to refer to Communists. [Eds.]

Why has this change in size and complexity occurred in America? It has not taken place in many areas of the technologically advanced world (the average West German refrigerator is about a yard high and less than a yard wide, yet refrigeration technology in Germany is quite advanced). Do we really need (or even want) all that space and cold?

The benefits of a large refrigerator are apparent: a saving of time (one grocery-shopping trip a week instead of several), a saving of money (the ability to buy expensive, perishable items in larger, cheaper quantities), a feeling of security (if the car breaks down or if famine strikes, the refrigerator is well stocked). The costs are there, too, but they are not so obvious.

Cost number one is psychological. Ever since the refrigerator began to grow, food has increasingly become something we buy to store rather than to eat. Few families go to market daily for their daily bread. The manna in the wilderness could be gathered for only one day at a time. The ancient distaste for making food a storage item is echoed by many modern psychiatrists who suggest that such psychosomatic disorders as obesity are often due to the patient's inability to come to terms with the basic transitoriness of life. Research into a relationship between excessive corpulence and the size of one's refrigerator has not been extensive, but we might suspect one to be there.

Another cost is aesthetic. In most of Europe, where grocery marketing is still a part of the daily rhythm, one can buy tomatoes, lettuce, and the like picked on the day of purchase. Many European families have modest refrigerators for storing small items (eggs, milk, butter) for a couple of days, but the concept of buying large quantities of food to store in the refrigerator is not widely accepted. Since fresh produce is easily available in Europe, most people buy it daily.

Which brings to mind another price the large refrigerator has cost us: the friendly neighborhood market. In America, time is money. A large refrigerator means fewer time-consuming trips to the grocery store. One member of a deep-freeze-owning family can do the grocery shopping once or twice a month rather than daily. Since shopping trips are infrequent, most people have been willing to forego the amenities of the little store around the corner in favor of the lower prices found in the supermarket.

If refrigerators weren't so large—that is, if grocery marketing were a daily affair—the "entertainment surcharge" of buying farm-fresh food in a smaller, more intimate setting might carry some weight. But as it is, there is not really that much difference between eggs bought from Farmer Brown's wife and eggs bought from the supermarket which in turn bought them from Eggs Incorporated, a firm operated out of Los Angeles that produces 200,000 eggs a day from

ADDITIONAL QUESTIONS FOR RESPONDING TO READING

1. What image do you get of the author as a person? Are you inclined to accept him as an authority? Why or why not?
2. Does Rodden's essay seem dated, or do his observations still hold true? What weaknesses, if any, do you find in his argument?
3. Does Rodden seem antiscience or hostile to technology? Explain.

TEACHING STRATEGIES

1. Recently, ideas similar to Rodden's have been accepted into mainstream thinking. Discuss such topics as energy-efficient appliances, recycling, and biodegradable soaps.
2. Discuss possible ways to counter Rodden's argument. If you were a manufacturer of refrigerators, would you try to appeal to people's logic or to their emotions? Or to both?

COLLABORATIVE ACTIVITIES

1. Ask students, working in small groups, to think of environmental concerns that once were considered radical that have been incorporated into our way of life. Follow with class discussion.

2. Ask each student group to do some research to determine how a particular news medium—television, radio, a weekly newsmagazine, a local newspaper, or a national newspaper—covers a particular environmental problem. How does coverage differ? Why?

chickens that are kept in gigantic warehouses lighted artificially on an eighteen-hour light-and-dark cycle and produce one-and-a-half times as many eggs—a special breed of chickens who die young and insane. Not much difference if you don't mind eating eggs from crazy chickens.

Chalk up Farmer and Mrs. Brown as cost number four of the big refrigerator. The small farmer can't make it in a society dominated by supermarkets and big refrigerators; make way for superfarmers, super yields, and pesticides (cost number five). 8

Cost number six of the big refrigerator has been the diminution of regional food differences. Of course the homogenization of American fare cannot be blamed solely on the availability of frozen food. Nonetheless, were it not for the trend toward turning regional specialties into frozen dinners, it might still be possible to experience novelty closer to home. 9

So much for the disadvantages of the big refrigerator. What about the advantages of the small one? First of all, it would help us to "think small," which is what we must learn anyway if the scary predictions of the Club of Rome[1] (*The Limits of Growth*) are true. The advent of smaller refrigerators would set the stage for reversing the "big-thinking" trends brought on with the big refrigerator, and would eventually change our lives. 10

Ivan Illich makes the point in *Tools for Conviviality* that any tool we use (the automobile, standardized public education, public-health care, the refrigerator) influences the individual, his society, and the relationship between the two. A person's automobile is a part of his identity. The average Volkswagen owner has a variety of characteristics (income, age, occupation) significantly different from those of the average Cadillac owner. American society, with more parking lots than parks, and with gridded streets rather than winding lanes, would be vastly different without the private automobile. Similar conclusions can be drawn about any of the tools we use. They change us. They change our society. Therefore, it behooves us to think well before we decide which tool to use to accomplish a given task. Do we want tools that usurp power unto themselves, the ones called "non-convivial" by Illich? 11

The telephone, a "convivial tool," has remained under control; it has not impinged itself on society or on the individual. Each year it has become more efficient, and it has not prevented other forms of communication (letter writing, visits). The world might be poorer 12

---

[1]A non-political group of individuals from fifty-one countries who are concurred about problems confronting society. The group periodically publishes reports, such as *The Limits of Growth*, which examine the effects of science and technology on society. [Eds.]

without the telephone, but it would not be grossly different. Telephones do not pollute, are not status symbols, and interact only slightly (if at all) with one's self-image.

So what about the refrigerator? Or back to the more basic problem 13 to which the refrigerator was a partial answer: what about our supply of food? When did we decide to convert the emotion-laden threat of starvation from a shared community problem (of societal structure: farm-market-home) to a personal one (of storage)? How did we decide to accept a thawed block taken from a supermarket's freezer as a substitute for the voluptuous shapes, smells, and textures of fresh fruits and vegetables obtained from complex individual sources?

The decision for larger refrigerators has been consistent with a 14 change in food-supply routes from highly diversified "trails" (from small farms to neighborhood markets) to uniform, standardized highways (from large farms to centrally located supermarkets). Desirable meals are quick and easy rather than rich and lesiurely. Culinary artistry has given way to efficiency, the efficiency of the big refrigerator.

People have a natural propensity for running good things into 15 the ground. Mass production has been a boon to mankind, but its reliance on homogeneity precludes its being a paradigm for all areas of human life. Our forebears and contemporaries have made it possible to mass-produce almost anything. An equally challenging task now lies with us: to choose which things of this world should be mass-produced, and how the standards of mass production should influence other standards we hold dear.

Should houses be mass-produced? Should education? Should 16 food? Which brings us back to refrigerators. How does one decide how large a refrigerator to buy, considering one's life, one's society, and the world, and not simply the question of food storage?

As similar questions are asked about more and more of the things 17 we mass-produce, mass production will become less of a problem and more of a blessing. As cost begins to be measured not only in dollars spent and minutes saved, but in total richness acquired, perhaps smaller refrigerators will again make good sense. A small step backward along some of the roads of "technological progress" might be a large step forward for mankind, and one our age is uniquely qualified to make.

RESPONDING TO READING

1. What biases does Rodden have about the environment? In what way do these biases show themselves? Which, if any, do you share?   **2.** Rodden concludes his essay by saying that a small step backward might result in a

WRITING SUGGESTION

Write an essay in which you agree or take issue with Rodden's idea that we must learn to "think small" in our relationship to the environment.

ANSWERS TO RESPONDING TO READING

1. Rodden indicates that we must learn to "think small," implying that humans make too many demands on the planet. He is concerned about overproduction of food (using chemicals) and about pollution. Personal opinions of his view will vary.

2. Answers will vary. Rodden implies that more intelligent use of resources might result from the production of smaller, more energy-efficient items. Some people might call this response a step backward, but actually it is a step forward—for example, the manufacturing of small energy-efficient automobiles in the present versus the large gas guzzlers of the past.

3. No. Rodden wants to show that smaller refrigerators would be part of a larger move toward "thinking small," which could eventually change our lives.

BACKGROUND ON READING

In an interview with *Contemporary Authors*, Lopez describes the relationship between the writer and "place": "I operate with a sense that I'm participating in something much larger than my own ability to see or comprehend. Because I believe that, when I go to a place, or when I'm interviewing a person, I'm always aware that there is more here than ever I could comprehend, and that the best way to pass on what is valuable to a reader is to make myself vulnerable or open to the moment or to the event or to the place" (*Contemporary Authors*, New Revision Series, vol. 23).

FOR OPENERS

Ask students to write a paragraph about a place with which they are very familiar. Discuss how places can have tremendous power to evoke memories and associations.

large step forward. Do you agree with this sentiment? Does it apply to other environmental issues? Explain. **3.** Does Rodden expect readers to take his title literally? Explain. Can you suggest another title that would convey the point of his essay in an interesting and eye-catching way?

Landscape and Narrative

BARRY LOPEZ

In much of his writing, Barry Lopez (1945–   ) uses natural history as a metaphor for larger themes, such as the interaction between people and the landscape. Lopez says, "By landscape I mean the complete lay of the land—the animals that are there, the trees, the vegetation, . . . the sounds common to the region." His most popular book, *Of Wolves and Men* (1979), is considered a complete portrait of the wolf. He is also the author of *Arctic Dreams: Imagination and Desire in a Northern Landscape* (1986) and has retold many Native American stories. In "Landscape and Narrative," from *Crossing Open Ground* (1988), Lopez shows how oral stories can animate the landscape in which they are set and how storytelling generates an "inexplicable renewal of enthusiasm" in listeners.

One summer evening in a remote village in the Brooks Range of Alaska, I sat among a group of men listening to hunting stories about the trapping and pursuit of animals. I was particularly interested in several incidents involving wolverine, in part because a friend of mine was studying wolverine[1] in Canada, among the Cree, but, too, because I find this animal such an intense creature. To hear about its life is to learn more about fierceness.   1

Wolverines are not intentionally secretive, hiding their lives from view, but they are seldom observed. The range of their known behavior is less than that of, say, bears or wolves. Still, that evening no gratuitous details were set out. This was somewhat odd, for wolverine easily excite the imagination; they can loom suddenly in the landscape with authority, with an aura larger than their compact physical dimensions, drawing one's immediate and complete attention. Wolverine also have a deserved reputation for resoluteness in the worst winters, for ferocious strength. But neither did these attributes induce the men to embellish.   2

---

[1]The largest members of the weasel family, wolverines are extremely fierce and will attack nearly every animal except human beings. [Eds.]

I listened carefully to these stories, taking pleasure in the sharply observed detail surrounding the dramatic thread of events. The story I remember most vividly was about a man hunting a wolverine from a snow machine in the spring. He followed the animal's tracks for several miles over rolling tundra in a certain valley. Soon he caught sight ahead of a dark spot on the crest of a hill—the wolverine pausing to look back. The hunter was catching up, but each time he came over a rise the wolverine was looking back from the next rise, just out of range. The hunter topped one more rise and met the wolverine bounding toward him. Before he could pull his rifle from its scabbard the wolverine flew across the engine cowl and the windshield, hitting him square in the chest. The hunter scrambled his arms wildly, trying to get the wolverine out of his lap, and fell over as he did so. The wolverine jumped clear as the snow machine rolled over, and fixed the man with a stare. He had not bitten, not even scratched the man. Then the wolverine walked away. The man thought of reaching for the gun, but no, he did not.

The other stories were like this, not so much making a point as evoking something about contact with wild animals that would never be completely understood.

When the stories were over, four or five of us walked out of the home of our host. The surrounding land, in the persistent light of a far northern summer, was still visible for miles—the striated, pitched massifs of the Brooks Range; the shy, willow-lined banks of the John River flowing south from Anaktuvuk Pass; and the flat tundra plain, opening with great affirmation to the north. The landscape seemed alive because of the stories. It was precisely these ocherous tones, this kind of willow, exactly this austerity that had informed the wolverine narratives. I felt exhilaration, and a deeper confirmation of the stories. The mundane tasks which awaited me I anticipated now with pleasure. The stories had renewed in me a sense of the purpose of my life.

This feeling, an inexplicable renewal of enthusiasm after story-telling, is familiar to many people. It does not seem to matter greatly what the subject is, as long as the context is intimate and the story is told for its own sake, not forced to serve merely as the vehicle for an idea. The tone of the story need not be solemn. The darker aspects of life need not be ignored. But I think intimacy is indispensable—a feeling that derives from the listener's trust and a storyteller's certain knowledge of his subject and regard for his audience. This intimacy deepens if the storyteller tempers his authority with humility, or when terms of idiomatic expression, or at least the physical setting for the story, are shared.

COLLABORATIVE ACTIVITY

Ask each student to relate a story about a personal experience to his or her small group, and have each group then nominate a student to tell his or her story to the class. Discuss the narratives on the basis of Lopez's criteria.

I think of two landscapes—one outside the self, the other within. 7 The external landscape is the one we see—not only the line and color of the land and its shading at different times of the day, but also its plants and animals in season, its weather, its geology, the record of its climate and evolution. If you walk up, say, a dry arroyo in the Sonoran Desert you will feel a mounding and rolling of sand and silt beneath your foot that is distinctive. You will anticipate the crumbling of the sedimentary earth in the arroyo[2] bank as your hand reaches out, and in that tangible evidence you will sense a history of water in the region. Perhaps a black-throated sparrow lands in a paloverde bush—the resiliency of the twig under the bird, that precise shade of yellowish-green against the milk-blue sky, the fluttering whir of the arriving sparrow, are what I mean by "the landscape." Draw on the smell of creosote bush, or clack stones together in the dry air. Feel how light is the desiccated dropping of the kangaroo rat. Study an animal track obscured by the wind. These are all elements of the land, and what makes the landscape comprehensible are the relationships between them. One learns a landscape finally not by knowing the name or identity of everything in it, but by perceiving the relationships in it—like that between the sparrow and the twig. The difference between the relationships and the elements is the same as that between written history and a catalog of events.

The second landscape I think of is an interior one, a kind of 8 projection within a person of a part of the exterior landscape. Relationships in the exterior landscape include those that are named and discernible, such as the nitrogen cycle, or a vertical sequence of Ordovician limestone, and others that are uncodified or ineffable, such as winter light falling on a particular kind of granite, or the effect of humidity on the frequency of a blackpoll warbler's burst of song. That these relationships have purpose and order, however inscrutable they may seem to us, is a tenet of evolution. Similarly, the speculations, intuitions, and formal ideas we refer to as "mind" are a set of relationships in the interior landscape with purpose and order; some of these are obvious, many impenetrably subtle. The shape and character of these relationships in a person's thinking, I believe, are deeply influenced by where on this earth one goes, what one touches, the patterns one observes in nature—the intricate history of one's life in the land, even a life in the city, where wind, the chirp of birds, the line of a falling leaf, are known. These thoughts are arranged, further, according to the thread of one's moral, intellectual, and spiritual development. The interior landscape responds to the character and

---

[2]Brook or stream. [Eds.]

subtlety of an exterior landscape; the shape of the individual mind is affected by land as it is by genes.

In stories like those I heard at Anaktuvuk Pass about wolverine, 9 the relationship between separate elements in the land is set forth clearly. It is put in a simple framework of sequential incidents and apposite detail. If the exterior landscape is limned[3] well, the listener often feels that he has heard something pleasing and authentic— trustworthy. We derive this sense of confidence I think not so much from verifiable truth as from an understanding that lying has played no role in the narrative. The storyteller is obligated to engage the reader with a precise vocabulary, to set forth a coherent and dramatic rendering of incidents—and to be ingenuous.

When one hears a story one takes pleasure in it for different 10 reasons—for the euphony of its phrases, an aspect of the plot, or because one identifies with one of the characters. With certain stories certain individuals may experience a deeper, more profound sense of well-being. This latter phenomenon, in my understanding, rests at the heart of storytelling as an elevated experience among aboriginal peoples. It results from bringing two landscapes together. The exterior landscape is organized according to principles or laws or tendencies beyond human control. It is understood to contain an integrity that is beyond human analysis and unimpeachable. Insofar as the story- teller depicts various subtle and obvious relationships in the exterior landscape accurately in his story, and insofar as he orders them along traditional lines of meaning to create the narrative, the narrative will "ring true." The listener who "takes the story to heart" will feel a pervasive sense of congruence within himself and also with the world.

Among the Navajo and, as far as I know, many other native 11 peoples, the land is thought to exhibit a sacred order. That order is the basis of ritual. The rituals themselves reveal the power in that order. Art, architecture, vocabulary, and costume, as well as ritual, are derived from the perceived natural order of the universe—from observations and meditations on the exterior landscape. An indige- nous philosophy—metaphysics, ethics, epistemology, aesthetics, and logic—may also be derived from a people's continuous attentiveness to both the obvious (scientific) and ineffable (artistic) orders of the local landscape. Each individual, further, undertakes to order his interior landscape according to the exterior landscape. To succeed in this means to achieve a balanced state of mental health.

I think of the Navajo for a specific reason. Among the various 12 sung ceremonies of this people—Enemyway, Coyoteway, Red

---

[3]Depicted. [Eds.]

Antway, Uglyway—is one called Beautyway. In the Navajo view, the elements of one's interior life—one's psychological makeup and moral bearing—are subject to a persistent principle of disarray. Beautyway is, in part, a spiritual invocation of the order of the exterior universe, that irreducible, holy complexity that manifests itself as all things changing through time (a Navajo definition of beauty, hózhóó). The purpose of this invocation is to recreate in the individual who is the subject of the Beautyway ceremony that same order, to make the individual again a reflection of the myriad enduring relationships of the landscape.

I believe story functions in a similar way. A story draws on relationships in the exterior landscape and projects them onto the interior landscape. The purpose of storytelling is to achieve harmony between the two landscapes, to use all the elements of story—syntax, mood, figures of speech—in a harmonious way to reproduce the harmony of the land in the individual's interior. Inherent in story is the power to reorder a state of psychological confusion through contact with the pervasive truth of those relationships we call "the land." 13

These thoughts, of course, are susceptible to interpretation. I am convinced, however, that these observations can be applied to the kind of prose we call nonfiction as well as to traditional narrative forms such as the novel and the short story, and to some poems. Distinctions between fiction and nonfiction are sometimes obscured by arguments over what constitutes "the truth." In the aboriginal literature I am familiar with, the first distinction made among narratives is to separate the authentic from the inauthentic. Myth, which we tend to regard as fictitious or "merely metaphorical," is as authentic, as real, as the story of a wolverine in a man's lap. (A distinction is made, of course, about the elevated nature of myth— and frequently the circumstances of myth-telling are more rigorously prescribed than those for the telling of legends or vernacular stories— but all of these narratives are rooted in the local landscape. To violate *that* connection is to call the narrative itself into question.) 14

The power of narrative to nurture and heal, to repair a spirit in disarray, rests on two things: the skillful invocation of unimpeachable sources and a listener's knowledge that no hypocrisy or subterfuge is involved. This last simple fact is to me one of the most imposing aspects of the Holocene history of man. 15

We are more accustomed now to thinking of "the truth" as something that can be explicitly stated, rather than as something that can be evoked in a metaphorical way outside science and Occidental culture. Neither can truth be reduced to aphorism or formulas. It is something alive and unpronounceable. Story creates an atmosphere 16 in which it becomes discernible as a pattern. For a storyteller to insist on relationships that do not exist is to lie. Lying is the opposite of story. (I do not mean to confuse ignorance with deception, or to imply that a storyteller can perceive all that is inherent in the land. Every storyteller falls short of a perfect limning of the landscape—perception and language both fail. But to make up something that is not there, something which can never be corroborated in the land, to knowingly set forth a false relationship, is to be lying, no longer telling a story.)

Because of the intricate, complex nature of the land, it is not always possible for a storyteller to grasp what is contained in a story. The intent of the storyteller, then, must be to evoke, honestly, some single aspect of all that the land contains. The storyteller knows that because different individuals grasp the story at different levels, the focus of his regard for truth must be at the primary one—with who was there, what happened, when, where, and why things occurred. The story will then possess similar truth at other levels—the integrity inherent at the primary level of meaning will be conveyed everywhere else. As long as the storyteller carefully describes the order before him, and uses his storytelling skill to heighten and emphasize certain relationships, it is even possible for the story to be more successful than the storyteller himself is able to imagine. 17

I would like to make a final point about the wolverine stories I heard at Anaktuvuk Pass. I wrote down the details afterward, concentrating especially on aspects of the biology and ecology of the animals. I sent the information on to my friend living with the Cree. When, many months later, I saw him, I asked whether the Cree had enjoyed these insights of the Nunamiut into the nature of the wolverine. What had they said? 18

"You know," he told me, "how they are. They said, "That could happen.' " 19

In these uncomplicated words the Cree declared their own knowledge of the wolverine. They acknowledged that although they themselves had never seen the things the Nunamiut spoke of, they accepted them as accurate observations, because they did not consider story a context for misrepresentation. They also preserved their own dignity by not overstating their confidence in the Nunamiut, a distant and unknown people. 20

Whenever I think of this courtesy on the part of the Cree I think of the dignity that is ours when we cease to demand the truth and realize that the best we can have of those substantial truths that guide our lives is metaphorical—a story. And the most of it we are likely to discern comes only when we accord one another the respect the Cree showed the Nunamiut. Beyond this—that the interior landscape 21

WRITING SUGGESTIONS

1. Write an essay about a place that has special meaning to you.
2. Analyze Lopez's criteria for a good narrative. Then write an essay in which you discuss whether or not Jack London's "To Build a Fire" (page 979) satisfies these criteria.

is a metaphorical representation of the exterior landscape, that the truth reveals itself most fully not in dogma but in the paradox, irony, and contradictions that distinguish compelling narratives—beyond this there are only failures of imagination: reductionism in science; fundamentalism in religion; fascism in politics.

Our national literatures should be important to us insofar as they 22 sustain us with illumination and heal us. They can always do that so long as they are written with respect for both the source and the reader, and with an understanding of why the human heart and the land have been brought together so regularly in human history.

RESPONDING TO READING

1. How, according to Lopez, does the storyteller help us to connect our "inner landscapes" with the natural world around us? Could you argue that television serves the same function as narrative, balancing the two types of landscape Lopez describes?   **2.** What value does Lopez put on stories? Do you think stories and storytellers are as important as he thinks they are?   **3.** In the last paragraph of his essay, Lopez makes a case for the importance of our national literatures. What does he mean by the term *national literatures*? Do you believe it is possible for a country as diverse as the United States to have a single "national literature"? Explain.

Sense of Place

BARBARA LAZEAR ASCHER

Feminist writer (see also page 386) Barbara Lazear Ascher explores the notion of place in our consciousness and culture in this selection from her book *The Habit of Loving* (1989).

I am uncertain whether it is the land or the people inhabiting the 1 land that gives one a sense of place. If you read *Far Away and Long Ago*, W. H. Hudson's moving autobiography of his boyhood in Argentina, you are quite certain it is the land. That the foundation for a sense of place is animism, a belief, not uncommon among children, that the earth and all that grows therein possess a soul, a spirit similar to one's own. Hudson's book is less biography than the story of mutual love shared with the trees, flowers, and birds of the pampas.

It may be the land that makes the primal claim, when a child, 2 locked in early muteness, has a natural affinity for the silent lives of trees and terrain. But it is the people that bring drama to a place. And it is drama that gives rise to the storytelling of later years. Stories that make it possible for the mind to return to a place long since departed.

When my sister and I reminisce, those of whom we speak could be characters created by Welty, Faulkner, or Hardy. Many of the children with whom we shared overheated classrooms came to school straight from the barnyard and morning chores. When it was "rest time," and Mrs. Murdoch played the piano and sang the sad song of Bobby Shaftoe going to sea, those weary laborers fell into deep sleep. Resting their heads on arms held in a fold by hands creased with brown.

We sometimes speak of the man in the hollow, who was a collector and would swap his things for your things. His refrigerator door for your car fender. Four worn tires for a picture frame buffed with gilt. Only weeds and rust claimed a plow that, in winter, protruded from snow like the rib cage of a fallen animal. And nobody ever had a swap for the claw-footed bathtub that rested among choke weed and Queen Anne's lace.

Unlike Hudson's, these memories comprise a one-sided love affair. If you, a stranger, were to pass through and ask the swapper if he remembers us, chances are he'd scratch his chin, do you the courtesy of repeating our names and feigning thought. He would appear to search the horizon the way one might investigate a row of books in a library stack. "Nope, can't say that I do," he'd say, and kick some gravel with his worn boot to dismiss you.

If you entered the schoolyard, a pasture where cows no longer graze, if you stopped at the swing set or baseball diamond, and asked after us, you might get a giggle and a quick shake of the head before losing your witness to a game of tag.

It's as if we were never there.

Sense of place is bolstered by a cruel, unrequited love. It takes hold insidiously as scents, scenes, and the corners of rooms become objects of eternal passion. When does the place where you rest your head become a matter for the heart to contend with? And how does the place you claim turn around and claim you?

"Former lives," a friend explains, and quickly adds, "Look, I'm not weird or from California or anything, I'm a very sensible down-to-earth person." But she thinks in a former life she lived near London's Covent Garden. She says it's the only way to explain her sense of peace when she's there as compared to the displacement she felt as a child. "I never felt at home where I lived in upstate New York. I remember, when I was eight years old, sitting on the back steps and thinking, 'I don't belong here.' "

3

4

5

6

7

8

9

ADDITIONAL QUESTIONS FOR RESPONDING TO READING

1. Is Ascher's tone appropriate for her purpose? Does it strike you as sentimental? Explain.
2. How is finding a sense of place analogous to falling in love?

TEACHING STRATEGY

Discuss the elements that Ascher says are involved in a sense of place. In what ways is Ascher's idea of "environment" different from those of other writers in this section? Why is having a "sense of place" so important?

COLLABORATIVE ACTIVITY

Assign groups the task of locating and bringing into class quotations by other writers addressing the "sense of place." In class discussion, try to classify the quotations into categories suggested by the class.

WRITING SUGGESTION

Ascher says that the sense of place "is bolstered by a cruel, unrequited love." What does she mean? Write an essay in which you support your explanation with examples from your own experience.

I remember when I was eight years old, sitting beneath the eaves 10 of my room and thinking, I do belong here. I belonged, not only in that room, but to the hills, pastures and the old apple tree outside my window. A tree with peeling bark and gnarled limbs that managed annual rejuvenations, bursts of energy each spring and fall bringing sweet and spicy perfumes. Scents set in a young girl's heart.

Scents that gave one a sense of place. 11

Beyond the tree, past the barn and pasture, set on the rise of a 12 distant hill was China. If I had read Blake,[1] I could just as easily have thought it was Jerusalem. Years later, when riding our horses there for picnics and the view, I would laugh at my earlier perspective. But it is that perspective that remains, somehow encompassing the mystery of what it means to be home.

When we left, twenty-four years ago, slamming the car doors, 13 and driving away through the twilight, we were uncertain whether to close our eyes to deny departure or to stare, to cling with vision as a young child outside a schoolyard might hold fast to a mother's skirts. The smell of hay and cows and barnyards grew heavy in the damp as cooling night fell like a curtain coming down. We would never again be on the other side. From then on we were audience.

The difference between being a home and not is that, if you are 14 not, you are always the outsider looking in: sometimes amused and entertained by what you see, but always displaced and alone, and a bit uncomfortable in your seat, even if you're surrounded by others sharing the darkened theater. It's brighter and warmer up there on the stage where people belong to each other and the scenery.

Eudora Welty is at home in Jackson. William Faulkner was at 15 home in Oxford. Although their gifts suggest that they would have written wherever they had been born and raised, I doubt their writings would shine with that peculiar and passionate energy had the authors not been born to places responsive to their spirits.

This bonding is described in Welty's essay, "Some Notes on River 16 Country." "A place that ever was lived in is like a fire that never goes out. It flares up, it smolders for a time, it is fanned or smothered by circumstance, but its being is intact, forever fluttering within it, the result of some original ignition."

No one is left to tell you, should you wander into the valley of 17 my home, that there was an ignition, a flame. But then, nobody ever saw it light. That happens in the intimate encounter of a young heart with a particular arch of a hill, or evening smells in rain or the sound of snow plows scraping a country road at two A.M. It is just like falling

---

[1]Ascher refers here to *Jerusalem*, a poem by English poet William Blake (1757–1827). [Eds.]

in love. If you try to remember how it happened, you may speak of being captivated by a graceful curve of hip, the melody of a voice, or the slant of eye. You will point to landmarks of the heart's path, but you'll be unable to re-create the journey.

RESPONDING TO READING

1. Do you agree with Ascher that most people have a sense of place? Do you believe a sense of place is possible in a country like the United States, where the population is highly mobile? Explain.   **2.** Is having a sense of place different from feeling a closeness with nature? If so, how?   **3.** What memories have created a sense of place for you? What does this place look like?

To Build a Fire

JACK LONDON

Jack London (1876–1916), born in San Francisco, left high school to become a sailor; he first bought his own boat and then signed aboard a sailing vessel for an expedition to the Pacific. At age twenty-one, after returning to California and graduating from high school, he journeyed to Alaska for the gold rush. London based his first short stories, *Son of Wolf* (1900), and the novel *Call of the Wild* (1903) on his experiences in Alaska. Many works followed these, including *Martin Eden* (1909), an autobiographical novel. The 1910 short story "To Build a Fire" tells of a battle between the frozen Yukon and a man's will to live.

Day had broken cold and gray, exceedingly cold and gray, when   1 the man turned aside from the main Yukon trail and climbed the high earth-bank, where a dim and little-travelled trail led eastward through the fat spruce timberland. It was a steep bank, and he paused for breath at the top, excusing the act to himself by looking at his watch. It was nine o'clock. There was no sun nor hint of sun, though there was not a cloud in the sky. It was a clear day, and yet there seemed an intangible pall over the face of things, a subtle gloom that made the day dark, and that was due to the absence of sun. This fact did not worry the man. He was used to the lack of sun. It had been days since he had seen the sun, and he knew that a few more days must pass before that cheerful orb, due south, would just peep above the sky line and dip immediately from view.

The man flung a look back along the way he had come. The Yukon   2 lay a mile wide and hidden under three feet of ice. On top of this ice were as many feet of snow. It was all pure white, rolling in gentle undulations where the ice jams of the freeze-up had formed. North and south, as far as his eye could see, it was unbroken white, save for a dark hairline that curved and twisted from around the spruce-covered island to the south, and that curved and twisted away into the north, where it disappeared behind another spruce-covered island. This dark hairline was the trail—the main trail—that led south five hundred miles to the Chilcoot Pass, Dyea, and salt water; and that led north seventy miles to Dawson, and still on to the north a thousand miles to Nulato, and finally to St. Michael, on Bering Sea, a thousand miles and half a thousand more.

But all this—the mysterious, far-reaching hairline trail, the absence of sun from the sky, the tremendous cold, and the strangeness and weirdness of it all—made no impression on the man. It was not because he was long used to it. He was a newcomer in the land, a *chechaquo*, and this was his first winter. The trouble with him was that he was without imagination. He was quick and alert in the things of life, but only in the things, and not in the significances. Fifty degrees below zero meant eighty-odd degrees of frost. Such fact impressed him as being cold and uncomfortable, and that was all. It did not lead him to meditate upon his frailty as a creature of temperature, and upon man's frailty in general, able only to live within certain narrow limits of heat and cold; and from there on it did not lead him to the conjectural field of immortality and man's place in the universe. Fifty degrees below zero stood for a bite of frost that hurt and that must be guarded against by the use of mittens, ear flaps, warm moccasins, and thick socks. Fifty degrees below zero was to him just precisely fifty degrees below zero. That there should be anything more to it than that was a thought that never entered his head.

As he turned to go on, he spat speculatively. There was a sharp, explosive crackle that startled him. He spat again. And again, in the air, before it could fall to the snow, the spittle crackled. He knew that at fifty below spittle crackled on the snow, but this spittle had crackled in the air. Undoubtedly it was colder than fifty below—how much colder he did not know. But the temperature did not matter. He was bound for the old claim on the left fork of Henderson Creek, where the boys were already. They had come over across the divide from the Indian Creek country, while he had come the roundabout way to take a look at the possibilities of getting out logs in the spring from the islands in the Yukon. He would be in to camp by six o'clock; a bit after dark, it was true, but the boys would be there, a fire would be going, and a hot supper would be ready. As for lunch, he pressed his hand against the protruding bundle under his jacket. It was also under his shirt, wrapped up in a handkerchief and lying against the naked skin. It was the only way to keep the biscuits from freezing. He smiled agreeably to himself as he thought of those biscuits, each cut open and sopped in bacon grease, and each enclosing a generous slice of fried bacon.

He plunged in among the big spruce trees. The trail was faint. A   5
foot of snow had fallen since the last sled had passed over, and he was glad he was without a sled, travelling light. In fact, he carried nothing but the lunch wrapped in the handkerchief. He was surprised, however, at the cold. It certainly was cold, he concluded, as he rubbed his numb nose and cheekbones with his mittened hand. He was a warm-whiskered man, but the hair on his face did not protect the high cheek-bones and the eager nose that thrust itself aggressively into the frosty air.

At the man's heels trotted a dog, a big native husky, the proper   6
wolf dog, gray-coated and without any visible or temperamental difference from its brother, the wild wolf. The animal was depressed by the tremendous cold. It knew that it was no time for travelling. Its instinct told it a truer tale than was told to the man by the man's judgment. In reality, it was not merely colder than fifty below zero; it was colder than sixty below, than seventy below. It was seventy-five below zero. Since the freezing point is thirty-two above zero, it meant that one hundred and seven degrees of frost obtained. The dog did not know anything about thermometers. Possibly in its brain there was no sharp consciousness of a condition of very cold such as was in the man's brain. But the brute had its instinct. It experienced a vague but menacing apprehension that subdued it and made it slink along at the man's heels, and that made it question eagerly every unwonted movement of the man as if expecting him to go into camp or to seek shelter somewhere and build a fire. The dog had learned fire, and it wanted fire, or else to burrow under the snow and cuddle its warmth away from the air.

The frozen moisture of its breathing had settled on its fur in a   7
fine powder of frost, and especially were its jowls, muzzle, and eyelashes whitened by its crystalled breath. The man's red beard and mustache were likewise frosted, but more solidly, the deposit taking the form of ice and increasing with every warm, moist breath he exhaled. Also, the man was chewing tobacco, and the muzzle of ice held his lips so rigidly that he was unable to clear his chin when he expelled the juice. The result was that a crystal beard of the color and solidity of amber was increasing its length on his chin. If he fell down it would shatter itself, like glass, into brittle fragments. But he did not mind the appendage. It was the penalty all tobacco chewers paid in that country, and he had been out before in two cold snaps. They had not been so cold as this, he knew, but by the spirit thermometer

TEACHING STRATEGIES

1. Discuss London's view of nature. Notice that he does not attempt to infuse nature with a particular personality. Compare and contrast London's concept of nature with that of others in this section—for example, Annie Dillard and John McPhee.

2. Occasionally, the narrator makes subjective comments: "The trouble with him was that he was without imagination. He was quick and alert in the things of life, but only in the things, and not in the significances" (paragraph 3); "The cold of space smote the unprotected tip of the planet, and he, being on that unprotected tip, received the full force of the blow" (paragraph 20). Relate these and similar passages to the story's theme.

at Sixty Mile he knew they had been registered at fifty below and at fifty-five.

He held on through the level stretch of woods for several miles, 8 crossed a wide flat of nigger heads,[1] and dropped down a bank to the frozen bed of a small stream. This was Henderson Creek, and he knew he was ten miles from the forks. He looked at his watch. It was ten o'clock. He was making four miles an hour, and he calculated that he would arrive at the forks at half-past twelve. He decided to celebrate that event by eating his lunch there.

The dog dropped in again at his heels, with a tail drooping dis- 9 couragement, as the man swung along the creek bed. The furrow of the old sled trail was plainly visible, but a dozen inches of snow covered the marks of the last runners. In a month no man had come up or down that silent creek. The man held steadily on. He was not much given to thinking, and just then particularly he had nothing to think about save that he would eat lunch at the forks and that at six o'clock he would be in camp with the boys. There was nobody to talk to; and, had there been, speech would have been impossible because of the ice muzzle on his mouth. So he continued monotonously to chew tobacco and to increase the length of his amber beard.

Once in a while the thought reiterated itself that it was very cold 10 and that he had never experienced such cold. As he walked along he rubbed his cheekbones and nose with the back of his mittened hand. He did this automatically, now and again changing hands. But, rub as he would, the instant he stopped his cheekbones went numb, and the following instant the end of his nose went numb. He was sure to frost his cheeks; he knew that, and experienced a pang of regret that he had not devised a nose strap of the sort Bud wore in cold snaps. Such a strap passed across the cheeks, as well, and saved them. But it didn't matter much, after all. What were frosted cheeks? A bit painful, that was all; they were never serious.

Empty as the man's mind was of thoughts, he was keenly obser- 11 vant, and he noticed the changes in the creek, the curves and bends and timber jams, and always he sharply noted where he placed his feet. Once, coming around a bend, be shied abruptly, like a startled horse, curved away from the place where he had been walking, and retreated several paces back along the trail. The creek he knew was frozen clear to the bottom—no creek could contain water in that arctic winter—but he knew also that there were springs that bubbled out from the hillsides and ran along under the snow and on top of the ice of the creek. He knew that the coldest snaps never froze these

---

[1]Knotted masses of roots projecting above the wet surface of a swamp. [Eds.]

springs, and he knew likewise their danger. They were traps. They hid pools of water under the snow that might be three inches deep, or three feet. Sometimes a skin of ice half an inch thick covered them, and in turn was covered by the snow. Sometimes there were alternate layers of water and ice skin, so that when one broke through he kept on breaking through for a while, sometimes wetting himself to the waist.

That was why he had shied in such panic. He had felt the give 12 under his feet and heard the crackle of a snow-hidden ice skin. And to get his feet wet in such a temperature meant trouble and danger. At the very least it meant delay, for he would be forced to stop and build a fire, and under its protection to bare his feet while he dried his socks and moccasins. He stood and studied the creek bed and its banks, and decided that the flow of water came from the right. He reflected awhile, rubbing his nose and cheeks, then skirted to the left, stepping gingerly and testing the footing for each step. Once clear of the danger, he took a fresh chew of tobacco and swung along at his four-mile gait.

In the course of the next two hours he came upon several similar 13 traps. Usually the snow above the hidden pools had a sunken, candied appearance that advertised the danger. Once again, however, he had a close call; and once, suspecting danger, he compelled the dog to go on in front. The dog did not want to go. It hung back until the man shoved it forward, and then it went quickly across the white, unbroken surface. Suddenly it broke through, floundered to one side, and got away to firmer footing. It had wet its forefeet and legs, and almost immediately the water that clung to it turned to ice. It made quick efforts to lick the ice off its legs, then dropped down in the snow and began to bite out the ice that had formed between the toes. This was a matter of instinct. To permit the ice to remain would mean sore feet. It did not know this. It merely obeyed the mysterious prompting that arose from the deep crypts of its being. But the man knew, having achieved a judgment on the subject, and he removed the mitten from his right hand and helped tear out the ice particles. He did not expose his fingers more than a minute, and was astonished at the swift numbness that smote them. It certainly was cold. He pulled on the mitten hastily, and beat the hand savagely across the chest.

At twelve o'clock the day was at its brightest. Yet the sun was 14 too far south on its winter journey to clear the horizon. The bulge of the earth intervened between it and Henderson Creek, where the man walked under a clear sky at noon and cast no shadow. At half-past twelve, to the minute, he arrived at the forks of the creek. He was pleased at the speed he had made. If he kept it up, he would certainly be with the boys by six. He unbuttoned his jacket and shirt and drew forth his lunch. The action consumed no more than a quarter of a minute, yet in that brief moment the numbness laid hold of the exposed fingers. He did not put the mitten on, but, instead, struck the fingers a dozen sharp smashes against his leg. Then he sat down on a snow-covered log to eat. The sting that followed upon the striking of his fingers against his leg ceased so quickly that he was startled. He had had no chance to take a bite of biscuit. He struck the fingers repeatedly and returned them to the mitten, baring the other hand for the purpose of eating. He tried to take a mouthful, but the ice muzzle prevented. He had forgotten to build a fire and thaw out. He chuckled at his foolishness, and as he chuckled he noted the numbness creeping into the exposed fingers. Also, he noted that the stinging which had first come to his toes when he sat down was already passing away. He wondered whether the toes were warm or numb. He moved them inside the moccasins and decided that they were numb.

He pulled the mitten on hurriedly and stood up. He was a bit 15 frightened. He stamped up and down until the stinging returned into the feet. It certainly was cold, was his thought. That man from Sulphur Creek had spoken the truth when telling how cold it sometimes got in the country. And he had laughed at him at the time! That showed one must not be too sure of things. There was no mistake about it, it *was* cold. He strode up and down, stamping his feet and threshing his arms, until reassured by the returning warmth. Then he got out matches and proceeded to make a fire. From the undergrowth, where high water of the previous spring had lodged a supply of seasoned twigs, he got his firewood. Working carefully from a small beginning, he soon had a roaring fire, over which he thawed the ice from his face and in the protection of which he ate his biscuits. For the moment the cold of space was outwitted. The dog took satisfaction in the fire, stretching out close enough for warmth and far enough away to escape being singed.

When the man had finished, he filled his pipe and took his com- 16 fortable time over a smoke. Then he pulled on his mittens, settled the ear flaps of his cap firmly about his ears, and took the creek trail up the left fork. The dog was disappointed and yearned back toward the fire. This man did not know cold. Possibly all the generations of his ancestry had been ignorant of cold, of real cold, of cold one hundred and seven degrees below freezing point. But the dog knew; all its ancestry knew, and it had inherited the knowledge. And it knew that it was not good to walk abroad in such fearful cold. It was the time to lie snug in a hole in the snow and wait for a curtain of cloud to be drawn across the face of outer space whence this cold came. On the other hand, there was no keen intimacy between the dog and the man. The one was the toil slave of the other, and the only caresses it had ever received were the caresses of the whip lash and of harsh and menacing throat sounds that threatened the whip lash. So the dog made no effort to communicate its apprehension to the man. It was not concerned in the welfare of the man; it was for its own sake that it yearned back toward the fire. But the man whistled, and spoke to it with the sound of whip lashes, and the dog swung in at the man's heels and followed after.

The man took a chew of tobacco and proceeded to start a new 17 amber beard. Also, his moist breath quickly powdered with white his mustache, eyebrows, and lashes. There did not seem to be so many springs on the left fork of the Henderson, and for half an hour the man saw no signs of any. And then it happened. At a place where there were no signs, where the soft, unbroken snow seemed to advertise solidity beneath, the man broke through. It was not deep. He wet himself halfway to the knees before the floundered out to the firm crust.

He was angry, and cursed his luck aloud. He had hoped to get 18 into camp with the boys at six o'clock, and this would delay him an hour, for he would have to build a fire and dry out his footgear. This was imperative at that low temperature—he knew that much; and he turned aside to the bank, which he climbed. On top, tangled in the underbrush about the trunks of several small spruce trees, was a high-water deposit of dry firewood—sticks and twigs, principally, but also larger portions of seasoned branches and fine, dry, last year's grasses. He threw down several large pieces on top of the snow. This served for a foundation and prevented the young flame from drowning itself in the snow it otherwise would melt. The flame he got by touching a match to a small shred of birch bark that he took from his pocket. This burned even more readily than paper. Placing it on the foundation, he fed the young flame with wisps of dry grass and with the tiniest dry twigs.

He worked slowly and carefully, keenly aware of his danger. 19 Gradually, as the flame grew stronger, he increased the size of the twigs with which he fed it. He squatted in the snow, pulling the twigs out from their entanglement in the brush and feeding directly to the flame. He knew there must be no failure. When it is seventy-five below zero, a man must not fail in his first attempt to build a fire— that is, if his feet are wet. If his feet are dry, and he fails, he can run along the trail for half a mile and restore his circulation. But the circulation of wet and freezing feet cannot be restored by running when it is seventy-five below. No matter how fast he runs, the wet feet will freeze the harder.

All this the man knew. The old-timer on Sulphur Creek had told 20
him about it the previous fall, and now he was appreciating the advice.
Already all sensation had gone out of his feet. To build the fire he
had been forced to remove his mittens, and the fingers had quickly
gone numb. His pace of four miles an hour had kept his heart
pumping blood to the surface of his body and to all the extremities.
But the instant he stopped, the action of the pump eased down. The
cold of space smote the unprotected tip of the planet, and he, being
on that unprotected tip, received the full force of the blow. The blood
of his body recoiled before it. The blood was alive, like the dog, and
like the dog it wanted to hide away and cover itself up from the fearful
cold. So long as he walked four miles an hour, he pumped the blood,
willy-nilly, to the surface; but now it ebbed away and sank down into
the recesses of his body. The extremities were the first to feel its
absence. His wet feet froze the faster, and his exposed fingers numbed
the faster, though they had not yet begun to freeze. Nose and cheeks
were already freezing, while the skin of all his body chilled as it lost
its blood.

But he was safe. Toes and nose and cheeks would be only touched 21
by the frost, for the fire was beginning to burn with strength. He was
feeding it with twigs the size of his finger. In another minute he
would be able to feed it with branches the size of his wrist, and then
he could remove his wet footgear, and, while it dried, he could keep
his naked feet warm by the fire, rubbing them at first, of course, with
snow. The fire was a success. He was safe. He remembered the advice
of the old-timer on Sulphur Creek, and smiled. The old-timer had
been very serious in laying down the law that no man must travel
alone in the Klondike after fifty below. Well, here he was; he had
had the accident; he was alone; and he had saved himself. Those old-
timers were rather womanish, some of them, he thought. All a man
had to do was to keep his head, and he was all right. Any man who
was a man could travel alone. But it was surprising, the rapidity with
which his cheeks and nose were freezing. And he had not thought
his fingers could go lifeless in so short a time. Lifeless they were, for
he could scarcely make them move together to grip a twig, and they
seemed remote from his body and from him. When he touched a
twig, he had to look and see whether or not he had hold of it. The
wires were pretty well down between him and his finger ends.

All of which counted for little. There was the fire, snapping and 22
crackling and promising life with every dancing flame. He started to
untie his moccasins. They were coated with ice; the thick German
socks were like sheaths of iron halfway to the knees; and the moccasin
strings were like rods of steel all twisted and knotted as by some

conflagration. For a moment he tugged with his numb fingers, then, realizing the folly of it, he drew his sheath knife.

But before he could cut the strings, it happened. It was his own 23 fault or, rather, his mistake. He should not have built the fire under the spruce tree. He should have built it in the open. But it had been easier to pull the twigs from the brush and drop them directly on the fire. Now the tree under which he had done this carried a weight of snow on its boughs. No wind had blown for weeks, and each bough was fully freighted. Each time he had pulled a twig he had communicated a slight agitation to the tree—an imperceptible agitation, so far as he was concerned, but an agitation sufficient to bring about the disaster. High up in the tree one bough capsized its load of snow. This fell on the boughs beneath, capsizing them. This process continued, spreading out and involving the whole tree. It grew like an avalanche, and it descended without warning upon the man and the fire, and the fire was blotted out! Where it had burned was a mantle of fresh and disordered snow.

The man was shocked. It was as though he had just heard his 24 own sentence of death. For a moment he sat and stared at the spot where the fire had been. Then he grew very calm. Perhaps the old-timer on Sulphur Creek was right. If he had only had a trail mate he would have been in no danger now. The trail mate could have built the fire. Well, it was up to him to build the fire over again, and this second time there must be no failure. Even if he succeeded, he would most likely lose some toes. His feet must be badly frozen by now, and there would be some time before the second fire was ready.

Such were his thoughts, but he did not sit and think them. He 25 was busy all the time they were passing through his mind. He made a new foundation for a fire, this time in the open, where no treacherous tree could blot it out. Next he gathered dry grasses and tiny twigs from the highwater flotsam. He could not bring his fingers together to pull them out, but he was able to gather them by the handful. In this way he got many rotten twigs and bits of green moss that were undesirable, but it was the best he could do. He worked methodically, even collecting an armful of the larger branches to be used later when the fire gathered strength. And all the while the dog sat and watched him, a certain yearning wistfulness in its eyes, for it looked upon him as the fire provider, and the fire was slow in coming.

When all was ready, the man reached in his pocket for a second 26 piece of birch bark. He knew the bark was there, and, though he could not feel it with his fingers, he could hear its crisp rustling as he fumbled for it. Try as he would, he could not clutch hold of it.

And all the time, in his consciousness, was the knowledge that each instant his feet were freezing. This thought tended to put him in a panic, but he fought against it and kept calm. He pulled on his mittens with his teeth, and threshed his arms back and forth, beating his hands with all his might against his sides. He did this sitting down, and he stood up to do it; and all the while the dog sat in the snow, its wolf brush of a tail curled around warmly over its forefeet, its sharp wolf ears pricked forward intently as it watched the man. And the man, as he beat and threshed with his arms and hands, felt a great surge of envy as he regarded the creature that was warm and secure in its natural covering.

After a time he was aware of the first faraway signals of sensations 27 in his beaten fingers. The faint tingling grew stronger till it evolved into a stinging ache that was excruciating, but which the man hailed with satisfaction. He stripped the mitten from his right hand and fetched forth the birch bark. The exposed fingers were quickly going numb again. Next he brought out his bunch of sulphur matches. But the tremendous cold had already driven the life out of his fingers. In his effort to separate one match from the others, the whole bunch fell in the snow. He tried to pick it out of the snow, but failed. The dead fingers could neither touch nor clutch. He was very careful. He drove the thought of his freezing feet, and nose, and cheeks, out of his mind, devoting his whole soul to the matches. He watched, using the sense of vision in place of that of touch, and when he saw his fingers on each side the bunch, he closed them—that is, he willed to close them, for the wires were down, and the fingers did not obey. He pulled the mitten on the right hand, and beat it fiercely against his knee. Then, with both mittened hands, he scooped the bunch of matches, along with much snow, into his lap. Yet he was no better off.

After some manipulation he managed to get the bunch between 28 the heels of his mittened hands. In this fashion he carried it to his mouth. The ice crackled and snapped when by a violent effort he opened his mouth. He drew the lower jaw in, curled the upper lip out of the way and scraped the bunch with his upper teeth in order to separate a match. He succeeded in getting one, which he dropped on his lap. He was no better off. He could not pick it up. Then he devised a way. He picked it up with his teeth and scratched it on his leg. Twenty times he scratched before he succeeded in lighting it. As it flamed he held it with his teeth to the birch bark. But the burning brimstone went up his nostrils and into his lungs, causing him to cough spasmodically. The match fell into the snow and went out.

The old-timer on Sulphur Creek was right, he thought in the 29 moment of controlled despair that ensued: after fifty below, a man should travel with a partner. He beat his hands, but failed in exciting any sensation. Suddenly he bared both hands, removing the mittens with his teeth. He caught the whole bunch between the heels of his hands. His arm muscles not being frozen enabled him to press the hand heels tightly against the matches. Then he scratched the bunch along his leg. It flared into flame, seventy sulphur matches at once! There was no wind to blow them out. He kept his head to one side to escape the strangling fumes, and held the blazing bunch to the birch bark. As he so held it, he became aware of sensation in his hand. His flesh was burning. He could smell it. Deep down below the surface he could feel it. The sensation developed into pain that grew acute. And still he endured it, holding the flame of the matches clumsily to the bark that would not light readily because his own burning hands were in the way, absorbing most of the flame.

At last, when he could endure no more, he jerked his hands 30 apart. The blazing matches fell sizzling into the snow, but the birch bark was alight. He began laying dry grasses and the tiniest twigs on the flame. He could not pick and choose, for he had to lift the fuel between the heels of this hands. Small pieces of rotten wood and green moss clung to the twigs, and he bit them off as well as he could with his teeth. He cherished the flame carefully and awkwardly. It meant life, and it must not perish. The withdrawal of blood from the surface of his body now made him begin to shiver, and he grew more awkward. A large piece of green moss fell squarely on the little fire. He tried to poke it out with his fingers, but his shivering frame made him poke too far, and he disrupted the nucleus of the little fire, the burning grasses and the tiny twigs separating and scattering. He tried to poke them together again, but in spite of the tenseness of the effort, his shivering got away with him, and the twigs were hopelessly scattered. Each twig gushed a puff of smoke and went out. The fire provider had failed. As he looked apathetically about him, his eyes chanced on the dog, sitting across the ruins of the fire from him, in the snow, making restless, hunching movements, slightly lifting one forefoot and then the other, shifting its weight back and forth on them with wistful eagerness.

The sight of the dog put a wild idea into his head. He remembered 31 the tale of the man, caught in a blizzard, who killed a steer and crawled inside the carcass, and so was saved. He would kill the dog and bury his hands in the warm body until the numbness went out of them. Then he could build another fire. He spoke to the dog, calling it to him; but in his voice was a strange note of fear that frightened the animal, who had never known the man to speak in such way before. Something was the matter, and its suspicious nature sensed danger— it knew not what danger, but somewhere, somehow, in its brain arose an apprehension of the man. It flattened its ears down at the sound of the man's voice, and its restless, hunching movements and the liftings and shiftings of its forefeet became more pronounced; but it would not come to the man. He got on his hands and knees and crawled toward the dog. This unusual posture again excited suspicion, and the animal sidled mincingly away.

The man sat up in the snow for a moment and struggled for 32 calmness. Then he pulled on his mittens, by means of his teeth, and got upon his feet. He glanced down at first in order to assure himself that he was really standing up, for the absence of sensation in his feet left him unrelated to the earth. His erect position in itself started to drive the webs of suspicion from the dog's mind; and when he spoke peremptorily, with the sound of whip lashes in his voice, the dog rendered its customary allegiance and came to him. As it came within reaching distance, the man lost his control. His arms flashed out to the dog, and he experienced genuine surprise when he discovered that his hands could not clutch, that there was neither bend nor feeling in the fingers. He had forgotten for the moment that they were frozen and that they were freezing more and more. All this happened quickly, and before the animal could get away, he encircled its body with his arms. He sat down in the snow, and in this fashion held the dog, while it snarled and whined and struggled.

But it was all he could do, hold its body encircled in his arms and 33 sit there. He realized that he could not kill the dog. There was no way to do it. With his helpless hands he could neither draw nor hold his sheath knife nor throttle the animal. He released it, and it plunged wildly away, with tail between its legs, and still snarling. It halted forty feet away and surveyed him curiously, with ears sharply pricked forward.

The man looked down at his hands in order to locate them, and 34 found them hanging on the ends of his arms. It struck him as curious that one should have to use his eyes in order to find out where his hands were. He began threshing his arms back and forth, beating the mittened hands against his sides. He did this for five minutes, violently, and his heart pumped enough blood up to the surface to put a stop to his shivering. But no sensation was aroused in the hands. He had an impression that they hung like weights on the ends of his arms, but when he tried to run the impression down, he could not find it.

A certain fear of death, dull and oppressive, came to him. This 35 fear quickly became poignant as he realized that it was no longer a mere matter of freezing his fingers and toes, or of losing his hands and feet, but that it was a matter of life and death with the chances against him. This threw him into a panic, and he turned and ran up the creek bed along the old, dim trail. The dog joined in behind and kept up with him. He ran blindly, without intention, in fear such as he had never known in his life. Slowly, as he plowed and floundered through the snow, he began to see things again—the banks of the creek, the old timber jams, the leafless aspens, and the sky. The running made him feel better. He did not shiver. Maybe, if he ran on, his feet would thaw out; and, anyway, if he ran far enough, he would reach camp and the boys. Without doubt he would lose some fingers and toes and some of his face; but the boys would take care of him, and save the rest of him when he got there. And at the same time there was another thought in his mind that said he would never get to the camp and the boys; that he would soon be stiff and dead. This thought he kept in the background and refused to consider. Sometimes it pushed itself forward and demanded to be heard, but he thrust it back and strove to think of other things.

It struck him as curious that he could run at all on feet so frozen 36
that he could not feel them when they struck the earth and took the weight of his body. He seemed to himself to skim along above the surface, and to have no connection with the earth. Somewhere he had once seen a winged Mercury, and he wondered if Mercury felt as he felt when skimming over the earth.

His theory of running until he reached camp and the boys had 37
one flaw in it: he lacked the endurance. Several times he stumbled, and finally he tottered, crumpled up, and fell. When he tried to rise, he failed. He must sit and rest, he decided, and next time he would merely walk and keep on going. As he sat and regained his breath, he noted that he was feeling quite warm and comfortable. He was not shivering, and it even seemed that a warm glow had come to his chest and trunk. And yet, when he touched his nose and cheeks, there was no sensation. Running would not thaw them out. Nor would it thaw out his hands and feet. Then the thought came to him that the frozen portions of his body must be extending. He tried to keep this thought down, to forget it, to think of something else; he was aware of the panicky feeling that it caused, and he was afraid of the panic. But the thought asserted itself, and persisted, until it produced a vision of his body totally frozen. This was too much, and he made another wild run along the trail. Once he slowed down to a walk, but the thought of the freezing extending itself made him run again.

And all the time the dog ran with him, at his heels. When he fell 38
down a second time, it curled its tail over its forefeet and sat in front of him, facing him, curiously eager and intent. The warmth and secu-

WRITING SUGGESTIONS

1. Write an essay that explains London's view of nature as reflected in "To Build a Fire," using the contrast between the man's and the dog's reactions as a central piece of supporting information.
2. Write an essay in which you discuss a time when you experienced nature at its worst.

ANSWERS TO RESPONDING TO READING

1. London's story reflects a "naturalistic" view in which all humans are subject to the same laws that apply to the rest of the universe. Answers will vary.
2. Answers will vary. Students might observe in London's setting and tone a bleakness that echoes the theme. In addition, the flat, unemotional tone devalues the position of people in relation to nature. In effect, human beings are inferior to nature; they are its victims, subject to its whims.
3. The man reduces his chances in the first place by trying to defy natural law by venturing into the extreme cold. The environment will not change for him, and his subsequent carelessness in judgment compounds his difficulties. Had he paid proper attention to the laws of nature and understood his own vulnerability, he might have lived.

rity of the animal angered him, and he cursed it till it flattened down its ears appeasingly. This time the shivering came more quickly upon the man. He was losing in his battle with the frost. It was creeping into his body from all sides. The thought of it drove him on, but he ran no more than a hundred feet, when he staggered and pitched headlong. It was his last panic. When he had recovered his breath and control, he sat up and entertained in his mind the conception of meeting death with dignity. However, the conception did not come to him in such terms. His idea of it was that he had been making a fool of himself, running around like a chicken with its head cut off—such was the simile that occurred to him. Well, he was bound to freeze anyway, and he might as well take it decently. With this new-found peace of mind came the first glimmerings of drowsiness. A good idea, he thought, to sleep off to death. It was like taking an anesthetic. Freezing was not so bad as people thought. There were lots worse ways to die.

He pictured the boys finding his body next day. Suddenly he found himself with them, coming along the trail and looking for himself. And, still with them, he came around a turn in the trail and found himself lying in the snow. He did not belong with himself any more, for even then he was out of himself, standing with the boys and looking at himself in the snow. It certainly was cold, was his thought. When he got back to the States he could tell the folks what real cold was. He drifted on from this to a vision of the old-timer on Sulphur Creek. He could see him quite clearly, warm and comfortable, and smoking a pipe. 39

"You were right, old hoss; you were right," the man mumbled to the old-timer of Sulphur Creek. 40

Then the man drowsed off into what seemed to him the most comfortable and satisfying sleep he had ever known. The dog sat facing him and waiting. The brief day drew to a close in a long, slow twilight. There were no signs of a fire to be made, and, besides, never in the dog's experience had it known a man to sit like that in the snow and make no fire. As the twilight drew on, its eager yearning for the fire mastered it, and with a great lifting and shifting of forefeet, it whined softly, then flattened its ears down in anticipation of being chidden by the man. But the man remained silent. Later the dog whined loudly. And still later it crept close to the man and caught the scent of death. This made the animal bristle and back away. A little longer it delayed, howling under the stars that leaped and danced and shone brightly in the cold sky. Then it turned and trotted up the trail in the direction of the camp it knew, where were the other food providers and fire providers. 41

RESPONDING TO READING

1. How would you characterize the story's view of the natural world? Have you felt this way toward nature? If so, under what circumstances? **2.** What effect do the story's repetitive, almost monotonous style and the narrator's matter-of-fact tone have on you? How do these elements affect your interpretation of the story? **3.** Is the man's fate inevitable—that is, does he ever have a chance, or is he doomed from the start? How does his attitude toward nature help determine his fate?

The Lake Isle of Innisfree

WILLIAM BUTLER YEATS

Poet and playwright William Butler Yeats (1865–1939) was an Irish nationalist and a distinguished man of letters, considered the leader of the Irish Literary Renaissance. Yeats helped found the famous Abbey Theatre in Dublin and also served as a government official. In 1924 he won the Nobel Prize for Literature. His lyric poetry draws on the romantic and has mystical overtones. In "The Lake Isle of Innisfree" Yeats, influenced by Thoreau's *Walden*, writes of seeking solitude in nature. The inspiration for this poem came from a fountain in a shop window in London. When Yeats saw the fountain, he remembered lake water. "From the sudden remembrance," he said, "came my poem 'Innisfree.' "

I will arise and go now, and go to Innisfree,
And a small cabin build there, of clay and wattles[1] made:
Nine bean-rows will I have there, a hive for the honeybee,
And live alone in the bee-loud glade.

And I shall have some peace there, for peace comes dropping
    slow   5
Dropping from the veils of the morning to where the cricket sings;
There midnight's all a glimmer, and noon a purple glow,
And evening full of the linnet's wings.

I will arise and go now, for always night and day
I hear lake water lapping with low sounds by the shore;   10
While I stand on the roadway, or on the pavements grey,
I hear it in the deep heart's core.

---

[1]Interlaced rods and twigs. [Eds.].

RESPONDING TO READING

1. What does Innisfree seem to represent to the speaker? Do you think he really intends to go there? Explain.   **2.** What view of nature does the speaker have? Do you hear or see Innisfree—or both? Do you believe he is painting an unrealistic picture of nature? Does the world he describes appeal to you?   **3.** When he wrote this poem, Yeats was influenced by *Walden*, Thoreau's account of his two-year retreat into the woods. One of the reasons Thoreau went into the woods was to leave behind a culture that he felt was becoming too materialistic. In what way do you think "The Lake Isle of Innisfree" addresses this subject?

Mother Earth: Her Whales

GARY SNYDER

Gary Snyder (1930–   ) is a poet of the American Northwest who sees a link between our culture and Asian and Eskimo cultures. His themes are often Zen Buddhism and ecology. In the 1950s, Snyder associated with artists of the "Beat" generation, such as Allen Ginsberg and Jack Kerouac. His poetry is influenced by the songs and dances of Great Basin Indian tribes as well as by four- and seven-line Chinese poems. Snyder is the author of *Riprap* (1979), *The Black Country* (1968), and *Turtle Island*—the Indian name for North America—(1974), from which the following poem about the environment is taken.

An owl winks in the shadows
A lizard lifts on tiptoe, breathing hard
Young male sparrow stretches up his neck,
          big head, watching—

The grasses are working in the sun. Turn it green.   5
Turn it sweet. That we may eat.
Grow our meat.

Brazil says "sovereign use of Natural Resources"
Thirty thousand kinds of unknown plants.
The living actual people of the jungle   10
          sold and tortured—
And a robot in a suit who peddles a delusion called "Brazil"
          can speak for *them*?

The whales turn and glisten, plunge
    and sound and rise again,   15
Hanging over subtly darkening deeps
Flowing like breathing planets
    in the sparkling whorls of
        living light—

And Japan quibbles for words on   20
    what kinds of whales they can kill?
A once-great Buddhist nation
    dribbles methyl mercury[1]
      like gonorrhea
        in the sea.   25

Père David's Deer,[2] the Elaphure,
Lived in the tule marshes of the Yellow River
Two thousand years ago—and lost its home to rice—
The forests of Lo-yang were logged and all the silt &
Sand flowed down, and gone, by 1200 AD—   30
Wild Geese hatched out in Sibera
      head south over basins of the Yang, the Huang,
      what we call "China"
On flyways they have used a million years.
Ah China, where are the tigers, the wild boars,   35
    the monkeys,
      like the snows of yesteryear
Gone in a mist, a flash, and the dry hard ground
Is parking space for fifty thousand trucks.
IS man most precious of all things?   40
—then let us love him, and his brothers, all those
Fading living beings—

North America, Turtle Island, taken by invaders
    who wage war around the world.
May ants, may abalone, otters, wolves and elk   45
Rise! and pull away their giving
    from the robot nations.

---

[1]Refers to mercury pollution. [Eds.]
[2]Asian deer known only from specimens in zoos. It once inhabited the swampy plains of China until it was displaced by agriculture. [Eds.]

ADDITIONAL QUESTIONS FOR RESPONDING TO READING

1. Examine the language used to describe the whales. What images are projected here?
2. According to Snyder, with whom should one find solidarity? Why?

TEACHING STRATEGY

    Analyze the distinct voices in the poem and the sharp contrast in their tones: the rhythmic, harmonious voice of nature and the brash, disjointed voice of "the robots." On the board, make lists of the subjects about which each of the voices speaks, and use this information to discover how the structure of the poem relates to its theme.

COLLABORATIVE ACTIVITY

Have small groups examine the poem as political satire. At what groups, traditions, and attitudes is Snyder aiming his criticism? Are there any other groups Snyder should have included? Explain.

WRITING SUGGESTION

Compare the attitude toward the environment expressed in Snyder's poem with your own attitude.

ANSWERS TO RESPONDING TO READING

1. Snyder's attitude is reverential and protective. He suggests that the human race has misused and abused nature, and he chastises the abusers.
2. Snyder's whales represent, among other things, natural flow and continuity. The recurring lines frame a diatribe of political criticism of the world's treatment of the environment. Whales are part of this picture, but here they have a symbolic rather than a literal function.
3. Answers will vary, but it is clear that at one level the poem is a plea to people to stop destroying nature. Although the poem is political in content and purpose, the imagery, allusions, and language qualify the work as poetry.

Solidarity. The People.
Standing Tree People!
Flying Bird People!   50
Swimming Sea People!
Four-legged, two-legged, people!

How can the head-heavy power-hungry politic scientist
Government   two-world   Capitalist-Imperialist
Third-world   Communist   paper-shuffling male   55
          non-farmer   jet-set   bureaucrats
Speak for the green of the leaf? Speak for the soil?

(Ah Margaret Mead[3] . . . do you sometimes dream of Samoa?)

The robots argue how to parcel out our Mother Earth
To last a little longer   60
          like vultures flapping
Belching, gurgling,
          near a dying Doe.

"In yonder field a slain knight lies—
We'll fly to him and eat his eyes   65
          with a down
     derry derry derry down down."

          An Owl winks in the shadow
          A lizard lifts on tiptoe
                breathing hard   70
          The whales turn and glisten
                plunge and
          Sound, and rise again
          Flowing like breathing planets

          In the sparkling whorls   75

          Of living light.

RESPONDING TO READING

1. How would you characterize the attitudes toward the environment expressed by this poem? Do you agree with them? Explain.   **2.** Why do you think Snyder describes whales as "flowing like breathing planets" (lines

---

[3]American anthropologist (see note p. 1058). [Eds.]

17 and 74)? Is the poem really about whales? Do you think the poem's title is misleading?   **3.** What do you think the poet's purpose was in writing this poem? Is this poetry or a political speech? Or is it both?

Traveling through the Dark

WILLIAM STAFFORD

William Stafford (1914–   ), a plain-talking poet of the western United States, was born in Hutchinson, Kansas, and earned an undergraduate degree from the University of Kansas and a doctorate from the University of Iowa. Although he hints at moral judgments in his poems, he tries to keep apart from trends and politics and to follow his own impulses. Stafford has said that writing is like fishing in that the writer must be willing to fail. Some of his many collections of verse are *Allegiances* (1970), *The Design of the Oriole* (1977), and *An Oregon Message* (1987). From *Stories That Could Be True* (1960) comes his poem "Traveling through the Dark," about an encounter between nature and technology.

Traveling through the dark I found a deer
dead on the edge of the Wilson River road.
It is usually best to roll them into the canyon:
that road is narrow; to swerve might make more dead.

By glow of the tail-light I stumbled back of the car   5
and stood by the heap, a doe, a recent killing;
she had stiffened already, almost cold.
I dragged her off; she was large in the belly.

My fingers touching her side brought me the reason—
her side was warm; her fawn lay there waiting,   10
alive, still, never to be born.
Beside that mountain road I hesitated.

The car aimed ahead its lowered parking lights;
under the hood purred the steady engine.
I stood in the glare of the warm exhaust turning red;   15
around our group I could hear the wilderness listen.

I thought hard for us all—my only swerving—
then pushed her over the edge into the river.

BACKGROUND ON AUTHOR

Stafford's poems generally have rural settings; as he observes in the poem "Passing Remark," "In scenery I like flat country. / In life I don't like much to happen" (quoted in Richard Ellmann and Robert O'Clair, eds., *The Norton Anthology of Modern Poetry*, 2nd ed.).

BACKGROUND ON READING

Stafford on his work: "When you make a poem you merely speak or write the language of every day, capturing as many bonuses as possible and economizing on the losses; that is, you come awake to what always goes on in language, and you use it to the limit of your ability and your power of attention at the moment."

FOR OPENERS

Ask students whether they have ever seen a dead animal lying beside the road. How did their reactions differ from those described in this poem? How do they account for any differences? Do they think most people react more emotionally to finding a deer (or a pet) then to finding another animal—say, a rabbit or a squirrel? Why?

ADDITIONAL QUESTION FOR RESPONDING TO READING

Why do you think Stafford's poem is titled "Traveling Through the Dark"?

TEACHING STRATEGIES

1. Consider the following ideas: the collision between (and interrelatedness of) nature and human civilization; the speaker's and the reader's identification with nature and with civilization.
2. Notice that Stafford's poem inconspicuously follows a formal plan: four stanzas with a rhyme scheme of abcb and a concluding couplet. His use of simple, direct language, off-rhyme (road / dead; engine / listen), and cutoff rhyme (killing / belly; waiting / hesitated; swerving / river) contribute to the poem's subtlety.

WRITING SUGGESTION

Write about a time when you, like the speaker in "Traveling Through the Dark," observed a conflict between nature and civilization.

ANSWERS TO RESPONDING TO READING

1. The conflict between, and paradoxical inter-relatedness of, nature and human civilization is exemplified by Stafford's encounter with the dead deer. When the two worlds clash, there is death. But humans cannot ignore the "listening" wilderness; because we have built a road in a natural world, we must constantly make decisions (sometimes difficult moral ones) that have the potential to affect both nature and civilization. In his poem, Stafford makes no explicit moral judgment, leaving the disturbing responsibility to the reader.

2. The speaker can hear both the engine purring and the wilderness listening, and he can see the deer in the red tail-light. He thinks but ultimately chooses not to save the fawn. Perhaps he decides that the two worlds cannot really come together; perhaps the thought of being responsible for the fawn's ultimate survival is overwhelming; perhaps he believes that his "swerving" would "make more dead"; perhaps he thinks the effort would simply be too much trouble. All of these ideas may come into play; the open-endedness of the poem is part of its appeal.

3. The possibility heightens the dramatic conflict, the sense of the speaker's being at a conjunction of life and death. The fawn is described in terms of life: "waiting, / alive, still, never to be born." The speaker's decision determines the fawn's fate. The ambiguity of the pronoun in the speaker's "hard for us all" brings the reader into the group standing in the road. Personal responses will vary.

RESPONDING TO READING

1. What ideas about nature does the dead deer suggest to the speaker? Do you share these ideas? **2.** Why does the speaker react the way he does? Why does he choose to abandon the unborn fawn? What are the implications of his choice? Would you react the same way? **3.** When the speaker sees the deer is pregnant, he hesitates. Although the poem does not explicitly state the reason for his hesitation, readers understand that the speaker considers cutting open the dead doe. How does this possibility affect your response to the poem? Why do you suppose the writer would want to elicit such a response?

WRITING: NATURE AND THE ENVIRONMENT

1. Many writers see contact with nature as having a beneficial effect on people, serving as a retreat from the pressures of civilization or helping to restore a lost innocence. Write an essay in which you describe the positive effects of nature on your life.

2. In his essay, Appletree Rodden discusses one way in which the environment can be preserved. Write an essay in which you discuss how a specific change in governmental policy, social behavior, or industrial policy would improve the environment.

3. Many of the essays in this chapter directly or indirectly criticize the encroachment of civilization on nature. For example, industrial development destroys the habitats of animals and transforms fields and woods into housing tracts and industrial parks. As Loren Eiseley says in ''The Brown Wasps'' as he contemplates a field that is about to be cleared for a shopping center, ''Thousands of obscure lives were about to perish, the spores of puffballs would go smoking off to new fields, and the bodies of little white-footed mice would be crunched under the inexorable wheels of the bulldozers'' (paragraph 11). Write an essay in which you use an extended description of the environment to make a comment on this issue.

4. The introduction to this chapter mentions a theme that is prevalent in much nature writing: the idea that human beings have somehow become separated from the natural world. How do two or three of the writers represented in this chapter try to reestablish a connection with nature? How successful are their attempts?

5. What responsibility do you believe each individual has for doing his or her part to save the planet? As you answer this question, you may consider what in particular is worth saving in the natural world and what forces you see as working to destroy it.

6. In ''The Grizzly'' John McPhee makes an effort to confront nature on its own terms. As a result, he does not romanticize the bear or describe its behavior in human terms. Write an essay in which you objectively describe an animal, place, or environment. Make sure that the picture you create does not contain your subjective reactions or any descriptions that romanticize your subject.

7. E. M. Forster in ''My Wood'' seems to have a definite opinion about owning property. Summarize Forster's views and discuss in what ways they are or are not consistent with your own.

8. Several of the selections in this chapter imply—or even state—that nature, if not respected, can turn on human beings. What situations have you experienced that called for you to meet a challenge in the natural world? How did you react?

9. What do Snyder's characterization of the whales, Stafford's of the deer, and McPhee's of the grizzly have in common? In what sense are they making a similar point about the role of animals?

12
MAKING CHOICES

CONFRONTING THE ISSUES

In "Lifeboat Ethics: The Case Against Helping the Poor," Garrett Hardin argues that the world's limited resources cannot be distributed to everyone who needs them. He uses the lifeboat metaphor to help make his case: If we let everyone climb aboard, the boat will sink and we will all drown. A few can be allowed into the boat, but the question of how those few will be chosen has no simple answer.

Ask your students to imagine they are on a lifeboat. To ensure their survival, the passengers can allow only one person to join them in relative safety. Those in need of rescue include the following:

- Bill McKay, twenty-seven. Outstanding athlete; last year's top NBA pick. Popular speaker at inner-city high schools, where he urges students to stay in school.
- Jenny Lang, twenty-five. High school dropout and single mother of four preschool children. She has no other family and depends on welfare for financial support.
- Frank Warfield, sixty-five. Philanthropist and Holocaust survivor who has been a generous contributor to numerous charities. Father of six, grandfather of fifteen. Has a heart condition.
- Jane Gordon, forty. Lawyer and advocate for the homeless and for battered wives. Volunteer literacy tutor, Special Olympics coordinator, gay rights advocate, and soup kitchen worker.
- Freddy Logan, twenty-two. Former gang member and cocaine addict, now employed and a part-time college student. Sole support of his fourteen-year-old brother, who looks up to him as a role model.
- Ana Garcia, thirty-five. Medical student. Single, no children. Recipient of a special community scholarship for Hispanic-Americans, she is a straight-A student who plans to practice in an impoverished area. She is the first person in her family to have graduated from college.
- John Ruscomb Tucker, eighteen. First-year student at Yale, where he plans to major in business. Only son of a U.S. senator who is often mentioned as a future presidential candidate.
- Elizabeth Pfam, fifteen. Daughter of a Vietnamese mother and an American GI father she never knew. Talented musician; enrolled in a program for intellectually gifted students. Came to the United States as a small child. Her mother, who still speaks little English, relies on Elizabeth to help her cope with American society.

Choice is fundamental to the lives of all human beings. The ability—and, in fact, the need—to make complex decisions is part of what characterizes us as human. On a practical level, we choose friends, mates, careers, and places to live. On a more theoretical level, we struggle to make the really important choices: the moral and ethical decisions that are a vital part of our everyday lives.

Many times complex questions have no easy answers; occasionally they have no answers at all. For example, should we act to save a suffering creature if that action may create an awkward or even dangerous situation? Should we stand up to authority even if our stand puts us at risk? Should we help less fortunate individuals if such help weakens our own social or economic position? Should we tell the truth even if the truth may hurt someone? Should we take the easy road or the hard one? These and other difficult questions are considered by writers whose works appear in this chapter.

Most of the time, the choice we, like these writers, face is the same: to act or not to act. To make a decision, we must understand the consequences, both long term and short term, of acting in a particular way or of choosing not to act. We must struggle with the possibility of compromise, with the possibility of making a morally or ethically objectionable decision in the interests of pragmatism. And we must learn to take responsibility for our decisions. Throughout the decision-making process, we face a difficult paradox: Often we must make practical decisions about the problems of daily life on the basis of abstract ideas of right and wrong.

In examining the difficult choices that confront us all, some writers are able to speak with confidence and certainty; others are tentative; still others are pessimistic about our ability to choose wisely, or to choose at all.

PREPARING TO READ AND WRITE

As you read and prepare to write about the selections in this chapter, consider the following questions:

- On what specific choices does the selection focus? Is the decision to be made moral? Ethical? Political?
- Does the writer introduce a dilemma—that is, a choice between two equally problematic alternatives?
- Is the writer's view of alternatives realistic or simplistic?
- Do you agree with the solution the writer presents? Are there additional alternatives that the writer does not consider?

- Does the choice with which the writer struggles apply only to a narrow, specific situation, or does it also have wider application?

- Is the writer emotionally involved with the issue under discussion? Does his or her involvement or lack of involvement affect your response to the selection? If so, how?

- What social, political, or religious ideas influence the writer's decision? In what ways?

- Does the decision under discussion cause the writer to examine his or her own values? The values of others? The values of the society at large?

- Does the writer believe the problem can be resolved?

- What choice or choices do you believe should be made in the circumstances described? Why?

After asking students to designate their choices by secret ballot, count the votes and discuss each candidate, beginning with the one deemed most deserving of rescue. As your students discuss the candidates and try to reach a consensus about who the most worthy one is, they will be forced to make moral judgments about the value to a society of money, education, youth, and family as well as to consider factors that may make someone undeserving—for example, health problems, antisocial habits, or unconventional lifestyles. Because students are likely to have varying ideas about the relative value of different individuals to society, they will be forced to defend (and perhaps to reconsider) their choices.

At the end of the class period, take another vote, again by secret ballot. Ask each student to indicate whether his or her vote has changed. If the discussion has been serious and honest, some votes certainly will be different.

The Deer at Providencia

ANNIE DILLARD

Like Thoreau, Annie Dillard (see also p. 34) writes prose that often reads like a journal of the mind, with perceptions that jar readers into seeing and thinking. In "The Deer at Providencia," published in 1982, Dillard moves the setting away from familiar territory to Ecuador. Her critically observant eye is at work as she describes a captured deer, whose "skin looked virtually hairless, . . . almost translucent, like a membrane." Then Dillard deftly turns to a consideration of the paradoxical nature of suffering.

BACKGROUND ON AUTHOR

Annie Dillard describes herself as "a poet and a walker with a background in theology and a penchant for quirky facts." Although Dillard explores the seemingly senseless and horrible aspects of nature, she also reasserts the human capacity to perceive the beauty as well as the violence in the universe.

FOR OPENERS

Consider the phrase "These things are not issues; they are mysteries" (paragraph 14) as it applies to the events described in the essay.

1   There were four of us North Americans in the jungle, in the Ecuadorian jungle on the banks of the Napo River in the Amazon watershed. The other three North Americans were metropolitan men. We stayed in tents in one riverside village, and visited others. At the village called Providencia we saw a sight which moved us, and which shocked the men.

2   The first thing we saw when we climbed the riverbank to the village of Providencia was the deer. It was roped to a tree on the grass clearing near the thatch shelter where we would eat lunch.

3   The deer was small, about the size of a whitetail fawn, but apparently full-grown. It had a rope around its neck and three feet caught in the rope. Someone said that the dogs had caught it that morning and the villagers were going to cook and eat it that night.

4   This clearing lay at the edge of the little thatched-hut village. We could see the villagers going about their business, scattering feed corn for hens about their houses, and wandering down paths to the river to bathe. The village headman was our host; he stood beside us as we watched the deer struggle. Several village boys were interested in the deer; they formed part of the circle we made around it in the clearing. So also did four businessmen from Quito who were attempting to guide us around the jungle. Few of the very different people standing in this circle had a common language. We watched the deer, and no one said much.

5   The deer lay on its side at the rope's very end, so the rope lacked slack to let it rest its head in the dust. It was "pretty," delicate of bone like all deer, and thin-skinned for the tropics. Its skin looked virtually hairless, in fact, and almost translucent, like a membrane. Its neck was no thicker than my wrist; it was rubbed open on the rope, and gashed. Trying to paw itself free of the rope, the deer had scratched its own neck with its hooves. The raw underside of its neck showed red stripes and some bruises bleeding inside the muscles. Now three of its feet were hooked in the rope under its jaw. It could

not stand, of course, on one leg, so it could not move to slacken the rope and ease the pull on its throat and enable it to rest its head.

Repeatedly the deer paused, motionless, its eyes veiled, with only its rib cage in motion, and its breaths the only sound. Then, after I would think, "It has given up; now it will die," it would heave. The rope twanged; the tree leaves clattered; the deer's free foot beat the ground. We stepped back and held our breaths. It thrashed, kicking, but only one leg moved; the other three legs tightened inside the rope's loop. Its hip jerked; its spine shook. Its eyes rolled; its tongue, thick with spittle, pushed in and out. Then it would rest again. We watched this for fifteen minutes.

Once three young native boys charged in, released its trapped legs, and jumped back to the circle of people. But instantly the deer scratched up its neck with its hooves and snared its forelegs in the rope again. It was easy to imagine a third and then a fourth leg soon stuck, like Brer Rabbit and the Tar Baby.

We watched the deer from the circle, and then we drifted on to lunch. Our palm-roofed shelter stood on a grassy promontory from which we could see the deer tied to the tree, pigs and hens walking under village houses, and black-and-white cattle standing in the river. There was even a breeze.

Lunch, which was the second and better lunch we had that day, was hot and fried. There was a big fish called *doncella*, a kind of catfish, dipped whole in corn flour and beaten egg, then deep fried. With our fingers we pulled soft fragments of it from its sides to our plates, and ate; it was delicate fish-flesh, fresh and mild. Someone found the roe, and I ate of that too—it was fat and stronger, like egg yolk, naturally enough, and warm.

There was also a stew of meat in shreds with rice and pale brown gravy. I had asked what kind of deer it was tied to the tree; Pepe had answered in Spanish, "*Gama*."[1] Now they told us this was *gama* too, stewed. I suspect the word means merely game or venison. At any rate, I heard that the village dogs had cornered another deer just yesterday, and it was this deer which we were now eating in full sight of the whole article. It was good. I was surprised at its tenderness. But it is a fact that high levels of lactic acid, which builds up in muscle tissues during exertion, tenderizes.

After the fish and meat we ate bananas fried in chunks and served on a tray; they were sweet and full of flavor. I felt terrific. My shirt was wet and cool from swimming; I had had a night's sleep, two decent walks, three meals, and a swim—everything tasted good.

---

[1]Doe. [Eds.]

ADDITIONAL QUESTIONS FOR RESPONDING TO READING

1. Do you think the act of writing this essay might have served any psychological or emotional purpose for the author?
2. How do you account for Dillard's *not* having left the village at the sight of the suffering deer? Does she lose your respect by remaining to watch?
3. What could Dillard have said to Pepe at the end of the essay to better express her feelings about the deer?

From time to time each one of us, separately, would look beyond our shaded roof to the sunny spot where the deer was still convulsing in the dust. Our meal completed, we walked around the deer and back to the boats.

That night I learned that while we were watching the deer, the others were watching me. 12

We four North Americans grew close in the jungle in a way that was not the usual artificial intimacy of travelers. We liked each other. We stayed up all that night talking, murmuring, as though we rocked on hammocks slung above time. The others were from big cities: New York, Washington, Boston. They all said that I had no expression on my face when I was watching the deer—or at any rate, not the expression they expected. 13

They had looked to see how I, the only woman, and the youngest, was taking the sight of the deer's struggles. I looked detached, apparently, or hard, or calm, or focused, still. I don't know. I was thinking. I remember feeling very old and energetic. I could say like Thoreau that I have traveled widely in Roanoke, Virginia.[2] I have thought a great deal about carnivorousness; I eat meat. These things are not issues; they are mysteries. 14

Gentlemen of the city, what surprises you? That there is suffering here, or that I know it? 15

We lay in the tent and talked, "If it had been my wife," one man said with special vigor, amazed, "she wouldn't have cared *what* was going on; she would have dropped *everything* right at that moment and gone in the village from here to there to there, she would not have *stopped* until that animal was out of its suffering one way or another. She couldn't *bear* to see a creature in agony like that." 16

I nodded. 17

Now I am home. When I wake I comb my hair before the mirror above my dresser. Every morning for the past two years I have seen in that mirror, beside my sleep-softened face, the blackened face of a burnt man. It is a wire-service photograph clipped from a newspaper and taped to my mirror. The caption reads: "Alan McDonald in Miami hospital bed." All you can see in the photograph is a smudged triangle of face from his eyelids to his lower lip; the rest is bandages. You cannot see the expression in his eyes; the bandages shade them. 18

---

[2]In *Walden* Henry David Thoreau (see p. 1018) says, "I have traveled a good deal in Concord." [Eds.]

TEACHING STRATEGY

Have your students look for images of isolation, of alienation, and of being an outsider. These images might serve to illustrate Dillard's sense that she is unable to intervene in the suffering and distress of another being.

COLLABORATIVE ACTIVITY

Ask students, working in groups, to list events that they consider to have been "unfair." In class discussion, try to agree on a definition of *fairness*. Would Alan McDonald's wife agree with the class's definition?

The story, headed MAN BURNED FOR SECOND TIME, begins: 19

> "Why does God hate me?" Alan McDonald asked from his hospital bed.
> "When the gunpowder went off, I couldn't believe it," he said. "I just couldn't believe it. I said, 'No, God couldn't do this to me again.' "

He was in a burn ward in Miami, in serious condition. I do not even know if he lived. I wrote him a letter at the time, cringing.

He had been burned before, thirteen years previously, by flaming   20
gasoline. For years he had been having his body restored and his face remade in dozens of operations. He had been a boy, and then a burnt boy. He had already been stunned by what could happen, by how life could veer.

Once I read that people who survive bad burns tend to go crazy;   21
they have a very high suicide rate. Medicine cannot ease their pain; drugs just leak away, soaking the sheets, because there is no skin to hold them in. The people just lie there and weep. Later they kill themselves. They had not known, before they were burned, that the world included such suffering, that life could permit them personally such pain.

This time a bowl of gunpowder had exploded on McDonald.   22

> "I didn't realize what had happened at first," he recounted. "And then I heard that sound from 13 years ago. I was burning. I rolled to put the fire out and I thought, 'Oh God, not again.'
> "If my friend hadn't been there, I would have jumped into a canal with a rock around my neck."

His wife concludes the piece, "Man, it just isn't fair."

I read the whole clipping again every morning. This is the Big   23
Time here, every minute of it. Will someone please explain to Alan McDonald in his dignity, to the deer at Providencia in his dignity, what is going on? And mail me the carbon.

> When we walked by the deer at Providencia for the last time, I   24
> said to Pepe, with a pitying glance at the deer, *"Pobrecito"*—"poor little thing." But I was trying out Spanish. I knew at the time it was a ridiculous thing to say.

RESPONDING TO READING

1. Do you believe Dillard could have done anything to free the deer? Why does she choose to do nothing? Does she seem to regret her decision not to act? Do you think she *should* regret it?   **2.** In paragraph 14 Dillard says, "I have thought a great deal about carnivorousness; I eat meat. These things

2. For Dillard the paradox of hating violence yet eating meat is no different from any other mystery in the world: it cannot be explained in neat, reasonable terms.
3. Both man and animal are "victims" in an often cruelly illogical universe. Thus there is a valid connection between the two situations.

BACKGROUND ON AUTHOR

Always an aggressive spokesperson for the poor, Orwell challenged the political orthodoxy, opposed imperialism and aristocratic privilege, and took the stand for English popular culture of the 1940s. He perceived the artist's role as an important one: Art, he believed, served to extend human sympathies, and the artist provided an intellectual commentary and helped to shape society.

FOR OPENERS

Consider the tension between power and powerlessness in the essay. Who (or what) seems to be in control?

are not issues; they are mysteries." What does she mean? Is this statement a rationalization? Do you find it to be a satisfactory explanation for her ability to eat and enjoy deer meat while she watches the trapped deer "convulsing in the dust" (paragraph 11)? Why or why not?   **3.** What connection does Dillard see between Alan McDonald and the deer at Providencia? Do you see this as a valid, logical association, or do you believe Dillard has exploited (or even invented) a connection?

Shooting an Elephant

GEORGE ORWELL

This careful account of a cruel incident with an elephant in Burma is George Orwell's (see also p. 61) most powerful criticism of imperialism and the impossible position of British police officers—himself among them—in the colonies. Orwell says about the incident, "It was perfectly clear to me what I ought to do," but then he thinks of "the watchful yellow faces behind," and he realizes that his choice is not so simple.

In Moulmein, in lower Burma, I was hated by large numbers of people—the only time in my life that I have been important enough for this to happen to me. I was sub-divisional police officer of the town, and in an aimless, petty kind of way anti-European feeling was very bitter. No one had the guts to raise a riot, but if a European woman went through the bazaars alone somebody would probably spit betel juice over her dress. As a police officer I was an obvious target and was baited whenever it seemed safe to do so. When a nimble Burman tripped me up on the football field and the referee (another Burman) looked the other way, the crowd yelled with hideous laughter. This happened more than once. In the end the sneering yellow faces of young men that met me everywhere, the insults hooted after me when I was at a safe distance, got badly on my nerves. The young Buddhist priests were the worst of all. There were several thousands of them in the town and none of them seemed to have anything to do except stand on street corners and jeer at Europeans.

All this was perplexing and upsetting. For at that time I had already made up my mind that imperialism was an evil thing and the sooner I chucked up my job and got out of it the better. Theoretically—and secretly, of course—I was all for the Burmese and all against their oppressors, the British. As for the job I was doing, I hated it more bitterly than I can perhaps make clear. In a job like that you see the dirty work of Empire at close quarters. The wretched prisoners huddling in the stinking cages of the lock-ups, the grey, cowed faces of the long-term convicts, the scarred buttocks of the men who had been flogged with bamboos—all these oppressed me with an intolerable sense of guilt. But I could get nothing into perspective. I was young and ill-educated and I had had to think out my problems in the utter silence that is imposed on every Englishman in the East. I did not even know that the British Empire is dying, still less did I know that it is a great deal better than the younger empires that are going to supplant it.[1] All I knew was that I was stuck between my hatred of the empire I served and my rage against the evil-spirited little beasts who tried to make my job impossible. With one part of my mind I thought of the British Raj[2] as an unbreakable tyranny, as something clamped down, in *saecula saeculorum*,[3] upon the will of prostrate peoples; with another part I thought that the greatest joy in the world would be to drive a bayonet into a Buddhist priest's guts. Feelings like these are the normal by-products of imperialism; ask any Anglo-Indian official, if you can catch him off duty.

One day something happened which in a roundabout way was enlightening. It was a tiny incident in itself, but it gave me a better glimpse than I had had before of the real nature of imperialism—the real motives for which despotic governments act. Early one morning the sub-inspector at a police station the other end of the town rang me up on the phone and said that an elephant was ravaging the bazaar. Would I please come and do something about it? I did not know what I could do, but I wanted to see what was happening and I got on to a pony and started out. I took my rifle, an old .44 Winchester and much too small to kill an elephant, but I thought the noise might be useful in *terrorem*. Various Burmans stopped me on the way and told me about the elephant's doings. It was not, of course, a wild elephant, but a tame one which had gone "must." It had been chained up, as tame elephants always are when their attack of "must"[4] is due, but on the previous night it had broken its chain and escaped. Its mahout, the only person who could manage it when it was in that state, had set out in pursuit, but had taken the wrong direction and was now twelve hours' journey away, and in the morning the elephant had suddenly reappeared in the town. The Burmese population had no weapons and were quite helpless against it. It had already destroyed somebody's bamboo hut, killed a cow, and raided some fruit-stalls and devoured the stock; also it had met the municipal

3

ADDITIONAL QUESTIONS FOR
RESPONDING TO READING

1. What is the tone of the essay? What would you judge to be the narrator's attitude toward his younger self and his past behavior?
2. How would you define what Orwell has called his "roundabout" way of coming to enlightenment? Is the concept oxymoronic?

---

[1]This essay was written in 1936, three years before the start of World War II; Stalin and Hitler were in power. [Eds.]

[2]Sovereignty. [Eds.]

[3]From time immemorial. [Eds.]

[4]Frenzy. [Eds.]

rubbish van and, when the driver jumped out and took to his heels, had turned the van over and inflicted violences upon it.

The Burmese sub-inspector and some Indian constables were 4 waiting for me in the quarter where the elephant had been seen. It was a very poor quarter, a labyrinth of squalid bamboo huts, thatched with palm-leaf, winding all over a steep hillside. I remember that it was a cloudy, stuffy morning at the beginning of the rains. We began questioning the people as to where the elephant had gone and, as usual, failed to get any definite information. That is invariably the case in the East; a story always sounds clear enough at a distance, but the nearer you get to the scene of events the vaguer it becomes. Some of the people said that the elephant had gone in one direction, some said that he had gone in another, some professed not even to have heard of any elephant. I had almost made up my mind that the whole story was a pack of lies, when we heard yells a little distance away. There was a loud, scandalized cry of "Go away, child! Go away this instant!" and an old woman with a switch in her hand came round the corner of a hut, violently shooing away a crowd of naked children. Some more women followed, clicking their tongues and exclaiming; evidently there was something that the children ought not to have seen. I rounded the hut and saw a man's dead body sprawling in the mud. He was an Indian, a black Dravidian coolie,[5] almost naked, and he could not have been dead many minutes. The people said that the elephant had come suddenly upon him round the corner of the hut, caught him with its trunk, put its foot on his back, and ground him into the earth. This was the rainy season and the ground was soft, and his face had scored a trench a foot deep and a couple of yards long. He was lying on his belly with arms crucified and head sharply twisted to one side. His face was coated with mud, the eyes wide open, the teeth bared and grinning with an expression of unendurable agony. (Never tell me, by the way, that the dead look peaceful. Most of the corpses I have seen looked devilish.) The friction of the great beast's foot had stripped the skin from his back as neatly as one skins a rabbit. As soon as I saw the dead man I sent an orderly to a friend's house nearby to borrow an elephant rifle. I had already sent back the pony, not wanting it to go mad with fright and throw me if it smelt the elephant.

The orderly came back in a few minutes with a rifle and five 5 cartridges, and meanwhile some Burmans had arrived and told us that the elephant was in the paddy fields below, only a few hundred yards away. As I started forward practically the whole population of

---

[5]An unskilled laborer. [Eds.]

the quarter flocked out of the houses and followed me. They had seen the rifle and were all shouting excitedly that I was going to shoot the elephant. They had not shown much interest in the elephant when he was merely ravaging their homes, but it was different now that he was going to be shot. It was a bit of fun to them, as it would be to an English crowd; besides they wanted the meat. It made me vaguely uneasy. I had no intention of shooting the elephant—I had merely sent for the rifle to defend myself if necessary—and it is always unnerving to have a crowd following you. I marched down the hill, looking and feeling a fool, with the rifle over my shoulder and an ever-growing army of people jostling at my heels. At the bottom, when you got away from the huts, there was a metalled road and beyond that a miry waste of paddy fields a thousand yards across, not yet ploughed but soggy from the first rains and dotted with coarse grass. The elephant was standing eight yards from the road, his left side towards us. He took not the slightest notice of the crowd's approach. He was tearing up bunches of grass, beating them against his knees to clean them and stuffing them into his mouth.

6   I had halted on the road. As soon as I saw the elephant I knew with perfect certainty that I ought not to shoot him. It is a serious matter to shoot a working elephant—it is comparable to destroying a huge and costly piece of machinery—and obviously one ought not to do it if it can possibly be avoided. And at that distance, peacefully eating, the elephant looked no more dangerous than a cow. I thought then and I think now that his attack of "must" was already passing off; in which case he would merely wander harmlessly about until the mahout came back and caught him. Moreover, I did not in the least want to shoot him. I decided that I would watch him for a little while to make sure that he did not turn savage again, and then go home.

7   But at that moment I glanced round at the crowd that had followed me. It was an immense crowd, two thousand at the least and growing every minute. It blocked the road for a long distance on either side. I looked at the sea of yellow faces above the garish clothes—faces all happy and excited over this bit of fun, all certain that the elephant was going to be shot. They were watching me as they would watch a conjurer about to perform a trick. They did not like me, but with the magical rifle in my hands I was momentarily worth watching. And suddenly I realized that I should have to shoot the elephant after all. The people expected it of me and I had got to do it; I could feel their two thousand wills pressing me forward, irresistibly. And it was at this moment, as I stood there with the rifle in my hands, that I first grasped the hollowness, the futility of the white man's dominion in the East. Here was I, the white man with his gun, standing in front

COLLABORATIVE ACTIVITY

Arrange a debate based on Orwell's dilemma. Have teams of students argue (1) that the first responsibility of any authority figure is to fulfill the duties required of a leader or (2) that an individual's primary obligation is to his or her own sense of justice and morality.

of the unarmed native crowd—seemingly the leading actor of the piece; but in reality I was only an absurd puppet pushed to and fro by the will of those yellow faces behind. I perceived in this moment that when the white man turns tyrant it is his own freedom that he destroys. He becomes a sort of hollow, posing dummy, the conventionalized figure of a sahib. For it is the condition of his rule that he shall spend his life in trying to impress the "natives," and so in every crisis he has got to do what the "natives" expect of him. He wears a mask, and his face grows to fit it. I had got to shoot the elephant. I had committed myself to doing it when I sent for the rifle. A sahib has got to act like a sahib; he has got to appear resolute, to know his own mind and do definite things. To come all that way, rifle in hand, with two thousand people marching at my heels, and then to trail feebly away, having done nothing—no, that was impossible. The crowd would laugh at me. And my whole life, every white man's life in the East, was one long struggle not to be laughed at.

But I did not want to shoot the elephant. I watched him beating   8 his bunch of grass against his knees, with that preoccupied grandmotherly air that elephants have. It seemed to me that it would be murder to shoot him. At that age I was not squeamish about killing animals, but I had never shot an elephant and never wanted to. (Somehow it always seems worse to kill a *large* animal.) Besides, there was the beast's owner to be considered. Alive, the elephant was worth at least a hundred pounds; dead, he would only be worth the value of his tusks, five pounds, possibly. But I had got to act quickly. I turned to some experienced looking Burmans who had been there when we arrived, and asked them how the elephant had been behaving. They all said the same thing: he took no notice of you if you left him alone, but he might charge if you went to close to him.

It was perfectly clear to me what I ought to do. I ought to walk   9 up to within, say, twenty-five yards of the elephant and test his behavior. If he charged, I could shoot; if he took no notice of me, it would be safe to leave him until the mahout came back. But also I knew that I was going to do no such thing. I was a poor shot with a rifle and the ground was soft mud into which one would sink at every step. If the elephant charged and I missed him, I should have about as much chance as a toad under a steam-roller. But even then I was not thinking particularly of my own skin, only of the watchful yellow faces behind. For at that moment, with the crowd watching me, I was not afraid in the ordinary sense, as I would have been if I had been alone. A white man mustn't be frightened in front of "natives"; and so, in general, he isn't frightened. The sole thought in my mind was that if anything went wrong those two thousand Burmans would see me pursued, caught, trampled on, and reduced to a grinning corpse like that Indian up the hill. And if that happened it was quite probable that some of them would laugh. That would never do. There was only one alternative. I shoved the cartridges into the magazine and lay down on the road to get a better aim.

The crowd grew very still, and a deep, low, happy sigh, as of 10 people who see the theatre curtain go up at last, breathed from innumerable throats. They were going to have their bit of fun after all. The rifle was a beautiful German thing with cross-hair sights. I did not then know that in shooting an elephant one would shoot to cut an imaginary bar running from ear-hole to ear-hole. I ought, therefore, as the elephant was sideways on, to have aimed straight at his ear-hole; actually I aimed several inches in front of this, thinking the brain would be further forward.

When I pulled the trigger I did not hear the bang or feel the kick— 11 one never does when a shot goes home—but I heard the devilish roar of glee that went up from the crowd. In that instant, in too short a time, one would have thought, even for the bullet to get there, a mysterious, terrible change had come over the elephant. He neither stirred nor fell, but every line of his body had altered. He looked suddenly stricken, shrunken, immensely old, as though the frightful impact of the bullet had paralysed him without knocking him down. At last, after what seemed a long time—it might have been five seconds, I dare say—he sagged flabbily to his knees. His mouth slobbered. An enormous senility seemed to have settled upon him. One could have imagined him thousands of years old. I fired again into the same spot. At the second shot he did not collapse but climbed with desperate slowness to his feet and stood weakly upright, with legs sagging and head dropping. I fired a third time. That was the shot that did for him. You could see the agony of it jolt his whole body and knock the last remnant of strength from his legs. But in falling he seemed for a moment to rise, for as his hind legs collapsed beneath him he seemed to tower upward like a huge rock toppling, his trunk reaching skywards like a tree. He trumpeted, for the first and only time. And then down he came, his belly towards me, with a crash that seemed to shake the ground even where I lay.

I got up. The Burmans were already racing past me across the 12 mud. It was obvious that the elephant would never rise again, but he was not dead. He was breathing very rhythmically with long rattling gasps, his great mound of a side painfully rising and falling. His mouth was wide open—I could see far down into caverns of pale pink throat. I waited a long time for him to die, but his breathing did not weaken. Finally I fired my two remaining shots into the spot where I thought his heart must be. The thick blood welled out of him like red velvet, but still he did not die. His body did not even jerk

1. Write an essay in which you explain how Orwell's dilemma is like and unlike Annie Dillard's in "The Deer at Providencia" (page 1004).
2. Have you, like Orwell, ever been in a situation in which you wanted to act in one way but were forced by circumstances to act in another? Tell about this incident in an essay.

when the shots hit him, the tortured breathing continued without a pause. He was dying, very slowly and in great agony, but in some world remote from me where not even a bullet could damage him further. I felt that I had got to put an end to that dreadful noise. It seemed dreadful to see the great beast lying there, powerless to move and yet powerless to die, and not even to be able to finish him. I sent back for my small rifle and poured shot after shot into his heart and down his throat. They seemed to make no impression. The tortured gasps continued as steadily as the ticking of a clock.

In the end I could not stand it any longer and went away. I heard 13 later that it took him half an hour to die. Burmans were bringing dahs[6] and baskets even before I left, and I was told they had stripped his body almost to the bones by the afternoon.

Afterwards, of course, there were endless discussions about the 14 shooting of the elephant. The owner was furious, but he was only an Indian and could do nothing. Besides, legally I had done the right thing, for a mad elephant has to be killed, like a mad dog, if its owner fails to control it. Among the Europeans opinion was divided. The older men said I was right, the younger men said it was a damn shame to shoot an elephant for killing a coolie, because an elephant was worth more than any damn Coringhee coolie. And afterwards I was very glad that the coolie had been killed; it put me legally in the right and it gave me a sufficient pretext for shooting the elephant. I often wondered whether any of the others grasped that I had done it solely to avoid looking a fool.

ANSWERS TO RESPONDING
TO READING

1. Although Orwell seems to imply that he feels some degree of self-recrimination for his failure to save the elephant, it could be argued that he had little choice in the matter. He himself may have been the greatest victim of imperialism.
2. Answers will vary.
3. The essay seems to be primarily directed at self-examination. In paragraph 2, Orwell alludes to his confusion, ambivalence, and inexperience. Orwell's own entrapment in the web of authority imposed by the imperialist system seems to be his most pressing concern.

RESPONDING TO READING

1. The central focus in this essay is Orwell's struggle to decide what action to take to control the elephant. Does he have a choice? What social and political factors influence his decision? Can you think of a time when social or political pressures caused you to act?   **2.** What do you think you would have done in Orwell's place? Why?   **3.** Orwell says that his encounter with the elephant, although "a tiny incident in itself," gave him an understanding of "the real nature of imperialism—the real motives for which despotic governments act" (paragraph 3). In light of this statement, do you think his purpose in this essay is to explore something within himself, something within the nature of British colonialism, or both?

---

[6]Large knives. [Eds.]

Late Night Thoughts on Listening to Mahler's Ninth Symphony

LEWIS THOMAS

In this essay Lewis Thomas (see also p. 253) reflects on his fears of nuclear war, prompted by his listening to the melancholy final movement of Mahler's classical piece.

1   I cannot listen to Mahler's Ninth Symphony with anything like the old melancholy mixed with the high pleasure I used to take from this music. There was a time, not long ago, when what I heard, especially in the final movement, was an open acknowledgment of death and at the same time a quiet celebration of the tranquility connected to the process. I took this music as a metaphor for reassurance, confirming my own strong hunch that the dying of every living creature, the most natural of all experiences, has to be a peaceful experience. I rely on nature. The long passages on all the strings at the end, as close as music can come to expressing silence itself, I used to hear as Mahler's idea of leave-taking at its best. But always, I have heard this music as a solitary, private listener, thinking about death.

2   Now I hear it differently. I cannot listen to the last movement of the Mahler Ninth without the door-smashing intrusion of a huge new thought: death everywhere, the dying of everything, the end of humanity. The easy sadness expressed with such gentleness and delicacy by that repeated phrase on faded strings, over and over again, no longer comes to me as old, familiar news of the cycle of living and dying. All through the last notes my mind swarms with images of a world in which the thermonuclear bombs have begun to explode, in New York or San Francisco, in Moscow and Leningrad, in Paris, in Paris, in Paris. In Oxford and Cambridge, in Edinburgh. I cannot push away the thought of a cloud of radioactivity drifting along the Engadin, from the Moloja Pass to Ftan, killing off the part of the earth I love more than any other part.

3   I am old enough by this time to be used to the notion of dying, saddened by the glimpse when it has occurred but only transiently knocked down, able to regain my feet quickly at the thought of continuity, any day. I have acquired and held in affection until very recently another sideline of an idea which serves me well at dark times: the life of the earth is the same as the life of an organism: the great round being possesses a mind: the mind contains an infinite number of thoughts and memories: when I reach my time I may find myself still hanging around in some sort of midair, one of those small

BACKGROUND ON AUTHOR

Thomas, a world-renowned specialist in cancer research and pathology, is also a writer and observer of the natural world, one who records his observations on everything from the behavior of a simple single cell to highly complex human social patterns and organizations. Much of Thomas's writing centers on the concept of symbiosis, the mutually beneficial relationship between organisms, and he is frequently critical of people's efforts to separate from the natural world.

BACKGROUND ON READING

In his earlier collection of essays, *The Lives of a Cell*, Thomas's general outlook was confident and his tone positive. "It is an illusion," he wrote, "to think that there is anything fragile about the life of the earth; surely this is the toughest membrane imaginable in the universe, opaque to probability, impermeable to death. We [human beings] are the delicate part, transient and vulnerable as cilia." The essay reprinted here clearly represents a profound change in Thomas's perspective. He seems now to be uttering a cry of warning, if not of despair.

The title of the essay provides a clue to the incident that provoked Thomas's reflections. Mahler's symphony once seemed to convey Thomas's own confidence in universal harmony and his certainty about life after death. But Thomas's mature experiences and his fears of nuclear disaster are now the feelings that he finds echoed in the music.

FOR OPENERS

Bring in a recording of Mahler's Ninth Symphony and play it for the class. Then play it a second time, asking students to freewrite as they listen.

thoughts, drawn back into the memory of the earth: in that peculiar sense I will be alive.

Now all that has changed. I cannot think that way anymore. Not while those things are still in place, aimed everywhere, ready for launching. 4

This is a bad enough thing for the people in my generation. We can put up with it, I suppose, since we must. We are moving along anyway, like it or not. I can even set aside my private fancy about hanging around in midair. 5

What I cannot imagine, what I cannot put up with, the thought that keeps grinding its way into my mind, making the Mahler into a hideous noise close to killing me, is what it would be like to be young. How do the young stand it? How can they keep their sanity? If I were very young, sixteen or seventeen years old, I think I would begin, perhaps very slowly and imperceptibly, to go crazy. 6

There is a short passage near the very end of the Mahler in which the almost vanishing violins, all engaged in a sustained backward glance, are edged aside for a few bars by the cellos. Those lower notes pick up fragments from the first movement, as though prepared to begin everything all over again, and then the cellos subside and disappear, like an exhalation. I used to hear this as a wonderful few seconds of encouragement: we'll be back, we're still here, keep going, keep going. 7

Now, with a pamphlet in front of me on a corner of my desk, published by the Congressional Office of Technology Assessment, entitled *MX Basing*, an analysis of all the alternative strategies for placement and protection of hundreds of these missiles, each capable of creating artificial suns to vaporize a hundred Hiroshimas, collectively capable of destroying the life of any continent, I cannot hear the same Mahler. Now, those cellos sound in my mind like the opening of all the hatches and the instant before ignition. 8

If I were sixteen or seventeen years old, I would not feel the cracking of my own brain, but I would know for sure that the whole world was coming unhinged. I can remember with some clarity what it was like to be sixteen. I had discovered the Brahms symphonies. I knew that there was something going on in the late Beethoven quartets that I would have to figure out, and I knew that there was plenty of time ahead for all the figuring I would ever have to do. I had never heard of Mahler. I was in no hurry. I was a college sophomore and had decided that Wallace Stevens[1] and I possessed a comprehensive understanding of everything needed for a life. The years stretched 9

---

[1]American poet (1879–1955). [Eds.]

ADDITIONAL QUESTIONS FOR RESPONDING TO READING

1. What factors contributed to Thomas's earlier serenity about death? What does he claim is now an unimaginable notion?
2. In paragraph 9, Thomas describes the way he remembers feeling at sixteen. Judging from your own experience, would you say that Thomas's memory of himself at sixteen is accurate? Or has memory softened reality?

away forever ahead, forever. My great-great grandfather had come from Wales, leaving his signature in the family Bible on the same page that carried, a century later, my father's signature. It never crossed my mind to wonder about the twenty-first century; it was just there, given, somewhere in the sure distance.

The man on television, Sunday midday, middle-aged and solid, 10 nice-looking chap, all the facts at his fingertips, more dependable looking than most high-school principals, is talking about civilian defense, his responsibility in Washington. It can make an enormous difference, he is saying. Instead of the outright death of eighty million American citizens in twenty minutes, he says, we can, by careful planning and practice, get that number down to only forty million, maybe even twenty. The thing to do, he says, is to evacuate the cities quickly and have everyone get under shelter in the countryside. That way we can recover, and meanwhile we will have retaliated, incinerating all of Soviet society, he says. What about radioactive fallout? he is asked. Well, he says. Anyway, he says, if the Russians know they can only destroy forty million of us instead of eighty million, this will deter them. Of course, he adds, they have the capacity to kill all two hundred and twenty million of us if they were to try real hard, but they know we can do the same to them. If the figure is only forty million this will deter them, not worth the trouble, not worth the risk. Eighty million would be another matter, we should guard ourselves against losing that many all at once, he says.

If I were sixteen or seventeen years old and had to listen to that, 11 or read things like that, I would want to give up listening and reading. I would begin thinking up new kinds of sounds, different from any music heard before, and I would be twisting and turning to rid myself of human language.

RESPONDING TO READING

1. Thomas uses his changing reactions to a symphony as a rhetorical device to help him express his fears about the dangers of nuclear weapons. Does this strategy help you to understand his points, or does it confuse you? Explain.   **2.** What choice does Thomas imply the human race confronts? In light of the recent changes in the government of the Soviet Union and of many Eastern European countries, do you believe we still have reason to be afraid of nuclear war?   **3.** Using your own outlook as a barometer, do you think Thomas is correct in assuming that a sixteen- or seventeen-year-old would be even more frightened than he is?

BACKGROUND ON AUTHOR

An individualist at heart, Thoreau considered himself "a mystic, a transcendentalist, and a natural philosopher to boot." Thoreau was a prolific reader who was chiefly interested in exploring the processes of the mind rather than in venturing into foreign settings, and he could legitimately claim to "have travelled a good deal in Concord." As a transcendentalist rather than a scientist, Thoreau's observations of nature were, he claimed, more true to the wideness of heaven than they were limited by the minute range of a microscope.

BACKGROUND ON READING

Thoreau's residence at Walden Pond was disturbed for one day when he was imprisoned for having refused to pay a poll tax to the government that supported the Mexican War. The essay, which outlines his belief in passive resistance, was originally delivered as a lecture. Thoreau's influential argument in support of the individual's obligation to his or her own highest code of ethics was later printed in Elizabeth Peabody's *Aesthetic Papers* (1849).

FOR OPENERS

"How does it become a man to behave toward this American government to-day? I answer, that he cannot without disgrace be associated with it." Is Thoreau being unpatriotic? Does his statement, made over one hundred years ago, seem dated? Is there any sense in which the statement applies today?

Civil Disobedience

HENRY DAVID THOREAU

American essayist, journalist, and intellectual Henry David Thoreau (1817–1862) was a social rebel who loved nature and solitude. A follower of transcendentalism, a philosophic and literary movement that flourished in New England, he contributed to *The Dial*, a publication that gave voice to the movement's romantic, idealistic, and individualistic beliefs. For three years, Thoreau lived in a cabin near Walden Pond in Concord, Massachusetts; his experiences there are recorded in his most famous book, *Walden* (1854). He left Walden, however, because he had "several more lives to live and could not spare any more for that one." A canoe excursion in 1839 resulted in the chronicle *A Week on the Concord and Merrimack Rivers*, and other experiences produced books about Maine and Cape Cod. The following impassioned and eloquent defense of civil disobedience, published in 1849, has influenced such leaders as Martin Luther King, Jr., and Mahatma Gandhi.

1   I heartily accept the motto,—"That government is best which governs least;" and I should like to see it acted up to more rapidly and systematically. Carried out, it finally amounts to this, which also I believe,—"That government is best which governs not at all;" and when men are prepared for it, that will be the kind of government which they will have. Government is at best but an expedient; but most governments are usually, and all governments are sometimes, inexpedient. The objections which have been brought against a standing army, and they are many and weighty, and deserve to prevail, may also at last be brought against a standing government. The standing army is only an arm of the standing government. The government itself, which is only the mode which the people have chosen to execute their will, is equally liable to be abused and perverted before the people can act through it. Witness the present Mexican war,[1] the work of comparatively a few individuals using the standing government as their tool; for, in the outset, the people would not have consented to this measure.

2   This American Government,—what is it but a tradition, though a recent one, endeavoring to transmit itself unimpaired to posterity, but each instant losing some of its integrity? It has not the vitality and force of a single living man; for a single man can bend it to his will. It is a sort of wooden gun to the people themselves. But it is

---

[1]In December 1845, the United States annexed Texas, leading to a war between the U.S. and Mexico (1846–48). Thoreau opposed this war, thinking it served the interests of slaveholders, who believed that the land won from Mexico would be slave territory. In protest, he refused to pay the Massachusetts poll tax and was arrested for his act of civil disobedience. [Eds.]

not the less necessary for this; for the people must have some complicated machinery or other, and hear its din, to satisfy that idea of government which they have. Governments show thus how successfully men can be imposed on, even impose on themselves, for their own advantage. It is excellent, we must all allow. Yet this government never of itself furthered any enterprise, but by the alacrity with which it got out of its way. *It* does not keep the country free. *It* does not settle the West. *It* does not educate. The character inherent in the American people has done all that has been accomplished; and it would have done somewhat more, if the government had not sometimes got in its way. For government is an expedient by which men would fain succeed in letting one another alone; and, as has been said, when it is most expedient, the governed are most let alone by it. Trade and commerce, if they were not made of India-rubber, would never manage to bounce over the obstacles which legislators are continually putting in their way; and, if one were to judge these men wholly by the effects of their actions and not partly by their intentions, they would deserve to be classed and punished with those mischievous persons who put obstructions on the railroads.

But, to speak practically and as a citizen, unlike those who call themselves no-government men, I ask for, not at once no government, but *at once* a better government. Let every man make known what kind of government would command his respect, and that will be one step toward obtaining it. 3

After all, the practical reason why, when the power is once in the hands of the people, a majority are permitted, and for a long period continue, to rule is not because they are most likely to be in the right, nor because this seems fairest to the minority, but because they are physically the strongest. But a government in which the majority rule in all cases cannot be based on justice, even as far as men understand it. Can there not be a government in which majorities do not virtually decide right and wrong, but conscience?—in which majorities decide only those questions to which the rule of expediency is applicable? Must the citizen ever for a moment, or in the least degree, resign his conscience to the legislator? Why has every man a conscience, then? I think that we should be men first, and subjects afterward. It is not desirable to cultivate a respect for the law, so much as for the right. The only obligation which I have a right to assume is to do at any time what I think right. It is truly enough said, that a corporation has no conscience; but a corporation of conscientious men is a corporation *with* a conscience. Law never made men a whit more just; and, by means of their respect for it, even the well-disposed are daily made the agents of injustice. A common and natural result of any undue respect for law is, that you may see a file of soldiers, 4

ADDITIONAL QUESTIONS FOR RESPONDING TO READING

1. What do you understand Thoreau to mean when he calls for a "man who is a man"? Why does he say there are so few "men" among Americans? Can he be accused of sexism?

2. Which of Thoreau's statements seem to you particularly surprising? Would you disagree with his advocacy of any specific actions? How does he reverse your expectations of what constitutes lawful behavior?

3. What is the dominant tone expressed in the essay? Is Thoreau primarily critical of America, or does the essay suggest a wider focus?

4. Thoreau's ideas influenced Gandhi, Martin Luther King, Jr., and Nelson Mandela. What specific ideas do you think appealed to these individuals? Which of Thoreau's ideas might contemporary advocates of political reform reject?

TEACHING STRATEGIES
1. Explain the key concepts of transcendentalism.
2. Thoreau's essay might serve as a model for various rhetorical devices. Look, for example, at his use of *paradox* and of *periodic* sentences (those in which the main idea is postponed until the end). Also, examine the effect of his rhetorical questions.

colonel, captain, corporal, privates, powder-monkeys, and all, marching in admirable order over hill and dale to the wars, against their wills, ay, against their common sense and consciences, which makes it very steep marching indeed, and produces a palpitation of the heart. They have no doubt that it is a damnable business in which they are concerned; they are all peaceably inclined. Now, what are they? Men at all? or small movable forts and magazines, at the service of some unscrupulous man in power? Visit the Navy-Yard, and behold a marine, such a man as an American government can make, or such as it can make a man with its black arts,—a mere shadow and reminiscence of humanity, a man laid out alive and standing, and already, as one may say, buried under arms with funeral accompaniments, though it may be,—

> "Not a drum was heard, not a funeral note,
>   As his corse to the rampart we hurried;
> Not a soldier discharged his farewell shot
>   O'er the grave where our hero we buried."[2]

The mass of men serve the state thus, not as men mainly, but as machines, with their bodies. They are the standing army, and the militia, jailers, constables, posse comitatus, etc. In most cases there is no free exercise whatever of the judgment or of the moral sense; but they put themselves on a level with wood and earth and stones; and wooden men can perhaps be manufactured that will serve the purpose as well. Such command no more respect than men of straw or a lump of dirt. They have the same sort of worth only as horses and dogs. Yet such as these even are commonly esteemed good citizens. Others—as most legislators, politicians, lawyers, ministers, and office-holders—serve the state chiefly with their heads; and, as they rarely make any moral distinctions, they are as likely to serve the Devil, without *intending* it, as God. A very few, as heroes, patriots, martyrs, reformers in the great sense, and *men*, serve the state with their consciences also, and so necessarily resist it for the most part; and they are commonly treated as enemies by it. A wise man will only be useful as a man, and will not submit to be "clay," and "stop a hole to keep the wind away,"[3] but leave that office to his dust at least:—

> "I am too high-born to be propertied,
> To be a secondary at control,
> Or useful serving-man and instrument
> To any sovereign state throughout the world."[4]

5

---

[2]From "The Burial of Sir John Moore at Corunna," by Irish poet Charles Wolfe (1791–1823). [Eds.]
[3]From *Hamlet* (Act V, scene i) by William Shakespeare. [Eds.]
[4]From *King John* (Act V, scene ii) by William Shakespeare. [Eds.]

He who gives himself entirely to his fellow-men appears to them useless and selfish; but he who gives himself partially to them is pronounced a benefactor and philanthropist.

How does it become a man to behave toward this American government to-day? I answer, that he cannot without disgrace be associated with it. I cannot for an instant recognize that political organization as *my* government which is the *slave's* government also.

All men recognize the right of revolution; that is, the right to refuse allegiance to, and to resist, the government, when its tyranny or its inefficiency are great and unendurable. But almost all say that such is not the case now. But such was the case, they think, in the Revolution of '75. If one were to tell me that this was a bad government because it taxed certain foreign commodities brought to its ports, it is most probable that I should not make an ado about it, for I can do without them. All machines have their friction; and possibly this does enough good to counterbalance the evil. At any rate, it is a great evil to make a stir about it. But when the friction comes to have its machine, and oppression and robbery are organized, I say, let us not have such a machine any longer. In other words, when a sixth of the population of a nation which has undertaken to be the refuge of liberty are slaves, and a whole country is unjustly overrun and conquered by a foreign army, and subjected to military law, I think that it is not too soon for honest men to rebel and revolutionize. What makes this duty the more urgent is the fact that the country so overrun is not our own, but ours is the invading army.

Paley,[5] a common authority with many on moral questions, in his chapter on the "Duty of Submission to Civil Government," resolves all civil obligation into expediency; and he proceeds to say, "that so long as the interest of the whole society requires it, that is, so long as the established government cannot be resisted or changed without public inconveniency, it is the will of God that the established government be obeyed, and no longer. . . . This principle being admitted, the justice of every particular case of resistance is reduced to a computation of the quantity of the danger and grievance on the one side, and of the probability and expense of redressing it on the other." Of this, he says, every man shall judge for himself. But Paley appears never to have contemplated those cases to which the rule of expediency does not apply, in which a people, as well as an individual, must do justice, cost what it may. If I have unjustly wrested a plank from a drowning man, I must restore it to him though I drown myself. This, according to Paley, would be inconvenient. But he that would save his life, in such a case, shall lose it. This people must

6

7

8

9

COLLABORATIVE ACTIVITY

Ask your students, working in groups, to analyze sections of the essay at the paragraph level. Can they isolate and then paraphrase each topic sentence? How do transitions connect sentences and paragraphs?

---

[5]William Paley (1743–1805), English clergyman and philosopher. [Eds.]

cease to hold slaves, and to make war on Mexico, though it cost them their existence as a people.

In their practice, nations agree with Paley; but does any one think   10 that Massachusetts does exactly what is right at the present crisis?

> "A drab of state, a cloth-o'-silver slut,
> To have her train borne up, and her soul trail in the dirt."[6]

Practically speaking, the opponents to a reform in Massachusetts are not a hundred thousand politicians at the South, but a hundred thousand merchants and farmers here, who are more interested in commerce and agriculture than they are in humanity, and are not prepared to do justice to the slave and to Mexico, *cost what it may*. I quarrel not with far-off foes, but with those who, near at home, coöperate with, and do the bidding of, those far away, and without whom the latter would be harmless. We are accustomed to say, that the mass of men are unprepared; but improvement is slow, because the few are not materially wiser or better than the many. It is not so important that many should be as good as you, as that there be some absolute goodness somewhere; for that will leaven the whole lump. There are thousands who are *in opinion* opposed to slavery and to the war, who yet in effect do nothing to put an end to them; who, esteeming themselves children of Washington and Franklin, sit down with their hands in their pockets, and say that they know not what to do, and do nothing; who even postpone the question of freedom to the question of free-trade, and quietly read the prices-current along with the latest advices from Mexico, after dinner, and, it may be, fall asleep over them both. What is the price-current of an honest man and patriot to-day? They hesitate, and they regret, and sometimes they petition; but they do nothing in earnest and with effect. They will wait, well disposed, for others to remedy the evil, that they may no longer have it to regret. At most, they give only a cheap vote, and a feeble countenance and Godspeed, to the right, as it goes by them. There are nine hundred and ninety-nine patrons of virtue to one virtuous man. But it is easier to deal with the real possessor of a thing than with the temporary guardian of it.

All voting is a sort of gaming, like checkers or backgammon, with   11 a slight moral tinge to it, a playing with right and wrong, with moral questions; and betting naturally accompanies it. The character of the voters is not staked. I cast my vote, perchance, as I think right; but I am not vitally concerned that that right should prevail. I am willing

---

[6]From Act IV, scene IV of Cyril Tourneur's *The Revenger's Tragedy* (1607). [Eds.]

to leave it to the majority. Its obligation, therefore, never exceeds that of expediency. Even voting *for the right* is *doing* nothing for it. It is only expressing to men feebly your desire that it should prevail. A wise man will not leave the right to the mercy of chance, nor wish it to prevail through the power of the majority. There is but little virtue in the action of masses of men. When the majority shall at length vote for the abolition of slavery, it will be because they are indifferent to slavery, or because there is but little slavery left to be abolished by their vote. *They* will then be the only slaves. Only *his* vote can hasten the abolition of slavery who asserts his own freedom by his vote.

I hear of a convention to be held at Baltimore, or elsewhere, for the selection of a candidate for the Presidency, made up chiefly of editors, and men who are politicians by profession; but I think, what is it to any independent, intelligent, and respectable man what decision they may come to? Shall we not have the advantage of his wisdom and honesty, nevertheless? Can we not count upon some independent votes? Are there not many individuals in the country who do not attend conventions? But no: I find that the respectable man, so called, has immediately drifted from his position, and despairs of his country, when his country has more reason to despair of him. He forthwith adopts one of the candidates thus selected as the only *available* one, thus proving that he is himself *available* for any purposes of the demagogue. His vote is of no more worth than that of any unprincipled foreigner or hireling native, who may have been bought. O for a man who is a *man*, and, as my neighbor says, has a bone in his back which you cannot pass your hand through! Our statistics are at fault: the population has been returned too large. How many *men* are there to a square thousand miles in this country? Hardly one. Does not America offer any inducement for men to settle here? The American has dwindled into an Odd Fellow,—one who may be known by the development of his organ of gregariousness, and a manifest lack of intellect and cheerful self-reliance; whose first and chief concern, on coming into the world, is to see that Almshouses[7] are in good repair; and, before yet he has lawfully donned the virile garb, to collect a fund for the support of the widows and orphans that may be; who, in short, ventures to live only by the aid of the Mutual Insurance company, which has promised to bury him decently. 12

It is not a man's duty, as a matter of course, to devote himself to the eradication of any, even the most enormous wrong; he may still properly have other concerns to engage him; but it is his duty, at least, to wash his hands of it, and, if he gives it no thought longer, 13

---

[7]Poorhouses; county homes that provided for the needy. [Eds.]

not to give it practically his support. If I devote myself to other pursuits and contemplations, I must first see, at least, that I do not pursue them sitting upon another man's shoulders. I must get off him first, that he may pursue his contemplations too. See what gross inconsistency is tolerated. I have heard some of my townsmen say, "I should like to have them order me out to help put down an insurrection of the slaves, or to march to Mexico;—see if I would go;" and yet these very men have each, directly by their allegiance, and so indirectly, at least, by their money, furnished a substitute. The soldier is applauded who refuses to serve in an unjust war by those who do not refuse to sustain the unjust government which makes the war; is applauded by those whose own act and authority he disregards and sets at naught; as if the state were penitent to that degree that it hired one to scourge it while it sinned, but not to that degree that it left off sinning for a moment. Thus, under the name of Order and Civil Government, we are all made at last to pay homage to and support our own meanness. After the first blush of sin comes its indifference; and from immoral it becomes, as it were, *un*moral, and not quite unnecessary to that life which we have made.

The broadest and most prevalent error requires the most disinterested virtue to sustain it. The slight reproach to which the virtue of patriotism is commonly liable, the noble are most likely to incur. Those who, while they disapprove of the character and measures of a government, yield to it their allegiance and support are undoubtedly its most conscientious supporters, and so frequently the most serious obstacles to reform. Some are petitioning the state to dissolve the Union, to disregard the requisitions of the President. Why do they not dissolve it themselves,—the union between themselves and the state,—and refuse to pay their quota into its treasury? Do not they stand in the same relation to the state that the state does to the Union? And have not the same reasons prevented the state from resisting the Union which have prevented them from resisting the state? 14

How can a man be satisfied to entertain an opinion merely, and enjoy *it*? Is there any enjoyment in it, if his opinion is that he is aggrieved? If you are cheated out of a single dollar by your neighbor, you do not rest satisfied with knowing that you are cheated, or with saying that you are cheated, or even with petitioning him to pay you your due; but you take effectual steps at once to obtain the full amount, and see that you are never cheated again. Action from principle, the perception and the performance of right, changes things and relations; it is essentially revolutionary, and does not consist wholly with anything which was. It not only divides states and churches, it divides families; ay, it divides the *individual*, separating the diabolical in him from the divine. 15

Unjust laws exist: shall we be content to obey them, or shall we 16
endeavor to amend them, and obey them until we have succeeded,
or shall we transgress them at once? Men generally, under such a
government as this, think that they ought to wait until they have
persuaded the majority to alter them. They think that, if they should
resist, the remedy would be worse than the evil. But it is the fault of
the government itself that the remedy *is* worse than the evil. *It* makes
it worse. Why is it not more apt to anticipate and provide for reform?
Why does it not cherish its wise minority? Why does it cry and resist
before it is hurt? Why does it not encourage its citizens to be on the
alert to point out its faults, and *do* better than it would have them?
Why does it always crucify Christ, and excommunicate Copernicus
and Luther, and pronounce Washington and Franklin rebels?

One would think, that a deliberate and practical denial of its 17
authority was the only offense never contemplated by government;
else, why has it not assigned its definite, its suitable and proportionate
penalty? If a man who has no property refuses but once to earn nine
shillings for the state, he is put in prison for a period unlimited by
any law that I know, and determined only by the discretion of those
who placed him there; but if he should steal ninety times nine shillings
from the state, he is soon permitted to go at large again.

If the injustice is part of the necessary friction of the machine of 18
government, let it go, let it go: perchance it will wear smooth,—
certainly the machine will wear out. If the injustice has a spring, or
a pulley, or a rope, or a crank, exclusively for itself, then perhaps
you may consider whether the remedy will not be worse than the
evil; but if it is of such a nature that it requires you to be the agent
of injustice to another, then, I say, break the law. Let your life be a
counter friction to stop the machine. What I have to do is to see, at
any rate, that I do not lend myself to the wrong which I condemn.

As for adopting the ways which the state has provided for rem- 19
edying the evil, I know not of such ways. They take too much time,
and a man's life will be gone. I have offer affairs to attend to. I came
into this world, not chiefly to make this a good place to live in, but
to live in it, be it good or bad. A man has not everything to do, but
something; and because he cannot do *everything*, it is not necessary
that he should do *something* wrong. It is not my business to be petitioning the Governor or the Legislature any more than it is theirs to
petition me; and if they should not hear my petition, what should I
do then? But in this case the state has provided no way: its very
Constitution is the evil. This may seem to be harsh and stubborn and
unconciliatory; but it is to treat with the utmost kindness and consideration the only spirit that can appreciate or deserve it. So is all
change for the better, like birth and death, which convulse the body.

I do not hesitate to say, that those who call themselves Aboli-   20
tionists should at once effectually withdraw their support, both in
person and property, from the government of Massachusetts, and
not wait till they constitute a majority of one, before they suffer the
right to prevail through them. I think that it is enough if they have
God on their side, without waiting for that other one. Moreover, any
man more right than his neighbors constitutes a majority of one
already.

I meet this American government, or its representative, the state   21
government, directly, and face to face, once a year—no more—in the
person of its tax-gatherer; this is the only mode in which a man
situated as I am necessarily meets it; and it then says distinctly, Recognize me; and the simplest, the most effectual, and, in the present
posture of affairs, the indispensablest mode of treating with it on this
head, of expressing your little satisfaction with and love for it, is to
deny it then. My civil neighbor, the tax-gatherer, is the very man I
have to deal with,—for it is, after all, with men and not with parchment that I quarrel,—and he has voluntarily chosen to be an agent
of the government. How shall he ever know well what he is and does
as an officer of the government, or as a man, until he is obliged to
consider whether he shall treat me, his neighbor, for whom he has
respect, as a neighbor and well-disposed man, or as a maniac and
disturber of the peace, and see if he can get over this obstruction to
his neighborliness without a ruder and more impetuous thought or
speech corresponding with his action. I know this well, that if one
thousand, if one hundred, if ten men whom I could name,—if ten
honest men only,—say if *one* HONEST man, in this State of Massachusetts, *ceasing to hold slaves*, were actually to withdraw from this copart-
nership, and be locked up in the county jail therefor, it would be the
abolition of slavery in America. For it matters not how small the
beginning may seem to be: what is once well done is done forever.
But we love better to talk about it: that we say is our mission. Reform
keeps many scores of newspapers in its service, but not one man. If
my esteemed neighbor, the State's ambassador, who will devote his
days to the settlement of the question of human rights in the Council
Chamber, instead of being threatened with the prisons of Carolina,
were to sit down the prisoner of Massachusetts, that State which is
so anxious to foist the sin of slavery upon her sister,—though at
present she can discover only an act of inhospitality to be the ground
of a quarrel with her,—the Legislature would not wholly waive the
subject the following winter.

Under a government which imprisons any unjustly, the true place   22
for a just man is also a prison. The proper place to-day, the only place
which Massachusetts has provided for her freer and less desponding

spirits, is in her prisons, to be put out and locked out of the State by her own act, as they have already put themselves out by their principles. It is there that the fugitive slave, and the Mexican prisoner on parole, and the Indian come to plead the wrongs of his race should find them; on that separate, but more free and honorable ground, where the State places those who are not *with* her, but *against* her,— the only house in a slave State in which a free man can abide with honor. If any think that their influence would be lost there, and their voices no longer afflict the ear of the State, that they would not be as an enemy within its walls, they do not know by how much truth is stronger than error, nor how much more eloquently and effectively he can combat injustice who has experienced a little in his own person. Cast your whole vote, not a strip of paper merely, but your whole influence. A minority is powerless while it conforms to the majority; it is not even a minority then; but it is irresistible when it clogs by its whole weight. If the alternative is to keep all just men in prison, or give up war and slavery, the State will not hesitate which to choose. If a thousand men were not to pay their tax-bills this year, that would not be a violent and bloody measure, as it would be to pay them, and enable the State to commit violence and shed innocent blood. This is, in fact, the definition of a peaceable revolution, if any such is possible. If the tax-gatherer, or any other public officer, asks me, as one has done, "But what shall I do?" my answer is, "If you really wish to do anything, resign your office." When the subject has refused allegiance, and the officer has resigned his office, then the revolution is accomplished. But even suppose blood should flow. Is there not a sort of blood shed when the conscience is wounded? Through this wound a man's real manhood and immortality flow out, and he bleeds to an everlasting death. I see this blood flowing now.

I have contemplated the imprisonment of the offender, rather than the seizure of his goods,—though both will serve the same purpose,—because they who assert the purest right, and consequently are most dangerous to a corrupt State, commonly have not spent much time in accumulating property. To such the State renders comparatively small service, and a slight tax is wont to appear exorbitant, particularly if they are obliged to earn it by special labor with their hands. If there were one who lived wholly without the use of money, the State itself would hesitate to demand it of him. But the rich man—not to make any invidious comparison—is always sold to the institution which makes him rich. Absolutely speaking, the more money, the less virtue; for money comes between a man and his objects, and obtains them for him; and it was certainly no great virtue to obtain it. It puts to rest many questions which he would otherwise be taxed to answer; while the only new question which it puts is the hard but superfluous one, how to spend it. Thus his moral ground is taken from under his feet. The opportunities of living are diminished in proportion as what are called the "means" are increased. The best thing a man can do for his culture when he is rich to endeavor to carry out those schemes which he entertained when he was poor. Christ answered the Herodians according to their condition. "Show me the tribute-money," said he;—and one took a penny out of his pocket;—if you use money which has the image of Caesar on it, which he has made current and valuable, that is, *if you are men of the State,* and gladly enjoy the advantages of Caesar's government, then pay him back some of his own when he demands it. "Render therefore to Caesar that which is Caesar's, and to God those things which are God's,"—leaving them no wiser than before as to which was which; for they did not wish to know.

When I converse with the freest of my neighbors, I perceive that, 24 whatever they may say about the magnitude and seriousness of the question, and their regard for the public tranquility, the long and the short of the matter is, that they cannot spare the protection of the existing government, and they dread the consequences to their property and families of disobedience to it. For my own part, I should not like to think that I ever rely on the protection of the State. But, if I deny the authority of the State when it presents its tax-bill, it will soon take and waste all my property, and so harass me and my children without end. This is hard. This makes it impossible for a man to live honestly, and at the same time comfortably, in outward respects. It will not be worth the while to accumulate property; that would be sure to go again. You must hire or squat somewhere, and raise but a small crop, and eat that soon. You must live within yourself, and depend upon yourself always tucked up and ready for a start, and not have many affairs. A man may grow rich in Turkey even, if he will be in all respects a good subject of the Turkish government. Confucius said: "If a state is governed by the principles of reason, poverty and misery are subjects of shame; if a state is not governed by the principles of reason, riches and honors are the subjects of shame." No: until I want the protection of Massachusetts to be extended to me in some distant Southern port, where my liberty is endangered, or until I am bent solely on building up an estate at home by peaceful enterprise, I can afford to refuse allegiance to Massachusetts, and her right to my property and life. It costs me less in every sense to incur the penalty of disobedience to the State than it would to obey. I should feel as if I were worth less in that case.

Some years ago, the State met me in behalf of the Church, and 25 commanded me to pay a certain sum toward the support of a clergyman whose preaching my father attended, but never I myself.

"Pay," it said, "or be locked up in the jail." I declined to pay. But, unfortunately, another man saw fit to pay it. I did not see why the schoolmaster should be taxed to support the priest, and not the priest the schoolmaster; for I was not the State's schoolmaster, but I supported myself by voluntary subscription. I did not see why the lyceum should not present its tax-bill, and have the State to back its demand, as well as the Church. However, at the request of the selectmen, I condescended to make some such statement as this in writing:— "Know all men by these presents, that I, Henry Thoreau, do not wish to be regarded as a member of any incorporated society which I have not joined." This I gave to the town clerk; and he has it. The State, having thus learned that I did not wish to be regarded as a member of that church, has never made a like demand on me since; though it said that it must adhere to its original presumption that time. If I had known how to name them, I should have then signed off in detail from all the societies which I never signed on to; but I did not know where to find a complete list.

I have paid no poll-tax for six years. I was put into a jail once on 26 this account, for one night; and, as I stood considering the walls of solid stone, two or three feet thick, the door of wood and iron, a foot thick, and the iron grating which strained the light, I could not help being struck with the foolishness of that institution which treated me as if I were mere flesh and blood and bones, to be locked up. I wondered that it should have concluded at length that this was the best use it could put me to, and had never thought to avail itself of my services in some way. I say that, if there was a wall of stone between me and my townsmen, there was a still more difficult one to climb or break through before they could get to be as free as I was. I did not for a moment feel confined, and the walls seemed a great waste of stone and mortar. I felt as if I alone of all my townsmen had paid my tax. They plainly did not know how to treat me, but behaved like persons who are underbred. In every threat and in every compliment there was a blunder; for they thought that my chief desire was to stand the other side of that stone wall. I could not but smile to see how industriously they locked the door on my meditations, which followed them out again without let or hindrance, and *they* were really all that was dangerous. As they could not reach me, they had resolved to punish my body; just as boys, if they cannot come at some person against whom they have a spite, will abuse his dog. I saw that the State was half-witted, that it was timid as a lone woman with her silver spoons, and that it did not know its friends from its foes, and I lost all my remaining respect for it, and pitied it.

Thus the State never intentionally confronts a man's sense, intel- 27 lectual or moral, but only his body, his senses. It is not armed with superior wit or honesty, but with superior physical strength. I was not born to be forced. I will breathe after my own fashion. Let us see who is the strongest. What force has a multitude? They only can force me who obey a higher law than I. They force me to become like themselves. I do not hear of *men* being *forced* to live this way or that by masses of men. What sort of life were that to live? When I meet a government which says to me, "Your money or your life," why should I be in haste to give it my money? It may be in a great strait, and not know what to do: I cannot help that. It must help itself; do as I do. It is not worth the while to snivel about it. I am not responsible for the successful working of the machinery of society. I am not the son of the engineer. I perceive that, when an acorn and a chestnut fall side by side, the one does not remain inert to make way for the other, but both obey their own laws, and spring and grow and flourish as best they can, till one, perchance, overshadows and destroys the other. If a plant cannot live according to its nature, it dies; and so a man.

The night in prison was novel and interesting enough. The prisoners in their shirt-sleeves were enjoying a chat and the evening air in the doorway, when I entered. But the jailer said, "Come, boys, it is time to lock up;" and so they dispersed, and I heard the sound of their steps returning into the hollow apartments. My room-mate was introduced to me by the jailer as "a first-rate fellow and a clever man." When the door was locked, he showed me where to hang my hat, and how he managed matters there. The rooms were whitewashed once a month; and this one, at least, was the whitest, most simply furnished, and probably the neatest apartment in the town. He naturally wanted to know where I came from, and what brought me there; and, when I had told him, I asked him in my turn how he came there, presuming him to be an honest man, of course; and, as the world goes, I believe he was. "Why," said he, "they accuse me of burning a barn; but I never did it." As near as I could discover, he had probably gone to bed in a barn when drunk, and smoked his pipe there; and so a barn was burnt. He had the reputation of being a clever man, had been there some three months waiting for his trial to come on, and would have to wait as much longer; but he was quite domesticated and contented, since he got his board for nothing, and thought that he was well treated. 28

He occupied one window, and I the other; and I saw that if one stayed there long, his principal business would be to look out the window. I had soon read all tracts that were left there, and examined where former prisoners had broken out, and where a grate had been sawed off, and heard the history of the various occupants of that room; for I found that even here there was a history and a gossip 29 which never circulated beyond the walls of the jail. Probably this is the only house in the town where verses are composed, which are afterward printed in a circular form, but not published. I was shown quite a long list of verses which were composed by some young men who had been detected in an attempt to escape, who avenged themselves by signing them.

I pumped my fellow-prisoner as dry as I could, for fear I should 30 never see him again; but at length he showed me which was my bed, and left me to blow out the lamp.

It was like traveling into a far country, such as I had never 31 expected to behold, to lie there for one night. It seemed to me that I never had heard the town-clock strike before, nor the evening sounds of the village; for we slept with the windows open, which were inside the grating. It was to see my native village in the light of the Middle Ages, and our Concord was turned into a Rhine stream, and visions of knights and castles passed before me. They were the voices of old burghers that I heard in the streets. I was an involuntary spectator and auditor of whatever was done and said in the kitchen of the adjacent village-inn,—a wholly new and rare experience to me. It was a closer view of my native town. I was fairly inside of it. I never had seen its institutions before. This is one of its peculiar institutions; for it is a shire town.[8] I began to comprehend what its inhabitants were about.

In the morning, our breakfasts were put through the hole in the 32 door, in small oblong-square tin pans, made to fit, and holding a pint of chocolate, with brown bread, and an iron spoon. When they called for the vessels again, I was green enough to return what bread I had left; but my comrade seized it, and said that I should lay that up for lunch or dinner. Soon after he was let out to work at haying in a neighboring field, whither he went every day, and would not be back till noon; so he bade me good-day, saying that he doubted if he should see me again.

When I came out of prison,—for some one interfered, and paid 33 that tax,—I did not perceive that great changes had taken place on the common, such as he observed who went in a youth and emerged a tottering and gray-headed man; and yet a change had to my eyes come over the scene,—the town, and State, and country,—greater than any that mere time could effect. I saw yet more distinctly the State in which I lived. I saw to what extent the people among whom I lived could be trusted as good neighbors and friends; that their friendship was for summer weather only; that they did not greatly

---

[8]County seat. [Eds.]

propose to do right; that they were a distinct race from me by their prejudices and superstitions, as the Chinamen and Malays are; that in their sacrifices to humanity they ran no risks, not even to their property; that after all they were not so noble but they treated the thief as he had treated them, and hoped, by a certain outward observance and a few prayers, and by walking in a particular straight though useless path from time to time, to save their souls. This may be to judge my neighbors harshly; for I believe that many of them are not aware that they have such an institution as the jail in their village.

It was formerly the custom in our village; when a poor debtor 34 came out of jail, for his acquaintances to salute him, looking through their fingers, which were crossed to represent the grating of a jail window, "How do ye do?" My neighbors did not thus salute me, but first looked at me, and then at one another, as if I had returned from a long journey. I was put into jail as I was going to the shoemaker's to get a shoe which was mended. When I was let out the next morning, I proceeded to finish my errand, and, having put on my mended shoe, joined a huckleberry party, who were impatient to put themselves under my conduct; and in half an hour,—for the horse was soon tackled,—was in the midst of a huckleberry field, on one of our highest hills, two miles off, and then the State was nowhere to be seen.

This is the whole history of "My Prisons." 35

I have never declined paying the highway tax, because I am as 36 desirous of being a good neighbor as I am of being a bad subject; and as for supporting schools, I am doing my part to educate my fellow-countrymen now. It is for no particular item in the tax-bill that I refuse to pay it. I simply wish to refuse allegiance to the State, to withdraw and stand aloof from it effectually. I do not care to trace the course of my dollar, if I could, till it buys a man or a musket to shoot one with,—the dollar is innocent,—but I am concerned to trace the effects of my allegiance. In fact, I quietly declare war with the State, after my fashion, though I will still make what use and get what advantage of her I can, as is usual in such cases.

If others pay the tax which is demanded of me, from a sympathy 37 with the State, they do but what they have already done in their own case, or rather they abet injustice to a greater extent than the State requires. If they pay the tax from a mistaken interest in the individual taxed, to save his property, or prevent his going to jail, it is because they have not considered wisely how far they let their private feelings interfere with the public good.

This, then, is my position at present. But one cannot be too much 38
on his guard in such a case, lest his action be biased by obstinacy or
an undue regard for the opinions of men. Let him see that he does
only what belongs to himself and to the hour.

I think sometimes, Why, this people mean well, they are only 39
ignorant; they would do better if they knew how: why give your
neighbors this pain to treat you as they are not inclined to? But I think
again, This is no reason why I should do as they do, or permit others
to suffer much greater pain of a different kind. Again, I sometimes
say to myself, When many millions of men, without heat, without ill
will, without personal feeling of any kind, demand of you a few
shillings only, without the possibility, such is their constitution, of
retracting or altering their present demand, and without the possibility, on your side, of appeal to any other millions, why expose
yourself to this overwhelming brute force? You do not resist cold and
hunger, the winds and the waves, thus obstinately; you quietly submit
to a thousand similar necessities. You do not put your head into the
fire. But just in proportion as I regard this as not wholly a brute force,
but partly a human force, and consider that I have relations to those
millions as to so many millions of men, and not of mere brute or
inanimate things, I see that appeal is possible, first and instantaneously, from them to the Maker of them, and, secondly, from them
to themselves. But if I put my head deliberately into the fire, there
is no appeal to fire or to the Maker of fire, and I have only myself to
blame. If I could convince myself that I have any right to be satisfied
with men as they are, and to treat them accordingly, and not accordingly, in some respects, to my requisitions and expectations of what
they and I ought to be, then, like a good Mussulman[9] and fatalist, I
should endeavor to be satisfied with things as they are, and say it is
the will of God. And, above all, there is this difference between
resisting this and a purely brute or natural force that I can resist this
with some effect; but I cannot expect, like Orpheus,[10] to change the
nature of the rocks and trees and beasts.

I do not wish to quarrel with any man or nation. I do not wish 40
to split hairs, to make the fine distinctions, or set myself up as better
than my neighbors. I seek rather, I may say, even an excuse for
conforming to the laws of the land. I am but too ready to conform to
them. Indeed, I have reason to suspect myself on this head; and each
year, as the tax-gatherer comes round, I find myself disposed to

---

[9]Moslem. [Eds.]
[10]Legendary Greek poet and musician who played the lyre so beautifully that wild beasts
were transfixed by his music and rocks and trees moved. [Eds.]

review the acts and position of the general and State governments, and the spirit of the people, to discover a pretext for conformity.

> "We must affect our country as our parents,
> And if at any time we alienate
> Our love or industry from doing it honor,
> We must respect effects and teach the soul
> Matter of conscience and religion,   5
> And not desire of rule or benefit."[11]

I believe that the State will soon be able to take all my work of this sort out of my hands, and then I shall be no better a patriot than my fellow-countrymen. Seen from a lower point of view, the Constitution, with all its faults, is very good; the law and the courts are very respectable; even this State and this American government are, in many respects, very admirable, and rare things, to be thankful for, such as a great many have described them; but seen from a point of view a little higher, they are what I have described them; seen from a higher still, and the highest, who shall say what they are, or that they are worth looking at or thinking of at all?

However, the government does not concern me much, and I shall 41 bestow the fewest possible thoughts on it. It is not many moments that I live under a government, even in this world. If a man is thought-free, fancy-free, imagination-free, that which *is not* never for a long time appearing *to be* to him, unwise rulers or reformers cannot fatally interrupt him.

I know that most men think differently from myself; but those 42 whose lives are by profession devoted to the study of these or kindred subjects content me as little as any. Statesmen and legislators, standing so completely within the institution, never distinctly and nakedly behold it. They speak of moving society, but have no resting-place without it. They may be men of a certain experience and discrimination, and have no doubt invented ingenious and even useful systems, for which we sincerely thank them; but all their wit and usefulness lie within certain not very wide limits. They are wont to forget that the world is not governed by policy and expediency. Webster[12] never goes behind government, and so cannot speak with authority about it. His words are wisdom to those legislators who contemplate no essential reform in the existing government; but for thinkers, and those who legislate for all time, he never once glances at the subject. I know of those whose serene and wise speculations on this theme would soon reveal the limits of his mind's range and

---

[11]From *The Battle of Alcazar* (1594), a play by George Peele (1558?–97?). [Eds.]
[12]Daniel Webster (1782–1852), legendary American orator, lawyer, and statesman. [Eds.]

hospitality. Yet, compared with the cheap professions of most reformers, and the still cheaper wisdom and eloquence of politicians in general, his are almost the only sensible and valuable words, and we thank Heaven for him. Comparatively, he is always strong, original, and, above all, practical. Still, his quality is not wisdom, but prudence. The lawyer's truth is not Truth, but consistency or a consistent expediency. Truth is always in harmony with herself, and is not concerned chiefly to reveal the justice that may consist with wrong-doing. He well deserves to be called, as he has been called, the Defender of the Constitution. There are really no blows to be given to him but defensive ones. He is not a leader, but a follower. His leaders are the men of '87. "I have never made an effort," he says, "and never propose to make an effort; I have never countenanced an effort, and never mean to countenance an effort, to disturb the arrangement as originally made, by which the various States came into the Union." Still thinking of the sanction which the Constitution gives to slavery, he says, "Because it was a part of the original compact,—let it stand." Notwithstanding his special acuteness and ability, he is unable to take a fact out of its merely political relations, and behold it as it lies absolutely to be disposed of by the intellect,— what, for instance, it behooves a man to do here in America to-day with regard to slavery,—but ventures, or is driven, to make some such desperate answer as the following, while professing to speak absolutely, and as a private man,—from which what new and singular code of social duties might be inferred? "The manner," says he, "in which the governments of those States where slavery exists are to regulate it is for their own consideration, under their responsibility to their constituents, to the general laws of propriety, humanity, and justice, and to God. Associations formed elsewhere, springing from a feeling of humanity, or any other cause, have nothing whatever to do with it. They have never received any encouragement from me, and they never will."

They who know of no purer sources of truth, who have traced 43 up its stream no higher, stand, and wisely stand, by the Bible and the Constitution, and drink at it there with reverence and humility; but they who behold where it comes trickling into this lake or that pool, gird up their loins once more, and continue their pilgrimage toward its fountain-head.

No man with a genius for legislation has appeared in America. 44 They are rare in the history of the world. There are orators, politicians, and eloquent men, by the thousand; but the speaker has not yet opened his mouth to speak who is capable of settling the much-vexed questions of the day. We love eloquence for its own sake, and not for any truth which it may utter, or any heroism it may inspire. Our

WRITING SUGGESTIONS

1. Do you agree that only "a very few" "heroes, patriots, martyrs, reformers in the great sense" have served their country with their consciences—and that they have been treated as enemies? Write about one such figure who is especially meaningful to you.
2. Thoreau asserts that when an individual acts on his own principles, the far-reaching gesture divides states and churches, families, and even the individual from himself. Do you see this division occurring in society today? Write about any such division you see.
3. Thoreau suggests that his night in jail prompted him to view familiar things from an entirely new perspective. Describe an experience that made you see things differently.

legislators have not yet learned the comparative value of free-trade and of freedom, of union, and of rectitude, to a nation. They have no genius or talent for comparatively humble questions of taxation and finance, commerce and manufacturers and agriculture. If we were left solely to the wordy wit of legislators in Congress for our guidance, uncorrected by the seasonable experience and the effectual complaints of the people, America would not long retain her rank among the nations. For eighteen hundred years, though perchance I have no right to say it, the New Testament has been written; yet where is the legislator who has wisdom and practical talent enough to avail himself of the light which it sheds on the science of legislation?

The authority of government, even such as I am willing to submit 45 to,—for I will cheerfully obey those who know and can do better than I, and in many things even those who neither know nor can do so well,—is still an impure one: to be strictly just, it must have the sanction and consent of the governed. It can have no pure right over my person and property but what I concede to it. The progress from an absolute to a limited monarchy, from a limited monarchy to a democracy, is a progress toward a true respect for the individual. Even the Chinese philosopher was wise enough to regard the individual as the basis of the empire. Is a democracy, such as we know it, the last improvement possible in government? Is it not possible to take a further step towards recognizing and organizing the rights of man? There will never be a really free and enlightened State until the State comes to recognize the individual as a higher and independent power, from which all its own power and authority are derived, and treats him accordingly. I please myself with imagining a State at last which can afford to be just to all men, and to treat the individual with respect as a neighbor; which even would not think it inconsistent with its own repose if a few were to live aloof from it, not meddling with it, nor embraced by it, who fulfilled all the duties of neighbors and fellow-men. A State which bore this kind of fruit, and suffered it to drop off as fast as it ripened, would prepare the way for a still more perfect and glorious State, which also I have imagined, but not yet anywhere seen.

RESPONDING TO READING

1. What moral or political choice does each of the following statements imply?

" 'That government is best which governs least' . . ." (paragraph 1).

"All men recognize the right of revolution . . ." (paragraph 8).

"All voting is a sort of gaming, like checkers or backgammon . . ." (paragraph 11).

ANSWERS TO RESPONDING TO READING

1. All the phrases, aimed ostensibly at the American political structure, reflect Thoreau's sense that the individual's obligation is to the highest form of morality, a morality that transcends government.

   a. "That government is best. . . ." implies a political choice in favor of the right and competency of the individual to serve as the highest possible authority in any government.

   b. "All men recognize. . . ." A government is subject to its people; therefore, when individuals are in conflict with their government, they must obey their own sense of moral obligation. The phrase implies both a moral and a political choice.

   c. "All voting. . . ." Behind the statement lies Thoreau's belief that his fellow citizens do not take their right to vote seriously enough, that they do not see each vote as a vital moral decision.

   d. "Under a government. . . ." Thoreau implies that our failure to act against injustice incriminates us. If political injustice exists at all in this country, the only way for the truly moral individual to behave is to demonstrate opposition and to face political imprisonment for a moral issue.

   e. "I did not see why. . . ." The inequities of the tax system are both a political and a moral issue. The paying of taxes is not simply a passive duty that we perform in order to avoid breaking the law. Thoreau urges us to comprehend the real consequences of our actions: to whom are we giving that support and for what cause?

2. Answers will vary.
3. Answers will vary.

"Under a government which imprisons any unjustly, the true place for a just man is also a prison" (paragraph 22).

"I did not see why the schoolmaster should be taxed to support the priest, and not the priest the schoolmaster . . ." (paragraph 25).

2. Do you believe civil disobedience is ever necessary? If so, under what circumstances? Would you engage in it? Why or why not?   **3.** Do you see any negative short- or long-term consequences of conforming to the law, however unjust, rather than disobeying it? If so, give some examples of such consequences.

Letter from Birmingham Jail

MARTIN LUTHER KING, JR.

Martin Luther King, Jr. (see also p. 474) was one of the most forceful advocates of nonviolent civil disobedience in America. The following letter, written in 1963, is his eloquent and impassioned response to a public statement by eight fellow clergymen in Birmingham, Alabama, who appealed to the citizenry of the city to "observe the principles of law and order and common sense."

MY DEAR FELLOW CLERGYMEN:[1]

While confined here in the Birmingham city jail, I came across   1 your recent statement calling my present activities "unwise and untimely." Seldom do I pause to answer criticism of my work and ideas. If I sought to answer all the criticisms that cross my desk, my secretaries would have little time for anything other than such correspondence in the course of the day, and I would have no time for constructive work. But since I feel that you are men of genuine good will and that your criticisms are sincerely set forth, I want to try to answer your statement in what I hope will be patient and reasonable terms.

---

[1]This response to a published statement by eight fellow clergymen from Alabama (Bishop C. C. J. Carpenter, Bishop Joseph A. Durick, Rabbi Milton L. Grafman, Bishop Paul Hardin, Bishop Holan B. Harmon, the Reverend George M. Murray, the Reverend Edward V. Ramage and the Reverend Earl Stallings) was composed under somewhat constricting circumstances. Begun on the margins of the newspaper in which the statement appeared while I was in jail, the letter was continued on scraps of writing paper supplied by a friendly Negro trusty, and concluded on a pad my attorneys were eventually permitted to leave me. Although the text remains in substance unaltered, I have indulged in the author's prerogative of polishing it for publication.

I think I should indicate that I am here in Birmingham, since you 2
have been influenced by the view which argues against "outsiders
coming in." I have the honor of serving as president of the Southern
Christian Leadership Conference, an organization operating in every
southern state, with headquarters in Atlanta, Georgia. We have some
eighty-five affiliated organizations across the South, and one of them
is the Alabama Christian Movement for Human Rights. Frequently
we share staff, educational, and financial resources with our affiliates.
Several months ago the affiliate here in Birmingham asked us to be
on call to engage in a nonviolent direct-action program if such were
deemed necessary. We readily consented, and when the hour came
we lived up to our promise. So I, along with several members of my
staff, am here because I was invited here. I am here because I have
organizational ties here.

But more basically, I am in Birmingham because injustice is here. 3
Just as the prophets of the eighth century B.C. left their villages and
carried their "thus saith the Lord" far beyond the boundaries of their
home towns, and just as the Apostle Paul left his village of Tarsus
and carried the gospel of Jesus Christ to the far corners of the Greco-
Roman world, so am I compelled to carry the gospel of freedom
beyond my own home town. Like Paul, I must constantly respond
to the Macedonian call for aid.

Moreover, I am cognizant of the interrelatedness of all commu- 4
nities and states. I cannot sit idly by in Atlanta and not be concerned
about what happens in Birmingham. Injustice anywhere is a threat
to justice everywhere. We are caught in an inescapable network of
mutuality, tied in a single garment of destiny. Whatever affects one
directly, affects all indirectly. Never again can we afford to live with
the narrow, provincial "outside agitator" idea. Anyone who lives
inside the United States can never be considered an outsider anywhere within its bounds.

You deplore the demonstrations taking place in Birmingham. But 5
your statement, I am sorry to say, fails to express a similar concern
for the conditions that brought about the demonstrations. I am sure
that none of you would want to rest content with the superficial kind
of social analysis that deals merely with effects and does not grapple
with underlying causes. It is unfortunate that demonstrations are
taking place in Birmingham, but it is even more unfortunate that the
city's white power structure left the Negro community with no alternative.

In any nonviolent campaign there are four basic steps: collection 6
of the facts to determine whether injustices exist; negotiation; self-
purification; and direct action. We have gone through all these steps
in Birmingham. There can be no gainsaying the fact that racial injustice

engulfs this community.   Birmingham is probably the most thoroughly segregated city in the United States. Its ugly record of brutality is widely known. Negroes have experienced grossly unjust treatment in the courts. There have been more unsolved bombings of Negro homes and churches in Birmingham than in any other city in the nation. These are the hard, brutal facts of the case. On the basis of these conditions, Negro leaders sought to negotiate with the city fathers. But the latter consistently refused to engage in good-faith negotiation.

Then, last September, came the opportunity to talk with leaders 7 of Birmingham's economic community. In the course of the negotiations, certain promises were made by the merchants—for example, to remove the stores' humiliating racial signs. On the basis of these promises, the Reverend Fred Shuttlesworth and the leaders of the Alabama Christian Movement for Human Rights agreed to a moratorium on all demonstrations. As the weeks and months went by, we realized that we were the victims of a broken promise. A few signs, briefly removed, returned; the others remained.

As in so many past experiences, our hopes had been blasted, and 8 the shadow of deep disappointment settled upon us. We had no alternative except to prepare for direct action, whereby we would present our very bodies as a means of laying our case before the conscience of the local and the national community. Mindful of the difficulties involved, we decided to undertake a process of self-purification. We began a series of workshops on nonviolence, and we repeatedly asked ourselves: "Are you able to accept blows without retaliating?" "Are you able to endure the ordeal of jail?" We decided to schedule our direct-action program for the Easter season, realizing that except for Christmas, this is the main shopping period of the year. Knowing that a strong economic-withdrawal program would be the by-product of direct action, we felt that this would be the best time to bring pressure to bear on the merchants for the needed change.

Then it occurred to us that Birmingham's mayoral election was 9 coming up in March, and we speedily decided to postpone action until after election day. When we discovered that the Commissioner of Public Safety, Eugene "Bull" Connor, had piled up enough votes to be in the run-off, we decided again to postpone action until the day after the run-off so that the demonstrations could not be used to cloud the issues. Like many others, we wanted to see Mr. Connor defeated, and to this end we endured postponement after postponement. Having aided in this community need, we felt that our direct-action program could be delayed no longer.

You may well ask, "Why direct action? Why sit-ins, marches, and 10 so forth? Isn't negotiation a better path?" You are quite right in calling

ADDITIONAL QUESTIONS FOR RESPONDING TO READING

1. King writes that the South has been bogged down in a "tragic effort to live in monologue rather than dialogue." What does he mean? In what ways does this "letter" serve as a dialogue?
2. What steps are taken to prepare for direct action? Do you understand the necessity for each of these steps?
3. Who are the people who are affected by segregation, according to King? Do you agree with his assessment? Do all parties suffer to the same extent?

for negotiation. Indeed, this is the very purpose of direct action. Nonviolent direct action seeks to create such a crisis and foster such a tension that a community which has constantly refused to negotiate is forced to confront the issue. It seeks so to dramatize the issue that it can no longer be ignored. My citing the creation of tension as part of the work of the nonviolent-resister may sound rather shocking. But I must confess that I am not afraid of the word "tension." I have earnestly opposed violent tension, but there is a type of constructive, nonviolent tension which is necessary for growth. Just as Socrates felt that it was necessary to create a tension in the mind so that individuals could rise from the bondage of myths and half-truths to the unfettered realm of creative analysis and objective appraisal, so must we see the need for nonviolent gadflies to create the kind of tension in society that will help men rise from the dark depths of prejudice and racism to the majestic heights of understanding and brotherhood.

The purpose of our direct-action program is to create a situation 11 so crisis-packed that it will inevitably open the door to negotiation. I therefore concur with you in your call for negotiation. Too long has our beloved Southland been bogged down in a tragic effort to live in monologue rather than dialogue.

One of the basic points in your statement is that the action that 12 I and my associates have taken in Birmingham is untimely. Some have asked: "Why didn't you give the new city administration time to act?" The only answer that I can give to this query is that the new Birmingham administration must be prodded about as much as the outgoing one, before it will act. We are sadly mistaken if we feel that the election of Albert Boutwell as mayor will bring the millennium to Birmingham. While Mr. Boutwell is a much more gentle person than Mr. Connor, they are both segregationists, dedicated to maintenance of the status quo. I have hoped that Mr. Boutwell will be reasonable enough to see the futility of massive resistance to desegregation. But he will not see this without pressure from devotees of civil rights. My friends, I must say to you that we have not made a single gain in civil rights without determined legal and nonviolent pressure. Lamentably, it is an historical fact that privileged groups seldom give up their privileges voluntarily. Individuals may see the moral light and voluntarily give up their unjust posture; but, as Reinhold Niebuhr[2] has reminded us, groups tend to be more immoral than individuals.

We know through painful experience that freedom is never vol- 13 untarily given by the oppressor; it must be demanded by the

---

[2]American religious and social thinker (1892–1971). [Eds.]

oppressed. Frankly, I have yet to engage in a direct-action campaign that was "well timed" in the view of those who have not suffered unduly from the disease of segregation. For years now I have heard the word "Wait!" It rings in the ear of every Negro with piercing familiarity. This "Wait" has almost always meant "Never." We must come to see, with one of our distinguished jurists, that "justice too long delayed is justice denied."

We have waited for more than 340 years for our constitutional 14 and God-given rights. The nations of Asia and Africa are moving with jetlike speed toward gaining political independence, but we still creep at horse-and-buggy pace toward gaining a cup of coffee at a lunch counter. Perhaps it is easy for those who have never felt the stinging darts of segregation to say, "Wait." But when you have seen vicious mobs lynch your mothers and fathers at will and drown your sisters and brothers at whim; when you have seen hate-filled policemen curse, kick, and even kill your black brothers and sisters; when you see the vast majority of your twenty million Negro brothers smothering in an airtight cage of poverty in the midst of an affluent society; when you suddenly find your tongue twisted and your speech stammering as you seek to explain to your six-year-old daughter why she can't go to the public amusement park that has just been advertised on television, and see tears welling up in her eyes when she is told that Funtown is closed to colored children, and see ominous clouds of inferiority beginning to form in her little mental sky, and see her beginning to distort her personality by developing an unconscious bitterness toward white people; when you have to concoct an answer for a five-year-old son who is asking, "Daddy, why do white people treat colored people so mean?"; when you take a cross-country drive and find it necessary to sleep night after night in the uncomfortable corners of your automobile because no motel will accept you; when you are humiliated day in and day out by nagging signs reading "white" and "colored"; when your first name becomes "nigger," your middle name becomes "boy" (however old you are) and your last name becomes "John," and your wife and mother are never given the respected title "Mrs."; when you are harried by day and haunted by night by the fact that you are a Negro, living constantly at tiptoe stance, never quite knowing what to expect next, and are plagued with inner fears and outer resentments; when you are forever fighting a degenerating sense of "nobodiness"—then you will understand why we find it difficult to wait. There comes a time when the cup of endurance runs over, and men are no longer willing to be plunged into the abyss of despair. I hope, sirs, you can understand our legitimate and unavoidable impatience.

You express a great deal of anxiety over our willingness to break 15 laws. This is certainly a legitimate concern. Since we so diligently

---

COLLABORATIVE ACTIVITY

Ask students, working in groups, to identify passages from the essay in which King moves from a general discussion of the movement to a specific recounting of personal details. Ask whether the shift into a personal tone is effective and what its impact is.

urge people to obey the Supreme Court's decision of 1954 outlawing segregation in the public schools, at first glance it may seem rather paradoxical for us consciously to break laws. One may well ask: "How can you advocate breaking some laws and obeying others?" The answer lies in the fact that there are two types of laws: just and unjust. I would be the first to advocate obeying just laws. One has not only a legal but a moral responsibility to obey just laws. Conversely, one has a moral responsibility to disobey unjust laws. I would agree with St. Augustine that "an unjust law is no law at all."

Now, what is the difference between the two? How does one 16 determine whether a law is just or unjust? A just law is a man-made code that squares with the moral law or the law of God. An unjust law is a code this is out of harmony with the moral law. To put it in the terms of St. Thomas Aquinas:[3] An unjust law is a human law that is not rooted in eternal law and natural law. Any law that uplifts human personality is just. Any law that degrades human personality is unjust. All segregation statutes are unjust because segregation distorts the soul and damages the personality. It gives the segregator a false sense of superiority and the segregated a false sense of inferiority. Segregation, to use the terminology of the Jewish philosopher Martin Buber,[4] substitutes an "I-it" relationship for an "I-thou" relationship and ends up relegating persons to the status of things. Hence segregation is not only politically, economically, and sociologically unsound, it is morally wrong and sinful. Paul Tillich[5] has said that sin is separation. Is not segregation an existential expression of man's tragic separation, his awful estrangement, his terrible sinfulness? Thus it is that I can urge men to obey the 1954 decision of the Supreme Court, for it is morally right; and I can urge them to disobey segregation ordinances, for they are morally wrong.

Let us consider a more concrete example of just and unjust laws. 17 An unjust law is a code that a numerical or power majority group compels a minority group to obey but does not make binding on itself. This is *difference* made legal. By the same token, a just law is a code that a majority compels a minority to follow and that it is willing to follow itself. This is *sameness* made legal.

Let me give another explanation. A law is unjust if it is inflicted 18 on a minority that, as a result of being denied the right to vote, had no part in enacting or devising the law. Who can say that the legislature of Alabama which set up that state's segregation laws was democratically elected? Throughout Alabama all sorts of devious

---

[3]Italian philosopher and theologian (1225–74). [Eds.]
[4]Austrian existentialist philosopher and Judaic scholar (1878–1965). [Eds.]
[5]American philosopher and theologian (1886–1965). [Eds.]

methods are used to prevent Negroes from becoming registered voters, and there are some counties in which, even though Negroes constitute a majority of the population, not a single Negro is registered. Can any law enacted under such circumstances be considered democratically structured?

Sometimes a law is just on its face and unjust in its application. 19 For instance, I have been arrested on a charge of parading without a permit. Now, there is nothing wrong in having an ordinance which requires a permit for a parade. But such an ordinance becomes unjust when it is used to maintain segregation and to deny citizens the First-Amendment privilege of peaceful assembly and protest.

I hope you are able to see the distinction I am trying to point out. 20 In no sense do I advocate evading or defying the law, as would the rabid segregationist. That would lead to anarchy. One who breaks an unjust law must do so openly, lovingly, and with a willingness to accept the penalty. I submit that an individual who breaks a law that conscience tells him is unjust, and who willingly accepts the penalty of imprisonment in order to arouse the conscience of the community over its injustice, is in reality expressing the highest respect for law.

Of course, there is nothing new about this kind of civil disobe- 21 dience. It was evidenced sublimely in the refusal of Shadrach, Meshach, and Abednego to obey the laws of Nebuchadnezzar, on the ground that a higher moral law was at stake.[6] It was practiced superbly by the early Christians, who were willing to face hungry lions and the excruciating pain of chopping blocks rather than submit to certain unjust laws of the Roman Empire. To a degree, academic freedom is a reality today because Socrates practiced civil disobedience.[7] In our own nation, the Boston Tea Party represented a massive act of civil disobedience.

We should never forget that everything Adolf Hitler did in Ger- 22 many was "legal" and everything the Hungarian freedom fighters[8] did in Hungary was "illegal." It was "illegal" to aid and comfort a Jew in Hitler's Germany. Even so, I am sure that, had I lived in Germany at the time, I would have aided and comforted my Jewish brothers. If today I lived in a Communist country where certain prin-

---

[6]In the Book of Daniel, Nebuchadnezzar commanded the people to worship a golden statue or be thrown into a furnace of blazing fire. When Shadrach, Meshach, and Abednego refused to worship any god but their own, they were bound and thrown into a blazing furnace, but the fire had no effect on them. Their escape led Nebuchadnezzar to make a decree forbidding blasphemy against their god. [Eds.]

[7]The ancient Greek philosopher Socrates was tried by the Athenians for corrupting their youth through his use of questions to teach. When he refused to change his methods of teaching, he was condemned to death. [Eds.]

[8]The anti-Communist uprising of 1956 was quickly crushed by the Russian army. [Eds.]

ciples dear to the Christian faith are suppressed, I would openly advocate disobeying that country's anti-religious laws.

I must make two honest confessions to you, my Christian and 23 Jewish brothers. First, I must confess that over the past few years I have been gravely disappointed with the white moderate. I have almost reached the regrettable conclusion that the Negro's great stumbling block in his stride toward freedom is not the White Citizen's Counciler or the Ku Klux Klanner, but the white moderate, who is more devoted to "order" than to justice; who prefers a negative peace which is the absence of tension to a positive peace which is the presence of justice; who constantly says, "I agree with you in the goal you seek, but I cannot agree with your methods of direct action"; who paternalistically believes he can set the timetable for another man's freedom; who lives by a mythical concept of time and who constantly advises the Negro to wait for a "more convenient season." Shallow understanding from people of good will is more frustrating than absolute misunderstanding from people of ill will. Lukewarm acceptance is much more bewildering than outright rejection.

I had hoped that the white moderate would understand that law 24 and order exist for the purpose of establishing justice and that when they fail in this purpose they become the dangerously structured dams that block the flow of social progress. I had hoped that the white moderate would understand that the present tension in the South is a necessary phase of the transition from an obnoxious negative peace, in which the Negro passively accepted his unjust plight, to a substantive and positive peace, in which all men will respect the dignity and worth of human personality. Actually, we who engage in nonviolent direct action are not the creators of tension. We merely bring to the surface the hidden tension that is already alive. We bring it out in the open, where it can be seen and dealt with. Like a boil that can never be cured so long as it is covered up but must be opened with all its ugliness to the natural medicines of air and light, injustice must be exposed, with all the tension its exposure creates, to the light of human conscience and the air of national opinion, before it can be cured.

In your statement you assert that our actions, even though 25 peaceful, must be condemned because they precipitate violence. But is this a logical assertion? Isn't this like condemning a robbed man because his possession of money precipitated the evil act of robbery? Isn't this like condemning Socrates because his unswerving commitment to truth and his philosophical inquiries precipitated the act by the misguided populace in which they made him drink hemlock? Isn't this like condemning Jesus because his unique God-consciousness and never-ceasing devotion to God's will precipitated the evil act of crucifixion? We must come to see that, as the federal courts have consistently affirmed, it is wrong to urge an individual to cease his efforts to gain his basic constitutional rights because the quest may precipitate violence. Society must protect the robbed and punish the robber.

I had also hoped that the white moderate would reject the myth 26 concerning time in relation to the struggle for freedom. I have just received a letter from a white brother in Texas. He writes: "All Christians know that the colored people will receive equal rights eventually, but it is possible that you are in too great a religious hurry. It has taken Christianity almost two thousand years to accomplish what it has. The teachings of Christ take time to come to earth." Such an attitude stems from a tragic misconception of time, from the strangely irrational notion that there is something in the very flow of time that will inevitably cure all ills. Actually, time itself is neutral; it can be used either destructively or constructively. More and more I feel that the people of ill will have used time much more effectively than have the people of good will. We will have to repent in this generation not merely for the hateful words and actions of the bad people, but for the appalling silence of the good people. Human progress never rolls in on wheels of inevitability; it comes through the tireless efforts of men willing to be co-workers with God, and without this hard work, time itself becomes an ally of the forces of social stagnation. We must use time creatively, in the knowledge that the time is always ripe to do right. Now is the time to make real the promise of democracy and transform our pending national elegy into a creative psalm of brotherhood. Now is the time to lift our national policy from the quicksand of racial injustice to the solid rock of human dignity.

You speak of our activity in Birmingham as extreme. At first I 27 was rather disappointed that fellow clergymen would see my nonviolent efforts as those of an extremist. I began thinking about the fact that I stand in the middle of two opposing forces in the Negro community. One is a force of complacency, made up in part of Negroes who, as a result of long years of oppression, are so drained of self-respect and a sense of "somebodiness" that they have adjusted to segregation; and in part of a few middle-class Negroes who, because of a degree of academic and economic security and because in some ways the profit by segregation, have become insensitive to the problems of the masses. The other force is one of bitterness and hatred, and it comes perilously close to advocating violence. It is expressed in the various black nationalist groups that are springing up across the nation, the largest and best-known being Elijah Muhammad's Muslim movement. Nourished by the Negro's frustration over the continued existence of racial discrimination, this movement is made up of people who have lost faith in America, who have absolutely repudiated Christianity, and who have concluded that the white man is an incorrigible "devil."

I have tried to stand between these two forces, saying that we 28 need emulate neither the "do-nothingism" of the complacent nor the hatred and despair of the black nationalist. For there is the more excellent way of love and nonviolent protest. I am grateful to God that, through the influence of the Negro church, the way of nonviolence became an integral part of our struggle.

If this philosophy had not emerged, by now many streets of the 29 South would, I am convinced, be flowing with blood. And I am further convinced that if our white brothers dismiss as "rabblerousers" and "outside agitators" those of use who employ nonviolent direct action, and if they refuse to support our nonviolent efforts, millions of Negroes will, out of frustration and despair, seek solace and security in black-nationalist ideologies—a development that would inevitably lead to a frightening racial nightmare.

Oppressed people cannot remain oppressed forever. The 30 yearning for freedom eventually manifests itself, and that is what has happened to the American Negro. Something within has reminded him of his birthright of freedom, and something without has reminded him that it can be gained. Consciously or unconsciously, he has been caught up by the *Zeitgeist*,[9] and with his black brothers of Africa and his brown and yellow brothers of Asia, South America, and the Caribbean, the United States Negro is moving with a sense of great urgency toward the promised land of racial justice. If one recognizes this vital urge that has engulfed the Negro community, one should readily understand why public demonstrations are taking place. The Negro has many pent-up resentments and latent frustrations, and he must release them. So let him march; let him make prayer pilgrimages to the city hall; let him go on freedom rides—and try to understand why he must do so. If his repressed emotions are not released in nonviolent ways, they will seek expression through violence; this is not a threat but a fact of history. So I have not said to my people, "Get rid of your discontent." Rather, I have tried to say that this normal and healthy discontent can be channeled into the creative outlet of nonviolent direct action. And now this approach is being termed extremist.

But though I was initially disappoined at being categorized as an 31 extremist, as I continued to think about the matter I gradually gained a measure of satisfaction from the label. Was not Jesus an extremist

---

[9]The spirit of the times. [Eds.]

for love: "Love your enemies, bless them that curse you, do good to them that hate you, and pray for them which despitefully use you, and persecute you." Was not Amos an extremist for justice: "Let justice roll down like waters and righteousness like an ever-flowing stream." Was not Paul an extremist for the Christian gospel: "I bear in my body the marks of the Lord Jesus." Was not Martin Luther an extremist: "Here I stand; I cannot do otherwise, so help me God." And John Bunyan: "I will stay in jail to the end of my days before I make a butchery of my conscience." And Abraham Lincoln: "This nation cannot survive half slave and half free." And Thomas Jefferson: "We hold these truths to be self-evident, that all men are created equal. . . ." So the question is not whether we will be extremists, but what kind of extremists we will be. Will we be extremists for hate or for love? Will we be extremists for the preservation of injustice or for the extension of justice? In that dramatic scene on Calvary's hill three men were crucified. We must never forget that all three were crucified for the same thing—the crime of extremism. Two were extremists for immorality, and thus fell below their environment. The other, Jesus Christ, was an extremist for love, truth, and goodness, and thereby rose above his environment. Perhaps the South, the nation, and the world are in dire need of creative extremists.

I had hoped that the white moderate would see this need. Perhaps 32 I was too optimistic; perhaps I expected too much. I suppose I should have realized that few members of the oppressor race can understand the deep groans and passionate yearnings of the oppressed race, and still fewer have the vision to see that injustice must be rooted out by strong, persistent, and determined action. I am thankful, however, that some of our white brothers in the South have grasped the meaning of this social revolution and committed themselves to it. They are still all too few in quantity, but they are big in quality. Some—such as Ralph McGill, Lillian Smith, Harry Golden, James McBridge Dabbs, Ann Braden, and Sarah Patton Boyle—have written about our struggle in eloquent and prophetic terms. Others have marched with us down nameless streets of the South. They have languished in filthy, roach-infested jails, suffering the abuse and brutality of policemen who view them as "dirty nigger-lovers." Unlike so many of their moderate brothers and sisters, they have recognized the urgency of the moment and sensed the need for powerful "action" antidotes to combat the disease of segregation.

Let me take note of my other major disappointment. I have been 33 so greatly disappointed with the white church and its leadership. Of course, there are some notable exceptions. I am not unmindful of the fact that each of you has taken some significant stands on this issue. I commend you, Reverend Stallings, for your Christian stand on this past Sunday, in welcoming Negroes to your worship service on a nonsegregated basis. I commend the Catholic leaders of this state for integrating Spring Hill College several years ago.

But despite these notable exceptions, I must honestly reiterate 34 that I have been disappointed with the church. I do not say this as one of those negative critics who can always find something wrong with the church. I say this as a minister of the gospel, who loves the church; who was nurtured in its bosom; who has been sustained by its spiritual blessings and who will remain true to it as long as the cord of life shall lengthen.

When I was suddenly catapulted into the leadership of the bus 35 protest in Montgomery, Alabama, a few years ago, I felt we would be supported by the white church. I felt that the white ministers, priests, and rabbis of the South would be among our strongest allies. Instead, some have been outright opponents, refusing to understand the freedom movement and misrepresenting its leaders; all too many others have been more cautious than courageous and have remained silent behind the anesthetizing security of stainedglass windows.

In spite of my shattered dreams, I came to Birmingham with the 36 hope that the white religious leadership of this community would see the justice of our cause and, with deep moral concern, would serve as the channel through which our just grievances could reach the power structure. I had hoped that each of you would understand. But again I have been disappointed.

I have heard numerous southern religious leaders admonish their 37 worshipers to comply with a desegregation decision because it is the law, but I have longed to hear white ministers declare: "Follow this decree because integration is morally right and because the Negro is your brother." In the midst of blatant injustices inflicted upon the Negro, I have watched white churchmen stand on the sideline and mouth pious irrelevancies and sanctimonious trivialities. In the midst of a mighty struggle to rid our nation of racial and economic injustice, I have heard many ministers say: "Those are social issues, with which the gospel has no real concern." And I have watched many churches commit themselves to a completely otherworldly religion which makes a strange, un-Biblical distinction between body and soul, between the sacred and the secular.

I have traveled the length and breadth of Alabama, Mississippi, 38 and all the other southern states. On sweltering summer days and crisp autumn mornings I have looked at the South's beautiful churches with their lofty spires pointing heavenward. I have beheld the impressive outlines of her massive religious-education buildings. Over and over I have found myself asking: "What kind of people worship here? Who is their God? Where were their voices when the lips of Governor Barnett dripped with words of interposition and nullification? Where were they when Governor Wallace gave a clarion call for defiance and hatred? Where were their voices of support when bruised and weary Negro men and women decided to rise from the dark dungeons of complacency to the bright hills of creative protest?"

Yes, these questions are still in my mind. In deep disappointment 39 I have wept over the laxity of the church. But be assured that my tears have been tears of love. There can be no deep disappointment where there is not deep love. Yes, I love the church. How could I do otherwise? I am in the rather unique position of being the son, the grandson, and the great-grandson of preachers. Yes, I see the church as the body of Christ. But, oh! How we have blemished and scarred that body through social neglect and through fear of being nonconformists.

There was a time when the church was very powerful—in the 40 time when the early Christians rejoiced at being deemed worthy to suffer for what they believed. In those days the church was not merely a thermometer that recorded the ideas and principles of popular opinion; it was a thermostat that transformed the mores of society. Whenever the early Christians entered a town, the people in power became distrubed and immediately sought to convict the Christians for being "disturbers of the peace" and "outside agitators." But the Christians pressed on, in the conviction that they were "a colony of heaven," called to obey God rather than man. Small in number, they were big in commitment. They were too God-intoxicated to be "astronomically intimidated." By their effort and example they brought an end to such ancient evils as infanticide and gladiatorial contests.

Things are different now. So often the contemporary church is a 41 weak, ineffectual voice with an uncertain sound. So often it is an archdefender to the status quo. Far from being distrubed by the presence of the church, the power structure of the average community is consoled by the church's silent—and often even vocal—sanction of things as they are.

But the judgment of God is upon the church as never before. If 42 today's church does not recapture the sacrificial spirit of the early church, it will lose its authenticity, forfeit the loyalty of millions, and be dismissed as an irrelevant social club with no meaning for the twentieth century. Every day I meet young people whose disappointment with the church has turned into outright disgust.

Perhaps I have once again been too optimistic. Is organized reli 43 gion too inextricably bound to the status quo to save our nation and the world? Perhaps I must turn my faith to the inner spiritual church, the church within the church, as the true *ekklesia*[10] and the hope of

---

[10]The Greek word for the early Christian church. [Eds.]

the world. But again I am thankful to God that some noble souls from the ranks of organized religion have broken loose from the paralyzing chains of conformity and joined us as active partners in the struggle for freedom. They have left their secure congregations and walked the streets of Albany, Georgia, with us. They have gone down the highways of the South on tortuous rides for freedom. Yes, they have gone to jail with us. Some have been dismissed from their churches, have lost the support of their bishops and fellow ministers. But they have acted in the faith that right defeated is stronger than evil triumphant. Their witness has been the spiritual salt that has preserved the true meaning of the gospel in these troubled times. They have carved a tunnel of hope through the dark mountain of disappointment.

I hope the church as a whole will meet the challenge of this 44 decisive hour. But even if the church does not come to the aid of justice, I have no despair about the future. I have no fear about the outcome of our struggle in Birmingham, even if our motives are at present misunderstood. We will reach the goal of freedom in Birmingham and all over the nation, because the goal of America is freedom. Abused and scorned though we may be, our destiny is tied up with America's destiny. Before the pilgrims landed at Plymouth, we were here. Before the pen of Jefferson etched the majestic words of the Declaration of Independence across the pages of history, we were here. For more than two centuries our forebears labored in this country without wages; they made cotton king; they built the homes of their masters while suffering gross injustice and shameful humiliation—and yet out of a bottomless vitality they continued to thrive and develop. If the inexpressible cruelties of slavery could not stop us, the opposition we now face will surely fail. We will win our freedom because the sacred heritage of our nation and the eternal will of God are embodied in our echoing demands.

Before closing I feel impelled to mention one other point in your 45 statement that has troubled me profoundly. You warmly commended the Birmingham police force for keeping "order" and "preventing violence." I doubt that you would have so warmly commended the police force if you had seen its dogs sinking their teeth into unarmed, nonviolent Negroes. I doubt that you would so quickly commend the policemen if you were to observe their ugly and inhumane treatment of Negroes here in the city jail; if you were to watch them push and curse old Negro women and young Negro girls; if you were to see them slap and kick old Negro men and young boys; if you were to observe them, as they did on two occasions, refuse to give us food because we wanted to sing our grace together. I cannot join you in your praise of the Birmingham police department.

It is true that the police have exercised a degree of discipline in   46
handling the demonstrators. In this sense they have conducted themselves rather "nonviolently" in public. But for what purpose? To
preserve the evil system of segregation. Over the past few years I
have consistently preached that nonviolence demands that the means
we use must be as pure as the ends we seek. I have tried to make
clear that it is wrong to use immoral means to attain moral ends. But
now I must affirm that it is just as wrong, or perhaps even more so,
to use moral means to preserve immoral ends. Perhaps Mr. Connor
and his policemen have been rather nonviolent in public, as was Chief
Pritchett in Albany, Georgia, but they have used the moral means of
nonviolence to maintain the immoral end of racial injustice. As T. S.
Eliot has said, "The last temptation is the greatest treason: To do the
right deed for the wrong reason."

I wish you had commended the Negro sit-inners and demon-   47
strators of Birmingham for their sublime courage, their willingness
to suffer, and their amazing discipline in the midst of great provocation. One day the South will recognize its real heroes. They will be
the James Merediths,[11] with the noble sense of purpose that enables
them to face jeering and hostile mobs, and with the agonizing loneliness that characterizes the life of the pioneer. They will be old,
oppressed, battered Negro women, symbolized in a seventy-two-
year-old woman in Montgomery, Alabama, who rose up with a sense
of dignity and with her people decided not to ride segregated buses,
and who responded with ungrammatical profundity to one who
inquired about her weariness: "My feets is tired, but my soul is at
rest." They will be the young high school and college students, the
young ministers of the gospel and a host of their elders, courageously
and nonviolently sitting in at lunch counters and willingly going to
jail for conscience' sake. One day the South will know that when
these disinherited children of God sat down at lunch counters, they
were in reality standing up for what is best in the American dream
and for the most sacred values in our Judaeo-Christian heritage,
thereby bringing our nation back to those great wells of democracy
which were dug deep by the founding fathers in their formulation of
the Constitution and the Declaration of Independence.

Never before have I written so long a letter. I'm afraid it is much   48
too long to take your precious time. I can assure you that it would
have been much shorter if I had been writing from a comfortable
desk, but what else can one do when he is alone in a narrow jail cell,

---

[11]First African-American to enroll at the University of Mississippi. [Eds.]

WRITING SUGGESTION

Write a newspaper editorial in support of King's position.

other than write long letters, think long thoughts, and pray long prayers?

If I have said anything in this letter that overstates the truth and indicates an unreasonable impatience, I beg you to forgive me. If I have said anything that understates the truth and indicates my having a patience that allows me to settle for anything less than brotherhood, I beg God to forgive me. 49

I hope this letter finds you strong in the faith. I also hope that circumstances will soon make it possible for me to meet each of you, not as an integrationist or a civil-rights leader but as a fellow clergyman and a Christian brother. Let us all hope that the dark clouds of racial prejudice will soon pass away and the deep fog of misunderstanding will be lifted from our fear-drenched communities, and in some not too distant tomorrow the radiant stars of love and brotherhood will shine over our great nation with all their scintillating beauty. 50

Yours for the cause of Peace and Brotherhood,
MARTIN LUTHER KING, JR.

**ANSWERS TO RESPONDING
TO READING**

1. The clergymen have admonished King for being what they consider "extremist" and impatient. King argues that time must be used constructively because oppressed people eventually fight back. Nonviolent action offers the only alternative to violence because it offers a creative outlet for discontent.
2. Some people might argue that recent events in Eastern Europe fulfill King's prophetic statement.
3. King was a powerful and moving orator. His writing style utilizes his strengths as a speaker, and his rhetorical devices and use of direct address draw the reader into a sense of close communication with a compassionate, vital, and intelligent individual.

RESPONDING TO READING

1. What decision do the clergymen he addresses believe King should rethink? Do you believe King would be justified in arguing that he has no other alternative? Would you accept this argument?   **2.** In paragraph 30 King says, "Oppressed people cannot remain oppressed forever." Do you think world events of the last few years confirm or challenge this sentiment? Explain.   **3.** Throughout this letter King uses elaborate diction and a variety of rhetorical devices: He addresses his audience directly; makes frequent use of balance and parallelism, understatement, and metaphor; and makes many allusions to religious and political figures. Do these rhetorical devices enhance his argument, or do they get in the way? What effect do you think they were intended to have on the letter's original audience of clergymen? What effect do they have on you?

BACKGROUND ON AUTHOR

Robert Coles is considered a leading authority on the psychological effects of poverty and racial discrimination in the United States. He has been noted for his unorthodox methods of working with children; in trying to explore their frustrations, hopes, and dilemmas, he frequently turns to examining the artwork of the very young.

I Listen to My Parents and I Wonder What They Believe

ROBERT COLES

Robert Coles (see also p. 671), an advocate of social reform, first published this article in 1980. In all his work, he has listened to and tried to understand children. Here Coles talks about the ethical dilemmas children face and the responsibility parents have to set standards.

No so long ago children were looked upon in a sentimental fashion as ''angels'' or as ''innocents.'' Today, thanks to Freud and his followers, boys and girls are understood to have complicated inner lives; to feel love, hate, envy and rivalry in various and subtle mixtures; to be eager participants in the sexual and emotional politics of the home, neighborhood and school. Yet some of us parents still cling to the notion of childhood innocence in another way. We do not see that our children also make ethical decisions every day in their own lives, or realize how attuned they may be to normal currents and issues in the larger society.

In Appalachia I heard a girl of eight whose father owns coal fields (and gas stations, a department store and much timberland) wonder about ''life'' one day: ''I'll be walking to the school bus, and I'll ask myself why there's some who are poor and their daddies can't find a job, and there's some who are lucky like me. Last month there was an explosion in a mine by daddy owns, and everyone became upset. Two miners got killed. My daddy said it was their own fault, because they'll be working and they get careless. When my mother asked if there was anything wrong with the safety down in the mine, he told her no and she shouldn't ask questions like that. Then the Government people came and they said it was the owner's fault—Daddy's. But he has a lawyer and the lawyer is fighting the Government and the union. In school, kids ask me what I think, and I sure do feel sorry for the two miners and so does my mother—I know that. She told me it's just not a fair world and you have to remember that. Of course, there's no one who can be sure there won't be trouble; like my daddy says, the rain falls on the just and the unjust. My brother is only six and he asked Daddy awhile back who are the 'just' and the 'unjust,' and Daddy said there are people who work hard and they live good lives, and there are lazy people and they're always trying to sponge off others. But I guess you have to feel sorry for anyone who has a lot of trouble, because it's poured-down, heavy rain.''

Listening, one begins to realize that an elementary-school child is no stranger to moral reflection—and to ethical conflict. This girl was torn between her loyalty to her particular background, its values and assumptions, and to a larger affiliation—her membership in the nation, the world. As a human being whose parents were kind and decent to her, she was inclined to be thoughtful and sensitive with respect to others, no matter what their work or position in society. But her father was among other things a mineowner, and she had already learned to shape her concerns to suit that fact of life. The result: a moral oscillation of sorts, first toward nameless others all over the world and then toward her own family. As the girl put it later, when she was a year older: ''You should try to have 'good

FOR OPENERS

Does everyone need to believe in something? From where do we get our system of beliefs? Family? Friends? Somewhere else?

ADDITIONAL QUESTIONS FOR RESPONDING TO READING

1. To whom might children turn when parents disagree over moral issues? Is parental disagreement over such issues necessarily harmful to a child?

2. If many parents today avoid moral instruction, what other lessons, according to Coles, are children getting?

3. How do you respond to Coles's assertion that we all need "a faith that addresses itself to the meaning of this life"? Do you find this need in yourself?

TEACHING STRATEGY

In paragraph 1, Coles observes that children "make ethical decisions every day in their own lives." Do your students agree that this is so? What kinds of ethical decisions have they made? Do they think their parents are aware of the ethical stances they have taken?

thoughts' about everyone, the minister says, and our teacher says that too. But you should honor your father and mother most of all; that's why you should find out what they think and then sort of copy them. But sometimes you're not sure if you're on the right track."

Sort of copy them. There could be worse descriptions of how children acquire moral values. In fact, the girl understood how girls and boys all over the world "sort of" develop attitudes of what is right and wrong, ideas of who the just and the unjust are. And they also struggle hard and long, and not always with success, to find out where the "right track" starts and ends. Children need encouragement or assistance as they wage that struggle. 4

In home after home that I have visited, and in many classrooms, I have met children who not only are growing emotionally and intellectually but also are trying to make sense of the world morally. That is to say, they are asking themselves and others about issues of fair play, justice, liberty, equality. Those last words are abstractions, of course—the stuff of college term papers. And there are, one has to repeat, those in psychology and psychiatry who would deny elementary-school children access to that "higher level" of moral reflection. But any parent who has listened closely to his or her child knows that girls and boys are capable of wondering about matters of morality, and knows too that often it is their grown-up protectors (parents, relatives, teachers, neighbors) who are made uncomfortable by the so-called "innocent" nature of the questions children may ask or the statements they may make. Often enough the issue is not the moral capacity of children but the default of us parents who fail to respond to inquiries put to us by our daughters and sons—and fail to set moral standards for both ourselves and our children. 5

Do's and don't's are, of course, pressed upon many of our girls and boys. But a moral education is something more than a series of rules handed down, and in our time one cannot assume that every parent feels able—sure enough of her own or his own actual beliefs and values—to make even an initial explanatory and disciplinary effort towards a moral education. Furthermore, for many of us parents these days it is a child's emotional life that preoccupies us. 6

In 1963, when I was studying school desegregation in the South, I had extended conversations with Black and white elementary-school children caught up in a dramatic moment of historical change. For longer than I care to remember, I concentrated on possible psychiatric troubles, on how a given child was managing under circumstances of extreme stress, on how I could be of help—with "support," with reassurance, with a helpful psychological observation or interpretation. In many instances I was off the mark. These children weren't "patients"; they weren't even complaining. They were worried, all 7 right, and often enough they had things to say that were substantive—that had to do not so much with troubled emotions as with questions of right and wrong in the real-life dramas taking place in their worlds.

Here is a nine-year-old white boy, the son of ardent segregationists, telling me about his sense of what desegregation meant to Louisiana in the 1960s: "They told us it wouldn't happen—never. My daddy said none of us white people would go into schools with the colored. But then it did happen, and when I went to school the first day I didn't know what would go on. Would the school stay open or would it close up? We didn't know what to do; the teacher kept telling us that we should be good and obey the law, but my daddy said the law was wrong. Then my mother said she wanted me in school even if there were some colored kids there. She said if we all stayed home she'd be a 'nervous wreck.' So I went.

"After a while I saw that the colored weren't so bad. I saw that there are different kinds of colored people, just like with us whites. There was one of the colored who was nice, a boy who smiled, and he played real good. There was another one, a boy, who wouldn't talk with anyone. I don't know if it's right that we all be in the same school. Maybe it isn't right. My sister is starting school next year, and she says she doesn't care if there's 'mixing of the races.' She says they told her in Sunday school that everyone is a child of God, and then a kid asked if that goes for the colored too and the teacher said yes, she thought so. My daddy said that it's true, God made everyone—but that doesn't mean we all have to be living together under the same roof in the home or the school. But my mother said we'll never know what God wants of us but we have to try to read His mind, and that's why we pray. So when I say my prayers I ask God to tell me what's the right thing to do. In school I try to say hello to the colored, because they're kids, and you can't be mean or you'll be 'doing wrong,' like my grandmother says."

Children aren't usually long-winded in the moral discussions they have with one another or with adults, and in quoting this boy I have pulled together comments he made to me in the course of several days. But everything he said was of interest to me. I was interested in the boy's changing racial attitudes. It was clear he was trying to find a coherent, sensible moral position too. It was also borne in on me that if one spends days, weeks in a given home, it is hard to escape a particular moral climate just as significant as the psychological one.

In many homes parents establish moral assumptions, mandates, priorities. They teach children what to believe in, what not to believe in. They teach children what is permissible or not permissible—and

COLLABORATIVE ACTIVITY

Divide students into groups of four. Assign students to interview children of various ages about their attitudes about race relations in their schools. Then, ask student groups to discuss the differences in the children's responses. In class discussion, consider when and how ethical stances develop.

why. They may summon up the Bible, the flag, history, novels, aphorisms, philosophical or political sayings, personal memories—all in an effort to teach children how to behave, what and whom to respect and for which reasons. Or they may neglect to do so, and in so doing teach their children *that*—a moral abdication, of sorts—and in this way fail their children. Children need and long for words of moral advice, instruction, warning, as much as they need words of affirmation or criticism from their parents about other matters. They must learn how to dress and what to wear, how to eat and what to eat; and they must also learn how to behave under X or Y or Z conditions, and why.

All the time, in 20 years of working with poor children and rich 12 children, Black children and white children, children from rural areas and urban areas and in every region of this country, I have heard questions—thoroughly intelligent and discerning questions—about social and historical matters, about personal behavior, and so on. But most striking is the fact that almost all those questions, in one way or another, are moral in nature: Why did the Pilgrims leave England? Why didn't they just stay and agree to do what the king wanted them to do? . . . Should you try to share all you've got or should you save a lot for yourself? . . . What do you do when you see others fighting— do you try to break up the fight, do you stand by and watch or do you leave as fast as you can? . . . Is it right that some people haven't got enough to eat? . . . I see other kids cheating and I wish I could copy the answers too; but I won't cheat, though sometimes I feel I'd like to and I get all mixed up. I go home and talk with my parents, and I ask them what should you do if you see kids cheating—pay no attention, or report the kids or do the same thing they are doing?

Those are examples of children's concerns—and surely millions 13 of American parents have heard versions of them. Have the various "experts" on childhood stressed strongly enough the importance of such questions—and the importance of the hunger we all have, no matter what our age or background, to examine what we believe in, are willing to stand for, and what we are determined to ask, likewise, of our children?

Children not only need our understanding of their complicated 14 emotional lives; they also need a constant regard for the moral issues that come their way as soon as they are old enough to play with others and take part in the politics of the nursery, the back yard and the schoolroom. They need to be told what they must do and what they must not do. They need control over themselves and a sense of what others are entitled to from them—co-operation, thoughtfulness, an attentive ear and eye. They need discipline not only to tame their excesses of emotion but discipline also connected to stated and clarified moral values. They need, in other words, something to believe in that is larger than their own appetites and urges and, yes, bigger than their "psychological drives." They need a larger view of the world, a moral context, as it were—a faith that addresses itself to the meaning of this life we all live and, soon enough, let go of.

Yes, it is time for us parents to begin to look more closely at what 15 ideas our children have about the world; and it would be well to do so before they become teen-agers and young adults and begin to remind us, as often happens, of how little attention we did pay to their moral development. Perhaps a nine-year-old girl from a well-off suburban home in Texas put it better than anyone else I've met:

> I listen to my parents, and I wonder what they believe in more than 16
> anything else. I asked my mom and my daddy once: What's the thing that means most to you? They said they didn't know but I shouldn't worry my head too hard with questions like that. So I asked my best friend, and she said she wonders if there's a God and how do you know Him and what does He want you to do—I mean, when you're in school or out playing with your friends. They talk about God in church, but is it only in church that He's there and keeping an eye on you? I saw a kid steal in a store, and I know her father has a lot of money—because I hear my daddy talk. But stealing's wrong. My mother said she's a 'sick girl,' but it's still wrong what she did. Don't you think?

There was more—much more—in the course of the months I 17 came to know that child and her parents and their neighbors. But those observations and questions—a "mere child's'—reminded me unforgettably of the aching hunger for firm ethical principles that so many of us feel. Ought we not begin thinking about this need? Ought we not all be asking ourselves more intently what standards we live by—and how we can satisfy our children's hunger for moral values?

RESPONDING TO READING

1. Coles observes that "an elementary-school child is no stranger to moral reflection—and to ethical conflict" (paragraph 3). What conflicts does he cite as examples? What additional moral and ethical struggles did you confront as a child?   **2.** Do you believe children in the 1990s are more or less likely to be torn by ethical dilemmas than their earlier counterparts? Why?   **3.** Coles believes that it is the responsibility of parents to set moral and ethical standards for children, to help them "to make sense of the world morally" (paragraph 5). According to Coles, how successful are parents? Do you agree with him?

WRITING SUGGESTIONS

1. Do you believe your parents transmitted moral values to you, or did they offer a "moral abdication"? What benefits and drawbacks did their message offer to you? Write an essay dealing with these questions.
2. What moral values do you intend to transmit to your children? Write a letter to your unborn children telling them what your hopes for them are.

ANSWERS TO RESPONDING TO READING

1. Children experience conflicts when they see (and try to understand) suffering in others. They also face conflicting loyalties when they learn that various authority figures, including their parents, have different moral codes.
2. Answers will vary.
3. Coles acknowledges that many parents do "teach children what to believe in, what not to believe in" (paragraph 11), but he also realizes that many do not. In these cases, children learn precisely what the parents teach: "a moral abdication."

A Life for a Life: What That Means Today

MARGARET MEAD

During her distinguished career, anthropologist Margaret Mead (1901–1978) was a pioneer in field studies, a teacher, a curator of ethnology at the American Museum of Natural History, and a leading American intellectual and public figure. She first gained renown for her classic of cultural anthropology, *Coming of Age in Samoa* (1928), a study of the behavior of adolescent girls. Mead is also author of *Growing Up in New Guinea* (1930), *Sex and Temperament in Primitive Societies* (1935), *Male and Female: A Study of the Sexes in a Changing World* (1949), *Continuities in Cultural Evolution* (1964), and the autobiographical *Blackberry Winter: My Early Years* (1972). In the following essay, from *Aspects of the Present*, written with Rhoda Metraux (and published posthumously in 1980), Mead expands her interest to social problems and adds her thoughtful comments to the debate over capital punishment.

BACKGROUND ON AUTHOR

Mead has been credited with revolutionizing anthropology by enriching it with elements from other disciplines, such as psychology and economics. As a woman in what was originally a man's field, Mead was certainly breaking down barriers; she was daring, too, in publishing her work in a form that nonspecialists could understand. Although she was criticized by some professionals for what has been termed her unscientific thinking, her work has been taken seriously since her initial study of adolescent Samoan girls in the 1920s. Particularly startling and popular with both students and general readers has been her suggestion that Americans had something to learn from the Samoan culture.

FOR OPENERS

What are your students' opinions about capital punishment? Do they see it as a violation of basic human rights? A necessary evil? Something else?

1   As Americans we have declared ourselves to be champions of human rights in the world at large. But at home . . .

2   At home the Congress and the majority of our state legislatures have been hurrying to pass new laws to ensure that persons convicted of various violent crimes (but not the same ones in all states) may be—or must be—executed.

3   In my view, it is a sorry spectacle to see a great nation publicly proclaiming efforts to modify violence and to protect human rights in distant parts of the world and at the same time devoting an inordinate amount of time and energy at every level of government to ensure that those men and women convicted of capital offenses will be condemned to death and executed. Decisions to carry out such vengeful, punitive measures against our own people would reverberate around the world, making a cold mockery of our very real concern for human rights and our serious efforts to bring about peace and controlled disarmament among nations.

4   If we do in fact take seriously our chosen role as champions of human rights, then certainly we must also reinterpret drastically the very ancient law of "a life for a life" as it affects human beings in our own society today. I see this as a major challenge, especially for modern women.

5   But first we must understand where we are now.

6   In the late 1960s we lived through a kind of twilight period when without any changes in our laws, men and women were condemned to death but the sentences were not carried out. Those who had been condemned where left to sit and wait—often for years.

In 1972 there was a brief period when it seemed that capital punishment had finally been abolished in the whole United States, as it has been in most of the modern countries of western Europe and in many other countries. For then, in the case of *Furman v. Georgia*, the Supreme Court of the United States ruled that existing laws whereby certain convicted criminals were condemned to death were haphazard and arbitrary in their application and constituted cruel and unusual punishment, which is prohibited by the Eighth Amendment to the Constitution. True, the Court was divided; even the five justices who supported the ruling were quite sharply divided in their reasoning. Nevertheless, *Furman v. Georgia* saved the lives of 631 persons in prisons across the country who were under sentence of death.   7

It seemed that we had passed a watershed.   8

But we were quickly disillusioned. The Supreme Court had not yet abolished capital punishment; the justices merely had ruled out the discriminatory manner in which the current laws were applied. As Justice William O. Douglas pointed out in his concurring opinion, the existing system allowed "the penalty to be discriminatorily and disproportionately applied to the poor, the Blacks and the members of unpopular groups."   9

In response, lawmakers in many states—often pushed by their constituents and by law-enforcement agencies—tried to meet the objections by means of new and contrasting laws. Some of these laws made the death penalty mandatory: no exceptions or mitigating circumstances were possible. Others made the death penalty discretionary, that is, they provided very specific guidelines for defining mitigating circumstances that should be taken into account. The reason was that experts differed radically in their opinions as to what the justices of the Supreme Court would find acceptable in revised laws.   10

In their haste, these lawmakers missed their chance to think in quite other terms.   11

Meanwhile, of course, cases were tried and a few women and many men were once more condemned. In July, 1976, the principles underlying the new laws were tested as the Supreme Court of the United States announced rulings in five of these cases, upholding three discretionary death-penalty statutes and ruling against two that imposed mandatory capital punishment. As a result, the death sentences of 389 persons in 19 states were later reduced to life imprisonment.   12

But the lawmaking and the convictions have continued. At the end of 1977, the number of condemned prisoners in the death rows of penitentiaries in the 33 states that then had capital punishment laws amounted to 407—five women and 402 men—divided almost   13

ADDITIONAL QUESTIONS FOR RESPONDING TO READING

1. What specific proposals does Mead appear to offer to alleviate the "violence" of capital punishment? How practical are her suggestions?
2. What does she say is the likely outcome of our ambivalence toward capital punishment? Do you agree with her assessment?

evenly between white Americans and Black or Hispanic Americans. Two were Native Americans—Indians—and concerning six, even this meager background information was lacking. Most were poor and ill educated, too unimportant to be permitted to enter into plea bargaining and too poor to hire the expensive legal talent that makes possible very different treatment in the courts for more affluent and protected individuals.

In early 1977 one man, Gary Gilmore, whose two attempts at 14 suicide were given extravagant publicity, finally was executed in the midst of glaring national publicity in the mass media. Looking back at this one sordidly exploited event, can anyone picture how we would react if, without discussion, it were suddenly decided to execute *all* the death row prisoners who were without resources to prolong their lives?

What we are much more likely to do, I think, is to seesaw between 15 the old, old demand for drastic retribution for crimes against human beings that very rightly rouse us to anger, fear and disgust and our rather special American belief that almost everyone (except the suspected criminal we catch on the run and kill forthwith) is entitled to a second chance. So we make harsh laws, convict some of the people who break them—and then hesitate. What next?

Every month the number of those convicted, sentenced and 16 waiting grows. Violent criminals, they become the victims of our very ambiguous attitudes toward violence and our unwillingness to face the true issues.

The struggle for and against the abolition of capital punishment 17 has been going on in our country and among enlightened peoples everywhere for well over a century. In the years before the Civil War the fight to end the death penalty was led in America by men like Horace Greeley, who also was fighting strongly to abolish slavery, and by a tiny handful of active women like New England's Dorothea Dix, who was fighting for prison reform. In those years three states— Michigan in 1847, Rhode Island in 1852 and Wisconsin in 1853— renounced the use of capital punishment, the first jurisdictions in the modern world to do so.

Both sides claim a primary concern for human rights. Those who 18 demand that we keep—and carry out—the death penalty speak for the victims of capital crimes, holding that it is only just that murderers, kidnappers, rapists, hijackers and other violent criminals should suffer for the harm they have done and so deter others from committing atrocious crimes.

In contrast, those who demand that we abolish capital punish- 19 ment altogether are convinced that violence breeds violence—that the death penalty carried out by the State against its own citizens in effect legitimizes willful killing. Over time, their concerns has been part of a much more inclusive struggle for human rights and human dignity. They were among those who fought against slavery and they have been among those who have fought for the civil rights of Black Americans, of immigrants and of ethnic minorities and Native Americans, for the rights of prisoners of war as well as for the prisoners in penitentiaries, for the rights of the poor, the unemployed and the unemployable, for women's rights and for the rights of the elderly and of children.

Now, I believe, we can—if we will—put this all together and 20 realize that in our kind of civilization "a life for a life" need not mean destructive retribution, but instead the development of new forms of community in which, because all lives are valuable, what is emphasized is the prevention of crime and the protection of all those who are vulnerable.

The first step is to realize that in our society we have permitted 21 the kinds of vulnerability that characterize the victims of violent crime and have ignored, where we could, the hostility and alienation that enter into the making of violent criminals. No rational person condones violent crime, and I have no patience with sentimental attitudes toward violent criminals. But it is time that we open our eyes to the conditions that foster violence and that ensure the existence of easily recognizable victims.

Americans respond generously—if not always wisely—to the 22 occurrence of natural catastrophes. But except where we are brought face to face with an unhappy individual or a family in trouble, we are turned off by the humanly far more desperate social catastrophes of children who are trashed by the schools—and the local community—where they should be learning for themselves what it means and how it feels to be a valued human being. We demean the men and women who are overwhelmed by their inability to meet their responsibilities to one another or even to go it alone, and we shut out awareness of the fate of the unskilled, the handicapped and the barely tolerated elderly. As our own lives have become so much more complex and our social ties extraordinarily fragile, we have lost any sense of community with others whose problems and difficulties and catastrophes are not our own.

We do know that human lives are being violated—and not only 23 by criminals. But at least we can punish criminals. That is a stopgap way. But it is not the way out of our dilemma.

We also know that in any society, however organized, security 24 rests on accepted participation—on what I have called here a sense of community in which everyone shares.

Up to the present, the responsibility for working and maintaining 25 the principles on which any code of law must depend and for the practical administration of justice has been primarily a male preoc-

COLLABORATIVE ACTIVITY

Divide the class into two teams, one that supports the death penalty and one that opposes it. Give the teams 20 minutes to prepare their arguments in support of their respected positions, and then stage a debate on the issue.

WRITING SUGGESTIONS

1. Recently a California public television station requested permission to videotape the execution of a convicted double murderer in the California gas chamber. The prison warden objected because of fear that inmates watching the execution on television might become violent. A federal district court ruled the prohibition of cameras at executions to be reasonable and valid. What do you think of this idea? What are the moral and ethical implications of such a practice? Write an essay explaining your views.

2. Write a letter from an inmate condemned to death to a judge with the power to commute his or her sentence to life in prison. Explain the reasons for the crime, and argue that the death penalty is cruel and unusual punishment. (Alternatively, you may reply to such an appeal, arguing that the death penalty is fair and necessary.)

cupation. At best, women working within this framework have been able sometimes to modify and sometimes to mitigate the working of the system of law.

Now, however, if the way out is for us to place the occurrence 26 of crime and the fate of the victim and of the criminal consciously within the context of our way of living and our view of human values, then I believe liberated women have a major part to play and a wholly new place to create for themselves in public life as professional women, as volunteers and as private citizens concerned with the quality of life in our nation. For it is women who have constantly had to visualize in personal, human terms the relationships between the intimate details of living and the setting in which living takes place. And it is this kind of experience that we shall need in creating new kinds of community.

Women working in new kinds of partnership with men should 27 be able to bring fresh thinking into law and the administration of justice with a greater awareness of the needs of individuals at different stages of life and the potentialities of social institutions in meeting those needs. What we shall be working toward is a form of deterrence based not on fear of punishment—which we know is ineffective, even when the punishment is the threat of death—but on a shared way of living.

It will be a slow process at best to convince our fellow citizens 28 that justice and a decline in violence can be attained only by the development of communities in which the elderly and children, families and single persons, the gifted, the slow and the handicapped can have a meaningful place and live with dignity and in which rights and responsibilities are aspects of each other. And I believe that we can make a start only if we have a long view, but know very well that what we can do today and tomorrow and next year will not bring us to utopia. We cannot establish instant security: we can only build for it step by step.

We must also face the reality that as far as we can foresee there 29 will always be a need for places of confinement—prisons of different kinds, to be frank—where individuals will have to be segregated for short periods, for longer periods or even, for some, for a whole lifetime. The fear that the violent person will be set free in our communities (as we all know happens all too often under our present system of law) is an important component in the drive to strengthen—certainly not to abolish—the death penalty. For their own protection as well as that of others, the few who cannot control their violent impulses and, for the time being, the larger number who have become hopelessly violent must be sequestered.

But we shall have to reconsider the whole question of what it 30 means to be confined under some form of restraint, whether for a short period, or for a lifetime. Clearly, prisons can no longer be set apart from the world. Prisoners must have some real and enduring relationship to a wider community if they are to have and exercise human rights. Whether as a way station or as a permanent way of living for a few persons, prison life must in some way be meaningful.

There is today a Prisoners Union, organized by former prisoners 31
as well as a variety of local unions within many prisons. We shall have to draw on the knowledge and experience of groups of this kind. Here again I believe that women, who have not been regularly and professionally involved in traditional prison practices, may be freer to think and construct new practices than male experts working alone.

The tasks are urgent and difficult. Realistically we know we 32
cannot abolish crime. But we can abolish crude and vengeful treatment of crime. We can abolish—as a nation, not just state by state—capital punishment. We can accept the fact that prisoners, convicted criminals, are hostages to our own human failures to develop and support a decent way of living. And we can accept the fact we are responsible to them, as to all living beings, for the protection of society, and especially responsible for those among us who need protection for the sake of society.

RESPONDING TO READING

1. Mead opens her essay with a paradox: The United States expresses concern about human rights violations in other countries, yet it continues capital punishment at home. Do you agree that the existence of capital punishment makes "a cold mockery of our very real concern for human rights and our serious efforts to bring about peace and controlled disarmament among nations" (paragraph 3), or do you think Mead is overstating or misrepresenting the case?   **2.** What do you think Mead means when she says, in paragraph 4, that the capital punishment issue is "a major challenge, especially for modern women"? (Consider, too, her comments about women's responsibilities in paragraphs 26–27). Does bringing gender into the discussion help or hinder her argument? Is she guilty of sexism?   **3.** In paragraph 20 Mead introduces her own interpretation of a "a life for a life," which, she says, "need not mean destructive retribution, but instead the development of new forms of community." Can she be accused of being too idealistic, too removed from the realities of the modern world? Is this "sense of community in which everyone shares" (paragraph 24) a realistic alternative to the need for capital punishment in the United States, especially in light of the current wave of homicides associated with illegal drugs? Why or why not?

ANSWERS TO RESPONDING TO READING

1. Mead would seem to belong to the group she describes in paragraph 19. Her sense that there is a broad discrepancy between our world image as peacemakers and our domestic concern with the execution of those convicted of capital crimes suggests that she believes "violence breeds violence." Students' responses to her stance will vary.

2. Mead may be contradicting herself. Although she sees women as traditionally involved in visualizing "in personal, human terms the relationships between the intimate details of living and the setting in which living takes place," she also says that it is only by creating a community of a new and untraditional order that America can find a way out of the cycle of violence. But this new vision would also seem to require a break from seeing women in their traditional roles and a movement toward a genuinely "communal" effort on the part of all Americans.

3. Mead may be correct in stressing that there is a need to create these communities, for in the United States today such communities do not exist in any real sense. Some students may believe Mead is idealistic, but she, like Martin Luther King, may feel that we cannot afford to wait for the right time to heal these ills.

Lifeboat Ethics: The Case Against Helping the Poor

GARRETT HARDIN

Garrett Hardin (1915–   ) is a biologist who writes on morality and ethics in his field. He often tells people what they do not want to hear about such subjects as ecology and the scarcity of resources. He has written *Stalking the Wild Taboo* (1973) and *Filters Against Folly: How to Survive Despite Economists, Ecologists, and the Merely Eloquent* (1985). In this essay, which appeared in 1974 in *Psychology Today*, Hardin uses the metaphor of the earth as a lifeboat to illustrate the rights of both the needy and the rich in the problem of distributing the world's food.

BACKGROUND ON READING

Hardin's argument that wealthy nations have no obligation to support the poor is provocative and even shocking. Presented with clarity and incisiveness, Hardin's essay provides insight into the long-term consequences of our actions, especially in light of the massive ongoing starvation taking place in many African countries. In confronting the future depletion of our resources we need to ask ourselves whether Hardin's "lifeboat ethics" do indeed offer the only strategy for survival.

FOR OPENERS

Can Hardin's argument be applied to helping the sick? The elderly? What dangers face a society that gives no aid to its weakest citizens?

1   Environmentalists use the metaphor of the earth as a "spaceship" in trying to persuade countries, industries and people to stop wasting and polluting our natural resources. Since we all share life on this planet, they argue, no single person or institution has the right to destroy, waste, or use more than a fair share of its resources.

2   But does everyone on earth have an equal right to an equal share of its resources? The spaceship metaphor can be dangerous when used by misguided idealists to justify suicidal policies for sharing our resources through uncontrolled immigration and foreign aid. In their enthusiastic but unrealistic generosity, they confuse the ethics of a spaceship with those of a lifeboat.

3   A true spaceship would have to be under the control of a captain, since no ship could possibly survive if its course were determined by committee. Spaceship Earth certainly has no captain; the United Nations is merely a toothless tiger, with little power to enforce any policy upon its bickering members.

4   If we divide the world crudely into rich nations and poor nations, two thirds of them are desperately poor, and only one third comparatively rich, with the United States the wealthiest of all. Metaphorically each rich nation can be seen as a lifeboat full of comparatively rich people. In the ocean outside each lifeboat swim the poor of the world, who would like to get in, or at least to share some of the wealth. What should the lifeboat passengers do?

5   First, we must recognize the limited capacity of any lifeboat. For example, a nation's land has a limited capacity to support a population and as the current energy crisis has shown us, in some ways we have already exceeded the carrying capacity of our land.

6   So here we sit, say 50 people in our lifeboat. To be generous let us assume it has room for 10 more, making a total capacity of 60. Suppose the 50 of us in the lifeboat see 100 others swimming in the

water outside, begging for admission to our boat or for handouts. We have several options: we may be tempted to try to live by the Christian ideal of being "our brother's keeper," or by the Marxist ideal of "to each according to his needs." Since the needs of all in the water are the same, and since they can all be seen as "our brothers," we could take them all into our boat, making a total of 150 in a boat designed for 60. The boat swamps, everyone drowns. Complete justice, complete catastrophe.

7   Since the boat has an unused excess capacity of 10 more passengers, we could admit just 10 more to it. But which 10 do we let in? How do we choose? Do we pick the best 10, the neediest 10, "first come, first served"? And what do we say to the 90 we exclude? If we do let an extra 10 into our lifeboat, we will have lost our "safety factor," an engineering principle of critical importance. For example, if we don't leave room for excess capacity as a safety factor in our country's agriculture, a new plant disease or a bad change in the weather could have disastrous consequences.

8   Suppose we decide to preserve our small safety factor and admit no more to the lifeboat. Our survival is then possible although we shall have to be constantly on guard against boarding parties.

9   While this last solution clearly offers the only means of our survival, it is morally abhorrent to many people. Some say they feel guilty about their good luck. My reply is simple: "Get out and yield your place to others." This may solve the problem of the guilt-ridden person's conscience, but it does not change the ethics of the lifeboat. The needy person to whom the guilt-ridden person yields his place will not himself feel guilty about his good luck. If he did, he would not climb aboard. The net result of conscience-stricken people giving up their unjustly held seats is the elimination of that sort of conscience from the lifeboat.

10   This is the basic metaphor within which we must work out our solutions. Let us now enrich the image, step by step, with substantive additions from the real world, a world that must solve real and pressing problems of overpopulation and hunger.

11   The harsh ethics of the lifeboat become even harsher when we consider the reproductive differences between the rich nations and the poor nations. The people inside the lifeboats are doubling in numbers every 87 years; those swimming around outside are doubling on the average, every 35 years, more than twice as fast as the rich. And since the world's resources are dwindling, the difference in prosperity between the rich and the poor can only increase.

12   As of 1973, the U.S. had a population of 210 million people, who were increasing by 0.8 percent per year. Outside our lifeboat, let us imagine another 210 million people (say the combined populations

ADDITIONAL QUESTIONS FOR RESPONDING TO READING

1. What does the environmentalists' metaphor of the spaceship suggest? How do the ethics of the spaceship differ from those of the lifeboat?
2. How are liberal thinkers characterized in this essay? Do you agree with Hardin's portrayal?
3. What would seem to be Hardin's basic view of human nature? Is it at all hopeful? Explain.

TEACHING STRATEGY

Students are likely to find Hardin's attitude cold and arrogant. Rather than focusing at once on the essay's emotionally charged issues, you might begin by examining the logic with which Hardin presents his argument.

of Colombia, Ecuador, Venezuela, Morocco, Pakistan, Thailand and the Philippines), who are increasing at a rate of 3.3 percent per year. Put differently, the doubling time for this aggregate population is 21 years, compared to 87 years for the U.S.

Now suppose the U.S. agreed to pool its resources with those 13 seven countries, with everyone receiving an equal share. Initially the ratio of Americans to non-Americans in this model would be one-to-one but consider what the ratio would be after 87 years, by which time the Americans would have doubled to a population of 420 million. By then, doubling every 21 years, the other group would have swollen to 354 billion. Each American would have to share the available resources with more than eight people.

But, one could argue, this discussion assumes that current pop- 14 ulation trends will continue, and they may not. Quite so. Most likely the rate of population increase will decline much faster in the U.S. than it will in the other countries, and there does not seem to be much we can do about it. In sharing with "each according to his needs," we must recognize that needs are determined by population size, which is determined by the rate of reproduction, which at present is regarded as a sovereign right of every nation, poor or not. This being so, the philanthropic load created by the sharing ethic of the spaceship can only increase.

The fundamental error of spaceship ethics, and the sharing it 15 requires, is that it leads to what I call "the tragedy of the commons." Under a system of private property, the men who own property recognize their responsibility to care for it, for if they don't they will eventually suffer. A farmer, for instance, will allow no more cattle in a pasture than its carrying capacity justifies. If he overloads it, erosion sets in, weeds take over, and he loses the use of the pasture.

If a pasture becomes a commons open to all, the right of each to 16 use it may not be matched by a corresponding responsibility to protect it. Asking everyone to use it with discretion will hardly do, for the considerate herdsman who refrains from overloading the commons suffers more than a selfish one who says his needs are greater. If everyone would restrain himself all would be well; but it takes only one less than everyone to ruin a system of voluntary restraint. In a crowded world of less than perfect human beings, mutual ruin is inevitable if there are no controls. This is the tragedy of the commons.

One of the major tasks of education today should be the creation 17 of such an acute awareness of the dangers of the commons that people will recognize its many varieties. For example, the air and water have become polluted because they are treated as commons. Further growth in the population or per-capita conversion of natural resources into pollutants will only make the problem worse. The same holds true for the fish of the oceans. Fishing fleets have nearly disappeared in many parts of the world, technological improvements in the art of fishing are hastening the day of complete ruin. Only the replacement of the system of the commons with a responsible system of control will save the land, air, water and oceanic fisheries.

18   In recent years there has been a push to create a new commons called a World Food Bank, an international depository of food reserves to which nations would contribute according to their abilities and from which they would draw according to their needs. This humanitarian proposal has received support from many liberal international groups, and from such prominent citizens as Margaret Mead, U.N. Secretary General Kurt Waldheim, and Senators Edward Kennedy and George McGovern.

19   A world food bank appeals powerfully to our humanitarian impulses. But before we rush ahead with such a plan, let us recognize where the greatest political push comes from, lest we be disillusioned later. Our experience with the "Food for Peace program," or Public Law 480, gives us the answer. This program moved billions of dollars worth of U.S. surplus grain to food-short, population-long countries during the past two decades. But when P.L. 480 first became law, a headline in the business magazine *Forbes* revealed the real power behind it: "Feeding the World's Hungry Millions: How It Will Mean Billions for U.S. Business."

20   And indeed it did. In the years 1960 to 1970, U.S. taxpayers spent a total of $7.9 billion on the Food for Peace program. Between 1948 and 1970, they also paid an additional $50 billion for other economic-aid programs, some of which went for food and food-producing machinery and technology. Though all U.S. taxpayers were forced to contribute to the cost of P.L. 480, certain special interest groups gained handsomely under the program. Farmers did not have to contribute the grain; the Government, or rather the taxpayers, bought it from them at full market prices. The increased demand raised prices of farm products generally. The manufacturers of farm machinery, fertilizers and pesticides benefited by the farmers' extra efforts to grow more food. Grain elevators profited from storing the surplus until it could be shipped. Railroads made money hauling it to ports, and shipping lines profited from carrying it overseas. The implementation of P.L. 480 required the creation of a vast Government bureaucracy, which then acquired its own vested interest in continuing the program regardless of its merits.

21   Those who proposed and defended the Food for Peace program in public rarely mentioned its importance to any of these special interests. The public emphasis was always on its humanitarian effects. The combination of silent selfish interests and highly vocal humani-

COLLABORATIVE ACTIVITY

If you have not done the "Confronting the Issues" exercise (page 1002) with your class, do it now, with students working in groups to decide who should be allowed into the boat.

tarian apologists made a powerful and successful lobby for extracting money from taxpayers. We can expect the same lobby to push now for the creation of a World Food Bank.

However great the potential benefit to selfish interests, it should   22
not be a decisive argument against a truly humanitarian program. We must ask if such a program would actually do more good than harm, not only momentarily but also in the long run. Those who propose the food bank usually refer to a current "emergency" or "crisis" in terms of world food supply. But what is an emergency? Although they may be infrequent and sudden, everyone knows that emergencies will occur from time to time. A well-run family, company, organization or country prepares for the likelihood of accidents and emergencies. It expects them, it budgets for them, it saves for them.

What happens if some organizations or countries budget for acci-   23
dents and others do not? If each country is solely responsible for its own well-being, poorly managed ones will suffer. But they can learn from experience. They may mend their ways, and learn to budget for infrequent but certain emergencies. For example, the weather varies from year to year, and periodic crop failures are certain. A wise and competent government saves out of the production of the good years in anticipation of bad years to come. Joseph taught this policy to Pharoah in Egypt more than 2,000 years ago. Yet the great majority of the governments in the world today do not follow such a policy. They lack either the wisdom or the competence, or both. Should those nations that do manage to put something aside be forced to come to the rescue each time an emergency occurs among the poor nations?

"But it isn't their fault!" Some kind-hearted liberals argue, "How   24
can we blame the poor people who are caught in an emergency? Why must they suffer for the sins of their governments?" The concept of blame is simply not relevant here. The real question is, what are the operational consequences of establishing a world food bank? If it is open to every country every time a need develops, slovenly rulers will not be motivated to take Joseph's advice. Someone will always come to their aid. Some countries will deposit food in the world food bank, and others will withdraw it. There will be almost no overlap. As a result of such solutions to food shortage emergencies, the poor countries will not learn to mend their ways, and will suffer progressively greater emergencies as their populations grow.

On the average, poor countries undergo a 2.5 percent increase in   25
population each year; rich countries, about 0.8 percent. Only rich countries have anything in the way of food reserves set aside, and even they do not have as much as they should. Poor countries have none. If poor countries received no food from the outside, the rate of their population growth would be periodically checked by crop

failures and famines. But if they can always draw on a world food bank in time of need, their population can continue to grow unchecked, and so will their "need" for aid. In the short run, a world food bank may diminish that need, but in the long run it actually increases the need without limit.

Without some system of worldwide food sharing, the proportion 26 of people in the rich and poor nations might eventually stabilize. The overpopulated poor countries would decrease in numbers, while the rich countries that had room for more people would increase. But with a well-meaning system of sharing, such as a world food bank, the growth differential between the rich and the poor countries will not only persist, it will increase. Because of the higher rate of population growth in the poor countries of the world, 88 percent of today's children are born poor, and only 12 percent rich. Year by year the ratio becomes worse, as the fast-reproducing poor outnumber the slow-reproducing rich.

A world food bank is thus a commons in disguise. People will 27 have more motivation to draw from it than to add to any common store. The less provident and less able will multiply at the expense of the abler and more provident, bringing eventual ruin upon all who share in the commons. Besides, any system of "sharing" that amounts to foreign aid from the rich nations to the poor nations will carry the taint of charity, which will contribute little to the world peace so devoutly desired by those who support the idea of a world food bank.

As past U.S. foreign-aid programs have amply and depressingly 28 demonstrated, international charity frequently inspires mistrust and antagonism rather than gratitude on the part of the recipient nation [see "What Other Nations Hear When the Eagle Screams," by Kenneth J. and Mary M. Gergen, *Psychology Today*, June 1974].

The modern approach to foreign aid stresses the export of tech- 29 nology and advice, rather than money and food. As an ancient Chinese proverb goes: "Give a man a fish and he will eat for a day; teach him how to fish and he will eat for the rest of his days." Acting on this advice, the Rockefeller and Ford Foundations have financed a number of programs for improving agriculture in the hungry nations. Known as the "Green Revolution," these programs have led to the development of "miracle rice" and "miracle wheat," new strains that offer bigger harvests and greater resistance to crop damage. Norman Borlaug, the Nobel Prize winning agronomist who, supported by the Rockefeller Foundation, developed "miracle wheat," is one of the most prominent advocates of a world food bank.

Whether or not the Green Revolution can increase food produc- 30 tion as much as its champions claim is a debatable but possibly irrelevant point. Those who support this well-intended humanitarian effort should first consider some of the fundamentals of human ecology. Ironically, one man who did was the late Alan Gregg, a vice president of the Rockefeller Foundation. Two decades ago he expressed strong doubts about the wisdom of such attempts to increase food production. He likened the growth and spread of humanity over the surface of the earth to the spread of cancer in the human body, remarking that "cancerous growths demand food, but, as far as I know, they have never been cured by getting it."

Every human born constitutes a draft on all aspects of the environment: food, air, water, forests, beaches, wildlife, scenery and solitude. Food can, perhaps, be significantly increased to meet a growing demand. But what about clean beaches, unspoiled forests, and solitude? If we satisfy a growing population's need for food, we necessarily decrease its per capita supply of the other resources needed by men.   31

India, for example, now has a population of 600 million, which increases by 15 million each year. This population already puts a huge load on a relatively impoverished environment. The country's forests are now only a small fraction of what they were three centuries ago, and floods and erosion continually destroy the insufficient farmland that remains. Every one of the 15 million new lives added to India's population puts an additional burden on the environment, and increases the economic and social costs of crowding. However humanitarian our intent, every Indian life saved through medical or nutritional assistance from abroad diminishes the quality of life for those who remain, and for subsequent generations. If rich countries make it possible, through foreign aid, for 600 million Indians to swell to 1.2 billion in a mere 28 years, as their current growth rate threatens, will future generations of Indians thank us for hastening the destruction of their environment? Will our good intentions be sufficient excuse for the consequences of our actions?   32

My final example of a commons in action is one for which the public has the least desire for rational discussion—immigration. Anyone who publicly questions the wisdom of current U.S. immigration policy is promptly charged with bigotry, prejudice, ethnocentrism, chauvinism, isolationism or selfishness. Rather than encounter such accusations, one would rather talk about other matters, leaving immigration policy to wallow in the crosscurrents of special interests that take no account of the good of the whole, or the interests of posterity.   33

Perhaps we still feel guilty about things we said in the past. Two generations ago the popular press frequently referred to Dagos, Wops, Polacks, Chinks and Krauts, in articles about how America was being "overrun" by foreigners of supposedly inferior genetic   34 stock [see "The Politics of Genetic Engineering: Who Decides Who's Defective?" *Psychology Today*, June 1974]. But because the implied inferiority of foreigners was used then as justification for keeping them out, people now assume that restrictive policies could only be based on such misguided notions. There are other grounds.

Just consider the numbers involved. Our Government acknowledges a net inflow of 400,000 immigrants a year. While we have no hard data on the extent of illegal entries, educated guesses put the figure at about 600,000 a year. Since the natural increase (excess of births over deaths) of the resident population now runs about 1.7 million per year, the yearly gain from immigration amounts to at least 19 percent of the total annual increase, and may be as much as 37 percent if we include the estimate for illegal immigrants. Considering the growing use of birth-control devices, the potential effect of educational campaigns by such organizations as Planned Parenthood Federation of America and Zero Population Growth, and the influence of inflation and the housing shortage, the fertility rate of American women may decline so much that immigration could account for all the yearly increase in population. Should we not at least ask if that is what we want?

For the sake of those who worry about whether the "quality" of the average immigrant compares favorably with the quality of the average resident, let us assume that immigrants and nativeborn citizens are of exactly equal quality, however one defines that term. We will focus here only on quantity; and since our conclusions will depend on nothing else, all charges of bigotry and chauvinism become irrelevant.

World food banks *move food to the people*, hastening the exhaustion of the environment of the poor countries. Unrestricted immigration, on the other hand, *moves people to the food*, thus speeding up the destruction of the environment of the rich countries. We can easily understand why poor people should want to make this latter transfer, but why should rich hosts encourage it?

As is the case of foreign-aid programs, immigration receives support from selfish interests and humanitarian impulses. The primary selfish interest in unimpeded immigration is the desire of employers for cheap labor, particularly in industries and trades that offer degrading work. In the past, one wave of foreigners after another was brought into the U.S. to work at wretched jobs for wretched wages. In recent years the Cubans, Puerto Ricans and Mexicans have had this dubious honor. The interests of the employers of cheap labor mesh well with the guilty silence of the country's liberal intelligentsia. White Anglo-Saxon Protestants are particularly reluctant to call for a closing of the doors to immigration for fear of being called bigots.

WRITING SUGGESTIONS

1. Write an essay in which you use personal experience to illustrate the tension between following one's conscience (doing the right thing) and struggling for one's own survival.
2. Write a letter to your U.S. senator arguing for or against U.S. aid to Somalia, Ethiopia, the Sudan, or Chad. As you make your case, support or refute Hardin's arguments.

But not all countries have such reluctant leadership. Most edu- 39 cated Hawaiians, for example, are keenly aware of the limits of their environment, particularly in terms of population growth. There is only so much room on the islands, and the islanders know it. To Hawaiians, immigrants from the other 49 states present as great a threat as those from other nations. At a recent meeting of Hawaiian government officials in Honolulu, I had the ironic delight of hearing a speaker, who like most of his audience was of Japanese ancestry, ask how the country might practically and constitutionally close its door to further immigration. One member of the audience countered: "How can we shut the doors now?" We have many friends and relatives in Japan that we'd like to bring here some day so that they can enjoy Hawaii too." The Japanese-American speaker smiled sympathetically and answered: "Yes, but we have children now, and someday we'll have grandchildren too. We can bring more people here from Japan only by giving away some of the land that we hope to pass on to our grandchildren some day. What right do we have to do that?"

At this point, I can hear U.S. liberals asking: "How can you justify 40 slamming the door once you're inside?" You say that immigrants should be kept out. But aren't we all immigrants, or the descendants of immigrants? If we insist on staying, must we not admit all others?" Our craving for intellectual order leads us to seek and prefer symmetrical rules and morals: a single rule for me and everybody else; the same rule yesterday, today and tomorrow. Justice, we feel, should not change with time and place.

We Americans of non-Indian ancestry can look upon ourselves 41 as the descendants of thieves who are guilty morally, if not legally, of stealing this land from its Indian owners. Should we then give back the land to the now living American descendants of those Indians? However morally or logically sound this proposal may be, I, for one, am unwilling to live by it and I know no one else who is. Besides, the logical consequence would be absurd. Suppose that, intoxicated with a sense of pure justice, we should decide to turn our land over to the Indians. Since all our other wealth has also been derived from the land, wouldn't we be morally obliged to give that back to the Indians too?

Clearly, the concept of pure justice produces an infinte regression 42 to absurdity. Centuries ago, wise men invented statutes of limitations to justify the rejection of such pure justice, in the interest of preventing continual disorder. The law zealously defends property rights. Drawing a line after an arbitrary time has elapsed may be unjust, but the alternatives are worse.

We are all the descendants of thieves, and the world's resources 43 are inequitably distributed. But we must begin the journey to tomorrow from the point where we are today. We cannot remake the past. We cannot safely divide the wealth equitably among all peoples so long as people reproduce at different rates. To do so would guarantee that our grandchildren, and everyone else's grandchildren, would have only a ruined world to inhabit.

To be generous with one's own possessions is quite different from   44
being generous with those of posterity. We should call this point to the attention of those who, from a commendable love of justice and equality, would institute a system of the commons, either in the form of a world food bank, or of unrestricted immigration. We must convince them if we wish to save at least some parts of the world from environmental ruin.

RESPONDING TO READING

1. Hardin presents his problem as one with no comfortable solution: One alternative, welcoming all who wish to come into the lifeboat, is "complete justice, complete catastrophe" (paragraph 6); the other, retaining the crucial "safety factor," is both "the only means of our survival" and "morally abhorrent to many people" (paragraphs 8–9). Does Hardin see these two alternatives as ethically and practically unacceptable? Do you? Is it really an either/or situation, or is there a middle ground? Are there some solutions he ignores?   **2.** Does Hardin's use of the lifeboat image make his arguments clearer and present the problem he describes more vividly? Or do you find it to be simplistic, distracting, or irrelevant? Explain your conclusion.   **3.** Hardin asks, "But does everyone on earth have an equal right to an equal share of its resources" (paragraph 2)? That is, are some people more—or less—deserving than others? How would a homeless person answer these questions? How would you answer them?

The Perils of Obedience

STANLEY MILGRAM

Social psychologist Stanley Milgram (1932–1984) is best known for experiments that study aggression and human conformity, especially obedience. He has said that "it is only the person dwelling in isolation who is not forced to respond, with defiance or submission, to the commands of others." Milgram uses Nazi Germany as a tragic example of submission to obedience. The following selection is from his book, *Obedience to Authority* (1974). In this essay, Milgram's descriptions of some of his experiments on obedience raise perplexing moral questions.

Times Literary Supplement of June 7, 1974, wrote: "If it is immoral to find out about ourselves in a way we do not like, these experiments are certainly immoral. But then, as the experiments show, morality—at least in its public form—may have quite a lot to answer for."

In this essay, Milgram challenges our conventional notions of obedience. For Milgram, obedience is not simply a positive, binding element in society. Instead, he sees it as leading to the denial of responsibility and to the blind submissiveness that permits the perpetuation of social evils.

FOR OPENERS

How does obedience function in society? Does it preserve the social fabric, or does it actually corrupt or even undermine the society?

Obedience is as basic an element in the structure of social life as 1
one can point to. Some system of authority is a requirement of all communal living, and it is only the person dwelling in isolation who is not forced to respond, with defiance or submission, to the commands of others. For many people, obedience is a deeply ingrained behavior tendency, indeed a potent impulse overriding training in ethics, sympathy, and moral conduct.

The dilemma inherent in submission to authority is ancient, as 2
old as the story of Abraham,[1] and the question of whether one should obey when commands conflict with conscience has been argued by Plato, dramatized in *Antigone*,[2] and treated to philosophic analysis in almost every historical epoch. Conservative philosophers argue that the very fabric of society is threatened by disobedience, while humanists stress the primacy of the individual conscience.

The legal and philosophic aspects of obedience are of enormous 3
import, but they say very little about how most people behave in concrete situations. I set up a simple experiment at Yale University to test how much pain an ordinary citizen would inflict on another person simply because he was ordered to by an experimental scientist. Stark authority was pitted against the subjects' strongest moral imperatives against hurting others, and, with the subjects' ears ringing with the screams of the victims, authority won more often than not. The extreme willingness of adults to go to almost any lengths on the command of an authority constitutes the chief finding of the study and the fact most urgently demanding explanation.

In the basic experimental design, two people come to a psy- 4
chology laboratory to take part in a study of memory and learning. One of them is designated as a "teacher" and the other a "learner." The experimenter explains that the study is concerned with the effects of punishment on learning. The learner is conducted into a room, seated in a kind of miniature electric chair; his arms are strapped to prevent excessive movement, and an electrode is attached to his wrist. He is told that he will be read lists of simple word pairs, and that he will then be tested on his ability to remember the second word of a pair when he hears the first one again. Whenever he makes an error, he will receive electric shocks of increasing intensity.

The real focus of the experiment is the teacher. After watching 5
the learner being strapped into place, he is seated before an impressive shock generator. The instrument panel consists of thirty lever switches set in a horizontal line. Each switch is clearly labeled with

---

[1]Abraham, commanded by God to sacrifice his son Isaac, is ready to do so until an angel stops him. [Eds.]

[2]In Plato's *Apology* the philosopher Socrates provokes and accepts the sentence of death rather than act against his conscience; the heroine of Sophocles' *Antigone* risks a death sentence in order to give her brother a proper burial. [Eds.]

a voltage designation ranging from 15 to 450 volts. The following designations are clearly indicated for groups of four switches, going from left to right: Slight Shock, Moderate Shock, Strong Shock, Very Strong Shock, Intense Shock, Extreme Intensity Shock, Danger: Severe Shock. (Two switches after this last designation are simply marked XXX.)

When a switch is depressed, a pilot light corresponding to each 6 switch is illuminated in bright red; an electric buzzing is heard; a blue light, labeled "voltage energizer," flashes; the dial on the voltage meter swings to the right; and various relay clicks sound off.

The upper left-hand corner of the generator is labeled SHOCK GEN- 7 ERATOR, TYPE ZLB, DYSON INSTRUMENT COMPANY, WALTHAM, MASS. OUTPUT 15 VOLTS-450 VOLTS.

Each subject is given a sample 45-volt shock from the generator 8 before his run as teacher, and the jolt stregthens his belief in the authenticity of the machine.

The teacher is a genuinely naïve subject who has come to the 9 laboratory for the experiment. The learner, or victim, is actually an actor who receives no shock at all. The point of the experiment is to see how far a person will proceed in a concrete and measurable situation in which he is ordered to inflict increasing pain on a protesting victim.

Conflict arises when the man receiving the shock begins to show 10 that he is experiencing discomfort. At 75 volts, he grunts; at 120 volts, he complains loudly; at 150, he demands to be released from the experiment. As the voltage increases, his protests become more vehement and emotional. At 285 volts, his response can be described only as an agonized scream. Soon thereafter, he makes no sound at all.

For the teacher, the situation quickly becomes one of gripping 11 tension. It is not a game for him; conflict is intense and obvious. The manifest suffering of the learner presses him to quit; but each time he heistates to administer a shock, the experimenter orders him to continue. To extricate himself from this plight, the subject must make a clear break with authority.[3]

The subject, Gretchen Brandt,[4] is an attractive thirty-one-year-old 12 medical technician who works at the Yale Medical School. She had emigrated from Germany five years before.

On several occasions when the learner complains, she turns to 13 the experimenter coolly and inquires, "Shall I continue"? She promptly returns to her task when the experimenter asks her to do

ADDITIONAL QUESTIONS FOR RESPONDING TO READING

1. According to Milgram, what is the dichotomy between conservative philosophers and humanists? In which camp would you place Milgram? In which camp would you place yourself?
2. According to Milgram, why would obedient subjects who believed they were inflicting pain consider themselves "on the side of the angels"?
3. What, according to Milgram, is the most extreme consequence of blind obedience? What pernicious effects does submission have on the individual who is submissive?

---

[3]The ethical problems of carrying out an experiment of this sort are too complex to be dealt with here, but they receive extended treatment in the book from which this article is adapted. [The book is *Obedience to Authority* (New York: Harper and Row, 1974)—Eds.]

[4]Names of subjects described in this piece have been changed.

TEACHING STRATEGIES

1. Remind students of the connection between Milgram's experiment and the killing of Jews in Nazi Germany, where soldiers committed unspeakable crimes and defended themselves by insisting they were "obeying orders." Ask students at what point an individual has a moral obligation to say no, even if it means defying an order. (You might also discuss the My Lai incident during the Vietnam War and consider what other options Lieutenant William Calley and the other soldiers had.)

2. Milgram's essay seems to follow the general model of a scientific study. You might list for your students the various divisions of the formal science or social science paper: introduction, identification of the problem, statement of the hypothesis, methodology, results, discussion, and conclusion. Then ask them to identify each component in Milgram's essay. (Remind them that a formal paper would be preceded by an abstract and would include internal headings and a list of references.)

so. At the administration of 210 volts, she turns to the experimenter, remarking firmly, "Well, I'm sorry, I don't think we should continue."

EXPERIMENTER: The experiment requires that you go on until he has learned all the word pairs correctly.

BRANDT: He has a heart condition, I'm sorry. He told you that before.

EXPERIMENTER: The shocks may be painful but they are not dangerous.

BRANDT: Well, I'm sorry, I think when shocks continue like this, they are dangerous. You ask him if he wants to get out. It's his free will.

EXPERIMENTER: It is absolutely essential that we continue . . .

BRANDT: I'd like you to ask him. We came here of our free will. If he wants to continue I'll go ahead. He told you he had a heart condition. I'm sorry. I don't want to be responsible for anything happening to him. I wouldn't like it for me either.

EXPERIMENTER: You have no other choice.

BRANDT: I think we are here on our own free will. I don't want to be responsible if anything happens to him. Please understand that.

She refuses to go further and the experiment is terminated.   14

The woman is firm and resolute throughout. She indicates in the   15 interview that she was in no way tense or nervous, and this corresponds to her controlled appearance during the experiment. She feels that the last shock she administered to the learner was extremely painful and reiterates that she "did not want to be responsible for any harm to him."

The woman's straightforward, courteous behavior in the experi-   16 ment, lack of tension, and total control of her own action seem to make disobedience a simple and rational deed. Her behavior is the very embodiment of what I envisioned would be true for almost all subjects.

Before the experiments, I sought predictions about the outcome   17 from various kinds of people—psychiatrists, college sophomores, middle-class adults, graduate students and faculty in the behavioral sciences. With remarkable similarity, they predicted that virtually all subjects would refuse to obey the experimenter. The psychiatrists specifically predicted that most subjects would not go beyond 150 volts, when the victim makes his first explicit demand to be freed. They expected that only 4 percent would reach 300 volts, and that only a pathological fringe of about one in a thousand would administer the highest shock on the board.

These predictions were unequivocally wrong. Of the forty sub-   18 jects in the first experiment, twenty-five obeyed the orders of the experimenter to the end, punishing the victim until they reached the most potent shock available on the generator. After 450 volts were administered three times, the experimenter called a halt to the sessions. Many obedient subjects then heaved sighs of relief, mopped their brows, rubbed their fingers over their eyes, or nervously fumbled cigarettes. Others displayed only minimal signs of tension from beginning to end.

When the very first experiments were carried out, Yale undergraduates were used as subjects, and about 60 percent of them were fully obedient. A colleague of mine immediately dismissed these findings as having no relevance to "ordinary" people, asserting that Yale undergraduates are a highly aggressive, competitive bunch who step on each other's necks on the slightest provocation. He assured me that when "ordinary" people were tested, the results would be quite different. As we moved from the pilot studies to the regular experimental series, people drawn from every stratum of New Haven life came to be employed in the experiment: professionals, white-collar workers, unemployed persons, and industrial workers. *The experimental outcome was the same as we had observed among the students.*

Moreover, when the experiments were repeated in Princeton, Munich, Rome, South Africa, and Australia, the level of obedience was invariably somewhat *higher* than found in the investigation reported in this article. Thus one scientist in Munich found 85 percent of his subjects obedient.

Fred Prozi's reactions, if more dramatic than most, illuminate the conflicts experienced by others in less visible form. About fifty years old and unemployed at the time of the experiment, he has a good-natured, if slightly dissolute, appearance, and he strikes people as a rather ordinary fellow. He begins the session calmly but becomes tense as it proceeds. After delivering the 180-volt shock, he pivots around in his chair and, shaking his head, addresses the experimenter in agitated tones:

PROZI: I can't stand it. I'm not going to kill that man in there. You hear him hollering?

EXPERIMENTER: As I told you before, the shocks may be painful, but . . .

PROZI: But he's hollering. He can't stand it. What's going to happen to him?

EXPERIMENTER (his voice is patient, matter-of-fact): The experiment requires that you continue, Teacher.

PROZI: Aaah, but, unh, I'm not going to get that man sick in there—know what I mean?

EXPERIMENTER: Whether the learner likes it or not, we must go on, through all the word pairs.

PROZI: I refuse to take the responsibility. He's in there hollering!

EXPERIMENTER: It's absolutely essential that you continue, Prozi.

19

20

21

COLLABORATIVE ACTIVITY

Ask students to work in groups to identify individuals whom they consider to be authority figures and to be prepared to explain why each individual is so perceived. Under what specific circumstances could they imagine defying each of these authority figures?

PROZI (indicating the unused questions): There's too many left here, I mean, Jeez, if he gets them wrong, there's too many of them left. I mean, who's going to take the responsibility if anything happens to that gentleman?

EXPERIMENTER: I'm responsible for anything that happens to him. Continue, please.

PROZI: All right. (Consults list of words.) The next one's "Slow—walk, truck, dance, music." Answer, please. (A buzzing sound indicates the learner has signaled his answer.) Wrong. A hundred and ninety-five volts. "Dance." (Zzumph!)

LEARNER (yelling): Let me out of here! My heart's bothering me! (Teacher looks at experimenter.)

EXPERIMENTER: Continue, please.

LEARNER: (screaming): Let me out of here! You have no right to keep me here! Let me out of here, my heart's bothering me, let me out!

PROZI (shakes head, pats the table nervously): You see, he's hollering. Hear that? Gee, I don't know.

EXPERIMENTER: The experiment requires . . .

PROZI (interrupting): I know it does, sir, but I mean—hunh! He don't know what he's getting in for. He's up to 195 volts! (Experiment continues, through 210 volts, 225 volts, 240 volts, 255 volts, 270 volts, at which point Prozi, with evident relief, runs out of word-pair questions.)

EXPERIMENTER: You'll have to go back to the beginning of that page and go through them again until he's learned them all correctly.

PROZI: Aw, no. I'm not going to kill that man. You mean I've got to keep going up with the scale? No sir. He's hollering in there. I'm not going to give him 450 volts.

EXPERIMENTER: The experiment requires that you go on.

LEARNER: Ohhh. I absolutely refuse to answer anymore. (Shouting urgently now.) Let me out of here! You can't hold me here! Get me out. Get-me-out-of-here!

EXPERIMENTER: Continue. The next word is "Green," please.

PROZI: "Green—grass, hat, ink, apple." (Nothing happens. No answering buzz. Just gloomy silence.)

PROZI: I don't think he is going to answer.

EXPERIMENTER: If the learner doesn't answer in a reasonable time, about four or five seconds, consider the answer wrong. And follow the same procedures you have been doing for wrong answers. Say, "Wrong," tell him the number of volts, give him the punishment, read him the correct answer. Continue, please.

PROZI: "Green—grass, hat, ink, apple." Answer, please. (More silence. Subject just sits there.)

EXPERIMENTER: Go on with the procedure, please.

PROZI: Three hundred and fifteen volts. The answer is "ink." (Zzumph!)

LEARNER: Ohh. Oooohh.

PROZI (relieved to hear response): Next one . . .

LEARNER: I absolutely refuse to answer.

PROZI: You got to. You get a shock if you don't answer. (Experiment continues with learner refusing to answer, and, finally, failing even to grunt or groan. At 375 volts, the subject stands up.)

PROZI: I think something's happening to that fellow in there. I don't get no answer. He was hollering at less voltage. Can't you check in and see if he's all right, please?

EXPERIMENTER (with same detached calm): Not once we've started. Please continue, Teacher.

PROZI (sits down, sighs deeply): "Cool—day, shade, water, paint." answer, please. Are you all right in there? Are you all right?

EXPERIMENTER: Please continue, Teacher. Continue, please. (Subject pushes lever. Zzumph!)

PROZI (swiveling around in his chair): Something's happened to that man in there. (Swiveling back.) Next one. "Low—dollar, necklace, moon, paint." (Turning around again.) Something's happened to that man in there. You better check in on him, sir. He won't answer or nothing.

EXPERIMENTER: Continue. Go on, please.

PROZI: You accept all responsibility?

EXPERIMENTER: The responsibility is mine. Correct. Please go on. (Subject returns to his list, starts running through words as rapidly as he can read them, works through to 450 volts.)

PROZI: That's that.

EXPERIMENTER: Continue using the 450 switch for each wrong answer. Continue, please.

PROZI: But I don't get anything!

EXPERIMENTER: Please continue. The next word is "white."

PROZI: Don't you think you should look in on him, please?

EXPERIMENTER: Not once we've started the experiment.

PROZI: What if he's dead in there? (Gestures toward the room with the electric chair.) I mean, he told me he can't stand the shock, sir. I don't mean to be rude, but I think you should look in on him. All you have to do is look in on him. All you have to do is look in the door. I don't get no answer, no noise. Something might have happened to the gentleman in there, sir.

EXPERIMENTER: We must continue. Go on, please.

PROZI: You mean keep giving him what? Four-hundred-fifty volts, what he's got now?

EXPERIMENTER: That's correct. Continue. The next word is "white."

PROZI (now at a furious pace): "White—cloud, horse, rock, house."
Answer, please. The answer is "horse." Four hundred and fifty volts.
(Zzumph!) Next word, "Bag—paint, music, clown, girl." The answer
is "paint." Four hundred and fifty volts. (Zzumph!) Next word is
"Short—sentence, movie . . ."
EXPERIMENTER: Excuse me, Teacher. We'll have to discontinue the
experiment.

Morris Braverman, another subject, is a thirty-nine-year-old social 22
worker. He looks older than his years because of his bald head and
serious demeanor. His brow is furrowed, as if all the world's burdens
were carried on his face. He appears intelligent and concerned.

When the learner refuses to answer and the experimenter 23
instructs Braverman to treat the absence of an answer as equivalent
to a wrong answer, he takes his instruction to heart. Before administering 300 volts he asserts officiously to the victim, "Mr. Wallace,
your silence has to be considered as a wrong answer." Then he administers the shock. He offers halfheartedly to change places with the
learner, then asks the experimenter. "Do I have to follow these
instructions literally?" He is satisfied with the experimenter's answer
that he does. His very refined and authoritative manner of speaking
is increasingly broken up by wheezing laughter.

The experimenter's notes on Mr. Braverman at the last few shocks 24
are:

Almost breaking up now each time gives shock. Rubbing face to hide 25
laughter.
Squinting, trying to hide face with hand, still laughing. 26
Cannot control his laughter at this point no matter what he does. 27
Clenching fist, pushing it onto table. 28

In an interview after the session, Mr. Braverman summarizes the 29
experiment with impressive fluency and intelligence. He feels the
experiment may have been designed also to "test the effects on the
teacher of being in an essentially sadistic role, as well as the reactions
of a student to a learning situation that was authoritative and punitive." When asked how painful the last few shocks administered to
the learner were, he indicates that the most extreme category on the
scale is not adequate (it read EXTREMELY PAINFUL) and places his mark
at the edge of the scale with an arrow carrying it beyond the scale.

It is almost impossible to convey the greatly relaxed, sedate quality 30
of his conversation in the interview. In the most relaxed terms, he
speaks about his severe inner tension.
EXPERIMENTER: At what point were you most tense or nervous?
MR. BRAVERMAN: Well, when he first began to cry out in pain, and I
realized this was hurting him. This got worse when he just blocked

and refused to answer. There was I. I'm a nice person, I think, hurting somebody, and caught up in what seemed a mad situation . . . and in the interest of science, one goes through with it.

When the interviewer pursues the general question of tension, 31 Mr. Braverman spontaneously mentions his laughter.

"My reactions were awfully peculiar. I don't know if you were 32 watching me, but my reactions were giggly, and trying to stifle laughter. This isn't the way I usually am. This was a sheer reaction to a totally impossible situation. And my reaction was to the situation of having to hurt somebody. And being totally helpless and caught up in a set of circumstances where I just couldn't deviate and I couldn't try to help. This is what got me."

Mr. Braverman, like all subjects, was told the actual nature and 33 purpose of the experiment, and a year later he affirmed in a questionnaire that he had learned something of personal importance: "What appalled me was that I could possess this capacity for obedience and compliance to a central idea, i.e., the value of a memory experiment, even after it became clear that continued adherence to this value was at the expense of violation of another value, i.e., don't hurt someone who is helpless and not hurting you. As my wife said, 'You can call yourself Eichmann.' I hope I deal more effectively with any future conflicts of values I encounter."

One theoretical interpretation of this behavior holds that all 34 people harbor deeply aggressive instincts continually pressing for expression, and that the experiment provides institutional justification for the release of these impulses. According to this view, if a person is placed in a situation in which he has complete power over another inividual, whom he may punish as much as he likes, all that is sadistic and bestial in man comes to the fore. The impulse to shock the victim is seen to flow from the potent aggressive tendencies, which are part of the motivational life of the individual, and the experiment, because it provides social legitimacy, simply opens the door to their expression.

It becomes vital, therefore, to compare the subject's performance 35 when he is under orders and when he is allowed to choose the shock level.

The procedure was identical to our standard experiment, except 36 that the teacher was told that he was free to select any shock level on any of the trials. (The experimenter took pains to point out that the teacher could use the highest levels on the generator, the lowest, any in between, or any combination of levels.) Each subject proceeded for thirty critical trials. The learner's protests were coordinated to standard shock levels, his first grunt coming at 75 volts, his first vehement protest at 150 volts.

The average shock used during the thirty critical trials was less 37
than 60 volts—lower than the point at which the victim showed the
first signs of discomfort. Three of the forty subjects did not go beyond
the very lowest level on the board, twenty-eight went no higher than
75 volts, and thirty-eight did not go beyond the first loud protest at
150 volts. Two subjects provided the exception, administering up to
325 and 450 volts, but the overall result was that the great majority
of people delivered very low, usually painless, shocks when the choice
was explicitly up to them.

This condition of the experiment undermines another commonly 38
offered explanation of the subjects' behavior—that those who
shocked the victim at the most severe levels came only from the
sadistic fringe of society. If one considers that almost two-thirds of
the participants fall into the category of "obedient" subjects, and that
they represented ordinary people drawn from working, managerial,
and professional classes, the argument becomes very shaky. Indeed,
it is highly reminiscent of the issue that arose in connection with
Hannah Arendt's 1963 book, *Eichmann in Jerusalem*. Arendt contended
that the prosecution's effort to depict Eichmann as a sadistic monster
was fundamentally wrong, that he came closer to being an uninspired
bureaucrat who simply sat at his desk and did his job. For asserting
her views, Arendt became the object of considerable scorn, even cal-
umny. Somehow, it was felt that the monstrous deeds carried out by
Eichmann required a brutal, twisted personality, evil incarnate. After
witnessing hundreds of ordinary persons submit to the authority in
our own experiments, I must conclude that Arendt's conception of
the banality of evil comes closer to the truth than one might dare
imagine. The ordinary person who shocked the victim did so out of
a sense of obligation—an impression of his duties as a subject—and
not from any peculiarly aggressive tendencies.

This is, perhaps, the most fundamental lesson of our study: ordi- 39
nary people, simply doing their jobs, and without any particular hostility on their part, can become agents in a terrible destructive process.
Moreover, even when the destructive effects of their work become
patently clear, and they are asked to carry out actions incompatible
with fundamental standards of morality, relatively few people have
the resources needed to resist authority.

Many of the people were in some sense against what they did to 40
the learner, and many protested even while they obeyed. Some were
totally convinced of the wrongness of their actions but could not bring
themselves to make an open break with authority. They often derived
satisfaction from their thoughts and felt that—within themselves, at
least—they had been on the side of the angels. They tried to reduce
strain by obeying the experimenter but "only slightly," encouraging

the learner, touching the generator switches gingerly. When interviewed, such a subject would stress that he had "asserted my humanity" by administering the briefest shock possible. Handling the conflict in this manner was easier than defiance.

The situation is constructed so that there is no way the subject 41
can stop shocking the learner without violating the experimenter's definitions of his own competence. The subject fears that he will appear arrogant, untoward, and rude if he breaks off. Although these inhibiting emotions appear small in scope alongside the violence being done to the learner, they suffuse the mind and feelings of the subject, who is miserable at the prospect of having to repudiate the authority to his face. (When the experiment was altered so that the experimenter gave his instructions by telephone instead of in person, only a third as many people were fully obedient through 450 volts.) It is a curious thing that a measure of compassion on the part of the subject—an unwillingness to "hurt" the experimenter's feelings—is part of those binding forces inhibiting his disobedience. The withdrawal of such deference may be as painful to the subject as to the authority he defies.

The subjects do not derive satisfaction from inflicting pain, but 42
they often like the feeling they get from pleasing the experimenter. They are proud of doing a good job, obeying the experimenter under difficult circumstances. While the subjects administered only mild shocks on their own initiative, one experimental variation showed that, under orders, 30 percent of them were willing to deliver 450 volts even when they had to forcibly push the learner's hand down on the electrode.

Bruno Batta is a thirty-seven-year-old welder who took part in 43
the variation requiring the use of force. He was born in New Haven, his parents in Italy. He has a rough-hewn face that conveys a conspicuous lack of alertness. He has some difficulty in mastering the experimental procedure and needs to be corrected by the experimenter several times. He shows appreciation for the help and willingness to do what is required. After the 150-volt level, Betta has to force the learner's hand down on the shock plate, since the learner himself refuses to touch it.

When the learner first complains, Mr. Batta pays no attention to 44
him. His face remains impassive, as if to dissociate himself from the learner's disruptive behavior. When the experimenter instructs him to force the learner's hand down, he adopts a rigid, mechanical procedure. He tests the generator switch. When it fails to function he immediately forces the learner's hand onto the shock plate. All the while he maintains the same rigid mask. The learner, seated alongside

him, begs him to stop, but with robotic impassivity he continues the procedure.

What is extraordinary is his apparent total indifference to the   45
learner; he hardly takes cognizance of him as a human being. Meanwhile, he relates to the experimenter in a submissive and courteous fashion.

At the 330-volt level, the learner refuses not only to touch the   46
shock plate but also to provide any answers. Annoyed, Batta turns to him, and chastises him: "You better answer and get it over with. We can't stay here all night." These are the only words he directs to the learner in the course of an hour. Never again does he speak to him. The scene is brutal and depressing, his hard, impassive face showing total indifference as he subdues the screaming learner and gives him shocks. He seems to derive no pleasure from the act itself, only quiet satisfaction at doing his job properly.

When he administers 450 volts, he turns to the experimenter and   47
asks, "Where do we go from here, Professor?" His tone is deferential and expresses his willingness to be a cooperative subject, in contrast to the learner's obstinacy.

At the end of the session he tells the experimenter how honored   48
he has been to help him, and in a moment of contrition, remarks, "Sir, sorry it couldn't have been a full experiment."

He has done his honest best. It is only the deficient behavior of   49
the learner that has denied the experimenter full satisfaction.

The essence of obedience is that a person comes to view himself   50
as the instrument for carrying out another person's wishes, and he therefore no longer regards himself as responsible for his actions. Once this critical shift of viewpoint has occurred, all of the essential features of obedience follow. The most far-reaching consequence is that the person feels responsible to the authority directing him but feels no responsibility *for* the content of the actions that the authority prescribes. Morality does not disappear—it acquires a radically different focus: the subordinate person feels shame or pride depending on how adequately he has performed the actions called for by authority.

Language provides numerous terms to pinpoint this type of   51
morality: *loyalty, duty, discipline* all are terms heavily saturated with moral meaning and refer to the degree to which a person fulfills his obligations to authority. They refer not to the "goodness" of the person per se but to the adequacy with which a subordinate fulfills his socially defined role. The most frequent defense of the individual who has performed a heinous act under command of authority is that he has simply done his duty. In asserting this defense, the individual is not introducing an alibi concocted for the moment but is reporting

honestly on the psychological attitude induced by submission to authority.

For a person to feel responsible for his actions, he must sense that the behavior has flowed from "the self." In the situation we have studied, subjects have precisely the opposite view of their actions—namely, they see them as originating in the motives of some other person. Subjects in the experiment frequently said, "If it were up to me, I would not have administered shocks to the learner."

Once authority has been isolated as the cause of the subject's behavior, it is legitimate to inquire into the necessary elements of authority and how it must be perceived in order to gain his compliance. We conducted some investigations into the kinds of changes that would cause the experimenter to lose his power and to be disobeyed by the subject. Some of the variations revealed that:

- *The experimenter's physical presence has a marked impact on his authority*. As cited earlier, obedience dropped off sharply when orders were given by telephone. The experimenter could often induce a disobedient subject to go on by returning to the laboratory.

- *Conflicting authority severely paralyzes action*. When two experimenters of equal status, both seated at the command desk, gave incompatible orders, no shocks were delivered past the point of their disagreement.

- *The rebellious action of others severely undermines authority*. In one variation, three teachers (two actors and a real subject) administered a test and shocks. When the two actors disobeyed the experimenter and refused to go beyond a certain shock level, thirty-six of forty subjects joined their disobedient peers and refused as well.

Although the experimenter's authority was fragile in some respects, it is also true that he had almost none of the tools used in ordinary command structures. For example, the experimenter did not threaten the subjects with punishment—such as loss of income, community ostracism, or jail—for failure to obey. Neither could he offer incentives. Indeed, we should expect the experimenter's authority to be much less than that of someone like a general, since the experimenter has no power to enforce his imperatives, and since participation in a psychological experiment scarcely evokes the sense of urgency and dedication found in warfare. Despite these limitations, he still managed to command a dismaying degree of obedience.

I will cite one final variation of the experiment that depicts a dilemma that is more common in everyday life. The subject was not

WRITING SUGGESTION

Is "obeying orders" a valid excuse for carrying out an immoral or unethical act? Write an essay in which you answer this question in light of the results of Milgram's findings.

ANSWERS TO RESPONDING TO READING

1. The dilemma inherent in submission is that when we defy authority we risk disrupting the social order. But submission allows us to abnegate our responsibility, which in turn allows corruption to be perpetuated. The experiments showed that ordinary people rarely have the inner resources to be defiant: Most of us are anxious to please authority figures, and our desires to be obedient outweigh our sympathies with the sufferings of others.
2. Most of us are taught to obey authority. The subjects were able to deny their own responsibility in inflicting pain, and their compliance seems normal.
3. Answers will vary.

ordered to pull the lever that shocked the victim, but merely to perform a subsidiary task (administering the word-pair test) while another person administered the shock. In this situation, thirty-seven of forty adults continued to the highest level of the shock generator. Predictably, they excused their behavior by saying that the responsibility belonged to the man who actually pulled the switch. This may illustrate a dangerously typical arrangement in a complex society: it is easy to ignore responsibility when one is only an intermediate link in a chain of action.

The problem of obedience is not wholly psychological. The form 59 and shape of society and the way it is developing have much to do with it. There as a time, perhaps, when people were able to give a fully human response to any situation because they were fully absorbed in it as human beings. But as soon as there was a division of labor things changed. Beyond a certain point, the breaking up of society into people carrying out narrow and very special jobs takes away from the human quality of work and life. A person does not get to see the whole situation but only a small part of it, and is thus unable to act without some kind of overall direction. He yields to authority but in doing so is alienated from his own actions.

Even Eichmann was sickened when he toured the concentration 60 camps, but he had only to sit at a desk and shuffle papers. At the same time the man in the camp who actually dropped Cyclon-b into the gas chambers was able to justify *his* behavior on the ground that he was only following orders from above. Thus there is a fragmentation of the total human act; no one is confronted with the consequences of his decision to carry out the evil act. The person who assumes responsibility has evaporated. Perhaps this is the most common characteristic of socially organized evil in modern society.

RESPONDING TO READING

1. What is the "dilemma inherent in submission to authority" (paragraph 2)? How do Milgram's experiments illustrate this dilemma? Why do you suppose virtually no one predicted that the subjects would continue to obey the orders of the experimenter? Is this what you would have predicted?   **2.** Do you see the subjects as ordinary people—cooperative, obedient, and eager to please—or that they are weak individiuals, too timid to defy authority? Explain. Did you ever submit to authority even though you thought you should not have? What were the consequences of your act?   **3.** Milgram says, "The most frequent defense of the individual who has performed a heinous act under command of authority is that he has simply done his duty." In your opinion, can such a defense ever excuse a "heinous act"? If so, under what circumstances?

The Ones Who Walk Away from Omelas

URSULA K. LE GUIN

Science fiction and fantasy writer Ursula K. Le Guin (1929–   )
has written fiction, screenplays, poetry, and essays. Le Guin's
interest in Eastern philosophy and Jungian psychology has influenced many of her books, in which she creates complex characters
with psychological depth. In her book of essays *The Language of the
Night* (1979), she says that "the use of imaginative fiction is to deepen
your understanding of your world, and your fellow men, and your
own feelings, and your destiny." Le Guin is the author of *The Left
Hand of Darkness* (1969), *The Lathe of Heaven* (1971), *The Dispossessed*
(1974), and the volume of poetry *Hard Words* (1981), among many
other books. In the 1975 story "The Ones Who Walk Away from
Omelas," Le Guin creates a scenario that offers a test of conscience
and a social commentary on our own society.

BACKGROUND ON AUTHOR

After 1970, Ursula K. Le Guin's work began
to reflect her increasing concern with feminism
and her opposition to the so-called technological imperative. In recent writing, she has
tended to move away from her earlier interest in
fantasy and science fiction and toward nonfiction prose.

With a clamor of bells that set the swallows soaring, the Festival 1
of Summer came to the city Omelas, bright-towered by the sea. The
rigging of the boats in harbor sparkled with flags. In the streets
between houses with red roofs and painted walls, between old moss-
grown gardens and under avenues of trees, past great parks and
public buildings, processions moved. Some were decorous: old people
in long stiff robes of mauve and grey, grave master workmen, quiet,
merry women carrying their babies and chatting as they walked. In
other streets the music beat faster, a shimmering of gong and tam-
bourine, and the people went dancing, the procession was a dance.
Children dodged in and out, their high calls rising like the swallows'
crossing flights over the music and the singing. All the processions
wound towards the north side of the city, where on the great water-
meadow called the Green Fields boys and girls, naked in the bright
air, with mud-stained feet and ankles and long, lithe arms, exercised
their restive horses before the race. The horses wore no gear at all
but a halter without bit. Their manes were braided with streamers of
silver, gold, and green. They flared their nostrils and pranced and
boasted to one another; they were vastly excited, the horse being the
only animal who had adopted our ceremonies as is own. Far off to
the north and west the mountains stood up half encircling Omelas
on her bay. The air of morning was so clear that the snow still
crowning the Eighteen Peaks burned with white-gold fire across the
miles of sunlit air, under the dark blue of the sky. There was just
enough wind to make the banners that marked the racecourse snap
and flutter now and then. In the silence of the broad green meadows
one could hear the music winding through the city streets, farther

FOR OPENERS

Discuss: "If you're not part of the solution,
you're part of the problem." How does this statement apply to Le Guin's story? To our lives?

**ADDITIONAL QUESTIONS FOR
RESPONDING TO READING**

1. Is the juxtaposition between Le Guin's fairy-
   tale narrative and the events she describes
   jarring? Is it effective?
2. Do *you* "believe"?
3. What implicit statement does Le Guin seem
   to be making about the role of art in society?
4. What is the nature of the evil Le Guin
   describes? Does every society conceal some
   evil? What is ours?

TEACHING STRATEGY

Give students some background on utopian societies—actual ones, such as Brook farm and the Oneida Community, and fictional ones, such as Plato's *Republic* and More's *Utopia*.

and nearer and ever approaching, a cheerful faint sweetness of the air that from time to time trembled and gathered together and broke out into the great joyous clanging of the bells.

Joyous! How is one to tell about joy! How describe the citizens 2 of Omelas?

They were not simple folk, you see, though they were happy. 3 But we do not say the words of cheer much any more. All smiles have become archaic. Given a description such as this one tends to make certain assumptions. Given a description such as this one tends to look next for the King, mounted on a splendid stallion and surrounded by his noble knights, or perhaps in a golden litter borne by great-muscled slaves. But there was no king. They did not use swords, or keep slaves. They were not barbarians. I do not know the rules and laws of their society, but I suspect that they were singularly few. As they did without monarchy and slavery, so they also got on without the stock exchange, the advertisement, the secret police, and the bomb. Yet I repeat that these were not simple folk, not dulcet shepherds, noble savages, bland utopians. They were not less complex than us. The trouble is that we have a bad habit, encouraged by pedants and sophisticates, of considering happiness as something rather stupid. Only pain is intellectual, only evil interesting. This is the treason of the artist: a refusal to admit the banality of evil and the terrible boredom of pain. If you can't lick 'em, join 'em. If it hurts, repeat it. But to praise despair is to condemn delight, to embrace violence is to lose hold of everything else. We have almost lost hold; we can no longer describe a happy man, nor make any celebration of joy. How can I tell you about the people of Omelas? They were not naïve and happy children—though their children were, in fact, happy. They were mature, intelligent, passionate adults whose lives were not wretched. O miracle! but I wish I could describe it better. I wish I could convince you. Omelas sounds in my words like a city in a fairy tale, long ago and far away, once upon a time. Perhaps it would be best if you imagined it as your own fancy bids, assuming it will rise to the occasion, for certainly I cannot suit you all. For instance, how about technology? I think that there would be no cars or helicopters in and above the streets; this follows from the fact that the people of Omelas are happy people. Happiness is based on a just discrimination of what is necessary, what is neither necessary nor destructive, and what is destructive. In the middle category, however—that of the unnecessary but undestructive, that of comfort, luxury, exuberance, etc.—they could perfectly well have central heating, subway trains, washing machines, and all kinds of marvelous devices not yet invented here, floating light-sources, fuelless power, a cure for the common cold. Or they could have none of that: It doesn't matter. As you like it. I incline to think that people from towns up and down the coast have been coming in to Omelas during the last days before the Festival on very fast little trains and double-decked trams, and that the train station of Omelas is actually the handsomest building in town, though plainer than the magnificent Farmers' Market. But even granted trains, I fear that Omelas so far strikes some of you as goody-goody. Smiles, bells, parades, horses, bleh. If so, please add an orgy. If an orgy would help, don't hesitate. Let us not, however, have temples from which issue beautiful nude priests and priestesses already half in ectasy and ready to copulate with any man or woman, lover or stranger, who desires union with the deep god-head of the blood, although that was my first idea. But really it would be better not to have any temples in Omelas—at least not manned temples. Religion yes, clergy no. Surely the beautiful nudes can just wander about, offering themselves like divine soufflés to the hunger of the needy and the rapture of the flesh. Let them join the processions. Let tambourines be struck above the copulations, and the glory of desire be proclaimed upon the gongs, and (a not unimportant point) let the offspring of these delightful rituals be beloved and looked after by all. One thing I know there is none of in Omelas is guilt. But what else should there be? I thought at first there were no drugs, but that is puritanical. For those who like it, the faint insistent sweetness of *drooz* may perfume the ways of the city, *drooz* which first brings a great lightness and brilliance to the mind and limbs, and then after some hours a dreamy languor, and wonderful visions at last of the very arcana and inmost secrets of the Universe, as well as exciting the pleasure of sex beyond all belief; and it is not habit-forming. For more modest tastes I think there ought to be beer. What else, what else belongs in the joyous city? The sense of victory, surely, the celebration of courage. But as we did without clergy, let us do without soldiers. The joy built upon successful slaughter is not the right kind of joy; it will not do; it is fearful and it is trivial. A boundless and generous contentment, a magnanimous triumph felt not against some outer enemy but in communion with the finest and fairest in the souls of all men everywhere and the splendor of the world's summer: This is what swells the hearts of the people of Omelas, and the victory they celebrate is that of life. I really don't think many of them need to take *drooz*.

Most of the processions have reached the Green Fields by now. 4 A marvelous smell of cooking goes forth from the red and blue tents of the provisioners. The faces of small children are amiably sticky; in the benign grey beard of a man a couple of crumbs of rich pastry are entangled. The youths and girls have mounted their horses and are beginning to group around the starting line of the course. An old

COLLABORATIVE ACTIVITY

Ask students, working in groups, to list their criteria for a perfect society. In class discussion, consider the possible limitations of the societies they propose.

woman, small, fat, and laughing, is passing out flowers from a basket, and tall young men wear her flowers in their shining hair. A child of nine or ten sits at the edge of the crowd, alone, playing on a wooden flute. People pause to listen, and they smile, but they do not speak to him, for he never ceases playing and never sees them, his dark eyes wholly rapt in the sweet, thin magic of the tune.

He finishes, and slowly lowers his hands holding the wooden flute. 5

As if that little private silence were the signal, all at once a trumpet sounds from the pavilion near the starting line: imperious, melancholy, piercing. The horses rear on their slender legs, and some of them neigh in answer. Sober-faced, the young riders stroke the horses' necks and soothe them, whispering, "Quiet, quiet, there my beauty, my hope. . . ." They begin to form in rank along the starting line. The crowds along the racecourse are like a field of grass and flowers in the wind. The Festival of Summer has begun. 6

Do you believe? Do you accept the festival, the city, the joy? No? Then let me describe one more thing. 7

In a basement under one of the beautiful public buildings of Omelas, or perhaps in the cellar of one of its spacious private homes, there is a room. It has one locked door, and no window. A little light seeps in dustily between cracks in the boards, secondhand from a cobwebbed window somewhere across the cellar. In one corner of the little room a couple of mops, with stiff, clotted, foul-smelling heads, stand near a rusty bucket. The floor is dirt, a little damp to the touch, as cellar dirt usually is. The room is about three paces long and two wide: a mere broom closet or disused tool room. In the room a child is sitting. It could be a boy or a girl. It looks about six, but actually is nearly ten. It is feeble-minded. Perhaps it was born defective, or perhaps it has become imbecile through fear, malnutrition, and neglect. It picks its nose and occasionally fumbles vaguely with its toes or genitals, as it sits hunched in the corner farthest from the bucket and the two mops. It is afraid of the mops. It finds them horrible. It shuts its eyes, but it knows the mops are still standing there; and the door is locked; and nobody ever comes, except that sometimes—the child has no understanding of time or interval—sometimes the door rattles terribly and opens, and a person, or several people, are there. One of them may come in and kick the child to make it stand up. The others never come close, but peer in at it with frightened, disgusted eyes. The food bowl and the water jug are hastily filled, the door is locked, the eyes disappear. The people at the door never say anything, but the child, who has not always lived in the tool room, and can remember sunlight and its mother's voice, sometimes speaks. "I will be good," it says. "Please let me out. I will 8 be good!" They never answer. The child used to scream for help at night, and cry a good deal, but now it only makes a kind of whining, "eh-haa-, ch-haa," and it speaks less and less often. It is so thin there are no calves to its legs; its belly protrudes; it lives on a half-bowl of corn meal and grease a day. It is naked. Its buttocks and thighs are a mass of festered sores, as it sits in its own excrement continually.

They all know it is there, all the people of Omelas. Some of them   9
have come to see it, others are content merely to know it is there. They all know that it has to be there. Some of them understand why, and some do not, but they all understand that their happiness, the beauty of their city, the tenderness of their friendships, the health of their children, the wisdom of their scholars, the skill of their makers, even the abundance of their harvest and the kindly weathers of their skies, depend wholly on this child's abominable misery.

This is usually explained to children when they are between eight   10
and twelve, whenever they seem capable of understanding; and most of those who come to see the child are young people, though often enough an adult comes, or comes back, to see the child. No matter how well the matter has been explained to them, these young spectators are always shocked and sickened at the sight. They feel digust, which they had thought themselves superior to. They feel anger, outrage, impotence, despite all the explanations. They would like to do something for the child. But there is nothing they can do. If the child were brought up into the sunlight out of that vile place, if it were cleaned and fed and comforted, that would be a good thing, indeed; but if it were done, in that day and hour all the prosperity and beauty and delight of Omelas would wither and be destroyed. Those are the terms. To exchange all the goodness and grace of every life in Omelas for that single, small improvement: to throw away the happiness of thousands for the chance of the happiness of one: that would be to let guilt within the walls indeed.

The terms are strict and absolute; they may not even be a kind   11
word spoken to the child.

Often the young people go home in tears, or in a tearless rage,   12
when they have seen the child and faced this terrible paradox. They may brood over it for weeks or years. But as time goes on they begin to realize that even if the child could be released, it would not get much good of its freedom: a little vague pleasure of warmth and food, no doubt, but little more. It is too degraded and imbecile to know any real joy. It has been afraid too long ever to be free of fear. Its habits are too uncouth for it to respond to humane treatment. Indeed, after so long it would probably be wretched without walls about it to protect it, and darkness for its eyes, and its own excrement to sit in. Their tears at the bitter injustice dry when they begin to perceive the

WRITING SUGGESTION

Describe an ideal community that you find "believable." What elements of our society would you eliminate in your ideal?

ANSWERS TO RESPONDING TO READING

1. The narrator seems almost to be testing readers, piling on more and more horrible detail to see how much readers can bear. If they "believe," she suggests, they must acknowledge that "civilization" is by definition evil and that they, as citizens, are somehow accomplices.
2. Answers will vary. The narrator does not overtly criticize either those who stay or those who leave. Those who stay are willing to maintain the social network at the expense of the child, and those who leave have learned that they are helpless and have chosen to try to escape from that knowledge.
3. It might be argued that every society has a child in a closet, but Le Guin's attitude seems to be that the best course is to keep our knowledge of the child firmly before us. The greatest challenge, she implies, is not to walk away from society and its problems, but to allow our compassion for the child to serve as the source of "splendor" in our lives.

terrible justice of reality, and to accept it. Yet it is their tears and anger, the trying of their generosity and the acceptance of their helplessness, which are perhaps the true source of the splendor of their lives. Theirs is no vapid, irresponsible happiness. They know that they, like the child, are not free. They know compassion. It is the existence of the child, and their knowledge of its existence, that makes possible the nobility of their architecture, the poignancy of their music, the profundity of their science. It is because of the child that they are so gentle with children. They know that if the wretched one were not there snivelling in the dark, the other one, the flute-player, could make no joyful music as the young riders line up in their beauty for the race in the sunlight of the first morning of summer.

Now do you believe in them? Are they not more credible? But 13 there is one more thing to tell, and this is quite incredible.

At times one of the adolescent girls or boys who go to see the 14 child does not go home to weep or rage, does not, in fact, go home at all. Sometimes also a man or woman much older falls silent for a day or two, and then leaves home. These people go out into the street, and walk down the street alone. They keep walking, and walk straight out of the city of Omelas, through the beautiful gates. They keep walking across the farmlands of Omelas. Each one goes alone, youth or girl, man or woman. Night falls; the traveler must pass down village streets, between the houses with yellow-lit windows, and on out into the darkness of the fields. Each alone, they go west or north, towards the mountains. They go on. They leave Omelas, they walk ahead into the darkness, and they do not come back. The place they go towards is a place even less imaginable to most of us than the city of happiness. I cannot describe it at all. It is possible that it does not exist. But they seem to know where they are going, the ones who walk away from Omelas.

RESPONDING TO READING

1. Why do you think the narrator keeps asking readers whether or not they "believe," whether they accept what she is saying as the truth? *Do you "believe"?* What do you find most unbelievable? What do you find most believable? **2.** Are the ones who walk away from Omelas any less morally responsible for the child's welfare than those who keep the child imprisoned? Or do you believe there is a difference between actively doing something "wrong" and passively allowing it to happen? **3.** Why does the logic of the story require that the child be present? Why must the child suffer? Might it be argued that every society has its own equivalent of the child locked in the closet and that we are all guilty of failing to act to save the child? Explain.

Three Thousand Dollars

DAVID LIPSKY

David Lipsky (1965–   ), a native of New York City, published his first short story, "Three Thousand Dollars," in *The New Yorker* while a junior in college. Lipsky's later short stories have been published in the *Mississippi Review*, the *Boston Globe Magazine*, and *The Best American Short Stories of 1986*. *Three Thousand Dollars: Stories* (1989) is a collection of his work. In the following story, published in 1986, Lipsky describes a conflict that arises between a young man and his parents.

My mother doesn't know that I owe my father three thousand dollars. What happened was this: My father sent me three thousand dollars to pay my college tuition. That was the deal he and my mom had made. We'd apply for financial aid without him, to get a lower tuition, and then he'd send me a check, and then I'd put the check in my bank account and write one of my own checks out to the school. This made sense not because my father is rich but because he makes a lot more money than my mother does—she's a teacher—and if we could get a better deal using her income instead of his, there was no reason not to. Only, when the money came, instead of giving it to the school, I spent it. I don't even know what I spent it on—books and things, movies. The school never called me in about it. They just kept sending these bills to my mother, saying we were delinquent in our payments. That's how my father found out. My mother kept sending him the bills, he kept looking on them for the money he'd sent me, and I kept telling him that the school's computer was making an error and that I'd drop by the office one day after class and clear it up.

So when I came home to New York for the summer my mother was frantic, because the school had called her and she couldn't understand how we could owe them so much money. I explained to her, somehow, that what we owed them was a different three thousand dollars—that during the winter the school had cut our financial aid in half. My mother called my father to ask him to send us the extra money, and he said that he wanted to talk to me.

I waited till the next day so I could call him at his office. My stepmother's in finance, and she gets crazy whenever money comes up—her nightmare, I think, is of a river of money flowing from my father to me without veering through her—so I thought it would be better to talk to him when she wasn't around. My father has his own advertising agency in Chicago—Paul Weller Associates. I've seen him at his job when I've visited him out there, and he's pretty good. His company does all the ads for a big midwestern supermarket chain,

2

3

and mostly what he does is supervise on these huge sets while camera crews stand around filming fruit. It's a really big deal. The fruit has to look just right. My father stands there in a coat and tie, and he and a bunch of other guys keep bending over and making sure that the fruit is O.K.—shiny-looking. There are all these other people standing around with water vapor and gloss. One word from my father and a thousand spray cans go off.

When he gets on the phone, I am almost too nervous to talk to 4 him, though his voice is slow and far off, surrounded by static. I ask him to please send more money. He says he won't. I ask why, and he says because it would be the wrong thing to do. He doesn't say anything for a moment and then I tell him that I agree with him, that I think he is right not to send the money. He doesn't say anything to acknowledge this, and there is a long pause during which I feel the distance between us growing.

Just before he gets off the phone, he says, "What I'm really curious 5 about, Richard, is what your mother thinks of all this," and this wakes me up, because he doesn't seem to realize that I haven't told her yet. I was afraid to. Before I came home, I thought of about twenty different ways of telling her, but once she was right there in front of me it just seemed unbearable. What I'm afraid of now is that my father will find that out, and then he will tell her himself. "I mean," he says, "if I were her, I probably couldn't bear having you in the house. What is she planning to do? Isn't the school calling you up? I can't imagine she has the money to pay them. Isn't she angry at you, Rich?"

I say, "She's pretty angry." 6

"I hope so," my father says. "I hope she's making you feel terrible. 7 When I talked to her on the phone yesterday—and we only talked for a couple of seconds—she seemed mostly concerned with getting me to give you this money, but I hope that deep down she's really upset about this. Tell her it's no great tragedy if you don't go back to school in the fall. You can get a job in the city and I'll be happy to pay your tuition again next year. I'm sorry, but it just doesn't feel right for me to keep supporting you while you keep acting the way you've been acting, which to me seems morally deficient."

My mother is tall, with light hair and gray, watery eyes. She is 8 a jogger. She has been jogging for six years, and as she's gotten older her body has gotten younger looking. Her face has gotten older, though. There are lines around her lips and in the corners of her eyes, as if she has taken one of those statues without arms or a head and put her own head on top of it. She teaches art at a grammar

TEACHING STRATEGY

In class discussion, ask students what they believe parents owe their children—and what children owe their parents. Do they see either Richard or his parents (or both) as having violated an unwritten contract?

school a few blocks up from our house, and the walls of our apartment are covered with her drawings. That's the way she teaches. She stands over these kids while she has them drawing a still life or a portrait or something, and if they're having trouble she sits down next to them to show them what to do, and usually she ends up liking her own work so much that she brings it home with her. We have all these candlesticks and clay flowerpots that she made during class. She used to teach up in Greenwich, Connecticut, which is where we lived before she and my dad got divorced, right before I started high school. Every summer, she and a bunch of other teachers rent a house together in Wellfleet; she will be leaving New York to go up there in six days, so I only have to keep her from finding out until then.

When I get off the phone, she is in the living room reading the newspaper. She gives me this ready-for-the-worst look and asks, "What did he say?" 9

I explain to her that I will not be going back to college in September. Instead, I will be staying in the apartment and working until I have paid the school the rest of the money. 10

My mother gets angry. She stands up and folds the paper together and stuffs it into the trash. "Not in this apartment," she says. 11

"Why not?" I ask, "It's big enough." 12

"A boy your age should be in college. Your friends are in college. Your father went to college. I'd better call him back." She walks to the phone, which sits on the windowsill. 13

"Why?" I ask quickly. "He said he wasn't going to do it." 14

"Well, of course, that's what he'd say to you. He knows you're afraid of him." She sees I'm going to protest this. "Who could blame you? Who wouldn't be afraid of a man who won't even support his own son's education?" 15

"He said he doesn't have the money." 16

"And you believe him?" she asks. "With two Volvos and a town house and cable TV? Let him sell one of his cars if he has to. Let him stop watching HBO. Where are his priorities? 17

"I'm not his responsibility." 18

"Oh no. You're just his son, that's all; I forgot. Why are you protecting him?" 19

I look up, and my mother's eyes widen a little—part of her question—and it feels as if she is seeing something in my face, so I realize I'd better get out of the room. "I'm not protecting him," I say. "It's just that you always want everything to be somebody's fault. It's the school's fault. It's nobody's fault. It's no great tragedy if I don't go back to school in the fall; you're the only person who thinks so. Why can't you just accept things, like everybody else?" I walk into my 20

COLLABORATIVE ACTIVITY

At work, Richard's father is described as dynamic and powerful: "One word from my father and a thousand spray cans go off" (paragraph 3). His mother is seen as patient and nurturing: "She stands over these kids . . . and if they're having trouble she sits down next to them to show them what to do" (paragraph 8). Have students work in groups to identify other differences between Richard's parents. In class discussion, consider how these differences help to explain their different styles of parenting.

bedroom, shutting the door behind me. I lie on my bed and look up at the ceiling, where the summer bugs have already formed a sooty layer inside the bottom of my light fixture. My ears are hot.

Our apartment is small. There are only the two bedrooms, the 21 living room, the bathroom, and the kitchen, and so if you want to be alone it's pretty impossible. My mother comes in after a few minutes. She has calmed down. She walks over to the air conditioner and turns it on, then waves her hand in front of the vents to make sure that cold air is coming out. I sit up and frown at her.

She sits down next to me and puts her arm around my shoulders. 22 "I'm sorry you're so upset," she says. As she talks she rubs the back of my neck. "But I just think that there are a lot of things we can do before you have to go and look for a full-time job. There are relatives we can call. There are loans we can take out. There are a lot of avenues open to us."

"O.K., Mom." 23

"I know it must be pretty hard on you, having a father like this." 24 She gives me time to speak, then says, "I mean, a man who won't even pay for his son's school."

"It's not that," I say, "It's not even that I'm that upset. It's just 25 that I don't want us to be beholden to him anymore. I don't even like him very much."

My mom laughs. "What's to like?" she says. 26

I laugh with her. "It's just that he's so creepy." 27

"You don't have to tell me. I was married to him." 28

"Why did you marry him?" I ask. 29

"He was different when I met him." 30

"How different could he be?" 31

Mom laughs, shaking her head. Her eyes blank a little, remem- 32 bering. She was twenty when she met my father—a year older than I am now. I imagine her in a green flannel skirt and blue knee socks. "I don't know," she says, looking past me. "Not very." We laugh together again. "I don't know. I wanted to get away from my parents, I guess."

"Who could blame you?" I say, but I can tell from a shift in her 33 face that I have pushed too far. Her father died two years back.

"What do you mean?" she asks, turning back to me. 34

"I don't know," I say. "I mean, you were young." 35

She nods, as if this fact, remembering it, comes as something of 36 a surprise to her. She blinks, "I was young," she says.

I get a job working at a B. Dalton bookstore. The manager has to 37 fill our some forms, and when he asks me how long I will be working—for the whole year or just the summer—I say, "Just for the summer," without thinking, and by the time I realize, he has already written it down and it doesn't seem worth the trouble of making him go back and change it. Still, I go through the rest of the day with the feeling that I've done something wrong. It's the store on Fifth Avenue, and it's not a bad place to work. I am sent to the main floor, to the middle register, where old women come in pairs and shuffle through the Romance section. I eat lunch in a little park a block from the store, where a man-made waterfall keeps tumbling down and secretaries drink diet soda. There is a cool breeze, because of the water. It is the second week of the summer, and on returning from lunch I am told I will have Wednesday off, because it is the Fourth of July.

38   Riding the bus home, I begin thinking that maybe my mother called my father anyway. It's terrible. The bus keeps stopping and people keep piling in, and meanwhile I am imagining their conversation going on. If I could make the bus go faster, maybe I could get home in time to stop them. I try to make mental contact with the bus driver by concentrating. I think, Skip the next stop; but he, out of loyalty to the other passengers or simple psychic deafness, doesn't, and instead the bus keeps stopping and people keep getting off and on. Walking into our building, I get the feeling everyone knows. Even the people on the elevator scowl. Maybe if I had told my mother myself, I would have softened it somehow. What would upset her now is not only the money—although the money would be a big part of it—but also that I tried to put something over on her. I am almost afraid to open our door. "Hello," I call, stepping inside.

39   As it turns out, my mother isn't home. There is a note on the table. She has gone shopping. I look at the note for a while, to see if I can figure anything out from it. For example, it is a short note. Would she usually write a longer one? It isn't signed "Love" or anything—just "Mom," in the scratchy way she draws her pictures.

40   I hang my jacket in the closet and then turn on my mom's answering machine. There is one hang-up, and then a message from my father. It makes my whole body go cold. His voice sounds farther away than when we talked the last time. "Richard?" he says. His voice is slow. "This is your father. I just wanted to call to see how things were going. I had an interesting discussion with your mother this afternoon, and we can talk about it later, if you'd like to. Call back if you get a chance." Then there is the clatter of his phone being hung up, and then a little electronic squawk as the connection is broken, which the machine has recorded. I play it again, but there is no way of telling just what he and Mom talked about. I walk into the bathroom and splash cold water on my face and look in the mirror. Then I try reading my mom's note again, but all I can really make it say is that she has gone to the supermarket.

My mother comes home, carrying two big bags of groceries. She   41
pushes the door open with her shoulder. "Can you give me a hand?"
she says.

I stand up and take the bags from her and carry them into the   42
kitchen. They are heavy even for me. I hold them close to my chest,
where the edges brush against my nose, giving me their heavy, dusty
smell. My mom stands in the dining area. She rests one hand on the
table. She is wearing running shorts and a T-shirt that on the front
says "Perrier" and on the back has the name and date of a race she
ran. "Any messages?" she asks me.

I look at her, but I can't tell anything from her face, either. She   43
looks angry, but that could be just because it was hot outside, or
because there was too long a line at the supermarket. "I didn't look,"
I answer, "Don't you even say hello anymore?"

"Hello," she says. She picks up her note and holds it so I can   44
see. "You could throw this away, you know," she says. "Or are you
saving it for any particular reason?"

"No, you can throw it away."   45

"That's nice. How about you throw it away?"   46

"I'm unloading the groceries right now."   47

She puts the note back down on the table and then walks into   48
the living room. I unload the rest of the groceries. There is a box of
spaghetti, Tropicana orange juice, brown rice, pita bread, a few plain
Dannon yogurts. I put everything away and then I fold up the bags
and stuff them into the broom closet, where we save them for garbage.

In the living room I hear my mom turn on the machine. There is   49
a hang-up and then my father's message begins again. "Richard?"
he says. "This is your father." I walk into the living room. Mom is
standing over the machine, one hand on the buttons. "Oh, God,"
she says, in a bored way when she hears his voice, and she shuts it
off. Then she turns around and looks at me. I am standing near the
wall. "Why do you have that funny look on your face, Richard?" she
asks.

I shrug. "How was your day?" I say.   50

"Bad." She steps over her chair and sits down on the sofa. From   51
the way she arranged herself, I can tell she is upset. She keeps her
arms folded across her stomach, and there is something compressed
and angry about her face. The way her lips are pressed together—
and also something around her eyes. "You want to make me some
tea?"

"What happened?" I ask.   52

"Nothing happened. I ran. I went shopping. I spoke to your   53
father."

I pull a chair over from the table and sit down across from her.   54
I count to five and then ask, "What did he say?"

She shakes her head and laughs through her nose. "Oh, God.   55
He was awful, Richard. Just awful. Right when we got on the phone,
he started asking if you'd found a job, and then when I asked him
if he was planning to pay the rest of your tuition he laughed and said
of course not. He said it was time for you to learn to take care of
yourself. He said it was going to be good for you. I couldn't talk to
him. Really, Richard, he was awful. I mean it. Just awful."

"I told you not to call him."   56

"Well, then, I was stupid, Richard."   57

"Are you going to call him again?"   58

"How do I know if I'm going to call him again? Not if he keeps   59
acting that way on the phone to me. But I can't pay the school myself."
Her lips go back to being tight, and she pulls her arms closer together,
so that each hand curls under the opposite elbow.

It occurs to me that what's pressing down on her face is the money   60
we owe the school. "Did the school call again?" I guess.

She nods. "Yesterday."   61

"Don't call him," I say.   62

"Thanks, Richard. You want to get me some tea?"   63

"How about 'please'?"   64

"How about throwing that note away? Or are you planning to   65
leave it there till Christmas?"

The next day, I get the same feeling that she has called my father   66
again. I go outside during lunch to phone her. It is very hot, and the
undersides of my arms are soggy. I have to walk about two blocks
down Fifth Avenue before I can find a free phone, and then when I
dial our number there is no answer. I think I may have dialed the
number wrong, because even if no one is home there should still be
the machine, but when I try again there is still no answer. As I hang
up, I catch my reflection in the shiny front of the phone for a second
and I look awful, sweaty. The rest of the day is terrible. I can hardly
work. I keep ringing up the paperbacks as Calendars and the children's books as Software. On the way home, I think that even if my
father didn't tell her I will have to tell her myself. I'm afraid that if I
don't something awful will happen, like we'll never speak to each
other again or something. But when I get home she is sitting on the
sofa, reading the newspaper with her feet up on a chair, and when
I walk into the living room she smiles at me, and it just doesn't seem
like the right time. I take off my tie and blazer and then pour myself
a glass of milk and sit down next to her. She smells like Ben Gay—

a strong, wintergreenish smell—which is what she rubs on her legs
after running.

"How was your day?" she asks me. She has a mug of tea on the   67
cushion next to her, and when I sit down she folds the newspaper
and picks up the mug.

"Fine," I say. Then I ask, "Did you go somewhere? I tried calling   68
around noon, but there was no answer."

"I drove up to Greenwich," she says.   69

"Why didn't you turn on the machine?"   70

"What are you, the police inspector? I didn't feel like it, that's   71
why."

"But why'd you drive up to Greenwich?"   72

She laughs, "I feel like I should have one of those big lights on   73
me." She brings her arms very close to her sides and speaks very
quickly, like a suspect: "I don't know. I don't know why I went up
to Greenwich." She drinks from her cup, which she holds with both
hands. Then she shakes her head and laughs.

We eat dinner. When we lived in Greenwich, she used to teach   74
art in the summers, too. They had a summer day program, with a
bunch of little kids running around—I was in it, too, when I was
younger—and she used to take them out into the fields and have
them draw trees and flowers. She hated it. While we were eating, I
get the idea that maybe this is what she went up there for, to talk to
someone about this job. Dinner is cool things: tuna fish and pita bread
and iced coffee. My mother has a salad. We don't talk for a while.
All we do is crunch.

"Why'd you go up to Greenwich?" I ask her again.   75

She looks up at me, a little angry. The rule, I know, is that we   76
don't talk about something once she has clearly finished talking about
it. "I felt like it," she says. Then she forks some more salad into her
mouth, and maybe thinks that her response is off key, because she
says, "I had a great idea while I was up there, though."

"What?"   77

"I thought we could go up tomorrow. You know, for the Fourth   78
of July. See the fireworks. I thought it'd be a lot of fun."

"It sounds great."   79

"Yes," she says, "I thought you'd like that."   80

I sleep late the next day, and when I wake up she has gone   81
jogging. She has left me a note saying so, which I throw away. She
comes back sweaty and happy, drinking a bottle of club soda, and I
ask her why she isn't drinking tea, and we joke, and it all feels very
nice, until I remember about Dad and the money and her job and

then I feel awful again, because it seems as if all our talking and joking is going on in midair, without anything underneath it to hold it up. We eat lunch, and then my mom makes some sandwiches and we get into our car and drive up the thruway to Connecticut. It's fun seeing the place where you used to live. We drive by our old house, and it looks the same, though there are some toys in the back yard and some lawn furniture—chairs and a big wooden table—which we didn't own. I get this funny feeling while we are in the car that we could still be living inside, as a family; that my father could walk out on the lawn and wave to us, or that if we stayed long enough we might see ourselves going past a window or walking over to sit at that big table. When we get to the high school, cars are everywhere, loading and unloading, families carrying big plastic coolers filled with food. I ask my mother if it was always this popular. "Yes," she says. "You just don't remember." We have to drive up the street about two blocks to find a space. By the time we have taken our own cooler out of the trunk, two more cars have already parked in front of us.

The fireworks are always held at the same place. The people sit   82
on the athletic field and the fireworks are set off from behind the baseball diamond about a hundred yards away. Thousands of people are sitting on blankets or walking around and talking to each other. It's like a scene from one of those movies where the dam bursts and everyone is evacuated to a municipal building, only instead of all their belongings the people here are carrying pillows and Cokes and Twinkies. We find a spot right in the middle of the field. Some kids are playing a game of tag. They keep running through the crowd, laughing, screaming, just barely missing the people on the ground, which of course is part of the fun. When one of the kids brushes against my mother's shoulder I can see that she wants to stop him, give him a talking to, but I ask her not to. I remember when I would have been playing, too.

There is a black platform in the center of the baseball field, and   83
after about three-quarters of an hour a presentation begins. A fireman and a policeman and a man from the Chamber of Commerce walk back and forth to the microphone and give each other awards, for safety and diligence and community service. Then they step down and a group of boys and girls collect onstage, most of them blond, all of them in robes. The man from the Chamber of Commerce, wearing his silver community-service medal, introduces them as the Royal Danish Boys and Girls Choir, "all the way from Holland." Then he leaves the stage, and though I imagine that the children will sing Danish folk songs, or maybe European anthems, what they sing is a medley of Broadway show tunes, in English, designed around the

theme of a foreigner's impressions of America: "Oklahoma!" and "Getting to Know You" and "Gary, Indiana," though it is hard to make out the exact words through their accents.

By the time they have finished, the sky has turned dark blue, 84 with the moon hanging just to one side. The policeman and the fireman return with the man from the Chamber of Commerce. "Good evening," he says. His voice echoes all over the field. "We'd like to welcome all of you to this year's celebration of the Greenwich, Connecticut, Fourth of July. In keeping with the spirit of this very special day, we'd like all of you to rise for the singing of our national anthem." My mother and I stand to sing, and there is something nice about being part of this wave of people, of voices. During the last line, there is a popping sound like a champagne bottle opening, and a yellow streak rises over the platform, nosing its way into the sky. The words "and the home, of the, brave" are lost in a chorus of "Oh"s. We sit down again, en masse. I hand my mother her sweater. I can barely see her, but her voice comes from where I know she should be: "Thank you." The fireworks go off over the outfield, sometimes one, sometimes two or three at a time. Each one leaves a little shadow of smoke that the next one, bursting, illuminates. Some bloom like flowers; others are simply midair explosions, flashes. A few burst and then shoot forward, like the effect in *Star Wars* when the ship goes into hyperspace. Some are designed to fool us: One pops open very high in the air, sending out a circle of streamers like the frame of an umbrella; the crowd begins to "Ooh." Then one of these streamers, falling, pops open itself, sending out another series, and the rest of the crowd goes "Ah." Finally, one of those pops right over our heads, giving off a final shower of color, and the crowd whistles and applauds. The display gets more and more elaborate, until, for the last few minutes, there are ten or twenty rockets in the air at once, bursting and unfolding simultaneously. Everyone starts cheering, and the noises keep booming over us, making us duck our heads. The air smells like sulfur.

In the car, I am close to sleep. My mother is driving, outside it 85 is dark, and I feel safe. The roads are crowded at first, but farther away from the school the traffic gets thinner, until we are driving alone down mostly empty roads. We seem to drive for a long time before joining up with the highway, where we become again simply one car among many.

"I'm working this summer," my mother announces after a little 86 while.

I know, but I ask "Where" anyway. 87

"Here," she says, "At the school. I got my old job back." 88

"Mom." 89

She stops me. "I thought about it, and I decided that it really was 90
important for me to have you in school right now. It was my decision
to make, and I made it."

I turn to look at her. Her face is lit up by the meters in the 91
dashboard. It's a surprise to remember that she had a body to go with
her voice. I look at her profile, at her cheek and at the skin underneath
her chin beginning to sag. I remember how frightened she had been
when we first moved to the city, how odd it had felt being in a house
without my father's voice filling it, and how when we drove up to
college for the first time last fall and she saw my name on top of my
registration folder she walked out of the reception hall. I found her
outside, on the main green, crying. "I can't believe we did it, we
pulled it off," she said, meaning college.

"I just don't want to be a burden," I say now. 92

"You are," she says. "But it's O.K. I mean, I'm your mother, and 93
you're supposed to be my burden." She turns back to look at me in
the dark. "I am your mother, aren't I?"

"As far as I know." 94

She laughs, and then we don't talk for a while. She turns on the 95
air conditioner. I close my eyes and lean my head against the window.
Every so often we hit a bump, which makes the window jiggle, which
makes my teeth click together. "I'm sorry you have to work," I say.

"Look, you should be. Don't ask me to get rid of your guilt for 96
you. If you feel guilty, that's fine. This was just important to me,
that's all."

Her using the word "guilt" frightens me. I sit up and open my 97
eyes. "What did Dad say to you on the phone?" I ask.

"Nothing. He said he wasn't going to pay for you. He said that 98
he was doing the right thing. He said you understood. Do you?"

"No." 99

She nods, driving. "That's what I told your father. He said you 100
should call him, if you want to. Do you?"

I laugh, "No." 101

She nods again. "I told him that, too." 102

She seems ready to stop talking, but I keep going. I want her to 103
tell me that it's O.K., that she missed working outdoors, that she
missed the little kids, missed Connecticut. "I just feel bad because
now you can't go to Wellfleet for the summer."

My mother says, "Let's not talk." 104

We drive. Through the windshield everything looks purple and 105
slick—the road and the taillights of the cars passing us and the
slender, long-necked lights hanging over the highway. We seem
sealed in, as if we are traveling under water.

WRITING SUGGESTION

Write a story in which Richard tells a psychologist why—and how—he spent the money.

**ANSWERS TO RESPONDING
TO READING**

1. Answers will vary. Richard misuses the money without fully realizing the consequences of his actions. He may do so because he does not really want to go to college, because he is trying to get his father to pay attention to him, or because he is subconsciously trying to punish his parents (and his stepmother, who is "in finance" and "gets crazy whenever money comes up") for the divorce. He lies because he is ashamed to tell his mother that he has let her down and perhaps also because he hopes the continued confusion about the money will force his parents to talk to each other.

2. How the money was spent does not really matter, to Richard or to readers. The money seems trivial in comparison with the consequences of its misuse for both Richard and his parents. The money serves the symbolic function of highlighting the emotional divisiveness and the barely submerged resentment in the family.

3. Students may blame Richard's parents because both seem more concerned with emerging victorious from the divorce than with doing what is best for Richard. His father is involved with his career and his new wife; his mother is preoccupied with the demands of building a new life for herself and surviving financially. They may also be blamed for permitting their stubbornness to keep them from communicating with each other.

BACKGROUND ON AUTHOR

When Robert Frost died in 1963, the public mourned a gentle writer of simple pastoral lyrics. However, more recent readers have seen that beneath the surface simplicity of Frost's poems lies a deeper ambiguity: A biographer portrayed him as a difficult man, a distant husband, and an indifferent parent.

FOR OPENERS

What exactly is "the road less travelled by"? Give some concrete examples of such roads in our lives. What well-known individuals have taken such roads?

My mother reaches over and turns off the air conditioner. "There 106 is something I want to talk to you about, Richard," she says.

"What?" I ask. 107

She keeps her face turned toward the highway. "If anything like 108 this ever happens again, I want you to tell me immediately. Don't make it so I have to find out myself. This whole thing wouldn't have happened if you had told me about it in the spring. We could have gotten loans and things. As it is, we're stuck."

I don't say anything. 109

"If you ever have anything to tell me," she says, "tell me when 110 it happens. O.K.? We're very close. You can tell me anything you want to, O.K.?"

She looks over at me. I try to keep my face from showing anything, 111 and when I can't do that I look away, at my feet under the dashboard. It is an offer. I can tell her or not. The funny thing is, I can feel that she doesn't really want me to. If she has guessed, she doesn't want me to confirm it. And though I am relieved, it seems to be that if I don't tell her now I never will, and this thing will always be between us, this failure, my father's voice embedded in static.

I look up. We are passing under the George Washington Bridge. 112
"O.K.," I say. 113

RESPONDING TO READING

1. In this story Richard chooses to misuse money given to him and to lie about what he has done. What motivates these two actions? Under what circumstances, if any, could you see yourself acting as he did? **2.** Richard claims that he does not know how he spent the three thousand dollars— "books and things, movies" (paragraph 1), he says. Do you believe him? Does it matter how he spent the money? How do you think he could have spent it? **3.** To what extent, if any, are Richard's parents to blame for his actions? Is his transgression more or less serious because he steals from and lies to his parents rather than anonymous strangers? Do you think your parents' reactions to this story might be different from yours?

The Road Not Taken

ROBERT FROST

Robert Frost (1874–1963), four-time Pulitzer Prize-winning poet of rural New England, lived most of his life in New Hampshire and taught at Amherst College and Dartmouth College. His language is familiar and accessible—but not simple—and his poems are often symbolic and rich in symbols and allusions. Frost read a poem, "The

Gift Outright," that he composed for the occasion at the inauguration of President John F. Kennedy. Some of Frost's more famous poems are "Birches," "Mending Wall," and "Stopping by the Woods on a Snowy Evening." "The Road Not Taken" is about uncertainty and the difficulty of choice.

> Two roads diverged in a yellow wood,
> And sorry I could not travel both
> And be one traveller, long I stood
> And looked down one as far as I could
> To where it bent in the undergrowth;   5
>
> Then took the other, as just as fair,
> And having perhaps the better claim,
> Because it was grassy and wanted wear;
> Though as for that the passing there
> Had worn them really about the same,   10
>
> And both that morning equally lay
> In leaves no step had trodden black.
> Oh, I kept the first for another day!
> Yet knowing how way leads on to way,
> I doubted if I should ever come back.   15
>
> I shall be telling this with a sigh
> Somewhere ages and ages hence:
> Two roads diverged in a wood, and I—
> I took the one less travelled by,
> And that has made all the difference.   20

RESPONDING TO READING

1. What is the difference between the two paths the speaker considers? Why does he make the choice he does?   **2.** Is the poem simply about two paths in the wood, or does it suggest something more—something about the nature of choice itself, or about the kinds of difficult choices to be made in life? What makes you think so? To what larger choices might the speaker be alluding? What choices in your own life might be seen as concrete examples of Frost's two paths?   **3.** What does the speaker mean by "That has made all the difference" (line 20)? Have you ever made a choice that made "all the difference"? In what way did it make a difference? How does the speaker feel about his choice?

ADDITIONAL QUESTIONS FOR RESPONDING TO READING

1. During which season does the journey take place? Why does the season seem appropriate to the poem?
2. Chart the poem's rhyme scheme and meter. How are they consistent with the poem's subject and theme?

TEACHING STRATEGY

Have your students look for concrete descriptions. Beyond the concrete images, what abstract or symbolic associations can they draw?

COLLABORATIVE ACTIVITY

In groups, ask students to discuss whether the poem is really about the road the speaker chose, which "made all the difference," or, as the title suggests, about the road *not* taken.

WRITING SUGGESTION

What two roads diverged in your life? Which path did you take? Why? Was it the right choice? Describe your decision and its consequences.

ANSWERS TO RESPONDING TO READING

1. Ultimately the difference between the two paths is slight. Nevertheless, the speaker says he made his choice because one of the paths "was grassy and wanted wear." The choice might suggest that the speaker took the less conventional, more adventurous route. On the other hand, the poet may be suggesting that even those actions that have significant consequences may begin with almost arbitrary decisions.
2. A journey is a conventional poetic symbol for the span of a lifetime, and here Frost seems to evoke some significant turning points in an individual's life. Lines 2 and 3 suggest that some aspect of the poet's identity is at stake: that in order to remain whole, he must choose one or two possible options. Line 12 may emphasize the solitary nature of the process of making really critical life decisions. And the final stanza suggests that the incident is significant enough to linger in the speaker's memory for "ages and ages."
3. A somewhat arbitrary choice has had multiple consequences. Just as in life, the speaker here cannot know all the possible results of his decision, yet he accepts it.

Ethics

LINDA PASTAN

Linda Pastan (1932–   ) has published poetry in the collections *Aspects of Eve* (1975) and *Waiting for My Life* (1981), as well as in many poetry journals. Her poem "Ethics" is from *Waiting for My Life*. In it, the speaker ponders a difficult ethical question and the dubious ability of the young to understand art or life.

In ethics class so many years ago
our teacher asked this question every fall:
if there were a fire in a museum
which would you save, a Rembrandt painting
or an old woman who hadn't many   5
years left anyhow? Restless on hard chairs
caring little for pictures or old age
we'd opt one year for life, the next for art
and always half-heartedly. Sometimes
the woman borrowed my grandmother's face   10
leaving her usual kitchen to wander
some drafty, half-imagined museum.
One year, feeling clever, I replied
why not let the woman decide herself?
Linda, the teacher would report, eschews   15
the burdens of responsibility.
This fall in a real museum I stand
before a real Rembrandt, old woman,
or nearly so, myself. The colors
within this frame are darker than autumn,   20
darker even than winter—the browns of earth,
though earth's most radiant elements burn
through the canvas. I know now that woman
and painting and season are almost one
and all beyond saving by children.   25

RESPONDING TO READING

1. Reading this poem for the first time, a student suggested that the obvious solution would be for the rescuer to carry the old woman and the woman to carry the painting. Do you think this is a reasonable response to the poem, or did the students miss (or sidestep) the point? What is your response?   **2.** Does the fact that the students would "opt one year for life, the next for art / and always half-heartedly" (lines 8–9) suggest to you that

---

BACKGROUND ON AUTHOR

While a senior at Radcliffe College, Linda Pastan won a poetry contest in *Mademoiselle* magazine. The contest runner-up was Sylvia Plath.

FOR OPENERS

Is there a satisfactory answer to the question the poem asks?

TEACHING STRATEGY

Study this poem's irregular meter and note its absence of rhyme. How do these features suit the poem's subject matter?

COLLABORATIVE ACTIVITY

Divide the class into groups. Ask groups to devise an ethical dilemma like the one Pastan proposes and to examine the choices and the probable consequences of each. Then ask each group to present its findings to the class for discussion and (if possible) resolution. Remind them that a dilemma has two *unacceptable* alternatives.

ADDITIONAL QUESTIONS FOR RESPONDING TO READING

1. How does Pastan's use of punctuation affect the sense of the poem?
2. What is the mature poet's attitude toward the real Rembrandt? How does she seem to have felt as a child?

WRITING SUGGESTION

Write an essay in which you make a cause for saving either the woman or the painting.

they are indifferent? That the question is trivial? That it has no answer? Is the choice really between life and art?   **3.** What does the speaker mean by "woman / and painting and season are almost one / and all beyond saving by children" (lines 23–25)? Do you agree? Would your interpretation change if the poem ended with the word *saving*?

ANSWERS TO RESPONDING TO READING

1. The student sidestepped the issue in the same way the poet does as a child ("Why not let the woman decide herself?"). The poem centers on the speaker's mature sense that these issues are finally more profound than any child—or adult—can comprehend.
2. For the children, the question is trivial because it cannot be answered in the concrete terms children prefer.
3. Now, in the "fall" of her own life, the poet recognizes a profound value in being alive that she could not understand as a child. If the phrase *by children* were deleted, the poem would conclude more pessimistically. The ending of the poem, as it stands, leaves open the possibility that, at the very least, human beings have the potential to learn that life, art, and the seasons have an abstract value that words cannot suggest.

WRITING: MAKING CHOICES

1. The question of whether or not to act to end another's suffering—possibly at one's own expense—is explored, implicitly or explicitly, in "The Deer at Providencia," "Shooting an Elephant," "Lifeboat Ethics: The Case Against Helping the Poor" and "The Ones Who Walk Away from Omelas." What are your own feelings about this subject?

2. Write an essay in which you formulate your own system of beliefs about the issues you see as most important in your life. Be careful to develop your ideas beyond the kinds of abstractions Robert Coles calls "the stuff of college term papers" (paragraph 5); give specific examples drawn from your own experience. You might begin by listing the things that are most important to you and then move on to consider what you would do or risk to gain or keep them.

3. Thoreau says, "Unjust laws exist: shall we be content to obey them, or shall we endeavor to amend them, and obey them until we have succeeded, or shall we transgress them at once?" (paragraph 16). Choose a law that you consider unjust, and write an essay in which you tell why you feel obligated to disobey it.

4. Garrett Hardin says, "We are all the descendants of thieves, and the world's resources are inequitably distributed. But we must begin the journey to tomorrow from the point where we are today. We cannot remake the past" (paragraph 43). Although his comments refer to problems of overpopulation and world hunger, they could also apply to inequalities among different racial or ethnic groups. Do you agree with such a position? Use material in the selections of Orwell, King, and Mead to help you make your decision and to support your conclusion.

5. Milgram observes that his study shows that "ordinary people, simply doing their jobs, and without any particular hostility on their part, can become agents in a terrible destructive process" (paragraph 39). Citing examples from your own experience, explain how this process works.

6. King, Milgram, and Thoreau all consider the difficulties of resisting majority rule, standing up to authority, and protesting against established rules and laws. What issues do you believe ordinary people need to stand up for? Why?

7. Describe an experience in which you stood up to authority. What motivated you? Was your resistance successful? Would you do the same thing again?

8. The writers represented in this chapter present some pessimistic scenarios. Hardin sees an overpopulated, underfed world; Thomas predicts the possibility of a world destroyed by nuclear weapons; King sees a world corrupted by prejudice. What world problems are you most pessimistic about? Why?

Acknowledgments

GORDON ALLPORT "The Language of Prejudice" from *The Nature of Prejudice* by Gordon Allport, © 1979 by Addison-Wesley Publishing Company. Reprinted by permission of Addison-Wesley Publishing Co., Inc., Reading, MA.

MAYA ANGELOU "Graduation" from *I Know Why the Caged Bird Sings* by Maya Angelou. Copyright © 1969 by Maya Angelou. Reprinted by permission of Random House, Inc.

BARBARA LAZEAR ASCHER Excerpts from *The Habit of Loving* by Barbara Ascher. Copyright © 1986, 1987, 1989 by Barbara Lazear Ascher. Reprinted by permission of Random House, Inc.

ISAAC ASIMOV "My Built-in Doubter" from *Fact and Fancy* by Isaac Asimov. Copyright © 1962 by Isaac Asimov. Copyright © 1958 by Strut and Smith Pub., Inc. Copyright © 1958, 1959, 1960, 1961 by Mercury Press, Inc. "The Eureka Phenomenon," copyright © 1971 by Mercury Press, Inc. from *The Left Hand of the Electron* by Isaac Asimov. Used by permission of Doubleday, a division of Bantam Doubleday Dell Publishing Group, Inc.

MARGARET ATWOOD "Pornography." Reprinted by permission of Margaret Atwood, © 1983 by Margaret Atwood.

W. H. AUDEN "Moon Landing" from *W. H. Auden: Collected Poems* by W. H. Auden, edited by E. Mendelson. Copyright © 1969 by W. H. Auden. Reprinted by permission of Random House, Inc. and reprinted by permission of Faber and Faber Ltd. from *Collected Poems* by W. H. Auden.

JAMES BALDWIN "Stranger in the Village" from *Notes of a Native Son* by James Baldwin, copyright © 1955, renewed 1983, by James Baldwin. Used by permission of Beacon Press.

TONI CADE BAMBARA "The Lesson" from *Gorilla, My Love* by Toni Cade Bambara. Copyright © 1972 by Toni Cade Bambara. Reprinted by permission of Random House, Inc.

CHARLES BAXTER "Gryphon," from *Through the Safety Net* by Charles Baxter. Copyright © 1985 by Charles Baxter. Used by permission of Viking Penguin, a division of Penguin Books USA Inc.

CAROLINE BIRD "College Is a Waste of Time and Money" from *The Case Against College* by Caroline Bird. Reprinted by permission of the author.

SISSELA BOK Excerpt from *Lying: Moral Choice in Public and Private Life* by Sissela Bok. Copyright © 1978 by Sissela Bok. Reprinted by permission of Pantheon Books, a Division of Random House, Inc.

DAVID BRADLEY "Harvest Home" by David Bradley, copyright © 1989 by David Bradley, from *Family Portraits* by Carolyn Anthony. Used by permission of Doubleday, a division of Bantam Doubleday Dell Publishing Group, Inc.

JUDY BRADY "I Want a Wife," *Ms.*, December 1971. Reprinted by permission of the author.

GWENDOLYN BROOKS "The Chicago *Defender* Sends a Man to Little Rock, Fall 1957" from *Blacks* by Gwendolyn Brooks. Copyright © 1987 by Gwendolyn Brooks. Reprinted by permission of the author.

ROY CAMPANELLA II "Roy Campanella" from *Cult Baseball Players: The Greats, the Flakes, the Weird and the Wonderful* edited by Daniel Peary. Copyright © 1989 by Roy Campanella II. Reprinted by permission of the author.

RACHEL CARSON "The Obligation to Endure" from *Silent Spring* by Rachel Carson. Copyright © 1962 by Rachel L. Carson. Reprinted by permission of Houghton Mifflin Co.

RAYMOND CARVER "My Father's Life," *Esquire*, 1984. Copyright © 1984 by Raymond Carver. Reprinted by permission of Tess Gallagher.

BRUCE CATTON "Grant and Lee: A Study in Contrasts" from *The American Story* edited by Earl Schenck Miers. Copyright U.S. Capitol Historical Society, all rights reserved.

STUART CHASE "Gobbledygook" from *Power of Words*, copyright 1954 and renewed 1982 by Stuart Chase, reprinted by permission of Harcourt Brace Jovanovich, Inc.

ROBERT COLES Adapted from "The Children of Affluence" from *Privileged Ones, Volume V of Children of Crises* by Robert Coles. Copyright © 1977 by Robert Coles. First appeared in *The Atlantic*. By permission of Little, Brown and Company. "I Listen to My Parents and Wonder What They Believe," *Redbook*, February 1980. Reprinted by permission of the author.

NORMAN COUSINS "Who Killed Benny Paret?" *Saturday Review*, May 5, 1962. Reprinted by permission of Omni Publications International, Inc.

JOAN DIDION "Salvador" from *Salvador* by Joan Didion. Copyright © 1983 by Joan Didion. Reprinted by permission of Simon & Schuster, Inc. "Marrying Absurd," "On Going Home," and "On Keeping a Notebook" from *Slouching Towards Bethlehem* by Joan Didion. Copyright © 1966, 1967, 1968 by Joan Didion. Reprinted by permission of Farrar, Straus and Giroux, Inc.

ANNIE DILLARD "Sight into Insight," *Harper's* Magazine, 1974. Copyright © 1974 by Annie Dillard. "The Joys of Reading," *The New York Times*, May 16, 1982. Copyright © 1982 by Annie Dillard. Reprinted by permission of the author and her agent Blanche C. Gregory, Inc. "Il Faut Travailler" and "The French and Indian War" from *An American Childhood* by Annie Dillard. Copyright © 1987 by Annie Dillard. "The Deer at Providencia" from *Teaching A Stone to Talk* by Annie Dillard. Copyright © 1982 by Annie Dillard. Reprinted by permission of HarperCollins Publishers.

LOREN EISELEY Excerpt from *The Immense Journey* by Loren Eiseley. Copyright © 1957 by Loren Eiseley. Reprinted by permission of Random House, Inc. "The Brown Wasps" reprinted with permission of Charles Scribner's Sons, an imprint of Macmillan Publishing Company from *The Night Country* by Loren Eiseley. Copyright © 1971 Loren Eiseley.

TREY ELLIS "Remember My Name," *The Village Voice*, June 13, 1989. Reprinted by permission of the author and *The Village Voice*.

LOUISE ERDRICH "Dear John Wayne" from *Jacklight* poems by Louise Erdrich. Copyright © 1984 by Louise Erdrich. Reprinted by permission of Henry Holt and Company, Inc.

E. M. FORSTER "My Wood" from *Abinger Harvest*, copyright 1936 and renewed 1964 by E. M. Forster, reprinted by permission of Harcourt Brace Jovanovich, Inc.

JOHN HOPE FRANKLIN "The Moral Legacy of the Founding Fathers," *University of Chicago Magazine*, Vol. XLVII, No. 4, Spring 1975. Reprinted by permission of *University of Chicago Magazine*.

ROBERT FROST "The Road Not Taken" from *The Poetry of Robert Frost* edited by Edward Connery Lathem. Copyright 1916, © 1969 by Holt, Rinehart and Winston. Copyright 1944 by Robert Frost. Reprinted by permission of Henry Holt and Company, Inc.

PAUL FUSSELL "The Middle Class" from *Class* by Paul Fussell. Copyright © 1983 by Paul Fussell. Reprinted by permission of Summit Books.

WILLIAM GOLDING "Thinking as a Hobby," *Holiday Magazine*, August 1961. Reprinted by permission of Curtis Brown, Ltd. Copyright © 1961 by William Golding. Renewed.

DORIS KEARNS GOODWIN "Fathers, Daughters, and the Magic of Baseball" from *Diamonds Are Forever: Artists and Writers on Baseball* by Doris Kearns Goodwin. Reprinted by permission of the author.

STEPHEN JAY GOULD "Nasty Little Facts," with permission from *Natural History*, February 1985; Copyright the American Museum of Natural History, 1985. "Dusty Rhodes" from *Cult Baseball Players: The Greats, the Flakes, the Weird and the Wonderful* edited by Daniel Peary. Reprinted by permission of the author. "Women's Brains" is reprinted from *The Panda's Thumb, More Reflections in Natural History*, by Stephen Jay Gould, by permission of W. W. Norton & Company, Inc. Copyright © 1980 by Stephen Jay Gould.

JEFF GREENFIELD "The Black and White Truth about Basketball," *Esquire*, 1975. Reprinted by permission of Sterling Lord Literistic, Inc. Copyright © 1975 by Jeff Greenfield.

EDWARD T. HALL "The Arab World" from *The Hidden Dimension* by Edward T. Hall. Copyright © 1966, 1982 by Edward T. Hall. Used by permission of Doubleday, a division of Bantam Doubleday Dell Publishing Group, Inc.

GARRETT HARDIN "Lifeboat Ethics: The Case Against Helping the Poor," *Psychology Today*, September 1974.

MARIE HART "Sport: Women Sit in the Back of the Bus," *Psychology Today*, 1971.

ROBERT HAYDEN "Those Winter Sundays" is reprinted from *Angle of Ascent, New and Selected Poems*, by Robert Hayden, by permission of Liveright Publishing Corporation. Copyright © 1975, 1972, 1970, 1966 by Robert Hayden.

LILIANA HEKER "The Stolen Party" by Liliana Heker, translated by Alberto Manguel. Reprinted from *Other Fires* by Alberto Manguel by permission of Clarkson N. Potter, Inc., a division of Crown Publishers, Inc. Copyright © 1985 by Alberto Manguel. Copyright © 1982 by Liliana Heker. Permission given by Lucinda Vardey Agency, Ltd. on behalf of Liliana Heker and Alberto Manguel.

LINDA HOGAN "Heritage." Reprinted by permission of Greenfield Review Press.

JOHN HOLT "School Is Bad for Children." Reprinted from *The Saturday Evening Post* © 1969.

JOYCE HOWE "Indelible Marks: Growing Up in a Chinese Laundry," *The Village Voice*, February 1983. Reprinted by permission of the author.

ROBERT HUFF "Rainbow," from *Colonel Johnson's Ride and Other Poems*, Wayne State University Press, copyright 1959 by Robert Huff. Reprinted by permission of the author.

ALDOUS HUXLEY "Propaganda Under a Dictatorship" from *Brave New World Revisited* by Aldous Huxley. Copyright © 1958 by Aldous Huxley. Reprinted by permission of HarperCollins Publishers, Mrs. Laura Huxley, and Chatto and Windus Ltd.

JAMAICA KINCAID Excerpt from *A Small Place* by Jamaica Kincaid. Copyright © 1988 by Jamaica Kincaid. Reprinted by permission of Farrar, Straus and Giroux, Inc.

MARTIN LUTHER KING, JR. "Letter from Birmingham Jail" from *Why We Can't Wait* by Martin Luther King, Jr. Copyright © 1963, 1964 by Martin Luther King, Jr. Reprinted by permission of HarperCollins Publishers. "I Have a Dream." Reprinted by permission of Joan Daves. Copyright © 1963 by Martin Luther King, Jr.

MAXINE HONG KINGSTON Excerpt from *The Woman Warrior* by Maxine Hong Kingston. Copyright © 1975, 1976 by Maxine Hong Kingston. Reprinted by permission of Alfred A. Knopf, Inc.

PERRI KLASS "India," reprinted by permission of the Putnam Publishing Group from *A Not Entirely Benign Procedure*. Copyright © 1987 by Perri Klass.

ELISABETH KÜBLER-ROSS "On the Fear of Death" reprinted with permission of Macmillan Publishing Company from *On Death and Dying* by Elisabeth Kübler-Ross. Copyright © 1969 by Elisabeth Kübler-Ross.

ROBIN LAKOFF "You Are What You Say," *Ms.*, July 1974. Reprinted with permission, *Ms.* Magazine © 1974.

URSULA K. LE GUIN "The Ones Who Walk Away from Omelas" from *The Wind's Twelve Quartets* by Ursula K. Le Guin. Copyright © 1973 by Ursula K. Le Guin; first appeared in *New Dimensions 3*; reprinted by permission of the author and the author's agent, Virginia Kidd.

JOSEPH LELYVELD Excerpt from *Move Your Shadow: South Africa, Black and White* by Joseph Lelyveld. Copyright © 1985 by Joseph Lelyveld. Reprinted by permission of Times Books, a Division of Random House, Inc.

DORIS LESSING "Being Prohibited," *The New Statesman*, April 21, 1956. Copyright © 1957 by Doris Lessing. Reprinted by permission of Jonathan Clowes Ltd., London, on behalf of Doris Lessing.

BARRY LOPEZ "Landscape and Narrative" is reprinted with permission of Charles Scribner's Sons, an imprint of Macmillan Publishing Company from *Crossing Open Ground* by Barry Lopez. Copyright © 1984, 1988 Barry Holstun Lopez. (First appeared under a different title in *Harper's*, December 1984).

SHIRLEY GEOK-LIN LIM "Modern Secrets" from *Crossing the Peninsula and Other Poems* by Shirley Geok-Lin Lim. Reprinted by permission of the author.

DAVID LIPSKY "Three Thousand Dollars" from *Three Thousand Dollars: and Other Stories* by David Lipsky. Copyright © 1989 by David Lipsky. Reprinted by permission of Summit Books, a division of Simon & Schuster, Inc.

NORMAN MAILER "The Language of Men" from *The Language of Men* by Normal Mailer. Copyright 1953 by Normal Mailer. Reprinted by permission of the author and the author's agents, Scott Meredith Literary Agency, Inc., 845 Third Avenue, New York, New York 10022.

BERNARD MALAMUD "A Summer's Reading" from *The Magic Barrel* by Bernard Malamud. Copyright © 1956, 1958, 1984 by Bernard Malamud. Reprinted by permission of Farrar, Straus and Giroux, Inc.

WILLIAM MANCHESTER "Okinawa: The Bloodiest Battle of All," *The New York Times*, June 14, 1987. Reprinted by permission of Don Congdon Associates, Inc. Copyright © 1987 by William Manchester.

PAULE MARSHALL "From the Poets in the Kitchen," *The New York Times*, January 1983. Reprinted by permission of the author.

BOBBIE ANN MASON "Shiloh" from *Shiloh and Other Stories* by Bobbie Ann Mason. Copyright © 1982 by Bobbie Ann Mason. Reprinted by permission of HarperCollins Publishers.

JOHN MCMURTRY "Kill 'Em! Crush 'Em! Eat 'Em Raw!" Reprinted by permission from *Maclean's*, October 1971.

JOHN MCPHEE Excerpt from "The Grizzly" from *Coming Into the Country* by John McPhee. Copyright © 1976, 1977 by John McPhee. Reprinted by permission of Farrar, Straus and Giroux, Inc.

MARGARET MEAD AND RHODA METRAUX "A Life for a Life: What That Means Today" from *Aspects of the Present* by Margaret Mead and Rhoda Metraux. Copyright © 1980 by Catherine Bateson Kassajian and Rhoda Metraux. By permission of William Morrow and Co., Inc.

CHARLES L. MEE, JR. "The Summer Before Salk," *Esquire*, December 1983. Copyright © 1983 by Charles L. Mee, Jr. Reprinted by permission of the Wallace Literary Agency, Inc. First appeared in *Esquire*.

STANLEY MILGRAM "The Perils of Obedience" from *Obedience to Authority* by Stanley Milgram. Copyright © 1974 by Stanley Milgram. Reprinted by permission of HarperCollins Publishers.

JESSICA MITFORD "The American Way of Death" from *The American Way of Death* by Jessica Mitford. Reprinted by permission of Jessica Mitford. All rights reserved. Copyright © 1963, 1978 by Jessica Mitford.

1114 ACKNOWLEDGMENTS

N. SCOTT MOMADAY "The Way to Rainy Mountain." First published in *The Reporter*, 26 January 1967. Reprinted from *The Way to Rainy Mountain* © 1969, The University of New Mexico Press.

LORRIE MOORE "How to Become a Writer" from *Self-Help* by Lorrie Moore. Copyright © 1985 by M. L. Moore. Reprinted by permission of Alfred A. Knopf, Inc.

PAT MORA "Sonrisas." Reprinted with permission of the publisher from *Borders*, by Pat Mora (Houston: Arte Publico Press, University of Houston, 1986).

ALICE MUNRO "Boys and Girls" from *Dance of the Happy Shades*. Copyright © 1986 by Alice Munro. Reprinted by arrangement with Virginia Barber Literary Agency, Inc. All rights reserved.

ALLEEN PACE NILSEN "Sexism in English: A 1990s Update," © Alleen Pace Nilsen, 1990. Reprinted by permission of the author.

JOYCE CAROL OATES "On Boxing," *The Ontario Review*, 1985. Reprinted by permission of the author and Blanche C. Gregory, Inc. Copyright © 1985 by The Ontario Review, Inc. "Where Are You Going" from *Wheel of Love* by Joyce Carol Oates. Copyright © 1965 by Joyce Carol Oates. Reprinted by permission of John Hawkins & Associates, Inc.

TILLIE OLSEN "I Stand Here Ironing," from *Tell Me A Riddle* by Tillie Olsen. Copyright © 1956, 1957, 1960, 1961 by Tillie Olsen. Used by permission of Delacorte Press/Seymour Lawrence, a division of Bantam Doubleday Dell Publishing Group, Inc.

GEORGE ORWELL "Politics and the English Language" by George Orwell from his volume *Shooting An Elephant and Other Essays*, copyright 1946 by Sonia Brownell Orwell and renewed 1974 by Sonia Orwell; "Shooting an Elephant" by George Orwell from his volume *Shooting an Elephant and Other Essays*, copyright 1950 by Sonia Brownell Orwell and renewed 1978 by Sonia Pitt-Rivers; "Why I Write" and "Marrakech" from *Such, Such Were the Joys* by George Orwell, copyright 1953 by Sonia Brownell Orwell and renewed 1981 by Mrs. George K. Perutz, Mrs. Miriam Gross, Dr. Michael Dickson, Executors of the Estate of Sonia Brownell Orwell, reprinted by permission of Harcourt Brace Jovanovich, Inc., and the estate of the late Sonia Brownell Orwell and Martin Secker & Warburg Ltd.

LINDA PASTAN "Ethics" is reprinted from *Waiting for My Life, Poems by Linda Pastan*, by permission of W. W. Norton & Company, Inc. Copyright © 1981 by Linda Pastan.

NOEL PERRIN "The Androgynous Man," *The New York Times*, February 5, 1984. Copyright © 1984 by The New York Times Company. Reprinted by permission.

ANN PETRY "Like a Winding Sheet" from *Miss Muriel and Other Stories* by Ann Petry. Reprinted by permission of Russell & Volkening as agents for the author. Copyright © 1971 by Ann Petry.

MARGE PIERCY "The Secretary Chant" from *Circles on the Water* by Marge Piercy. Copyright © 1969, 1971, 1973 by Marge Piercy. Reprinted by permission of Alfred A. Knopf, Inc.

APPLETREE RODDEN "Why Smaller Refrigerators Can Preserve the Human Race," *Harper's Magazine*, January 1975. Copyright © 1974 by *Harper's Magazine*. All rights reserved. Reprinted from the January 1975 issue by special permission.

RICHARD RODRIGUEZ "Aria" from *Hunger of Memory* by Richard Rodriguez. Copyright © 1982 by Richard Rodriguez. Reprinted by permission of David R. Godine, Publisher. "The Fear of Losing a Culture," *Time*, July 11, 1988. Reprinted by permission of Georges Borchardt, Inc. for the author. Copyright © 1988 by Richard Rodriguez.

MURRAY ROSS "Football Red and Baseball Green." Reprinted by permission of the author.

PHILIP ROTH "Safe at Home" from *The Facts: A Novelist's Autobiography* by Philip Roth. Copyright © 1988 by Philip Roth. Reprinted by permission of Farrar, Straus and Giroux, Inc.

JIM SAGEL "Baca Grande" from *Hispanics in the United States, An Anthology of Creative Literature*, Vol. II, edited by Francisco Jimenez and Gary D. Keller, 1982. Copyright Bilingual Press/ Editorial Bilinque, Arizona State University, Tempe, AZ.

SCOTT RUSSELL SANDERS "Under the Influence," *Harper's Magazine*, November 1989. Copyright © 1989 by *Harper's Magazine*. All rights reserved. Reprinted from the November issue by special permission. "The Men We Carry in Our Minds" from *The Paradise of Bombs*, by Scott Russell Sanders. Copyright © 1984 by Scott Russell Sanders; first appeared in *Milkweed Chronicle*; reprinted by permission of the author and the author's agent, Virginia Kidd.

JONATHAN SCHELL Excerpt from *The Fate of the Earth* by Jonathan Schell. Copyright © 1982 by Jonathan Schell. Reprinted by permission of Alfred A. Knopf, Inc. Originally appeared in *The New Yorker*.

RICHARD SELZER "A Mask on the Face of Death," *Life* Magazine, August 1987. Reprinted by permission of Georges Borchardt, Inc. for the author. Copyright © 1987 by Richard Selzer.

IRWIN SHAW "The Eighty-Yard Run" from *Selected Short Stories of Irwin Shaw*. Reprinted with permission. © Irwin Shaw.

GARY SNYDER "Mother Earth: Her Whales" from *Turtle Island*. Copyright © 1972 by Gary Snyder. Reprinted by permission of New Directions Publishing Corporation.

GARY SOTO "One Last Time" from *Living Up the Street*, by Gary Soto. Copyright © 1985 by Gary Soto. Published by Strawberry Hill Press, Portland, Oregon.

WOLE SOYINKA "Telephone Conversation" by Wole Soyinka. Copyright 1960 by Wole Soyinka. Reprinted by permission of Brandt & Brandt Literary Agents, Inc.

WILLIAM STAFFORD "Traveling Through the Dark" from *Stories that Could Be True*. Copyright by William Stafford. Published by Harper & Row, 1977. Reprinted by permission of the author.

BRENT STAPLES Brent Staples is a member of The New York Times Editorial Board where he writes on politics and culture. "Just Walk on By: A Black Man Ponders His Power to Alter Public Space," *Ms.*, September 1986. Reprinted by permission of the author.

SHELBY STEELE "On Being Black and Middle Class." Copyright © 1990 by Shelby Steele. From the book *The Content of Our Character* and reprinted with permission from St. Martin's Press, Inc., New York, NY. "The Recoloring of Campus Life," *Harper's Magazine*, February 1989. Copyright © 1989 by *Harper's Magazine*. All rights reserved. Reprinted from the February issue by special permission.

GLORIA STEINEM "The Good News Is: These Are Not the Best Years of Your Life," *Ms.*, September 1979. Reprinted by permission of the author.

ROBERT STONE "A Higher Horror of Whiteness," *Harper's Magazine*, December 1986. Reprinted by permission of Donadio & Ashworth. Copyright © 1986 by Robert Stone.

ANDREW SUKNASKI "The Bitter Word" from *Wood Mountain Poems* by Andrew Suknaski. Reprinted by permission of the author.

STUDS TERKEL Excerpt from *Hard Times* by Studs Terkel. Copyright © 1970 by Studs Terkel. Reprinted by permission of Pantheon Books, a Division of Random House, Inc.

LEWIS THOMAS "Debating the Unknowable," *The Atlantic Monthly*, July 1981. Reprinted by permission of Abigail Thomas, Agent. "Late Night Thoughts on Listening to Mahler's Ninth," copyright © 1982 by Lewis Thomas from *Late Night Thoughts on Listening to Mahler's Ninth* by Lewis Thomas; and "Notes on Punctuation," copyright © 1979 by Lewis Thomas, from *The Medusa and the Snail* by Lewis Thomas. Used by permission of Viking Penguin, a division of Penguin Books USA Inc.

CALVIN TRILLIN "It's Just Too Late," by Calvin Trillin. Appears in his book, entitled *Killings*, published by Ticknor & Fields. Copyright © 1984 by Calvin Trillin. Originally appeared in *The New Yorker*.

BARBARA TUCHMAN "The Black Death" from *A Distant Mirror* by Barbara Tuchman. Copyright © 1978 by Barbara Tuchman. Reprinted by permission of Alfred A. Knopf, Inc. "An Inquiry into the Persistence of Unwisdom in Government," *Esquire*, 1980. Reprinted by permission of Russell & Volkening as agents for the author. Copyright © 1980 by Barbara Tuchman.

JOHN UPDIKE "Ex-Basketball Player" from *The Carpentered Hen and Other Tame Creatures* by John Updike. Copyright © 1982 by John Updike. Reprinted by permission of Alfred A. Knopf, Inc.

ALICE WALKER "Everyday Use" from *In Love & Trouble: Stories of Black Women*, copyright © 1973 by Alice Walker; "Beauty When the Other Dancer is the Self" from *In Search of Our Mothers' Gardens*, copyright © 1983 by Alice Walker; "The Civil Rights Movement: What Good Was It?" from *In Search of Our Mothers' Gardens*, copyright © 1967 by Alice Walker; "Saving the Life that is Your Own: The Importance of Models in the Artist's Life" from *In Search of Our Mothers' Gardens*, copyright © 1976 by Alice Walker; "In Search of Our Mothers' Gardens" from *In Search of Our Mothers' Gardens*, copyright © 1974 by Alice Walker; "Women" from *Revolutionary Petunias*, copyright © 1970 by Alice Walker, reprinted by permission of Harcourt Brace Jovanovich, Inc.

EUDORA WELTY "One Writer's Beginnings," reprinted by permission of the publishers from *One Writer's Beginnings* by Eudora Welty, Cambridge, Mass.: Harvard University Press, copyright © 1983, 1984 by Eudora Welty.

E. B. WHITE "Once More to the Lake" from *Essays of E. B. White*. Copyright 1941 by E. B. White. Reprinted by permission of HarperCollins Publishers.

VIRGINIA WOOLF "If Shakespeare Had a Sister" from *A Room of One's Own* by Virginia Woolf, copyright 1929 by Harcourt Brace Jovanovich, Inc. and renewed 1957 by Leonard Woolf, reprinted by permission of the publisher, The Estate of Virginia Woolf, and The Hogarth Press.

STANTON L. WORMLEY, JR. "About Men: Fighting Back," *The New York Times*, March 10, 1985. Copyright © 1985 by The New York Times Company. Reprinted by permission.

RICHARD WRIGHT "The Library Card" from *Black Boy* by Richard Wright. Copyright 1937, 1942, 1944, 1945 by Richard Wright. Reprinted by permission of HarperCollins Publishers.

MALCOLM X Excerpt from *The Autobiography of Malcolm X* by Malcolm X, with Alex Haley. Copyright © 1964 by Alex Haley and Malcolm X. Copyright © 1965 by Alex Haley and Betty Shabazz. Reprinted by permission of Random House, Inc.

W. B. YEATS "The Lake Isle of Innisfree" from *The Poems of W. B. Yeats: A New Edition*, edited by Richard J. Finneran (New York: Macmillan, 1983).

WILLIAM ZINSSER "College Pressures," *Blair & Ketchum's Country Journal*, Vol. VI, No. 4, April 1979. Copyright © 1979 by William K. Zinsser. Reprinted by permission of the author.

TOPICAL CLUSTERS

HEROES AND ROLE MODELS

EXILES

TEENAGE WASTELAND

THE GENERATION GAP

FATHERS AND SONS

FATHERS AND DAUGHTERS

MOTHERS AND DAUGHTERS

MOTHERS AND SONS

MARRIAGE

WOMEN IN A MAN'S WORLD

DOMESTIC ABUSE

SUBSTANCE ABUSE

SUCCESS AND FAILURE

VIOLENCE IN SPORTS

BIAS IN SPORTS

THE AMERICAN DREAM

Political Repression

War

Saving the Planet

Humans and Animals

The Limitations of Science

Death and Dying

Apocalypse

Index of Authors and Titles